QuickPass™
More Than a Textbook

P9-BJH-520

- ## More online resources
  Go to **Civics ONLINE** at <u>glencoe.com</u>.

- ## More convenient
  Enter a **QuickPass**™ chapter code to go directly to the chapter resources you need.

Student QuickPass™

> Key in chapter number.

Enter student code CIV3093c1 to access these resources:

- StudentWorks™ Plus Online
- Section Spotlight Video
- Chapter Overview
- Study Central™
- Study-to-Go
- Chapter Audio
- In Motion Animations
- Student Web Activity
- Self-Check Quiz
...and more

Teacher QuickPass™

> Key in chapter number.

Enter teacher code CIV1360c1T to access these resources:

- All student materials
- Web resources
- Teacher resources
...and more

You can easily launch a wide range of digital products from your computer's desktop with the McGraw-Hill Social Studies widget.

Civics Today

Features and Benefits

Dynamic Instructional Strategies
... presents clear and comprehensive coverage of Civics.
- Each engaging section introduction includes **Guide to Reading, Content and Academic Vocabulary,** and **Real World Civics.**
- **TIME® Reports, Political Cartoons,** and **Teens in Action** features bring real-life to your classroom.

A Strong Reading Strand
... encourages active reading and learning for students of all reading levels.
- The **Reading Social Studies** feature at the beginning of each unit allows students to learn and practice new content-area reading skills.
- **Main Idea** and **Civics & You** at the beginning of each main heading give students a focus and a reason for reading, and **Reading Checks** assess their comprehension.
- The **Reading Essentials and Note-Taking Guide** ancillary benefits all students by combining a concise version of the text, at a lower reading level, with a 2-column note-taking guide.

Differentiated Instruction
... makes *Civics Today* accessible to students of all learning levels.
- Differentiated Instruction activities and strategies can be found in the **Teacher Wraparound Edition,** the **Unit Resource** ancillaries, the **Teacher's Guide to Differentiated Instruction** ancillary, and online at **glencoe.com.**
- **Reading and Study Skills Foldables™** are 3-D kinesthetic exercises that help students organize and process key concepts as they read.
- **Civics Today Graphic Novel** is one motivating tool among many for differentiating instruction and engaging all learners in civics content.

Standardized Test Practice
... gives students the opportunity to practice for state and national exams.
- **Chapter Assessments** in *standardized test format* allow students to practice the skills they need for high-stakes state and national exams while reviewing chapter content.
- A remediation guide on each chapter assessment page guides students to the exact page where each question's content was covered.

A Variety of Activities and Features
... are essential for student success and to get students excited about Civics.
- **Landmark Supreme Court Case Studies** allows students to sharpen their critical thinking skills.
- The **Issues to Debate** feature challenges students to interpret and discuss opposing views of an issue.
- Integrated economics instruction and the **Financial Literacy** feature give students real-life economics information.
- **Historical Documents** and the **Analyzing Primary Sources** features offer students practice in using the tools of social scientists.

Teacher Resources
... provide convenient strategies to help both new and experienced teachers.
- *TeacherWorks™ Plus* contains the Interactive Teacher Edition, all ancillaries and transparencies, *editable* blackline masters, and a powerful, easy-to-use lesson planner.
- The **Teacher Wraparound Edition** now contains the **Brackets and Letters System,** identifying reading, differentiated instruction, writing support, critical thinking, and skill practice activities and strategies at the *exact* point-of-use.

Technology
... provides time-saving aids to help you reduce preparation time and engage students creatively.
- *StudentWorks™ Plus* includes the Interactive Student Edition, all student workbooks, and *full audio of the entire text* in English, with a Spanish audio summary. *StudentWorks™ Plus* is available on disc and online at **glencoe.com.**
- *ExamView® Assessment Suite* allows you to make customized tests using a huge databank of questions, including DBQs, that can be modified for all students.
- *Civics Today* at **glencoe.com** provides chapter-based, interactive activities and Web-based resources that will engage your students.
- *Study Central™* is an online, *section-based* homework helper that offers more content, skills practice, and vocabulary development.
- *Study-To-Go™* provides content and vocabulary review activities for portable electronic devices.
- *Presentation Plus! with MindJogger Checkpoint* DVD contains a PowerPoint™ presentation of the textbook, all program transparencies, and the interactive MindJogger quiz game.
- The *Civics Today* Section Spotlight Video Program offers interesting and diverse content extension.

Teacher Wraparound Edition

GLENCOE
CIVICS TODAY

CITIZENSHIP, ECONOMICS, & YOU

Richard C. Remy, Ph.D. • **John J. Patrick, Ed.D.**
David C. Saffel, Ph.D. • **Gary E. Clayton, Ph.D.**

Richard C. Remy, Ph.D., is professor emeritus in the College of Education at The Ohio State University, and Senior Consultant on Civic Education with the Mershon Center for International Security and Public Policy at Ohio State. He received his Ph.D. in political science from Northwestern University. His books include: *United States Government: Democracy in Action, Building Civic Education for Democracy in Poland, American Government and National Security*, and *Lessons on the Constitution*. In the 1990s Dr. Remy created and codirected a long-term project with the Polish Ministry of National Education and the Center for Citizenship Education, Warsaw to develop new civic education programs for Polish students, teachers, and teacher educators.

John J. Patrick, Ed.D., is a professor emeritus of Education at Indiana University, Bloomington. He is the author or coauthor of many publications about civics and government, such as *The Oxford Guide to the United States Government, The Supreme Court of the United States: A Student Companion, The Bill of Rights: A History in Documents, Founding the Republic,* and *Constitutional Debates on Freedom of Religion*. He is a member of the Standing Committee on Civics for the National Assessment of Educational Progress (NAEP). Since 1992 he has been involved in several international Civic education projects involving post-Communist countries. In 2002 he received Indiana University's John W. Ryan Award for distinguished achievements in International Programs. In 2003 he received the Sagamore of the Wabash award from the Governor of Indiana in recognition of his long-term contributions to civic education in Indiana. In 2005, he was the original recipient of the Indiana State Bar Association's civic eduation award.

David C. Saffell, Ph.D., received his Ph.D. degree in political science from the University of Minnesota. He has taught at Ohio Northern University since 1972, serving as chair of the Social Science Division for 15 years. Professor Saffell is coauthor of *State of Local Government: Politics and Public Policies,* 7th edition, published by McGraw-Hill. He has authored and edited several other books dealing with American government.

Gary E. Clayton, Ph.D., currently teaches economics at Northern Kentucky University. He received his Ph.D. in Economics from the University of Utah, has taught economics and finance at several universities and internationally, and has authored a number of books. Dr. Clayton appeared on numerous radio and television programs and was a guest commentator for NPR's *Marketplace*. Dr. Clayton has a long-standing interest in economic education. He has participated in numerous economic education workshops, and is a National Council on Economic Education Kazanjian award winner. Dr. Clayton most recently received a year 2000 Leavey Award for Excellence in Private Enterprise Education from the Freedoms Foundation at Valley Forge, and is the recipient of a national teaching award from the National Council on Economic Education. Most recently Dr. Clayton was the recipient of NKU's 2005 Frank Sinton Milburn Outstanding Professor Award.

Contributing Author

Dinah Zike, M.Ed., is an award winning author, educator, and inventor known for designing three-dimensional hands-on manipulatives and graphic organizers known as Foldables™. Foldables are used nationally and internationally by teachers, parents, and educational publishing companies. Dinah has developed over 150 supplemental educational books and materials. She is the author of *The Big Book of Books and Activities,* which was awarded *Learning Magazine*'s Teachers' Choice Award. In 2004, Dinah was honored with the CESI Science Advocacy Award. Dinah received her M.Ed. from Texas A&M, College Station, Texas.

The *McGraw·Hill* Companies

 Glencoe

TIME Reports and TIME Teens in *Action* © Time Inc. Prepared by TIME Learning Ventures in collaboration with Glencoe/McGraw-Hill. TIME and the red border design are trademarks of Time Inc. used under license.

ExamView® is a registered trademark of FSCreations, Inc. References to components of the *ExamView*® Assessment Suite are made in this publication.

Send all inquiries to: Glencoe/McGraw-Hill, 8787 Orion Place, Columbus, OH 43240-4027

(Teacher Wraparound Edition) ISBN: 978-0-07-892136-0   (Student Edition) ISBN: 978-0-07-880309-3
                MHID: 0-07-892136-8   MHID: 0-07-880309-8

Printed in the United States of America.
1 2 3 4 5 079/043 13 12 11 10 09

Academic Consultants

Brandon Bartels, Ph.D.
Assistant Professor of Political Science
Stony Brook University
Stony Brook, New York

Jody Baumgartner, Ph.D.
Assistant Professor of Political Science
East Carolina University
Greenville, North Carolina

Jeff Biddle, Ph.D.
Professor of Economics
Michigan State University
East Lansing, Michigan

Nancy Lind, Ph.D.
Associate Department Chair, Professor
  of Political Science
Illinois State University
Normal, Illinois

Scott McClurg, Ph.D.
Assistant Professor of Political Science
Southern Illinois University
Carbondale, Illinois

Carrie Meyer, Ph.D.
Associate Professor of Economics
George Mason University
Fairfax, Virginia

Emmanuel Oritsejafor, Ph.D.
Associate Professor of Political Science
North Carolina Central University
Durham, North Carolina

Bassam Yousif, Ph.D.
Associate Professor of Economics
Indiana State University
Terre Haute, Indiana

Teacher Reviewers

Cliff Avant
Bleckley County High School
Cochran, Georgia

Lori Braunstein
Aurora Central High School
Aurora, Colorado

Heather Bridges
Mills University Studies High School
Little Rock, Arkansas

Nathan Bruck
Greenfield-Central High School
Greenfield, Indiana

Dorothea Bryant
Huron High School
Ann Arbor, Michigan

Michael Clark
Hall High School
Little Rock, Arkansas

Brad Donovan
Willapa Valley High School
Menlo, Washington

Jennifer Goss
Fleetwood Area High School
Fleetwood, Pennsylvania

Jeanne Hamacher
Lake Park High School
Roselle, Indiana

Jodi Howell
West Albany High School
Albany, Oregon

Annette King
Colquitt County High School
Moultrie, Georgia

Vanessa Lal Steinkamp
Adlai Stevenson High School
Lincolnshire, Illinois

Brian Myatt
Oneida High School
Oneida, New York

Bill Schreier
Wheaton Warrenville South
  High School
Wheaton, Illinois

Russell Sousa
Fort Myers High School
Fort Myers, Florida

Brian Stevens
Coldwater High School
Coldwater, Michigan

Diane Stewart
Chester County High School
Henderson, Tennessee

John Sullivan
Belmont High School
Belmont, Massachusetts

Stephen Venezia
Marblehead High School
Marblehead, Massachusetts

Table of Contents

▼ U.S. Capitol,
Washington, D.C.

▼ Replica of the United States
Constitution

Joint session ▼
of Congress

TABLE OF CONTENTS

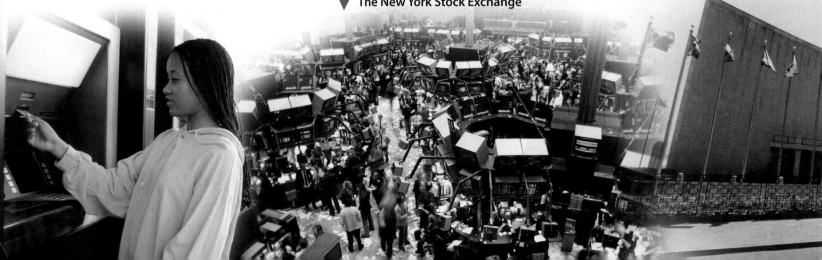

▼ Convenient ATM banking

▼ The New York Stock Exchange

▼ United Nations
Headquarters in
New York City

Appendix

TIME™ Features

TIME™ Political Cartoons

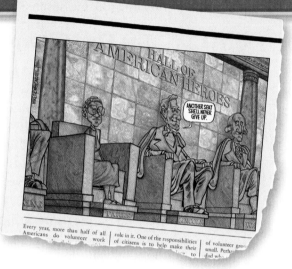

TIME™ Teens in *Action*

FEATURES

American Biography

Issues to Debate

LANDMARK SUPREME COURT CASE STUDIES

Financial Literacy

Reading Social Studies

Analyzing Primary Sources

Historical Documents

Skills Handbook

Charts and Graphs

Primary Sources

Ed. = Editor   Tr. = Translator   V = Volume

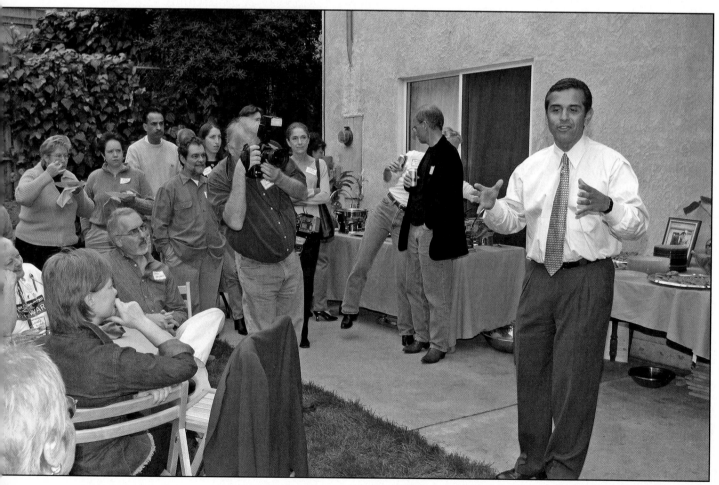

Scavenger Hunt

Civics Today contains a wealth of information. The trick is to know where to look in the text to access all this information. If you complete this Scavenger Hunt exercise with your teacher or parents, you will see how the textbook is organized, and how to get the most out of your reading and study time. Let's get started!

1 How many units and how many chapters are in the book?
8 units; 27 chapters

2 What topic does Unit 4 cover?
State and Local Government

3 Where can you quickly find a definition of the word *communism*?
in the Glossary/Glosario

4 What is the topic of the *Real World Civics* item on page 292?
making polling places accessible for handicapped voters

5 What is the topic of "Analyzing Primary Sources" at the end of Unit 2?
The Federal Branch of Government

6 What does the Web site call-out found on page 439 tell you to do?
complete the Student Web Activity at glencoe.com

7 How are the content vocabulary words *microeconomics*, *scarcity*, and *trade-off* in Chapter 18 called out?
They are boldfaced and highlighted yellow.

8 Who is the topic of Teens in *Action* on page 152?
Geneva Johnson

9 What does the Foldables™ exercise on page 655 ask you to do?
Make a Foldable to take notes on the Federal Reserve.

10 Where do you find graphic data about all of the United States, including the presidents?
in the Appendix

Understanding the BIG Ideas

The 30 BIG IDEAS will help you understand the information in *Civics Today: Citizenship, Economics, & You.* The big ideas—found in each chapter—are based on the national standards for Civic Education and Economic Education. They help you organize important ideas, recognize trends, and see connections and patterns in the information you will be reading.

Civics

★ As American citizens, we make a commitment to the nation and to the values and principles that are part of United States democracy.

★ Citizens possess certain rights. With citizenship, there are also certain responsibilities expected of all Americans.

★ People form governments to establish order, provide security, and accomplish common goals.

★ Political and economic institutions evolve to help individuals and groups accomplish their goals.

★ Political, social, religious, and economic changes influence the way Americans think and act.

★ Political principles and major events shape how people form governments.

★ A constitution reflects the values and goals of the society that creates it.

★ The Constitution of the United States establishes and protects fundamental rights and liberties.

★ For government to be effective, citizens must fulfill their civic duties and responsibilities.

★ Citizen participation is essential to the foundation and preservation of the U.S. political system.

★ The Constitution gives the legislative branch—Congress—the power to make laws.

★ The Constitution gives the executive branch the power to execute, or implement, the law.

★ Under our federal system, the executive, legislative, and judicial branches share the responsibility of governing the nation.

★ The judicial branch is charged with interpreting the law.

★ The right to vote is one of the fundamental rights of citizens in a democratic society.

★ A successful democracy is built on an informed electorate.

★ A democratic society requires the active participation of its citizens.

★ In a democratic society, various forces shape people's ideas.

★ Under our federal system, power is shared between the national government and the state governments.

Economics

★ Scarcity requires individuals and groups to make choices about using goods and services to satisfy their wants.

★ Throughout history, civilizations have developed systems of laws to meet their needs.

★ An economic system is the way a society organizes the production and consumption of goods and services.

★ The basis of the market economy is voluntary exchange. In the American economy, the exchange usually involves money in return for a good or service.

★ Free enterprise is the freedom of individuals and businesses to operate and compete with a minimum of government interference or regulation.

★ You and everyone around you are consumers and, as such, play an important role in the economic system.

★ We all make economic choices. Opportunity cost, scarcity, and supply and demand influence the decisions we make.

★ Supply and demand in a market interact to determine price and the quantities bought and sold.

★ Market economies rest upon the fundamental principle of individual freedom for consumers, producers, and workers.

★ The exchange of goods and services helps create economic interdependence among peoples in different places and different countries.

★ Economic, social, and political changes create new traditions, values, and beliefs.

Civics Today: Citizenship, Economics, and You
to the National Standards

The following Scope and Sequence chart illustrates how *Civics Today: Citizenship, Economics, and You* meets the content standards for Civics and Government as outlined in the *National Standards for Civics and Government.*

Standard	Student Edition Chapter
I. What are civic life, politics, and government?	
A. What is civic life? What is politics? What is government? Why are government and politics necessary? What purposes should government serve?	Chapters 1, 5, 9, 12, 13
B. What are the essential characteristics of limited and unlimited government?	Chapters 2, 3, 4, 15, 17, 23, 27
C. What are the nature and purposes of constitutions?	Chapters 1, 3, 4
D. What are alternative ways of organizing constitutional governments?	Chapters 3, 4, 27
II. What are the foundations of the American political system?	
A. What is the American idea of constitutional government?	Chapters 1, 3, 4, 5, 15, 17
B. What are the distinctive characteristics of American society?	Chapters 1, 5, 9, 11, 14, 15, 23, 25
C. What is American political culture?	Chapters 9, 10, 11, 14
D. What values and principles are basic to American constitutional democracy?	Chapters 1, 2, 3, 4, 5
III. How does the government established by the Constitution embody the purposes, values, and principles of American democracy?	
A. How are power and responsibility distributed, shared, and limited in the government established by the United States Constitution?	Chapters 3, 4, 6, 7, 8, 12
B. How is the national government organized and what does it do?	Chapters 3, 6, 7, 8, 12
C. How are state and local governments organized and what do they do?	Chapters 12, 13, 14
D. What is the place of law in the American constitutional system?	Chapters 15, 16, 17
E. How does the American political system provide for choice and opportunities for participation?	Chapters 3, 4, 5, 6, 7, 9, 10, 17

Standard	Student Edition Chapter
IV. What is the relationship of the United States to other nations and to world affairs?	
A. How is the world organized politically?	Chapters 26, 27
B. How do the domestic politics and constitutional principles of the United States affect its relations with the world?	Chapters 3, 9, 18, 19, 27
C. How has the United States influenced other nations, and how have other nations influenced American politics and society?	Chapters 9, 23, 26, 27
V. What are the roles of the citizen in American democracy?	
A. What is citizenship?	Chapters 1, 5, 9, 10
B. What are the rights of citizens?	Chapters 3, 4, 5, 15, 16, 17
C. What are the responsibilities of citizens?	Chapter 5
D. What civic dispositions or traits of private and public character are important to the preservation and improvement of American constitutional democracy?	Chapters 1, 3, 4, 5, 14, 15, 17
E. How can citizens take part in civic life?	Chapters 5, 9, 10, 14, 15, 17

Civics Today: Citizenship, Economics, and You to the NCEE Content Standards

The United States Congress has designated economics as one of the nine core subjects to be taught in America's schools. As a result, the National Council on Economic Education (NCEE) developed the *Voluntary National Content Standards in Economics* for use in economics curricula. *Civics Today: Citizenship, Economics, and You* provides coverage for the 20 voluntary content standards.

NCEE Standard	Civics Today: Citizenship, Economics, and You Chapter and Section Coverage
Standard 1: Scarcity **Productive resources are limited. Therefore, people cannot have all the goods and services they want; as a result, they must choose some things and give up others.** **Related concepts:** Capital Resources, Choice, Consumer Economics, Consumers, Goods, Human Resources, Natural Resources, Opportunity Cost, Producers, Production, Productive Resources, Scarcity, Services, Wants, Entrepreneurship, Inventors, Entrepreneur, Factors of Production	**Chapter 18** **What Is Economics?** **Section 1:** How Economic Systems Work **Section 2:** Making Economic Decisions
Standard 2: Marginal Cost/Benefit **Effective decision making requires comparing the additional costs of alternatives with the additional benefits. Most choices involve doing a little more or a little less of something; few choices are "all or nothing" decisions.** **Related concepts:** Decision Making, Profit Motive, Benefit, Costs, Marginal Analysis, Profit, Profit Maximization, Cost/Benefit Analysis	**Chapter 18** **What Is Economics?** **Section 1:** How Economic Systems Work **Section 2:** Making Economic Decisions **Chapter 19** **The American Economy** **Section 1:** Economic Resources **Chapter 20** **Personal Finance and Economics** **Section 1:** Managing Your Money **Section 2:** Planning and Budgeting **Section 3:** Saving and Investing **Section 4:** Achieving Your Financial Goals
Standard 3: Allocation of Goods and Services **Different methods can be used to allocate goods and services. People, acting individually or collectively through government, must choose which methods to use to allocate different kinds of goods and services.** **Related concepts:** Economic Systems, Market Structure, Supply, Command Economy, Market Economy, Traditional Economy	**Chapter 19** **The American Economy** **Section 1:** Economic Resources **Chapter 20** **Personal Finance and Economics** **Section 3:** Saving and Investing **Chapter 21** **Demand and Supply** **Section 1:** Demand **Section 2:** Factors Affecting Demand **Section 3:** Supply and the Supply Curve **Section 4:** Demand and Supply at Work **Chapter 26** **Comparing Economic Systems** **Section 2:** Economic Systems

NCEE Standard	Civics Today: Citizenship, Economics, and You Chapter and Section Coverage
Standard 4: Role of Incentives People respond predictably to positive and negative incentives. **Related concepts:** Choice, Incentive	**Chapter 18 What Is Economics?** **Section 1:** How Economic Systems Work **Chapter 19 The American Economy** **Section 1:** Economic Resources **Section 2:** Economic Activity **Section 3:** Capitalism and Free Enterprise **Chapter 23 Government and the Economy** **Section 2:** Measuring the Economy **Chapter 24 Money and Banking** **Section 2:** The Federal Reserve System
Standard 5: Gain from Trade Voluntary exchange occurs only when all participating parties expect to gain. This is true for trade among individuals or organizations within a nation, and among individuals or organizations in different nations. **Related concepts:** Barriers to Trade, Barter, Exports, Imports, Voluntary Exchange, Exchange, Exchange Rate	**Chapter 19 The American Economy** **Section 1:** Economic Resources **Section 2:** Economic Activity **Section 3:** Capitalism and Free Enterprise **Chapter 20 Personal Finance and Economics** **Section 3:** Saving and Investing **Chapter 26 Comparing Economic Systems** **Section 1:** International Trade **Section 2:** Economic Systems
Standard 6: Specialization and Trade When individuals, regions, and nations specialize in what they can produce at the lowest cost and then trade with others, both production and consumption increase. **Related concepts:** Division of Labor, Production, Productive Resources, Specialization, Factor Endowments, Gains from Trade, Relative Price, Transaction Costs, Factors of Production, Full Employment	**Chapter 19 The American Economy** **Section 2:** Economic Activity **Chapter 26 Comparing Economic Systems** **Section 1:** International Trade **Section 2:** Economic Systems
Standard 7: Markets - Price and Quantity Determination Markets exist when buyers and sellers interact. This interaction determines market prices and thereby allocates scarce goods and services. **Related concepts:** Market Structure, Markets, Price Floor, Price Stability, Quantity Demanded, Quantity Supplied, Relative Price, Exchange Rate	**Chapter 19 The American Economy** **Section 1:** Economic Resources **Section 2:** Economic Activity **Section 3:** Capitalism and Free Enterprise **Chapter 21 Demand and Supply** **Section 1:** Demand **Section 2:** Factors Affecting Demand **Section 3:** Supply and the Supply Curve **Section 4:** Demand and Supply at Work

NCEE Standard	*Civics Today: Citizenship, Economics, and You* **Chapter and Section Coverage**
Standard 8: Role of Price in Market System Prices send signals and provide incentives to buyers and sellers. When supply or demand changes, market prices adjust, affecting incentives. **Related concepts:** Non-price Determinants, Price Floor, Price Stability, Supply, Determinants of Demand, Determinants of Supply, Law of Demand, Law of Supply, Price Ceiling, Substitute Good, Price	**Chapter 19 The American Economy** Section 1: Economic Resources Section 2: Economic Activity Section 3: Capitalism and Free Enterprise **Chapter 21 Demand and Supply** Section 1: Demand Section 2: Factors Affecting Demand Section 3: Supply and the Supply Curve Section 4: Demand and Supply at Work
Standard 9: Role of Competition Competition among sellers lowers costs and prices, and encourages producers to produce more of what consumers are willing and able to buy. Competition among buyers increases prices and allocates goods and services to those people who are willing and able to pay the most for them. **Related concepts:** Market Structure, Non-price Competition, Levels of Competition	**Chapter 19 The American Economy** Section 1: Economic Resources Section 2: Economic Activity Section 3: Capitalism and Free Enterprise **Chapter 21 Demand and Supply** Section 1: Demand Section 2: Factors Affecting Demand Section 3: Supply and the Supply Curve Section 4: Demand and Supply at Work
Standard 10: Role of Economic Institutions Institutions evolve in market economies to help individuals and groups accomplish their goals. Banks, labor unions, corporations, legal systems, and not-for-profit organizations are examples of important institutions. A different kind of institution, clearly defined and enforced property rights, is essential to a market economy. **Related concepts:** Legal and Social Framework, Mortgage, Borrower, Interest, Labor Union, Legal Forms of Business, Legal Foundations of a Market Economy, Nonprofit Organization, Property Rights, Banking	**Chapter 20 Personal Finance and Economics** Section 1: Managing Your Money Section 4: Achieving Your Financial Goals **Chapter 22 Business and Labor** Section 1: Types of Businesses Section 2: The American Labor Force Section 3: Businesses in Our Economy **Chapter 24 Money and Banking** Section 1: What is Money? Section 2: The Federal Reserve System Section 3: How Banks Operate
Standard 11: Role of Money Money makes it easier to trade, borrow, save, invest, and compare the value of goods and services. **Related concepts:** Exchange, Money Management, Money Supply, Currency, Definition of Money, Money, Characteristics of Money, Functions of Money	**Chapter 24 Money and Banking** Section 1: What Is Money? Section 2: The Federal Reserve System Section 3: How Banks Operate

NCEE Standard	Civics Today: Citizenship, Economics, and You Chapter and Section Coverage
Standard 12: Role of Interest Rates Interest rates, adjusted for inflation, rise and fall to balance the amount saved with the amount borrowed, which affects the allocation of scarce resources between present and future uses. **Related concepts:** Interest Rate, Monetary Policy, Real vs. Nominal, Risk, Investing, Savers, Savings	**Chapter 24 Money and Banking** **Section 1:** What Is Money? **Section 2:** The Federal Reserve System **Section 3:** How Banks Operate
Standard 13: Role of Resources in Determining Income Income for most people is determined by the market value of the productive resources they sell. What workers earn depends, primarily, on the market value of what they produce and how productive they are. **Related concepts:** Human Resources, Derived Demand, Functional Distribution of Income, Labor, Labor Market, Marginal Resource Product, Personal Distribution of Income, Wage, Aggregate Demand (AD), Aggregate Supply (AS), Demand, Prices of Inputs, Functional Distribution	**Chapter 19 The American Economy** **Section 1:** Economic Resources **Section 2:** Economic Activity **Section 3:** Capitalism and Free Enterprise **Chapter 21 Demand and Supply** **Section 1:** Demand **Section 2:** Factors Affecting Demand **Section 3:** Supply and the Supply Curve **Section 4:** Demand and Supply at Work
Standard 14: Profit and the Entrepreneur Entrepreneurs are people who take the risks of organizing productive resources to make goods and services. Profit is an important incentive that leads entrepreneurs to accept the risks of business failure. **Related concepts:** Taxation, Costs, Costs of Production, Entrepreneur, Risk, Taxes, Cost/Benefit Analysis, Innovation, Entrepreneurship, Inventors	**Chapter 19 The American Economy** **Section 1:** Economic Resources **Chapter 20 Personal Finance and Economics** **Section 1:** Managing Your Money **Section 4:** Achieving Your Financial Goals **Chapter 22 Business and Labor** **Section 1:** Types of Businesses **Section 3:** Businesses in Our Economy
Standard 15: Growth Investment in factories, machinery, new technology, and in the health, education, and training of people can raise future standards of living. **Related concepts:** Incentive, Interest Rate, Opportunity Cost, Production, Technological Changes, Trade-off, Trade-offs Among Goals, Human Capital, Intensive Growth, Investment, Physical Capital, Productivity, Risk, Standard of Living, Economic Efficiency, Economic Equity, Economic Freedom, Economic Growth, Economic Security, Investing, Business, Businesses and Households, Factors of Production, Health and Nutrition, Savers, Savings, Stock Market	**Chapter 19 The American Economy** **Section 1:** Economic Resources **Section 2:** Economic Activity **Section 3:** Capitalism and Free Enterprise **Chapter 20 Personal Finance and Economics** **Section 3:** Saving and Investing **Section 4:** Achieving Your Financial Goals

NCEE Standard	*Civics Today: Citizenship, Economics, and You* Chapter and Section Coverage
Standard 16: Role of Government There is an economic role for government in a market economy whenever the benefits of a government policy outweigh its costs. Governments often provide for national defense, address environmental concerns, define and protect property rights, and attempt to make markets more competitive. Most government policies also redistribute income. **Related concepts:** Externalities, Income, Natural Monopoly, Redistribution of Income, Role of Government, Taxation, Transfer Payments, Bonds, Distribution of Income, Income Tax, Maintaining Competition, Monopolies, Negative Externality, Non-clearing Markets, Positive Externality, Property Rights, Public Goods, Maintaining Regulation, Taxes, Regulation, Government Expenditures, Government Revenues	**Chapter 19** **The American Economy** **Section 3:** Capitalism and Free Enterprise **Chapter 23** **Government and the Economy** **Section 1:** The Role of Government **Section 2:** Measuring the Economy **Section 3:** Government, the Economy, and You **Chapter 24** **Money and Banking** **Section 2:** The Federal Reserve System **Chapter 25** **Government Finances** **Section 1:** The Federal Government **Section 2:** State and Local Governments **Section 3:** Managing the Economy
Standard 17: Using Cost/Benefit Analysis to Evaluate Government Programs Costs of government policies sometimes exceed benefits. This may occur because of incentives facing voters, government officials, and government employees, because of actions by special interest groups that can impose costs on the general public, or because social goals other than economic efficiency are being pursued. **Related concepts:** Cost/Benefit Analysis, Benefit, Costs, Special Interest Group, Barriers to Trade	**Chapter 23** **Government and the Economy** **Section 1:** The Role of Government **Section 2:** Measuring the Economy **Section 3:** Government, the Economy, and You **Chapter 25** **Government Finances** **Section 1:** The Federal Government **Section 2:** State and Local Governments **Section 3:** Managing the Economy
Standard 18: Macroeconomy-Income/Employment, Prices A nation's overall levels of income, employment, and prices are determined by the interaction of spending and production decisions made by all households, firms, government agencies, and others in the economy. **Related concepts:** Gross Domestic Product (GDP), Macroeconomic Indicators, Nominal Gross Domestic Product (GDP), Per Capita Gross Domestic Product (GDP), Potential Gross Domestic Product (GDP), Real Gross Domestic Product (GDP), Circular Flow	**Chapter 19** **The American Economy** **Section 1:** Economic Resources **Section 2:** Economic Activity **Section 3:** Capitalism and Free Enterprise **Chapter 23** **Government and the Economy** **Section 1:** The Role of Government **Section 2:** Measuring the Economy **Section 3:** Government, the Economy, and You **Chapter 25** **Government Finances** **Section 1:** The Federal Government **Section 3:** Managing the Economy

NCEE Standard	*Civics Today: Citizenship, Economics, and You* Chapter and Section Coverage
Standard 19: Unemployment and Inflation Unemployment imposes costs on individuals and nations. Unexpected inflation imposes costs on many people and benefits some others because it arbitrarily redistributes purchasing power. Inflation can reduce the rate of growth of national living standards because individuals and organizations use resources to protect themselves against the uncertainty of future prices. **Related concepts:** Types of Unemployment, Causes of Inflation, Consumer Price Index (CPI), Deflation, Labor Force, Unemployment, Unemployment Rate, Inflation	**Chapter 19** **The American Economy** **Section 3:** Capitalism and Free Enterprise **Chapter 23** **Government and the Economy** **Section 1:** The Role of Government **Section 2:** Measuring the Economy **Section 3:** Government, the Economy, and You **Chapter 24** **Money and Banking** **Section 3:** How Banks Operate
Standard 20: Monetary and Fiscal Policy Federal government budgetary policy and the Federal Reserve System's monetary policy influence the overall levels of employment, output, and prices. **Related concepts:** Inflation, National Debt, Tools of the Federal Reserve, Discount Rate, Federal Budget, Fiscal Policy, Monetary Policy, Open Market Operations, Reserve Requirements, Budget, Budget Deficit, Central Banking System, Budget Surplus, Causes of Inflation	**Chapter 19** **The American Economy** **Section 3:** Capitalism and Free Enterprise **Chapter 23** **Government and the Economy** **Section 1:** The Role of Government **Section 2:** Measuring the Economy **Section 3:** Government, the Economy, and You **Chapter 24** **Money and Banking** **Section 2:** The Federal Reserve System **Section 3:** How Banks Operate **Chapter 25** **Government Finances** **Section 1:** The Federal Government **Section 3:** Managing the Economy

To Teachers:

Welcome to the the Teacher Wraparound Edition of *Civics Today: Citizenship, Economics, and You*. We have created this teacher edition based on input from experienced teachers and educational consultants. Our goal is to provide you with teaching strategies and activities, which are labeled for you at point-of-use. The following pages will show the structure of the Teacher Wraparound Edition.

Student-Based Instruction

Point-of-Use
- Strategies and activities apply directly to student content.

Differentiated Instruction
- Leveled activities and options for differentiated instruction help meet the needs of all your students, including English language learners.

Review and Reinforcement
- Reading and critical thinking skills are reinforced throughout the lesson.

Assessment and Intervention
- Chapter Assessments provide standardized test practice.
- Assessments gauge student mastery of content.
- Additional resources provide intervention options.

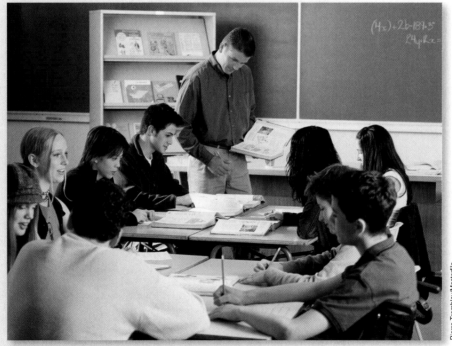

Pierre Tremblay/Masterfile

Planning and Teaching the Unit

Planning pages appear at the beginning of each unit.

Pacing Chart

Provides time management suggestions for teaching the unit

Author Note

Highlights author's ideas for teaching the unit

Teacher to Teacher

Includes activities from the classrooms of successful teachers

---

Unit 1 Planning Guide

Introducing Unit 1

UNIT PACING CHART

Unit 1	Chapter 1	Chapter 2	Chapter 3	Chapter 4	Chapter 5
Day 1 Unit Opener, Reading Social Studies	Chapter Opener, Section 1	Chapter Opener, Section 1	Chapter Opener, Section 1	Chapter Opener, Section 1, Issues to Debate	Chapter Opener, Section 1, Financial Literacy
Day 2	Section 2	Section 2	Section 2	Section 2	Section 2, Chapter Review
Day 3	Section 3, Chapter Review, and Visual Summary	Section 3	Section 3	Landmark Supreme Court Case Studies	Chapter Assessment
Day 4	Chapter Assessment	Section 4	Section 4	Section 3, Financial Literacy	TIME Reports
Day 5		Visual Summary, Chapter Review	Chapter Review, Visual Summary	Section 4, Chapter Review, Visual Summary	Analyzing Primary Sources
Day 6		Chapter Assessment	Chapter Assessment	Chapter Assessment	
Day 7		The Declaration of Independence	Constitution of the United States		
Day 8		The Declaration of Independence	Constitution of the United States		
Day 9			Constitution of the United States		
Day 10			Constitution of the United States		

Teacher to Teacher

Jan Rabin,
Northside High School,
Roanoke, Virginia

Government During the Revolution The objective of this activity is to describe the shortcomings and inadequacies of the Articles of Confederation. Students are to brainstorm and list the difficulties that the Continental Army encountered while fighting the war. The class can be divided into groups, with each group assigned two problems that George Washington and the troops encountered. Because the Articles of Confederation was the only national government available during this time, students are to attempt to solve each of the difficulties within the framework of the Articles. The group will examine the areas of each problem, as well as the difficulties caused for the soldiers. Each group will be asked to share their conclusions at the end of the study, as well as their conclusion concerning the effectiveness of the Articles of Confederation in solving the wartime problems.

1A

Author Note

Dear Social Studies Teacher:

During a recent trip to Washington, D. C., I visited the Charters of Freedom exhibit at the National Archives. I was filled with pride and awe while looking at the original copies of the Constitution and Bill of Rights, and my commitment to teach young Americans about these documents was renewed and strengthened.

We Americans are justly proud of our 1787 Constitution and 1791 Bill of Rights, which constitute the world's oldest, continuously in use, written frame of government. Our constitutional government has stood the test of time, even though based on two ideas in perpetual tension, majority rule and minority rights. President Thomas Jefferson recognized this constitutional paradox in his First Inaugural Address, "All, too, will bear in mind this sacred principle, that though the will of the majority is in all cases to prevail, that will to be rightful must be reasonable; that the minority possess their equal rights, which equal law must protect and to violate would be oppression."

Civic educators, like you and me, must remember that our Constitution will yield justice only if we balance and blend majority rule with minority rights in our responses to ongoing public issues. At what point should majority rule be limited by law in order to protect constitutionally guaranteed minority rights? And conversely, at what point should certain rights of minorities be constitutionally limited in favor of the majority will?

Public issues raised by the ongoing tensions between constitutionally based majority rule and the constitutionally guaranteed rights of individuals in the minority should be confronted openly, fairly, critically, and civilly in the social studies classroom. I urge you to engage your students in this kind of learning experience to prepare them for the continuing challenges of citizenship in our democratic republic.

John J. Patrick
Author

1B

Be an Active Citizen

Provides questions and activities to engage students in unit content

Unit Objectives

Lists objectives for student learning

Launching the Unit

Activates prior knowledge and stimulates discussion about unit themes

---

UNIT 1 Introduction

Unit Objectives

After studying this unit, students will be able to:
- Explain the role of government in everyday life.
- Understand the history of our country's government.
- Describe the principles in the Constitution.
- Discuss the freedoms guaranteed by the Bill of Rights.
- Know the difference between the duties and responsibilities of citizens.

Did You Know?

Every ten years, the United States government conducts the census, or the official counting of the population. The results of the first census in 1790 showed the U.S. population at 3.9 million. On October 17, 2006, the U.S. population officially reached the 300-million mark.

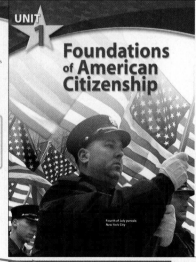

UNIT 1
Foundations of American Citizenship

Fourth of July parade,
New York City

★ Chapter 1 The American People
★ Chapter 2 Roots of American Democracy
★ Chapter 3 The Constitution
★ Chapter 4 The Bill of Rights
★ Chapter 5 Citizenship and Government in a Democracy

CITIZENSHIP Be an Active Citizen

Find out the purposes of government firsthand. Contact a government leader, such as a state representative, a city council member, or a school board member, and ask how the government he or she represents serves American citizens.

UNIT 1 Introduction

Be an Active Citizen

CITIZENSHIP Do your students know who represents them in Congress? Have your students do research at www.senate.gov and www.house.gov to discover who their senators and representatives are. These Web sites also contain links to the home page of the members of Congress. Have students find information on the party affiliations, biographical history, and bills introduced or fought for by each member of Congress.

Activity: Launching the Unit

Foundations of American Citizenship
Ask: What is a citizen? (A citizen is literally a person who owes loyalty to and is entitled to the protection of a state, nation, and/or government. A citizen of the United States is guaranteed rights through the Constitution and its amendments. There are certain legal duties required of citizens, as well as civic obligations that citizens may engage in to enrich their communities.) Students may have heard the term "citizen" before but may not know all of the rights and roles involved in citizenship. Have your students make a list of the characteristics they believe constitute citizenship. After they have completed the unit, have them review their lists and discuss what aspects they may have overlooked. **OL**

More About the Photo

Today's Fourth of July celebrations have roots in the celebrations of colonial times. The first organized Fourth of July celebration was in Philadelphia in 1777. It featured food, music, and a military parade, complete with cannon and other artillery fire to celebrate the event. There was even a small fireworks display at night! The festivities have become more elaborate today. Corporate giant Macy's has sponsored the New York City 4th of July Parade for over 30 years. A recent Independence Day fireworks display featured 30,000 fireworks, all coordinated via computer to the accompanying music.

1

Planning the Chapter

Chapter Planning Guides provide a snapshot of the scope of resources available for each chapter.

Incorporating Resources

Utilizes a structured lesson plan for additional resources

Leveled Activities

Organizes resources by ability levels

*Spanish Resources

Indicates resources for English Language Learners

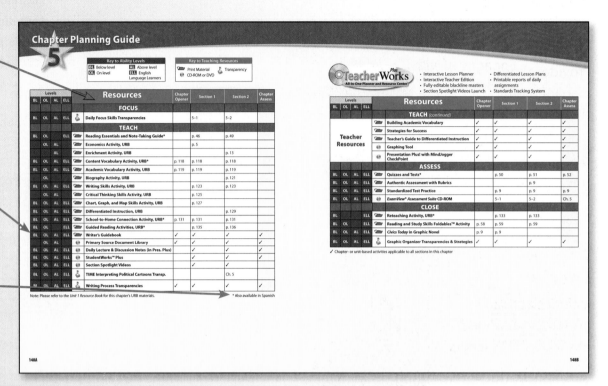

Additional Resources

Identifies resources for supplementing the chapter

Understanding Brackets

Lists the different prompts for side wrap activities for ease of reference

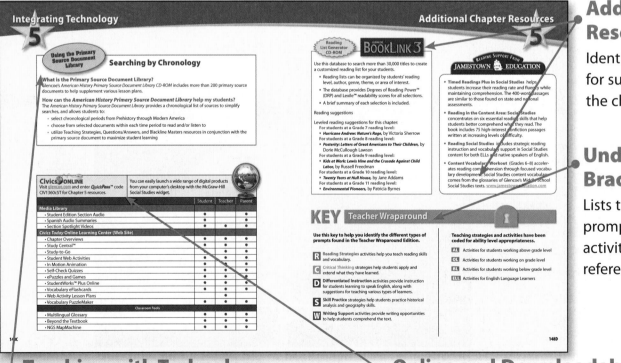

Teaching with Technology

Explains how to incorporate different Glencoe technology resources in the classroom

Online and Downloadable Learning

Engages students and parents with online and downloadable content

Teaching the Chapter

The **Big Ideas** at the beginning of the chapter help you teach the most important chapter contents.

Why It Matters

Engages students with questions and activities to introduce the chapter

Foldables

Dinah Zike's Foldables help students organize information and prepare for assessments

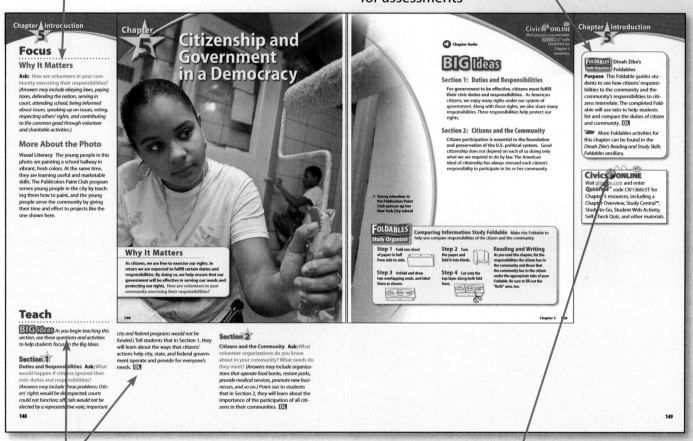

BIG Ideas

Big Ideas are major themes, issues, concepts, questions, or ideas that help students organize information and understand civic and economic themes.

Civics Online

Provides additional chapter resources

Lesson Structure

Each lesson in *Civics Today: Citizenship, Economics, and You* is presented in a structured lesson plan: Focus, Teach, Assess, and Close.

FOCUS

Includes a Bellringer activity to help your students think about the lesson topic

Guide to Reading

Provides pre-reading strategies to improve comprehension

Spotlight Video

Engages students with the content using a short video

Resource Manager

Provides a list of teacher edition and supplemental resources that supports lesson content and reinforce skills

TEACH

Stimulates learning and interest using leveled activities

ASSESS

Identifies assessment resources

CLOSE

Gauges comprehension of section content

Answers

Lists the answers to Student Edition questions

Understanding the Letters and Brackets

Letters*

The letters on the reduced Student Edition page identify the type of strategy or activity. See the key below to learn about the different types of strategies and activities.

Brackets

Brackets on the reduced Student Edition page correspond to teaching strategies and activities in the Teacher Wraparound Edition. As you teach the section, the brackets show you exactly where to teach these strategies and activities.

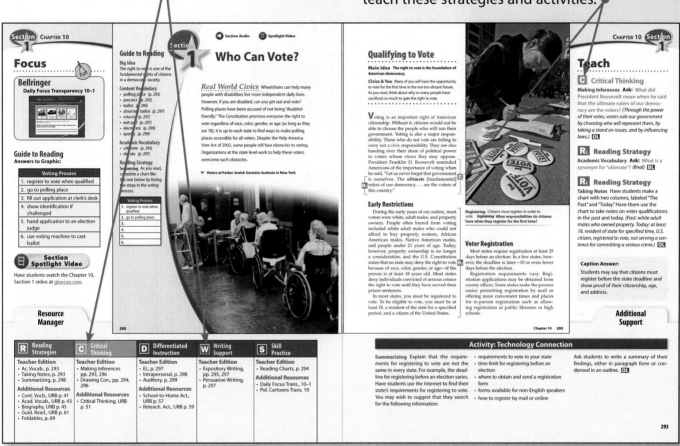

KEY for Using the Teacher Wraparound Edition

R **Reading Strategies** activities help you teach reading skills and vocabulary.

C **Critical Thinking** strategies help students apply and extend what they have learned.

D **Differentiated Instruction** activities provide differentiated instruction for students learning to speak English, along with suggestions for teaching various types of learners.

S **Skill Practice** strategies help students practice historical analysis and geography skills.

W **Writing Support** activities provide writing opportunities to help students comprehend the text.

* Letters are followed by a number when there is more than one of the same type of strategy or activity on the page.

Hands-On Chapter Projects

Extend student learning with unique interactive projects in each chapter. The Hands-On Chapter Projects allow students to take concepts and put them to practical use. Activities are progressive and require teamwork. Students conceptualize, plan, and execute their vision in a hands-on approach that makes civics and economics come alive.

Steps

Each lesson includes a self-contained activity, with one lesson building on knowledge gained from previous lessons.

Hands-On

Students utilize diverse learning styles and creativity and work cooperatively to create a final project for each lesson.

Results

The Hands-On Project culminates in a discussion or summary activity that ties the other activities in the chapter together.

Differentiated Instruction

Each section of the Teacher Wraparound Edition of *Civics Today: Citizenship, Economics, and You* provides differentiated instruction activities to meet the diverse needs of every student.

Differentiated Activities

Innovative ideas meet each student's interests and learning styles through point-of-use activities

Supplemental Resources

Provides suggestions for incorporating additional resources based on students' different learning abilities

Leveled Activities

Extends instruction beyond the text by suggesting activities related to content on the page

Dynamic Features

Use the creative features in the textbook to dig deep into the fascinating issues and people covered in the text.

Issues to Debate

Teaches students to analyze different points of view on current issues in civics

Additional Reading

Supplemental reading suggestions provide opportunities for students to connect with each unit

Analyzing Primary Sources

Helps students interpret and analyze primary source documents

Financial Literacy

Presents students with answers to real-life economic questions

Chapter Summary and Assessment

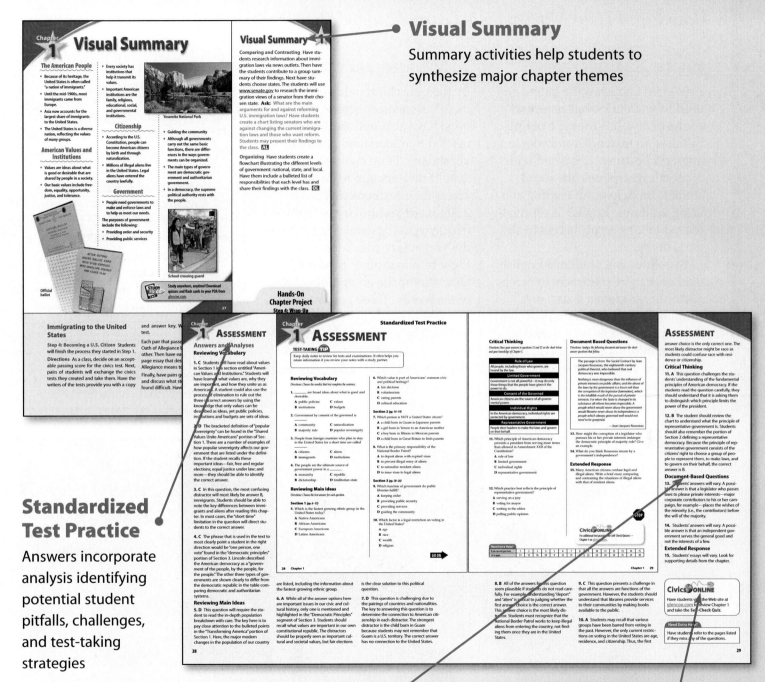

Visual Summary

Summary activities help students to synthesize major chapter themes

Standardized Test Practice

Answers incorporate analysis identifying potential student pitfalls, challenges, and test-taking strategies

Document-Based Questions

Extends answers and analysis through document and graphic assessment

Civics Online

Provides additional assessment opportunities

Academic Vocabulary

How Can I Help My Students Learn Academic Vocabulary?

What Is Academic English?

Academic English is the language used in academics, business, and courts of law. It is the type of English used in textbooks and contains linguistic features associated with academic disciplines like social studies. Proficiency in reading and using academic English is especially related to long-term success in all parts of life.

By reinforcing academic English, teachers can help learners to access authentic, academic texts—not simplified texts that dummy down the content. In this way, they can provide information that will help build their students' background knowledge rapidly.

What Is Academic Vocabulary?

By the time children have completed elementary school, they must have acquired the knowledge needed to understand academic vocabulary. How many words should they acquire to be able to access their textbooks? A basic 2,000-word vocabulary of high-frequency words makes up 87% of the vocabulary of academic texts. Eight hundred other academic words comprise an additional 8% of the words. Three percent of the remaining words are technical words. The remaining 2% are low-frequency words. There may be as many as 123,000 low-frequency words in academic texts.

Why Should Students Learn Academic Vocabulary?

English learners who have a basic 2,000-word vocabulary are ready to acquire most general words found in their texts.

Knowledge of academic words and of general words can significantly boost student's comprehension level of academic texts. Students who learn and practice these words before they graduate from high school are likely to master academic material with more confidence and speed. They waste less time and effort in guessing words or consulting dictionaries than those who only know the basic 2,000 words that characterize general conversation.

Superstudio/Getty Images

How Do I Include Academic Vocabulary and Academic English in My Teaching?

Teachers can provide students with rich samples of academic vocabulary and help students understand and attend to the academic English of their text.

To develop academic English, learners must have already acquired basic proficiency in the grammar of everyday English.

Academic English should be taught within contexts that make sense. In terms of instruction, teaching academic English includes providing students with access to core curriculum—in this case Social Studies.

Academic English arises not only from knowledge of a linguistic code and cognition but also from social practices in which academic English is used to accomplish communicative goals. The acquisition of academic vocabulary and grammar is necessary to advance the development of academic English.

Tips for Teaching Academic Vocabulary:

✔ **Expose Students to Academic Vocabulary**
You do not need to call attention to words students are learning because they will acquire them subconsciously.

✔ **Do Not Correct Students' Mistakes When Using the Vocabulary Words**
All vocabulary understanding and spelling errors are developmental and will disappear once the student reads more.

✔ **Help Students Decode the Words Themselves** Once they learn the alphabet, they should be able to decode words. Decoding each word they don't recognize will help them more than trying to focus on sentence structure. Once they can recognize the words, they can read "authentic" texts.

✔ **Do Not Ignore the English Learner in This Process** They can learn academic vocabulary before they are completely fluent in oral English.

✔ **Helping Students Build Academic Vocabulary Leads to Broader Learning** Students who have mastered the basic academic vocabulary are ready to continue acquiring words from the rest of the groups. To help determine which words are in the 2,000-word basic group, refer to *West's General Service List of English Words*, 1953. The list is designed to serve as a guide for teachers and as a checklist and goal list for students. For additional information about the list, visit:

http://jbauman.com/aboutgsl.html

Guidelines for Teaching Academic Vocabulary

1. Direct and planned instruction	4. Practice
2. Models—that have increasingly difficult language	5. Motivation
3. Attention to form—pointing out linguistic features of words	6. Instructional feedback
	7. Assessment—on a regular basis

Classroom Activity

Writing About Modern America

Give students a brief writing assignment. Ask them to write a short essay about one of the topics listed below in the left column. Have students use as many of the academic vocabulary words in the right column as they can in their essay. When completed, ask student volunteers to share their writing. Note what academic vocabulary words they use.

Topic	Academic Vocabulary
The challenges of reducing poverty in America	sufficient
	minimum
	medical
	income
Recent technological advances	innovate
	technology
	media
	potential
	data
	transmit

Meeting the Diverse Needs of Our Students

by Douglas Fisher, Ph.D.

Today's classroom contains students from a variety of backgrounds with a variety of learning styles, strengths, and challenges. As teachers we are facing the challenge of helping students reach their educational potential. With careful planning, you can address the needs of all students in the social studies classroom. The basis for this planning is universal access. When classrooms are planned with universal access in mind, fewer students require specific accommodations.

What Is a Universal Access Design for Learning?

Universal design was first conceived in architectural studies when business people, engineers, and architects began making considerations for physical access to buildings. The idea was to plan the environment in advance to ensure that everyone had access. As a result, the environment would not have to be changed later for people with physical disabilities, people pushing strollers, workers who had injuries, or others for whom the environment would be difficult to negotiate. The Center for Universal Design at www.design.ncsu.edu/cud defines Universal Design as:

The design of products and environments to be usable by all people, to the greatest extent possible, without the need for adaptation or specialized design.

Universal Design and Access in Education

Researchers, teachers, and parents in education have expanded the development of built-in adaptations and inclusive accommodations from architectural space to the educational experience, especially in the area of curriculum.

In 1998, the National Center to Improve the Tools of Educators (NCITE),

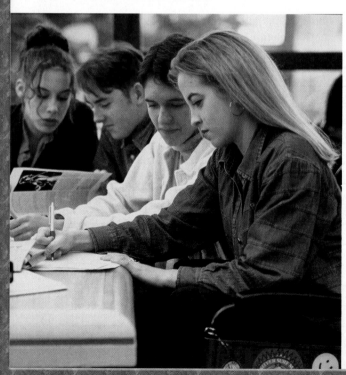

with the partnership of the Center for Applied Special Technology (CAST), proposed an expanded definition of universal design focused on education: *In terms of learning, universal design means the design of instructional materials and activities that allows the learning goals to be achievable by individuals with wide differences in their abilities to see, hear, speak, move, read, write, understand English, attend, organize, engage, and remember.*

How Does Universal Design Work in Education?

Universal design and access, as they apply to education and schooling, suggest the following:

✔ **Inclusive Classroom Participation** Curriculum should be designed with all students and their needs in mind. The Glencoe/McGraw-Hill social studies texts and materials were designed with a wide range of students in mind. For example, understanding that English learners and students who struggle with reading would be using this textbook, vocabulary is specifically taught and reinforced. Similarly, the teacher-support materials provide multiple instructional points to be used depending on the needs of the students in the class. Further, the text is written such that main ideas are identified for all learners. Activating prior knowledge is also taken into consideration

by the text. Connections between what students know and think about are made within the text.

✔ **Maximum Text Readability** In universally designed classrooms that provide access for all students, texts use direct language, clear noun-verb agreements, and clear construct-based wording. In addition to these factors, the Glencoe social studies text uses embedded definitions for difficult terms, provides for specific instruction in reading skills, uses a number of visual representations, and includes note-taking guides.

✔ **Adaptable and Accommodating** The content in this textbook can be easily translated, read aloud, or otherwise changed to meet the needs of students in the classroom. The section and end-of-chapter assessments provide students with multiple ways of demonstrating their content knowledge while also ensuring that they have practice with thinking in terms of multiple-choice questions. Critical thinking and analysis skills are also practiced.

How Is Differentiated Instruction the Key to Universal Access?

To differentiate instruction, teachers must acknowledge student differences in background knowledge and current reading, writing, and English language skills. They must also consider student learning styles and preferences, interests, and needs, and react accordingly. There are a number of general guidelines for differentiating instruction in the classroom to reach all students, including:

✔ **Link Assessment With Instruction** Assessments should occur before, during, and after instruction to ensure that the curriculum is aligned with what students do and do not know. Using assessments in this way allows you to plan instruction for whole groups, small groups, and individual students. Backward planning, where you establish the assessment before you begin instruction, is also important.

✔ **Clarify Key Concepts and Generalizations** Students need to know what is essential and how this information can be used in their future learning. In addition, students need to develop a sense of the **Big Ideas**—ideas that transcend time and place.

✔ **Emphasize Critical and Creative Thinking** The content, process, and products used or assigned in the classroom should require that students think about what they are learning. While some students may require support, additional motivation, varied tasks, materials, or equipment, the overall focus on critical and creative thinking allows for all students to participate in the lesson.

✔ **Include Teacher- and Student-Selected Tasks** A differentiated classroom includes both teacher- and student-selected activities and tasks. At some points in the lesson or day, the teacher must provide instruction and assign learning activities. In other parts of the lesson, students should be provided choices in how they engage with the content. This balance increases motivation, engagement, and learning.

How Do I Support Individual Students?

The vast majority of students will thrive in a classroom based on universal access and differentiated instruction. However, wise teachers recognize that no single option will work for all students and that there may be students who require unique systems of support to be successful.

Classroom Activity

Display a map of imperialism in Africa around 1914. Discuss with students the map's general information and have them list each country under the European power that controlled it.

To differentiate this activity:

- Have students imagine they are living in the early 1900s. Have them write a letter to a British newspaper about colonial rule in Africa.
- Have students record the number of African countries under European rule. Have them take the data and create a bar graph that shows which European powers were the most active colonizers at the time.
- Have students compose a song or poem about European rule in Africa, from an African's point of view.
- Have students choose a country of modern Africa to research. Have them write a three-page paper discussing how that country was affected by colonialism and how it has changed since the days of European rule.

Tips For Instruction

The following tips for instruction can support your efforts to help all students reach their maximum potential.

✔ Survey students to discover their individual differences. Use interest inventories of their unique talents so you can encourage contributions in the classroom.

✔ Be a model for respecting others. The student with learning differences is especially sensitive to correction and criticism, particularly when it comes from a teacher.

✔ Expand opportunities for success. Provide a variety of instructional activities that reinforce skills and concepts.

✔ Establish measurable objectives and decide how you can best help students who meet them.

✔ Celebrate successes and make note of and praise "work in progress."

✔ Keep it simple. Avoid overwhelming students with too many goals at one time.

✔ Assign cooperative group projects that challenge all students to contribute to solving a problem or creating a product.

How Do I Reach Students With Learning Disabilities?

✔ Provide support and structure. Clearly specify rules, assignments, and responsibilities.

✔ Practice skills frequently. Use games and drills to help maintain student interest.

✔ Incorporate many modalities into the learning process. Provide opportunities to say, hear, write, read, and act out important concepts and information.

✔ Link new skills and concepts to those already mastered.

✔ If possible, allow students to record answers on audiotape.

✔ Allow extra time to complete assessments and assignments.

✔ Let students demonstrate proficiency with alternative presentations, including oral reports, role plays, art projects, and musical presentations.

✔ Provide outlines, notes, or tape recordings of lecture material.

✔ Pair students with helpers, and provide class time for interaction.

How Do I Reach Students With Behavioral Challenges?

✔ Provide a structured environment with clear-cut schedules, rules, seat assignments, and safety procedures.

✔ Reinforce appropriate behavior and model it for students.

✔ Cue distracted students back to the task through verbal signals and teacher proximity.

Comstock/CORBIS

How Do I Reach Students With Physical Challenges?

✔ Set goals that can be achieved in the short term. Work for long-term improvement in the big areas.

✔ Openly discuss with the student any uncertainties you have about when to offer aid.

✔ Ask parents or therapists and students what special devices or procedures are needed and whether any special safety precautions need to be taken.

✔ Welcome students with physical challenges into all activities, including field trips, special events, and projects.

✔ Provide information to assist class members and adults in their understanding of support needed.

How Do I Reach Students with Visual Impairments?

✔ Facilitate independence. Modify assignments as needed.

✔ Teach classmates how and when to serve as visual guides.

✔ Limit unnecessary noise in the classroom if it distracts the student with visual impairments.

✔ Provide tactile models.

✔ Foster a spirit of inclusion. Describe people and events as they occur in the classroom. Remind classmates that the student with visual impairments cannot interpret gestures.

✔ Provide taped lectures and reading assignments for use outside the classroom.

✔ Team the student with a sighted peer for written work.

How Do I Reach Students With Hearing Impairments?

✔ Seat students where they can see your lip movements easily and where they can avoid any visual distractions.

✔ Avoid standing with your back to the window or light source.

✔ Use an overhead projector so you can maintain eye contact while writing information for students.

✔ Seat students where they can see speakers.

✔ Write all assignments on the board, or hand out instructions.

✔ If the student has a manual interpreter, allow both student and interpreter to select the most favorable seating arrangements.

✔ Teach students to look directly at each other when they speak.

How Do I Reach English Learners?

✔ Remember, students' ability to speak English does not reflect their academic abilities.

✔ Try to incorporate the students' cultural experience into your instruction. The help of a bilingual aide may be effective.

✔ Avoid any references in your instruction that could be construed as cultural stereotypes.

✔ Preteach important vocabulary and concepts.

✔ Encourage students to preview text before they begin reading, noting headings.

✔ Remind students not to ignore graphic organizers, photographs, and maps since there is much information in these visuals.

✔ Use memorabelia and photographs to build background knowledge and understanding. An example of this would be foreign currency or a raw cotton ball to reinforce its importance in history.

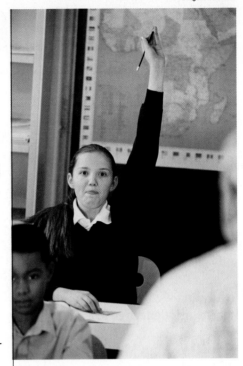

How Do I Reach Gifted Students?

✔ Make arrangements for students to take selected subjects early and to work on independent projects.

✔ Ask "what if" questions to develop high-level thinking skills. Establish an environment safe for risk taking in your classroom.

✔ Emphasize concepts, theories, ideas, relationships, and generalizations about the content.

✔ Promote interest in the past by inviting students to make connections to the present.

✔ Let students express themselves in alternate ways such as creative writing, acting, debates, simulations, drawing, or music.

✔ Provide students with a catalog of helpful resources, listing such things as agencies that provide free and inexpensive materials, appropriate community services and programs, and community experts who might be called upon to speak to your students.

✔ Assign extension projects that allow students to solve real-life problems related to their communities.

Douglas Fisher is a professor at San Diego State University, San Diego, CA.

Classroom Activity

Students respond eagerly to a subject when they can relate it to their own experiences. With the growing number of students who come from other world regions, explaining geography through a global theme (such as volcanoes) can give them a worldwide as well as a regional perspective. To develop this awareness, display a large world map. Have students use the library or the Internet to research the latitude and longitude of 15 major volcanoes around the world. Ask them to mark these locations on the map and answer the following questions:

- What patterns do you see in volcanic activity?
- What causes volcanic activity?
- Where in the world are volcanoes most active?

As a follow-up, suggest students go to http://volcano.und.nodak.edu/vwdocs/kids/legends.html to find legends about the origins of some of the world's volcanoes. Encourage students to share what they find with the class.

Backward Mapping

How Can My Instruction Help Students Succeed in a Standards-Based System?

by Emily M. Schell, Ed.D.

Content standards articulate what students should know and be able to do in every social studies classroom. Effective instructional planning based in the standards and maximizing available resources is essential for meaningful teaching and learning of social studies. Planning instruction with educational goals in mind makes for the most effective teaching.

How Do I Map My Curriculum?

Mapping the curriculum from beginning to end, and from the end to the beginning—backward mapping—makes for solid instruction. Mapping out the curriculum allows teachers to achieve several goals. These goals include a better understanding of the standards and content-specific objectives, organization and pacing of the curriculum, and focused assessment related to specific goals and objectives.

✔ **Begin the Process of Curriculum Mapping** To begin, teachers analyze the body of content standards for one grade level. They then compare and contrast these standards to additional sources of information that support effective teaching and learning at that grade level and in that subject area. This process works best with same-grade colleagues who bring varying perspectives and expertise to teaching this subject. As a result of this collaboration, strengths and weaknesses of the standards become apparent. Teachers will have a better understanding of

the standards and identify concerns and questions for follow-up while mapping.

✔ **Analyze the Organization of the Standards-Based Content** Most social studies teachers agree with researchers that history is best taught in chronological order. However, some grade-level standards either do not or cannot present the content in chronological order. Rich discussions about themes and concepts tend to emerge, and teachers identify meaningful methods for presenting complex and overlapping information. In this way students will see the connections that transcend chronology.

✔ **Identify the Content and Order of Teaching** A plan is developed to present certain content first, then second, then third and so on. Folding in content that is either missing from the standards or essential in building background knowledge with students enters the curriculum map as well. Outside resources brought into the classroom are good supplements.

✔ **Separate Overlapping Units** Identify areas of instruction for the topics, themes, big ideas, or concepts. It is at this stage that backward planning is introduced for the development of instructional units, which will support the grade-level curriculum map. The instruction must support the planned assessment.

✔ **Map Curriculum at Each Grade Level** Curriculum planning should be

shared among grade levels. Teachers will have a better understanding of what knowledge and skills students bring to their coursework if they take into consideration what has been learned previously.

How Do I Use Backward Mapping?

After a year-long course of study is mapped out, each unit must be further developed through backward mapping. You will start with the end in mind—knowing your curricular goals and objectives at the outset, which are often found in the content standards and articulated in the curriculum maps.

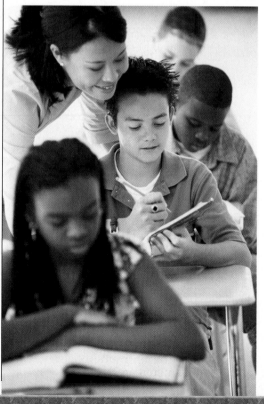

Creatas/PunchStock

Once goals have been determined, teachers develop assessments that will show progress toward those goals and objectives. In the final step of this backward mapping process, teachers determine meaningful teaching and learning strategies and identify useful resources that support the assessment.

To use backward mapping in developing your units of instruction, consider the following steps:

Step One: Know Your Targets

First, identify exactly what students must know and do in this unit. Analyze content standards and any other resources that support curricular goals and objectives for this unit. As you plan, ask yourself:

✔ What do I want my students to know as a result of this unit?
✔ What skills will students develop during the course of this unit?
✔ How do I describe these goals clearly and concisely to my students so they understand where we should be at the end of this unit?
✔ What essential knowledge will students need to access to make sense of this information?
✔ Do my instructional goals align with strategies identified in the curriculum map?
✔ Have I introduced any Big Ideas that are pertinent to this content?

Step Two: Identify and Develop Assessments

✔ Second, consider the multiple forms of formal and informal assessments that will help you determine to what degree each student has achieved the stated goals and objectives seen in Step One. Some assessments are embedded throughout the instructional unit, while others come at the end of the unit. Some assessments are performance-based, while others are not. Some are authentic applications of information and skills, while others require the formal recall of information. Ask yourself:

✔ What do I want to know and see from each student?
✔ What are the best methods for students to demonstrate what they know and can do based on the goals and objectives?
✔ How many assessments do I need to determine what students know and can do?
✔ How will I balance informal and formal assessments?
✔ How will I assess students with diverse learning styles, skills, and abilities?
✔ How can I prepare and support students?
✔ How will these assessments promote student progress in social studies?
✔ At what time(s) during the unit will I administer these assessments?

Step Three: Develop Meaningful Instruction

After the assessments for the unit have been determined, consider the meaningful and effective teaching strategies that will support learning and student achievement on assessments. While developing lesson plans for instruction, ask yourself:

✔ How will students learn what they are expected to know?
✔ How will I engage students in the studies of this unit?
✔ In what ways might students relate or connect to this information?
✔ What research-based strategies will be most effective with my students and in these studies?
✔ How will I differentiate my instruction to meet the diverse needs of my students?
✔ How will I scaffold or provide access to the curriculum for my English learners?
✔ What vocabulary requires attention in this unit?
✔ How much time will I have to effectively teach this unit?
✔ How will I use the textbook and other resources to support the goals and objectives for this unit?
✔ What lessons will I develop?
✔ In what sequence will I teach these lessons during this unit?
✔ How will these lessons support the assessments from Step Two?

Step Four: Locate and Manage Resources

Effective teaching and learning of social studies requires the use of multiple forms of text and varied resources. Consider what you have available in your classroom, including your textbook, and identify resources you will add in order to teach this unit successfully. Ask yourself:

✔ What parts of the textbook are required for the lessons determined in Step Three?
✔ What ancillary materials are needed for the lessons in this unit?
✔ What Web sites will I recommend to students to support these lessons?
✔ Do I need to contact guest speakers or obtain outside resources?
✔ What literature resources are available to support this unit?

Emily Schell is Visiting Professor, San Diego State University; and Social Studies Education Director, SDSU City Heights Educational Collaborative, San Diego, CA

Test-Taking Strategies

How Can I Help My Students Succeed on Tests?

It's not enough for students to learn social studies facts and concepts—they must be able to show what they know in a variety of test-taking situations.

How Can I Help My Students Do Well on Objective Tests?

Objective tests may include multiple choice, true/false, and matching questions. Applying the following strategies can help students do their best on objective tests.

Multiple-Choice Questions

✔ Students should read the directions carefully to learn what answer the test requires—the best answer or the right answer. This is especially important when answer choices include "all of the above" or "none of the above."

✔ Advise students to watch for negative words in the questions, such as not, except, unless, never, and so forth. If the question contains a negative, the correct answer choice is the one that does not fit.

✔ Students should try to mentally answer the question before reading the answer choices.

✔ Students should read all the answer choices and cross out those that are obviously wrong. Then they should choose an answer from those that remain.

True/False Questions

✔ It is important that students read the entire question before answering. For an answer to be true, the entire statement must be true. If one part of a statement is false, the answer should be marked False.

✔ Remind students to watch for words like all, never, every, and always. Statements containing these words are often false.

Matching Questions

✔ Students should read through both lists before they mark any answers.

✔ Unless an answer can be used more than once, students should cross out each choice as they use it.

✔ Using what they know about grammar can help students find the right answer. For instance, when matching a word with its definition, the definition is often the same part of speech (noun, verb, adjective, and so forth) as the word.

How Can I Help My Students Do Well on Essay Tests?

Essay tests require students to provide thorough and well-organized written responses, in addition to telling what they know. Help students use the following strategies on essay tests.

✔ **Analyze** To analyze means to systematically and critically examine all parts of an issue or event.

✔ **Classify or Categorize** To classify or categorize means to put people, things, or ideas into groups, based on a common set of characteristics.

✔ **Compare and Contrast** To compare is to show how things are similar, or alike. To contrast is to show how things are different.

✔ **Describe** To describe means to present a sketch or impression. Rich details, especially details that appeal to the senses, flesh out a description.

✔ **Discuss** To discuss means to systematically write about all sides of an issue or event.

✔ **Evaluate** To evaluate means to make a judgment and support it with evidence.

✔ **Explain** To explain means to clarify or make plain.

✔ **Illustrate** To illustrate means to provide examples or to show with a picture or other graphic.

✔ **Infer** To infer means to read between the lines or to use knowledge and experience to draw conclusions, make a generalization, or form a prediction.

✔ **Justify** To justify means to prove or to support a position with specific facts and reasons.

✔ **Predict** To predict means to tell what will happen in the future, based on an understanding of prior events and behaviors.

✔ **State** To state means to briefly and concisely present information.

✔ **Summarize** To summarize means to give a brief overview of the main points of an issue or event.

✔ **Trace** To trace means to present the steps or stages in a process or event in sequential or chronological order.

Read the Question

The key to writing successful essay responses lies in reading and interpreting questions correctly. Teach

students to identify and underline key words in the questions, and to use these words to guide them in understanding what the question asks. Help students understand the meaning of some of the most common key words, listed in the chart on the previous page.

Plan and Write the Essay

After students understand the question, they should follow the writing process to develop their answer. Encourage students to follow the steps below to plan and write their essays.

1. **Map out an answer.** Make lists, webs, or an outline to plan the response.

↓

2. **Decide on an order** in which to present the main points.

↓

3. **Write an opening statement** that directly responds to the essay question.

↓

4. **Write the essay.** Expand on the opening statement. Support key points with specific facts, details, and reasons.

↓

5. **Write a closing statement** that brings the main points together.

↓

6. **Proofread** to check for spelling, grammar, and punctuation.

How Can I Help My Students Prepare for Standardized Tests?

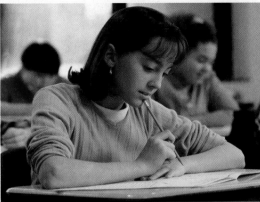

Students can follow the steps below to prepare for standardized assessments they are required to take.

✔ **Read About the Test** Students can familiarize themselves with the format of the test, the types of questions that will be asked, and the amount of time they will have to complete the test. Emphasize that it is very important for students to budget their time during test-taking.

✔ **Review the Content** Consistent study throughout the school year will help students build social studies knowledge and understanding. If there are specific objectives or standards that are tested on the exam, help students review these facts or skills to be sure they are proficient.

✔ **Practice** Provide practice, ideally with real released tests, to build students' familiarity with the content, format, and timing of the real exam. Students should practice all the types of questions they will encounter on the test—multiple choice, short answer, true or false, and extended response.

✔ **Pace** Students should pace themselves differently depending on how the test is administered. If the test is timed, students should not allow themselves to become stuck on any one question. As students practice, they should try to increase the number of questions they can answer correctly.

Classroom Activity

Below is an example of an activity to incorporate assessment review in the classroom. Frequently reviewing graded tests is a great way for students to assess their test-taking skills. It also gives teachers the opportunity to teach test-taking strategies and review content. As the class rereads each test question, guide students to think logically about their answer choices. Show students how to:

1. Read each question carefully to determine its meaning.
2. Look for key words in the question to support their answers.
3. Recognize synonyms in the answer choices that may match phrases in the question.
4. Narrow down answer choices by eliminating ones that don't make sense.
5. Anticipate the answer before looking at the answer choices.
6. Circle questions of which they are unsure and go back to them later. Sometimes a clue will be found in another question on the test.

Unit 1 Planning Guide

	Unit 1	Chapter 1	Chapter 2	Chapter 3	Chapter 4	Chapter 5
Day 1	Unit Opener, Reading Social Studies	Chapter Opener, Section 1	Chapter Opener, Section 1	Chapter Opener, Section 1	Chapter Opener, Section 1, Issues to Debate	Chapter Opener, Section 1, Financial Literacy
Day 2		Section 2	Section 2	Section 2	Section 2	Section 2, Chapter Review
Day 3		Section 3, Chapter Review, and Visual Summary	Section 3	Section 3	Landmark Supreme Court Case Studies	Chapter Assessment
Day 4		Chapter Assessment	Section 4	Section 4	Section 3, Financial Literacy	TIME Reports
Day 5			Visual Summary, Chapter Review	Chapter Review, Visual Summary	Section 4, Chapter Review, Visual Summary	Analyzing Primary Sources
Day 6			Chapter Assessment	Chapter Assessment	Chapter Assessment	
Day 7			The Declaration of Independence	Constitution of the United States		
Day 8			The Declaration of Independence	Constitution of the United States		
Day 9				Constitution of the United States		
Day 10				Constitution of the United States		

UNIT PACING CHART

Teacher to Teacher

Jan Rabin, Northside High School, Roanoke, Virginia

Government During the Revolution The objective of this activity is to describe the shortcomings and inadequacies of the Articles of Confederation. Students are to brainstorm and list the difficulties that the Continental Army encountered while fighting the war. The class can be divided into groups, with each group assigned two problems that George Washington and the troops encountered. Because the Articles of Confederation was the only national government available during this time, students are to attempt to solve each of the difficulties within the framework of the Articles. The group will examine the areas of the Articles that could be used to solve each problem, as well as the difficulties caused for the soldiers. Each group will be asked to share their conclusions at the end of the study, as well as their conclusion concerning the effectiveness of the Articles of Confederation in solving the wartime problems.

Author Note

Dear Social Studies Teacher:

During a recent trip to Washington, D. C., I visited the Charters of Freedom exhibit at the National Archives. I was filled with pride and awe while looking at the original copies of the Constitution and Bill of Rights, and my commitment to teach young Americans about these documents was renewed and strengthened.

We Americans are justly proud of our 1787 Constitution and 1791 Bill of Rights, which constitute the world's oldest, continuously in use, written frame of government. Our constitutional government has stood the test of time, even though based on two ideas in perpetual tension, majority rule and minority rights. President Thomas Jefferson recognized this constitutional paradox in his First Inaugural Address, "All, too, will bear in mind this sacred principle, that though the will of the majority is in all cases to prevail, that will to be rightful must be reasonable; that the minority possess their equal rights, which equal law must protect and to violate would be oppression."

Civic educators, like you and me, must remember that our Constitution will yield justice only if we balance and blend majority rule with minority rights in our responses to ongoing public issues. At what point should majority rule be limited by law in order to protect constitutionally guaranteed minority rights? And conversely, at what point should certain rights of minorities be constitutionally limited in favor of the majority will?

Public issues raised by the ongoing tensions between constitutionally based majority rule and the constitutionally guaranteed rights of individuals in the minority should be confronted openly, fairly, critically, and civilly in the social studies classroom. I urge you to engage your students in this kind of learning experience to prepare them for the continuing challenges of citizenship in our democratic republic.

John J. Patrick

Author

Unit Objectives

After studying this unit, students will be able to:

- Explain the role of government in everyday life.
- Understand the history of our country's government.
- Describe the principles in the Constitution.
- Discuss the freedoms guaranteed by the Bill of Rights.
- Know the difference between the duties and responsibilities of citizens.

Did You Know?

Every ten years, the United States government conducts the census, or the official counting of the population. The results of the first census in 1790 showed the U.S. population at 3.9 million. On October 17, 2006, the U.S. population officially reached the 300-million mark.

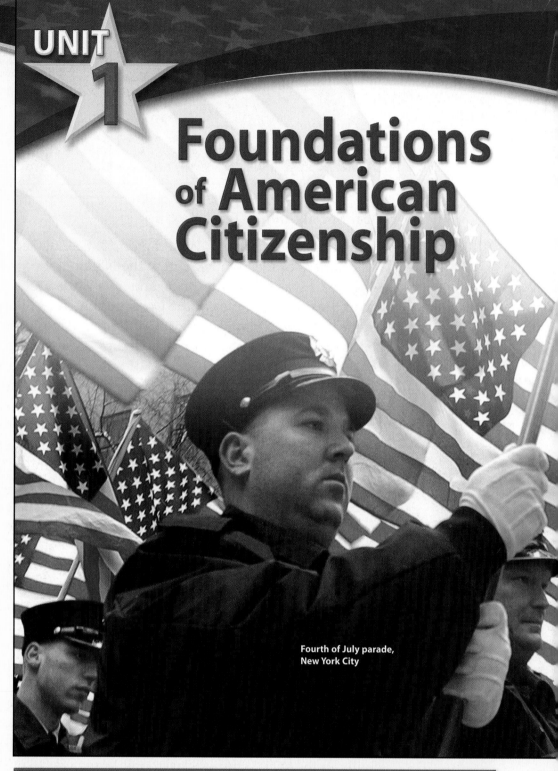

UNIT ★ 1

Foundations of American Citizenship

Fourth of July parade, New York City

Activity: Launching the Unit

Foundations of American Citizenship
Ask: What is a citizen? *(A citizen is literally a person who owes loyalty to and is entitled to the protection of a state, nation, and/or government. A citizen of the United States is guaranteed rights through the Constitution and its amendments. There are certain legal duties required of citizens, as well as civic obligations that citizens may engage in to enrich their communities.)* Students may have heard the term "citizen" before but may not know all of the rights and roles involved in citizenship. Have your students make a list of the characteristics they believe constitute citizenship. After they have completed the unit, have them review their lists and discuss what aspects they may have overlooked. **OL**

CITIZENSHIP Be an Active Citizen

Find out the purposes of government firsthand. Contact a government leader, such as a state representative, a city council member, or a school board member, and ask how the government he or she represents serves American citizens.

1

Be an Active Citizen

CITIZENSHIP Do your students know who represents them in Congress? Have your students do research at www.senate.gov and www.house.gov to discover who their senators and representatives are. These Web sites also contain links to the home page of the members of Congress. Have students find information on the party affiliations, biographical history, and bills introduced or fought for by each member of Congress.

Online Current Events Update

Visit Glencoe's *Online Current Events Update* at www.glencoe.com to find news reports, features, maps, graphs, and photos of current events that shape our lives. Students can also make connections between historical events and current events by using the interactive time line.

More About the Photo

Today's Fourth of July celebrations have roots in the celebrations of colonial times. The first organized Fourth of July celebration was in Philadelphia in 1777. It featured food, music, and a military parade, complete with cannon and other artillery fire to celebrate the event. There was even a small fireworks display at night! The festivities have become more elaborate today. Corporate giant Macy's has sponsored the New York City 4th of July Parade for over 30 years. A recent Independence Day fireworks display featured 30,000 fireworks, all coordinated via computer to the accompanying music.

Why Making Connections Is Important

When readers connect the text, they relate the information to events in their lives or to other material they have read. By making connections, students can improve comprehension, retain more information, and enjoy reading. When reading textbooks, students might connect to the text by relating the material to prior knowledge or to events occurring in the news rather than to personal experience. Regardless, whenever students make a real connection to the text, they will appreciate that events that happened hundreds of years ago still have meaning in the present.

Learn It!

Write the following sentence on the board: "The Anti-Federalists argued that the new Constitution would take away the liberties Americans had fought to win from Great Britain." Ask students if this sentence reminds them of any current news stories. Explain to students that when they can relate foreign ideas to something they already know about, they can more easily understand the new idea. Tell students that by connecting text with current affairs or personal experience, the text takes on meaning. **OL**

UNIT 1 Reading Social Studies

Making Connections

① Learn It!

As a reader, you are constantly making connections between what you are reading and what you already know. The more connections you make, the better you are able to comprehend. You may make connections between the text and an experience you have had in your life (text-to-self), the text and another text (text-to-text), or the text and something that happened in school, your community, or the world (text-to-world).

- Read the paragraph below.
- Which statements in the paragraph create a connection in your mind?
- Think about any connections related to the text, such as the examples given below.

> Conflicts are unavoidable when people live together in a community. Governments make laws to prevent conflicts and to settle those conflicts that do arise.
>
> —*from page 22*

Graphic Organizer

Statement from text	Connection
Conflicts are unavoidable when people live together in a community.	Our neighbors got into a big argument once about loud music.
Governments make laws to prevent conflicts.	My uncle once went to court to settle a conflict he had with a company.

Reading Tip
Be an active reader by seeking connections through the people, places, things or events that make up your own background experiences.

Reading Strategy | Taking Notes

Making Connections One way students can connect with the text is to ask questions about the people or events they are reading about. For example, a reader might ask: "Have I ever felt this way?" "What would I do if I were in this situation?" "What part of this experience can I relate to?" "Do I know anyone who had a similar experience?" "Didn't I hear something about this on the news?" As students read, encourage them to write notes that tie in personal experience to the text. Ask students to choose a paragraph from one of the sections in Chapter 1 and see if they can write a question that connects with the text. **OL**

② Practice It!

Read the following paragraph from this unit.

- Draw a graphic organizer like the one shown below.
- In the left-hand column, write at least three statements from the paragraph with which you can make a connection. You do not need to copy the entire sentence.
- In the right-hand column, write your connections beside each statement.

> Throughout our nation's history, people still in their teens have bravely fought for our country. By law, however, they were not old enough to vote for the leaders who sent them into battle. Although the Constitution did not specify, or mention, a minimum age for voters, most states set the minimum at 21.
>
> That standard finally changed in 1971, a year when many young Americans were fighting in the Vietnam War.
>
> *—from page 137*

Statement from text	Connection

③ Apply It!

Your mind will be busy making connections as you read the chapters in this unit. At the end of each chapter, create a graphic organizer such as the one above to help you tie your connections to an important concept from the chapter. Use your organizer to help you remember important facts as you study for tests.

Read to Write Activity

Read the section titled *New Taxes and a Tea Party* in Chapter 2, Section 4, page 53. As you read, jot down any statement with which you make a connection. Write a paragraph about one connection you made and how it relates to the text.

---

② Practice It!

Statement from Text:

1. Throughout our nation's history, people still in their teens have bravely fought for our country.
2. By law, however, they were not old enough to vote for the leaders who sent them into battle.
3. Although the Constitution did not specify a minimum age for voters, most states set the minimum at 21.
4. The standard finally changed in 1971, a year when many young Americans were fighting in the Vietnam War.

Connection: *(Answers will vary.)*

1. Students may have a relative or friend who is in the military, or perhaps a parent joined at a young age.
2. Students may know of people who have voted for a leader based on the politicians' view of war.
3. Students may comment that they have read that not many young people vote.
4. Students may know something about Vietnam or someone who fought there.

Ask students how they would feel in this situation. How do their feelings compare with those who wanted to change the law? **OL**

③ Apply It!

Bring to class a copy of "I Have a Dream" by Martin Luther King, Jr. First, have students create a list of things they know about the text. As they read, have them take notes about other similar texts as well as similar personal experiences. After they have written their notes, have volunteers discuss the process. **OL**

📖 Reading Strategy   Read to Write

Keeping a Journal When making connections with a text, students do not always have to relate the text to personal experience. The connection can be from information they are familiar with or from what others think about an idea. Taxes may not be important to students right now, but they hear parents and others talk about taxes. Students may also connect to smaller concepts, such as a boycotting a product that is expensive or being subjected to "Intolerable Acts."

Have students keep a journal of connections they make to major ideas in Chapters 1–3. After reading Unit 1, ask students to evaluate whether these journals improved their comprehension and interest in reading. **AL**

Chapter Planning Guide

1

Levels					Resources	Chapter Opener	Section 1	Section 2	Section 3	Chapter Assessment
BL	OL	AL	ELL							
					FOCUS					
BL	OL	AL	ELL	🖨	Daily Focus Skills Transparencies		1–1	1–2	1–3	
					TEACH					
BL	OL		ELL	📁	Reading Essentials and Note-Taking Guide*		p. 1	p. 4	p. 7	
	OL	AL		📁	Citizenship/Decision-Making Activity, URB		p. 3	p. 3	p. 3	
BL	OL		ELL	📁	Reading Skills Activity, URB			p. 7		
BL	OL	AL	ELL	📁	Speaking and Listening Skills Activity, URB			p. 9		
BL	OL	AL	ELL	📁	Content Vocabulary Activity, URB*		p. 21	p. 21	p. 21	
BL	OL	AL	ELL	📁	Academic Vocabulary Activity, URB		p. 23	p. 23	p. 23	
	OL			📁	Biography Activity, URB		p. 25			
BL	OL	AL	ELL	📁	Writing Skills Activity, URB		p. 29	p. 29	p. 27	
	OL	AL		📁	Critical Thinking Skills Activity, URB		p. 31			
BL	OL	AL	ELL	📁	Chart, Graph, and Map Skills Activity, URB		p. 33			
BL	OL	AL	ELL	📁	Differentiated Instruction, URB		p. 35	p. 35		
BL	OL	AL	ELL	📁	School-to-Home Connection Activity, URB*		p. 37	p. 37	p. 37	
BL	OL		ELL	📁	Guided Reading Activities, URB*		p. 41	p. 42	p. 43	
BL	OL	AL	ELL	📁	Writer's Guidebook	✓	✓	✓	✓	✓
	OL	AL		💿	Primary Source Document Library	✓	✓	✓	✓	✓
BL	OL	AL	ELL	💿	Daily Lecture & Discussion Notes (in Pres. Plus)		✓	✓	✓	✓
BL	OL	AL	ELL	💿	StudentWorks™ Plus		✓	✓	✓	✓

Note: Please refer to the *Unit 1 Resource Book* for this chapter's URB materials.

* Also available in Spanish

Teacher Works **Plus**
All-In-One Planner and Resource Center

- Interactive Lesson Planner
- Interactive Teacher Edition
- Fully editable blackline masters
- Section Spotlight Videos Launch

- Differentiated Lesson Plans
- Printable reports of daily assignments
- Standards Tracking System

Levels BL OL AL ELL		Resources	Chapter Opener	Section 1	Section 2	Section 3	Chapter Assessment
		TEACH (continued)					
BL OL AL ELL	💿	Section Spotlight Videos		✓	✓	✓	
BL OL AL ELL	🖨	TIME Interpreting Political Cartoons Transp.				Ch. 3	
BL OL AL ELL	🖨	Writing Process Transparencies	✓	✓	✓	✓	✓
Teacher Resources	📁	Building Academic Vocabulary	✓	✓	✓	✓	✓
	📁	Strategies for Success	✓	✓	✓	✓	✓
	📁	Teacher's Guide to Differentiated Instruction	✓	✓	✓	✓	✓
	💿	Graphing Tool	✓	✓	✓	✓	✓
	💿	Presentation Plus! with MindJogger CheckPoint	✓	✓	✓	✓	✓
		ASSESS					
BL OL AL ELL	📁	Quizzes and Tests*		p. 3	p. 4	p. 5	p. 6
BL OL AL ELL	📁	Authentic Assessment with Rubrics		p. 5			
BL OL AL ELL	📁	Standardized Test Practice		p. 1	p. 1	p. 1	p. 1
BL OL AL ELL	💿	*ExamView® Assessment Suite* CD-ROM		1–1	1–2	1–3	Ch. 1
		CLOSE					
BL ELL	📁	Reteaching Activity, URB		p. 39	p. 39	p. 39	
BL OL ELL	📁	Reading and Study Skills Foldables™ Activity	p. 50	p. 51		p. 51	
BL OL AL ELL	🖨	Graphic Organizer Transparencies & Strategies	✓	✓	✓	✓	✓

✓ Chapter- or unit-based activities applicable to all sections in this chapter

Integrating Technology

1

Using QuickPass™

Navigating the Glencoe Web Site

What is a QuickPass™ code?

A *QuickPass™* code is a shortcut that takes students and teachers from <u>glencoe.com</u> directly to the numerous on-line resources for each chapter in this book. You can enter a QuickPass™ code at <u>glencoe.com</u> or with the McGraw-Hill Social Studies widget.

How can a QuickPass™ code help my students and me?

QuickPass™ codes are found for each chapter of the textbook on the Chapter Opener pages. QuickPass™ codes will help you and your students

- find links directly to all of Glencoe's resources for a particular chapter. QuickPass™ codes in the Student Edition go directly to student resources, while codes in the Teacher Wraparound Edition go to teacher resources. The *T* at the end of the code indicates a teacher version
- locate links to other Web sites related to the chapter's subject matter, as well as other social studies areas
- find, in state-specific books, links to state resources

Find a QuickPass™ code on the Chapter Opener pages of the textbook. Visit <u>glencoe.com</u> and enter a *QuickPass™* code to go directly to resources for each chapter.

Civics ONLINE

Visit <u>glencoe.com</u> and enter *QuickPass™* code CIV1360c1T for Chapter 1 resources.

You can easily launch a wide range of digital products from your computer's desktop with the McGraw-Hill Social Studies widget.

	Student	Teacher	Parent
Media Library			
• Student Edition Section Audio	●		●
• Spanish Audio Summaries	●		●
• Section Spotlight Videos	●	●	●
***Civics Today* Online Learning Center (Web Site)**			
• Chapter Overviews	●	●	●
• Study Central™	●	●	●
• Study-to-Go	●	●	●
• Student Web Activities	●	●	●
• In Motion Animation	●	●	●
• Self-Check Quizzes	●	●	●
• ePuzzles and Games	●	●	●
• StudentWorks™ Plus Online	●	●	●
• Vocabulary eFlashcards	●	●	●
• Web Activity Lesson Plans		●	
• Vocabulary PuzzleMaker	●	●	●
Classroom Tools			
• Multilingual Glossary	●	●	●
• Beyond the Textbook	●	●	●
• NGS MapMachine	●	●	●

GLENCOE BOOKLINK 3

Use this database to search more than 30,000 titles to create a customized reading list for your students.

- Reading lists can be organized by students' reading level, author, genre, theme, or area of interest.
- The database provides Degrees of Reading Power™ (DRP) and Lexile™ readability scores for all selections.
- A brief summary of each selection is included.

Leveled reading suggestions for this chapter:

For students at a Grade 7 reading level:
- *We Are Americans: Voices of the Immigrant Experience,* by Dorothy Hoobler and Thomas Hoobler

For students at a Grade 8 reading level:
- *Bound for America: The Story of the European Immigrants,* by Milton Meltzer

For students at a Grade 9 reading level:
- *Deported Aliens,* by Rob Staeger

For students at a Grade 10 reading level:
- *Immigration,* by Philip Brooks

For students at a Grade 11 reading level:
- *Jews in America,* by Hasia R. Diner

READING SUPPORT FROM JAMESTOWN EDUCATION

- **Timed Readings Plus in Social Studies** helps students increase their reading rate and fluency while maintaining comprehension. The 400-word passages are similar to those found on state and national assessments.

- **Reading in the Content Area: Social Studies** concentrates on six essential reading skills that help students better comprehend what they read. The book includes 75 high-interest nonfiction passages written at increasing levels of difficulty.

- **Reading Social Studies** includes strategic reading instruction and vocabulary support in Social Studies content for both ELLs and native speakers of English.

- **Content Vocabulary Workout** (Grades 6–8) accelerates reading comprehension through focused vocabulary development. Social Studies content vocabulary comes from the glossaries of Glencoe's Middle School Social Studies texts. www.jamestowneducation.com

KEY Teacher Wraparound

Use this key to help you identify the different types of prompts found in the Teacher Wraparound Edition.

R **Reading Strategies** activities help you teach reading skills and vocabulary.

C **Critical Thinking** strategies help students apply and extend what they have learned.

D **Differentiated Instruction** activities provide instruction for students learning to speak English, along with suggestions for teaching various types of learners.

S **Skill Practice** strategies help students practice historical analysis and geography skills.

W **Writing Support** activities provide writing opportunities to help students comprehend the text.

Teaching strategies and activities have been coded for ability level appropriateness.

AL Activities for students working above grade level

OL Activities for students working on grade level

BL Activities for students working below grade level

ELL Activities for English Language Learners

Focus

Why It Matters

Ask: What does "equal rights" mean to you? *(Answers may include the idea that all citizens have the right to vote, the right to own property, the right to an education, the right to run for elected office, and the right to free speech.)*

More About the Photo

Visual Literacy The Pledge of Allegiance was originally written by Francis Bellamy. Bellamy wrote the pledge for the National Public School Celebration. On October 12, 1892, the American flag was proudly displayed at every school, and 12 million students recited his words. The words have been modified three times. In 1923, the Daughters of the American Revolution revised the first line from "I pledge allegiance to *my Flag*" to "*the Flag of the United States . . .*" In 1924, the phrase "of America" was added. On Flag Day 1954, President Eisenhower approved the phrase "under God." During most naturalization ceremonies, new citizens recite the pledge.

Teach

BIG Ideas *As you begin teaching each section, use these questions and activities to help students focus on the Big Ideas.*

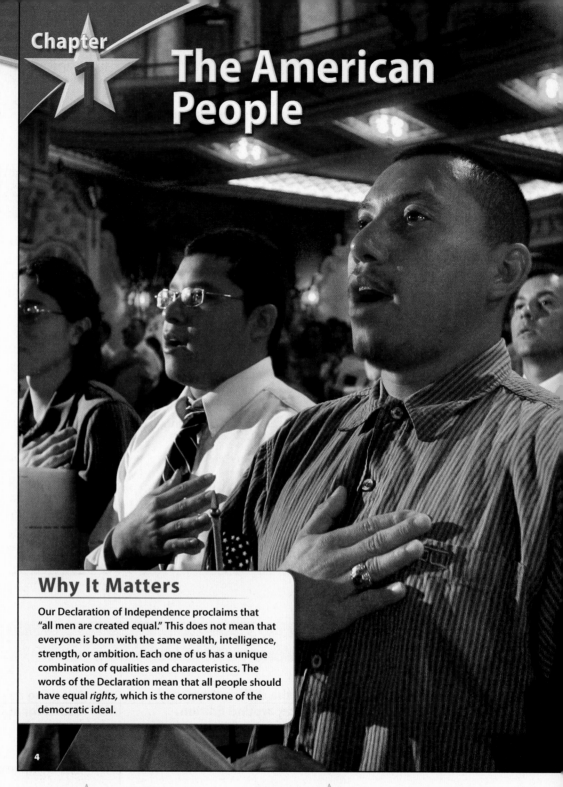

Chapter
1
The American People

Why It Matters

Our Declaration of Independence proclaims that "all men are created equal." This does not mean that everyone is born with the same wealth, intelligence, strength, or ambition. Each one of us has a unique combination of qualities and characteristics. The words of the Declaration mean that all people should have equal *rights,* which is the cornerstone of the democratic ideal.

4

Section 1

The Diversity of Americans Ask: Why do you think people from other countries migrate to the United States? *(Some come to avoid harsh governments or to gain more personal freedom and a better life.)* Point out that in Section 1, students will learn about the shared values and ideals that are universal for U.S. citizens. **OL**

Section 2

Who Are America's Citizens? Ask: How do people become American citizens? *(A person who is born in the United States is a citizen. People may also apply for citizenship and complete a naturalization process.)* Tell students that in Section 2, they will learn about immigration and naturalization. Illegal immigration, a topic that has recently come under scrutiny by the federal government, is also discussed. **OL**

Civics ONLINE
Visit glencoe.com and enter
QuickPass™ code
CIV3093c1 for
Chapter 1
resources.

Chapter Introduction
1

Chapter Audio

BIG Ideas

Section 1: The Diversity of Americans

As American citizens, we make a commitment to the nation and to the values and principles that are part of United States democracy. In addition to the common values and civic unity, the United States benefits from its rich diversity.

Section 2: Who Are America's Citizens?

Citizens possess certain rights. With citizenship, Americans also have certain responsibilities. In the United States, there are two ways to become a citizen: by birth and by a process called naturalization.

Section 3: Government and the People

People form governments to establish order, provide security, and accomplish common goals. Democratic governments perform necessary functions so citizens can live together peacefully.

Jorge and Carlos Urbina, and others, take the oath of allegiance to become American citizens

FOLDABLES™ Dinah Zike's
Study Organizer Foldables

Purpose This Foldable guides the student to understand the process of becoming a citizen, either by birth or by naturalization. The completed Foldable will use tabs to help them compare and contrast the differing processes and rights as allowed by law. **OL**

More Foldables activities for this chapter can be found in the *Dinah Zike's Reading and Study Skills Foldables* ancillary.

Civics ONLINE

Visit glencoe.com and enter *QuickPass*™ code CIV1360c1T for Chapter 1 resources, including a Chapter Overview, Study Central™, Study-to-Go, Student Web Activity, Self-Check Quiz, and other materials.

FOLDABLES™ Study Organizer

Comparing Information Study Foldable Make the following Foldable to help you compare information about citizenship and government in a democracy.

Step 1 Use one sheet of paper folded in half the long way.

Step 2 Fold in half again to create cutting lines.

Step 3 Cut the folded top sheet in half to create two tabs.

Step 4 Label the tabs as shown.

Citizenship

Birth   Naturalized

Reading and Writing As you read the chapter, note details about the processes of becoming a citizen from birth or by naturalization.

Chapter 1   5

Section 3

Government and the People Ask: What services does our government provide to its citizens? *(It creates and enforces laws; it supports services, such as schools, the postal service, and welfare; and it manages relations with foreign governments.)* Explain that in Section 3, students will learn about the role of government, including federal, state, and local functions. **OL**

Focus

Bellringer

Daily Focus Transparency 1–1

Guide to Reading

Answers to Graphic:

Migration to cities → Changes in population

Immigration → Changes in population

Increase in number of children → Changes in population

Population in South and West growing → Changes in population

Migration from South to North → Changes in population

Section Spotlight Video

To generate student interest and provide a springboard for class discussion, access the Chapter 1, Section 1 video at glencoe.com or on the video DVD.

Resource Manager

Guide to Reading

Big Idea

As American citizens, we make a commitment to the nation and to the values and principles that are part of United States democracy.

Content Vocabulary

- civics *(p. 7)*
- citizenship *(p. 7)*
- citizen *(p. 7)*
- service economy *(p. 10)*
- value *(p. 11)*
- popular sovereignty *(p. 12)*
- institution *(p. 13)*

Academic Vocabulary

- diverse *(p. 8)*
- ethnic *(p. 9)*
- principle *(p. 11)*

Reading Strategy

Identifying As you read, note on the diagram below the major changes in the population of the United States that have taken place since its beginning.

Changes in population

Section 1

The Diversity of Americans

Real World Civics Does your vote count? Enthusiastic young people like those pictured volunteered for the America Votes National Day of Action. Both political parties worked to register as many citizens as possible to vote, especially minorities and immigrants who might not feel that their voice matters. Why? When you do not vote, you let others speak for you.

▼ **Stacey Brayboy and Alvin Anderson prepare to canvass a neighborhood in Miami, Florida.**

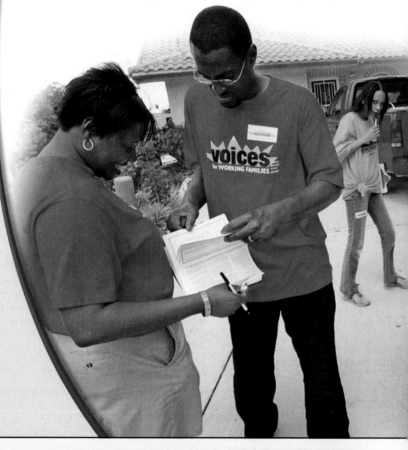

R Reading Strategies	**C** Critical Thinking	**D** Differentiated Instruction	**W** Writing Support	**S** Skill Practice
Teacher Edition • Inferring, p. 7 • Predicting, p. 8 • Outlining, p. 9 • Academic Vocab., p. 9 • Making Connections, p. 12 • Summarizing, p. 12 **Additional Resources** • Cont. Voc., URB p. 21 • Ac. Voc., URB p. 23	**Teacher Edition** • Analyzing Info., p. 7 • Making Generalizations, p. 9 • Drawing Con., p. 10 • Compare/Contrast, p. 11 • Analyzing Pri. Sources, p. 13 **Additional Resources** • Biographies, URB p. 25 • Crit. Think., URB p. 31	**Teacher Edition** • Interpersonal, p. 8 • Mathematics, p. 10 **Additional Resources** • Diff. Instr., URB p. 35 • Reteach. Act., URB p. 39	**Teacher Edition** • Personal Writing, p. 11 **Additional Resources** • Writing Skills, URB p. 27	**Teacher Edition** • Using Geo. Skills, p. 10 **Additional Resources** • Chart, Graph, and Map Skills, URB p. 33 • Daily Focus Trans., 1–1

What Is Civics?

Main Idea Civics is the study of the rights and duties of citizens.

Civics & You As an American citizen, did you know you have certain rights as well as responsibilities? Read to find out what it means to be a citizen of a country.

When Americans vote or serve on a jury, their actions are based on ideas that people had in the fourth century B.C. In examining how people act, Greek philosopher Aristotle wrote:

> " If liberty and equality, as is thought by some, are chiefly to be found in democracy, they will be best attained when all persons alike share in the government to the utmost. "
>
> —Aristotle, *Politics*

Ancient Roots

Civics is the study of the rights and duties of citizens. The concept of **citizenship** dates back more than 2,500 years to ancient Greece and Rome. In those days, only a few people could be **citizens**. Only men with property possessed the right to vote and to take part in government. **R**

Today gender and wealth are no longer requirements for citizenship. Indeed, most people are citizens of the country in which they live. Citizens have certain rights and duties. They are community members who owe loyalty to the government and are entitled to protection from it.

However, being a citizen means much more than just living in a country. American citizens who live abroad are still citizens of the United States. Citizens are a part of a country. They may share a common history, common customs, or common beliefs. They agree to follow a set of rules and to accept the government's authority. **C**

Reading Check Explaining As a citizen, what do you agree to do?

Diversity Native Americans from Taos, New Mexico, perform a dance that represents one of their cultural traditions. **Discussing** How do you think diversity has influenced our nation and its culture?

Teach

C Critical Thinking

Analyzing Information Have students reread Aristotle's quote and explain what he means. *(Aristotle believed that for a democracy to work, all people—not just a few—must be willing to take an active role in governing.)* **OL**

R Reading Strategy

Inferring Ask: Why do you think women were not given rights as citizens? *(They were considered inferior, uneducated, and uninformed, or they were viewed as property.)* **OL**

Reading Check Answer: Citizens agree to remain loyal to their government by abiding by rules and laws.

Caption Answer:

Students may say that diversity has influenced our clothing, food, music, language, and religion. Encourage students to provide specific examples. For example, the word *rodeo* was introduced by the Spanish.

Additional Support

Did You Know?

Legacy of Aristotle When the Framers of the U.S. Constitution proposed to create a new government, they relied on contemporary philosophers such as John Locke. However, most of their ideology was borrowed from the ancient Greek philosopher Aristotle.

Born in 384 B.C. Aristotle studied astronomy, mathematics, ethics, and law under the tutelage of the philosopher Plato. One of Aristotle's main interests was government. Interestingly, Aristotle was not very supportive of a true democracy. In his book *Politics*, he wrote that if all people— whether rich, poor, educated, or uneducated—could vote and hold office, the government might suffer.

However, Aristotle did have some hope for democracy. He believed that it is better for all of the people to govern rather than just a few of the best citizens. Our Constitution is founded on this principle: a government run by the people instead of by a select group.

D Differentiated Instruction

Interpersonal Have students work in small groups and discuss their family heritage. Some students may be first- or second-generation immigrants. Encourage them to discuss reasons their families immigrated to the United States. Invite students to share stories or experiences. **OL**

R Reading Strategy

Predicting Ask: Which part of the world do most U.S. immigrants come from at present? *(Latin America)* **OL**

Analyzing Graphs

Answers:
1. 2005
2. 1910

Immigrating to the United States

Step 1: Planning a New Start Pairs of students will choose a country from which they will immigrate to the United States. They will decide why they are leaving their homeland, where they plan to arrive in the United States, and what they plan to do upon their arrival.

A Changing Society

Main Idea American society has undergone many changes in the past, and these changes continue today.

Civics & You What would make you want to move to a new place? Read on to find out why people immigrated to the Americas.

On the back of every American coin, you will find the Latin words *E pluribus unum,* meaning "Out of many, one." This phrase reminds us that the many **diverse,** or different, citizens of the United States have joined together to make a single, strong nation. For all our differences, we are linked by shared values and experiences. More than 300 million people live in the United States today. All of us are descendants from families that immigrated at one time or another. Most scholars believe that even the first Native Americans arrived here thousands of years ago by crossing over a "land bridge" that once connected Asia and North America.

A Nation of Immigrants

Until the mid-1900s, most immigrants came from Europe. The first Europeans to settle permanently in North America arrived from Spain during the 1500s. They lived in what is now Florida, California, and the Southwest. By the time the United States won its independence from England, the Spanish had founded Tucson, Albuquerque, San Antonio, and San Diego.

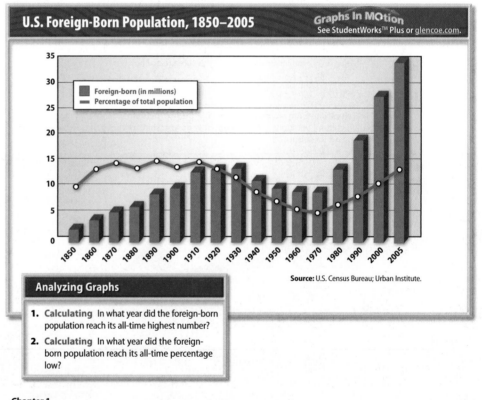

U.S. Foreign-Born Population, 1850–2005

Graphs In MOtion
See StudentWorks™ Plus or glencoe.com.

Legend: Foreign-born (in millions); Percentage of total population

Source: U.S. Census Bureau; Urban Institute.

Analyzing Graphs

1. **Calculating** In what year did the foreign-born population reach its all-time highest number?
2. **Calculating** In what year did the foreign-born population reach its all-time percentage low?

Directions Write the Big Idea on the board. Assign pairs of students a region of the world. Tell pairs of students to research information to describe their "homeland." Pairs should write a descriptive summary about who they are—describing their customs, their language, and their lives. They should also say why they are leaving their homeland, and create a list of things they have to do before leaving their homeland. Pairs should determine where they plan to live once they arrive in the United States. They will need to research criteria that new immigrants need before arrival in the U.S, such as how to obtain a green card or resident card.

Summarizing Have pairs share what they learned about the Big Idea while planning their immigration. Pairs will use this information about immigration in Section 2 to decide how they plan to achieve their goal of becoming a naturalized citizen. **OL**

(Project continued in Section 2)

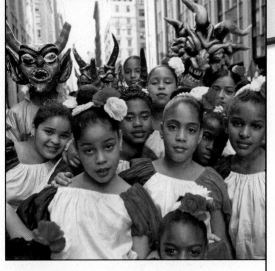

Early Immigration Beginning in the 1600s, people from France and England came to North America. The French settled primarily in Canada, but they also clustered around the Mississippi River. English immigrants settled mainly along the east coast of North America, creating the thirteen colonies that became the United States. During the late 1600s and the 1700s, immigrants from Germany, the Netherlands, Ireland, Scotland, and Sweden joined these English settlers.

After Independence After the United States gained its independence, it became known throughout Europe as a land of promise. The number of immigrants grew from 600,000 in the 1830s to more than 2 million by the 1850s. Between 1860 and 1890, more than 10 million Europeans—many of them from Denmark, Norway, and Sweden—streamed into this country.

A Shift in Immigration Another flood of immigrants—about 22 million—reached our shores between 1890 and 1924. Most of them came from southern and eastern Europe, from countries such as Italy, Greece, Poland, and Russia.

During the past 50 years, immigration from Europe to the United States has lagged far behind immigration from the rest of the world. Asia now accounts for the largest share of foreign newcomers, followed by Latin America.

Enslaved Africans Among the early immigrants to America were some who did not come willingly. Western and central Africans were taken by force from their homes, shipped across the Atlantic Ocean, and sold as slaves in the Caribbean Islands and North and South America. Between 1619 and 1808, before it became illegal to bring enslaved persons into the United States, some 500,000 people were brought to the country in this way. Most African Americans today are descendants of enslaved persons. Others are immigrants from various countries in Africa and the Caribbean region.

R1 **Immigration Patterns** Until the mid-1900s most American immigrants came from Europe. Today the largest numbers of immigrants, like these girls taking part in the Latino celebration of Cinco de Mayo in New York City, have come from Spanish-speaking countries. ***Speculating*** Why do people from other countries want to live in the United States?

A Diverse Population

The American population is extraordinarily diverse in terms of **ethnic,** or racial, backgrounds. Many Americans today do not identify themselves as members of a single ethnic group. However, whites of European descent number more than 234 million. There are about 37 million African Americans, over 12 million Asians and Pacific Islanders, and almost 2.8 million Native Americans. More than 39 million people are Latinos—people of any race who trace their ancestry to the Spanish-speaking countries of the Western Hemisphere.

Religious Diversity Our ethnic diversity is matched by religious diversity. More than 200 million people practice some form of Christianity. Jews, Muslims, Buddhists, and many other religious groups are also free to worship according to their conscience. Those who do not practice any religion are equally at home here.

Chapter 1   9

D Differentiated Instruction

Mathematical Ask: By how much did the population grow between 1830 and 1930? *(108 million)* **OL**

C Critical Thinking

Drawing Conclusions Tell students that moving to the city was quite a change for people who lived on farms or in rural areas. **Ask:** How was life in cities different for people who moved from rural areas? *(They had more encounters with strangers and different cultures; they had a more rigid work environment; they had to purchase food items instead of growing them; they had more access to new inventions, such as electricity, automobiles, and telephones.)* **AL**

S Skill Practice

Using Geography Skills Ask students to identify the countries or region in which immigrants have the shortest distances to travel to reach America. *(Canada and Latin America)* **OL**

Analyzing Maps

Answers:
1. 10.1 percent
2. Australia & Oceania

Additional Support

Teacher Tip

Economics Connection This activity requires students to understand economic terms. Before beginning, define and discuss the terms *blue-collar workers, white-collar workers,* and *industrialization.*

Many Traditions As people with different beliefs and backgrounds have made lives for themselves in the United States, many of their "old country" traditions have become part of the American culture. The American culture is a rich blend of varied influences.

Transforming America

Between 1830 and 1930, the nation's population grew from about 12 million people to about 120 million people. About 40 million of those new Americans were immigrants.

Over the years, the American population has changed in many ways. In the mid-1800s, for example, people began moving from rural areas to cities. The higher wages paid in the

cities attracted workers. Many of those moving to the cities found work in newly opened factories. These workers became known as blue-collar workers. Others found jobs in offices, schools, stores, and other nonfactory settings and were called white-collar workers. By 1920 more than half of all Americans lived in towns or cities.

Another significant change was the shift to service industry jobs. In the past few decades, manufacturing has lost ground to what we call the **"service economy."** Many Americans now earn a living by providing services—practicing law or medicine, programming computers, teaching, and so forth. There are also more women and at-home workers in the labor force than ever before.

United States Immigration, 2007

Maps In MOtion
See StudentWorks™ Plus or glencoe.com.

32.2%
11.5%
36.4%
9.0%
10.1%
0.6%

Africa
Asia
Australia & Oceania
Europe
Canada and Middle America
South America
United States

0   1,500   3,000 Miles
0   1,500   3,000 kilometers
Robinson projection

Source: U.S. Department of Homeland Security, Office of Immigration Statistics.

Analyzing Maps

1. **Analyzing** What is the percentage of immigrants coming to the United States from South America?
2. **Identifying** Which region accounts for the smallest percentage of immigrants?

Activity: Economic Connections

Making Connections Discuss how a marked increase in immigration might change a country's economic base. **Ask:** How did migration to the United States and to urban areas affect the American economy? *(More urban residents meant more demand for services, so jobs were created. Population growth increased the demand for more food. Farmers grew crops*

for themselves and to sell in local stores and restaurants.) Form three groups—blue-collar workers, white-collar workers, and farmers. Have each group create a poster that illustrates the kind of job they could get in the mid-1800s, including the skills they would need and their income. Students should use at least three Internet sources, as well as library sources. **AL**

Cultural Diversity Americans enjoy foods, music, sports, and holiday traditions brought to the United States by immigrants from around the world. This Chicago parade marks the Chinese New Year. *Analyzing* Why is it important for American citizens to share cultural traditions?

The places where we live are changing too. For example, shortly after the Civil War, African Americans, freed from slavery, headed for northern cities, seeking jobs and a new way of life. The result was a migration, or mass movement, of African Americans from the South to the North. For much of our history, the Northeast was the most populous part of the country. Today, the South claims that distinction, and the population there and in the West is growing faster than in any other regions.

The population is changing in other ways, including the following:

- The average age of citizens is climbing upward as people live longer and have fewer children.
- Record numbers of Americans are now earning college and graduate degrees.
- Latinos, commonly referred to as Hispanic Americans, are the fastest-growing ethnic group.

Indeed, if current patterns continue, Latinos and other minority groups, taken as a whole, will soon be in the majority.

Reading Check **Summarizing** In what ways is the American population changing?

American Values and Institutions

Main Idea Americans share key values, and these values are reflected in the important institutions of American life.

Civics & You What do you think makes a person an American? Read to find out about the values we share and how they have shaped the character of the American people.

Even though American society is more diverse than ever, certain shared ideas help unite Americans of different backgrounds. Two of these important ideas are our values and our institutions.

What Are Values?

Do you agree with most of your classmates on what is good and what is bad? The general **principles,** or beliefs, you use to make these judgments are your **values.** Values are broad ideas about what is good or desirable, and are shared by people in a society. Values are important because they influence the way we act.

Chapter 1   11

11

R1 Reading Strategy

Making Connections Review the list of values students included in their writing activity. Have students state which values are the most important. Discuss if the values are interconnected or if some can be merged. **OL**

This **Reading Skill** (Making Connections) was introduced in this unit.

R2 Reading Strategy

Summarizing Pair students and have them write one paragraph summarizing why common civic and political heritages are important to American unity. Have students share their summaries with the class. **OL**

TIME™ Political Cartoons

Answers:

1. The flag represents the United States.

2. The magnified section reveals immigrants as the stitching.

3. Answers may vary, but students may say the artist is saying that America is made from immigrants. Without immigrants to this nation, it would not be the United States.

Additional Support

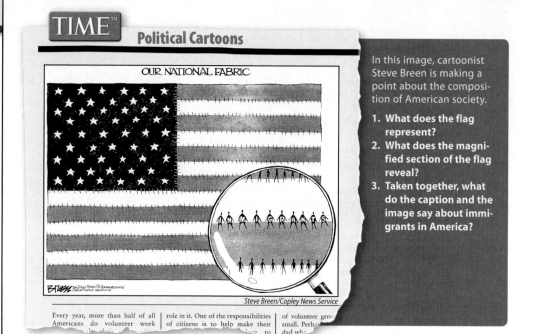

TIME™ Political Cartoons

OUR NATIONAL FABRIC

Steve Breen/Copley News Service

In this image, cartoonist Steve Breen is making a point about the composition of American society.

1. **What does the flag represent?**

2. **What does the magnified section of the flag reveal?**

3. **Taken together, what do the caption and the image say about immigrants in America?**

Basic American Values

Everyone's list of basic American values will include different ideas. However, some values would appear on almost every list. These include freedom, equality, opportunity, justice, democracy, unity, respect, and tolerance. Some of these values, such as equality and opportunity, and respect and tolerance, are linked. Can you think of other values to include on this list?

Shared Values Unite Americans

Another important effect of having a set of shared values is the unity it builds among Americans. For example, one very important source of American unity is a common civic and political heritage based on the country's founding documents. These key documents include the Declaration of Independence, the U.S. Constitution of 1787, and the Bill of Rights of 1791. American ideals of individual rights to "life, liberty, and the pursuit of happiness" are in these founding documents. So are such values as **popular sovereignty** (government by consent of the governed) through

- fair, free, and regular elections;
- equal justice under the law;
- majority rule through the people's representatives in government.

A second significant source of unity is a single language, English, which generally is accepted as the primary means of communication in education, government, and business. Americans are free to speak any language. However, some people think that the United States is strengthened by the common and public use of one language, which can be used by diverse groups of Americans to communicate freely with one another. Can you think of other values that have helped unite Americans throughout history?

Activity: Collaborative Learning

Making Generalizations Remind students that America is a country with a diverse cultural background. **Ask:** How can people who are so different come together and create a democracy that has been working for more than 200 years? (*Our values are similar—we all want freedom of speech and religion and other rights.*) Have groups of students identify what values are and make a list of examples (*friendship, compassion, honesty, human rights, respect and so on*). Next, have students create a Venn diagram consisting of personal values and social values that they would be willing to defend. **Ask:** Which of these values would you fight for if someone wanted to take them away? Have groups share their conclusions with the class. **OL**

American Institutions

Each society has its own social **institutions.** These are not buildings or places but sets of ideas that people have about relationships, obligations, roles, and functions. As in every society, the most important institution in American life is the *family.* The family is the core of social life: it produces new generations, socializes the young, offers care and affection, and provides economic support. Parents and caregivers are also transmitters of values, both personal and national, to their children.

Other important institutions in American life, which also reflect our nation's shared values, are religious, educational, and social. *Religious institutions,* such as churches, temples, and mosques, can promote social unity and provide a sense of meaning and belonging. *Educational institutions* at all levels reflect our society's culture, history, and learning, create a common identity, and promote personal growth and development. *Social institutions,* such as clubs and volunteer service organizations, can be another way we share our common values.

The different parts of our government are also institutions. *Governmental institutions* were created, and have developed over time, based on important shared American values. As Abraham Lincoln explained in his first Inaugural Address in 1861:

> " *This country, with its institutions, belongs to the people who inhabit it. Whenever they shall grow weary of the existing government, they can exercise their constitutional right of amending it, or their revolutionary right to dismember, or overthrow it.* "

— Abraham Lincoln, *First Inaugural Address*

With these words, Lincoln underscored the most important concept of American government: the people, not the government, are in control.

✔ **Reading Check** Identifying What are some types of important American institutions?

C Critical Thinking

Analyzing Primary Sources Ask: What does President Lincoln suggest citizens do if they are unhappy with their government? *(They can change it through the democratic process or start a revolution.)* **OL**

✔ **Reading Check** Examples include the family and religious, educational, and social institutions.

Assess

Civics ONLINE

Study Central™ provides summaries, interactive games, and online graphic organizers to help students review content.

Close

Personal Journal Have students write about their heritage, culture, and customs and what it means to them to be part of American society. **OL**

Section 1 Review

Vocabulary

1. **Define** the following terms and use them correctly in sentences: *civics, citizenship, citizen, service economy, value, popular sovereignty, institution.*

Main Ideas

2. **Describing** What do people of a nation share as citizens?

3. **Explaining** What impact do American values have on society?

Critical Thinking

4. **BIG Ideas** What do you think is the most important source of American unity? Explain your answer.

5. **Sequencing** On a diagram similar to the one below, identify the period when various ethnic groups immigrated to the United States.

To 1500	
1600–1700	
1800–1900	
2000–today	

CITIZENSHIP Activity

6. **Expository Writing** Review the discussion of values in this section. Is there a value not listed that you think should be included? What is it? Why would you include it?

Civics ONLINE

Study Central™ To review this section, go to glencoe.com.

Section 1 Review

Answers

1. Sentences should use vocabulary words according to their definitions in the section and in the Glossary.

2. Citizens share a common history, common customs, and common values. They agree to follow a set of rules and accept the government's authority.

3. Values influence the way Americans think and act, how they vote, and how they create rules of order.

4. Answers will vary but may include values such as freedom, equality under the law, democracy, respect, and tolerance.

5. **to 1500:** Spain; **1600–1700:** France, England, Germany, Ireland, Scotland, Sweden, Netherlands; **1800–1900:** Denmark, Norway, Sweden, Italy, Greece, Poland, Russia; **2000–today:** Latin America, Asia

6. Answers may include specific values such as fairness, patriotism, faith, privacy, free enterprise, honesty, integrity, and a work value. Ask volunteers to share their responses and to lead a class discussion.

Focus

Bellringer
Daily Focus Transparency 1–2

Guide to Reading
Answers to Graphic:

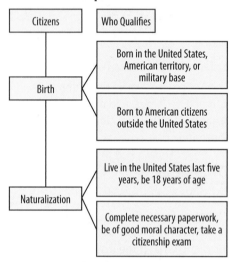

| Citizens | Who Qualifies |

Birth → Born in the United States, American territory, or military base

Birth → Born to American citizens outside the United States

Naturalization → Live in the United States last five years, be 18 years of age

Naturalization → Complete necessary paperwork, be of good moral character, take a citizenship exam

Section Spotlight Video

Have students watch the Chapter 1, Section 2 video at <u>glencoe.com</u>.

Resource Manager

Guide to Reading

Big Idea
Citizens possess certain rights. With citizenship, Americans also have certain responsibilities.

Content Vocabulary
- naturalization *(p. 15)*
- alien *(p. 16)*
- immigrant *(p. 16)*
- deport *(p. 19)*

Academic Vocabulary
- deny *(p. 17)*
- obtain *(p. 17)*
- priority *(p. 18)*

Reading Strategy
Defining As you read, complete a diagram like the one below that shows the different paths to U.S. citizenship and who qualifies for each.

🔊 **Section Audio**   📽 **Spotlight Video**

Who Are America's Citizens?

Real World Civics What does your U.S. citizenship mean to you? The aircraft carrier USS *Midway* set the scene for Navy sailor Hugston Brooks from Liberia and 80 other Marine and Navy service members from 25 countries to become U.S. citizens on Veterans Day in 2004. The San Diego ceremony was held during a military celebration of Veterans Day. For many people around the world, becoming a U.S. citizen is a lifelong dream. With nearly 12,500 noncitizen active-duty sailors, the Navy now provides a streamlined route to naturalized citizenship for many recruits.

▼ **U.S. Navy sailor Hugston Brooks**

R **Reading Strategies**	**C** **Critical Thinking**	**D** **Differentiated Instruction**	**W** **Writing Support**	**S** **Skill Practice**
Teacher Edition • Outlining, p. 15 • Organizing, p. 17 • Academic Vocab., p. 17 • Questioning, p. 18 **Additional Resources** • Reading Skills, URB p. 7 • Cont. Voc., URB p. 21 • Act. Voc., URB p. 23	**Teacher Edition** • Making Generalizations, p. 16 **Additional Resources** • Quizzes and Tests, p. 4	**Teacher Edition** • Interpersonal, p. 16 **Additional Resources** • Speak./Listen., URB p. 9 • Diff. Instr., URB p. 35 • Reteach. Act., URB p. 39	**Teacher Edition** • Persuasive Writing, p. 15 **Additional Resources** • Cit./Dec.-Making Act., URB p. 3 • Writing Skills, URB p. 27	**Teacher Edition** • Making Inferences, p. 19 **Additional Resources** • Daily Focus Trans., 1–2

Path to Citizenship

Main Idea In the United States, there are two ways to become a citizen: by birth and by a process called naturalization.

Civics & You What should people who want to become U.S. citizens know about our country? Read to find out about the process of becoming a citizen.

You learned that citizens are community members who owe loyalty to the government and are entitled to protection from it. Every country has rules about how people gain citizenship. The U.S. Constitution establishes two ways to become a citizen: by birth and, for foreign-born people who choose to become citizens, by a legal process called **naturalization.**

Citizenship by Birth

If you were born in any of the 50 states or the District of Columbia, you automatically became an American citizen at birth. The same is true if you were born outside the country but in American territory, such as Puerto Rico or Guam, or on a U.S. military base overseas. Even if you were born elsewhere, you could still claim American citizenship if your parents are both citizens or if one is a citizen who has lived in the United States. Children born on American soil to non-U.S. citizens also acquire U.S. citizenship at birth. **R**

Americans may hold dual citizenship. This means that they enjoy rights in the United States and in another country. For example, a child born abroad to American parents may be both a U.S. citizen and a citizen of the country of his or her birth. **W**

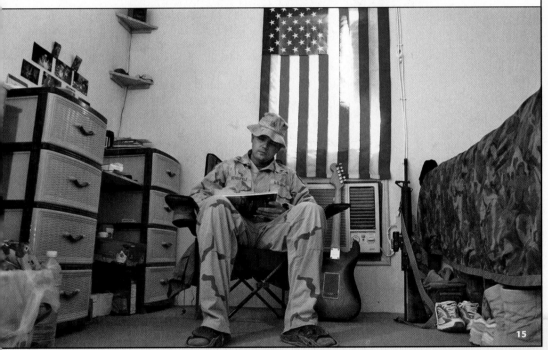

Shared Opportunities Both native-born and naturalized citizens can vote in America. In his room at Camp Eagle in Baghdad, Iraq, U.S. Army Sergeant George Scheufele fills out an absentee ballot for a presidential election. *Defining* **U.S. citizens are encouraged to vote. Is this more a right or responsibility of citizenship? Explain.**

Did You Know?

The Case of Puerto Rico The United States includes twelve territories and two commonwealths: the Northern Marianas (in the Pacific Ocean) and Puerto Rico.

On July 25, 1952, Puerto Rico was adopted as a U.S. commonwealth. As a commonwealth, it governs its internal affairs and has its own constitution. The governor of Puerto Rico, who is elected every four years, controls executive power. The chief of state is the president of the United States. Although Puerto Ricans enjoy many of the rights and responsibilities of U.S. citizens, they are not allowed to vote in presidential elections.

Unless Puerto Rico becomes a state, this is a right they will not get. Yet it is a right many Puerto Ricans wish they had (Puerto Ricans are noted for having the highest voter participation in the world). These voters believe that their voices would make a difference.

C Critical Thinking

Making Generalizations Ask: Why do you think many aliens decide to become American citizens after they stay in the country for a while? *(They feel they can make a better living; they enjoy the many freedoms Americans have.)* **OL**

D Differentiated Instruction

Interpersonal Ask: Do people feel the same way about immigration today as they did 100 years ago? *(Answers will vary, but most will state that in the past, Americans were more receptive to immigration.)* **OL**

Caption Answer:
1. An immigrant signs a Declaration of Intention.
2. The Declaration is filed with USCIS.
3. After living in the United States for five years, the immigrant files an application for citizenship.
4. A USCIS official interviews the applicant.
5. The applicant passes a citizenship exam.
6. The USCIS grants the application, and the applicant pledges an oath of allegiance in a naturalization ceremony.

Differentiated Instruction

The Naturalization Process

Several million noncitizens, or **aliens,** live in the United States. Some come to study, to work, or to visit relatives. They remain citizens of their own countries and eventually return home. Other aliens plan to settle here and become naturalized citizens. More than half a million **immigrants**—people who move permanently to a new country—gain American citizenship each year.

Beginning the Process Aliens who want to become United States citizens must first

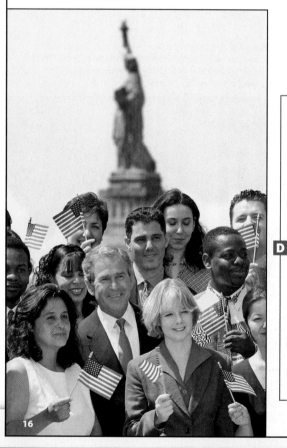

Naturalized Citizens President George W. Bush poses with new American citizens at their swearing in on Ellis Island, New York. ***Reviewing*** What are the steps that aliens must take to become citizens of the United States?

sign a statement saying just that. This Declaration of Intention is then filed with the U.S. Citizenship and Immigration Services (USCIS), an agency of the national government. For most aliens, the next step comes after living in the United States at least five years. (Aliens who are married to citizens wait only three years.) During this time, many immigrants take special classes to prepare for citizenship. Then, if they are at least 18 years old and have lived for at least three months in the state where they seek naturalization, they may file an application for citizenship.

Interview and Examination After the paperwork is checked, the alien has an interview with a USCIS official. Agency officials want to be sure the alien meets the necessary requirements and is of good moral character. The applicant must also take a citizenship exam that consists of questions about reading, writing, and speaking English and basic facts about the history and government of the United States. Afterward, the USCIS makes its decision.

Oath of Allegiance If the application is granted, the final step in naturalization is attending a ceremony and pledging an oath of allegiance. The alien swears to be loyal to this country above all others, to obey the Constitution and other laws, and to perform military or other duties if needed. Then the person signs a document and is declared a citizen of the United States. If he or she has children under 18, they automatically become naturalized citizens, too.

Native Americans For a long time, most Native Americans were excluded from citizenship. A few groups became citizens through treaties with the federal government. Later, Congress offered citizenship to individual Native Americans who gave up their traditional culture. Not until 1924 did Congress make all Native Americans citizens of the United States.

Biography Activity 1, URB p. 25

Elizabeth Jennings

Objective:	To learn about protecting civil rights
Focus:	Have students define "segregation" and "civil rights."
Teach:	Have students discuss groups who were segregated during the mid-1800s.
Assess:	Students should create a list of more American citizens who fought for civil rights.
Close:	Lead a discussion on how individuals can still fight for rights protected under the Constitution.

Differentiated Instruction Strategies

BL List two reasons why Jennings won her case.

AL Create a timeline of significant changes in the civil rights movement.

ELL Define "segregation" and "desegregation" and illustrate each word.

A Lifelong Privilege

Whether they are naturalized or native-born, most Americans keep their citizenship forever. Only the federal government can both grant citizenship and take it away. State governments can **deny,** or refuse, a convicted criminal some of the privileges of citizenship, such as voting, but they do not have the power to deny citizenship itself.

The government may strip naturalized citizens of citizenship if it was improperly **obtained,** or gained. Citizens can lose citizenship in three ways: through denaturalization, through expatriation, or by being convicted of certain crimes. Native-born U.S. citizens can lose citizenship only through their own actions and cannot be denaturalized.

Denaturalization The loss of citizenship through fraud or deception during the naturalization process is called denaturalization. For example, former Nazis who engaged in war crimes during World War II and later lied about their wartime activities were denaturalized after they entered the United States or when they applied for citizenship.

Expatriation The simplest way to lose citizenship is through expatriation, or giving up one's citizenship by leaving one's native country to live in a foreign country. Expatriation may be voluntary or involuntary. For example, a person who becomes a naturalized citizen of another country automatically loses his or her American citizenship. Involuntary expatriation would occur in the case of a child whose parents become citizens of another country.

Punishment For a Crime A person may lose citizenship when convicted of certain federal crimes that involve extreme disloyalty. These crimes include treason, participation in a rebellion, and attempts to overthrow the government through violent means.

Reading Check Summarizing Describe the two methods of obtaining U.S. citizenship.

TIME™ Teens in *Action*

Chris Garrett

Meet Chris Garrett, a 16-year-old who lives near Key West, Florida. Thanks to his work to protect our natural resources, Chris has received an Environmental Hero Award from the National Oceanic & Atmospheric Administration—and a Congressional Certificate of Recognition.

QUESTION: How do you make a difference?

ANSWER: I helped start Team Panda—a youth conservation organization sponsored by the World Wildlife Fund. There are now 16 students in the group helping to preserve the environment.

Q: Do you work with elected officials?

A: Definitely. Much of our work is geared to changing government policies to help further conservation efforts. Elected officials want to hear what students have to say. It's really great to see officials making huge decisions that will protect our environment because we got involved.

Q: What inspires you?

A: I believe the more we give to help others, the more we gain for ourselves. And growing up in the Florida Keys, you learn the environment is very special and it's important to preserve it.

Q: What would you tell other teens who want to help conserve the environment?

Team Panda members

A: Find an organization that's dedicated to conservation and that sounds appealing to you. Or start your own.

Making a Difference — **CITIZENSHIP**

What do you think motivated Chris to start Team Panda?

Chapter 1   17

R₁ Reading Strategy

Organizing Draw three columns on the board. Have students state three ways in which any American citizen can lose his or her citizenship. *(Denaturalization, Expatriation, Federal Crime)* Have students provide details that explain each process. **OL**

R₂ Reading Strategy

Academic Vocabulary Have students write two sentences using the words "deny" and "obtained." Remind students both words are verbs. They may choose verb tense. Challenge students to use both words in one sentence. **BL ELL**

TIME™ Teens in *Action*

Answers:
Student answers might suggest that Chris was motivated due to his concern for the environment and his drive to do something. Instead of expecting others to provide a solution, Chris became proactive and initiated a group.

Reading Check **Answer:** being native-born or through naturalization

Hands-On Chapter Project
Step 2

Immigrating to the United States

Step 2: Applying for Citizenship Pairs of students continue their work toward becoming U.S. citizens that they began in Section 1.

Directions Write the Big Idea on the board. Tell the pairs that now they will begin their naturalization process. Students can find the information they need at www.uscitizenship.info. Students should fill out the eligibility worksheet and application form found in the guide on the government site. Have students create a flowchart illustrating the steps they must take to prepare for the day of the naturalization ceremony. **OL**

(Project continued in Section 3)

R Reading Strategy

Questioning After students read the first sentence, ask them to list reasons the number of immigrants is restricted. **OL**

Caption Answer:

The process to apply for entry into the United States is slow. Also, some immigrants might not qualify for entry, so they choose to enter illegally.

Aliens in America

Main Idea Even though the United States controls the admission of aliens to this country, each year millions of people enter America illegally.

Civics & You Why do you think so many people want to come to the United States? Read to find out why our country is such a magnet to people around the world.

R The United States restricts the number of immigrants who can enter the country. Millions apply, but only about one million are admitted each year. Traditionally, the relatives of U.S. citizens and people with needed job skills receive the highest **priority,** or first consideration. Family members still get special consideration, but because of the Immigration Act of 1990, emphasis has shifted toward welcoming "those who want to work and produce and contribute," as one member of Congress put it. The new policy benefits people with particular skills, talents, or the money to invest in our economy.

Illegal Aliens

Despite immigration limits, more than 12 million aliens are living in the United States illegally. Some were refused permission to immigrate; others never applied for permission because they feared a long, slow process or being turned down.

Illegal aliens come to the United States in a variety of ways. A few enter the country as temporary visitors but never leave. Others risk arrest by illegally crossing our borders with Mexico and Canada. Other illegal aliens are foreigners who have stayed in the United States after their legal permits expired.

Whatever the method, the reason is usually the same. "I came for work and for a better life," explained one Mexican immigrant. Yet illegal aliens often have a difficult time in the United States. Many have no

Border Security A U.S. Immigration and Naturalization Service agent searches a Mexican fishing boat for people who may be entering the country illegally. *Discussing* Why do people enter the United States illegally?

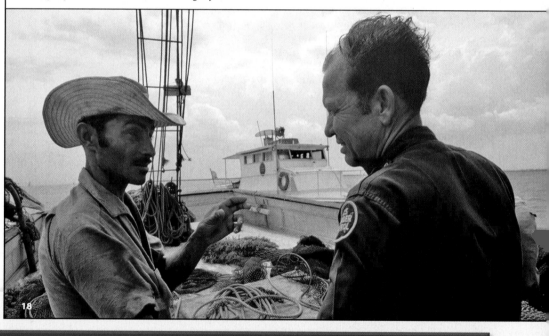

18

Differentiated Instruction

Leveled Activities

BL Reading Skills Activity 1, URB pp. 7–8

AL Writing Skills Activity 1, URB pp. 27–30

ELL Guided Reading Activity 1–2, URB p. 42

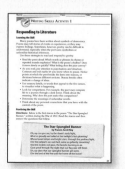

friends or family here, no place to live, and no sure way to earn money. It is against the law to hire illegal aliens, and those who do find work usually receive little pay and no benefits. Every day they live with the fear that government officials will discover and deport them—send them back to their own countries.

The United States Border Patrol is the law-enforcement unit of the USCIS. Its primary responsibility is to detect and prevent the illegal entry of aliens into the United States. The Border Patrol guards the 6,000 miles of Mexican and Canadian international land borders and 2,000 miles of coastal waters surrounding the Florida Peninsula and the island of Puerto Rico.

Legal Aliens

United States law classifies aliens into different categories. A resident alien is a person from a foreign country who has established permanent residence in the United States. Resident aliens may stay in the United States as long as they wish without becoming American citizens. A nonresident alien is a person from a foreign country who expects to stay in the United States for a short, specified period. A Turkish journalist who has come to report on a presidential election is an example of a nonresident alien. Refugees are another category. Refugees are people fleeing their country to escape persecution.

Aliens who have entered the United States legally lead lives much like those of American citizens. Aliens may hold jobs, own property, attend public schools, and receive other government services. They pay taxes and are entitled to legal protection.

Aliens do not have full political rights, however. They may not vote in elections or run for office. They may not serve on juries or work in most government jobs. In addition, unlike U.S. citizens, aliens must carry identification cards at all times.

✓ **Reading Check** **Contrasting** How do the rights of legal aliens differ from those of U.S. citizens?

Skill Practice

Making Inferences **Ask:** How do citizens take advantage of illegal aliens? *(They employ them for less than minimum wage; they do not treat them as equals.)* What do you think happens when illegal aliens are caught by the border patrol? *(They are put in jail until they can be deported to their home country.)* **OL**

✓ **Reading Check** **Answer:** Unlike U.S. citizens, legal aliens cannot vote, run for elections, serve on a jury, or hold a government job. Also, they must carry an I.D. card describing them as aliens.

Assess

Civics ONLINE

Study Central™ provides summaries, interactive games, and online graphic organizers to help students review content.

Close

Summarizing Have students work in small groups. Using their graphic organizers, have them create a two-minute oral presentation about how one can become a U.S. citizen and how the privilege may be revoked. **OL**

Section 2 Review

Section 2 Review

Vocabulary

1. **Explain** how each of the following terms relates to citizenship in the United States: *naturalization, alien, immigrant, deport.*

Main Ideas

2. **Explaining** What is dual citizenship? How can an American obtain dual citizenship?

3. **Analyzing** Why do you think the United States puts a limit on the number of immigrants who may enter the country?

Critical Thinking

4. **Synthesizing** If you were a government official, how would you prevent illegal aliens from entering the United States?

5. **BIG Ideas** On a chart like the one below, list the sequence of steps in the naturalization process.

Naturalization
Step 1 _____
Step 2 _____
Step 3 _____

CITIZENSHIP Activity

6. **Descriptive Writing** Interview an American who became a citizen through the naturalization process. Write a one-page paper in which you answer these questions: What reasons brought him or her to the United States? Why did he or she want to become an American citizen?

Civics ONLINE

Study Central™ To review this section, go to glencoe.com.

Chapter 1 19

Answers

1. Definitions for the vocabulary words are found in the section and in the Glossary.

2. Dual citizenship is when a person has U.S. rights as well as rights of another country. A child who is born in a foreign country to American citizens may obtain dual citizenship.

3. to make sure there are enough jobs, to restrict economic strain, to control population explosion

4. Answers may include hiring more border patrol officers, building a fence, and severely punishing those who hire illegal aliens.

5. an immigrant signs a Declaration of Intention; the Declaration is filed with USCIS; the immigrant files an application for citizenship after living in U.S. for five years; the USCIS interviews the applicant; the applicant passes a citizenship exam; the USCIS grants the application; the applicant pledges an oath of allegiance

6. Interviews will vary. Papers should answer why the person came to America in the first place, and why he or she wanted to become a citizen.

Focus

Bellringer
Daily Focus Transparency 1–3

Guide to Reading
Answers to Graphic:

Types of Government	Description
1. Democracy	Government is run by the people, and there are free elections.
2. Monarchy	Government is run by a hereditary ruler (king or queen).
3. Dictatorship	Government is ruled by one leader who is considered oppressive.
4. Totalitarianism	Government is run by scare tactics and violence. Citizens cannot express opinions.

Section Spotlight Video

To generate student interest and provide a springboard for class discussion, access the Chapter 1, Section 3 video at glencoe.com or on the video DVD.

Resource Manager

Guide to Reading

Big Idea
People form governments to establish order, provide security, and accomplish common goals.

Content Vocabulary
- government (p. 21)
- public policy (p. 22)
- budget (p. 22)
- democracy (p. 23)
- direct democracy (p. 23)
- representative democracy (p. 24)
- republic (p. 24)
- monarchy (p. 24)
- majority rule (p. 25)
- authoritarian (p. 25)
- totalitarian (p. 26)

Academic Vocabulary
- community (p. 21)
- enforce (p. 21)
- constrain (p. 25)

Reading Strategy
Organizing Create a chart like the one below. Then list the different types of government and a brief description of each.

Types of Government	Description
1. Democracy	
2.	
3.	
4.	

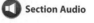 Section Audio Spotlight Video

Government and the People

Real World Civics Curious teens scramble over rocks as they near the spectacular Fiery Furnace in Arches National Park and are careful to leave the park the way they found it. This park is one of nearly 400 national parks in 49 states to which lawmakers are considering cutting services. About 118 million people visit these precious gems for fun, recreation, inspiration, and renewal. However, rising costs for maintenance and staffing, which is provided by the national government, may cause some national parks to reduce tours and public access, cut back on hours, and in some cases close parkland.

▼ **Ranger Clay Parcels leads a group through the Fiery Furnace of Arches National Park in Moab, Utah.**

R Reading Strategies	C Critical Thinking	D Differentiated Instruction	W Writing Support	S Skill Practice
Teacher Edition • Academic Vocab., p. 21 • Reading Charts, p. 22 • Inferring, p. 23 • Making Connections, p. 25 • Det. Importance, p. 26 **Additional Resources** • Guided Read., URB p. 43 • RENTG, p. 7	**Teacher Edition** • Det. Cause/Effect, p. 21 • Drawing Con., p. 23 • Compare/Contrast, p. 24 • Making Generalizations, p. 25 **Additional Resources** • Quizzes and Tests, p. 5 • Pol. Cartoons Trans. 1	**Teacher Edition** • Interpersonal, p. 21 • Visual/Spatial, p. 23 • Adv. Learners, p. 24 • Below Grade Level, p. 25 **Additional Resources** • Diff Instr., URB p. 35 • Reteach. Act., URB p. 39	**Teacher Edition** • Personal Writing, p. 26 **Additional Resources** • Writing Skills, URB p. 27	**Teacher Edition** • Making Inferences, p. 22 **Additional Resources** • Daily Focus Trans., 1–3 • Stan. Test, p. 1

The Need for Government

Main Idea The different levels of government provide many different services.

Civics & You When was the last time a government provided you with a service? Read to find out how local, state, and national governments serve the public.

A **government** is the ruling authority for a **community,** or society. Any organization that has the power to make and **enforce,** or carry out, laws and decisions for its members acts as a government.

For hundreds of years, people have formed governments. The earliest Native Americans had tribal councils. Thomas Hobbes, an English political thinker during the 1600s, believed that without government, life would be "solitary, poor, nasty, brutish, and short." If each of us could do just as he or she pleased, fighting probably would be common, and survival would depend on strength and skill.

Think about trying to play basketball with no rules or referees. The game would probably be a chaotic free-for-all. Similarly, if there were no government to make and enforce laws, we would live in a state of confusion, violence, and fear. Government can make it possible for people to live together peacefully and productively.

What Governments Do

The most important purpose of a government is to provide laws, or rules of conduct. These laws help prevent conflicts between individuals, groups, or nations and help settle any conflicts that do occur.

Government Services This fire station protects the community and also serves as a place where these citizens can cast their votes in their neighborhoods. *Identifying* What other types of public services does government provide?

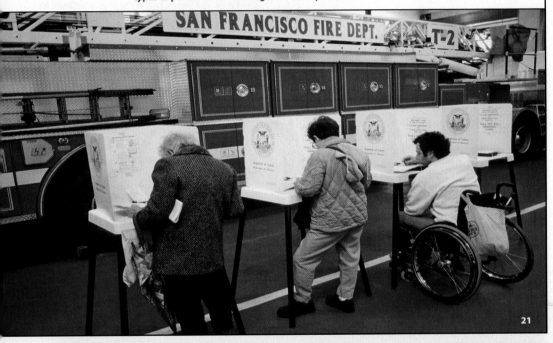

Teach

R Reading Strategy

Academic Vocabulary Have students create a word web for "community" and "enforce," listing synonyms for each word. *(community: group of people, village, town, neighborhood; enforce: uphold, defend, put into practice)* **BL**

D Differentiated Instruction

Interpersonal Have students list a few basketball (or football) rules. Ask them what rules they would change. See if the class can come to an agreement on amending the rules. Have them consider how difficult it is to change laws. **AL**

C Critical Thinking

Determining Cause and Effect Ask: Why must communities form governments? *(to install some kind of order)* What kinds of problems could arise when forming a government? (People do not always think alike, so what rules get set may be difficult to decide.) **OL**

Caption Answer:
They provide education, programs to help the disabled, police protection, road construction, and parks.

Additional Support

Activity: Interdisciplinary Connection

Literature and History Have students find the following primary sources, either in the library or on the Internet: The Magna Carta, The Articles of Confederation, and *The Forgotten Founders* by Bruce E. Johansen (located at www.ratical.org/many worlds/6Nations/FF.html). Have students write down phrases or sentences that they feel represent our American democracy. Discuss that when our democracy was crafted, the Founders used many sources to outline a system they believed would be fair to all citizens. Ask the students to create a collage that represents our government at work and to include in their artwork the phrases they collected. **OL**

R Reading Strategy

Reading Charts **Ask:** What are the four main functions of government? (*keeping order, providing security, providing services, and guiding the community*) Which do you think is most important? (*Answers will vary. Have students support their answers with an example.*) **OL**

S Skill Practice

Making Inferences **Ask:** Can you name a few examples of public policy that affect you personally? (*Students may cite examples that relate to school policy, such as state exams, drug testing, and driver's education.*) **OL**

Analyzing Charts

Answers:
1. provide services
2. Courts decide if the accused are guilty and what punishment should be applied to the guilty.

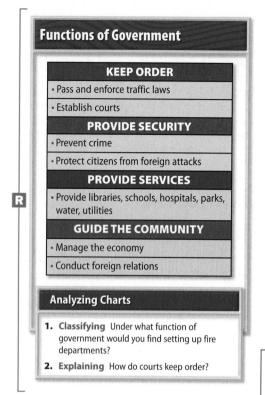

Functions of Government

KEEP ORDER
• Pass and enforce traffic laws
• Establish courts

PROVIDE SECURITY
• Prevent crime
• Protect citizens from foreign attacks

PROVIDE SERVICES
• Provide libraries, schools, hospitals, parks, water, utilities

GUIDE THE COMMUNITY
• Manage the economy
• Conduct foreign relations

Analyzing Charts

1. **Classifying** Under what function of government would you find setting up fire departments?

2. **Explaining** How do courts keep order?

Keep Order Conflicts are unavoidable when people live together in a community. Governments make laws to help prevent conflicts and to settle those conflicts that do arise.

Governments have the power to enforce the laws. For example, to make sure that drivers obey traffic regulations, police officers are empowered to ticket or arrest violators. Courts decide whether those accused of crimes are guilty and how they should be punished if found guilty.

Provide Security Along with the need for law and order come concerns about community security—defending citizens and their land from enemies. For this reason, governments set up armed forces and agencies that watch for likely sources of trouble.

Provide Public Services Governments provide many services that would not be available otherwise. Governments create and manage libraries, schools, hospitals, parks, and recreation centers. Government workers build and repair streets, erect bridges, collect garbage, and deliver the mail.

Many government services are aimed at keeping the public healthy and safe. Local communities set up fire departments and ambulance services. States license drivers and doctors. Other government agencies protect us from dangerous medicines and spoiled food. Government inspectors check for safety problems in everything from factories to amusement park rides.

Governments also give help to needy people. For example, in each of the 50 states, poor families and people who are out of work can receive food, aid, or cash. Government agencies also supply affordable housing, health care, job training, and special programs for people with disabilities.

Guide the Community Another function of government is to formulate **public policy,** or a course of government action to achieve community goals. When government leaders decide they want to protect consumers, for example, or strengthen national security, they are setting public policy goals. When they pass laws or develop guidelines to reach these goals, they are making public policy.

Most public policy decisions involve financial planning. Governments have limited amounts of money, and they must use it wisely. Creating a **budget,** or a plan for collecting and spending money, is key to the success of the community.

Another part of guiding the community is developing relations with the community's neighbors and other outsiders. Governments often take responsibility for communicating and cooperating with other governments on matters of trade, travel, and military agreements for the benefit of their citizens.

Differentiated Instruction

Citizenship and Decision-Making Activity 1, URB p. 3-4

You Have Rights!

Objective: To gain an understanding of rights and freedoms protected in the Bill of Rights

Focus: Students evaluate the First Amendment and how it is practiced.

Teach: Discuss the importance of the First Amendment and list examples.

Assess: Have students write a paragraph explaining why the First Amendment is important to them.

Close: Create a chart of the issues students chose to write about in their editorials.

Differentiated Instruction Strategies

BL Provide a list of situations in which people are protected by the First Amendment.

AL Create a poster that illustrates the Bill of Rights in action.

ELL Draw a postcard that illustrates the First Amendment in practice.

Levels of Government

Many levels of government exist, each representing a particular collection of people. Each of the 50 states has its own government; so do most counties, cities, and towns. The students in your school may have their own student government.

National Government Although each of the above is a government, when most people talk about "the government," they are talking about the national government—the government of an entire country. In the United States, the national government is made up of three branches of government. These branches are the legislative, the executive, and the judicial branches. A national government is different from other levels of government in two important ways.

First, a national government has the highest level of authority over its citizens. A city or state government cannot make any laws that would go against the laws of the national government. The national government, however, has the power to make whatever laws it feels would benefit the country. Second, a national government provides the basic framework for citizenship.

State and Local Government The national government makes and enforces laws for the entire country. Each state decides matters for the people in that state.

The level of government closest to Americans is local government. Local governments include counties, cities, and towns. Your school may have a student government, and if you choose to belong to a club like Girl Scouts or 4-H, you respect that organization's governing body, too.

However, state and local governments, as well as governments of organizations, cannot take actions that go against the laws and authority of the national government.

✔ **Reading Check** Describing How do governments keep order and provide security?

Types of Government

Main Idea The people are the ultimate rulers of democratic countries, while in totalitarian states, a single person or small group holds all the power.

Civics & You Did you know there is more than one type of democracy? Read to find out about other kinds of democracies.

Democratic Government

The foundations of **democracy** are more than 2,500 years old. Democracy began in the ancient Greek city of Athens. Athens had a **direct democracy**—all the citizens met to debate government matters and vote firsthand. Direct democracy is not practical for most countries today because of their large areas and populations.

Public Safety Government inspectors regularly check amusement park rides to ensure that they meet safety requirements. *Identifying* In what other ways does the government protect your health and safety?

Hands-On Chapter Project
Step 3

Immigrating to the United States

Step 3: Learning about the United States Pairs of students continue their work toward becoming U.S. citizens that they began in Section 1.

Directions Write the Big Idea on the board. Discuss that those who are seeking to become naturalized citizens must know about the heritage of the United States. They must pass a civics test that assesses their knowledge about America's history and its government. Tell the pairs that they will be taking a 20-question civics test written by their classmates. Each pair will create an exam based on test questions from

the USCIS Guide. Students may use the Education & Resources section of www. uscis.gov. Have pairs begin creating a test and preparing their own study guides. Allow pairs to quiz each other periodically in order to prepare for their exam. **OL**
(Project continued on the Visual Summary page)

C Critical Thinking

Comparing and Contrasting Ask: How is a representative democracy different from a direct democracy? *(A representative democracy elects people to represent the majority, whereas each person has a first-hand say in a direct democracy.)* **OL**

D Differentiated Instruction

Gifted and Talented Have students investigate when Great Britain became a modern constitutional monarchy and the effect it had on its citizens. Have them present an oral report to the class, using a timeline to assist with their presentation. **AL**

Analyzing Charts

Answers:
1. the people, the citizens, the voters
2. the law

Civics ONLINE

Objectives and answers to the **Student Web Activity** can be found at glencoe.com under the Web Activity Lesson Plan for this chapter.

Differentiated Instruction

What Is a Republic? Many countries have a **representative democracy** instead. The citizens choose a smaller group to represent them, make laws, and govern on their behalf. For most Americans today, the terms representative democracy, **republic,** and constitutional republic mean the same thing: a system of limited government in which the people are the ultimate source of governmental power. The United States is the oldest representative democracy in the world.

Constitutional Monarchy Another kind of democracy is the constitutional monarchy. The word **monarchy** describes a government

with a hereditary ruler—a king, queen, or other royal figure who inherits this position of power. In most countries with monarchs, the power of the hereditary ruler is limited by the country's constitution and laws.

Modern constitutional monarchies generally follow democratic practices. The monarchs are heads of state only, presiding at ceremonies and serving as symbols of unity. The queen of Great Britain and the emperor of Japan are two examples of constitutional monarchs.

Democratic Principles

Abraham Lincoln described our democracy as a "government of the people, by the people, for the people." His words make three important points. First, the power of the government comes from the citizens. Second, Americans themselves, acting through their representatives, run their government. Third, the purpose of the government is to make the United States a better place for those who live here.

Voting and Democracy All genuine democracies have free, fair, and competitive elections. Everyone's vote must carry the same weight. This principle is often expressed in the phrase "one person, one vote." All candidates have the right to express their views freely to the public, and citizens are free to support any candidate or issue.

The legal requirements for voting must be kept to a minimum. For example, our voting laws center on age, residence, and citizenship, while other factors, such as wealth, race, and ethnic and religious background, cannot be used to restrict voting. Finally, citizens may vote freely by secret ballot, without fearing punishment for their voting decisions.

Principles of American Democracy

RULE OF LAW
- All people, including those who govern, are bound by the law.

LIMITED GOVERNMENT
- Government is not all-powerful—it may do only those things that the people have given it the power to do.

CONSENT OF THE GOVERNED
- American citizens are the source of all government power.

INDIVIDUAL RIGHTS
- In the American democracy, individual rights are protected by government.

REPRESENTATIVE GOVERNMENT
- People elect government leaders to make the laws and govern on their behalf.

Analyzing Charts

1. **Identifying** Who is the source of power in direct and representative democracies?
2. **Explaining** What binds the governed together in a democracy?

Civics ONLINE

Student Web Activity Visit glencoe.com and complete the Chapter 1 Web Activity.

Leveled Activities

BL Content Vocabulary, Activity 1, URB pp. 21–22

OL Speaking/Listening Activity 1, URB pp. 9–11

ELL Chart/Graph/ Map Activity 1, URB pp. 33–34

Comparing Democratic and Authoritarian Systems

	Selection of Leaders	Extent of Government Power	Means of Ensuring Compliance	Political Parties
Democracy	Leaders are chosen in fair elections with universal suffrage	The government is limited in power by the constitution and laws; citizens' rights and freedoms are protected	The government relies on the rule of law	Multiple parties exist
Authoritarianism (including absolute monarchy, dictatorship, and totalitarianism)	Rulers inherit their positions or take power by force	Rulers have unlimited power; the government may impose an official ideology and control all aspects of political, economic, and civic life	The government relies on state control of the media, propaganda, military or police power, and terror	Power lies with a single party

Analyzing Charts

1. **Explaining** Why do you think dictators control their military and police forces?

2. **Comparing** How do the leaders gain their positions of power in each form of government?

Voters Have Choices Competitive elections and competing political parties are an important element in democracies. A political party is a group of individuals with broad, common interests who organize to support candidates for office and determine public policy. Competing political parties give voters a choice among candidates. Also, parties out of power serve as watchdogs of parties in power.

Majority Rule Another principle of our democracy is **majority rule.** French philosopher Jean-Jacques Rousseau promoted this idea in the late 1700s. According to this principle, citizens agree that when differences of opinion arise, they will abide by what most people want. At the same time, they respect the rights of those in the minority.

Respect for minority rights is sometimes difficult, though, especially if society is under a great deal of stress. For example, after the terrorist attacks of 2001, President George W. Bush realized that many Americans might turn their anger against Muslims in the United States. He explained that Islam is a peaceful religion and urged Americans to treat Muslim Americans fairly.

Authoritarian Government

In democratic regimes, the people rule. In **authoritarian** regimes, power is held by an individual or a group not accountable to the people.

Absolute Monarchy Until about the 1600s, monarchs were mostly absolute monarchs. That is, they had unlimited authority to rule as they wished. Many countries still have monarchs, but absolute monarchy is almost nonexistent today. In the Middle East, however, the king of Saudi Arabia and the emir of Qatar might still be considered "absolute." Their power is technically unrestricted, although they do consult with advisers and are **constrained,** or bound, by Islamic law.

R Reading Strategy

Making Connections Ask: What can citizens do if their ideals are in the minority? *(Citizens can write editorials and write to their representatives; or they can demonstrate peacefully to let their voices be heard.)* What would you do if you felt the majority was wrong? *(Students may suggest they would write letters or start a grass-roots organization to get their ideas across to the majority.)* **AL**

C Critical Thinking

Making Generalizations Have students explain why citizens in an absolute monarchy have fewer rights than those in a democracy. **OL**

D Differentiated Instruction

Below Grade Level Have students create a Venn diagram listing differences and similarities between an absolute monarchy and a constitutional monarchy. **BL ELL**

Analyzing Charts

Answers:
1. to ensure their positions of power
2. In a democracy, leaders are elected. In an authoritarian system, the leader inherits the power or takes it by force.

Additional Support

Activity: Collaborative Learning

Drawing Conclusions Help students understand that government is a necessary organization for living in a peaceful community. Group students together and have each group write and perform a skit that illustrates why communities need a government. Assign a certain type of government for each group *(democracy, monarchy, dictatorship, and so on).* **Ask:** Why is the type of government important to the people? Explain to students that government is important for order, but only a few types of governments allow its citizens equal rights under the law. **OL**

W Writing Support

Personal Writing Have students write one paragraph describing their thoughts about monarchies or totalitarian states. **AL**

✓**Reading Check** **Answer:** one in which the government controls most aspects of people's lives

Assess

Civics ONLINE

Study Central™ provides summaries, interactive games, and online graphic organizers to help students review content.

Close

Analyzing Information Tell students that though there are many democracies throughout the world, presently there are countries ruled by dictators. **Ask:** Why are dictatorships able to exist in modern societies? *(Dictators take control by force, using military tactics to uphold their position. Many citizens do not have the means to rebel. Citizens are misinformed and believe their quality of life will improve. Some countries, such as Cuba, believe that democracy is detrimental to the people.)* **OL**

Section 3 Review

Dictatorships Another form of authoritarian government is a dictatorship. Dictators, like absolute monarchs, exercise complete control over the state. Unlike absolute monarchs, who usually acquire their power through inheritance, dictators usually take power by force. At times, when a crisis situation demands a strong leader, authorities may place them in charge. To stay in power, most dictators rely on the police and military. They often tamper with elections or refuse to hold them. They also limit freedoms of speech, assembly, and the press.

Scores of dictators have ruled throughout history. Those who seek only personal gain are often overthrown quickly. With the help of the United States, Panamanian dictator Manuel Noriega was overthrown in 1989. Other dictators endure for decades. Fidel Castro led Cuba from 1959 until he retired in 2008. Saddam Hussein ruled Iraq from 1979 until he was overthrown in 2003. Hussein was convicted of crimes against humanity and executed in 2007.

Totalitarianism Many dictators impose totalitarian rule on their people. In a **totalitarian** state, the government's control extends to almost all aspects of people's lives. Totalitarian leaders ban political opposition. They regulate what industries and farms produce. They suppress individual freedom, dictating what people should believe and with whom they may interact. The people lack the power to limit their rulers.

W To enforce their ideology, or ideas about life and society, totalitarian leaders control the media and use propaganda, scare tactics, and violence. Three of the most notorious totalitarian regimes arose in the 1920s and 1930s. They were Nazi Germany under Adolf Hitler, Fascist Italy under Benito Mussolini, and the Soviet Union under Joseph Stalin. Today, the nations of China, Cuba, and North Korea are usually considered totalitarian states.

✓**Reading Check** **Describing** What is a totalitarian government?

Section 3 Review

Vocabulary

1. **Write** complete sentences that demonstrate the meaning of each of the following terms: *government, public policy, budget, democracy, direct democracy, representative democracy, republic, monarchy, majority rule, authoritarian, totalitarian.*

Main Ideas

2. **Identifying** Name three public services that governments provide.

3. **Comparing** What is the difference between rulers in a democracy and rulers in a totalitarian state?

Critical Thinking

4. **BIG Ideas** What do you think would happen if there were no governments anywhere in the world? Describe such a situation, then explain why governments are necessary.

5. **Organizing** On a diagram like the one below, write the functions of government.

```
      Government
    ┌──┬──┬──┐
    □  □  □  □
```

6. **Analyzing Visuals** Review the principles of American democracy on page 24. How does the American government carry out the principle of consent of the governed?

CITIZENSHIP Activity

7. **Descriptive Writing** In a one-page essay, explain how you think your life would be different if you were living in a country ruled by a monarch.

Civics ONLINE

Study Central™ To review this section, go to glencoe.com.

Answers

1. Sentences should use vocabulary words according to their definitions in the section and in the Glossary.

2. Answers will vary. Responses may include managing libraries, schools, hospitals, parks; building streets and bridges; delivering the mail; setting up fire departments, ambulance services, police protection, and so on.

3. In a democracy, a ruler is elected by its people and must answer to them. In a totalitarian state, a ruler assumes control by force and dictates what the people should believe.

4. Answers will vary, but students should suggest that there would be chaos, fighting, and fear. Some form of governing body is needed so that people maintain order.

5. keeping order; providing security; providing services; guiding the community

6. The citizens of America are the source of governmental power. They run their own government through representatives.

7. Essays will vary but should include how difficult it would be for the people to express their opinions and engage in most freedoms if the ruling monarch were oppressive.

The American People

- Because of its heritage, the United States is often called "a nation of immigrants."
- Until the mid-1900s, most immigrants came from Europe.
- Asia now accounts for the largest share of immigrants to the United States.
- The United States is a diverse nation, reflecting the values of many groups.

American Values and Institutions

- Values are ideas about what is good or desirable that are shared by people in a society.
- Our basic values include freedom, equality, opportunity, justice, and tolerance.

- Every society has institutions that help it transmit its values.
- Important American institutions are the family, religious, educational, social, and governmental institutions.

Citizenship

- According to the U.S. Constitution, people can become American citizens by birth and through naturalization.
- Millions of illegal aliens live in the United States. Legal aliens have entered the country lawfully.

Government

- People need governments to make and enforce laws and to help us meet our needs.

The purposes of government include the following:

- Providing order and security
- Providing public services

Yosemite National Park

- Guiding the community
- Although all governments carry out the same basic functions, there are differences in the ways governments can be organized.
- The main types of government are democratic government and authoritarian government.
- In a democracy, the supreme political authority rests with the people.

School crossing guard

Official ballot

STUDY TO GO Study anywhere, anytime! Download quizzes and flash cards to your PDA from glencoe.com.

Comparing and Contrasting Have students research information about immigration laws via news outlets. Then have the students contribute to a group summary of their findings. Next have students choose states. The students will use www.senate.gov to research the immigration views of a senator from their chosen state. **Ask:** What are the main arguments for and against reforming U.S. immigration laws? Have students create a chart listing senators who are against changing the current immigration laws and those who want reform. Students may present their findings to the class. **AL**

Organizing Have students create a flowchart illustrating the different levels of government: national, state, and local. Have them include a bulleted list of responsibilities that each level has and share their findings with the class. **OL**

Hands-On Chapter Project
Step 4: Wrap-Up

Immigrating to the United States

Step 4: Becoming a U.S. Citizen Students will finish the process they started in Step 1.

Directions As a class, decide on an acceptable passing score for the civics test. Next, pairs of students will exchange the civics tests they created and take them. Have the writers of the tests provide you with a copy

and answer key. Writers may grade their test.

Each pair that passes its test may take the Oath of Allegiance by reciting it to each other. Then have each pair write a one-page essay that describes what the Oath of Allegiance means to them.

Finally, have pairs get into small groups and discuss what steps of the process they found difficult. Have them look at their

flowcharts from Section 2 and determine if they would recommend any changes to the process. For example, do they think the civics test is too easy or too difficult? To finalize the project, have groups use their essays to discuss the meaning of the Oath of Allegiance and the responsibilities and rights they have as naturalized U.S. citizens. **OL**

Answers and Analyses

Reviewing Vocabulary

1. C Students will have read about values in Section 1 in a section entitled "American Values and Institutions." Students will have learned what values are, why they are important, and how they unite us as Americans. A student could also use the process of elimination to rule out the three incorrect answers by using the knowledge that only values can be described as ideas, yet public policies, institutions and budgets are sets of ideas.

2. D The bracketed definition of "popular sovereignty" can be found in the "Shared Values Unite Americans" portion of Section 1. There are a number of examples of how popular sovereignty affects our government that are listed under the definition. If the student recalls these important ideas—fair, free and regular elections; equal justice under law; and more—they should be able to identify the correct answer.

3. C In this question, the most confusing distractor will most likely be answer B, immigrants. Students should be able to note the key differences between immigrants and aliens after reading this chapter. In most cases, the "short time" limitation in the question will direct students to the correct answer.

4. C The phrase that is used in the text to most clearly point a student in the right direction would be "one person, one vote" found in the "democratic principles" portion of Section 3. Lincoln described the American democracy as a "government of the people, by the people, for the people." The other three types of governments are shown clearly to differ from the democratic republic in the table comparing democratic and authoritarian systems.

Reviewing Main Ideas

5. D This question will require the student to read the in-depth population breakdown with care. The key here is to pay close attention to the bulleted points in the "Transforming America" portion of Section 1. Here, the major modern changes in the population of our country

TEST-TAKING TIP

> Keep daily notes to review for tests and examinations. It often helps you retain information if you review your notes with a study partner.

Reviewing Vocabulary

Directions: Choose the word(s) that best completes the sentence.

1. _____ are broad ideas about what is good and desirable.

  A public policies   **C** values

  B institutions   **D** budgets

2. Government by consent of the governed is _____.

  A community   **C** naturalization

  B majority rule   **D** popular sovereignty

3. People from foreign countries who plan to stay in the United States for a short time are called _____.

  A citizens   **C** aliens

  B immigrants   **D** institutions

4. The people are the ultimate source of government power in a _____.

  A monarchy   **C** republic

  B dictatorship   **D** totalitarian state

Reviewing Main Ideas

Directions: Choose the best answer for each question.

Section 1 *(pp. 6–13)*

5. Which is the fastest growing ethnic group in the United States today?

  A Native Americans

  B African Americans

  C European Americans

  D Latino Americans

6. Which value is part of Americans' common civic and political heritage?

  A fair elections

  B volunteerism

  C caring parents

  D cultural education

Section 2 *(pp. 14–19)*

7. Which person is NOT a United States citizen?

  A a child born in Guam to Japanese parents

  B a girl born in Yemen to an American mother

  C a boy born in Illinois to Mexican parents

  D a child born in Great Britain to Irish parents

8. What is the primary responsibility of the National Border Patrol?

  A to deport aliens with expired visas

  B to prevent illegal entry of aliens

  C to naturalize resident aliens

  D to issue visas to legal aliens

Section 3 *(pp. 20–26)*

9. Which function of government do public libraries fulfill?

  A keeping order

  B providing public security

  C providing services

  D guiding the community

10. Which factor is a legal restriction on voting in the United States?

  A age

  B race

  C wealth

  D religion

GO ON

are listed, including the information about the fastest-growing ethnic group.

6. A While all of the answer options here are important issues in our civic and cultural history, only one is mentioned and highlighted in the "Democratic Principles" segment of Section 3. Students should recall what values are important in our own constitutional republic. The distractors should be properly seen as important cultural and societal values, but fair elections

is the clear solution to this political question.

7. D This question is challenging due to the pairings of countries and nationalities. The key to answering this question is to determine the connection to American citizenship in each distractor. The strongest distractor is the child born in Guam because students may not remember that Guam is a U.S. territory. The correct answer has no connection to the United States.

Critical Thinking

Directions: Base your answers to questions 11 and 12 on the chart below and your knowledge of Chapter 1.

Rule of Law
All people, including those who govern, are bound by the law.

Limited Government
Government is not all powerful—it may do only those things that the people have given it the power to do.

Consent of the Governed
American citizens are the source of all governmental power.

Individual Rights
In the American democracy, individual rights are protected by government.

Representative Government
People elect leaders to make the laws and govern on their behalf.

11. Which principle of American democracy prevents a president from serving more terms than allowed in Amendment XXII of the Constitution?

   A rule of law

   B limited government

   C individual rights

   D representative government

12. Which practice best reflects the principle of representative government?

   A serving on a jury

   B voting for mayor

   C writing to the editor

   D polling public opinion

Document Based Questions

Directions: Analyze the following document and answer the short-answer questions that follow.

> The passage is from *The Social Contract* by Jean Jacques Rousseau, the eighteenth-century political theorist, who believed that real democracy was impossible.
>
> *Nothing is more dangerous than the influence of private interests on public affairs; and the abuse of the laws by the government is a lesser evil than the corruption of the legislator [lawmaker], which is the infallible result of the pursuit of private interests. For when the State is changed in its substance all reform becomes impossible. A people which would never abuse the government would likewise never abuse its independence; a people which always governed well would not need to be governed.*
>
> —Jean Jacques Rousseau

13. How might the corruption of a legislator who pursues his or her private interests endanger the democratic principle of majority rule? Give an example.

14. What do you think Rousseau means by a government's independence?

Extended Response

15. Many American citizens confuse legal and illegal aliens. Write a brief essay comparing and contrasting the situations of illegal aliens with that of resident aliens.

STOP

For additional test practice, use Self-Check Quizzes—Chapter 1 on glencoe.com.

Need Extra Help?

If you missed question. . .	1	2	3	4	5	6	7	8	9	10	11	12	13	14	15
Go to page. . .	11	12	16	24	9	12	15	19	22	24	24	24	25	24	18

ASSESSMENT

answer choice is the only correct one. The most likely distractor might be race as students could confuse race with residence or citizenship.

Critical Thinking

11. A This question challenges the students' understanding of the fundamental principles of American democracy. If the students read the question carefully, they should understand that it is asking them to distinguish which principle limits the power of the president.

12. B The student should review the chart to understand what the principle of representative government is. Students should also remember the portion of Section 2 defining a representative democracy. Because the principle of representative government consists of the citizens' right to choose a group of people to represent them, to make laws, and to govern on their behalf, the correct answer is B.

Document-Based Questions

13. Students' answers will vary. A possible answer is that a legislator who passes laws to please private interests—major corporate contributors to his or her campaign, for example—places the wishes of the minority (i.e., the contributors) before the will of the majority.

14. Students' answers will vary. A possible answer is that an independent government serves the general good and not the interests of a few.

Extended Response

15. Students' essays will vary. Look for supporting details from the chapter.

---

8. B All of the answers for this question seem plausible if students do not read carefully. For example, understanding "deport" and "alien" is critical to judging whether the first answer choice is the correct answer. This answer choice is the most likely distractor. Students must recognize that the National Border Patrol works to keep illegal aliens from entering the country, not finding them once they are in the United States.

9. C This question presents a challenge in that all the answers are functions of the government. However, the students should understand that libraries provide services to their communities by making books available to the public.

10. A Students may recall that various groups have been barred from voting in the past. However, the only current restrictions on voting in the United States are age, residence, and citizenship. Thus, the first

Civics ONLINE

Have students visit the Web site at glencoe.com to review Chapter 1 and take the **Self-Check Quiz**.

Need Extra Help?

Have students refer to the pages listed if they miss any of the questions.

Chapter Planning Guide

2

Levels BL	OL	AL	ELL		Resources	Chapter Opener	Section 1	Section 2	Section 3	Section 4	Chapter Assess
					FOCUS						
BL	OL	AL	ELL	🖨	**Daily Focus Skills Transparencies**		2–1	2–2	2–3	2–4	
					TEACH						
BL	OL		ELL	📁	**Reading Essentials and Note-Taking Guide***		p. 10	p. 13	p. 16	p. 19	
	OL	AL		📁	**Primary Source Reading, URB**		p. 15				
BL	OL	AL	ELL	📁	**Content Vocabulary Activity, URB***	p. 45	p. 45	p. 45	p. 45	p. 45	
BL	OL	AL	ELL	📁	**Academic Vocabulary Activity, URB**	p. 47	p. 47	p. 47	p. 47	p. 47	
	OL			📁	**Biography Activity, URB**					p. 49	
BL	OL	AL	ELL	📁	**Writing Skills Activity, URB**		p. 51	p. 51	p. 51	p. 51	
	OL	AL		📁	**Critical Thinking Skills Activity, URB**			p. 55			
BL	OL	AL	ELL	📁	**Chart, Graph, and Map Skills Activity, URB**					p. 57	
BL	OL	AL	ELL	📁	**Differentiated Instruction, URB**		p. 59				
BL	OL	AL	ELL	📁	**School-to-Home Connection Activity, URB***	p. 61	p. 61	p. 61	p. 61	p. 61	
BL	OL		ELL	📁	**Guided Reading Activities, URB***		p. 65	p. 66	p. 67	p. 68	
BL	OL			📁	**Focus on American History**		p. 16	p. 16	p. 21	p. 29	
BL	OL	AL	ELL	📁	**Writer's Guidebook**	✓	✓	✓	✓	✓	✓
	OL	AL		💿	**Primary Source Document Library**	✓	✓	✓	✓	✓	✓
BL	OL	AL	ELL	💿	**Daily Lecture & Discussion Notes (in Pres. Plus)**		✓	✓	✓	✓	✓
BL	OL	AL	ELL	💿	**StudentWorks™ Plus**		✓	✓	✓	✓	✓
BL	OL	AL	ELL	💿	**Section Spotlight Videos**		✓	✓	✓	✓	
BL	OL	AL	ELL	🖨	**TIME Interpreting Political Cartoons Transp.**					Ch. 2	
BL	OL	AL	ELL	🖨	**Writing Process Transparencies**	✓	✓	✓	✓	✓	✓

Note: Please refer to the *Unit 1 Resource Book* for this chapter's URB materials.

* Also available in Spanish

- Interactive Lesson Planner
- Interactive Teacher Edition
- Fully editable blackline masters
- Section Spotlight Videos Launch
- Differentiated Lesson Plans
- Printable reports of daily assignments
- Standards Tracking System

Levels					Resources	Chapter Opener	Section 1	Section 2	Section 3	Section 4	Chapter Assess
BL	OL	AL	ELL								
					TEACH *(continued)*						
Teacher Resources				📁	**Building Academic Vocabulary**	✓	✓	✓	✓	✓	✓
				📁	**Strategies for Success**	✓	✓	✓	✓	✓	✓
				📁	**Teachers Guide to Differentiated Instruction**	✓	✓	✓	✓	✓	✓
				💿	**Graphing Tool**	✓	✓	✓	✓	✓	✓
				💿	**Presentation Plus! with MindJogger CheckPoint**	✓	✓	✓	✓	✓	✓
					ASSESS						
BL	OL	AL	ELL	📁	**Quizzes and Tests***		p. 14	p. 15	p. 16	p. 17	p. 18
BL	OL	AL	ELL	📁	**Authentic Assessment with Rubrics**		p. 6	p. 6	p. 6	p. 6	
BL	OL	AL	ELL	📁	**Standardized Test Practice**		p. 3	p. 3	p. 3	p. 3	p. 3
BL	OL	AL	ELL	💿	*ExamView®* **Assessment Suite CD-ROM**		2–1	2–2	2–3	2–4	Ch. 2
					CLOSE						
BL			ELL	📁	**Reteaching Activity, URB***	p. 63	p. 63	p. 63	p. 63	p. 63	
BL	OL		ELL	📁	**Reading and Study Skills Foldables™ Activity**	p. 53	p. 53			p. 53	
BL	OL	AL	ELL	📁	*Civics Today* **in Graphic Novel**	p. 1				p. 1	
BL	OL	AL	ELL	🖨	**Graphic Organizer Transparencies & Strategies**	✓	✓	✓	✓	✓	✓

✓ Chapter- or unit-based activities applicable to all sections in this chapter

Integrating Technology

2

Using the Media Library

Section Spotlight Videos

What is the Media Library?

The Media Library is an online tool that includes videos that highlight a theme or concept in each section of the textbook.

How can the Media Library help my students?

The Media Library helps you:

- activate students' prior knowledge as they begin to study each section
- teach section content using digital media
- connect section content with students' lives

Visit glencoe.com and enter a **QuickPass**™ code to go directly to resources for each chapter.

Civics ONLINE

Visit glencoe.com and enter **QuickPass**™ code CIV1360c2T for Chapter 2 resources.

You can easily launch a wide range of digital products from your computer's desktop with the McGraw-Hill Social Studies widget.

	Student	Teacher	Parent
Media Library			
• Student Edition Section Audio	●		●
• Spanish Audio Summaries	●		●
• Section Spotlight Videos	●	●	●
***Civics Today* Online Learning Center (Web Site)**			
• Chapter Overviews	●	●	●
• Study Central™	●	●	●
• Study-to-Go	●	●	●
• Student Web Activities	●	●	●
• In Motion Animation	●	●	●
• Self-Check Quizzes	●	●	●
• ePuzzles and Games	●	●	●
• StudentWorks™ Plus Online	●	●	●
• Vocabulary eFlashcards	●	●	●
• Web Activity Lesson Plans		●	
• Vocabulary PuzzleMaker	●	●	●
Classroom Tools			
• Multilingual Glossary	●	●	●
• Beyond the Textbook	●	●	●
• NGS MapMachine	●	●	●

Reading List Generator CD-ROM

GLENCOE BOOKLINK 3

Use this database to search more than 30,000 titles to create a customized reading list for your students.

- Reading lists can be organized by students' reading level, author, genre, theme, or area of interest.
- The database provides Degrees of Reading Power™ (DRP) and Lexile™ readability scores for all selections.
- A brief summary of each selection is included.

Leveled reading suggestions for this chapter:

For students at a Grade 7 reading level:
- *A Journey to the New World: The Diary of Remember Patience Whipple, Mayflower, 1620,* by Kathryn Lasky

For students at a Grade 8 reading level:
- *John Winthrop, Oliver Cromwell, and the Land of Promise,* by Marc Aronson

For students at a Grade 9 reading level:
- *Founding Mothers: Women of America in the Revolutionary War,* by Linda Grant De Pauw

For students at a Grade 10 reading level:
- *On Liberty,* by John Stuart Mill

For students at a Grade 11 reading level:
- *Thomas Jefferson,* by Joyce Appleby

READING SUPPORT FROM JAMESTOWN EDUCATION

- **Timed Readings Plus in Social Studies** helps students increase their reading rate and fluency while maintaining comprehension. The 400-word passages are similar to those found on state and national assessments.

- **Reading in the Content Area: Social Studies** concentrates on six essential reading skills that help students better comprehend what they read. The book includes 75 high-interest nonfiction passages written at increasing levels of difficulty.

- **Reading Social Studies** includes strategic reading instruction and vocabulary support in Social Studies content for both ELLs and native speakers of English.

- **Content Vocabulary Workout** (Grades 6–8) accelerates reading comprehension through focused vocabulary development. Social Studies content vocabulary comes from the glossaries of Glencoe's Middle School Social Studies texts. www.jamestowneducation.com

KEY Teacher Wraparound

Use this key to help you identify the different types of prompts found in the Teacher Wraparound Edition.

R **Reading Strategies** activities help you teach reading skills and vocabulary.

C **Critical Thinking** strategies help students apply and extend what they have learned.

D **Differentiated Instruction** activities provide instruction for students learning to speak English, along with suggestions for teaching various types of learners.

S **Skill Practice** strategies help students practice historical analysis and geography skills.

W **Writing Support** activities provide writing opportunities to help students comprehend the text.

Teaching strategies and activities have been coded for ability level appropriateness.

AL Activities for students working above grade level

OL Activities for students working on grade level

BL Activities for students working below grade level

ELL Activities for English Language Learners

Focus

Why It Matters

Ask: What does "limited and representative government" mean to you? *(Answers may include the idea that government should limit its power by not intruding into the lives of its citizens, but at the same time, it should represent and protect their rights.)*

More About the Photo

Visual Literacy The Lincoln Memorial was designed by New York architect Henry Bacon. It was dedicated in 1922, 57 years after President Lincoln's death. Located on the National Mall in Washington, D.C., the memorial is built in the style of a Greek temple. The 36 Doric columns outside the memorial represent the U.S. states that existed when our 16th president died. The centerpiece of this symbol of American democracy is a 19-foot-tall statue of Lincoln carved from white marble by Daniel Chester French. Engraved on the wall behind it are the words "In this temple, as in the hearts of the people for whom he saved the union, the memory of Abraham Lincoln is enshrined forever."

Teach

BIG Ideas *As you begin teaching each section, use these questions and activities to help students focus on the Big Ideas.*

Section 1

Our English Heritage Ask: Why did the colonists hold on to their country's ideas about government? *(The ideas had been developing for centuries; except for the lack of religious freedom, the colonists*

Chapter
2
Roots of American Democracy

Why It Matters

The American colonies were settled by individuals from many nations. Nonetheless, the majority of American settlers came from England. Many of the rights that American citizens enjoy can be traced to the political and legal traditions of England. When English people began settling in the Americas, they brought with them a tradition of limited and representative government.

30

believed the ideas were worth implementing.) Point out that in Section 1, students will learn about the heritage and values the U.S. shares with England. **OL**

Section 2

The English Colonies Ask: Why did the colonists settle in America? *(Some came to escape religious persecution; others came for economic opportunities; slaves, prisoners, and criminals were brought here.)* Tell students that in Section 2, they will learn about the people who established the thirteen colonies and their reasons for doing so. **OL**

Chapter Audio

Civics ONLINE
Visit glencoe.com and enter
QuickPass™ code
CIV3093c2 for
Chapter 2
resources.

Chapter Introduction
2

BIG Ideas

Section 1: Our English Heritage

Political and economic institutions evolve to help individuals and groups accomplish their goals. The English colonists brought with them ideas about government that had been developing in England for centuries.

Section 2: The English Colonies

Political, social, religious, and economic changes influence the way Americans think and act. The English established thirteen colonies along the East Coast of North America.

Section 3: Colonial Society

Political, social, religious, and economic changes influence the way Americans think and act. The English colonists created a prosperous economy and learned to govern themselves.

◀ The Lincoln Memorial is an important symbol of American democracy.

Section 4: Birth of a Democratic Nation

Political principles and major events shape how people form governments. The Declaration of Independence explained why the colonies were founding a new nation.

FOLDABLES™
Study Organizer

Sequencing Information Study Foldable Make the following Foldable to help you sequence information about the roots of American democracy.

Step 1 Fold the paper in half from side to side.

Step 3 Cut the top layer of the paper only along the fold lines.

Reading and Writing As you read the chapter write details of the sequence of events that unfolded as democracy developed in America under the tabs.

Step 2 Turn the paper and fold it in half and in half again.

Step 4 Label each tab as shown.

Chapter 2 31

FOLDABLES™
Study Organizer **Dinah Zike's Foldables**

Purpose This Foldable guides the student to understand the sequence of events that led to the birth of America as a democratic nation. The completed Foldable uses tabs to sequence information and to list details that led to the Declaration of Independence. **OL**

📁 More Foldables activities for this chapter can be found in the *Dinah Zike's Reading and Study Skills Foldables* ancillary.

Civics ONLINE

Visit glencoe.com and enter *QuickPass™* code CIV1360c2T for Chapter 2 resources, including a Chapter Overview, Study Central™, Study-to-Go, Student Web Activity, Self-Check Quiz, and other materials.

★ Section 3

Colonial Society Ask: How did geography affect the livelihood of colonists in different regions? *(Settlers in the New England, Middle, and Southern Colonies had to make the best use of natural resources and opportunities in each area.)* Explain that in Section 3, students will learn about the different economies that developed in each area. The developing American identity is also discussed. **OL**

★ Section 4

Birth of a Democratic Nation Ask: What caused the colonists to rebel against British control? *(To help pay off debts incurred during the French and Indian War [1754–1763], the British imposed harsh and unfair trade and tax policies on the colonists.)* Explain that in Section 4, students will learn about the events that led colonists to use traditional English political rights to begin their struggle for independence. **OL**

Focus

Bellringer

Daily Focus Transparency 2–1

Guide to Reading

Answers to Graphic:

Greek Law — Common Law
Roman Law
Statutory Law — American Law — Equity Law
Constitutional Law

Section Spotlight Video

To generate student interest and provide a springboard for class discussion, access the Chapter 2, Section 1 video at glencoe.com or on the video DVD.

Resource Manager

Guide to Reading

Big Idea
Political and economic institutions evolve to help individuals and groups accomplish their goals.

Content Vocabulary
- Enlightenment *(p. 33)*
- monarch *(p. 33)*
- legislature *(p. 33)*
- precedent *(p. 34)*
- common law *(p. 34)*
- natural rights *(p. 34)*
- social contract *(p. 35)*
- colony *(p. 36)*
- joint-stock company *(p. 36)*
- charter *(p. 36)*
- compact *(p. 36)*

Academic Vocabulary
- document *(p. 33)*
- authority *(p. 33)*
- grant *(p. 33)*

Reading Strategy
Organizing As you read, complete a web diagram like the one below by listing six sources of American law.

American Law

Our English Heritage

Real World Civics For many of us, town meetings seem like something from another century—and for the most part they are. The first settlers in this country, most of whom were English, brought with them their traditional forms of government, which relied on local involvement. Town meetings are a form of direct democracy, giving citizens a clear voice in decision making. The purpose of the town meeting has not changed in over 200 years.

▼ **Town meeting in Bridgeport, Vermont**

R Reading Strategies	**C** Critical Thinking	**D** Differentiated Instruction	**W** Writing Support	**S** Skill Practice
Teacher Edition • Predicting, p. 33 • Identifying, p. 35 • Analyzing Information, p. 36 **Additional Resources** • Pri. Source Read., URB p. 15 • Cont. Vocab., URB p. 45 • Acad. Vocab., URB p. 47 • Guid. Read., URB p. 65	**Teacher Edition** • Ident. Cent., p. 33 • Analyzing Pri. Sources, p. 35 • Predicting, p. 36 **Additional Resources** • Quizzes and Tests, p. 14	**Teacher Edition** • English Learners, p. 34 • Logical/Math., p. 36 • Gifted/Talented, p. 37 **Additional Resources** • Diff. Instr., URB p. 59 • Teacher's Guide to Differentiated Instruction, p. 3	**Teacher Edition** • Personal Writing, p. 34 **Additional Resources** • Authentic Assessment, p. 6	**Teacher Edition** • Visual Literacy, p. 34 • Using Geo. Skills, p. 37 **Additional Resources** • Daily Focus Trans., 2–1

What Influenced Colonial Government?

Main Idea Science and the influence of reason led to new innovations in political thought.

Civics & You What helps people get along with each other? Do they need rules, a strong leader, or to share the same goals? Read to learn how thinkers in Europe answered these questions.

Many of the rights that American citizens enjoy today can be traced to the political and legal traditions of England and to the ideas of a cultural movement called the **Enlightenment.** When English people began settling here in the 1600s, they brought with them a history of limited and representative government. They also brought with them new ideas about law, society, and the rights people possessed.

For centuries, England had been ruled by a **monarch**—a king or queen. However, noble families also had considerable power. The monarch gave them ownership and control of vast lands in exchange for their loyalty, tax payments, and promises of military support.

The Magna Carta

In 1215, nobles rebelled against King John, who had treated them harshly. They forced the king to sign an agreement called the Magna Carta (Latin for "Great Charter"). This **document,** or deed, protected the nobles' privileges and **authority,** or control. It also **granted,** or allowed, certain rights to all landholders—rights that eventually came to apply to all English people. These rights included equal treatment under the law and trial by one's peers. The Magna Carta limited the power of the monarch by guaranteeing that no one would be above the law, not even the king or queen. 📖 (See the Appendix to read this document.)

Parliament

Kings who followed John met regularly with nobles and church officials to get their advice. Gradually, this group grew in size and power, expanding to include representatives of the common people. By the late 1300s, it had developed into a **legislature**—a lawmaking body—known as Parliament.

For the next few centuries, English monarchs cooperated with Parliament. In the mid-1600s, however, serious power struggles began. In 1688, Parliament removed King James II from the throne and invited his daughter Mary and her husband William to rule instead. In doing so, Parliament demonstrated that it was now stronger than the monarch.

This peaceful transfer of power, known as the Glorious Revolution, changed government in England. From that time on, no ruler would have more power than Parliament.

Authority From the end of the seventeenth century on, English monarchs, such as George III, shared the powers of government with Parliament. ***Describing*** How did the authority of English monarchs change?

33

Teach

C Critical Thinking

Identifying Central Issues Have students briefly state the central issue addressed by the Magna Carta and the Glorious Revolution. *(In both cases, monarchs surrendered power to the people.)* **OL**

R Reading Strategy

Predicting Ask: What might have happened to King John if he had refused to sign the Magna Carta? *(He probably would have been removed from the throne or possibly even killed.)* **OL**

Caption Answer:

Students may say that the Glorious Revolution in 1688 peacefully and permanently transferred power from the monarch to Parliament. Encourage students to name the king that Parliament removed from the throne and his replacement. *(King James II was replaced by his daughter Mary and her husband William.)*

Additional Support

Did You Know?

Parliament The word "parliament" is formed from two root words in French and Latin. The French word is "parler," which means to talk. The Latin word is "parliamentum." It is the word for the conversations monks used to engage in every evening after dinner.

Great Britain's parliament consists of the Monarch, the House of Lords, and the House of Commons. Today, the House of Lords has 700 members. The House of Commons has 646 elected MPs, or Members of Parliament.

D Differentiated Instruction

English Learners Point out the words "equity law" and "statutory" law in the chart. Tell students that the word "equity" means "fair or just." Explain that "statutory" comes from the word "statute." Statutes are the laws passed by legislatures. Equity laws are the laws used in courts. **Ask:** Why do we need different kinds of laws? *(Different laws address different situations or solve different problems.)* **ELL**

S Skill Practice

Visual Literacy Ask: How are constitutional and equity law different? *(Constitutional law is our most important source of law. Equity law is used in courts to resolve disputes.)* **OL**

W Writing Support

Personal Writing Have students write a paragraph or poem explaining what the word "liberty" means to them. They may include personal experiences, an anecdote, or an example. **OL**

Analyzing Charts

Answers:
1. because it is based on the Roman practice of writing their senate's laws
2. constitutional law

Differentiated Instruction

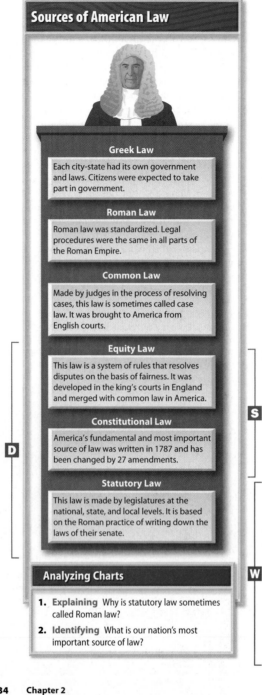

Sources of American Law

Greek Law
Each city-state had its own government and laws. Citizens were expected to take part in government.

Roman Law
Roman law was standardized. Legal procedures were the same in all parts of the Roman Empire.

Common Law
Made by judges in the process of resolving cases, this law is sometimes called case law. It was brought to America from English courts.

Equity Law
This law is a system of rules that resolves disputes on the basis of fairness. It was developed in the king's courts in England and merged with common law in America.

Constitutional Law
America's fundamental and most important source of law was written in 1787 and has been changed by 27 amendments.

Statutory Law
This law is made by legislatures at the national, state, and local levels. It is based on the Roman practice of writing down the laws of their senate.

Analyzing Charts

1. **Explaining** Why is statutory law sometimes called Roman law?
2. **Identifying** What is our nation's most important source of law?

English Bill of Rights To clarify this relationship, Parliament drew up the English Bill of Rights in 1689. This document further restricted the monarch's power. It also guaranteed free elections to Parliament, the right to a fair trial, and the elimination of cruel and unusual punishments.

Common Law

In its earliest days, England had no written laws. People developed rules to live by, however, and these customs came to have the force of law. In addition, as a court system developed, the courts' decisions became the basis of a body of law. When judges were asked to decide a case, they would look for a **precedent,** or a ruling in an earlier case that was similar. The judge would then make a consistent ruling.

This system of law is known as **common law.** It rests on court decisions rather than regulations written by lawmakers. Although England's system of common law came about without being planned, it worked well and has remained in place to this day. Our own laws about property, contracts, and personal injury are based on English common law.

Philosophical Influences

John Locke (1632–1704) was an English writer who supported the Glorious Revolution. Locke argued that people were born free, equal, and independent. They also possessed rights, called **natural rights,** to life, liberty, and property that no government could take away. In *The Second Treatise of Government,* Locke wrote:

> " *All mankind . . . being all equal and independent, no one ought to harm another in his life, health, liberty, or possessions.* "
>
> —John Locke, *The Second Treatise of Government*

Leveled Activities

BL Academic Vocabulary Activity 2, URB p. 47

OL Critical Thinking Skills Activity 2, URB pp. 55–56

AL Primary Source Reading 1A, URB pp. 15–16

ELL Differentiated Instruction Activity 2, pp. 59–60

What Is a Social Contract? Locke also believed that if a government tried to take away people's natural rights, it was breaking the social contract. A **social contract** is an agreement among the people in a society. They agree to give up part of their freedom to a government in exchange for protection of natural rights. The people agree to obey the government as long as it protects their rights.

French philosopher Jean-Jacques Rousseau (1712–1778) wrote in *The Social Contract,* published in 1762, that "man is born free, yet everywhere he is found in chains." Rousseau was referring to the large number of people **C** in Europe living under oppressive governments. He argued that the people alone had the right to determine how they should be governed.

Separation of Powers A French writer, Baron de Montesquieu (1689–1755), developed the idea about dividing the branches of government into different parts to balance

each other so that no one part can become too strong or threaten individual rights. His ideas on the separation of powers, along with Locke's ideas on the social contract and natural rights, became cornerstones of the Declaration of Independence and the U.S. Constitution.

Ideas of Enlightenment Locke and Montesquieu are considered Enlightenment thinkers. Building on the scientific discoveries of the 1600s, these thinkers believed that God had created an orderly universe. The laws of this universe could be discovered through the use of human reason. **R** Enlightenment thinkers argued that the laws that governed nature also applied to human life and society. As you will read, the ideas of the Enlightenment had a profound effect on Americans.

Reading Check Evaluating Why was the English Bill of Rights important to English citizens?

Social Contract The Mayflower Compact, signed by the Pilgrims in 1620, stands as the first example of many colonial plans for self-government. *Explaining* Why is the Mayflower Compact considered a social contract?

C Critical Thinking

Analyzing Primary Sources French philosopher Jean Jacques Rousseau wrote in 1762 that "man is born free, yet everywhere he is found in chains."
Ask: Do you think he approved or disapproved of this situation? Why? *(He disapproved. Using the word "yet" after the word "free" implies his disapproval.)* **OL**

For additional practice on this skill (Analyzing Primary Sources), see the **Skills Handbook.**

R Reading Strategy

Identifying Ask: What does the word "enlightenment" mean? *(the promotion of reasoning and the spread of knowledge)* **OL**

Reading Check **Answer:** It restricted the monarch's power, guaranteed free elections and the right to fair trials, and eliminated cruel and unusual punishments.

Caption Answer:

Students may say that the Mayflower Compact was a written set of rules for self-government that the Pilgrims drew up for themselves.

Critical Thinking Skills Activity 2, URB pp. 55-56

Assessing and Interpreting Sources

Objective: To understand Locke's reasoning

Focus: Have students seek Locke's reasons for limiting government involvement in religion.

Teach: Explain that Locke is writing from a nation with a state religion.

Assess: Identify over which parts of life Locke believes government should have some control.

Close: Outline Locke's reasons for government not controlling worship.

Differentiated Instruction Strategies

BL Ask: What are "civil interests," according to Locke?

AL Connect Locke's final claim in the excerpt with the need for religious tolerance.

ELL Pair English learners with more proficient readers for help with archaic language.

D Differentiated Instruction

Logical/Mathematical Ask: How many years passed between the founding of Jamestown and the formation of the House of Burgesses? *(twelve years; Jamestown, 1607; House of Burgesses, 1619)* **BL**

R Reading Strategy

Analyzing Information Have students explain in their own words how a joint-stock company is organized. *(Each person owns part of the company and gets a share of the profits.)* **OL**

C Critical Thinking

Predicting Ask: What might have happened if the Pilgrims had not signed the Mayflower Compact? ? *(Without rules, the colony probably would have fallen into chaos.)* **OL**

For additional practice on this skill (Predicting), see the **Skills Handbook**.

Caption Answer:

They were elected by the men who owned property.

Hands-On Chapter Project
Step 1

Colonial Traditions of Self-Government

Main Idea The American colonists accepted the idea of representative government.

Civics & You What do you do when you face a difficult problem? Do you try to solve it yourself? Do you ask other people for help? Read to learn about the development of representative government in the colonies.

In the 1600s and 1700s, England established colonies in America. A **colony** is a group of people in one place who are ruled by a parent country elsewhere.

The Capitol at Williamsburg Williamsburg was the capital of Virginia from 1699 to 1780. Those who met here included Patrick Henry, George Washington, Thomas Jefferson, and George Mason. *Explaining* How were the members of the House of Burgesses chosen?

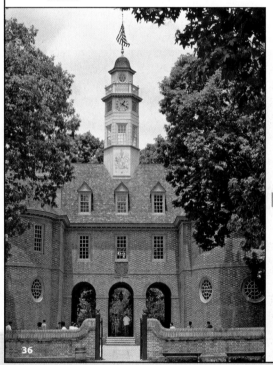

36

The early colonists remained loyal subjects of England, with a strong sense of English political traditions. They accepted common law and believed that the ruler was not above the law. They also expected to have a voice in government and other basic rights.

Representative Government

The first permanent English settlement in North America was Jamestown, in what is now Virginia. It was founded in 1607 by the Virginia Company, a group of London merchants. Jamestown was organized as a **joint-stock company,** which provided investors partial ownership and a share in future profits. The merchants also received a charter from King James I. A **charter** is a written document granting land and the authority to set up colonial governments.

At first Jamestown was managed by a governor and council appointed by the Virginia Company. In 1619, however, the colonists formed the House of Burgesses, the first representative assembly, or legislature, in the English colonies. The House of Burgesses had little power, but it marked the beginning of self-government in colonial America.

The Mayflower Compact In 1620, shortly after the House of Burgesses was formed, another group of colonists from England, known as the Pilgrims, arrived in America. They built a settlement called Plymouth hundreds of miles north of Virginia. Today Plymouth is in Massachusetts, a part of New England.

Even before their ship, the *Mayflower*, reached America, the Plymouth colonists realized they needed rules to govern themselves if they were to survive in a new land. They drew up a written plan for government. Forty-one of the men aboard signed the Mayflower Compact. (See the Appendix to read this document.) A **compact** is an agreement, or contract, among a group of people.

Conducting a Community Meeting

Step 1: Electing a Leader Groups of students will research traditional New England town meetings in order to plan and conduct a classroom community meeting.

Directions Write the Big Idea on the board. Assign students to groups. Tell each group to first elect a leader to direct their group. Explain that the leader will make sure that everyone has input into developing the

agenda for the meeting and will see to it that when the meeting is held, everyone will have an opportunity to speak. After the majority in each group agrees on a leader, have the groups research the kinds of issues addressed at traditional New England town meetings as well as how the meetings are organized and run.

Summarizing Have groups share what they learned about the Big Idea while researching New England town meetings. For guidance, students may refer to "Plan-

ning an Interactive Town Meeting," www.democracy2000.org/meetingplan.htm, "Town Meeting." Encourage them to also discover additional historical sources on their own. Groups will use this information about town meetings in Section 2 to decide what to put on the agendas for their school or classroom community meetings. **OL**

(Project continued in Section 2)

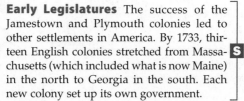

Town Meetings The Mayflower Compact established a tradition of direct democracy. Throughout the colonial period—and in New England today—citizens held town meetings to address local problems and issues. These town meetings developed into the local town government. Although anyone in the town could attend and express an opinion, voting was limited to men who had been granted land by the town.

Fundamental Orders of Connecticut D
By 1639 a number of Pilgrims were being persecuted for their religious beliefs. They left Massachusetts and colonized the area that is now Connecticut. There, they developed America's first written constitution—the Fundamental Orders of Connecticut. This document called for an assembly of elected representatives from each town to make laws. It also called for the popular election of a governor and judges.

Early Legislatures The success of the Jamestown and Plymouth colonies led to other settlements in America. By 1733, thirteen English colonies stretched from Massachusetts (which included what is now Maine) in the north to Georgia in the south. Each new colony set up its own government. **S**

Each colony had a governor, who was elected by the colonists or appointed by the English king. Each colony also had a legislature, with representatives elected by the free adult males.

As years passed, the colonial governments took on more responsibility while the king and Parliament dealt with matters in Great Britain (the country was renamed the United Kingdom of Great Britain in 1707 when England unified with Scotland). The colonists in America soon grew used to making their own decisions.

✓ **Reading Check** Concluding How did Great Britain's tending to matters in that country affect the colonists?

Section 1 Review

Vocabulary

1. **Write** complete sentences using each of these key terms: *Enlightenment, monarch, legislature, precedent, common law, natural rights, social contract, colony, joint-stock company, charter, compact.*

Main Ideas

2. **Explaining** Describe two influences that changed colonial thought.

3. **Hypothesizing** Why were colonists so eager to put self-government into practice?

Critical Thinking

4. **BIG Ideas** Explain the reasons for and the effects of the English Bill of Rights by completing a graphic organizer like the one that follows.

```
        Reasons
         for:
           ↑
English Bill of Rights
           ↓
        Effects
      on English
      Government:
```

5. **Drawing Conclusions** Explain the significance of the Glorious Revolution.

6. **Comparing** Read the Mayflower Compact in the Appendix. What ideas do you see in the compact that also exist in the government of the United States?

CITIZENSHIP Activity

7. **Persuasive Writing** Imagine you are an English noble in favor of the Magna Carta. Write a letter to the king explaining why he should sign the document.

Civics ONLINE

Study Central™ To review this section, go to <u>glencoe.com</u>.

Gifted and Talented Have students choose either the Mayflower Compact or the Fundamental Orders of Connecticut and research one or more men who helped write the documents. Have students present their findings in an oral report. **AL**

S **Skill Practice**

Using Geography Skills Ask students to find Jamestown, Virginia, and Plymouth, Massachusetts, on a map. **OL**

✓ **Reading Check** **Answer:** They began governing themselves with little input from Great Britain.

Assess
. . . .

Civics ONLINE

Study Central™ provides summaries, interactive games, and online graphic organizers to help students review.

Close
. . . .

Identifying Without referring to the text, have students name as many documents as they can that influenced the colonists' political thinking. **OL**

Section 1 Review

Answers

1. Sentences should use vocabulary words according to their definitions in the section and in the Glossary.

2. the Enlightenment, social contracts, and natural rights

3. The British were living far away in a different type of society, and the colonists thought they were better suited to govern themselves.

4. Reasons for: power struggles with King James II; Effects: restricted monarch's power; guaranteed free elections; guaranteed the right to a fair trial; eliminated cruel and unusual punishment

5. It changed government in England by proving that Parliament was more powerful than the monarch.

6. Answers may include just and equal laws that all would obey for the common good. Ask volunteers to share their responses and to lead a class discussion.

7. Answers will vary but may include the ideas that nobles had privileges and authority; landowners had rights; the power of the monarch should be limited; and no one should be above the law, not even the king or the queen.

Focus

Guide to Reading
Answers to Graphic:

Charters from the king
Economic gain
Prisoners sent over
Reasons for Immigrating
Slaves wanted by plantation owners
Religious ideals

Section Spotlight Video

To generate student interest and provide a springboard for class discussion, access the Chapter 2, Section 2 video at glencoe.com or on the video DVD.

Resource Manager

Guide to Reading

Big Idea
Political, social, religious, and economic changes influence the way Americans think and act.

Content Vocabulary
- proprietary colony *(p. 39)*
- royal colony *(p. 39)*
- religious dissenters *(p. 41)*
- Puritans *(p. 41)*
- Pilgrims *(p. 41)*
- toleration *(p. 41)*
- indentured servant *(p. 42)*
- plantation *(p. 43)*
- triangular trade *(p. 43)*

Academic Vocabulary
- acquire (p. 39)
- decade (p. 39)

Reading Strategy
Identifying On a web diagram like the one below, identify reasons that people immigrated to the English colonies.

Reasons for Immigrating
Religious ideals

Section 2

The English Colonies

Real World Civics During the American Revolution, the drum and fife called the soldiers to action! Julie Phelps keeps the tradition alive. She practices the fife, whose shrill notes strengthened soldiers' orders to march, turn, change formation, or halt. The fife, and its companion the drum, have marched to war with soldiers since the twelfth century. During the Revolutionary War, the fife and drum were well known to colonist-soldiers. The rat-a-tat tat-a-pan of the drums provided a beat for marching and for signaling battle. So, even though colonists worked to escape from English rule, they brought an English military custom into battle.

▼ **Julie Phelps, playing the fife, keeps tradition alive**

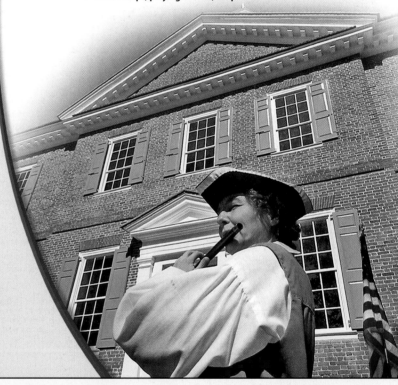

R Reading Strategies	**C** Critical Thinking	**D** Differentiated Instruction	**W** Writing Support	**S** Skill Practice
Teacher Edition • Organizing, p. 39 • Identifying, p. 40 • Summarizing, p. 42 • Questioning, p. 43 **Additional Resources** • Cont. Vocab., URB p. 45 • Guid. Read., URB p. 66 • RENTG, p. 13	**Teacher Edition** • Making Inferences, p. 39 • Draw. Conclusions, p. 41 • Making Comparisons, p. 42 **Additional Resources** • Crit. Think., URB p. 55 • Quizzes and Tests, p. 15	**Teacher Edition** • Gifted & Talented, p. 41 • Below Grade Level, p. 43 **Additional Resources** • School-to-Home Conn., URB p. 61 • Reteach. Act., URB p. 63	**Teacher Edition** • Descriptive Writing, p. 41 **Additional Resources** • Authentic Assessment, p. 6	**Teacher Edition** • Hypothesizing, p. 40 **Additional Resources** • Daily Focus Trans., 2–2 • Stan. Test., p. 3

Settling the Colonies

Main Idea The English established thirteen colonies along the East Coast of North America.

Civics & You How far would you travel to live in a new place? What would it be like if you did not know what to expect? Read to learn about the early settlements in North America.

Although several European nations had claims in North America, it was the English who eventually dominated the continent. By 1733, there were thirteen colonies along the eastern seaboard under English control. These colonies had been founded in a variety of ways and for a variety of reasons. Despite these differences, the colonies had one thing in common—their English heritage.

New England Colonies

Nine years after the Pilgrims arrived at Plymouth, another group of investors received a royal charter to start a colony north of Plymouth. In 1630, about 900 men, women, and children landed at Massachusetts Bay and built a town they called Boston. During the 1630s, more than 15,000 people journeyed to the new colony of Massachusetts. By the mid-1600s, the New England colonies of Rhode Island, Connecticut, and New Hampshire had been founded.

The Middle Colonies

A second group of colonies grew up south of New England. Known as the Middle Colonies, they included New York, New Jersey, Pennsylvania, and Delaware.

The first of these, New York, was originally the Dutch colony of New Netherland. An English fleet seized the important harbor town of New Amsterdam on Manhattan Island in 1664. The English King Charles II gave the colony to his brother, the Duke of York.

The newly **acquired,** or obtained, colony of New York became a **proprietary colony,** in which the owner, or proprietor, owned the land and controlled the government. The Duke of York gave the southern part of his colony to two men, who named it New Jersey. For several **decades,** or ten-year spans, New Jersey was a proprietary colony. In 1702, it became a **royal colony,** one owned and ruled directly by the king.

Another proprietary colony was started in 1680. William Penn received a large parcel of land west of the Delaware River from King Charles. Penn saw his colony, Pennsylvania, as a place to put his Quaker ideals of peace, equality, and justice to work. By offering freedom of religion, Penn drew many settlers to his new city of Philadelphia. In 1704, the southernmost three counties of the colony separated and became known as Delaware.

Southern Colonies

A third set of colonies formed in the South after Jamestown, Virginia, was founded as a joint-stock colony in 1607 (it became a royal colony in 1624). North of Virginia, Maryland was founded in 1734. To Virginia's south, another group of proprietors started Carolina. The two parts of Carolina developed differently, and they officially became two royal colonies, North and South Carolina, in 1729.

Boston By the 1660s, Boston was one of the largest cities in the English colonies. *Specifying* **In what year did the first English settlers come to Boston?**

Teach

C Critical Thinking

Making Inferences Ask: Why were the first colonies established on the eastern seaboard? *(That's where new colonists arrived by ship.)* **OL**

R Reading Strategy

Organizing As students read, have them fill in time lines of the key dates and events related to settling each of these areas: New England, Middle, and Southern colonies. **OL**

Caption Answer:

Settlers arrived in 1630.

Additional Support

Did You Know?

Pennsylvania William Penn, who founded the colony of Pennsylvania, did not name it after himself. He wanted to call it "New Wales" or "Sylvania." However, King Charles II asked William Penn to name the colony after his father who shared the same name.

King Charles owed the elder Penn money, but Mr. Penn died before the king could repay it. To settle the debt, he gave the younger William Penn a charter for land in the New World that became the colony of Pennsylvania.

A Quaker, Penn set out to create a godly society that welcomed all religions. His goal was to create an ideal place that would be a model for—not just the other colonies—but for the rest of the world.

S Skill Practice

Hypothesizing Have students study the map and series of key events. **Ask:** Why do you think major governmental meetings were held in Philadelphia? (*because of its central location and prominence*) **OL**

R Reading Strategy

Identifying Ask: What was one reason the colony of Georgia was established? (*as a debtor's haven or as a military barrier*) **OL**

Analyzing Maps

Answers:

1. New Jersey, Pennsylvania, New York, Delaware
2. Connecticut, the Fundamental Orders of Connecticut

✔ **Reading Check** **Answer:** In proprietary colonies, the owner owned the land and controlled the government. The king owned the land and ruled royal colonies.

Differentiated Instruction

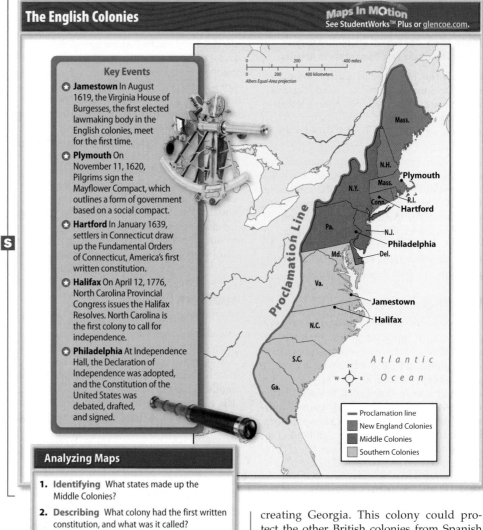

The English Colonies

Maps In MOtion
See StudentWorks™ Plus or glencoe.com.

Key Events

⭐ **Jamestown** In August 1619, the Virginia House of Burgesses, the first elected lawmaking body in the English colonies, meet for the first time.

⭐ **Plymouth** On November 11, 1620, Pilgrims sign the Mayflower Compact, which outlines a form of government based on a social compact.

⭐ **Hartford** In January 1639, settlers in Connecticut draw up the Fundamental Orders of Connecticut, America's first written constitution.

⭐ **Halifax** On April 12, 1776, North Carolina Provincial Congress issues the Halifax Resolves. North Carolina is the first colony to call for independence.

⭐ **Philadelphia** At Independence Hall, the Declaration of Independence was adopted, and the Constitution of the United States was debated, drafted, and signed.

Legend: Proclamation line — New England Colonies ■ Middle Colonies ■ Southern Colonies □

Analyzing Maps

1. **Identifying** What states made up the Middle Colonies?
2. **Describing** What colony had the first written constitution, and what was it called?

Georgia The last English colony founded in America was Georgia. A group led by James Oglethorpe received a charter to create a colony where English debtors and poor people could make a fresh start. In Great Britain, debtors were often thrown into prison. The British government had another reason for creating Georgia. This colony could protect the other British colonies from Spanish attack. Great Britain had been at war in the early 1700s, and new conflicts over territory in North America were always breaking out. Located between Spanish Florida and South Carolina, Georgia could serve as a military barrier.

✔ **Reading Check** **Comparing** How did proprietary and royal colonies differ?

Leveled Activities

BL Critical Thinking Skills 2, URB pp. 55–56

OL Guided Reading Activity 2-2, URB p. 66

AL Primary Source Reading 1B, URB pp. 17–18

ELL Writing Skills Activity 2, URB pp. 51–54

People of the Colonies

Main Idea Throughout the colonies, people adapted their traditions to the new conditions of life in America.

Civics & You Would you be willing to move across the ocean to unexplored, possibly dangerous territory to gain certain freedoms or perhaps just to get a new start on life? Read to find out why English settlers came to North America.

English colonists settled in America for different reasons. Some immigrated to escape religious persecution in England. Others came in search of economic gain. Still others, such as criminals, prisoners, and enslaved Africans, did not come willingly. Colonists' reasons for immigration helped shape the types of colonies they created.

Why Did Colonists Immigrate?

Many colonists in New England and the Middle Colonies were **religious dissenters,** those who followed a faith other than the official religion of England, the Anglican religion. For example, the founders of Massachusetts were called **Puritans,** because they wanted to reform, or purify, the Anglican Church.

Religious Havens These Puritans also considered themselves **Pilgrims,** or people on a religious journey. The rulers of Massachusetts did not believe in **toleration,** or acceptance, of other religions.

D

New York City Colonists settled where economic opportunities were available. New York became a leading center for commerce and trade. **Explaining** What natural feature made New York an economic center?

C

W

D Differentiated Instruction

Gifted and Talented Have students investigate the reforms the Puritans wanted the Anglican Church to make. Have them present an oral report to the class, using a chart to list the issues. **AL**

C Critical Thinking

Drawing Conclusions Have students look carefully at the picture. **Ask:** How could you tell these people lived in a city, even if the streets and buildings were not shown? *(They are dressed in nice clothes, so clearly are not doing work such as fishing or farming common to rural areas.)* **OL**

W Writing Support

Descriptive Writing Have students imagine they are using the painting on this page to describe life in New York City to a relative in England. Have them write a descriptive letter based on this painting that would make that person want to visit. **OL**

Caption Answer:

its harbor

Hands-On Chapter Project
Step 2

Conducting a Community Meeting

Step 2: Setting an Agenda Groups of students report on their research on traditional New England town meetings that they began in Section 1.

Directions Write the Big Idea on the board. Have students share what they have learned so far. Tell each group to elect a "town clerk" to take notes on their ideas. Based on their knowledge, they will develop and reach consensus on an agenda, known in colonial times as a warrant. They will publicly post the warrant so that all citizens know the issues relevant to their own school or classroom community that will be discussed.

Summarizing Have groups share their ideas for the content and design of their warrants. Groups will use the information about the practical content of town meetings they learned in Section 1 to decide what issues to put on their school or classroom agendas. **OL**

(Project continued in Section 3)

R   Reading Strategy

Summarizing Pair students and have them write one paragraph summarizing where different immigrant groups settled and why each settled in a particular area. **OL**

C   Critical Thinking

Making Comparisons Ask: How were the lives of slaves and indentured servants the same? How were they different? *(Both groups were poor and worked hard. Once the indentured servants worked off their debts to colonists who paid for their passage, they were free. The slaves were owned by their masters.)* **OL**

For additional practice on this skill (Making Comparisons), see the **Skills Handbook**.

Analyzing Maps

Answers:
1. English
2. Middle Colonies

Differentiated Instruction

Differentiated Instruction Activity 2, URB pp. 59–60

42

Dominant Immigrant Groups in the Colonies

- English
- Scotch-Irish
- German
- Dutch
- African
- - - - Colony boundaries

Analyzing Maps

1. **Locating** What immigrant group was predominant along the Atlantic Coast?

2. **Describing** In what regions did German immigrants settle?

In the late 1600s, devout Puritans in Salem and other Massachusetts towns held trials of people accused of witchcraft. In the town of Salem alone, 19 residents were convicted and hanged, and five died in prison before the trials were discontinued in 1693.

Other groups sought religious freedom. The Quakers founded Pennsylvania as a safe place to practice their religion. A proprietor named George Calvert founded Maryland in 1634 as a safe home for Catholics. In 1636, a minister named Thomas Hooker led his church congregation to Connecticut, south of Massachusetts, in search of religious freedom. Another minister, Roger Williams, was forced to leave Massachusetts for his religious views and his belief that it was wrong to take land from Native Americans. In 1644, Williams received a charter to found the colony of Rhode Island. Rhode Island became the first place in America to welcome people of all faiths.

Economic Opportunity Especially in the South, many settlers came to the colonies for economic reasons. Early Virginians struggled until they began successfully to raise and sell their tobacco crop. Carolina was strongly influenced by immigrants from the English colony of Barbados in the West Indies. There, many settlers became involved in growing rice and indigo, a valuable blue dye.

The system of **indentured servants** made it possible for poor people to come to the colonies. Colonists in America agreed to pay the cost of transporting the servants to the colonies and promised to provide food, clothing, and shelter to them until their indentures, or labor contracts, expired.

Conflict Over Land Throughout the colonies, the spread of settlements led to conflicts with Native Americans over land. In some colonies, such as Pennsylvania, relations were fairly peaceful. In Virginia, they were not. In the 1640s, Virginia Governor William Berkeley agreed to keep settlers from taking Native American land. A planter named Nathaniel Bacon disagreed strongly with this policy and led attacks on the colonial government. Bacon's Rebellion showed that many settlers were not willing to be restricted by government policy.

The Mayflower Compact

Objective: To understand this document's significance

Focus: Have students discuss the challenges the Pilgrims faced.

Teach: Review the Mayflower Compact with students.

Assess: Underline phrases in the compact that establish self-government.

Close: Discuss the physical conditions under which the compact was written.

Differentiated Instruction Strategies

BL Ask: Why did the Pilgrims come to the New World?

AL Have students write and perform a skit in which the Pilgrims decide to write the compact.

ELL Discuss with students the formal language and serious tone common to important historical documents such as this.

The Beginnings of Slavery

In the Southern Colonies, a form of large-scale agriculture developed, based on the **plantation,** or large estate. This system for growing tobacco, rice, and indigo demanded more workers than immigration and the system of indentured servants could provide. Southern farmers began using enslaved Africans. Enslaved workers, unlike indentured servants, did not have to be freed and therefore would never need their own land.

At first it was not clear that enslaved Africans were to be treated differently from white indentured servants. Gradually, legal distinctions were adopted. Indentured servants retained the rights of English people and the protection of the law. Africans were protected by no law or tradition.

The trade in enslaved Africans was at the heart of what came to be called the **triangular trade**—the pattern of trade that developed among the Americas, Africa, and Europe. The colonists shipped rum to Africa, where traders exchanged it for enslaved people and gold. The enslaved were shipped to the West Indies and traded for sugar and molasses, which was used to make rum in America. The Africans' horrendous journey across the Atlantic was known as the Middle Passage. A young African, Olaudah Equiano, described the voyage:

" *I was soon put down under the decks . . . . The closeness of the place, and the heat of the climate, added to the number in the ship, which was so crowded that each had scarcely room to turn himself, almost suffocated us . . . . The shrieks of the women, and the groans of the dying, rendered [made] the whole a scene of horror.* "

—Olaudah Equiano, *The Interesting Narrative of the Life of Olaudah Equiano*

 Reading Check **Evaluating** How did the system of indentured servants help both business owners and workers?

 Reading Strategy

Questioning After students read the first two sentences, ask them why indentured servants and immigrants were not sufficient for the Southern Colonies. **OL**

D Differentiated Instruction

Below Grade Level Have students draw a large triangle and label the points the Americas, Africa, and Europe. Have them use arrows and pictures to illustrate the triangular trade. **BL**

Reading Check **Answer:** business owners did not have to pay the workers; the workers got their passage paid to the colonies and were eventually free.

Assess

Civics ONLINE

Study Central™ provides summaries, interactive games, and online graphic organizers to help students review content.

Close

Outlining Have students outline the section. They should highlight the differences of the three colony groupings. **OL**

Section 2 Review

 Section 2 Review

Vocabulary

1. **Write** a paragraph in which you use the following terms: *proprietary colony, royal colony, religious dissenters, Puritans, Pilgrims,* and *toleration.* Then write a second paragraph using these terms: *indentured servant, plantation,* and *triangular trade.*

Main Ideas

2. **Identify** the Southern Colonies and their location.

3. **Describe** three main reasons why colonists came to America. Which do you think was most important? Why?

Critical Thinking

4. **BIG Ideas** Use a graphic organizer similar to the one below to discuss the reasons the colony was founded.

Colony	Why was it founded?
New York	
Pennsylvania	
Georgia	

5. **Analyzing** Why did slavery become more prevalent in the Southern Colonies than in New England?

6. **Explaining** What was the main reason immigrants settled in the Southern Colonies?

CITIZENSHIP Activity

7. **Descriptive Writing** Pretend you have decided to move from England to America in the 1700s. Write a letter to your family and friends explaining why you have chosen to settle in a particular colony.

Civics ONLINE

Study Central™ To review this section, go to glencoe.com.

Chapter 2   43

Answers

1. Sentences should use vocabulary words according to their definitions in the section and in the Glossary.

2. Maryland, Virginia, North Carolina, South Carolina, Georgia

3. They came for religious freedom or economic reasons or were brought against their will as enslaved Africans, prisoners, or criminals. Others chose to come as indentured servants. Answers for the most important reason they came will vary.

4. **New York:** founded as a royal colony by the Duke of York, brother of King Charles II; **Pennsylvania:** founded by William Penn to offer religious freedom to all; **Georgia:** founded as a proprietary colony as a place for debtors to get a fresh start also served as a military barrier

5. More workers were needed for the plantations there, and slaves were cheap labor.

6. Immigrants settled there to grow tobacco, rice, and indigo.

7. Letters will vary but should include factual information about the chosen colony.

Focus

Bellringer
Daily Focus Transparency 2–3

Guide to Reading
Answers to Graphic:

New England	general farming, fishing, sewing clothes, lumbering, running small businesses, milling grain, making rum, and working as shopkeepers, blacksmiths, shoemakers, ship-builders, fur trappers, and whalers
Middle Colonies	growing wheat and other cash crops, working in sawmills, mines, and ironworks
Southern Colonies	growing tobacco, rice, indigo, and grain on plantations, raising cattle, naval stores

Section Spotlight Video

Have students watch the Chapter 2, Section 3 video at glencoe.com.

Resource Manager

Guide to Reading

Big Idea
Political, social, religious, and economic changes influence the way Americans think and act.

Content Vocabulary
• Tidewater *(p. 46)*
• egalitarianism *(p. 48)*

Academic Vocabulary
• adapt *(p. 45)*
• assist *(p. 48)*

Reading Strategy
Organizing Use a graphic organizer like the one below to describe the differences in the economies of the New England, Middle, and Southern Colonies.

Economic Differences

New England — Southern Colonies — Middle Colonies

Colonial Society

Real World Civics Six U.S. presidents graduated from Harvard University, a remarkable record for a school founded before the Revolutionary War and designed to train ministers. Most early schools in America were established on the ideals of freedom of religion and freedom of education. In 1940, John F. Kennedy, one of those Harvard graduates, prepared to leave college to visit Britain, where his father was the U.S. Ambassador. Kennedy later returned to the United States during the early rumblings of World War II and went on to be, in just over two decades, the 35th president of the United States.

▼ **A youthful John F. Kennedy**

R Reading Strategies	**C** Critical Thinking	**D** Differentiated Instruction	**W** Writing Support	**S** Skill Practice
Teacher Edition • Outlining, p. 45 • Monitoring, p. 46 • Summarizing, p. 47 • Academic Vocab., p. 47 • Organizing, p. 48 **Additional Resources** • Guid. Read. URB, p. 67 • RENTG, p. 16	**Teacher Edition** • Analyzing Pri. Sources, p. 47 • Analyzing Info., p.48 • Sequencing Events, p. 49 **Additional Resources** • Quizzes and Tests, p. 16	**Teacher Edition** • Interpersonal, p. 45 **Additional Resources** • Diff. Instr., URB p. 59 • Graphic Novel, p. 1	**Teacher Edition** • Expository Writing, p. 46 **Additional Resources** • Authentic Assessment, p. 6	**Teacher Edition** • Using Geo. Skills, p. 45 **Additional Resources** • Daily Focus Trans., 2–3

The Economy

Main Idea The people in the colonies developed different ways of living.

Civics & You Is your community or region known for any special product, either agricultural or manufactured? Read to find out how the economies of the New England, Middle, and Southern Colonies differed.

From the beginning, geography played a key role in how colonies developed. Colonists in the different regions had to **adapt,** or adjust, to the climate, soil, terrain, availability of rivers and harbors, natural resources, and other factors.

New England

Most people in New England, including farmers, lived in towns. Farms were small and located on the towns' outskirts. Long winters and rocky, infertile soil made large-scale farming difficult. Other New Englanders worked in small businesses, milling grain, sewing clothes, or making furniture. Some worked as blacksmiths, shoemakers, or shopkeepers.

Shipbuilding was an important industry. The region's forests provided wood for boats, and fishing and whaling also employed many New Englanders. The Puritan religion of early New England emphasized hard work, modest living, and personal virtues such as honesty, thriftiness, and obedience. These personal characteristics became known as the Puritan ethic.

The Middle Colonies

In contrast to New England, the soil and climate in New York, Pennsylvania, New Jersey, and Delaware were more suited to agriculture. Farmers in the Middle Colonies grew large amounts of wheat and other cash crops, which they sold in markets and overseas. This foreign trade spurred the growth of busy ports, such as New York and Philadelphia. Industries such as sawmills, mines, and ironworks were developed to take advantage of the region's abundant natural resources. Industry and agriculture also improved through the ideas and energy of immigrants from Germany, Holland, Sweden, and other European countries.

American Economy, c. 1750

General farming
Tobacco
Rice and indigo
Cattle
Fish
Fur trapping
Grain
Ironworks
Lumber
Rum
Shipbuilding
Naval stores
Whaling
---- Colony boundaries

Mass.
N.H.
N.Y.   Mass.   R.I.
New England Colonies
Pa.   Conn.
N.J.
Md.   Del.   Middle Colonies
Va.
N.C.
Southern Colonies
S.C.
Ga.
Atlantic Ocean
Gulf of Mexico

0   200   400 miles
0   200   400 kilometers
Albers Equal-Area projection

Analyzing Maps

1. **Describing** On what crops did the economy of the Southern Colonies depend?
2. **Locating** What colonies produced rice and indigo?

Chapter 2   **45**

Teach

D Differentiated Instruction

Interpersonal Have students discuss among themselves the way the economies of a region can affect peoples' lives. Ask them to consider food, clothing, shelter, and transportation, as well as economic effects. **OL**

R Reading Strategy

Outlining Have students use the map and words on this page to complete their graphic organizers. **Ask:** Which two areas are best suited to agriculture? *(the Middle and Southern Colonies)* **OL**

S Skill Practice

Using Geography Skills Ask: In which colony was fur trapping practiced? *(New Hampshire)* **OL**

Analyzing Maps

Answers:
1. tobacco, rice, and indigo
2. the Southern Colonies

Additional Support

Did You Know?

Scots-Irish Heritage The Middle Colonies were settled mainly by poor Scots-Irish immigrants who were drawn to the New World in search of religious freedom and a better standard of living. The number of Scots-Irish immigrants in colonial times was second only to the English. Beginning in 1717, they arrived in large groups until the beginning of the Revolutionary War.

Most settled in the Middle Colonies. Many got off ships in Philadelphia and stayed on in Pennsylvania. The majority were skilled workers who quickly found jobs. Those who came as indentured servants were also skilled. After working off their debts, they readily found work and lived successful lives.

Later, some traveled south on the Great Philadelphia Road, through the Shenandoah Valley and made their way to North and South Carolina, where they settled the frontier. Presidents Andrew Jackson and Ronald Reagan trace their roots to the Scots-Irish immigrants who came to America and built a better life.

R Reading Strategy

Monitoring Remind students to check their comprehension of the text. Students should be asking questions such as "What is the Tidewater?" and "What types of crops were grown there?" **BL ELL**

W Writing Support

Expository Writing Have students write brief magazine articles about the Tidewater regions of Virginia and North Carolina. Tell students to write their articles for first graders and to explain how their vocabulary level and tone will be adapted for beginning readers. **OL**

✔ **Reading Check** **Answer:** The South had the right conditions: a warm climate, a long growing season, rich soil, and large tracts of land available.

Caption Answer:

Crops on large plantations required massive amounts of labor. By not paying enslaved workers, plantation owners could save money.

Differentiated Instruction

Chart, Graph, and Map Act. 2, URB pp. 57-58

The Southern Colonies

A warm climate, long growing season, and rich soil spurred the growth of large-scale agriculture in the Southern Colonies. In Maryland, Virginia, and North Carolina, tobacco was the leading crop. Rice dominated in South Carolina and Georgia. Both crops were grown in the **Tidewater,** areas of flat, low plains, near the seacoast of Virginia and North Carolina. The region's rivers made it easy to transport the harvested tobacco and rice, along with other products such as indigo and grain, to the coast for shipment to overseas markets. Charleston, South Carolina, became a leader in trade, thanks to its excellent harbor.

Tidewater crops required very large amounts of labor. Owners of plantations, the large estates of the Southern Colonies, came to depend on enslaved African workers. Smaller-scale agriculture also existed, mainly in inland areas. Independent small farmers grew tobacco, corn, and other crops and were less dependent on enslaved workers.

Small farmers outnumbered the large plantation owners. The plantation owners, however, had greater wealth and more influence. They controlled the economic and political life of the region. Because large-scale agriculture was dominant in the South, the region did not develop much industry or commerce. It traded its many agricultural products for the manufactured goods it needed.

✔ **Reading Check** **Explaining** Why did the plantation system develop in the South but not in the New England or the Middle Colonies?

The Southern Economy Large-scale farming grew in South Carolina and in many parts of the South. *Explaining* Why did slavery become the labor system for large plantations?

Reading a Time Line

Objective: To practice reading a time line

Focus: Review with students the purposes of time lines.

Teach: Have students explain why each event is important enough to appear on the time line.

Assess: Ask students to explain their placement of events on the second time line

Close: Have students create a time line of important events in the school.

Differentiated Instruction Strategies

BL Ask students to decide on a useful and descriptive title for each time line.

AL What cause-and-effect relationships can you infer from events on the first time line?

ELL Remind students that time lines can be arranged horizontally, with dates running from left to right, or vertically, with dates running from top to bottom.

An American Identity

Main Idea The colonies continued to grow and developed their own culture and beliefs.

Civics & You What are some things you consider truly American? Read to find out how the colonists began to form a culture that was different from other cultures.

In 1760, an English traveler in America, Andrew Burnaby, wrote that the colonies were as different from one another as "fire and water." He felt their differences in character, manners, religion, and interests would prevent them from ever uniting. Burnaby noted:

> "In short, such is the difference of character, manners, religion, and interest of the different colonies that if they were left to themselves, there would soon be a civil war from one end of the continent to another."
>
> —Andrew Burnaby, *Burnaby's Travels Through North America*

But in spite of the opinion of Burnaby and others, by the mid-1700s, colonists were already developing an American identity.

Religion

The desire for religious freedom was the reason many settlers first came to America, and religion remained a key element of the emerging American identity. In several colonies, such as Massachusetts, religious leaders were often also the leaders of the government. Puritans passed laws that supported their beliefs about religion and society, and they had the power to expel those who did not share these beliefs.

In other colonies, however, religion became separate from government, and toleration became the official policy. In colonies

Religion Revival Massachusetts minister Jonathan Edwards preached throughout the colonies urging renewed faith. *Explaining* What was the Great Awakening?

such as Pennsylvania and Rhode Island, toleration of other religions drew settlers of many different faiths. Religious tolerance gradually spread to other colonies during the 1700s.

The Great Awakening While some Americans turned away from religion in the 1700s, others renewed their faith. In the 1720s, a powerful religious revival known as the Great Awakening swept through the colonies. Fiery preachers stressed the importance of a personal religious experience and questioned the commitment and authority of some established religious leaders. Congregations were torn apart, and new religious groups, such as Baptists and Methodists, grew strong. In the South, enslaved workers found hope in Christianity, which strongly influenced the development of a new African American culture.

Education

Religious feeling also led to the founding of America's first colleges and schools. Colleges such as Harvard in Massachusetts, Princeton in New Jersey, and William and Mary in Virginia were created for the

C Critical Thinking

Analyzing Primary Sources After students read the first sentence, ask them to clarify Burnaby's use of figurative language by explaining the differences between fire and water. **OL**

For additional practice on this skill (Analyzing Primary Sources), see the **Skills Handbook.**

R₁ Reading Strategy

Summarizing Pair students and have them write one paragraph summarizing the different attitudes toward religion in the colonies. Have students share their summaries with the class. **OL**

R₂ Reading Strategy

Academic Vocabulary Tell students: Rewrite the sentence, using a synonym for the word "expel." *(Sentences should include the words "force out," "remove," or something similar.)* **BL ELL**

Caption Answer:

The Great Awakening was a powerful religious revival that swept through the colonies during the 1720s.

Leveled Activities

BL School-to-Home Activity 2, URB p. 61

OL Speaking/Listening Skills 1, URB pp. 9–11

AL Critical Thinking Skills Activity 2, URB pp. 55–56

ELL Guided Reading Activity 2-3, URB p. 67

47

R Reading Strategy

Organizing Draw two columns on the board and head one "Men" and the other "Women." Ask students to list the different duties and rights of the sexes in colonial society. *(Men were family heads, could vote and own property, and managed all community and church affairs; wives looked after family and household but could not run businesses or own property; widows and unmarried women could do so, but no women could vote. In towns women could work as maids, cooks, nurses, teachers, seamstresses, and shopkeepers.)* **OL**

C Critical Thinking

Analyzing Information Ask: Why were widows and unmarried women allowed to run businesses and own property? *(because they had to support themselves)* **OL**

TIME™ Teens in *Action*

Answer:

Student answers might suggest Bita was motivated by the poverty she saw in Iran to help immigrant children in her city for whom English was a second language. She has a passion for languages and believes education is a way to battle poverty.

Hands-On Chapter Project
Step 3

TIME™ Teens in *Action*

Bita Emrani

Bita Emrani, 17, who lives in Greensboro, North Carolina, knows the power of words. To help immigrants and disadvantaged kids in her area, she started a program called English Learning with Love (ELL).

QUESTION: Why did you create a language-tutoring program?

ANSWER: I started ELL in 2005 after a visit to Iran. I was haunted by the poverty there and decided to help the disadvantaged in my own city. I think education is an important way to battle poverty. Plus, I have a real passion for languages (I'm bilingual in Persian and English and able to get by in Spanish).

Q: What does ELL do?

A: ELL is an English for Speakers of Other Languages (ESOL) program and it's held after school in three local elementary schools. We help newcomers to the area become members of the community by working to improve their English. ELL works with about 30 to 35 students.

Q: Who are the tutors?

A: I recruit high school kids who volunteer their time to help. These teens discover that they can have a huge impact on their community.

Q: What difference do you see in the participants after they take the program?

A: ELL has not only improved kids' English, but it's also improved their attitude toward learning.

Q: What does the future hold for you?

A: I want to pursue a degree in public policy. I'd also like to volunteer for a nonprofit international medical organization, such as Doctors Without Borders.

ACTION FACT: Emrani loves learning dances from other countries.

Making a Difference   **CITIZENSHIP**

Why did Bita start the ELL program?

purpose of training ministers. Religious groups also set up schools for children to make sure that people could read the Bible for themselves. In some colonies, taxes were levied to pay for public education. Not all colonial Americans enjoyed the benefits of education, however. Slave codes—strict laws governing the treatment of enslaved people—made it illegal to teach enslaved workers to read or write.

Family Life

The family formed the foundation of colonial society. Men were the formal heads of their families, which were often large. Wives looked after children and worked on household chores. On farms, men and women often worked together, **assisted,** or helped, by older children.

In towns, women sometimes held jobs outside the home. They worked as maids, cooks, nurses, teachers, shopkeepers, or seamstresses. Families often arranged for their sons to work as apprentices, or learning assistants, to craft workers who taught them a trade. Married women had few rights, while widows and unmarried women could run businesses and own property. Women, however, could not vote, and men managed all community and church affairs.

Ideas About Government

In spite of the inequalities that existed in colonial America between whites and African Americans and between men and women, a new spirit was growing. The Enlightenment reinforced the idea of natural rights and individualism. The Great Awakening encouraged Christians to question traditional authority and to rely on their own insights about God. Together these two powerful influences helped create a spirit of **egalitarianism,** or equality. One element of this spirit of egalitarianism was the belief of many colonists that they possessed all the traditional rights of native English people.

Planning and Conducting a Community Meeting

Step 3: Creating a Warrant Groups of students will continue their work on conducting a community meeting. A representative from each group will report on the agendas they developed for a school community meeting. Representatives chosen from each group will prepare a warrant.

Directions Write the Big Idea on the board. Have the town clerk from each group share

what issues students have decided to display on their warrants. The warrant will take the form of a poster. Students should decorate the poster in old-fashioned lettering and include drawings of school landmarks or illustrations that reflect the content of their warrants.

Summarizing Have groups share their ideas for their warrants. Groups will use their warrants to conduct their own town meetings in Section 4. **OL**

(Project continued in Section 4)

Americans viewed the growth of the power of Parliament in the 1700s with approval. They considered the British legislature the protector of the people's rights against royal power. At the same time, America's colonies were governed by officials appointed by the British crown, a decision in which Americans had no say. British trade and tax policies protected British interests at the expense of American businesses.

Government in the Colonies The English government had permitted new patterns of land ownership, new types of worship, and new kinds of government in its colonies. Once established, these practices became fixed principles. The colonists became used to self-government and gradually came to think of it as their right.

By 1733, all thirteen English colonies had been established, each with its own constitution. The Massachusetts Body of Liberties, adopted in 1641, protected individual rights and became part of colonial law. In 1683 the Pennsylvania Frame of Government

was passed. This document, along with the 1701 Pennsylvania Charter of Privileges, established part of the basis for the U.S. Constitution and the Bill of Rights. By the time the colonies gained independence in 1776, each colony had its own representative government, one that had been operating for more than 100 years.

Growing Discontent Yet, by the mid-1700s, many Americans felt they did not possess the rights of English citizens. They read Enlightenment writings in which the rights of the individual were proclaimed. Yet many British policies toward the colonies did not follow these ideals. In particular, colonists accepted John Locke's idea that government derives its power from the consent of the people. As the century wore on, Americans looked for answers to the problem of a distant and unresponsive British government. To a growing number, one answer seemed to make the most sense: independence.

Reading Check Concluding How did religious beliefs influence American ideas about government?

Section 3 Review

Vocabulary

1. **Write** a paragraph about life in the Southern Colonies using these terms: *Tidewater, egalitarianism.*

Main Ideas

2. **Identifying** What were the main crops grown in the Southern Colonies?

3. **Describing** What was the purpose of the first colleges?

Critical Thinking

4. **Determining Cause and Effect** How did the geography of the New England and the Middle Colonies contribute to their economic development?

5. **BIG Ideas** Use a graphic organizer similar to the one below to show the effects of the Great Awakening on the American colonies.

Great Awakening

6. **Analyzing Visuals** Study the map on page 45 that shows the economic activity of the colonies. On what crops did the economy of the Middle Colonies depend?

CITIZENSHIP Activity

7. **Expository Writing** Describe the founding of at least two colonies in a short essay.

Civics ONLINE

Study Central™ To review this section, go to glencoe.com.

Sequencing Events Have students work in pairs to find the dates each of these documents were adopted and then put the documents in sequential order: Declaration of Independence, Pennsylvania Charter of Privileges, Pennsylvania Framer of Government, Massachusetts Body of Liberties. *(1. Massachusetts Body of Liberties, 1641; 2. Pennsylvania Framer of Government, 1683; 3. Pennsylvania Charter of Privileges, 1701; 4. Declaration of Independence, 1776)* **BL**

Reading Check **Answer:** It encouraged Christians to question authority and to rely on their own insights.

Assess

Civics ONLINE

Study Central™ provides summaries, interactive games, and online graphic organizers to help students review content.

Close

Summarizing Have students use their graphic organizers to create a two-minute presentation about the differences among the three regions and how these differences affected each region's citizens. **OL**

Section 3 Review

Answers

1. Definitions for the vocabulary words are found in the section and in the Glossary.

2. tobacco, indigo, and rice

3. to train ministers

4. Bad soil and a cold climate made New England unsuited to extensive farming. Fishing and whaling were also popular jobs. The fertile land of the Middle Colonies was suited for farming wheat and other crops; their fine seaports spurred trade, and the region's natural resources supported sawmills, mines, and ironworks.

5.

Great Awakening

| congregations torn apart | new religious groups became stronger | enslaved workers found hope in Christianity |

6. grain

7. Essays will vary. Papers should include accurate, factual information.

Focus

Bellringer
Daily Focus Transparency 2–4

Guide to Reading
Answers to Graphic:

Colonial Response

| Boycotted goods. | Threw British tea in harbor. | Declared their independence. |

Section Spotlight Video

To generate student interest and provide a springboard for class discussion, access the Chapter 2, Section 4 video at glencoe.com or on the video DVD.

Resource Manager

Guide to Reading
Political principles and major events shape how people form governments.

Content Vocabulary
- mercantilism *(p. 51)*
- boycott *(p. 52)*
- repeal *(p. 52)*
- delegate *(p. 54)*
- independence *(p. 54)*

Academic Vocabulary
- challenge *(p. 54)*
- restore *(p. 54)*

Reading Strategy
Determining Cause and Effect As you read, complete a chart like the one below by explaining how the colonists responded to British actions.

Colonial Response

Section 4

Birth of a Democratic Nation

Real World Civics The air was hot and muggy, the sun beating down at midday, and the windows were tightly shut. As July 1776 began, dozens of men sat around these tables in Independence Hall in Philadelphia debating Thomas Jefferson's Declaration of Independence. They were British subjects living in a British colony, so each man agreeing to this document was committing treason against his country. Treason was punishable by death. Yet 56 men signed the Declaration, which outlines the reason why America should declare itself a new and independent nation. On the Fourth of July, these men announced to the world : "We mutually pledge to each other our lives, our fortunes and our sacred honor," in the hope that they one day would be free.

▼ **Room where Declaration of Independence was signed**

R Reading Strategies	C Critical Thinking	D Differentiated Instruction	W Writing Support	S Skill Practice
Teacher Edition	**Teacher Edition**	**Teacher Edition**	**Teacher Edition**	**Teacher Edition**
• Predicting, p. 51	• Drawing Conclusions, p. 51	• Gifted/Talented, p. 54	• Personal Writing, p. 52	• Identifying Points of View, p. 55
• Summarizing, p. 52	• Analyzing Info., p. 53	**Additional Resources**	• Persuasive Writing, p. 56	**Additional Resources**
• Academic Vocab., p. 53	• Compare/Contrast, p. 54	• School-to-Home Conn., URB p. 61	**Additional Resources**	• Chart, Map, and Graph Skills, URB p. 57
• Setting a Purpose, p. 54	**Additional Resources**	• Reteach. Act., URB p. 63	• Writing Skills Act., URB p. 51	• Daily Focus Trans., 2–4
• Indentifying, p. 55	• Biographies, URB p. 49	• Graphic Novel, p. 1	• Authentic Assessment, p. 6	• Pol. Cartoons Trans. 2
Additional Resources	• Quizzes and Tests, p. 17			
• Guid. Read., URB p. 68				
• RENTG, p. 19				

New York Harbor New York served as an economic center of activity for the Northern Colonies, receiving ships from all over the world. *Analyzing* How did the British policy of salutary neglect affect the colonies?

Colonial Resistance

Main Idea The American colonists began to fight against British control.

Civics & You Have you ever stopped buying a product, perhaps because the manufacturer changed the product or raised its price? Read to find out why American colonists refused to buy British products.

Separated from Great Britain by more than 3,000 miles (4,828 km) of vast ocean and left largely to their own devices, the American colonists gained valuable experience in self-government. They learned how to manage their own affairs. This policy of loose control by the British was known as salutary, or healthy, neglect. Under this policy, the British did not insist on strict enforcement of laws.

Mercantilism Around 1760, when George III took the throne, Britain's policy toward the American colonies began to change. The British adopted a program called mercantil-ism. **Mercantilism** is the theory that a country's power depends on its wealth. A nation should sell more goods to other countries than it buys. A favorable balance of trade—more exports and fewer imports—brings money into the country. For mercantilism to be successful, Great Britain needed the colonies to be a source of cheap, raw materials. The Navigation Acts were a series of laws, passed in the early 1660s, that put the theory of mercantilism into practice.

Growing Tensions

Since the late 1600s, the British and the French had battled for supremacy in Europe and other parts of the world. After several wars in Europe, the fighting spilled over into North America. At a conference in Albany, New York, in 1754, the colonies debated a plan for a federal union. The plan, proposed by a committee led by Benjamin Franklin, was rejected. However, the Albany Plan showed that many colonists were already thinking about joining together for their common defense.

Chapter 2 **51**

Teach

R Reading Strategy

Predicting Ask: According to the theory of mercantilism, what would happen if a country bought more goods than it sold to other countries? *(It would not become powerful or wealthy.)* **OL**

For additional practice on this skill (Predicting), see the **Skills Handbook**.

C Critical Thinking

Drawing Conclusions Ask: Who benefited most from mercantilism: the colonies or Great Britain? *(Great Britain)* **BL**

Caption Answer:

They learned how to govern themselves and to manage their own affairs.

Additional Support

Activity: Interdisciplinary Connection

Literature and History Have students find the following primary source, either in the library or on the Internet. It explains the Albany Plan of Union drafted by Benjamin Franklin, which proposed that each colony would elect delegates to an American con-tinental assembly run by a royal governor. (The library reference is *Papers of Benjamin Franklin, vol. 5 [1959]*, pp. 387–92 by Leonard Larrabee, ed. The online reference for this source is located at http://www.constitution.org/bcp/albany.htm). Have students briefly summarize the major points in Franklin's plan and tell why the British government did not support it. *(British officials realized it would give too much power to the colonies.)* **AL**

R Reading Strategy

Summarizing Have students use a tape recorder to dictate a brief summary of events before and after the Stamp Act of 1765. Then have each student listen to a partner's recording and provide feedback of the completeness of the summary. **OL**

W Writing Support

Personal Writing Have students write a paragraph describing their thoughts about whether the colonists' response to the Stamp Act was reasonable. **OL**

TIME™ Political Cartoons

Answers:

1. America (the colonies)

2. the king

3. The horse (America) is trying to throw off its master (the king).

4. opposition to the Stamp Act

Differentiated Instruction

Biography Activity 2,
URB pp. 49–50

TIME™

Political Cartoons

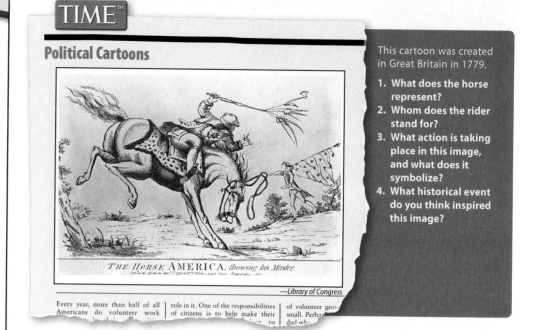

THE HORSE AMERICA, *throwing his Master.*

—Library of Congress

This cartoon was created in Great Britain in 1779.

1. What does the horse represent?

2. Whom does the rider stand for?

3. What action is taking place in this image, and what does it symbolize?

4. What historical event do you think inspired this image?

Every year, more than half of all Americans do volunteer work ... role in it. One of the responsibilities of citizens is to help make their ... of volunteer grou... small. Perha... dad who ...

From 1754 to 1763, Great Britain fought a long, costly war against France—the French and Indian War—winning French territory in North America. In order to prevent conflict with Native Americans over land, colonial settlers were forbidden to settle west of the Appalachian Mountains without permission from the British government. This Proclamation of 1763 enraged many farmers and others who wanted the land. To pay off its heavy war debts, Britain placed steep taxes and new restrictions on the American colonies. The Stamp Act of 1765 required colonists to attach expensive tax stamps to all newspapers and legal documents. The Quartering Act required the colonies to provide barracks and supplies to British troops.

Worsening Relations

In protest, many colonists decided to **boycott,** or refuse to buy, British goods. Organizations known as the Sons of Liberty were formed throughout the colonies in opposition to the Stamp Act.

Stamp Act Congress In October of 1765, nine of the thirteen colonies sent representatives to the Stamp Act Congress held in New York City. The representatives prepared a declaration against the new British actions, which was sent to King George III. This action marked the first time that a majority of the colonies joined together to oppose British rule. As a result, the British Parliament **repealed,** or cancelled, the Stamp Act.

The same day it repealed the Stamp Act, Parliament passed the Declaratory Act of 1766, which stated that Parliament had the right to tax and make decisions for the American colonies "in all cases." Then, in 1767, Parliament passed a set of laws that came to be known as the Townshend Acts. One of the Townshend Acts legalized the use of writs of assistance to assist customs officers in arresting smugglers.

52 Chapter 2

Richard Henry Lee

Objective: To identify Lee's contributions to the early governing documents of the United States

Focus: Have students identify Lee's contributions to the Continental Congress, the Declaration of Independence, and the Constitution.

Teach: Review the Stamp and Townshend acts, and why they angered Lee.

Assess: Explain Lee as "a chief architect" of the nation.

Close: Write a paragraph on Lee's importance.

Differentiated Instruction Strategies

BL Ask: Who is considered "the father of our country," and how did Lee help shape this man's career of service to the nation?

AL Explain the logic behind Lee's comparison of "bad government" and suicide.

ELL What was the result of Lee opposing a strong national government?

The writs were general search warrants that enabled customs officers to enter any location to look for evidence of smuggling. Angered by these laws, colonists caused trouble for British officials. The worst incident of violence took place in Boston. On March 5, 1770, British soldiers fired into a crowd, killing five. The shootings became known as the Boston Massacre.

New Taxes and a Tea Party

The colonists resented the new taxes. Because they had no representatives in Parliament, as people living in Great Britain did, the colonists believed that Parliament had no right to tax them. They summed up their feelings with the slogan "No taxation without representation!"

In 1773 Parliament passed another measure. The Tea Act gave the British East India Company the right to ship tea to the colonies without paying most of the taxes usually placed on tea. This made the East India Company tea cheaper than any other tea in the colonies, giving the British company an advantage over colonial merchants. In December 1773, a group of angry colonists dressed as Native Americans dumped 342 chests of British tea into Boston Harbor. In reaction to this protest, known as the Boston Tea Party, Parliament passed the Coercive Acts, which Americans called the Intolerable Acts. These laws restricted the colonists' civil rights, including the right to trial by jury.

Reading Check Explaining Why were the colonists angry about the new taxes?

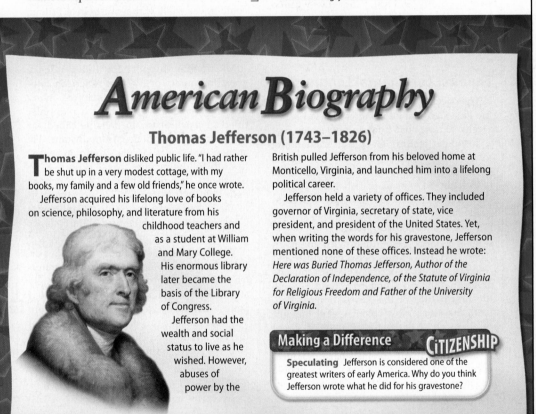

American Biography

Thomas Jefferson (1743–1826)

Thomas Jefferson disliked public life. "I had rather be shut up in a very modest cottage, with my books, my family and a few old friends," he once wrote. Jefferson acquired his lifelong love of books on science, philosophy, and literature from his childhood teachers and as a student at William and Mary College. His enormous library later became the basis of the Library of Congress.

Jefferson had the wealth and social status to live as he wished. However, abuses of power by the British pulled Jefferson from his beloved home at Monticello, Virginia, and launched him into a lifelong political career.

Jefferson held a variety of offices. They included governor of Virginia, secretary of state, vice president, and president of the United States. Yet, when writing the words for his gravestone, Jefferson mentioned none of these offices. Instead he wrote: *Here was Buried Thomas Jefferson, Author of the Declaration of Independence, of the Statute of Virginia for Religious Freedom and Father of the University of Virginia.*

Making a Difference   CiTIZENSHIP

Speculating Jefferson is considered one of the greatest writers of early America. Why do you think Jefferson wrote what he did for his gravestone?

Chapter 2   53

Hands-On Chapter Project
Step 4

Planning and Conducting a Community Meeting

Step 4: Conducting the Meeting Groups of students will conduct a school community meeting based on the format followed in traditional New England town meetings. Depending on the number of groups, each meeting may last 10 or 15 minutes.

Directions Write the Big Idea on the board. Have the town clerk from each group read what has been posted on their warrants. The group leaders, in turn, will open the meetings and act as moderators. The town clerk for each group will record the proceedings. After the meeting, all members of each group will review the notes and make suggestions for the writing of the minutes.

Later, the town clerk will write the minutes and distribute them to all group members.

Summarizing To finalize the project, have groups review and discuss their research, their warrants, and their meetings. Have each member write a one-paragraph evaluation of each step of the process they used to plan and conduct their community meeting. **OL**

(Project continued on the Visual Summary page)

R Reading Strategy

Setting a Purpose Have students create a K-W-L chart and write what they know about the Continental Congresses in the K column and what they want to know about them in the W column. After they read the section, have students complete the L column with what they learned. **BL**

C Critical Thinking

Comparing and Contrasting Ask: What different things happened in the First and Second Continental Congresses? *(In the first Congress in 1774, delegates sent a document to the king demanding that their rights be restored. In the second Congress, they decided to officially announce their independence.)* **OL**

D Differentiated Instruction

Gifted and Talented Have students investigate which other delegates assisted Jefferson in drafting the Declaration of Independence. Have them present an oral report to the class, using photographs and background information about each of these delegates. **AL**

> **Reading Check Answer:** to determine the best course of action in dealing with Great Britain

Differentiated Instruction

Moving Toward Independence

Main Idea The colonists began to take steps toward independence from Great Britain.

Civics & You How might you protest a new community or school rule that you believed was unfair? Read to find out how Americans protested British measures.

R The colonial governments banded together to fight the Intolerable Acts. In September 1774, twelve of the colonies sent **delegates,** or representatives, to Philadelphia to discuss their concerns. These representatives—from every colony except Georgia—wanted to establish a political body to represent American interests and **challenge,** or question, British control.

The First Continental Congress

The meeting in Philadelphia, known as the First Continental Congress, lasted seven weeks. During that time, the delegates sent a document to King George III demanding that the rights of the colonists be **restored,** or given back. They also made plans to extend the boycott of British goods. When the Congress ended, the delegates vowed to hold another meeting if their demands were not met by the following year.

C King George responded with force. In April 1775, two battles between British and colonial soldiers took place in Massachusetts at Lexington and Concord. These became the first battles of the Revolutionary War. Until this time, most colonists still thought of themselves as loyal subjects of Great Britain. Now, with British soldiers shooting at Americans, many colonists began to question their attachment to Britain. More people began talking about **independence,** or self-reliance and freedom from outside control.

Years after the first battle, Ralph Waldo Emerson wrote this poem to immortalize the colonists who fought at Concord:

> *By the rude bridge that arched the flood, Their flag to April's breeze unfurled, Here once the embattled farmers stood; And fired the shot heard round the world.*
>
> —Ralph Waldo Emerson, "The Concord Hymn"

The Second Continental Congress

In May 1775, colonial leaders met at the Second Continental Congress in Philadelphia. Not every member of the Congress favored independence. Some believed the colonists could never win a war against Great Britain. Others were still loyal to their home country. The Congress spent many months debating the best course of action.

Meanwhile, support for independence grew. In January of 1776, an American colonist named Thomas Paine inspired many other colonists by publishing a pamphlet titled *Common Sense.* In it Paine called for complete independence from Britain. He argued that it was simply "common sense" to stop following the "royal brute," King George III. Paine called the colonists' actions a struggle for freedom. By 1776 more than half of the delegates of the Second Continental Congress agreed with Paine that the colonies must break away from Britain.

D The Congress, acting now as a government for the colonies, appointed a committee to write a document that would officially announce the independence of the United States. Thomas Jefferson, a delegate from Virginia, did most of the work. His draft of the Declaration explained why the United States of America should be a free nation.

> **Reading Check Explaining** Why did colonists gather at the Second Continental Congress?

Leveled Activities

BL Reading Skills Activity 1, pp. 7–8

OL Biography Activity 2, URB pp. 49–50

ELL Writing Skills Activity 2, URB pp. 51–54

Citizen Warriors Many women, including Molly Pitcher, fought side by side with other colonial soldiers during the American Revolution. *Comparing* **How does the colonial fighting force compare with the makeup of modern army groups?**

The Declaration of Independence

Main Idea The Declaration of Independence used traditional English political rights to call for independence for the colonies.

Civics & You Why do you think governments are formed? Read to find out how the writer of the Declaration of Independence addressed this question.

The Declaration argued that the British government did not look after the interests of the colonists. The authors included a long list of abuses by King George III and called him **S** a "Tyrant . . . unfit to be the Ruler of a free People." However, the document was much more than a list of complaints.

Democratic Ideals

The second paragraph of the Declaration of Independence set forth the colonists' beliefs about the rights of individuals. It said:

> " *We hold these truths to be self-evident, that all men are created equal, that they are endowed by their Creator with certain unalienable Rights, that among these are Life, Liberty and the pursuit of Happiness.* "
> —The Declaration of Independence **R**

Civics ONLINE
Student Web Activity Visit glencoe.com and complete the Chapter 2 Web Activity.

S Skill Practice

Identifying Points of View Have pairs of students either take the side of the king and Parliament in their decisions to tax the colonists and pass various acts, or the side of the colonists in rebelling against the king and his decisions. **OL**

R Reading Strategy

Identifying Ask: What is a synonym for "unalienable rights"? *(absolute rights)* What is a synonym for "pursuit"? *("hunt" or "quest")* **OL**

Caption Answer:

Answers will vary. Colonial fighting forces often had to use their own weapons or even farm tools to fight in hand-to-hand combat. Students may suggest that modern armies fight with body armor and use tanks, planes, and bombs as weapons. Hand-to-hand combat is uncommon.

Civics ONLINE

Objectives and answers to the **Student Web Activity** can be found at glencoe.com under the Web Activity Lesson Plan for this chapter.

Additional Support

Chapter 2   55

Did You Know?

Revolutionary Women Women also risked their lives fighting in the American Revolution. The image in your textbook shows Molly Pitcher in the midst of a battle. Molly Pitcher's real name was Mary Ludwig Hays McCauley. During the Philadelphia Campaign in New Jersey, Mary joined her husband, a gunner in the Pennsylvania Artillery. She even spent the winter with the Army at Valley Forge.

Mary became known as "Molly Pitcher" after the Battle of Monmouth. This battle occurred in New Jersey on a very hot summer day in 1778. Mary bravely brought pitchers of water to the soldiers during the fighting. Some accounts of the battle say that Mary even took her husband's place at a cannon after he became ill or injured.

W Writing Support

Persuasive Writing Have students write one paragraph telling some reasons a government should feel responsible for protecting the rights of its people. **OL**

Reading Check **Answer:** to protect the rights of its people

Assess

Civics ONLINE

Study Central™ provides summaries, interactive games, and online graphic organizers to help students review content.

Close

Summarizing Have students work in small groups to rephrase, in their own words, the excerpt from the Declaration of Independence at the top of the page. Suggest they use a dictionary or thesaurus, if necessary. **Ask:** How do modern Americans peacefully show they want a change in government? *(They vote in local, state, and national elections.)* **OL**

Section 4 Review

The paragraph quoted from the Declaration went on to say:

> "*. . . to secure these rights, Governments are instituted among Men, deriving their just powers from the consent of the governed, That whenever any Form of Government becomes destructive of these ends, it is the Right of the People to alter or abolish it, and to institute new Government. . . .*"
>
> —The Declaration of Independence

W In other words, the purpose of a government is to protect the rights of the people. Moreover, government is based on the consent, or agreement, of the people. It only has the powers that the governed give it. The people are also entitled to change a government if it disregards their rights or their combined wishes.

These ideas were not new. Remember as you read earlier, the ideas about democracy and freedom originated with the ancient Greeks. Jefferson was influenced by John Locke and other writers. As you learned earlier, Locke wrote that good government is based on a social contract between the people and the rulers. Locke also wrote that all people should equally enjoy the rights to life, liberty, and property.

An Uncertain Future

The Second Continental Congress approved the Declaration of Independence, with a few changes, on July 4, 1776. The American colonies were now independent states—at least in theory. True freedom, though, would not come until the war ended and Great Britain officially recognized the United States as an independent nation.

Reading Check **Summarizing** According to the Declaration, what is the purpose of government?

 Review

Vocabulary

1. **Write** complete sentences that include these groups of terms: *merchant, boycott, repeal; delegates,* and *independence.*

Main Ideas

2. **Explaining** Why did Great Britain show control by raising taxes on the American colonists after 1763? What effect did this have on the colonists?

3. **Identifying** What British legislation prompted colonists to hold the First Continental Congress in a show of independence?

Critical Thinking

4. **Persuasive Writing** Assume the role of a British government official in 1774, and write a press release explaining why the Coercive Acts (Intolerable Acts) were necessary.

5. **BIG Ideas** In a web diagram like the one below, list the ideas of government found in the Declaration of Independence.

Ideas

CITIZENSHIP Activity

6. **Expository Writing** Read the Declaration of Natural Rights in the Declaration of Independence (second, third, and fourth paragraphs). Select what you think is the single most important idea and explain in a paragraph how that idea affects your life today.

 Civics ONLINE

Study Central™ To review this section, go to glencoe.com.

Answers

1. Sentences should use vocabulary words according to their definitions in the section and in the Glossary.

2. Britain raised taxes to pay off its heavy debt incurred during its war with France. The increase in taxes enraged the colonists.

3. the Coercive Acts, which the colonists called the Intolerable Acts

4. Press releases will vary, but most students will say the Coercive Acts were necessary to regain control and to restore order after the colonists protested the Tea Act by dumping chests of tea in Boston Harbor.

5. men are created equal; people have unalienable rights; governments derive power with citizens' consent; governments must protect citizens' rights; citizens have the right to throw off despotic governments and to set up new ones

6. Essays will vary, but should include how the idea affects their daily lives.

Visual Summary

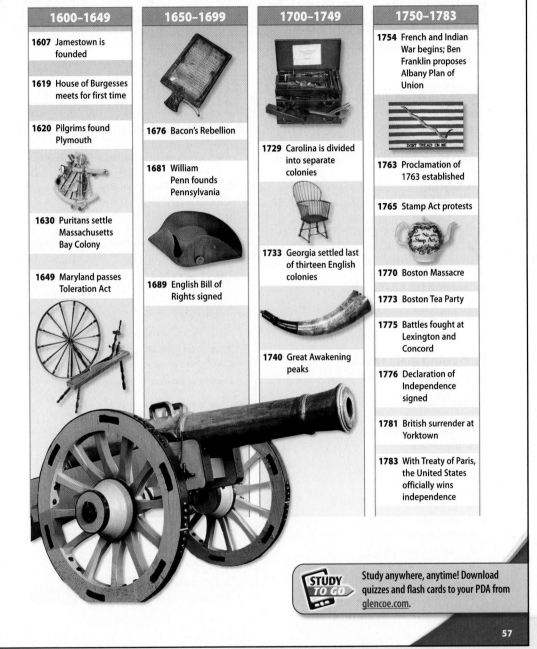

1600–1649	1650–1699	1700–1749	1750–1783
1607 Jamestown is founded			**1754** French and Indian War begins; Ben Franklin proposes Albany Plan of Union
1619 House of Burgesses meets for first time	**1676** Bacon's Rebellion		
1620 Pilgrims found Plymouth	**1681** William Penn founds Pennsylvania	**1729** Carolina is divided into separate colonies	**1763** Proclamation of 1763 established
1630 Puritans settle Massachusetts Bay Colony			**1765** Stamp Act protests
1649 Maryland passes Toleration Act	**1689** English Bill of Rights signed	**1733** Georgia settled last of thirteen English colonies	**1770** Boston Massacre
			1773 Boston Tea Party
			1775 Battles fought at Lexington and Concord
		1740 Great Awakening peaks	**1776** Declaration of Independence signed
			1781 British surrender at Yorktown
			1783 With Treaty of Paris, the United States officially wins independence

STUDY TO GO Study anywhere, anytime! Download quizzes and flash cards to your PDA from glencoe.com.

Visual Summary 2

Reading a Time Line Have students consider the total amount of time represented by the time line. **Ask:** How many years passed between the founding of Jamestown and the signing of the Treaty of Paris? *(176)* Reinforce that the development of the American democracy was a slow process. **BL**

Making Decisions Have students work in small groups and discuss what kinds of laws are important in an orderly society. **Ask:** If you were a leader charged with building the foundation for a new society, what three common laws would be most important to institute in an attempt to create a fair and balanced community? Students should think of the laws that would frame and reasonably maintain their ideal society. Remind students that common laws are those based on customs and rules by which to live. To get students thinking, offer these examples: treating all people with respect, punishing people who break laws, holding elections for leaders. **AL**

Hands-On Chapter Project
Step 5: Wrap-Up

Planning and Conducting a Community Meeting

Step 5: Reviewing the Meeting Students will analyze the process they started in Step 1.

Directions: Have the town clerk for each group distribute minutes of the meeting to all group members. After the students have read the minutes, have the groups meet to discuss any concerns. Make sure all the group members agree with what is written. If there is disagreement, the group members should submit proposed changes to the town clerk. Group members will vote on whether to amend the minutes.

To finalize the project, have groups review and discuss their research, their warrants, and their meetings. Have each member write a one-paragraph evaluation of each step of the process they used to plan and conduct their community meeting. **OL**

Answers and Analyses

Reviewing Vocabulary

1. B Students will have read about natural rights in Section 1 in a section entitled "Philosophical Influences" and about social contracts in the subsection "What Is a Social Contract?" A student could eliminate the three incorrect answers by using the knowledge that none of the other answers are items that can be taken away.

2. C Students will have read this in Section 2 in a section entitled "The Middle Colonies." The Duke was given the colony by his brother, King Charles II. Since he owned the colony, he was its proprietor. Knowing that "proprietary" is related to the word that means "owner" in the question should help students logically rule out the other answers.

3. D The text states in a section entitled "Why Did Colonists Immigrate?" that the founders of Massachusetts were Puritans, so named because they wanted to purify the Church of England.

4. B The text states this directly in Section 3 in a section entitled "Colonial Resistance": "The Navigation Acts were a series of laws passed in the early 1660s that put the theory of mercantilism into practice." The most confusing distractor would most likely be answer D, triangular trade. Students should be able to remember that triangular trade was a trading pattern that developed among the Americas, Africa, and Europe and included the slave trade.

Reviewing Main Ideas

5. C This question will require that students understand the relationships among the most obvious answer selections. From their reading, they should recall that the Magna Carta restricted the monarch's power and included equal treatment and trial by peers. It was followed by the English Bill of Rights, which further restricted the monarchy and banned cruel and unusual punishment.

6. C This is stated directly in the text in a section entitled "Town Meetings": "The Mayflower Compact established a tradition of direct democracy." The most likely

---

TEST-TAKING **TIP**

> Get eight or more hours of sleep the night before a test.

Reviewing Vocabulary

Directions: Choose the word(s) that best completes the sentence.

1. If a government tried to take away a people's _____, it was breaking the social contract.

  A legislature   **C** charter

  B natural rights   **D** compact

2. The Duke of York owned and governed the _____ of New York.

  A Tidewater   **C** proprietary colony

  B royal colony   **D** joint-stock company

3. The founders of Massachusetts were _____.

  A enslaved people   **C** indentured servants

  B plantation owners   **D** religious dissenters

4. The Navigation Acts put _____ into practice.

  A toleration   **C** egalitarianism

  B mercantilism   **D** triangular trade

Reviewing Main Ideas

Directions: Choose the best answer for each question.

Section 1 (pp. 32–37)

5. Which innovation allowed rights to land holders in England?

  A Magna Carta

  B common law

  C English Bill of Rights

  D Locke's social contract

6. Which institution or document established a tradition of direct democracy in New England?

  A Virginia Company

  B House of Burgesses

  C Mayflower Compact

  D Fundamental Orders of Connecticut

Section 2 (pp. 38–43)

7. Which English colony became the first to welcome people of all faiths?

  A Massachusetts   **C** Pennsylvania

  B Rhode Island   **D** Maryland

8. Why did Southern farmers begin using enslaved Africans?

  A Africans were more willing workers than Europeans.

  B Long indentures placed huge financial burdens on planters.

  C Plantations demanded more workers than immigration provided.

  D The triangular trade was more humane than indentured servitude.

Section 3 (pp. 44–49)

9. What about the Middle Colonies spurred the growth of ports such as New York and Philadelphia?

  A soil and climate suited to cash crops

  B rivers for easy transport to the coast

  C abundant wood for use in shipbuilding

  D an ideal location for fishing and whaling

10. How would you characterize the Great Awakening of the 1700s?

  A a religious revival

  B a political upheaval

  C an economic revolution

  D an educational movement

Section 4 (pp. 50–56)

11. Which legislation passed by Parliament restricted colonists' right to trial by jury?

  A Stamp Act

  B Townsend Acts

  C Declaratory Act of 1766

  D Coercive Acts

GO ON

---

distractor is the House of Burgesses, the first representative assembly in the colonies and the beginning of self-government.

7. B Because all the answer choices are the names of colonies, all seem plausible if students do not read carefully. Careful reading reveals that the Puritans in Massachusetts did not believe in accepting other religions. Pennsylvania was founded by the Quakers as a safe place to practice their religion. Maryland was founded as a safe place for

Catholics. Only Rhode Island, founded by Roger Williams, welcomed people of all faiths.

8. C All the answers for this question except D seem plausible if students do not read carefully. Africans had no choice about working, which is quite different from being more willing to work than Europeans. Since indentured servants were not paid, they placed no financial burden on planters other than costs for room and

12. Who published *Common Sense*, a pamphlet calling for complete independence from Britain?

  A Benjamin Franklin

  B Thomas Paine

  C Thomas Jefferson

  D John Locke

Critical Thinking

Directions: Base your answers to questions 13 and 14 on the cartoon below and your knowledge of Chapter 2.

13. What does the cartoonist imply by using darker print for the word *men*?

  A Women are excluded.

  B All people are included.

  C All slaves are excluded.

  D Male slaves are included.

14. Why does the cartoonist include a washerwoman?

  A to contrast rulers and workers in the colonies

  B to suggest gender inequality in colonial times

  C to show the industriousness of colonial women

  D to imply the protection of even poor people's rights

Document-Based Questions

Directions: Analyze the document and answer the short-answer questions that follow.

This passage from the Declaration of Independence includes some of the colonists' complaints about King George III.

> He has combined with others to subject us to a jurisdiction foreign to our constitution, and unacknowledged by our laws; giving his Assent to their Acts of pretended Legislation:
>
> For quartering large bodies of troops among us:
>
> For protecting them, by a mock Trial, from punishment for any Murders which they should commit on the Inhabitants of these States:
>
> For cutting off our Trade with all parts of the world:
>
> For imposing Taxes on us without our Consent:
>
> For depriving us in many cases, of the benefits of Trial by Jury:
>
> For transporting us beyond Seas to be tried for pretended offences:
>
> —the Declaration of Independence

15. The Declaration refers to King George combining with "others" and "giving his assent to their Acts of pretended Legislation." Who are these others?

16. Choose two of the complaints. What legislation or event from the chapter is related to each complaint?

Extended Response

17. The colonists tried other means of resolving their differences with the British before declaring their independence. Write a brief essay describing their efforts.

Civics ONLINE

For additional test practice, use Self-Check Quizzes— Chapter 2 on glencoe.com.

If you missed questions...	1	2	3	4	5	6	7	8	9	10	11	12	13	14	15	16	17
Go to page...	35	39	41	51	33	37	39	43	45	47	53	54	48	48	55	51	51

Need Extra Help?

Chapter 2 **59**

ASSESSMENT

First Continental Congress to discuss independence in 1774 would help them choose the correct answer.

12. B This is a straightforward question that requires a careful reading of the text. Because all the answers are the names of men who wrote important documents, students need to have kept straight who wrote what.

Critical Thinking

13. A The answer is clearly that women are excluded, because the men are gathered around the Declaration while a woman is depicted scrubbing a floor.

14. B Scrubbing the floors is not a good answer because it is presented in the context of men doing the important work of declaring independence. Students' knowledge from the text would equip them to know that none of the colonists were "rulers" as such. Also, there is no discussion of poor people's rights in the text.

Document-Based Questions

15. Members of Parliament

16. Students answers will vary. Possible answers are that the Coercive or Intolerable Acts caused the quartering of troops in colonists' homes and that the "Murders which they should commit" refers to the Boston Massacre.

Extended Response

17. Students' essays will vary. Look for supporting details from the chapter.

---

board. Students' recollection of the account by Olaudah Equiano in "The Beginning of Slavery" in Section 2 would clearly rule out triangular trade as a humane practice.

9. A A careful reading of facts about each colonial region in the section entitled "The Economy" in Section 3 is required to select the right answer. It was the rivers of the Southern Colonies that made for easy transport. The other two answers describe attributes of the New England colonies.

10. A This question challenges students' understanding of the difference between what the Great Awakening *was* and what happened as a *result* of the religious revival that swept through the colonies. The other answers all reflect the aftermath of the Great Awakening, not the definition of the event itself.

11. D Because they are acts that occurred in rapid sequence, all of the answers seem plausible if students do not read carefully. Knowing the sequence of acts that led the

Civics ONLINE

Have students visit the Web site at glencoe.com to review Chapter 2 and take the **Self-Check Quiz**.

Need Extra Help?

Have students refer to the pages listed if they miss any of the questions.

59

R Reading Strategy

Activating Prior Knowledge Have students review the events that led to the drafting of the Declaration of Independence. *(Colonists were unhappy about British government policies, especially taxation. They reacted by staging the Boston Tea Party and protesting in other ways. Representatives from each colony met at the First Continental Congress and the Second Continental Congress to act on their concerns.)* **BL**

C Critical Thinking

Analyzing Primary Sources **Ask:** Why do you think some words in the middle of sentences are capitalized? *(These words and phrases were important parts of the Declaration. The writer wanted to emphasize them.)* **OL**

For additional practice on this skill (Analyzing Primary Sources), see the **Skills Handbook**.

Additional Support

The Declaration of Independence

In Congress, July 4, 1776. The unanimous Declaration
of the thirteen united States of America,

Words spelled as originally written.

What It Means

The Preamble The Declaration of Independence has four parts. The Preamble explains why the Continental Congress drew up the Declaration.

impel: force

What It Means

Natural Rights The second part, the Declaration of Natural Rights, lists the rights of the citizens. It goes on to explain that, in a republic, people form a government to protect their rights.

endowed: provided

usurpations: unjust uses of power
despotism: unlimited power

What It Means

List of Grievances The third part of the Declaration lists the colonists' complaints against the British government. Notice that King George III is singled out for blame.

[Preamble]

When in the Course of human events, it becomes necessary for one people to dissolve the political bands which have connected them with another, and to assume among the Powers of the earth, the separate and equal station to which the Laws of Nature and of Nature's God entitle them, a decent respect to the opinions of mankind requires that they should declare the causes which **impel** them to the separation.

[Declaration of Natural Rights]

We hold these truths to be self-evident, that all men are created equal, that they are **endowed** by their Creator with certain unalienable Rights, that among these are Life, Liberty, and the pursuit of Happiness.

That to secure these rights, Governments are instituted among Men, deriving their just powers from the consent of the governed,

That whenever any Form of Government becomes destructive of these ends, it is the Right of the People to alter or to abolish it, and to institute new Government, laying its foundation on such principles and organizing its powers in such form, as to them shall seem most likely to effect their Safety and Happiness. Prudence, indeed, will dictate that Governments long established should not be changed for light and transient causes; and accordingly all experience hath shown, that mankind are more disposed to suffer, while evils are sufferable, than to right themselves by abolishing the forms to which they are accustomed. But when a long train of abuses and **usurpations,** pursuing invariably the same Object evinces a design to reduce them under absolute **Despotism,** it is their right, it is their duty, to throw off such Government, and to provide new Guards for their future security.

[List of Grievances]

Such has been the patient sufferance of these Colonies; and such is now the necessity which constrains them to alter their former Systems of Government. The history of the present King of Great Britain is a history of repeated injuries and usurpations, all having in direct object the establishment of an absolute Tyranny

60

Activity: Interdisciplinary Connection

Language Arts Have students discuss the reading difficulty presented by the Declaration of Independence. Tell them that Thomas Jefferson was selected to be the author because he was known to be a powerful writer. However, the document was not submitted exactly as Jefferson wrote it. Benjamin Franklin and John Adams made edits to a draft. **Ask:** If you were Jefferson's editor, how would you rewrite the Declaration of Natural Rights part of the document for modern readers? Advise students to use simple sentences to explain their ideas. Have them share their writing with the class. **AL**

over these States. To prove this, let Facts be submitted to a candid world.

He has refused his Assent to Laws, the most wholesome and necessary for the public good.

He has forbidden his Governors to pass Laws of immediate and pressing importance, unless suspended in their operation till his Assent should be obtained; and when so suspended, he has utterly neglected to attend to them.

He has refused to pass other Laws for the accommodation of large districts of people, unless those people would **relinquish** the right of Representation in the Legislature, a right **inestimable** to them and formidable to tyrants only.

relinquish: give up
inestimable: priceless

He has called together legislative bodies at places unusual, uncomfortable, and distant from the depository of their Public Records, for the sole purpose of fatiguing them into compliance with his measures.

He has dissolved Representative Houses repeatedly, for opposing with manly firmness his invasions on the rights of the people.

He has refused for a long time, after such dissolutions, to cause others to be elected; whereby the Legislative Powers, incapable of **Annihilation**, have returned to the People at large for their exercise; the State remaining in the mean time exposed to all the dangers of invasion from without, and **convulsions** within.

annihilation: destruction

convulsions: violent disturbances

He has endeavoured to prevent the population of these States; for that purpose obstructing the **Laws for Naturalization of Foreigners;** refusing to pass others to encourage their migrations hither, and raising the conditions of new Appropriations of Lands.

Laws for Naturalization of Foreigners: process by which foreign-born persons become citizens

He has obstructed the Administration of Justice, by refusing his Assent to Laws for establishing Judiciary Powers.

He has made Judges dependent on his Will alone, for the **tenure** of their offices, and the amount and payment of their salaries.

tenure: term

He has erected a multitude of New Offices, and sent hither swarms of Officers to harass our people, and eat out their substance.

He has kept among us, in times of peace, Standing Armies without the Consent of our legislature.

He has affected to render the Military independent of and superior to the Civil Power.

He has combined with others to subject us to a jurisdiction foreign to our constitution, and unacknowledged by our laws; giving his Assent to their acts of pretended legislation:

C Critical Thinking

Making Inferences Ask: Why might holding government meetings in strange and inconvenient places make the colonists more likely to accept King George's policies? *(Answers will vary but most should say that the king was trying to make it so difficult for legislators to meet that they would simply give up.)* **OL**

R Reading Strategy

Using Context Clues The word "hither" is used twice on this page. **Ask:** How can you figure out the meaning of hither using the words around it? *(Hither means "here" or "to this place." Answers will vary, but students might say they used their understanding of the words "naturalization" and "migrations" for the first reference. For the second reference, they could use the idea of officers being "sent" from Britain to harass "our people.")* **AL**

Activity: Technology Connection

Using the Declaration of Independence Today Tell students that although the Declaration of Independence was written hundreds of years ago, it is still relevant in today's society. Have pairs of students search an Internet news database, such as Google News www.news.google.com or Lexis-Nexis, using the search term Declaration of Independence. Tell students to pick three news stories that reference the Declaration and note the context in which the document is mentioned. Have the pairs share their findings during a class discussion. **OL**

D Differentiated Instruction

English Learners Point out the bold word "quartering" in the sentence. Tell students that the word has more than one meaning. It can refer to lodging or housing people, usually soldiers, as it does in this sentence. **Ask:** Can you think of another meaning for "quartering" that relates to math? *("Quartering" can also mean "dividing something into four equal parts.")* **ELL**

R Reading Strategy

Identifying Have students name some of the "domestic insurrections" to which Jefferson refers. *(Answers will vary, but might include the boycott of British goods, the Boston Massacre, or the Boston Tea Party.)* **OL**

Additional Support

D **quartering:** lodging

render: make

abdicated: given up

perfidy: violation of trust

R **insurrections:** rebellions

petitioned for redress: asked formally for a correction of wrongs

unwarrantable jurisdiction: unjustified authority

For **quartering** large bodies of troops among us:

For protecting them, by a mock Trial, from Punishment for any Murders which they should commit on the Inhabitants of these States:

For cutting off our Trade with all parts of the world:

For imposing taxes on us without our Consent:

For depriving us in many cases, of the benefits of Trial by Jury:

For transporting us beyond Seas to be tried for pretended offences:

For abolishing the free System of English Laws in a neighbouring Province, establishing therein an Arbitrary government, and enlarging its Boundaries so as to **render** it at once an example and fit instrument for introducing the same absolute rule into these Colonies:

For taking away our Charters, abolishing our most valuable Laws, and altering fundamentally the Forms of our Governments:

For suspending our own Legislature, and declaring themselves invested with Power to legislate for us in all cases whatsoever.

He has **abdicated** Government here, by declaring us out of his Protection and waging War against us.

He has plundered our seas, ravaged our Coasts, burnt our towns, and destroyed the lives of our people.

He is at this time transporting large armies of foreign mercenaries to compleat the works of death, desolation and tyranny, already begun with circumstances of Cruelty & **perfidy** scarcely paralleled in the most barbarous ages, and totally unworthy the Head of a civilized nation.

He has constrained our fellow Citizens taken Captive on the high Seas to bear Arms against their Country, to become the executioners of their friends and Brethren, or to fall themselves by their Hands.

He has excited domestic **insurrections** amongst us, and has endeavoured to bring on the inhabitants of our frontiers, the merciless Indian Savages, whose known rule of warfare, is an undistinguished destruction of all ages, sexes and conditions.

In every stage of these Oppressions We have **Petitioned for Redress** in the most humble terms: Our repeated Petitions have been answered only by repeated injury. A Prince, whose character is thus marked by every act which may define a Tyrant, is unfit to be the ruler of a free People.

Nor have We been wanting in attention to our British brethren. We have warned them from time to time of attempts by their legislature to extend an **unwarrantable jurisdiction** over us. We have reminded them of the circumstances of our emigration and settlement here. We have appealed to their native justice and magnanimity, and we have conjured them by the ties of our common kindred to disavow these usurpations, which, would inevitably interrupt our connections and correspondence. They

---

Activity: US/World Connections

Tracing the Influence of the Declaration of Independence Tell students that France's Declaration of the Rights of Man and of the Citizen was as important to the French Revolution as the Declaration of Independence was to the American Revolution. The French document was written by the Marquis de Lafayette and was partly inspired by the American Declaration. In fact, Thomas Jefferson was the United States minister to France at the time of the document's drafting. Lafayette and Jefferson were friends and often discussed Lafayette's work.

Have students read the translation of the document online at www.constitution.org/fr/fr_drm.htm. As they read, students should note differences and similarities between the ideas in the two documents. Have students share their findings with the class. As a class, make a Venn diagram that shows how the two documents are the same and different. **AL**

too have been deaf to the voice of justice and of **consanguinity**. We must, therefore, acquiesce in the necessity, which denounces our Separation, and hold them, as we hold the rest of mankind, Enemies in War, in Peace Friends.

[Resolution of Independence by the United States]

We, therefore, the Representatives of the united States of America, in General Congress, Assembled, appealing to the Supreme Judge of the world for the **rectitude** of our intentions, do, in the Name, and by Authority of the good People of these Colonies, solemnly publish and declare, That these United Colonies are, and of Right ought to be Free and Independent States; that they are Absolved from all Allegiance to the British Crown, and that all political connection between them and the State of Great Britain, is and ought to be totally dissolved; and that as Free and Independent States, they have full Power to levy War, conclude Peace, contract Alliances, establish Commerce, and to do all other Acts and Things which Independent States may of right do.

And for the support of this Declaration, with a firm reliance on the Protection of Divine Providence, we mutually pledge to each other our Lives, our Fortunes and our sacred Honor.

John Hancock
  President from
  Massachusetts

Georgia
Button Gwinnett
Lyman Hall
George Walton

North Carolina
William Hooper
Joseph Hewes
John Penn

South Carolina
Edward Rutledge
Thomas Heyward, Jr.
Thomas Lynch, Jr.
Arthur Middleton

Maryland
Samuel Chase
William Paca
Thomas Stone
Charles Carroll
  of Carrollton

Virginia
George Wythe
Richard Henry Lee
Thomas Jefferson
Benjamin Harrison
Thomas Nelson, Jr.
Francis Lightfoot Lee
Carter Braxton

Pennsylvania
Robert Morris
Benjamin Rush
Benjamin Franklin
John Morton
George Clymer
James Smith
George Taylor
James Wilson
George Ross

Delaware
Caesar Rodney
George Read
Thomas McKean

New York
William Floyd
Philip Livingston
Francis Lewis
Lewis Morris

New Jersey
Richard Stockton
John Witherspoon
Francis Hopkinson
John Hart
Abraham Clark

New Hampshire
Josiah Bartlett
William Whipple
Matthew Thornton

Massachusetts
Samuel Adams
John Adams
Robert Treat Paine
Elbridge Gerry

Rhode Island
Stephen Hopkins
William Ellery

Connecticut
Samuel Huntington
William Williams
Oliver Wolcott
Roger Sherman

consanguinity: originating from the same ancestor

What It Means

Resolution of Independence The final section declares that the colonies are "Free and Independent States" with the full power to make war, to form alliances, and to trade with other countries.

rectitude: rightness

What It Means

Signers of the Declaration The signers, as representatives of the American people, declared the colonies independent from Great Britain. Most members signed the document on August 2, 1776.

The Declaration of Independence

C Critical Thinking

Analyzing Primary Sources Ask: Why didn't Jefferson capitalize the word "united" in the phrase "united States of America"? (*The United States of America did not exist when the Declaration was written. Jefferson was simply using the word to say that the colonies were united in their feelings.*) **OL**

For additional practice on this skill (Analyzing Primary Sources), see the **Skills Handbook**.

R Reading Strategy

Summarizing Pair students together and have them write two-sentence summaries of the final section of the Declaration. **OL**

Did You Know?

Independence of Youth Edward Rutledge of South Carolina was the youngest man to sign the Declaration of Independence. He was 26 in August of 1776. Rutledge was also the youngest in his family. He had seven siblings. Rutledge's older brother John was his mentor, and he also attended the Second Continental Congress.

Despite his age, Rutledge was an influential member of the Congress. However, he was initially opposed to independence for the colonies. He even worked to delay the vote for declaring independence. When a vote finally took place, only the South Carolina and New Hampshire delegations voted no. After Rutledge realized that he

was in the minority, he encouraged the South Carolina legislators to reconsider their vote and to now support independence.

Chapter Planning Guide

3

Levels					Resources	Chapter Opener	Section 1	Section 2	Section 3	Section 4	Chapter Assess
BL	OL	AL	ELL		**FOCUS**						
BL	OL	AL	ELL	🖨	**Daily Focus Skills Transparencies**		3–1	3–2	3–3	3–4	
					TEACH						
BL	OL		ELL	📁	**Reading Essentials and Note-Taking Guide***		p. 22	p. 25	p. 28	p. 31	
BL	OL	AL	ELL	📁	**Content Vocabulary Activity, URB***		p. 71	p. 71	p. 71	p. 71	
BL	OL	AL	ELL	📁	**Academic Vocabulary Activity, URB**		p. 73	p. 73	p. 73	p. 73	
	OL			📁	**Biography Activity, URB**					p. 75	
BL	OL	AL	ELL	📁	**Writing Skills Activity, URB**				p. 77		
	OL	AL		📁	**Critical Thinking Skills Activity, URB**			p. 79			
BL	OL	AL	ELL	📁	**Chart, Graph, and Map Skills Activity, URB**		p. 81	p. 81			
BL	OL	AL	ELL	📁	**Differentiated Instruction, URB**		p. 83	p. 83	p. 83	p. 83	
BL	OL	AL	ELL	📁	**School-to-Home Connection Activity, URB***		p. 85	p. 85	p. 85	p. 85	
BL	OL		ELL	📁	**Guided Reading Activities, URB***		p. 89	p. 90	p. 91	p. 92	
BL	OL	AL	ELL	📁	**The Living Constitution Study Guide***	✓	✓	✓	✓	✓	
BL	OL			📁	**Focus on American History**		p. 55	p. 55	p. 55	p. 55	
BL	OL	AL	ELL	📁	**Writer's Guidebook**	✓	✓	✓	✓	✓	✓
	OL	AL		💿	**Primary Source Document Library**	✓	✓	✓	✓	✓	✓
BL	OL	AL	ELL	💿	**Daily Lecture & Discussion Notes (in Pres. Plus)**		✓	✓	✓	✓	✓
BL	OL	AL	ELL	💿	**StudentWorks™ Plus**		✓	✓	✓	✓	✓
BL	OL	AL	ELL	💿	**Section Spotlight Videos**		✓	✓	✓	✓	
BL	OL	AL	ELL	🖨	**TIME Interpreting Political Cartoons Transp.**					Ch. 3	
BL	OL	AL	ELL	🖨	**Writing Process Transparencies**	✓	✓	✓	✓	✓	✓

Note: Please refer to the *Unit 1 Resource Book* for this chapter's URB materials.

* Also available in Spanish

Teacher**Works** *Plus*
All-In-One Planner and Resource Center

- Interactive Lesson Planner
- Interactive Teacher Edition
- Fully editable blackline masters
- Section Spotlight Videos Launch
- Differentiated Lesson Plans
- Printable reports of daily assignments
- Standards Tracking System

Levels					Resources	Chapter Opener	Section 1	Section 2	Section 3	Section 4	Chapter Assess
BL	OL	AL	ELL								
					TEACH (continued)						
Teacher Resources				📁	**Building Academic Vocabulary**	✓	✓	✓	✓	✓	✓
				📁	**Strategies for Success**	✓	✓	✓	✓	✓	✓
				📁	**Teachers Guide to Differentiated Instruction**	✓	✓	✓	✓	✓	✓
				💿	**Graphing Tool**	✓	✓	✓	✓	✓	✓
				💿	**Presentation Plus! with MindJogger CheckPoint**	✓	✓	✓	✓	✓	✓
					ASSESS						
BL	OL	AL	ELL	📁	**Quizzes and Tests***		p. 26	p. 27	p. 28	p. 29	p. 30
BL	OL	AL	ELL	📁	**Authentic Assessment with Rubrics**			p. 7			
BL	OL	AL	ELL	📁	**Standardized Test Practice**		p. 5	p. 5	p. 5	p. 5	p. 5
BL	OL	AL	ELL	💿	*ExamView*® *Assessment Suite* CD-ROM		3–1	3–2	3–3	3–4	Ch. 3
					CLOSE						
BL			ELL	📁	**Reteaching Activity, URB***		p. 87	p. 87	p. 87	p. 87	
BL	OL		ELL	📁	**Reading and Study Skills Foldables™**	p. 55		p. 55			
BL	OL	AL	ELL	🖐	**Graphic Organizer Transparencies & Strategies**	✓	✓	✓	✓	✓	✓

✓ Chapter- or unit-based activities applicable to all sections in this chapter

3

Using ExamView® Assessment Suite

QuickTest

What is ExamView® Assessment Suite?

ExamView® Assessment Suite is a powerful assessment tool that enables you to quickly create and customize tests for your students. Tests can be either printed or administered online.

How can ExamView® help my students?

ExamView® QuickTest allows you to create your own test questions or choose from an existing, fully editable bank of questions customized for this book. The flexibility of ExamView® allows you to develop testing materials that:

- focus on specific skills or competencies
- can be translated to Spanish in one click
- are leveled for different abilities
- address state or national standards

Civics ONLINE

Visit glencoe.com and enter *QuickPass*™ code CIV1360c3T for Chapter 3 resources.

You can easily launch a wide range of digital products from your computer's desktop with the McGraw-Hill Social Studies widget.

	Student	Teacher	Parent
Media Library			
• Student Edition Section Audio	●		●
• Spanish Audio Summaries	●		●
• Section Spotlight Videos	●	●	●
***Civics Today* Online Learning Center (Web Site)**			
• Chapter Overviews	●	●	●
• Study Central™	●	●	●
• Study-to-Go	●	●	●
• Student Web Activities	●	●	●
• In Motion Animation	●	●	●
• Self-Check Quizzes	●	●	●
• ePuzzles and Games	●	●	●
• StudentWorks™ Plus Online	●	●	●
• Vocabulary eFlashcards	●	●	●
• Web Activity Lesson Plans		●	
• Vocabulary PuzzleMaker	●	●	●
Classroom Tools			
• Multilingual Glossary	●	●	●
• Beyond the Textbook	●	●	●
• NGS MapMachine	●	●	●

Reading List Generator CD-ROM

GLENCOE BOOKLINK 3

Use this database to search more than 30,000 titles to create a customized reading list for your students.

- Reading lists can be organized by students' reading level, author, genre, theme, or area of interest.
- The database provides Degrees of Reading Power™ (DRP) and Lexile™ readability scores for all selections.
- A brief summary of each selection is included.

Leveled reading suggestions for this chapter:

For students at a Grade 7 reading level:
- *A Convention of Delegates: The Creation of the Constitution,* by Denis J. Hauptly

For students at a Grade 8 reading level:
- *The Great Declaration: A Book for Young Americans,* by Henry Steele Commager

For students at a Grade 9 reading level:
- *How They Chose These Words,* by Walter Isaacson

For students at a Grade 10 reading level:
- *American Values,* by Mary E. Williams

For students at a Grade 11 reading level:
- *American Sphinx: The Character of Thomas Jefferson,* by Joseph J. Ellis

READING SUPPORT FROM JAMESTOWN EDUCATION

- **Timed Readings Plus in Social Studies** helps students increase their reading rate and fluency while maintaining comprehension. The 400-word passages are similar to those found on state and national assessments.

- **Reading in the Content Area: Social Studies** concentrates on six essential reading skills that help students better comprehend what they read. The book includes 75 high-interest nonfiction passages written at increasing levels of difficulty.

- **Reading Social Studies** includes strategic reading instruction and vocabulary support in Social Studies content for both ELLs and native speakers of English.

- **Content Vocabulary Workout** (Grades 6–8) accelerates reading comprehension through focused vocabulary development. Social Studies content vocabulary comes from the glossaries of Glencoe's Middle School Social Studies texts. www.jamestowneducation.com

KEY Teacher Wraparound

Use this key to help you identify the different types of prompts found in the Teacher Wraparound Edition.

R **Reading Strategies** activities help you teach reading skills and vocabulary.

C **Critical Thinking** strategies help students apply and extend what they have learned.

D **Differentiated Instruction** activities provide instruction for students learning to speak English, along with suggestions for teaching various types of learners.

S **Skill Practice** strategies help students practice historical analysis and geography skills.

W **Writing Support** activities provide writing opportunities to help students comprehend the text.

Teaching strategies and activities have been coded for ability level appropriateness.

AL Activities for students working above grade level

OL Activities for students working on grade level

BL Activities for students working below grade level

ELL Activities for English Language Learners

Focus

Why It Matters

Ask: Why do many people claim that the Constitution is the United States' most important document? *(It outlines our type of government—one that is run by the people. It also outlines our freedoms and rights, such as those of speech and religion, as well as the right to bear arms, the right to petition, and the right to a trial by jury.)*

More About the Photo

Visual Literacy The National Constitution Center is a nonprofit organization that was created to increase the public's understanding of our Constitution. The center's museum, solely dedicated to the Constitution, includes multimedia exhibits, photographs, films, and artifacts that detail the Constitution's history as well as its relevance to modern society. This photograph depicts an actor who provides an orientation to the major principles of the Constitution.

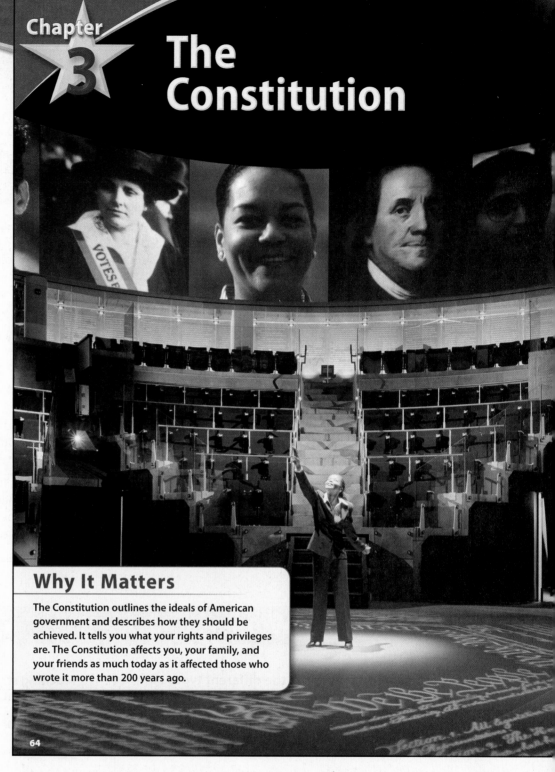

Chapter
3

The Constitution

Why It Matters

The Constitution outlines the ideals of American government and describes how they should be achieved. It tells you what your rights and privileges are. The Constitution affects you, your family, and your friends as much today as it affected those who wrote it more than 200 years ago.

64

Teach

BIG Ideas *As you begin teaching each section, use these questions and activities to help students focus on the Big Ideas.*

Section 1

The Nation's First Governments
Ask: What kinds of freedoms and what form of government do you think the colonists wanted to outline in their first constitutions? *(They wanted to have freedom of religion and a government run by*

the people.) Tell students that in Section 1, they will learn how the thirteen colonies established a form of government and created policies that would be the backbone of the Constitution. **OL**

Section 2

The Road to the Constitution Ask: What kinds of obstacles do you think the Framers faced when writing the Constitution? *(Each delegate would want to serve his constituents. They might have argued and disagreed about major issues.)* Point out that in Section 2, students will discover what occurred during the proceedings of the Constitutional Convention and learn about the compromises that were made. **OL**

Chapter Audio

Civics ONLINE
Visit glencoe.com and enter
QuickPass™ code
CIV3093c3 for
Chapter 3
resources.

Chapter Introduction
3

BIG Ideas

Section 1: The Nation's First Governments

Political principles and major events shape how people form governments. Americans faced the task of forming independent governments at both the state and national levels.

Section 2: The Road to the Constitution

Political principles and major events shape how people form governments. American leaders decided that a new constitution was needed.

Section 3: The Structure of Our Constitution

A constitution reflects the values and goals of the society that creates it. The Constitution is this nation's fundamental law.

Section 4: Principles Underlying the Constitution

A constitution reflects the values and goals of the society that creates it. The Constitution sets forth the basic principles of government.

◄ The National Constitution Center in Philadelphia provides an interactive tour of important events in our nation's history.

FOLDABLES
Study Organizer

Sequencing Information Study Foldable Make the following Foldable to help you analyze information about the Constitution.

Step 1 Mark the midpoint of a sheet of paper. Then fold in the outside edges to touch the midpoint.

Step 2 Fold paper in half from top to bottom.

Step 3 Open and cut along the inside fold lines to form four tabs. Label your Foldable as shown.

Reading and Writing As you read the chapter, note details about the Constitution, showing each major idea of the document under the tabs.

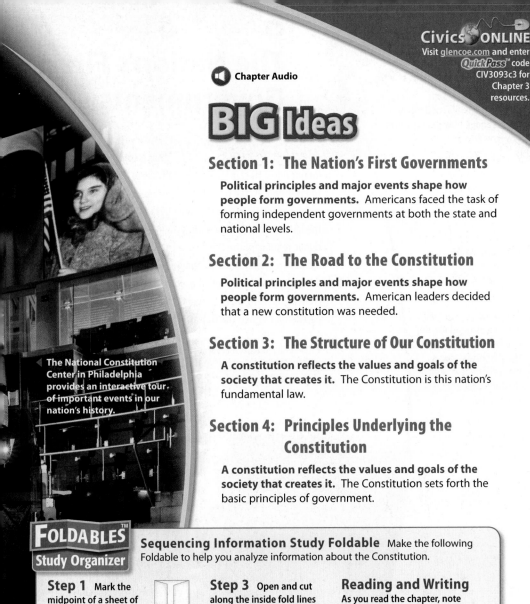

FOLDABLES
Study Organizer
Dinah Zike's Foldables

Purpose This Foldable guides the student in analyzing the Constitution. The completed Foldable will use tabs that show major ideas outlined in the Constitution. The details that support each main idea are listed inside. **OL**

📁 More Foldables activities for this chapter can be found in the *Dinah Zike's Reading and Study Skills Foldables* ancillary.

Civics ONLINE

Visit glencoe.com and enter *QuickPass*™ code CIV1360c3T for Chapter 3 resources, including a Chapter Overview, Study Central™, Study-to-Go, Student Web Activity, Self-Check Quiz, and other materials.

Section 3

The Structure of Our Constitution
Ask: Why do you think the Constitution has survived as the basis for our government for more than two hundred years? *(It is an outline for how our government should be run that allows for wide interpretation and amendment.)* Explain that in Section 3, students will learn about the three main parts of the Constitution, including the process of constitutional amendment. **OL**

Section 4

Principles Underlying the Constitution
Ask: What main principles of government does the Constitution outline? *(It outlines a government that is run by the people, both statewide and nationally. It operates under a system of checks and balances so that no part of the national government can have too much power.)* Tell students that Section 4 provides an overview of the three branches of government, separation of powers, and the system of checks and balances. **OL**

Focus

Section 1

Bellringer
Daily Focus Transparency 3–1

Guide to Reading
Answers to Graphic:

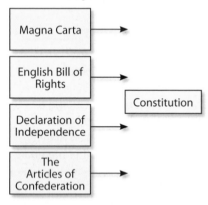

- Magna Carta
- English Bill of Rights
- Declaration of Independence
- The Articles of Confederation

→ Constitution

Section Spotlight Video

Have students watch the Chapter 3, Section 1 video at glencoe.com.

Resource Manager

Guide to Reading

Big Idea
Political principles and major events shape how people form governments.

Content Vocabulary
- constitution (p. 67)
- bicameral (p. 67)
- confederation (p. 68)
- ratify (p. 68)

Academic Vocabulary
- convert (p. 67)
- area (p. 69)
- impact (p. 69)

Reading Strategy
Comparing As you read, create a diagram like the one below identifying four important documents of government that preceded the Constitution.

☐ →
☐ → Constitution
☐ →
☐ →

The Nation's First Governments

Real World Civics It has a crack—and it no longer rings. The Liberty Bell, on display in Philadelphia today, brings to the minds of every American student what independence and freedom mean. Tradition tells us that the Liberty Bell last rang in July 1776, to announce the first public reading of the Declaration of Independence. This was a time when there was no television, radio, or Internet; it announced to the people that John Hancock and Benjamin Franklin, William Ellery, Josiah Bartlett, and the other 52 people had signed the Declaration.

▼ **Several students marvel at the Liberty Bell in Philadelphia, Pennsylvania**

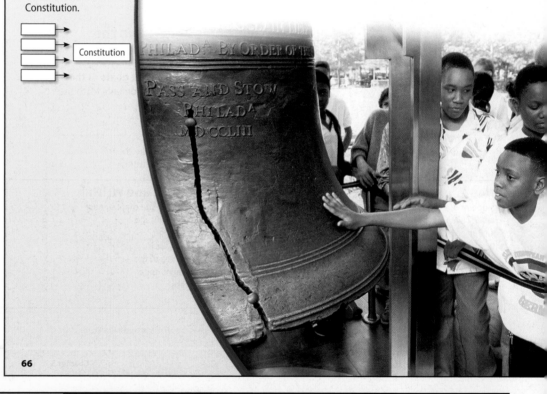

R Reading Strategies	**C** Critical Thinking	**D** Differentiated Instruction	**W** Writing Support	**S** Skill Practice
Teacher Edition • Inferring, p. 68 • Identifying, p. 69 **Additional Resources** • Cont. Vocab., URB p. 71 • Ac. Vocab, URB p. 73 • Guid. Read., URB p. 89 • RENTG, p. 22	**Teacher Edition** • Analyzing Info., p. 67 • Drawing Con., p. 70 **Additional Resources** • Living Const., p. 1 • Quizzes and Tests, p. 26	**Teacher Edition** • Interpersonal, p. 68 **Additional Resources** • Diff. Instr., URB p. 83 • School-to-Home Conn., URB p. 85 • Teacher's Guide to Differentiated Instruction, p. 4	**Teacher Edition** • Expository Writing, p. 69	**Teacher Edition** • Analyzing Visuals, p. 68 **Additional Resources** • Chart, Graph, and Map Skills, URB p. 81 • Daily Focus Trans., 3–1 • Stan. Test, p. 5

The First State Constitutions

Main Idea Americans faced the task of forming independent governments at both the state and national levels.

Civics & You Would you be surprised to learn that the Constitution of the United States was not our first plan of government? Read to find out about the nation's first constitution.

Even before the Declaration of Independence was signed, American colonists discussed the possibility of independence, and American leaders began preparing new state constitutions to replace the old colonial charters. In May of 1776, the Second Continental Congress urged colonists to form state governments,

> " as shall . . . best conduce [contribute] to the happiness and safety of their constituents [voters]. "
> —Continental Congress

In January 1776, New Hampshire became the first colony to organize as a state and craft a detailed, written plan for government, or **constitution.** Within a few years, every former colony had a new constitution or had **converted,** or changed, its colonial charters into a state constitution.

From Colonies to States

The states set up similar systems of government. Each state had a legislature to create laws. Most of these legislatures were **bicameral,** like the English Parliament; that is, they were divided into two parts, or houses. The members of each house or state legislature were chosen by different methods.

Each state also had a governor, who was elected either by the legislature or by the citizens. The governor's job was to carry out the laws. Finally, each state had judges and courts to decide what the laws meant and how they applied to each new situation.

Preserving Rights

Many of the new state governments were based upon ideals expressed in the Declaration of Independence. American ideals of individual rights to "life, liberty, and the pursuit of happiness" are in the Declaration. Most state constitutions included a bill of rights, guaranteeing certain basic freedoms and legal protections to the state's citizens. Some of these rights, such as trial by jury and protection of personal property, can be traced back to the Magna Carta and the English Bill of Rights.

Reading Check Describing What documents did the new state constitutions replace?

Early Statehood New Hampshire's state capitol building is one of the oldest in the country.
Discussing Why were state governments based on the ideals of the Declaration of Independence?

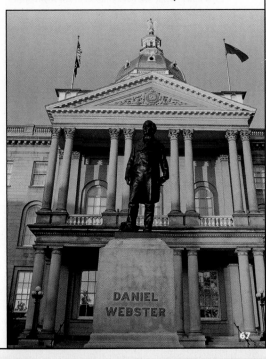

DANIEL WEBSTER

67

Teach

C Critical Thinking

Analyzing Information Although not stated in the U.S. Constitution, the phrase "life, liberty, and the pursuit of happiness" is often quoted as the American way of life. Have students discuss what this phrase means to them. *(Answers may include the freedom to live life without judgment, the freedom to achieve one's goals and dreams, or the various freedoms guaranteed in the Bill of Rights.)* **OL**

Reading Check **Answer:** the old colonial charters

Caption Answer:

Students may say that the American Revolution was fought to ensure individual rights for liberty and freedom. Thus, it would make sense that each state's government would emphasize personal freedoms and legal protection as outlined in the Declaration of Independence.

Differentiated Instruction

Creating a Venn Diagram

CHART, GRAPH, AND MAP SKILLS ACTIVITY 3

Creating a Venn Diagram

Chart, Graph, and Map Skills Activity 3, URB pp. 81–82

Objective:	To compare and contrast different documents	
Focus:	Students compare and contrast the Articles with the Constitution.	
Teach:	Review main principles of the two documents.	
Assess:	Have students use the Venn diagram to explain which document is a better plan of government.	
Close:	Create a T-Chart that summarizes each document's plan of government.	

Differentiated Instruction Strategies

BL Tell why the Articles of Confederation needed revising.

AL Explain why the Framers needed to compromise during the writing of the Constitution.

ELL Define "constitution" and use it in a sentence.

S Skill Practice

Analyzing Visuals **Ask:** How are the property lines in the photo different from what those in a township would look like? *(The property lines of a township would be perfectly square because it is divided into 36 sections that are all the same size.)* **AL**

D Differentiated Instruction

Interpersonal Have students create a list of powers they think a government should have. Write ideas on the board and hold a discussion. Vote on powers that everyone agrees with and create a separate list. **OL**

R Reading Strategy

Inferring **Ask:** Why did the states refuse to give Congress the power to tax? *(The colonies had been excessively taxed by the British, and this was one of their reasons for revolution.)* **OL**

Caption Answers:

A township is six miles square, or 36 sections. A section is one square mile.

Differentiated Instruction

The Articles of Confederation

Main Idea The weaknesses of the Articles of Confederation created problems for the new country.

Civics & You You make a plan but the plan is not working—what do you do? Find out what action American leaders took when their plan of government was not working.

Although each state was well prepared to govern itself when independence was declared, a state could not do some things on its own. It could not raise and maintain a large army, for example, and Americans realized that 13 small, separate forces would be no match for the mighty British army. Americans concluded that if they wanted to

S **Land Ordinance** Some Midwestern boundaries still reflect those drawn by the Ordinance of 1785. *Explaining* What are the dimensions of townships? Of sections?

68

win the war with Great Britain, they needed a single, strong army under central control.

For this and other reasons, the Second Continental Congress made plans for a union of the states. In 1777 the Congress detailed these plans in a document called the Articles of Confederation, the first constitution of the United States of America.

D **Forming a Confederation** A **confederation** is a group of individual state governments that band together for a common purpose. The Articles of Confederation established a system for cooperation, or "league of friendship," among independent states. By 1781 all 13 states had **ratified,** or approved, the Articles of Confederation.

The Articles set up a one-house legislature in which each state had one vote. This Confederation Congress, as it came to be called, was the only government body with control over the army and authority to deal with foreign countries on behalf of the states. These central powers were quite limited, though.

R As a result of the colonial experience under the British government, the 13 states refused to give the Confederation Congress two important powers. It had no power to enforce its laws and no power to tax. The Articles allowed the Congress to ask the states for money but not to demand it. The Congress could not, in fact, require the states to do anything.

Accomplishments

The Confederation Congress laid the foundations for the administration of the national government. It also provided for the systematic growth and development of the United States.

Ordinance of 1785 When the American Revolution began, only a few thousand white settlers lived west of the Appalachian Mountains. By the 1790s, their numbers had increased to about 120,000.

Leveled Activities

BL **Guided Reading Activity 3-1, URB p. 89**

OL **Differentiated Instruction Activity 3, URB pp. 83–84**

AL **Primary Source Reading 1A, URB pp. 15–16**

Through the Ordinance of 1785, Congress created a system for surveying—taking a detailed measurement of an area of land—and selling the western lands. It arranged the land into townships six miles square. Each township was divided into 36 sections of each one square mile. The Ordinance of 1785 at first applied only to what was then called the Northwest Territory—present-day Ohio, Indiana, Illinois, Michigan, and Wisconsin. It established a system of land surveying and settlement that we still use today.

Northwest Ordinance Once the policy for settlement of western lands was established, Congress turned to the problem of governing this **area,** or region. In 1787, the Northwest Ordinance, perhaps the most significant achievement of Congress under the Articles, was passed. It laid the basis for the organization of new territorial governments and set a precedent for the method of admitting new states to the Union. The Northwest Ordinance also included a specific provision outlawing slavery:

> "*There shall be neither slavery nor involuntary servitude in said territory.*"
>
> —the Northwest Ordinance

This provision would have an important **impact,** or effect, on the history of America in the 1800s. The Confederation's western ordinances had an enormous effect on American expansion and development. The Ordinance of 1785 and the Northwest Ordinance opened the way for settlement of the Northwest Territory in a stable and orderly manner.

Weaknesses of the Articles

It soon became clear that the Articles had some serious problems. To begin with, the Congress could not pass a law unless nine states voted in favor of it. Any attempt to amend, or change, the Articles required a unanimous vote of all 13 states. These strict voting requirements made it difficult for the Congress to accomplish anything.

Even when the Congress managed to pass laws, it could not enforce them. Unlike the state constitutions, the Articles did not provide for a governor or for courts. If a state decided to ignore a law, the Congress could do nothing about it.

A Time of Crisis

The United States was able to overcome the weaknesses of the Articles. The states secured their independence by winning the Revolutionary War against Great Britain. A peace agreement called the Treaty of Paris was signed in 1783.

Weaknesses of the Articles of Confederation

LACK OF POWER AND MONEY
- Congress had no power to collect taxes.
- Congress had no power to regulate trade.
- Congress had no power to enforce its laws.

LACK OF CENTRAL POWER
- No single leader or group directed government policy.
- No national court system existed.

RULES TOO RIGID
- Congress could not pass laws without the approval of 9 states.
- The Articles could not be changed without the agreement of all 13 states.

Analyzing Charts

1. **Discussing** Did Congress have the power to enforce its laws? Explain.
2. **Analyzing** Why was it so difficult to pass laws under the Articles of Confederation?

Chapter 3   **69**

R **Reading Strategy**

Identifying Ask: When new territories were created under the Northwest Ordinance, what practice was prohibited by law? *(slavery)* **BL**

W **Writing Support**

Expository Writing Have students write a paragraph explaining how the weakness of the central government under the Articles of Confederation contributed to economic weakness. *(Answers should cite the government's powerlessness to regulate trade, lack of ability to collect taxes, and large debt as contributors to a weak economy.)* **OL**

Analyzing Charts

Answers:
1. No. Congress created laws, but if a state chose not to follow the law, Congress had no power to do anything about it.
2. It was difficult because Congress needed the approval of 9 of the 13 states to pass a law.

Hands-On Chapter Project
Step 1

Creating a Constitution

Step 1: Revising the Articles of Confederation Form groups of four. Groups will read the Articles of Confederation and write a declaration stating suggested changes.

Directions Write the Big Idea on the board. Assign groups to one of the thirteen states. Then, have groups read the Articles of Confederation and discuss its weaknesses. Students must research facts about their assigned state during the late 1780s, including main sources of income, the name of the state governor and his ideals, and the debt incurred during the Revolutionary War. Based on this information, have each group create a two- to three-sentence declaration that states why they believe the Articles are in need of revision.

Summarizing Have groups share what they learned about the Big Idea during their research. Their research will be useful in Section 2, as they will be required to take a more personal approach toward creating a new constitution. **OL**

(Project continued in Section 2)

C Critical Thinking

Drawing Conclusions Ask: Why would citizens who had just won a revolution be so willing to take arms against their new government? *(The states were assuming powers that were extreme—taking a man's property and livelihood. These are the principles the colonists fought for, and they were not willing to give them up to a state that claimed this power.)* **AL**

✓ Reading Check Answer: It had to pay off the money it had borrowed to finance the Revolutionary War.

Assess

Civics ONLINE

Study Central™ provides summaries, interactive games, and online graphic organizers to help students review content.

Close

Making Connections Have students clip newspaper articles about taxes or trade regulations. Have them discuss how the stories would have been written if the Articles were still in effect. **BL ELL**

Section 1 Review

Debt Independence, however, did not put an end to the struggles of the United States. For one thing, the country faced serious financial troubles. Unable to collect taxes, the Congress had borrowed money to pay for the Revolutionary War. It had run up a debt that would take years to repay.

The state governments had also fallen into deep debt. They taxed their citizens heavily as a result, driving many farmers out of business and sparking widespread resentment. The states also taxed goods imported from other states and foreign countries, hurting trade. The Confederation Congress had no power to remedy these problems.

Shays's Rebellion Even worse, the Congress could do nothing about the public's insecurity. Americans feared that the government could not protect their safety. During 1786 and 1787, riots broke out in several states. Daniel Shays, a farmer who had fallen into debt because of heavy state taxes, led one of the most alarming disturbances. When Massachusetts courts threatened to take his farm as payment for his debts, Shays felt the state had no right to punish him for a problem it had created. Many others agreed. Shays armed about 1,200 farmers in an attack on a federal arsenal. Although the rebellion, known as Shays's Rebellion, was quickly stopped, it sent a wake-up call throughout the country.

Many political leaders, merchants, and others began arguing for a stronger national government. As George Washington wrote,

> **"** *I do not conceive we can exist long as a nation, without having lodged somewhere a power which will pervade the whole Union.* **"**
>
> —George Washington's papers

In 1787, only 12 of the states sent delegates to a meeting in Philadelphia to revise the Articles of Confederation.

✓ Reading Check Explaining What financial troubles did the young nation face?

Section 1 Review

Vocabulary

1. **Write** a paragraph in which you use each of the following vocabulary terms: *constitution, bicameral, confederation, ratify.*

Main Ideas

2. **Explaining** Why did the colonies decide they needed a national government in addition to state governments?

3. **Describing** What problems did the colonists come up against because of the weaknesses of the Articles of Confederation?

Critical Thinking

4. **BIG Ideas** Why was the Ordinance of 1785 important?

5. **Categorizing** On a graphic organizer like the one below, list the characteristics of bicameral legislatures—the one adopted by most colonies.

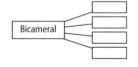

Bicameral

6. **Analyzing** Why did the states approve the Articles of Confederation despite its many weaknesses?

CITIZENSHIP Activity

7. **Expository Writing** Imagine you are on a committee to write a new state constitution. List three freedoms you want attached to your state's constitution. Explain why it is important to guarantee these rights.

Civics ONLINE

Study Central™ To review this section, go to glencoe.com.

Answers

1. Paragraphs should use vocabulary words according to their definitions in the section and in the Glossary.

2. States could not do things on their own, such as raising an army, and they needed a strong militia with central leadership to win their independence from Great Britain.

3. Any changes to the Articles required a unanimous vote, making it almost impossible for Congress to accomplish anything. Also, Congress had no power to enforce laws, to collect debts, or to arbitrate trade.

4. It provided a standard by which land was surveyed and arranged in new territories.

5. **Bicameral legislatures:**
   divided in two houses;
   members chosen by different methods;
   state governor elected;
   state judges and courts interpreted laws

6. Answers may include that colonists needed a central government to win their independence. They were anxious to create a government that was different from their experience under British rule.

7. Answers will vary. Students' lists should explain the importance of the rights they listed.

Guide to Reading

Big Idea
Political principles and major events shape how people form governments.

Content Vocabulary
- Constitutional Convention (p. 73)
- Great Compromise (p. 75)
- Three-Fifths Compromise (p. 75)
- Electoral College (p. 76)
- Federalists (p. 77)
- federalism (p. 77)
- Anti-Federalists (p. 78)

Academic Vocabulary
- process (p. 72)
- despite (p. 73)

Reading Strategy
Identifying As you read, compare the Virginia Plan to the New Jersey Plan by completing a Venn diagram like the one below.

🔊 Section Audio   🎬 Spotlight Video

The Road to the Constitution

Real World Civics When the U.S. Constitution was ratified in 1787, there were no parades, no wild celebration, and certainly no bulletproof glass to shield the president. But in 1987, then president Ronald Reagan had to be protected from harm when he led the celebration for the 200th birthday of the Constitution. He asked Americans to think back to the time when the document was drafted. The colonies were surrounded by unfriendly powers, some colonies had unbearably high taxes, others had crushing debts, and still others were involved in trade disagreements.

▼ **Americans celebrate the 200th birthday of the Constitution outside the Capitol**

71

Focus

Bellringer
Daily Focus Transparency 3–2

Guide to Reading
Answers to Graphic:

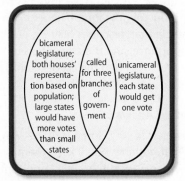

bicameral legislature; both houses' representation based on population; large states would have more votes than small states

called for three branches of government

unicameral legislature, each state would get one vote

 Section Spotlight Video

Have students watch the Chapter 3, Section 2 video at glencoe.com.

Resource Manager

Reading Strategies	Critical Thinking	Differentiated Instruction	Writing Support	Skill Practice
Teacher Edition • Using Context Clues, p. 72 • Det. Importance, p. 73 • Outlining, pp. 74, 75, 78 • Identifying, p. 78 **Additional Resources** • Cont. Vocab., URB p. 71 • Ac. Vocab, URB p. 73 • Guid. Read., URB p. 90 • RENTG, p. 25	**Teacher Edition** • Drawing Con., p. 73 • Analyzing Pri. Sources, p. 74 • Making Inferences, p. 75 • Ident. Cent. Issues, p. 76 • Pred. Consequences, p. 77 **Additional Resources** • Crit. Think., URB p. 79	**Teacher Edition** • ELL, p. 73 • Visual/Spatial, p. 75 **Additional Resources** • School-to-Home Conn., URB p. 85 • Teacher's Guide to Differentiated Instruction, p. 4	**Teacher Edition** • Descriptive Writing, p. 72 • Personal Writing, p. 76	**Teacher Edition** • Visual Literacy, p. 77 **Additional Resources** • Chart, Graph, and Map Skills, URB p. 81 • Daily Focus Trans., 3–2

Teach

R Reading Strategy

Using Context Clues Have students use information from the first paragraph to determine what a Constitutional Convention is. **Ask:** What is a convention? *(a meeting with a specific purpose)* **Ask:** What was the purpose of the Constitutional Convention? *(to meet and draft a new plan of government that would replace the flawed Articles of Confederation)* **BL**

W Writing Support

Descriptive Writing Have students write an introductory paragraph for a newspaper article that describes May 25, 1787, its importance, and the credentials of those who attended the convention. **OL**

Caption Answer:

Answers will vary. Some students will say that nothing would keep them away from waiting for such important news. During the time, getting the most accurate version of news meant waiting to hear it from the source.

Additional Support

The Philadelphia Convention

Main Idea American leaders decided to create a new plan of government.

Civics & You Why is it important for a nation to establish a set of laws? Read to find out the issues American leaders faced in organizing a new plan of government.

Ten years of living under the Articles of Confederation had shown Americans that the loose association of 13 independent states was not working. By early 1787, it was clear that the national government had to be strengthened. Each state was asked to send delegates to a convention in Philadelphia to fix the flaws. This meeting was to become the Constitutional Convention. Only Rhode Island chose not to take part, because its leaders opposed a stronger central government.

New Government Colonial reenactors perform a scene at Independence Hall. *Explaining* Would you have waited outside the hall for word of your new government? Why or why not?

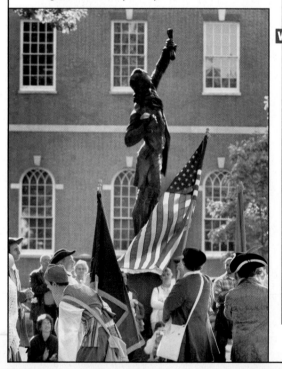

The Work Begins

The convention began in Philadelphia's Independence Hall on May 25, 1787. Rain fell heavily during the opening week, leaving the roads to the city choked with mud. Many delegates had to travel long distances and arrived late. Once all were assembled, however, they were an extraordinary group.

The Delegates Most of the 55 men present were well-educated lawyers, merchants, college presidents, physicians, generals, governors, and planters with considerable political experience. Eight of the delegates had signed the Declaration of Independence. Seven had been governors of their states, and 41 were or had been members of the Continental Congress. Native Americans, African Americans, and women were not considered part of the political **process,** or movement, so none attended.

Benjamin Franklin of Pennsylvania, 81, was the oldest delegate. He was famous as a diplomat, writer, inventor, and scientist. Most delegates, however, were still young men in their thirties or forties with great careers ahead of them. Two delegates, George Washington and James Madison, would go on to become presidents of the United States. Nineteen would become U.S. senators, and 13 served in the House of Representatives. Four men would become federal judges, and four others would become Supreme Court justices.

A few notable leaders were not at the convention. Thomas Jefferson and John Adams were both in Europe as representatives of the American government—Jefferson in Paris and Adams in London. Patrick Henry, a prominent Virginian leader during the American Revolution, was also missing. Although elected as a delegate, Henry was against the convention and did not attend.

Activity: Technology Connection

Making Connections Have students use the Internet to find out which delegates who attended the Constitutional Convention went on to become U.S. Senators, representatives to the House of Representatives, federal judges, and Supreme Court judges. Once students have their lists, assign small groups. Have each group write a news story that reviews the lives of these delegates. They may want to begin with background information, describing the Constitutional Convention, and then switch to "present" time, providing details about their "current" political careers. Make sure they include important decisions or legislation the delegates supported as public servants. **OL**

Key Decisions

The delegates unanimously chose George Washington to preside over the convention. Widely respected for his leadership during the American Revolution, Washington would now call on speakers and make sure that the meetings ran in an orderly, efficient manner. **R** At the start, he reminded the delegates of the importance of their task. He warned that if they could not come up with an acceptable plan of government, "perhaps another dreadful conflict is to be sustained."

Operating Procedures At the very start of the convention, the delegates made several important decisions. They agreed that each state would have one vote, no matter how many delegates represented that state. They also agreed that a simple majority—in this case, seven votes—would decide any issue.

The delegates decided to keep the work of the convention secret. This was a key decision because it made it possible for the delegates to talk freely. The public was not allowed to attend meetings, the doors were guarded, and the windows were kept tightly shut **despite,** or in spite of, the summer heat. **C** Each delegate promised not to tell outsiders what was going on inside.

Because of this secrecy, we have virtually no written records of the convention. The only details we have came from a notebook kept by James Madison, a delegate from Virginia.

Need for a New Constitution The Congress gave delegates the job of revising the Articles of Confederation. The call to revise the Articles of Confederation came while the young nation faced difficult problems. Many Americans believed that the Confederation **D** government was too weak to deal with these challenges. Many national leaders had become dissatisfied with the weaknesses of the Confederation. They quickly agreed, that changing the Articles was not enough. They decided instead to dispose of the Articles and

Who Were the Delegates?

- Practically all of the 55 delegates had experience in colonial and state government.

- Eight delegates had signed the Declaration of Independence.

- Forty-four of the delegates had been members of the Continental Congress.

- Virtually every individual had taken part in the American Revolution, and at least 29 served in the military.

- George Washington and James Madison became president of the United States.

- The delegates ranged in age from Jonathan Dayton (left) of New Jersey, aged 26, to Benjamin Franklin (above), aged 81.

Analyzing Charts

Inferring Why do you think delegates came from so many different backgrounds and professions?

write a new constitution. All the delegates set out to strengthen the national government by creating a new plan of government. Thus the meeting in Philadelphia came to be known as the **Constitutional Convention.**

✔ **Reading Check** **Explaining** Why did the delegates decide to keep the work of the Constitutional Convention a secret?

Chapter 3 73

R Reading Strategy

Determining Importance Discuss the leadership qualities of George Washington. Have students paraphrase his quote. **OL**

C Critical Thinking

Drawing Conclusions **Ask:** Do you think it was necessary to keep delegates' meetings so secretive that they did not keep minutes? *(Students may say secrecy was necessary to avoid public pressure and future political repercussions.)* **AL**

D Differentiated Instruction

English Learners Explain to students that "revising" means "to change the wording." The delegates thought the Articles required more than a revision. "Dispose" means to "do away with." **ELL**

Analyzing Charts

Answer:

to better represent the interests of a diverse population

✔ **Reading Check** **Answer:** They wanted to speak freely and not worry about public reaction.

Hands-On Chapter Project
Step 2

Creating a Constitution

Step 2: Voicing Individual Concerns Groups of students continue their work toward creating a constitution.

Directions Tell groups they will make their declarations more personal. Write each of the following positions on pieces of paper and place them in a cup: a shopkeeper, a female citizen who is the town's seamstress, a soldier from the Revolutionary War, and a newspaper writer. Have each group member choose an identity and then discuss how a new constitution would affect them personally. Groups may need to research their occupations. Have students discuss any concerns with the group. Once individuals in each groups have listed legitimate concerns or needs, have them create a biographical note card. **OL**

(Project continued in Section 3)

C Critical Thinking

Analyzing Primary Sources Remind students that the Constitutional Convention was extremely important to the success of the new nation. Have them discuss the meaning of George Mason's words. *(Mason meant he would prefer to die trying to create a plan for a new government rather than fail to come up with a plan. He was not willing to give up the fight for his new country.)* **OL**

R Reading Strategy

Outlining Have students outline or list key ideas of the Virginia Plan. They may use this list to complete their section graphic organizer. *(a president, courts, congress with two houses, representation based on state's population)* **BL**

Caption Answers:

The Declaration of Independence was signed there. The Second Continental Congress met there, and the Articles of Confederation were drafted there as well. It was already a symbol of American independence. It was the logical place to hold the Constitutional Convention.

Creating the Constitution

Main Idea Many of the provisions of the Constitution were arrived at through a series of compromises.

Civics & You Have you and a rival ever set aside your differences to work for a common cause? This happened when the delegates resolved their differences to create the Constitution.

The delegates to the Constitutional Convention were determined to create a framework of government that all states could accept. Everyone knew that failure could mean disaster. According to James Madison's notes of the Convention, George Mason of Virginia said the following:

" [I] would bury [my] bones in this city rather than [leave] . . . the Convention without any thing being done. "
—George Mason, remarks at the Constitutional Convention

On May 29, 1787, shortly after the convention began, the Virginia delegates proposed a plan for the new government. James Madison had designed what became known as the Virginia Plan.

The Virginia Plan

The Virginia Plan described a federal government very similar to the one we have today. It included a president, courts, and a congress with two houses. Representation in each house of congress would be based on each state's population. Large states would have more votes than smaller states.

Birthplace of the Nation Independence Hall was originally built to serve as the Pennsylvania state capitol. ***Speculating*** **What other important event occurred here? Why do you think it was chosen as the site of the Constitutional Convention?**

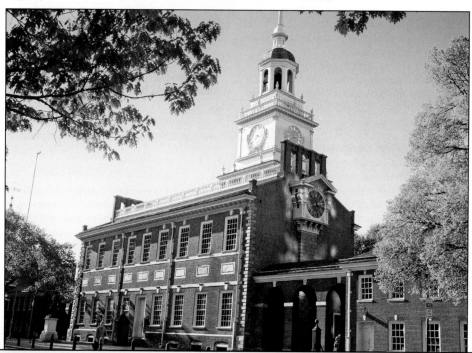

74

Differentiated Instruction

Leveled Activities

BL Guided Reading Activity 3–2, URB p. 90

OL Speaking/Listening Skills Activity1, URB pp. 9–11

AL Crit. Thinking Skills Activity 3, URB p. 79–80

ELL Chart, Graph, and Map Act. 3, URB pp. 81–82

The Virginia Plan appealed to delegates from the more heavily populated states such as Massachusetts, Pennsylvania, and New York, as well as Virginia. The small states, however, feared that a government dominated by the large states would ignore their interests.

The New Jersey Plan

R After two weeks of heated discussion, delegates from the smaller states submitted their own plan. On June 15, William Paterson presented an alternative plan. The New Jersey Plan called for a government similar to the one under the Articles of Confederation. It included a one-house congress in which states would have equal representation and therefore equal votes. Under this plan, Congress could set taxes and regulate trade—powers it did not have under the Articles.

Delegates from Delaware, New Jersey, and Maryland approved of this plan. It made their states equal in power to the big states. Of course, the large states would not accept this plan. They thought larger states should have more power than smaller states. **C**

The Great Compromise

For six weeks the delegates debated the merits of the two plans. A committee headed by Roger Sherman of Connecticut finally came up with an answer. The committee proposed that Congress have two houses—a Senate and a House of Representatives—that would be structured differently from each other. Each state would have equal representation in the Senate, which would please the smaller states. In the House, representation would be based on population, which would **D** please the larger states.

No group was completely happy, but this was a solution with which all could live. Historians call Sherman's plan the Connecticut Compromise, or the **Great Compromise.** (A compromise is a way of resolving disagreements in which each side gives up something but gains something else.)

Counting Population The delegates decided representation in a new government would be based on population but could not decide how to count the many slaves in America. *Explaining* What compromise answered this question?

The Three-Fifths Compromise

Although the Great Compromise settled the structure of Congress, other questions remained. At the time of the Constitutional Convention, more than 550,000 African Americans, mostly in the South, were enslaved. The Southern states wanted to count these people as part of their populations to increase their voting power in the House of Representatives. The Northern states, which had few enslaved persons, opposed the idea. They argued that because enslaved persons were not allowed to vote or otherwise participate in government, they should not be used to give Southern states a stronger voice in Congress.

In the **Three-Fifths Compromise,** delegates agreed that every five enslaved persons would count as three free persons. Thus three-fifths of the slave population in each state would be used in determining representation in Congress.

Did You Know?

Life of a Patriot Roger Sherman was a shoemaker as a boy in Massachusetts. Although he had no formal training, he was determined to learn and read widely. After his father's death, he moved to Connecticut where he bought a store, learned surveying, and was appointed to serve in local offices.

In time, the self-educated Sherman became a practicing attorney and earned a reputation as a political leader. He was known for his shrewd negotiating skills. Sherman also found time to publish an essay on monetary theory, a series of almanacs that contained his own astronomical calculations, and poetry.

In 1761, Sherman stopped practicing law and returned to manage his store, but he remained politically active. In 1766, Sher-man became an associate judge on the state superior court of Connecticut. He was a strong supporter of the Patriot cause and served in the Continental Congress. Sherman helped draft the Declaration of Independence and the Articles of Confederation. Sherman eventually served in the U.S. House of Representatives and later became a senator.

C Critical Thinking

Identifying Central Issues Ask: How did the compromise over trade regulations satisfy both Northern and Southern interests? *(Exports were not taxed, which pleased Southerners. However, Congress could regulate trade between the states, which Northerners wanted.)* **OL**

W Writing Support

Personal Writing Explain that some states do not require their Electoral College representatives, or electors, to vote for the candidate who wins the popular vote in presidential elections. However, most electors pledge to vote for the winner in their states. Because of this difference, the candidate who gets the most votes nationwide may not become the president of the United States. Ask students to write a paragraph stating their views on the constitutional compromise that became the Electoral College. **AL**

American Biography

Answer: Some students may say that some people use their personal liberty to hurt the personal liberty of others. We should all use good judgment and control when exercising our rights.

Additional Support

Teacher Tip

This activity requires students to write in a format that might be unfamiliar to them. Using professionally-written editorials, help students analyze how editorial writers include statements of opinion supported by factual details to persuade readers of an issue's importance.

American Biography

James Madison (1751–1836)

Even in his day, **James Madison** was known as the "Father of the Constitution." Madison protested: "You give me credit to which I have no claim. . . . It ought to be regarded as the work of many heads and many hands."

When it came to creating a constitution, however, Madison had few equals. Madison, though, at first opposed the addition of a bill of rights. He feared that future governments might honor only those rights listed in the bill. When some leaders continued to insist on a bill of rights, Madison finally agreed.

To make sure the amendments did not weaken the new government, he helped write them himself. Then, as the U.S. representative from Virginia, Madison pushed the amendments through Congress, fulfilling the Constitution's promise to create a "more perfect union."

At the Constitutional Convention, Madison served his nation well. In the years to come, the nation would call on him again. In 1801 he became President Thomas Jefferson's secretary of state. In 1808 Madison was elected the fourth president of the United States.

Making a Difference   CITIZENSHIP

James Madison wrote that "Liberty may be endangered by the abuse of liberty, but also by the abuse of power." **Explaining** Put this statement in your own words.

Other Compromises Northern and Southern delegates to the convention compromised on trade matters, too. The Northern states felt that Congress should be able to regulate both foreign trade and trade between the states. The Southern states, however, feared that Congress would use this power to tax exports—goods sold to other countries. If this happened, the Southern economy would suffer because it depended heavily on exports of tobacco, rice, and other products.

Southerners also feared that Congress might stop slave traders from bringing enslaved people into the United States. Thus, Southern delegates objected because Southern plantations depended on the labor of slaves. Again a compromise among the delegates would settle the issue.

After some discussion, the Southern states agreed that Congress could regulate trade between the states, as well as with other countries. In exchange, the North agreed that Congress could not tax exports, nor could it interfere with the slave trade before 1808.

The delegates also compromised on issues concerning their new government. Some delegates thought members of Congress should choose the president; others believed that the people should vote to decide the presidency. The solution was the **Electoral College,** a group of people who would be named by each state legislature to select the president and vice president. The Electoral College system is still used today, but the voters in each state, not the legislatures, now choose electors.

Activity: Interdisciplinary Connection

Language Arts The Constitution was created through compromise. Have students write a newspaper editorial that details the four important compromises and states the writer's opinion about whether the Constitution should be ratified. Show students examples of professional newspaper editorials before they begin writing. Student editorials should include reasons to support the opinions. Students may use facts, examples, anecdotes, or emotional appeal to support their positions. **OL**

Balancing Viewpoints [S]

Main Idea Writing the new Constitution and getting the American people to approve it was not an easy task.

Civics & You Did you ever work on a committee in which many people had to decide on one solution to a problem? That is a similar situation to what faced the writers of the new U.S. Constitution.

Throughout the summer, the delegates to the Constitutional Convention hammered out the details of the new government. As their work drew to an end, some delegates headed home, but 42 remained out of the original 55. On September 17, 1787, they gathered for the last time. A committee headed by Gouverneur Morris had put its ideas in writing, and the Constitution was ready to be signed. All but three delegates signed their names at the bottom.

The delegates at Philadelphia had produced the Constitution, but its acceptance depended upon the will of the American people. The next step was to win ratification, or approval, of the Constitution. The delegates had decided that each state would set up a ratifying convention to vote "yes" or "no." When at least nine of the 13 states had ratified it, the Constitution would become the supreme law of the land. [C]

Who Were the Federalists? Americans reacted to the proposed Constitution in different ways. Supporters of the document called themselves **Federalists.** They chose this name to emphasize that the Constitution would create a system of **federalism,** a form of government in which power is divided between the federal, or national, government and the states.

Civics ONLINE
Student Web Activity Visit glencoe.com and complete the Chapter 3 Web Activity.

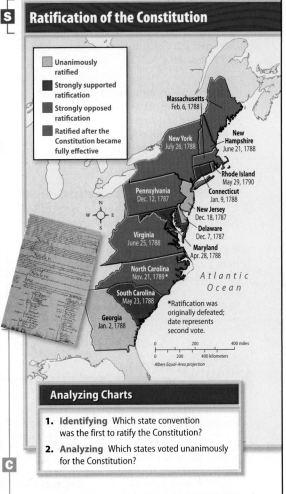

Ratification of the Constitution

- Unanimously ratified
- Strongly supported ratification
- Strongly opposed ratification
- Ratified after the Constitution became fully effective

Massachusetts Feb. 6, 1788
New York July 26, 1788
New Hampshire June 21, 1788
Rhode Island May 29, 1790
Pennsylvania Dec. 12, 1787
Connecticut Jan. 9, 1788
New Jersey Dec. 18, 1787
Delaware Dec. 7, 1787
Virginia June 25, 1788
Maryland Apr. 28, 1788
North Carolina Nov. 21, 1789*
South Carolina May 23, 1788
Georgia Jan. 2, 1788

*Ratification was originally defeated; date represents second vote.

Atlantic Ocean

0   200   400 miles
0   200   400 kilometers
Albers Equal-Area projection

Analyzing Charts

1. **Identifying** Which state convention was the first to ratify the Constitution?
2. **Analyzing** Which states voted unanimously for the Constitution?

To win support, the Federalists reminded Americans of the flaws in the Articles of Confederation. They argued that the United States would not survive without a strong national government. Supporters of the Federalists included large landowners who wanted the property protection a strong national government could provide. The Federalists claimed that only a strong national government could protect the new nation from enemies abroad and solve the country's internal problems.

[C] Critical Thinking

Predicting Consequences Explain to students that just because the delegates agreed on the Constitution, it could not become law until individual states ratified, or approved, it. **Ask:** Do you think the Constitution was ratified quickly by most of the states? Why or why not? *(Some students may say that the states were eager to create a strong union and would ratify without delay. Others may say that it would be difficult to get every state to agree on a plan.)* **AL**

[S] Skill Practice

Visual Literacy Have students use the states and dates to create a time line of the ratification of the Constitution. **OL**

Civics ONLINE

Objectives and answers to the **Student Web Activity** can be found at glencoe.com under the Web Activity Lesson Plan for this chapter.

Analyzing Charts

Answers:
1. Delaware; December 7, 1787
2. Delaware, New Jersey, and Georgia

Differentiated Instruction

Critical Thinking Skills Activity 3, URB pp. 79–80

Understanding Historical Perspective

Objective:	To identify and analyze Alexander Hamilton's writing
Focus:	Students analyze the context and purpose of *Federalist, No. 30.*
Teach:	Discuss how ideas are influenced by social and political situations.
Assess:	List historical events that prompted Hamilton to write.
Close:	Create a graphic organizer that illustrates the three branches of government.

Differentiated Instruction Strategies

BL Explain why it is important to note the date of any text.

AL Draw a political cartoon that illustrates how Hamilton feels about the Constitution.

ELL Find one example of how Hamilton's attitude is shaped by events of his time.

R Reading Strategy

Identifying Ask: What compromise did the Federalists make to get the Constitution approved? *(They agreed to a bill of rights.)* Which state was last to ratify the Constitution? *(Rhode Island)* **BL**

✓**Reading Check** **Answer:** They felt it ignored the will of the people and the state and that it favored the wealthy. It lacked protection of individual freedoms.

Assess

Civics ONLINE

Study Central™ provides summaries, interactive games, and online graphic organizers to help students review content.

Close

Outlining Have pairs use their graphic organizers and notes to create a road map that illustrates the origins of the Constitution, including why it was needed, how the meetings were held, and compromises that were made. The road map could show dead ends (for example with the Virginia Plan and the New Jersey Plan). Have students display their road maps. **OL ELL**

Section 2 Review

The Federalist Papers In a series of essays known as *The Federalist*, Alexander Hamilton, James Madison, and John Jay defended the Constitution. Madison argued in *The Federalist*, No. 10:

> " *A Republic, by which I mean a Government in which the scheme of representation takes place . . . promises the cure for which we are seeking. . . .*"
>
> —James Madison, The Federalist, No. 10

Who Were the Anti-Federalists? Those who opposed the Constitution were called **Anti-Federalists.** Their main argument was that the new Constitution would take away the liberties Americans had fought to win from Great Britain. They believed the new Constitution would create a strong national government, ignore the will of the states and the people, and favor the wealthy few over the common people.

Perhaps the strongest criticism of the Constitution was that it lacked a bill of rights to protect individual freedoms. Many feared they would lose the liberties gained during the Revolution. Several state conventions took a stand and announced they would not ratify the Constitution without the addition of a bill of rights.

Launching a New Nation The Federalists eventually agreed with the Anti-Federalists that a bill of rights was necessary. They promised that if the Constitution was adopted, the new government would add a bill of rights to it.

That promise helped turn the tide. Several states had already voted for ratification. On June 21, 1788, New Hampshire became the ninth state to do so, and the Constitution took effect. In time, the four remaining states ratified the Constitution, the last being Rhode Island in 1790. The 13 independent states were now one nation, the United States of America.

✓**Reading Check** **Explaining** Why did Anti-Federalists oppose the Constitution?

Section 2 Review

Vocabulary

1. **Write** short paragraphs about the Constitutional Convention using these terms: *Great Compromise, Three-Fifths Compromise, Electoral College, Federalists, federalism, Anti-Federalists.*

Main Ideas

2. **Explaining** Why did delegates think the Articles of Confederation needed to be replaced?

3. **Describing** What issue did the Three-Fifths Compromise solve?

4. **Analyzing** What was the biggest obstacle the delegates faced when getting the Constitution approved?

Critical Thinking

5. **BIG Ideas** Why was the Electoral College established? What power did it have?

6. **Comparing** On a graphic organizer like the one below, list the details of the Great Compromise that many delegates supported.

Great Compromise

CITIZENSHIP Activity

7. **Expository Writing** Conduct a survey of at least 10 adults in which you ask them whether they favor continuing the Electoral College or amending the Constitution to have the presidency determined by the popular vote. Ask respondents to explain their answers. Then, summarize your findings in a short paper.

Civics ONLINE

Study Central™ To review this section, go to glencoe.com.

Answers

1. Paragraphs should use vocabulary words according to their definitions in the section and in the Glossary.

2. The Articles were too weak, and they were not working. The delegates wanted the states to function as a stronger union.

3. It solved the question of how slaves were to be counted in a population. The compromise established that every five enslaved persons counted as three free persons.

4. The constitution originally did not have a bill of rights. Many feared they could lose the liberties they had gained during the Revolution.

5. It was established as a compromise. Some wanted the people to vote for president; others wanted Congress to choose. It has the power to choose the president through electors representing each state.

6. Congress has two houses; the House of Representatives; Representation in the House based on state population; the Senate; each state has equal representation in Senate.

7. Surveys and summaries will vary. Invite students to share survey responses with the class.

Guide to Reading

Big Idea
A constitution reflects the values and goals of the society that creates it.

Content Vocabulary
- Preamble *(p. 80)*
- legislative branch *(p. 80)*
- executive branch *(p. 80)*
- judicial branch *(p. 81)*
- amendment *(p. 82)*

Academic Vocabulary
- consist *(p. 80)*
- assume *(p. 84)*

Reading Strategy
Categorizing As you read, complete the diagram below listing the major powers the Constitution allows each branch.

U.S. Constitution
→ Legislative Executive Judicial

Section 3
The Structure of Our Constitution

Real World Civics What does the word government mean to you? The military? Many, many documents? Laws and rules? Lynne Cheney, wife of former Vice President Dick Cheney, supports the idea that school children need to know the government is made up of living, breathing people who represent their right to freedom. Mrs. Cheney, hosting a Constitution Day party for dozens of Washington, D.C., second graders, stressed the importance of knowing history and that, "One of the important [history] lessons we can learn is that freedom isn't inevitable."

▼ **Lynne Cheney hosts Constitution Day in Washington, D.C.**

Teach

W Writing Support

Personal Writing Have students write the phrase, "We the People of the United States." Have them free-write for two minutes, writing words or phrases they associate with this phrase. Then have them choose partners and exchange ideas. Have pairs write a few sentences that summarize their ideas. As a class, use students' ideas to discuss the meaning of these important words. **OL**

D Differentiated Instruction

Auditory/Musical Have small groups of students practice reading the entire Preamble *(found on page 95)* several times. Groups will choose whether to make a recording for the class, record the words with musical background, or perform an oral reading for the class. **OL**

R Reading Strategy

Activating Prior Knowledge Ask: How many branches of government do we have? *(three)* What are they? *(the legislative, the executive, and the judicial)* **OL**

Differentiated Instruction

Writing Skills Activity 3, URB pp. 77–78

The Sections of the Constitution

Main Idea The Constitution is a remarkable document that serves as an adaptable blueprint for governing the United States.

Civics & You Have you ever read some instructions that did not make sense? Did you wish they were better organized so you could follow them? Read how the Constitution was organized.

Although the main purpose of the Constitution is to provide a framework for government, it does much more than that. It is the highest authority in the nation. It is the basic law of the United States. The powers of the branches of government come from it. Like the American flag, the Constitution is a symbol of our nation. It represents our system of government and our basic ideals, such as liberty and freedom.

The Constitution has three main parts. First is the **Preamble,** an introduction that states the goals and purposes of the government. Next are seven articles that describe the structure of the government. Third are 27 amendments, or additions and changes, to the Constitution.

The Preamble

The Preamble **consists,** or is expressed by, a single concise sentence that begins and ends as follows:

> **W** " *We the People of the United States . . . do ordain and establish this Constitution for the United States of America.* "
>
> —Preamble of the U.S. Constitution

These carefully chosen words make clear that the power of government comes from the people. The government depends on the people for its power and exists to serve them. The middle part of the Preamble states six purposes of the government:

1. "To form a more perfect Union"—to unite the states so they can operate as a single nation, for the good of all
2. "To establish Justice"—to make certain that all citizens are treated equally
3. "To insure domestic Tranquility"—to maintain peace and order, keeping citizens and their property safe from harm
D 4. "To provide for the common defense"—to be ready militarily to protect the country and its citizens from attack
5. "To promote the general Welfare"— to help people live healthy, happy, and prosperous lives
6. "To secure the Blessings of Liberty to ourselves and our Posterity"—to guarantee the basic rights of all Americans, including future generations (posterity)

The Articles

The seven articles that follow the Preamble are identified by the Roman numerals I through VII. The first three articles describe the powers and responsibilities of each branch of government.

Article I Article I outlines the lawmaking powers of the **legislative branch,** or Congress. The Article states that Congress, made up of two houses—the Senate and the House of Representatives—will have all lawmaking authority. The article then describes **R** how members of each house will be chosen and what rules they must follow in making laws. You will learn more about Congress in Chapter 6.

Article II Article II provides for an **executive branch,** or law-enforcing branch of government headed by a president and vice president. Article II explains how these leaders are to be elected and how they can be removed from office.

Identifying Parts of Speech and Types of Sentences

Objective: To identify parts of speech in the Constitution

Focus: Students identify parts of speech and sentence structure.

Teach: Review the eight parts of speech and four different sentence types.

Assess: Identify more parts of speech from the Constitution.

Close: Create a chart of the parts of speech using the Second Amendment.

Differentiated Instruction Strategies

BL Write a declarative sentence about the Constitution and identify the parts of speech.

AL Write several different types of sentences about the Constitution, trying to use as many parts of speech as possible.

ELL Write an interrogative sentence and identify the nouns.

Article II goes on to list the president's powers, including the power to command the armed forces and to make treaties with other nations. You will learn more about the executive branch in Chapter 7.

Article III The **judicial branch** is the part of government that interprets the laws and sees that they are fairly applied. Article III calls for "one Supreme Court" and such lower courts as Congress deems appropriate. Article III then lists the powers of the federal courts and describes the kinds of cases they may hear. You will read about our federal judiciary in Chapter 8.

Articles IV–VII Article IV of the Constitution explains the relationship between the states and the national government. Article V specifies under what conditions the Constitution can be changed. Article VI contains a key statement declaring the Constitution the "supreme Law of the Land." **R**

In Article VII, the Framers dealt with practical matters. The Constitution would take effect, they wrote, when nine states ratified it.

Reading Check Describing What is the main purpose of Article I of the U.S. Constitution?

Comparing Governments

Charts In MOtion
See StudentWorks™ Plus or glencoe.com.

ARTICLES OF CONFEDERATION

Organization

- Strong independent states with weak central government
- One-house legislature with equal representation for each state

Congress
- Declare war
- Make treaties
- Coin and borrow money
- Make laws although not empowered to enforce them
- No power to tax
- No power to regulate trade

No executive branch
No judicial branch

CONSTITUTION

- Strong central government with certain powers reserved to states
- Two-house legislature: House of Representatives with representation based on state population; Senate, with equal representation for all states

Powers

Congress
- Declare war
- Make treaties
- Coin and borrow money
- Make nation's laws
- Tax
- Regulate trade

President
- Commander in chief of armed forces
- Carries out the nation's laws

Supreme Court and lower federal court
- Interpret the law

S

Analyzing Charts

1. **Explaining** How was the power to make laws limited under the Articles?
2. **Identifying** What branches of government did the Constitution add?

R Reading Strategy

Organizing Have students outline or create a graphic organizer of the Constitution and its seven articles. Students can use their outlines as study guides. **BL** **ELL**

S Skill Practice

Comparing and Contrasting Under the Articles of Confederation, Congress did not have the power to enforce laws. Congress does not have the power to enforce laws under the Constitution either. **Ask:** Which branch of government enforces laws under the Constitution? *(The president carries out the nation's laws.)* **OL**

Reading Check **Answer:** to outline the lawmaking powers of the legislative branch, or Congress

Analyzing Charts

Answers:
1. Congress did not have the power to enforce laws, nor was there a system to interpret the laws.
2. Executive (president) and Judicial (Supreme Court)

Hands-On Chapter Project
Step 3

Creating a Constitution

Step 3: Writing and Compromising Groups continue their work toward creating a constitution.

Directions Write the Big Idea on the board. Have each group chose a delegate to send to a constitutional convention. Groups may vote openly or secretly. Let them decide on the method.

Next, all delegates meet as a group. The delegates will take the note cards created in Step 2 to the meeting and work to write a constitution, making sure that they protect the rights of their group (or state). Have them write their constitution on poster paper and sign it.

The citizens of each group will work together to write a letter to the editor of a newspaper commenting on the secrecy of the Constitutional Convention and voicing their opinions based on their note card. Glue all groups (states) articles on poster board. **OL**

(Project continued in Section 4)

C Critical Thinking

Determining Cause and Effect Explain to students that the Constitution is a plan, an outline for our government. The Framers knew it would have to be changed, but they didn't want it to happen constantly. **Ask:** Why would the Framers of the Constitution purposely make the amendment process difficult? *(The Framers worked a long time to write the Constitution. They wanted the process to be difficult so that any changes would be debated thoroughly and justly, not haphazardly.)* **AL**

R Reading Strategy

Determining Importance Ask: What might have happened if the Constitution did not allow for amendments? *(There might have been another revolution. Women and African Americans would not tolerate being ignored. Even though the process allowed these changes, there were still protests, but they could have been worse.)* **OL**

TIME™ Teens in *Action*

Answer:

The first three words of the Constitution, "We the People," mean that citizens rule our government. Kushal knows that voting is how people can take an active role in government.

Differentiated Instruction

TIME™ Teens in *Action*

We the People

We caught up with Kushal Kadakia, 17, in his hometown of Fremont, California. He had just taken part in a competition called "We the People."

QUESTION: What is We the People?

ANSWER: It's the first three words of the United States Constitution—but it's also a civics competition.

Q: How does that work?

A: Teams of students compete in a simulated congressional testimony. There are question-and-answer sessions on constitutional principles. It promotes an understanding of the Constitution and how it applies to historical and current events. According to We the People's Web site, www.civiced.org, the program started in 1987 and served more than 28 million students.

Q: How did your team do?

A: We finished fourth in California. But beyond the awards, We the People has motivated many of us to become involved with politics by making us more aware of how our government functions.

Q: Is that important?

A: Very! Look at voter apathy. People don't vote because they don't think it will make a difference. Kids who take part in We the People learn how important it is to assume an active role in the government process!

Kushal encourages voting

ACTION FACT: Kadakia is a huge sports fan and runs cross-country and track.

Making a Difference **CITIZENSHIP**

Why does Kushal believe voting is an important responsibility?

Amending the Constitution

Main Idea The Framers wrote the Constitution so that it could be adapted to meet changing needs.

Civics & You How do you think the Constitution and our government have changed over time? Read to find out how the Framers planned for change.

A ny change in the Constitution is called an **amendment.** Would it surprise you to know that thousands of amendments to the Constitution have been considered over the years? Only 27 have become law because the Framers deliberately made the amendment process difficult. After months of debate and compromise, they knew how delicately balanced the Constitution was. Changing even one small detail could have dramatic effects throughout the government. Therefore, the Framers made sure the Constitution could not be altered without the overwhelming support of the people.

At the same time, the ability to amend the Constitution is necessary. Constitutional amendments safeguard many of our freedoms. For example, the abolition of slavery and the right of women to vote were added as amendments. If the Constitution could not have been amended to protect the rights of African Americans, women, and other oppressed groups, it—and our government—might not have survived.

Amendment Process The process for amending the Constitution, as outlined in Article V, involves two steps: proposal and ratification. An amendment may be proposed in either of two ways. The first method—used for all amendments so far—is by congressional action. A vote of two-thirds of the members of both houses of Congress is required. The second method is by a national convention requested by two-thirds of the state legislatures.

Leveled Activities

BL Guided Reading, Activity 3-3, URB p. 91

OL Writing Skills Activity 3, URB pp. 77–78

AL Citizenship/Decision-Making Activity 1, URB p. 3

ELL Reteaching Activity 3, p. 87

Ratifying an Amendment Once a national amendment has been proposed, three-fourths of the states must ratify it. The states have two ways to do this: by a vote of either the state legislature or by a special state convention. Only one amendment, the Twenty-first Amendment, has been ratified by means of state conventions.

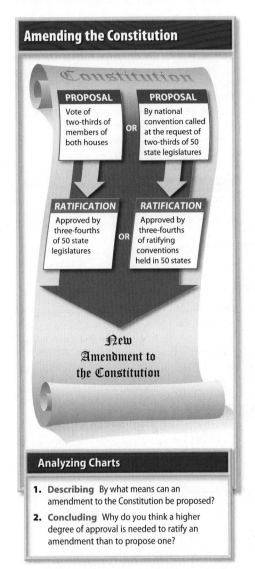

Amending the Constitution

Constitution

PROPOSAL
Vote of two-thirds of members of both houses

OR

PROPOSAL
By national convention called at the request of two-thirds of 50 state legislatures

RATIFICATION
Approved by three-fourths of 50 state legislatures

OR

RATIFICATION
Approved by three-fourths of ratifying conventions held in 50 states

New Amendment to the Constitution

Analyzing Charts

1. **Describing** By what means can an amendment to the Constitution be proposed?
2. **Concluding** Why do you think a higher degree of approval is needed to ratify an amendment than to propose one?

Interpreting the Constitution

The writers of the Constitution knew that the world would change in ways they could not predict. For this reason, they attempted to keep the document as general as possible. Although they went into great detail about some matters, they left other matters open to interpretation.

The Necessary and Proper Clause
Article I lists the powers of Congress. In this article, the Constitution gives Congress the power "to make all Laws which shall be necessary and proper" to carry out its duties. The necessary and proper clause allows Congress to exercise powers not specifically listed in the Constitution. These powers are known as "implied powers." Much of what the federal government does today—from licensing television stations to regulating air pollution—is based on the implied powers of Congress.

Of course, not everyone agrees which laws are "necessary and proper" and which laws are not. Some people feel Congress should be allowed to make any laws the Constitution does not specifically forbid. These people believe in a loose interpretation of the Constitution. Others believe in a strict interpretation. They feel Congress should make only the kinds of laws mentioned by the Constitution.

Court Decisions The final authority for interpreting the Constitution rests with the Supreme Court. Over the years, the Supreme Court has interpreted the Constitution in different ways—sometimes strictly, sometimes loosely. With each new interpretation, our government changes.

Legislative and Presidential Actions The actions of Congress and the executive branch have also caused new interpretations of the Constitution. The Constitution allows the House of Representatives to impeach, or accuse, federal officials, while the Senate determines the person's guilt or innocence.

Chapter 3   83

Activity: Collaborative Learning

Drawing Conclusions Organize the class into seven groups. Assign each group one of the seven articles of the U.S. Constitution. Each group will write and perform a skit that illustrates their article in action. Encourage students to use current events, reminding students that the Constitution is alive and working today. Students may use the Internet or library to find current news events related to their article. **OL**

R Reading Strategy

Academic Vocabulary Explain to students that "assume" is a word with different meanings. In this sentence it means the vice president "took on the role" of president. Have students write another sentence with "assume(d)" as it is used in this context. **ELL**

✔ **Reading Check** **Answer:** to safeguard the freedoms of Americans and to ensure that the document remains relevant

Assess

Civics ONLINE

Study Central™ provides summaries, interactive games, and online graphic organizers to help students review content.

Close

Making Predictions Have students work in small groups and discuss what kind of changes the Constitution might go through in the future. Have them consider current political affairs. **Ask:** Do you think the Constitution will survive another 200 years? **OL**

Section **3** Review

How have actions by the president informally amended the Constitution? In 1841 William Henry Harrison became the first president to die in office. Vice President John Tyler **assumed,** or accepted, the powers of the president according to the provisions in the Constitution. The Constitution, however, was unclear on whether Tyler automatically became president or whether he was merely acting as president until the next election. Tyler went ahead and took the presidential oath. Not until 1967, when the Twenty-fifth Amendment was ratified, was Tyler's action officially part of the Constitution.

There are other examples as well. Nowhere in the Constitution does it state that the president should propose bills or budgets to Congress. Yet since the presidency of Woodrow Wilson (1913–1921), each year the president proposes hundreds of bills to Congress. Presidents interpret the Constitution in other ways, too. Not only does the president make agreements with other countries without congressional approval, the president also requests legislation from Congress. The Constitution does not direct the president to take these actions.

Interpretation Through Custom The interpretation of the Constitution has also changed through customs that have developed. For example, although the Constitution does not mention political parties, they are an important part of today's political system. These days, parties help organize the government and conduct elections.

The Constitution in the present day is quite different from the document written in 1787. In the next 200 years, it will probably go through many more changes. However, the basic structure and principles of our government—a delicate balance among three branches—will no doubt remain.

✔ **Reading Check** **Inferring** Why are amendments to the Constitution necessary?

Section 3 Review

Vocabulary

1. **Write** a paragraph about the Constitution in which you use these terms: *Preamble, legislative branch, executive branch, judicial branch, amendment.*

Main Ideas

2. **Explaining** Why has the Constitution been called a blueprint for governing the United States?

3. **Describing** How are the states involved in the process of ratifying an amendment?

Critical Thinking

4. **BIG Ideas** Why have only 27 amendments been added to the Constitution?

5. **Summarizing** Complete the chart below by listing important details of each part of the Constitution.

Part	Details
Preamble	
Articles	
Amendments	

Analyzing Visuals

6. **Comparing** Review the chart on page 81. How does the power to tax differ under both forms of government?

CITIZENSHIP Activity

7. **Creative Writing** One responsibility of being an American citizen is to become involved in the affairs of one's community. Make a poster showing how students can get involved in their community.

Civics ONLINE

Study Central™ To review this section, go to glencoe.com.

Answers

1. Sentences should use vocabulary words according to their definitions in the section and in the Glossary.

2. It describes the principles that are the basis for our system of government. Our government was built using the Constitution as a guide.

3. The legislatures of states can propose an amendment by joining together to call for a national convention. Ratifying conventions held in all 50 states may approve an amendment if three-fourths agree. Also, amendments proposed by Congress must be approved by three-fourths of state legislatures.

4. The Framers did not want changes to be easy, so the process they outlined requires many steps as well as consensus.

5. **Preamble:** explain why the Constitution was written; the government exists to serve the people;
Articles: establish the three branches of government; identify how amendments can be added;
Amendments: necessary to ensure the rights of all Americans, difficult to add

6. In the Articles of Confederation, Congress had no power to tax. This power was granted to Congress in the Constitution.

7. Ask students to explain their posters. Display student posters in your classroom.

Guide to Reading

Big Idea
A constitution reflects the values and goals of the society that creates it.

Content Vocabulary
• popular sovereignty *(p. 86)*
• rule of law *(p. 87)*
• separation of powers *(p. 88)*
• checks and balances *(p. 88)*
• expressed powers *(p. 89)*
• reserved powers *(p. 89)*
• concurrent powers *(p. 89)*

Academic Vocabulary
• ensure *(p. 87)*
• assign *(p. 88)*

Reading Strategy
Organizing List information about the way the Constitution divides powers by completing a graphic organizer like the one below.

Section 4

🔊 **Section Audio**   🎬 **Spotlight Video**

Principles Underlying the Constitution

Real World Civics When young people leave home to go to college, where do they vote? At home or in the city where they go to school for nine months of the year? Young Han, a student at Hamilton College in Utica, New York, believed that state and federal law should grant him the right to vote in the town where he lived while going to school. The county election board in Utica did not agree, claiming that students living in dorms were not permanent residents. Han organized the national Student Voting Rights campaign to fight for college students who wanted to vote at the location of their colleges.

▼ **Young Han, founder of Student Voting Rights, a grass roots voting campaign**

85

Focus

Bellringer
Daily Focus Transparency 3–4

Guide to Reading
Answers to Graphic:

Divided Powers → expressed powers / reserved powers / concurrent powers

🎬 **Section Spotlight Video**

To generate student interest and provide a springboard for class discussion, access the Chapter 3, Section 4 video at glencoe.com or on the video DVD.

Resource Manager

R Reading Strategies	**C** Critical Thinking	**D** Differentiated Instruction	**W** Writing Support	**S** Skill Practice
Teacher Edition	**Teacher Edition**	**Teacher Edition**	**Teacher Edition**	**Teacher Edition**
• Outlining, p. 86	• Compare/Contrast, pp. 86, 89	• Visual/Spatial, p. 90	• Expository Writing, p. 88	• Analyzing Visuals, p. 87
• Academic Vocab., p. 87	• Analyzing Pri. Sources, p. 87	**Additional Resources**		• Visual Literacy, p. 88
• Reading Charts, p. 89	• Ident. Cent. Issues, p. 90	• School-to-Home Conn., URB p. 86		**Additional Resources**
Additional Resources	**Additional Resources**	• Reteach. Act., URB p. 87		• Daily Focus Trans., 3–4
• Cont. Vocab., URB p. 71	• Biographies, URB p. 75			• Pol. Cartoons Trans. 3
• Ac. Vocab., URB p. 73	• Quizzes and Tests, p. 29			
• Guid. Read., URB p. 92				

R Reading Strategy

Outlining Have students draw five columns on a sheet of paper and label them: popular sovereignty, the rule of law, separation of powers, checks and balances, and federalism. As they read, have them write notes or include a drawing to help them understand the main idea of each concept. **OL**

C Critical Thinking

Comparing and Contrasting Ask: How is the word "republic" interpreted today as opposed to how the Framers of the Constitution used the word? *(Today, the word has a more general meaning: a representative government with an elected leader. The Framers defined a republic as a true representative democracy).* **OL**

TIME™ Political Cartoons

Answers:

1. The figure is Uncle Sam, and he is holding the U.S. Constitution.
2. The pencil represents the security of the United States.
3. Answers may vary, but students may say the artist means that by balancing the freedoms guaranteed by the Constitution with the security of the country, some freedoms might be limited.

Differentiated Instruction

Biography Activity 3, URB pp. 75–76

Major Principles of Government

Main Idea The Constitution sets forth the basic principles of government.

Civics & You What principles do you live by? Read to discover how the basic principles of the Constitution have remained the same for more than 200 years.

R While the Constitution may seem filled with many details about how our nation should be governed, these details fall under five fundamental principles of government: popular sovereignty; the rule of law; separation of powers; checks and balances; and federalism. These principles are the foundation on which our government is built.

C Article IV of the Constitution guarantees the American people "a Republican Form of Government." Today the word *republic* can mean any representative government headed by an elected president or similar leader rather than a leader who inherits the position. To the Framers of the Constitution, though, a republic was a representative democracy. In a representative democracy, the power belongs to the people, who express their will through elected representatives. This idea was important to the early English colonists who came to America.

Popular Sovereignty

The idea that the power of government lies with the people is called **popular sovereignty.** (*Sovereignty* means "the right to rule"; *popular*, in this case, means "the population or public.") The Declaration of Independence is really a statement about popular sovereignty. It says that governments should draw their powers "from the consent of the governed." The same idea is echoed in the "We the People" phrase with which the Constitution begins.

TIME™ Political Cartoons

SO... WHERE DO I DRAW THE LINE?

—Scott Stantis/Copley News Service

In this image, cartoonist Scott Stantis is making a comment on security and liberty in the United States.

1. **What figure is depicted, and what document is he holding?**
2. **What does the pencil stand for?**
3. **What do you think the figure means when he asks, "So . . . where do I draw the line?"**

Every year, more than half of all Americans do volunteer work ... role in it. One of the responsibilities of citizens is to help make their ... of volunteer gro... small. Perha... dad wh...

George Mason

Objective: To identify George Mason's contributions to the Constitution

Focus: Have students discuss Virginia's role as a Southern state.

Teach: Define "compromise" and create a list of compromises Mason made for the Constitution.

Assess: Write a paragraph about Mason's contribution to individual rights.

Close: Create a biography of Mason's contributions to the country.

Differentiated Instruction Strategies

BL List some of Mason's positions as a public servant.

AL Research the economy of Virginia during Mason's life, and discover why so many Virginians supported slavery.

ELL Create a list of words that describe Mason's commitment to freedom and individual rights.

Further, the Constitution includes several provisions that protect and **ensure,** or guarantee, the sovereignty of the people. Under the Constitution, the will of the people is expressed most strongly through elections. By a majority vote, citizens decide who will represent them in Congress. Through the Electoral College, they also choose the president and vice president.

Elected officials are always accountable to the people. Elections are regularly scheduled, and voters can reject and replace representatives who serve them poorly.

Rule of Law

The Framers firmly believed that the government should be strong, but not too strong. They therefore included in the Constitution the principle of limited government, which means that government can do only what the people allow it to do.

As James Madison put it,

"*In framing a government which is to be administered by men over men, the great difficulty lies in this: you must first enable the government to control the governed; and in the next place oblige it to control itself.*"

—James Madison, *The Federalist,* No. 51

To limit the power of both the federal government and the states, the Constitution specifies what they may and may not do. English monarchs, prior to the Magna Carta, had unlimited government. There were few restrictions on what they did.

Under the Constitution, the government is also limited by the **rule of law.** This means that the law applies to everyone, even those who govern. No one may break the law or escape its reach.

Foundations of Rights

Charts In MOtion
See StudentWorks™ Plus or glencoe.com.

RIGHTS AND FREEDOMS	Magna Carta (1215)	English Bill of Rights (1689)	Virginia Declaration of Rights (1776)	Bill of Rights (1791)
Trial by jury	✪	✪	✪	✪
Due process	✪	✪	✪	✪
Private property	✪		✪	✪
No unreasonable searches or seizures	✪		✪	✪
No cruel punishment	✪	✪	✪	✪
No excessive bail or fines		✪	✪	✪
Right to bear arms		✪		✪
Right to petition		✪		✪
Freedom of speech				✪
Freedom of the press			✪	✪
Freedom of religion			✪	✪

Analyzing Charts

1. **Identifying** Which documents granted freedom of religion?
2. **Analyzing** Which rights or freedoms were included in all four documents?

R Reading Strategy

Academic Vocabulary Explain to students the difference between "insure" (to contract a payment in case of a loss) and "ensure" (to give a guarantee or to make sure). The words are often used interchangeably, but "insure" is usually reserved for the business of insurance companies. Have students write a sentence using each word correctly. **OL**

C Critical Thinking

Analyzing Primary Sources Have students reread Madison's quote and paraphrase what he means. *(Creating a government that both limits the power of government branches and limits the behavior of people is a challenge. The government must have enough power to be effective but not overpowering.)* **AL**

S Skill Practice

Anaylzing Visuals **Ask:** Which freedom does only the Bill of Rights guarantee? *(freedom of speech)* **OL**

Analyzing Charts

Answers:
1. Virginia Declaration of Rights, Bill of Rights
2. trial by jury, due process, no cruel punishment

Additional Support

Activity: U.S./World Connections

Making Connections Organize the class into small groups. Have groups bring newspapers and current newsmagazines to class, ones they can cut up. Begin by having a discussion of personal freedoms and basic human rights. Then have students cut out articles that relate to personal freedoms, such as those granted by our Bill of Rights.

Each group will create a scrapbook, adding comments about how a particular freedom was challenged, abused, or enforced. Encourage students to find international articles, noting whether other countries have the same freedoms granted to citizens as those granted to Americans by the Bill of Rights. Have groups share their work with the class and discuss which freedoms affect people's lives on an everyday basis. **Ask:** Which rights do you think are most important for all people? **OL**

S Skill Practice

Visual Literacy Have students look at the chart, the questions, and the headings. **Ask:** What are the different powers or branches of government? *(Executive, Legislative, and Judicial)* What do the arrows on the chart represent? *(They illustrate which branch can check on another.)* **BL**

W Writing Support

Expository Writing Have students use the chart to write a paragraph explaining which branch of government they think has more power. Ask volunteers to read their paragraphs aloud, and see if the class agrees. **OL**

Analyzing Charts

Answers:
1. It can declare presidential actions unconstitutional.
2. It appoints judges.

Reading Check **Answer:** to guard against any person or group gaining too much power

---

Hands-On Chapter Project
Step 4

Creating a Constitution

Step 4: Approving the Constitution and Creating Amendments Groups continue their work toward creating a constitution.

Directions Delegates will return to their original groups with a copy of the constitution. Each group (or state) will decide if the constitution should be approved. If approved without suggestions for amend-ments, the group should outline an argument stating reasons no changes are necessary.

If groups do want to add amendments before approval, they will outline an amendment that they feel needs to be added. The arguments should be presented in such a way that they are as persuasive as possible. Students will present their arguments in the final step as a song, poem, letter, or political commercial. Have students begin working on how they will present their arguments. **OL**

(Project continued on the Visual Summary page)

A System of Checks and Balances

UNITED STATES CONGRESS

LEGISLATIVE BRANCH

Can impeach president;
Can override veto;
Can reject appointments;
Can refuse to approve treaties

Can impeach judges;
Can reject appointment of judges

Can veto legislation

Can declare acts of legislature unconstitutional

Can appoint judges

Can declare presidential actions unconstitutional

EXECUTIVE BRANCH

JUDICIAL BRANCH

Analyzing Charts

1. **Describing** How can the judicial branch check the power of the executive branch?
2. **Describing** How can the executive branch check the power of the judicial branch?

Separation of Powers

To protect against abuse of power and the possibility of one person or group gaining too much power, the Framers divided the federal government into three branches, each with different functions. The Framers were influenced by the ideas of French philosopher Baron de Montesquieu.

Montesquieu believed that the best way to safeguard the liberty of the people was to clearly separate the legislative, executive, and judicial functions of government and **assign,** or appoint, each to a separate branch of government. This division of authority is called **separation of powers.**

Checks and Balances

Even with the separation of powers, the Framers feared that one branch of government could dominate the other two. In order to prevent any one of the three branches from becoming too powerful, the Framers of the Constitution also included a system of **checks and balances.** Under this system, each branch of government is able to check, or limit, the power of the others. Look at the chart of checks and balances on this page and you can see how this is done.

Reading Check **Explaining** Why did the Framers divide the government into three branches?

The Principle of Federalism

Main Idea The Constitution created a federal system of government. Under federalism, power is divided between national and state governments.

Civics & You As you read, think about how the writers of the Constitution divided powers between the federal and state governments.

Further limits on government arise from our Federal system. Under federalism, as you read in Section 3, power is shared by the national government and the states. Each level of government—national and state—has independent authority over people at the same time. Americans must obey both federal and state laws.

Three Types of Power

In setting up a federal system, the writers of the Constitution divided the powers of government into three types. The powers specifically granted to the national government are called the enumerated powers, or **expressed powers.** You will read more about them in Chapter 6. Powers that the Constitution does not give to the national government are kept by the states. These **reserved powers,** as they are called, include regulating trade within state borders, establishing schools, and making rules for marriage and divorce.

In some areas, the authority of the states and the national government overlaps. Powers that both levels of government can exercise are **concurrent powers.** Examples include the power to collect taxes, borrow money, and set up courts and prisons.

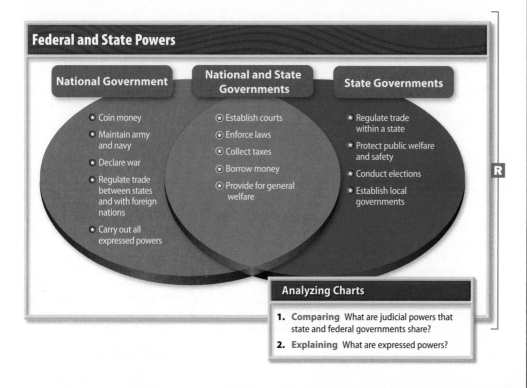

Federal and State Powers

National Government
- Coin money
- Maintain army and navy
- Declare war
- Regulate trade between states and with foreign nations
- Carry out all expressed powers

National and State Governments
- Establish courts
- Enforce laws
- Collect taxes
- Borrow money
- Provide for general welfare

State Governments
- Regulate trade within a state
- Protect public welfare and safety
- Conduct elections
- Establish local governments

Analyzing Charts
1. **Comparing** What are judicial powers that state and federal governments share?
2. **Explaining** What are expressed powers?

C Critical Thinking

Comparing and Contrasting Have students provide examples of federal laws and state laws. *(Answers will vary. Discrimination laws, child labor laws, and consumer protection laws are covered under federal legislation. State laws include speed limits, legal driving age, and helmet laws.)* **AL**

R Reading Strategy

Reading Charts Have students look at the chart and provide examples of expressed powers *(coining money, declaring war)*, reserved powers *(conduct elections)*, and concurrent powers *(collecting taxes and providing for general welfare)*. **OL**

Analyzing Charts

Answers:
1. establishing courts and enforcing laws
2. Powers given to the federal government: coining money, maintaining army and navy, declaring war, regulating trade between states and with foreign nations, carrying out all expressed powers.

Differentiated Instruction

Chapter 3 **89**

Leveled Activities

BL Content Vocabulary Activity 3, URB p. 72

OL Guided Reading 3–4, URB p. 92

AL Economics Activity 1, URB pp. 5–6

ELL Academic Vocabulary Activity 3, p. 74

D Differentiated Instruction

Visual/Spatial Have students write or draw words and phrases that support the idea that the Constitution is "durable and adaptable." Invite students to share their work with the class. **OL**

✓ **Reading Check** **Answer:** powers the Constitution gives to state governments

Assess

Civics ONLINE

Study Central™ provides summaries, interactive games, and online graphic organizers to help students review content.

Close

Identifying Central Issues Discuss with students how a system of checks and balances creates an equitable government. **Ask:** Do you think the Framers of the Constitution created an effective form of government? **OL**

Section 4 Review

The Supremacy Clause

In a federal system, the laws of a state and the laws of the nation may conflict. To deal with this possibility, the Framers included the supremacy clause. Found in Article VI, the supremacy clause states that the Constitution and other laws and treaties made by the national government "shall be the supreme Law of the Land."

Because the Constitution is the highest law, the national government is not supposed to act in violation of it. Likewise, states may do nothing that goes against either the Constitution or federal law.

Thomas Jefferson admired the Constitution. He wrote,

❝ *I am persuaded no constitution was ever before so well calculated as ours for . . . self-government.* ❞

—Thomas Jefferson's letter to James Madison

The Constitution Today

The entire system of federal government in the United States rests on a single document: the Constitution. It has served as the "supreme law of the land" for more than 200 years. The Constitution is both durable and adaptable. The principles that underpin it—popular sovereignty, the rule of law, separation of powers, checks and balances, and federalism—ensure government restraint as well as power. The Constitution gives our chosen representatives enough power to defend our country's freedom and to keep order. At the same time, it sets limits so that Americans need never fear tyranny. The United States Constitution stands as a powerful symbol of American values and a source of pride and unity.

✓ **Reading Check** **Explaining** What are reserved powers?

Section 4 Review

Vocabulary

1. **Write** at least three paragraphs about the U.S. Constitution using the group of words that follow: *popular sovereignty, rule of law, separation of powers, checks and balances, expressed powers, reserved powers, concurrent powers.*

Main Ideas

2. **Identifying Central Issues** Why did the Framers include the principles they did in writing the Constitution?

3. **Explaining** How is the power to govern shared under the principle of federalism?

Critical Thinking

4. **BIG Ideas** What are the five principles of government embodied in the United States Constitution?

5. **Summarizing** Give an explanation of each of the listed Constitutional principles in a graphic organizer like the one below.

Popular Sovereignty	
Rule of Law	
Separation of Powers	
Checks and Balances	

6. **Analyzing** In what ways has the system of checks and balances helped avoid conflict between the branches of government?

CITIZENSHIP Activity

7. **Expository Writing** Part of your responsibility as an American citizen is to be informed about what the government is doing and to voice your opinion about its actions. Draft a speech you would give at a schoolwide meeting, outlining your views on an issue your school or community is currently facing.

Civics ONLINE

Study Central™ To review this section, go to glencoe.com.

Answers

1. Paragraphs should use vocabulary words according to their definitions in the section and in the Glossary.

2. They wanted to create a government that had enough power to maintain a republic, but they also wanted a government that could not be so strong that it would undermine personal freedoms.

3. The power is divided between the national government and state governments.

4. popular sovereignty, rule of law, separation of powers, check and balances, federalism

5. **Popular sovereignty:** The people rule the government.
   Rule of Law: The government is allowed to do only what the people approve.
   Separation of Powers: Having three branches of government eliminates the possibility of one person or group assuming too much power.
   Checks and Balances: Each branch of government limits the power of others.

6. Each branch has different powers and the ability to restrain the power of the other two branches. This setup instills a spirit of cooperation.

7. Drafts will vary. Encourage students to develop their speeches and present them to the class. Consider inviting other school personnel to listen to the speeches.

Visual Summary

Constitutional Convention, 1787

The Constitution

The Constitution is this nation's fundamental law. It established that our nation is a republic that includes:

- an elected president;
- a bicameral legislature;
- a system of courts.

The Constitution is made up of three parts:

- the Preamble
- the Articles
- the Amendments

Independence Hall

The Constitution sets forth the five basic principles upon which the American system of government rests.

1. popular sovereignty
2. the rule of law
3. separation of powers
4. checks and balances
5. federalism

In setting up a federal system, the writers of the Constitution divided the powers of government into three types:

- **Enumerated powers** are those powers the Constitution specifically gives to the national government.
- **Reserved powers** are those that the Constitution gives to the states.
- **Concurrent powers** are those that the national and state governments share.

The Supremacy Clause

Found in Article VI, the supremacy clause states that the Constitution and the laws of the national government are the "supreme law of the land." In any conflict between national law and state law, the national law has the higher authority.

Amending the Constitution

Any change in the Constitution is called an amendment. The Constitution has 27 amendments.

Viewing the Declaration of Independence

 STUDY TO GO Study anywhere, anytime! Download quizzes and flash cards to your PDA from glencoe.com.

91

Identifying Central Issues Have students create a children's book that describes and illustrates the principles of the U.S. Constitution. **Ask:** What are the main ideas presented in the Constitution? Students may work with a partner and divide sections of the book. Each book should include a review of three parts of the Constitution and its five basic principles of government. Each main idea should have a heading and include at least three details. Encourage students to use drawings, symbols, and charts to help explain their text. **AL**

Questioning Have students create a list of at least five questions about the three types of power the government has. Students may use the Internet, newspapers, or the library to find the answers to their questions. **OL**

Personal Writing Have students skim the 27 amendments to the Constitution. Then have students choose one amendment they feel is important to them. Students will research the history behind the amendment. When they have completed their research, ask students to write a personal essay that expresses their opinions about the subject and the process of adding their chosen amendment. **AL**

Hands-On Chapter Project
Step 5: Wrap-Up

Creating a Constitution

Step 5: Presenting Amendments and Final Approval of Constitution Groups finalize their work toward creating a constitution.

Directions Have each group present their amendment proposal or argument for no changes to the class. Students may sing, recite a poem, or reenact a political commercial. After each performance, have each group cast a secret ballot as to whether the amendment should be added.

Once all groups have performed their arguments and all ballots are in, have delegates from each group oversee the results. Approval must be gained from three-fourths of the groups (states). Have delegates announce what amendments were added to the constitution.

Finally, have the class prepare its constitution on a poster board, complete with amendments. Have all delegates sign the document and display it in class. **OL**

Answers and Analyses
Reviewing Vocabulary

1. A In this question, the most likely distractor is answer B, constitutional convention. Students should know that the Second Continental Congress first sought a unification of states, as was set forth in the Articles of Confederation. After they discovered the weakness of the Articles, they decided to create a new and improved plan of government as outlined in the Constitution.

2. D The phrase "enslaved persons" should lead students to the correct answer. Students may find the word "Compromise" in choice C distracting. However, the Great Compromise deals with a Congress with two houses.

3. B Each state has control over its educational system, thus the correct answer is reserved power. Expressed powers (A) are those granted to the federal government, also called enumerated powers (D). Concurrent powers are exercised by both state and national governments (B).

4. B The executive branch is headed by the president and vice president. The judicial branch (A) is headed by the Supreme Court justices, and the legislative branch (C) is run by House representatives and senators.

Reviewing Main Ideas

5. B This question will require the student to know about English Parliament, which was bicameral, as well as the Magna Carta and the English Bill of Rights, which guaranteed a trial by jury and protected personal property. Each state in America had a state constitution, or plan of government.

6. C This question requires that students understand the accomplishment of the Articles: to lay forth the foundations for systematic growth. These provisions were outlined in the Ordinance of 1785 and the Northwest Ordinance. The other choices highlight weaknesses of the Articles: they did not allow Congress to collect taxes to pay off war debts, nor did they allow Congress the power to enforce laws in individual states.

TEST-TAKING TIP

> Note the kinds of topics and ideas covered in a test to determine what to study for the next examination.

Reviewing Vocabulary
Directions: Choose the word(s) that best completes the sentence.

1. The Second Continental Congress made plans for a _____.

  A confederation   **C** bill of rights

  B constitutional convention   **D** territorial government

2. The agreement about how to represent enslaved persons was known as the _____.

  A rule of law   **C** Great Compromise

  B Electoral College Compromise   **D** Three-Fifths Compromise

3. According to the Constitution, establishing schools is a(n) _____.

  A expressed power   **C** concurrent power

  B reserved power   **D** enumerated power

4. The president and vice president head the _____.

  A judicial branch   **C** legislative branch

  B executive branch   **D** all three branches

Reviewing Main Ideas
Directions: Choose the best answer for each question.

Section 1 (pp.66–70)

5. How were most early state governments different from the British government?

  A They guaranteed trial by jury.

  B They had written constitutions.

  C They had bicameral legislatures.

  D They protected private property.

6. What was a significant achievement under the Articles of Confederation?

  A payment of all Revolutionary War debts

  B economic security for American farmers

  C establishment of a plan for organizing territories

  D uniform enforcement of laws throughout the states

Section 2 (pp. 71–78)

7. Which proposal at the Constitutional Convention described a system with a president, courts, and bicameral legislature?

  A Albany Plan

  B Virginia Plan

  C New Jersey Plan

  D Connecticut Compromise

8. Which person defended the Constitution in *The Federalist*?

  A John Jay

  B John Tyler

  C Roger Sherman

  D Baron de Montesquieu

Section 3 (pp. 79–84)

9. What does Article I of the Constitution outline?

  A the purposes of the federal government

  B the lawmaking powers of the legislative branch

  C the law-enforcing powers of the executive branch

  D the relationship of the state and national governments

GO ON ➡

---

7. B This question is challenging as students need to identify a proposal, not a compromise. Students should know the two proposals: the Virginia Plan and the New Jersey Plan. However, the New Jersey Plan called for a one-house congress. The Albany Plan (A) is completely unrelated.

8. A This question requires that students know details about each individual. Tyler was the first vice president who assumed the presidency when President Harrison died in office. Sherman is credited for creating the Great Compromise. Montesquieu was a French philosopher who influenced the Framers in including separation of powers.

9. B This question presents a challenge in that all the answers are outlined in the Constitution. Students must be able to recall that lawmaking authority was given to Congress in Article 1.

Section 4 (pp. 85–90)

10. Which principle divides the functions of government among three branches?

   A federalism

   B rule of law

   C popular sovereignty

   D separation of powers

11. What does the supremacy clause state?

   A The Constitution is the highest law of the land.

   B Only the national government can raise an army.

   C States keep powers not given to the federal government.

   D The federal and state governments share the power to tax.

Critical Thinking

Directions: Base your answers to questions 12 and 13 on the diagram below and your knowledge of Chapter 3.

Amending the Constitution	
Proposal By	Proposal By
2/3 vote of Congress	Conventions called by 3/4 of states
Ratification	Ratification
By 2/3 of state legislatures	By 3/4 of state conventions

12. Either process for amending the Constitution involves representatives from _____.

   A half of the states

   B states who entered the union before 1900

   C all of the states

   D states with populations over 12 million

13. Of those asked, how many state legislatures must approve an amendment for it to be ratified?

   A three-fifths

   B two-thirds

   C all

   D half

Document-Based Questions

Directions: Analyze the following document and answer the short-answer questions that follow.

The preamble to the United States Constitution describes the writers' vision for a new kind of government.

> *We the People of the United States, in Order to form a more perfect Union, establish Justice, insure domestic Tranquility, provide for the common defence, promote the general Welfare, and secure the Blessings of Liberty to ourselves and our Posterity, do ordain and establish this Constitution for the United States of America.*
>
> —Preamble of the U.S. Constitution

14. What is meant by the phrase to "promote the general Welfare"?

15. Which phrase indicates the source of the government's power? Explain.

Extended-Response Question

16. Write a brief essay explaining why leaders of the United States decided to replace the Articles of Confederation.

Civics ONLINE

For additional test practice, use Self-Check Quizzes—Chapter 3 on glencoe.com.

Need Extra Help?

If you missed question...	1	2	3	4	5	6	7	8	9	10	11	12	13	14	15	16
Go to page...	68	75	89	80	67	68	74	78	80	88	90	82	83	80	80	69

Chapter 3   93

ASSESSMENT

13. B Students will need to read the chart and the question carefully so that they will not confuse the ratio of necessary state legislatures with the ratio of necessary state conventions.

Document-Based Questions

14. Students' answers may vary. A possible answer is to help people live happy, healthy, and prosperous lives.

15. The phrase is "We the People of the United States." Students' explanations will vary. A possible answer is that elected officials are bound to represent the wishes of the people who elected them.

Extended Response

16. Students' essays will vary. Look for supporting details from the chapter.

---

10. D This question asks that the students look for a system of division. Students might choose A, federalism, but this refers to a division between the national government and state government. Separation of powers divides our three governing branches.

11. A The student should focus on the word supremacy. Although statements in choices B, C, and D are all correct, none of them relates to the supreme power the Framers wanted to assign. They wanted to make sure that the Constitution would be the supreme law of the nation.

Critical Thinking

12. C Students will need to have familiarity with the chapter to know that all states in the union are involved in the amendment process.

Civics ONLINE

Have students visit the Web site at glencoe.com to review Chapter 3 and take the **Self-Check Quiz**.

Need Extra Help?

Have students refer to the pages listed if they miss any of the questions.

R Reading Strategy

Setting a Purpose Prepare students to read by explaining that the Constitution has archaic language. As it was written in the 18th century, the wording and some of the ideas may seem odd to readers today. Some of the vocabulary is difficult, and a number of the words may be unfamiliar. Point out that the notes in the margin (**What It Means**) are useful, as they explicate main ideas, provide background information, and explain certain words or phrases. **OL**

Resource Manager

The **Constitution** of the **United States**

The Constitution of the United States is truly a remarkable document. It was one of the first written constitutions in modern history. The Framers wanted to devise a plan for a strong central government that would unify the country, as well as preserve the ideals of the Declaration of Independence. The document they wrote created a representative legislature, the office of president, a system of courts, and a process for adding amendments. For over 200 years, the flexibility and strength of the Constitution has guided the nation's political leaders. The document has become a symbol of pride and a force for national unity.

R The entire text of the Constitution and its amendments follows. For easier study, those passages that have been set aside or changed by the adoption of amendments are printed in blue. Also included are explanatory notes that will help clarify the meaning of each article and section.

U.S. Capitol

R **Reading Strategies**	C **Critical Thinking**	D **Differentiated Instruction**	W **Writing Support**	S **Skill Practice**
Teacher Edition	**Teacher Edition**	**Teacher Edition**	**Teacher Edition**	**Teacher Edition**
• Set. Purpose, p. 94	• Contrasting, p. 96	• Visual/Spatial, p. 97	• Expository Writing, pp. 100, 106, 117	• Naming, p. 95
• Analyzing Text, p. 95	• Making Gen., pp. 97, 112	• Below Grade Level, p. 98	• Descriptive Writing, p. 104	• Recognizing Bias, p. 110
• Identifying, pp. 96, 108	• Drawing Con., pp. 98, 99, 105, 112	• Auditory/Musical, p. 99		
• Specifying, p. 96	• Hypothesizing, p. 102	• Logical/Mathematical, p.101		
• Summarizing, p. 100	• Defending, pp. 103, 109	• Intrapersonal, p. 108		
• Det. Importance, p. 101	• Analyzing Info., p. 107	• Gifted/Talented, p. 111		
• Outlining, pp. 102, 116	• Debating, p. 114	• English Learners, p. 113		
• Act. Prior Know., p. 103	• Ident. Cent. Issues, p. 114			
• Inferring, p. 114	• Evaluating, p. 116			
• Calculating, p. 115				

Preamble

We the People of the United States, in Order to form a more perfect Union, establish Justice, insure domestic Tranquility, provide for the common defence, promote the general Welfare, and secure the Blessings of Liberty to ourselves and our Posterity, do ordain and establish this Constitution for the United States of America.

Article I

Section 1

All legislative Powers herein granted shall be vested in a Congress of the United States, which shall consist of a Senate and House of Representatives.

Section 2

[1.] The House of Representatives shall be composed of Members chosen every second Year by the People of the several States, and the Electors in each State shall have the Qualifications requisite for Electors of the most numerous Branch of the State Legislature.

[2.] No person shall be a Representative who shall not have attained the Age of twenty five Years, and been seven Years a Citizen of the United States, and who shall not, when elected, be an Inhabitant of that State in which he shall be chosen.

[3.] Representatives and direct Taxes shall be apportioned among the several States which may be included within this Union, according to their respective Numbers, which shall be determined by adding to the whole Number of free Persons, including those bound to Service for a Term of Years, and excluding Indians not taxed, three fifths of all other Persons. The actual Enumeration shall be made within three Years after the first Meeting of the Congress of the United States, and within every subsequent Term of ten Years, in such Manner as they shall by Law direct. The Number of Representatives shall not exceed one for every thirty Thousand, but each State shall have at Least one Representative; and until such enumeration shall be made, the State of New Hampshire shall be entitled to chuse three; Massachusetts eight, Rhode-Island and Providence Plantations one, Connecticut five, New-York six, New Jersey four, Pennsylvania eight, Delaware one, Maryland six, Virginia ten, North Carolina five, South Carolina five, and Georgia three.

The Preamble introduces the Constitution and sets forth the general purposes for which the government was established. The Preamble also declares that the power of the government comes from the people.

The printed text of the document shows the spelling and punctuation of the parchment original.

R

What It Means

Article I. The Legislative Branch The Constitution contains seven divisions called articles. Each article covers a general topic. For example, Articles I, II, and III create the three branches of the national government—the legislative, executive, and judicial branches. Most of the articles are divided into sections.

What It Means

Representation The number of representatives from each state is based on the size of the state's population. Each state is entitled to at least one representative. *What are the qualifications for members of the House of Representatives?*

S

Vocabulary

preamble: introduction

constitution: principles and laws of a nation

enumeration: census or population count

R Reading Strategy

Analyzing Text Structure Point out that many of the capitalized words do not follow standardized rules of capitalization. **Ask:** Why do you think the Framers capitalized certain words? *(They wanted to place more emphasis on those words; it was the style during the period.)* **OL**

S Skill Practice

Naming Have students research to find out how many state representatives their state has, who they are, and what each has done while in office. **OL**

What It Means

Answer: Members of the House must be at least 25 years old, a U.S. citizen for at least seven years, and be an inhabitant of the state from which he or she was elected.

Additional Support

Activity: Technology Connection

Making Connections Have students use Internet sources to find out how many representatives each state currently has. Then have them organize the information into a chart or map. Students may chart their information by listing the states with the most representatives first, create a chart that shows representatives by political parties, or they may use a map to illustrate their results. Encourage students to be creative in how they display the information. **OL**

R₁ Reading Strategy

Identifying Ask: How is the Speaker of the House chosen? *(by its own members)* Have students find out who currently holds the job of Speaker of the House of Representatives. **OL**

C Critical Thinking

Contrasting Ask: What qualifications do senators have that are different from House representatives? *(Members of the Senate must be at least 30 years old versus 25 for the House, and a U.S. citizen for at least nine years versus seven years for representatives. Senators are elected every six years; representatives must be elected every two.)* **OL**

R₂ Reading Strategy

Specifying Ask: When does the vice president get to vote in the Senate? *(When there is a tie).* Tell students that this rarely occurs, so the vice president seldom has a vote and only in the case of a tie. **OL**

What It Means

Answer: the Senate

Additional Support

What It Means

Electing Senators Originally, senators were chosen by the state legislators of their own states. The Seventeenth Amendment changed this, so that senators are now elected by the people. There are 100 senators, 2 from each state. The vice president serves as president of the Senate.

▲ John Adams, the first vice president

What It Means

Impeachment One of Congress's powers is the power to impeach—to accuse government officials of wrongdoing, put them on trial, and if necessary remove them from office. *Which body has the power to decide the official's guilt or innocence?*

Vocabulary

impeachment: bringing charges against an official

president pro tempore: presiding officer of Senate who serves when the vice president is absent

indictment: charging a person with an offense

[4.] When vacancies happen in the Representation from any State, the Executive Authority thereof shall issue Writs of Election to fill such Vacancies.

[5.] The House of Representatives shall chuse their Speaker and other Officers; and shall have the sole Power of Impeachment.

Section 3

[1.] The Senate of the United States shall be composed of two Senators from each State, chosen by the Legislature thereof, for six Years; and each Senator shall have one Vote.

[2.] Immediately after they shall be assembled in Consequence of the first Election, they shall be divided as equally as may be into three Classes. The Seats of the Senators of the first Class shall be vacated at the Expiration of the second Year, of the second Class at the Expiration of the fourth Year, and of the third Class at the Expiration of the sixth Year, so that one third may be chosen every second Year; and if Vacancies happen by Resignation, or otherwise, during the Recess of the Legislature of any State, the Executive thereof may make temporary Appointments until the next Meeting of the Legislature, which shall then fill such Vacancies.

[3.] No Person shall be a Senator who shall not have attained to the Age of thirty Years, and been nine Years a Citizen of the United States, and who shall not, when elected, be an Inhabitant of that State for which he shall be chosen.

[4.] The Vice President of the United States shall be President of the Senate, but shall have no Vote, unless they be equally divided.

[5.] The Senate shall chuse their other Officers, and also a President pro tempore, in the Absence of the Vice President, or when he shall exercise the Office of the President of the United States.

[6.] The Senate shall have the sole Power to try all Impeachments. When sitting for that Purpose, they shall be on Oath or Affirmation. When the President of the United States is tried, the Chief Justice shall preside: And no Person shall be convicted without the Concurrence of two thirds of the Members present.

[7.] Judgment in Cases of Impeachment shall not extend further than to removal from Office, and disqualification to hold and enjoy any Office of honor, Trust or Profit under the United States: but the Party convicted shall nevertheless be liable and subject to Indictment, Trial, Judgment and Punishment, according to Law.

Activity: Interdisciplinary Connection

History Begin a discussion of the impeachment clause. Tell students that only two sitting presidents have been impeached: Andrew Johnson and William Clinton. The House started impeachment proceedings on President Richard Nixon, but he resigned before the vote took place.

Have students work in groups to research both impeachments. Although neither President Johnson nor President Clinton was convicted by the Senate, the impeachment is part of their historical record. Have students discuss how this affects each president's place in history. **OL**

Section 4

[1.] The Times, Places and Manner of holding Elections for Senators and Representatives, shall be prescribed in each State by the Legislature thereof; but the Congress may at any time by Law make or alter such Regulations, except as to the Places of chusing Senators.

[2.] The Congress shall assemble at least once in every Year, and such Meeting shall be on the first Monday in December, unless they shall by Law appoint a different Day.

Section 5

[1.] Each House shall be the Judge of the Elections, Returns and Qualifications of its own Members, and a Majority of each shall constitute a Quorum to do Business; but a smaller Number may adjourn from day to day, and may be authorized to compel the Attendance of absent Members, in such Manner, and under such Penalties as each House may provide.

[2.] Each House may determine the Rules of its Proceedings, punish its Members for disorderly Behaviour, and, with the Concurrence of two thirds, expel a Member.

[3.] Each House shall keep a Journal of its Proceedings, and from time to time publish the same, excepting such Parts as may in their Judgment require Secrecy; and the Yeas and Nays of the Members of either House on any question shall, at the Desire of one fifth of those Present, be entered on the Journal.

[4.] Neither House, during the Session of Congress, shall, without the Consent of the other, adjourn for more than three days, nor to any other Place than that in which the two Houses shall be sitting.

D

Section 6

[1.] The Senators and Representatives shall receive a Compensation for their Services, to be ascertained by Law, and paid out of the Treasury of the United States. They shall in all Cases, except Treason, Felony and Breach of the Peace, be privileged from Arrest during their Attendance at the Session of their respective Houses, and in going to and returning from the same; and for any Speech or Debate in either House, they shall not be questioned in any other Place.

C

[2.] No Senator or Representative shall, during the Time for which he was elected, be appointed to any civil Office under the Authority of the United States, which shall have been created, or the Emoluments whereof shall have been encreased during such time; and no Person holding any Office under the United States, shall be a Member of either House during his Continuance in Office.

What It Means

Congressional Salaries To strengthen the federal government, the Founders set congressional salaries to be paid by the United States Treasury rather than by members' respective states. Originally, members were paid $6 per day. In 2006, all members of Congress received a base salary of $165,200.

Vocabulary

quorum: minimum number of members that must be present to conduct sessions

adjourn: to suspend a session

immunity privilege: members cannot be sued or prosecuted for anything they say in Congress

emoluments: salaries

D Differentiated Instruction
===

Visual/Spatial Have students record a congressional session, either in the House or the Senate. These sessions are shown on *C-Span*. Have students research the business conducted during the session, and explain the proceedings to the class. **AL**

C Critical Thinking
===

Making Generalizations Ask: Why do you think members of Congress enjoy immunity from criminal arrest? *(This clause was meant to protect members of Congress from getting sued by individuals and being removed from the floor where they work for their constituents. The idea was that representatives and senators should not be summoned and removed from his or her seat while giving the people a voice in legislation. This clause does not protect them from criminal offenses.)* **AL**

Activity: Collaborative Learning

Describing In this activity, students will use the Internet and other sources to find out what representatives and senators do on a daily basis. Form small groups and instruct students to begin their research with a list of questions, such as, Do new senators or representatives get training? What do they do? What kind of work constitutes a typical day? How long does it take to learn all the rules, and so on.

Next, students will conduct their research. Encourage students to write to their state representatives or senators to get a personal answer to questions. Have students document the results of their research in a poster. **OL**

The Constitution
of the United States

C Critical Thinking

Drawing Conclusions Ask: Why do you think the issue of tax laws was so important to the framers of the Constitution. *(The colonies had been overtaxed by the monarchy, leading to the Revolutionary War. They wanted to make sure that the people could have a say in this important matter.)* **AL**

D Differentiated Instruction

Below Grade Level Have students create a flow chart summarizing Section 7, Clause 2. Working with a partner, have pairs draw five boxes and write five general statements to summarize the section.

What It Means

Answer: If two-thirds of the House of Representatives and two-thirds of the Senate approve a vetoed bill, it can become a law.

What It Means

Answer: Article 1, Section 8, Clause 11

Additional Support

What It Means

Where Tax Laws Begin All tax laws must originate in the House of Representatives. This ensures that the branch of Congress that is elected by the people every two years has the major role in determining taxes.

What It Means

How Bills Become Laws A bill may become a law only by passing both houses of Congress and by being signed by the president. The president can check Congress by rejecting—vetoing—its legislation. *How can Congress override the president's veto?*

What It Means

Powers of Congress Expressed powers are those powers directly stated in the Constitution. Most of the expressed powers of Congress are listed in Article I, Section 8. These powers are also called enumerated powers because they are numbered 1–18. *Which clause gives Congress the power to declare war?*

Vocabulary

bill: draft of a proposed law

revenue: income raised by government

resolution: legislature's formal expression of opinion

naturalization: procedure by which a citizen of a foreign nation becomes a citizen of the United States.

Section 7

[1.] All Bills for raising Revenue shall originate in the House of Representatives; but the Senate may propose or concur with Amendments as on other Bills.

[2.] Every Bill which shall have passed the House of Representatives and the Senate, shall, before it become a Law, be presented to the President of the United States; If he approve he shall sign it, but if not he shall return it, with his Objections to that House in which it shall have originated, who shall enter the Objections at large on their Journal, and proceed to reconsider it. If after such Reconsideration two thirds of that House shall agree to pass the Bill, it shall be sent, together with the Objections, to the other House, by which it shall likewise be reconsidered, and if approved by two thirds of that House, it shall become a Law. But in all such Cases the Votes of both Houses shall be determined by yeas and Nays, and the Names of the Persons voting for and against the Bill shall be entered on the Journal of each House respectively. If any Bill shall not be returned by the President within ten Days (Sundays excepted) after it shall have been presented to him, the Same shall be a Law, in like Manner as if he had signed it, unless the Congress by their Adjournment prevent its Return, in which Case it shall not be a Law.

[3.] Every Order, Resolution, or Vote to which the Concurrence of the Senate and House of Representatives may be necessary (except on a question of Adjournment) shall be presented to the President of the United States; and before the Same shall take Effect, shall be approved by him, or being disapproved by him, shall be repassed by two thirds of the Senate and House of Representatives, according to the Rules and Limitations prescribed in the Case of a Bill.

Section 8

[1.] The Congress shall have the Power To lay and collect Taxes, Duties, Imposts and Excises, to pay the Debts and provide for the common Defence and general Welfare of the United States; but all Duties, Imposts and Excises shall be uniform throughout the United States;

[2.] To borrow Money on the credit of the United States;

[3.] To regulate Commerce with foreign Nations, and among the several States, and with the Indian Tribes;

[4.] To establish an uniform Rule of Naturalization, and uniform Laws on the subject of Bankruptcies throughout the United States;

[5.] To coin Money, regulate the Value thereof, and of foreign Coin, and fix the Standard of Weights and Measures;

[6.] To provide for the Punishment of counterfeiting the Securities and current Coin of the United States;

[7.] To establish Post Offices and post Roads;

Activity: Technology Connection

Categorizing Explain to students that both houses of Congress have committees that do most of the work preparing bills. Have students use the Internet to locate the names of the various committees in the House of Representatives and in the Senate. Students should also find out how many committees a member can serve on. Have students share their results with the class. Ask students to say which committee they would like to serve on if they served in Congress. **OL**

[8.] To promote the Progress of Science and useful Arts, by securing for limited Times to Authors and Inventors the exclusive Right to their respective Writings and Discoveries;

[9.] To constitute Tribunals inferior to the supreme Court;

[10.] To define and punish Piracies and Felonies committed on the high Seas, and Offences against the Law of Nations;

[11.] To declare War, grant Letters of Marque and Reprisal, and make Rules concerning Captures on Land and Water;

[12.] To raise and support Armies, but no Appropriation of Money to that Use shall be for a longer Term than two Years;

[13.] To provide and maintain a Navy;

[14.] To make Rules for the Government and Regulation of the land and naval Forces;

[15.] To provide for calling forth the Militia to execute the Laws of the Union, suppress Insurrections and repel Invasions;

[16.] To provide for organizing, arming, and disciplining, the Militia, and for governing such Part of them as may be employed in the Service of the United States, reserving to the States respectively, the Appointment of the Officers, and the Authority of training the Militia according to the discipline prescribed by Congress;

[17.] To exercise exclusive Legislation in all Cases whatsoever, over such District (not exceeding ten Miles square) as may, by Cession of particular States, and the Acceptance of Congress, become the Seat of Government of the United States, and to exercise like Authority over all Places purchased by the Consent of the Legislature of the State in which the Same shall be, for the Erection of Forts, Magazines, Arsenals, dock-Yards, and other needful Buildings, —And

[18.] To make all Laws which shall be necessary and proper for carrying into Execution the foregoing Powers, and all other Powers vested by this Constitution in the Government of the United States, or in any Department or Officer thereof.

Section 9

[1.] The Migration or Importation of such Persons as any of the States now existing shall think proper to admit, shall not be prohibited by the Congress prior to the Year one thousand eight hundred and eight, but a Tax or duty may be imposed on such Importation, not exceeding ten dollars for each Person.

[2.] The Privilege of the Writ of Habeas Corpus shall not be suspended, unless when in Cases of Rebellion or Invasion the public Safety may require it.

[3.] No Bill of Attainder or ex post facto Law shall be passed.

[4.] No Capitation, or other direct, Tax shall be laid, unless in Proportion to the Census or Enumeration herein before directed to be taken.

[5.] No Tax or Duty shall be laid on Articles exported from any State.

What It Means

Elastic Clause The final enumerated power is often called the "elastic clause." This clause gives Congress the right to make all laws "necessary and proper" to carry out the powers expressed in the other clauses of Article I. It is called the elastic clause because it lets Congress "stretch" its powers to meet situations the Founders could never have anticipated.

What does the phrase "necessary and proper" in the elastic clause mean? Almost from the beginning, this phrase was a subject of dispute. The issue was whether a strict or a broad interpretation of the Constitution should be applied. The dispute was first addressed in 1819, in the case of *McCulloch* v. *Maryland*, when the Supreme Court ruled in favor of a broad interpretation.

What It Means

Habeas Corpus A writ of habeas corpus issued by a judge requires a law official to bring a prisoner to court and show cause for holding the prisoner. A bill of attainder is a bill that punished a person without a jury trial. An "ex post facto" law is one that makes an act a crime after the act has been committed. *What does the Constitution say about bills of attainder?*

Vocabulary

tribunal: a court
insurrection: rebellion

D ## Differentiated Instruction

Auditory/Musical Have students work in groups to write a skit or song that illustrates the powers of Congress. Their skits or songs may be similar to those on children's educational programs. Have students present oral presentations. **AL**

C ## Critical Thinking

Drawing Conclusions Lead a discussion about which powers of Congress are most important. List choices on the board and prioritize them according to class opinion. **OL**

What It Means

Answer: no bills of attainder shall be passed

Activity: Interdisciplinary Connection

History Discuss with students that on many occasions when the United States has intervened militarily, Congress has not issued a declaration of war. These "undeclared wars" are typically called conflicts, for example, the Vietnam Conflict. Other wars, the Korean, Gulf, and Iraq wars, have all been fought on the President's authority. Have students work in groups to discuss their view on these military actions. **Ask:** Should the executive branch have the power to use military force without a declaration of war from Congress? If Congress authorizes military appropriations, is that acceptable? **OL**

Teach

R Reading Strategy

Summarizing Section 10 outlines the limits placed on the states. Have students summarize these restrictions. *(States cannot make their own money, declare war, tax goods from other states, or maintain navies).* **OL**

W Writing Support

Expository Writing Article II describes the executive branch. Have students write a paragraph explaining why the Framers of the Constitution wanted the office of presidency to have limited powers. *(Students should note the Framers' fear of a single leader with uncontrolled powers, as was the case with British monarchies.)* **OL**

**Additional
Support**

[6.] No Preference shall be given by any Regulation of Commerce or Revenue to the Ports of one State over those of another: nor shall Vessels bound to, or from, one State, be obliged to enter, clear, or pay Duties in another.

[7.] No Money shall be drawn from the Treasury, but in Consequence of Appropriations made by Law; and a regular Statement and Account of the Receipts and Expenditures of all public Money shall be published from time to time.

[8.] No Title of Nobility shall be granted by the United States: And no Person holding any Office of Profit or Trust under them, shall, without the Consent of the Congress, accept of any present, Emolument, Office, or Title, of any kind whatever, from any King, Prince, or foreign State.

What It Means

Limitations on the States Section 10 lists limits on the states. These restrictions were designed, in part, to prevent an overlapping in functions and authority with the federal government.

Section 10

[1.] No State shall enter into any Treaty, Alliance, or Confederation; grant Letters of Marque and Reprisal; coin Money; emit Bills of Credit; make any Thing but gold and silver Coin a Tender in Payment of Debts; pass any Bill of Attainder, ex post facto Law, or Law impairing the Obligation of Contracts, or grant any Title of Nobility.

[2.] No State shall, without the Consent of the Congress, lay any Imposts or Duties on Imports or Exports, except what may be absolutely necessary for executing its inspection Laws: and the net Produce of all Duties and Imposts, laid by any State on Imports and Exports, shall be for the Use of the Treasury of the United States; and all such Laws shall be subject to the Revision and Controul of the Congress.

[3.] No State shall, without the Consent of Congress, lay any Duty of Tonnage, keep Troops, or Ships of War in time of Peace, enter into any Agreement or Compact with another State, or with a foreign Power, or engage in War, unless actually invaded, or in such imminent Danger as will not admit of delay.

What It Means

Article II. The Executive Branch Article II creates an executive branch to carry out laws passed by Congress. Article II lists the powers and duties of the presidency, describes qualifications for office and procedures for electing the president, and provides for a vice president.

Article II

Section 1

[1.] The executive Power shall be vested in a President of the United States of America. He shall hold his Office during the Term of four Years, and, together with the Vice President, chosen for the same Term, be elected, as follows.

[2.] Each State shall appoint, in such Manner as the Legislature thereof may direct, a Number of Electors, equal to the whole Number of Senators and Representatives to which the State may be entitled in the Congress: but no Senator or Representative, or Person holding an Office of Trust or Profit under the United States, shall be appointed an Elector.

Vocabulary
appropriations: funds set aside for a specific use
emolument: payment
impost: tax
duty: tax

Activity: Interdisciplinary Connection

Language Arts The Constitution outlines the basic qualifications of the president of the United States and how elections should be run. It does not, however, provide a list of traits the president should have.

Have students write a newspaper article in which they describe the perfect president. Articles should include personality traits, work experience, and principles that they think a person should have to run as president. Ask students if any past or current presidents measure up to the standards they have created. **OL**

[3.] The Electors shall meet in their respective States, and vote by Ballot for two Persons, of whom one at least shall not be an Inhabitant of the same State with themselves. And they shall make a List of all the Persons voted for, and of the Number of Votes for each; which List they shall sign and certify, and transmit sealed to the Seat of the Government of the United States, directed to the President of the Senate. The President of the Senate shall, in the Presence of the Senate and House of Representatives, open all the Certificates, and the Votes shall then be counted. The Person having the greatest Number of Votes shall be the President, if such Number be a Majority of the whole Number of Electors appointed; and if there be more than one who have such Majority, and have an equal Number of Votes, then the House of Representatives shall immediately chuse by Ballot one of them for President; and if no person have a Majority, then from the five highest on the List the said House shall in like Manner chuse the President. But in chusing the President, the Votes shall be taken by States, the Representation from each State having one Vote; A quorum for this Purpose shall consist of a Member or Members from two thirds of the States, and a Majority of all the States shall be necessary to a Choice. In every Case, after the Choice of the President, the Person having the greatest Number of Votes of the Electors shall be the Vice President. But if there should remain two or more who have equal Votes, the Senate shall chuse from them by Ballot the Vice President.

[4.] The Congress may determine the Time of chusing the Electors, and the Day on which they shall give their Votes; which Day shall be the same throughout the United States.

[5.] No Person except a natural born Citizen, or a Citizen of the United States, at the time of the Adoption of this Constitution, shall be eligible to the Office of President; neither shall any Person be eligible to that Office who shall not have attained to the Age of thirty five Years, and been fourteen Years a Resident within the United States.

[6.] In Case of the Removal of the President from Office, or of his Death, Resignation, or Inability to discharge the Powers and Duties of the said Office, the Same shall devolve on the Vice President, and the Congress may by Law provide for the Case of Removal, Death, Resignation or Inability, both of the President and Vice President, declaring what Officer shall then act as President, and such Officer shall act accordingly, until the Disability be removed, or a President shall be elected.

[7.] The President shall, at stated Times, receive for his Services, a Compensation, which shall neither be encreased nor diminished during the Period for which he shall have been elected, and he shall not receive within that Period any other Emolument from the United States, or any of them.

D

What It Means

Previous Elections The Twelfth Amendment, added in 1804, changed the method of electing the president stated in Article II, Section 3. The Twelfth Amendment requires that the electors cast separate ballots for president and vice president.

What It Means

Qualifications The president must be a citizen of the United States by birth, at least 35 years of age, and a resident of the United States for 14 years.

R

What It Means

Vacancies If the president dies, resigns, is removed from office by impeachment, or is unable to carry out the duties of the office, the vice president becomes president. The Twenty-fifth Amendment sets procedures for presidential succession.

What It Means

Salary Originally, the president's salary was $25,000 per year. The president's current salary is $400,000 plus a $50,000 nontaxable expense account per year. The president also receives living accommodations in two residences—the White House and Camp David.

Chapter 3 The Constitution **101**

R Reading Strategy

Outlining Have students outline the powers of the president. (*He is the commander-in-chief of the armed forces, he can pardon criminals, make treaties with other nations, pick judges and other members of the government [with Senate approval], make suggestions to Congress, act as head of state by receiving ambassadors and other heads of state, and make sure all federal laws are carried out.*) **OL**

C Critical Thinking

Hypothesizing Ask students to offer ideas on why the Framers wanted the president to be the commander-in-chief of the armed forces and state militia rather than a commander in the military. (*They wanted to make sure the people had a voice in the military actions, so they gave the power to an elected official. They feared a strong, nonelected military leader could overthrow the government.*) **OL**

Additional Support

What It Means

The Cabinet Mention of "the principal officer in each of the executive departments" is the only suggestion of the president's cabinet to be found in the Constitution. The cabinet is an advisory body, and its power depends on the president. Section 2, Clause 1 also makes the president—a civilian—the head of the armed services. This established the principle of civilian control of the military.

What It Means

Presidential Powers An executive order is a command issued by a president to exercise a power which he or she has been given by the U.S. Constitution or by a federal statute. In times of emergency, presidents sometimes have used the executive order to override the Constitution and Congress. During the Civil War, President Lincoln suspended many fundamental rights, such as closing down newspapers that opposed his policies and imprisoning people who disagreed with him. Lincoln said that these actions were justified to preserve the Union.

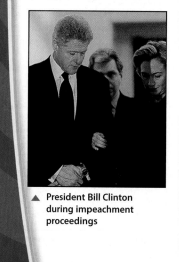

▲ **President Bill Clinton during impeachment proceedings**

[8.] Before he enter on the Execution of his Office, he shall take the following Oath or Affirmation:—"I do solemnly swear (or affirm) that I will faithfully execute the Office of President of the United States, and will to the best of my Ability, preserve, protect and defend the Constitution of the United States."

R Section 2

[1.] The President shall be Commander in Chief of the Army and Navy of the United States, and of the Militia of the several States, when called into the actual Service of the United States; he may require the Opinion, in writing, of the principal Officer in each of the executive Departments, upon any Subject relating to the Duties of their respective Offices, and he shall have Power to grant Reprieves and Pardons for Offences against the United States, except in Cases of Impeachment.

[2.] He shall have Power, by and with the Advice and Consent of the Senate, to make Treaties, provided two thirds of the Senators present concur; and he shall nominate, and by and with the Advice and Consent of the Senate, shall appoint Ambassadors, other public Ministers and Consuls, Judges of the supreme Court, and all other Officers of the United States, whose Appointments are not herein otherwise provided for, and which shall be established by Law: but the Congress may by Law vest the Appointment of such inferior Officers, as they think proper, in the President alone, in the Courts of Law, or in the Heads of Departments.

[3.] The President shall have Power to fill up all Vacancies that may happen during the Recess of the Senate, by granting Commissions which shall expire at the End of their next Session.

Section 3

He shall from time to time give to the Congress Information of the State of the Union, and recommend to their Consideration such Measures as he shall judge necessary and expedient; he may, on extraordinary Occasions, convene both Houses, or either of them, and in Case of Disagreement between them, with Respect to the Time of Adjournment, he may adjourn them to such Time as he shall think proper; he shall receive Ambassadors and other public Ministers; he shall take Care that the Laws be faithfully executed, and shall Commission all the Officers of the United States.

Did You Know?

Inauguration Traditions The President of the United States takes office on January 20th following the November elections, as stated in the Twentieth Amendment. Yet it has been tradition that has set the protocol for transfer of power. For example, George Washington placed his hand on the Bible during his oath, and the practice has been repeated by nearly every president.

Ceremonies typically occur in front of the U.S. Capitol building; however, if the ceremony falls on a Sunday, it is traditionally conducted in private and the public ceremony occurs the next day. Although not required by law, the President is usually sworn in by the Chief Justice of the Supreme Court. Previous presidents are not required to be present, and in the past, some have boycotted the inauguration.

Section 4

The President, Vice President and all civil Officers of the United States, shall be removed from Office on Impeachment for, and Conviction of, Treason, Bribery, or other high Crimes and Misdemeanors.

Article III
Section 1

The judicial Power of the United States, shall be vested in one supreme Court, and in such inferior Courts as the Congress may from time to time ordain and establish. The Judges, both of the supreme and inferior Courts, shall hold their Offices during good Behaviour, and shall, at stated Times, receive for their Services, a Compensation, which shall not be diminished during their Continuance in Office.

C

Section 2

[1.] The judicial Power shall extend to all Cases, in Law and Equity, arising under this Constitution, the Laws of the United States, and Treaties made, or which shall be made, under their Authority;—to all Cases affecting Ambassadors, other public Ministers and Consuls;—to all Cases of admiralty and maritime Jurisdiction;—to Controversies to which the United States shall be a Party;—to Controversies between two or more States;—between a State and Citizens of another State;—between Citizens of different States,—between Citizens of the same State claiming Lands under Grants of different States, and between a State, or the Citizens thereof, and foreign States, Citizens or Subjects.

R

[2.] In all Cases affecting Ambassadors, other public Ministers and Consuls, and those in which a State shall be Party, the supreme Court shall have original Jurisdiction. In all the other Cases before mentioned, the supreme Court shall have appellate Jurisdiction, both as to Law and Fact, with such Exceptions, and under such Regulations as the Congress shall make.

[3.] The Trial of all Crimes, except in Cases of Impeachment, shall be by Jury; and such Trial shall be held in the State where the said Crimes shall have been committed; but when not committed within any State, the Trial shall be at such Place or Places as the Congress may by Law have directed.

What It Means

Article III. The Judicial Branch The term *judicial* refers to courts. The Constitution set up only the Supreme Court, but provided for the establishment of other federal courts. The judiciary of the United States has two different systems of courts. One system consists of the federal courts, whose powers derive from the Constitution and federal laws. The other includes the courts of each of the 50 states, whose powers derive from state constitutions and laws.

What It Means

Statute Law Federal courts deal mostly with "statute law," or laws passed by Congress, treaties, and cases involving the Constitution itself.

What It Means

The Supreme Court A Court with "original jurisdiction" has the authority to be the first court to hear a case. The Supreme Court has "appellate jurisdiction" and mostly hears cases appealed from lower courts.

Vocabulary

original jurisdiction: authority to be the first court to hear a case

appellate jurisdiction: authority to hear cases that have been appealed from lower courts

---

C Critical Thinking

Defending **Say:** As long as judges are on good behavior, and they usually are, they can serve. This is interpreted as serving for life. Do you think Supreme Court justices should serve such long terms? How does this affect our laws? *(Answers will vary. Appointment of Supreme Court justices does not occur frequently. Thus, many of their decisions cannot be reversed. Students may consider this advantageous or detrimental.)* **OL**

R Reading Strategy

Activating Prior Knowledge **Ask:** What powers does the Supreme Court have over the executive branch? *(It can declare presidential actions unconstitutional.)* Over the legislative branch? *(It can declare acts of legislation unconstitutional.)* **OL**

Activity: Interdisciplinary Connection

History Until the late 1900s, all Supreme Court justices were white males. Lead a discussion on how this may have influenced Supreme Court decisions. Point out that the first African American justice was Thurgood Marshall, and the first woman was Sandra Day O'Connor.

Next, have students research the names of other minorities to serve in Congress. Charts should include dates and states.

Ask students to speculate why they think it took so long for Americans to support a minority or female presidential candidate. **OL**

W Writing Support

Descriptive Writing Have students write two or three examples in which all states have to honor the laws of other states. *(If a couple is divorced in New York, they are also considered divorced in Florida. If a person was convicted of robbing a bank in Texas, he is a still a criminal in Nevada.)* **OL**

Additional Support

What It Means

Article IV. Relations Among the States Article IV explains the relationship of the states to one another and to the national government. This article requires each state to give citizens of other states the same rights as its own citizens, addresses admitting new states, and guarantees that the national government will protect the states.

What It Means

New States Congress has the power to admit new states. It also determines the basic guidelines for applying for statehood. Two states, Maine and West Virginia, were created within the boundaries of another state. In the case of West Virginia, President Lincoln recognized the West Virginia government as the legal government of Virginia during the Civil War. This allowed West Virginia to secede from Virginia without obtaining approval from the Virginia legislature.

Vocabulary

treason: violation of the allegiance owed by a person to his or her own country, for example, by aiding an enemy

Section 3

[1.] Treason against the United States, shall consist only in levying War against them, or in adhering to their Enemies, giving them Aid and Comfort. No Person shall be convicted of Treason unless on the Testimony of two Witnesses to the same overt Act, or on Confession in open Court.

[2.] The Congress shall have Power to declare the Punishment of Treason, but no Attainder of Treason shall work Corruption of Blood, or Forfeiture except during the Life of the Person attainted.

Article IV

Section 1

Full Faith and Credit shall be given in each State to the public Acts, Records, and judicial Proceedings of every other State. And the Congress may by general Laws prescribe the Manner in which such Acts, Records and Proceedings shall be proved, and the Effect thereof.

Section 2

[1.] The Citizens of each State shall be entitled to all Privileges and Immunities of Citizens in the several States.

[2.] A Person charged in any State with Treason, Felony, or other Crime, who shall flee from Justice, and be found in another State, shall on Demand of the executive Authority of the State from which he fled, be delivered up, to be removed to the State having Jurisdiction of the Crime.

[3.] No Person held to Service of Labour in one State, under the Laws thereof, escaping into another, shall, in Consequence of any Law or Regulation therein, be discharged from such Service or Labour, but shall be delivered up on Claim of the Party to whom such Service or Labour may be due.

Section 3

[1.] New States may be admitted by the Congress into this Union; but no new State shall be formed or erected within the Jurisdiction of any other State; nor any State be formed by the Junction of two or more States, or Parts of States, without the Consent of the Legislatures of the States concerned as well as of the Congress.

[2.] The Congress shall have Power to dispose of and make all needful Rules and Regulations respecting the Territory or other Property belonging to the United States; and nothing in this Constitution shall be so construed as to Prejudice any Claims of the United States, or of any particular State.

Activity: Collaborative Learning

Geography Ask students to draw a current map of the United States and write the names of states and the dates in which they became states. In addition, have students locate, copy, or recreate maps of the 13 colonies, the Western Land Claims of 1754, Louisiana Purchase Territory, the Florida purchase, the Texas annexation, and the Oregon Territory. Have them discuss the importance of these acquisitions. Then, have students work in groups and create a States Quiz Game. Have groups challenge each other. **AL**

Section 4

The United States shall guarantee to every State in this Union a Republican Form of Government, and shall protect each of them against Invasion; and on Application of the Legislature, or of the Executive (when the Legislature cannot be convened) against domestic Violence.

Article V

The Congress, whenever two thirds of both Houses shall deem it necessary, shall propose Amendments to this Constitution, or, on the Application of the Legislatures of two thirds of the several States, shall call a Convention for proposing Amendments, which, in either Case, shall be valid to all Intents and Purposes, as Part of this Constitution, when ratified by the Legislatures of three fourths of the several States, or by Conventions in three fourths thereof, as the one or the other Mode of Ratification may be proposed by the Congress; Provided that no Amendment which may be made prior to the Year One thousand eight hundred and eight shall in any Manner affect the first and fourth Clauses in the Ninth Section of the first Article; and that no State, without its Consent, shall be deprived of its equal Suffrage in the Senate.

Article VI

[1.] All Debts contracted and Engagements entered into, before the Adoption of this Constitution, shall be as valid against the United States under this Constitution, as under the Confederation.

[2.] This Constitution, and the Laws of the United States which shall be made in Pursuance thereof; and all Treaties made, or which shall be made, under the Authority of the United States, shall be the supreme Law of the Land; and the Judges in every State shall be bound thereby, any Thing in the Constitution or Laws of any State to the Contrary notwithstanding.

[3.] The Senators and Representatives before mentioned, and the Members of the several State Legislatures, and all executive and judicial Officers, both of the United States and of the several States, shall be bound by Oath or Affirmation, to support this Constitution; but no religious Test shall ever be required as a Qualification to any Office or public Trust under the United States.

What It Means

Republic Government can be classified in many different ways. The ancient Greek Philosopher Aristotle classified government based on the question: Who governs? According to Aristotle, all governments belong to one of three major groups: (1) autocracy—rule by one person; (2) oligarchy—rule by a few persons; or (3) democracy—rule by many persons. A republic is a form of democracy in which the people elect representatives to make the laws and conduct government.

What It Means

Article V. The Amendment Process Article V spells out the ways that the Constitution can be amended, or changed. All of the 27 amendments were proposed by a two-thirds vote of both houses of Congress. Only the Twenty-first Amendment was ratified by constitutional conventions of the states. All other amendments have been ratified by state legislatures. *What is an amendment?*

What It Means

Article VI. National Supremacy Article VI contains the "supremacy clause." This clause establishes that the Constitution, laws passed by Congress, and treaties of the United States "shall be the supreme Law of the Land." The "supremacy clause" recognized the Constitution and federal laws as supreme when in conflict with those of the states.

Vocabulary

amendment: a change to the Constitution

ratification: process by which an amendment is approved

C Critical Thinking

Drawing Conclusions Point out that several states did not want to approve the Constitution because it lacked a bill of rights. All delegates agreed to add this later. **Ask:** How did the Framers know that the Constitution may need amendments? *(They could not foresee every problem that could arise in the future. They knew their work would need improvements, such as the slavery issue.)* **OL**

What It Means

Answer: a change to the Constitution

Activity: Interdisciplinary Connection

Art The first seven articles of the Constitution provide our country with a framework for our national government. Have students create a collage that illustrates the main ideas set forth in Articles I-VII of the Constitution. Students can clip pictures from magazines or make drawings to represent the articles. Ask students to explain their work to the class. **OL**

W Writing Support

Expository Writing Explain to students that this last Article guaranteed that the people of the United States, not just the delegates, approved the plan of government they outlined. Have students write a short essay addressing the following questions: How difficult would it be in present times to have the majority of states approve a plan of government? Do you think people today would accept the Articles set forth in the Constitution? Which Article would you not accept? **AL**

Additional Support

Article VII

The Ratification of the Conventions of nine States, shall be sufficient for the Establishment of this Constitution between the States so ratifying the Same.

W   Done in Convention by the Unanimous Consent of the States present the Seventeenth Day of September in the Year of our Lord one thousand seven hundred and Eighty seven and of the Independence of the United States of America the Twelfth. In witness whereof We have hereunto subscribed our Names,

Signers

George Washington, President and Deputy from Virginia

New Hampshire
John Langdon
Nicholas Gilman

Massachusetts
Nathaniel Gorham
Rufus King

Connecticut
William Samuel Johnson
Roger Sherman

New York
Alexander Hamilton

New Jersey
William Livingston
David Brearley
William Paterson
Jonathan Dayton

Pennsylvania
Benjamin Franklin
Thomas Mifflin
Robert Morris
George Clymer
Thomas FitzSimons
Jared Ingersoll
James Wilson
Gouverneur Morris

Delaware
George Read
Gunning Bedford, Jr.
John Dickinson
Richard Bassett
Jacob Broom

Maryland
James McHenry
Daniel of St. Thomas Jenifer
Daniel Carroll

Virginia
John Blair
James Madison, Jr.

North Carolina
William Blount
Richard Dobbs Spaight
Hugh Williamson

South Carolina
John Rutledge
Charles Cotesworth Pinckney
Charles Pinckney
Pierce Butler

Georgia
William Few
Abraham Baldwin

Attest: William Jackson, **Secretary**

◀ Re-creating colonial response to the signing at Independence Hall

Activity: Collaborative Learning

History and Language Arts Create a sign-up sheet that lists the signers of the Constitution. Have students each select one signer from the list. Students will write a short biographical report, providing details such as family life, education, personal experience, and so on. Make sure students include information related to the Constitutional Convention, such as why they were invited to the convention. Students should include any input their historical person had into the content of the Constitution. **OL**

Amendment I

Congress shall make no law respecting an establishment of religion, or prohibiting the free exercise thereof; or abridging the freedom of speech, or of the press; or the right of the people peaceably to assemble, and to petition the Government for a redress of grievances.

Amendment II

A well regulated Militia, being necessary to the security of a free State, the right of the people to keep and bear Arms, shall not be infringed.

Amendment III

No Soldier shall, in time of peace be quartered in any house, without the consent of the Owner, nor in time of war, but in a manner to be prescribed by law.

Amendment IV

The right of the people to be secure in their persons, houses, papers, and effects, against unreasonable searches and seizures, shall not be violated, and no Warrants shall issue, but upon probable cause, supported by Oath or affirmation, and particularly describing the place, to be searched, and the persons or things to be seized.

Amendment V

No person shall be held to answer for a capital, or otherwise infamous crime, unless on a presentment or indictment of a Grand Jury, except in cases arising in the land or naval forces, or in the Militia, when in actual service in time of War or public danger; nor shall any person be subject for the same offence to be twice put in jeopardy of life or limb; nor shall be compelled in any criminal case to be a witness against himself, nor be deprived of life, liberty, or property, without due process of law; nor shall private property be taken for public use without just compensation.

What It Means

The Amendments This part of the Constitution consists of amendments, or changes. The Constitution has been amended 27 times throughout the nation's history.

What It Means

Bill of Rights The first 10 amendments are known as the Bill of Rights (1791). These amendments limit the powers of government. The First Amendment protects the civil liberties of individuals in the United States. The amendment freedoms are not absolute, however. They are limited by the rights of other individuals. *What freedoms does the First Amendment protect?*

What It Means

Rights of the Accused This amendment contains important protections for people accused of crimes. One of the protections is that government may not deprive any person of life, liberty, or property without due process of law. This means that the government must follow proper constitutional procedures in trials and in other actions it takes against individuals. *According to Amendment V, what is the function of a grand jury?*

Vocabulary

quarter: to provide living accommodations

warrant: document that gives police particular rights or powers

probable cause: police must have a reasonable basis to believe a person is linked to a crime

The Constitution of the United States

C Critical Thinking

Analyzing Information Read several newspaper articles or headlines to the class that presently address freedoms guaranteed in the Bill of Rights. Discuss how the Constitution protects people. Ask students to start collecting articles and watching newscasts that deal with the first 10 amendments. Encourage students to discuss the particulars of the situation and whether they feel the people are being protected by the Bill of Rights. **OL**

What It Means

Answer: freedom of religion, freedom of speech, freedom to peaceably assemble, and freedom to petition the government for a redress of grievances

What It Means

Answer:
"Presentment" or "indictment" means to formally charge a person with committing a crime. The grand jury evaluates whether there is enough evidence to bring an accused person to trial.

Differentiated Instruction

Putting the Constitution to Work/The Bill of Rights

The Living Constitution, Review 3, pp. 47–48

Objective:	To understand our rights as protected in the Constitution
Focus:	Have students read the Bill of Rights
Teach:	Discuss why the Constitution was drafted and the history behind the Bill of Rights.
Assess:	Develop a quiz show about the Bill of Rights. Teams can help create questions and answers.
Close:	Create a poster illustrating the Bill of Rights

Differentiated Instruction Strategies

BL List two rights listed in the First Amendment that affect you on a daily basis.

AL Select one of the first ten amendments and research historic Supreme Court rulings.

ELL Choose five words that represent freedom and illustrate their definitions.

Teach

D Differentiated Instruction

Intrapersonal Some groups have tried to challenge the Bill of Rights. For example, some special interests groups have tried to restrict the purchase of handguns; some lawyers have complained that too much media coverage has stripped the rights of their clients. Have students search the Web and find examples of people or groups who want to weaken the Bill of Rights. Have students present their findings to the class and discuss their views on the topic. **OL**

R Reading Strategy

Identifying Ask: Why did the Framers want to include Amendment IX? *(They worried that some people would use the bill of rights to limit freedoms. This amendment makes sure that rights not specified in the Constitution are protected as well.)* **OL**

What It Means

Answer: A "speedy" trial ensures than an accused person will not be held in jail for a lengthy period as a means of punishing the accused without a trial.

Additional Support

What It Means

Rights to a Speedy, Fair Trial A basic protection is the right to a speedy, public trial. The jury must hear witnesses and evidence on both sides before deciding the guilt or innocence of a person charged with a crime. This amendment also provides that legal counsel must be provided to a defendant. In 1963, the Supreme Court ruled, in *Gideon v. Wainwright*, that if a defendant cannot afford a lawyer, the government must provide one to defend him or her. **Why is the right to a "speedy" trial important?** **D**

What It Means

Powers of the People This amendment prevents government from claiming that the only rights people have are those listed in the Bill of Rights.

What It Means

Powers of the States The final amendment of the Bill of Rights protects the states and the people from an all-powerful federal government. It establishes that powers not given to the national government—or denied to the states—by the Constitution belong to the states or to the people.

What It Means

Suits Against States The Eleventh Amendment (1795) limits the jurisdiction of the federal courts. The Supreme Court had ruled that a federal court could try a lawsuit brought by citizens of South Carolina against a citizen of Georgia. This case, *Chisholm v. Georgia*, decided in 1793, raised a storm of protest, leading to passage of the Eleventh Amendment.

Amendment VI

In all criminal prosecutions, the accused shall enjoy the right to a speedy and public trial, by an impartial jury of the State and district wherein the crime shall have been committed, which district shall have been previously ascertained by law, and to be informed of the nature and cause of the accusation; to be confronted with the witnesses against him; to have compulsory process for obtaining Witnesses in his favor, and to have the assistance of counsel for his defence.

Amendment VII

In Suits at common law, where the value in controversy shall exceed twenty dollars, the right of trial by jury shall be preserved, and no fact tried by a jury, shall be otherwise reexamined in any Court of the United States, than according to the rules of common law.

Amendment VIII

Excessive bail shall not be required, nor excessive fines imposed, nor cruel and unusual punishments inflicted.

Amendment IX

The enumeration in the Constitution, of certain rights, shall not be construed to deny or disparage others retained by the people.

Amendment X

The powers not delegated to the United States by the Constitution, nor prohibited by it to the States, are reserved to the States respectively, or to the people.

Amendment XI

The Judicial power of the United States shall not be construed to extend to any suit in law or equity, commenced or prosecuted against any one of the United States by Citizens of another State, or by Citizens or Subjects of any Foreign State.

Activity: Collaborative Learning

Identifying Central Issues Allow students to form small groups. Have groups create a set of four to five scenarios or situations that illustrate the freedoms or rights in the first 10 amendments. (You may want to assign particular amendments to each group.) Each group will read or reenact the scenario, and the class will decide to which amendment the situation applies. **OL**

Amendment XII

The electors shall meet in their respective states and vote by ballot for President and Vice-President, one of whom, at least, shall not be an inhabitant of the same state with themselves; they shall name in their ballots the person voted for as President, and in distinct ballots the person voted for as Vice-President, and they shall make distinct lists of all persons voted for as President, and of all persons voted for as Vice-President, and of the number of votes for each, which lists they shall sign and certify, and transmit sealed to the seat of the government of the United States, directed to the President of the Senate;—The President of the Senate shall, in the presence of the Senate and House of Representatives, open all the certificates and the votes shall then be counted;—The person having the greatest number of votes for President, shall be the President, if such number be a majority of the whole number of Electors appointed; and if no person have such majority, then from the persons having the highest numbers not exceeding three on the list of those voted for as President, the House of Representatives shall choose immediately, by ballot, the President. But in choosing the President, the votes shall be taken by states, the representation from each state having one vote; a quorum for this purpose shall consist of a member or members from two-thirds of the states, and a majority of all the states shall be necessary to a choice. And if the House of Representatives shall not choose a President whenever the right of choice shall devolve upon them, before the fourth day of March next following, then the Vice-President shall act as President, as in the case of the death or other constitutional disability of the President. The person having the greatest number of votes as Vice-President, shall be the Vice-President, if such number be a majority of the whole number of Electors appointed, and if no person have a majority, then from the two highest numbers on the list, the Senate shall choose the Vice-President; a quorum for the purpose shall consist of two-thirds of the whole number of Senators, and a majority of the whole number shall be necessary to a choice. But no person constitutionally ineligible to the office of President shall be eligible to that of Vice-President of the United States.

What It Means

Elections The Twelfth Amendment (1804) corrects a problem that had arisen in the method of electing the president and vice president. This amendment provides for the Electoral College to use separate ballots in voting for president and vice president. *If no candidate receives a majority of the electoral votes, who elects the president?*

C

Vocabulary

common law: law established by previous court decisions

bail: money that an accused person provides to the court as a guarantee that he or she will be present for a trial

majority: more than half

devolve: to pass on

C Critical Thinking

Defending Explain that the Electoral College was created as a compromise. Some delegates wanted the president to be elected by popular vote; others wanted Congress to elect the president. Have students discuss how they think the president should be elected. Write ideas on the board. Have the class vote on a method. The method must receive two-thirds vote of the class. **OL**

What It Means

Answer: the House of Representatives

Did You Know?

Too Close to Call? The 1888 presidential election was extremely close. The Democratic candidate, President Glover Cleveland, won the popular election by 95,713 votes, but he lost the Electoral College vote by 65 votes. As a result, Benjamin Harrison was elected as the 23rd president of the United States.

Today, a president must have the majority of electoral votes, 270, to be elected. In situations where no candidate has the majority of electoral votes, the House of Representatives decides. This has only happened twice. The House voted in Thomas Jefferson in 1801 and John Quincy Adams in 1825.

S **Skill Practice**

S **Skill Practice**

Recognizing Bias Discuss that the Fourteenth Amendment was written to protect the rights of freed slaves, which the government attempted to do in the Thirteenth Amendment. Begin a discussion about segregation in public schools, the civil rights movement, and the Fourteenth Amendment. Have students research these issues outside of class and prepare a report, poster, or poem that illustrates the slow struggle for freedom. **OL**

For additional practice on this skill (Recognizing Bias), see the **Skills Handbook**.

Additional Support

What It Means

Abolition of Slavery Amendments Thirteen (1865), Fourteen (1868), and Fifteen (1870) often are called the Civil War amendments because they grew out of that great conflict. The Thirteenth Amendment outlaws slavery.

What It Means

Rights of Citizens The Fourteenth Amendment (1868) originally was intended to protect the legal rights of the freed slaves. Today it protects the rights of citizenship in general by prohibiting a state from depriving any person of life, liberty, or property without "due process of law." In addition, it states that all citizens have the right to equal protection of the law in all states.

What It Means

Representation in Congress This section reduced the number of members a state had in the House of Representatives if it denied its citizens the right to vote. Later civil rights laws and the Twenty-fourth Amendment guaranteed the vote to African Americans.

Vocabulary

apportionment: distribution of seats in House based on population

abridge: to reduce

Amendment XIII

Section 1

Neither slavery nor involuntary servitude, except as a punishment for crime whereof the party shall have been duly convicted, shall exist within the United States, or any place subject to their jurisdiction.

Section 2

Congress shall have power to enforce this article by appropriate legislation.

Amendment XIV

Section 1

All persons born or naturalized in the United States, and subject to the jurisdiction thereof, are citizens of the United States and of the State wherein they reside. No State shall make or enforce any law which shall abridge the privileges or immunities of citizens of the United States; nor shall any State deprive any person of life, liberty, or property, without due process of law; nor deny to any person within its jurisdiction the equal protection of the laws.

S

Section 2

Representatives shall be apportioned among the several States according to their respective numbers, counting the whole number of persons in each State, excluding Indians not taxed. But when the right to vote at any election for the choice of electors for President and Vice President of the United States, Representatives in Congress, the Executive and Judicial officers of a State, or the members of the Legislature thereof, is denied to any of the male inhabitants of such State, being twenty-one years of age, and citizens of the United States, or in any way abridged, except for participation in rebellion, or other crime, the basis of representation therein shall be reduced in the proportion which the number of such male citizens shall bear to the whole number of male citizens twenty-one years of age in such State.

Section 3

No person shall be a Senator or Representative in Congress, or elector of President and Vice President, or hold any office, civil or military, under the United States, or under any State, who, having previously taken an oath, as a member of Congress, or as an officer of the United States, or as a member of any State legislature, or as an executive or judicial officer of any State, to support the Constitution

Activity: Technology Connection

Drawing Conclusions Have students use the Internet and use several government sources to find out how the Supreme Court interpreted Amendment XIV over the years, beginning with Gitlow case in 1925 (*Gitlow v. New York*). Have students research the following cases: *Near* v. *Minnesota, DeJonge* v. *Oregon, Wolf* v. *Colorado, Pointer* v. *Texas,* and *Benton* v. *Maryland.* Students will present their findings in a chart. **Ask:** Should all the protections and rights covered under the Bill of Rights apply to state governments as well as the national government? Do you think the framers of the Constitution wanted the states to grant all of the rights stated in the Bill of Rights? **AL**

of the United States, shall have engaged in insurrection or rebellion against the same, or given aid or comfort to the enemies thereof. But Congress may by a vote of two-thirds of each House, remove such disability.

Section 4

The validity of the public debt of the United States, authorized by law, including debts incurred for payment of pensions and bounties for service in suppressing insurrection or rebellion, shall not be questioned. But neither the United States nor any State shall assume or pay any debt or obligation incurred in aid of insurrection or rebellion against the United States, or any claim for the loss or emancipation of any slave; but all such debts, obligations and claims shall be held illegal and void.

Section 5

The Congress shall have power to enforce, by appropriate legislation, the provisions of this article.

Amendment XV

Section 1

The right of citizens of the United States to vote shall not be denied or abridged by the United States or by any State on account of race, color, or previous condition of servitude.

Section 2

The Congress shall have power to enforce this article by appropriate legislation.

Amendment XVI

The Congress shall have power to lay and collect taxes on incomes, from whatever source derived, without apportionment among the several States and without regard to any census or enumeration.

Amendment XVII

Section 1

The Senate of the United States shall be composed of two Senators from each State, elected by the people thereof, for six years; and each Senator shall have one vote. The electors in each State shall have the qualifications requisite for electors of the most numerous branch of the State legislatures.

What It Means

Public Debt The public debt acquired by the federal government during the Civil War was valid and could not be questioned by the South. However, the debts of the Confederacy were declared to be illegal. *Could former slaveholders collect payment for the loss of their slaves?*

What It Means

Right to Vote The Fifteenth Amendment (1870) prohibits the government from denying a person's right to vote on the basis of race. Despite the law, many states denied African Americans the right to vote by such means as poll taxes, literacy tests, and white primaries. During the 1950s and 1960s, Congress passed successively stronger laws to end racial discrimination in voting rights.

What It Means

Election of Senators The Seventeenth Amendment (1913) states that the people, instead of state legislatures, elect United States senators. *How many years are in a Senate term?*

Vocabulary

insurrection: rebellion against the government

emancipation: freedom from slavery

D Differentiated Instruction

Gifted and Talented Have students investigate *Pollock* v. *Farmers' Loan and Trust Company* (1895). Students should then discuss the case with the class and explain how Amendment Sixteen changes Article 1, Section 8, Clause 1 and Article 1, Section 9, Clause 4. **AL**

What It Means

Answer: Former slaveholders could not collect compensation for the loss of their slaves.

What It Means

Answer: six years

Activity: Economics Connection

Making Decisions Explain to students that as population increases, so does government spending and so do taxes. Have students create a line graph. One line will show how the average income of Americans has increased since 1915. A second line will indicate tax increases. Ask students to show their charts to family members or friends and note personal reactions. Have students share responses with the class. **Ask:** Do you agree that income tax is necessary? Should everyone pay the same rate or should it be a progressive tax (rates rise with income), as it is now? **AL**

C1 Critical Thinking

Drawing Conclusions Have students discuss what they know about the Prohibition. Encourage them to voice their opinions about the government banning alcoholic beverages. Write pros and cons on the board. **Ask:** Why do you think the Eighteenth Amendment was difficult to enforce? *(Answers will vary. Students will say that based on what they know or have seen in the media, powerful people, including government officials, made huge profits selling illegal liquor.)* **OL**

C2 Critical Thinking

Making Generalizations Point out that when the Nineteenth Amendment was ratified, some women chose not to exercise this right. **Ask:** Why do you think women chose not to participate in elections? *(Answers will vary. Some may say that they felt intimidated; family members discouraged them from voting.)* **OL**

Additional Support

▲ Dumping illegal liquor

What It Means

Prohibition The Eighteenth Amendment (1919) prohibited the production, sale, or transportation of alcoholic beverages in the United States. Prohibition proved to be difficult to enforce. This amendment was later repealed by the Twenty-first Amendment.

What It Means

Woman Suffrage The Nineteenth Amendment (1920) guaranteed women the right to vote. By then women had already won the right to vote in many state elections, but the amendment put their right to vote in all state and national elections on a constitutional basis.

Section 2

When vacancies happen in the representation of any State in the Senate, the executive authority of such State shall issue writs of election to fill such vacancies: *Provided,* That the legislature of any State may empower the executive thereof to make temporary appointments until the people fill the vacancies by election as the legislature may direct.

Section 3

This amendment shall not be so construed as to affect the election or term of any Senator chosen before it becomes valid as part of the Constitution.

▶ Amendment XVIII

Section 1

After one year from ratification of this article, the manufacture, sale, or transportation of intoxicating liquors within, the importation thereof into, or the exportation thereof from the United States and all territory subject to the jurisdiction thereof for beverage purposes is hereby prohibited.

C1 Section 2

The Congress and the several States shall have concurrent power to enforce this article by appropriate legislation.

Section 3

This article shall be inoperative unless it shall have been ratified as an amendment to the Constitution by the legislatures of the several States, as provided in the Constitution, within seven years from the date of the submission hereof to the States by the Congress.

▶ Amendment XIX

Section 1

The right of citizens of the United States to vote shall not be denied or abridged by the United States or by any State on **C2** account of sex.

Section 2

Congress shall have power by appropriate legislation to enforce the provisions of this article.

Activity: Collaborative Learning

Auditory/Musical Have students work in groups of at least four—two reporters, an interviewer, an interviewee. Each group will create a newscast, depicting public reaction to the Nineteenth Amendment. Remind students the amendment was ratified in 1920. Students may be creative and dress for the period. They may either present their newscast live in front of the class or record it. **OL**

Amendment XX

Section 1

The terms of the President and Vice President shall end at noon on the 20th day of January, and the terms of the Senators and Representatives at noon on the 3d day of January, of the years in which such terms would have ended if this article had not been ratified; and the terms of their successors shall then begin.

Section 2

The Congress shall assemble at least once in every year, and such meeting shall begin at noon on the 3d day of January, unless they shall by law appoint a different day.

Section 3

If, at the time fixed for the beginning of the term of the President, the President elect shall have died, the Vice President elect shall become President. If a President shall not have been chosen before the time fixed for the beginning of his term, or if the President elect shall have failed to qualify, then the Vice President elect shall act as President until a President shall have qualified; and the Congress may by law provide for the case wherein neither a President elect nor a Vice President elect shall have qualified, declaring who shall then act as President, or the manner in which one who is to act shall be selected, and such person shall act accordingly until a President or Vice President shall have qualified.

Section 4

The Congress may by law provide for the case of the death of any of the persons from whom the House of Representatives may choose a President whenever the right of choice shall have devolved upon them, and for the case of the death of any of the persons from whom the Senate may choose a Vice President whenever the right of choice shall have devolved upon them.

Section 5

Section 1 and 2 shall take effect on the 15th day of October following the ratification of this article.

D

What It Means

"Lame-Duck" Amendments The Twentieth Amendment (1933) sets new dates for Congress to begin its term and for the inauguration of the president and vice president. Under the original Constitution, elected officials who retired or who had been defeated remained in office for several months. For the outgoing president, this period ran from November until March. Such outgoing officials had little influence and accomplished little, and they were called lame ducks because they were so inactive. *What date was fixed as Inauguration Day?*

What It Means

Succession This section provides that if the president-elect dies before taking office, the vice president-elect becomes president.

Vocabulary

president elect: individual who is elected president but has not yet begun serving his or her term

The Constitution of the United States

D Differentiated Instruction

English Learners Idiomatic phrases, such as "lame duck," are often difficult to translate. Point out that "lame" is an adjective meaning *weak* or *powerless*. A lame duck is a wild bird that has been wounded by a hunter and cannot travel with the other wild birds. An elected official is called a lame duck when someone else has been elected to replace him or her, and the official will soon leave office. The expression was originally used to refer to bankrupted business investors who could not meet their financial obligations. **Ask:** How did the Twentieth Amendment address the problem of "lame ducks?" *(It shortened the waiting period between election day and the beginning of the new term.)* **ELL** **BL**

What It Means

Answer: January 20

Activity: Interdisciplinary Connection

Art and History Have groups find current or historical political cartoons that address lame duck sessions or presidents. Have each group make a scrapbook of cartoons and share the final product with the class. Students should discuss the meaning of the cartoon. Encourage students to create their own political cartoons to add to their books. **OL**

C₁ Critical Thinking

Debating Have students discuss the reasons behind the Prohibition and whether the Eighteenth Amendment should have been added to the Constitution in first place. Remind students how difficult it is to amend the Constitution. Invite students to discuss what control the government should have over personal habits, such as consuming alcohol or eating fatty foods. **Ask:** Do people need the national government to protect them from bad habits? **OL**

C₂ Critical Thinking

Identifying Central Issues Section 2 of the Twenty-first Amendment allowed states to continue their ban on alcohol, if they so desired. Presently, some states have strict laws on the sale of alcohol. Have students research to find out which states are more restrictive. **OL**

R Reading Strategy

Inferring Ask: What does the Twenty-second Amendment say about our view of the President? *(It says that the people do not want to give long-term power to one individual.)* **OL**

Additional Support

What It Means

Repeal of Prohibition The Twenty-first Amendment (1933) repeals the Eighteenth Amendment. It is the only amendment ever passed to overturn an earlier amendment. It is also the only amendment ratified by special state conventions instead of state legislatures.

What It Means

Term Limit The Twenty-second Amendment (1951) limits presidents to a maximum of two elected terms. It was passed largely as a reaction to Franklin D. Roosevelt's election to four terms between 1933 and 1945.

Section 6

This article shall be inoperative unless it shall have been ratified as an amendment to the Constitution by the legislatures of three-fourths of the several States within seven years from the date of its submission.

Amendment XXI

Section 1

C₁ The eighteenth article of amendment to the Constitution of the United States is hereby repealed.

Section 2

C₂ The transportation or importation into any State, Territory, or possession of the United States for delivery or use therein of intoxicating liquors, in violation of the laws thereof, is hereby prohibited.

Section 3

This article shall be inoperative unless it shall have been ratified as an amendment to the Constitution by conventions in the several States, as provided in the Constitution, within seven years from the date of the submission hereof to the States by the Congress.

Amendment XXII

Section 1

No person shall be elected to the office of the President more than twice, and no person who had held the office of President, or acted as President, for more than two years of a term to which some other person was elected President shall be elected to the office of the President more than once. But this Article shall not apply to any person holding the office of President when this Article was proposed by the Congress, and shall not prevent any person who may **R** be holding the office of President, or acting as President, during the term within which this Article becomes operative from holding the office of President or acting as President during the remainder of such term.

Section 2

This article shall be inoperative unless it shall have been ratified as an amendment to the Constitution by the legislatures of three-fourths of the several States within seven years from the date of its submission to the States by the Congress.

Activity: Collaborative Learning

Monitoring Organize the class into small groups. Have groups review all of the amendments and create a 20-item True/False Quiz. Have students prepare the tests with an answer key for your approval. Then have groups exchange quizzes. Decide as a class what the reward will be for achieving the highest score. **OL**

Amendment XXIII

Section 1

The District constituting the seat of Government of the United States shall appoint in such manner as the Congress may direct:

A number of electors of President and Vice President equal to the whole number of Senators and Representatives in Congress to which the District would be entitled if it were a State, but in no event more than the least populous State; they shall be in addition to those appointed by the States, but they shall be considered, for the purposes of the election of President and Vice President, to be electors appointed by a State; and they shall meet in the District and perform such duties as provided by the twelfth article of amendment.

Section 2

The Congress shall have power to enforce this article by appropriate legislation.

Amendment XXIV

Section 1

The right of citizens of the United States to vote in any primary or other election for President or Vice President, for electors for President or Vice President, or for Senator or Representative in Congress, shall not be denied or abridged by the United States or any State by reason of failure to pay any poll tax or other tax.

Section 2

The Congress shall have power to enforce this article by appropriate legislation.

Amendment XXV

Section 1

In case of the removal of the President from office or his death or resignation, the Vice President shall become President.

Section 2

Whenever there is a vacancy in the office of the Vice President, the President shall nominate a Vice President who shall take the office upon confirmation by a majority vote of both Houses of Congress.

What It Means

Electors for the District of Columbia The Twenty-third Amendment (1961) allows citizens living in Washington, D.C., to vote for president and vice president, a right previously denied residents of the nation's capital. The District of Columbia now has three presidential electors, the number to which it would be entitled if it were a state.

What It Means

Abolition of Poll Tax The Twenty-fourth Amendment (1964) prohibits poll taxes in federal elections. Prior to the passage of this amendment, some states had used such taxes to keep low-income African Americans from voting. In 1966 the Supreme Court banned poll taxes in state elections as well.

What It Means

The Vice President The Twenty-fifth Amendment (1967) established a process for the vice president to take over leadership of the nation when a president is disabled. It also set procedures for filling a vacancy in the office of vice president.

This amendment was used in 1973, when Vice President Spiro Agnew resigned from office after being charged with accepting bribes. President Richard Nixon then appointed Gerald R. Ford as vice president in accordance with the provisions of the Twenty-fifth Amendment. A year later, President Nixon resigned during the Watergate scandal and Ford became president. President Ford then had to fill the vice presidency, which he had left vacant upon assuming the presidency. He named Nelson A. Rockefeller as vice president. Thus individuals who had not been elected held both the presidency and the vice presidency. *Whom does the president inform if he or she cannot carry out the duties of the office?*

R Reading Strategy

Calculating Ask: How many years after the Fifteenth Amendment was ratified did it take to ensure that African Americans would not lose their voting rights due to an inability to pay poll taxes? *(94 years)* **BL**

What It Means

Answer: the President pro tempore of the Senate and the Speaker of the House of Representatives

Activity: Interdisciplinary Connection

Language Arts Imagine you are a resident of Washington D.C. You have only recently been allowed to vote in Presidential Elections (1963). Yet, presently, you do not have representation in Congress. No one represents the District of Columbia in the House or in the Senate. Write a letter to the Supreme Court or to the president, urging them to support you in your fight to win representation in Congress. **OL**

▲ Lyndon B. Johnson is sworn into office after the assassination of President John F. Kennedy.

What It Means

Voting Age The Twenty-sixth Amendment (1971) lowered the voting age in both federal and state elections to 18.

Section 3

Whenever the President transmits to the President pro tempore of the Senate and the Speaker of the House of Representatives his written declaration that he is unable to discharge the powers and duties of his office, and until he transmits to them a written declaration to the contrary, such powers and duties shall be discharged by the Vice President as Acting President.

Section 4

Whenever the Vice President and a majority of either the principal officers of the executive departments or of such other body as Congress may by law provide, transmit to the President pro tempore of the Senate and the Speaker of the House of Representatives their written declaration that the President is unable to discharge the powers and duties of his office, the Vice President shall immediately assume the power and duties of the office of Acting President.

R Thereafter, when the President transmits to the President pro tempore of the Senate and the Speaker of the House of Representatives his written declaration that no inability exists, he shall resume the powers and duties of his office unless the Vice President and a majority of either the principal officers of the executive department or of such other body as Congress may by law provide, transmit within four days to the President pro tempore of the Senate and the Speaker of the House of Representatives their written declaration that the President is unable to discharge the powers and duties of his office. Thereupon Congress shall decide the issue, assembling within forty-eight hours for that purpose if not in session. If the Congress, within twenty-one days after receipt of the latter written declaration, or, if Congress is not in session, within twenty-one days after Congress is required to assemble, determines by two-thirds vote of both Houses that the President is unable to discharge the powers and duties of his office, the Vice President shall continue to discharge the same as Acting President; otherwise, the President shall resume the power and duties of his office.

►Amendment XXVI

Section 1

C The right of citizens of the United States, who are eighteen years of age or older, to vote shall not be denied or abridged by the United States or by any State on account of age.

Activity: U.S./World Connections

Assessing On a few occasions, the President of the United States has died, been assassinated, or been disabled. Have students research the times in which the Vice President of the United States has had to assume power. **Ask: How did the people in the United States react? How did the world react?** Have students write a one page report answering the questions. **AL**

Section 2

The Congress shall have power to enforce this article by appropriate legislation.

Amendment XXVII

No law, varying the compensation for the services of Senators and Representatives, shall take effect, until an election of representatives shall have intervened.

▼ Joint meeting of Congress

What It Means

Congressional Pay Raises The Twenty-seventh Amendment (1992) makes congressional pay raises effective during the term following their passage. James Madison offered the amendment in 1789, but it was never adopted. In 1982 Gregory Watson, then a student at the University of Texas, discovered the forgotten amendment while doing research for a school paper. Watson made the amendment's passage his crusade.

W

W **Writing Support**

Expository Writing **Ask:** Why is the Twenty-seventh Amendment important? *(because members of Congress have to get reelected to receive raises)* **OL**

Activity: Collaborative Learning

Making Decisions Have students work with a partner. Students will review the amendments and discuss their meanings. Have students create a T-chart. One column will include a list of amendments they think should be repealed. Students should state the reasons why they think the amendments should be repealed. The second column will include a list of rights they think should be added as amendments with the reason why. Finally, have students write a statement that explains why people still challenge the Constitution in present times. Share evaluations with the class. **OL**

Chapter Planning Guide

4

Levels (BL OL AL ELL)					Resources	Chapter Opener	Section 1	Section 2	Section 3	Section 4	Chapter Assess
FOCUS											
BL	OL	AL	ELL	🖨	**Daily Focus Skills Transparencies**		4–1	4–2	4–3	4–4	
TEACH											
BL	OL		ELL	📁	**Reading Essentials and Note-Taking Guide***		p. 34	p. 37	p. 40	p. 43	
BL	OL	AL	ELL	📁	**Content Vocabulary Activity, URB***		p. 95	p. 95	p. 95	p. 95	
BL	OL	AL	ELL	📁	**Academic Vocabulary Activity, URB**		p. 97	p. 97	p. 97	p. 97	
	OL			📁	**Biography Activity, URB**					p. 99	
BL	OL	AL	ELL	📁	**Writing Skills Activity, URB**					p. 101	
	OL	AL		📁	**Critical Thinking Skills Activity, URB**		p. 103				
BL	OL	AL	ELL	📁	**Chart, Graph, and Map Skills Activity, URB**		p. 105				
BL	OL	AL	ELL	📁	**Differentiated Instruction, URB**		p. 107	p. 107	p. 107	p. 107	
BL	OL	AL	ELL	📁	**School-to-Home Connection Activity, URB***		p. 109	p. 109	p. 109	p. 109	
BL	OL		ELL	📁	**Guided Reading Activities, URB***		p. 113	p. 114	p. 115	p. 116	
	OL	AL		📁	**Supreme Court Cases**			pp. 105, 129, 131	p. 39	pp. 11, 73	
BL	OL			📁	**Focus on American History**		p. 49	p. 49	p. 49		
BL	OL	AL	ELL	📁	**Writer's Guidebook**	✓	✓	✓	✓	✓	✓
	OL	AL		💿	**Primary Source Document Library**	✓	✓	✓	✓	✓	✓
BL	OL	AL	ELL	💿	**Daily Lecture & Discussion Notes (in Pres. Plus)**		✓	✓	✓	✓	✓
BL	OL	AL	ELL	💿	**StudentWorks™ Plus**		✓	✓	✓	✓	✓
BL	OL	AL	ELL	💿	**Section Spotlight Videos**		✓	✓	✓	✓	
BL	OL	AL	ELL	🖨	**TIME Interpreting Political Cartoons Transp.**					Ch. 4	
BL	OL	AL	ELL	🖨	**Writing Process Transparencies**	✓	✓	✓	✓	✓	✓

Note: Please refer to the *Unit 1 Resource Book* for this chapter's URB materials.

* Also available in Spanish

Teacher**Works** *Plus*
All-In-One Planner and Resource Center

- Interactive Lesson Planner
- Interactive Teacher Edition
- Fully editable blackline masters
- Section Spotlight Videos Launch
- Differentiated Lesson Plans
- Printable reports of daily assignments
- Standards Tracking System

Levels					Resources	Chapter Opener	Section 1	Section 2	Section 3	Section 4	Chapter Assess
BL	OL	AL	ELL								
					TEACH (continued)						
				📁	**Building Academic Vocabulary**	✓	✓	✓	✓	✓	✓
Teacher Resources				📁	**Strategies for Success**	✓	✓	✓	✓	✓	✓
				📁	**Teachers Guide to Differentiated Instruction**	✓	✓	✓	✓	✓	✓
				💿	**Graphing Tool**	✓	✓	✓	✓	✓	✓
				💿	**Presentation Plus! with MindJogger CheckPoint**	✓	✓	✓	✓	✓	✓
					ASSESS						
BL	OL	AL	ELL	📁	**Quizzes and Tests***		p. 38	p. 39	p. 40	p. 41	p. 42
BL	OL	AL	ELL	📁	**Authentic Assessment with Rubrics**			p. 8			
BL	OL	AL	ELL	📁	**Standardized Test Practice**		p. 7	p. 7	p. 7	p. 7	p. 7
BL	OL	AL	ELL	💿	*ExamView® Assessment Suite* **CD-ROM**		4–1	4–2	4–3	4–4	Ch. 4
					CLOSE						
BL			ELL	📁	**Reteaching Activity, URB***		p. 111	p. 111	p. 111	p. 111	
BL	OL		ELL	📁	**Reading and Study Skills Foldables™**	p. 56	p. 57			p. 57	
BL	OL	AL	ELL	🖱️	**Graphic Organizer Transparencies & Strategies**	✓	✓	✓	✓	✓	✓

✓ Chapter- or unit-based activities applicable to all sections in this chapter

4

Using Widgets

Technology Tools

What is a widget?
The Glencoe Social Studies widget is an application for your computer desktop that acts as a one-stop launching pad for both software- and online-based programs.

How can the widget help my students and me?
The widget is a convenient way for you and your students to access Glencoe's technology offerings. Some of the features of the widget include:

- customizable links to frequently used Glencoe Web pages
- pre-loaded software links that instantly recognize the Glencoe DVD- and CD-based programs installed
- QuickPass™ entry for fast access to chapter content and activities

Visit glencoe.com to download the free student and teacher versions of the Glencoe Social Studies widget.

Civics ONLINE
Visit glencoe.com and enter **QuickPass**™ code CIV1360c4T for Chapter 4 resources.

You can easily launch a wide range of digital products from your computer's desktop with the McGraw-Hill Social Studies widget.

	Student	Teacher	Parent
Media Library			
• Student Edition Section Audio	●		●
• Spanish Audio Summaries	●		●
• Section Spotlight Videos	●	●	●
***Civics Today* Online Learning Center (Web Site)**			
• Chapter Overviews	●	●	●
• Study Central™	●	●	●
• Study-to-Go	●	●	●
• Student Web Activities	●	●	●
• In Motion Animation	●	●	●
• Self-Check Quizzes	●	●	●
• ePuzzles and Games	●	●	●
• StudentWorks™ Plus Online	●	●	●
• Vocabulary eFlashcards	●	●	●
• Web Activity Lesson Plans		●	
• Vocabulary PuzzleMaker	●	●	●
Classroom Tools			
• Multilingual Glossary	●	●	●
• Beyond the Textbook	●	●	●
• NGS MapMachine	●	●	●

GLENCOE BookLink 3

Use this database to search more than 30,000 titles to create a customized reading list for your students.

- Reading lists can be organized by students' reading level, author, genre, theme, or area of interest.
- The database provides Degrees of Reading Power™ (DRP) and Lexile™ readability scores for all selections.
- A brief summary of each selection is included.

Leveled reading suggestions for this chapter:

For students at a Grade 7 reading level:
- *Dred and Harriet Scott: A Family's Struggle for Freedom,* by Gwenyth Swain

For students at a Grade 8 reading level:
- *Growing Up King: An Intimate Memoir,* by Dexter Scott King and Ralph Wiley

For students at a Grade 9 reading level:
- *Profiles in Courage,* by John F. Kennedy

For students at a Grade 10 reading level:
- *The Power of One: Daisy Bates and the Little Rock Nine,* by Judith Bloom Fradin

For students at a Grade 9 reading level:
- *To Establish Justice: Citizenship and the Constitution,* by Patricia McKissack

READING SUPPORT FROM JAMESTOWN EDUCATION

- **Timed Readings Plus in Social Studies** helps students increase their reading rate and fluency while maintaining comprehension. The 400-word passages are similar to those found on state and national assessments.

- **Reading in the Content Area: Social Studies** concentrates on six essential reading skills that help students better comprehend what they read. The book includes 75 high-interest nonfiction passages written at increasing levels of difficulty.

- **Reading Social Studies** includes strategic reading instruction and vocabulary support in Social Studies content for both ELLs and native speakers of English.

- **Content Vocabulary Workout** (Grades 6–8) accelerates reading comprehension through focused vocabulary development. Social Studies content vocabulary comes from the glossaries of Glencoe's Middle School Social Studies texts. www.jamestowneducation.com

KEY Teacher Wraparound

Use this key to help you identify the different types of prompts found in the Teacher Wraparound Edition.

R **Reading Strategies** activities help you teach reading skills and vocabulary.

C **Critical Thinking** strategies help students apply and extend what they have learned.

D **Differentiated Instruction** activities provide instruction for students learning to speak English, along with suggestions for teaching various types of learners.

S **Skill Practice** strategies help students practice historical analysis and geography skills.

W **Writing Support** activities provide writing opportunities to help students comprehend the text.

Teaching strategies and activities have been coded for ability level appropriateness.

AL Activities for students working above grade level

OL Activities for students working on grade level

BL Activities for students working below grade level

ELL Activities for English Language Learners

Focus

Why It Matters

Ask: Why is freedom of speech so important to being an American? *(Answers may include the idea that citizens who are free to share ideas often arrive at better decisions than those who are afraid to speak up.)*

More About the Photo

Visual Literacy Students see in this photograph a march of people demanding rights for immigrants to the United States. Throughout its history, the United States has been a destination for people seeking shelter from political oppression, wanting to practice their religions freely, or simply grabbing hold of the chance to start a new and better life. However, immigration is a topic of heated debate. Questions about how many immigrants should be allowed to come to the United States, under what conditions they may come, and the extent of access they should have to services in the United States has provoked discussion, argument, and protest around the nation.

Teach

BIG Ideas *As you begin teaching each section, use these questions and activities to help students focus on the Big Ideas.*

Section 1

The First Amendment Ask: What does it mean to live in a free country? *(It means you may live a life in which you are able to develop your own beliefs and to express yourself.)* Point out that in Section 1 students will learn about basic freedoms guaranteed to all Americans. **OL**

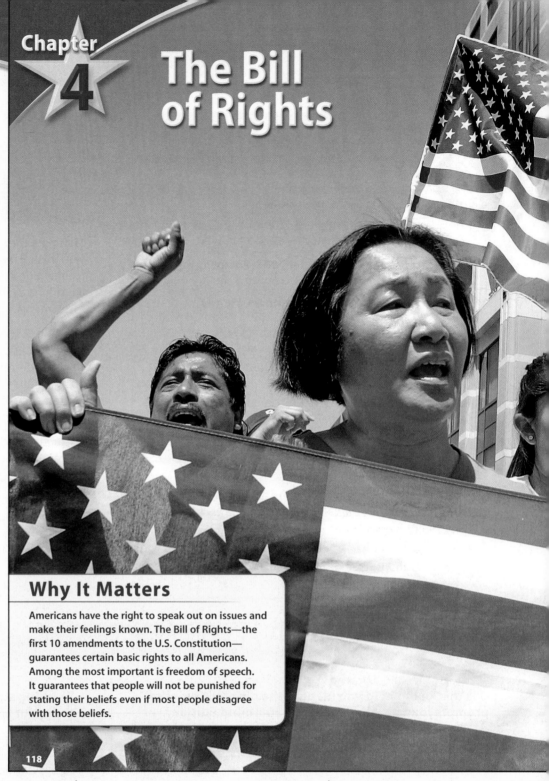

Chapter 4
The Bill of Rights

Why It Matters

Americans have the right to speak out on issues and make their feelings known. The Bill of Rights—the first 10 amendments to the U.S. Constitution—guarantees certain basic rights to all Americans. Among the most important is freedom of speech. It guarantees that people will not be punished for stating their beliefs even if most people disagree with those beliefs.

118

Section 2

The Bill of Rights Ask: What rights might citizens want other than to express themselves? *(Answers may include the idea that citizens want to feel safe in their homes and to be treated fairly if accused of a crime.)* Tell students that in Section 2 they will learn about amendments that guarantee fair legal treatment. **OL**

Section 3

Extending the Bill of Rights Ask: What additional rights might citizens want beyond freedom of expression and fair legal treatment? *(They want to be treated equally and to be able to vote and otherwise participate in the government.)* Explain that in Section 3 students will learn about amendments that guarantee voting rights to all. **OL**

Civics ONLINE
Visit glencoe.com and enter
QuickPass™ code
CIV3093c4 for
Chapter 4
resources.

Chapter Introduction
4

🔊 Chapter Audio

BIG Ideas

Section 1: The First Amendment

The Constitution of the United States establishes and protects fundamental rights and liberties. The First Amendment protects five basic freedoms that are essential to the American way of life.

Section 2: The Bill of Rights

The Constitution of the United States establishes and protects fundamental rights and liberties. The first 10 amendments to the Constitution describe the rights of American citizens.

Section 3: Extending the Bill of Rights

A constitution reflects the values and goals of the society that creates it. Some Americans have not always enjoyed the full rights of United States citizens.

Section 4: The Civil Rights Struggle

Political, social, religious, and economic changes influence the way Americans think and act. In the 1950s and 1960s, many African Americans began an organized fight for their rights as citizens.

◀ Rally for immigrant rights, Oakland, California

FOLDABLES Dinah Zike's
Study Organizer **Foldables**

Purpose This Foldable helps students organize the rights guaranteed by each amendment in the Bill of Rights. The completed Foldable will use tabs to help students match each amendment with the rights it guarantees. **OL**

📁 More Foldables activities for this chapter can be found in the *Dinah Zike's Reading and Study Skills Foldables* ancillary.

Civics ONLINE

Visit glencoe.com and enter *QuickPass*™ code CIV1360c4T for Chapter 4 resources, including a Chapter Overview, Study Central™, Study-to-Go, Student Web Activity, Self-Check Quiz, and other materials.

FOLDABLES™
Study Organizer

Organizing Information Study Foldable Make the following Foldable to help you organize information about the Bill of Rights.

Step 1 Fold a sheet of paper in half from side to side.

Step 2 Turn the paper and fold it in fifths.

Step 3 Unfold and cut the top layer only along both folds. Then cut each of the five tabs in half. This will make 10 tabs.

Step 4 Label your Foldable as shown.

1st Amendment
2nd Amendment
3rd Amendment
4th Amendment
5th Amendment
6th Amendment
7th Amendment
8th Amendment
9th Amendment
10th Amendment

Reading and Writing As you read, select key facts about each amendment to the Constitution and write them under the tabs of your Foldable.

Chapter 4   119

Section 4

The Civil Rights Struggle Ask: Why would the struggle for civil rights be included in a chapter than explains the Bill of Rights? *(Even though the Bill of Rights gave Americans the right to vote, it took many years and many court rulings before this right could be freely practiced by everyone.)* Explain that in Section 4 students will learn about the changes that had to occur in America before all citizens of age could vote. **OL**

Focus

Guide to Reading
Answers to Graphic:

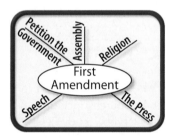

Petition the Government · Assembly · Religion · First Amendment · Speech · The Press

Section Spotlight Video

To generate student interest and provide a springboard for class discussion, access the Chapter 4, Section 1 video at glencoe.com or on the video DVD.

Resource Manager

Guide to Reading

Big Idea
The Constitution of the United States establishes and protects fundamental rights and liberties.

Content Vocabulary
- civil liberties *(p. 121)*
- censorship *(p. 122)*
- petition *(p. 123)*
- slander *(p. 124)*
- libel *(p. 124)*

Academic Vocabulary
- media *(p. 122)*
- imply *(p. 123)*

Reading Strategy
Identifying As you read, identify the main rights outlined in the First Amendment.

First Amendment

Section 1

The First Amendment

Real World Civics Today it is not unusual to see a minority or a woman delivering the news on national television. This was not always the case. Former CNN correspondent Maria Hinojosa led a panel discussion among important artists of color about this issue. Even though the Bill of Rights gives Americans the right to free speech, free press, and free expression, it did not ensure these opportunities would be given to all Americans. Hinojosa's career success, and that of other minorities, represented an acceptance of multicultural voices in mainstream media, music, and the arts that is relatively recent in American history.

▼ **Latina CNN correspondent, Maria Hinojosa, speaks on a panel about multicultural music in Washington, D.C.**

R Reading Strategies	**C** Critical Thinking	**D** Differentiated Instruction	**W** Writing Support	**S** Skill Practice
Teacher Edition • Making Connections, p. 121 • Indentifying, p. 122 **Additional Resources** • Foldables, URB p. 57 • Cont. Vocab.,URB p. 95 • Acad. Vocab., URB p. 97 • Guide Read., URB p. 113	**Teacher Edition** • Pred. Consequences, p. 122 • Making Generalizations, p. 123 **Additional Resources** • Critical Thinking, URB p. 103 • Quizzes and Tests, p. 38	**Teacher Edition** • Interpersonal, p. 123 **Additional Resources** • Diff. Instr., URB p. 107	**Teacher Edition** • Personal Writing, p. 121 • Persuasive Writing, p. 124	**Teacher Edition** • Analyzing Visuals, p. 123 **Additional Resources** • Chart, Map, and Graph Skills, URB p. 105 • Daily Focus Trans., 4–1

First Amendment Freedoms

Main Idea Soon after ratification of the Constitution, the First Amendment was added to guarantee basic freedoms essential to American democracy.

Civics & You As you learn about the First Amendment, think about how life in the United States might be different if we did not have these rights.

The Founders of the United States believed that protecting individual rights and providing for the safety and well-being of citizens were important purposes of government. The Constitution might not have been ratified had the Bill of Rights not been promised. Added in 1791, the 10 amendments in the Bill of Rights place strict limits on how the national government can use its power over the people.

Civil Liberties The Bill of Rights protects our **civil liberties**—the freedoms we have to think and to act without government interference or fear of unfair treatment. These civil liberties are the cornerstone of our democracy. They ensure that each of us can develop our own beliefs, express ourselves freely, meet openly with others, and have our views on public matters heard by those who govern.

The First Amendment to the Constitution protects five basic freedoms: freedom of religion, freedom of speech, freedom of the press, freedom of assembly, and freedom to petition the government.

Freedom of Religion

Intolerance of different beliefs in their homelands forced many colonists to come to America in the first place. The First **R** Amendment safeguards religious freedom in two ways. First, the amendment prohibits

Congress from establishing an official religion in the United States. This is known as the establishment clause. In 1802 President Thomas Jefferson referred to the First Amendment's establishment clause as a "wall of separation between church and state."

This makes the United States different from countries in which a state religion is established. It also makes us different from nations that have in the past strongly discouraged the practice of religion at all, such as the former Soviet Union and People's Republic of China. **W**

The First Amendment

Freedom of Assembly

THE FIRST AMENDMENT

Freedom of Speech

Freedom of Religion

DAILY NEWS

Freedom of the Press

Freedom to Petition the Government

Analyzing Charts

1. **Identifying** What rights are listed in the First Amendment?

2. **Explaining** What is meant by the "press" in this amendment?

Teach

R Reading Strategy

Making Connections Ask: What famous ship brought colonists seeking religious freedom to Massachusetts in the New World? (*The Mayflower brought Pilgrims to Plymouth in 1620.*) **OL**

This **Reading Skill** (Making Connections) was introduced in this unit.

W Writing Support

Personal Writing Have students write a paragraph they believe would convince other nations of the importance of religious freedom. They may include personal experiences, an anecdote, or an example. **OL**

Analyzing Graphs

Answers:
1. freedom of religion, speech, the press, and assembly, and the right to petition the government
2. The "press" includes all printed material and the media.

Differentiated Instruction

Distinguishing Fact from Opinion

Critical Thinking Skills Activity 4, URB pp. 103–104

Objective:	To identify statements of fact and opinion
Focus:	Have students read the content of the ruling.
Teach:	Ask students to paraphrase each section of the excerpt.
Assess:	Have students discuss the basis for Rehnquist's opinions in the ruling.
Close:	Write definitions for "fact" and "opinion" and review how to distinguish the two.

Differentiated Instruction Strategies

BL Have students discuss how a teacher's or coach's effectiveness would be affected by accusations of dishonesty.

AL Have students make an inference as to why this case was brought to court.

ELL Define legal terms such as "respondent" and "proceeding" before students read.

C Critical Thinking

Predicting Consequences Ask: Are there any times when free speech should be illegal? Explain your answer. *(Answers may include times when speech may cause danger for the country, start a riot, or cause violence. Answers may also include the idea that there are no situations in which free speech should be illegal.)* **AL**

R Reading Strategy

Identifying Ask: Why do you think the Bill of Rights refers to "the press" even though the amendment covers other kinds of media? *(At the time those documents were written, the only media available were created by a printing press. Today, the concept applies to all media, regardless of how they are created.)* **OL** **ELL**

Caption Answer:

Many of the people who braved the journey to the American colonies did so because they were not allowed to practice their religions in the nations from which they came. The Framers wanted to be sure this would not happen in their new nation.

Second, this amendment guarantees Americans the right to practice their faith as they wish. The government may not favor one religion over another or treat people differently because of their personal beliefs.

Freedom of Speech

In some countries, people can be jailed for criticizing the government or for expressing their ideas, even if they do so in private conversations. The First Amendment guarantees that we can say what is on our minds, in public or in private, without fear of punishment by the government.

Face-to-face discussions, telephone conversations, lectures, and radio and TV broadcasts are covered by the guarantee of free speech; so are other forms of expression besides the spoken word. As interpreted by the Supreme Court, "speech" can mean Internet communication, art, music, and even clothing.

Freedom of the Press

The First Amendment allows Americans to express themselves in print as well as in speech. When the Bill of Rights was written, "the press" referred to printed publications such as books, newspapers, and magazines. Today the press includes many other sources of **media,** such as radio, television, and computer networks.

Freedom of the press ensures that the American people are exposed to a wide variety of viewpoints. The government cannot practice **censorship;** that is, it cannot ban printed materials or films merely because they contain alarming or offensive ideas. It also cannot censor information before it is published or broadcast.

Buddhist New Year Buddhist monks in San Francisco's Chinatown celebrate the 2006 Chinese New Year by bringing families together, sharing food, and praying for good health and prosperity. A Sikh woman (inset) prays during a weekly religious ceremony. *Inferring* Why do you think the Framers included freedom of religion in the First Amendment?

122

Hands-On Chapter Project
Step 1

Bill of Rights for Our School

Step 1: Determining the Rights of Teachers, Students, and Other Workers in the School Groups of students will work together to determine a list of rights for each school group—teachers, students, and other workers (administrators, custodial staff, and so on) in order for the school to fulfill its mission.

Directions Write the Big Idea on the board. Point out the phrase "essential to the American way of life." Remind students that our rights make up a code of behavior in our country, our state, our community, and our schools. Sometimes these rights are unstated. Tell students that they will be making clear the rights of the people who spend their days in the school for all to read and follow.

Identifying Central Issues Assign small groups a segment of the school population. Each group should answer these questions: What does this school group need to get their jobs done? What does this group do to help others in the school succeed? Tell students that they will use this information in Section 2 to codify the rights of people at their schools. **OL**

(Project continued in Section 2)

The Zenger Case In 1733, publisher John Peter Zenger, in his paper the *New-York Weekly Journal*, was arrested and imprisoned for criticizing the governor of New York. Andrew Hamilton, Zenger's lawyer, argued that only a press free to criticize the government could prevent that government from abusing its power. Zenger was acquitted. At the time, the case attracted little attention, but today it is regarded as a landmark in the development of free press in America.

After the American Revolution, several states provided for the freedom of the press in their state constitutions. Later, the First Amendment of the U.S. Constitution provided for a free press in American society as a whole. The mass media—newspapers, magazines, television, radio, and the Internet—however, are not totally free of government regulation.

Many reasonable restrictions can be placed on rights of the media. For example, no person has the right to use printed words to injure another person's character or reputation. Supreme Court rulings allowed the press to be limited when the printed materials might threaten national security. Laws also prohibit the printing and distribution of obscene materials.

Freedom of Assembly

The First Amendment protects our right to gather in groups for any reason, so long as the assemblies are peaceful. We have the right to attend meetings, parades, political rallies, and public celebrations. Governments may make rules about when and where such activities can be held, but they cannot ban them.

The Supreme Court has decided that freedom of assembly **implies,** or suggests, freedom of association. Thus the First Amendment also protects our right to form and join social clubs, political parties, labor unions, and other organizations. Even if we never assemble with fellow members, we have the right to belong to such groups.

A POPULAR TRIUMPH CELEBRATED.

Freedom of the Press Supporters celebrate John Peter Zenger's acquittal. ***Explaining*** Why is the Zenger case significant?

Freedom to Petition

Finally, the First Amendment guarantees all Americans the right to petition the government. A **petition** is simply a formal request. Often we use the word to refer to a specific kind of document—a brief, or written statement signed by hundreds or thousands of people. Even a simple letter or e-mail written by an individual, however, could be considered a petition.

The right to petition means the right to express one's ideas to the government. If you want to complain about overcrowded schools, for example, or suggest that a skating park be built in your community, you can write to your elected representatives. If enough people express similar views, government leaders may take action.

Reading Check Summarizing What is meant by a "petition" in freedom to petition?

Chapter 4 123

W Writing Support

Persuasive Writing Have students write several paragraphs in response to the following question: In your opinion, when, if ever, is it appropriate for the government to limit First Amendment freedoms? **AL**

✔ Reading Check **Answer:** First Amendment freedoms are limited because some people may abuse their rights.

Assess

Civics ONLINE

Study Central™ provides summaries, interactive games, and online graphic organizers to help students review content.

Close

Personal Journal Have students write about their appreciation of the freedoms they enjoy because of the First Amendment. **OL**

Section ★ 1 Review

First Amendment Limits

Main Idea All constitutional rights are limited. These limitations are necessary to ensure our other rights are protected.

Civics & You The First Amendment protects free speech, but does it protect speech that damages a person's character or reputation? Read to find out what limits are placed on our First Amendment W freedoms.

The First Amendment guarantees Americans the right to express their thoughts and opinions. However, this is not an absolute freedom. Freedom of speech, for example, does not include the right to endanger our government or other Americans. You do not have freedom to provoke a riot. You are not free to speak or write in a way that immediately leads to criminal activities or efforts to overthrow the government by force.

Citizens should use their civil liberties responsibly, which means they should not interfere with the rights of others. For example, you are free to talk with your friends in the street, but you must not block traffic. You may campaign for causes, but you may not disturb your neighbors with blaring loudspeaker broadcasts. You may criticize government officials, but you may not spread lies that harm a person's reputation. Spreading W spoken lies is a crime called **slander.** It is called **libel** if lies are printed.

The First Amendment was never intended to allow Americans to do whatever they please. The rights of one individual must be balanced against the rights of others and against the rights of the community. When there is a conflict, the rights of the community often come first. Otherwise, the society would break apart.

✔ Reading Check **Explaining** Why are your First Amendment rights limited?

Section 1 Review

Vocabulary

1. **Define** the following terms and use them in sentences related to the First Amendment: *civil liberties, censorship, petition, slander, libel.*

Main Ideas

2. **Analyzing** Why was the First Amendment added to the Constitution immediately?

3. **Explaining** What is the difference between libel and slander?

Critical Thinking

4. **BIG Ideas** Which First Amendment right do you think is the most important? Explain your view.

5. **Classifying** In a chart like the one below, list two limitations to our First Amendment freedoms.

Limitations to First Amendment Freedoms
1.
2.

6. **Analyzing** Why do you think the right to petition is considered an important basic freedom?

CITIZENSHIP Activity

7. **Persuasive Writing** How do you think the First Amendment's freedom of the press protections should be applied during wartime? Do you think that the government should be allowed to censor press coverage or that the press should be allowed to report on what it sees? Write an essay expressing your view. Give reasons to support your answers.

Civics ONLINE

Study Central™ To review this section, go to glencoe.com.

Answers

1. Sentences should use vocabulary words according to their definitions in the section and in the Glossary.

2. Many people, including some of the Founders of the new nation, felt that the Constitution did not go far enough to protect the rights of individuals. Before they would approve the Constitution, they insisted that a Bill of Rights follow as soon as possible.

3. Slander occurs when spoken lies are spread about a person. Libel occurs when the lies are printed or published.

4. Answers may include any First Amendment right as long as the student provides a reasonable explanation of why it is the most important right.

5. Answers may include the limits on speech that prevent endangering others and encourage criminal activity.

6. Answers may include the idea that the colonists lacked this important method of airing grievances and requesting change, so they guaranteed it for the new government and its citizens.

7. Essays should clearly define the student's position on the issue of freedom of the press during wartime and give reasons to support the position.

Is the Patriot Act an infringement of privacy?

A terrorist attack shocked the United States on September 11, 2001. Congress quickly responded to the Attorney General's call for changes in the law to combat terrorism. President George W. Bush signed the Patriot Act as a new tool to fight "a threat like no other our Nation has ever seen." Later, some members of Congress and concerned citizens said some parts of the act violated the Fourth Amendment's protection against unreasonable searches and seizures. Before most searches, officers must obtain a warrant from a judge, showing "probable cause" and describing the place to be searched and the persons or things to be seized. The Patriot Act made exceptions to these requirements. Section 215 permitted the FBI to go before the Foreign Intelligence Surveillance Court for an order to search for "any tangible things" connected to a terrorism suspect.

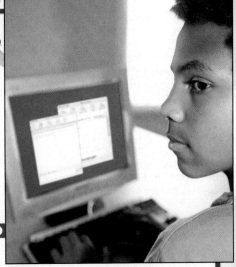

Schools place restrictions on computers to protect students from visiting undesirable Internet sites. Some consider this a form of surveillance.

YES

In November 2003, the American Civil Liberties Union contended that the Patriot Act contains "flaws that threaten your fundamental freedoms by giving the government the power to access to your medical records, tax records, information about the books you buy or borrow without probable cause, and the power to break into your home and conduct secret searches without telling you for weeks, months, or indefinitely." In 2004 the ACLU filed a lawsuit to overturn a Patriot Act provision that gave the government authority to obtain customer records from Internet service providers and other businesses without a warrant.

—American Civil Liberties Union

NO

Senator Orrin Hatch of Utah voted for the Patriot Act and defended it when Congress voted to renew most of its provisions. In 2003 he said, "The Patriot Act has not eroded any of the rights we hold dear as Americans. I would be the first to call for corrective action, were that the case. Yet not one of the civil liberties groups has cited one instance of abuse of our constitutional rights. . . . We should not undermine or limit our law enforcement and intelligence agencies' efforts by imposing requirements that go above and beyond those required by the Constitution. That would only have the effect of protecting terrorists and criminals while endangering the lives of innocent Americans."

—Senator Orrin Hatch

Debating the Issue

1. **Describing** How does the Fourth Amendment attempt to protect Americans' privacy?

2. **Describing** What must an officer of the law do to obtain a warrant for a search?

3. **Explaining** Why were some people concerned about the provisions in Section 215?

4. **Concluding** Were the concerns of people who opposed some provisions of the Patriot Act justified? Explain.

Chapter 4   125

D Differentiated Instruction

English Learners Ask: What might give a police officer probable cause to pull over a driver and to search the driver's car? *(In many cities, if an officer sees someone driving in a way that suggests the driver is under the influence of illegal substances, then the officer may stop the driver and would have probable cause to search the car for illegal substances.)* **OL**

Debating the Issue

Answers:

1. The Fourth Amendment protects Americans from unreasonable searches and seizures of their belongings.

2. The officer must obtain a warrant from a judge, explaining the reasons for the search and naming the place that will be searched.

3. Under this section, FBI agents can search without getting a warrant from a judge if they suspect a connection to terrorist activities.

4. Answers will include students' knowledge of incidents, such as the banking of phone records, that have been reported in recent media. Students' conclusions will vary.

Additional Support

Activity: U.S./World Connections

Making Connections Ask: How have the privacy rights of international travelers been changed by the need to detect and deter terrorist activities? Have students gather media reports on the changing requirements for international travel. Tell them to check the Web sites of airlines that carry international passengers to review the restrictions on travelers. Then ask them to describe to the class the losses of privacy that have resulted from the need to deter terrorist activity and the movement of terrorists. **OL**

Focus

Bellringer
Daily Focus Transparency 4–2

Guide to Reading
Answers to Graphic:

- no second trial for same crime
- speedy and public trial

Protections

- no cruel or unusual punishments for those found guilty
- right to trial by jury and defense by lawyer

Section Spotlight Video

Have students watch the Chapter 4, Section 2 video at glencoe.com.

Resource Manager

Guide to Reading

Big Idea
The Constitution of the United States establishes and protects fundamental rights and liberties.

Content Vocabulary
- search warrant (p. 127)
- indictment (p. 128)
- grand jury (p. 128)
- double jeopardy (p. 128)
- due process (p. 128)
- eminent domain (p. 128)
- bail (p. 129)

Academic Vocabulary
- proportion (p. 129)
- involve (p. 131)

Reading Strategy
Summarizing On a graphic organizer like the one below, discuss four ways that the Bill of Rights protects the rights of the accused.

speedy and public trial

Protections

The Bill of Rights

Real World Civics Some dogs are pets and some dogs perform a civic duty during a legal search. Below, police officer Tom Kolbert and his K-9 partner, Reggie, check student lockers in a Cheektowaga, New York, high school for contraband. Most dogs have a sense of smell that is 1,000 times more sensitive than a human's. With proper training, sniffer dogs can detect explosives, weapons, and illegal drugs. The Supreme Court holds that an individual's right to privacy does not extend to illegal activities and has ruled that K-9 searches are legal.

▼ **A drug-sniffing dog and police officer search lockers**

KNOWLEDGE IS POWER

R **Reading Strategies**	C **Critical Thinking**	D **Differentiated Instruction**	W **Writing Support**	S **Skill Practice**
Teacher Edition • Making Connections, p. 129 **Additional Resources** • Cont. Vocab.,URB p. 95 • Acad. Vocab., URB p. 97 • Guide Read., URB p. 114 • RENTG, p. 37	**Teacher Edition** • Making Inferences, p. 129 • Drawing Con., p. 131 **Additional Resources** • Quizzes and Tests, p. 39	**Teacher Edition** • English Learners, p. 127 • Advanced Learners, p. 128 • Visual/Spatial, pp. 128, 130 **Additional Resources** • Diff. Instr., URB p. 107 • Reteach. Act., URB p. 111	**Teacher Edition** • Personal Writing, p. 127 • Narrative Writing, p. 130 **Additional Resources** • Auth. Assess., URB p. 4	**Teacher Edition** • Interpreting Charts, p. 127 **Additional Resources** • Daily Focus Trans., 4–2

Protecting the Rights of the Accused

Main Idea In addition to the important civil liberties protected by the First Amendment, the other nine amendments in the Bill of Rights guarantee the right to fair legal treatment, as well as other freedoms.

Civics & You How well do you know what constitutional protections you enjoy as a United States citizen? Read about your rights under the Bill of Rights.

The First Amendment freedoms are among our most important civil liberties. Equally precious, however, is the right to fair legal treatment. This is the subject of several amendments in the Bill of Rights.

Suppose someone accuses you of committing a crime. In some countries, government agents might ransack your home, drag you off to jail, beat you, and hold a trial without even letting you respond to the charges. In the United States, the Fourth, Fifth, Sixth, and Eighth Amendments help prevent such a scenario from occurring.

The Fourth Amendment

The Fourth Amendment protects Americans "against unreasonable searches and seizures." No soldier, government agent, or police officer can search your home or take your property without probable, or a valid, cause.

If law enforcement officers believe you have committed a crime, they can ask a judge to issue a **search warrant.** This is a court order allowing law enforcement officers to search a suspect's home or business and take specific items as evidence. Judges do not give out search warrants easily. They must be convinced that a search will probably turn up evidence of criminal activity.

Rights of the Accused

FIFTH AMENDMENT

- No trial may be held unless a person is formally charged, or indicted, by the grand jury.
- A person found not guilty may not be put on trial again for the same crime.
- Accused persons may not be forced to testify against themselves.
- Every person is entitled to due process of law.
- No one may be deprived of their property by the government without compensation.

SIXTH AMENDMENT

- The accused must be informed of the nature of the charges.
- The accused must be allowed a speedy and public trial by an impartial jury.
- If possible, the trial must be held in the area where the crime took place.
- The accused must be permitted to hear and question all witnesses.
- The accused is entitled to a lawyer and to call witnesses for his or her defense.

Analyzing Charts

1. **Identifying** Which amendment guarantees that if you are arrested, you will be informed of the charges against you?
2. **Explaining** What is due process of law?

Chapter 4   127

Teach

W Writing Support

Personal Writing Have students write a paragraph about how life might be different where there aren't rights such as those we have in the United States. **OL**

D Differentiated Instruction

English Learners Explain that "seizures," in this context, means the taking away of a person's property. Make sure that students do not mistake the word for its medical use. Have students write sentences using the word correctly. **ELL**

S Skill Practice

Interpreting Charts Have students rephrase each bulleted item so that it applies to them. For the first bullet a student might say, "I can't be put on trial unless I've been formally charged with a crime or indicted by a grand jury." **OL**

Analyzing Charts

Answers:
1. the Sixth Amendment
2. It is the process by which all parties follow the law carefully so that everyone's rights are protected.

Differentiated Instruction

Leveled Activities

128

D₁ Differentiated Instruction

Advanced Learners Remind students that under the nation's laws, a person accused of a crime is innocent until proven guilty. **Ask:** How would an accused person's experience be different if guilt, rather than innocence, were assumed? *(Answers may include the idea that the jury would be biased against the accused before evidence was presented, that the trial was simply for show, and so on.)* **AL**

D₂ Differentiated Instruction

Visual/Spatial Have students recall trial scenes they have seen in movies and on TV shows in which the accused person says, under questioning, "I plead the Fifth." Have students discuss the situation in which this occurs and the accused's unwillingness to answer a question. **OL**

Caption Answer:

The warrant prohibits law enforcement personnel from searching and taking away your property without cause.

Additional Support

Teacher Tip

Invite a law enforcement officer or an attorney to explain the rights of both the accused and the accuser and to explain how the Sixth Amendment is interpreted in modern courts.

Legal Searches Reasonable searches can take place when the county police have cause to suspect a crime has been committed. *Analyzing* How does a search warrant help protect the rights of a person accused of a crime?

If warrants were issued frivolously, the Fourth Amendment would give us little sense of security. Anytime of the day or night, the police could invade our privacy and confiscate our possessions.

The Fifth Amendment

The Fifth Amendment protects the rights of people accused of crimes. It states that no one can be put on trial for a serious federal crime without an **indictment**—a formal charge by a group of citizens called a **grand jury,** who review the evidence against the accused.

D₁ A person who is indicted is not necessarily guilty of a crime. An indictment simply indicates the grand jury's belief that an individual *may* have committed a crime.

The Fifth Amendment also protects people from **double jeopardy.** This means that people who are accused of a crime and judged not guilty may not be put on trial again for the same crime.

D₂ In addition, the Fifth Amendment protects an accused person's right to remain silent. Throughout history, innocent people have been threatened, tortured, or bullied into confessing to crimes they did not commit. To prevent this, the Fifth Amendment states that people cannot be forced to testify against themselves. This is called protection against self-incrimination.

The Fifth Amendment goes on to say that no one may be denied life, liberty, or property "without due process of law." **Due process** means following established legal procedures. It also includes the idea that the laws themselves must be reasonable.

The Fifth Amendment also protects a citizen's property rights. It limits the government's power of eminent domain. **Eminent domain** is the right of the government to take private property—usually land—for public use.

For example, if your home lies in the path of a proposed highway, the government may legally take the land and destroy your house. The Fifth Amendment limits this power and requires the government to pay a fair price for the property.

The Sixth Amendment

The Sixth Amendment guarantees additional rights to people accused of crimes. It requires that they be told the exact nature of the charges against them. It also requires that the accused be allowed a trial by jury, although they may ask to be tried by only a judge instead.

If an accused person asks for a jury trial, the trial must be speedy and public, and jurors must be impartial. If possible, the trial should be held in the same area in which the crime took place.

Activity: Collaborative Learning

Comparing and Contrasting Remind students that both the rights of the accused and the rights of the accuser—often a victim of a crime—must be respected. **Ask:** How does the law provide for the rights of both accuser and accused? *(The law establishes a process by which a trial can determine guilt or innocence of the accused, while ensuring that the accuser is able to seek justice in court.)* Have groups of students make a list of the rights of a person who has been affected by a crime. **Ask:** Do you think that the law favors the accused or the accuser? Why? Have groups share their thoughts with the class. **OL**

Accused individuals have the right to hear and question all witnesses against them. They must also be permitted to call witnesses in their own defense. Finally, they are entitled to have a lawyer. Since the Sixth Amendment was written, the Supreme Court has ruled that if an accused person cannot afford a lawyer, the government must provide one and pay his or her fees.

The Eighth Amendment

Although the Sixth Amendment guarantees a speedy trial, sometimes months go by before a case can be heard. During that time, the accused may have two choices: stay in jail or remain free by paying bail. **Bail** is a sum of money used as a security deposit. If the accused person comes to court for the trial, the bail is returned. If the person fails to appear, though, the bail is forfeited.

The judge decides how much bail a person must pay. The Eighth Amendment, however, forbids "excessive" bail—that is, an amount that is much too high. Excessive does not just refer to what a person can afford to pay. In determining bail, a judge considers various factors, including the type of crime committed, the record of the accused person, and the likelihood that the accused will appear in court. In some cases, bail may be denied, as when a defendant is likely to flee.

When a person is convicted of a crime, the Eighth Amendment protects him or her against having to pay excessive fines. Fines may vary, however, depending on the seriousness of the crime.

The Eighth Amendment forbids "cruel and unusual punishments." For many years, Americans have debated what kinds of punishment are cruel and unusual. It is generally agreed that punishment should be in **proportion,** or balanced, to the crime committed. For example, a sentence of life imprisonment for stealing a loaf of bread would be too harsh. People disagree strongly, however, about whether the death penalty for very serious crimes is cruel and unusual punishment.

Reading Check Identifying Which amendment protects a person accused of a crime from double jeopardy?

Gun Ownership Individuals may own firearms if laws are obeyed. At this firing range in Massachusetts, gun owners are trained on weapon safety. *Speculating* Why did the Framers think the right to bear arms was an important right to protect?

129

C Critical Thinking

Making Inferences Ask: Why is it important that the accused be allowed to hear and question witnesses against them? *(For the trial to be fair, the accused must be able to have all the information presented against him or her so that he or she has the opportunity to refute it.)* **AL**

R Reading Strategy

Making Connections Ask: What does "skipping bail" mean? What are the consequences of missing a court date? *("Skipping bail" means failing to show up for a trial. Bail is then forfeited.)* **ELL OL**

Reading Check **Answer:** The Fifth Amendment protects a person accused of a crime from double jeopardy.

Caption Answer:

Answers may include the idea that citizens have the right to defend their personal safety or that the Founders lived in a time before a national militia existed and that they wanted to have an armed population in case of conflict.

Differentiated Instruction

Primary Source Reading 1-A, URB pp. 15–16

Democracy in America

Objective:	To identify characteristics of American government
Focus:	Have students identify the traits of democracy that impress Tocqueville.
Teach:	Discuss the responsibilities and compensation of those who govern in a democracy.
Assess:	Explain why putting officials in "unpaid offices" creates problems for the governed.
Close:	Write a bulleted memo outlining proper behavior in and out of office.

Differentiated Instruction Strategies

BL Guide students to paraphrase each paragraph of the excerpt.

AL How does the way U.S. citizens govern themselves follow logically from the idea that government is a "necessary evil"?

ELL Read aloud Tocqueville's words so that his candid, first-person expression aids in comprehension.

W Writing Support

Narrative Writing Point out to students that this paragraph is about a time when freedom of expression played a role in their lives. Advise them to write about the event as if it were a story, with a beginning problem, a middle in which they face the problem, and an end in which the problem is solved. **BL**

D Differentiated Instruction

Visual/Spatial Show the class several editorial cartoons that comment on the Second Amendment. Ask students to state in their own words the point of each cartoon. **OL**

TIME™ Teens in Action

Answer:

Student paragraphs should narrate an event that demonstrates the importance of freedom of expression.

Civics ONLINE

Objectives and answers to the **Student Web Activity** can be found at glencoe.com under the Web Activity Lesson Plan for this chapter.

Hands-On Chapter Project
Step 2

TIME™ Teens in Action

Jackie Fernandez

You can probably find Jackie Fernandez, 17, of Alexandria, Virginia, in a local bookstore. She is one of the writers of a new book published by Bill Rhatican, her AP government teacher at West Potomac High School.

QUESTION: Can you tell us about the book?

ANSWER: It's called *The Constitution: Written in Sand or Etched in Stone?* The book is a collection of essays written by students about the U.S. Constitution and the Bill of Rights.

Q: What's your essay in the book about?

A: Fanfiction, or fictional stories about characters from books and movies that are already copyrighted. For example, if I wanted to write a story about what the character Yoda did between *Star Wars: Episode III* and the original Star Wars movies—that would be fanfiction.

Q: How does this relate to the Bill of Rights?

A: I think the First Amendment protects the fanfiction author's freedom of speech, while the Fifth Amendment protects the original creator's right to property. In other words, one part of the Bill of Rights allows me to write about Yoda, but another part of the Bill of Rights protects the person who thought Yoda up. So fanfiction is both condemned and protected by the Bill of Rights.

Q: Is the Bill of Rights a "living" document?

A: Yes! If the Bill of Rights wasn't "alive," it wouldn't be applicable to modern-day inventions.

Q: How will it feel to see the book in stores?

A: Amazing. I've always wanted to be published. It's like a dream come true!

Making a Difference   CITIZENSHIP

W Write a paragraph on how freedom of expression has taken place in your life.

Other Protections

Main Idea In addition to the First Amendment freedoms and due process guarantees, the Bill of Rights includes other protections for American citizens.

Civics & You Several of the first 10 amendments deal with the rights of people accused of committing a crime. Why do you think the constitution protects the rights of the accused?

There is debate over what rights, exactly, are guaranteed by the Second Amendment. Some argue that it provides only for each state to maintain "a well-regulated militia" by allowing the members of those militias to carry arms. When the Second Amendment was written, a militia was a small, local army made of volunteer soldiers.

D Other people hold that the Second Amendment guarantees the right of all individual citizens to "keep and bear arms" without the interference of the government. The courts have generally ruled that the government can pass laws to control, but not prevent, the possession of weapons. For example, federal and state laws determine who can be licensed to own firearms.

The Third Amendment

One cause of the American Revolution was the colonists' resentment of the law requiring them to house and feed British soldiers. The Third Amendment makes it unlikely that Americans will ever be forced to shelter the military again. The amendment says that, in peacetime, soldiers may not move into private homes without the consent of the homeowner.

Civics ONLINE

Student Web Activity Visit glencoe.com and complete the Chapter 4 Web Activity.

Bill of Rights for Our School

Step 2: Determining the Rights of Teachers, Students, and Other Workers in the School Groups of students will translate the answers to their questions into a "Bill of Rights" for their segment of the school population.

Directions On the board, draw a large Venn diagram consisting of three circles. Label the circles Students, Teachers, and Other Workers. Label the overlap Our School's Mission. Assign a note taker to copy what students will add to the Venn diagram. You will need this copy to complete the project. Then ask students, working in their original groups, to discuss the answers to the questions in Step 1.

Using Venn Diagrams Ask student groups to formulate rights for their segment of the student population, based on what that segment needs to succeed. Ask students to write a mission statement for the school, based on their segment's goals. Place these in the Venn diagram. Have the class collaborate to produce a single mission statement that takes into consideration the needs of the whole school population. **AL**

(Project continued in Section 3)

The Seventh Amendment

The Fifth, Sixth, and Eighth Amendments deal with people's rights in criminal cases. The Seventh Amendment concerns civil cases—lawsuits that **involve,** or contain, disagreements between people rather than crimes. The Seventh Amendment provides for the right to a jury trial in federal courts to settle all disputes about property worth more than $20. When both parties in a conflict agree, however, a judge rather than a jury may hear evidence and settle the case.

The Ninth Amendment

The Ninth Amendment states that all other rights not spelled out in the Constitution are "retained by the people." This amendment prevents the government from claiming that the only rights people have are those listed in the Bill of Rights. The Ninth Amendment makes it clear that citizens have other rights beyond those listed in the Constitution, and those rights may not be taken away.

The Tenth Amendment

The first eight amendments grant the people rights. The Ninth Amendment states that the rights guaranteed in the Constitution are not the only rights the people have.

Unlike the other amendments, the Tenth Amendment did not add anything to the ratified Constitution. The Tenth Amendment states that any powers the Constitution does not specifically give to the national government are reserved for the states and for the people. (This amendment is the source of many of the reserved powers you learned about in Chapter 3.) The amendment expresses the idea that the federal government is limited only to the powers it is granted in the Constitution.

In this way, the Tenth Amendment prevents Congress and the president from becoming too strong. The government of the United States can have only the powers the people give it.

Reading Check Describing What is the purpose of the Tenth Amendment?

C Critical Thinking

Drawing Conclusions Ask: What do the Ninth and Tenth Amendments suggest about the concerns of the Framers? *(The Framers were very concerned that a future government might try to limit or take away the rights of citizens and worked hard to secure these rights.)* **OL**

Reading Check Answer: The Tenth Amendment assigns powers not given to the federal government to the states and the people.

Assess

Civics ONLINE

Study Central™ provides summaries, interactive games, and online graphic organizers to help students review content.

Close

Summarizing Have students close their books and, as a class, recall as many of the rights guaranteed to citizens as they can. When students can no longer think of rights, have them check their books and add any rights that they missed. **OL**

Section 2 Review

Vocabulary

1. **Write** sentences related to the Bill of Rights using the following terms: *search warrant, indictment, grand jury, double jeopardy, due process, eminent domain, bail.*

Main Ideas

2. **Hypothesizing** Why do you think the Framers of the Constitution addressed the legal treatment of the accused in so many amendments?

3. **Explaining** How do the Ninth and Tenth Amendments limit the power of government?

Critical Thinking

4. **BIG Ideas** Which of the first 10 amendments do you think is the most important? Why?

5. **Organizing** In a web diagram similar to the one below, identify important rights in the Fifth Amendment.

Fifth Amendment

CITIZENSHIP Activity

6. **Persuasive Writing** Select an issue related to the amendments in this section, such as the death penalty or gun control. Write a letter to the editor of your local newspaper expressing your views on the issue.

Civics ONLINE

Study Central™ To review this section, go to glencoe.com.

Answers

1. Sentences should use vocabulary words according to their definitions in the section and in the Glossary.

2. They had experienced unfair treatment under British law and wanted to prevent similar abuses in their new government.

3. The Ninth and Tenth Amendments state that not all rights are covered by the Bill of Rights and secure all unspecified rights to the states and to the people.

4. Answers may include specific reasons to support any one of the amendments discussed.

5. No trial may be held unless a person is formally charged or indicted by a grand jury. A person found not guilty may not be put on trial again for the same crime. Accused persons may not be forced to testify against themselves. Every person is entitled to due process of law. No one may be deprived of their property by the government without compensation.

6. Letters should follow the standard format and adhere to the accepted tone. Letters should include a clear position and reasons to support that position.

Teach

Freedom of speech has long been one of the more debated protections of the First Amendment. Can citizens be members of the Communist Party? Can citizens burn an American flag to protest? These and many other questions of free speech have been controversial for decades.

Introduce the feature by telling students that during the late 1960s and early 1970s, issues of free speech became even more contentious as citizens carried out various protests against governmental policies. As students read page 132, point out that *Tinker* v. *Des Moines School District* raises these questions: What is speech? Is it feelings and beliefs expressed only in words? Or are symbols—black armbands, flags—also speech? Are actions, such as wearing an armband, speech?

ANALYZING THE COURT DECISION

Answers:

1. The lawyers argued that the wearing of the armbands constituted an expression of feeling and beliefs similar to actual speech.

2. Fortas's concept of "pure speech" extended the First Amendment protection to symbolic expressions of ideas that can also be spoken.

Additional Support

Tinker v. Des Moines School District

Public school officials set standards of behavior that students are expected to follow. Does this arrangement leave students with any rights? Sometimes the Supreme Court must decide.

Background of the Case

One night in December 1965, a group of public school students, led by high school sophomores Christopher Eckhardt and John Tinker, and eighth-grader Mary Beth Tinker, wore black armbands to protest the Vietnam War. As other students joined the armband protest, principals and members of the school board met the growing protest with a ban on armbands—to prevent "disturbing influences."

On December 16, 1965, Christopher, John, and Mary Beth were suspended for wearing their armbands to school. Their parents protested the suspensions in federal courts. They contended the students' First Amendment free-speech rights had been violated.

Lorena, Paul, and Mary Beth Tinker hear their case has been settled in their favor.

The Decision

On February 24, 1969, the United States Supreme Court in a 7–2 decision declared the school suspensions unconstitutional. Justice Abe Fortas, who wrote the majority opinion, first established that the students' action was "akin to pure speech." Even though their protest involved no speaking, it deserved "protection under the First Amendment." Then he wrote:

> ❝ It can hardly be argued that either students or teachers shed their constitutional rights to freedom of speech or expression at the schoolhouse gate. ❞
>
> —Justice Abe Fortas

Why It Matters

Supporters saluted the decision that "students are entitled to freedom of expression of their views." Critics predicted harmful consequences. Dissenter Justice Hugo Black suggested that the Court's decision was "the beginning of a new revolutionary era of permissiveness in this country fostered by the judiciary." He argued that no one has a complete right to freedom of speech and expression. Later decisions, such as *Bethel School District* v. *Fraser* (1986) and *Hazelwood School District* v. *Kuhlmeier* (1988), narrowed students' First Amendment rights while expanding the authority of school officials.

Analyzing the Court Decision

1. **Explaining** Why did the students' lawyers argue that the armbands were protected by the First Amendment?

2. **Inferring** How did Judge Fortas's concept of "pure speech" extend First Amendment free-speech rights?

Background

Tinker v. Des Moines School District
The event that led to the students' suspension and the eventual appeal to the Supreme Court of their suspensions occurred in December 1965, when Christopher Eckhardt and John and Mary Tinker decided to wear the armbands to silently protest the Vietnam War. They had previously participated in similar protests with their parents.

When the principals of the Des Moines schools heard of the plan, they developed a school policy to target it. The students knew that they faced suspension if they wore the armbands.

On December 16, the students wore their armbands and received their suspensions, which lasted until school began again in the new year. School officials claimed that the policy was necessary to prevent a breakdown in discipline, and a district court agreed. Because the 8th Circuit Court of Appeals was equally divided on the case, it went forward to the Supreme Court, which extended the First Amendment protection of speech to the symbolic action and reversed the lower courts' decisions.

Guide to Reading

Big Idea
A constitution reflects the values and goals of the society that creates it.

Content Vocabulary
- suffrage *(p. 135)*
- poll tax *(p. 137)*

Academic Vocabulary
- violate *(p 134)*
- specify *(p. 137)*

Reading Strategy
Explaining As you read, complete a graphic organizer like the one below to identify and explain the Civil War amendments.

13th Amendment · 14th Amendment
Civil War Amendments
15th Amendment

🔊 **Section Audio**   🎬 **Spotlight Video**

Extending the Bill of Rights

Real World Civics In the 1948 primary elections, thousands of African Americans across the country stood in line to exercise their right to vote for the first time since 1876. They faced possible violence, name calling—even losing their jobs. Although the Fifteenth Amendment guarantees the right to vote, some states created obstacles such as poll taxes, passing a literacy test, or proving property ownership to avoid letting minorities vote. In 1944, the Supreme Court ruled that these requirements, specifically designed to exclude African Americans, were illegal.

▼ **African American voters line up to receive ballots in Columbia, South Carolina, in 1948**

133

Focus

Bellringer
Daily Focus Transparency 4–3

Guide to Reading
Answers to Graphic:

13th Amendment · 14th Amendment
Civil War Amendments
15th Amendment

🎬 **Section Spotlight Video**

To generate student interest and provide a springboard for class discussion, access the Chapter 4, Section 3 video at glencoe.com or on the video DVD.

Resource Manager

R Reading Strategies	**C** Critical Thinking	**D** Differentiated Instruction	**W** Writing Support	**S** Skill Practice
Teacher Edition	**Teacher Edition**	**Teacher Edition**	**Teacher Edition**	**Teacher Edition**
• Using Word Parts, p. 134	• Predicting, p. 135	• Visual/Spatial, p. 136	• Personal Writing, p. 134	• Analyzing Charts, p. 135
• Act. Prior Know., p. 134	• Making Inferences, p. 137	**Additional Resources**	• Persuasive Writing, p. 137	**Additional Resources**
• Making Connections, p. 136	**Additional Resources**	• Diff. Instr., URB p. 107		• Daily Skills Trans., 4–3
Additional Resources	• Quizzes and Tests, p. 40			
• Cont. Vocab., URB p. 96				
• Acad. Vocab., URB p. 98				

Teach

R₁ Reading Strategy

Using Word Parts Ask: What other word besides "violate" begins with the root "viol"? Use the term in a sentence. *(Example: The book ended with a very violent scene.)* **BL** **ELL**

R₂ Reading Strategy

Activating Prior Knowledge Survey the class to see what they know about when voting rights were extended to African Americans, women, and people who have just turned eighteen. Tell them that they will learn more about these constitutional milestones as they complete the chapter. **OL**

W Writing Support

Personal Writing Have students write in their journals to answer why the Framers might have been surprised at the need to nationalize the Bill of Rights. **AL**

Caption Answer:

At various times after the Civil War, some states have tried to prevent women, people with disabilities, and other groups from voting.

Differentiated Instruction

Differentiated Instruction Activity 4, URB pp. 107–108

Civil War Amendments

Main Idea The Thirteenth, Fourteenth, and Fifteenth Amendments are called the Civil War amendments because they grew out of that war.

Civics & You In our country, freedom and the right to express our opinions are precious rights. Read to learn about efforts to extend these rights.

The Bill of Rights was intended originally to constrain only the national government. For many years, local and state governments were not bound by its terms. As a result, states sometimes used their reserved powers to pass laws that **violate,** or disobey, civil liberties. In most parts of the country, for example, women and African Americans could not vote. Before 1865, many states had laws that sanctioned the enslavement of African Americans, who were treated as property and had almost no rights at all.

Three amendments were passed after the Civil War to extend civil liberties to African Americans. However, the promise of these Civil War amendments was not fulfilled for almost 100 years. Many states were slow to change their customs; some actively resisted. The federal government and the Supreme Court often seemed indifferent.

The Thirteenth Amendment

The Thirteenth Amendment officially outlawed slavery in the United States and thus freed thousands of African Americans. It also outlawed any sort of forced labor, except as punishment for a crime.

The Fourteenth Amendment

Although the Thirteenth Amendment ensured the freedom of African Americans, it did not guarantee them full rights. After the Civil War, many Southern states passed "black codes" that excluded African Americans from certain jobs, limited their property rights, and restricted them in other ways.

To remedy this situation, the Fourteenth Amendment was enacted in 1868. It defined a United States citizen as anyone "born or naturalized in the United States," a definition that included most African Americans. The amendment also required every state to grant its citizens "equal protection of the laws." In recent years, this clause has been used to benefit women, people with disabilities, and other groups whose rights have not always been protected fairly.

The Fourteenth Amendment also forbids state governments from interfering with the "privileges or immunities of citizens of the United States." Further, state governments may not take an individual's "life, liberty, or property, without due process of law." These provisions made the Bill of Rights binding for state governments as well as the federal government. This is called the nationalization of the Bill of Rights.

The Supreme Court, however, ignored this interpretation of the Fourteenth Amendment until 1925. Then, in *Gitlow* v. *New York*, the Court ruled that the Fourteenth Amendment could safeguard free speech and a free press "from impairment by the states."

The Right to Vote Following the Civil War, African Americans across the South voted for the first time. Many states tried to make it difficult for them to exercise this right. *Identifying* Who else besides African Americans were prevented from voting after the Civil War?

Changing Education

Objective: To analyze the reasoning behind this landmark court ruling

Focus: Have students identify the goal of the plaintiffs.

Teach: Explain the background that led to the *Plessy* v. *Ferguson* ruling of "separate but equal" facilities.

Assess: Have students outline the arguments in each paragraph.

Close: Write a paragraph predicting the impact on public schools of this landmark ruling.

Differentiated Instruction Strategies

BL Give one reason that the court recognized the importance of educating all minors.

AL Is it still the case today that "separate educational facilities are inherently unequal"? Do all-male or all-female schools contradict this ruling?

ELL Who is the "we" of this ruling in phrases such as "We conclude" and "we hold"?

Constitutional Amendments

ELEVENTH AMENDMENT (1795)
• Places limits on suits against states

TWELFTH AMENDMENT (1804)
• Revises procedure for electing the president and vice president

THIRTEENTH AMENDMENT (1865)
• Abolishes slavery

FOURTEENTH AMENDMENT (1868)
• Defines United States citizenship; guarantees all citizens "equal protection of the laws"

FIFTEENTH AMENDMENT (1870)
• Prohibits restrictions on the right to vote based on race and color

SIXTEENTH AMENDMENT (1913)
• Gives Congress the power to levy an income tax

SEVENTEENTH AMENDMENT (1913)
• Enables voters to elect senators directly

EIGHTEENTH AMENDMENT (1917)
• Prohibits making, drinking, or selling alcoholic beverages (Prohibition)

NINETEENTH AMENDMENT (1920)
• Gives women the right to vote

TWENTIETH AMENDMENT (1933)
• Changes the dates of congressional and presidential terms

TWENTY-FIRST AMENDMENT (1933)
• Repeals Prohibition (Eighteenth Amendment)

TWENTY-SECOND AMENDMENT (1951)
• Limits presidents to two terms in office

TWENTY-THIRD AMENDMENT (1961)
• Gives residents of the District of Columbia the right to vote

TWENTY-FOURTH AMENDMENT (1964)
• Abolishes poll taxes

TWENTY-FIFTH AMENDMENT (1967)
• Establishes procedures for succession to the presidency

TWENTY-SIXTH AMENDMENT (1971)
• Sets voting age at 18 years

TWENTY-SEVENTH AMENDMENT (1992)
• Delays congressional pay raises until the term following their passage

Analyzing Charts

1. **Identifying** Which is the amendment that specifically deals with women's rights?

2. **Explaining** Why do you think the Framers made the amendment process so difficult?

Since the *Gitlow* case, the Supreme Court has used the Fourteenth Amendment to apply other rights in the Bill of Rights to the states. This "incorporation" of the Bill of Rights by the Fourteenth Amendment's due process clause means that U.S. citizens in every part of the country have the same basic rights.

The Fifteenth Amendment

The last of the Civil War amendments, the Fifteenth, says that no state may take away a person's voting rights on the basis of race, color, or previous enslavement. The amendment clearly aimed to guarantee **suffrage**—the right to vote—to African Americans. Still, many states found ways to keep African Americans away from the polls.

The Fifteenth Amendment, in reality, protected only men. The various states had the power to decide whether women could vote. Women, regardless of their race, could not vote in most federal or state elections.

Reading Check **Explaining** What did the Thirteenth Amendment outlaw in addition to slavery?

Chapter 4   135

S Skill Practice

Analyzing Charts Ask: What organizational pattern does this chart use? *(It is organized chronologically, from the earliest amendment to the most recent amendment.)* **BL**

C Critical Thinking

Predicting Ask: What would happen if different states had the power to apply the Bill of Rights as they saw fit? *(Answers may include the idea that some states would show less concern about citizens' rights than others and that the unfair treatment would more likely be found in some parts of the nation than in others.)* **AL**

For additional practice on this skill (Predicting), see the **Skills Handbook**.

Analyzing Charts

Answers:
1. the Nineteenth Amendment
2. A difficult process ensures that time and thought will be brought to bear on the question of changing the Constitution.

Reading Check **Answer:** any sort of forced labor

Differentiated Instruction

Leveled Activities

BL Reteaching Activity 4, URB p. 111

OL Guided Reading Activity 4-3, URB p. 115

ELL Content Vocabulary Activity 4, URB p. 96

R Reading Strategy

Making Connections Ask: What event of international importance preceded the ratification of the Nineteenth Amendment in 1920? *(World War I)* How might women's participation in World War I have contributed to the extension of suffrage? *(Women served in many capacities at home and abroad during the war and perhaps won the confidence of male voters.)* **AL**

D Differentiated Instruction

Visual/Spatial Ask: Where did Congress designate that the nation's new government be placed? *(between Maryland and Virginia)* **ELL BL**

Caption Answer:

Because men could be drafted for the military at age eighteen, the nation ratified the amendment allowing people of this age to vote as well.

Hands-On Chapter Project
Step 3

Bill of Rights for Our School

Step 3: Checking the Rights of Teachers, Students, and Other Workers in the School Groups of students will check the rights they have written to see whether one group's rights impinge on another group's rights.

Directions Tell students that in this step, they will begin to work together as a class. Hand out copies of the Venn diagram that students completed in Step 2.

Later Amendments

Main Idea Amendments added to the Constitution in the twentieth century deal with a wide range of topics.

Civics & You Our Constitution has endured for more than 200 years with only 27 amendments. Read to find out about the amendments added to the Constitution in the twentieth century.

Gradually, the Bill of Rights came to cover all Americans equally and to limit government power at all levels. Additional amendments to the Constitution and court rulings extended the rights of Americans to participate fully in the democratic process. A number of amendments deal with voting rights.

The Seventeenth Amendment

According to Article I of the Constitution, the people were to elect members of the House of Representatives, but the state legislatures were to choose members of the Senate. Ratified in 1913, the Seventeenth Amendment allows voters to elect their senators directly. This change in the election process gave Americans a greater voice in their government.

The Nineteenth Amendment

Although the Constitution did not guarantee women the right to vote, it did not explicitly deny them suffrage. As a result, states made their own laws on the matter, using the powers reserved to them under the Tenth Amendment. The territory of Wyoming permitted women to vote in 1869, and several other territories and states did so as well in the years that followed.

Anthony and Stanton However, national support for woman suffrage was slow in coming. Woman suffrage leaders Susan B. Anthony and Elizabeth Cady Stanton had

18-Year-Olds Get the Vote In 1971 President Richard Nixon, before a group of young people, signed the Twenty-sixth Amendment. ***Explaining*** **What role did the Vietnam War play in the passing of this amendment?**

insisted as early as 1848 that women belonged at the polls. Many who believed that women should not have the same rights as men opposed them, however. It was only in 1920 that the Nineteenth Amendment protected the right of women to vote in all national and state elections.

The Twenty-third Amendment

African Americans and women were not the only citizens who were denied voting rights for many years. Residents of our nation's capital, Washington, D.C., also fell into this group.

As you may know, "D.C.," stands for the District of Columbia, an area between Maryland and Virginia. Because the District is not a state, the people who lived there were not initially allowed to vote in national elections. The Twenty-third Amendment changed that in 1961. The amendment says that residents of the District of Columbia may vote for the president and vice president, just as other Americans do.

Interpersonal Have students read the three sets of rights—those for teachers, students, and other school workers—and note any instances in which one group's rights conflict with another's. Point out that, similarly, states' rights sometimes clash with federal law. Have students work out a compromise to any conflicts. For instance, students may want the right to after-school tutoring while teachers want the right to prepare lesson plans. At the end of this step, students should have a completed a school

mission statement (written in Step 2) and a list of rights that do not clash with each other. **OL**

(Project continued in Section 4)

The Twenty-fourth Amendment

Although the Fifteenth Amendment gave African Americans the right to vote, many had trouble exercising this right. One reason was that several Southern states had **poll taxes.** In other words, they required voters to pay a sum of money before casting a ballot. Because the tax had to be paid not only for the current year, but also for previous unpaid years as well, it was a financial burden for many. Because many African Americans could not afford the tax, they could not vote. Poor whites were in the same situation.

In 1964, the Twenty-fourth Amendment made poll taxes illegal in national elections. Two years later, the Supreme Court ruled that poll taxes were illegal in state elections as well. The elimination of the poll tax allowed many African American citizens to enjoy their full rights as voters for the first time.

The Twenty-sixth Amendment

Throughout our nation's history, people still in their teens have bravely fought for our country. By law, however, they were not old enough to vote for the leaders who sent them into battle. Although the Constitution did not **specify,** or mention, a minimum age for voters, most states set the minimum at 21.

That standard finally changed in 1971, a year when many young Americans were fighting in the Vietnam War. The Twenty-sixth Amendment guaranteed the right to vote to citizens 18 and older for all national and state elections. As a result, millions more Americans can exercise their right to vote and enjoy the rights of full citizenship.

Reading Check Explaining Who benefitted most from the passing of the Twenty-third Amendment?

C Critical Thinking

Making Inferences Ask: What does the requirement of a poll tax suggest about the people making the laws in the states that had poll taxes? *(They were wealthy enough to pay the poll tax and wanted to dilute the voices of poor citizens.)* **AL**

Reading Check **Answer:** People living in the District of Columbia benefited most from the Twenty-third Amendment.

Assess

Civics ONLINE

Study Central™ provides summaries, interactive games, and online graphic organizers to help students review content.

Close

Identifying Central Issues Have students work in groups to create a statement that generalizes the purpose of the Amendments studied in this section. **OL**

Section 3 Review

Vocabulary

1. **Write** sentences related to voting rights using the following terms: *suffrage, poll tax.*

Main Ideas

2. **Explaining** How was the promise of the Civil War amendments fulfilled in the mid-twentieth century?

3. **Identifying** One topic covered in the later amendments is the right to vote. Whose voting rights did the twentieth century amendments specifically address?

Critical Thinking

4. **BIG Ideas** How do you account for the fact that even though the Fifteenth Amendment guaranteed suffrage to African Americans, many were not allowed to vote?

5. **Explaining** On a chart like the one below, explain how each of these amendments extended voting rights.

Amendment	Effect
17th	Voters elect senators directly
19th	
23rd	
24th	
26th	

6. **Analyzing Visuals** Review the chart on page 135. Which amendment guaranteed the right to vote to citizens 18 and older?

CITIZENSHIP Activity

7. **Persuasive Writing** Because many 18- to 21-year-olds do not vote, some believe the Twenty-sixth Amendment should be repealed. Write a one-page essay expressing your views on this topic.

Civics ONLINE

Study Central™ To review this section, go to glencoe.com.

Section 3 Review

Answers

1. Sentences should use vocabulary words according to their definitions in the section and in the Glossary.

2. Succeeding amendments to the Constitution gradually removed state-imposed barriers to suffrage and employment rights.

3. These amendments addressed the rights to vote of women, residents of the District of Columbia, African Americans, poor whites, and people aged 18 to 21.

4. Until the Bill of Rights was nationalized, states could and often did ignore and pass laws that conflicted with the right to vote guaranteed in the Fifteenth Amendment.

5. **17th:** voters elect senators directly; **19th:** suffrage is extended to women of age; **23rd:** suffrage is extended to residents of the District of Columbia; **24th:** eliminated poll taxes, ensuring African Americans and poor whites would be able to exercise voting rights; **26th:** suffrage is extended to people aged 18–21

6. The Twenty-sixth Amendment guaranteed the right to vote to citizens 18 and older.

7. Essays should state a clear position on the issue and provide reasons to support that position.

S Skill Practice

Visual Literacy Ask: What is the cartoonist's opinion about credit cards? How do you know? *(The cartoonist's opinion is that using credit cards can cause people problems. The weight of overdue bills is weighing down the man with anxiety. The blush on his face and the disapproving look on the cashier's face indicate the embarrassment that uncontrolled credit spending produces.)* **OL**

D Differentiated Instruction

English Learners Ask: What is a "hard-and-fast" rule? *(It is a rule that applies and is useful in every instance.)* **ELL**

Analyzing Economics

1. Students should list three of these ways: Postpone purchases until you can pay cash. Keep track of credit card expenditures. Consider the cost of finance charges. Consider the time it will take to pay for an item. Control impulse buying.
2. Answers may include the idea that younger children should have cards so they can be trained to use them correctly or that younger children are not ready to have cards.

Additional Support

Cash or Credit?

Debbie is shopping and sees a jacket she really likes on sale for $300. However, she has a problem—no cash. Since she is 18, she has her own credit card. The card carries an 18 percent annual percentage rate on unpaid balances. Debbie calculates she can afford to pay $15 a month on the account. Should she buy the jacket or not?

How Credit Cards Work

Credit is using tomorrow's money to pay for something you get today. A credit card is a useful financial tool. It can be more convenient to use and carry than cash, and it offers valuable consumer protections under federal law.

Credit card advantages:
- Buy needed items now
- Do not have to carry cash
- Creates a record of purchases
- Consolidates bills into one payment

Credit card pitfalls:
- Higher cost of items (interest and finance charges)
- Financial problems may occur if you lose track of how much you are spending each month
- Leads to impulse buying

Credit has both advantages and disadvantages. By using it wisely, you emphasize the advantages.

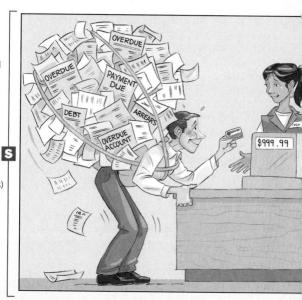

S

Checklist for Buying on Credit

D There are no hard-and-fast rules to tell you whether or not to buy on credit. Answer these questions to help you determine if you are making a wise decision:

1. Do I really require this item? Can I postpone purchasing the item until later?
2. If I pay cash, what will I be giving up that I could buy with this money?
3. Have I done comparison shopping for credit?
4. Can I afford to borrow or use credit now?

Analyzing Economics

1. **Describing** What are three ways to avoid credit card debt?
2. **Defending** To qualify for a personal credit card, a person must be 18 years old or older. Should the age restriction remain the same or be changed? Defend your response.

138 Chapter 4

Activity: Economics Connection

Logical/Mathematical Have students "do the math" to figure out how much Debbie will pay for the jacket if she can afford to pay $15 a month toward the credit card purchase and how long it will take her to pay for the jacket.

18% interest on a $300 purchase (300 × .18) is an extra $54, bringing the total cost of the jacket to $354. That might not sound like much, but Debbie can budget only $15 a month for this bill. 354 divided by $15 a month = 23.6 monthly payments.

Not only will the jacket cost 54 more dollars if Debbie uses her card, she will also be paying for the jacket for two years! Tell students that Debbie must also be disciplined to pay each monthly bill on time; otherwise, she'll have to pay late fees as well. **OL**

Guide to Reading

Big Idea
Political, social, religious, and economic changes influence the way Americans think and act.

Content Vocabulary
- discrimination (p. 140)
- segregation (p. 140)
- civil rights (p. 140)
- affirmative action (p. 143)
- racial profiling (p. 143)

Academic Vocabulary
- section (p. 140)
- gender (p. 141)

Reading Strategy
Identifying As you read, complete the chart below by filling in key laws achieved by the civil rights movement.

Important Laws
Civil Rights Acts of 1964

🔊 **Section Audio** 📽 **Spotlight Video**

Section 4
The Civil Rights Struggle

Real World Civics In September 1957, after weeks of violence, Little Rock Central High School accepted nine African American students—the only black students in the public high school. The teenagers, and their families, could not have imagined how their determination would affect the lives of millions of students who came after them. Now, more than 50 years later, their bravery is marked by *Testament,* a monument on the Arkansas State Capitol grounds. The former students, Elizabeth Eckford (right), Melba Pattillo Beals (left), and the other students were reunited for the dedication.

▼ **Elizabeth Eckford, right, unveils her *Testament* statue in 2005**

139

Teach

R Reading Strategy

Organizing Have students create a word web for section in which they list things that can easily be divided into sections. Challenge students to think of as many things as possible that can be divided into sections. (*Examples may include books [chapters], oranges [sections], houses [rooms], and so on.*) **BL** **ELL**

C Critical Thinking

Predicting Consequences **Ask:** How would this nation be different today had the struggle for civil rights failed? (*Answers may include the idea that unfair treatment would continue on a large scale and that resentment would build among those suffering discrimination.*) **OL**

TIME™ Political Cartoons

Answers:

1. The setting is the Lincoln Memorial in Washington, D. C.
2. Rosa Parks, Abraham Lincoln, and George Washington are depicted.
3. Answers may include the idea that Lincoln admires Parks for her courage and equates her actions with those of other Americans who have striven toward justice.

Differentiated Instruction

Writing Skills Activity 4, URB pp. 101–102

Struggle for Rights

Main Idea Although amendments to the Constitution guaranteed rights to Americans, African Americans and other groups still did not enjoy civil rights.

Civics & You What would you do if you were denied equal rights when using public transportation or while sitting in a movie theater? Read to find out how the civil rights movement reacted.

Despite the advances made after the Civil War, African Americans routinely faced **discrimination,** or unfair treatment based on prejudice against a certain group. Southern states, for example, passed so-called "Jim Crow" laws requiring African Americans and whites to be separated in most public places, such as schools. Later, African Americans had to ride in the back of buses and sit in separate **sections,** or parts, of restaurants and theaters. They even had to use separate public restrooms. The social separation of the races was known as **segregation.** African Americans in the North fared better. They could vote freely, and segregation was less noticeable. Even so, prejudice restricted opportunities for many. It would take more than 100 years for African Americans to secure their **civil rights**—the rights of full citizenship and equality under the law.

The *Brown* Decision An important gain came in 1948, when President Harry S. Truman ordered an end to segregation in the nation's armed forces. A bigger victory was the Supreme Court's decision in *Brown* v. *Board of Education of Topeka, Kansas* (1954). In this landmark case, the Supreme Court ruled that racial segregation in the public schools was unconstitutional. Segregation violated the Fourteenth Amendment's principle of equal protection under the law.

TIME™ Political Cartoons

Mike Thompson/Copley News Service

Cartoonist Mike Thompson created this image in 2005, when civil rights activist Rosa Parks died at the age of 92.

1. **What is the setting for this cartoon?**
2. **What figures are depicted?**
3. **How do you interpret the statement made by President Lincoln?**

Every year, more than half of all Americans do volunteer work ... role in it. One of the responsibilities of citizens is to help make their ... of volunteer grou... small. Perha... dad who...

Interpreting and Evaluating Visual Images

Objective: To interpret photographs from the civil rights movement

Focus: Have students describe in detail what they see in each photograph.

Teach: Provide context for each photograph, and note the difference in the dates.

Assess: Work through the bulleted list for each photograph.

Close: Create a two-column chart to compare and contrast the photographs.

Differentiated Instruction Strategies

BL Define photography jargon such as "point of view," "composition," "foreground," and "background."

AL Encourage students to use one of the photographs as a prompt for a poem or short story about the event.

ELL Have students compare civil rights issues in their countries of origin to the issues depicted in the photographs.

American Biography

Martin Luther King, Jr. (1929–1968)

Born in Atlanta, Georgia, in 1929, **Martin Luther King, Jr.,** riveted the country's conscience as a leader of the civil rights movement. He was selected as Man of the Year by *TIME* magazine in 1963. King received the Nobel Peace Prize in 1964, making him the youngest man and third African American ever to receive this international award. His words and efforts moved many to join in the struggle for equal rights. What drove him into this demanding role in history? The son of a Baptist minister, King attended Morehouse College and, when he was 18 years old, decided on a career in the ministry. By the time he first arrived in Montgomery in September 1954 as pastor of the Dexter Avenue Baptist Church, he had also met and married Coretta Scott.

From the beginning of the Montgomery bus boycott, King encouraged his followers to use nonviolent resistance. This meant that those who carried out the demonstrations should not fight with authorities. In spite of his stand on nonviolence, King often became the target of violence.

In April 1968, King was in Memphis, Tennessee, to support a strike of sanitation workers. There, the minister was shot and killed.

Making a Difference CITIZENSHIP

In what way does Dr. King's religious training show itself in his leadership of the civil rights movement?

Montgomery Bus Boycott In 1955, one year after the *Brown* decision, an African American woman named Rosa Parks was arrested for refusing to give up her seat to a white man on a Montgomery, Alabama, bus. Parks was arrested for violating Alabama's segregation laws. Her refusal and arrest spurred the local African American community to organize a boycott of the Montgomery bus system. A year later, the Supreme Court ruled that public bus segregation was unconstitutional. Both Parks and Dr. Martin Luther King, Jr., a leader of the boycott, gained national prominence.

D

Peaceful Protests A Baptist minister and stirring speaker, King believed in nonviolent resistance—the peaceful protest of unfair laws. He helped organize marches, boycotts, and demonstrations that opened many people's eyes to the need for change.

African American students began staging "sit-ins" at lunch counters that served only whites. White and African American "Freedom Riders" traveled together on buses to protest segregation. In his 1963 "I Have a Dream" speech, King inspired thousands with his hopes for racial equality.

Civil Rights Act of 1964 In response to the growing demand for government action, Congress passed the Civil Rights Act of 1964. This far-reaching law prohibited discrimination in public facilities, employment, education, and voter registration. It also banned discrimination not only by race and color but also by sex, or **gender,** religion, and national origin.

R

Reading Check **Describing** Through what means did Martin Luther King, Jr., hope to change unfair laws?

Chapter 4 141

Leveled Activities

C Critical Thinking

Analyzing Primary Sources **Ask:** Why is keeping a citizen of age from voting a "wrong . . . which no American, in his heart, can justify"? *(Answers may include the ideas that America was founded on this important right and that to deny the right to citizens is to deny the special nature of this nation.)* **AL**

S Skill Practice

Analyzing Charts **Ask:** Although this chart looks unorganized and rather thrown together, it has an organizational strategy that helps readers locate information. What is the chart designed to look like, and how is it organized? *(The chart is designed to look like a bulletin board with announcements randomly tacked up, yet it is organized chronologically by date of acts and can be read in two columns from left to right and top to bottom to put the dates in order.)* **OL**

Analyzing Charts

Answers:
1. The Americans with Disabilities Act of 1990 (ADA) protects the rights of disabled workers.
2. The Equal Pay Act of 1963 bans wage discrimination on the basis or race, gender, religion, or national origin.

Hands-On Chapter Project
Step 4

The Struggle Continues

Main idea The struggle for equality in America has persisted and has extended to include many groups.

Civics & You Regardless of your race, religion, or political beliefs, you have the right to be treated equally under the law. Read more about the efforts to fight discrimination.

Although the Fifteenth Amendment to the Constitution gave African American males the right to vote, that right was not always respected. By the 1960s, several states had found ways, such as the poll tax, to discourage African Americans from registering and voting.

Ratified in 1964, the Twenty-fourth Amendment outlawed poll taxes. The Voting Rights Act of 1965 took further steps to ensure that all citizens would have the opportunity to vote, regardless of race. As President Lyndon Johnson said when he signed the act,

> " *Millions of Americans are denied the right to vote because of their color. This law will ensure them the right to vote. The wrong is one which no American, in his heart, can justify.* "
> —President Lyndon B. Johnson

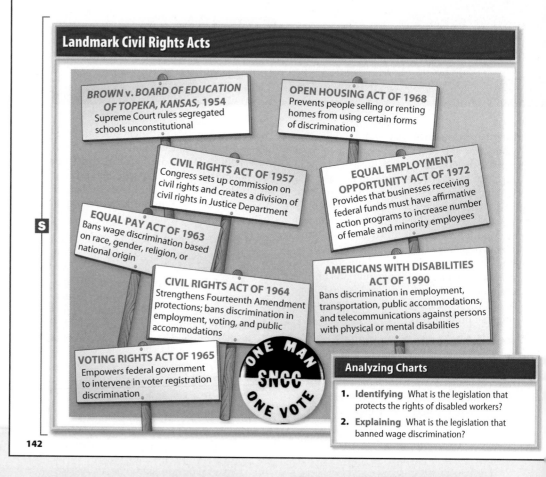

Landmark Civil Rights Acts

BROWN v. BOARD OF EDUCATION OF TOPEKA, KANSAS, 1954
Supreme Court rules segregated schools unconstitutional

OPEN HOUSING ACT OF 1968
Prevents people selling or renting homes from using certain forms of discrimination

CIVIL RIGHTS ACT OF 1957
Congress sets up commission on civil rights and creates a division of civil rights in Justice Department

EQUAL EMPLOYMENT OPPORTUNITY ACT OF 1972
Provides that businesses receiving federal funds must have affirmative action programs to increase number of female and minority employees

EQUAL PAY ACT OF 1963
Bans wage discrimination based on race, gender, religion, or national origin

CIVIL RIGHTS ACT OF 1964
Strengthens Fourteenth Amendment protections; bans discrimination in employment, voting, and public accommodations

AMERICANS WITH DISABILITIES ACT OF 1990
Bans discrimination in employment, transportation, public accommodations, and telecommunications against persons with physical or mental disabilities

VOTING RIGHTS ACT OF 1965
Empowers federal government to intervene in voter registration discrimination

ONE MAN SNCC ONE VOTE

Analyzing Charts
1. **Identifying** What is the legislation that protects the rights of disabled workers?
2. **Explaining** What is the legislation that banned wage discrimination?

Bill of Rights for Our School

Step 4: Producing the Document for Display Students will create a School Bill of Rights for display.

Directions Tell students that in this step, they will decide on a format for the Bill of Rights they have developed and choose a place to display it.

Visual/Spatial Congratulate students on their hard work during Steps 1, 2, and 3. Tell them that they are now ready to put their work in motion. Guide students in discussing how they want to publish their School Bill of Rights. Students may decide to use the computer to publish the document, or they may want to make it by hand so that it resembles the documents that survive from our nation's earliest days. Have students speak to the school's principal about an appropriate venue to display their Bill of Rights.

(Project continued on the Visual Summary page)

School Bill of Rights

Civil Rights Gains

In 2006, the United States Senate renewed the Voting Rights Act of 1965, hailing it as one of the most effective pieces of civil rights legislation in history. The civil rights laws of the 1960s were instrumental in opening more doors for minorities. African Americans, Latinos, and other minorities have made striking gains in educational achievement. They increasingly hold professional and managerial jobs and serve in government, yet whites still tend to have more opportunities.

Affirmative Action

In the 1970s, the federal government began **affirmative action** programs to try to make up for past discrimination. These programs encouraged the hiring and promoting of minorities and women in fields that were traditionally closed to them. Colleges, too, practiced affirmative action to help minority students gain admission.

From the start, affirmative action was controversial. Critics complained that giving preferential treatment to women and minorities amounted to discrimination against men and whites. The Supreme Court case of *Gratz* v. *Bollinger* (2003) centered on affirmative action. The Court struck down a University of Michigan point-based admission policy, stating that it gave excessive points to minority applicants.

The struggle for equal rights continues. Each year, the federal government receives more than 75,000 complaints of workplace discrimination. Many Americans and others are sometimes subject to **racial profiling** by law enforcement officers—being singled out as suspects because of the way they look. Some Americans even become the victims of hate crimes—acts of violence based on a person's race, color, national origin, gender, or disability.

Reading Check **Explaining** What is the purpose of affirmative action programs?

Section 4 Review

Vocabulary

1. **Write** a paragraph using the following terms to summarize the civil rights movement: *discrimination, segregation, civil rights, affirmative action, racial profiling.*

Main Ideas

2. **Identifying** List examples of the discrimination that African Americans faced after the Civil War.

3. **Describing** What other groups besides African Americans are struggling for equality under the law today?

Critical Thinking

4. **BIG Ideas** Why was the civil rights movement started?

5. **Identifying** Use the graphic organizer below to identify the areas of American life where affirmative action has been used.

Affirmative Action

6. **Analyzing Visuals** Reexamine the chart on page 142 that lists some landmark acts achieved by civil rights activists. What was the purpose of the Americans with Disabilities Act?

CITIZENSHIP Activity

7. **Persuasive Writing** Do you think that affirmative action laws are a fair way to change past discrimination? Write your opinion in a letter to the editor.

Civics ONLINE

Study Central™ To review this section, go to glencoe.com.

W Writing Support

Persuasive Writing Have students research online to find out more information on the *Gratz* v. *Bollinger* case. Students should then write several paragraphs about whether or not they think the Court ruling was correct. **OL**

Reading Check **Answer:** Affirmative action programs attempt to make up for past discrimination by encouraging the hiring and promoting of minorities and women in fields that were traditionally closed to them.

Assess

Civics ONLINE

Study Central™ provides summaries, interactive games, and online graphic organizers to help students review content.

Close

Identifying Central Issues **Ask:** How do the Bill of Rights and the amendments to the Constitution shape the character of this nation? **OL**

Section 4 Review

Answers

1. Sentences should use vocabulary words according to their definitions in the section and in the Glossary.

2. Answers may include examples of abridgement of rights to suffrage, fair employment, and access to public facilities.

3. Answers may include women, minorities, and disabled people.

4. The civil rights movement was started to ensure that all Americans received the rights guaranteed in the Bill of Rights, regardless of race, religion, gender, disability, or national origin.

5. gaining admission to college; promoting; hiring; opening fields traditionally closed

6. The ADA ensures that Americans with disabilities have equal access to employment, transportation, public facilities, and telecommunications.

7. Letters should include a clear position on the issue and give reasons to support that position.

Teach

Explain that in the years leading up to the Civil War, the federal government attempted to soothe growing tensions between states in which slavery was legal and states in which it was not by introducing the Missouri Compromise. The compromise ensured that as the nation grew, a rough balance between "slave states" and "free states" would hold so that neither kind of state would have undue influence over the nation's development.

ANALYZING THE COURT DECISION

Answers:

1. The court determined that Dred Scott was a not a citizen because he was a slave. Thus, his case was unconstitutional. The Constitution applied only to citizens.

2. Answers may include the idea that Justice Taney's view was influenced by the time in which he lived.

Additional Support

Dred Scott v. Sandford

Before the Civil War, Americans were asking: Are African Americans citizens of the United States? May Congress prohibit enslavement of African Americans in U.S. territories?

Background of the Case

Dred Scott, an enslaved African American, worked for a physician. A member of the military, the physician moved often, taking Scott with him. As a result, Scott lived for a time in the state of Illinois and in the territory of Wisconsin, both slave-free zones. Both zones were also north of the boundary set by Congress in the Missouri Compromise of 1820. The Missouri Compromise permitted slavery south of the line and prohibited slavery north of it.

By 1846, the physician died, and Scott was again living in Missouri. There he continued to work for the physician's widow and her brother John Sanford, who was from New York. Scott sued for his freedom. He claimed that his earlier residence in a free state and a free territory made him free. Missouri's courts denied Scott, however. In order to claim federal court jurisdiction, Scott's lawyers then stated that Scott was a citizen of Missouri bringing suit against Sanford, a citizen of New York.

Dred Scott

The Decision

The Supreme Court decided the case on March 6–7, 1857. Chief Justice Roger B. Taney spoke for the seven-justice majority. Taney first asserted his own view of the Framers' so-called original intent: "The only rights and privileges African Americans were meant to have were those granted by their so-called 'owners' or by the government. Therefore, Dred Scott could not be a citizen." He wrote further:

> ❝ [I]t is the opinion of the Court that the act of Congress which prohibited . . . [slaveholding] north of the line therein mentioned is . . . void; and that neither Dred Scott himself, nor any member of his family were made free by being carried into this territory. ❞
>
> —Chief Justice Roger B. Taney

The Court was saying that the suit of non-citizen Scott and the Missouri Compromise were unconstitutional. Therefore, Scott was not free.

Why It Matters

The ruling added to the tensions that led to the Civil War. In 1868, three years after the end of the war, the Fourteenth Amendment to the United States Constitution overruled the *Dred Scott* decision.

Analyzing the Court Decision

1. **Explaining** Why was Dred Scott not freed as a result of the Supreme Court's decision?

2. **Inferring** What is your opinion of Justice Taney's view of the Framers' "original intent"?

Background

Dred Scott v. Sandford Justice Taney was in fact a supporter of the slave states' position and wanted to protect the institution of slavery and the economic system that it supported. He wrote in his decision that African Americans "had no rights which the white man was bound to respect" and believed that the phrase from the Declaration of Independence declaring all men "equal" was not intended for African Americans.

The court's decision angered abolitionists. Now slavery would be permitted in every state in the nation. The abolitionist and former slave Frederick Douglass, on the other hand, believed that in time this decision would help bring an end to slavery because it riveted the nation's attention to this critical issue.

Visual Summary

Rights of Citizens

The Bill of Rights—the first 10 amendments to the U.S. Constitution—guarantees certain basic rights to all Americans. The Bill of Rights ensures constitutional guarantees of

- freedom of expression and belief;
- individual security; and
- equal and fair treatment before the law.

First North Carolina sit-in, 1960s

Limits on Rights

- An individual's rights must be balanced with the rights of others and the community's health and safety.

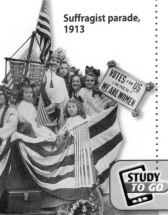

Suffragist parade, 1913

Equality Under the Law

- Limits on rights must be reasonable and apply equally to all.
- This is especially critical in the courtroom, which is where the right to due process comes into play.
- Due process means that government may not act unfairly or arbitrarily but must follow a set of reasonable, fair, and standard procedures.

Civil Rights

- Civil rights are the protections granted in the Constitution that recognize all citizens must be treated equally under the law.
- In the United States at one time, there were widespread segregation laws.

Civil Rights march on Washington, D.C., 1963

- In *Plessy* v. *Ferguson* (1896), the Supreme Court ruled that separate-but-equal facilities were constitutional.
- In *Brown* v. *Board of Education of Topeka* (1954), the Court ruled for complete desegregation.
- The civil rights movement made possible the passage of legislation guaranteeing basic civil rights for all Americans.

STUDY TO GO Study anywhere, anytime! Download quizzes and flash cards to your PDA from glencoe.com.

145

Identifying the Main Idea Draw students' attention to the two court cases summarized in the right-hand column. **Ask:** These cases' rulings are opposites. What does this tell you about the nature of the nation's law? *(Answer: The law is not static but changes gradually toward an ideal of equal and fair treatment for all citizens.)* **OL**

Analyzing Visuals Ask: Look at the three images on the page. What do the three events chronicled in these images have in common? *(Each image records a nonviolent demonstration—a sit-in, a peaceful march, and a parade. Each event was an attempt to bring an injustice to the attention of citizens and leaders so that the unjust situation would be changed. Each is an example of the process by which the law of the land is examined and reexamined.)* **AL**

Hands-On Chapter Project

Step 5: Wrap-Up

Bill of Rights for Our School

Step 5: Comparing Students' School Bill of Rights with Existing Documents Students will find out whether the school or district has a "bill of rights" and compare theirs to it.

Tell students that in this step, they will find out whether their school or district has already produced a similar document out-lining the rights of school personnel and students. They will examine how closely their document resembles the existing document and discuss differences.

Comparing and Contrasting Provide students with school or district documents that outline the rights of students and school personnel. Ask students to read this document and to correlate their School Bill of Rights to it. Guide them in discussing any differences they note. If the school or district does not have such a document, have students submit the document to the school's principal for consideration. **OL**

Answers and Analyses
Reviewing Vocabulary

1. C Slander and libel are distractors because they are made illegal by the First Amendment. Due process is guaranteed by the Fifth Amendment.

2. C If students understand that "domain" is control of something, they will more easily rule out the other options and relate control of property to eminent domain.

3. A Age requirements would affect everyone's right to vote—not just African Americans. If a person has civil rights, he or she will be able to vote. Only A names a strategy that Southern states used to abridge voting rights.

4. B Review with students the definitions of the options. Affirmative action tries to help minorities, so option D is incorrect. While A does apply to legal action, only B names an unfair action sometimes taken by law enforcement officials.

Reviewing Main Ideas

5. C Options A and D both describe violent and harmful actions made illegal under the law of nation. Option B describes another part of the Constitution. The Bill of Rights protects the natural rights of citizens. Only option C describes a right of citizens.

6. B Ask students to recall the five protections of the First Amendment. Options A, C, and D are permitted and protected acts under the First Amendment. Option B violates the protection of freedom of religion.

7. D Options A, B, and C are all rights guaranteed by the Constitution. Only option D is a guaranteed right of the accused in any and every case, criminal or civil.

8. D Review with students the sections that list amendments and help them locate the amendment in question.

9. C Review with students the sections that list amendments and help them locate the amendment in question. Option D deals with voting rights for

Chapter

4 ASSESSMENT

Standardized Test Practice

TEST-TAKING TIP

For effective recall at exam time, study in one-half-hour intervals for a week before the test.

Reviewing Vocabulary

Directions: Choose the word(s) that best completes the sentence.

1. The First Amendment guarantees the right to _____.

  A libel   **C** petition

  B slander   **D** due process

2. The right of the government to take private property for public use is called _____.

  A suffrage   **C** eminent domain

  B civil right   **D** double jeopardy

3. _____ in Southern states prevented many African Americans from voting.

  A poll taxes   **C** civil rights

  B age requirements **D** search warrants

4. Sometimes law enforcement officials single out suspects unfairly through _____.

  A indictments   **C** censorship

  B racial profiling **D** affirmative action

Reviewing Main Ideas

Directions: Choose the best answer for each question.

Section 1 *(pp.120–124)*

5. Which of the following does the Bill of Rights protect?

  A the right to provoke a riot for a good cause

  B the power of government to operate efficiently

  C the freedom to act without government interference

  D the choice to overthrow an unjust government by force

6. What does the First Amendment prohibit?

  A assembly of groups such as communists

  B establishment of an official state religion

  C criticism of the government or its officials

  D dissemination of alarming or offensive ideas

Section 2 *(pp. 126–131)*

7. How does the Fifth Amendment help accused persons?

  A by requiring a speedy trial

  B by requiring a search warrant

  C by guaranteeing a trial by jury

  D by protecting against self incrimination

8. Which amendment states that all rights not spelled out in the Constitution are "retained by the people"?

  A Second Amendment

  B Third Amendment

  C Seventh Amendment

  D Ninth Amendment

Section 3 *(pp. 133–137)*

9. Which amendment guaranteed African American men the right to vote?

  A Thirteenth Amendment

  B Fourteenth Amendment

  C Fifteenth Amendment

  D Nineteenth Amendment

10. Whose right to vote did the Twenty-sixth Amendment guarantee?

  A poor people in the South

  B women across the country

  C residents of Washington, D.C.

  D citizens 18 years old and older

GO ON ➡

women. Options A, B, and C were all "Civil War" amendments. Only option C deals with voting rights.

10. D Remind students that the Twenty-sixth Amendment is the most recent and occurred during the Vietnam War. Challenge them to use these historical connections to choose the correct answer.

11. C Students must remember that the *Brown* Supreme Court case happened in the 1950s. Ask students to remember when

Dr. King, Rosa Parks, and others began to peacefully protest for civil rights. Guide them to use this historical clue to determine the answer.

12. D The biggest clue in this question is that it is asking about voting. This automatically eliminates options A and B. The Voting Rights Act of 1965 dealt with discrimination, but it was passed after the ratification of the Twenty-fourth Amendment.

Section 4 *(pp. 139–143)*

11. Which sphere of American life was desegregated in the 1940s?

  A schools

  B work places

  C armed forces

  D lunch counters

12. Which measure outlawed poll taxes?

  A Civil Rights Act of 1957

  B Civil Rights Act of 1954

  C Voting Rights Act of 1965

  D Twenty-fourth Amendment

Critical Thinking

Directions: Base your answers to questions 13 and 14 on the table below and your knowledge of Chapter 4.

Rights and Freedoms in the Bill of Rights
Trial by jury
Due process
Private property
No unreasonable searches or seizures
No cruel punishment
No excessive bail or fines
Right to bear arms
Right to petition
Freedom of speech
Freedom of the press
Freedom of religion

13. Which amendment protects freedom of speech?

  A First Amendment

  B Fifth Amendment

  C Thirteenth Amendment

  D Twenty-fourth Amendment

14. Which right or freedom best reflects the humane intent of Anglo-American law?

  A the right to bear arms

  B the freedom of the press

  C the right to private property

  D the freedom from cruel punishment

Document-Based Questions

Directions: Analyze the following document and answer the short-answer questions that follow.

> **Amendment XXII**
>
> **Section 1**
>
> *No person shall be elected to the office of the President more than twice, and no person who had held the office of President, or acted as President, for more than two years of a term to which some other person was elected president shall be elected to the office of President more than once.*
>
> —the Constitution

15. A presidential term lasts four years. According to the Twenty-second Amendment, what is the longest time one person may serve as president?

16. Why do you think Congress and the state legislatures considered the Twenty-second Amendment necessary?

Extended-Response Question

17. Write a brief essay explaining how the Ninth and Tenth Amendments prevent the national government from becoming too strong.

STOP

Civics ONLINE

For additional test practice, use Self-Check Quizzes—Chapter 4 on glencoe.com.

Need Extra Help?																	
If you missed question…	1	2	3	4	5	6	7	8	9	10	11	12	13	14	15	16	17
Go to page…	121	128	134	143	121	124	128	131	135	137	140	142	122	129	135	135	131

ASSESSMENT

16. Students' answers will vary. A possible answer is that Congress and the states did not want a popular president to accumulate too much power over time.

Extended Response

17. Students' essays will vary but must include supporting examples from the chapter.

Critical Thinking

13. A While all options protect our freedoms, only the First Amendment protects our freedom of speech.

14. D Draw students' attention to the word "humane," and ask them to supply synonyms and antonyms for it. Then tell them to look for these words in the options. They will locate the antonym "cruel." Tell them to determine whether this option answers the question correctly.

Document-Based Questions

15. The maximum length of time that one can serve as president is ten years. If someone served as president for up to two years without being elected as president (if the president died in office, for example), that person can still serve two four-year terms as president.

Civics ONLINE

Have students visit the Web site at glencoe.com to review Chapter 4 and take the **Self-Check Quiz**.

Need Extra Help?

Have students refer to the pages listed if they miss any of the questions.

Chapter Planning Guide

5

Levels					Resources	Chapter Opener	Section 1	Section 2	Chapter Assess
BL	OL	AL	ELL						
					FOCUS				
BL	OL	AL	ELL	🖋	Daily Focus Skills Transparencies		5–1	5–2	
					TEACH				
BL	OL		ELL	📁	Reading Essentials and Note-Taking Guide*		p. 46	p. 49	
	OL	AL		📁	Economics Activity, URB		p. 5		
		AL		📁	Enrichment Activity, URB			p. 13	
BL	OL	AL	ELL	📁	Content Vocabulary Activity, URB*	p. 118	p. 118	p. 118	
BL	OL	AL	ELL	📁	Academic Vocabulary Activity, URB	p. 119	p. 119	p. 119	
	OL			📁	Biography Activity, URB			p. 121	
BL	OL	AL	ELL	📁	Writing Skills Activity, URB		p. 123	p. 123	
	OL	AL		📁	Critical Thinking Skills Activity, URB		p. 125		
BL	OL	AL	ELL	📁	Chart, Graph, and Map Skills Activity, URB		p. 127		
BL	OL	AL	ELL	📁	Differentiated Instruction, URB			p. 129	
BL	OL	AL	ELL	📁	School-to-Home Connection Activity, URB*	p. 131	p. 131	p. 131	
BL	OL		ELL	📁	Guided Reading Activities, URB*		p. 135	p. 136	
BL	OL	AL	ELL	📁	Writer's Guidebook	✓	✓	✓	✓
	OL	AL		💿	Primary Source Document Library	✓	✓	✓	✓
BL	OL	AL	ELL	💿	Daily Lecture & Discussion Notes (in Pres. Plus)		✓	✓	✓
BL	OL	AL	ELL	💿	StudentWorks™ Plus		✓	✓	✓
BL	OL	AL	ELL	💿	Section Spotlight Videos		✓	✓	
BL	OL	AL	ELL	🖋	TIME Interpreting Political Cartoons Transp.			Ch. 5	
BL	OL	AL	ELL	🖋	Writing Process Transparencies	✓	✓	✓	✓

Note: Please refer to the *Unit 1 Resource Book* for this chapter's URB materials.

* Also available in Spanish

TeacherWorks *Plus*
All-In-One Planner and Resource Center

- Interactive Lesson Planner
- Interactive Teacher Edition
- Fully editable blackline masters
- Section Spotlight Videos Launch

- Differentiated Lesson Plans
- Printable reports of daily assignments
- Standards Tracking System

Levels					Resources	Chapter Opener	Section 1	Section 2	Chapter Assess
BL	OL	AL	ELL						
					TEACH *(continued)*				
				📁	**Building Academic Vocabulary**	✓	✓	✓	✓
				📁	**Strategies for Success**	✓	✓	✓	✓
Teacher Resources				📁	**Teacher's Guide to Differentiated Instruction**	✓	✓	✓	✓
				💿	**Graphing Tool**	✓	✓	✓	✓
				💿	**Presentation Plus! with MindJogger CheckPoint**	✓	✓	✓	✓
					ASSESS				
BL	OL	AL	ELL	📁	**Quizzes and Tests***		p. 50	p. 51	p. 52
BL	OL	AL	ELL	📁	**Authentic Assessment with Rubrics**			p. 9	
BL	OL	AL	ELL	📁	**Standardized Test Practice**		p. 9	p. 9	p. 9
BL	OL	AL	ELL	💿	*ExamView®* **Assessment Suite CD-ROM**		5–1	5–2	Ch. 5
					CLOSE				
BL			ELL	📁	**Reteaching Activity, URB***		p. 133	p. 133	
BL	OL		ELL	📁	**Reading and Study Skills Foldables™ Activity**	p. 58	p. 59	p. 59	
BL	OL	AL	ELL	📁	*Civics Today* **in Graphic Novel**	p. 9	p. 9		
BL	OL	AL	ELL	🖋	**Graphic Organizer Transparencies & Strategies**	✓	✓	✓	✓

✓ Chapter- or unit-based activities applicable to all sections in this chapter

5

Using the Primary Source Document Library

Searching by Chronology

What is the Primary Source Document Library?

Glencoe's *American History Primary Source Document Library CD-ROM* includes more than 200 primary source documents to help supplement various lesson plans.

How can the *American History Primary Source Document Library* help my students?

The *American History Primary Source Document Library* provides a chronological list of sources to simplify searches, and allows students to:

- select chronological periods from Prehistory through Modern America
- choose from selected documents within each time period to read and/or listen to
- utilize Teaching Strategies, Questions/Answers, and Blackline Masters resources in conjunction with the primary source document to maximize student learning

Civics ONLINE
Visit glencoe.com and enter *QuickPass*™ code CIV1360c5T for Chapter 5 resources.

You can easily launch a wide range of digital products from your computer's desktop with the McGraw-Hill Social Studies widget.

TeacherWorks

	Student	Teacher	Parent
Media Library			
• Student Edition Section Audio	●		●
• Spanish Audio Summaries	●		●
• Section Spotlight Videos	●	●	●
***Civics Today* Online Learning Center (Web Site)**			
• Chapter Overviews	●	●	●
• Study Central™	●	●	●
• Study-to-Go	●	●	●
• Student Web Activities	●	●	●
• In Motion Animation	●	●	●
• Self-Check Quizzes	●	●	●
• ePuzzles and Games	●	●	●
• StudentWorks™ Plus Online	●	●	●
• Vocabulary eFlashcards	●	●	●
• Web Activity Lesson Plans		●	
• Vocabulary PuzzleMaker	●	●	●
Classroom Tools			
• Multilingual Glossary	●	●	●
• Beyond the Textbook	●	●	●
• NGS MapMachine	●	●	●

BOOKLINK 3

Reading List Generator CD-ROM

Use this database to search more than 30,000 titles to create a customized reading list for your students.

- Reading lists can be organized by students' reading level, author, genre, theme, or area of interest.
- The database provides Degrees of Reading Power™ (DRP) and Lexile™ readability scores for all selections.
- A brief summary of each selection is included.

Reading suggestions

Leveled reading suggestions for this chapter:

For students at a Grade 7 reading level:
- *Hurricane Andrew: Nature's Rage,* by Victoria Sherrow

For students at a Grade 8 reading level:
- *Posterity: Letters of Great Americans to Their Children,* by Dorie McCullough Lawson

For students at a Grade 9 reading level:
- *Kids at Work: Lewis Hine and the Crusade Against Child Labor,* by Russell Freedman

For students at a Grade 10 reading level:
- *Twenty Years at Hull House,* by Jane Addams

For students at a Grade 11 reading level:
- *Environmental Pioneers,* by Patricia Byrnes

READING SUPPORT FROM
JAMESTOWN EDUCATION

- **Timed Readings Plus in Social Studies** helps students increase their reading rate and fluency while maintaining comprehension. The 400-word passages are similar to those found on state and national assessments.

- **Reading in the Content Area: Social Studies** concentrates on six essential reading skills that help students better comprehend what they read. The book includes 75 high-interest nonfiction passages written at increasing levels of difficulty.

- **Reading Social Studies** includes strategic reading instruction and vocabulary support in Social Studies content for both ELLs and native speakers of English.

- **Content Vocabulary Workout** (Grades 6–8) accelerates reading comprehension through focused vocabulary development. Social Studies content vocabulary comes from the glossaries of Glencoe's Middle School Social Studies texts. www.jamestowneducation.com

KEY Teacher Wraparound

Use this key to help you identify the different types of prompts found in the Teacher Wraparound Edition.

R **Reading Strategies** activities help you teach reading skills and vocabulary.

C **Critical Thinking** strategies help students apply and extend what they have learned.

D **Differentiated Instruction** activities provide instruction for students learning to speak English, along with suggestions for teaching various types of learners.

S **Skill Practice** strategies help students practice historical analysis and geography skills.

W **Writing Support** activities provide writing opportunities to help students comprehend the text.

Teaching strategies and activities have been coded for ability level appropriateness.

AL Activities for students working above grade level

OL Activities for students working on grade level

BL Activities for students working below grade level

ELL Activities for English Language Learners

Focus

Why It Matters

Ask: How are volunteers in your community exercising their responsibilities? *(Answers may include obeying laws, paying taxes, defending the nation, serving in court, attending school, being informed about issues, speaking up on issues, voting, respecting others' rights, and contributing to the common good through volunteer and charitable activities.)*

More About the Photo

Visual Literacy The young people in this photo are painting a school hallway in vibrant, fresh colors. At the same time, they are learning useful and marketable skills. The Publicolors Paint Club program serves young people in the city by teaching them how to paint, and the young people serve the community by giving their time and effort to projects like the one shown here.

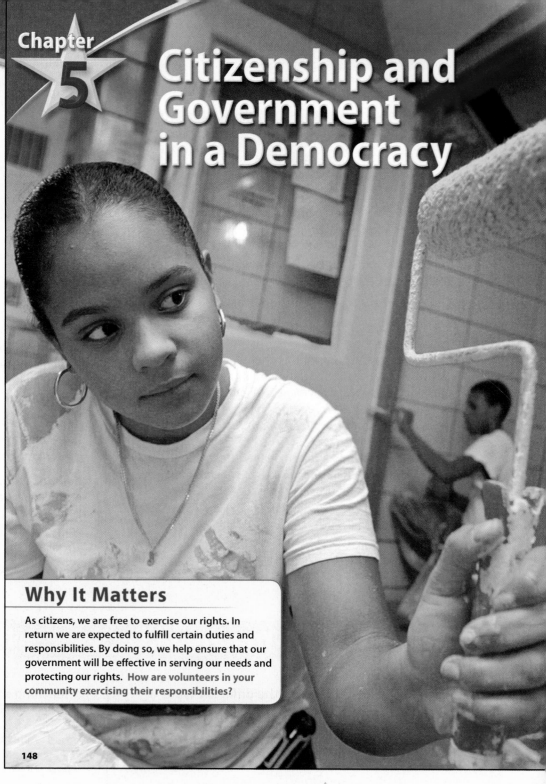

Chapter
5

Citizenship and Government in a Democracy

Why It Matters

As citizens, we are free to exercise our rights. In return we are expected to fulfill certain duties and responsibilities. By doing so, we help ensure that our government will be effective in serving our needs and protecting our rights. **How are volunteers in your community exercising their responsibilities?**

148

Teach

BIG Ideas *As you begin teaching this section, use these questions and activities to help students focus on the Big Ideas.*

Section 1

Duties and Responsibilities Ask: What would happen if citizens ignored their civic duties and responsibilities? *(Answers may include these problems: Others' rights would be disrespected; courts could not function; officials would not be elected by a representative vote; important*

city and federal programs would not be funded.) Tell students that in Section 1, they will learn about the ways that citizens' actions help city, state, and federal government operate and provide for everyone's needs. **OL**

Section 2

Citizens and the Community Ask: What volunteer organizations do you know about in your community? What needs do they meet? *(Answers may include organizations that operate food banks, restore parks, provide medical services, promote new businesses, and so on.)* Point out to students that in Section 2, they will learn about the importance of the participation of all citizens in their communities. **OL**

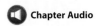 Chapter Audio

Civics ONLINE
Visit glencoe.com and enter
QuickPass™ code
CIV3093c5 for
Chapter 5
resources.

Chapter Introduction
5

BIG Ideas

Section 1: Duties and Responsibilities

For government to be effective, citizens must fulfill their civic duties and responsibilities. As American citizens, we enjoy many rights under our system of government. Along with those rights, we also share many responsibilities. These responsibilities help protect our rights.

Section 2: Citizens and the Community

Citizen participation is essential to the foundation and preservation of the U.S. political system. Good citizenship does not depend on each of us doing only what we are required to do by law. The American ideal of citizenship has always stressed each citizen's responsibility to participate in his or her community.

◀ **Young volunteer in the Publicolors Paint Club spruces up her New York City school**

 FOLDABLES
Study Organizer **Dinah Zike's Foldables**

Purpose This Foldable guides students to see how citizens' responsibilities to the community and the community's responsibilities to citizens interrelate. The completed Foldable will use tabs to help students list and compare the duties of citizen and community. **OL**

More Foldables activities for this chapter can be found in the *Dinah Zike's Reading and Study Skills Foldables* ancillary.

Civics ONLINE

Visit glencoe.com and enter *QuickPass*™ code CIV1360c5T for Chapter 5 resources, including a Chapter Overview, Study Central™, Study-to-Go, Student Web Activity, Self-Check Quiz, and other materials.

 FOLDABLES
Study Organizer

Comparing Information Study Foldable Make this Foldable to help you compare responsibilities of the citizen and the community.

Step 1 Fold one sheet of paper in half from side to side.

Step 2 Turn the paper and fold it into thirds.

Reading and Writing
As you read this chapter, list the responsibilities the citizen has to the community and those that the community has to the citizen under the appropriate tabs of your Foldable. Be sure to fill out the "Both" area, too.

Step 3 Unfold and draw two overlapping ovals, and label them as shown.

Step 4 Cut only the top layer along both fold lines.

Chapter 5 **149**

Focus

Bellringer

Daily Focus Transparency 5–1

Guide to Reading

Answers to Graphic:

Duties of Citizens

- defend the nation
- pay taxes
- attend school
- serve in court
- obey laws

Section Spotlight Video

To generate student interest and provide a springboard for class discussion, access the Chapter 5, Section 1 video at glencoe.com or on the video DVD.

Resource Manager

Guide to Reading

Big Idea
For government to be effective, citizens must fulfill their civic duties and responsibilities.

Content Vocabulary
- responsibility *(p. 151)*
- duty *(p. 151)*
- draft *(p. 152)*
- tolerance *(p. 154)*

Academic Vocabulary
- global *(p. 151)*
- income *(p. 152)*

Reading Strategy
Summarizing Information
As you read, on a web diagram like the one below, list the legal duties of U.S. citizens.

Duties of Citizens

attend school

🔊 **Section Audio**   🎬 **Spotlight Video**

Duties and Responsibilities

Real World Civics Kirk Bauer is no stranger to a challenge. As a young soldier in Vietnam in 1969, Bauer lost his leg to a grenade blast. Today, after years of surgeries and rehabilitation, Bauer is the executive director of Disabled Sports USA, an organization dedicated to providing sports rehabilitation to persons with permanent disabilities. Because Bauer was introduced to skiing by other Vietnam veterans, he has focused his energy on providing rehabilitation opportunities for veterans injured in conflicts in Iraq and Afghanistan.

▼ **Kirk Bauer competes at the Hartford Ski Spectacular in Breckenridge, Colorado.**

R Reading Strategies	**C** Critical Thinking	**D** Differentiated Instruction	**W** Writing Support	**S** Skill Practice
Teacher Edition • Act. Prior Know., p. 153 **Additional Resources** • Cont. Vocab., URB p. 118 • Acad. Vocab., URB p. 119 • Guide Read., URB p. 135 • Foldables, URB p. 59	**Teacher Edition** • Pred. Consequences, p. 152 **Additional Resources** • Economics Activity, URB p. 5 • Crit. Thinking Act., URB p. 125 • Quizzes and Tests, p. 50	**Teacher Edition** • Visual/Spatial, p. 151 • English Learners, p. 153 **Additional Resources** • School-to-Home Act., URB p. 131 • Reteach. Act., URB p. 133 • Graphic Novel, p. 9	**Teacher Edition** • Expository Writing, p. 154 **Additional Resources** • Writing Skills, URB p. 123	**Teacher Edition** • Analyzing Charts, p. 153 **Additional Resources** • Chart, Graph, and Map Skills, URB p. 127 • Daily Focus Trans., 5–1

Duties of Citizens

Main Idea The privilege of U.S. citizenship brings with it certain duties and responsibilities.

Civics & You Are you a good citizen? What are the duties and the responsibilities of citizenship? Read on to find out why American citizens have a responsibility to their communities, the environment, and the law.

What comes to mind when you hear the word "community"? Do you think of your neighborhood or perhaps your town? Actually, each of us belongs to many communities—our school or workplace; our church, synagogue, or mosque; our state; and our country. On the broadest level, we are also members of the **global,** or worldwide, community becoming more connected than ever before with people around the world.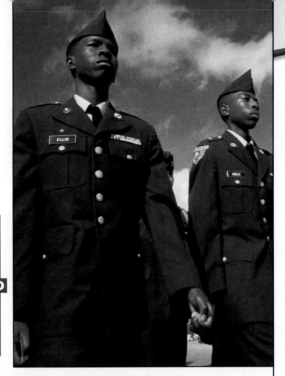

We all play a part in making our communities safe and successful. All of us have certain responsibilities to fulfill. **Responsibilities** are things we should do; they are obligations that we fulfill voluntarily. As American citizens, we also have legal duties that we are required to perform. **Duties** are things that we are required to do.

National, state, and local governments require Americans to perform certain duties established by laws. If we fail to perform them, we are subject to legal penalties, such as fines or imprisonment.

Some countries require much from their citizens. In some countries, for example, citizens must serve in the armed forces for a period of time each year. The United States government asks much less of its citizens than many other countries. Nonetheless, the government does require its citizens to perform the following duties.

Student Web Activity Visit glencoe.com and complete the Chapter 5 Web Activity.

Duties As citizens of the United States, we all have certain duties, such as defending the nation.
Explaining Why is it important to fulfill our duties as citizens?

Obey Laws

This is a citizen's most important duty. Our laws are designed for specific purposes—to help people get along, to prevent accidents, to see that resources are used fairly, and so on. If we do not obey the law, then communities cannot maintain order or protect our health, safety, and property.

Pay Taxes

Another duty of citizens is to pay taxes. Taxes provide most of the money government needs to keep functioning. Without taxes, the federal government could not pay its employees, maintain armed forces to defend the country, and help those in need. Your local community probably could not hire police or firefighters, and your state could not pave roads or maintain prisons.

Chapter 5 151

Teach

D Differentiated Instruction

Visual/Spatial Have students create a graphic organizer to represent the communities in which they participate. Guide them to begin by drawing a small circle in the center of a page; they should label this circle "family." Have students add concentric circles to represent larger communities to which they belong: at school in their community, and in state, nation, and world. **BL**

Caption Answer:

Students may say that if we do not fulfill our duties as citizens, we will no longer be able to enjoy the rights and freedoms that citizens of our nation are guaranteed.

Civics ONLINE

Objectives and answers to the **Student Web Activity** can be found at glencoe.com under the Web Activity Lesson Plan for this chapter.

Hands-On Chapter Project
Step 1

Serving in Your Community

Step 1: Researching Volunteer Opportunities Groups of students will gather information on opportunities for young people to serve their communities. They will find information on specific organizations, events, and skills and use this information to create a Student Volunteer Information Center.

Directions Write the "Why It Matters" question from page 148 on the board. Assign small groups of students to research community services that are provided by volunteers. Students can use references such as phone books, city Web sites and newspapers, and the Chamber of Commerce. Students can also interview by phone the organizers of volunteer agencies. Tell students to look for information on specific community events, such as park cleanup days, as well. Remind students to keep an accurate record of the information they find.

Collating Ask groups of students to share the information they have found with other groups. Together, the class should create a database of volunteer organizations, eliminating overlapping information and checking accuracy of information. **OL**

(Project continued in Section 2)

C Critical Thinking

Predicting Consequences Ask: What would happen if most people used excuses *(both long and short term)* to avoid serving on juries when called? *(Courts could not try cases quickly. Prisons would overfill when courts fell behind. Justice and the rule of law would be weakened because people could not be tried and, if guilty, punished for breaking the law.)* **AL**

> ✓ **Reading Check Answer:** Taxes pay for many needs, from federal highways to local schools.

TIME™ Teens in *Action*

Answers:

Students' paragraphs should note that Geneva's community benefits from the business seminars, which promote new businesses in the area, and that the art gallery adds a cultural dimension to the community.

Differentiated Instruction

The federal government and some states and cities collect **income,** or earnings, in the form of taxes—a percentage of what people earn. Most states and some cities collect taxes on the sale of goods and services. Your school district collects taxes on the residential and commercial property within the district.

Defend the Nation

Under the law, men aged 18 to 25 are required to register with the government in case the country needs to **draft,** or call up, men for military service. Since the end of the Vietnam War, there has been no draft, and America's military has been made up of volunteers. The draft is typically used only in the event of war or extreme national emergency.

Serve in Court

The Constitution guarantees the right to a trial by jury. Every adult citizen must be prepared to serve on a jury. People can be **C** excused from jury duty if they have a valid reason, but service is usually rewarding. People involved in court cases depend on their fellow citizens to reach a fair verdict. Another duty of citizens is to serve as witnesses at a trial if called to do so.

Attend School

All young people have access to free public schools and, in most states, are required to attend school until the age of 16. This benefits both you and the government because you need knowledge and skills to be a good citizen. In school you not only gain an understanding of history, government, and other important subjects, but you also learn to think through problems, to form opinions, and to express your views clearly.

> ✓ **Reading Check Explaining** Why must all citizens pay taxes?

TIME™ Teens in *Action*

Bring It On!

Geneva Johnson, 17, runs a group in New York City that gives hope and guidance to inner-city kids.

Geneva Johnson was 14 when she and her two siblings watched in horror as a stranger shot a man waiting for a parking space outside their Bronx apartment. "We were so scared," she says. "We just hit the floor." Living in a neighborhood so dangerous her parents forbade her to use the local playground, Johnson was determined to give other kids options—and hope.

To do that, Johnson founded Bring It On! (www.bringitonnyc.org). It is a youth group that tries to fire up the dreams and ambitions of underprivileged kids. Although she gets some money as donations from corporations and local businesses, Johnson also contributes money from her own pocket. With siblings Jeremiah, 18, and Christina, 14, she runs a neighborhood art gallery. For the 50 or so members of Bring It On!—most are from her Eastchester Heights neighborhood—Johnson runs seminars on starting up businesses and ways to make money. Johnson also hosts monthly panels called You Go Girl Go!! where women who have overcome obstacles tell their stories to girls.

Geneva Johnson helps inner-city kids create art in New York City.

Making a Difference ——— CITIZENSHIP

Write a paragraph explaining how Geneva Johnson's project has helped others and Geneva herself.

Tax Revenues

Objective: To understand the system of paying taxes

Focus: Guide students to understand why they pay taxes.

Teach: Discuss the taxes listed in each column and elicit examples of what each pays for.

Assess: Have students explain direct and indirect taxes.

Close: Have students make a poster encouraging people to pay their taxes.

Differentiated Instruction Strategies

BL If people did not pay their taxes, what programs and services might suffer?

AL Choose a state that does not have state income taxes and explain how it pays for programs and services.

ELL Compare the way the United States funds programs and services with the way another country does.

Civic Responsibilities

Main Idea The voluntary responsibilities of U.S. citizens include participating in the political process and being informed.

Civics & You As a citizen, what do you think is your most important responsibility? Read to find out what voluntary actions are part of good citizenship.

Be Informed

Keep in mind that government decisions affect your life. The state legislature, for example, might pass a law changing the rate of sales tax you pay. Your school board might vote to start the school day earlier. Your town council might set aside funds for a new recreation center. You have a responsibility to know what the government is doing so that you can voice your opinions on matters about which you feel strongly.

Speak Up and Vote

Our government is based on the principle of "consent of the governed." This means that people are the source of all governmental power; that is, government exists to serve you. If you expect public officials to act in your interests, you can make your concerns known by contacting your elected representatives, working for a particular cause, or, above all, by voting.

Voting is one of American citizens' most important responsibilities. By electing leaders and voting on proposed measures, Americans give their consent to the government. As former President Franklin D. Roosevelt said,

> ❝ *The ultimate rulers of our democracy are not a President and Senators and Congressmen and Government officials but the voters of this country.* ❞
>
> —Franklin D. Roosevelt, *Address at Marietta*

Citizens' Duties and Responsibilities

RIGHTS
• **Security**—protection by government
• **Equality**—equal treatment under the law
• **Liberty**—rights guaranteed under the Constitution

DUTIES
• Obey the law
• Pay taxes
• Defend the nation
• Serve in court
• Attend school

RESPONSIBILITIES
• Be informed and vote
• Participate in your community and government
• Respect the rights and property of others
• Respect different opinions and ways of life

Analyzing Charts

1. **Recognizing** Is voting a right or a responsibility of American citizens?

2. **Comparing** How do duties differ from responsibilities?

In the United States today, all citizens of at least 18 years of age have the right to vote. Each Election Day, citizens have the chance to shape the future of our communities, states, and nation by voting. Thoughtful voters study the candidates and issues carefully before marking their ballots. They also regularly check on what their elected leaders are doing. If an official's performance falls short, it is up to the voters to choose someone else in the next election. Voting responsibly ensures that leadership is changed in a peaceful and orderly manner.

Chapter 5   153

R Reading Strategy

Activate Prior Knowledge Ask: What changes to laws have affected life in your community? (*Answers may include such changes as the required number of school days, graduated driver's license plans, and so on.*) **OL**

D Differentiated Instruction

English Learners Explain the phrase "consent of the governed" to students. Tell them that "the governed" are all the citizens of the United States. Their "consent" is their agreement to abide by the laws of the nation as created by elected officials. **BL**

S Skill Practice

Analyzing Charts Ask: What labels could you add to the chart to help you use it more easily? (*Answers may include labels explaining that rights are guaranteed by the Constitution, duties are required by law, and responsibilities are voluntary.*) **OL**

Analyzing Charts

Answers:
1. Voting is both a responsibility and a right.
2. Citizens must perform duties, or they break the law. Citizens may choose to carry out responsibilities.

Leveled Activities

BL School-to-Home Activity 5, URB p. 131	**OL** Crit. Thinking Activity 5, URB pp. 125–126	**AL** Economic Activity 1, URB pp. 5–6	**ELL** Acad. Vocab. Activity 5, URB pp. 119–120

W Writing Support

Expository Writing Have students write several paragraphs explaining why it is important for citizens to contribute their time and efforts to their communities. Students should consider what their communities would be like if no one ever became involved or volunteered or donated to charity. **OL**

✓ Reading Check **Answer:** When you are informed about your government, you understand the laws you must follow, the rights you have, and the responsibilities you must uphold.

Assess

Civics ONLINE

Study Central™ provides summaries, interactive games, and online graphics organizers to help students review content.

Close

Comparing and Contrasting Have students discuss three rights, three duties, and three responsibilities of American citizenship. Ask them their reasons for assigning each item to the proper category. **OL**

Section ⭐ 1 Review

Respect Others' Rights

In order for you to enjoy your rights, you have a responsibility to respect the rights of others. For example, if you own a dog, you have an obligation to keep it from becoming a nuisance to your neighbors. In a democratic society like ours, with such a diverse population, it is especially important to respect the civil liberties of others. Although you may disagree with people or disapprove of their lifestyles, they have an equal right to their beliefs and practices. Respecting and accepting others, regardless of their beliefs, practices, or differences, is called **tolerance.** Treating others politely and respectfully is thus part of being a good citizen. Many of our laws encourage people to respect each other's rights.

You also have a responsibility to respect public and private property. Some people might claim that "no one gets hurt" when they litter in a park or paint graffiti on a school wall, yet such public property belongs to us all, and we all pay if it is damaged.

Contribute to the Common Good

Responsible citizens show concern for others as well as for themselves. They are willing to give time, effort, and money to improve community life for all.

The members of a community must be actively concerned with promoting the health and welfare of every one of its members so that each member can contribute to the common good, or the things that benefit all members of the community. For example, everyone benefits from having safe streets, good schools, and a clean environment.

Think about what your community would be like if no one donated to charities, volunteered in after-school programs, or lent a hand at the local health clinic. What if no one ever spoke out about community problems? Communities and governments need people to participate.

✓ Reading Check **Explaining** Why is being informed about your government an important responsibility?

Section 1 Review

Vocabulary

1. Define *responsiblity, duty, draft,* and *tolerance.* Use them in sentences related to U.S. citizenship.

Main Ideas

2. Identify three duties of U.S. citizens.

3. Describing What are the responsibilities of American citizens?

Critical Thinking

4. BIG Ideas Why are citizens' responsibilities to their communities an important part of our democratic system?

5. Explaining Why is it important to respect the rights of others?

6. Describing On a graphic organizer like the one below, describe three ways you can express your views and influence government.

Vote

Influencing Government

CITIZENSHIP Activity

7. Expository Writing What do you think would happen if the legal duties of citizens became voluntary? Write a paragraph explaining your answers.

Civics ONLINE

Study Central™ To review this section, go to glencoe.com.

Answers

1. Sentences should use vocabulary words according to their definitions in the section and in the Glossary.

2. Students will list three of these duties: obey the law, pay taxes, defend the nation, serve in court, attend school.

3. Students will list some or all of these responsibilities: be informed and vote, participate in the community and government, respect the rights and properties of others; practice tolerance; volunteer or otherwise contribute to the common good.

4. Answers may include these reasons: citizens better their communities through volunteerism; citizens reinforce rights through respecting the law and practicing tolerance; citizens improve government and law by being informed and voting.

5. In a democracy, people believe many ideas and live in many ways. By respecting the rights of everyone citizens strengthen the rights that all citizens are privileged to share. When citizens do not respect others' rights, the rights of all people are jeopardized.

6. Citizens can express their views and influence government in these ways: vote, be informed, contact elected representatives to speak up about issues.

7. Students' paragraphs should demonstrate an understanding of citizens' duties, as opposed to rights and responsibilities, and should predict consequences were these duties to become voluntary.

Federal Revenues and Expenditures

"The only constants in life are death and taxes." Perhaps you have heard someone utter that line. At the federal level, there are three major taxes: the individual income tax, the corporate income tax, and the Social Security tax. Many people do not know how their tax dollars are being used. Where does the money go?

Where Your Tax Dollars Go

S

National Defense
17.2%

Medicare
12.0%

Net Interest
7.2%

Other
14.2%

Social Security
21.1%

Income Security
14.0%

Health Benefits
10.4%

Education and Other Health Services
3.9%

Where Your Tax Dollars Come From

 D

Individual Income Taxes
45.4%

Corporate Income Taxes
11.5%

Other Taxes
3.8%

Social Security Taxes, other Retirement, Insurance
39.3%

Source: Department of the Treasury; Congressional Budget Office, 2006.

Analyzing Economics

1. **Concluding** Should we be required to pay taxes? Why or why not?
2. **Prioritizing** How would you change the top diagram if you were able to assign how your tax money would be spent? Why?

S Skill Practice

Reading Graphs Ask: How could you convert the information in this visual into a useful graph? *(Answers may include drawing a bar graph or circle graph that represents the same information in a different format.)* **AL**

D Differentiated Instruction

Visual/Spatial Ask: Why did the author use dollar bills instead of a more standard graph? *(Answers may include the conclusion that the author used dollar bills to make a visual impact and to help readers understand the importance of the topic.)* **OL**

Analyzing Economics

Answers:
1. Yes, we should. Without income from taxes, many important and necessary programs, such as education and national defense, would not be adequately funded.
2. Answers may include various options depending on which programs students would prioritize. Students should explain their prioritizations.

Additional Support

Activity: US/World Connections

Comparing and Contrasting Tell students that many countries require citizens to pay taxes but that each country divides income tax in different ways. Have students use the Internet to study the division of income tax in two other countries.

Students can examine two questions: In other nations, what percentage of each earned dollar goes to taxes? Do other nations use income tax in the same ways as the United States does?

Ask students to produce charts that answer these questions. Lead students in a discussion in which they compare and contrast the uses of income tax in the countries they researched. **AL**

Focus

Bellringer
Daily Focus Transparency 5–2

Guide to Reading
Answers to Graphic:

- Taking Action
  - volunteer for national service
  - volunteer in community
  - donate money
  - donate time

Section Spotlight Video

To generate student interest and provide a springboard for class discussion, access the Chapter 5, Section 2 video at glencoe.com or on the video DVD.

Resource Manager

Guide to Reading

Big Idea
Citizen participation is essential to the foundation and preservation of the U.S. political system.

Content Vocabulary
- bureaucracy *(p. 157)*
- welfare *(p. 158)*
- volunteerism *(p. 158)*

Academic Vocabulary
- percent *(p. 158)*
- register *(p. 160)*
- domestic *(p. 160)*
- annual *(p. 162)*

Reading Strategy
Organizing Information
As you read, complete a graphic organizer like the one below in which you list ways that people can take action and contribute to their community.

- Taking Action
  - donate time

Section 2

Citizens and the Community

Real World Civics The "Dragon Slayers" are teen members of the Aniak Volunteer Fire Department in Alaska. All members must undergo extensive training. In addition to fire fighting, the teens are trained as medics. Contributing to their tiny community located near Anchorage is uppermost in the minds of these young people. All volunteers must vow to abstain from drugs and alcohol and maintain passing grades in school.

▼ The group's volunteers—the youngest is 13—serve on the only emergency medical team within 10,000 square miles of Aniak, Alaska.

R Reading Strategies	**C** Critical Thinking	**D** Differentiated Instruction	**W** Writing Support	**S** Skill Practice
Teacher Edition • Und. Q/A Relationships, p. 157 • Understanding Word Parts, p. 158 • Academic Vocab., p. 160 **Additional Resources** • Cont. Vocab., URB p. 118 • Foldables, URB p. 59	**Teacher Edition** • Det. Cause/Effect, p. 157 • Making Inferences, p. 160 **Additional Resources** • Enrichment Activity, URB p. 13 • Biography Act, URB p. 121 • Quizzes and Tests, p. 51	**Teacher Edition** • Auditory/Musical, p. 158 • Interpersonal, p. 159 • English Learners, p. 161 **Additional Resources** • Diff. Instr. Act., URB p. 129 • School-to-Home Act., URB p. 131	**Teacher Edition** • Personal Writing, p. 159 **Additional Resources** • Writing Skills Act., URB p. 123 • Auth. Assess., p. 9	**Teacher Edition** • Analyzing Graphs, p. 161 • Using Venn Diagrams, p. 162 **Additional Resources** • Daily Focus Trans., 5–2 • Pol. Cartoons Trans. 5

Civic Responsibility Volunteer crews rescue a Mississippi family trapped by flooding caused by 2005's Hurricane Katrina. *Explaining* Why is it important that citizens support their communities?

Citizen Involvement

Main Idea By volunteering, we make our communities better places to live, gain new opportunities to solve problems, and learn new things.

Civics & You Have you volunteered to help out at school or in your community? Read on to find out why it is important for citizens to volunteer.

Why do volunteers such as the Dragon Slayers do so much work without pay? John Gatus, a retired steamfitter who volunteers in an anti-gang neighborhood patrol, explains his reason:

R

> *Volunteer work brings real change, change you can be a part of, change you can see with your own eyes.*
>
> —John Gatus, as quoted in "America's Voluntary Spirit"

Every year, more than half of all Americans do volunteer work to help make their communities better places to live. A community is a group of people who share the same interests and concerns. These volunteers include more than 14 million students in grades 6 through 12. Without the efforts of so many private citizens, many pressing social needs simply would not be met.

In the United States, federal, state, and local government provides many different services. We rely on government for everything from local police protection to national defense, from collecting household trash to ensuring clean water and air nationwide.

Citizens, though, also share responsibility for meeting community needs. The government, after all, has limited resources. In addition, governments are **bureaucracies**— **C** complex systems with many departments, many rules, and many people in the chain of command.

Chapter 5 157

Teach

R Reading Strategy

Understanding Question/Answer Relationships Ask: Why do the authors begin this section of the chapter with a question, and why don't they answer the question themselves? *(The question gets readers thinking about an unusual activity: working for no pay. The answer comes from someone else, someone who has first-hand experience with volunteering. This answer is more persuasive than an answer from the authors.)* **AL**

C Critical Thinking

Determining Cause and Effect Ask: How might a bureaucracy slow down the response to community needs? *(With so many people in the chain of command, and so many departments involved, much time is needed to decide on, approve, coordinate, staff, fund, and carry out a response.)* **OL**

Caption Answer:

Answers may include that people enjoy and benefit from supporting their communities, that some community needs will not be met if people do not volunteer time and money, and that some needs are more easily and quickly met by people rather than by government.

Differentiated Instruction

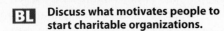

Enrichment Activity

Enrichment Activity 1,
URB pp. 13–14

Objective: To understand the services provided by charitable organizations

Focus: Have students recall events in recent or local news when charitable organizations helped people in need.

Teach: Review the charitable organizations on the list.

Assess: Guide students as they navigate the Web sites of the organizations.

Close: Have each student present a recruitment tool for an organization.

Differentiated Instruction Strategies

BL Discuss what motivates people to start charitable organizations.

AL Where can potential donors go to find the answer to questions about how charitable organization use their funds?

ELL The Red Cross functions in many countries. Find out where it exists around the world, and make a list of the names it uses in other nations.

D **Differentiated Instruction**

Auditory/Musical Have students study the presidential quotes on this page. Then ask them to practice reading each quote as if they were using it in a speech to inspire citizens to volunteer. Have students read the quotes aloud to the class, and discuss what makes each presentation compelling to listeners. **OL**

D Differentiated Instruction

Auditory/Musical Have students study the presidential quotes on this page. Then ask them to practice reading each quote as if they were using it in a speech to inspire citizens to volunteer. Have students read the quotes aloud to the class, and discuss what makes each presentation compelling to listeners. **OL**

R Reading Strategy

Understanding Word Parts Explain to students that in the word "percent," "per" means "of each" and that "cent" means "hundred." A percentage tells how many of one hundred are included, affected, or involved. Remind students that this sign—%—means the same thing as the word "percent." **ELL** **BL**

TIME™ Political Cartoons

Answers:

1. Hurricane Katrina.
2. the outpouring of help from many groups and individuals from around the nation
3. It is powerful and beneficial.

✔ **Reading Check** **Answer:** offering your time to others without payment

Hands-On Chapter Project
Step 2

Serving in Your Community

Step 2: Researching Volunteer Opportunities Groups of students will gather information on ways for young people to serve their communities through volunteerism.

Directions Write the Main Idea from page 157 on the board. Have students use the information they gathered in Step 1 to create a Student Volunteer Information Center. Students can exhibit the information they have collected on a bulletin board. If possi-

ble, allow students to use computer tools to present their information clearly.

Extending Have students brainstorm ways to make their display more user-friendly. Can they print information sheets that classmates can take home with them? Can they create a page within the school's Web site and post updated information about volunteer opportunities? Can they interview students who volunteer and include their comments in their display? **OL**

(Project continued on the Visual Summary page)

TIME™

Political Cartoons

Marshall Ramsey/Copley News Service

In 2005, Hurricane Katrina dealt devastating blows to communities in Louisiana and Mississippi. Cartoonist Marshall Ramsey shows help arriving.

1. **Based only on the first panel of the cartoon, what would you imagine Ramsey sees as "the most powerful force in nature"?**
2. **Looking at the second panel, what event do you think inspired this cartoon, which was drawn in the summer of 2005?**
3. **How does Ramsey feel about volunteerism?**

Every year, more than half of all Americans do volunteer work ... role in it. One of the responsibilities of citizens is to help make their ... of volunteer gro... small. Perha... ...dad who...

Because of this, government cannot always respond quickly or efficiently to problems. In many cases, the best solutions come from private citizens. Good citizens are concerned about the **welfare**—the health, prosperity, and happiness—of all members of the community.

In 1961 President John F. Kennedy issued a challenge: "Ask not what your country can do for you; ask what you can do for your country." President George W. Bush in 2005 noted that we can show "the world the true values of America through the gathering momentum of a million acts of responsibility and decency and service."

Donating Time and Money

People help their communities in many ways, working independently or as part of volunteer groups both large and small. Neighbors might gather to spend a Saturday cleaning up a highway or preparing holiday baskets for needy families. Retirees mentor schoolchildren, record books for the blind, and lead museum tours. You and your fellow students might visit nursing home patients, volunteer in an animal shelter, or collect canned goods for a local food pantry.

Giving your time to work on community projects is the core of **volunteerism**—the practice of offering your time and services to others without payment. However, Americans may also support worthy causes by contributing money. Annually, individual Americans give more than $250 billion to charity. Much of this money comes from small donations by average citizens. The typical American donates about 2 **percent**, or portion of an amount in hundredths, of his or her income to charity.

✔ **Reading Check** **Defining** What is volunteerism?

American Biography

Marian Wright Edelman (1939–)

Marian Wright Edelman once told an interviewer that she "never for a moment lacked a purpose worth fighting, living, or dying for." At first, Edelman found her purpose in the civil rights movement of the 1950s and 1960s. Then, in 1973, she organized the Children's Defense Fund (CDF). The CDF's mission is to institute programs to keep children healthy, in school, and out of trouble.

Edelman, the youngest of five children, credits her parents with teaching her to help other people. "Working for the community was as much a part of our existence as eating and sleeping," Edelman recalled. With her parents' support, she obtained a law degree and went on to become the first African American woman to practice law in Mississippi. She also served as a leader in the NAACP Legal Defense and Education Fund.

Edelman's work with the CDF earned her the reputation as "the children's crusader." Today the CDF is the leading lobby on behalf of children, especially the more than 12 million children who live in poverty. In 2000, Edelman received the Presidential Medal of Freedom, the nation's highest civilian award. In 2005, Edelman and the CDF responded to the destruction along the Gulf Coast caused by Hurricane Katrina by aiding hurricane survivors and helping displaced families locate their loved ones.

Making a Difference — CITIZENSHIP

Edelman wrote that "service is the rent we pay to be living." *Explaining* How does this apply to Edelman's life and work?

Volunteers in Action

Main Idea Young people can make a difference by volunteering.

Civics & You Is it okay to want some benefits for yourself from volunteering? Think about this question as you read. **W**

Responsible citizens are concerned about the welfare of the community as a whole. They may be concerned about the environment, or surroundings of the community, or about the quality of life.

Safeguarding these things may require government action. It could mean cleaning up a toxic waste dump that is polluting the water, adding more police officers to combat drug trafficking, or building more parks.

Having concern for our communities is not enough, however. Our concern must be supported by our action. No community or government has the money or resources to provide for the welfare of all its people or to solve all its problems. It counts on volunteers to help.

Community Involvement

Community involvement tends to be rooted in individual action and informal groups. People are more likely to participate when they feel a connection to a cause or know others involved. Thus they join their Neighborhood Watch or become active at their child's school. They reach out to the community through their religious congregations or their work through service clubs such as the Lions and Kiwanis. **D** Some people, however, volunteer through more formal channels.

Chapter 5 159

W **Writing Support**

Personal Writing Allow students to free-write for five minutes to answer this question: If I worked as a volunteer, how would I benefit from spending my time and effort to help others? **OL**

D **Differentiated Instruction**

Interpersonal Ask: If you could interview a representative of a service club such as the Lions or Kiwanis, what questions would you ask? *(Answers may include questions about what the organization does, who can belong, and what segments of the community it serves.)* **OL**

American Biography

Answer: Edelman paid her "rent to be living" by using her skills, education, and passion to improve the lives of children by creating the Children's Defense Fund.

Differentiated Instruction

Leveled Activities

OL **Content Vocabulary Activity 5, URB p. 118**

AL **Enrichment Activity 1, URB pp. 13–14**

AL **Writing Skills Activity 5, URB pp. 123–124**

ELL **Reteaching Activity 5, URB p. 133**

Charitable Organizations

More than 1 million charities are officially **registered,** or recorded, with the federal government. Many are small and locally based. These organizations often work on one or two projects, such as helping the victims of **domestic,** or home, abuse or preserving a historic building. Other organizations are large national charities serving millions of people.

School-Based Programs

More than half of all United States middle and high schools now arrange community service for students in grades 6 through 12. Several hundred school districts in various states even require it. In Atlanta, Chicago, and the entire state of Maryland, for example, high school students must volunteer a set number of hours to earn a graduation diploma.

National Service Programs

During his Inaugural Address in 1961, President John F. Kennedy challenged Americans to work together to fight poverty, disease, and war in the poorest corners of the world. Less than two months later, Kennedy signed an executive order establishing the Peace Corps.

Since that time, the Peace Corps has sent more than 180,000 Americans to 138 countries, where they advise farmers, teach children and young adults, help start small businesses, and fight the spread of AIDS.

AmeriCorps Here in the United States, AmeriCorps members help meet the nation's needs in education, public safety, health, and the environment. More than 50,000 Americans participate each year in AmeriCorps. In return for a year of full-time service, organization members receive an allowance to live on and money to help pay for college.

Global Responsibility Peace Corps volunteers learn about installing toilet bowls in preparation for work in Western Samoa. ***Explaining*** Why is it important that people support communities around the world?

160

Activity: Interdisciplinary Connection

Language Arts Have students locate President Kennedy's 1961 Inaugural Address at the Miller Center of Public Affairs Web site at http://millercenter.virginia.edu/scripps/diglibrary/prezspeeches/kennedy/jfk_1961_0120.html. Read the brief speech with students, and ask them to write out the sentences and phrases that they find particularly persuasive.

Then have students listen to the recording at the same Web site of Kennedy giving the speech. Ask them to discuss how Kennedy's presentation of the speech affects their opinion of its persuasiveness. **OL**

American Volunteers in Action

Graphs In MOtion
See StudentWorks™ Plus or glencoe.com.

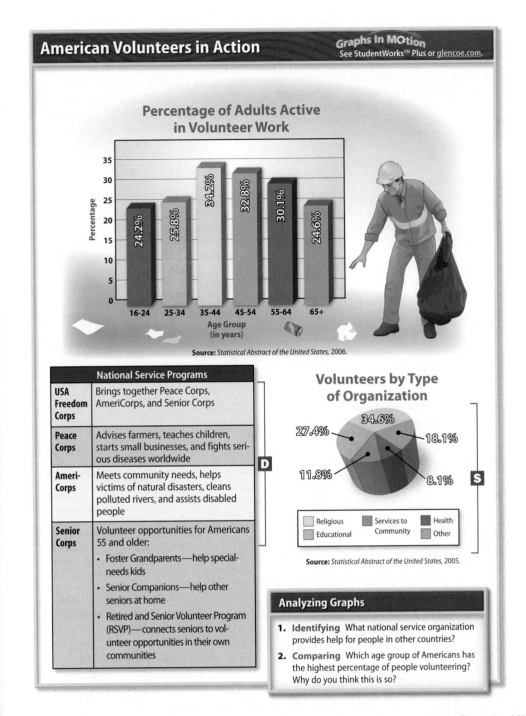

Percentage of Adults Active in Volunteer Work

Age Group (in years)	Percentage
16-24	24.2%
25-34	25.8%
35-44	34.2%
45-54	32.8%
55-64	30.1%
65+	24.6%

Source: *Statistical Abstract of the United States,* 2006.

National Service Programs

USA Freedom Corps	Brings together Peace Corps, AmeriCorps, and Senior Corps
Peace Corps	Advises farmers, teaches children, starts small businesses, and fights serious diseases worldwide
Ameri-Corps	Meets community needs, helps victims of natural disasters, cleans polluted rivers, and assists disabled people
Senior Corps	Volunteer opportunities for Americans 55 and older: • Foster Grandparents—help special-needs kids • Senior Companions—help other seniors at home • Retired and Senior Volunteer Program (RSVP)—connects seniors to volunteer opportunities in their own communities

Volunteers by Type of Organization

34.6%
27.4%
18.1%
11.8%
8.1%

- Religious
- Educational
- Services to Community
- Health
- Other

Source: *Statistical Abstract of the United States,* 2005.

Analyzing Graphs

1. **Identifying** What national service organization provides help for people in other countries?

2. **Comparing** Which age group of Americans has the highest percentage of people volunteering? Why do you think this is so?

D Differentiated Instruction

English Learners Point out the word "Corps" in the name of each national service programs. Model the correct pronunciation for the word to show students that the *p* and *s* are silent and that the word is a homophone with "core." Explain that "corps" means "body or group of people." **ELL** **BL**

S Skill Practice

Analyzing Graphs **Ask:** What is the rectangular box beneath the circle graph, and how do you use it? *(The box provides a key for understanding the graph. Each colored rectangle corresponds to a colored wedge in the graph. By matching colors, readers know what type of organization provides which percentage of volunteers; for example, 34.6 percent of volunteers works through religious organizations.)* **OL**

Analyzing Graphs

Answers:
1. The Peace Corps provides help for people in other countries.
2. People 35–44 years old have the highest percentage of volunteers, followed closely by people 45–54. These people in general have the money, time, and desire to volunteer.

Activity: Technology Connection

Using Online Applications Some high school graduates choose to spend time working for AmeriCorps before beginning college, trade school, or a career. AmeriCorps volunteers may work in another state—some are currently working on the Gulf Coast, rebuilding the structures destroyed by Katrina. Others may work in their home cities with organizations such as Big Brothers.

Have students go online to http://www.americorps.gov/ to find out what the requirements for and benefits of joining AmeriCorps are. Have them print an application and work as a group to complete it and to discuss the process of using online applications. **OL**

S Skill Practice

Using Venn Diagrams Have students use the information about the volunteer programs in the text and in the graphs to create a three-part Venn diagram summarizing the information about the programs. **OL**

✓ **Reading Check** **Answer:** Senior Corps

Assess

Civics ONLINE

Study Central™ provides summaries, interactive games, and online graphic organizers to help students review content.

Close

Personal Writing Have students write journal entries about volunteering. Students should answer these questions: What have I learned about volunteering? What would I enjoy about volunteering? What might I dislike about volunteering? **OL**

Section 2 Review

Senior Corps The Senior Corps provides volunteer opportunities to Americans aged 55 or older. These senior citizens take part in three main programs. Foster Grandparents work one-on-one with children with special needs. Senior Companions help other seniors meet their daily needs while living independently in their own homes. The Retired and Senior Volunteer Program provides seniors with volunteer opportunities in their communities.

S USA Freedom Corps On January 29, 2002, in his **annual,** or yearly, State of the Union address, President Bush asked Americans to join together and help, saying, "If you aren't sure how to help, I've got a good place to start."

Bush described a new program, called USA Freedom Corps. The program brings together the Peace Corps, AmeriCorps, and Senior Corps. Freedom Corps was designed to focus on three areas of need: responding to national emergencies, rebuilding our communities, and extending American compassion throughout the world.

Voluntary Spirit

Americans have a long history of volunteering. When Alexis de Tocqueville, a French political writer, visited America in the 1830s, he was amazed to see citizens pitching in to solve community problems rather than relying on the government. He explained it as "self-interest rightly understood." In other words, by banding together to serve the community, we really serve ourselves. For example, more than 50,000 Americans participate each year in AmeriCorps. Most work through local and national organizations such as Habitat for Humanity.

✓ **Reading Check** **Identifying** What organization provides opportunities for volunteers 55 years of age or older?

Section 2 Review

Vocabulary

1. **Define** *bureaucracy, welfare,* and *volunteerism.* Use each of these terms in sentences.

Main Ideas

2. **Explaining** Why is it important for citizens to volunteer?

3. **Describing** Provide at least two examples of useful services provided by volunteer groups and organizations in a community.

Critical Thinking

4. **BIG Ideas** Explain why citizens have a responsibility to turn their concerns for their community into action.

5. **Identifying** On a graphic organizer like the one below, list channels through which an individual can volunteer.

CITIZENSHIP Activity

6. **Expository Writing** Do research or contact a local volunteer organization that was mentioned in Section 2 of this chapter. Find out what projects or problems they are working on in your community and how they use volunteers. Write a one-page essay in which you provide answers to these questions.

Civics ONLINE

Study Central™ To review this section, go to glencoe.com.

162 Chapter 5

Answers

1. Sentences should use vocabulary words according to their definitions in the section and in the Glossary.
2. Volunteers meet many needs that governments cannot meet or cannot meet quickly.
3. Examples will vary but may be drawn from the section or from students' experiences.
4. Answers will include the ideas that it is not enough to be concerned about problems, that the government relies on people to act on their concerns; and that volunteering benefits both the served and those serving.
5. Students will add these channels to the graphic organizer: community involvement, charities, national service programs.
6. Student interviews should be prepared in advance with at least three questions and may be conducted in person, by phone, or online. Essays should be a page in length and should include answers to the questions suggested by the prompt: what projects or problems the organization is working on and how the organization uses volunteers.

Visual Summary

Citizenship

- The combination of rights, responsibilities, and duties characterizes what it means to be a citizen of a free democratic society.
- As citizens, we are free to exercise our rights.
- In return, we are expected to fulfill certain duties and responsibilities.

Why Should I Participate?

- A key part of being a good citizen is taking an active and engaged role in your community.
- A well-planned project gives you opportunities to practice your rights and responsibilities as a citizen.
- You make a difference by participating. Your efforts are needed, valued, and respected.
- When you share your knowledge and skills to help others, you develop new skills and cultivate new knowledge.

Registering to vote

Our Duties

Duties are things we are required to do by law.

- One of the duties of all Americans is to obey the law.
- Americans have a duty to pay taxes.
- Another duty of citizenship is to defend the nation.

Neighborhood crime prevention

NEIGHBORHOOD CRIME WATCH

TAKE A BITE OUT OF **CRIME**

WE IMMEDIATELY REPORT ALL SUSPICIOUS ACTIVITIES TO OUR POLICE DEPARTMENT

IN COOPERATION WITH OUR LOCAL POLICE DEPARTMENT

Our Responsibilities

Responsibilities are things we should do. Civic responsibilities include:

- being informed;
- speaking up and voting;
- respecting others' rights;
- respecting diversity; and
- contributing to the common good.

Active Citizens

- Participate in community service
- Do their part to make their schools, communities, and the world a better place

City street cleanup

STUDY TO GO Study anywhere, anytime! Download quizzes and flash cards to your PDA from glencoe.com.

163

Analyzing Primary Sources On the board, write the quote from John F. Kennedy given on page 158: "Ask not what your country can do for you; ask what you can do for your country." Tell students that, in fact, our country does much for us, and we should do what we can for our country. **Ask:** What does our country do for us? What must we do for our country? What can we do for our country, if we choose to? Have students create a three-column chart that summarizes the main ideas that answer these three questions. **OL**

For additional practice on this skill (Analyzing Primary Sources), see the **Skills Handbook**.

Analyzing Visuals Ask: Look at the images on the page. Which images remind viewers about citizens' rights? Which tell about citizens' duties? Which tell about citizens' responsibilities? (The image of a person voting reminds viewers that citizens have the right to elect their government and the responsibility to be informed, to voice concerns, and to vote. The image of the crime prevention program reminds viewers that citizens have personal and property rights, the duty to obey the law, and the responsibility to respect others' rights. The image of city street cleanup reminds viewers of citizens' responsibilities to volunteer to improve their communities.) **BL ELL**

Hands-On Chapter Project
Step 3: Wrap-Up

Serving in Our Community

Step 3: Researching Volunteer Opportunities Once students have created their display of volunteer opportunities, tell them that in doing the project, they have served as volunteers by gathering and publicizing information. Have students discuss the ways they have helped their community by producing the display.

Directions With the school administration's permission, have students wrap up this project by planning, staffing, and implementing a small volunteer project around their school, such as a trash pickup walk. Students can create an announcement for the project and distribute it to other students. They can document the work done during the project with cameras and brief interviews. Then they can add an "Our Students Serve!" section to their display.

Wrap up the project by asking students to discuss these questions: What was the most enjoyable part of volunteering? What was the hardest part? Would we undertake another volunteer project in the future? **OL**

Chapter 5 ASSESSMENT
Answers and Analyses
Reviewing Vocabulary

1. A Students have read about many duties, but only one applies specifically to men of a certain age group: military duty. Remind students that all citizens must, depending on their ages, go to school and serve on juries and that volunteering is a responsibility, not a duty.

2. A To show tolerance is a responsibility of citizenship, so students may be distracted by D. Also, tolerance can be a compassionate act (C). However, the key to the item is the word "different." Good citizens respect and accept different ways of living and believing.

3. B Because this is a voluntary action, students can rule out A and D. Students may be drawn to C, civic responsibility, because the action benefits members of a community. However, the action is something a volunteer does to serve someone else without pay. The reader does not benefit personally from the action.

4. B Review the definitions of the options with students. They may be unsure of D, congregation. Once students are clear on the definitions, the correct answer will be clear.

Reviewing Main Ideas

5. B Point out to students that options A, C, and D all fall under the heading of option B, to obey laws. When citizens obey the nation's laws, they carry out all their duties.

6. A Ask students what kind of information newspapers contain and why people read them. Then guide them to rule out options B, C, and D—newspapers do not cause people to respect others, to speak up and vote, or to contribute to the common good. However, being informed by keeping up with the news may lead to all these activities.

7. B Picking up trash shows that you respect others' right to a clean environment. Students may be distracted by option D. A better example of contributing to the common good might be planting community gardens.

8. B Options A, C, and D name activities undertaken by federal or local government. Only B names an activity for which volunteers are responsible.

9. B The Freedom Corps is a national program managed by the federal government. Option A is a privately run organization, and options C and D name local groups.

10. B Point out to students that they can rule out option A because this group aids Americans, as its name suggests. Option D is not a national program. Then remind students that the Peace Corps was established to carry aid and goodwill to other nations.

Chapter 5 ASSESSMENT

TEST-TAKING TIP

When reviewing for a test, pay special attention to bold type, questions, and summary paragraphs in your text.

Reviewing Vocabulary

Directions: Choose the word(s) that best completes the sentence.

1. Men 18 to 25 years of age are required to register in case the country needs to draft them for _____.

  A military duty   **C** jury duty

  B volunteer service   **D** school attendance

2. Listening to a neighbor in a different political party shows _____.

  A tolerance   **C** compassion

  B obedience   **D** responsibility

3. Recording books for the blind is an example of _____.

  A civic duty   **C** civic responsibility

  B volunteerism   **D** government activity

4. Your neighborhood is a kind of _____.

  A charity   **C** bureaucracy

  B community   **D** congregation

Reviewing Main Ideas

Directions: Choose the best answer for each question.

Section 1 (pp. 150–154)

5. What is the most important civic duty of Americans?

  A to pay taxes

  B to obey laws

  C to serve in court

  D to attend school

6. Which civic responsibility does reading the metropolitan section of a newspaper fulfill?

  A being informed

  B respecting others

  C speaking up and voting

  D contributing to the common good

7. When was the last time the United States instituted a military draft?

  A World War II

  B World War I

  C Korean War

  D Vietnam War

Section 2 (pp. 156-162)

8. Which service do volunteers perform?

  A ensuring clean water

  B mentoring schoolchildren

  C collecting household trash

  D providing for national defense

9. Which group is a national charity?

  A United Way

  B Freedom Corps

  C church food pantry

  D Neighborhood Watch

10. Which national service program sends volunteers overseas?

  A AmeriCorps

  B Peace Corps

  C Senior Corps

  D Foster Grandparents

GO ON

Critical Thinking

Directions: Base your answers to questions 11 and 12 on the table below and your knowledge of Chapter 5.

Reason for Not Voting in Last Presidential Election	Percent Who Sited Reason
Not registered	31
Didn't like candidates	10
Not interested in politics	8
No particular reason	8
Illness	7
Inconvenient	7
Working	7
Other reasons	7
Not a citizen	6
Out of town	5
Couldn't get to the polls	3
Didn't get absentee ballot	1

11. Which generalization can you make based on this chart?

A Political parties are nominating uninspiring candidates.

B Most people in this survey are shirking their civic duty.

C Most people in this survey are neglecting an important civic responsibility.

D The sample is too small to draw any valid conclusions about why people do not vote.

12. Which prediction is supported by the chart?

A Fast-track naturalization laws could double voter turnout.

B Providing shuttle buses to the polls would not increase voter participation.

C Improving the absentee voting system might raise voter turnout by 10 percent.

D Declaring voting day a national holiday could boost voter participation up to 7 percent.

Document-Based Questions

Directions: Analyze the following document and answer the short-answer questions that follow.

The following paragraph is the current oath for commissioned officers in the United States Army.

> *I, (name), having been appointed an officer in the Army of the United States, as indicated above in the grade of (rank) do solemnly swear (or affirm) that I will support and defend the Constitution of the United States against all enemies, foreign or domestic, that I will bear true faith and allegiance to the same; that I take this obligation freely, without any mental reservations or purpose of evasion; and that I will well and faithfully discharge the duties of the office upon which I am about to enter; So help me God.*
>
> —United States Army

13. Which of the five civic duties does an army officer perform?

14. Give an example of domestic enemies of the Constitution of the United States.

Extended-Response Question

15. Anthropologist Margaret Mead wrote: "Never doubt that a small group of thoughtful, committed citizens can change the world. Indeed, it is the only thing that ever has." Write a brief essay explaining why you agree or disagree with Mead's statement. Use examples from the chapter to support your opinion.

STOP

Civics ONLINE
For additional test practice, use Self-Check Quizzes—Chapter 5 on glencoe.com.

Need Extra Help?

If you missed question...	1	2	3	4	5	6	7	8	9	10	11	12	13	14	15
Go to page...	152	154	158	159	151	153	152	158	160	160	153	153	151	151	157

ASSESSMENT

Document-Based Questions

13. An army officer defends the nation.

14. Students' answers will vary. A possible answer is partisan groups that try to intimidate voters at the polls.

Extended Response

15. Students' essays will vary but must include supporting examples from the chapter.

Critical Thinking

11. C Remind students that a generalization is a conclusion drawn based on evidence. The only option supported by the evidence in the chart is C. The chart gives no information about the quality of candidates (A); option B mentions a civic duty, but voting is a responsibility; and option D contradicts the chart, which lists specific reasons people do not vote.

12. D "Inconvenient," "Working," and "Out of town" account for 19 percent of the reasons for not voting. If voting day were a national holiday, some of the people who gave these excuses might be able to vote. The chart does not support the other options.

Civics ONLINE

Have students visit the Web site at glencoe.com to review Chapter 5 and take the **Self-Check Quiz.**

Need Extra Help?

Have students refer to the pages listed if they miss any of the questions.

Analyzing Primary Sources

Focus

C Critical Thinking

Predicting Consequences Alexis de Tocqueville was a French aristocrat sent to America to study the United States penal system. **Ask:** What view would people living in other countries have of U.S. citizens after reading de Tocqueville's report? *(They would probably view U.S. citizens as committed to their democratic values and willing to lend a hand to fellow citizens.)* **OL**

R Reading Strategy

Questioning Ask: If "no constitution, no law, no court" can save liberty, why do we have constitutions, laws, and courts? *(Answers may include the idea that even when people agree to promote and maintain liberty, they must decide what laws to enforce and how to punish those who break the laws.)* **AL**

Additional Reading

Analyzing Primary Sources

Active Citizenship

Reading Focus

Have you ever thought about the things that bind people together? What values and beliefs do they share? The American ideal of citizenship has always stressed each citizen's responsibility to participate in political life.

Read to Discover

As you read, think about the following:

- What are the things that unite people in a common cause?
- What values and beliefs do people in a society share?

Reader's Dictionary

self-interest: a concern for one's own advantage or well-being

complacency: self-satisfaction

disinterested: free of bias; impartial

ruthless: without mercy

unbridled: uncontrolled

abridged: cut short

servitude: lack of personal freedom

Democracy in America

In *Democracy in America,* Alexis de Tocqueville vividly described nineteenth-century American life, politics, and morals.

> The Americans, on the other hand, are fond of explaining almost all the actions of their lives by the principle of **self-interest** rightly understood; they show with **complacency** how an enlightened regard for themselves constantly prompts them to assist one another and inclines them willingly to sacrifice a portion of their time and property to the welfare of the state. In this respect I think they frequently fail to do themselves justice, for in the United States as well as elsewhere people are sometimes seen to give way to those **disinterested** and spontaneous impulses that are natural to man; but the Americans seldom admit that they yield to emotions of this kind; they are more anxious to do honor to their philosophy than to themselves.
>
> —Alexis de Tocqueville, *Democracy in America*

The Spirit of Liberty

In his essay "The Spirit of Liberty," United States Circuit Court Judge Learned Hand promoted the ideal of ethical and committed citizens.

> What do we mean when we say that first of all we seek liberty? I often wonder whether we do not rest our hopes too much upon constitutions, upon laws, and upon courts. These are false hopes; believe me, these are false hopes. Liberty lies in the hearts of men and women; when it dies there, no constitution, no law, no court can save it; no constitution, no law, no court can even do much to help it. And what is this liberty which must lie in the hearts of men and women? It is not the **ruthless,** the **unbridled** will; it is not freedom to do as one likes. That is the denial of liberty, and leads straight to its overthrow. A society in

---

Posterity: Letters of Great Americans to Their Children by Dorie McCullough Lawson provides a collection of personal letters written by famous Americans, giving insight into their private lives.

Kids at Work: Lewis Hine and the Crusade Against Child Labor by Russell Freedman is a photo essay book depicting the harsh working conditions for children working in factories in the early 20th century.

Environmental Pioneers by Patricia Byrnes highlights Americans who have dedicated their lives to protecting the environment.

which men recognize no check upon their freedom soon becomes a society where freedom is the possession of only a savage few; as we have learned to our sorrow.

—Judge Learned Hand, "The Spirit of Liberty"

The Right to Vote

Many groups struggled to win the right to vote. Several amendments to the U.S. Constitution deal with suffrage.

The right of citizens of the United States to vote shall not be denied or **abridged** by the United States or by any State on account of race, color, or previous condition of **servitude.**

—Fifteenth Amendment (1870)

The right of citizens of the United States to vote shall not be denied or abridged by the United States or by any State on account of sex.

—Nineteenth Amendment (1920)

The right of citizens of the United States to vote in any primary or other election . . . shall not be denied or abridged . . . by reason of failure to pay any poll tax or other tax.

—Twenty-fourth Amendment (1964)

The right of citizens of the United States, who are eighteen years of age or older, to vote shall not be denied or abridged by the United States or by any State on account of age.

—Twenty-sixth Amendment (1971)

Photographs as Primary Sources
What does this photograph tell you about women's rights in the early 1900s? For what right is this woman campaigning?

R Reading Strategy

Making Connections Tell students that while the Fifteenth Amendment formally ended voting discrimination on the basis of race, some states managed to pass laws restricting the voting rights of people of color. **Ask: How is the Twenty-fourth Amendment connected to these state laws?** (*The Twenty-fourth Amendment prevented states from restricting citizens' right to vote by requiring them to pay a tax.*) **OL**

Caption Answers:
women did not have all the rights enjoyed by men; the right to vote

DBQ Document-Based Questions

Answers:

1. When individuals act in their own best interests, they are inclined to donate some of their money and effort to benefit their group.
2. If people did not first believe in the importance of liberty, no laws could create or enforce liberty.
3. Answers will vary. Some students might predict that voter turnout would be higher.
4. Paragraphs should include logical arguments based on how students think people would react.

DBQ Document-Based Questions

1. **Connecting** What connections did de Tocqueville make between the interests of individuals and the interests of groups?

2. **Responding** What do you think Judge Hand meant when he said, "Liberty lies in the hearts of men and women"?

3. **Predicting** How do you think people would respond to a compulsory voting law in the United States? Explain.

4. **Evaluating and Connecting** The privilege of U.S. citizenship brings with it certain responsibilities. Some responsibilities, such as obeying laws, are required. Other responsibilities, such as participating in political life, are voluntary. Make a list of the voluntary responsibilities you found in these readings. Then write a paragraph in response to the question: What do you think would happen if the voluntary responsibilities you listed became required by law?

167

Did You Know?

The Twenty-sixth Amendment Prior to 1970, the voting age for federal elections was 21. During the Vietnam War, many young men were drafted into combat at 18 years of age. Therefore, a man old enough to fight in a war for the country was not old enough to vote for the president. Congress passed a law in 1970 to lower the voting age for federal elections, but the Supreme Court ruled that it was unconstitutional for the federal law to set parameters for state elections. It was left up to the states to decide if they wanted to lower the voting age for their own elections. To avoid this, Congress proposed the Twenty-sixth Amendment to set the voting age at 18 for federal and state elections. The amendment was ratified in 107 days—the shortest ratification period in U.S. history.

Teach

TIME REPORTS

D₁ Differentiated Instruction

Intrapersonal Ask: What circumstances might prompt you to give your time, money, or effort to help others?
(Answers will include ideas of wanting to help out, feeling good because one is able to help, being moved by others' situations, and so on.) **BL**

D₂ Differentiated Instruction

Advanced Learners Ask: What have you heard or read about generous acts in response to recent world events?
(Answers will include information students have gleaned about donations prompted by recent catastrophes, including those that appear in the text.) **AL**

Additional Support

A Nation of Givers

Through charities, churches, and foundations, Americans put their money where their cause is

Comstock

D₁ Every year, nearly two-thirds of all Americans donate money to charity. Some citizens contribute only a few dollars, while others give away millions. On average, each American contributes $1,894.

All those donations add up. Americans donated a total of $248.5 billion to U.S. charities in 2004. Of this amount, about a third went to religious groups; less than 10% was donated to organizations that directly help the poor (see "Donation Nation" at right).

So why is the U.S. the most generous nation on earth? Its tax code encourages private giving in place of spending more public money on social programs. But tax breaks can't account for all the generosity. **D₂** The deduction for charitable giving cost the government $40 billion in 2004. Americans gave away more than six times that amount.

The Top Three

The largest total philanthropic gifts by individuals in 2004

$3.35 billion

Bill and Melinda Gates
The Microsoft chairman and his wife's pledge to the Gates Foundation—which committed more than $1 billion to global health alone in 2004—increased its endowment to nearly $32 billion, by far the largest in the world.

$2.55 billion

Susan T. Buffett
The wife of Berkshire Hathaway founder Warren Buffett left 31,707 shares of company stock largely to her foundation dedicated to college scholarships and medical research.

$550 million

John M. Templeton
The former investor pledged the money to his foundation to investigate the relationship among science, religion, and health.

Generosity's Deep Roots

Wealthy Americans have been creating ways to give away their time and money for generations

Culver Pictures

1873
Johns Hopkins (1795-1873), a railroad investor and merchant, leaves $7 million to found a university and hospital.

1907
Margaret Olivia Slocum Sage (1828-1918), a banking heiress, creates the Russell Sage Foundation, which offers grants to improve living conditions. Her total gift is estimated at $80 million.

Time Life Pictures/Getty Images

1911
Andrew Carnegie (1835-1919), a Scottish-born steel baron, defines charity as a moral imperative and gives away more than $350 million in his lifetime through the Carnegie Corporation.

Background

The American Red Cross Much of the money that U.S. citizens donate when disasters occur goes to the American Red Cross, a national organization that has existed since 1900. The American Red Cross assists in times of catastrophe, training and sending workers where need arises. Red Cross medical teams have served in every war since World War I, and its workers have brought water, food, and medical aid to people in need, both in the United States and abroad.

In addition to disaster relief programs, the Red Cross coordinates a national program that supplies nearly half of the nation's need for blood. Red Cross programs also prepare people to care for themselves and others in times of need, through courses on first aid, safety, and disaster preparedness.

The Red Cross works with the federal government but is led and staffed by volunteers. It is heavily dependent on the generosity that U.S. citizens have demonstrated for over a century.

Donation Nation

About two-thirds of Americans give to charity each year. The average gifts:

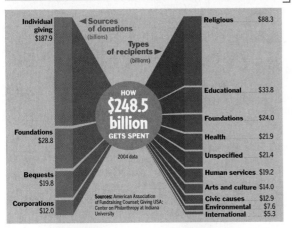

Most generous region

Most likely to give to religious causes

Highest percentage of donors: 82%

$2,252

$2,146

$1,648

$1,903

$1,615 $1,404

$2,204

$1,986

$1,927

Lowest percentage of donors: 61%

U.S. average: $1,894

Regional figures are from 2002 data, the most recent available

Individual giving $187.9

◀ Sources of donations (billions)

Types of recipients ▶ (billions)

HOW $248.5 billion GETS SPENT

2004 data

Foundations $28.8

Bequests $19.8

Corporations $12.0

Sources: American Association of Fundraising Counsel; Giving USA; Center on Philanthropy at Indiana University

Religious $88.3

Educational $33.8

Foundations $24.0

Health $21.9

Unspecified $21.4

Human services $19.2

Arts and culture $14.0

Civic causes $12.9

Environmental $7.6

International $5.3

Star Power

Big names are changing the face of philanthropy

$1.78 billion Tsunami relief

$3.12 billion Hurricane relief

U.S. contributions to disaster relief through Dec. 2005

Former Presidents and rivals **George H.W. Bush** and **Bill Clinton** formed an unlikely partnership that turned into a friendship, raising millions after the Asian tsunami and the devastating hurricanes in the U.S.

The Bono Effect? Since 2001, development aid for poor nations has increased from $67 billion to $80 billion and is projected to rise 60% by 2010. Many European countries are committed to giving 0.7% of their gross domestic product for aid; the U.S. currently gives only 0.1%.

1913
John D. Rockefeller (1839-1937) is the founder of Standard Oil and the richest man of his time. His $450 million in contributions to public health through the Rockefeller Foundation sets a precedent for the Gates Foundation.

1919
Madam C.J. Walker (1867-1919), an African American self-made millionaire, supports social and educational institutions with the profits from her hair-care and cosmetics business.

1936
Henry Ford (1863-1947), the automotive pioneer, establishes the Ford Foundation in Dearborn, Michigan, with $25,000. Now a nationwide force, it has more than $11 billion in assets.

Bettmann/Corbis

1977
John D. (1897-1978) and **Catherine T. MacArthur** (1909-1981) start their namesake foundation with the vast wealth from his insurance company, Bankers Life. Today the foundation's assets are estimated at $5 billion.

169

S Skills Practice

Analyzing Visuals Guide students to locate their state on the map. **Ask:** How does your state compare to other states or areas of the nation in amounts donated? *(Answers will vary depending on students' state.)* **OL**

Did You Know?

Bono is the leader of the band U2. Born Paul Hewson in Dublin, Ireland, Bono has used his considerable celebrity to help less fortunate people around the world. He plays an active role in combating world poverty and promoting AIDS awareness in Africa. He was nominated for the Nobel Peace Prize in 2003 for his humanitarian efforts.

Reading Strategy   Read to Write

Organizing Have students analyze the chart titled "How $248.5 Billion Gets Spent." The right side of the chart gives a breakdown of where the money donated by U.S. citizens goes. Ask students if, given the chance, they would assign money to different activities. Would they assign more to education? Give more help to solve social problems or to support medical research? Have students reapportion the money in their own charts as they think it should be spent. Then ask students to write a paragraph explaining the rationale for their decisions. **OL**

UNIT PACING CHART

	Unit 2	Chapter 6	Chapter 7	Chapter 8
Day 1	Unit Opener, Reading Social Studies	Chapter Opener, Section 1	Chapter Opener, Section 1	Chapter Opener, Section 1
Day 2		Section 2, Issues to Debate	Section 2	Section 2
Day 3		Section 3	Section 3	Section 3
Day 4		Section 4, Chapter Review, Visual Summary	Section 4, Chapter Review, Visual Summary	Section 4, Landmark Supreme Court Case Studies
Day 5		Chapter Assessment	Chapter Assessment	Chapter Review, Visual Summary
Day 6			TIME Reports	Chapter Assessment
Day 7				Analyzing Primary Sources

Teacher to Teacher

Frank Hobby, Lake Norman High School, Mooresville, North Carolina

Congressional Committee Assignment Divide the class into four or five groups to act as congressional committees. Each committee is assigned the task of writing a bill. (I find writing a bill on a school rule that should be implemented works the best.) After about ten minutes, each committee will exchange bills with another. The committee is free to make any changes to the bill as long as a majority of the committee agrees to the change. After about five minutes, the bills are exchanged again and the process is repeated until all committees have input on each bill. The bills are finally given to the original committee so that they may see the changes. Students will understand the active role that congressional committees play in the legislative process. This activity could continue with a debate and vote on each bill, with the class acting as a chamber of Congress. A majority vote would be needed to pass.

Author Note

Dear Social Studies Teacher:

Our national government as described in Unit 2 is based on a key constitutional principle—the separation of powers. As we know, the Founders gave each of the three branches powers that can be used to check and balance the actions of the other branches. A national government organized in this way divides responsibilities for making public policy. As the daily headlines constantly remind us, nothing in this arrangement requires the president and Congress to cooperate with each other. Inevitably the Supreme Court becomes involved in adjudicating disputes between the contending branches and thereby continuously adjusts the balance of power among the branches.

The practical impact of separation of powers is clearly evident in the national government's efforts to respond to threats to our national security from international terrorism. The wars in Iraq and Afghanistan, the Patriot Act, the creation of special prisons for suspected terrorists, and countless other public policies dramatically illustrate how this principle can put the separate branches of government at odds with each other. The war in Iraq is an example. In 2003, as part of the war on terror, Congress authorized the president to use force against Iraq. However, as the Iraq war continued over several years, Congress then searched for ways to limit or control the president's conduct of that war.

Throughout our history, separation of powers has helped us maintain a national government strong enough to be effective and yet constrained enough to safeguard our individual liberties. The threats posed by international terrorism are creating new challenges for this time-honored principle. Only time will tell if this principle will continue to serve us as well in the future as it has in the past.

Richard C. Remy

Author

Unit Objectives

After studying this unit, students will be able to:

- Identify the structure and functions of the legislative branch, or Congress.

- Analyze the duties, qualifications, and powers of the president and other members of the executive branch.

- Recognize the structure and authority of federal courts and relate Supreme Court decisions to the United States Constitution.

Did You Know?

One person is officially responsible for the entire United States Capitol Complex, which includes the Capitol, the congressional office buildings, the Library of Congress buildings, the Supreme Court building, the U.S. Botanic Garden, the Capitol Power Plant, and other buildings. That person—the Architect of the Capitol—oversees the maintenance, operation, development, and preservation of every existing building and any others that may be added. The Capitol Architect reports to Congress and becomes an official of the legislative branch when the Senate confirms the appointment. Although the nation has had an Architect of the Capitol since George Washington selected Dr. William Thornton in 1793, the job has grown dramatically.

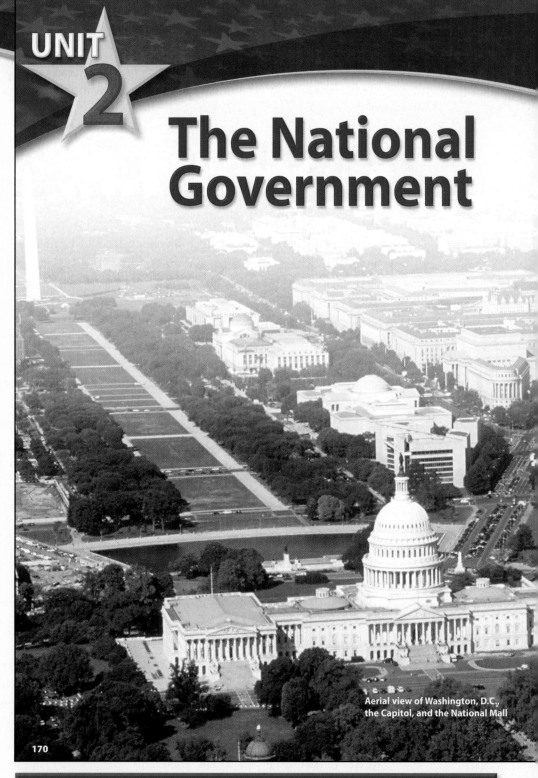

UNIT 2
The National Government

Aerial view of Washington, D.C., the Capitol, and the National Mall

170

Activity: Launching the Unit

The National Government Ask: What are the branches of the national government and what duties does each branch have? *(The national, or federal, government consists of three branches as described by the Constitution: the legislative branch (Congress), the executive branch (the president, the cabinet, and federal agencies), and the judicial branch (the U.S. Supreme Court and other courts of the federal court system). The legislative branch passes laws, the executive branch enforces laws, and the judicial branch reviews laws for constitutionality. Each branch has many duties within these broad descriptions, as well as other duties that serve the American people.)* **OL**

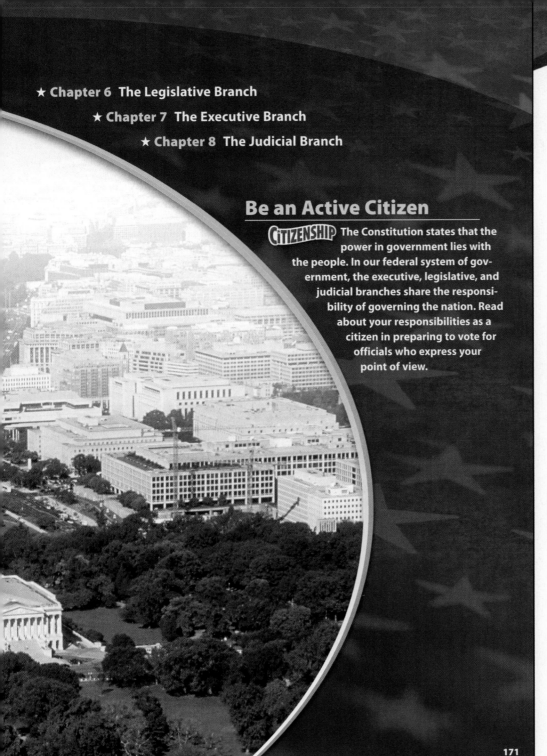

Be an Active Citizen

CITIZENSHIP The Constitution states that the power in government lies with the people. In our federal system of government, the executive, legislative, and judicial branches share the responsibility of governing the nation. Read about your responsibilities as a citizen in preparing to vote for officials who express your point of view.

171

Be an Active Citizen

CITIZENSHIP Do your students know the decision-making process that precedes a constituent's and a legislator's vote? Organize students into three groups. Present them with scenarios 1, 2, and 5 from www.ncsl.org/public/trust/democracylesson/Democracy LessonPlan_RepresentationHandoutB.htm as well as the modified chart on this sheet. Have groups consider each point as they formulate their group's vote on each scenario and complete the chart. Reconvene the class. Present students with the same scenarios from a legislator's viewpoint (see www.ncsl.org/public/trust/democracylesson/DemocracyLessonPlan_RepresentationHandoutC.htm). Discuss factors that cause legislators to depart from the views of their constituents.

Online Current Events Update

Visit Glencoe's *Online Current Events Update* **at** www.glencoe.com **to find news reports, features, maps, graphs, and photos of current events that shape our lives. Students can also make connections between historical events and current events by using the interactive time line.**

More About the Photo

Visual Literacy In 1793, construction began on the Capitol. For over a century, this was the only building created for the national legislature. It housed not only Congress but also the Supreme Court, district courts, and the Library of Congress. As the nation grew, so did the Capitol. By 1892, the Capitol had reached its current appearance and size with the exception of the east front extension in the late 1950s/early 1960s and the infill areas of the courtyard in the early 1990s. In 1897, the crowded Capitol saw the departure of the Library of Congress. It now resides in the Thomas Jefferson Building. The House and Senate soon got their own buildings, with later additions. Add to that a federal judiciary building, a power plant, a botanic garden, and others to create today's massive Capitol Complex.

Why Finding the Main Idea Is Important

Locating the main idea and its supporting details is an essential skill for understanding many kinds of writing, from textbooks to essays to news articles. By identifying supporting details, students are better able to remember key information about the content. When they analyze persuasive writing, they can use the skill as a step toward determining whether the details an author provides are adequate to support the author's arguments.

① Learn It!

Read the following statement aloud: "The power of the U.S. government is divided between the three separate branches." Have volunteers provide details that support the statement. Tell students that details can answer such questions as *why, when,* and *how.* **OL**

Finding the Main Idea

① Learn It!

Main ideas are the most important ideas in a paragraph, section, or chapter. Supporting details are facts or examples that explain the main idea.

- Read the paragraph below. Notice how the main idea is identified.
- The sentences that follow are the supporting details.

Main Idea

Supporting Details

> Our Constitution explains not only what Congress may do but also what it may *not* do. Some limitations are imposed by the Bill of Rights. The purpose of the Bill of Rights was to limit or deny certain powers to the federal government. For example, Congress may not pass laws that restrict freedom of speech, or ban freedom of religion.
>
> —*from page 188*

Web Diagram

A web diagram can organize the main idea and supporting details.

Our Constitution explains not only what Congress may do but also what it may *not* do.

- Some limitations are imposed by the Bill of Rights.
- The purpose of the Bill of Rights was to limit or deny certain powers to the federal government.
- For example, Congress may not pass laws, restrict freedom of speech, or ban freedom of religion.

Reading Tip

Often, the first sentence in a paragraph will contain a main idea. However, main ideas can also appear in the middle or at the end of a paragraph.

📖 Reading Strategy ⟨ Organizing Information

Finding the Main Idea Students can use clues in a written document to help them identify main ideas. Headings and subheadings often provide such clues by indicating a topic or theme that applies to the information grouped under that topic. Remind students that, as in the sample paragraph on this page, the first sentence of a paragraph often—though not always—states the main idea. Ask students to chose a paragraph from one of the section in Chapter 6 and identify the main idea. **ELL**

② Practice It!

Read the paragraph. Draw a graphic organizer like the one below to show the main idea and supporting details.

People contribute to their communities in countless ways, working independently or as part of volunteer groups both large and small. Perhaps you know a mom or dad who is active in the PTA (Parent Teacher Association) or leads a Scout troop. Your friends and you might spend a Saturday cleaning up a highway or preparing holiday baskets for needy families. Retirees mentor school children, record books for the blind, and lead museum tours.

▲ A volunteer highway cleanup crew

③ Apply It!

Identify one main idea and its supporting details for:

- **Chapter 7; Section 2**
- **Chapter 8; Section 3**

Read to Write Activity

Read the Main Idea on page 185. Use it as a topic sentence and add supporting details to create a complete paragraph.

② Practice It!

Main idea: The president is commander in chief of the nation's armed forces.
Supporting details: The president can use force to back up foreign policy; the president is head of the army, navy, air force, marines, and coast guard; the top commanders of all branches of service are subordinate to the president.
Now have students close their books and ask a volunteer to summarize the main idea and details in his or her own words. **OL**

③ Apply It!

Bring to class a collection of news articles and opinion essays from newspapers and news-magazines. Divide the class into small groups and have each group analyze a different piece of writing to identify the main idea and supporting details. After they have finished the work, have the class discuss the process. **OL**

📖 Reading Strategy ‹ Read to Write

Summarizing In writing summaries, students read a text to identify the most important ideas and concepts and only the most essential details. Have students write a brief summary of a subsection of this chapter. Then have students exchange summaries and compare their partners' work to the original. Ask students to comment on whether their partners' writing adequately summarizes the original. **AL**

Chapter Planning Guide

6

Key to Ability Levels
BL Below level **AL** Above level
OL On level **ELL** English Language Learners

Key to Teaching Resources
📁 Print Material 🖐 Transparency
💿 CD-ROM or DVD

Levels					Resources	Chapter Opener	Section 1	Section 2	Section 3	Section 4	Chapter Assess
BL	OL	AL	ELL								
FOCUS											
BL	OL	AL	ELL	🖐	Daily Focus Skills Transparencies		6–1	6–2	6–3	6–4	
TEACH											
BL	OL		ELL	📁	Reading Essentials and Note-Taking Guide*		p. 52	p. 55	p. 58	p. 61	
BL	OL	AL	ELL	📁	Content Vocabulary Activity, URB*		p. 21	p. 21	p. 21	p. 21	
BL	OL	AL	ELL	📁	Academic Vocabulary Activity, URB		p. 23	p. 23	p. 23	p. 23	
	OL			📁	Biography Activity, URB				p. 25		
BL	OL	AL	ELL	📁	Writing Skills Activity, URB				p. 27		
	OL	AL		📁	Critical Thinking Skills Activity, URB			p. 29			
BL	OL	AL	ELL	📁	Chart, Graph, and Map Skills Activity, URB			p. 31		p. 31	
BL	OL	AL	ELL	📁	Differentiated Instruction, URB		p. 33				
BL	OL	AL	ELL	📁	School-to-Home Connection Activity, URB*		p. 35	p. 35	p. 35	p. 35	
BL	OL		ELL	📁	Guided Reading Activities, URB*		p. 39	p. 40	p. 41	p. 42	
BL	OL	AL	ELL	📁	Writer's Guidebook	✓	✓	✓	✓	✓	✓
	OL	AL		💿	Primary Source Document Library	✓	✓	✓	✓	✓	✓
BL	OL	AL	ELL	💿	Daily Lecture & Discussion Notes (in Pres. Plus)		✓	✓	✓	✓	✓
BL	OL	AL	ELL	💿	StudentWorks™ Plus		✓	✓	✓	✓	✓
BL	OL	AL	ELL	💿	Section Spotlight Videos		✓	✓	✓	✓	
BL	OL	AL	ELL	🖐	TIME Interpreting Political Cartoons Transp.				Ch. 6		
BL	OL	AL	ELL	🖐	Writing Process Transparencies	✓	✓	✓	✓	✓	✓

Note: Please refer to the *Unit 2 Resource Book* for this chapter's URB materials.

* Also available in Spanish

- Interactive Lesson Planner
- Interactive Teacher Edition
- Fully editable blackline masters
- Section Spotlight Videos Launch
- Differentiated Lesson Plans
- Printable reports of daily assignments
- Standards Tracking System

Levels					Resources	Chapter Opener	Section 1	Section 2	Section 3	Section 4	Chapter Assess
BL	OL	AL	ELL								
					TEACH *(continued)*						
					Building Academic Vocabulary	✓	✓	✓	✓	✓	✓
					Strategies for Success	✓	✓	✓	✓	✓	✓
Teacher Resources					**Teacher's Guide to Differentiated Instruction**	✓	✓	✓	✓	✓	✓
					Graphing Tool	✓	✓	✓	✓	✓	✓
					Presentation Plus! with MindJogger CheckPoint	✓	✓	✓	✓	✓	✓
					ASSESS						
BL	OL	AL	ELL		**Quizzes and Tests***		p. 64	p. 65	p. 66	p. 67	p. 68
BL	OL	AL	ELL		**Authentic Assessment with Rubrics**				p. 10		
BL	OL	AL	ELL		**Standardized Test Practice**		p. 11	p. 11	p. 11	p. 11	p. 11
BL	OL	AL	ELL		*ExamView® Assessment Suite* **CD-ROM**		6–1	6–2	6–3	6–4	Ch. 6
					CLOSE						
BL			ELL		**Reteaching Activity, URB**		p. 37	p. 37	p. 37	p. 37	
BL	OL		ELL		**Reading and Study Skills Foldables™ Activity**	p. 60	p. 61	p. 61			
BL	OL	AL	ELL		*Civics Today* **in Graphic Novel**	p. 15		p. 15			
BL	OL	AL	ELL		**Graphic Organizer Transparencies & Strategies**	✓	✓	✓	✓	✓	✓

✓ Chapter- or unit-based activities applicable to all sections in this chapter

Using the Media Library

Section Based Audio

What is the Media Library?

The Media Library is an online tool that includes audio recordings of every section of the textbook.

How can the Media Library help my students?

The Section Based Audio recordings on the Media Library help students to:

- improve their content comprehension by reading (in their textbook) and listening to section content simultaneously
- practice reading skills
- review important concepts
- improve listening comprehension

Visit glencoe.com and enter a *QuickPass*™ code to go directly to resources for each chapter.

Civics ONLINE
Visit glencoe.com and enter *QuickPass*™ code CIV1360c6T for Chapter 6 resources.

You can easily launch a wide range of digital products from your computer's desktop with the McGraw-Hill Social Studies widget.

	Student	Teacher	Parent
Media Library			
• Student Edition Section Audio	●		●
• Spanish Audio Summaries	●		●
• Section Spotlight Videos	●	●	●
***Civics Today* Online Learning Center (Web Site)**			
• Chapter Overviews	●	●	●
• Study Central™	●	●	●
• Study-to-Go	●	●	●
• Student Web Activities	●	●	●
• In Motion Animation	●	●	●
• Self-Check Quizzes	●	●	●
• ePuzzles and Games	●	●	●
• StudentWorks™ Plus Online	●	●	●
• Vocabulary eFlashcards	●	●	●
• Web Activity Lesson Plans		●	
• Vocabulary PuzzleMaker	●	●	●
Classroom Tools			
• Multilingual Glossary	●	●	●
• Beyond the Textbook	●	●	●
• NGS MapMachine	●	●	●

Reading List Generator CD-ROM

GLENCOE BookLink 3

Use this database to search more than 30,000 titles to create a customized reading list for your students.

- Reading lists can be organized by students' reading level, author, genre, theme, or area of interest.
- The database provides Degrees of Reading Power™ (DRP) and Lexile™ readability scores for all selections.
- A brief summary of each selection is included.

Leveled reading suggestions for this chapter:

For students at a Grade 7 reading level:
- *You Want Women to Vote, Lizzie Stanton?* by Jean Fritz

For students at a Grade 8 reading level:
- *Marian Wright Edelman: Defender of Children's Rights,* by Steven Otfinoski

For students at a Grade 9 reading level:
- *The Story of Rachel Carson and the Environmental Movement,* by Leila M. Foster

For students at a Grade 10 reading level:
- *The Great Depression and the New Deal: America's Economic Collapse and Recovery,* by Anne E. Schraff

For students at a Grade 11 reading level:
- *Thurgood Marshall, Champion of Justice,* by G.S. Prentzas

READING SUPPORT FROM JAMESTOWN EDUCATION

- **Timed Readings Plus in Social Studies** helps students increase their reading rate and fluency while maintaining comprehension. The 400-word passages are similar to those found on state and national assessments.

- **Reading in the Content Area: Social Studies** concentrates on six essential reading skills that help students better comprehend what they read. The book includes 75 high-interest nonfiction passages written at increasing levels of difficulty.

- **Reading Social Studies** includes strategic reading instruction and vocabulary support in Social Studies content for both ELLs and native speakers of English.

- **Content Vocabulary Workout** (Grades 6–8) accelerates reading comprehension through focused vocabulary development. Social Studies content vocabulary comes from the glossaries of Glencoe's Middle School Social Studies texts. www.jamestowneducation.com

KEY Teacher Wraparound

Use this key to help you identify the different types of prompts found in the Teacher Wraparound Edition.

R **Reading Strategies** activities help you teach reading skills and vocabulary.

C **Critical Thinking** strategies help students apply and extend what they have learned.

D **Differentiated Instruction** activities provide instruction for students learning to speak English, along with suggestions for teaching various types of learners.

S **Skill Practice** strategies help students practice historical analysis and geography skills.

W **Writing Support** activities provide writing opportunities to help students comprehend the text.

Teaching strategies and activities have been coded for ability level appropriateness.

AL Activities for students working above grade level

OL Activities for students working on grade level

BL Activities for students working below grade level

ELL Activities for English Language Learners

Focus

Why It Matters

Ask: Why might your positions on the issues differ from your classmates'? *(Answers may include the idea that people have different interests and needs. While someone may feel unemployment is a serious national problem, others may view national health care as more important.)*

More About the Photo

Visual Literacy The nation's capital—Washington, D.C.—is actually a donated parcel of land. Although both Maryland and Virginia ceded land for the building of a capital, President George Washington selected the Maryland parcel in 1791. Pierre Charles L'Enfant, the French engineer selected to design the city, called the rise on which the capitol is located "a pedestal waiting for a monument."

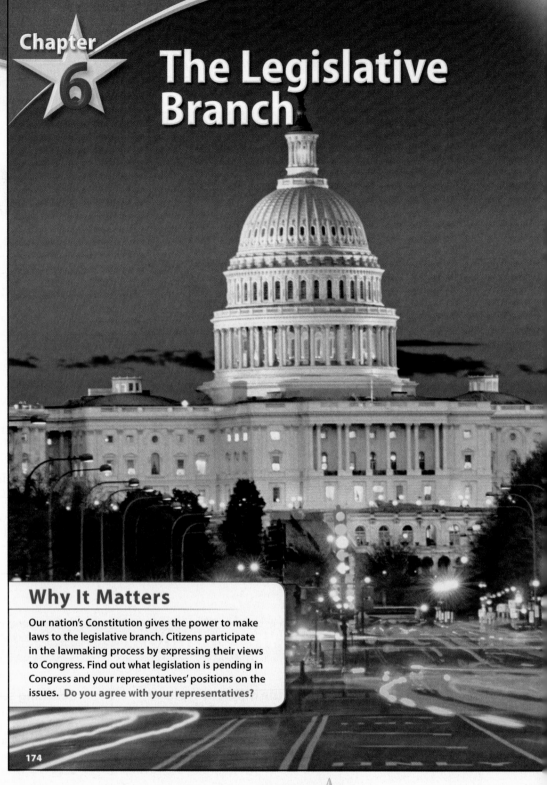

Chapter

6 The Legislative Branch

Why It Matters

Our nation's Constitution gives the power to make laws to the legislative branch. Citizens participate in the lawmaking process by expressing their views to Congress. Find out what legislation is pending in Congress and your representatives' positions on the issues. **Do you agree with your representatives?**

174

Teach

BIG Ideas *As you begin teaching each section, use these questions and activities to help students focus on the Big Ideas.*

Section 1

How Congress Is Organized Ask: Why do you think much of the work in Congress is done in committees? *(By assigning tasks to different committees, research and discussion on a variety of issues can proceed more efficiently.)* Point out that in Section 1, students will learn about the various types of congressional committees. **OL**

Section 2

Powers of Congress Ask: Why might the Framers of the Constitution have limited the powers of Congress? *(The Founders did not want Congress to be like the British Parliament, a legislature that was not responsible to the voters.)* Tell students that in Section 2, they will learn about the powers of Congress. Constitutional limitations, including the system of checks and balances, are also discussed. **OL**

 Chapter Audio

Civics ONLINE
Visit glencoe.com and enter
QuickPass™ code
CIV3093c6 for
Chapter 6
resources.

BIG Ideas

Section 1: How Congress Is Organized

The Constitution gives the legislative branch—Congress—the power to make laws. In Congress, members of each party select their own leaders and work mainly in committees to carry out their duties.

Section 2: Powers of Congress

The Constitution gives the legislative branch—Congress—the power to make laws. While the Constitution limits the powers of Congress, it also gives Congress the powers it needs to conduct its business and to accomplish its goals.

Section 3: Representing the People

The Constitution gives the legislative branch—Congress—the power to make laws. Congress employs many staffers who help with the workload.

Section 4: How a Bill Becomes a Law

The Constitution gives the legislative branch—Congress—the power to make laws. Several complex steps are involved in taking an idea and turning it into a law.

The U.S. Capitol, Washington, D.C.

FOLDABLES™
Study Organizer

Summarizing Information Study Foldable Make the following Foldable to help you summarize information about the national government of the United States.

Step 1 Collect three sheets of paper and place them on top of each other about an inch apart.

Step 2 Fold up the bottom edges of the paper to form six tabs.

This makes all tabs the same size.

Step 3 When all the tabs are the same size, crease the paper to hold the tabs in place and staple the sheets together. Label each tab as shown.

Presidential Action
Voting on a Bill
Floor Debate and Action
Committee Action
Bill Introduced
How a Bill Becomes a Law

Reading and Writing
As you read the chapter, write the details of the different stages that a bill goes through to become a law as it passes through Congress.

FOLDABLES™
Study Organizer Dinah Zike's Foldables

Purpose This Foldable guides students to understand the congressional process that makes a bill into law. The completed Foldable will use tabs to help them identify the steps in the process. **OL**

📁 More Foldables activities for this chapter can be found in the *Dinah Zike's Reading and Study Skills Foldables* ancillary.

Civics ONLINE
Visit glencoe.com and enter
QuickPass™ code CIV1360c6T for Chapter 6 resources, including a Chapter Overview, Study Central™, Study-to-Go, Student Web Activity, Self-Check Quiz, and other materials.

Section 3

Representing the People Ask: Why does the Constitution outline requirements for representatives and senators? *(Because these lawmakers have great power and responsibility, they must have a certain level of maturity and firsthand knowledge of their constituents.)* Explain that in Section 3, students will learn about the qualifications and duties of legislators, their staff, and support agencies. **OL**

Section 4

How a Bill Becomes a Law Ask: Why should there be many steps before a bill becomes a law? *(When a bill becomes a law, every American citizen is required to obey it. It is important that a bill is discussed, researched, and sometimes revised to make the best law possible.)* Explain that in Section 4, students will learn about the roles of committees, the full Congress, and the president in the lawmaking process. **OL**

Focus

Guide to Reading
Answers to Graphic:

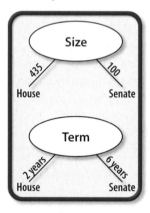

Size
435 — House
100 — Senate

Term
2 years — House
6 years — Senate

Section
Spotlight Video

Have students watch the Chapter 6, Section 1 video at glencoe.com.

Resource Manager

 Section Audio   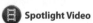 **Spotlight Video**

Guide to Reading

Big Idea
The Constitution gives the legislative branch—Congress—the power to make laws.

Content Vocabulary
- bicameral *(p. 177)*
- census *(p. 179)*
- constituent *(p. 179)*
- gerrymander *(p. 179)*
- majority party *(p. 180)*
- minority party *(p. 180)*
- standing committee *(p. 181)*
- seniority *(p. 182)*

Academic Vocabulary
- occur *(p. 178)*
- adjust *(p. 179)*

Reading Strategy
Comparing and Contrasting Create graphic organizers similar to the ones below. As you read, fill in the information about the House of Representatives and the Senate.

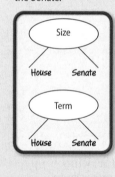

Size — House / Senate
Term — House / Senate

Section
1

How Congress Is Organized

Real World Civics Politics in Illinois—the heartland of America—are the same as everywhere else in the country. Members of Congress speak to and listen to the people they represent so they can do their jobs in Washington. Here, as a senator, Barack Obama speaks to constituents at a town hall meeting in Carrollton, Illinois. Members of Congress meet with their constituents to find out how they feel about important issues.

▼ **Former Illinois U.S. senator Barack Obama**

A Bicameral Legislature

Main Idea Congress is the legislative, or lawmaking, branch of government.

Civics & You What type of person would you choose to represent you in government? Read to find out how congressional leadership is determined.

The Framers wanted to establish a Congressional voting body, but one of the conflicts at the Constitutional Convention in 1787 concerned state representation. While delegates from the smaller states wanted equal representation, delegates from the larger states wanted representation to be based on population, which would give them a greater voice in government. As you will recall **D**

from Chapter 3, the Great Compromise established Congress as a two-part, or **bicameral,** body. In the Upper House, the Senate, each state would have an equal number of representatives—two. In the lower house, the House of Representatives, each state's population would determine its representation.

The Framers of the U.S. Constitution intended to make the legislative branch of government more powerful than any other branch. In fact, Congress is described in the first part of the Constitution, Article I. As James Madison said, Congress is "the First Branch of this Government." **C**

Every year, inside the U.S. Capitol in Washington, D.C., 535 of our fellow citizens gather to make new laws and address countless issues facing our country. These are our elected representatives, the members of Congress.

Joint Session A special session of Congress in New York City marks only the second time in 200 years that Congress has met outside the nation's capital. *Explaining* Why did the Framers establish a bicameral legislature?

Activity: Technology Connection

Ask: What is the purpose of a convention? *(At a convention, representatives of larger groups of people meet for a common purpose, such as deciding on issues and candidates, and writing statements for the group as a whole.)* Have groups use www.archives.gov/national-archives-experience/charters/ charters.html to research and chart plans presented at the Constitutional Convention. In their charts, have students include the Virginia, New Jersey, and British (Hamilton's) plans with the description from each plan for the legislative, executive, and judicial branches. **OL**

Teach

D Differentiated Instruction

Visual/Spatial Show students a map of the thirteen original states. Ask them to identify which plan for representation people in each state might have favored. *(Students should link small states with the plan for equal representation. They should link large states with population-based representation.)* **BL**

C Critical Thinking

Making Inferences Ask: Why did the Framers intend Congress to be the most powerful branch in the federal government? *(It is the branch most representative of the people of the country.)* **AL**

Caption Answer:

Answers will vary, but students may note that because of the difference in service terms, qualifications, perspectives, and leadership, a two-house system is more likely to voice various viewpoints and to protect the interests of minorities.

Additional Support

C Critical Thinking

Making Inferences Ask: Why is it important that the government calendar is established by law? *(Congressional leaders might avoid meeting and, therefore, neglect the business of the country.)* **AL**

R Reading Strategy

Identifying Ask: What crises might lead Congress to meet in special session? *(declaring war, a terrorist attack, the death of a president, and so on)* **OL**

Analyzing Maps

Answers:
1. California
2. Gained: AZ, CA, CO, FL, GA, NV, NC, TX. Lost: CT, IL, IN, MI, MS, NY, OH, OK, PA, WI. The South and West gained representatives, and the North lost representatives. People may be leaving the cold North for warmer climates.

Civics ONLINE

Objectives and answers to the **Student Web Activity** can be found at glencoe.com under the Web Activity Lesson Plan for this chapter.

Hands-On Chapter Project
Step 1

Mock Senate

Step 1: Writing Bills Divide students into four groups. Each group will write a bill to introduce on the Senate floor. The bills should focus on issues that affect teens and families or other issues to which students relate.

Directions Write the Big Idea on the board. Identify two groups as Republicans and two as Democrats. Tell groups to research bill ideas at www.gpoaccess.gov/bills/

Congressional Apportionment, Selected Years

1790

1850

1950

Analyzing Maps

1. **Identifying** Which state has the most electoral votes today?
2. **Analyzing** Which states gained representatives in 2000? Which states lost representatives? Did any particular region of the country gain or lose seats? Explain.

Terms of Congress

The government calendar is set by law. Each Congress lasts for a meeting period, or a term, of two years. Each term of Congress starts on January 3rd of odd-numbered years (unless a different day is appointed) and lasts for two years.

Each "new" Congress is given a number to identify its two-year term. For example, the first Congress met in 1789, and the 111th Congress is in session from January 2009 to January 2011.

Congressional Sessions

Each term of Congress is divided into two sessions, or meetings. A typical session of Congress today lasts from January until November or December. Congress may also meet during special sessions or in times of crisis. A joint session **occurs,** or takes place, when the House and Senate meet together.

Civics ONLINE

Student Web Activity Visit glencoe.com and complete the Chapter 6 Web Activity.

Index.html. Groups should then research the issue they have selected: its history, facts, existing controversies, and the population most affected (such as the elderly, teens, criminals, and so on). Remind students to consider the powers given to Congress as they propose solutions. Have groups write their bills, using current bills found at the Library of Congress Web site, thomas.loc.gov/home/textonly.html, as models.

Writing Have groups write their bills using the two-page blank bill found at congress.indiana.edu/pdf/Best%20Practices%20Conrad%20a.pdf. Number the bills using the Senate numbering system. Groups will use their bills in Section 2. **OL**

(Project continued in Section 2)

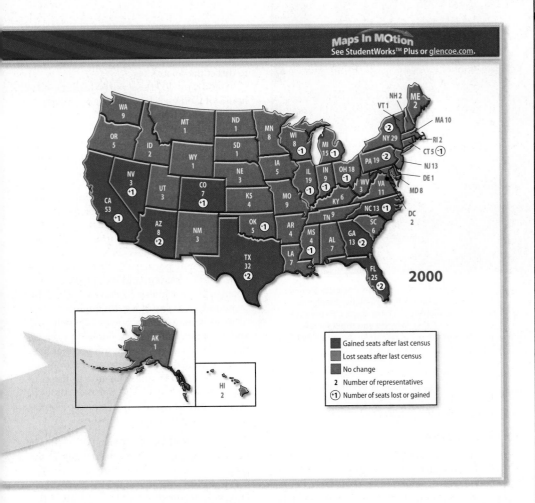

Maps In MOtion
See StudentWorks™ Plus or glencoe.com.

2000

Gained seats after last census
Lost seats after last census
No change
2 Number of representatives
(1) Number of seats lost or gained

W Writing Support

Persuasive Writing Distribute copies of editorials to groups of students. Explain that editors often call attention to local or state problems through this type of persuasive writing. Have groups identify a local or state problem that needs to be addressed by the national legislature. Using the editorials as models, have each group write an editorial about the problem it identified. **OL**

D Differentiated Instruction

Verbal/Linguistic Ask: Which English word helps explain the meaning of "constituent"? What does this word mean? (constitute; It means "to make up, form, or compose.") **AL**

S Skill Practice

Illustrating Have students reread the description of a gerrymander in the text. Ask students to sketch a gerrymander. **ELL**

The House of Representatives

The House of Representatives, the larger body of Congress, has 435 voting members allotted to the states according to population. The Constitution guarantees each state at least one representative, no matter how small its population. After each 10-year **census,** or population count taken by the Census Bureau, Congress **adjusts,** or changes, the number of representatives given to each state. Representatives serve two-year terms and usually focus on concerns in their districts. **W**

Congressional Districts Each state is divided into one or more congressional districts, with one representative elected from each district. State legislatures must draw the boundaries so that the districts include roughly the same number of **constituents,** **D** or people represented. Sometimes states abuse this process by gerrymandering. A **gerrymander** is an oddly shaped district designed to increase the voting strength of a **S** particular group. Laws have reduced but not eliminated gerrymandering.

Chapter 6   179

Did You Know?

A New Lizard The term "gerrymander" was invented in 1812 by a political cartoonist for a Boston newspaper. The first part of the term comes from the name of a former Massachusetts governor—Elbridge Gerry. Gerry and his political supporters used their influence to reshape voting districts so Gerry's party would have a political advantage in elections. The second part of the term—"mander"—comes from an amphibian known as the salamander. The cartoonist jokingly pointed out that gerrymanders were so oddly shaped that they resembled salamanders.

Additional Support

D Differentiated Instruction

Logical/Mathematical Ask: How many senators are likely to be elected every two years? *(no more than 33)* **BL**

C Critical Thinking

Analyzing Remind students that Article I, Section 2, Clause 5, of the United States Constitution does not state that the Speaker has to be a member of the House. **Ask:** What is the benefit of having a House member as Speaker? *(Answers may include that the Speaker may be better equipped to handle the presidency in the event of the president's and vice president's deaths or incapacity, and the Speaker would have the authority to cast votes on legislation.)* **AL**

Caption Answer:

Answers may include that women have not been in Congress for as many years as men, and it may take time for the balance to swing.

✔ **Reading Check** **Answer:** Article I

Differentiated Instruction

Biography Activity 6, URB p. 25

180

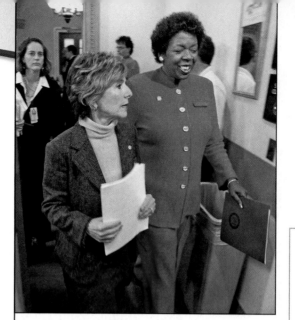

House and Senate Cooperation Senator Barbara Boxer (left) and former Representative Stephanie Tubbs Jones (right), both Democrats, collaborated often. *Speculating* Why do you think female members of Congress remain in the minority?

For example, if most of a state's representatives are Republican, they might draw the lines so that as many districts as possible have more Republican than Democratic voters.

The Senate

The Senate has 100 members—2 from each of the 50 states. Each senator represents his or her entire state rather than a particular district. Senators serve six-year terms, but the elections are staggered so that no more than one-third of the senators are up for reelection at any one time. This ensures a certain amount of stability and continuity.

If a senator dies or resigns before the end of the term, the state legislature may authorize the governor to appoint someone to fill the vacancy until the next election.

Leaders in Congress

In both the House and the Senate, the political party to which more than half the members belong is known as the **majority**

---

party. The other party is called the **minority party.** At the beginning of each term, the party members in each house choose leaders to direct their activities.

In addition to these party leaders, each house of Congress has one overall leader. In the House of Representatives, this leader is the Speaker of the House. Members of the majority party choose the Speaker at a caucus, or closed meeting. The rest of the House then approves the choice of Speaker.

Role of the Speaker As presiding officer of the House and the leader of the majority party, the Speaker has great power. The Speaker steers legislation through the House and leads floor debates (in which all representatives may participate). If anything happens to the president and vice president, the Speaker is next in line to become president, provided he or she is legally qualified.

Speakers rely on their powers of persuasion and the power of their positions to exercise influence. On a typical day, the Speaker may talk with dozens of members of Congress. Often the Speaker does this just to listen to requests for a favor. The Speaker, though, expects something in return—the representatives' support on important issues.

Congressional Leadership Leadership in the Senate closely parallels leadership in the House, but the Senate has no speaker. The vice president presides in the Senate but may only vote to break a tie. The president pro tempore—meaning "for the time being"—usually acts as chairperson of the Senate. He or she is from the majority party and is usually its most senior member.

Other powerful leaders are the floor leaders. The majority and minority floor leaders in each house speak for their parties on issues, push bills along, and try to sway votes. Party "whips" help the floor leaders. They make sure legislators are present for key votes.

✔ **Reading Check** **Identifying** Which article of the Constitution describes Congress?

Nancy Pelosi

Objective: Read about a woman who is making political history

Focus: Have students define the role of Speaker of the House.

Teach: Discuss which parties control the House and Senate.

Assess: Create a time line showing Pelosi's political career.

Close: Lead a discussion on how different today's Congress is from the one of the Founders.

Differentiated Instruction Strategies

BL List two factors that you think most influenced Nancy Pelosi's career in politics.

AL Write a letter from Jane Addams to Nancy Pelosi about the change for women.

ELL Define "commitment" and "dedication." Give examples for each word.

Committee Work

Main Idea Much of the actual work of legislating is performed by committees and subcommittees within Congress.

Civics & You Have you served on a committee? What are their advantages and disadvantages? Read to find out about congressional committees.

Each house of Congress must consider thousands of bills, or proposed laws, in the course of a session. To make it possible to handle so many bills at one time, each house has developed a system of committees.

Congressional Committees

Congress has three types of committees: standing committees, select committees, and joint committees. **Standing committees** are permanent committees. For example, both the Senate and the House have standing committees to deal with agriculture, commerce, and veterans' affairs.

The House and Senate sometimes form temporary committees to deal with special issues. These select committees meet for a limited time until they complete their assigned task. Occasionally, the Senate and the House form joint committees, which include members of both houses. Joint committees meet to consider specific issues.

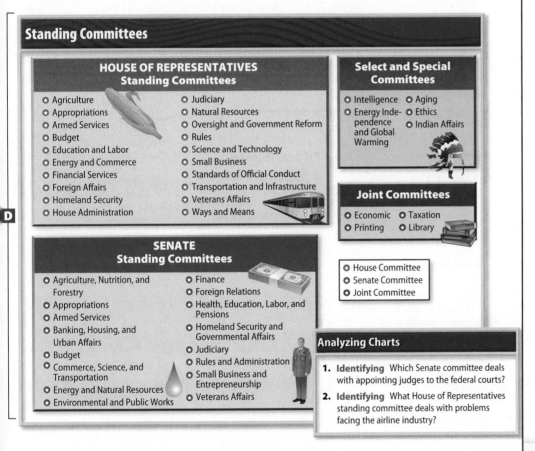

Standing Committees

HOUSE OF REPRESENTATIVES Standing Committees

- Agriculture
- Appropriations
- Armed Services
- Budget
- Education and Labor
- Energy and Commerce
- Financial Services
- Foreign Affairs
- Homeland Security
- House Administration
- Judiciary
- Natural Resources
- Oversight and Government Reform
- Rules
- Science and Technology
- Small Business
- Standards of Official Conduct
- Transportation and Infrastructure
- Veterans Affairs
- Ways and Means

SENATE Standing Committees

- Agriculture, Nutrition, and Forestry
- Appropriations
- Armed Services
- Banking, Housing, and Urban Affairs
- Budget
- Commerce, Science, and Transportation
- Energy and Natural Resources
- Environmental and Public Works
- Finance
- Foreign Relations
- Health, Education, Labor, and Pensions
- Homeland Security and Governmental Affairs
- Judiciary
- Rules and Administration
- Small Business and Entrepreneurship
- Veterans Affairs

Select and Special Committees

- Intelligence
- Energy Independence and Global Warming
- Aging
- Ethics
- Indian Affairs

Joint Committees

- Economic
- Printing
- Taxation
- Library

- House Committee
- Senate Committee
- Joint Committee

Analyzing Charts

1. **Identifying** Which Senate committee deals with appointing judges to the federal courts?
2. **Identifying** What House of Representatives standing committee deals with problems facing the airline industry?

CHAPTER 6 Section 1

R Reading Strategy

Using Context Clues Ask: Which words from the text explain the term "bills"? *(proposed laws)* **ELL**

D Differentiated Instruction

Special Education Ask: Which standing committees of the House and Senate study the same topics? *(Agriculture/ Agriculture, Nutrition, and Forestry; Appropriations/Appropriations; Armed Services/ Armed Services; Budget/Budget; Energy and Commerce/Energy and Natural Resources; Judiciary/Judiciary; Veterans Affairs/Veterans Affairs; Small Business/ Small Business and Entrepreneurship)*

C Critical Thinking

Comparing and Contrasting Ask: What is the main difference between standing and joint committees? *(Members of standing committees belong to the same congressional house; members of joint committees belong to both houses of Congress.)* **BL**

Analyzing Charts

Answers:
1. Judiciary
2. Transportation and Infrastructure

Leveled Activities

BL Academic Vocabulary Activity 6, URB pp. 23–24

OL Biography Activity 6, URB pp. 25–26

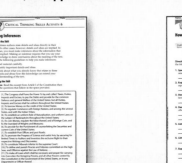

AL Critical Thinking Activity 6, URB pp. 29–30

ELL Guided Reading Activity 6–1, URB p. 39

Critical Thinking

Predicting Consequences Explain to students that incumbents are occasionally defeated when trying to get reelected. **Ask:** How will this affect the district or state the legislator represents? *(If the defeated incumbent had been a senior member of Congress and a member of important standing committees, it is unlikely that the newly elected junior legislator will automatically serve on the incumbent's committees.)* **AL**

Reading Check Answer: A standing committee is permanent; a select committee is temporary.

Assess

Civics ONLINE

Study Central™ provides summaries, interactive games, and online graphic organizers to help students review content.

Close

Identifying Have students work in pairs to list the various leaders in Congress. Have students include a brief description of the responsibilities and powers of each leadership position. **BL**

Section 1 Review

Committee Assignments

When senators and representatives first come to Congress, they try to get assigned to important committees that affect the people who elected them. For example, members of Congress from farm areas might want to serve on agriculture committees. Those with many factories in their districts might be interested in serving on labor committees.

What Is The Seniority System? Party leaders make committee assignments. In doing so, they consider members' preferences, expertise, and loyalty to the party. Another key factor is **seniority,** or years of service. The senators and representatives who have been in Congress longest usually get the preferred committee spots. The longest-serving committee member from the majority party traditionally becomes chairperson. Chairpersons decide when and if a committee will meet, what bills will be studied, and who will serve on which subcommittees.

Some people think the seniority system is a good idea. They say it prevents fights over committee jobs and ensures that chairpersons will have experience. Other people complain that talented people may be overlooked in favor of those who have simply been around for a while. There has been so much criticism of the seniority system over the years that both political parties have moved slightly away from it. The senior majority party member on a committee still usually wins the role of chairperson, but it is no longer guaranteed.

Reading Check Explaining What is the difference between a standing committee and a select committee?

Vocabulary

1. **Write** sentences or short paragraphs in which you use the following terms: *bicameral, census, constituent, gerrymander, majority party, minority party, standing committee,* and *seniority.*

Main Ideas

2. **Describing** Why are the two houses of Congress good places to discuss issues that might require new laws?

3. **Explaining** Why is so much of the business of Congress conducted in committees?

Critical Thinking

4. **BIG Ideas** In what ways do the Senate and House of Representatives work together to pass bills into laws?

5. **Identifying** On a graphic organizer like the one below, identify the different types of committees established in Congress.

6. **Analyzing Visuals** Review the maps on pages 178–179. How many representatives did North Carolina have in 1790? In 1950? In 2000? What does this tell you about how North Carolina's population has changed?

CITIZENSHIP Activity

7. **Persuasive Writing** Do you think that government by committee makes the role of individual members of Congress less important? Express your opinion on this question in a one-page essay.

Civics ONLINE

Study Central™ To review this section, go to glencoe.com.

Answers

1. Sentences should use vocabulary words according to their definitions in the section and in the Glossary.
2. The Constitution gives Congress the sole authority to make national laws.
3. Committees make it possible for Congress to handle a great number of bills at one time.
4. Answers may include that joint committees allow the houses to work out their differences on various bills.

5.

6. 10; 12; 13. North Carolina's population has grown.

7. Student essays may include that individual members of committees work to accomplish goals that benefit their constituents and, consequently, remain important figures in the legislative process.

What Is a Lemon Law? R

You save money for your first car, and you find a great deal. From the beginning, however, problems start. It stalls at traffic lights. You take it in for repair. In most cases, the manufacturer's warranty will provide the coverage you need to have your car repaired at no cost to you. However, what if your car spends more time in the repair shop than on the road? In some cases, the dealer may be unable to fix your car's problem. Did you get a "lemon"?

What Is a Lemon? A "lemon" is a vehicle that has a defect that the dealer has not fixed within a reasonable number of chances.

State Lemon Laws State lemon laws provide some protection. In most states, to qualify as a lemon, the problem has to be serious enough that it "substantially impairs the use, value, or safety" of the vehicle, and the vehicle has not been properly repaired within a "reasonable number of attempts." **S**

In North Carolina, for example, this reasonable number is four attempts or if the car has been out of service awaiting repair for a total of 20 or more business days during any 12-month period of the warranty. Most state lemon laws stipulate that a manufacturer must provide a refund or replacement for a defective new vehicle when a substantial defect cannot be fixed.

Checklist for Buying a Vehicle

Your best protection against a lemon happens <u>before</u> you buy. These tips will help you:

- Have a reliable technician thoroughly inspect the vehicle—whether it is new or used.
- Check what is covered by the service warranty. A used car may still be covered under the original manufacturer's warranty. Also, some dealers offer their own limited warranties for used cars.
- Check various dealers for the reputation of their service departments. Your warranty usually allows you to take your car to any dealer selling that make of car.

 Analyzing Economics

1. **Describing** What is the purpose of a lemon law?
2. **Specifying** Write three questions you should ask yourself before you buy a vehicle.

Financial Literacy

Teach

R Reading Strategy

Activating Prior Knowledge Explain that slang words, such as "lemon," often borrow connotations, or suggested meanings, from the original meaning of the word. **Ask:** How does your knowledge of lemons help you understand the word's meaning in this passage? *(A lemon is sour, so people don't want to taste it. A "lemon" vehicle doesn't work properly, so people can't or don't want to use it.)* **ELL**

S Skill Practice

Visual Literacy Ask: What is the cartoonist suggesting about the car in the illustration? *(It won't work because it has lemons, instead of an engine, under the hood.)* **BL**

 Analyzing Economics

1. A lemon law protects consumers who have purchased a faulty vehicle.

2. Answers may include the following: Is this car reliable? If it is a used vehicle, what do its service records say about its condition? What does the vehicle's warranty cover?

Additional Support

Activity: Economics Connection

Appreciating Lemon Laws To help students better understand why state governments have enacted vehicle lemon laws, invite the manager of an auto repair facility to visit the classroom. In advance of the visit, give the manager and students the following list of items that might need repair or replacement in a "lemon" vehicle: fuel pump, oil pump, water pump, ignition, alternator, radiator, head gasket, exhaust system, braking system, and axle. Ask the manager to be prepared to (1) explain the significance of each item on the list, and (2) supply approximate repair and replacement costs, broken down into parts and labor, for each item.

After students have taken notes on the speaker's comments, have students work in pairs to calculate the number of hours a teen would have to work to pay for each repair/replacement at an hourly wage of $6.50 after taxes. Reconvene the class and invite volunteers to share their calculations. Ask students to draw conclusions about why legislators responded to this consumer need. **OL**

Focus

Bellringer
Daily Focus Transparency 6–2

Guide to Reading
Answers to Graphic:

Legislative Powers
- money
- commerce
- military and foreign policy

Section Spotlight Video

To generate student interest and provide a springboard for class discussion, access the Chapter 6, Section 2 video at glencoe.com or on the video DVD.

Resource Manager

Guide to Reading

Big Idea
The Constitution gives the legislative branch—Congress—the power to make laws.

Content Vocabulary
- expressed powers *(p. 185)*
- implied powers *(p. 185)*
- elastic clause *(p. 185)*
- impeach *(p. 187)*
- writ of habeas corpus *(p. 188)*
- bill of attainder *(p. 188)*
- ex post facto law *(p. 188)*

Academic Vocabulary
- regulate *(p. 185)*

Reading Strategy
Explaining As you read, complete a graphic organizer like the one below to explain the main areas of Congressional legislative powers.

Legislative Powers

Section 2

Powers of Congress

Real World Civics Who represents the people of America and protects their safety around the world? Congress. Powers granted to Congress by Article I, Section 8, of the Constitution include the ability to raise an army and a navy and to declare war. All men between the ages of 18 and 25 are required to register for military service, even though there is currently no active draft. Many young men and women choose to enlist voluntarily in the military, which makes the draft unnecessary.

▼ These young marines are training at Camp Pendleton in California, the busiest military base in the country

---

R **Reading Strategies**	C **Critical Thinking**	D **Differentiated Instruction**	W **Writing Support**	S **Skill Practice**
Teacher Edition • Organizing, p. 185 • Identifying, p. 188 **Additional Resources** • Cont. Vocab., URB p. 21 • Guid. Read., URB p. 40 • RENTG, p. 55	**Teacher Edition** • Making Inferences, p. 187 • Ident. Central Issues, p. 189 • Compare/Contrast, p. 189 **Additional Resources** • Crit. Think., URB p. 29 • Quizzes and Tests, p. 65	**Teacher Edition** • Interpersonal, p. 186 • Gifted/Talented, p. 187 **Additional Resources** • School-to-Home Conn., URB p. 35 • Graphic Novel, p. 15 • Teacher's Guide to Differentiated Instruction, p. 7	**Teacher Edition** • Personal Writing, p. 186	**Teacher Edition** • Defining Soc. Studies Terms, p. 185 **Additional Resources** • Chart, Graph, and Map Skills, URB p. 31 • Daily Focus Trans., 6–2

Legislative Powers

Main Idea The Constitution provides that all powers to make laws for the United States government shall be given to Congress.

Civics & You Did you know that no government agency can spend money without the approval of Congress? Read to find out about the legislative powers of Congress.

Most of the powers delegated to the Congress are enumerated, or clearly listed, in Article I, Section 8. These are called **expressed powers.** There are 18 separate clauses enumerating different powers specifically given to Congress. Clause 5, for example, says, "The Congress shall have the Power . . . To coin Money."

Certain powers are given to the national government even though they are not expressly presented in the Constitution.

Their constitutional basis is found in Article I, Section 8, Clause 18, which states that Congress shall have the power to do whatever is "necessary and proper" to carry out the expressed powers. The powers that Congress has because of Clause 18 are called **implied powers** because they are not stated explicitly in the Constitution. Clause 18 is often called the **elastic clause** because it has allowed Congress to stretch its powers to meet new needs. For instance, you will not find the power to create an air force written in the Constitution. However, the elastic clause has allowed Congress to do so as part of its expressed powers to support armies.

Most of Congress's powers are related to making laws. Some of the most important legislative powers involve raising and spending money, **regulating** (or managing) commerce, and dealing with foreign countries.

Reading Check **Explaining** Why is the "necessary and proper" clause also called the elastic clause?

Congress Funds Defense Military weaponry stored on the deck of the USS *Harry S. Truman* is supplied by funds from Congress. **Specifying** How is maintaining an air force an example of an implied power of Congress?

185

D Differentiated Instruction

Interpersonal Explain to students that during the Vietnam War, Americans were sharply divided on the issue of the draft. **Ask:** If our government stopped using an all-volunteer army and restarted the draft, how might people's reactions today compare to those of the Vietnam War era? *(Answers may include that Americans still will be on both sides of the issue.)* **OL**

W Writing Support

Personal Writing Have students write a paragraph expressing which of the expressed powers listed in the chart they believe to be the most important and why. **OL**

Analyzing Charts

Answers:
1. Clause 11
2. Expressed powers are specifically stated in the Constitution. Implied powers are those that can be assumed from the Constitution.

Differentiated Instruction

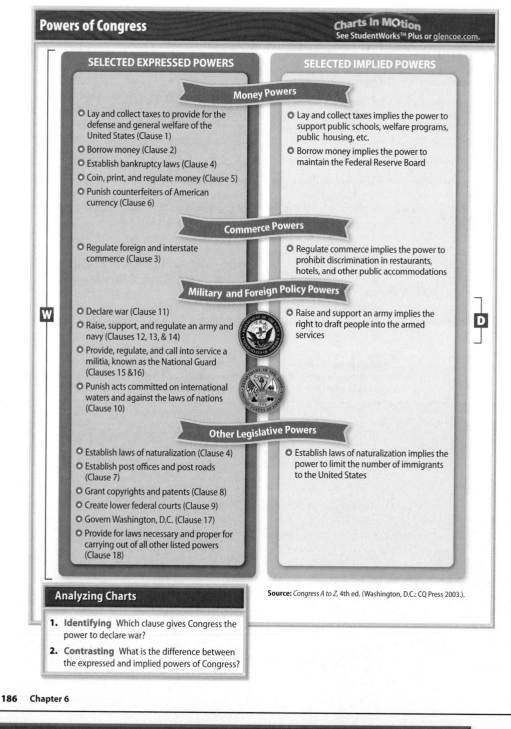

Powers of Congress

Charts In MOtion See StudentWorks™ Plus or glencoe.com.

SELECTED EXPRESSED POWERS

Money Powers
- Lay and collect taxes to provide for the defense and general welfare of the United States (Clause 1)
- Borrow money (Clause 2)
- Establish bankruptcy laws (Clause 4)
- Coin, print, and regulate money (Clause 5)
- Punish counterfeiters of American currency (Clause 6)

Commerce Powers
- Regulate foreign and interstate commerce (Clause 3)

Military and Foreign Policy Powers
- Declare war (Clause 11)
- Raise, support, and regulate an army and navy (Clauses 12, 13, & 14)
- Provide, regulate, and call into service a militia, known as the National Guard (Clauses 15 &16)
- Punish acts committed on international waters and against the laws of nations (Clause 10)

Other Legislative Powers
- Establish laws of naturalization (Clause 4)
- Establish post offices and post roads (Clause 7)
- Grant copyrights and patents (Clause 8)
- Create lower federal courts (Clause 9)
- Govern Washington, D.C. (Clause 17)
- Provide for laws necessary and proper for carrying out of all other listed powers (Clause 18)

SELECTED IMPLIED POWERS

- Lay and collect taxes implies the power to support public schools, welfare programs, public housing, etc.
- Borrow money implies the power to maintain the Federal Reserve Board

- Regulate commerce implies the power to prohibit discrimination in restaurants, hotels, and other public accommodations

- Raise and support an army implies the right to draft people into the armed services

- Establish laws of naturalization implies the power to limit the number of immigrants to the United States

Source: *Congress A to Z*, 4th ed. (Washington, D.C.: CQ Press 2003.).

Analyzing Charts

1. **Identifying** Which clause gives Congress the power to declare war?
2. **Contrasting** What is the difference between the expressed and implied powers of Congress?

Leveled Activities

BL Guided Reading Activity 6–2, URB p. 40

OL Writing Skills Activity 6, URB pp. 27–28

AL Differentiated Instruction Activity 6, pp. 33–34

ELL School-to-Home Connection 6, URB pp. 35–36

Nonlegislative Powers

Main Idea The Constitution gives Congress a number of nonlegislative duties.

Civics & You Has a friend ever asked you to check over something after it was completed? Congress often checks over other departments of government as part of its nonlegislative powers.

As the legislative branch, the most important duty of Congress is to make laws. Congress also holds a number of duties besides lawmaking. Among Congress's most important nonlegislative powers are those it uses to check the other branches of government. Some of these are set forth in the Constitution; others have developed over time. One such power is to propose amendments to the Constitution.

The Senate has the power to approve or reject the president's nominees for various offices, including Supreme Court justices, federal judges, and ambassadors.

The Constitution also allows Congress to remove from office any federal official who has committed serious wrongdoing. The House has the sole authority to **impeach,** or accuse officials of misconduct in office. If a majority of the House votes to impeach a public official, the Senate then has the power to hold a trial and to act as a jury and decide the official's guilt or innocence. A two-thirds vote is necessary to convict and to remove a person from office.

The House uses its impeachment power sparingly, most often with federal judges. Only two presidents have been impeached: Andrew Johnson in 1868 and Bill Clinton in 1998. Both presidents were tried by the Senate and acquitted (they were not removed from office).

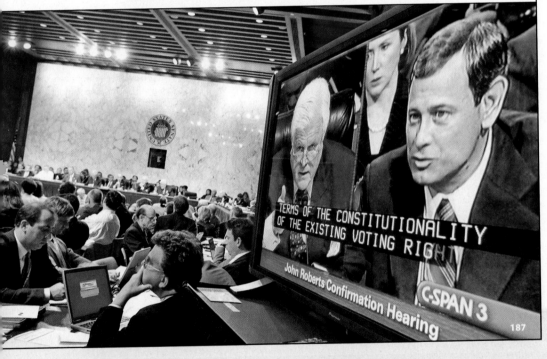

Senate Approval The Constitution gives the Senate the power to approve Supreme Court justices such as John G. Roberts, Jr., in an open hearing. *Hypothesizing* Why do you think the Framers did not leave judicial appointments to the president alone?

Mock Senate

Step 2: Introducing and Marking Up Bills in Committee Groups of students continue the law-making process they began in Section 1.

Directions Have each group choose one member to introduce the bill. Ask groups to identify the standing committee to which their bills will be sent. Each group will then become a standing committee. Do not assign a bill to its originating group.

Deliberation Have students read and research the bill. Senate committees have the power to kill bills, but for the purpose of this activity, committees are to revise their assigned bills to prepare them for consideration on the Senate floor. Have committees prepare a new bill that reflects their mark-ups, using the blank-bill template at congressindiana.edu/pdf/Best%20Practices %20Conrad%20a.pdf. Students will be using these bills in Step 3. **OL**

(Project continued in Section 3)

D Differentiated Instruction

Gifted and Talented Have students work in pairs to list questions they would ask a Supreme Court nominee. Have students group their questions in the following categories: personal convictions, legal knowledge, and professional background. **AL**

C Critical Thinking

Making Inferences Draw columns on the board and assign them the headings "House" and "Senate." Have students describe each legislature's responsibilities in the impeachment process. Record their responses in the appropriate columns. **Ask:** Why is the impeachment process divided between the two houses of Congress? *(Answers may include that separating the accusation from the trial better ensures the fairness of the outcome.)* **OL**

Caption Answer:

Answers may include that Senate confirmation ensures that the justice is worthy and not unduly influenced by the president's views.

Hands-On Chapter Project
Step 2

R Reading Strategy

Identifying Ask: Of the powers denied to Congress, which relate to court or criminal proceedings? *(writ of habeas corpus, bills of attainder, ex post facto laws)* **BL**

✓**Reading Check** **Answer:** The president can veto a congressional bill, and the Supreme Court can review a law's constitutionality.

Assess

Civics ONLINE

Study Central™ provides summaries, interactive games, and online graphic organizers to help students review content.

Close

Illustrating Have students illustrate a power of Congress and write a paragraph on the importance of that power in their everyday lives. **OL**

Section 2 Review

Power Limitations

Our Constitution explains not only what Congress may do but also what it may *not* do. Some limitations are imposed by the Bill of Rights. The purpose of the Bill of Rights was to limit or deny certain powers to the federal government. For example, Congress may not pass laws that restrict freedom of speech or ban freedom of religion.

According to Article I of the Constitution, Congress may not favor one state over another, tax interstate commerce, or tax exports. Article I also forbids Congress from enacting laws that would interfere with the legal rights of individuals. Congress cannot suspend the **writ of habeas corpus.** This is a court order that requires police to bring a prisoner to court to explain why they are holding the person. Congress is also banned from passing **bills of attainder,** or laws that punish a person without a jury trial.

Further, Congress may not pass **ex post facto laws.** These are laws that make an act a crime after the act has been committed.

The Constitution also reserves many powers for the states. Congress cannot interfere with these powers, such as the right to regulate public school systems. The Bill of Rights and other amendments also deny Congress certain powers.

Checks and Balances Other restrictions come from the Constitution's system of checks and balances. The Supreme Court can declare laws established by Congress as unconstitutional. The president can veto bills passed by Congress before they become laws. If both houses of Congress can muster a two-thirds vote, they can override the president's action.

✓**Reading Check** **Concluding** How does the Bill of Rights limit Congress's powers?

Section 2 Review

Vocabulary

1. **Explain** how each of the following terms relates to Congress: *expressed powers, implied powers, elastic clause, impeach, writ of habeas corpus, bill of attainder, ex post facto law.*

Main Ideas

2. **Hypothesizing** Why do you think Congress, rather than the states, is given most law-making powers?

3. **Describe** three nonlegislative powers given to Congress.

Critical Thinking

4. **Comparing** What do writs of habeas corpus, bills of attainder, and ex post facto laws have in common?

5. **BIG Ideas** In a graphic organizer like the one below, list the different offices for which Congress has the right to approve appointees.

Approve or Disapprove

6. **Analyzing Visuals** Reexamine the powers of Congress on page 186. Which clause gives Congress the power to borrow money?

CITIZENSHIP Activity

7. **Persuasive Writing** Should representatives always vote the way their constituents want, or should they vote according to their own best judgment? Write an essay in which you express your view. Give reasons for your answer.

Civics ONLINE

Study Central™ To review this section, go to glencoe.com.

Answers

1. Answers should include the following ideas: Expressed powers are those specifically given to Congress by the Constitution. Implied powers are those assumed by Congress through Constitutional interpretation. The elastic clause permits Congress to stretch its powers to meet new needs. Congress has the power to impeach and try a federal official due to misconduct in office. Congress is denied the power to suspend the writ of habeas corpus, to pass a bill of attainder, or to enact an ex post facto law.

2. Answer may include that national legislation must take precedence over state legislation to unify the country.

3. approve or reject presidential nominees for official appointments, impeach federal officials, remove federal officials from office

4. Answers will probably state that all are powers denied to Congress by the Constitution.

5. ambassadors, federal judges, Supreme Court justices

6. Clause 2

7. Answers will vary. Some students may feel that legislators are elected to represent their constituents and should vote as their constituents direct. Others may feel legislators are more qualified and more informed to make voting decisions than their constituents.

Does a public library have the right to censor Internet information?

In its early stages of development, the Internet raised a number of issues. Hackers can access private information. Many people are concerned about spyware, adware, and offensive sites. Congress first addressed the issue of offensive Internet sites in the Communications Decency Act of 1996. The Supreme Court ruled that law an unconstitutional violation of free speech. In December 2000, Congress passed the Children's Internet Protection Act (CIPA) to address concerns about access to offensive Internet content on school and library computers. Almost immediately, civil liberties groups challenged the law.

On the Internet Students in Brownsville, Texas, work together on a project with information they are obtaining from Internet research.

YES

In 2003 the Supreme Court ruled that the Children's Internet Protection Act was constitutional. The act allows the federal government to withhold funds from schools and public libraries that do not have a safety policy to "block or filter Internet access to pictures that: (a) are obscene, or (b) are harmful to minors, for computers are accessed by minors." Chief Justice Rehnquist wrote, "A library's need to exercise judgment in making collection decisions depends on its traditional role in identifying suitable and worthwhile material; it is no less entitled to play that role when it collects material from the Internet than when it collects material from any other source."

—William Rehnquist, October 2002

NO

One interest group that opposed the new law was the Online Policy Group, Inc. It filed a "friend of the court" brief with the Supreme Court during the CIPA case. The group said that blocking of information was similar to "prior restraint," because it allowed prepublication censorship and gave local officials the authority to make such judgments: "Indeed, commercial blocking software is even more troubling because it effectively delegates censorship decisions to private individuals, who . . . have no obligation to uphold the Constitution or narrowly tailor (fit) their censorship to comply with the First Amendment."

—*Brief of Amici Curiae* Online Policy Group, Inc., 2002

Debating the Issue

1. **Identifying** What are three important issues related to the use of the Internet?

2. **Naming** What was the first attempt by Congress to address the issue of offensive Internet sites?

3. **Explaining** How did Congress attempt to control the use of the Internet by schools and public libraries?

4. **Concluding** Is the censorship of some Internet sites similar to a library's decision to purchase certain books and exclude others?

Chapter 6   189

Focus

Guide to Reading
Answers to Graphic:

Requirements	
Senator	Congressperson
at least 30 years old	at least 25 years old
live in the represented state	live in the represented state
a U.S. citizen for at least 9 years	a U.S. citizen for at least 7 years

Section Spotlight Video

To generate student interest and provide a springboard for class discussion, access the Chapter 6, Section 3 video at glencoe.com or on the video DVD.

Resource Manager

Guide to Reading

Big Idea
The Constitution gives the legislative branch—Congress—the power to make laws.

Content Vocabulary
- franking privilege (p. 192)
- lobbyist (p. 192)
- casework (p. 195)
- pork-barrel project (p. 196)

Academic Vocabulary
- draft (p. 193)
- complex (p. 193)
- estimate (p. 193)

Reading Strategy
Analyzing On a chart like the one below, write the basic requirements for running for Congress.

Requirements

Section Audio **Spotlight Video**

Section 3

Representing the People

Real World Civics Shake up in the halls of Congress! The results of the 2006 national election made it possible for the first woman Speaker of the House—Nancy Pelosi of California—to lead the 110th Congress in 2007. Also, after 12 years of Republican control, in 2007 the Democrats held majorities in both the House of Representatives and the Senate. This Democratic hold on Congress, however, was only by a narrow margin. The Democrats did not have enough votes to override President George W. Bush's vetoes of their legislation, and the President did not have enough Republican votes to carry out his legislative plans. It was apparent that little would be accomplished until after the 2008 elections.

▼ **Rep. Nancy Pelosi celebrates 2007 Democratic control of Congress**

R Reading Strategies	**C** Critical Thinking	**D** Differentiated Instruction	**W** Writing Support	**S** Skill Practice
Teacher Edition • Academic Vocab., p. 192 • Predicting, p. 193 • Sequencing Info., p. 194 • Using Word Parts, p. 195 **Additional Resources** • Cont. Vocab., URB p. 22 • Guid. Read., URB p. 41 • RENTG, p. 58	**Teacher Edition** • Drawing Con., p. 192 • Making Generalizations, p. 194 **Additional Resources** • Biography, URB p. 25 • Quizzes and Tests, p. 66	**Teacher Edition** • Intrapersonal, p. 193 **Additional Resources** • School-to-Home Conn., URB p. 35 • Teacher's Guide to Differentiated Instruction, p. 8	**Teacher Edition** • Expository Writing, p. 191 **Additional Resources** • Writing Skills Act., URB p. 27	**Teacher Edition** • Assessing, p. 191 • Defending, p. 196 **Additional Resources** • Daily Focus Trans., 6–3 • Pol. Cartoons Trans. 6

Qualifications and Privileges

Main Idea The Constitution sets forth the qualifications for election to the House and to the Senate.

Civics & You Have you applied for a job? What set of qualifications did you need for the job? Read to find out about the qualifications for Congress.

Each American is represented by a congressperson and two senators. Many others help these elected representatives. Thousands of people work full-time for Congress, keeping the wheels of government turning.

Qualifications The legal qualifications for our congressional representatives are spelled out in the Constitution. To run for senator, you must be at least 30 years old, live in the state you plan to represent, and have been a U.S. citizen for at least nine years **S** before being elected. Members of the House of Representatives must be at least 25 years old, live in the state they represent, and have been a U.S. citizen for at least seven years before being elected.

Makeup of Congress The members of Congress have more in common than legal qualifications. Nearly half are lawyers. Almost all have college degrees. They also **W** tend to be "joiners." Members of Congress are more likely than the average citizen to be active in community organizations.

Campaign Trail Many members of the House, such as Representative Harold Ford, Jr., of Tennessee, run for the Senate later in their careers. *Identifying* What qualities do you think representatives and senators have in common?

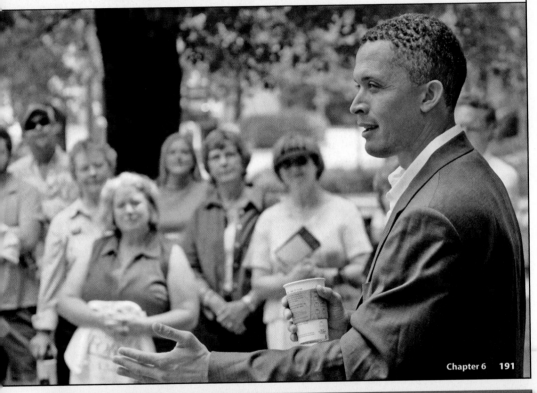

Chapter 6 **191**

Teach

S Skill Practice

Assessing Ask: Why are legal qualifications for members of Congress necessary? *(Answers may include that the age requirement builds a more experienced legislature, the residency requirement ensures that legislators understand their constituency, and the citizenship requirement permits naturalized citizens to run for office but not until they understand American culture and government.)* **OL**

W Writing Support

Expository Writing With students, discuss the various features of a written personal profile: objective/reason for running for Congress, educational background, work experience, outside interests, and professional organizations. Have students work in pairs to write a personal profile for a successful congressional candidate. **AL**

> **Caption Answer:**
> Many are lawyers, college-educated, and active in community organizations.

Additional Support

Activity: Collaborative Learning

Connecting Ask: How many people are needed to run your school and school district? What roles do they play? *(Students will most likely respond that many people are employed by the district, such as teachers, aides, administrators, cooks, custodians, and so on.)* Explain to students that school districts, like Congress, establish budgets that must cover the costs of their employees.

Provide students with a directory that shows school and district personnel. Have students work in pairs to list the various jobs that affect their lives every day.

Have partners create a word web with their names in the center circle. Ask students to complete outer circles with school and district positions that contribute to their lives as students. **OL**

C Critical Thinking

Drawing Conclusions Ask: Why are members of Congress given the use of a gymnasium and a medical clinic? *(to keep them in good health so they can serve the country)* **ELL**

R Reading Strategy

Academic Vocabulary Draw a wheel-like organizer on the board with Lobbyist in the center and Health, Education, Agriculture and Transportation on the spokes. Have student groups name an issue in each area that might be lobbied by a private group. **AL**

Caption Answer:

Answers may include that members of Congress send informational mailings to constituents; they also return to their states to meet with constituents.

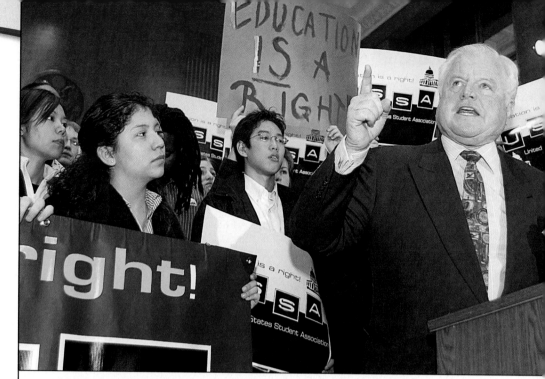

Representing Voters Senator Ted Kennedy from Massachusetts responds to students lobbying for funds for higher education. *Explaining* How do members of Congress keep voters informed about issues that the members are supporting?

Salary Members of Congress receive an annual salary, currently $169,300 for both senators and representatives. Further, they receive free office space, parking, and trips to their home states. Senators and representatives can send job-related mail without paying postage. This is called the **franking privilege.** Members of Congress also have low-cost life insurance and the use of a gymnasium, special restaurants, and a medical clinic.

Other Privileges The Constitution also grants senators and representatives immunity, or legal protection, in certain situations. This allows them to say and do what they believe is right without fear of interference from outsiders. The guarantee of immunity does not mean that members of Congress are free to break the law.

Behind-the-Scene Helpers

Serving in Congress is a full-time job. To get help with their workload, members of Congress hire a staff of clerks, secretaries, and special assistants.

Personal Staff The personal staffs of members of Congress run offices in Washington, D.C., as well as one or more offices in the congressional member's home district. Why are personal staffs needed? These workers gather information on new bills and issues. They handle requests for help from voters. They deal with news reporters and **lobbyists**—people hired by private groups to influence government decision makers. They also work for the re-election of the congressional member, even though the law requires them to do this on their own time.

192 Chapter 6

Differentiated Instruction

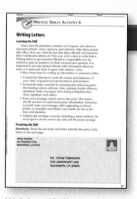

Writing Skills Activity 6, URB pp. 27-28

Writing Letters

Objective:	To learn how to address and write a formal letter
Focus:	Students identify the parts and formatting of formal letters.
Teach:	Discuss the importance of traditional letter writing.
Assess:	Have students give reasons for writing to members of Congress.
Close:	Create a chart of the topics students chose to write about in their letters to Congress.

Differentiated Instruction Strategies

BL Tell why it is important to thank the person who reads your letter.

AL Explain why members of Congress now ask their constituents to send e-mails instead of letters sent through the U.S. Postal Service.

ELL Define the words "concise" and "constituents."

In addition to professional staffers, many members of Congress hire students from their home states or districts to serve as interns and pages. Interns typically help with research and office duties; pages deliver messages and run other errands. This experience gives young people a firsthand look at the political process. One former congressional intern commented, "I felt like I had a backstage pass to the greatest show in the world."

Committee Staff Congressional committees also need staffs. Committee staff members do many of the various day-to-day lawmaking chores of Congress. They **draft,** or outline, bills, gather information, organize committee hearings, and negotiate with lobbyists. In short, they keep the long and **complex,** or difficult, lawmaking process moving.

Support Services Congress has created several agencies to support its work. The Library of Congress is one of the largest libraries in the world. Did you know that one copy of every book published in the United States is kept there? The Library of Congress is an important source of information for members of Congress and their staffs.

Finance and Budget The General Accounting Office (GAO) is the investigative arm of Congress in financial issues. It reviews the spending activities of federal agencies, studies federal programs, and recommends ways to improve the financial performance of the government.

The Congressional Budget Office (CBO) provides Congress with information and analysis for making budgetary decisions. It makes no policy recommendations but rather **estimates,** or guesses, the costs and possible economic effects of programs. It also helps Congress come up with—and stick to—a budget plan.

Reading Check **Explaining** Why are members of Congress granted some immunity?

TIME™ Teens in *Action*

Sarah Seufer

Take a page from this teen's book! Sarah Beth Seufer, 18, of Newland, North Carolina, took part in the United States House of Representatives Page Program. Here is what she had to say about her experiences living and working in Washington, D.C.

QUESTION: How did you become involved?
ANSWER: Last summer, after submitting an application, I was nominated by my congressional representative to the office of the Speaker of the House. I was chosen to be a Cloakroom Page. It was my responsibility to answer phone calls related to the activities on the House floor, and to relay messages to representatives.

Pages and representatives leaving a House session

Q: Did you have a good time?
A: I've always loved learning about American government—seeing it in action was incredible! The goal is that pages will return home from Washington, D.C., with a newfound sense of American history and politics.
ACTION FACT: Seufer wants to become a lawyer and eventually run for public office.

Making a Difference **CITIZENSHIP**
What steps did Sarah take to become a page?

Chapter 6 **193**

CHAPTER 6 **Section** **3**

D **Differentiated Instruction**

Intrapersonal Have students form groups to brainstorm the characteristics the House Page Program looks for in student volunteers. Ask groups to prepare a résumé for a fictitious student applicant using a résumé template in a word processing program. **OL**

R **Reading Strategy**

Predicting Ask: From the descriptions of the page and intern programs, what careers might many of these students pursue? *(Answers may include law, politics, government service, and so on.)* **OL**

Reading Check **Answer:** It allows members of Congress to say and do what they think is right without fearing interference from outsiders.

TIME™ Teens in *Action*
Answer:
She submitted an application and received a congressional nomination.

Hands-On Chapter Project
Step 3

Mock Senate

Step 3: Debating Bills on the Senate Floor Groups of students continue to follow legislation through the Senate.

Directions At this point, the class reconvenes as the body of the Senate. Students will act as senators; you will preside as president of the Senate. Political party affiliations should reflect current Senate distribution. Distribute the worksheet entitled *Mock Senate Debate Notes,* which can be found at congress.indiana.edu/pdf/ Best%20Practices%20Conrad%20a.pdf. Debate each bill in numerical order, asking volunteers to share their comments. Instruct students to take notes on the debate using the debate notes worksheet. Have students cast their votes in the Senate method of your choice. Tell students that all bills will be passed and forwarded to the House of Representatives. Students will work on compromise bills in conference committees in Step 4. **OL**

(Project continued in Section 4)

C Critical Thinking

Making Generalizations **Ask:** What usually determines how members of Congress vote? *(They reflect their constituents' interests and concerns.)* **OL**

R Reading Strategy

Sequencing Information **Ask:** What are the four steps in the lawmaking process? *(write and introduce bills, take part in committee work, listen to others' input about a bill, vote on the bill)* **BL**

American Biography

Answer:
Most answers will reflect Ros-Lehtinen's support of human rights and her family's flight from Castro's communist Cuba.

American Biography
Ileana Ros-Lehtinen (1952–)

In 1822, Joseph Marion Hernandez of Florida became the first Latino to serve in Congress. In 1989, **Ileana Ros-Lehtinen** was the first Cuban American to be elected to the United States Congress. Born in 1952, Ileana and her family fled Cuba in 1959 after Fidel Castro's Communist revolution. After completing her studies, she began her career as an educator. She founded a private school, Eastern Academy, where she served as a teacher and administrator.

Ros-Lehtinen entered politics in 1982, serving as a Republican member of the Florida House of Representatives and later in the state senate. Since 1989 she has served in the United States House of Representatives, representing Florida's Eighteenth Congressional District.

Ros-Lehtinen has been one of the leaders in defending the U.S. embargo on Cuba. She also plays a leading role promoting the spread of human rights to countries like Lebanon, Syria, Iran, Saudi Arabia, and China. Ros-Lehtinen was part of a congressional delegation that visited Iraq to understand how the war has affected Iraqi women and their families and to encourage them to get "involved in all levels of their government."

Making a Difference CITIZENSHIP

Ileana Ros-Lehtinen was an educator before she turned to politics. **Explaining** Why do you think Ros-Lehtinen is such a strong supporter of the U.S. embargo on Cuba?

Congress at Work

Main Idea The 535 members of Congress have several different but closely related roles.

Civics & You What do you think is the most important work for members of Congress? Read on to find out about the three major jobs of Congress.

C The basic job of senators and representatives is to represent the people of their states and districts. They are responsible for reflecting and translating into action their constituents' interests and concerns. Congress does its work in regular time periods, or sessions, that begin each January 3 and continue through most of the year.

Lawmaking

In carrying out the responsibility of representing the people of their states and districts, members of Congress perform three major jobs. Making laws is perhaps the best known task of Congress.

Congress considers several different kinds of legislation each year. Most pieces of legislation are in the form of bills. Bills are drafts of laws presented to the House and Senate for enactment. Members of the Senate and the House of Representatives write and **R** introduce bills, take part in committee work, listen to the input of people for and against a bill, and then vote on the floor of the House or Senate. You will learn more about this process in Section 4 of this chapter.

Differentiated Instruction

Leveled Activities

BL Chart, Graph, and Map Skills Activity 6, URB p. 31

OL Citizenship and Decision-Making Activity 2, URB p. 3

AL Enrichment Activity 2, URB pp. 13–14

ELL Speaking and Listening Skills Activity 2, pp. 9–12

Casework

Members of Congress often act as trouble-shooters for people from their home districts and states who request help in dealing with the federal government. This help is called **casework.** Over the course of a year, some congressional offices receive as many as 10,000 requests for information or services.

What drives representatives to help their constituents? Senator Olympia Snowe of Maine explains:

> ❝Out of my experiences in life has grown a conviction that no pursuit is as valuable as, or worthier than, the simple idea of helping others—of enabling individuals to improve their lives, to soften the hardest days and brighten the darkest.❞
>
> —Olympia Snowe quoted in *Nine and Counting: The Women of the Senate*

Most requests for help are handled by the senator's or representative's office staff. If a staffer cannot get results, the senator or representative usually steps in. Senator Dianne Feinstein of California said,

> ❝It's one of the most important things we do . . . . We respond to constituents. . . . I insist on responding promptly, because it's a matter of accountability to our constituency.❞
>
> —Dianne Feinstein quoted in *Nine and Counting: The Women of the Senate*

Why do lawmakers spend so much of their time on casework? First, casework helps lawmakers to get reelected. Helping voters increases popular support. Second, casework helps lawmakers get a closer look at how well the executive branch is handling programs such as Social Security or veterans' benefits. Third, casework provides a way to help average citizens deal with federal agencies.

TIME™ Political Cartoons

Michael Ramirez/Copley News Service

With this 2006 cartoon, Michael Ramirez is making a point about earmarking—the Congressional practice of setting aside specific funds for a special project in a spending bill, often without public review.

1. **How is Congress depicted in this cartoon?**
2. **Why do you think Ramirez chose this symbol?**
3. **How is earmarking represented?**
4. **Do you think Ramirez supports or opposes earmarking? Explain.**

Every year, more than half of all Americans do volunteer work ... role in it. One of the responsibilities of citizens is to help make their ... of volunteer grou... small. Perhap... dad wh...

S Skill Practice

Defending Ask: What defense can be given for pork-barrel projects? *(Answers may include that these projects benefit Americans living in a particular state or district.)* **OL**

✓ **Reading Check Answer:** making laws, doing casework for constituents, bringing federal projects and money to their districts and states

Assess

Civics ONLINE

Study Central™ provides summaries, interactive games, and online graphic organizers to help students review content.

Close

Describing Ask: What pork-barrel project might benefit your district or state? *(Answers may include references to highway funds, new bridges, new government-employment opportunities and so on.)* Have students work in groups to write a rider to a Senate bill that describes a pork-barrel project for their district or state. **OL**

Section 3 Review

Helping the District or State

Besides providing services for their constituents, members of Congress also try to bring federal government projects and money to their districts and states. Lawmakers do this in several ways.

Public Works Every year through public works bills, Congress appropriates billions of dollars for a variety of local projects. These projects might include things such as post offices, dams, military bases, veterans' hospitals, and mass transit system projects. Such government projects can bring jobs and money into a state or district.

Grants and Contracts Lawmakers also try to make sure their districts or states get their fair share of the available federal grants and contracts which are funded through the federal budget. Federal grants and contracts are very important to lawmakers and their districts or states. These contracts are a crucial source of money and jobs and can greatly affect the economy of a state.

All members of Congress work to give their constituents a share in the money the national government spends every year. A contract to make army uniforms, for example, might mean lots of money for a local business. Government projects and grants that primarily benefit the home district or state are known as **pork-barrel projects.** To understand this term, think of a member of Congress dipping into the "pork barrel" (the federal treasury) and pulling out a piece of "fat" (a federal project for his or her district).

Using Influence Lawmakers do not have direct control over grants and contracts. Instead, agencies of the executive branch, such as the Department of Labor, award federal grants and contracts.

Lawmakers, however, may try to influence agency decisions. They may pressure agency officials to give a favorable hearing to their state's requests. Lawmakers may also encourage their constituents to contact agency officials in order to make their needs known.

✓ **Reading Check Describing** What are the three major jobs of a congressperson?

Section 3 Review

Vocabulary

1. **Write** a true and a false statement for each term below. Beside each false statement, explain why it is false: *franking privilege, lobbyist, casework, pork-barrel project.*

Main Ideas

2. **Explaining** What are the qualifications for members of the House of Representatives and the Senate?

3. **Summarizing** What action does Congress take after a bill is introduced in Congress?

Critical Thinking

4. **Analyzing** Why do you think the Constitution did not include other qualifications for members of Congress?

5. **BIG Ideas** On a graphic organizer like the one below, write the major responsibilities Congress has in the lawmaking process.

CITIZENSHIP Activity

6. **Creative Writing** Describe the job of a member of the House or Senate by creating a want ad for a congressperson. In the ad, include qualifications, benefits and salary, and skills needed. Also include facts that demonstrate the typical responsibilities of members.

Civics ONLINE

Study Central™ To review this section, go to glencoe.com.

Answers

1. Each sentence should contain one of the listed vocabulary terms in either a true or false statement. Each false statement should be followed by an explanation of why the statement is false.

2. House: age 25, citizen 7 years or more, resident of the state/district. Senate: age 30, citizen 9 years or more, resident of the state.

3. Both houses of Congress assign introduced bills to a standing committee for discussion.

4. Answers may include the idea that the Framers kept requirements to a minimum to

allow more citizens to serve in Congress.

5. take part in committee work; listen to the input of people for and against the bill; vote on the floor

6. **Member of the House of Representatives:** 25 years of age, a minimum of 7 years of citizenship, residency in the state. **Senate:** 30 years of age, a minimum of 9 years of citizenship, residency in the state. Benefits and salary: $165,200 yearly salary; free office space, parking, trips to their home states, franking privilege, low-cost life insurance,

access to special restaurants, gymnasium, and medical clinic for all members of Congress. Answers regarding needed skills may include a thorough understanding of the legislative process and the U.S. system of government, an ability to communicate effectively with fellow legislators and constituents, an ability to read and comprehend large amounts of information in an efficient manner, and an ability to consider proposed legislation in an unbiased manner.

Guide to Reading

Big Idea
The Constitution gives the legislative branch—Congress—the power to make laws.

Content Vocabulary
- joint resolution *(p. 198)*
- special-interest group *(p. 199)*
- filibuster *(p. 200)*
- cloture *(p. 200)*
- voice vote *(p. 202)*
- standing vote *(p. 202)*
- roll-call vote *(p. 202)*
- veto *(p. 202)*
- pocket veto *(p. 202)*

Academic Vocabulary
- element *(p. 198)*
- category *(p. 198)*

Reading Strategy
Sequencing Information
As you read, create a graphic organizer similar to the one below to track the major steps an idea takes to become a law.

Section 4
How a Bill Becomes a Law

Real World Civics For most of our nation's history, African Americans throughout the South were prevented from voting by local officials. President Lyndon B. Johnson had assured Dr. Martin Luther King, Jr., that he would push for a Voting Rights Act in time. In March of 1965, Dr. King decided to change things himself by marching from Selma to Montgomery, Alabama, demanding the right to vote. When Dr. King's original 600 marchers reached Montgomery, they had become 25,000 strong. Less than five months later, President Johnson signed a law assuring every citizen the right to vote. Passing laws such as the Voting Rights Act is one of Congress's most important roles.

▼ **Dr. Martin Luther King, Jr., (center), wife Coretta, and others in the 1965 peace march**

197

Focus

Bellringer
Daily Focus Transparency 6–4

Guide to Reading
Answers to Graphic:

```
        Bill to Law
             │
             ▼
standing committee considers bill
             │
             ▼
   full house debates bill
             │
             ▼
 passed bill sent to other house
             │
             ▼
bill passed by both houses sent to president
```

🎬 **Section Spotlight Video**

Have students watch the Chapter 6, Section 4 video at glencoe.com.

Additional Support

R Reading Strategies	**C** Critical Thinking	**D** Differentiated Instruction	**W** Writing Support	**S** Skill Practice
Teacher Edition • Using Context Clues, p. 198 • Visualizing, p. 199 • Det. Importance, p. 200 **Additional Resources** • Cont. Vocab., URB p. 22 • Ac. Vocab., URB p. 23 • Guid. Read., URB p. 42 • RENTG, p. 61	**Teacher Edition** • Compare/Contrast, p. 198 • Det. Cause/Effect, p. 201 • Making Inferences, p. 201 **Additional Resources** • Quizzes and Tests, p. 67	**Teacher Edition** • English Learners, p. 202 **Additional Resources** • School-to-Home Conn., URB p. 35 • Reteach Act., URB p. 37 • Teacher's Guide to Differentiated Instruction, p. 8	**Teacher Edition** • Personal Writing, p. 200	**Teacher Edition** • Evaluating, p. 199 • Synthesizing, p. 201 **Additional Resources** • Chart, Graph, and Map Skills, URB p. 31 • Daily Focus Trans., 6–4

Section CHAPTER 6

4

Focus

R Reading Strategy

Using Context Clues Ask: Which words from the text explain resolutions? *(formal statements expressing lawmakers' opinions or decisions)* **ELL**

C Critical Thinking

Comparing and Contrasting Ask: In what way is a joint resolution different from other resolutions? *(It is passed by both houses of Congress.)* **BL**

Caption Answer:

Federal park lands are held in reserve for the nation, not the individual states in which they are located.

✓ **Reading Check Answer:** Answers may include the idea that bills are written on complicated, important issues on which members of Congress might have varying opinions.

Bills Congress Considers

Main Idea Congress considers several different kinds of legislation each year. Most pieces of legislation are in the form of bills.

Civics & You How do you think Congress should make decisions about bills? What factors should have the greatest influence on its decision making?

Have you heard people say there are two things you should never watch being made—sausages and laws? Strange **elements,** or factors, may go into the final product, and the process requires patience. More than 10,000 bills are often introduced during each term of Congress, yet only several hundred pass all the hurdles and become law.

Bills generally fall into two **categories,** or types. Private bills concern individual people or places. They usually deal with people's claims against the government. Public bills apply to the entire nation and involve general matters such as taxation.

Along with bills, Congress considers different kinds of resolutions, or formal statements expressing lawmakers' opinions or decisions. Many resolutions do not have the force of law. **Joint resolutions,** however, which are passed by both houses of Congress, do become laws if signed by the president. Congress uses joint resolutions to propose constitutional amendments and to designate money for a special purpose.

✓ **Reading Check Analyzing** Why might public bills take months to debate?

Protecting Parkland Part of the money Congress designates for the upkeep of federal parks goes to Yellowstone National Park, which is visited by thousands each year. *Analyzing* Why do you think the power for funding of federal parkland is not given to the states?

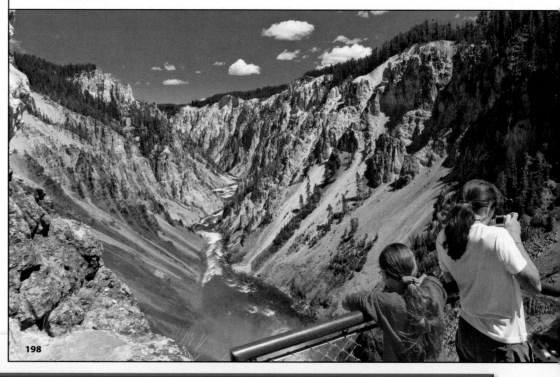

198

Differentiated Instruction

Leveled Activities

OL Economics Activity 2, URB pp. 5–6

AL Reading Skills Activity 2, URB pp. 7–8

ELL Guided Reading Activity 6-4, pp. 42

Presidential Signing The majority of bills passed by Congress are signed into law by the president. In 1962, President John F. Kennedy signed a bill designating the home of abolitionist Frederick Douglass as a national monument as his descendants looked on. *Speculating* Why might a president refuse to sign a bill?

From Bill to Law

Main Idea To become a law, a bill must be passed in identical form by both chambers of Congress.

Civics & You As a bill is considered, both houses of Congress keep a check on it. Read to find out why the houses must agree on each law.

Every bill starts with an idea. The ideas for new bills come from private citizens, the White House, or from **special-interest groups**—organizations made up of people with common interests.

Whatever its source, a senator or representative must introduce a bill before Congress will consider it. Every bill is given a title and a number when it is submitted. For example, during the first session of Congress, the first bill introduced is called S.1 in the Senate and H.R.1 in the House.

Committee Action

After a bill is introduced, it is sent to the standing committee that is related to the subject of the bill. Standing committees have life-and-death power over bills. The committee can (1) pass the bill, (2) mark up a bill with changes and suggest that it be passed, (3) replace the original bill with a new bill, (4) ignore the bill and let it die (which is called "pigeonholing" the bill), or (5) kill the bill outright by majority vote.

Debating a Bill

Bills approved in committee are ready for consideration by the full House or Senate. When bills do reach the floor of the House or Senate, the members argue their pros and cons and discuss amendments. The House accepts only amendments relevant to the bill. The Senate, however, allows riders—completely unrelated amendments—to be tacked onto the bill.

Chapter 6   199

R **Reading Strategy**

R Reading Strategy

Determining Importance **Ask:** Why is cloture important to the lawmaking process? *(Cloture restricts each speaker's comments to one hour, which allows other legislators to address the floor and continue discussion on a bill.)* **BL**

W Writing Support

Personal Writing Ask students to write one-page personal essays explaining their views on the current gender distribution in Congress. **OL**

✔ Reading Check **Answer:** A rider is an unrelated addition to a bill. Senators may attach riders to pass legislation that might fail to pass if introduced as separate bills.

Analyzing Charts

Answers:

1. A majority vote passes legislation, so the party with more members usually gets more legislation passed.
2. Students may state that men have been in Congress from the beginning, so that tradition lends itself to having more men in Congress now.

Differentiated Instruction

Rules of Debate In the House, the Rules Committee sets the terms for debate. It usually puts time limits on the discussion, for example, to speed up action. The Senate, because it is smaller, has fewer rules. Senators can speak as long as they wish. At times they take advantage of this custom to **filibuster,** or talk a bill to death. One member can speak—holding the floor for hour after hour, delaying a vote until the bill's sponsor withdraws the measure.

R The Senate can end a filibuster if three-fifths of the members vote for **cloture.** Under this procedure, no one may speak for more than one hour. Senators rarely resort to cloture, though. In 1964, during debate on the Civil Rights Act, the Senate waited out a 74-day filibuster by senators opposed to the legislation.

✔ Reading Check **Speculating** What is a rider to a bill? Why do you think Senators attach riders to bills?

Profile of the 111th Congress*

Party Affiliation

Senate: Republican 41, Democrat 56, Independent 2, Undecided 1

House: Republican 177, Democrat 256, Undecided 2

RACIAL DIVERSITY IN CONGRESS		
Ethnicity	House	Senate
African American	42	0
Asian American	6	2
Hispanic American	28	3

AVERAGE AGE	
House	Senate
56	62

Senate: 83 Men, 17 Women

House: 361 Men, 74 Women

Source: www.opencrs.com, Membership of the 111th Congress: A Profile.
*Totals may change due to undecided races as of November 30, 2008.

Analyzing Charts

1. **Explaining** Why is it important which political party has the most members in the House or Senate?
2. **Analyzing** Why do you think there are so many more men than women in Congress?

200   Chapter 6

Chart, Graph, and Map Skills Activity 6, URB p. 31–32

Analyzing a Diagram

Objective: Understand the basic process of impeachment

Focus: Have students identify the diagram's format.

Teach: Discuss the definition of "impeachment."

Assess: Have groups design diagrams identifying roles played during impeachment.

Close: Have groups share their diagrams.

Differentiated Instruction Strategies

BL Tell who serves as jury and judge during an impeachment process.

AL Research the process for presidential impeachment in other countries and compare them to U.S. impeachment procedures.

ELL Define "proceedings" and "presides" and come up with synonyms for each word.

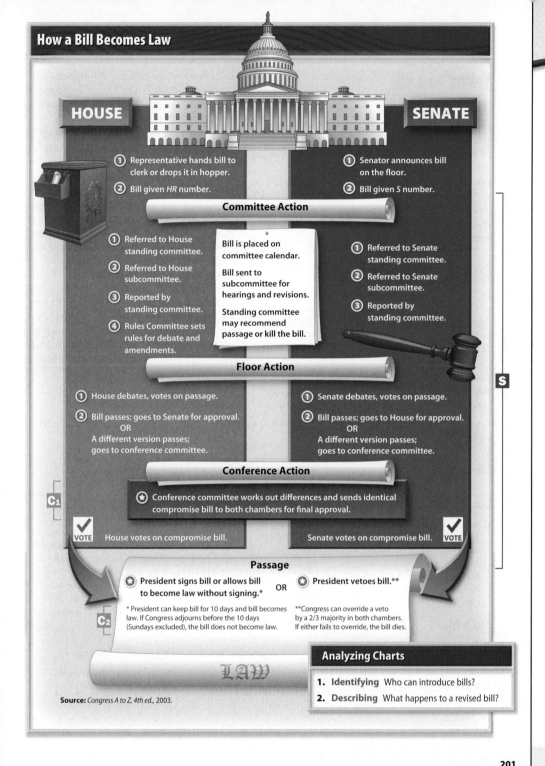

How a Bill Becomes Law

HOUSE

SENATE

① Representative hands bill to clerk or drops it in hopper.

② Bill given *HR* number.

① Senator announces bill on the floor.

② Bill given *S* number.

Committee Action

① Referred to House standing committee.

② Referred to House subcommittee.

③ Reported by standing committee.

④ Rules Committee sets rules for debate and amendments.

Bill is placed on committee calendar.

Bill sent to subcommittee for hearings and revisions.

Standing committee may recommend passage or kill the bill.

① Referred to Senate standing committee.

② Referred to Senate subcommittee.

③ Reported by standing committee.

Floor Action

① House debates, votes on passage.

② Bill passes; goes to Senate for approval.
OR
A different version passes; goes to conference committee.

① Senate debates, votes on passage.

② Bill passes; goes to House for approval.
OR
A different version passes; goes to conference committee.

Conference Action

★ Conference committee works out differences and sends identical compromise bill to both chambers for final approval.

✓VOTE House votes on compromise bill.

Senate votes on compromise bill. ✓VOTE

Passage

★ President signs bill or allows bill to become law without signing.*

OR

★ President vetoes bill.**

* President can keep bill for 10 days and bill becomes law. If Congress adjourns before the 10 days (Sundays excluded), the bill does not become law.

**Congress can override a veto by a 2/3 majority in both chambers. If either fails to override, the bill dies.

LAW

Source: *Congress A to Z, 4th ed.,* 2003.

Analyzing Charts

1. **Identifying** Who can introduce bills?
2. **Describing** What happens to a revised bill?

201

S Skill Practice

Synthesizing Ask: From the diagram, what are the four main steps from bill to law? *(committee action, floor action, conference action, passage)* **ELL**

C₁ Critical Thinking

Determining Cause and Effect Ask: Why are conference committees made up of both Senators and Representatives? *(Conference committees can then draft a bill that both houses will accept.)* **OL**

C₂ Critical Thinking

Making Inferences Ask: Why might the President hold a bill for 10 days, allowing it to become law? *(The President may not personally agree with the bill but may believe it is necessary or it will pass with Congressional override.)* **AL**

Analyzing Charts

Answers:
1. Senators and Representatives
2. The president signs it into law, holds it for ten days, or vetoes it.

Hands-On Chapter Project
Step 4

Mock Senate

Step 4: Drafting a Compromise Bill Groups of students near the end of the lawmaking process in their mock Senate.

Directions Before class, revise each bill as if it were the version of the bill passed by the House of Representatives. Be sure to include some significant differences that must be resolved in committee. Have students return to their original groups, which are now conference committees. Give each "committee" one of the bills they previously passed, as well as the corresponding "House" version. Direct committee members to underline the differences between the bills on their copies. Ask committees to discuss compromises that will be acceptable to both houses. Have committees draft a new compromise bill. **OL**

(Project continued on the Visual Summary page)

D Differentiated Instruction

English Learners Ask: From the description of a pocket veto, why is this term appropriate? *(Because the bill is shelved and forgotten about, it's as if it has been placed in someone's pocket, out of sight.)* **ELL**

 Reading Check Answer: A conference committee is formed when two versions of the same bill are passed, and they submit a revised bill.

Assess

. . . .

Civics ONLINE

Study Central™ provides summaries, interactive games, and online graphic organizers to help students review.

Close

. . . .

Sequencing List the following steps of the legislative process on the board: The full House or Senate debates the bill. The bill is numbered and named. The conference committee drafts a compromise bill. The bill is introduced. Both houses pass the identical bill. The bill is referred to a standing committee. The bill is sent to the president. Ask students to copy and correctly order the steps. **OL**

Section 4 Review

Voting on a Bill

After a bill is debated, it is brought to a vote. Voting in the House is done in one of three ways. The simplest is a **voice vote,** in which those in favor say "Yea" and those against say "No." The Speaker determines which side has the most voice votes. In a **standing vote,** those in favor of a bill stand to be counted, and then those against it stand to be counted. The third method is a recorded vote, in which members' votes are recorded electronically.

The Senate has three methods of voting: a voice vote, a standing vote, and a roll call. In a **roll-call vote,** senators respond "Aye" or "No" as their names are called. A simple majority of all members that are present is needed to pass a bill. If a bill passes in one house, it is sent to the other. If either the Senate or the House rejects a bill, it dies.

The Senate and House must pass a bill in identical form before it becomes law. When two versions of the same bill are passed, a conference committee with members from both houses work out the differences and submit a revised bill. The House and Senate must either accept it without amendments or completely reject it.

Action by the President After a bill is approved, it goes to the president. One of four things may then happen. The president may sign the bill and declare it a new law. The president may **veto,** or refuse to sign, the bill. The president may also do nothing for 10 days. At that point, if Congress is in session, the bill becomes law without the president's signature. If Congress has adjourned, the bill dies. Killing legislation in this way is called a **pocket veto.**

If the president vetoes a bill, Congress has one last chance to save it. As you read earlier, Congress can override the veto with a two-thirds vote of each house. This is not an easy task, though. From 1789 through May 2008, Congress overturned only 108 vetoes.

 Reading Check Explaining When is a conference committee formed and what is its purpose?

 Section 4 Review

Vocabulary

1. **Define** the following terms and use them in sentences that relate to the lawmaking process: *joint resolution, special-interest group, filibuster, cloture, voice vote, standing vote, roll-call vote, veto, pocket veto.*

Main Ideas

2. **Contrasting** What is the difference between public and private bills? What are resolutions?

3. **Hypothesizing** Why do you think a bill has to pass both houses of Congress to reach the president's desk?

Critical Thinking

4. **Explaining** Why is the action of a standing committee so important to the passage of a bill?

5. **BIG Ideas** On a web diagram like the one below, write the different actions the president can take when deciding on the passage of a bill.

President's Action

CITIZENSHIP Activity

6. **Persuasive Writing** Do you think it is necessary for a bill to go through so many steps to become a law? Write a one-page essay in which you express your view. Make sure you include reasons to defend your view.

Civics ONLINE

Study Central™ To review this section, go to glencoe.com.

Answers

1. Sentences should use vocabulary words according to their definitions in the section and in the Glossary.

2. A public bill addresses a national or general concern whereas a private bill focuses on individual people and places.

3. The focuses of the House and Senate are slightly different (district vs. state). Both sets of perspectives need consideration.

4. A standing committee can pass, change, ignore, or kill a bill.

5. sign into law; veto; do nothing for 10 days

6. Answers may include the idea that it is important that laws be just and well-considered because they bind every resident of the United States.

Visual Summary

Comparing the House and the Senate

The Congress of the United States was created by Article I, Section 1, of the Constitution, providing that "All legislative Powers herein granted shall be vested in a Congress of the United States, which shall consist of a Senate and a House of Representatives."

HOUSE*	SENATE
Members chosen from local districts	Members chosen from an entire state
Two-year term	Six-year term
A representative must be at least 25 years of age and must have been a citizen of the United States for at least 7 years	A senator must be at least 30 years of age and must have been a citizen of the United States for at least 9 years
House members must be residents of the state from which they are chosen	Senate members must be residents of the state from which they are chosen
435 voting members; the number representing each state is determined by population	Composed of 100 members; 2 from each state
Originally elected by voters	Originally (until 1913) elected by state legislatures
May impeach federal officials	May convict federal officials of impeachable offenses
More formal rules	Fewer rules and restrictions
Debate limited	Debate extended
Floor action controlled	Unanimous consent rules
Less prestige and less individual notice	More prestige and media attention
Originates bills for raising revenues	Power of "advice and consent" on presidential appointments and treaties
Local or narrow leadership	National leadership
The Speaker of the House is the presiding officer	The vice president of the United States is the presiding officer

*Some of these differences, such as terms of office, are provided for in the Constitution, while others, such as debate rules, are not.

STUDY TO GO Study anywhere, anytime! Download quizzes and flash cards to your PDA from glencoe.com.

Visual Summary 6

Making Connections Tell students that the actions of Congress affect the lives of all Americans. Have students work in pairs to research information on the Internet about bills currently debated or recently passed in the House and Senate. Direct students to thomas.loc.gov for current legislation. Then have the students identify two bills (or laws) that directly affect their lives. **Ask:** Why might people in this classroom disagree about the personal importance of a bill or law? *(Everyone has different opinions.)* Have students create a chart listing the bill or law name, its number, and the effects it has on students' lives. **OL**

Evaluating Ask: Based on the information in the chart, which would you rather be—a congressperson or a senator? *(Opinions will vary.)* Have students work in groups to write a poem to identify their choice and explain their reasoning. **AL**

Hands-On Chapter Project
Step 5: Wrap-Up

Mock Senate

Step 5: Evaluating the Activity Students will finish the process they started in Step 1.

Directions Tell students that both the Senate and House passed the compromise bills they wrote in Step 4. The bills are now on the president's desk awaiting signature. Distribute an evaluation form to each student. Have students complete the evaluations on their own. Reconvene the class and then ask volunteers to share their comments about the class as a model Senate.

Evaluation Evaluations can be modeled after the following.

1. Were the bill sponsors prepared to answer questions during floor debate? Were they able to support their views with facts and logic?
2. Were you prepared to question or challenge other bill sponsors? What helped you prepare? What else might you have done?
3. Did you change any of your votes as a result of the floor debate? Which one(s)? What persuaded you to vote differently?
4. How well did your group work together? Did you display qualities of successful Senate members? Explain. **OL**

6 ASSESSMENT

Answers and Analyses

Reviewing Vocabulary

1. D Students may incorrectly select constituents since voters elect House members who, in turn, choose the Speaker if they are members of the majority party. Lobbyists are not members of the House but, rather, outsiders representing special interest groups that attempt to influence how legislators vote. Standing committees receive bills for consideration at the Speaker's direction. Only majority party members choose the Speaker of the House.

2. D The franking privilege is the right of legislators to mail official correspondence free of charge. Students may confuse the remaining three answers as they refer to rights denied to Congress. An ex post facto law is one that outlaws an act after it has been committed, while a bill of attainder is a congressional act that convicts and punishes an accused person without benefit of a trial. The third limit of power—suspension of the writ of habeas corpus—refers to an individual's right to hear official charges in court.

3. D Gerrymandering is the practice of oddly configuring districts for political advantage. Special-interest groups are private groups that attempt to influence how legislators vote. Only two answers describe acts/responsibilities of Congress: pork-barrel projects and casework. Through casework, members of Congress help constituents resolve their problems with government agencies. Pork-barrel projects, which bring money and other benefits to states, are authorized by the addition of unrelated provisions to existing bills.

4. A Students may be confused since all answers list congressional voting methods. Roll-call votes are time-consuming because each member's name must be called and his/her vote cast. Standing votes are not simple because each standing member must be identified and counted. Computerized votes require complicated technology. Voice votes are simplest because the volume of the responses indicates the wishes of the majority.

---

6 ASSESSMENT

TEST-TAKING TIP

Answer the questions you know first and go back to those for which you need more time.

Directions: Choose the word(s) that best completes the sentence.

1. _____ choose the Speaker of the House.
- **A** Lobbyists
- **B** Constituents
- **C** Standing committees
- **D** Majority party members

2. _____ requires police to bring a prisoner to court to explain why they are holding him or her.
- **A** A bill of attainder
- **B** The franking privilege
- **C** An ex post facto law
- **D** A writ of habeas corpus

3. Members of Congress bring government funds to their state through _____.
- **A** casework
- **B** special-interest groups
- **C** gerrymandering
- **D** pork-barrel projects

4. The simplest way to vote in the House and the Senate is a _____.
- **A** voice vote
- **B** standing vote
- **C** roll-call vote
- **D** computerized vote

Reviewing Main Ideas

Directions: Choose the best answer for each question.

Section 1 *(pp. 176–182)*

5. The House and Senate meet as one body in _____.
- **A** a standing committee
- **B** odd-numbered years
- **C** caucuses
- **D** a joint session

6. The _____ is the most powerful leader in the House of Representatives.
- **A** Speaker of the House
- **B** president pro tempore
- **C** vice president
- **D** minority leader

Section 2 *(pp. 184–188)*

7. Which of the following legislative powers is implied by the elastic clause?
- **A** coining money
- **B** creating an air force
- **C** regulating foreign trade
- **D** establishing post offices

8. What nonlegislative power resides in the House of Representatives?
- **A** trying public officials
- **B** impeaching federal judges
- **C** establishing bankruptcy laws
- **D** approving presidential nominees

Section 3 *(pp. 190–196)*

9. Which of the following is a requirement for representatives in the House?
- **A** be at least 30 years old
- **B** live in the state they represent
- **C** live in the district they represent
- **D** be U.S. citizens for at least 9 years

10. What is NOT a major responsibility of representatives?
- **A** writing and introducing bills
- **B** voting on the floor of the House
- **C** troubleshooting for people in their district
- **D** providing analysis for the IRS

GO ON

Reviewing Main Ideas

5. D There are no scheduled meetings between the houses of Congress between regular sessions or after each census. The Constitution provides instructions for handling the death or resignation of a senator, so no meeting is necessary. Of the four answers, only the State of the Union address presents the opportunity for members of both houses to meet.

6. A Remind students that the Speaker is a member of the majority party. Members of a minority party have less power than those of a majority party to pass legislation. While leading members on joint committees are influential, their power is not equal to the chairpersons of standing committees, who determine the order in which their committees will consider bills.

Section 4 (pp. 197–202)

11. What is the term for ignoring a bill and letting it die?

A earmarking

B cloture

C gerrymandering

D pigeonholing

12. What may happen to a bill in the House after the bill leaves committee?

A Representatives add riders to the bill.

B The House clerk assigns a number to the bill.

C Representatives add amendments related to the bill.

D Representatives vote for cloture to limit debate on the bill.

Critical Thinking

Directions: Base your answers to questions 13 and 14 on the cartoon below and your knowledge of Chapter 6.

13. Determine the cartoonist's point of view. How would he describe politicians?

A extremely ruthless

B easily manipulated

C scrupulously honest

D fiercely independent

14. Analyze the symbols in the cartoon. What does the wagon most likely represent?

A casework

B legislation

C franking privileges

D campaign contributions

Document-Based Questions

Directions: Analyze the following document and answer the short-answer questions that follow.

Article 1, Section 7, U.S. Constitution

In this section of the Constitution the passing of a bill is discussed.

> *Every bill which shall have passed the House of Representatives and the Senate, . . . [and] Every order, resolution, or vote to which the concurrence of the Senate and House of Representatives may be necessary (except on a question of adjournment) shall be presented to the President. . .*
>
> —U.S. Constitution

15. Why do you think the Framers decided that all three arms of the government—the House of Representatives, the Senate, and the president—must be made aware of all bills and issues discussed in Congress?

16. What issue is the exception to this plan of review?

Extended Response

17. Write a brief essay describing two ways a president might stop a bill from becoming law.

For additional test practice, use Self-Check Quizzes—Chapter 6 on glencoe.com.

Need Extra Help?

If you missed question...	1	2	3	4	5	6	7	8	9	10	11	12	13	14	15	16	17
Go to page...	180	188	196	202	178	180	185	187	191	194	199	201	192	195	201	202	202

ASSESSMENT

constituents. The fourth answer, providing analysis for the IRS, is not.

11. D The practice of earmarking is the power of Congress to identify how funds will be allocated to one or more projects. Students may confuse the three remaining answers, as all refer to types of congressional legislation.

12. C Students who select answers A and D confuse the House with the Senate. Only senators add riders or use cloture to end filibuster. Students who select answer B have incorrectly sequenced the legislative process, as bills are numbered before going to committee.

Critical Thinking

13. B Students who identify the cartoonist's viewpoint of easily manipulated politicians recognize that the oxen (politicians) are directionless and are guided by the whip (or influence) of lobbyists.

14. B Students who correctly identify legislation realize that lobbyists try to influence congressional voting on legislation. Casework is not a lobbyist's concern. Franking privileges are not influenced by lobbyists. Campaign contributions are not the job (or load) of Congress.

Document-Based Questions

15. Answers will vary, but students may note that it forces everyone to be involved in the process, thus creating more steps in the process and eliminating unnecessary laws. It also serves as another form of checks and balances.

16. adjournment of Congress

Extended Response

17. Student essays will vary but should accurately describe a direct veto and a pocket veto.

7. B Of the answers, three are expressed powers: coining money, regulating foreign trade, and establishing post offices. Only creation of an air force is implied by the elastic clause, since the Constitution expressly empowers Congress to maintain a military (army and navy).

8. B Two powers refer to the Senate: trying public officials and approving presidential nominees. A third—establishing bankruptcy laws—is a legislative power.

9. B Two answers refer to Senate requirements: at least 30 years old and citizenship of 9 years or more. A third is not a requirement of either house—live in the district they represent. Only the requirement that members of the House live in the state they represent is accurate.

10. D Three answers are, indeed, House responsibilities: writing and introducing bills, voting on the House floor, and troubleshooting (or doing casework) for their

Civics ONLINE

Have students visit the Web site at glencoe.com to review Chapter 6 and take the **Self-Check Quiz.**

Need Extra Help?

Have students refer to the pages listed if they miss any of the questions.

Chapter Planning Guide

7

Levels (BL / OL / AL / ELL)		Resources	Chapter Opener	Section 1	Section 2	Section 3	Section 4	Chapter Assess
		FOCUS						
BL OL AL ELL	🖐	Daily Focus Skills Transparencies		7–1	7–2	7–3	7–4	
		TEACH						
BL OL — ELL	📁	Reading Essentials and Note-Taking Guide*		p. 64	p. 67	p. 70	p. 72	
OL AL	📁	Economics Activity, URB					p. 5	
AL	📁	Enrichment Activity, URB					p. 13	
OL AL	📁	Primary Source Reading, URB		p. 15	p. 15	p. 15	p. 15	
BL OL AL ELL	📁	Content Vocabulary Activity, URB*	p. 45	p. 45	p. 45	p. 45	p. 45	
BL OL AL ELL	📁	Academic Vocabulary Activity, URB	p. 47	p. 47	p. 47	p. 47	p. 47	
OL	📁	Biography Activity, URB				p. 49	p. 49	
BL OL AL ELL	📁	Writing Skills Activity, URB		p. 51				
OL AL	📁	Critical Thinking Skills Activity, URB				p. 53		
BL OL AL ELL	📁	Chart, Graph, and Map Skills Activity, URB		p. 55				
BL OL AL ELL	📁	Differentiated Instruction, URB			p. 57			
BL OL AL ELL	📁	School-to-Home Connection Activity, URB*	p. 59	p. 59	p. 59	p. 59	p. 59	
BL OL — ELL	📁	Guided Reading Activities, URB*		p. 63	p. 64	p. 65	p. 66	
BL OL AL ELL	📁	Writer's Guidebook	✓	✓	✓	✓	✓	✓
OL AL	💿	Primary Source Document Library	✓	✓	✓	✓	✓	✓
BL OL AL ELL	💿	Daily Lecture & Discussion Notes (in Pres. Plus)		✓	✓	✓	✓	✓
BL OL AL ELL	💿	StudentWorks™ Plus		✓	✓	✓	✓	✓
BL OL AL ELL	💿	Section Spotlight Videos		✓	✓	✓	✓	
BL OL AL ELL	🖐	TIME Interpreting Political Cartoons Transp.				Ch. 7		
BL OL AL ELL	🖐	Writing Process Transparencies	✓	✓	✓	✓	✓	✓

Note: Please refer to the *Unit 2 Resource Book* for this chapter's URB materials.

* Also available in Spanish

TeacherWorks *Plus*
All-In-One Planner and Resource Center

- Interactive Lesson Planner
- Interactive Teacher Edition
- Fully editable blackline masters
- Section Spotlight Videos Launch
- Differentiated Lesson Plans
- Printable reports of daily assignments
- Standards Tracking System

Levels					Resources	Chapter Opener	Section 1	Section 2	Section 3	Section 4	Chapter Assess
BL	OL	AL	ELL								
					TEACH *(continued)*						
				📁	**Building Academic Vocabulary**	✓	✓	✓	✓	✓	✓
Teacher Resources				📁	**Strategies for Success**	✓	✓	✓	✓	✓	✓
				📁	**Teachers Guide to Differentiated Instruction**	✓	✓	✓	✓	✓	✓
				💿	**Graphing Tool**	✓	✓	✓	✓	✓	✓
				💿	**Presentation Plus! with MindJogger CheckPoint**	✓	✓	✓	✓	✓	✓
					ASSESS						
BL	OL	AL	ELL	📁	**Quizzes and Tests***		p. 76	p. 77	p. 78	p. 79	p. 80
BL	OL	AL	ELL	📁	**Authentic Assessment with Rubrics**					p. 11	
BL	OL	AL	ELL	📁	**Standardized Test Practice**		p. 13	p. 13	p. 13	p. 13	p. 13
BL	OL	AL	ELL	💿	*ExamView*® **Assessment Suite CD-ROM**		7–1	7–2	7–3	7–4	Ch. 7
					CLOSE						
BL			ELL	📁	**Reteaching Activity, URB***		p. 61	p. 61	p. 61	p. 61	
BL	OL		ELL	📁	**Reading and Study Skills Foldables™ Activity**	p. 62			p. 63	p. 63	
BL	OL	AL	ELL	📁	*Civics Today* **in Graphic Novel**	p. 21	p. 21				
BL	OL	AL	ELL	🖨	**Graphic Organizer Transparencies & Strategies**	✓	✓	✓	✓	✓	✓

✓ Chapter- or unit-based activities applicable to all sections in this chapter

Using the Glencoe Web site

Self-Check Quiz

What is the Glencoe Web site?
The Glencoe Web site offers in-depth overviews that summarize and reinforce the content of each chapter.

How can the Glencoe Web site help my students?
Glencoe's Web site offers Self-Check Quizzes to give students a quick and easy way to check how much they have learned and to identify areas needing improvement. When using the Web site's Self-Check Quizzes, students can:

- view their results immediately
- view the correct answers
- e-mail their results to you or themselves
- receive feedback on each question for where students can go to review topics they missed or had trouble answering

Visit glencoe.com or enter a *QuickPass*™ code to go directly to student resources for the chapter.

Civics ONLINE
Visit glencoe.com and enter *QuickPass*™ code CIV1360c7T for Chapter 7 resources.

You can easily launch a wide range of digital products from your computer's desktop with the McGraw-Hill Social Studies widget.

	Student	Teacher	Parent
Media Library			
• Student Edition Section Audio	●		●
• Spanish Audio Summaries	●		●
• Section Spotlight Videos	●	●	●
***Civics Today* Online Learning Center (Web Site)**			
• Chapter Overviews	●	●	●
• Study Central™	●	●	●
• Study-to-Go	●	●	●
• Student Web Activities	●	●	●
• In Motion Animation	●	●	●
• Self-Check Quizzes	●	●	●
• ePuzzles and Games	●	●	●
• StudentWorks™ Plus Online	●	●	●
• Vocabulary eFlashcards	●	●	●
• Web Activity Lesson Plans		●	
• Vocabulary PuzzleMaker	●	●	●
Classroom Tools			
• Multilingual Glossary	●	●	●
• Beyond the Textbook	●	●	●
• NGS MapMachine	●	●	●

Reading List Generator CD-ROM

BookLink 3

Use this database to search more than 30,000 titles to create a customized reading list for your students.

- Reading lists can be organized by students' reading level, author, genre, theme, or area of interest.
- The database provides Degrees of Reading Power™ (DRP) and Lexile™ readability scores for all selections.
- A brief summary of each selection is included.

Leveled reading suggestions for this chapter:

For students at a Grade 7 reading level:
- *The White House: An Illustrated History,* by Catherine O'Neill Grace

For students at a Grade 8 reading level:
- *Our Country's Presidents,* by Ann Bausum

For students at a Grade 9 reading level:
- *You Are the President,* by Nathan Aaseng

For students at a Grade 10 reading level:
- *America's Third-Party Presidents,* by Nathan Aaseng

For students at a Grade 11 reading level:
- *Presidential Leadership: Rating the Best and the Worst in the White House,* by James Taranto

Reading Support from Jamestown Education

- **Timed Readings Plus in Social Studies** helps students increase their reading rate and fluency while maintaining comprehension. The 400-word passages are similar to those found on state and national assessments.

- **Reading in the Content Area: Social Studies** concentrates on six essential reading skills that help students better comprehend what they read. The book includes 75 high-interest nonfiction passages written at increasing levels of difficulty.

- **Reading Social Studies** includes strategic reading instruction and vocabulary support in Social Studies content for both ELLs and native speakers of English.

- **Content Vocabulary Workout** (Grades 6–8) accelerates reading comprehension through focused vocabulary development. Social Studies content vocabulary comes from the glossaries of Glencoe's Middle School Social Studies texts. www.jamestowneducation.com

KEY Teacher Wraparound

Use this key to help you identify the different types of prompts found in the Teacher Wraparound Edition.

R **Reading Strategies** activities help you teach reading skills and vocabulary.

C **Critical Thinking** strategies help students apply and extend what they have learned.

D **Differentiated Instruction** activities provide instruction for students learning to speak English, along with suggestions for teaching various types of learners.

S **Skill Practice** strategies help students practice historical analysis and geography skills.

W **Writing Support** activities provide writing opportunities to help students comprehend the text.

Teaching strategies and activities have been coded for ability level appropriateness.

AL Activities for students working above grade level

OL Activities for students working on grade level

BL Activities for students working below grade level

ELL Activities for English Language Learners

Focus

Why It Matters

Ask: What does each president have the obligation and the opportunity to do? *(Answers may include the idea that each president is obligated to follow and honor the traditions that have shaped the presidency and that each has the opportunity to shape the office for those who will follow and to respond to current national needs.)*

More About the Photo

Visual Literacy The 2008 Republican National Convention, held in St. Paul, Minnesota, convened on September 1. The convention was only the second Republican convention held in St. Paul since 1892. The presidential nominee, Senator John McCain, came as no surprise to the delegates. His vice presidential choice may have. Governor Sarah Palin of Alaska was nominated at this convention as the first female Republican candidate for Vice President.

Teach

BIG Ideas *As you begin teaching each section, use these questions and activities to help students focus on the Big Ideas.*

Section 1

The President and the Vice President
Ask: What qualities are needed in the person who is president of the United States? *(Answers may include the idea that the person must be able to lead, to learn*

206

Chapter

7

The Executive Branch

Why It Matters

The Framers did not state specifically in the Constitution what the role of the president should be. The nation's first president, George Washington, established many traditions that shaped the presidency. Every president since Washington has followed and built upon these traditions, refining the president's role within the government.

Delegates to the 2008 National Republican Convention prepare to nominate their candidate for president.

206

---

quickly, and to make difficult decisions.) Point out that in Section 1 students will learn who can run for president, how the president is elected, and what Americans expect of their presidents. **AL**

Section 2

The President's Job Ask: What do you know about the president's roles and responsibilities? *(Answers may include implementing or vetoing legislation, acting as commander in chief, and representing the nation abroad.)* Tell students that in Section 2 they will learn about the ways the president serves the nation. **OL**

Chapter Audio

Civics ONLINE
Visit glencoe.com and enter
QuickPass™ code
CIV3093c7 for
Chapter 7
resources.

Chapter Introduction
7

BIG Ideas

Section 1: The President and Vice President

The Constitution gives the executive branch the power to execute, or implement, the law. The president holds one of the most powerful and important elective offices in the world.

Section 2: The President's Job

The Constitution gives the executive branch the power to execute, or implement, the law. The president fills many different roles.

Section 3: Making Foreign Policy

Under our federal system, the executive, legislative, and judicial branches share the responsibility of governing the nation. The president and Congress have important roles in making foreign policy.

Section 4: Presidential Advisers and Executive Agencies

The Constitution gives the executive branch the power to execute, or implement, the law. Thousands of employees and advisers help the president.

FOLDABLES
Study Organizer

Organizing Information Study Foldable Make the following Foldable to help you organize information about the U.S. president and the executive branch of government.

Step 1 Fold a sheet of paper in half from top to bottom with edges evenly together.

Step 2 Then fold the paper in half from side to side.

Step 3 Label the Foldable as shown.

Roles of the President

Reading and Writing
As you read the chapter, record the different roles the president plays in government as he or she fulfills the requirements of this office.

FOLDABLES **Dinah Zike's**
Study Organizer **Foldables**

Purpose This Foldable helps students learn and record the roles presidents fill as they serve the nation. The completed Foldable will form a booklet to help students review the responsibilities of the office of president. **OL**

More Foldables activities for this chapter can be found in the *Dinah Zike's Reading and Study Skills Foldables* ancillary.

Civics ONLINE
Visit glencoe.com and enter *QuickPass*™ code CIV1360c7T for Chapter 7 resources, including a Chapter Overview, Study Central™, Study-to-Go, Student Web Activity, Self-Check Quiz, and other materials.

Section 3

Making Foreign Policy Ask: Why is it important for the president to maintain good relationships with foreign nations? *(Answers may include the need for cooperation among nations in trade, in solving global problems, and in policing the world.)* Explain that in Section 3 students will learn about the tools the president uses to shape foreign policy. **AL**

Section 4

Presidential Advisers and Executive Agencies Ask: Who are the president's advisers? *(Answers may include the First Lady, the cabinet, and other bureaucrats.)* Explain that in Section 4 students will learn about the people who advise the president. **OL**

Focus

Bellringer
Daily Focus Transparency 7–1

Guide to Reading
Answers to Graphic:

```
Office of the
President

   terms          qualifications

• limited to      • at least 35 years
  two terms          old
  (or a maxi-     • native-born Amer-
  mum of ten         ican citizen
  years)          • resident of United
                     States for at least
                     14 years
```

Section Spotlight Video

To generate student interest and provide a springboard for class discussion, access the Chapter 7, Section 1 video at glencoe.com or on the video DVD.

Resource Manager

Guide to Reading

Big Idea
The Constitution gives the executive branch the power to execute, or implement, the law.

Content Vocabulary
• Electoral College *(p. 210)*
• elector *(p. 210)*

Academic Vocabulary
• display *(p. 210)*
• outcome *(p. 210)*

Reading Strategy
Describing As you read this section, describe the qualifications and terms of office for the president by completing the graphic organizer below.

```
Office of the
President

terms      qualifications
```

Section 1

The President and Vice President

Real World Civics Any child born in the United States can grow up to be president. It is considered to be the most powerful job in the world. Would you want it? Barack Obama did. After serving in the U.S. Senate representing Illinois, he decided to run for the presidency in 2008. After becoming the nominee of his party, he chose Senator Joseph Biden as his running mate. Together they campaigned in a history-making election. Barack Obama succeeded at becoming the first African American elected to the U.S. presidency.

▼ **Barack Obama (right) and Joe Biden claim the nominations for president and vice president at the 2008 Democratic convention.**

R Reading Strategies	**C** Critical Thinking	**D** Differentiated Instruction	**W** Writing Support	**S** Skill Practice
Teacher Edition • Making Connections, pp. 209, 211, 212 • Ac. Voc., p. 210 **Additional Resources** • Pri. Source Act., URB p. 15 • Cont. Vocab., URB p. 45 • Ac. Voc., URB p. 47 • Guid. Read., URB p. 63	**Teacher Edition** • Making Inferences, p. 209 • Pred. Consequences, p. 213 **Additional Resources** • Quizzes and Tests, p. 76	**Teacher Edition** • Adv. Learners, p. 210 • EL, p. 212 **Additional Resources** • Reteach. Act., URB p. 61 • School-to-Home Conn., URB p. 59 • Graphic Novel, p. 21	**Teacher Edition** • Personal Writing, p. 210 **Additional Resources** • Writing Skills Act., URB p. 51	**Teacher Edition** • Interp. Graphics, p. 211 **Additional Resources** • Chart, Map, and Graph Activity, URB p. 55 • Daily Focus Trans., 7–1

The Office of the President

Main idea As the head of the executive branch of our federal government, the president holds one of the most powerful and important elective offices in the world.

Civics & You What qualifications do you think a president should have? Read this section to find out what Americans have come to expect from their presidents.

The president heads the executive branch of the United States government. The presidency is the top political job in the country. Because of the power and global influence of the United States, the president is generally considered to hold the most important job in the world. Our country's first president was George Washington. Just as the nation has grown tremendously since that time, so has the office of the presidency.

The U.S. Constitution lists only three rules about who, by law, can become president of the United States. A person must be (1) at least 35 years old, (2) a native-born American citizen, and (3) a resident of the United States for at least 14 years.

Characteristics of Presidents Almost all our presidents have shared similar characteristics. So far, every American president has been male. All but one have been Protestant Christians. Most have had a college education. Many have been lawyers. Most came from states with large populations.

Only in the past few decades has the presidency become a possibility for a wider group of Americans. John F. Kennedy became the first Catholic president in 1960. In 1984 the Democratic Party nominated Geraldine Ferraro as its first female vice-presidential candidate. In 2000 the Democrats nominated Connecticut senator Joseph Lieberman as the first Jewish candidate for vice president. The first African American president, Barack Obama, was elected in 2008.

President for Life Former presidents are often called upon to attend official ceremonies as former presidents Carter, Bush, Clinton, and Ford do here. *Identifying* What would happen if a person who came to this country as an immigrant wanted to run for president?

209

Teach

C Critical Thinking

Making Inferences Ask: Why is having won earlier elections a characteristic of most presidents? *(Candidates who have won earlier elections have greater name recognition than newcomers to politics and refer to their experiences governing as they campaign.)* **OL**

R Reading Strategy

Making Connections Ask: What American ideal does this widening field of presidential candidates reflect? *(It reflects the ideal of equal opportunity for all, regardless of race, religion, or gender.)* **AL**

Caption Answer:
Under current Constitutional requirements, the immigrant could not run for president.

Differentiated Instruction

Creating a Double-Bar Graph

CHART, GRAPH, AND MAP SKILLS ACTIVITY 7

Creating a Double-Bar Graph

Chart, Graph, and Map Skills Activity 7, URB pp. 55–56

Objective: To identify the uses of and interpret double-bar graphs

Focus: Have students suggest tasks that require comparing and contrasting numerical information.

Teach: Guide students to interpret the graph using the bulleted instructions.

Assess: Check accuracy of students' graphs.

Close: Have students rephrase the instructions for creating double-bar graphs.

Differentiated Instruction Strategies

BL For which president did the electoral and popular votes vary most? For which were they closest?

AL What other kinds of graphs could you use to express the information in the graph you created on page 56?

ELL Which is the x-axis of the graph—the left-to-right line or the bottom-to-top line? Which is the y-axis?

D Differentiated Instruction

Advanced Learners Have students look up the word "college" in a dictionary. **Ask:** Which definition of "college" helps you understand the term "electoral college"? *(The definition of college as a body or group of people considered by tradition or law to be a unit will help students understand the term.)* **AL**

R Reading Strategy

Academic Vocabulary Ask: What synonyms for "display" fit this context? *(Answers may include "present" and "show.")* **ELL BL**

W Writing Support

Personal Writing Have students write several paragraphs to answer this question: Does every vote count in a presidential election? Explain. *(Students should realize that because the votes of the Electoral College actually elect the president, rather than the popular votes, every vote does not count.)* **OL**

Analyzing Maps

Answers:
1. the South
2. California, New York, Florida

Hands-On Chapter Project
Step 1

The Role of the Cabinet

Step 1: Determining the Makeup of the Cabinet The class will research the president's cabinet to learn what positions it is made of.

Directions Tell students that later in the chapter, they will learn about the people that advise the president. In this step of the project, they will use books and Internet sources to find out and record the positions

on the cabinet. Before they begin, explain the use of the title "Secretary" and the meaning of the word "cabinet" in this context.

Identifying Have students use library books or Internet sources such as http://www.whitehouse.gov/government/cabinet.html to learn about the fifteen cabinet positions. Tell students to list the areas of expertise and the person who currently serves in the position. **OL**

(Project continued in Section 2)

Presidential Elections

Presidential elections take place every four years in years evenly divisible by the number four—for example, 2000, 2004, and 2008. The Constitution provides for an indirect method **D** of election called the **Electoral College.** The Constitution says that each state "shall appoint" **electors,** who then vote for one of the major candidates. Although the ballot **R** will **display,** or show, the names of the presidential candidates, you are actually voting for a list of presidential electors pledged to that candidate.

Each state has as many electoral votes as the total of its U.S. senators and representatives. (Washington, D.C., has three electoral votes.) The Electoral College includes 538 **W** electors. In almost every state, the Electoral College is a "winner-take-all" system. Even

if a candidate wins the popular vote by just a tiny majority, that candidate usually gets all of the state's electoral votes. Thus, the electoral votes of a few small states can decide the **outcome,** or result, of a close election.

To be elected, a candidate must receive half of the 538 electoral votes available, or 270 votes to win. If no candidate gets an electoral college majority, the House of Representatives votes on the candidates, with each state delegation casting only a single vote. This has happened twice—in 1800 and in 1824.

Although the winning presidential candidate is usually announced on the same evening as the popular election, the formal election by the Electoral College does not take place until December. The electors meet in each state capital to cast their ballots. Then Congress officially counts the electoral votes.

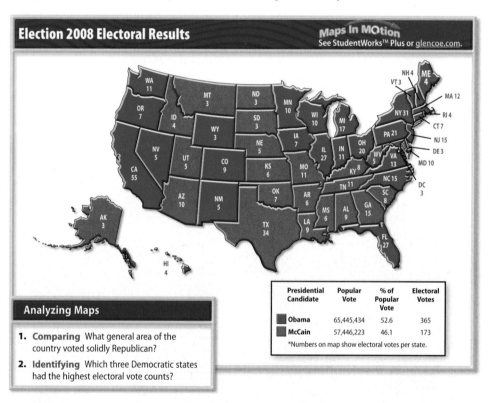

Election 2008 Electoral Results

Maps In MOtion
See StudentWorks™ Plus or glencoe.com.

Presidential Candidate	Popular Vote	% of Popular Vote	Electoral Votes
Obama	65,445,434	52.6	365
McCain	57,446,223	46.1	173

*Numbers on map show electoral votes per state.

Analyzing Maps

1. **Comparing** What general area of the country voted solidly Republican?
2. **Identifying** Which three Democratic states had the highest electoral vote counts?

210

Presidential Succession

Graphs In MOtion
See StudentWorks™ Plus or glencoe.com.

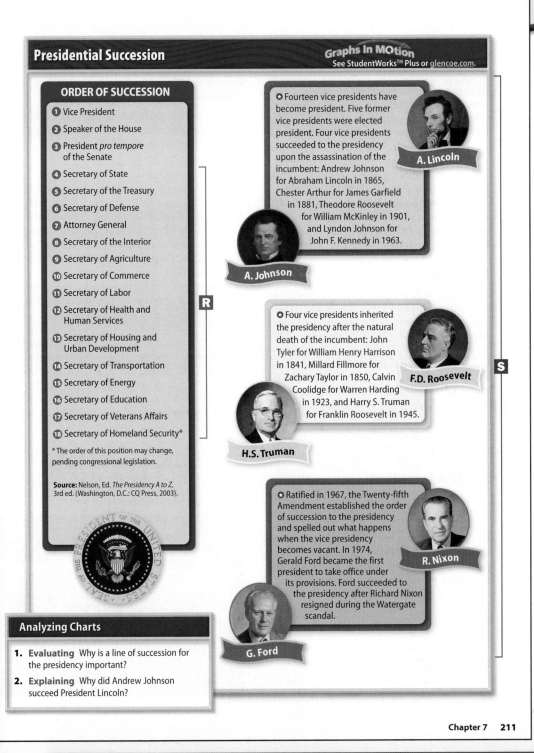

ORDER OF SUCCESSION

1. Vice President
2. Speaker of the House
3. President *pro tempore* of the Senate
4. Secretary of State
5. Secretary of the Treasury
6. Secretary of Defense
7. Attorney General
8. Secretary of the Interior
9. Secretary of Agriculture
10. Secretary of Commerce
11. Secretary of Labor
12. Secretary of Health and Human Services
13. Secretary of Housing and Urban Development
14. Secretary of Transportation
15. Secretary of Energy
16. Secretary of Education
17. Secretary of Veterans Affairs
18. Secretary of Homeland Security*

* The order of this position may change, pending congressional legislation.

Source: Nelson, Ed. *The Presidency A to Z,* 3rd ed. (Washington, D.C.: CQ Press, 2003).

R

Fourteen vice presidents have become president. Five former vice presidents were elected president. Four vice presidents succeeded to the presidency upon the assassination of the incumbent: Andrew Johnson for Abraham Lincoln in 1865, Chester Arthur for James Garfield in 1881, Theodore Roosevelt for William McKinley in 1901, and Lyndon Johnson for John F. Kennedy in 1963.

A. Lincoln

A. Johnson

Four vice presidents inherited the presidency after the natural death of the incumbent: John Tyler for William Henry Harrison in 1841, Millard Fillmore for Zachary Taylor in 1850, Calvin Coolidge for Warren Harding in 1923, and Harry S. Truman for Franklin Roosevelt in 1945.

F.D. Roosevelt

H.S. Truman

S

Ratified in 1967, the Twenty-fifth Amendment established the order of succession to the presidency and spelled out what happens when the vice presidency becomes vacant. In 1974, Gerald Ford became the first president to take office under its provisions. Ford succeeded to the presidency after Richard Nixon resigned during the Watergate scandal.

R. Nixon

G. Ford

Analyzing Charts

1. **Evaluating** Why is a line of succession for the presidency important?
2. **Explaining** Why did Andrew Johnson succeed President Lincoln?

Chapter 7   211

R Reading Strategy

Making Connections Ask: Who are the people listed in numbers 4 through 18 in the order of succession? *(They are the secretaries of the president's cabinet.)* **OL**

S Skill Practice

Interpreting Graphics Ask: How does each box in the right-hand column relate to the box captioned "Order of Succession" in the left-hand column? *(The top and middle boxes in the right-hand column give examples of times when an order of succession was needed. The bottom box explains when and why the order of succession was established.)* **AL**

Analyzing Charts

Answers:
1. It ensures a smooth transfer of authority in case of the death or incapacitation of a president.
2. Lincoln was assassinated while still in office, so Johnson assumed the position and responsibilities of president.

Differentiated Instruction

Leveled Activities

BL School-to-Home Activity 7, URB pp. 59–60

OL Writing Skills Activity 7, URB pp. 51–52

AL Chart/Graph/Map Activity 7, URB pp. 55–56

ELL Guided Reading Activity 7-1, URB p. 63

R **Reading Strategy**

Making Connections **Ask:** What important international event occurred during Franklin D. Roosevelt's terms in office? *(World War II)* **OL**

D **Differentiated Instruction**

English Learners Tell students that Camp David can serve as a retreat for the president but often serves as a private place where the president, his or her advisors, and decision makers from other nations meet to consider pressing problems and suggest solutions. Ask students to discuss if they think this more informal meeting place is necessary. **ELL**

✔ Reading Check **Answer:** 10 years

Caption Answer:
Early presidents did not travel the long distances that today's presidents cover, nor did they have the technology to travel quickly that today's presidents enjoy.

Additional Support

Term of Office

Presidents serve four-year terms. Originally the Constitution placed no limits on how many terms a president could serve. The nation's first president, George Washington, served for eight years and then refused to run for a third term. Following Washington's example, no president served more than two **R** terms until 1940, when Franklin D. Roosevelt ran for and won a third term. In 1944 Roosevelt won a fourth term. The Twenty-second Amendment, ratified in 1951, limits each president to two elected terms in office, or a maximum of 10 years if the presidency began during another president's term.

Salary and Benefits

The president receives a salary of $400,000 per year, plus money for expenses and travel. The president lives and works in the White House. A domestic staff of more than 80 people takes care of the president's family.

The president has use of Camp David, an estate in the Catoctin Mountains of Maryland, about 60 miles north of Washington, D.C. **D** When presidents travel, they command a fleet of special cars, helicopters, and airplanes. For long trips, the president uses *Air Force One*, a specially equipped jet.

The Vice President

The vice president is elected with the president through the Electoral College system. The qualifications for the office are the same as those for the presidency. The Constitution gives little authority to the vice president. Article I states that the vice president shall preside over the Senate and vote in that body in case of a tie. If the president dies, is removed from office, falls seriously ill, or resigns, the vice president becomes president.

✔ Reading Check **Identifying** What is the maximum number of years that a U.S. president can serve?

Presidential Succession

Main Idea The office of the president has an established order of succession.

Civics & You Do you know what happens when a president dies or is forced to leave office? Read to find out how the Constitution answers this question.

In 1841 William Henry Harrison became the first president to die in office. His death raised many questions. While the Constitution says that the vice president should assume the "powers and duties" of the presidency, no one was sure what that meant. Should the vice president remain as vice president while doing the president's job? Should the vice president become president? Should a special election be called to elect a new president?

Vice President John Tyler settled these questions. He declared himself president, took the oath of office, and served out the remainder of Harrison's term. Since Tyler's time, eight other vice presidents have taken over the presidency following the death or resignation of a president.

Executive Travel President Bush walks from the White House to *Marine One* to fly to a fund-raiser within an hour. **Speculating How might this be different than an early president's travel?**

Did You Know?

Presidential Term Limits George Washington established the two-term tradition that became law with the ratification of the Twenty-second Amendment to the Constitution. As president, Washington discussed problems thoroughly and listened to the advice of people from different parties. He considered himself separate from party influence. Washington's administration was marked by ceremony. Some critics accused him of behaving as if he were a king whose power would last his life. However, Washington had to be pressed into serving a second term as president and refused to stand for a third term. In 1796, worn out from service and impatient with partisan politics, Washington submitted his Farewell Address to the nation and retired to his farm, where he worked until his death on December 12, 1799. Advanced students may wish to read Washington's Farewell Address, which they can access at http://www.britannica.com/eb/article-9116980/Document-George Washington-Farewell-Address, and to summarize his final words of advice to the nation for the class.

Presidential Succession Act

In 1947 Congress passed the Presidential Succession Act, which indicates the line of succession after the vice president. According to this law, if both the president and vice president die or leave office, the Speaker of the House becomes president. Next in line is the president pro tempore of the Senate, then the secretary of state and other members of the cabinet.

Twenty-fifth Amendment

Remaining questions about presidential succession were answered by the passage of a constitutional amendment. The Twenty-fifth Amendment, ratified in 1967, says that if the president dies or leaves office, the vice president becomes president. The new president then chooses another vice president. Both the Senate and House of Representatives must approve the choice. This amendment also gives the vice president a role in determining whether a president is disabled and unable to do the job. Should that occur, the vice president would serve as acting president until the president is able to go back to work.

The Twenty-fifth Amendment has been used only three times. In 1973 Vice President Spiro Agnew resigned. President Richard Nixon replaced him with Gerald Ford, a representative from Michigan, and Congress approved the nomination. When Nixon resigned from the presidency in 1974, Ford became the new president. Ford then nominated Nelson A. Rockefeller, former governor of New York, to be his vice president. In 1985 President Ronald Reagan informed Congress that he would need to undergo surgery and would be unable to carry out his presidential duties. As a result, Vice President George H.W. Bush served as acting president for about eight hours.

C

✓ **Reading Check Describing** What was the purpose of the Twenty-fifth Amendment?

C Critical Thinking

Predicting Consequences Ask: What would happen if the president were temporarily unconscious because of injury or illness? *(The vice president would assume the president's responsibilities until the president was well again.)* **OL**

✓ **Reading Check Answer:** It provides a process for choosing a new vice president in the event that the former vice president has succeeded to the office of president, and gives the vice president a role in deciding whether the president is unable to serve because of incapacitation.

Assess

Civics ONLINE

Study Central™ provides summaries, interactive games, and online graphic organizers to help students review content.

Close

Summarizing Have students develop a summary of the history of the office of president, based on what they learned in this section. **OL**

Section 1 Review

Vocabulary

1. **Write** complete sentences about the United States presidency using each of the following terms: *Electoral College, elector.*

Main Ideas

2. **Analyzing** Why do you think the president is elected rather than appointed by Congress?

3. **Identifying** Who are the first four officers in the line of succession to the presidency? Who is last in line?

Critical Thinking

4. **Analyzing** Candidates for president are not usually drawn to the office because of the salary. Why do you think these people run for office?

5. **BIG Ideas** In a graphic organizer like the one below, identify the main qualifications for running for the office of president of the United States.

Running for President

CITIZENSHIP Activity

6. **Expository Writing** What qualifications or characteristics do you think a president should have? Which of the recent presidents, if any, have had these qualifications or characteristics? Write a one-page essay in which you answer these questions.

Civics ONLINE

Study Central™ To review this section, go to <u>glencoe.com</u>.

Section 1 Review

Chapter 7 **213**

Answers

1. Sentences should use vocabulary words according to their definitions in the section and in the Glossary.

2. The president, or executive branch, should serve as a check on the legislative branch. Congress might appoint a president who would support their legislation. This would erode the balance of power among the three branches of government.

3. The first four officers are the vice president, the Speaker of the House, the President pro tempore of the Senate, and the Secretary of State. Last in line is the Secretary of Homeland Security.

4. Answers will vary, but may include that candidates want to serve the nation and to shape policy.

5 Answers that complete the graphic organizer include the three constitutional requirements of minimum age of 35, native-born status, and residency in the U.S. for at least 14 years.

6. Student essays should identify necessary qualifications and characteristics and provide examples of recent presidents who displayed these traits.

Focus

Bellringer
Daily Focus Transparency 7–2

Guide to Reading
Answers to Graphic:

Chief Executive
- receive leaders of foreign countries
- help the economy prosper
- carry out laws
- serve as commander in chief
- make treaties with other nations
- appoint federal officials

Section Spotlight Video

To generate student interest and provide a springboard for class discussion, access the Chapter 7, Section 2 video at glencoe.com or on the video DVD.

Resource Manager

Guide to Reading

Big Idea
The Constitution gives the executive branch the power to execute, or implement, the law.

Content Vocabulary
- executive order *(p. 216)*
- pardon *(p. 217)*
- reprieve *(p. 217)*
- amnesty *(p. 217)*

Academic Vocabulary
- require *(p. 215)*
- impact *(p. 216)*
- policy *(p. 217)*

Reading Strategy
Summarizing As you read, in a chart like the one below, list the different duties that are part of the president's role as chief executive.

Chief Executive — Carry out laws

🔊 **Section Audio**   🎬 **Spotlight Video**

The President's Job

Real World Civics The president is the commander in chief of the U.S. armed forces. He or she is also one of the most important hosts of one of the most impressive houses in the world—the White House. The president must maintain good relationships with other world leaders and often entertains dignitaries. Here President Bill Clinton hosts Spain's King Juan Carlos in 2000, engaging in a ceremonial troop review of U.S. Marines. The south lawn of the White House is a popular location for such honorary troop reviews and other greetings of foreign leaders.

▼ **Former president Clinton honors the king of Spain**

R Reading Strategies	**C** Critical Thinking	**D** Differentiated Instruction	**W** Writing Support	**S** Skill Practice
Teacher Edition • Read. Pri. Sources., p. 215 • Ac. Voc., p. 216 **Additional Resources** • Cont. Vocab., URB p. 45 • Ac. Voc., URB p. 47 • Guid. Read., URB p. 64 • RENTG, p. 67	**Teacher Edition** • Ident. Cent. Issues., p. 215 • Pred. Consequences, p. 217 **Additional Resources** • Quizzes and Tests, p. 77	**Teacher Edition** • Adv. Learners, p. 216 **Additional Resources** • Diff. Instr. Act., URB p. 57 • School-to-Home Conn., URB p. 59 • Reteach. Act., URB p. 61	**Teacher Edition** • Creative Writing, p. 218	**Teacher Edition** • Creating a Cause-and-Effect Chart, p. 217 **Additional Resources** • Daily Focus Trans., 7–2

Constitutional Powers

Main Idea The source for the president's authority is Article II of the Constitution.

Civics & You What qualifications or characteristics do you think a president should have? Which of the recent presidents, if any, have had these qualifications or characteristics?

Fewer than 50 men have been able to say what it feels like to be president of the United States. Some former presidents' thoughts are revealing.

" The presidency has made every man who occupied it, no matter how small, bigger than he was; and no matter how big, not big enough for its demands. "

—Lyndon B. Johnson

Duties of the President

Although the president is the head of just one of the three branches of government, he or she, with the exception of the vice president, is the only official of the federal government 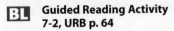 elected by the entire nation. As a result, the president stands as a symbol not only of the federal government, but of the entire nation as well. Even so, the thirty-eighth president, Gerald Ford, pointed out that not even the president can do the impossible.

" You know, the President of the United States is not a magician who can wave a wand or sign a paper that will instantly end a war, cure a recession, or make bureaucracy disappear. "

—Gerald Ford

The president is the most powerful public official in the United States. The U.S. Constitution is the basis of the president's power. Article II says,

" Executive Power shall be invested in a President. . . . "

Thus, the president's main job is to execute, or carry out, the laws passed by Congress.

The Constitution also gives the president the power to

- veto, or reject, bills passed in Congress.
- call Congress into special session.
- serve as commander in chief of the armed forces.
- receive leaders and other officials of foreign countries.
- make treaties with other countries (with Senate approval).
- appoint heads of executive agencies, federal court judges, ambassadors, and other top government officials (also subject to Senate approval).
- pardon or reduce the penalties against people convicted of federal crimes.

Because the Constitution **requires,** or calls for, the president to give Congress information about the "state of the union," the president gives several speeches to Congress each year. The most important is the State of the Union address, in which the president discusses the most important issues facing the nation.

The constitutional duties of the nation's first president, George Washington, and those of a modern president are much the same. For example, the Constitution makes the president the commander in chief of the nation's armed forces. In Washington's administration this meant calling out a militia of 15,000 volunteers. Today the president oversees a military divided into five major units and makes the decision on how to deploy troops stationed around the world.

Reading Check **Analyzing** What are the powers of the president as expressed in the Constitution?

Chapter 7 215

Teach

R Reading Strategy

Reading Primary Sources Have students explain the ideas expressed in the quotes on this page. **Ask:** How do these quotes reshape your opinion of presidential power? *(Answers may include the ideas that the office makes great demands on the person who holds it and that it is unrealistic to think that one person can do the job perfectly at all times.)* **AL**

C Critical Thinking

Identifying Central Issues **Ask:** To make treaties and appoint officials, the president must have Senate approval. Of what fact of American government is this relationship an example? *(It is an example of the system of checks and balances.)* **OL**

Reading Check **Answer:** The Constitution gives the president the power to execute laws, to veto bills, to call special sessions of Congress, to command the military, to receive leaders of other nations, to make treaties with other nations (with Senate approval), to appoint officials (with Senate approval), and to pardon or reduce the sentences of federal convicts.

Differentiated Instruction

Leveled Activities

BL **Guided Reading Activity 7-2, URB p. 64**

OL **Differentiated Instruction Activity 7, URB pp. 57–58**

ELL **Content Vocabulary Activity 7, URB p. 45**

215

Roles of the President

Main Idea The president fills many roles that are important to the functioning of the United States government.

Civics and You The Constitution grants broad powers to the president. Do you think the president has too much power? Read about the president's many roles.

The Constitution holds one person—the president—responsible for carrying out the duties of the executive branch. As the nation has grown, the duties and responsibilities of the executive branch have grown.

Chief Executive

The most important job of the president is to carry out the nation's laws. To do this, the president is in charge of 15 cabinet departments and the approximately 3 million civilians who work for the federal government. The president appoints the heads of the cabinet departments and of other large government agencies, with the Senate's approval.

Use of Executive Orders Presidents have several tools to influence how laws are carried out. One is the executive order. An **executive order** is a rule or command that has the force of law. Only Congress has the authority to make laws. Issuing executive orders, however, is generally considered to fall under the president's constitutional duty to "take care that the laws are faithfully executed."

Many executive orders deal with simple administrative problems. Some, however, have had a great **impact,** or influence. President Harry S. Truman, for instance, used an executive order in 1948 to racially integrate the armed forces. This gave Americans of all races the opportunity to serve in the armed forces.

TIME™ Teens in *Action*

Shauna Fleming

What is it like to meet the president of the United States? Just ask Shauna Fleming, 17, of Orange, California. She received the President's Volunteer Service Award for her work as founder of "A Million Thanks."

QUESTION: What does A Million Thanks do?
ANSWER: Our goal is to collect thank-you letters for the U.S. military. I started the campaign in 2004 and have collected 2 million letters so far.
Q: Why did you start it?
A: I saw a need for a morale boost for our troops. We've sent millions of letters and e-mails to U.S military men and women stationed all over the world. If you put all the paper together, it would weigh 8,000 pounds and fill two large semi trucks. Our Web site has had over 4 million hits and thousands of great responses from soldiers who received letters.
Q: Because of your work, you were invited to the White House. What was that like?
A: I've met some of the most powerful people in the world. But the highlight has to be meeting President George W. Bush in a private meeting with my family in the Oval Office. I presented the president with the one millionth thank-you letter received by my campaign. I discussed many things with him and he even gave us a tour of the office, pointing out objects that were important to him.

Making a Difference **CITIZENSHIP**
What qualities does Shauna display that makes her volunteer work successful?

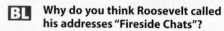

First Fireside Chat

Objective: To understand Roosevelt's use of Fireside Chats to inform and reassure U.S. citizens

Focus: Discuss why people wanted to withdraw their money from banks.

Teach: Read aloud Roosevelt's words.

Assess: Ask how the bank holiday helped the government begin to repair the economy.

Close: Role-play the discussion a family might have after Roosevelt speech.

Differentiated Instruction Strategies

BL Why do you think Roosevelt called his addresses "Fireside Chats"?

AL What media might Roosevelt have used today? How might these media change the way citizens perceive the message?

ELL Use the Reader's Dictionary words in sentences that will help you learn and remember what each word means.

Power of Appointment The Constitution gives the president the power to appoint judges to the Supreme Court and other federal courts. This is an important power because the Supreme Court has the final authority to determine whether a law is constitutional. Because the power to interpret laws is important, most presidents try to appoint Supreme Court justices who share views similar to their own.

The Constitution also gives the president the power to grant pardons. A **pardon** is a declaration of forgiveness and freedom from punishment. The president may also issue a **reprieve,** an order to delay a person's punishment until a higher court can hear the case, or grant **amnesty,** a pardon toward a group of people.

Chief Diplomat

The president directs the foreign **policy,** or strategy, of the United States, making key decisions about how the United States acts toward other countries in the world.

Commander in Chief

The Constitution makes the president commander in chief of the armed forces of the United States. This role gives presidents

the ability to back up their foreign policy decisions with force, if necessary. The president is in charge of the army, navy, air force, marines, and coast guard. The top commanders of all these branches of service are subordinate to the president.

The president shares with Congress the power to make war. The Constitution gives Congress the power to declare war, but only the president can order American soldiers into battle. Congress has declared war five times: the War of 1812, the Mexican War, the Spanish-American War, World War I, and World War II. Presidents, however, have sent troops into action overseas more than 150 times since 1789. For example, although Congress never declared war in Korea or in Vietnam, American troops were involved in conflicts in those countries because they were sent there by U.S. presidents.

In 1973, after the Vietnam War, Congress passed the War Powers Resolution. According to this law, the president must notify Congress within 48 hours when troops are sent into battle. These troops must be brought home after 60 days unless Congress gives its approval for them to remain longer or declares war.

Legislative Leader

Only members of Congress have the power to introduce bills for consideration, but in practice Congress expects the executive branch to propose the legislation it would like to see enacted.

Every president has a legislative program. These are new laws that the president wants Congress to pass. The president makes speeches to build support for this program and meets with key senators and representatives to try to persuade them to support the proposed laws.

European Union President Bush and advisers meet with leaders in Europe to discuss trade. **Identifying** What official role of the president is this an example of?

Civics ONLINE

Student Web Activity Visit glencoe.com and complete the Chapter 7 Web Activity.

The Role of the Cabinet

Step 2: Proposing a Problem Groups of students will suggest problems about which the president's cabinet might advise him or her.

Directions Explain to students that the president must choose experts in many subjects to advise him or her. The leaders of

these advisers sit on the cabinet, each in charge of a department that gathers information.

Identifying Central Issues Ask student groups to think about important problems facing the nation today. These problems may be national or international in scope. Encourage each group to generate two or three problems. Then have students write

their lists of problems on the board and, as a class, choose the one they think is most in need of executive leadership. Students will use this central issue problem in Step 3 of the project. **OL**

(Project continued in Section 3)

Section 2 Review

W Writing Support

Creative Writing Refer students to Differentiated Instruction Activity 7 (URB p. 57) for an example of a typical presidential day in office for Gerald Ford. Encourage them to write an agenda of daily activities that reflects the nation's needs and issues today. **OL**

✓Reading Check **Answer:** the laws he or she hopes to see enacted during his or her administration

Assess

Civics ONLINE

Study Central™ provides summaries, interactive games, and online graphic organizers to help students review content.

Close

Personal Writing Have students write about the current president to produce an assessment of how well he or she is carrying out the roles and responsibilities of the president. **OL**

Section 2 Review

The president and Congress have often disagreed over what new laws Congress should adopt. One reason for this is that presidents represent the entire United States, while members of Congress represent only the people of their states or districts.

The difference in the lengths of time that presidents and members of Congress can hold office also contributes to this conflict. While presidents can serve no more than two elected terms, members of Congress can be elected over and over again for decades. Therefore, many members of Congress may not want to move as quickly on programs as the president does.

Head of State

The president is the living symbol of the nation. In this role, the president aids diplomacy by greeting visiting kings and queens, prime ministers, and other foreign leaders. The president also carries out ceremonial functions for Americans, such as lighting the national Christmas tree and giving medals to the country's heroes.

Economic Leader

Every president tries to help the country's economy prosper. Voters expect the president to deal with such problems as unemployment, rising prices, and high taxes. One key task the president must accomplish each year as economic leader is to plan the federal government's budget. The president meets with budget officials to decide what programs to support and what programs to cut back. Budget decisions have a great effect on the national economy.

Party Leader

The president is generally regarded as the leader of his or her political party. Members of the president's party work hard to elect the president. In turn, the president gives speeches to help fellow party members who are running for office as members of Congress, governors, and mayors. The president also helps the party raise money.

✓Reading Check Defining What is a president's legislative program?

Section 2 Review

Vocabulary

1. **Define** the following terms and use them in complete sentences related to the presidency: *executive order, pardon, reprieve, amnesty.*

Main Ideas

2. **Identifying** According to the Constitution, what is the president's duty to Congress?

3. **Describing** As commander in chief, what responsibilities does the president have? Which is most important?

Critical Thinking

4. **Drawing Conclusions** Which of the roles of the president do you think is the most important? Least important? Why?

5. **BIG Ideas** In a web diagram like the one below, classify the roles filled by the president as leader of his or her party.

fund-raiser

Party Leader

CITIZENSHIP Activity

6. **Creative Writing** Imagine a typical day in the life of a United States president. Prepare an agenda for the president's day. Be sure to keep the duties of the president in mind when creating the agenda.

Civics ONLINE

Study Central™ To review this section, go to glencoe.com.

Answers

1. Sentences should use vocabulary words according to their definitions in the section and in the Glossary.

2. The president must give Congress information on the state of the union in several yearly addresses.

3. The president oversees the four major units of the military and makes the important decisions about where and when to deploy troops around the world.

4. Answers may include any of the roles discussed in the section, supported by the students' reasons.

5. The web should include these roles: fundraiser, speaker in support of candidates, supporter of legislation party members want, and maker of appointments that reflect party interests.

6. Agendas should follow a standard format, with times and activities listed chronologically, and should reflect students' understanding of the roles and responsibilities of the president.

Guide to Reading

Big Idea
Under our federal system, the executive, legislative, and judicial branches share the responsibility of governing the nation.

Content Vocabulary
- foreign policy *(p. 220)*
- national security *(p. 220)*
- treaty *(p. 222)*
- executive agreement *(p. 222)*
- ambassador *(p. 222)*
- trade sanction *(p. 223)*
- embargo *(p. 223)*

Academic Vocabulary
- method *(p. 222)*
- target *(p. 223)*

Reading Strategy
Comparing and Contrasting As you read, complete a graphic organizer like the one below showing the president's four goals in foreign policy.

Section Audio *Spotlight Video*

Making Foreign Policy

Real World Civics The president's long arm of foreign policy stretches around the world in the form of U.S. ambassadors. The president cannot be everywhere spreading good will. So he or she appoints ambassadors to major countries to maintain diplomatic relationships with other governments. Great Britain has been one of the United States's closest allies. Here, Prince Charles, accompanied by U.S. Ambassador William S. Farish, signs a book of condolences following the terrorist attacks on New York City and the Pentagon in 2001. Ambassadorships are often awarded to people for their hard work and support of the president.

▼ **Prince Charles of Wales signs Remembrance Book with U.S. Ambassador Farish in London**

219

Focus

Bellringer
Daily Focus Transparency 7–3

Guide to Reading
Answers to Graphic:

- promote democracy around the world
- promote national security
- **President**
- promote world peace
- promote international trade

Section Spotlight Video

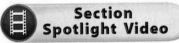

To generate student interest and provide a springboard for class discussion, access the Chapter 7, Section 3 video at glencoe.com or on the video DVD.

Resource Manager

Teach

S Skill Practice

Visual Literacy Tell students that the cartoon includes several allusions. Point out that its title, "Poseidon," refers to the Greek god of the sea, who caused storms and other oceanic events. It may also refer to disaster movies about doomed ships. Have students discuss the implications of these allusions and what effect the visual presentation of these allusions has on the viewer. **ELL BL**

D Differentiated Instruction

Visual/Spatial Have students develop a graphic organizer that shows how the four goals of foreign policy are interrelated and interdependent. **OL**

TIME™ Political Cartoons

Answers:

1. George W. Bush; he is holding a flag with a "W," his political nickname, on it.
2. the many problems that Bush's administration must confront
3. Bush's policies on immigration, Iraq, and gas prices have had a negative effect on his approval ratings.

Differentiated Instruction

Primary Source Reading 2-B, URB pp. 17–18

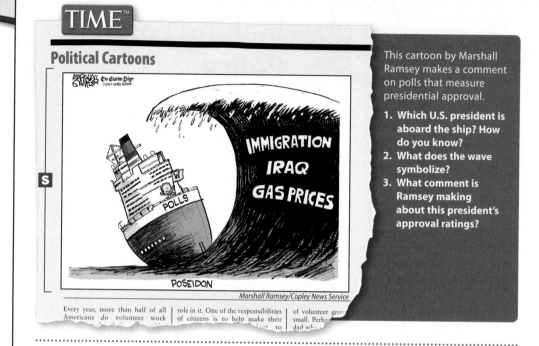

TIME™
Political Cartoons

This cartoon by Marshall Ramsey makes a comment on polls that measure presidential approval.

1. **Which U.S. president is aboard the ship? How do you know?**
2. **What does the wave symbolize?**
3. **What comment is Ramsey making about this president's approval ratings?**

Marshall Ramsey/Copley News Service

The President and Foreign Policy

Main Idea As commander in chief and chief diplomat, the president leads the nation's armed forces and directs U.S. foreign policy.

Civics & You Just as the president very often has to deal with people outside our country, you have to deal with people outside your family. Think about times when that has been a challenge for you. What did you do?

A nation's plan for dealing with other nations is called its **foreign policy.** The president directs the foreign policy of the United States, making the key decisions about the relations the United States has with other countries in the world. The primary goal of American foreign policy is **national security,** the ability to keep the country safe from attack or harm. This goal is vital. No government can effectively meet other important goals, such as better health care or cleaning up the environment, if the nation is under attack.

Another important goal is international trade. In today's economy, trade with other nations is vital to economic prosperity. Trade creates markets for American products and jobs for American workers.

A third goal is promoting world peace. Even a war far from the United States can disrupt trade and put national security at risk. When other nations are at peace, the United States runs no risk of being drawn into a foreign war.

A fourth goal of foreign policy is to promote democracy around the world. Promoting democracy and basic human rights in other countries encourages peace and thus helps protect our own national security.

220 Chapter 7

9/11 Commission Testimony

Objective: To understand how the federal government reviews its actions

Focus: Explain some features of transcripts: bracketed words, ellipses, dashes.

Teach: Have two students read the roles of Rice and Ben-Veniste.

Assess: Ask students to simplify Rice's answer to Ben-Veniste's question with one sentence.

Close: Discuss which speaker "won" this round of the testimony.

Differentiated Instruction Strategies

BL Tell what the F.B.I. is and what it does.

AL How is reading a transcript of testimony about an event different from reading a report about an event?

ELL Who speaks most in this excerpt? Who speaks least? Why do you think one speaker says much more than the other?

American Biography

Condoleezza Rice (1954–)

Condoleezza Rice juggles numbers of missiles and tanks as confidently as any general. An expert on Russia and arms control, Rice launched her foreign policy career while only a teenager.

Born in Birmingham, Alabama, Rice lived through the early years of the civil rights movement. While Rice was in junior high school, her father took a job in Denver, Colorado. There she skipped two grades and entered college at age 15. Rice had many interests and was not sure about a future career. As Rice shopped for a major, she sat in on a lecture about the former Soviet Union.

All the governmental maneuvers by the Communists fascinated her. Rice was hooked. A talented piano player, Rice once joked, "I was saved from [becoming] a music major by Russia."

Rice went on to earn a Ph.D. and by her late 20s was teaching political science at Stanford University in California. In 2001 President Bush appointed Rice as the first woman to head the National Security Council. In 2005 he appointed her to serve as Secretary of State. Rice became the first African American woman to hold that position. At her confirmation hearing, Rice stated "we must use American diplomacy to help create a balance of power in the world that favors freedom. And the time for diplomacy is now."

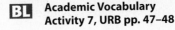

Making a Difference — CITIZENSHIP

What positions has Rice held in the federal government?

"I make American foreign policy," President Harry S. Truman declared in 1948. The president is indeed a very important foreign-policy decision maker. Americans and others throughout the world look to the president to represent our country in foreign affairs.

Foreign-Policy Bureaucracy The president, along with White House assistants, works with a large foreign-policy bureaucracy in the executive branch. This bureaucracy includes the State Department, the **R** Defense Department, the Central Intelligence Agency, and the National Security Council. These agencies assist the president in foreign affairs. They can carry out presidential decisions around the world and give the president valuable information. At the same time, presidents must make the final decision. President Harry S. Truman noted,

> "No one who has not had the responsibility can really understand what it is like to be President, not even his closest aides. . . . [H]e is never allowed to forget that he is President."
>
> —Harry S. Truman

Congress v. the President

The president is chief diplomat and commander in chief, but Congress has the power to declare war, to prohibit certain military **C** actions, and to spend—or withhold—money for defense. The Constitution does not clearly spell out how the legislative and the executive branches can use their powers. As a result, there has always been competition between Congress and the president over who controls foreign policy.

R Reading Strategy

Questioning Many people and groups gather information and advise the president on foreign affairs. **Ask:** What questions might readers ask to find out how these groups work toward the same goal? *(Answers may include questions about whether and how groups share information, what areas of expertise groups cover, and when and how the heads of each group report to the president.)* **OL**

C Critical Thinking

Predicting Ask: What might happen if a president wanted to send troops into a military action but Congress disagreed with the president's decision? Of what are these divided powers an example? *(Answers may include that both sides of the issue would reach a compromise, or Congress would refuse to fund the military action. This is an example of checks and balances.)* **AL**

For additional practice on this skill (Predicting), see the **Skills Handbook**.

American Biography

Answer:
Rice headed the National Security Council and served as Secretary of State.

Leveled Activities

BL Academic Vocabulary Activity 7, URB pp. 47–48

OL Biography Activity 7, URB pp. 49–50

AL Primary Source Reading 2B, URB pp. 17–18

ELL Reteaching Activity 7, URB p. 61

R **Reading Strategy**

Academic Vocabulary Ask: What is a "method"? *(A method is a way of doing something, a process or a series of steps to follow to accomplish something.)* **BL** **ELL**

D **Differentiated Instruction**

Advanced Learners Have students find out why the United States has refused to acknowledge and send ambassadors to certain countries at this time. Ask students to present this information to the class in a chart naming the unrecognized government and nation and the reason that the U.S. has withheld recognition. Students may also want to research examples of nations who have recently gained recognition. **AL**

Caption Answer:
When the president makes treaties, he or she deals directly or indirectly with leaders and representatives of other nations. He or she has the opportunity to generate goodwill and to benefit both the United States and other nations.

In this struggle, one branch or the other has controlled foreign policy at various times. After World War II, Congress lost much of its control over foreign policy to the president. Then, in the late 1960s and early 1970s, during the Vietnam conflict, Congress regained some of its war powers. In starting the American war on global terrorism in 2001, President George W. Bush tipped the balance back toward the presidency.

Tools of Foreign Policy

R The president and Congress have several approaches they can use to carry out American foreign policy. These **methods,** or procedures, include creating treaties; appointing ambassadors; and directing foreign aid, international trade, and military forces.

Treaties and Executive Agreements
Formal agreements between the governments of two or more countries are called **treaties.**

Some treaties are based on defense. One of the most important is the North Atlantic Treaty Organization (NATO), a mutual defense treaty between the United States, Canada, and the nations of Europe.

The Senate must approve a treaty by a two-thirds vote. However, the president can bypass the Senate by making an **executive agreement.** This is an agreement between the president and the leader of another country. Most agreements deal with fairly routine matters.

D **Appointing Ambassadors** An official representative of a country's government is an **ambassador.** The president appoints about 150 ambassadors, who must be confirmed by the Senate. Ambassadors are sent only to those countries where the United States recognizes, or accepts, the legal existence of the government. If the government of a certain country is thought to hold power illegally,

Teamwork President George W. Bush's advisers—namely his cabinet, who often met at his retreat, Camp David—helped him announce decisions about foreign policy. *Hypothesizing* Why is the president's power to make treaties through executive power an important part of his foreign policy powers?

222

Hands-On Chapter Project
Step 3

The Role of the Cabinet

Step 3: Determining which cabinet members can advise the president on the problem. Groups of students will investigate the areas of expertise of cabinet members and decide which should advise the president on the problem.

Directions Organize the class into five groups, and assign three cabinet departments to each group.

Interpersonal Have students use library books or online sources such as http://www.whitehouse.gov/government/cabinet.html to learn the area of expertise of each secretary and his or her department. Students should list the areas of national and international interest for which each secretary is responsible. Then the whole class should review the issue that students chose in Step 2. Ask the class to determine which secretaries should be assigned to gather information and then to advise the president on the problem. Students should be prepared to explain why they have included or excluded a secretary. **OL**

(Project continued in Section 4)

the president can refuse to recognize that government.

Foreign Aid Foreign aid is money, food, military assistance, or other supplies given to help other countries. One of this nation's greatest examples of foreign aid was the Marshall Plan, a program created to help restore Western Europe after World War II.

International Trade As the leader of a great economic power, the president can make agreements with other nations about what products may be traded and the rules for such trading. Sometimes trade measures include trade sanctions, or efforts to punish another nation by imposing trade barriers. Another punishing tool is the embargo, which is an agreement among a group of nations that prohibits them from trading with a target nation. Congress takes the lead in other areas, such as tariffs—taxes on imported goods—and membership in international trade groups, such as the North **W**

American Free Trade Agreement (NAFTA) and the World Trade Organization (WTO).

Military Force As commander in chief of the armed forces, presidents may use the military to carry out some foreign-policy decisions. Numerous times in the history of the United States, presidents have sent troops to troublesome spots on the globe, even though Congress had not declared war. This is a powerful tool of foreign policy, but one that must be used with great care. President George Washington summoned troops to put down the Whiskey Rebellion in 1794. President Bill Clinton ordered cruise missiles to be launched at terrorist facilities in Afghanistan and Sudan in 1998. In 2003 President George W. Bush ordered the American armed forces to invade Iraq and remove the nation's dictator Saddam Hussein.

✓ **Reading Check** **Concluding** What foreign policy tools does the president have to deal with international terrorism?

Section 3 Review

Vocabulary

1. **Define** the following terms and use them in sentences related to U.S. foreign policy: *foreign policy, national security, treaty, executive agreement, ambassador, trade sanction, embargo.*

Main Ideas

2. **Describing** In what way is the president the country's chief diplomat? What duties does this include?

3. **Defining** Why are trade sanctions and embargoes considered tools of foreign policy?

Critical Thinking

4. **Analyzing** Should Congress or the president have more power in conducting foreign affairs? Explain your answer.

5. **BIG Ideas** Compare and contrast the responsibilities and roles of the president and Congress on a chart like the one below.

Foreign Policy	
President	Congress

CITIZENSHIP Activity

6. **Expository Writing** Interview several adults, all of whom have different jobs, about the North American Free Trade Agreement (NAFTA). Find out why they think it is good or bad foreign policy. Share your results in an essay.

Civics ONLINE

Study Central™ To review this section, go to glencoe.com.

W **Writing Support**

Expository Writing You may wish to provide a brief history of NAFTA for students who are not aware of it. Information can be found at http://www.law.duke.edu/lib/researchguides/nafta.html. Have students write a paragraph describing the main reason NAFTA came about. **OL**

✓ **Reading Check** **Answer:** Presidents can issue trade sanctions, embargoes, and tariffs; reward nations who work against terrorism with foreign aid; and can take military action.

Assess

Civics ONLINE

Study Central™ provides summaries, interactive games, and online graphic organizers to help students review.

Close

Predicting Consequences Have students discuss how legislation and foreign policy are different when both the president and Congress belong to the same party and when they do not. **OL**

Section 3 Review

Answers

1. Definitions for the vocabulary words are found in the section and in the Glossary.

2. He or she appoints ambassadors to foreign nations, makes treaties with other nations, and may offer aid to needy nations.

3. They are used against nations considered dangerous to the United States. They are intended to pressure the nation into changing its policies.

4. Answers may show a preference for Congressional or presidential power or a preference for a balance of power; answers should

be supported with reasons.

5. **President:** chief diplomat; commander in chief with power to send troops; chief shaper of foreign policy

   Congress: checks presidential power to appoint officials and ambassadors; has power to declare war and to fund military action; advises on foreign policy

6. Student essays should show a basic understanding of NAFTA and include the accurate opinions of several adults.

Focus

Bellringer
Daily Focus Transparency 7–4

Guide to Reading
Answers to Graphic:

President's Cabinet	
No. of Depts.	15
Dept. Head's Role	inform president on issues
Newest Dept.	Homeland Security
Cabinet Meets When	whenever president determines the need

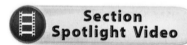

Section Spotlight Video

Have students watch the Chapter 7, Section 4 video at glencoe.com.

Resource Manager

Guide to Reading

Big Idea
The Constitution gives the executive branch the power to execute, or implement, the law.

Content Vocabulary
- cabinet *(p. 226)*
- federal bureaucracy *(p. 228)*
- independent agency *(p. 229)*
- government corporation *(p. 229)*
- political appointee *(p. 229)*
- civil service worker *(p. 229)*
- civil service system *(p. 229)*
- spoils system *(p. 230)*
- merit system *(p. 230)*

Academic Vocabulary
- monitor *(p. 225)*
- role *(p. 225)*

Reading Strategy
Categorizing As you read, complete a chart similar to the one below to categorize information about the president's cabinet.

President's Cabinet	
No. of Depts.	
Dept. Head's Role	
Newest Dept.	
Cabinet Meets When	

Section 4

Presidential Advisers and Executive Agencies

Real World Civics What is the proper role of the First Lady? At one time, the spouse of the president served as a ceremonial hostess at White House events. Eleanor Roosevelt changed all that when she became active in political causes during her husband's presidencies in the 1940s. Jacqueline Kennedy, Lady Bird Johnson, Rosalynn Carter and Barbara Bush continued to revolutionize the role of the First Lady. Here President George H.W. Bush celebrates Thanksgiving with the U.S. Marines in Saudi Arabia during the Persian Gulf War in 1990. Now, First Ladies are seen as advisers to their husbands, as well as having their own agendas as public figures.

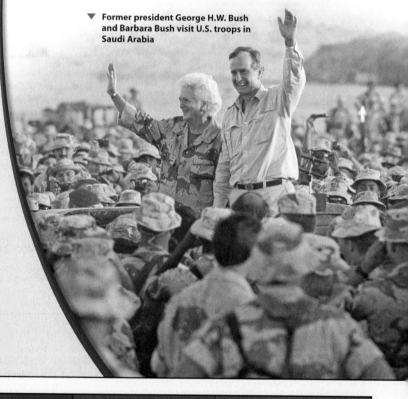

▼ Former president George H.W. Bush and Barbara Bush visit U.S. troops in Saudi Arabia

---

R Reading Strategies	**C** Critical Thinking	**D** Differentiated Instruction	**W** Writing Support	**S** Skill Practice
Teacher Edition • Using Word Parts, p. 226 • Making Connections, p. 229 • Using Context Clues, p. 230 **Additional Resources** • Cont. Vocab., URB p. 46 • Ac. Voc., URB p. 48 • Guid. Read., URB p. 66	**Teacher Edition** • Making Inferences, p. 225 • Det. Cause/Effect, p. 227 • Drawing Con., p. 228 • Making Comparisons, p. 229 **Additional Resources** • Biography Act., URB p. 49 • Quizzes and Tests, p. 79	**Teacher Edition** • ELL, pp. 225, 228 **Additional Resources** • Econ. Act., URB p. 5 • Reteach. Act., URB p. 61	**Teacher Edition** • Expository Writing, p. 229 **Additional Resources** • Enrich. Act., URB p. 13	**Teacher Edition** • Analyzing Charts, pp. 226, 227 **Additional Resources** • Daily Focus Trans., 7–4

Organization of the Federal Branch

Main Idea The executive branch is made up of the top advisers and assistants who help the president carry out major duties.

Civics & You The executive branch has grown tremendously over the years. What advantages and disadvantages can you see in having a large executive staff?

The executive branch is organized like a pyramid. The president, as chief executive, is at the very top of the pyramid. Directly below the president are a number of powerful officials, usually handpicked by the president. Below these are many levels of lesser officials and managers. In general, the people at the top of the pyramid are the ones who set goals and make important decisions.

In 1801 President Thomas Jefferson did his job with the help of a few advisers, a messenger, and a part-time secretary. Today thousands of highly trained specialists, secretaries, and clerks assist the president. Most of these people work in the Executive Office of the President (EOP). These people are often referred to as a president's administration.

Franklin D. Roosevelt's administration created the EOP in 1939 to help the president do his job. The office has been growing ever since. Currently it has about 2,000 employees and a budget of more than $100 million.

The Executive Office

The core of the Executive Office of the President is the White House Office, which is comprised of about 500 people who work directly for the president. Among them are 10 to 12 people who serve as the president's closest political advisers. The most powerful among this group is the chief of staff. Other top advisers are the deputy chief of staff and the press secretary. (The press secretary pro- vides the public with news about and statements from the president.) As a group, such advisers make up the White House staff.

Management and Budget

The Office of Management and Budget (OMB) prepares the federal budget and **monitors,** or oversees, spending in hundreds of government agencies. The director of the OMB works closely with the president. The federal budget is the clearest statement of the administration's plans and goals for the coming year.

National Security Council (NSC)

The National Security Council (NSC) helps the president direct United States military and foreign policy. It handles matters affecting the security of the country. It includes the vice president, the secretaries of state and defense, and the chairman of the Joint Chiefs of Staff, which includes the top commander from each of the armed services. The National Security Advisor heads the NSC. The NSC also super- vises the Central Intelligence Agency (CIA), which gathers information about the govern- ments of other countries.

Other Offices

The Office of Administration provides administrative services to the executive offices of the president. The Office also responds to individuals who are seeking records under the Freedom of Information Act.

The Council of Economic Advisers (CEA) helps the president carry out the **role,** or position, of economic leader. The president names the CEA's members, and the Senate approves them. The CEA's primary duty involves giving the president advice about complex economic matters such as employ- ment, inflation, and foreign trade.

Reading Check Identifying What are the duties of a president's press secretary?

Teach

D Differentiated Instruction

English Learners Explain that the idiom "hand-picked" means "chosen individually and personally." Help students remember the idiom by explaining that it is a meta- phor comparing choosing officials to picking only the best fruits, one at a time, from a tree or a vine. **ELL**

C Critical Thinking

Making Inferences Ask: Why might the president need information about other countries' governments? *(Answers may include that other governments, seeking to forward their own agendas and to benefit their own people, might act in ways detri- mental to the United States.)* **AL**

Reading Check **Answer:** provides the public with news about and state- ments from the president

Differentiated Instruction

225

Biography Activity 7, URB pp. 49–50

Tom Ridge

Objective: To identify events that led to Tom Ridge becom- ing the first Secretary of Homeland Security

Focus: Discuss organizations that investigate attacks against America.

Teach: Underline examples of the challenges of Ridge's work.

Assess: Characterize Ridge based on the three quotes in the biography.

Close: Write a paragraph about how changes in national security affect you.

Differentiated Instruction Strategies

BL How long did Ridge serve as Secre- tary of Homeland Security?

AL What does Ridge's comment on leav- ing office suggest about his service as Secretary of Homeland Security?

ELL What is the president's cabinet, and how do the cabinet secretaries aid the president?

225

R Reading Strategy

Using Word Parts Draw students' attention to the words "coordinate" and "counterterrorism" in this challenging sentence. **Ask:** What prefix begins each word, and what does each prefix mean? *("Co-" begins the first word and means "with or together." "Counter-" begins the second word and means "against.")* Then guide students in developing definitions for each word by adding the prefix meaning to the root. **BL**

S Skill Practice

Analyzing Charts Ask: What do the longer brackets above each row of offices indicate? *(They indicate that these offices are on the same level and often work together.)* **OL**

Analyzing Charts

Answers:
1. the Office of the United States Trade Representative
2. The National Security Council, the Foreign Intelligence Advisory Board

The Cabinet

Main Idea The cabinet is an advisory group chosen by the president to help accomplish the work of the executive branch.

Civics & You Some presidents have followed their cabinets' opinion on many matters. Other presidents have not. Do you think strong presidents rely more or less on their cabinets' advice?

The EOP is only a small part of the president's administration. Many more people work in the cabinet. The **cabinet** is a group of presidential advisers that includes the heads of the 15 top-level executive departments. The head of the Department of Justice is called the attorney general; all the other department heads are called secretaries. The president may also ask the vice president and other top officials to join the cabinet.

Department of Homeland Security

On November 25, 2002, President Bush signed the Homeland Security Act of 2002. The act created the Department of Homeland Security to improve the nation's defenses against terrorism and coordinate counterterrorism intelligence. It is the first new department established since the Department of Veterans Affairs was created in 1989.

Cabinet Responsibilities

As cabinet members, the secretaries advise the president on issues related to their departments. The secretary of agriculture, for instance, might keep the president and White

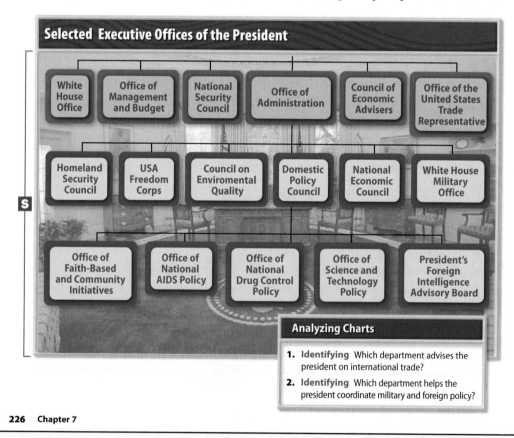

Selected Executive Offices of the President

- White House Office
- Office of Management and Budget
- National Security Council
- Office of Administration
- Council of Economic Advisers
- Office of the United States Trade Representative
- Homeland Security Council
- USA Freedom Corps
- Council on Enviromental Quality
- Domestic Policy Council
- National Economic Council
- White House Military Office
- Office of Faith-Based and Community Initiatives
- Office of National AIDS Policy
- Office of National Drug Control Policy
- Office of Science and Technology Policy
- President's Foreign Intelligence Advisory Board

Analyzing Charts

1. **Identifying** Which department advises the president on international trade?
2. **Identifying** Which department helps the president coordinate military and foreign policy?

Differentiated Instruction

Leveled Activities

BL Guided Reading Activity 7-4, URB p. 66

OL Economics Activity 2, URB pp. 5–6

AL Enrichment Activity 2, URB pp. 13–14

ELL Content Vocabulary Activity 7, URB p. 46

The President's Cabinet

Department of State (1789)
Plans and carries out the nation's foreign policy
Department of the Treasury (1789)
Collects, borrows, spends, and prints money
Department of Defense (1789 as War Department; renamed in 1949)
Manages the armed forces
Department of Justice (1870)
Responsible for all aspects of law enforcement
Department of the Interior (1849)
Manages and protects nation's public lands and natural resources
Department of Agriculture (1889)
Assists farmers and consumers of farm products
Department of Commerce (1903)
Supervises trade, promotes U.S. business, tourism
Department of Labor (1913)
Deals with working conditions, wages of U.S. workers

Department of Health and Human Services (1953)
Works for the well-being and health of all Americans
Department of Housing and Urban Development (1965)
Deals with the special needs and problems of cities
Department of Transportation (1966)
Manages nation's highways, railroads, airlines, and sea traffic
Department of Energy (1977)
Directs overall energy plan for the nation
Department of Education (1979)
Provides advice and funding for schools
Department of Veterans Affairs (1989)
Directs services for armed forces veterans
Department of Homeland Security (2002)
Oversees America's defenses against terrorist attacks

Analyzing Charts

1. **Identifying** Which department manages public lands? In what year was this department created?

2. **Analyzing** Why might the president call on the secretary of transportation to deal with drug smuggling along the Pacific coast?

House staff informed about matters of concern to American farmers. Cabinet secretaries often make important policy decisions.

No mention of the cabinet appears in the Constitution. Instead, this body developed when George Washington began to meet regularly with the heads of the first four executive departments. These were the attorney general and the secretaries of state, war, and the treasury.

The cabinet meets whenever the president determines that it is necessary. This may be as often as once a week or hardly at all. Many presidents have not relied heavily on their cabinets and have felt free to ignore cabinet advice. As heads of executive agencies, these department secretaries must spend most of their time coordinating those departments' activities. Department heads of the cabinet must be approved by the Senate.

227

C Critical Thinking

Determining Cause and Effect Ask: Why is the date that the Department of Housing and Urban Development (HUD) was created important? *(It was created during the time of the civil rights movement and it began with a focus on developing minority housing and guarding minority housing rights.)* **AL**

S Skill Practice

Analyzing Charts Ask: What strategy was used to organize this chart, and how does this strategy help readers? *(The chart is arranged chronologically, from the department first created in 1789, to the most recently created department in 2002. This strategy helps readers understand how the cabinet developed over more than two centuries.)* **OL**

Analyzing Charts

Answers:

1. The Department of the Interior manages public lands and was created in 1849.

2. This secretary manages traffic at sea, including illegal traffic.

Hands-On Chapter Project
Step 4

The Role of the Cabinet

Step 4: Producing a Memo to the Cabinet Students will create a memo calling for investigation of the problem.

Directions Tell students that in this step, they will compose a memo from the president's personal secretary to the cabinet secretaries whose areas of expertise will help the president address the problem.

Personal Writing Guide students to create a memo from the president's secretary to the cabinet secretaries, who advise the president to address the problem. Ask students to decide on a task to assign each secretary, in line with his or her area of expertise. Have students include an action plan in the memo, stating the steps to fix the problem. **OL**

(Project continued on the Visual Summary page)

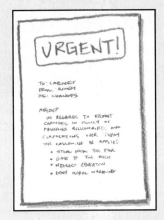

C Critical Thinking

Drawing Conclusions Ask: If vice presidents have historically had little authority, why is the office important to voters and to the nation? *(Answers may include the idea that the vice president will assume presidential duties in the event of the president's death or incapacitation.)* **OL**

D Differentiated Instruction

English Learners Draw students' attention to the woman in the photograph. Explain that her raised right hand signifies her willingness to pledge truthfully and that her left hand rests on a Bible to signify her honesty. Ask students to describe similar ceremonies in their home cultures. **ELL**

✔Reading Check Answer: The cabinet meets whenever the president finds it necessary to hear the advice of the secretaries.

Caption Answer:
Such people are not merely employees but civil servants who have undertaken to work for the national good.

Additional Support

Teacher Tip

This activity requires students to access the Internet. Supervise access, directing students to government-run sites appropriate to the activity. Preteach the words "résumé," "qualification," "application," and "references" before students begin the exercise.

Vice President and First Lady

Most presidents have delegated little authority to their vice presidents. Recently, however, some have tried to give their vice presidents more responsibility. Vice President Al Gore, for example, served as a close adviser to President Bill Clinton on environmental issues, and Vice President Dick Cheney advised President George W. Bush closely on foreign policy issues.

The Constitution does not mention the spouse of a president. First Ladies, though, have served the country in many ways. Eleanor Roosevelt worked tirelessly for the young and the disadvantaged. Nancy Reagan spoke out for drug abuse prevention, Hillary Clinton worked to improve health care for all Americans, and Laura Bush promoted education and reading. Today First Ladies have an office in the White House.

✔Reading Check Stating When does the cabinet meet?

The Federal Bureaucracy

Main Idea The federal bureaucracy has grown over the years and assumes an important role in making public policy.

Civics & You With every new administration, new people are named to hold positions within the federal bureaucracy. Why might it be a problem for new people to always be taking these jobs?

Below the cabinet departments are hundreds of agencies that deal with everything from setting standards for the hot dogs you eat to running the space shuttle program. About 3 million civilians work in these many departments and agencies. Taken together, the agencies and employees of the executive branch are often called the **federal bureaucracy.** The people who work for these organizations are called bureaucrats, or civil servants.

Federal Staffing President Bush watches as Trade Representative Susan Schwab is sworn into office as a new member of the federal civil servant corps. *Explaining* Why do you think such position holders are sworn in rather than simply hired like other government workers?

228

Activity: Technology Connection

Applications What does it take to become a bureaucrat, or civil servant, and what kinds of jobs do bureaucrats do? Have students research civil service careers at http://www.usajobs.gov/. Guide students to choose a job they are interested in and to find out what qualifications they would need as young adults applying for that job. Provide students with a simple job application form to practice filling out. Discuss the importance of beginning to gather references, knowledge, and experience as soon as possible. **OL**

The Bureaucracy in Action

The executive branch of government must carry out the many programs that Congress has created to serve the American people. Executive departments and agencies do this by performing three basic jobs. First, they turn new laws into action by deciding how to apply the laws to daily life. When Congress writes new laws, it often uses very general language. Federal agencies then must develop specific rules and procedures to put the laws into practice.

Second, departments and agencies administer the day-to-day operations of the federal government. Agencies deliver the mail, collect taxes, send out Social Security checks, and perform thousands of other services.

Regulatory Functions Third, with authority from Congress, federal agencies regulate various activities. They regulate, or police, the activities of broadcasting companies, labor unions, banks, airlines, nuclear power plants, and many other enterprises and organizations.

In doing these jobs, federal agencies help shape government policy. By deciding how to run a government program or what to do in a certain situation, federal agencies often determine what government policy will be.

Independent Agencies

The executive branch includes hundreds of **independent agencies.** They are called independent because they are not part of the cabinet. In general, however, these agencies can be divided into three types: executive agencies, government corporations, and regulatory commissions.

Executive Agencies These are independent agencies responsible for dealing with certain specialized areas within the government. The National Aeronautics and Space Administration (NASA) is an example. It operates the United States space program.

Government Corporations More than 50 independent agencies are **government corporations.** These are like private businesses, except that the government rather than individuals owns and operates them. With Senate approval, the president chooses a board of directors and a general manager to run each corporation. Like private businesses, these corporations charge fees for their services and products, but they are not supposed to make a profit. The United States Postal Service, for example, is a government corporation.

Regulatory Boards and Commissions These units differ from other independent agencies. They do not have to report to the president, who appoints the members but cannot fire them. Only Congress can remove them through impeachment.

Regulatory commissions are supposed to protect the public. They make and enforce rules for certain industries or groups. For instance, the Federal Communications Commission (FCC) makes broadcasting rules for the nation's television and radio stations.

Government Workers

Every executive department has thousands of employees. The top leadership jobs generally go to **political appointees**—people whom the president has chosen because they have proven executive ability or were important supporters of the president's election campaign. Their employment usually ends when the president leaves office.

About 90 percent of all national government employees are **civil service workers.** Unlike political appointees, civil service workers usually have permanent employment. These are people, ranging from clerks to doctors and lawyers, employed by the federal government through the **civil service system**—the practice of hiring government workers on the basis of open, competitive examinations and merit.

W Writing Support

Expository Writing Ask students to write about what they think could happen if the government didn't place any emphasis on regulating businesses. *(Students may include the idea that consistency is helpful for interstate and international businesses and that, if unregulated, some businesses would cease to be vigilant about issues of quality and safety.)* **OL**

R Reading Strategy

Making Connections Make sure that students remember what impeachment is. **Ask:** What does it mean to impeach someone? *(It means to charge that person with misconduct in office and to prove this charge in court, resulting in the person's removal from that office.)* **OL**

C Critical Thinking

Making Comparisons Ask: What are the two reasons that political appointees receive their jobs? Which reason, in your opinion, is the sounder reason to hire someone into a position? *(Appointees receive their jobs because they have proven executive abilities or because they supported the president's election campaign strongly. Opinions as to which reason is sounder will vary but should be supported.)* **AL**

For additional practice on this skill (Making Comparisons), see the **Skills Handbook**.

Did You Know?

Funding the Government Every federal department, office, and agency requires funds to operate. Congress must design a budget that will divide the tax dollars, and the president must sign the budget. If the government overspends its revenue (income from taxes), the budget is in deficit. If the government does not use all its revenue, the budget may have a surplus.

Occasionally Congress and the executive branch cannot agree on how much money to allocate to each office, department, or agency. When a compromise cannot be reached, the previous year's budget may be extended for days or weeks by a temporary spending bill. In a few instances, disagreement on how to spend the nation's revenue has been so intense that no budget was

approved or extended, and many nonessential federal groups had to shut down for a day or two. This happened, for example, in November 1995, when about 800,000 federal employees nationwide were briefly "off work."

R Reading Strategy

Using Context Clues Ask: Based on the paragraph, what must people in a merit system do to succeed and advance? *(They must perform well, meet or surpass standards, and have skills and abilities suited to their jobs.)* **OL**

✓ **Reading Check Answer:** to protect the public by making and enforcing rules for certain industries and groups

Assess

Civics ONLINE

Study Central™ provides summaries, interactive games, and online graphic organizers to help students review content.

Close

Analyzing Text Structure Remind students that the executive branch is organized in a pyramid shape with the president at the top. Then ask them to discuss how the order of sections in this chapter helps them understand the pyramid shape of the executive branch. **OL**

Section ⭐ 4 Review

Development of the Civil Service System

Originally, the executive branch was small enough for presidents to be able to choose most of their employees personally. Early presidents tried to appoint the most qualified people to federal jobs. They also, however, tended to appoint members of their own party, who shared similar views.

The Spoils System Before 1883 a great many federal jobs fell under the **spoils system.** In this system, government jobs went to people as a reward for their political support. Each newly elected president would sweep out most of the old federal workers and replace them with his own political supporters and friends. The idea was "To the victor belong the spoils [jobs]." Public dissatisfaction with abuses of the spoils system, and public outrage over the assassination of President James Garfield in 1881 by a man who was refused a job under the system, led Congress to pass the Pendleton Act.

The Merit System The Pendleton Act, also known as the Civil Service Reform Act of 1883, created the civil service system and placed limits on the number of jobs a new president could hand out to friends and backers. The Office of Personnel Management (OPM) directs the civil service system today. It sets standards for federal jobs, and it gives demanding written tests to people who want those jobs. The civil service system is a **merit system.** Government officials hire new workers from lists of people who have passed the tests or otherwise met civil service standards.

✓ **Reading Check Describing** What is the purpose of regulatory commissions?

Section **Review**
4

Vocabulary

1. Write complete sentences related to the federal government using the following vocabulary terms: *cabinet, federal bureaucracy, independent agency, government corporation, political appointee, civil service worker, civil service system, spoils system, merit system.*

Main Ideas

2. Discuss the role of the Office of Management and Budget.

3. Describing Name three cabinet departments and describe their main duties.

4. Comparing Why has the federal bureaucracy grown over the years?

Critical Thinking

5. Making Inferences What part of the EOP do you think is the most important? Why?

6. BIG Ideas In the Venn diagram below, compare and contrast the types of workers employed by the federal government under the civil service system and those who are political employees.

Civil Service — Both — Political Employees

7. Analyzing Visuals Review the cabinet departments of the executive branch on page 227. Why are there so many cabinet departments under the president of the United States?

CITIZENSHIP Activity

8. Creative Writing Imagine that you are on a presidential commission looking into establishing a new executive department. Decide on an important issue facing the country today. Think of a new executive department to deal with this issue. Present your suggestion in a one-page report.

Civics ONLINE

Study Central™ To review this section, go to glencoe.com.

Answers

1. Sentences should use vocabulary words according to their definitions in the section and in the Glossary.

2. It works closely with the president to prepare the federal budget and monitors federal spending.

3. Answers may include the names of any of the fifteen cabinet departments and brief descriptions of their main duties.

4. The nation and its needs have grown in number and complexity.

5. Answers may include any group within the EOP as long as reasons are given for that group's importance.

6. Civil Service: jobs are gained through competition and merit; jobs make up about 90 percent of federal employment; jobs are longer-lived

Political Employees: jobs may be gained through merit or through support of president; jobs are shorter-lived

Both: jobs are paid by the federal budget; jobs involve carrying out government tasks

7. Each cabinet department deals with a different national need and requires special expertise.

8. Students' reports should use formal language, identify an unaddressed or inadequately addressed need, suggest a department to meet that need, and provide reasons for establishing the department.

Visual Summary

The Presidency

- The president is head of the executive branch of the federal government and is our nation's top political leader.

- The source for the president's authority is Article II of the Constitution, which says that "the executive power shall be vested in the president of the United States of America."

John F. Kennedy, 1940 Harvard yearbook

Electing the President

- Presidents are elected through an indirect method called the Electoral College.

Responsibilities

- According to the Constitution, the president's main job is to carry out the laws passed by Congress.

- As head of the executive branch of government, the president must make decisions that affect the lives of all Americans.

Roles of the President

In carrying out the responsibilities of the office, the president must play a number of different roles. These roles are:

- Chief executive
- Chief diplomat
- Commander in chief
- Legislative leader
- Head of state
- Economic leader
- Party leader

President Lyndon B. Johnson

Tools of Foreign Policy

The president and Congress use many tools to carry out American foreign policy. These tools include:

- Treaties and executive agreements
- Appointing ambassadors
- Foreign aid
- International trade
- Military force

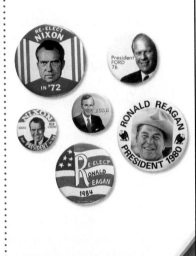

President's official helicopter

Organization of the Federal Government

- President
- Vice president
- Executive Office of the President
- Executive departments
- Federal bureaucracy

STUDY TO GO Study anywhere, anytime! Download quizzes and flash cards to your PDA from glencoe.com.

231

Visual Summary 7

Finding the Main Idea Ask: Who is the single most important elected official in the country, and why? *(The president is the most important elected official because of his or her position as the living symbol of the nation and his or her many roles and responsibilities within the executive branch.)* **BL**

This **Reading Skill** (Finding the Main Idea) was introduced in this unit.

Analyzing Visuals Ask: Look at the images on the page. What do they tell you about the history of the office of the president of the United States through the 2004 election? *(They make it clear that through that election, only white men have been elected to the office.)* **OL**

Hands-On Chapter Project
Step 5: Wrap-Up

The Role of the Cabinet

Step 5: Extending the Project Students will find out who currently heads each cabinet department and consider playing the role of secretary.

Directions Remind students that each president appoints a cabinet and that cabinet members may retire during a president's term. Thus, the makeup of the cabinet shifts often. Have students return to the Web sites they have used in the project to see who is currently serving on the cabinet.

Analyzing Information Challenge interested students to complete the memos in Step 4 by taking on the roles of the secretaries whose advice is needed. Small groups of students can research the issue from the points of view of relevant departments. Students can then hold a mock cabinet meeting, in which one student plays the role of the president and others the roles of the secretaries offering their expertise and research. **OL**

1. B Review the definition of each term with students. Point out the shared roots of "electing" and "Electoral."

2. C Options A and B are distractors because they refer to a president's power to grant freedom for a punishment. Option C, a reprieve, refers to the president's ability to delay a sentence until a higher court can hear the case. This is the correct answer.

3. A All of the incorrect answers relate to the correct answer. Point out to students that B is a goal of foreign policy, C is a tool of foreign policy, and D includes people working to carry out foreign policy. All belong under the heading Foreign Policy.

4. B Encourage students to think about how many people are employed as cabinet members (15), as ambassadors (one per nation), or as political appointees (presidential favorites). Students may recall the statistic that about 90 percent of federal employees are civil service workers.

Reviewing Main Ideas

5. C Ask students to recall how the terms of Washington and Lincoln ended (in retirement after two terms and in assassination during the second term). Remind them that by the time George W. Bush became president, presidents could serve only two terms.

6. D Students may confuse their answer with the Twenty-second Amendment, which limits the terms a president may serve. Help students distinguish between the similar Twenty-second and Twenty-fifth Amendments.

7. B Option A is a power reserved to Congress. Option C denies the interaction of the three branches of government. Option D is a power reserved to the Supreme Court. Only Option A is the president's constitutional power.

TEST-TAKING TIP

When taking a test, watch for *usually, never, most,* and other qualifying words that indicate under what circumstances an answer is correct.

Reviewing Vocabulary

Directions: Choose the word(s) that best completes the sentence.

1. The Constitution provides an indirect method of electing a president called the _____.

  A merit system   **C** spoils system

  B Electoral College   **D** executive agreement

2. The president can delay the punishment of a person by issuing a (n) _____.

  A pardon   **C** reprieve

  B amnesty   **D** executive order

3. The nation's plan for dealing with other nations is called its _____.

  A foreign policy   **C** trade sanctions

  B national security   **D** federal bureaucracy

4. Most national government employees are _____.

  A ambassadors   **C** cabinet members

  B civil service workers   **D** political appointees

Reviewing Main Ideas

Directions: Choose the best answer for each question.

Section 1 *(pp. 208–213)*

5. Which president was elected to four terms?

  A George Washington

  B Abraham Lincoln

  C Franklin Roosevelt

  D George W. Bush

6. Why was the Twenty-fifth Amendment passed?

  A to create the Electoral College

  B to limit presidents to two terms

  C to establish the order of presidential succession

  D to clarify when a vice president becomes president

Section 2 *(pp. 214–218)*

7. Which of the following powers does the Constitution give the president?

  A to declare war on other nations

  B to appoint judges to federal courts

  C to ignore laws passed by Congress

  D to strike down unconstitutional laws

8. How does a president fulfill the role of economic leader?

  A by planning the federal budget

  B by meeting with foreign leaders

  C by raising funds for his or her party

  D by proposing legislation to Congress

Section 3 *(pp. 219–223)*

9. Which of the following is NOT a primary goal of American foreign policy?

  A world peace

  B national security

  C better health care

  D international trade

Section 4 *(pp. 224–230)*

10. What part of the Executive Office of the President supervises the Central Intelligence Agency?

  A Office of Administration

  B National Security Council

  C Council of Economic Advisers

  D Office of Management and Budget

11. What is the responsibility of the Department of the Interior?

  A school funding

  B natural resources

  C problems of cities

  D trade, business, and tourism   **GO ON ►**

8. A Ask students in what way Options B, C, and D could benefit the nation's economy. These options may or may not deal with finances, but only Option A is a role that directly impacts the national economy.

9. C Remind students of the graphic organizer they completed. Point out that three of the goals listed here are sweeping goals affecting many nations. One, Option C, is very specific and is a national policy matter, not a goal of foreign policy.

10. B Remind students that the CIA gathers information about other nations' governments in order to keep the United States safe. Ask them which option uses a word that means "safe" or "safety." In addition, answers A, C, and D all deal with organizational, clerical, scheduling, and mostly financial matters outside the realm of safety or security for the nation.

Critical Thinking

Directions: Choose the best answer for each question.

Base your answers to questions 12 and 13 on the chart below and your knowledge of Chapter 7.

Order of Succession

1 Vice President
2 Speaker of the House
3 President *pro tempore* of the Senate
4 Secretary of State
5 Secretary of the Treasury
6 Secretary of Defense
7 Attorney General
8 Secretary of the Interior
9 Secretary of Agriculture
10 Secretary of Commerce
11 Secretary of Labor
12 Secretary of Health and Human Services
13 Secretary of Housing and Urban Development
14 Secretary of Transportation
15 Secretary of Energy
16 Secretary of Education
17 Secretary of Veterans Affairs
18 Secretary of Homeland Security

12. How many office holders listed on the chart are elected officials?

  A none   **B** one

  C three   **D** eighteen

13. The offices in the line of succession are ordered according to the dates they were created. What would it take to change that order?

  A an executive order

  B a law passed by Congress

  C a Supreme Court decision

  D a Constitutional Amendment

Document-Based Questions

Directions: Analyze the following document and answer the short-answer questions that follow.

The passage below is from George Washington's Farewell Address given at his retirement.

> *Observe good faith and justice toward all nations. Cultivate peace and harmony with all. . . .*
>
> *In the execution of such a plan, nothing is more essential than that permanent, inveterate antipathies [deep-rooted hatred] against particular nations and passionate attachments for others should be excluded, and that in place of them just and amicable feelings toward all should be cultivated. . . .*
>
> —George Washington, "Washington Bids Farewell"

14. Which role of the president does Washington discuss in the passage?

15. Which member of the cabinet would most likely assist Washington's successor in achieving the goals described in the passage?

Extended Response

16. Which do you think is the most effective foreign diplomacy tool: foreign aid, trade sanctions, or military force? Write a brief essay giving reasons for your choice.

STOP

Civics ONLINE
For additional test practice, use Self-Check Quizzes—Chapter 7 on glencoe.com.

Need Extra Help?

If you missed question. . .	1	2	3	4	5	6	7	8	9	10	11	12	13	14	15	16
Go to page. . .	210	217	220	229	212	213	215	218	220	225	227	227	213	216	216	222

ASSESSMENT

13. B In 1947 Congress passed the Presidential Succession Act, which set the line of succession to the presidency. Because Congress created this act, it is reasonable to assume that they can change it.

Document-Based Questions

14. Chief diplomat; Washington talks about "Cultivating peace and harmony with all. . ." as part of his advice as he leaves office.

15. The secretary of state; Washington continues to talk about the need to get along with all nations, which is the realm of the secretary of state.

Extended Response

16. Students' essays will vary but must include supporting examples from the chapter.

---

11. B Remind students that in this use, "interior" means the land contained within the United States, with all its resources, both above- and belowground.

Critical Thinking

12. C Although each president is allowed to choose his or her advisors, the vice president and two members of Congress—the Speaker of the House and the president pro tempore of the Senate—are elected.

Civics ONLINE

Have students visit the Web site at glencoe.com to review Chapter 7 and take the **Self-Check Quiz**.

Need Extra Help?

Have students refer to the pages listed if they miss any of the questions.

Teach

C Critical Thinking

Analyzing Primary Sources Ask: What do Ford's and Truman's quotes reveal about life in the White House? *(Ford's remark reminds readers that life in the White House is paid for by taxes and that the White House is home only temporarily to any family. Truman's remark implies that at times a president may wish to escape the challenging and exhausting duties and decisions of the presidency but that such escape is not possible.)* **OL**

For additional practice on this skill (Analyzing Primary Sources), see the **Skills Handbook**.

R Reading Strategy

Making Connections Ask: What advantage to citizens across the nation is there in spending more than $1 million to build a scale model of the White House? *(The model can be taken around the nation so that people who will never travel to Washington, D.C., to visit the actual White House can enjoy the beauty of this national treasure.)* **OL**

Additional Support

TIME
REPORTS

The White House

An intricate model takes visitors behind the scenes at 1600 Pennsylvania Avenue

C Described by former President Gerald Ford as "the best public housing in the world" and by former President Harry S. Truman as a "glamorous prison," the White House was first occupied by President John Adams in 1800. Two centuries later, the White House is a village of 6,000 busy souls: On a typical day, the President and First Lady, journalists, cooks, cops, gardeners, and tourists operate in harmony on 18 acres.

In 1962, John and Jan Zweifel of Orlando, Florida, set out to bring the White House to the American people by constructing the detailed model shown at right. Except for the location of the library, which was pushed forward for show purposes, the Zweifels' White House is a faithful recreation of the original, down to TVs, furniture, and paintings. The Zweifels contact the White House every few weeks to find out if anything has changed. The 60-foot by 20-foot, **R** 10-ton model, which includes the East and West wings (not shown), took more than 500,000 hours to construct and cost more than $1 million. It is built on a scale of 1 inch to 1 foot.

1 SITTING ROOM
Generally claimed by the First Lady, this room has an unusual distinction: It was allocated one of the building's first indoor toilets in 1801.

2 MASTER BEDROOM
Nancy Reagan, who served as First Lady from 1981 to 1989, decorated this bedroom in hand-painted paper that was imported from China.

3 PRESIDENT'S STUDY
Franklin Delano Roosevelt used this study as a bedroom; the Reagans liked to have quiet dinners here in front of the television.

4 YELLOW OVAL ROOM
One of the most historic rooms in the house, it took on the color yellow during the tenure of First Lady Dolley Madison.

5 TREATY ROOM
Originally a large bedroom, this room served as Bill Clinton's office in the residence.

6 LINCOLN BEDROOM
Abraham Lincoln signed the Emancipation Proclamation here.

7 LINCOLN SITTING ROOM
William McKinley's war room during the Spanish-American War.

8 STATE DINING ROOM
Gilbert Stuart's portrait of George Washington (which was later used on the one-dollar bill) hung here when the British torched the mansion in 1814. (The portrait survived the fire.)

9 RED ROOM
John Adams's breakfast room was where Rutherford B. Hayes took the oath of office in 1877.

234

Background

The Miniature White House John Zweifel enjoyed building miniatures even as a teen, and his skills have been put to the test by the White House model. What works in the real White House often works in the model: chandeliers light up, phones ring, televisions turn on and off, and—yes—the toilets flush. Curtains and carpets are faithfully reproduced, stitch by stitch.

Over forty years, through his own time, work, and financial support, and with the help of thousands of volunteer craftspeople, the Zweifels have created a model considered one the world's finest miniature buildings. It has toured all fifty states.

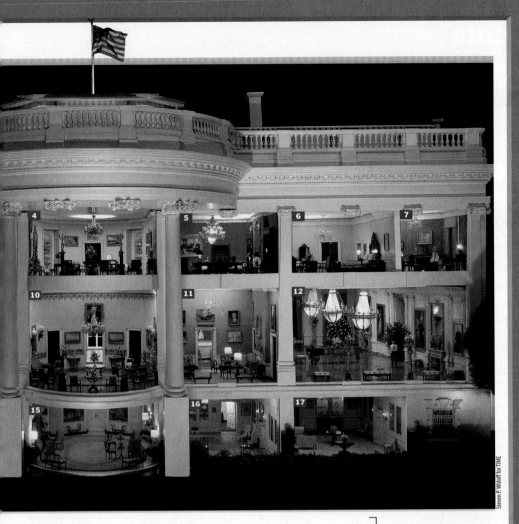

Steven P. Widoff for TIME

10 BLUE ROOM
Where Grover Cleveland married Frances Folsom, in 1886.

11 GREEN ROOM
Thomas Jefferson's dining room is now used for receptions.

12 EAST ROOM
The largest room in the mansion, it was used by First Lady Abigail Adams to dry the family wash.

13 LIBRARY
Placed here by the replica designers, the presidential library is actually located behind the Vermeil Room.

14 MAP ROOM
Decorated with Chippendale furniture imported from England, this room was inspired by Winston Churchill's World War II map room.

15 DIPLOMATIC RECEPTION ROOM
Site from which F.D.R. broadcast his fireside chats (though the fireplace at that time was fake).

16 CHINA ROOM
Edith Wilson, First Lady from 1915 to 1921, used this area to display china.

17 VERMEIL (ver-MAY) ROOM
This room takes its name from a display of vermeil (gilded silver).

A Long Road

The Zweifels' quest to create a replica of the White House took decades. After going on hundreds of public tours of the mansion, they finally persuaded President Gerald Ford to let them look behind the scenes.

S Skill Practice

Analyzing Visuals Ask: Why do the numbered descriptions include more than just the room's name? *(They include historical facts to demonstrate that the White House is not just a fine building or the president's home, but a place in which history has repeatedly been made.)* **OL**

Did You Know?

The White House is one of the nation's most popular tourist destinations, with more than a million visitors a year. The guided tours of the White House, however, reveal only part of the building. Government, after all, is going on at all times in this building, as is the daily life of the president's family. Even people who have toured the White House see new areas and behind-the-scenes details in the Zweifels' model.

235

Reading Strategy ◆ Read to Write

Writing a Letter Have students write a letter, either individually or as a class, asking the Zweifels to travel to their school and to display the model. Encourage students to persuade the Zweifels to make this trip by discussing how viewing the model would enrich their current studies. Students may also suggest activities to take place while the model is on display, such as speeches or celebrations. **OL**

Chapter Planning Guide

8

Key to Ability Levels
BL Below level	**AL** Above level
OL On level	**ELL** English Language Learners

Key to Teaching Resources
📁 Print Material	🖨 Transparency
💿 CD-ROM or DVD	

Levels					Resources	Chapter Opener	Section 1	Section 2	Section 3	Section 4	Chapter Assess
BL	OL	AL	ELL								
					FOCUS						
BL	OL	AL	ELL	🖨	**Daily Focus Skills Transparencies**		8–1	8–2	8–3	8–4	
					TEACH						
BL	OL		ELL	📁	**Reading Essentials and Note-Taking Guide***		p. 75	p. 78	p. 81	p. 84	
	OL	AL		📁	**Citizenship/Decision-Making Activity, URB**				p. 3	p. 3	
BL	OL		ELL	📁	**Reading Skills Activity, URB**		p. 7				
BL	OL	AL	ELL	📁	**Speaking and Listening Skills Activity, URB**					p. 9	
BL	OL	AL	ELL	📁	**Content Vocabulary Activity, URB***	p. 69	p. 69	p. 69	p. 69	p. 69	
BL	OL	AL	ELL	📁	**Academic Vocabulary Activity, URB**	p. 71	p. 71	p. 71	p. 71	p. 71	
	OL			📁	**Biography Activity, URB**				p. 73		
BL	OL	AL	ELL	📁	**Writing Skills Activity, URB**		p. 75	p. 75			
	OL	AL		📁	**Critical Thinking Skills Activity, URB**				p. 77	p. 77	
BL	OL	AL	ELL	📁	**Chart, Graph, and Map Skills Activity, URB**			p. 79		p. 79	
BL	OL	AL	ELL	📁	**Differentiated Instruction, URB**				p. 81		
BL	OL	AL	ELL	📁	**School-to-Home Connection Activity, URB***		p. 83	p. 83	p. 83	p. 83	
BL	OL		ELL	📁	**Guided Reading Activities, URB***		p. 87	p. 88	p. 89	p. 90	
	OL	AL		📁	**Supreme Court Cases**		✓	✓	✓	✓	
BL	OL	AL	ELL	📁	**Writer's Guidebook**	✓	✓	✓	✓	✓	✓
	OL	AL		💿	**Primary Source Document Library**	✓	✓	✓	✓	✓	✓
BL	OL	AL	ELL	💿	**Daily Lecture & Discussion Notes (in Pres. Plus)**		✓	✓	✓	✓	✓
BL	OL	AL	ELL	💿	**StudentWorks™ Plus**		✓	✓	✓	✓	✓
BL	OL	AL	ELL	💿	**Section Spotlight Videos**		✓	✓	✓	✓	
BL	OL	AL	ELL	🖨	**TIME Interpreting Political Cartoons Transp.**				Ch. 8		
BL	OL	AL	ELL	🖨	**Writing Process Transparencies**	✓	✓	✓	✓	✓	✓

Note: Please refer to the *Unit 2 Resource Book* for this chapter's URB materials.

* Also available in Spanish

- Interactive Lesson Planner
- Interactive Teacher Edition
- Fully editable blackline masters
- Section Spotlight Videos Launch
- Differentiated Lesson Plans
- Printable reports of daily assignments
- Standards Tracking System

Levels					Resources		Chapter Opener	Section 1	Section 2	Section 3	Section 4	Chapter Assess
BL	OL	AL	ELL									
					TEACH (continued)							
				📁	**Building Academic Vocabulary**		✓	✓	✓	✓	✓	✓
				📁	**Strategies for Success**		✓	✓	✓	✓	✓	✓
Teacher Resources				📁	**Teacher's Guide to Differentiated Instruction**		✓	✓	✓	✓	✓	✓
				💿	**Graphing Tool**		✓	✓	✓	✓	✓	✓
				💿	**Presentation Plus! with MindJogger CheckPoint**		✓	✓	✓	✓	✓	✓
					ASSESS							
BL	OL	AL	ELL	📁	**Quizzes and Tests***			p. 88	p. 89	p. 90	p. 91	p. 92
BL	OL	AL	ELL	📁	**Authentic Assessment with Rubrics**				p. 12	p. 12		
BL	OL	AL	ELL	📁	**Standardized Test Practice**			p. 15	p. 15	p. 15	p. 15	p. 15
BL	OL	AL	ELL	💿	*ExamView® Assessment Suite* **CD-ROM**			8–1	8–2	8–3	8–4	Ch. 8
					CLOSE							
BL			ELL	📁	**Reteaching Activity, URB***			p. 85	p. 85	p. 85	p. 85	
BL	OL		ELL	📁	**Reading and Study Skills Foldables™ Activity**		p. 64		p. 65		p. 65	
BL	OL	AL	ELL	🖥	**Graphic Organizer Transparencies & Strategies**		✓	✓	✓	✓	✓	✓

✓ Chapter- or unit-based activities applicable to all sections in this chapter

Using Study Central™

Build Vocabulary

What is Study Central™?

Study Central™ is an interactive, online tool that helps students understand and remember textbook content section-by-section. It can be used alongside lessons or before a test.

How can Study Central™ help my students?

The Build Vocabulary tab on the Study Central™ Web site allows students to reinforce the content vocabulary and academic vocabulary in each section of a chapter. Build Vocabulary helps students:

- strengthen vocabulary skills
- reinforce their understanding of the content and academic vocabulary in each section

Visit glencoe.com or enter a *QuickPass*™ code to go directly to resources for each chapter.

Civics ONLINE
Visit glencoe.com and enter *QuickPass*™ code CIV1360c8T for Chapter 8 resources.

You can easily launch a wide range of digital products from your computer's desktop with the McGraw-Hill Social Studies widget.

	Student	Teacher	Parent
Media Library			
• Student Edition Section Audio	●		●
• Spanish Audio Summaries	●		●
• Section Spotlight Videos	●	●	●
***Civics Today* Online Learning Center (Web Site)**			
• Chapter Overviews	●	●	●
• Study Central™	●	●	●
• Study-to-Go	●	●	●
• Student Web Activities	●	●	●
• In Motion Animation	●	●	●
• Self-Check Quizzes	●	●	●
• ePuzzles and Games	●	●	●
• StudentWorks™ Plus Online	●	●	●
• Vocabulary eFlashcards	●	●	●
• Web Activity Lesson Plans		●	
• Vocabulary PuzzleMaker	●	●	●
Classroom Tools			
• Multilingual Glossary	●	●	●
• Beyond the Textbook	●	●	●
• NGS MapMachine	●	●	●

GLENCOE BOOKLINK 3

Use this database to search more than 30,000 titles to create a customized reading list for your students.

- Reading lists can be organized by students' reading level, author, genre, theme, or area of interest.
- The database provides Degrees of Reading Power™ (DRP) and Lexile™ readability scores for all selections.
- A brief summary of each selection is included.

Leveled reading suggestions for this chapter:

For students at a Grade 7 reading level:
- *Roe v. Wade: The Right to Choose,* by Simone Payment

For students at a Grade 8 reading level:
- *Demanding Justice: A Story about Mary Ann Shadd Clay,* by Jeri Chase Ferris

For students at a Grade 9 reading level:
- *The March of the Mill Children,* by Judith Pinkerton Josephson

For students at a Grade 10 reading level:
- *The Supreme Court of the United States,* by David Heath

For students at a Grade 11 reading level:
- *Great Justices of the Supreme Court,* by Nathan Aeseng

READING SUPPORT FROM JAMESTOWN EDUCATION

- **Timed Readings Plus in Social Studies** helps students increase their reading rate and fluency while maintaining comprehension. The 400-word passages are similar to those found on state and national assessments.

- **Reading in the Content Area: Social Studies** concentrates on six essential reading skills that help students better comprehend what they read. The book includes 75 high-interest nonfiction passages written at increasing levels of difficulty.

- **Reading Social Studies** includes strategic reading instruction and vocabulary support in Social Studies content for both ELLs and native speakers of English.

- **Content Vocabulary Workout** (Grades 6–8) accelerates reading comprehension through focused vocabulary development. Social Studies content vocabulary comes from the glossaries of Glencoe's Middle School Social Studies texts. www.jamestowneducation.com

KEY Teacher Wraparound

Use this key to help you identify the different types of prompts found in the Teacher Wraparound Edition.

R **Reading Strategies** activities help you teach reading skills and vocabulary.

C Critical Thinking strategies help students apply and extend what they have learned.

D **Differentiated Instruction** activities provide instruction for students learning to speak English, along with suggestions for teaching various types of learners.

S **Skill Practice** strategies help students practice historical analysis and geography skills.

W **Writing Support** activities provide writing opportunities to help students comprehend the text.

Teaching strategies and activities have been coded for ability level appropriateness.

AL Activities for students working above grade level

OL Activities for students working on grade level

BL Activities for students working below grade level

ELL Activities for English Language Learners

Focus

Why It Matters

Ask: What would our country be without a judicial system or a way of enforcing our laws? *(Answers may include the idea that without a judicial system to uphold the Constitution, citizens would not have equal justice under the law.)*

More About the Photo

Visual Literacy What makes this picture interesting is that Chief Justice Roberts' son is a young boy. Before Roberts was appointed to the Supreme Court, the average age of the justices was 70. Chief Justice John Roberts, Jr., 50, replaced William Rehnquist, 80, who had died after serving 33 years as an associate and later as chief justice. From 1780 to 1970, a justice on the Supreme Court served, on average, almost 15 years. Since 1970, the average has increased to about 25 years. Some people wonder if there should be term limits for Supreme Court justices, claiming that the Framers of the Constitution did not intend for anyone to hold such a powerful office for life.

Teach

BIG Ideas *As you begin teaching each section, use these questions and activities to help students focus on the Big Ideas.*

Section 1

The Federal Courts Ask: Why does there have to be a federal court system? *(The federal court system guarantees that citizens in all states have equal justice under the law. There may be special cases that state courts alone cannot resolve.)*

236

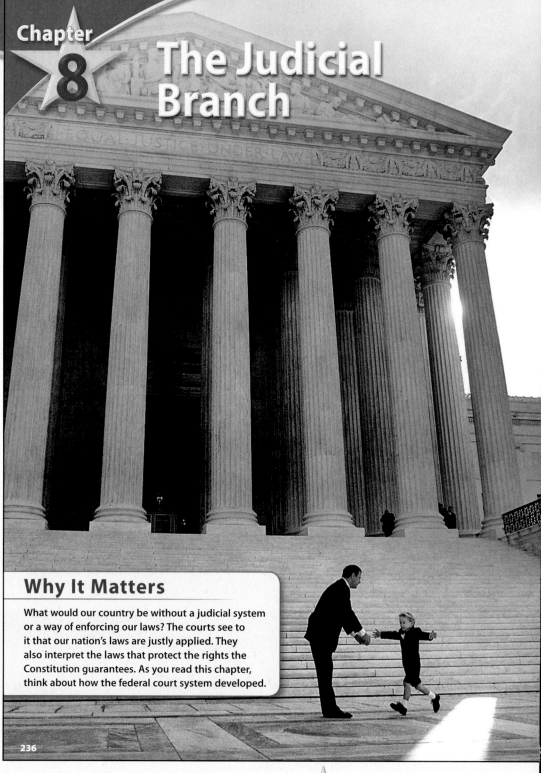

Chapter
8
The Judicial Branch

Why It Matters

What would our country be without a judicial system or a way of enforcing our laws? The courts see to it that our nation's laws are justly applied. They also interpret the laws that protect the rights the Constitution guarantees. As you read this chapter, think about how the federal court system developed.

236

Point out that in Section 1, students will learn how the judicial branch upholds the Constitution and enforces our nation's laws. **OL**

Section 2

How Federal Courts Are Organized
Ask: How many types of courts are there in the federal system? *(There are three types of federal courts: district courts, courts of appeals, and the Supreme Court.)* Tell students that in Section 2, they will learn about the organization of the federal court system and the role of federal judges and other court officials. **OL**

Chapter Audio

Civics ONLINE
Visit glencoe.com and enter
QuickPass™ code
CIV3093c8 for
Chapter 8
resources.

Chapter Introduction
8

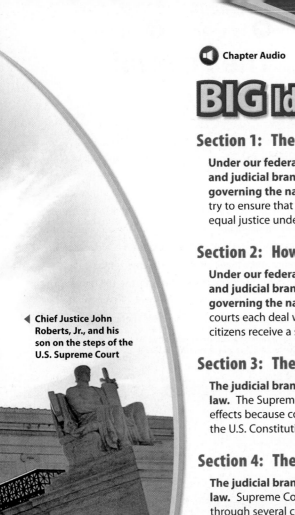

◀ Chief Justice John
Roberts, Jr., and his
son on the steps of the
U.S. Supreme Court

BIG Ideas

Section 1: The Federal Courts

Under our federal system, the executive, legislative, and judicial branches share the responsibility of governing the nation. Three levels of federal courts try to ensure that everyone in the United States receives equal justice under the law.

Section 2: How Federal Courts Are Organized

Under our federal system, the executive, legislative, and judicial branches share the responsibility of governing the nation. The different levels of federal courts each deal with a different caseload, ensuring all citizens receive a speedy trial or day in court.

Section 3: The Supreme Court

The judicial branch is charged with interpreting the law. The Supreme Court's decisions have wide-ranging effects because court justices interpret the meaning of the U.S. Constitution.

Section 4: The Supreme Court at Work

The judicial branch is charged with interpreting the law. Supreme Court justices weigh many factors and go through several complex steps before making a decision.

FOLDABLES™
Study Organizer

Sequencing Information Study Foldable Make the following Foldable to help you analyze and sequence key influences and responsibilities of the judicial branch of government.

Step 1 Fold a sheet of paper in half from the long way with edges evenly together.

Step 2 Turn the paper and fold it into thirds.

Reading and Writing
As you read the chapter, compare and note the details of the responsibilities of each level of the court system from least influence to greatest influence.

Step 3 Unfold and cut along the two folds on the front flap to make three tabs.

Step 4 Label as shown, including arrows.

Supreme
Court ↑
Appeals
Court ↑
District
Courts

Chapter 8   237

FOLDABLES™ Dinah Zike's
Study Organizer Foldables

Purpose This Foldable guides students into understanding the differences between what they know or think they know about the federal judicial system and what they are learning. The completed Foldable will help them write their comparisons as well as help them prepare for assessment. **OL**

More Foldables activities for this chapter can be found in the *Dinah Zike's Reading and Study Skills Foldables* ancillary.

Civics ONLINE

Visit glencoe.com and enter *QuickPass*™ code CIV1360c8T for Chapter 8 resources, including a Chapter Overview, Study Central™, Study-to-Go, Student Web Activity, Self-Check Quiz, and other materials.

Section 3

The Supreme Court Ask: Why is it called the Supreme Court? *(It is called the Supreme Court because it is the highest court in the land. It has the final say on any appealable case.)* Explain that in Section 3, students will learn how the Supreme Court is organized, how justices are appointed, and the limits of its power. **OL**

Section 4

The Supreme Court at Work Ask: Does the Supreme Court hear every case that comes before it? *(No, the justices must select which cases to hear.)* Explain that in Section 4, students will learn how the Supreme Court functions, how cases are heard, and the factors that influence decisions. **OL**

Focus

Guide to Reading
Answers to Graphic:

U.S. Courts

| District Courts |
↓
| Courts of Appeals |
↓
| Supreme Court |

Section Spotlight Video

To generate student interest and provide a springboard for class discussion, access the Chapter 8, Section 1 video at glencoe.com or on the video DVD.

Resource Manager

Guide to Reading

Big Idea
Under our federal system, the executive, legislative, and judicial branches share the responsibility of governing the nation.

Content Vocabulary
- circuit (p. 240)
- jurisdiction (p. 240)
- exclusive jurisdiction (p. 242)
- concurrent jurisdiction (p. 242)

Academic Vocabulary
- acknowledge (p. 239)
- circumstance (p. 242)

Reading Strategy
Organizing As you read, complete a graphic organizer like the one below to identify the three levels of courts in the U.S. justice system.

U.S. Courts

 Section Audio   Spotlight Video

The Federal Courts

Real World Civics Can you imagine being forced to live in a strange place simply because of your nationality? That is exactly what happened to these young boys during World War II. During the United States war with Japan, President Roosevelt ordered Japanese Americans to be sent to internment camps so that they could not spy on America. More than half of those interned in the "camps" were naturalized American citizens. By the 1980s the U.S. admitted it had acted too harshly, apologized to those who had been wrongly interned, and paid them damages.

▼ **Young Japanese children interned at Manzanar War Relocation Center in California during World War II**

R Reading Strategies	**C** Critical Thinking	**D** Differentiated Instruction	**W** Writing Support	**S** Skill Practice
Teacher Edition • Inferring, p. 239 • Making Connections, p. 240 • Predicting, p. 241 **Additional Resources** • Read. Skills, URB p. 7 • Cont. Vocab., URB p. 69 • Guid. Read., URB p. 87 • RENTG., p. 75	**Teacher Edition** • Pred. Consequences, p. 239 • Ident. Cent. Issues, p. 240 **Additional Resources** • Quizzes and Tests, p. 88	**Teacher Edition** • English Learners, p. 240 • Special Ed., p. 242 **Additional Resources** • School-to-Home Act., URB p. 83 • Reteach. Act., URB p. 85	**Teacher Edition** • Personal Writing, p. 241 **Additional Resources** • Writing Skills Act., URB p. 75	**Teacher Edition** • Using Geo. Skills, p. 241 **Additional Resources** • Daily Focus Trans., 8–1

Right to Trial The judicial system provides fair trials to all accused, even if the crimes involve attacks against the United States, as in the case of accused al-Qaeda conspirator Zacarias Moussaoui. *Predicting* What difficulties might arise in finding a fair jury to judge a crime such as terrorism?

Equal Justice for All

Main Idea The courts that make up the judicial branch try to ensure that our nation's laws are justly enforced.

Civics & You Do you think a society could exist without a court system that determines in a fair manner if laws have been broken? Read about the powers of the courts as established in the Constitution.

A native-born citizen, Mitsuye Endo was fired from a California state job in 1942 and sent to a relocation center like the boys discussed on the previous page. Her lawyer **R** challenged the War Relocation Board's right to intern a loyal American citizen.

Endo took the matter to the Supreme Court and won her case. In 1944, the Court ruled that Endo "should be given her liberty." Justice William O. Douglas proclaimed that

> *"A citizen who is concededly loyal presents no problem of espionage or sabotage. Loyalty is a matter of the heart and mind not of race, creed, or color."*
>
> —*Ex parte Endo,* 1944

C

Later the United States government would **acknowledge,** or admit to, the injustice of the internment camps and apologize. Shortly after the Court made its decision in the *Ex parte Endo* case, many detained Japanese Americans were released and returned home.

Chapter 8   239

Teach

R Reading Strategy

Inferring Ask: Why do you think the Japanese Americans were interned without a trial? *(The United States was at war with Japan, so anyone of Japanese ancestry was considered a threat.)* **OL**

C Critical Thinking

Predicting Consequences Have students reread the quotation from Justice William O. Douglas, *Ex parte Endo, 1944.* **Ask:** What would the outcome have been if the other justices had not shared his view? *(Justice Douglas believed that being Japanese did not make one a traitor or a threat to the United States during World War II. Without this basic belief, the court would not have decided as it did, and most Japanese Americans would have been denied the basic liberties of all citizens.)* **OL**

> **Caption Answer:**
> Students may say that it would be difficult to find an impartial jury for someone accused of terrorism. Whenever there is a climate of anger or fear, it is difficult for most people to be fair or free of prejudices.

Differentiated Instruction

Differentiated Instruction Activity 8, URB p. 81

Selecting Supreme Court Justices

Objective:	To understand the process of selecting Supreme Court justices
Focus:	Have students read Senator Frist's speech about Chief Justice Roberts.
Teach:	Discuss the importance of Senate confirmation hearings.
Assess:	Discuss students' answers to the questions posed on page 81.
Close:	Make a list of ideal qualities for a Supreme Court justice.

Differentiated Instruction Strategies

BL Tell what the Senate's role is in selecting a Supreme Court justice.

AL Why would the Judiciary Committee not recommend a nominee?

ELL Explain the phrase "he will check political views at the door to the Court."

D Differentiated Instruction

English Learners Point out the word "parties" in the second paragraph. **Ask:** What two meanings does this word have? *(Most often, it refers to festive gatherings. In a court of law, however, it refers to a person, persons, or group involved in a legal proceeding.)* **ELL**

C Critical Thinking

Identifying Central Issues Ask: What sort of case might be presented to the Supreme Court that does not involve a decision of guilt or innocence? *(a civil court case whereby one party is pressing for protection under the Constitution)* **AL**

R Reading Strategy

Making Connections Ask: If there is a system of federal courts, why does there have to be a parallel system of state courts? *(Students may point out that the state courts were in place before the federal system and that a parallel system of state and federal courts provides another form of checks and balances.)* **OL**

> ✓ **Reading Check** **Answer:** Every accused person has the right to a public trial and a lawyer. A person is innocent until proven guilty and has the right to appeal, or ask for a review.

Differentiated Instruction

Role of the Courts

Federal courts, such as the Supreme Court, make up the third branch of the U.S. government. Courts use the law to settle civil disputes and to decide the guilt or innocence of people accused of crimes.

Whether a civil dispute is between two private parties (people, companies, or organizations), between a private party and the government, or between the United States and a state or local government, both sides come before a court. Each side presents its position. The court then applies the law to the facts that have been presented and makes a decision in favor of one or the other. The courts also hold criminal trials in which witnesses present evidence and a jury or a judge delivers a verdict.

Equal Treatment

The United States Supreme Court is at the top of the federal court system. If you visit the Court, you will see the words "Equal Justice Under Law" on the face of its marble building. Our legal system is based on this important ideal. The goal of the legal system is to treat every person the same. Under the Constitution, every person accused of breaking the law has the right to have a public trial and a lawyer. If an accused person cannot afford a lawyer, the court will appoint and pay for one. Each person is presumed innocent until proven guilty and has the right to ask for a review of his or her case if, in that person's view, the courts have made a mistake.

The ideal of equal justice is difficult to achieve. Judges and juries are not free from personal prejudices or the prejudices of their communities. Poor people do not have the money to spend on the best available legal help, unlike wealthy citizens and large companies. Nonetheless, American courts try to uphold the ideal of equal justice.

> ✓ **Reading Check** **Describing** Under the Constitution, what rights does every accused person have?

Federal Courts

Main Idea The Constitution gives the federal courts the authority to hear and decide certain types of cases.

Civics & You Do you know anyone who has had to go to court or has served on a jury? Read to learn about what kinds of cases are heard in federal courts.

From 1781 to 1789, when the United States was governed by the Articles of Confederation, there was no national court system. Each state had its own laws and its own courts. There was no way to guarantee that people would receive equal justice in all the states.

To deal with this problem, the writers of the Constitution provided for a federal judiciary. Article III of the Constitution established a national Supreme Court. It also gave Congress the power to establish lower federal courts.

Over the years, Congress has created two kinds of lower courts. In 1789 it passed the Judiciary Act, which established federal district courts and circuit courts of appeals. Much later, in 1891, Congress created a system of federal appeals courts and the **circuits** or districts they serve. Thus, the federal court system has three levels—the district courts at the lower level, the appeals courts in the middle, and the Supreme Court at the top.

Our federal court system exists alongside 50 separate state court systems. Each state has its own laws and courts. The state courts get their powers from state constitutions and laws. You will read more about state courts in Chapter 12.

Federal Court Jurisdiction

Article III of the Constitution gives federal courts **jurisdiction**—the authority to hear and decide a case—only in cases that involve one of the following:

Leveled Activities

Federal Judicial Circuits

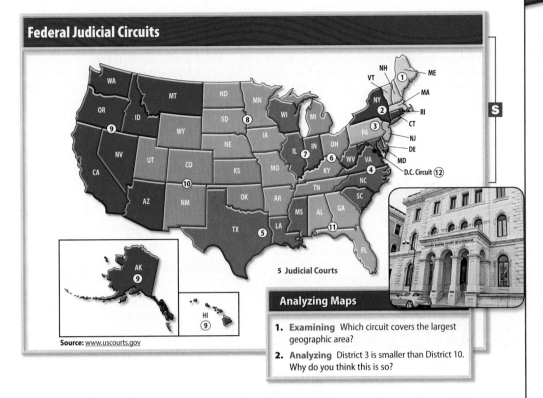

Source: www.uscourts.gov

5 Judicial Courts

Analyzing Maps

1. **Examining** Which circuit covers the largest geographic area?

2. **Analyzing** District 3 is smaller than District 10. Why do you think this is so?

S **Skill Practice**

Using Geography Skills Ask students to identify the states within each district. Using what they know about each state's population, what generalization could they make about how the states were divided into circuits. *(With the exception of the 9th district, the districts vary in land area but have similar populations.)* **OL**

W **Writing Support**

Personal Writing Have students write a paragraph or poem explaining what constitutional right means to them. They may include personal anecdotes. **OL**

R **Reading Strategy**

Predicting Ask: What could happen if there were no federal court to help California and Colorado resolve their dispute over rights to a precious resource such as water? *(Students may point out that without federal court involvement, states could fight.)* **BL**

Analyzing Maps

Answers:

1. District 9

2. The population density of District 3 is greater.

The Constitution For example, if a person believes a constitutional right, such as freedom of speech, has been violated, that person has a right to be heard in a federal court. **W**

Federal Laws Federal courts try people accused of federal crimes such as kidnapping, tax evasion, and counterfeiting. Federal courts also hear civil cases that involve federal laws.

Disputes Between States Disagreements between state governments are resolved in federal courts. If Colorado and California, for example, disagree over rights to water in the Colorado River, it is a federal case. **R**

Citizens from Different States Lawsuits between citizens of different states also come under the federal courts. For example, Ms.

Jones of Maine may bring suit in a federal court against Mr. Smith of Iowa for not fulfilling his part of a business agreement.

The Federal Government The U.S. government, for example, could take a company to court for failing to live up to a contract to deliver supplies to a government department. Individuals or companies can also take the government to court. For instance, if a United States Army van struck your car or the Department of the Interior failed to pay your company for equipment, you could sue the government.

Foreign Governments and Treaties In any dispute between a foreign government and the United States government, an American company, or an American citizen, the case will be heard in a federal court.

Chapter 8 241

A Day in Court

Step 1: Getting Started During a mock trial, students will assume the roles and responsibilities of people involved in Mitsuye Endo's court case, starting at the district level, through the appeals court, and ultimately to the Supreme Court.

Directions Write the Big Idea on the board. Divide the class into thirds. To each group assign one of the levels of federal courts. Explain that they will be working on Mitsuye Endo's case.

Setting a Purpose Tell groups to research the Executive Orders that Roosevelt enacted that made possible the internment of

Mitsuye Endo. Groups will use this information in Section 2 to decide how they plan to present their cases in court. **OL**

(Project continued in Section 2)

Hands-On Chapter Project
Step 1

Differentiated Instruction

Special Education Draw an 8-legged spider word map on the board with "federal jurisdiction" in the body. Then read aloud pages 241–242 describing the eight kinds of court cases over which federal courts have jurisdiction. Invite volunteers to write the type of each case on one of the spider legs. **Ask:** If a driver hits and hurts a pedestrian and flees the scene but is later caught by the police, does the case go to a state court or a federal district court? *(state court)* **BL**

Reading Check **Answer:** Article III

Assess

Civics ONLINE

Study Central™ provides summaries, interactive games, and online graphic organizers to help students review content.

Close

Summarizing Have students work in small groups. Using their graphic organizers, they can present a two-minute overview of the federal court system. **OL**

Section 1 Review

Admiralty and Maritime Laws These laws concern crimes and accidents outside territorial waters. For example, a case involving disagreement over the rights of property recovered from a shipwreck would be tried in federal court.

U.S. Diplomats If, for example, an American diplomat working in the U.S. embassy in France is accused of breaking an American law, the case would go to a federal court.

Types of Jurisdiction

For most of the areas just described, federal courts have **exclusive jurisdiction,** which means that only the federal courts may hear and decide cases. In the dual court system, federal courts have jurisdiction over cases involving federal laws, while state courts have jurisdiction over cases involving state laws. Most U.S. court cases involve state law and are tried in state courts.

Under some **circumstances,** or instances, however, both federal and state courts have jurisdiction, a situation known as **concurrent jurisdiction.** Either court may try crimes that violate both state and federal law. Concurrent jurisdiction also applies when citizens of different states are involved in a dispute concerning at least $50,000. In such a case, a person may sue in either a federal court or a state court. If the person being sued insists, however, the case must be tried in a federal court. Such appeals might eventually reach the United States Supreme Court.

Reading Check Identifying Which article of the Constitution lists the jurisdiction of federal courts?

Section 1 Review

Vocabulary

1. **Define** *jurisdiction*. Then explain the difference between *exclusive* and *concurrent jurisdiction*.

Main Ideas

2. **Explaining** What is meant by the words that are inscribed on the United States Supreme Court building: "Equal Justice Under Law."

3. **Describing** Why do you think federal courts rule on disputes between states? What would be an example of such a case?

Critical Thinking

4. **Describing** How did the federal court system develop?

5. **BIG Ideas** On a chart like the one below, write four kinds of cases for which federal courts have jurisdiction and give an example of each kind of case.

Kinds of Cases	Examples
Cases involving the Constitution	Person believes First Amendment right is violated

6. **Analyzing Visuals** Study the map of federal judicial circuits and districts on page 241. In which judicial circuit is your state?

CITIZENSHIP Activity

7. **Expository Writing** Do research on the United States Supreme Court in the library or online. Select a famous case decided by the Supreme Court. Of the eight kinds of cases for which federal courts have jurisdiction, under which kind does your case fall? Write a paragraph explaining your choice.

Study Central™ To review this section, go to glencoe.com.

Answers

1. Sentences should use vocabulary words according to their definitions in the section and in the Glossary.

2. It is the goal of the legal system to treat everyone the same.

3. Unlike either state's court, the Supreme Court can guarantee a fair trial when, for example, two states have a boundary dispute or are fighting over access to a shared resource, such as water.

4. The Constitution provided for the development of a federal court system. Article III established a Supreme Court and also gave Congress the power to establish the lower federal courts.

5. **Involving federal laws:** kidnapping, tax evasion, counterfeiting; **Foreign governments and treaties:** any dispute between a foreign government and the U.S. government or an American company or citizen; **Admiralty and maritime law:** any crime or accident outside territorial waters; **Involving federal government:** contract disputes between the federal government and a company

6. Answers will vary based on state.

7. Answers will vary depending on the court case selected.

Guide to Reading

Big Idea
Under our federal system, the executive, legislative, and judicial branches share the responsibility of governing the nation.

Content Vocabulary
- district court *(p. 244)*
- original jurisdiction *(p. 244)*
- appeals court *(p. 244)*
- appellate jurisdiction *(p. 244)*
- remand *(p. 245)*
- opinion *(p. 245)*
- precedent *(p. 245)*

Academic Vocabulary
- affect *(p. 244)*
- submit *(p. 246)*

Reading Strategy
Analyzing As you read, take notes on a Venn diagram like the one below to compare the similarities and differences between two branches of the courts.

District Courts — Both — Courts of Appeals

Section Audio **Spotlight Video**

How Federal Courts Are Organized

Real World Civics For more than one hundred years, the Supreme Court justices have carried on the tradition of the "conference handshake." When they gather before taking the bench, each justice shakes hands with each of the other eight. Chief Justice Melvin Fuller instituted this practice in the late 1800s. It serves as a reminder that their differences of opinion do not prevent the justices from working harmoniously toward a common purpose.

▼ **Newly appointed Supreme Court Justice Samuel Alito, Jr., receives congratulations from Attorney General Alberto Gonzales.**

243

Focus

Bellringer
Daily Focus Transparency 8–2

Guide to Reading
Answers to Graphic:

District Courts	Both	Courts of Appeals
94 districts, At least one in each state, Original jurisdiction, Where all federal cases begin, Trial courts for criminal and civil cases, Decides guilt or innocence, Witnesses, Juries	Federal courts Cover set geographic areas Judges	12 circuits, Appellate jurisdiction, Review decisions made in district courts, No guilt or innocence decisions, Review federal regulatory agency rulings, No juries, 13th Court of Appeals has nationwide jurisdiction

 Section Spotlight Video

Have students watch the Chapter 8, Section 2 video at <u>glencoe.com</u>.

Resource Manager

R Reading Strategies	**C** Critical Thinking	**D** Differentiated Instruction	**W** Writing Support	**S** Skill Practice
Teacher Edition • Outlining, p. 244 • Predicting, p. 246 **Additional Resources** • Cont. Vocab., URB p. 69 • Guid. Read., URB p. 88 • RENTG., p. 78	**Teacher Edition** • Compare/Contrast, p. 245 • Making Inferences, p. 246 **Additional Resources** • Quizzes and Tests, p. 89	**Teacher Edition** • English Learner, p. 246 **Additional Resources** • School-to-Home Act., URB p. 83 • Teacher's Guide to Differentiated Instruction, p. 10	**Teacher Edition** • Persuasive Writing, p. 247 **Additional Resources** • Writing Skills Act., URB p. 75	**Teacher Edition** • Categorizing/Analyzing Info., p. 244 **Additional Resources** • Chart, Map, and Graph Skills, URB p. 79 • Daily Focus Trans., 8–2

Hands-On Chapter Project
Step 2

The Lower Federal Courts

Main Idea There are three types of federal courts: district courts, courts of appeals, and the Supreme Court.

Civics & You What makes the U.S. court system effective? Read to learn how the federal court system is organized.

At the top of the federal court system is the Supreme Court. Below the Supreme Court are two lower courts—the district courts and the appeals courts.

Media Coverage The media often film trials as they happen. Federal court buildings are located in each state and trials must be held in the state where the crime was committed. *Analyzing* In what way can extensive media coverage help ensure a fair trial?

244

U.S. District Courts

District courts are the federal courts in which trials are held and lawsuits are begun. There are 94 district courts in all. Every state has at least one district court, and some states have more. All federal cases must begin in a district court, because district courts have **original jurisdiction,** the authority to hear cases for the first time. District courts are responsible for determining the facts of a case; they are the trial courts for both criminal and civil federal cases. Thus, in a criminal case, a district court will decide if a person is guilty or innocent based on the evidence presented. District courts are the only federal courts in which witnesses testify and juries hear cases and reach verdicts.

U.S. Courts of Appeals

Above the district courts in the federal court system are the United States courts of appeals. These courts are also referred to as federal appeals courts, circuit courts of appeals, or appellate courts. The job of the **appeals courts** is to review decisions made in lower district courts. This is referred to as **appellate jurisdiction,** or the authority of a court to hear a case appealed from a lower court.

Lawyers usually appeal when they feel that the district court judge in their case followed the wrong procedure or did not apply the law. Some appeals may be based on new evidence that could **affect,** or impact, the verdict. Appeals courts may also review federal regulatory agency rulings if those involved believe the agency acted unfairly.

Organization Today, each of the 12 United States courts of appeals has jurisdiction over a circuit, or particular geographic area. In addition, a thirteenth appeals court, the Court of Appeals for the Federal Circuit, has nationwide jurisdiction to hear special cases, such as those involving patent law or international trade. This court's headquarters is in Washington, D.C., but it can hear cases in other parts of the country.

A Day in Court

Step 2: Preparing the Case Groups of students continue their work that they began in Section 1 to prepare for the mock trials.

Directions Tell the groups that they must research their local district or appellate courts. Refer them to the Web site, http://www.uscourts.gov/courtlinks/. They can use their zip codes to locate the nearest court. Each group should use the Web site as an online resource to help them prepare for their day in court. Have students identify the chief judge and the clerk of courts. **Ask:** What other information can you get from this government Web site that might help you prepare your case? *(There are instructions to the jury and forms for filing both civil and criminal cases, local and federal rules are explained, appellate and district courts are distinguished, and so on.)* **OL**

(Project continued in Section 3)

United States Court System

U.S. SUPREME COURT

(Judges/No Jury)

○ Jurisdiction: Limited original jurisdiction and appellate jurisdiction

U.S. COURTS OF APPEALS

(Judges/No Jury)

○ Jurisdiction: Appellate

U.S. DISTRICT COURTS

(Judges and Juries)

○ Jurisdiction: Original

Analyzing Charts

1. **Explaining** Who provides the decision in the courts of appeals?

2. **Analyzing** What is the difference between appellate and original jurisdiction?

Making a Decision

Appeals courts do not hold trials. Instead, these courts may decide an appeal in one of three ways: by upholding the original decision, by reversing that decision, or by **remanding** the case, that is, by sending the case back to the lower court to be tried again. A panel of three or more judges reviews the record of the case being appealed and listens to arguments. The judges then meet and make a decision by majority vote.

The judges do not decide the guilt or innocence of a defendant in a criminal case or which side should win in a civil lawsuit. They rule on only whether the defendant's rights have been protected and on whether he or

she received a fair trial. Unless appealed to the Supreme Court, decisions of the courts of appeals are final.

Announcing the Decision

When an appeals court makes a decision, one judge writes an opinion for the court. The **opinion** offers a detailed explanation of the legal thinking behind the court's decision. The opinion sets a precedent for all courts and agencies within the district.

A **precedent** gives guidance to other judges by offering a model upon which to base their own decisions on similar cases. A precedent does not have the force of law, but it is a very powerful argument to use in court. Judges and courts follow precedents in nearly all cases.

Early Precedents

Certain judicial principles were established early in the nation's history. Neither any federal court nor the Supreme Court may initiate action. A judge or justice may not seek out an issue and ask both sides to bring it to court. The courts must wait for litigants, or people engaged in a lawsuit, to come before them.

Judicial precedents derive their force from a common law principle. This principle states that the decisions of the highest court in the jurisdiction are binding on all lower courts in the jurisdiction. Thus, all courts in the United States are bound by precedent to follow the decisions of the United States Supreme Court. Furthermore, each panel of judges on the courts of appeals for a circuit is bound to follow the prior appellate decisions of the same circuit. You will read more about this precedent in Section 4.

Reading Check Explaining Why are precedents important to the enforcement of laws?

Civics ONLINE

Student Web Activity Visit glencoe.com and complete the Chapter 8 Web Activity.

C Critical Thinking

Comparing and Contrasting Ask: If you were watching a session of a courts of appeals, what differences might you notice compared to a district court? *(There is no jury, there is a panel of three or more judges hearing the case, and there are no witnesses testifying.)* **OL**

Analyzing Charts

Answers:

1. A panel of three or more judges decides the case.

2. Original jurisdiction is the authority to hear cases for the first time. Appellate jurisdiction is the authority to hear a case appealed from the lower district court.

Reading Check Answer: A precedent gives judges a model upon which to base their own decisions.

Civics ONLINE

Objectives and answers to the **Student Web Activity** can be found at glencoe.com under the Web Activity Lesson Plan for this chapter.

Differentiated Instruction

Interpreting a Flowchart

Chart, Graph, and Map Skills Activity 8, URB p. 79–80

Objective:	To gain an understanding of processes in the federal court system
Focus:	Students will analyze a sequence of events as displayed on flowcharts.
Teach:	Discuss how a legal case ends up before the Supreme Court.
Assess:	Check for students' ability to interpret the flowchart on page 80.
Close:	Have students present the information in the flowchart as a series of steps.

Differentiated Instruction Strategies

BL With a reading partner, compare and contrast the flowcharts on pages 79 and 80. How are rectangles used differently?

AL Write an outline for an oral argument about a case to present before the Supreme Court.

ELL Define and draw an "octagon." Tell why this symbol was used in the flowchart.

D Differentiated Instruction

English Learners Point out the words "solicit," "refurbish," and "distribute." Help students use context clues to figure out the meaning of each word. **Ask:** What does Clayton's Backyard Crew do with the gently used bikes? *(They fix them and then hand them out to children.)* **ELL BL**

C Critical Thinking

Making Inferences Ask: How might letting the president select federal judges offset the checks and balances of government? *(The courts could become stacked in favor of the executive branch.)* **OL**

R Reading Strategy

Predicting Ask: What is the practice of senatorial courtesy? What might happen to a court nomination if this wasn't followed? *(judges might not be accepted by the Senate)* **OL**

TIME™ Teens in Action

Answer:
Students may point out that community-based volunteer work keeps us all actively involved in society and we have a responsibility to do things the government cannot do.

Differentiated Instruction

TIME™ Teens in Action

Clayton G. Lillard

Clayton G. Lillard, 17, from San Antonio, Texas, decided to do something good for kids who had a parent in prison. So he started Clayton's Backyard Crew.

QUESTION: What does your group do?

ANSWER: Clayton's Backyard Crew is made up of volunteers, usually teenagers. Each year we solicit donations for gently used bicycles and cash donations for new bikes and parts. We refurbish the used bikes and distribute them to children whose parents are in prison.

Q: When do you hand out the bikes?

A: Each year I deliver the bikes on my birthday, December 23. I get to play Santa—it's amazing!

Q: How did the group start?

A: In 1999, my mom and I saw two bikes in the trash. I thought I'd fix them up and give them to needy children. Then we set a goal of giving out 25 bikes. I contacted the radio stations and they put out the word. The response from the community was overwhelming. We ended up getting 100 bikes the first year.

Q: How many bikes have you given away?

A: About 800 bikes. Parents in prison really miss their children at Christmas, and the children are really sad with their parents gone during the holidays. On one occasion, we delivered bikes to two brothers. We told them the bikes were from their father in prison. One boy jumped up and down with joy. He kept shouting, "I knew he wouldn't forget me, I just knew he wouldn't forget me!" It brought tears to everyone's eyes.

For more info, check out www.claytonsbackyardcrew.com.

ACTION FACT: Music is Lillard's passion—water polo and swimming play big parts in his life as well.

Making a Difference — CITIZENSHIP

Why does a community need organizations like Clayton's Backyard Crew?

Federal Judges

Main Idea Federal judges interpret the laws and protect the rights the Constitution guarantees.

Civics & You What qualifications do you think are important in selecting a person for a position of responsibility? Read on to find out about how federal judges are selected.

The chief decision makers in the judicial branch are the federal judges. There are more than 650 judges who preside over the district courts. Each district court has at least two judges. Some district courts in high-population areas have more judges because there are more cases to hear. Each appeals court has from 6 to 28 judges. The Supreme Court has nine justices.

Selection of Federal Judges

Article II, Section 2, of the Constitution provides that the president, with the advice and consent of the Senate, will appoint all federal judges. The Constitution, however, sets no particular qualifications for federal judges. In general, presidents want to appoint judges who share their ideas about politics and justice. Thus, presidents usually choose people who belong to their political parties.

When naming judges, presidents usually follow a practice called senatorial courtesy. Under this system, a president **submits,** or presents, the name of a candidate to the senators from the candidate's state before submitting it to the entire Senate for approval. If either or both senators object to the candidate, the president usually withdraws the name and nominates another candidate. The practice of senatorial courtesy usually applies only to the selection of judges to the district courts and other trial courts, not to the selection of judges to courts of appeals or the Supreme Court.

Leveled Activities

BL Academic Vocabulary Activity 8, URB p. 71

AL Writing Skills Activity 8, URB pp. 75–76

OL Chart, Graph, and Map Skills 8, URB pp. 79–80

ELL Guided Reading Activity 8–2, URB p. 88

Tenure Once appointed, federal judges may have their jobs for life. A judge can be removed from office only through the process of impeachment. The writers of the Constitution gave federal judges this sort of job security because they wanted judges to be able to decide cases free from public or political pressures.

Other Court Officials

Judges do not work alone. They have help from clerks, secretaries, court reporters, probation officers, and other workers.

Magistrates Each district court has magistrate judges. These officials take care of much of a judge's routine work. They issue court orders, such as search and arrest warrants, in federal cases. They hear preliminary evidence in a case to determine whether the case should be brought to trial. They also decide whether people under arrest should be held in jail or released on bail. Magistrates may also hear minor cases.

U.S. Attorneys Each judicial district has a United States attorney and one or more deputies. U.S. attorneys are government lawyers who prosecute people accused of breaking federal laws. They look into complaints of crime, prepare formal charges, and then present evidence in court. It is the U.S. attorney's job to represent the nation in civil cases in which the government is involved. U.S. attorneys are appointed to four-year terms by the president, with consent of the Senate.

U.S. Marshals Each federal judicial district also has a United States marshal. Marshals and their staffs make arrests, collect fines, and take convicted persons to prison. They protect jurors, keep order in federal courts, and serve legal papers, including subpoenas. A subpoena is a court order requiring someone to appear in court.

✓ **Reading Check** Defining What is senatorial courtesy?

W Writing Support

Persuasive Writing Have students write a paragraph stating their position on life tenure for federal judges. **OL**

✓ **Reading Check** **Answer:** When the president wants to appoint someone as a federal judge, the senators of the candidate's home state may reject or accept the candidate before the full Senate votes.

Assess

Civics ONLINE

Study Central™ provides summaries, interactive games, and online graphic organizers to help students review content.

Close

Summarizing Have students work in small groups to create a two-minute oral presentation about the organization of the federal courts. **OL**

Section 2 Review

Vocabulary

1. **Write** sentences using each of the following key terms: *district court, original jurisdiction, appeals court, appellate jurisdiction, remand, opinion, precedent.*

Main Ideas

2. **Describing** What are the responsibilities of judges in district courts?

3. **Explaining** Why do federal judges serve for life? Who appoints them to these terms?

Critical Thinking

4. **Analyzing** A judge who shares a president's views when first appointed may rule differently on cases later. Why?

5. **BIG Ideas** On a graphic organizer like the one below, identify the people who help federal court judges with their duties.

6. **Analyzing Visuals** Review the organization of the U.S. courts system on page 245. What type of jurisdiction do U.S. Courts of Appeals have? Explain what this means.

CITIZENSHIP Activity

7. **Creative Writing** Write a job description for a federal district judge. Include the qualifications you believe federal judges should have.

Civics ONLINE

Study Central™ To review this section, go to glencoe.com.

Answers

1. Sentences should use vocabulary words according to their definitions in the section and in the Glossary.

2. Judges in district courts hear the facts of a case in order to decide guilt or innocence.

3. Federal judges serve for life because the Constitution provides such job security. The president appoints federal judges with Senate approval.

4. Once the president who appointed a judge is no longer in office, that judge is less inclined to be influenced by the president's agenda. Also, a person's attitudes and beliefs change with time and experience.

5.

6. Courts of Appeals have appellate jurisdiction, meaning they have the authority to hear a case appealed from a lower district court. They have the power to uphold or reverse a lower court's decision; they can also remand a case—send it back to the lower court to be tried again. They do not determine guilt or innocence but whether or not the trial was fair and the ruling just.

7. Job descriptions and qualifications will vary. Papers should list any sources that students used.

Focus

Bellringer
Daily Focus Transparency 8–3

Guide to Reading
Answers to Graphic:

Powers of the Supreme Court

- **Judicial Review**
- **Interpreting Laws**

It can review any federal, state, or local law or action to see if it is constitutional.

It can nullify or cancel laws found unconstitutional.

Section Spotlight Video

Have students watch the Chapter 8, Section 3 video at glencoe.com.

Resource Manager

🔊 **Section Audio**   📺 **Spotlight Video**

Guide to Reading

Big Idea
The judicial branch is charged with interpreting the law.

Content Vocabulary
- judicial review *(p. 252)*
- constitutional *(p. 252)*

Academic Vocabulary
- philosophy *(p. 250)*
- conflict *(p. 252)*

Reading Strategy
Summarizing On a graphic organizer similar to the one below, describe the powers of the Supreme Court and give an example of each.

Powers of the Supreme Court

Judicial Review

Section 3

The Supreme Court

Real World Civics How many people are appointed to a job for life? U.S. Supreme Court justices are. William O. Douglas served on the Court for 36 years, longer than any other justice. John Marshall served longest as chief justice, 34 years. Since justices can serve a lifetime, many different groups want a say in their confirmation. When Justice Sandra Day O'Connor announced she was stepping down in 2005, the White House saw its chance to select a judge who supports President Bush's views. Samuel Alito, Jr., was confirmed and sworn in following a tough confirmation battle in the Senate.

▼ **Justices Souter, Thomas, and Ginsburg attending the swearing in of Justice Alito**

R **Reading Strategies**	C **Critical Thinking**	D **Differentiated Instruction**	W **Writing Support**	S **Skill Practice**
Teacher Edition • Identifying, p. 249 • Questioning, p. 250 • Making Connections, p. 251 • Summarizing, p. 252 **Additional Resources** • Cont. Vocab., URB p. 70 • Guid. Read., URB p. 89 • RENTG, p. 81	**Teacher Edition** • Pred. Conseq., p. 250 • Compare/Contrast, p. 252 **Additional Resources** • Cit./Dec.-Making, URB p. 3 • Biographies, URB p. 73 • Crit. Think., URB p. 77 • Quizzes and Tests, p. 90	**Teacher Edition** • Adv. Learners, p. 249 **Additional Resources** • Diff. Instr., URB p. 81 • School-to-Home Act., URB p. 83 • Teacher's Guide to Diff. Instruction, p. 10	**Teacher Edition** • Personal Writing, p. 253 **Additional Resources** • Cit./Decision-Making, URB p. 3	**Teacher Edition** • Creating a Time Line, p. 251 **Additional Resources** • Daily Focus Trans., 8–3 • Pol. Cartoons Trans. 8

Jurisdiction and Powers

Main Idea The Supreme Court is composed of nine justices: the chief justice of the United States and eight associate justices.

Civics & You What qualities do you think a judge should have? Read on to find out how the justices of the Supreme Court are selected.

Chief Justice of the Supreme Court John G. Roberts, Jr., summarized his view of the Court's role in the following way:

" *What Daniel Webster termed, 'the miracle of our Constitution' is not something that happens in every generation. But every generation in its turn must accept the responsibility of supporting and defending the Constitution, and bearing true faith and allegiance to it.* "

—Chief Justice John G. Roberts, Jr.

As Justice Roberts noted, all Americans are called upon to support the Constitution. It stands above all other courts. The Supreme Court's main job is to decide whether laws are allowable under the U.S. Constitution.

Jurisdiction

Like the federal government, the power of the Supreme Court is limited. Article III of the U.S. Constitution established the boundaries of federal judicial power.

The Supreme Court has original jurisdiction in only two instances. It can preside over cases that involve diplomats from foreign countries and in disputes between states. In all other instances, the Supreme Court hears cases that have been appealed from lower district courts or federal regulatory agencies.

The Supreme Court does not hear all the cases it receives. It chooses the cases it hears. It has final authority in any case involving the Constitution, acts of Congress, and treaties with other nations. The decisions of the Court are binding on all lower courts. When the Court refuses to hear a case, the decision of the lower court stands.

The Supreme Court Seated left to right: Anthony Kennedy, John Paul Stevens, Chief Justice John G. Roberts, Jr., Antonin Scalia, David Souter. Standing left to right: Stephen Breyer, Clarence Thomas, Ruth Bader Ginsburg, Samuel Alito, Jr. *Describing* **Why do you think Congress keeps the number of justices an uneven number?**

249

Teach

R Reading Strategy

Identifying Have students create word webs for "philosophy" and "conflict," listing synonyms for each word. *(Philosophy: beliefs, values, viewpoint, thinking, ideas, way of life. Conflict: war, disagreement, clash, dispute, difference, argument.)* **ELL BL**

D Differentiated Instruction

Advanced Learners Chief Justice Roberts made this comment when being sworn into office. Have students explain the importance of Daniel Webster in American history. **Ask:** Who was Daniel Webster and what would he have thought of Chief Justice Roberts' comment? *(Daniel Webster, 1782–1852, was a leading American statesman, administrator, and diplomat. Webster would have agreed with Roberts. Webster sacrificed his own ideals—and political career—by supporting the Compromise Measure of 1850 because he believed that to not allow enactment of the Fugitive Slave Law would contradict the Constitution.)* **AL**

Caption Answer:
there will always be a tie-breaker on close decisions

Additional Support

Activity: Interdisciplinary Connection

Literature and History Have students find and read the short story "The Devil and Daniel Webster," by Steven Vincent Benét. It is available either online or through a local library. Originally published by the *Saturday Evening Post* in 1938, it tells the story of how Daniel Webster helps a New Hampshire man who has sold his soul to the devil get out of the contract. The short story won the 1938 *O. Henry* literary award. In 1939, it was adapted for a folk music opera, and in 1941 the story was adapted for screenplay and released as a film. Students can work in small groups to interpret the political significance of the short story as it relates to fundamental freedoms in the United States and our notion of equal justice under the law. **Ask:** What does Webster, as defense attorney, demand for his client? *(the right to trial by a jury of his peers)* **OL**

R Reading Strategy

Questioning Students can prepare themselves to learn new material by asking questions on the topic. One tip is to change a subtitle into a question. **Ask:** What questions can you ask yourself about 'Organization and Duties'? *(What is the organization of the Supreme Court? What are the duties of the justices?)* What question can you ask yourself about 'Selecting the Justices'? *(How are Supreme Court justices selected?)* **BL ELL**

C Critical Thinking

Predicting Consequences Ask: What would result if, when appointing new justices, the president repeatedly rejected advice from members of the Senate? *(Students' answers will vary. Certainly a lack of cooperation and compromise on the president's part could make it difficult for the president to get his or her programs approved in the future.)* **OL**

American Biography

Answer:

As the first woman to be appointed to the Supreme Court, Justice O'Connor had to deflect any sexism directed at her. The source of her influence and authority was her intellect.

Differentiated Instruction

American Biography

Sandra Day O'Connor (1930–)

When a Supreme Court vacancy opened up in 1981, President Ronald Reagan decided to fulfill his campaign promise to name the first woman justice. He chose **Sandra Day O'Connor**, an Arizona appeals court judge.

Unlike most Supreme Court justices, O'Connor also had broad political experience. After earning a law degree in 1952, she found that most law firms would not hire a woman—except as a legal secretary. She went into public service, had three sons, and practiced law privately. Appointed to a state senatorial vacancy in 1969, she successfully ran for the position and became its first woman majority leader in 1972. O'Connor won the election for superior court judge in 1974 and was later appointed to the appeals court.

Her nomination to the Supreme Court had strong support, but was opposed by some because she had supported the Equal Rights Amendment (ERA) and refused to back an antiabortion amendment. Others, however, praised her legal judgment.

O'Connor's years on the Court marked her as a conservative jurist; however, she often occupied the Court's "middle ground," by casting the deciding vote on many controversial issues.

Making a Difference CITIZENSHIP

Justice O'Connor once said, "The power I exert on the Court depends on the power of my arguments, not on my gender." **Explain** What is the meaning of this statement?

Organization and Duties

R The Supreme Court is made of eight associate justices led by a chief justice. Congress sets this number and has the power to change it. The justices are important political decision makers. Their rulings often affect citizens as much as do presidential or congressional decisions.

The main duty of justices is to hear and rule on cases. They choose which cases to hear from among the thousands appealed to the Court each year, then decide the case itself and issue a written explanation for the decision, called the Court's opinion.

Selecting the Justices

The president appoints Supreme Court justices, with the approval of the Senate. Vacancies in the Court open up due to the resignation or death of a justice. In 2005, for example, President Bush appointed John G. Roberts, Jr., as chief justice, following the death of Chief Justice William Rehnquist. He also selected Samuel Alito, Jr., to replace Sandra Day O'Connor, who resigned.

C Presidents are careful to choose nominees who are likely to be approved by the Senate. The president's decision is often influenced by the attorney general and other Justice Department officials, other Supreme Court justices, the American Bar Association, and interest groups, such as labor and civil rights groups.

Senators typically give the president advice in appointing new justices, which he is free to accept or ignore. The Senate also has rejected nominees based on doubts about the qualifications or the legal **philosophy** (system of beliefs) of the persons nominated.

Thurgood Marshall

Biography Activity 8, URB p. 73–74

Objective: To identify legal cases that created Marshall's legacy

Focus: Have students identify the importance of Marshall to the civil rights movement.

Teach: Discuss how Marshall's personal life affected his professional career.

Assess: List the important events and accomplishments in Marshall's life.

Close: Write a paragraph summarizing Marshall's importance in the desegregation movement.

Differentiated Instruction Strategies

BL Ask: Why do you think Marshall fought for racial justice?

AL Ask: As a Supreme Court justice, why would Marshall have supported the federal government over the states?

ELL Ask: What is racial segregation? Give an example.

Background of the Justices

Supreme Court justices are always lawyers, although there is no legal requirement that they must be lawyers. They have had careers practicing or teaching law, serving as judges in lower courts, or holding other public positions prior to appointment.

Political support and agreement with the president's ideas are important factors in who gets appointed. Of course, once appointed, a justice may make rulings with which the president does not agree.

The first African American justice, Thurgood Marshall, joined the Court in 1967. The first female justice, Sandra Day O'Connor, was appointed in 1981.

✔ **Reading Check** **Identifying** Who makes up the Supreme Court?

Powers of the Court

Main Idea The Supreme Court is the final court to which anyone can appeal a legal decision.

Civics & You How do you feel when someone makes a decision that you feel is against the law? Read to find out about the Supreme Court and the constitutionality of the law.

The Supreme Court enjoys a great deal of power and prestige. The legislative and executive branches of government must follow the Supreme Court's rulings. The fact that the Supreme Court is removed from politics and from the influences of special-interest groups makes it more likely that the parties involved in a case will get a fair hearing.

Special Rulings The Supreme Court ruled on whether these residents of Washington, D.C., burning their federal tax statements could vote in federal elections. **Identifying** Which branches of the federal government must follow Supreme Court rulings?

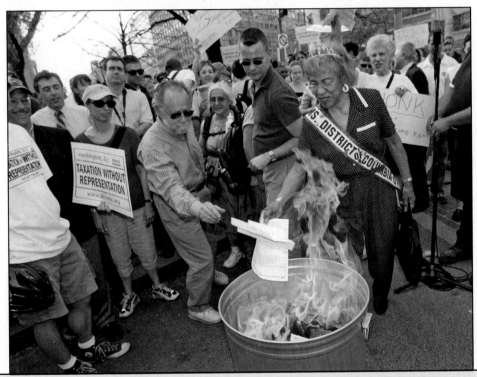

251

Hands-On Chapter Project
Step 3

A Day in Court

Step 3: Path to the Supreme Court Groups continue their work preparing cases that they began in Section 1.

Directions Discuss how this case will reach the Supreme Court. **Ask:** Where does a case first get heard? *(All cases are first heard in a U.S. District Court.)* **OL**

Mitsuye Endo was forced to leave her job and her home, was detained in a prison camp for months, and was never charged for violating any law. Write "habeas corpus" and explain that it comes from Latin: "You (should) have the body." Discuss what it meant for Endo to petition for a writ of habeas corpus. *(It gave her the right to a court hearing.)* **Ask:** Why is the right to petition for a writ of habeas corpus often referred to as the "centerpiece of our liberty"? *(Students should recognize the right to be released from unlawful imprisonment.)* **OL**

(Project continued in Section 4)

R Reading Strategy

Summarizing Have students work in pairs to rewrite the quotation in their own words. Remind them to use synonyms for the words "emphatically," "province," "expound," and "interpret."
Ask: When Chief Justice Marshall says the "judicial department," what is he really talking about? *(the Supreme Court)* **BL** **ELL**

C Critical Thinking

Comparing and Contrasting Ask: Both the Judiciary Act of 1798 and the case of *Marbury* v. *Madison* gave the Supreme Court the power of judicial review. How were they different? *(The Judiciary Act granted the Supreme Court the power of judicial review for acts of state governments only, whereas* Marbury v. Madison *gave the Supreme Court power of judicial review over any laws that Congress enacted.)* **OL**

TIME™ Political Cartoons

Answers:
1. The setting is the Supreme Court; depicted is a panel of three judges.
2. The Supreme Court is the ultimate authority in determining the constitutionality of a law.
3. The law is nullified.

Differentiated Instruction

Judicial Review

One of the most important powers of the Supreme Court is the power of judicial review. **Judicial review** means that the Court can review any federal, state, or local law or action to see if it is **constitutional,** or allowed by the Constitution. If the Court decides a law is unconstitutional, it has the power to nullify, or cancel, that law or action. Chief Justice John Marshall described the great power of judicial review when he said,

> **"** It is emphatically the province and duty of the judicial department to say what the law is. Those who apply the rule to particular cases, must of necessity expound and interpret that rule. If two laws conflict with each other, the courts must decide on the operation of each. **"**
>
> —Chief Justice John Marshall

Marbury v. Madison The Constitution does not give the Supreme Court the power of judicial review. A provision of the Judiciary Act of 1789 gave the Court the power of judicial review for acts of state governments. In 1803 the case of *Marbury* v. *Madison* established that the Supreme Court had the power to decide whether laws passed by Congress were constitutional.

(📖 See Landmark Supreme Court Case Studies on page 260 for information about this case.)

John Marshall's opinion set forth three principles of judicial review:

- The Constitution is the supreme law of the land.
- If there is a **conflict,** or a disagreement, between the Constitution and any other law, the Constitution rules.
- The judicial branch has a duty to uphold the Constitution. Thus, it must be able to determine when a law conflicts with the Constitution and to nullify unconstitutional laws.

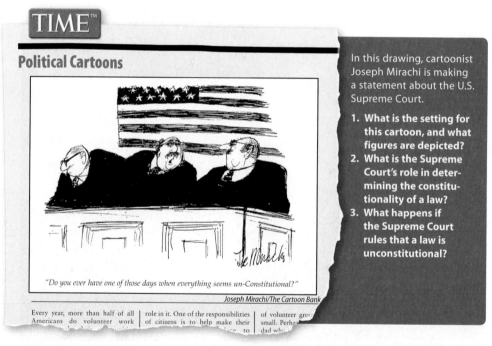

TIME™

Political Cartoons

"Do you ever have one of those days when everything seems un-Constitutional?"

Joseph Mirachi/The Cartoon Bank

In this drawing, cartoonist Joseph Mirachi is making a statement about the U.S. Supreme Court.

1. **What is the setting for this cartoon, and what figures are depicted?**
2. **What is the Supreme Court's role in determining the constitutionality of a law?**
3. **What happens if the Supreme Court rules that a law is unconstitutional?**

Every year, more than half of all Americans do volunteer work... role in it. One of the responsibilities of citizens is to help make their... of volunteer grou... small. Perha... dad wh...

Leveled Activities

BL Academic Vocabulary Activity 8, URB p. 72

OL Biography Activity 8, URB pp. 73–74

OL Critical Thinking Skills Activity 8, URB pp. 77–78

ELL Differentiated Instruction, URB pp. 81–82

The power of judicial review is an important check on the legislative and executive branches of government. It prevents them [W] from straying too far from the Constitution when they make and carry out laws.

Limits on the Supreme Court

Under the system of checks and balances, there are limits on the power of the federal courts, including the Supreme Court. The Court depends on the executive branch as well as state and local officials, such as governors or police officers, to enforce its decisions.

The executive branch usually follows Court rulings, but there have been exceptions. President Andrew Jackson refused to obey a Court ruling in the case of *Worcester* v. *Georgia*, in which Chief Justice John Marshall ordered the state of Georgia to stop violating federal land treaties with the Cherokee Nation in 1832. Because most citizens agreed with President Jackson, there was no public pressure to force him to uphold the Court's decision.

Congress can get around a Court ruling by passing a new law or changing a law ruled unconstitutional by the Court. Congress and state legislatures can also try to undo Court rulings by adopting a new amendment to the Constitution.

Another limit is the fact that the Court can only hear and make rulings on the cases that come to it. All cases submitted to the Court must be actual legal disputes. A person cannot simply ask the Court to decide whether a law is constitutional. The Court will not rule on a law or action that has not been challenged on appeal. The Court also accepts only cases that involve a federal question.

Traditionally, the Court has refused to deal with political questions because it believes that these are issues the executive or legislative branch of the government should resolve. However, in the 2000 presidential election, the Supreme Court for the first time heard two cases involving the recounting of votes in the state of Florida.

✓ Reading Check **Explaining** How does the Supreme Court receive the cases it considers?

 Review

Vocabulary

1. **Write** a true statement *and* a false statement for the terms: *judicial review, constitutional.* Beside each false statement explain why it is false.

Main Ideas

2. **Describe** the selection process for Supreme Court justices.

3. **Analyzing** What is the significance of the case of *Marbury* v. *Madison* and how it relates to Congress?

Critical Thinking

4. **Interpreting** Former Chief Justice Charles Evans Hughes once said, "The Constitution is what the judges say it is." Explain the meaning of this statement.

5. **BIG Ideas** On a graphic organizer like the one below, list the kinds of laws that can be reviewed in judicial review and what they are reviewed for.

Laws Reviewed

CITIZENSHIP Activity

6. **Expository Writing** Select one Supreme Court Justice, either past or current. Research more about and write a report on the justice.

Civics ONLINE

Study Central™ To review this section, go to glencoe.com.

W Writing Support

Personal Writing Have students write one paragraph expressing their thoughts about the power of judicial review. **OL**

✓ Reading Check **Answer:** It must be a case that was challenged on appeal or that involves a federal question.

Assess

Civics ONLINE

Study Central™ provides summaries, interactive games, and online graphic organizers to help students review content.

Close

Analyzing Information Tell students that in *Worcester* v. *Georgia*, the Supreme Court ruled that the state of Georgia did not have jurisdiction over the Cherokees and thus had no right to force them off their lands. President Jackson refused to enforce the ruling, leading to the eviction of the Cherokee nation. **Ask:** Does our president today have the right to refuse to follow a Supreme Court ruling? Why or why not? *(Yes; the Supreme Court has no way to enforce its rulings.)* **OL**

Section 3 Review

Answers

1. Sentences should use vocabulary words according to their definitions in the section and in the Glossary.

2. In order to become a Supreme Court justice one must be appointed by the president and confirmed by the Senate.

3. *Marbury* v. *Madison* gives the Supreme Court judicial review over Congress and the laws it enacts.

4. Answers should refer to the authority of the Supreme Court when it comes to interpreting the Constitution and determining the constitutionality of any law whether enacted by a state or by Congress.

5.

| Executive branch: strays from Constitution | Act of Congress: unconstitutional | Act of State: conflicts with the Constitution |

Laws Reviewed

6. Students' choice of justices will vary. They should cite all research sources and reference material at the end of their report.

Focus

Bellringer
Daily Focus Transparency 8–4

Guide to Reading
Answers to Graphic:

Supreme Court Decisions

Dissenting Opinions → Oppose majority's decision

Concurring Opinions → Agree with majority's decision → Different reason for decision

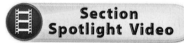

Section Spotlight Video

Have students watch the Chapter 8, Section 4 video at glencoe.com.

Resource Manager

Guide to Reading

Big Idea
The judicial branch is charged with interpreting the law.

Content Vocabulary
- docket *(p. 255)*
- brief *(p. 256)*
- majority opinion *(p. 256)*
- unanimous opinion *(p. 256)*
- concurring opinion *(p. 256)*
- dissenting opinion *(p. 256)*
- stare decisis *(p. 257)*

Academic Vocabulary
- communicate *(p. 256)*
- attitude *(p. 257)*

Reading Strategy
Contrasting As you read, use a graphic organizer similar to the one below to take notes on the differences between dissenting opinions and concurring opinions.

Supreme Court Decisions

Dissenting Opinions | Concurring Opinions

 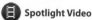

The Supreme Court at Work

Real World Civics At times, the Supreme Court has changed its mind due to changing social conditions. In the 1890s, the Supreme Court ruled that segregation in America was legal. But in the 1950s, nine African American students won a lower court case to desegregate Central High School in Little Rock, Arkansas. In 1958, Thurgood Marshall, a lawyer for the National Association for the Advancement of Colored People (NAACP), helped convince the Supreme Court that Little Rock had to proceed with integration.

▼ **Thurgood Marshall with Little Rock students on the steps of the Supreme Court building in Washington, D.C., in 1958**

254

R Reading Strategies	**C** Critical Thinking	**D** Differentiated Instruction	**W** Writing Support	**S** Skill Practice
Teacher Edition • Taking Notes, p. 255 • Using Context Clues, p. 255 • Act. Prior Know., p. 256 • Making Connections, p. 257 **Additional Resources** • Cont. Vocab., URB p. 70 • Guid. Read., URB p. 90 • Foldables, p. 65	**Teacher Edition** • Ident. Cent. Issues, p. 256 • Analyzing Info., p. 257 • Det. Cause/Effect, p. 258 **Additional Resources** • Crit. Think., URB p. 77 • Quizzes and Tests, p. 91	**Teacher Edition** • Visual/Spatial, p. 257 **Additional Resources** • Speak/Listen Skills Act., URB p. 9 • School-to-Home Act., URB p. 84 • Reteach. Act., URB p. 85	**Teacher Edition** • Narrative Writing, p. 259 **Additional Resources** • Cit./Dec.-Making, URB p. 3	**Teacher Edition** • Reading a Graph, p. 255 **Additional Resources** • Chart, Map, and Graph Skills, URB p. 79 • Daily Focus Trans., 8–4

Court Procedures

Main Idea The Supreme Court is not required to hear all cases presented before it and carefully chooses the cases it will consider.

Civics & You In a dispute, why might it be helpful to have an impartial third party decide who is right and who is wrong? Read to find out the process the Supreme Court uses to make an unbiased decision.

The Supreme Court meets for about nine months each year. Each term begins the first Monday in October and runs as long as the business before the Court requires. A term is named after the year in which it begins. The 2009 term, for example, began in October 2009 and ended in July 2010. Special sessions may be called to deal with urgent matters that cannot wait until the next term. Between terms the justices study new cases and catch up on other Court work.

How Cases Reach the Court

An important task of Supreme Court justices is to decide whether to hear a case. The justices review a list of possible cases and consider their merits. The Court will accept a case if four of the nine justices agree to do so. Accepted cases go on the Court **docket,** or calendar.

Caseload The number of cases handled in a given period is called the caseload. Thousands of cases are filed with the Supreme Court each year. Nearly 8,900 cases were appealed to the Supreme Court in 2006. The Court may decide several hundred cases, but, for example, it gave full hearings and written opinions in only 67 cases in 2006.

In the opinions that accompany this small number of cases, the Court sets out general principles that apply to the nation as well as to the specific parties in the case. It is mainly through these cases that the Court interprets the law and shapes public policy.

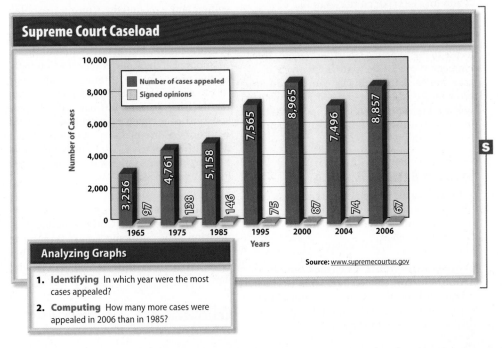

Supreme Court Caseload

Number of cases appealed | Signed opinions

Year	Number of cases appealed	Signed opinions
1965	3,256	97
1975	4,761	138
1985	5,158	146
1995	7,565	75
2000	8,965	87
2004	7,496	74
2006	8,857	67

Source: www.supremecourtus.gov

Analyzing Graphs

1. **Identifying** In which year were the most cases appealed?
2. **Computing** How many more cases were appealed in 2006 than in 1985?

Chapter 8 255

Differentiated Instruction

Selecting Cases

Supreme Court justices decide to hear only certain kinds of cases. They usually decide to hear a case if it involves a significant constitutional question. In most instances, such questions center around the Bill of Rights and other amendments and deal with issues such as freedom of speech, equal protection of the laws, and fair trial.

The justices always choose cases that involve a real dispute between two adversaries, or opposing sides. In other words, the cases must deal with real people and events.

Supreme Court justices also tend to select cases that involve legal, rather than political issues, as well as those that affect the entire country rather than isolated individuals or groups.

You have already learned that nearly all cases come to the Supreme Court on appeal from a lower court. Most of the appeals reach the Court by a request for a writ of certiorari (Latin for "to make more certain").

Writ of Certiorari A writ of certiorari directs a lower court to send its records on a case to the Supreme Court for review. This happens if one of the parties involved in a case claims that the lower court made an error in the case. Sometimes a lower court will ask the Supreme Court to make a ruling in a case because it is not sure how to apply the law to the case.

Steps in Decision Making

Every case the Supreme Court accepts goes through a series of steps: written arguments, oral arguments, conference, opinion writing, and announcement.

Written Arguments Once the Court takes a case, the lawyers for each side prepare a brief. A **brief** is a written document that explains one side's position on the case. The justices then study the briefs.

Oral Arguments Next, lawyers for each side present oral arguments. Each side gets only 30 minutes to summarize its case. The justices often ask the lawyers very tough questions about the case.

Conference On Fridays the justices get together to make their first decisions about the cases they have been studying. These meetings take place in secret; no audience is present and no meeting minutes are kept. The chief justice presides over the discussion of the case. A majority—at least five votes when all nine justices are participating—decides a case. At least six justices must be present for a decision.

Opinion Writing Once the Court has reached a decision on a case, one justice gets the job of writing the majority opinion. A **majority opinion** presents the views of the majority of the justices on a case. The opinion states the facts of the case, announces the ruling, and explains the Court's reasoning in reaching the decision. Written opinions are important. They set a precedent for lower courts to follow, and they also **communicate,** or announce, the Court's view to Congress, to the president, to interest groups, and to the public. The justice who agrees with the majority decision but has different reasons writes a **concurring opinion.** Justices who oppose the majority decision issue a **dissenting opinion.** The Court may also issue a **unanimous opinion** in which all the justices vote the same way.

Announcement When the opinion writing is completed, the Court announces its decision. The Supreme Court and other courts around the country use the written opinions to guide their decisions regarding new cases.

✔**Reading Check** **Explaining** Why are the Court's written opinions important?

Leveled Activities

Reasons for Decisions

Main Idea The law, social conditions, and legal and personal views are among the factors that influence the decisions of the Supreme Court.

Civics & You The Supreme Court hears cases appealed to it by everyone from prisoners in jail to presidents. What influences the justices' decisions?

Many factors, such as precedents, the social atmosphere in the country, and the justices' own legal and personal views, influence justices when they decide a case that comes before the Court.

The Law Law is the foundation for deciding cases that come before the Supreme Court. A guiding principle for all judges is called **stare decisis,** a Latin term that means "let the decision stand." By following precedent, courts make the law predictable.

At the same time, the law needs to be flexible to adapt to changing times. Social conditions, public ideas and **attitudes,** or feelings, and technology change over the years. As the highest court in the land, the Supreme Court is in a position to overrule outdated precedents.

The Supreme Court sometimes reviews a case to clarify the meaning of the Constitution for an important issue. This happened with disputes over manually recounting the Florida ballots in the presidential election of 2000. The dispute led the Court to address a question involving the Fourteenth Amendment: did all recounted votes have to be treated equally? In *Bush* v. *Gore* (2000), the Court ordered the recount to stop. This decision ensured that George W. Bush would receive Florida's electoral votes and win the election.

Changing Social Conditions Although the Supreme Court is somewhat protected from public and political pressures, the social situation can also influence Court decisions. When social conditions change, the Court may make new interpretations of the law.

Constitutional Question Demonstrators gathered outside the Supreme Court building in Washington, D.C., while justices considered the recount question of the 2000 presidential election. *Analyzing* Why did the Supreme Court rule on the issue rather than a state court?

257

C Critical Thinking

Determining Cause and Effect Ask:
Why do some historians believe that what happened during WWII had such a significant impact for social change that both the civil rights movement and the women's movement started because of it? *(During WWII, African Americans serving in the armed forces tolerated segregation and second-class treatment. Upon their return, they found themselves denied access to decent housing and jobs being offered to white veterans. During the war, many women had to assume the roles and jobs of men. When the war ended, most of the women were forced to give up their jobs to men, and many faced societal pressure to marry. As a result, both groups yearned for fuller participation in and respect from society.)* **AL**

Analyzing Charts

Answers:
1. *Brown* v. *Board of Education*, 1954, overturned *Plessy* v. *Ferguson*, 1896.
2. These decisions reflect a new interpretation of the Constitution due to changing social conditions and, as such, either set long-reaching precedents or overturned previous rulings.

Hands-On Chapter Project
Step 4

A Day in Court

Step 4: A Court Procedures Groups continue their work preparing the cases that they began in Section 1.

Directions Discuss court procedures for each group to present its case. Explain that one must apply to the Supreme Court for a *writ of certiorari*. If at least three justices

---

Landmark Decisions of the Supreme Court

FEDERAL POWER

- *Marbury* v. *Madison* (1803) established the Supreme Court's power of judicial review
- *McCulloch* v. *Maryland* (1819) ruled that in a conflict between national and state power, the national government is supreme
- *Gibbons* v. *Ogden* (1824) established that Congress has sole authority to regulate interstate commerce

CIVIL LIBERTIES

- *Brown* v. *Board of Education* (1954) overturned *Plessy* v. *Ferguson* (1896), which said African Americans could be provided with "separate but equal" public facilities; began school integration
- *Reed* v. *Reed* (1971) held that a state law that discriminated against women was unconstitutional
- *Roe* v. *Wade* (1973) legalized a woman's right to an abortion under certain circumstances
- *Bush* v. *Gore* (2000) ruled that Florida recount of presidential votes violated Fourteenth Amendment; recount stopped and Bush became president

FIRST AMENDMENT RIGHTS

- *Brandenburg* v. *Ohio* (1969) expanded the protection of political speech unless it is linked to immediate lawless behavior
- *Near* v. *Minnesota* (1931) ruled against censorship of information, defining "prior restraint" of written material as unconstitutional
- *DeJonge* v. *Oregon* (1937) reinforced peaceable assembly and association protection of the First Amendment
- *Engel* v. *Vitale* (1962) held that a public school district's practice of starting the day with prayer violates the establishment clause
- *United States* v. *Eichman* (1990) struck down Federal Flag Protection Act; held that flag burning is expressive speech

RIGHTS OF THE ACCUSED

- *Gideon* v. *Wainwright* (1963) declared that a person accused of a major crime had the right to legal counsel during a trial
- *Miranda* v. *Arizona* (1966) ruled that at the time of arrest suspects cannot be questioned until informed of their rights
- *Hamdan* v. *Rumsfeld* (2006) ruled that special military courts for foreign prisoners violated U.S. military law and international laws

Analyzing Charts

1. **Analyzing** What earlier decision did *Brown* v. *Board of Education* overturn?
2. **Concluding** Why do you think these decisions are called "landmark" decisions?

In the 1890s, many restaurants, schools, and trains were separate for whites or for African Americans. In Louisiana, Homer Plessy, an African American, decided to sit in a section of a train marked "For Whites Only." When he refused to move, Plessy was arrested.

Plessy was convicted of violating Louisiana's segregation law. The Supreme Court upheld the Louisiana law as constitutional in *Plessy* v. *Ferguson.* "Legislation is powerless to eradi-

cate racial instincts or to abolish distinctions," the Court concluded. The Court ruled that the equal protection clause of the Fourteenth Amendment permitted "separate but equal" facilities for whites and for African Americans. The "separate but equal" doctrine was used to justify segregation in many areas of American life for the next 50 years.

---

agree that the case merits review, then the Supreme Court will direct the lower court to send the records. Refer students to the government Web site for further research. http://www.uscourts.gov/outreach/topics/hamdan/procedures.html.

Ask: What has to happen in order for Mitsuye Endo's case to be reviewed by the Supreme Court? *(Her lawyers must first peti-*

tion the Supreme Court to review her case. Then, if all goes well, the Supreme Court presents a writ of certiorari to the lower court.) How many justices must vote to hear and rule on a case? *(Four out of nine justices must vote to hear a case.)* **OL**

(Project continued on the Visual Summary page)

Reversing *Plessy* However, by the 1950s, society's views on racial segregation were beginning to change. World War II made it harder to support segregation openly because many African Americans had fought and died for American ideals. In addition, civil rights groups were demanding an end to racial discrimination. In 1954, in the case of *Brown* v. *Board of Education of Topeka, Kansas,* the Court overturned the precedent of "separate but equal."

On May 17, 1954, Chief Justice Earl Warren read the decision of the unanimous Court:

> **"** *We conclude that in the field of public education the doctrine of 'separate but equal' has no place. Separate educational facilities are inherently unequal.* **"**

The justices ruled that racially separate schools are unequal simply because they are separate. The Court found that segregation was a violation of the equal protection clause of the Fourteenth Amendment.

Differing Legal Views Justices have varying views of the law and the proper role of the courts in our society. Some justices, for example, believe that the Court should be very active and hear many different kinds of cases. Others believe that the Court should hesitate to use the power of judicial review to promote new ideas or policies. Political checks limit the extent to which courts can exercise judicial review. **W**

Personal Beliefs Finally, justices are human beings. Each sees the world based on his or her own life experiences. Justice Benjamin Cardozo once said,

> **"** *We may try to see things as objectively as we please. Nonetheless, we can never see them with any eyes except our own.* **"**
>
> —Benjamin Cardozo,
> *The Nature of the Judicial Process* (1921)

✔ **Reading Check** **Summarizing** Why do you think the Court relies on the concept of stare decisis?

Section 4 Review

Vocabulary

1. **Define** the following terms and use them in sentences that relate to the Supreme Court: *docket, brief, majority opinion, concurring opinion, dissenting opinion, unanimous opinion, stare decisis.*

Main Ideas

2. **Describing** What are the steps of a writ of certiorari?

3. **Explaining** Why does the Supreme Court sometimes reverse its earlier decisions?

Critical Thinking

4. **Concluding** Do you think it is a good idea that Supreme Court justices are appointed for life? Explain your answer.

5. **BIG Ideas** On a web diagram like the one below, identify the factors that must be part of a majority decision made by the Supreme Court.

6. **Analyzing Visuals** Review the chart on page 258. Which ruling guarantees you the right to be informed of your rights if you are arrested?

CITIZENSHIP Activity

7. **Expository Writing** Read more about *Brown* v. *Board of Education of Topeka, Kansas.* Summarize the facts in the case.

Civics ONLINE

Study Central™ To review this section, go to glencoe.com.

Chapter 8   **259**

W **Writing Support**

Narrative Writing Have students write a monologue from the point of view of one of the justices as he or she prepares to deliver a decision at the Supreme Court. **AL**

✔ **Reading Check** **Answer:** Relying on the concept of stare decisis ensures stability in that the Court will follow legal precedents.

Assess

Civics ONLINE

Study Central™ provides summaries, interactive games, and online graphic organizers to help students review content.

Close

Synthesizing Discuss with students how a nation's values are reflected in its laws. **Ask:** What factors do you believe most influence the decisions of the Supreme Court? *(Student responses will vary and may include legal precedent, the Constitution, public opinion, and so on.)* **OL**

Section 4 Review

Answers

1. Sentences should use vocabulary words according to their definitions in the section and in the Glossary.

2. The Supreme Court selects a case that at least four justices agree to review. If that case came to the Supreme Court on appeal, a writ of certiorari will direct the lower court to send its records to the Supreme Court for review.

3. A Supreme Court reverses earlier decisions when there are changes in social conditions or public attitudes.

4. Students' viewpoints and explanations will vary.

5.

6. *Miranda* v. *Arizona,* 1966, guarantees the right to be informed of your rights if you are arrested.

7. Summaries should include the salient facts of the case. Check that students list all references, whether online or in print.

259

Teach

When the new government of the United States was launched in 1789, it was not clear who had the authority to decide whether or not an act of Congress was unconstitutional because the Constitution did not specifically address this question. In 1803, the Supreme Court ruled in the case of *Marbury* v. *Madison* that the Court itself had this power.

Introduce the feature by stressing to students that President John Adams tried to keep his Federalist Party in power by appointing Federalists to judgeships. After students have read page 260, call on volunteers to explain the events that led to the Supreme Court ruling in *Marbury* v. *Madison*. Discuss with students how the ruling helped strengthen the national government at that time.

ANALYZING THE COURT DECISION

Answers:

1. It defined the role of the Supreme Court as the final authority on the meaning of the Constitution.

2. It refused because it ruled that the Constitution did not give the Court the authority to issue writs of mandamus, orders to perform a specified duties, to public officers.

Additional Support

Marbury v. Madison

By the early 1800s, the role of the judicial branch was unclear and its influence small. How did the Supreme Court establish its power of judicial review of Congress?

Background of the Case

As President John Adams' term expired in 1801, Congress passed a bill—the Judiciary Act of 1789—giving the president a chance to appoint 42 new justices of the peace in the District of Columbia. The Senate approved the new appointees, and the Secretary of State, James Madison, delivered the paperwork to all but four of the new judges before the next president—Thomas Jefferson—was sworn in. Because Jefferson wanted to stop any action by the previous officeholder, his first act as president was to stop delivery of those last four appointments. William Marbury was one of those who did not receive his appointment in time. He filed a suit in the Supreme Court under the Judiciary Act against the person who was to deliver the paperwork—James Madison. Marbury claimed he should have received his appointment as declared by Congress.

The Decision

The Supreme Court heard the case in 1803. Chief Justice John Marshall announced the ruling. He stated that Marbury's rights had been violated under the Judiciary Act. The Court further ruled, however, that the act gave the Supreme Court rights it should not have, according to the Constitution. Thus, they ruled that the law itself—the one that gave Marbury his appointment—was unconstitutional. Even though Marbury was ruled the winner, the Court could not force the president to give him the appointment because the law allowing the whole appointment was constitutionally false.

President Adams spent his last night in office signing commissions.

Marshall wrote:

> 66 *It is emphatically the province and duty of the judicial department to say what the law is. Those who apply the rule to particular cases, must of necessity expound and interpret the rule.* 99
>
> —Chief Justice John Marshall

Why It Matters

The Supreme Court claimed its right to declare acts of the legislative and executive branches unconstitutional for the first time in *Marbury* v. *Madison*. It defined its role as the final authority on what the Constitution means. By doing so, it established a model of judicial independence.

Analyzing the Court Decision

1. **Explaining** Why is *Marbury* v. *Madison* a landmark case?

2. **Describing** Why did the Supreme Court refuse to allow the appointment of the last judges?

Background

Marbury* v. *Madison The Constitution never set forth any process to declare an act of Congress unconstitutional. Through this Supreme Court decision, Chief Justice Marshall established that such a declaration, called judicial review, was within the Court's power. The Court also has the power to review presidential policies. During the Civil War, President Abraham Lincoln suspended some civil rights, especially for those who supported the Confederacy. In the case of *Ex parte Milligan* in 1866, the Court ruled that Lincoln's actions were unconstitutional. The Court said that the Constitution applied to everyone equally, even to the president during a time of war.

The Judicial Branch

- The Constitution provided for a Supreme Court of the United States as part of a court system that would balance the powers of the other two branches of government.

- The United States judiciary consists of parallel systems of federal and state courts.

Federal Court System

- District Courts are the federal courts where trials are held and lawsuits are begun.

- Courts of Appeals review decisions made in lower district courts.

- Once appointed, federal judges may have their jobs for life.

Chief Justice John Marshall

The Supreme Court

- The Supreme Court is the final authority in the federal court system.

- Most of the Supreme Court cases come from appeals of lower court decisions.

- Judicial review gives the Supreme Court the authority to determine the constitutionality of government laws and actions.

- The Supreme Court is made up of eight associate justices and a chief justice.

- The Supreme Court does not have unlimited powers. The Constitution provides that the legislative and executive branches of the national government have several ways to check the Supreme Court's power.

Decisions of the Court

- The Court's decisions are written in an opinion.

- When all justices unanimously agree on an opinion, it is written for the entire Court in a unanimous opinion.

- When there is not a unanimous opinion, a majority opinion is written.

- One or more dissenting opinions are usually written by those justices who do not agree with the majority.

Justice Samuel Alito, Jr., being sworn in

STUDY TO GO Study anywhere, anytime! Download quizzes and flash cards to your PDA from glencoe.com.

Visual Summary 8

Making Comparisons Have students work in small groups to research information about judicial review in another country. Then have each group report a summary of their findings to the class. **Ask:** What do nations with judicial review have in common? *(They are mostly European democracies or countries once under colonial rule of a European nation.)* **AL**

For additional practice on this skill (Making Comparisons), see the **Skills Handbook**.

Organizing Have students refer to "Decisions of the Court" to create a flowchart illustrating Supreme Court procedure. Have them include a bulleted list defining "opinion", "unanimous opinion", "majority opinion", "concurring opinion", and "dissenting opinion". **OL**

Hands-On Chapter Project
Step 5: Wrap-Up

A Day in Court

Step 5: Keep It Brief Students will finish the process they started in Step 1.

Directions Student lawyers prepare their briefs and present their arguments to the Court. Have the student justices confer, decide the ruling, and write their opinions.

After the opinions have been written, launch a class discussion about the decision. **Ask:** Was there a strong majority opinion for this case? Why or why not? *(Student answers will vary based on the decision of the case.)* Point out to students that Mitsuye Endo waited confined for more than two years without being charged of any crime. Mitsuye Endo believed in her cause, so she held firm during that time until she won her case. Ask students how they would react to waiting for so long to achieve such a lofty goal. Start a class discussion about what it takes to stand up for what you believe is right. **OL**

Reviewing Vocabulary

1. B Students will have read about concurrent jurisdiction at the very end of Section 1. Answer A, *appellate jurisdiction*, the right to hear appeals, is reserved for the Courts of Appeals and the Supreme Court. Answer C, *original jurisdiction*, refers to the first hearing of a case and could be in a state court or, in certain circumstances, in the Supreme Court. Answer D, exclusive jurisdiction, means only federal courts can hear or try a case.

2. D A sentence defining precedents is in Section 2 above the head "Precedents." Answer B is a distractor for students who confuse a decision with an opinion or think that either is synonymous with precedent. A student is clearly not paying attention if he or she selects answer A, circuit, the geographic district of the federal appeals court, or answer C, docket, the court calendar.

3. A After reading "Judicial Review" in Section 3, students should know the answer. B: Only appellate courts remand a case (Section 2). C: Briefs are written and studied; an argument is what can be rejected (Section 4). Answer D, hear an appeal, is another distractor because students know that cases are appealed to the Supreme Court.

4. D The words in the question that are most important are "all" and "same". Students need to understand that answer A, majority opinion, does not mean everyone agrees with the decision and that answer B, a concurring opinion, can agree with the majority but have a different reason. To chose C, dissenting opinion, indicates no grasp of section content.

Reviewing Main Ideas

5. A Section 1, "Equal Treatment," covers the constitutional right to a public trial and a lawyer. Students selecting B, civil trial, need to know that there are also criminal trials. Answer C is misleading because some students may have read, "Equal Justice Under Law." As for D, there is no Constitutional right to a Supreme Court hearing.

TEST-TAKING TIP

When answering multiple-choice questions, your first answer is usually correct. Do not change an answer unless you are absolutely certain your first answer is wrong.

Reviewing Vocabulary

Directions: Choose the word(s) that best completes the sentence.

1. A situation in which both federal and state courts have authority to hear a case is known as _____.

   A appellate jurisdiction

   B concurrent jurisdiction

   C original jurisdiction

   D exclusive jurisdiction

2. A past decision on which judges base their decisions in similar cases is a(n) _____.

   A circuit   **C** docket

   B opinion   **D** precedent

3. Judicial review gives the Supreme Court the power to _____.

   A declare a law unconstitutional

   B remand a case to a lower court

   C reject a brief

   D hear an appeal

4. When all the justices vote the same way, the Supreme Court issues a(n) _____.

   A majority opinion   **C** dissenting opinion

   B concurring opinion   **D** unanimous opinion

Reviewing Main Ideas

Directions: Choose the best answer for each question.

Section 1 *(pp. 238–242)*

5. According to the Constitution, what does every accused person have a right to?

   A a lawyer

   B a civil trial

   C the best legal help

   D a Supreme Court hearing

6. Which of the following cases would be tried in a federal court?

   A A state sues another state over water rights.

   B A Houstonian kills a person in Los Angeles.

   C An Illinois state worker is accused of forgery.

   D The U.S. ambassador to Russia breaks a Russian law.

Section 2 *(pp. 243–247)*

7. In which federal courts do juries try cases?

   A district courts

   B appellate courts

   C the Supreme Court

   D all levels of federal courts

Section 3 *(pp. 248–253)*

8. How might a president limit the powers of the Supreme Court?

   A submit an appeal to the Court

   B veto Court decisions

   C appoint federal judges

   D refuse to enforce a Supreme Court decision

Section 4 *(pp. 254–259)*

9. What kind of case does the Supreme Court usually decide to hear?

   A a case that concerns political issues

   B a case that involves the Bill of Rights

   C a case that poses hypothetical questions

   D a case that affects only a few individuals

10. What major factor influenced the Court to overturn the "separate but equal" precedent?

   A stare decisis

   B conservatism

   C racial prejudice

   D societal changes

GO ON ▶

6. A The key here is to pay close attention to the paragraphs in the "Federal Court Jurisdiction" on the last two pages of Section 1. Answers B and C are examples of criminal cases that would be tried in the state courts where the crime occurred. Answer D is an example of a case that no U.S. court, state or federal, would try.

7. A After reading "U.S. District Courts" and viewing the chart of the U.S. court system at the beginning of Section 2, it should be clear that only district courts have juries.

8. C This question pertains to the principle of checks and balances, whereby each branch of government exercises some control over the others. Review how the executive branch can limit the powers of the judicial branch.

Critical Thinking

Directions: Base your answers to questions 11 and 12 on the chart below and your knowledge of Chapter 8.

11. Which decision might lead you to infer that the Constitution protects your right to protest war by wearing a black armband?

A *Engle* v. *Vitale*

B *DeJonge* v. *Oregon*

C *Brandenberg* v. *Ohio*

D *United States* v. *Eichman*

First Amendment Rights

***Brandenburg* v. *Ohio* (1969)** expanded scope of political speech by protecting all political speech unless it is linked to immediate lawless behavior

***Near* v. *Minnesota* (1931)** ruled against censorship of information, defining "prior restraint" of written material as unconstitutional

***DeJonge* v. *Oregon* (1937)** reinforced peaceable assembly and association protection of the First Amendment

***Engle* v. *Vitale* (1962)** held that a public school district's practice of starting the day with prayer violates the establishment clause

***United States* v. *Eichman* (1990)** struck down Federal Flag Protection Act; held that flag burning is expressive speech

---

12. What First Amendment freedom did *Near* v. *Minnesota* uphold?

A freedom to petition

B freedom of religion

C freedom of the press

D freedom to assemble

Document Based Questions

Directions: Analyze the document and answer the short-answer questions that follow.

The following document is a summation of the Supreme Court's decision in *Reed* v. *Reed* (1971).

Facts of the Case
The Idaho Probate Code specified that "males must be preferred to females" in naming administrators of estates. After the death of their adopted son, both Sally and Cecil Reed sought to be named the administrator of their son's estate. According to the Probate Code, Cecil was appointed administrator and Sally challenged the law in court.

Question Presented
Did the Idaho Probate Code violate the Equal Protection Clause of the Fourteenth Amendment?

Conclusion
In a unanimous decision, the Court held that the law's dissimilar treatment of men and women was unconstitutional. The Court argued that "[t]o give a mandatory preference to members of either sex over members of the other . . . is to make the very kind of arbitrary legislative choice forbidden by the Equal Protection Clause of the Fourteenth Amendment. . .[T]he choice in this context may not lawfully be mandated solely on the basis of sex."

—Reed v. Reed

---

13. How many Supreme Court justices agreed with the decision in *Reed* v. *Reed*?

14. What is the main idea of the Court's conclusion?

Extended Response

15. Write a brief essay describing the procedure that Supreme Court justices follow in hearing important cases.

Civics ONLINE
For additional test practice, use Self-Check Quizzes—Chapter 8 on glencoe.com.

Need Extra Help?

If you missed question...	1	2	3	4	5	6	7	8	9	10	11	12	13	14	15
Go to page...	242	245	252	256	240	241	244	253	256	259	258	258	256	256	256

ASSESSMENT

Document-Based Questions

13. All the justices agreed with the decision in *Reed* v. *Reed.*

14. The Idaho Probate Court, in denying Sally Reed the right to be the administrator of her son's estate because she was a female, violated the Equal Protection Clause of the Fourteenth Amendment. It is unconstitutional to allow dissimilar treatment of men and women.

Extended Response

15. Students' essays will vary. Look for supporting details from the chapter.

---

9. B The job of the Court is to interpret the Constitution. Answers A and C deal with issues that are not concrete and thus would not attract the Court. The Court also works for the national good, negating answer D.

10. C Students may think choice D is also correct, but racial prejudice is a much more specific and direct response.

Critical Thinking

11. C The choice of the correct answer rests with the student's ability to correctly interpret the case summaries.

12. C Freedom of the press is the only correct response. Selecting any other answer indicates no understanding of either censorship or press.

Civics ONLINE

Have students visit the Web site at glencoe.com to review Chapter 8 and take the **Self-Check Quiz.**

Need Extra Help?

Have students refer to the pages listed if they miss any of the questions.

Analyzing Primary Sources

Focus

C Critical Thinking

Identifying Central Issues Have students discuss the significance of what Margaret Chase Smith wrote by applying her comments to their own life experiences. **Ask:** What does she mean when she writes "the exercise of these rights should not cost one single American citizen his reputation or his right to a livelihood"? *(Students' responses will vary but should all be germane to the basic principles of Americanism in the bulleted list.)* **AL**

Did You Know?

Senator Robert C. Byrd began his political career during the early years of World War II as a local butcher organizing for the KKK in West Virginia. In his autobiography, *A Senator's Shame*, he confessed deep remorse and embarrassment. He does not deny, however, that his experience as a young Klan leader is what launched a lifelong career in politics.

Additional Reading

Analyzing Primary Sources

The Federal Branch of Government

Reading Focus

Each of the excerpts are from persons who have served in the legislative, executive, or judicial branches. Each excerpt provides a view on the workings of that particular branch.

Read to Discover

As you read, think about

- how political and judicial leaders view their roles.
- what values and beliefs these leaders share.

Reader's Dictionary

character assassination: the slandering of a person with the goal of destroying his or her public image

exemplary: showing or illustrating by example

comity: a friendly social atmosphere

usurpation: taking hold of by force and without right

pervasive: spread throughout

The Role of Congress

Senator Margaret Chase Smith of Maine was a senator who believed in the idea of true Americanism—those who believe in the freedom of America. Robert Byrd, who has served longer than any other U.S. senator, argues that the American people need statespeople in Congress, not politicians.

Those of us who shout the loudest about Americanism in making **character assassinations** are all too frequently those who, by our own words and acts, ignore some of the basic principles of Americanism—

- The right to criticize
- The right to hold unpopular beliefs
- The right to protest
- The right of independent thought

C The exercise of these rights should not cost one single American citizen his reputation or his right to a livelihood nor should he be in danger of losing his reputation or livelihood merely because he happens to know someone who holds unpopular beliefs. Who of us doesn't? Otherwise none of us could call our souls our own. Otherwise thought control would have set in.

—from "Declaration of Conscience" by Margaret Chase Smith, June 1, 1950

In the real world, **exemplary** personal conduct can sometimes achieve much more than any political agenda. **Comity,** courtesy, charitable treatment of even our political opposites, combined with a concerted effort to not just occupy our offices, but to bring honor to them, will do more to inspire our people and restore their faith in us, their leaders, than millions of dollars of 30-second spots or glitzy puff-pieces concocted by spinmeisters.

—Address by Robert C. Byrd, September 15, 1998

264

Review suggested books before assigning them.

Secretaries of State: Making Foreign Policy, by Jason Richie describes the history of the secretary of state, highlighting eight men who held this important position, including John Quincy Adams and Henry Kissinger.

Choosing the Candidates, by George Sullivan outlines how presidential candidates today are chosen by means of party caucuses, primaries, and national conventions.

America's Courts on Trial: Questioning Our Legal System, by Elaine Pascoe notes that the Constitution guarantees every American the right to a fair trial, but after a number of recent controversial cases, some people question how fair the current system is.

The Role of the Executive Branch

Two presidents write about the power of the executive branch.

I have used every ounce of power there was in the office and I have not cared a rap for the criticisms of those who spoke of my '**usurpation** of power'; for I knew that the talk was all nonsense and that there was no usurpation . . . I have felt not merely that my action was right in itself, but that in showing the strength of, or in giving strength to, the executive, I was establishing a precedent of value.

—Theodore Roosevelt, letter to George Otto Trevelyan

[T]he government of the United States has become too big, too complex, and too **pervasive** in its influence on all our lives for one individual to pretend to direct the details of its important and critical programming. Competent assistants are mandatory; without them the Executive Branch would bog down.

—Dwight Eisenhower, letter to Henry Robinson Luce

The Role of the Supreme Court

Two justices write about the role of the Court.

A dissent in a court of last resort is an appeal to the brooding spirit of the law, to the intelligence of a future day, when a later decision may possibly correct the error into which the dissenting judge believes to court to have been betrayed.

—Chief Justice Charles Evans Hughes

[The Supreme Court is] somewhat of an umpire. It considers what the Congress proposes, or what the executive proposes, or what some individual claims, and rules upon these laws . . . by comparing them with the law as laid down by the Constitution . . . and then calls the strikes and the balls.

—Associate Justice Tom Clark

Photographs as Primary Sources
President Lyndon Johnson (right) discusses strategy with adviser Abe Fortas. What does this photograph tell you about Johnson's leadership style? Do you think his style was effective or not?

DBQ Document-Based Questions

1. **Explaining** Do you think Smith's stand was courageous? Explain.

2. **Comparing and Contrasting** How are the views expressed by Roosevelt and Eisenhower alike and how are they different?

3. **Explaining** What purpose does the dissenting opinion in a Supreme Court decision play?

4. **Evaluate and Connect** Select one of the passages that expresses a view that you agree with and select one with which you disagree. Write two paragraphs explaining your position.

265

Did You Know?

Judges as Umpires During his confirmation hearings for Chief Justice, Roberts echoed Associate Justice Tom Clark's baseball metaphor, "Nobody ever went to a ball game to see the umpire . . . It's my job to call balls and strikes and not to pitch or bat." Roberts's remarks revealed his intention to lead a Supreme Court that would have a limited role. The caseload of the Supreme Court during Roberts's first term was more striking. The court took 40 percent fewer cases than the preceding term, during which the Court had the lowest number of signed opinions since 1953. By having a hands-off approach, Chief Justice Roberts is essentially curtailing the power of the judicial branch, or—as the baseball metaphor would have it—he's benching the judges.

Unit 3 Planning Guide

UNIT PACING CHART

	Unit 3	Chapter 9	Chapter 10	Chapter 11
Day 1	Unit Opener, Reading Social Studies	Chapter Opener, Section 1	Chapter Opener, Section 1	Chapter Opener, Section 1, Financial Literacy
Day 2		Section 2	Section 2	Section 2, Issues to Debate
Day 3		Chapter Review, Visual Summary	Section 3, Chapter Review, Visual Summary	Section 3
Day 4		Chapter Assessment	Chapter Assessment	Section 4, Landmark Supreme Court Case Studies
Day 5			TIME Reports	Chapter Review, Visual Summary
Day 6				Chapter Assessment
Day 7				Analyzing Primary Sources

Teacher to Teacher

Anne McCanless
Providence
High School
Charlotte, North Carolina

Voting Eligibility Have a representative from the local Board of Elections speak to the class about laws that set out voting eligibility. Then, provide students with specific profiles of potential voters representing a cross-section of the population. Ask the class to examine the profiles to evaluate and determine which individuals are legally entitled to cast a ballot. As the students discuss both the laws and the profiles, the resource speaker contributes to the student discussion and provides insights into the workings of state voting laws. Students are encouraged to interact with the speaker. To complete the day, the students are asked to write a letter to the speaker explaining any ideas about the process of voting that they have learned.

Author Note

Dear Social Studies Teacher:

In 2006 I helped manage a campaign for the Oregon House of Representatives. The candidate was a neighbor of mine who had served on the Eugene City Council and had narrowly lost the 2004 mayoral election.

We had several advantages in the legislative race. Our candidate had strong name recognition and most people had a positive opinion of her as a moderate on the council. The incumbent Representative was retiring and the district had a history of supporting our candidate's party. Still, nearly one third of registered voters are Independents, and we didn't want to take anything for granted.

Our candidate went door-to-door throughout the district, starting in the spring when few potential voters were thinking about the election. Campaign volunteers met on Saturday mornings and, fortified with coffee and donuts, set off with voter lists to attach flyers to house door handles. Having won the primary, the process began again in August for the general election. Our candidate participated in meet-the-candidates forums and went to all media interviews that were available. One fundraiser was held.

At a time when there is distrust of most governmental officials, I was impressed that our candidate, as well as many other legislative candidates, was genuinely motivated to run because she wanted to help make life better in Oregon. Clearly people don't run for the salary, which in Oregon is about $16,000 a year. She wasn't beholden to interest groups (although endorsements were welcome), or to well-heeled contributors.

A central position of the campaign was that voters disliked partisan bickering in the legislature, and they wanted members who would not have rigid ideological positions. We believed that even on hot button issues, most voters held moderate positions.

Our candidate was elected, and we enjoyed the campaign experience. Maybe I am being naïve, but I came away feeling that many political candidates in Oregon seek office because they want to do the right thing.

David C. Saffell
Author

Unit Objectives

After studying this unit, students will be able to:

- Identify the origin, structure, function, and types of U.S. political parties.

- Explain voting requirements and responsibilities in elections at the local, county, state, and national levels.

- Recognize the influence of individual voters and political parties on American government.

Did You Know?

The Internet provides many great ways for Americans to take part in their government. For example, EnviroLink—www.envirolink.org— gives individuals and community groups detailed information on environmental issues as well as sug- gestions of how citizens can help. At www.neighborhoodsonline.net, Neighborhoods Online helps grass- roots organizations work to better their neighborhoods and commu- nities.

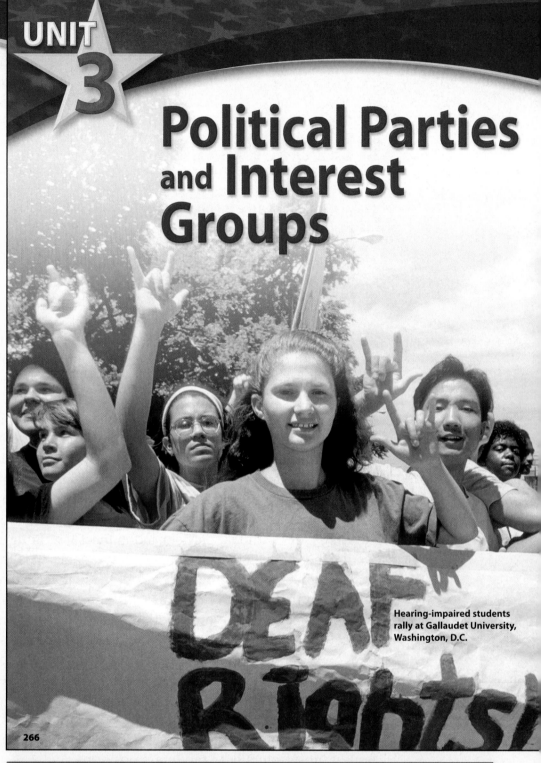

UNIT ★
3

Political Parties and Interest Groups

Hearing-impaired students rally at Gallaudet University, Washington, D.C.

266

Activity: Launching the Unit

Why Study Political Parties and Interest Groups? Ask: What are political parties and interest groups? How do they affect the lives of everyday Americans? *(Political parties are organizations of everyday citizens who share broad, common interests and orga- nize to win elections, to operate the govern- ment, and thereby to influence government policy. Interest groups are made up of citizens who work to influence government policy on a particular issue or cause. Both groups are examples of ways in which citizens participate in their government.)* **OL**

Be an Active Citizen

CITIZENSHIP The United States is the first modern nation in which citizens deliberately took governmental power into their own hands. They created a governmental system in which the people—rather than a monarch, a dictator, or ruling party—have ultimate power. To ensure the continuation of democracy in this country, Americans must constantly involve themselves in their government.

267

Be an Active Citizen

CITIZENSHIP Do your students understand the basic principles of democracy? To help them connect democratic ideals with American government, write the sentence opener "In a democracy…" on the board. Beneath the opener, list the following principles: *people give government its powers; human rights and freedoms are protected; the majority rules but minority rights are protected; free, fair, regular elections are held; citizens have responsibilities as well as rights; people have easy access to local government.* Have students work in groups to show everyday examples of democracy in action.

Online Current Events Update

Visit Glencoe's *Online Current Events Update* at www.glencoe.com to find news reports, features, maps, graphs, and photos of current events that shape our lives. Students can also make connections between historical events and current events by using the interactive time line.

More About the Photo

Visual Literacy Through the First Amendment to the U.S. Constitution, all Americans have freedom of speech and the right to peacefully assemble, or gather. Citizens have long used these rights to communicate to government leaders and the courts—either to encourage government attention to important issues, or to protest government policies and laws. University students in particular have used these freedoms to comment on important issues, such as immigration laws, environmental protection, and racial equality.

Why Summarizing Information **Is Important**

Summarizing information requires students to be able to identify main, or important, ideas. This skill helps students review and check their understanding of what they have read and learned. When they summarize, students identify and incorporate keywords from the text. They use the most precise language to keep summaries clear and concise. Summarizing also helps students communicate what they know clearly and efficiently.

 Learn It!

Photocopy and distribute the body of a short news article from a recent newspaper or magazine, being careful not to include the headline or title. Instruct students to underline keywords and main ideas as you read the article aloud. Have students suggest titles that summarize the main idea of the article. **OL**

Summarizing Information

① **Learn It!**

Summarizing is an important skill that helps you clarify text and understand key points, especially if the text is difficult.

- Read the paragraph below. What are the key points in the paragraph?
- In your mind, summarize the key points in complete thoughts.

> The Progressive Party promoted the direct primary to allow the people a more direct role in government. Two other Progressive ideas—the initiative and referendum—were intended to give voters more power to make laws. Although the Populists and the Progressives never won the presidency, the Democratic and Republican Parties adopted many of their ideas.
>
> —*from page 275*

Graphic Organizer

A graphic organizer can help to organize key points to summarize.

Key Points
- There are two major parties: Republican and Democratic
- Both parties have millions of supporters.
- Since 1860, one or the other has always held the presidency.
- Together they have held most seats in Congress.

Reading Tip
Reading a summary before reading the actual text will help with your comprehension of new concepts.

Summary
The Republican and Democratic Parties are the two major political parties. Both parties have millions of supporters. Since 1860, one or the other has always held the presidency. Together, they have also held most seats in Congress.

📖 **Reading Strategy** ⟨ **Organizing**

Summarizing Information Before writing summaries, students should reread the text, noting important words and ideas. Have students write a summary of the subsection Primary Elections in Chapter 9, Section 2. Tell students that good summaries answer questions such as *Who? What? When? Where?* and *Why?* Have students exchange their summaries with a partner. Ask students to comment on how well their partners summarized the main ideas of the selection. **OL**

② Practice It!

Read the following paragraph from this unit. Draw a graphic organizer like the one below to show key points and a summary.

> There are important reasons to exercise your right to vote. Voting gives citizens a chance to choose their government leaders. It gives them an opportunity to voice their opinions on past performances of public officials. If voters are dissatisfied, they can elect new leaders. Voting also allows citizens to express their opinions on public issues.
>
> —*from page 299*

Key Points

↓

Summary

Read to Write Activity

Read the section titled "Forming Public Opinion" pages 318–324. Then, write a paragraph that uses key points to summarize the argument *for* public opinion polling or *against* public opinion polling.

③ Apply It!

Identify one summary with supporting key points for:

- **Chapter 11, Section 2**

② Practice It!

Point out that paragraph divisions and subheads signal readers that a new idea is being introduced. Have students work in pairs to copy the subheads in Section 1 of Chapter 10. Under each subhead, ask students to write a summary statement of each paragraph in the section. **OL**

③ Apply It!

Have students work in groups to brainstorm ways in which political activity affects their lives. Ask groups to write a summary paragraph of their discussion. **OL**

Reading Strategy — Read to Write

Determining Importance Students can use selective underlining to identify keywords in the text. Have students work with partners to copy a paragraph from Chapter 9. Ask partners to underline keywords in the paragraph. Have students use the underlined words to write a brief summary of the paragraph. **ELL**

Chapter Planning Guide

9

Levels					Resources	Chapter Opener	Section 1	Section 2	Chapter Assess
BL	OL	AL	ELL						
					FOCUS				
BL	OL	AL	ELL	🖋	Daily Focus Skills Transparencies		9–1	9–2	
					TEACH				
BL	OL		ELL	📁	Reading Essentials and Note-Taking Guide*		p. 87	p. 90	
	OL	AL		📁	Economics Activity, URB		p .5		
		AL		📁	Enrichment Activity, URB		p. 13		
BL	OL	AL	ELL	📁	Content Vocabulary Activity, URB*		p. 21	p. 21	
BL	OL	AL	ELL	📁	Academic Vocabulary Activity, URB		p. 22	p. 22	
	OL			📁	Biography Activity, URB		p. 23		
BL	OL	AL	ELL	📁	Writing Skills Activity, URB		p. 25	p. 25	
	OL	AL		📁	Critical Thinking Skills Activity, URB			p. 27	
BL	OL	AL	ELL	📁	Chart, Graph, and Map Skills Activity, URB		p. 29		
BL	OL	AL	ELL	📁	Differentiated Instruction, URB		p. 31		
BL	OL	AL	ELL	📁	School-to-Home Connection Activity, URB*		p. 33	p. 33	
BL	OL		ELL	📁	Guided Reading Activities, URB*		p. 37	p. 38	
BL	OL	AL	ELL	📁	Writer's Guidebook	✓	✓	✓	✓
	OL	AL		💿	Primary Source Document Library	✓	✓	✓	✓
BL	OL	AL	ELL	💿	Daily Lecture & Discussion Notes (in Pres. Plus)		✓	✓	✓
BL	OL	AL	ELL	💿	StudentWorks™ Plus		✓	✓	✓
BL	OL	AL	ELL	💿	Section Spotlight Videos		✓	✓	
BL	OL	AL	ELL	🖋	TIME Interpreting Political Cartoons Transp.			Ch. 9	
BL	OL	AL	ELL	🖋	Writing Process Transparencies	✓	✓	✓	✓

Note: Please refer to the *Unit 3 Resource Book* for this chapter's URB materials.

* Also available in Spanish

- Interactive Lesson Planner
- Interactive Teacher Edition
- Fully editable blackline masters
- Section Spotlight Videos Launch

- Differentiated Lesson Plans
- Printable reports of daily assignments
- Standards Tracking System

Levels					Resources	Chapter Opener	Section 1	Section 2	Chapter Assess
BL	OL	AL	ELL						
					TEACH (continued)				
				📁	**Building Academic Vocabulary**	✓	✓	✓	✓
				📁	**Strategies for Success**	✓	✓	✓	✓
Teacher Resources				📁	**Teacher's Guide to Differentiated Instruction**	✓	✓	✓	✓
				💿	**Graphing Tool**	✓	✓	✓	✓
				💿	**Presentation Plus! with MindJogger CheckPoint**	✓	✓	✓	✓
					ASSESS				
BL	OL	AL	ELL	📁	**Quizzes and Tests***		p. 104	p. 105	p. 106
BL	OL	AL	ELL	📁	**Authentic Assessment with Rubrics**		p. 13		
BL	OL	AL	ELL	📁	**Standardized Test Practice**		p. 17	p. 17	p. 17
BL	OL	AL	ELL	💿	*ExamView® Assessment Suite* **CD-ROM**		9–1	9–2	Ch. 9
					CLOSE				
BL			ELL	📁	**Reteaching Activity, URB***		p. 35	p. 35	
BL	OL		ELL	📁	**Reading and Study Skills Foldables™**	p. 66	p. 67		
BL	OL	AL	ELL	🖎	**Graphic Organizer Transparencies & Strategies**	✓	✓	✓	✓

✓ Chapter- or unit-based activities applicable to all sections in this chapter

Using StudentWorks™ Plus CD-ROM

Daily Assignments and Grade Log

What is StudentWorks™ Plus CD-ROM?

StudentWorks™ Plus is a powerful learning and teaching tool that offers the entire textbook in an interactive, searchable format. It provides links to student workbooks, audio recordings of the textbook, audio summaries in Spanish, and videos for every section.

How can StudentWorks™ Plus help my students?

By using the Daily Assignments and Grade Log feature of StudentWorks™ Plus CD-ROM, students can take responsibility for individual tasks and improve their independent study skills. The Daily Assignments and Grade Log allows students to:

- record and track progress on daily assignments
- log results achieved, including grades
- sort assignments alphabetically or by category
- view and print the assignment and grade log

Civics ONLINE

Visit glencoe.com and enter *QuickPass*™ code CIV1360c9T for Chapter 9 resources.

You can easily launch a wide range of digital products from your computer's desktop with the McGraw-Hill Social Studies widget.

	Student	Teacher	Parent
Media Library			
• Student Edition Section Audio	●		●
• Spanish Audio Summaries	●		●
• Section Spotlight Videos	●	●	●
***Civics Today* Online Learning Center (Web Site)**			
• Chapter Overviews	●	●	●
• Study Central™	●	●	●
• Study-to-Go	●	●	●
• Student Web Activities	●	●	●
• In Motion Animation	●	●	●
• Self-Check Quizzes	●	●	●
• ePuzzles and Games	●	●	●
• StudentWorks™ Plus Online	●	●	●
• Vocabulary eFlashcards	●	●	●
• Web Activity Lesson Plans		●	
• Vocabulary PuzzleMaker	●	●	●
Classroom Tools			
• Multilingual Glossary	●	●	●
• Beyond the Textbook	●	●	●
• NGS MapMachine	●	●	●

Reading List Generator CD-ROM

GLENCOE BookLink 3

Use this database to search more than 30,000 titles to create a customized reading list for your students.

- Reading lists can be organized by students' reading level, author, genre, theme, or area of interest.
- The database provides Degrees of Reading Power™ (DRP) and Lexile™ readability scores for all selections.
- A brief summary of each selection is included.

Leveled reading suggestions for this chapter:

For students at a Grade 7 reading level:
- *Malcolm X: A Fire Burning Brightly,* by Walter Dean Myers

For students at a Grade 8 reading level:
- *The Day Martin Luther King, Jr., Was Shot,* by James Haskins

For students at a Grade 9 reading level:
- *The Day Women Got the Vote,* by George Sullivan

For students at a Grade 10 reading level:
- *Historic Speeches of African Americans,* by Warren J. Halliburton

For students at a Grade 11 reading level:
- *Separate But Not Equal,* by Jim Haskins

READING SUPPORT FROM JAMESTOWN EDUCATION

- **Timed Readings Plus in Social Studies** helps students increase their reading rate and fluency while maintaining comprehension. The 400-word passages are similar to those found on state and national assessments.

- **Reading in the Content Area: Social Studies** concentrates on six essential reading skills that help students better comprehend what they read. The book includes 75 high-interest nonfiction passages written at increasing levels of difficulty.

- **Reading Social Studies** includes strategic reading instruction and vocabulary support in Social Studies content for both ELLs and native speakers of English.

- **Content Vocabulary Workout** (Grades 6–8) accelerates reading comprehension through focused vocabulary development. Social Studies content vocabulary comes from the glossaries of Glencoe's Middle School Social Studies texts. www.jamestowneducation.com

KEY Teacher Wraparound

Use this key to help you identify the different types of prompts found in the Teacher Wraparound Edition.

R **Reading Strategies** activities help you teach reading skills and vocabulary.

C **Critical Thinking** strategies help students apply and extend what they have learned.

D **Differentiated Instruction** activities provide instruction for students learning to speak English, along with suggestions for teaching various types of learners.

S **Skill Practice** strategies help students practice historical analysis and geography skills.

W **Writing Support** activities provide writing opportunities to help students comprehend the text.

Teaching strategies and activities have been coded for ability level appropriateness.

AL Activities for students working above grade level

OL Activities for students working on grade level

BL Activities for students working below grade level

ELL Activities for English Language Learners

Focus

Why It Matters

Ask: Why might political parties have been a natural development in a growing country? *(Answers may include the idea that people had different ideas about how the new American government should work. Their ideas were sufficiently diverse to motivate people to form political parties.)*

More About the Photo

Visual Literacy Although networks had experimented with televised conventions four years earlier, 1952 marked the beginning of televised broadcasts of Democratic and Republican nominating conventions. That year, the Republicans met first. After viewing the convention on TV, Democratic Party officials hurriedly revised their convention, hoping to capture and hold viewers' attention. Over the years, both parties have continued to appeal to the television audience with patriotic decorations and stirring speeches.

Teach

 BIG Ideas *As you begin teaching each section, use these questions and activities to help students focus on the Big Ideas.*

Section 1

Development of American Political Parties Ask: How do political parties help citizens accomplish their goals? *(Individuals increase their political power by joining with others who share their*

Political Parties and Politics

Why It Matters

The Constitution makes no mention of political parties, but the first ones formed during the early years of the republic. Today, the United States has several political parties, although two—the Democrats and the Republicans—dominate American politics. Why do people join political parties? Why does America have a two-party system?

270

views.) Point out that in Section 1, students will learn about the evolution of political parties in the United States. **OL**

Section 2

Role of Political Parties Today Ask: In what way might political parties slow the decision-making process of government? *(If differing parties are unable to compromise on an issue such as national health care, nothing will be done.)* Tell students that in Section 2 they will learn how political parties work to elect candidates, inform and communicate with citizens, and operate and monitor government. **OL**

Civics ONLINE

Visit glencoe.com and enter **QuickPass**™ code CIV3093c9 for Chapter 9 resources.

🔊 **Chapter Audio**

BIG Ideas

Section 1: Development of Political Parties

Political and economic institutions evolve to help individuals and groups accomplish their goals. The United States has had a two-party system since its early days as a nation.

Section 2: Role of Political Parties Today

Political and economic institutions evolve to help individuals and groups accomplish their goals. Political parties play a large role in the decisions made by government.

◀ **Delegates cheer for the first African American presidential candidate at the 2008 Democratic Convention**

FOLDABLES™ **Dinah Zike's**
Study Organizer **Foldables**

Purpose This Foldable helps the student understand how political parties work at local, state, and national levels. The completed Foldable will use tabs to help them keep track of party duties and roles at different levels. **OL**

📁 More Foldables activities for this chapter can be found in the *Dinah Zike's Reading and Study Skills Foldables* ancillary.

Civics ONLINE

Visit glencoe.com and enter **QuickPass**™ code CIV1360c9T for Chapter 9 resources, including a Chapter Overview, Study Central™, Study-to-Go, Student Web Activity, Self-Check Quiz, and other materials.

FOLDABLES™
Study Organizer

Comparing Information Study Foldable Make the following Foldable to help you compare how political parties work.

Step 1 Fold a sheet of paper in half from the long way with edges evenly together.

Step 2 Turn the paper and fold it into thirds.

Reading and Writing As you read the chapter, compare and contrast the duties and roles of political parties at different levels.

Step 3 Unfold and draw two overlapping ovals. Cut the top layer along both fold lines.

Step 4 Label as shown.

Chapter 9 **271**

Focus

Bellringer
Daily Focus Transparency 9–1

Guide to Reading
Answers to Graphic:

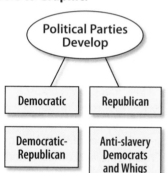

Political Parties Develop

Democratic — Republican

Democratic-Republican — Anti-slavery Democrats and Whigs

Section Spotlight Video

To generate student interest and provide a springboard for class discussion, access the Chapter 9, Section 1 video at glencoe.com or on the video DVD.

Resource Manager

Guide to Reading

Big Idea
Political and economic institutions evolve to help individuals and groups accomplish their goals.

Content Vocabulary
- political party (p. 273)
- two-party system (p. 273)
- third party (p. 274)
- platform (p. 277)
- plank (p. 277)

Academic Vocabulary
- stress (p. 273)
- promote (p. 274)

Reading Strategy
Comparing As you read, complete a web diagram similar to the one below by detailing the development of today's major political parties in the United States: the Democratic and Republican.

Political Parties Develop

Democratic Republican

Development of Political Parties

Real World Civics Despite the dominance of the two major political parties, third parties have often influenced American politics. Many important issues have been brought to the public's attention by third parties. Theodore Roosevelt's Progressive Party split the Republican Party, taking many of its votes and causing it to lose the election in 1912. Democratic candidate Woodrow Wilson was elected.

▼ **In 1912, Theodore Roosevelt became the presidential candidate for the newly formed Progressive Party**

R Reading Strategies	**C** Critical Thinking	**D** Differentiated Instruction	**W** Writing Support	**S** Skill Practice
Teacher Edition • Using Context Clues, p. 274 • Identifying, p. 275 • Making Connections, p. 275 • Using Word Parts, p. 276 **Additional Resources** • Cont. Vocab., URB p. 21 • Acad. Vocab., URB p. 22	**Teacher Edition** • Making Inferences, pp. 273, 276 • Compare/Contrast, p. 273 • Det. Cause/Effect, p. 274 • Drawing Con., p. 275 **Additional Resources** • Enrich. Act., URB p. 13 • Biography Act., URB p. 23	**Teacher Edition** • Logical/Math., p. 273 **Additional Resources** • Diff. Instr. Act., URB p. 31	**Teacher Edition** • Persuasive Writing, p. 277 **Additional Resources** • Writing Act., URB p. 25	**Teacher Edition** • Creating a Time Line, p. 274 **Additional Resources** • Chart, Graph, and Map Skills, URB p. 29 • Daily Focus Trans., 9–1

Political Participation As American citizens, each of us has the right to participate in the political process and express our opinions on government policy. Political parties are one of the major vehicles of participation in our political system. *Describing* What is the function of political parties?

Political Parties

Main Idea Political parties play a vital role in our democratic system.

Civics & You Many of us demand to have a say in the governmental decisions that affect us. Read on to find out how political parties help meet this demand.

A political party is an organization of individuals with broad, common interests who organize to win elections, to operate the government, and to thereby influence government policy. During most of American history there have been two major political parties. Other parties have sometimes run in elections, but they have seldom won. For these reasons, the United States is said to have a two-party system.

Growth of American Parties

The U.S. Constitution says nothing about political parties. In fact, many delegates to the Constitutional Convention were against them. In his Farewell Address of 1796, President George Washington warned against the "baneful [very harmful] effects of the spirit of the party." Even so, by the late 1790s, two rival political groups had organized in opposition to one another.

Secretary of State Thomas Jefferson led one group, and Secretary of the Treasury Alexander Hamilton led the other. They disagreed strongly about how the U.S. government should operate.

Hamilton believed that individual rights were at risk if the government was too weak, so he favored a strong national government. Jefferson wanted to limit the power of the national government. Contrary to Hamilton, he argued for more power for state governments, which were closer to the citizens.

The Democratic Party At first Jefferson's group was called the Democratic-Republican Party. From 1800 to 1816 Jefferson's party grew stronger, while Hamilton's, the Federalist Party, weakened. In 1824 all four presidential candidates had run as Democratic-Republicans. By 1828, however, the party had split. Those who supported candidate Andrew Jackson took the name Democratic Party to **stress,** or play up, their ties to the common people. In 1830 a new party, the Whigs (or National Republicans), rose to compete with the Democrats. The Whigs and the Democrats remained the two major parties until the 1850s.

Chapter 9   273

D Differentiated Instruction

Logical/Mathematics Ask: Why are two-party systems more efficient than multiparty systems? *(In a multiparty system, one party seldom gets the majority of the votes. Decisions are delayed until parties form coalitions to gain a majority.)* **AL**

C1 Critical Thinking

Making Inferences Ask: Why didn't Washington want political parties to form in the United States? *(He wanted Americans to unite to build the country and was afraid that political divisions would destroy the nation's future.)* **OL**

C2 Critical Thinking

Comparing and Contrasting Ask: How did Hamilton and Jefferson differ on their view of the national government? *(Hamilton supported a strong national government. Jefferson wanted more power for state governments.)* **OL**

Caption Answer:

Political parties work to win elections, operate the government, and influence government policy.

Hands-On Chapter Project
Step 1

Mock Nominating Conventions

Step 1: Creating Political Parties Organize students into four groups each representing a new political party. The parties will develop a name, a symbol, a slogan, and a platform. In Step 2, the parties will host conventions to nominate candidates.

Directions Write the Big Idea on the board. Help students identify issues that political parties address, such as unemployment, national health care, and so on.

Illustrating Have groups make posters inviting citizens to join their parties. Posters should include the party name, symbol, slogan, and platform statements on at least four issues. Students will use these posters at the "national conventions" in Step 2 of the activity. **OL**

(Project continued in Section 2)

S Skill Practice

Creating a Time Line Have students work with a partner to create a time line of American political party evolution. Instruct students to shade the span of each party, noting that parties will overlap during some years. **ELL**

C Critical Thinking

Determining Cause and Effect Ask: Why was the Republican Party able to make great strides in the 1854 congressional elections? *(The majority of Northern voters agreed that slavery must be kept out of the Northern territories.)* **BL**

R Reading Strategy

Using Context Clues Ask: Which words from the text explain third parties? *(smaller minor parties)* **BL**

Analyzing Charts

Answers:

1. National Republicans
2. 1856

Reading Check **Answer:** He feared that rival parties would hurt the government.

Differentiated Instruction

Biography Activity 9,
URB pp. 23–24

Evolution of American Political Parties

Federalist	1789–1820	Promoted a strong central government
Democratic-Republican	1796–1832	Formed to oppose Federalist policies
National Republican	1828–1836	Split from the Democratic-Republican Party to promote strong national government and oppose Andrew Jackson's campaign for presidency
Democratic	1832–Present	Party formed in support of Andrew Jackson
Whig	1834–1864	Included critics of Andrew Jackson, states' rights advocates, and supporters of internal improvements
Republican	1856–Present	Formed to oppose the Democratic Party's support of the institution of slavery

Analyzing Charts

1. **Identifying** According to the chart, which political party had the shortest life span?

2. **Sequencing** When did the modern Republican Party get its start?

The Republican Party In 1854 a group of Democrats and Whigs, many of whom opposed slavery, left their parties to form new ones. These parties took many different names, including the Fusion Party, the Peoples Party, and the Independent Party. The most popular name for the new coalition was the Republican Party.

Republicans did not agree on whether slavery should be abolished in the Southern states, but they did agree that it had to be kept out of the Northern territories. A large majority of Northern voters seemed to agree, enabling the Republican Party to make great strides in the congressional elections of 1854. In 1860 Abraham Lincoln won election as the first Republican president. Since then, Republicans and Democrats have been the major parties in our system.

Reading Check **Explaining** Why did Washington not want political parties to form?

Third Parties

Main Idea Throughout American history, additional parties have arisen to influence politics.

Civics & You As you read, think about how third parties influence American politics.

Throughout American history, smaller minor parties, sometimes called **third parties,** have competed for power in the nation's two-party system. While most Americans do not support third parties or vote for their candidates, third parties have influenced American politics in several important ways.

Third parties have often **promoted,** or advanced, ideas that were at first unpopular or hotly debated. The Populist Party of the 1890s, a combination of farmers and laborers, called for the direct election of senators and an eight-hour working day.

274 Chapter 9

Theodore Roosevelt

BIOGRAPHY ACTIVITY 9

Theodore Roosevelt (1858–1919)

Objective:	To gain understanding of what makes a president
Focus:	Find out what students know about third-party candidates.
Teach:	Discuss the Bull Moose Party's election results.
Assess:	Create a timeline showing Roosevelt's political career.
Close:	Ask students if they think a third party is necessary.

Differentiated Instruction Strategies

BL Tell a reading partner what you liked most about Roosevelt's life.

AL Write a paragraph describing Roosevelt's legacy.

ELL Define "candidate," "determination," "extensive" and "strenuous." Write a sentence for each word.

The Progressive Party promoted the direct primary to allow the people a more direct role in government. Two other Progressive ideas—the initiative and referendum—were intended to give voters more power to make laws. Although the Populists and the Progressives never won the presidency, the Democratic and the Republican Parties adopted many of their ideas. (You will read about the initiative and referendum in Chapter 10.)

Single-Issue Parties Some third parties form to promote a social, economic, or moral issue. For example, the Prohibitionist Party, formed in 1872, wanted to ban the sale of alcohol. A single-issue party usually does not last long. It may fade away when the issue is no longer important or if a major party adopts the issue.

Ideological Parties An ideology is a set of beliefs about human nature and government institutions. Ideological parties are those that support a particular philosophy or political doctrine. For example, the Socialist Labor Party and the Communist Party USA believe that our free enterprise system should be replaced by one in which government or workers own the factories, transportation, and resources. In contrast, an ideological party such as the Libertarian Party opposes government interference in private enterprise in order to increase individual freedoms.

Independent Candidates Sometimes third parties form around leaders with strong personalities who cannot get support from one of the two major parties. Such parties usually do not survive beyond the defeat of their candidates.

In 1992 wealthy business leader H. Ross Perot challenged both major-party candidates as an independent. Perot ran again in 1996, under the banner of the Reform Party.

Obstacles to Third Parties Third parties rarely win major elections because of the nation's two-party tradition. While the names of the Republican and Democratic candidates are automatically placed on the ballot in many states, third-party candidates must obtain a large number of voter signatures in order to get on the ballot. Third parties also often have trouble raising sufficient amounts of money to compete in campaigns against the major-party candidates.

Other Party Systems

Political parties exist in most countries. Two-party systems, however, are rare. The role that political parties play differs with each nation's political system.

Third Parties Former professional wrestler and Reform Party candidate Jesse Ventura was elected governor of Minnesota in 1998. *Explaining* Why are some political parties called third parties?

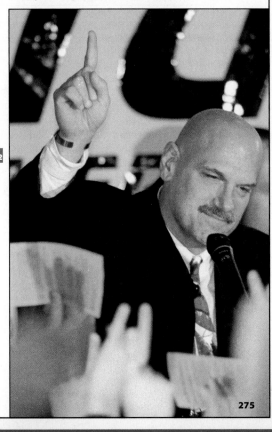

275

R₁ Reading Strategy

Identifying Ask: In what three ways did the Progressive Party contribute to increased voter participation in government? *(It promoted the direct primary, the initiative, and the referendum.)* **OL**

R₂ Reading Strategy

Making Connections Ask: On what national concern does the Libertarian Party primarily focus? *(government interference in private enterprise)* **OL**

C Critical Thinking

Drawing Conclusions Ask: Why do many states require third-party candidates to obtain many voter signatures before their names are placed on the ballot? *(to prove they have sufficient voter support to be viable candidates)* **AL**

Caption Answer:

Because the nation has two major parties, all smaller or minor parties are referred to as "third parties."

Leveled Activities

BL Content Vocabulary Activity 9, URB p. 21

OL Biography Activity 9, URB pp. 23–24

AL Enrichment Activity 3, URB pp. 13–14

ELL Academic Vocabulary Activity 9, URB p. 22

R Reading Strategy

Using Word Parts Ask: In the compound word "multiparty," what does "multi" mean? *(Answers may include many or several.)* ELL BL

C Critical Thinking

Making Inferences Ask: Why do some countries, such as Israel, have multiparty systems? *(Answers may include the idea that there is little consensus among citizens of these countries on issues affecting their country.)* OL

Analyzing Charts

Answers:

1. H. Ross Perot
2. George Wallace, John Anderson, and H. Ross Perot

✓ **Reading Check** **Answer:** Answers should include parties listed in the section.

Additional Support

Teacher Tip

Collaborative Learning activities are engaging and fun. Remember that they must be leveled appropriately and must be diverse to interest all students. Be sure that directions for the activity are clearly stated.

Leading Third-Party Presidential Candidates, 1952–2008

ELECTION YEAR	CANDIDATE	POLITICAL PARTY	VOTES (in thousands)
1952	Vincent Hallinan	Progressive	104
1956	T. Coleman Andrews	States' Rights	111
1960	Eric Hass	Socialist Labor	48
1964	Eric Hass	Socialist Labor	45
1968	George Wallace	American Independent	9,906
1972	John Schmitz	American	1,099
1976	Eugene McCarthy	Independent	757
1980	John Anderson	Independent	5,720
1984	David Bergland	Libertarian	228
1988	Ron Paul	Libertarian	432
1992	H. Ross Perot	Independent	19,742
1996	H. Ross Perot	Reform	8,085
2000	Ralph Nader	Green	2,883
2004	Ralph Nader	Independent	464
2008	Ralph Nader	Independent	698

Analyzing Charts

1. **Identifying** Which of the candidates listed was most successful in gaining popular votes?

2. **Comparing** Which third-party candidates received more than 5 million votes?

R **Multiparty Systems** Many democracies have multiparty systems. In these systems, three or more parties compete for control of the government. For example, Canada has three major parties, Germany has five, and Israel has more than 20.

C In multiparty systems, one party rarely wins enough support to control the government, so several parties often must work together. This is a situation that may easily break down and become politically unstable because of so many competing interests of the parties.

One-Party System Another type of party system is the one-party system. In such a system, the party and the government are nearly the same thing. In the People's Republic of China, for instance, only one party—the Communist Party—is allowed to exist, and only Communist candidates may run for office. As a result, only Communist Party members fill government positions. In a one-party system, the main job of party members is to recruit new members, maintain party discipline, and carry out the party's orders. Elections are an empty exercise because there are no rival candidates. One-party systems, obviously, are not democratic systems.

✓ **Reading Check** **Describing** Name three different types of third parties and explain why they were formed.

Activity: Collaborative Learning

Organizing Explain that the purpose of this activity is to understand how coalitions are necessary in multiparty systems. Organize the class into numbered groups. Give each group this list of school-related topics: class day (length and beginning/ending time), school uniforms, pass/fail versus letter grades, cafeteria versus fast food.

Have each group discuss and propose "legislation" on each topic. Reconvene the class. Ask each group to read its legislation on each issue, recording their proposals in a chart on the board. Have groups form coalitions to gain a majority vote on the issues. By a show of hands, have the class vote on the proposed legislation. OL

How the Parties Differ

Main Idea Political parties play a large role in the decisions made by government.

Civics & You People who share common goals often join political parties. Read on to find out about the basic differences between the major parties.

Competing political parties are a necessary part of democratic government. They are a key link between citizens and their elected officials. They give voters a choice among candidates and ideas.

A basic difference between the major parties is their belief in how much the government should be involved in the lives of Americans. For example, the Democrats tend to believe that the federal government should be more directly involved in regulating the economy and in providing housing, income, education, and jobs for the poor. The Republicans tend to believe that if they help the nation's economy grow, poor people will have a better chance of finding jobs on their **W** own. They favor less government regulation of the economy as the best way to promote the growth of production.

Sometimes the differences between the two major parties seem small. Both try to appeal to as many voters as possible. By adopting moderate and mainstream positions and avoiding extreme or radical positions, the major parties hope to attract votes and win elections. The parties are also similar because the majority of American people generally agree about many political and social issues.

One way to identify the differences between the parties is to read the political document, or platform, that each party writes at its presidential nominating convention, held every four years. The **platform** is a series of statements expressing the party's principles, beliefs, and positions on election issues. Each individual part of the platform is called a **plank.** The platform communicates to voters what the party claims it will do if it wins.

Reading Check Explaining Why do the two major parties seem so similar?

Writing Support

W **Writing Support**

Persuasive Writing Have students write brief essays explaining how they feel about government intervention in their lives. Remind students to support their views with specific details and clear, logical reasoning. **AL**

✓ Reading Check **Answer:** The majority of American people generally agree about many political and social issues.

Assess

Civics ONLINE

Study Central™ provides summaries, interactive games, and online graphic organizers to help students review content.

Close

Summarizing Organize students into groups. Ask each group to discuss the benefits and drawbacks of American political parties. Have each group write a brief report summarizing the major points of their discussion. **OL**

Section 1 Review

Vocabulary

1. **Write** sentences or short paragraphs about political parties in which you use the following terms: *political party, two-party system, third party, platform, plank.*

Main Ideas

2. **Identifying** What were the first two major political parties in the United States?

3. **Explaining** What are the characteristics of one-party systems?

Critical Thinking

4. **Comparing** Describe the basic differences between the views of Thomas Jefferson and Alexander Hamilton regarding how government should operate.

5. **BIG Ideas** In a diagram like the one below, identify at least three obstacles third parties face.

Obstacles to Third Parties

CITIZENSHIP Activity

6. **Expository Writing** Prepare for a debate on the following statement: The two-party system has outlived its usefulness. Choose either the pro or con side of the issue and prepare arguments for the side you choose. Pair up with a classmate who has prepared arguments opposing yours and debate the issue.

Civics ONLINE

Study Central™ To review this section, go to glencoe.com.

Chapter 9 277

Section 1 Review

Focus

Bellringer
Daily Focus Transparency 9–2

Guide to Reading
Answers to Graphic:

Political Party Functions
- inform citizens
- nominate candidates
- act as a watchdog
- operate the government

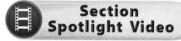

Section Spotlight Video

To generate student interest and provide a springboard for class discussion, access the Chapter 9, Section 2 video at glencoe.com or on the video DVD.

Resource Manager

Guide to Reading

Big Idea
Political and economic institutions evolve to help individuals and groups accomplish their goals.

Content Vocabulary
- national committee *(p. 279)*
- caucus *(p. 279)*
- precinct *(p. 281)*
- ward *(p. 281)*
- political machine *(p. 282)*
- direct primary *(p. 283)*
- closed primary *(p. 283)*
- open primary *(p. 283)*
- plurality *(p. 284)*
- majority *(p. 284)*
- petition *(p. 284)*

Academic Vocabulary
- range *(p. 279)*
- adjacent *(p. 281)*

Reading Strategy
Identifying As you read, identify four functions of political parties.

Political Party Functions — nominate candidates

Role of Political Parties Today

Real World Civics On the campaign trail, who manages travel for the candidates? Who makes sure there are facilities available? And who makes up the cheering crowds? The answer is the loyal members of each candidate's political party. The party supporters are whom the candidates want to reach out to, but also whom they depend upon. The heart of any campaign for national office is the support and organization of the major political parties.

▼ **John McCain and Sarah Palin reach out to supporters during the 2008 presidential campaign.**

R Reading Strategies	C Critical Thinking	D Differentiated Instruction	W Writing Support	S Skill Practice
Teacher Edition • Categorizing, p. 279 • Identifying, p. 279 • Using Context Clues, pp. 281, 284 • Using Word Parts, p. 284 • Act. Prior Know., p. 286 **Additional Resources** • Cont. Vocab., URB p. 21 • Ac. Vocab., URB p. 22	**Teacher Edition** • Making Comparisons, p. 279 • Det. Cause/Effect, p. 280 • Making Inferences, p. 281 • Analyzing Info., p. 283 • Ident. Cen. Issues, p. 285 **Additional Resources** • Crit. Thinking Act., URB p. 27	**Teacher Edition** • English Learners, p. 283 • Visual/Spatial, p. 284 **Additional Resources** • School-to-Home Act., URB p. 33 • Reteach. Act., URB p. 35	**Teacher Edition** • Persuasive Writing, p. 285 • Personal Writing, p. 285 **Additional Resources** • Enrichment Act., URB p. 13	**Teacher Edition** • Visual Literacy, p. 280 • Using Geo. Skills, p. 281 • Recog. Bias, p. 282 **Additional Resources** • Daily Focus Trans., 9–2 • Pol. Cartoons Trans. 9

National Conventions Every four years, political party delegates gather to select a ticket—candidates for president and vice president as they did in 1948 in Philadelphia. *Explaining* What is the first task for the delegates?

Organization of Political Parties

Main Idea Democrats and Republicans are organized into 50 state parties and thousands of local parties that operate independently of the national organization.

Civics & You Do you support one of the political parties? Political parties do everything they can to attract supporters.

The two major parties are organized at the local, state, and national levels. These levels are only loosely tied together. There is no chain of command that lets the national organization control state or local party leaders. All the levels, however, have roughly the same political beliefs, and they are united in their ultimate goal—to help the party win election to as many offices as possible.

National Organization

Each party has a **national committee** made of representatives from every state. This committee helps raise funds for presidential elections and organizes the party's national convention. A national party chairperson runs the committee. The chairperson's main jobs are to manage the office, to direct the committee staff, and to lead fund-raising efforts.

National Convention The national convention is one of the most important responsibilities of the national committee. Held once every four years, the national convention is where party members nominate their candidates for president and vice president of the United States. Each party chooses its delegates through a combination of presidential primary elections and **caucuses,** or meetings, of state and local party organizations.

The delegates' first job is to write the platform. This task can be difficult because each party includes members with a wide **range,** or variety, of positions on key issues.

Chapter 9   279

Teach

C Critical Thinking

Making Comparisons Ask: In what way are all levels of political parties similar? *(They share the common goal of helping the party win election to as many offices as possible.)* **BL**

For additional practice on this skill (Making Comparisons), see the **Skills Handbook.**

R1 Reading Strategy

Categorizing Ask: What is the purpose of a party's national committee? *(It helps raise funds for presidential elections and organizes the party's national convention.)* **BL**

R2 Reading Strategy

Identifying Ask: What are caucuses? *(meetings in which state and local party organizations choose delegates)* **ELL**

Caption Answer:

writing the platform

Additional Support

Activity: Economics Connection

Making Inferences Explain that the Bipartisan Campaign Reform Act of 2002 focused on soft money—contributions given for the general use of a political party but not necessarily to support a candidate. Tell students that the act limits or bans soft money contributions and spending. It also requires parties to disclose who contrib- uted more than $10,000 for campaign ads. Under the act, however, individuals are now allowed to contribute more to candidates and parties. Have student groups discuss and write paragraphs about why both parties might have supported this legislation. Ask groups to share their paragraphs with the class. **AL**

C Critical Thinking

Determining Cause and Effect Ask: Why do Americans usually know the names of presidential nominees before national conventions? *(Early primaries narrow the list of candidates.)* **BL**

S Skill Practice

Visual Literacy Ask: Who is the top-ranking nongovernment official in a political party? *(the national chairperson)* **ELL**

Analyzing Charts

Answers:
1. local; city, town, or county committee
2. Answers may include the idea that citizens are more directly involved in local committees, state committees coordinate the activities of local groups, and the national committee unifies the party nationwide.

Nominating the Candidate After the platform has been prepared and approved, delegates nominate the party's presidential candidate. The nominating speech for each candidate sets off a demonstration, as supporters parade around the convention hall. Historically, conventions were suspenseful events where delegates from around the country decided upon their presidential candidate. The conventions were a grand spectacle on television. Today the increasing use of early primary elections, where voters narrow down the list of candidates, has caused the nomination for president to be almost entirely decided by the time of the convention.

Campaign Committees The major parties also have campaign committees made up of members of Congress. These committees work to elect party members and raise money.

State and Local Organization

Each major party has 50 state committees or organizations. In some states the parties are well organized, have large staffs, and spend a lot of money each year. In others the organization is weak. State committees focus on electing party candidates to state offices—governor, attorney general, state legislators, and others. They also work to elect their parties' candidates to national offices.

Organization of Political Parties

Charts In MOtion
See StudentWorks™ Plus or glencoe.com.

National Convention → National Committee → Congressional Campaign Committee, Senatorial Campaign Committee

National Chairperson
National Committee
State Chairperson
State Committee
Local Chairperson
City, Town, or County Committee
Precinct Captain / Precinct Workers

Analyzing Charts

1. **Identifying** At what level of organization is a precinct? Who controls the precinct workers?
2. **Explaining** Why do you think political parties have three levels: national, state, and local?

Hands-On Chapter Project
Step 2

Mock Nominating Conventions

Step 2: Televising Conventions Provide students with crepe and construction paper to coordinate with their parties' chosen color schemes. Give each group a section of the classroom to decorate for their convention. Have them prominently display their posters.

Directions Ask each group to select one member as their party's presidential candidate. Show students a brief video of a national nominating convention in which the candidate is nominated and accepts the nomination. Allow groups time to practice this process.

Videotaping Videotape each group's nominating convention. Remind students that parties want conventions to impress television viewers and to persuade them to vote for their candidates. Students will review the videotapes in the final step of this convention activity. **OL**

(Project continued on the Visual Summary page)

Local party organizations consist of thousands of city, town, and county committees across the country. These committees include people elected by their fellow party members.

What Is a Precinct? Each city or county is divided into election districts or precincts. A **precinct** is a geographic area that contains a specific number of voters. A precinct may consist of an entire small town or, in a large city, a group of **adjacent,** or neighboring, neighborhoods. All voters in a precinct cast their ballots at the same voting place.

For each precinct, the local party committee appoints a precinct captain, whose job is to organize other party members during campaigns and encourage voters on Election Day. The volunteers distribute leaflets, register voters, and try to convince voters to support the party's candidates.

Several geographically connected precincts make up a larger election unit called a **ward.** Party members in each ward typically elect a volunteer to represent the ward at the local party's next level of organization—the county committee.

County Committees

Counties are the largest political units within a state. Both major parties have county committees. A county chairperson, who runs the committee, often has a great deal of political power in the county. If the county is large, state party leaders such as the governor or a U.S. senator may consult with the county chairperson about important appointments, such as judgeships.

Higher-level party leaders depend on precinct and ward leaders to build the party at the "grassroots," or neighborhood, level. These local leaders have to know what issues their neighbors are worried about and keep track of how local political sentiment is running. At election time they must "deliver the vote" for party candidates at every level of government.

TIME™ Teens in *Action*

Emily Nguyen

Emily Nguyen, 16, from Morristown, New Jersey, knows debate is a big part of politics. That is one reason she takes part in the Junior Statesmen of America (JSA).

QUESTION: What's JSA?

ANSWER: It's a group for high school students that promotes interest in government, politics, debate, law, and global affairs.

Q: How does it do all that?

A: JSA hosts discussions about contemporary issues, conventions for students, and summer school programs. The group encourages all teenagers to stand up and be heard with its motto "Democracy is not a spectator sport!"

Q: Sounds intense. But is it fun?

A: Yes! The chapter at my school is extremely active. We attend the triannual regional conventions, hold debates at our weekly meetings, organize community service projects—and take part in many other activities.

Q: How will it help your future?

A: Members of JSA learn leadership, managerial, and public speaking skills. JSA works solely to educate America's youth, with the knowledge that one day they will become lawmakers, lawyers, activists, and politicians.

Q: How can other teens get involved with JSA?

A: If there isn't a chapter at their school, students can visit www.jsa.org for more information.

ACTION FACT: Nguyen can often be found playing soccer with a team or refereeing youth soccer.

Making a Difference CITIZENSHIP

What is the motto of JSA?

Chapter 9 281

S Skill Practice

Using Geography Skills Obtain a voting precinct map for your school's attendance area from a local government office. Ask students to look at the map and to identify their voting precincts. **OL**

C Critical Thinking

Making Inferences Ask: What are the personality traits of a successful precinct captain? *(Answers may include the following traits: organized, cooperative, focused, enthusiastic, dedicated, hardworking, and so on.)* **ELL** **BL**

R Reading Strategy

Using Context Clues Ask: What is the "grassroots" level? *(the neighborhood level)* **BL**

TIME™ Teens in *Action*

Answer:

"Democracy is not a spectator sport!"

Additional Support

Activity: Technology Connection

Drawing Conclusions Tell students that the Election Assistance Commission is the government agency that disburses money to help states improve their voting systems and practices. Have students work in pairs to study the effects of the punch card system on the presidential election of 2000 at americanhistory.si.edu/vote/florida.html.

Instruct partners then to identify how government responded with the Help America Vote Act. Information on this act is available at www.eac.gov/about/help-america-vote-act. Have partners write a brief summary of the punch card problem and the government's solution. **OL**

S Skill Practice

Recognizing Bias Ask: Are people justified in thinking political machines are harmful? *(Answers may vary. Some students may argue that people assume parties who hold power for long periods of time will become unresponsive and less accountable. Others may feel that Tammany Hall and other political machines are good examples of the negative aspects of political machines.)* **OL**

TIME™ Political Cartoons

Answers:

1. as an armored truck
2. Armored trucks are known to carry large sums of money and are strong and well protected.
3. Even with campaign finance reform, special interests, or PACS, still donate a lot of money to political parties.
4. The cartoonist is pessimistic because, in the cartoon, the figure representing reform cannot stop the truck of special interests.

✔ **Reading Check Answer:** It lets the party handle local issues and build local support.

Differentiated Instruction

TIME™ Political Cartoons

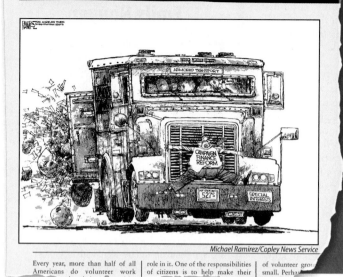

Michael Ramirez/Copley News Service

In this cartoon, Michael Ramirez makes a comment on the campaign-finance reform movement, whose aim is to regulate donations to political candidates.

1. How are "special interests" represented?
2. Why do you think Ramirez chose this symbol?
3. Why is money falling off the back of the truck?
4. Do you think Ramirez is optimistic or pessimistic that new campaign-finance reform measures will become law? Explain.

Every year, more than half of all Americans do volunteer work ... role in it. One of the responsibilities of citizens is to help make their ... of volunteer grou... small. Perhap... dad who...

Political Machines

Sometimes a local party organization becomes so powerful that, year after year, its candidates sweep almost every election. Such a strong party organization is called a **political machine.** One of the most famous—and notorious—political machines was New York City's Tammany Hall.

This organization ruled New York City in the late 1800s and early 1900s. Its leader, William Marcy "Boss" Tweed, and his friends grew rich from bribes and kickbacks—extra payments—given by building contractors seeking to do business with the city. Eventually, many members of the Tweed group ended up in prison.

At a time in American history when few social service agencies existed to help poor people and immigrants, political machines often served a useful purpose. The machines provided needy citizens with jobs, food, fuel, and help with medical care in return for their votes. Today most people think of political **S** machines as harmful. They believe when one party is in power for too long, it may become unresponsive to the needs of the community. Political leaders are less accountable to citizens when the leaders do not have to worry about getting reelected.

Joining a Political Party

You do not need to join a political party in the United States to vote. However, political parties offer every citizen a great way to get involved in politics. Political parties do everything they can to attract members, and they welcome whomever wishes to belong. Party membership involves no duties or obligations other than voting. If a member of a party chooses to do more, then he or she may contribute money, do volunteer work, or participate in other activities, especially during election campaigns. The parties depend on citizen involvement to accomplish their goals.

✔ **Reading Check Concluding** Why is it important to build grassroots support for a party?

Leveled Activities

BL Writing Skills Activity 9, URB pp. 25–26

OL Biography Activity 9, URB pp. 23–24

AL Differentiated Instruction Activity 9, URB pp. 31–32

ELL School-to-Home Conn. 9, URB pp. 33–34

Nominating Candidates

Main Idea Political parties nominate candidates to run for public office.

Civics & You Have you ever run for an office at school? Did you choose to run or did someone nominate you? Read to find out the role political parties play in selecting nominees for public office.

The individuals who take part in the work of political parties play an important role in the American system of government. They select candidates for office. They keep people informed and interested in the issues and the candidates. They try to see that party members elected to office do a good job. They keep an eye on the opposition party, publicly criticizing many of its actions. They also act as a link between different branches and levels of government.

The parties carry out these activities throughout the year. They are busiest, however, at election time. Political parties are the only organizations that select and present candidates for public office. They do this through the nomination process.

Primary Elections

Today major parties in all states nominate candidates at all levels of government. The method most commonly used today to nominate candidates is the direct primary. The **direct primary** is an election in which voters choose candidates to represent each party in a general election. In recent years, these elections have been very competitive, and the winner of the most primaries is often nominated by his or her party. There are two main forms of the direct primary: closed and open.

Most states hold a **closed primary,** in which only the declared members of a party are allowed to vote for that party's nominees. For example, only Republicans can vote in the Republican Party's primary.

Rules for how voters declare their party affiliation vary by state. In some states you must declare your party when you register. In others, you do not have to declare your party preference until you actually vote.

A few states hold an **open primary,** in which voters do not need to declare their party preference in order to vote for the party's nominees. In most open-primary states, you choose a party in the privacy of the voting booth.

Campaigning Candidates for president begin organizing their campaigns long before the election. Representative Dennis Kucinich of Ohio, campaigning for the 2004 Democratic nomination, talks to New Hampshire students before the state's primary election. *Explaining* Why do candidates bother to talk to students who cannot vote?

283

Did You Know?

Voting Fraud The earliest elections in the United States were conducted by voice votes or paper ballots. Some early ballots and ballot boxes, however, allowed voters to cheat. During the Civil War, for example, multiple party ticket ballots were printed on large sheets of paper in the Union states. Although they were supposed to have been cut apart, some people cast two or more votes at a time. A "stuffer's ballot box" from 1856 had a sliding false bottom and side. Hidden behind these panels were additional party ticket ballots that would eventually be counted with the legitimate votes. In addition, many state election laws actually allowed voters to change, or modify, the ballots. Called the "paster ballot," these ballots allowed voters to cover the name of a candidate and to paste over a slip of paper with another candidate's name.

R₁ Reading Strategy

Using Word Parts Ask: How does the meaning of "plural" contribute to the definition of "plurality"? *("Plural" refers to several or many. A plurality vote: many votes that fail to win a majority.)* **AL**

R₂ Reading Strategy

Using Context Clues Ask: Which words from the text explain the concept of a petition? *(papers declaring support for a candidate)* **ELL**

D Differentiated Instruction

Visual/Spatial Have students make drawings to illustrate the watchdog role of a political party. **BL**

> ✔ **Reading Check Answer:** In an open primary, voters do not have to declare a party affiliation in order to vote for that party's candidates. Closed primaries require voters to declare a party.

Civics ONLINE

Objectives and answers to the **Student Web Activity** can be found at glencoe.com under the Web Activity Lesson Plan for this chapter.

Differentiated Instruction

Critical Thinking Skills Activity 9, URB pp. 27–28

Closed Primaries People who support the closed primary believe that it helps keep the members of one party from crossing over into the other party's primary to try to promote weak candidates (who would then be easy to defeat). An argument against the closed primary is that it does not permit a truly secret ballot, since voters must first declare a party preference. It also prevents unaffiliated voters from taking part in primary elections in most states.

What Is a Plurality? Sometimes a political office can have more than one vacancy, and thus each party can nominate more than one candidate. Most offices, however, are open to only one winner. In these cases, the candidate who gets the *most* votes obtains a **plurality** (the largest number), and wins the election, even if this means less than 50 percent of the votes cast.

What Is a Majority? In a few states, however, the winner must have a **majority.** (A majority is more than 50 percent of the total votes.) If no candidate receives a majority, the party holds a runoff primary between the two leading candidates with the most votes. The winner then becomes the party's candidate in the general election.

Unaffiliated Candidates Candidates who are not affiliated with either of the two major parties can get on the ballot for the general election in most states by **petition.** If enough qualified voters sign papers declaring support for a candidate, he or she goes on the ballot for the general election.

> ✔ **Reading Check Contrasting** What is the difference between an open and a closed primary?

Civics ONLINE

Student Web Activity Visit glencoe.com and complete the Chapter 9 Web Activity.

Other Party Roles

Main Idea In addition to nominating candidates for office, political parties have many other responsibilities.

Civics & You Taking part in political parties is an important way for citizens to affect government decision making. Read to find out the impact of political parties on government.

Although the main purpose of political parties in the United States is to elect candidates to office, they also play an important role in helping the people of the United States practice self-government. The parties enable people to communicate with their government leaders and help ensure that government remains responsive to the people. The parties fulfill this role in a number of ways. Nominating candidates for office is just one of many tasks that political parties perform.

Political parties have several functions that help them fulfill their role in government. Political parties do the following:

- select and support candidates
- inform citizens
- carry the message of the people to the government
- operate the government
- act as a watchdog over government
- serve as a link between different levels and branches of government

Campaigning for Candidates After a political party nominates its candidates for office, it begins to campaign for them in the general election. The parties raise money for the campaign. They also help candidates inform voters about their ideas and views on public issues. A key role for party volunteers is to make sure party supporters are registered to vote and to ensure that on Election Day these voters go to the polls.

Interpreting Point of View

Objective: To understand how personal beliefs influence political positions

Focus: Students interpret what McCarthy must have felt about the war.

Teach: Discuss the historical context of the Vietnam War and its controversy.

Assess: Ask students what McCarthy would say about the war in Iraq.

Close: Have students explain the quote: "price . . . to pay for a military victory."

Differentiated Instruction Strategies

BL Reread the speech aloud with a partner. Look for clues about McCarthy's beliefs.

AL Explain why McCarthy was never elected president. Refer to the speech to support your argument.

ELL Define "casualties," "escalate," and "intensify." Write a sentence for each word.

Informing Citizens Running a campaign serves another important purpose in a democracy: it informs citizens about public issues and the way government works. To get their views across, party candidates make speeches, publish and distribute pamphlets, and place ads in newspapers and magazines and on television and radio. **W₁**

Carrying the People's Message In addition to presenting their views to the people, the parties listen to what the people have to say. Voters have ideas and concerns of their own and issues they want leaders to address.

Sometimes people in different areas feel very strongly about an issue. They may oppose a government policy or want stronger laws to protect the environment. A political movement that begins with the people **C**

is known as a grassroots movement. When a grassroots movement becomes strong enough, its ideas will probably be taken over by a political party.

Operating the Government Political parties play a key role in running and staffing the government. Congress and the state legislatures are organized and carry on their work on the basis of party affiliation. Party leaders in the legislature make every effort to see that their members support the party's position when considering legislation.

Many government jobs are civil service jobs gained on the basis of open, competitive examinations and merit. However, the president, governors, and some mayors have the **W₂** power to appoint their trusted supporters to many high-level jobs.

Spreading the Message Concerned citizens use various tactics to make the public aware of their concerns. These California citizens hand out information before a special election. *Explaining* What is a grassroots movement?

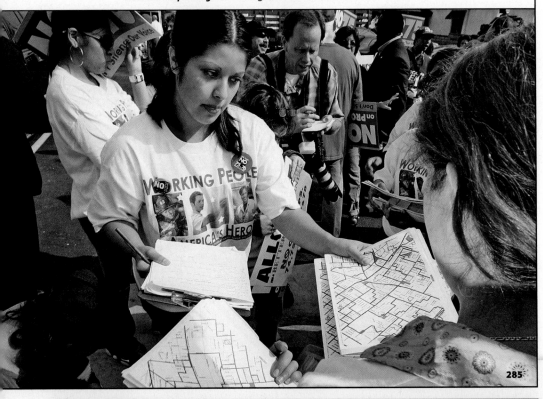

285

W₁ Writing Support

Persuasive Writing Ask students to work with a partner to write a political advertisement. Students may select any medium: newspaper, magazine, television, or radio. **OL**

C Critical Thinking

Identifying Central Issues Ask: What is the basis of a grassroots movement? *(strong feelings on the part of citizens regarding a particular policy, issue, or practice)* **OL**

W₂ Writing Support

Personal Writing Direct students to the "Plum Book" at www.gpoaccess. gov/plumbook/index.html, which lists approximately 8,000 federal government appointive positions. Have students write a letter to the president in which they ask for an appointment to a government job. **AL**

Caption Answer:

building party support at the neighborhood level

Activity: Interdisciplinary Connection

Science Invite a science teacher to class to inform students about environmental issues in which they might become politically active, such as the preservation of the world's rainforests, the concern over the melting polar caps, and so on. Ask students to form groups and select one issue of focus. Have groups use the Internet to research grassroots organizations that are actively involved in their issue. Have groups use a computer presentation program to describe grassroots efforts on their issue. **OL**

R Reading Strategy

Activating Prior Knowledge Ask: How does competition improve performance—in sports as in government? *(Answers may include the idea that competing for team positions makes players work harder, stay in shape, and try to please the coach. In the same way, when political parties compete for votes, they work harder to please voters with their actions and decisions.)* **OL**

✓ **Reading Check** **Answer:** To pass legislation, members of a political party agree to vote the same way.

Assess

Civics ONLINE

Study Central™ provides summaries, interactive games, and online graphic organizers to help students review content.

Close

Interpreting Have students work in groups. Ask groups to list five ways in which political parties benefit the lives of American citizens. **OL**

Section 2 Review

These supporters will usually be party members who believe in their party's ideas and want the opportunity to serve in government. If a chief executive has jobs to fill but does not have enough high-level supporters to fill them, he or she often seeks recommendations from party leaders.

Linking the Different Levels of Government Just as political parties carry the people's message to the government, they also help different levels and branches of government cooperate with one another. For example, suppose the mayor of Columbia, South Carolina, and the governor of South Carolina are both Democrats. They are likely to have similar goals and ideas. They may be personal friends. Perhaps they have worked together on election campaigns or party business in the past. These connections may make it easier for them to join forces to tackle

mutual problems. Likewise, when a majority of legislators belongs to the same party as a chief executive, cooperation between the two branches is likely to be better than if they belong to opposing parties.

Acting as a Watchdog Between elections, political parties act as "watchdogs" over government activities. The party that is out of power—the party that lost the election for president, governor, or Congress—watches the actions of the party in power for any mistakes or misuse of power. This opposition party may criticize the party in power and offer its own solutions to political problems. In this way, the opposition party hopes to attract voters. Competition between parties forces the party in power to pay attention to the will of the people.

✓ **Reading Check** Explaining What is a political party's connection to legislation?

Vocabulary

1. **Explain** the following terms by using each in a complete sentence: *national committee, caucus, precinct, ward, political machine, direct primary, closed primary, open primary, plurality, majority,* and *petition.*

Main Ideas

2. **Explaining** What is the purpose of a party's national convention?

3. **Explaining** In what way do political parties help manage the government?

4. **Identify** three ways in which parties and their candidates inform the public.

Critical Thinking

5. **Evaluating** In your opinion, which is a better system, the open primary or the closed primary? Explain.

6. **BIG Ideas** On a web diagram like the one below, write the campaigning roles that political party members play in supporting their party.

```
          raise money
Role of Campaigning
```

7. **Understanding Cause and Effect** The two major parties are criticized as being out of touch with the needs of many Americans. How might a successful third party affect the two major parties?

CITIZENSHIP Activity

8. **Creative Writing** Create a poster that presents a democratic and cost-efficient system for selecting nominees for president.

Civics ONLINE

Study Central™ To review this section, go to glencoe.com.

Answers

1. Sentences should use vocabulary words according to their definitions in the section and in the Glossary.

2. At a national convention the party decides on its platform and nominates its presidential candidate.

3. Party members serve in elected and appointed government positions. Parties serve as watchdogs over government and inform citizens of what is happening. They communicate citizens' concerns and needs to government officials.

4. Party candidates make speeches, publish and distribute pamphlets, and place informative ads.

5. Answers will vary. Students may argue that closed primaries give a true indication of party strength. Other students may argue that this system is more fair to voters who choose candidates based on individual merits, not party affiliation.

6. make sure party supporters are registered; raise money; ensure that voters go to the polls; help candidates reach out to voters

7. Answers may include that if a third party gains enough support, it may force the existing major parties to reevaluate their practices.

8. Posters will vary but should reflect a reasonable system of selecting presidential nominees.

Visual Summary

What Is a Political Party?

A political party is a group of individuals outside of government that organizes to win elections, to operate the government, and to determine policy.

Candidates are ready to answer questions

Students speak out on issues

Political Parties Form

- Shortly after our nation began, two political parties formed.
- The basic difference between the two parties today is their beliefs in how much the government should be involved in Americans' lives.
- In the United States, we have a two-party system, which means that two major parties—the Democrats and the Republicans—dominate national politics.

Organization

- Each party has a national committee and congressional campaign committees. Each party also has 50 state committees and many local party organizations.
- In the past, some local party organizations became so powerful that their candidates won almost every election. These were known as political machines.

What Political Parties Do

- Select candidates
- Inform the public
- Coordinate policy making
- Balance competing interests
- Run campaigns

Comparing Parties

- One way to compare political parties is to study their party platforms, which are declarations of each party's beliefs and positions on major issues.
- The platform is made of planks, which are the party's official positions on specific issues such as education, crime, and foreign policy.

The president leads his political party

 STUDY TO GO Study anywhere, anytime! Download quizzes and flash cards to your PDA from glencoe.com.

287

Visual Summary 9

Predicting Ask: What helps listeners predict how a candidate will respond to specific questions? *(Candidates will usually follow the party platform on major issues.)* **OL**

For additional practice on this skill (Predicting), see the **Skills Handbook**.

Making Connections Have students work with a partner to illustrate a political "machine." **Ask:** How do the traits of a real machine help you understand the functioning of a political machine? *(Answers may include the idea that all parts of a machine must work together in order to function.)* **BL**

Analyzing Text Structure Ask: In which section will readers learn about the functions of political parties? *(What Political Parties Do)* **ELL**

Hands-On Chapter Project
Step 3: Wrap-Up

Mock Convention

Step 3: Evaluating the Activity Students will finish the process they started in Step 1 by reviewing and evaluating the mock conventions.

Directions Reconvene the class as a whole. Again play portions of a real national nominating convention. Then play the video of each group's convention. Have students take notes on each convention. Students should create a chart that lists the party name, symbol, slogan, and platform of each group's political party. Ask students to volunteer constructive comments and positive feedback to evaluate how well each "party" conducted a national convention. **Ask:** Which "convention" was more informative: the class's or the actual national convention? Which was more entertaining? What could be done to the national conventions to make them more engaging? **OL**

Answers and Analyses

Reviewing Vocabulary

1. C Answer A is a general term and does not employ the academic vocabulary of the chapter. Students who choose B are confusing a platform—a party's combined beliefs on a series of issues—with its position on a single issue. Students who incorrectly select D confuse ideology, a broad statement of beliefs, with a single position. By selecting answer C, students acknowledge that a plank is a party's stand on a single issue.

2. B Petitions are documents voters sign so that third-party candidates can be listed on ballots. Political machines are local party organizations that are now viewed as harmful. National committees are groups of party members that coordinate the activities of national nominating conventions. Some states use caucuses rather than elections to select candidates for national conventions.

3. B Although both "ward" and "precinct" refer to political divisions, only a precinct defines where residents of an area go to vote. A ward is composed of several precincts. Members of political parties are distributed throughout the nation and vote according to their geographic location. Similarly, voters across the state vote according to their area of residence in a direct primary.

4. D Only in a closed primary are voters required to declare their party affiliations before they can vote. An open primary allows voters to vote without declaring a party affiliation. Both open and closed primaries are direct primaries. In general elections, each party has only one candidate.

Reviewing Main Ideas

5. D With Abraham Lincoln's election to the presidency in 1860, the country's major parties became Republican and Democratic. Although Republicans made great strides in the 1854 congressional elections, they were still not viewed as a major party. The Republican Party did not exist in 1824 and 1828.

TEST-TAKING TIP

Preconceived ideas about what will be on the test may lead you to assume the meaning of a question before you finish reading it. Read every word in each question to avoid wrong answers based on false assumptions.

Reviewing Vocabulary

Directions: Choose the word(s) that best completes the sentence.

1. A political party's belief, position, or principle on an election issue is called a(n) _____.

  A idea   **C** plank
  B platform   **D** ideology

2. Each party chooses its delegates to the national convention through a combination of elections and _____.

  A petitions   **C** political machines
  B caucuses   **D** national committees

3. All voters in a _____ cast their ballots at the same voting place.

  A ward   **C** political party
  B precinct   **D** direct primary

4. An election in which only the declared members of a party are allowed to vote for that party's nominees is a(n) _____.

  A direct primary   **C** open primary
  B general election **D** closed primary

Reviewing Main Ideas

Directions: Choose the best answers to the following questions.

Section 1 *(pp. 272–277)*

5. In what year did Democrats and Republicans become the major political parties in the United States?

  A 1824
  B 1828
  C 1854
  D 1860

6. Which third party would like to replace capitalism with worker-owned factories?

  A Reform Party
  B Libertarian Party
  C Communist Party
  D Prohibitionist Party

Section 2 *(pp. 278–286)*

7. What is the delegates' first job at a party's national convention?

  A nominating candidates
  B writing the party platform
  C raising large amounts of money
  D listening to nominating speeches

8. How do candidates unaffiliated with either of the two major parties get on the ballot in a general election?

  A by winning an open primary
  B by running in a direct primary
  C by collecting voters' signatures
  D by receiving a majority of votes

9. What political organization of the past used to win elections consistently?

  A idealogical party
  B whig party
  C precinct organization
  D political machine

GO ON

---

6. C Although all answers refer to third parties, only the Communist Party wishes to replace capitalism with worker-owned factories. The Prohibitionist Party was a single-issue party that faded out when prohibition ceased to be an issue. The Libertarian Party focuses on keeping government out of citizens' lives, while the Reform Party wished to enact social reform legislation in areas such as education and health care.

7. B Although all answers describe delegate activities, only three take place at the convention. Money-raising activities take place after the convention. Before candidates can be nominated, however, the party platform must be written.

8. C In order to run in or win a primary with a majority of the votes, an unaffiliated candidate must circulate petitions and collect enough voters' signatures to appear on the ballot.

Critical Thinking

Directions: Base your answers to questions 10 and 11 on the diagram below and your knowledge of Chapter 9.

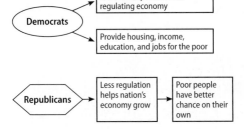

10. Consider how different persons might view the two major parties. Which voter would most likely support the Republican Party?

A a homeless senior

B a low-income student

C a corporate executive

D a government regulator

11. Compare the discussion of third parties in the chapter with the facts in the diagram. Which third party has goals similar to those of Republicans?

A Libertarian Party

B Communist Party

C Prohibitionist Party

D Socialist Labor Party

Document Based Questions

Directions: Analyze the following document and answer the short-answer questions that follow.

The following passage is from the keynote speech by senatorial candidate Barack Obama given at the Democratic National Convention in 2004.

> *For alongside our famous individualism, there's another ingredient in the American saga. A belief that we are connected as one people.*
>
> *If there's a child on the south side of Chicago who can't read, that matters to me, even if it's not my child. If there's a senior citizen somewhere who can't pay for their prescription and having to choose between medicine and the rent, that makes my life poorer, even if it's not my grandparent. If there's an Arab American family being rounded up without benefit of an attorney or due process, that threatens my civil liberties. It's that fundamental belief—I am my brother's keeper, I am my sister's keeper— that makes this country work. It's what allows us to pursue our individual dreams, yet still come together as a single American family. "E pluribus unum." Out of many, one.*
>
> —Barack Obama

12. What two priorities of the Democratic Party are alluded to in Obama's speech?

13. How does Obama suggest that the Democratic Party is the party of diversity? Back up your answer with proof from the passage.

Extended Response

14. Write a short description of the state and local organization of the political parties. Discuss the differences from state to state, the divisions of the organization, and the common focus in all the states.

STOP

Civics ONLINE

For additional test practice, use Self-Check Quizzes—Chapter 9 on glencoe.com.

Need Extra Help?

If you missed question...	1	2	3	4	5	6	7	8	9	10	11	12	13	14
Go to page...	277	279	281	283	274	275	279	284	282	277	275	279	279	280

ASSESSMENT

11. A Libertarians agree with the Republican view on minimal government intervention in the lives of its citizens. The Communist and Socialist Labor Parties disagree with capitalism, a system Republicans promote. Prohibitionists focused only on the issue of a ban on the use, manufacture, and sale of alcohol.

Document-Based Questions

12. education and public health care

13. Answers may include that the speaker models racial, ethnic, and gender diversity with his references to African Americans, Arab Americans, senior citizens, and women (sister).

Extended Response

14. Students' descriptions should model the information pictured in the chart on page 280 of the Student Edition. Stated differences may include using caucuses rather than elections to select convention delegates. Students should indicate that the common focus of all party levels is to work for the election of as many party candidates as possible.

9. D Ideological parties and precinct organizations are not outdated. While the Whig party no longer exists, it did not consistently win elections during its tenure. Political machines, such as Tammany Hall, were so powerful that they consistently won elections.

Critical Thinking

10. C Of the four answers, only the corporate executive is a reasonable answer since Republicans favor little government intervention in the nation's free market economy. Both the homeless senior and the low-income student might favor the Democratic Party, which believes that government must intervene with social assistance programs. Because Republicans favor deregulation, conceivably a government regulator would be out of a job.

Civics ONLINE

Have students visit the Web site at glencoe.com to review Chapter 9 and take the **Self-Check Quiz**.

Need Extra Help?

Have students refer to the pages listed if they miss any of the questions.

10

Key to Ability Levels

BL	Below level	AL	Above level
OL	On level	ELL	English Language Learners

Key to Teaching Resources

Print Material   Transparency

CD-ROM or DVD

Levels					Resources	Chapter Opener	Section 1	Section 2	Section 3	Chapter Assess
BL	OL	AL	ELL							
					FOCUS					
BL	OL	AL	ELL	🖳	Daily Focus Skills Transparencies		10–1	10–2	10–3	
					TEACH					
BL	OL		ELL	📁	Reading Essentials and Note-Taking Guide*		p. 93	p. 96	p. 99	
	OL	AL		📁	Citizenship/Decision-Making Activity, URB			p. 3	p. 3	
	OL	AL		📁	Economics Activity, URB				p. 5	
	OL	AL		📁	Primary Source Reading, URB				p. 15	
BL	OL	AL	ELL	📁	Content Vocabulary Activity, URB*	p. 41	p. 41	p. 41	p. 41	
BL	OL	AL	ELL	📁	Academic Vocabulary Activity, URB	p. 43	p. 43	p. 43	p. 43	
	OL			📁	Biography Activity, URB		p. 45			
BL	OL	AL	ELL	📁	Writing Skills Activity, URB				p. 47	
	OL	AL		📁	Critical Thinking Skills Activity, URB		p. 51		p. 51	
BL	OL	AL	ELL	📁	Chart, Graph, and Map Skills Activity, URB			p. 53	p. 53	
BL	OL	AL	ELL	📁	Differentiated Instruction, URB				p. 55	
BL	OL	AL	ELL	📁	School-to-Home Connection Activity, URB*	p. 57	p. 57	p. 57	p. 57	
BL	OL		ELL	📁	Guided Reading Activities, URB*		p. 61	p. 62	p. 63	
BL	OL	AL	ELL	📁	Writer's Guidebook	✓	✓	✓	✓	✓
	OL	AL		💿	Primary Source Document Library	✓	✓	✓	✓	✓
BL	OL	AL	ELL	💿	Daily Lecture & Discussion Notes (in Pres. Plus)		✓	✓	✓	✓
BL	OL	AL	ELL	💿	StudentWorks™ Plus		✓	✓	✓	✓
BL	OL	AL	ELL	💿	Section Spotlight Videos		✓	✓	✓	
BL	OL	AL	ELL	🖳	TIME Interpreting Political Cartoons Transp.		Ch. 10			
BL	OL	AL	ELL	🖳	Writing Process Transparencies	✓	✓	✓	✓	✓

Note: Please refer to the *Unit 3 Resource Book* for this chapter's URB materials.

* Also available in Spanish

- Interactive Lesson Planner
- Interactive Teacher Edition
- Fully editable blackline masters
- Section Spotlight Videos Launch
- Differentiated Lesson Plans
- Printable reports of daily assignments
- Standards Tracking System

Levels					Resources	Chapter Opener	Section 1	Section 2	Section 3	Chapter Assess
BL	OL	AL	ELL							
TEACH *(continued)*										
				📁	**Building Academic Vocabulary**	✓	✓	✓	✓	✓
Teacher Resources				📁	**Strategies for Success**	✓	✓	✓	✓	✓
				📁	**Teacher's Guide to Differentiated Instruction**	✓	✓	✓	✓	✓
				💿	**Graphing Tool**	✓	✓	✓	✓	✓
				💿	**Presentation Plus! with MindJogger CheckPoint**	✓	✓	✓	✓	✓
ASSESS										
BL	OL	AL	ELL	📁	**Quizzes and Tests***		p. 114	p. 115	p. 116	p. 117
BL	OL	AL	ELL	📁	**Authentic Assessment with Rubrics**			p. 14		
BL	OL	AL	ELL	📁	**Standardized Test Practice**		p. 19	p. 19	p. 19	p. 19
BL	OL	AL	ELL	💿	*ExamView®* **Assessment Suite CD-ROM**		10–1	10–2	10–3	Ch. 10
CLOSE										
BL			ELL	📁	**Reteaching Activity, URB***		p. 59	p. 59	p. 59	
BL	OL		ELL	📁	**Reading and Study Skills Foldables™ Activity**	p. 68	p. 69	p. 69		
BL	OL	AL	ELL	📁	*Civics Today* **in Graphic Novel**	p. 29		p. 29		
BL	OL	AL	ELL	🖪	**Graphic Organizer Transparencies & Strategies**	✓	✓	✓	✓	✓

✓ Chapter- or unit-based activities applicable to all sections in this chapter

Using PuzzleMaker™ 3.1

Online Crossword Puzzles

What is PuzzleMaker™ 3.1?

Glencoe's PuzzleMaker™ 3.1 is an interactive online tool that lets you create your own crossword puzzles for classroom use based on the glossary and using either content vocabulary, academic vocabulary, or both, for classroom use.

How can PuzzleMaker™ 3.1 help my students?

Completing the crossword puzzles helps students to:

- recall vocabulary terms based on puzzle clues
- reinforce their understanding of the vocabulary

Visit glencoe.com and enter a **QuickPass**™ code to go directly to resources for each chapter.

Civics ONLINE

Visit glencoe.com and enter **QuickPass**™ code CIV1360c10T for Chapter 10 resources.

You can easily launch a wide range of digital products from your computer's desktop with the McGraw-Hill Social Studies widget.

	Student	Teacher	Parent
Media Center			
• Student Edition Section Audio	●		●
• Spanish Summaries	●		●
• Section Spotlight Videos	●	●	●
***Civics Today* Online Learning Center (Web Site)**			
• Chapter Overviews	●	●	●
• Study Central™	●	●	●
• Study-to-Go	●	●	●
• Student Web Activities	●	●	●
• Concepts in Motion	●	●	●
• Self-Check Quizzes	●	●	●
• ePuzzles and Games	●	●	●
• StudentWorks™ Plus Online	●	●	●
• Vocabulary eFlashcards	●	●	●
• Web Activity Lesson Plans		●	
• Vocabulary PuzzleMaker	●	●	●
Classroom Tools			
• Multilingual Glossary	●	●	●
• Beyond the Textbook	●	●	●
• NGS MapMachine	●	●	●

Reading List Generator CD-ROM

GLENCOE BookLink 3

Use this database to search more than 30,000 titles to create a customized reading list for your students.

- Reading lists can be organized by students' reading level, author, genre, theme, or area of interest.
- The database provides Degrees of Reading Power™ (DRP) and Lexile™ readability scores for all selections.
- A brief summary of each selection is included.

Leveled reading suggestions for this chapter:

For students at a Grade 7 reading level:
- *Nobody Particular: One Woman's Fight to Save the Bays,* by Molly Bang

For students at a Grade 8 reading level:
- *With Courage and Cloth: Winning the Fight for a Woman's Right to Vote,* by Ann Bausum

For students at a Grade 9 reading level:
- *Elections in the United States,* by David Heath

For students at a Grade 10 reading level:
- *The Torchbearers,* by Rita Dove

For students at a Grade 11 reading level:
- *A Pocket History of the United States,* by Henry Steele Commager

READING SUPPORT FROM JAMESTOWN EDUCATION

- **Timed Readings Plus in Social Studies** helps students increase their reading rate and fluency while maintaining comprehension. The 400-word passages are similar to those found on state and national assessments.

- **Reading in the Content Area: Social Studies** concentrates on six essential reading skills that help students better comprehend what they read. The book includes 75 high-interest nonfiction passages written at increasing levels of difficulty.

- **Reading Social Studies** includes strategic reading instruction and vocabulary support in Social Studies content for both ELLs and native speakers of English.

- **Content Vocabulary Workout** (Grades 6–8) accelerates reading comprehension through focused vocabulary development. Social Studies content vocabulary comes from the glossaries of Glencoe's Middle School Social Studies texts. www.jamestowneducation.com

KEY Teacher Wraparound

Use this key to help you identify the different types of prompts found in the Teacher Wraparound Edition.

R **Reading Strategies** activities help you teach reading skills and vocabulary.

C **Critical Thinking** strategies help students apply and extend what they have learned.

D **Differentiated Instruction** activities provide instruction for students learning to speak English, along with suggestions for teaching various types of learners.

S **Skill Practice** strategies help students practice historical analysis and geography skills.

W **Writing Support** activities provide writing opportunities to help students comprehend the text.

Teaching strategies and activities have been coded for ability level appropriateness.

AL Activities for students working above grade level

OL Activities for students working on grade level

BL Activities for students working below grade level

ELL Activities for English Language Learners

Focus

Why It Matters

Ask: Why is it important for citizens in a democracy to exercise their right to vote? *(Answers may include these ideas: through voting, citizens have a voice in their government—in influencing its laws and in choosing who will represent them. It is the right to vote that makes a democracy a government of the people.)*

More About the Photo

Visual Literacy California's Governor Arnold Schwarzenegger is shown campaigning for his reelection in 2006, which he won in a landslide. Schwarzenegger, the Austrian-born bodybuilder and Hollywood movie star, first won the race for governor in 2003 in a special election called to remove Governor Gray Davis from office. In that election, Schwarzenegger defeated 134 other candidates and won 49 percent of the vote even though he had no prior experience in politics.

Teach

 As you begin teaching each section, use these questions and activities to help students focus on the Big Ideas.

Section 1

Who Can Vote? Ask: What are the requirements to vote in a U.S. election? *(You must be a U.S. citizen and not a convicted felon or legally insane. Most states require you to be a resident of the state for*

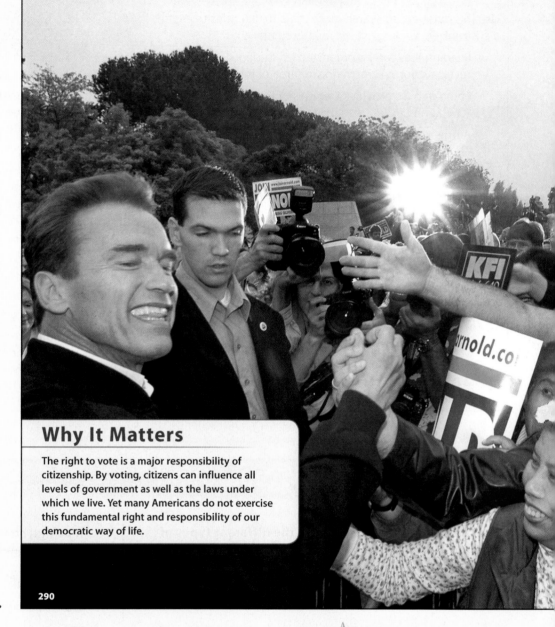

Chapter
10
Voting and Elections

Why It Matters

The right to vote is a major responsibility of citizenship. By voting, citizens can influence all levels of government as well as the laws under which we live. Yet many Americans do not exercise this fundamental right and responsibility of our democratic way of life.

290

a specified period and be registered to vote.) Tell students that in Section 1, they will learn how the right to vote became a right for all U.S. citizens. Ask students to think about, as they read, what it would be like if they would never be allowed to vote. **OL**

Section 2

Election Campaigns Ask: What different types of political elections are held in the United States? *(primary, general, and special)* Explain that in Section 2, students will learn about the types of political elections, the role of campaigns in elections, and the system for deciding votes in presidential elections. **OL**

Chapter Audio

Civics ONLINE
Visit glencoe.com and enter
QuickPass™ code
CIV3093c10 for
Chapter 10
resources.

Chapter Introduction
10

BIG Ideas

Section 1: Who Can Vote?

The right to vote is one of the fundamental rights of citizens in a democratic society. Voting is a basic political right of all U.S. citizens who meet certain qualifications set by law.

Section 2: Election Campaigns

A successful democracy is built on an informed electorate. The success of an election campaign depends on the people who organize it.

Section 3: Paying for Election Campaigns

A successful democracy is built on an informed electorate. The sophisticated vote-getting techniques that candidates use have made campaigning very expensive.

Governor Arnold Schwarzenegger campaigns in California

FOLDABLES™
Study Organizer

Evaluating Information Study Foldable Make the following Foldable to help you evaluate the voting process and who can vote, how election campaigns are run, and how campaigns are financed.

Step 1 Fold a sheet of paper in thirds as shown.

Step 2 Open up the paper and label each of the columns created by folds with these headings:
Who Can Vote?
Election Campaigns
Paying for Election Campaigns

Reading and Writing As you read the chapter, evaluate the information you read about the voting process, taking notes on the rules of voting and how election campaigns are run. Use your notes to understand the entire process of an election.

FOLDABLES™ Dinah Zike's
Study Organizer **Foldables**

Purpose This Foldable guides students to take notes that will help them understand and evaluate what they read. In the completed Foldable, students' notes are organized and recorded in three columns to aid them to understand and evaluate voting requirements, election campaigns, and campaign financing. **OL**

📁 More Foldables activities for this chapter can be found in the *Dinah Zike's Reading and Study Skills Foldables* ancillary.

Civics ONLINE
Visit glencoe.com and enter
QuickPass™ code CIV1360c10T for Chapter 10 resources, including a Chapter Overview, Study Central™, Study-to-Go, Student Web Activity, Self-Check Quiz, and other materials.

Chapter 10 291

Section 3

Paying for Election Campaigns Ask:
How are political campaigns funded?
(They are privately funded by groups and individuals and publicly funded with federal campaign funds.) Tell students that in Section 3 they will learn about the process of becoming a candidate, the role of political campaigns, how campaigns are financed, and why financing is an issue. **OL**

Focus

Bellringer
Daily Focus Transparency 10–1

Guide to Reading
Answers to Graphic:

Voting Process
1. register to vote when qualified
2. go to polling place
3. fill out application at clerk's desk
4. show identification if challenged
5. hand application to an election judge
6. use voting machine to cast ballot

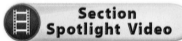
Section Spotlight Video

Have students watch the Chapter 10, Section 1 video at glencoe.com.

Resource Manager

Guide to Reading

Big Idea
The right to vote is one of the fundamental rights of citizens in a democratic society.

Content Vocabulary
- polling place *(p. 295)*
- precinct *(p. 295)*
- ballot *(p. 296)*
- absentee ballot *(p. 297)*
- returns *(p. 297)*
- exit poll *(p. 297)*
- electorate *(p. 299)*
- apathy *(p. 299)*

Academic Vocabulary
- ultimate *(p. 293)*
- devote *(p. 297)*

Reading Strategy
Sequencing As you read, complete a chart like the one below by listing the steps in the voting process.

Voting Process
1. register to vote when qualified
2. go to polling place
3.
4.
5.
6.

Section 1

Who Can Vote?

Real World Civics Wheelchairs can help many people with disabilities live more independent daily lives. However, if you are disabled, can you get out and vote? Polling places have been accused of not being "disabled-friendly." The Constitution promises everyone the right to vote regardless of race, color, gender, or age (as long as they are 18). It is up to each state to find ways to make polling places accessible for all voters. Despite the Help America Vote Act of 2002, some people still face obstacles to voting. Organizations at the state level work to help these voters overcome such obstacles.

▼ **Voters at Parker Jewish Geriatric Institute in New York**

R Reading Strategies	**C** Critical Thinking	**D** Differentiated Instruction	**W** Writing Support	**S** Skill Practice
Teacher Edition • Ac. Vocab., p. 293 • Taking Notes, p. 293 • Summarizing, p. 298 **Additional Resources** • Cont. Vocb., URB p. 41 • Acad. Vocab., URB p. 43 • Biography, URB p. 45 • Guid. Read., URB p. 61 • Foldables, p. 69	**Teacher Edition** • Making Inferences pp. 293, 296 • Drawing Con., pp. 294, 296 **Additional Resources** • Critical Thinking, URB p. 51	**Teacher Edition** • EL, p. 297 • Intrapersonal, p. 298 • Auditory, p. 299 **Additional Resources** • School-to-Home Act., URB p. 57 • Reteach. Act., URB p. 59	**Teacher Edition** • Expository Writing, pp. 295, 297 • Persuasive Writing, p. 297	**Teacher Edition** • Reading Charts, p. 294 **Additional Resources** • Daily Focus Trans., 10–1 • Pol. Cartoons Trans. 10

Qualifying to Vote

Main Idea The right to vote is the foundation of American democracy.

Civics & You Many of you will have the opportunity to vote for the first time in the not-too-distant future. As you read, think about why so many people have sacrificed so much to gain the right to vote.

Voting is an important right of American citizenship. Without it, citizens would not be able to choose the people who will run their government. Voting is also a major responsibility. Those who do not vote are failing to carry out a civic responsibility. They are also handing over their share of political power to voters whose views they may oppose. President Franklin D. Roosevelt reminded Americans of the importance of voting when he said, "Let us never forget that government is ourselves. The **ultimate** [fundamental] rulers of our democracy . . . are the voters of this country."

Early Restrictions

During the early years of our nation, most voters were white, adult males, and property owners. People often barred from voting included white adult males who could not afford to buy property, women, African American males, Native American males, and people under 21 years of age. Today, however, property ownership is no longer a consideration, and the U.S. Constitution states that no state may deny the right to vote because of race, color, gender, or age—if the person is at least 18 years old. Most states deny individuals convicted of serious crimes the right to vote until they have served their prison sentences.

In most states, you must be registered to vote. To be eligible to vote, you must be at least 18, a resident of the state for a specified period, and a citizen of the United States.

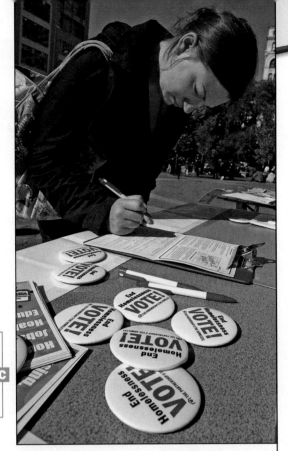

Registering Citizens must register in order to vote. *Explaining* What responsibilities do citizens have when they register for the first time?

Voter Registration

Most states require registration at least 25 days before an election. In a few states, however, the deadline is later—10 or even fewer days before the election.

Registration requirements vary. Registration applications may be obtained from county offices. Some states make the process easier, permitting registration by mail or offering more convenient times and places for in-person registration such as allowing registration at public libraries or high schools.

Teach

C Critical Thinking

Making Inferences Ask: What did President Roosevelt mean when he said that the ultimate rulers of our democracy are the voters? *(Through the power of their votes, voters rule our government by choosing who will represent them, by taking a stand on issues, and by influencing laws.)* **OL**

R1 Reading Strategy

Academic Vocabulary Ask: What is a synonym for "ultimate"? *(final)* **BL**

R2 Reading Strategy

Taking Notes Have students make a chart with two columns, labeled "The Past" and "Today." Have them use the chart to take notes on voter qualifications in the past and today. *(Past: white adult males who owned property. Today: at least 18, resident of state for specified time, U.S. citizen, registered to vote, not serving a sentence for committing a serious crime.)* **OL**

Caption Answer:

Students may say that citizens must register before the state deadline and show proof of their citizenship, age, and address.

Additional Support

Activity: Technology Connection

Summarizing Explain that the requirements for registering to vote are not the same in every state. For example, the deadline for registering before an election varies. Have students use the Internet to find their state's requirements for registering to vote. You may wish to suggest that they search for the following information:

- requirements to vote in your state
- time limit for registering before an election
- where to obtain and send a registration form
- forms available for non-English speakers
- how to register by mail or online

Ask students to write a summary of their findings, either in paragraph form or condensed in an outline. **OL**

S Skill Practice

Reading Charts **Ask:** What does the chart show? *(how the right to vote was extended between 1870 and 2006)* Have students note the chart's organization *(chronological)* and the type of items it includes *(Constitutional amendments, Congressional acts, Supreme Court rules, legislative acts)*. **Ask:** Which decade has the most listings for right-to-vote extensions: the 1920s, 1960s, 1970s, or 1990s? *(the 1960s)* **OL**

C Critical Thinking

Drawing Conclusions **Ask:** What do the actions taken in 1975, 1992, and 2006 indicate about the changing population of the United States? *(It indicates an increase in non-English-speaking citizens who need ballots they can read to protect their right to vote.)* **OL**

Analyzing Charts

Answers:

1. The Civil Rights Acts were needed because the voting rights of individuals were obstructed in various states.
2. the Twenty-sixth Amendment (The Amendments of 1970 gave them the right to vote in federal elections.)

Hands-On Chapter Project
Step 1

Running an Election Campaign

Step 1: Choosing a Candidate Form groups of students for the ongoing project. Try to distribute students skilled in art, writing, organization, and dramatics among the groups.

Directions Tell the groups that today they will "invent" the candidate they will support in a mock class election. Suggest that they begin by brainstorming.

Have students brainstorm to generate as many ideas as possible about their candidate's name, appearance, manner, qualifications, and positions on issues about which they care. One person could act as the recorder for the group. Those with an artistic bent might volunteer to make a quick sketch of the proposed candidate. Finally, have the group make a list of their decisions. **OL**

(Project continued in Section 2)

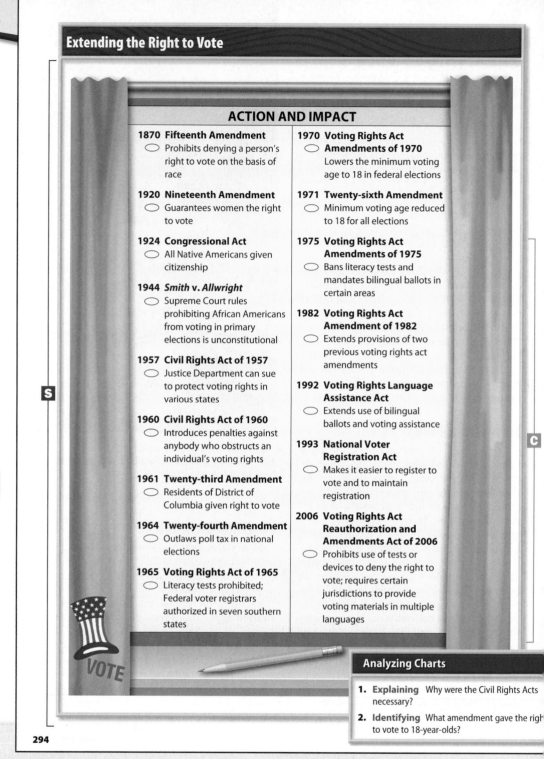

Extending the Right to Vote

ACTION AND IMPACT

1870 Fifteenth Amendment
○ Prohibits denying a person's right to vote on the basis of race

1920 Nineteenth Amendment
○ Guarantees women the right to vote

1924 Congressional Act
○ All Native Americans given citizenship

1944 *Smith v. Allwright*
○ Supreme Court rules prohibiting African Americans from voting in primary elections is unconstitutional

1957 Civil Rights Act of 1957
○ Justice Department can sue to protect voting rights in various states

1960 Civil Rights Act of 1960
○ Introduces penalties against anybody who obstructs an individual's voting rights

1961 Twenty-third Amendment
○ Residents of District of Columbia given right to vote

1964 Twenty-fourth Amendment
○ Outlaws poll tax in national elections

1965 Voting Rights Act of 1965
○ Literacy tests prohibited; Federal voter registrars authorized in seven southern states

1970 Voting Rights Act Amendments of 1970
○ Lowers the minimum voting age to 18 in federal elections

1971 Twenty-sixth Amendment
○ Minimum voting age reduced to 18 for all elections

1975 Voting Rights Act Amendments of 1975
○ Bans literacy tests and mandates bilingual ballots in certain areas

1982 Voting Rights Act Amendment of 1982
○ Extends provisions of two previous voting rights act amendments

1992 Voting Rights Language Assistance Act
○ Extends use of bilingual ballots and voting assistance

1993 National Voter Registration Act
○ Makes it easier to register to vote and to maintain registration

2006 Voting Rights Act Reauthorization and Amendments Act of 2006
○ Prohibits use of tests or devices to deny the right to vote; requires certain jurisdictions to provide voting materials in multiple languages

VOTE

Analyzing Charts

1. **Explaining** Why were the Civil Rights Acts necessary?
2. **Identifying** What amendment gave the right to vote to 18-year-olds?

294

American Biography

Carrie Chapman Catt (1859–1947)

Carrie Chapman Catt declared, "Everybody counts in a democracy." She worked to help women gain the right to vote. Catt felt that self-government would never be safe until "every responsible and law-abiding adult" possessed the vote.

Catt, born Carrie Clinton Lane, grew up along the Iowa frontier. She put herself through college by washing dishes, teaching, and working in the library. She went on to become one of the nation's first female school superintendents. In 1885 Lane married Leo Chapman and helped coedit his newspaper. Widowed a year later, she joined the suffrage movement. When her second husband, George Catt,

died in 1902, Carrie Chapman Catt went overseas to help spread the movement worldwide.

With the support of Susan B. Anthony, one of the founders of the suffrage movement, she led the campaign to add the Nineteenth Amendment to the Constitution when she returned to America. Victory came in 1920. To prepare some 20 million women for "political independence," Catt founded the League of Women Voters. Today the League honors its founder by educating all citizens on the importance of voting in a democracy.

Making a Difference   CITIZENSHIP

Carrie Catt was one of the earliest female education reformers. **Identifying** What organization did Catt found to prepare women for "political independence"?

W **Writing Support**

Expository Writing Have students write a list of instructions for first-time voters on how to register to vote. Remind them to include optional ways to register and what first-time voters will need to prove they are qualified to vote. *(They may register by mail, at state offices and agencies, or on renewing a driver's license. Some states allow voters to register on the Internet. They will need to show a driver's license or birth certificate as proof of age and citizenship.)* **BL**

American Biography

Answer: Carrie Catt founded the League of Women Voters to prepare women for "political independence."

Reading Check **Answer:** You must be a U.S. citizen, at least 18 years old, a resident of a state for a specified period, not a convicted felon or legally insane, and registered to vote.

How to Register The National Voter Registration Act requires states to let people register when they renew their drivers' licenses. Citizens may also mail in registrations or register at various state and welfare offices, and agencies that serve people with disabilities.

Registration forms ask for your name, address, age, and often your party preference. **W** You may register as a member of a political party or as an unaffiliated voter. If you register as a Democrat or a Republican, you may vote in primary elections in which you choose candidates for the general election.

To register, first-time voters must show proof of citizenship, address, and age using a driver's license or birth certificate. Voters are then assigned to an election district.

Reading Check **Identifying** What requirements must you meet to qualify to vote?

Steps in Voting

Main Idea Voting is a basic political right of all U.S. citizens who meet certain qualifications set by law.

Civics & You Once you take the initiative to vote, there is a process you must follow in order to cast your ballot.

Once the campaign is over, it is up to the voters to decide who will win or lose. On Election Day, voters go to the polling place in their precincts to cast their votes. A **polling place** is the location where voting is carried out, and a **precinct** is a voting district. Polling places are usually set up in town halls, schools, fire stations, community centers, and other public buildings.

Differentiated Instruction

Esther Hobart Morris

BIOGRAPHY ACTIVITY 10

Esther Hobart Morris (1814–1902)

Biography Activity 10,
URB pp. 45-46

Objective: To identify Morris's contributions to the women's rights movement

Focus: Have students identify Morris's role in the woman suffrage movement.

Teach: Discuss how life in the territories differed from life in the states.

Assess: List the important events and accomplishments in Morris's life.

Close: Write a paragraph summarizing Morris's importance in the history of voting rights for women.

Differentiated Instruction Strategies

BL Give one reason Morris became aware of the need for women's voting rights.

AL What qualities do you think Morris had that caused her to be appointed to a judicial position?

ELL Name one important thing Morris did to help women get the right to vote.

C1 Critical Thinking

Making Inferences **Ask:** What should you bring with you to the polling place in case your signature is challenged? *(Answers may include bringing your driver's license or birth certificate as proof of your identification.)* **OL**

C2 Critical Thinking

Drawing Conclusions Ask students to think about the present system that leaves the choice of election methods to the states. Then have them write a short paragraph about whether or not states should have this right. *(Students' opinions should be backed up by specific reasons or examples.)* **AL**

Caption Answer:

because African Americans were still being prevented from voting

---

The Right to Vote African Americans rallied to be allowed to vote in 1965 in Montgomery, Alabama. Led by Dr. Martin Luther King, Jr., they faced a line of police officers barring their way. **Explaining** Why did it require protests to allow African Americans to vote?

At the Polls

Polling places are generally open from early morning until 7 or 8 P.M. When you first arrive, you can study a sample ballot posted near the entrance. A **ballot** is the list of candidates on which you cast your vote. Once inside, you write your name and address and sign an application form at the clerk's table. The clerk reads your name aloud and passes the form to a challenger's table.

A challenger—there are challengers representing each party—looks up your registration form and compares the signature on it with the signature on your application. If the two do not appear to match, the challenger may ask you for additional identification. When the challenger is convinced that you are eligible to vote, he or she initials the application form and returns it to you.

Casting Your Vote

You then go to the voting booth where you hand the application form to an election judge. Judges oversee the operation of the voting booths, ensuring that everyone votes in secret and helping voters who are physically challenged, elderly, or unable to read.

Types of Voting Machines

You will cast your ballot by using a voting machine. The two most common types are the punch-card machine and the lever machine. Because election methods are left to the states, the kinds of voting machines used vary widely. Whatever machine you use, you will usually have a ballot with the candidates' names listed according to their political party and the office they are seeking.

"Butterfly Ballot" It is always important to read the ballot carefully. In the 2000 presidential election, many voters in Florida were confused by the "butterfly ballot," a paper ballot in which opposing candidates were listed across from each other instead of vertically. The 2000 election in Florida also proved that some machines were more reliable than others.

Differentiated Instruction

Leveled Activities

BL Academic Vocabulary Activity 10, URB p. 43

OL Biography Activity 10, URB, p. 45

AL Crit. Thinking Activity 10, URB pp. 51–52

ELL Content Vocabulary Activity 10, URB p. 41

Punch-Card Ballots Punch-card ballots, in which voters punched a hole next to the name of a candidate, were run through machines and misread much more often than computerized, scanned ballots. Since the 2000 election, many states are converting to upgraded voting machines.

The Secret Ballot

All types of voting machines allow voters to cast a secret ballot. We recognize the secret ballot as a protection of our right to make our electoral choices unhindered and without fear. Some machines also allow voters to vote for a straight ticket, which means voting for all the candidates in one political party. If you choose some candidates from one party and some from another, you are voting a split ticket. You may even decide to cast a write-in vote by writing in the name of someone who is not on the ballot.

Absentee Voting

Citizens who cannot get to the polls on Election Day can vote by **absentee ballot.** People who know they will be out of town that day, those who are too sick to get to the polls, and military personnel serving away from home often use absentee ballots. Voters must request an absentee ballot from their local election board sometime before Election Day. They mark this ballot and return it to the election board. On Election Day, or shortly thereafter, election officials open and count the absentee ballots.

Counting the Vote

When the polls close, election workers count the votes at the polling place and take the ballots and the results—called **returns**— to the election board. The board then collects

Civics ONLINE
Student Web Activity Visit glencoe.com and complete the Chapter 10 Web Activity.

and counts the returns for the entire city or county. If the voting machines are not computerized, gathering all the returns and tallying the results can take several hours or longer. Then the board sends the returns to the state canvassing authority. A few days after the election, the state canvassing authority certifies the election of the winner.

In a major election, the news media and party workers try to predict winners as soon as possible. One way they do this is to ask a sample of voters leaving selected polling places how they voted. This is known as an **exit poll.** Through exit polling, specialists can often predict the winners long before all the votes have been officially counted.

The Media and Elections

Major television networks always **devote,** or dedicate, the entire evening to covering the vote during presidential elections. They use computerized predictions based on the past voting history of key precincts. Through this process, the media "call" winners of Senate, House, and governors' seats, as well as the electoral vote in the race for president.

In some cases the networks make these **W₂** calls with as little as 10 percent of the vote counted. Their projections are usually correct, but some of the major networks were embarrassed by an early and incorrect call on the presidential vote in the 2000 election in the decisive state of Florida.

Some political commentators have criticized these early projections. The predictions usually come when millions of Americans in the Western time zones have yet to vote and the polls there are still open. These observers charge that such early projections **W₁** may persuade great numbers of West Coast voters not to bother going out to vote. This not only reduces overall voter turnout but also may affect the outcome of local, state, and congressional elections.

✓ **Reading Check** **Explaining** What does it mean to vote a split ticket?

Chapter 10 **297**

W₁ **Writing Support**

Expository Writing Have students write a list of what happens to voters' ballots once the polls close. Remind them to number the steps and to list them in order. **BL**

W₂ **Writing Support**

Persuasive Writing Ask students to take a position on whether to allow the media to make early election predictions. Then have them write several paragraphs in support of their view. Remind them to include details and examples in support of their arguments. *(Student paragraphs should be persuasive, take only one point of view, and include supporting details or examples.)* **AL**

Civics ONLINE
Objectives and answers to the **Student Web Activity** can be found at glencoe.com under the Web Activity Lesson Plan for this chapter.

✓ **Reading Check** **Answer:** When you vote a split ticket, you vote for candidates from more than one political party for different offices.

Additional Support

Activity: Collaborative Learning

Understanding Question-Answer Relationships Ask: What questions might people in our community have about voting? Brainstorm questions, such as: Where are the polling places? How do I use the voting machine? How do I cast my vote?

Organize students into groups. Each group will decide on a question and research its answer by using both the Internet and local

resources. They will then make a question-and-answer poster to summarize what they have learned.

Encourage ELL students to review their group's rough draft and to suggest changes for confusing words. The group might decide to make a second version of their poster in Spanish or another language. **OL**

Teacher Tip

Through this activity, students with different skills and abilities can work together. Each group will need students to research, write, and illustrate. In addition, ELL students could check students' writing for words that might be unclear to English Language Learners.

D Differentiated Instruction

Intrapersonal Ask students to ask themselves how well informed they are. Do they know what the public issues are and have opinions about them? If there is an election in the near future, do they know who the candidates are and for what they stand? Suggest that they write a few sentences for their eyes alone. They should rate themselves on their knowledge of public issues and candidates and cite at least one thing they can do to stay informed. **OL**

R Reading Strategy

Summarizing Pair students and have them write one paragraph summarizing why it is important for citizens in a democracy to stay informed. **OL**

TIME™ Political Cartoons

Answers:

1. members of the armed services who sacrificed their lives to protect the rights of U.S. citizens
2. Answers may vary. Students might say that the cartoonist disapproves of the man and his attitude.
3. Answers may include the opinion that the cartoonist is hoping to inspire people to get out and vote.

Additional Support

Why Your Vote Matters

Main Idea Through our vote, we directly participate in governing.

Civics & You Each person's vote counts. If you doubt it, think about how many elections have been decided by just a few votes.

Registering is only one part of getting ready to vote. It is equally important to prepare to vote. It is important to stay informed about candidates and public issues. Newspapers, TV, radio, newsmagazines, and the Internet carry useful information. Other good sources include the Voters' Information Bulletin, published by the League of Women Voters; literature distributed by each political party; and information published by interest groups, such as the American Conservative Union or the AFL-CIO Committee on Political Education.

Preparing to Vote As you read about candidates and the issues they support, read carefully to separate facts from opinions. Everyone has different reasons for supporting particular candidates. As you read about various candidates, answer the following questions to help you decide whom to support with your vote:

- Does the candidate stand for the things I think are important?
- Is the candidate reliable and honest?
- Does the candidate have relevant past experience?
- Will the candidate be effective in office?
- Does the candidate have a real chance of winning? Sometimes Americans vote for candidates, even though they do not have a real chance of winning the election, because they wish to show their support for a certain point of view.

TIME™

Political Cartoons

In this cartoon, Mike Thompson is making a statement about patriotism and sacrifice.

1. What do the tombstones stand for?
2. How do you think the cartoonist views the man in the upper-left section of the image?
3. What action does Thompson hope to inspire with this cartoon?

Mike Thompson/Copley News Service

Every year, more than half of all Americans do volunteer work ... role in it. One of the responsibilities of citizens is to help make their ... of volunteer grou... small. Perha... dad wh...

Did You Know?

Presidential Election Facts:

- George Washington was unanimously elected in 1789.
- In 1848 Wisconsin gave aliens the right to vote if they had resided there one year and if they intended to become citizens.
- The first literacy test for voting was adopted by Connecticut in 1855.
- In 1878 an act for the amendment giving women the right to vote was introduced

into Congress. It took Congress 42 years to adopt and ratify it.

- In the presidential election of 1960, Nixon received 49.5 percent of the popular vote; Kennedy received 49.7 percent—only two-tenths of a percent more.
- The Nixon-Kennedy debates for the 1960 election were the first presidential debates to be broadcast on television.

All the people who are eligible to vote are called the **electorate.** Each person's vote counts. If you doubt it, consider this. The 2000 presidential election was decided by about 500 votes in the state of Florida. In the 2006 mid-term elections, which party took control of Congress was decided by a few thousand votes.

Why Some People Do Not Vote

Despite the fact that voting gives Americans a chance to participate in their government, not everyone votes. Some citizens do not vote because they do not meet state voting requirements, or they have not reregistered after changing residences. Others do not think that any of the candidates represent their feelings on issues, or they think that their vote will not make a difference. Another reason is **apathy,** or lack of interest. Even among those who are registered to vote, many fail to do so.

Why Some People Do Vote

The citizens who do vote share some characteristics. These citizens generally have positive attitudes toward government and citizenship. Usually the more education a citizen has, the more likely it is that he or she will be a regular voter. Middle-aged citizens have the highest voting turnout rate of all age groups. The higher a person's income, the more likely he or she is to vote.

Reasons for Voting There are important reasons to exercise your right to vote. Voting gives citizens a chance to choose their government leaders. It gives them an opportunity to voice their opinions on past performances of public officials. If voters are dissatisfied, they can elect new leaders. Voting also allows citizens to express their opinions on public issues.

D

✓ **Reading Check** Summarizing What are two important reasons to exercise your right to vote?

Section 1 Review

Vocabulary

1. Write a true statement *and* a false statement for each term below. For each false statement explain why it is false. *polling place, precinct, ballot, absentee ballot, returns, exit poll, electorate,* and *apathy.*

Main Ideas

2. Identifying In the early days of our nation, what was the only group of people eligible to vote?

3. Explaining Why is the secret ballot important?

4. Identify three reasons that some citizens do not exercise their right to vote.

Critical Thinking

5. Drawing Conclusions Do you think the federal government should prohibit exit polls during presidential elections? Why or why not?

6. BIG Ideas On a graphic organizer like the one below, identify four different places a citizen may register to vote.

county offices

Registration

7. Making Inferences American statesman John Jay (1745–1829) said, "The people who own the country ought to govern it." Would Jay have supported or opposed the extension of voting rights? Explain.

CITIZENSHIP Activity

8. Creating Voter apathy is an issue in the United States today. Draw a political cartoon that depicts a reason people give for not voting.

Civics ONLINE

Study Central™ To review this section, go to glencoe.com.

Answers

1. Sentences should use vocabulary words according to their definitions in the section and in the Glossary.

2. Only white, adult, male property owners were permitted to vote.

3. The secret ballot allows us to vote without fear.

4. Answers may include the following: They do not meet state voting requirements. They

have not registered after changing addresses. They think their vote will not make a difference. They lack interest.

5. Answers will vary, but students must back up their opinions with reasons or examples.

6. county offices; public libraries; high schools; through the mail

7. Answers will vary. Students should conclude that John Jay believed voters should be

property owners and therefore would have been opposed to most extensions of voting rights.

8. Cartoons should be based on one of the reasons given in the text.

Focus

Bellringer
Daily Focus Transparency 10–2

Guide to Reading
Answers to Graphic:

Types of Elections

↓

general elections

↓

elections on issues

↓

special elections

Section Spotlight Video

To generate student interest and provide a springboard for class discussion, access the Chapter 10, Section 2 video at glencoe.com or on the video DVD.

Resource Manager

Guide to Reading

Big Idea
A successful democracy is built on an informed electorate.

Content Vocabulary
- Electoral College (p. 301)
- initiative (p. 301)
- proposition (p. 301)
- referendum (p. 301)
- recall (p. 301)
- elector (p. 303)
- winner-take-all system (p. 303)

Academic Vocabulary
- issue (p. 301)
- odd (p. 301)

Reading Strategy
Organizing As you read this section, complete a graphic organizer like the one below by listing the features of three types of elections.

Types of Elections

general elections

Election Campaigns

Real World Civics Candidates on the campaign trail face long days, trip delays, meals at odd times, uncomfortable sleeping conditions, and lots of handshaking. Senator Hillary Clinton ran for president in 2008 in a tough primary race for the democratic nomination. The road to the nominations is long. Campaigning often starts a year ahead of the first primary in New Hampshire, which is two years before the actual election.

▼ **Hillary Clinton campaigns in 2008**

R Reading Strategies	**C** Critical Thinking	**D** Differentiated Instruction	**W** Writing Support	**S** Skill Practice
Teacher Edition • Taking Notes, p. 301 • Sequencing Info., p. 301 **Additional Resources** • Cont. Vocab., URB p. 41 • Ac. Voc., URB p. 43 • Guid. Read., URB p. 62 • Foldables, p. 69	**Teacher Edition** • Making Inferences, p. 302 **Additional Resources** • Cit./Dec. Making Act., URB p. 3 • Graphic Novel, p. 29	**Teacher Edition** • English Learners, p. 302 **Additional Resources** • School-to-Home Act., URB p. 57 • Reteach. Act., URB p. 59	**Teacher Edition** • Expository Writing, p. 303	**Teacher Edition** • Reading a Graph, p. 303 **Additional Resources** • Chart/Graph/Map Skills, URB p. 53 • Daily Focus Trans., 10–2

Types of Elections

Main Idea There are different types of elections in the United States political system.

Civics & You Americans have been voting since the earliest colonial governments. As you read, identify the differences among the different types of elections.

The **Electoral College** is part of the process that Americans use to select their president. Americans also vote in many other elections. There are about half a million elected officials in the United States. In addition, Americans have many opportunities to vote on **issues,** or topics of concern, as well as candidates. Besides primary elections, there are three other types of elections in the United States: general elections, elections on issues, and special elections.

General Elections

Under the United States political system, every election is a two-part process. The first part is the nomination of candidates in a primary election. Primary races help to narrow the field of candidates. Then, in a general election, the voters choose candidates for various offices. General elections always take place on the first Tuesday after the first Monday in November. All seats in the U.S. House of Representatives and about one-third of the seats in the Senate are at stake in general elections every even-numbered year.

Presidential elections occur every four years. In these elections the ballot often includes candidates for governor, the state legislature, county government, and local offices. In some states, however, elections for mayor and other city offices take place in **odd**-numbered, or uneven, years.

For all races except the presidential race, the candidate who wins most of the popular vote is elected to office. If an election is very close, the loser has the right to demand a recount of the votes. Occasionally, a disputed election cannot be resolved through a recount and another election must be held. In the case of a national election, a dispute may be referred to Congress for settlement. If it is a presidential election and neither candidate wins a majority of electoral votes, the House of Representatives elects the president. This happened in the elections of 1800 and 1824.

Voting on Issues

In some elections at the state or local level, voters may decide on issues as well as candidates. The **initiative,** for example, is a way that citizens can propose new laws or state constitutional amendments. Citizens who want a new law gather signatures of qualified voters on a petition. If enough people sign the petition, the proposed law, or **proposition,** is put on the ballot at the next general election.

The **referendum** is a way for citizens to approve or reject a state or local law. Citizens in more than half the states have the right to petition to have a law referred, or sent back, to the voters for their approval at the next general election.

Special Elections

From time to time, state or local governments also hold certain kinds of special elections. Runoff elections may be held when none of the candidates for a particular office wins a majority of the vote in the general election. The runoff is held to determine the winner.

The **recall** is another type of special election. In a recall, citizens in some states can vote to remove a public official from office. Like the initiative, the recall starts with a petition. Voters may recall an official because they do not like his or her position on issues or because the official has been charged with wrongdoing.

Reading Check Comparing What is the difference between an initiative and a referendum?

Chapter 10 301

Teach

R1 Reading Strategy

Taking Notes Help students take notes for this page. Have students read the introductory paragraph. **Ask:** What information does it give about the topic, Types of Elections?*(The types are primary elections, general elections, elections on issues, and special elections.)* Demonstrate how to record that information in a modified outline form (omitting Roman numerals and letters). Continue in the same way for the rest of the page. **OL**

R2 Reading Strategy

Sequencing Information Have students reread the first paragraph under Voting on Issues. **Ask:** If citizens want to propose a new law, how do they go about getting it on the ballot? *(First they gather signatures of qualified voters on a petition for the new law. The signatures are then counted. If there are enough signatures, the law is put on the ballot in the next general election.)* **BL**

Reading Check Answer: An initiative proposes new laws; a referendum is a way to get rid of existing law.

Differentiated Instruction

Leveled Activities

BL Guided Reading Activities 10–2, URB p. 62

OL Chart/Graph/Map Activity 10, URB pp. 53–54

AL Citizenship/Decision-Making Activity 3, URB p. 3

ELL Content Vocabulary 10, URB pp. 41–42

D Differentiated Instruction

English Learners Check on students' understanding of figurative language used in the text. Ask them what each of these expressions means. Provide explanations as needed: *"behind-the-scenes* negotiations"; *"rounded up* support"; *"wrapped up* the nomination"; *"kick off* the campaign"; *"campaigns in full swing."* **ELL**

C Critical Thinking

Making Inferences Lead students in a discussion about how political parties and candidates use TV to convince voters. Have them consider whether the presence of TV cameras means that a candidate's appearance and manner can help decide an election. **AL**

TIME™ Teens in *Action*

Answer:

Student answers might suggest that Sam became involved in Kids Voting USA because he was committed to their goals and believed that the group could help him make a difference.

Differentiated Instruction

Citizenship and Decision-Making Activity 3, URB pp. 3-4

302

TIME™ Teens in *Action*

Kids Voting USA

One vote can make a difference—and Sam Hay, 18, of Charlotte, North Carolina, is spreading the word!

QUESTION: What is Kids Voting USA?

ANSWER: It's a group that teaches kids about citizenship and voting through classroom activities— and by asking them to go to the polls with their parents on Election Day. I'm on the Student Advisory Board of the group.

Q: Why is it so important to vote?

A: Many people think their vote doesn't matter, but it does. There have been elections where the winner has been decided by only a few votes. By taking part in our democracy you show our leaders what you think.

Q: How does getting kids involved in voting and politics affect parents?

A: Conversations at the dinner table may become more political if a child takes part in Kids Voting. To keep up, parents may follow politics closer.

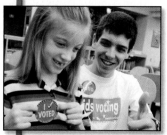

Q: How many kids do you reach?

A: Thousands in 27 states and the District of Columbia. The program reaches out to every student because voter apathy stretches across all ethnic and socioeconomic boundaries.

Making a Difference ━━ **CITIZENSHIP**

Why do you think Sam decided to become involved in Kids Voting USA?

302 Chapter 10

Presidential Elections

Main Idea Presidential elections have three major steps: (1) nomination of candidates, (2) the campaign, and (3) the vote.

Civics & You As you read, ask yourself: What issues are important for a candidate to address?

Candidates for president begin organizing their campaigns long before the election. In the past, both major parties held national conventions in the summer of the election year to choose their candidates. Delegates came to these conventions from each state, the District of Columbia, and U.S. territories.

These conventions were dramatic events full of behind-the-scenes negotiations. Backers of various candidates would move around the convention floor, promising future political favors to state delegations in hopes of stealing their votes away from a rival. The political dealings would be interrupted for suspenseful and colorful state-by-state roll-call votes to see if any contender had rounded up enough support to win the nomination.

In recent years, however, the conventions have lost their main purpose—choosing the nominee. So much campaigning now goes on in the primary elections that by convention time one contender has already wrapped up the nomination. The parties use the conventions mainly to kick off the campaign and to rally party members across the country for the work ahead. **D**

Campaigns

Presidential campaigns are usually in full swing by early September. Candidates travel across the country giving speeches, appearing on TV, and holding news conferences— even though there is seldom any real news to announce. **C**

Vote for Me!

Objective: To gain an understanding of how an election campaign is run

Focus: Students analyze how a political campaign presents a candidate.

Teach: Discuss the persuasive techniques listed in the chart on page 4.

Assess: Check for students' use of persuasive techniques in their campaign advertisements.

Close: Create a chart of persuasive techniques.

Differentiated Instruction Strategies

BL Give two reasons a person might choose to vote for a particular candidate.

AL Write a summary of the steps involved in running an election campaign.

ELL Write an advertising slogan that uses one of the techniques in the chart on page 4.

Candidates may face their opponents in televised debates. They meet with state and local political leaders, and they give pep talks to lower-level members of the party who are working for them.

Electoral Votes and the States

For all races except the presidential race, the candidate who wins a majority of the popular vote—votes cast directly by the people—is elected to office. In a presidential race, the voters are actually electing people called **electors,** who hold electoral votes and 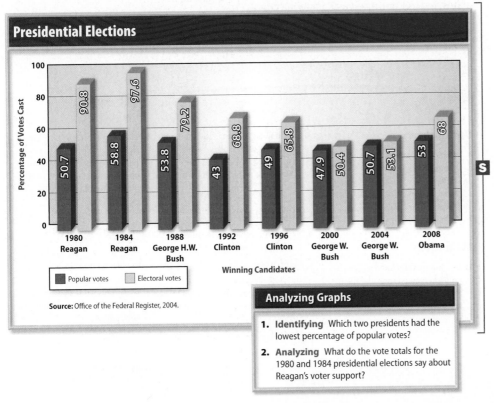 are part of the Electoral College system.

In every state, a slate, or list, of electors is pledged to each candidate. The purpose of the popular vote in each state is to choose one of these slates of electors. The candidate who wins the popular vote in a state usually receives all of the state's electoral votes. This is called the **winner-take-all system.**

The winning electors meet in their state capitals in December to cast the state's electoral votes for president and vice president. The electors send their votes to Congress, which counts them. Because every state has one elector for each of its U.S. senators and representatives, the total number of votes in the Electoral College is 538. (Washington, D.C., has three electoral votes.) The candidate who receives a majority of these votes—270 or more—wins the election.

Article II, Section 1, established the Electoral College. It was a compromise measure. Some of the Framers wanted the American people to have direct control over the new national government.

Presidential Elections

Percentage of Votes Cast

Year / Winning Candidate	Popular votes	Electoral votes
1980 Reagan	50.7	90.8
1984 Reagan	58.8	97.6
1988 George H.W. Bush	53.8	79.2
1992 Clinton	43	68.8
1996 Clinton	49	65.8
2000 George W. Bush	47.9	50.4
2004 George W. Bush	50.7	53.1
2008 Obama	53	68

Winning Candidates

■ Popular votes ☐ Electoral votes

Source: Office of the Federal Register, 2004.

Analyzing Graphs

1. **Identifying** Which two presidents had the lowest percentage of popular votes?
2. **Analyzing** What do the vote totals for the 1980 and 1984 presidential elections say about Reagan's voter support?

W Writing Support

Expository Writing Have students increase their understanding by writing an explanation of the Electoral College system, when it is used, and how it works. *(Answers will vary but should explain that the system is used in presidential races and that voters vote for electors who, in turn, are pledged to vote for a certain candidate.)* **OL**

S Skill Practice

Reading a Graph **Ask:** What does the graph compare? *(popular versus electoral votes for winners of presidential elections, 1976–2004)* What do the horizontal lines on the graph represent? *(percentage of the vote, with each line representing 20 percent more than the line below it)* In what two years were the popular and electoral votes most nearly equal? *(the years 2000 and 2004)* **OL**

Analyzing Graphs

Answers:
1. Clinton and George W. Bush
2. Reagan's voter support was exceptionally high. He won over 90 percent of the electoral vote in both elections.

Hands-On Chapter Project
Step 2

Running an Election Campaign

Step 2: Planning the Campaign Groups will plan the campaign and make a campaign poster for the candidate they developed in Step 1.

Directions Ask the groups to brainstorm ways to promote their candidates. Suggest that they develop campaign slogans to help voters remember their candidates. The group members might like to write a campaign song.

When the groups have developed a strategy and slogan, distribute poster-making supplies, and have each group make a campaign poster for its candidate.

Summarizing Ask groups to display their posters. **OL**

(Project continued in Section 3)

Reading Check Answer: electors who hold electoral votes and are part of the Electoral College

Assess

Civics ONLINE

Study Central™ provides summaries, interactive games, and online graphic organizers to help students review content.

Close

Summarizing Ask: How does a potential candidate become a party's presidential nominee and win the election? *(Answers should include these steps: A group within the party begins a campaign before the national convention. The candidate wins the nomination in the convention and is put on the ballot, and the campaign kicks off. The candidate wins the majority of electoral votes in the general presidential election and is elected.)* **OL**

Section 2 Review

Others strongly believed that the government must be able to function without having to give in to popular whims. The first group demanded a direct popular election of the president. Their opponents pushed to have Congress name the president. The compromise was to have the legislatures in each state choose presidential electors. Today, the voters in each state directly choose the electors.

Electoral College Issues

Some people think that the Electoral College should be changed or eliminated. They charge that large states—such as California and Texas, which have many more electoral votes than smaller states—have too much influence in deciding the election. One candidate might win five or six small states and yet not receive as many electoral votes as the candidate who wins just one large state.

If a candidate wins the largest number of popular votes in a state, that person receives all the state's electoral votes. Under the winner-take-all system, a candidate who loses the popular vote can still win the electoral vote and the presidency. This has happened four times in our nation's history, most recently in 2000. The winner-take-all system also makes it extremely difficult for third-party candidates to be represented in the electoral vote.

Ideas for Reform There have been several suggestions for reform. Under one plan, electoral votes would be based on the percentage of the popular vote. If a candidate won 54 percent of a state's popular vote, for example, he or she would also get 54 percent of the electoral votes. Any change in the Electoral College system requires a constitutional amendment.

Reading Check Inferring When you vote for the U.S. president, for whom are you actually voting?

Section 2 Review

Vocabulary

1. **Write** a paragraph that summarizes the key points of this section. Use all of the following terms: *Electoral College, initiative, proposition, referendum, recall, elector, winner-take-all system.*

Main Ideas

2. **Explaining** Why have national political conventions lost the main purpose of choosing nominees?

3. **Summarizing** How is the total of 538 Electoral College votes determined? What is the purpose of the popular vote in the Electoral College system?

Critical Thinking

4. **Explaining** What is a recall election? Describe the process.

5. **BIG Ideas** List and explain the steps involved in presidential elections by completing a graphic organizer like the one below.

6. **Making Generalizations** The right to vote belongs to every United States citizen. In your opinion, what do citizens forfeit if they do not exercise their right to vote?

CITIZENSHIP Activity

7. **Persuasive Writing** Should the Electoral College be kept, abolished, or reformed in some way? State your views in a letter to the editor of your local newspaper.

Civics ONLINE

Study Central™ To review this section, go to glencoe.com.

Answers

1. Definitions for the vocabulary words are found in the section and in the Glossary.

2. Because a large amount of campaigning is done in the primaries, the parties' presidential nominations are often clear before the convention.

3. Each state has one vote for each of its senators and representatives. Washington, D.C., has three votes. The popular vote determines which group of electors pledged to a candidate will win that state's electoral votes.

4. A recall election is held to vote on removing a local or state official from office. A petition is circulated. If it has enough signatures, a special recall election is held.

5. **Step 1:** Nomination of candidates
   Step 2: National campaign
   Step 3: Winning the electoral votes

6. Opinions will vary. Students should give reasons for their opinions.

7. The letters should be persuasive in tone, argue only one side of the issue, and include reasons or examples.

Guide to Reading

Big Idea
A successful democracy is built on an informed electorate.

Content Vocabulary
- propaganda *(p. 307)*
- political action committee (PAC) *(p. 308)*
- soft money *(p. 308)*
- incumbent *(p. 309)*

Academic Vocabulary
- image *(p. 307)*
- fee *(p. 307)*

Reading Strategy
Explaining Use a graphic organizer like the one below to explain the main part of the Federal Election Campaign Act (FECA).

FECA

Section 3

Paying for Election Campaigns

🔊 **Section Audio**   🎬 **Spotlight Video**

Real World Civics Citizens take action when they believe in an issue. Doris "Granny D" Haddock, 91, walked across the country to register voters and to protest the use of corporate money in political campaigns. Ms. Haddock, like many Americans, was concerned that within the current system only the rich can run for office. Inspired by Haddock and others, Senators Russell Feingold and John McCain teamed up in 2001 to present to Congress the McCain-Feingold bill to limit the money spent on campaigns. Although it passed, the 2004 presidential election cost nearly a billion dollars.

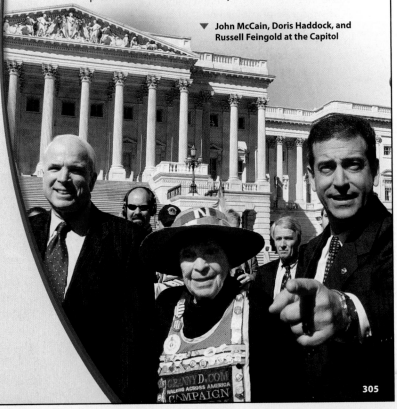

▼ **John McCain, Doris Haddock, and Russell Feingold at the Capitol**

305

Focus

Bellringer
Daily Focus Transparency 10–3

Guide to Reading
Answers to Graphic:

FECA

Requires public disclosure of a candidate's spending

Limits the amount individuals or groups can donate directly to a candidate or party

Tries to limit the amount other individuals or groups can spend

 Section Spotlight Video

Have students watch the Chapter 10, Section 3 video at glencoe.com.

Resource Manager

R Reading Strategies	**C** Critical Thinking	**D** Differentiated Instruction	**W** Writing Support	**S** Skill Practice
Teacher Edition • Identifying, p. 308 • Inferring, p. 309 **Additional Resources** • Cont. Vocab., URB p. 42 • Acad. Vocab., URB p. 43 • Guid. Read., URB p. 63	**Teacher Edition** • Contrasting, p. 306 • Assessing, p. 306 • Contrasting, p. 308 • Drawing Con., p. 309 **Additional Resources** • Critical Thinking, URB p. 51	**Teacher Edition** • Gifted/Talented, p. 306 **Additional Resources** • Diff. Instr. Act., URB p. 55 • School-to-Home Act., URB p. 57	**Teacher Edition** • Persuasive Writing, p. 310 **Additional Resources** • Writing Skills Activity, URB p. 47	**Teacher Edition** • Predicting Consequences, pp. 307, 308 **Additional Resources** • Economics Activity, URB p. 5 • Chart, Graph, and Map Skills, URB p. 53 • Daily Focus Trans., 10–3

C Critical Thinking

Contrasting Ask: How do the methods for soliciting votes differ in local elections and presidential elections? *(In local elections, candidates may solicit votes personally. In presidential elections, candidates primarily solicit votes through the media.)* **OL**

D Differentiated Instruction

Gifted and Talented Have pairs of students improvise a meeting between a local candidate who is soliciting votes to become mayor and a citizen whose vote is being solicited. Then have them reverse roles and reenact the encounter. Before they begin, suggest that "candidates" decide how to introduce themselves and what they will say about their positions on an issue. "Citizens" might consider what attitude they will assume towards the candidate—receptive, argumentative, indifferent. **AL**

Caption Answer:

Candidates for both local and national offices must make their positions on issues known to voters and must convince voters to like and trust them. Local candidates contact voters directly, whereas national candidates rely on the mass media.

Additional Support

Running for Office

Main Idea Running for public office is the first step in the election process.

Civics & You Would you run for public office if given the chance? As you read, ask yourself: What are the reasons an individual runs for public office?

Americans spend more than $3 billion on national, state, and local elections every four-year period. Former House Speaker Tip O'Neill once said, "There are four parts to any campaign. The candidate, the issues . . . , the campaign organization, and the money. Without money you can forget the other three."

It takes a great deal of money to run a successful campaign for a major office today. Once candidates are nominated, they spend weeks and even months campaigning.

The purpose of campaigns is to convince the public to vote for a particular candidate. Each campaign has a campaign organization. An organization for a local candidate may have only a few workers. Presidential campaigns, though, have thousands of workers.

Campaign workers must acquaint voters with the candidate's name, face, and positions on issues, and convince voters to like and trust the candidate. Campaign workers use several techniques to accomplish their goals.

Canvassing

When candidates or campaign workers travel through neighborhoods asking for votes or taking public opinion polls, they are canvassing. At the local level, candidates often go door-to-door to solicit votes and hand out campaign literature. At the national level, campaign organizations conduct frequent polls to find out how their candidates are doing. **C**

Endorsements

When a famous and popular person supports or campaigns for a candidate, it is an endorsement. The endorser may be a movie star, a famous athlete, a popular politician, or some other well-known individual. The idea behind endorsements is that if voters like the person making the endorsement, they may decide to vote for the candidate.

Running for Office Shepherd University student Frank Salzano campaigned and won election in 2006 to a seat on the Shepherdstown, West Virginia, town council. ***Comparing*** In what ways are running for local office and running for national office similar and in what ways are they different?

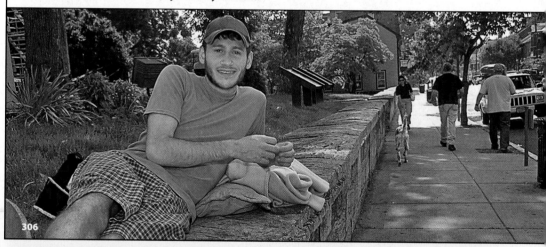

306

Activity: Economics Connection

Assessing Ask students to list expense items that would be involved in running a campaign for mayor. Have them review the list and group the items into categories, such as printing, TV and radio advertising, office supplies, transportation, and so on. Ask them to assign the percentage of the campaign budget they would allot to each one. Finally, have them convey those percentages visually in a pie chart or bar graph titled "Campaign Expenses." Assure students that there are no "right" or "wrong" answers for this activity. It is what they learn from the process of identifying and assessing expenses that is important. **OL ELL**

Grass Roots Mayor Antonio Villaraigosa, the first Latino mayor of Los Angeles since 1872, gained national attention for progress in his city. *Describing* Where do popular candidates like Villaraigosa get funds for their campaigns?

S Skill Practice

Predicting Consequences Ask: How do you think the widespread use of the Internet might affect future political campaigns? Will it affect their cost? Their ability to reach voters? Their ability to get feedback from voters? *(Opinions will vary, but students should supply reasons or examples to support their opinions. You might wish to point out that although Internet ads cost money, the cost of sending e-mails is minimal compared to the cost of postage.)* **AL**

For additional practice on this skill (Predicting), see the **Skills Handbook**.

Caption Answer:

Answers will vary, but students may suggest that he gets funds from people and groups who help finance his campaign.

Reading Check Answer: to try to influence voters to choose them over other candidates

Endorsements are a kind of propaganda technique. **Propaganda** is an attempt to promote a particular person or idea. Candidates use propaganda techniques to try to persuade or influence voters to choose them over another candidate.

Advertising and Image Molding

Campaign workers spend much time and money to create the right **image**, or impression, for a candidate. Much of that money goes to advertising. Political advertisements allow a party to present only its candidate's position or point of view. They also enable a candidate to attack an opponent without offering an opportunity to respond.

Candidates for a local election may use newspaper advertisements or posters, while state and national candidates spend a great deal of money advertising on television. Why? Television ads can present quick and dramatic images of a candidate and his or her ideas. Such television images tend to stay in the viewer's mind.

Campaign Expenses

The sophisticated vote-getting techniques that candidates use have made campaigning very expensive. Television commercials are a very effective way to win votes, but they cost tens of thousands of dollars per minute. Other campaign costs include airfare and other transportation, salaries of campaign staff members, and **fees,** or payments, to professional campaign consultants, such as public opinion pollsters. There are also computer, telephone, postage, and printing costs.

A small-town mayoral race may cost only a few hundred or a few thousand dollars. A state legislative or congressional race may cost several hundred thousand dollars or more. In recent elections, spending for each seat in Congress has averaged about $1.5 million. Some congressional candidates spent $15 million or more. A presidential race can cost hundreds of millions of dollars.

Reading Check *Describing* What is the purpose of election propaganda?

Campaign Finance

Economics Activity 3, URB pp. 5-6

Objective:	To compare and contrast sources of campaign funding
Focus:	Students contrast the sources of funds for candidates in 2006.
Teach:	Review limits imposed by the Bipartisan Campaign Reform Act of 2002.
Assess:	Have students write a paragraph about the Act of 2002 and its results.
Close:	Make a two-column chart to summarize sources of funding before and after the Act of 2002.

Differentiated Instruction

Differentiated Instruction Strategies

BL Tell why campaign funding reform was needed.

AL Explain how campaign financing was changed by the Campaign Reform Act of 2002.

ELL Tell how much you can give to a person's campaign fund and how much you can give to a political party.

C Critical Thinking

Contrasting Ask: What is the difference between "hard money" and "soft money"? *(Hard money is money individuals or groups are permitted to donate directly to a candidate or a political party. Soft money is money donated to a political party for general purposes, such as voter registration drives.)* **OL**

S Skill Practice

Predicting Consequences Ask: What might be a possible result of the Supreme Court's ruling in *Buckley* v. *Valeo* that allows candidates to spend an unlimited amount of their own money on their campaigns? *(Answers may include the opinion that it gives an unfair advantage to wealthy candidates by permitting them to spend a fortune to get elected.)* **OL**

R Reading Strategy

Identifying Ask: How does the federal government help fund national political campaigns? *(Through the Federal Election Campaign Fund, the government collects voluntary $3 donations from taxpayers that, under certain conditions, can be distributed among the major-party presidential candidates after the primaries.* **OL**

Hands-On Chapter Project
Step 3

Financing a Campaign

Main Idea Candidates spend considerable time and effort raising campaign funds.

Civics & You Have you read about campaign finance issues? As you read, think about questions you may have about campaign spending.

The methods used to finance election campaigns have been established by congressional legislation and Supreme Court decisions. In recent years, a push to reform how candidates raise money has led to many changes in the law.

Federal Election Campaign Act

In 1971 Congress passed the Federal Election Campaign Act (FECA) in an effort to place some controls on campaign financing. FECA and its amendments in 1974, 1976, and 1979 established many key rules for campaign finance. The law required public disclosure of each candidate's spending. It limited the amount—called hard money—that individuals or groups could donate directly to a candidate or a political party. It also tried to limit how much other individuals and groups could spend.

Federal Election Commission The 1974 amendment to FECA created the Federal Election Commission (FEC)—an independent agency of the executive branch—to administer all federal election laws and to monitor campaign spending. All candidates and political parties must keep records of campaign contributions. Candidates are now required to report all individual contributions that exceed $200 to the FEC.

Limiting Contributions In 1976 the Supreme Court ruled in *Buckley* v. *Valeo* that the government, through laws like FECA, could set limits on campaign contributions because of its need to keep corruption out of

elections. The Court did find, however, that it was a violation of free speech to limit how much of their own money candidates could spend on their election campaigns.

Public Funding

FECA also set up public funding for presidential elections by creating the Presidential Election Campaign Fund. This fund allows taxpayers, by checking a box on their federal income tax return, to designate $3 of their annual taxes to go to the fund. In general, major-party presidential candidates can qualify for some of this money to campaign in the primary elections if they have raised $100,000 on their own. After the national conventions, the two major-party candidates can receive equal shares of money from the fund, so long as they agree not to accept any other direct contributions. Third-party candidates can also qualify for this funding if their party received more than 5 percent of the popular vote in the previous presidential election.

Soft Money and PACS

Most campaign money comes from private sources rather than public funding. These sources include individual citizens, corporations, labor unions, interest groups, and **political action committees (PACs).** PACs are organizations set up by interest groups especially to collect money to support favored candidates. FECA limited direct donations from PACs and other private sources.

In the late 1970s, complaints grew that campaign finance legislation was making fund-raising difficult. Congress responded with new laws enabling political parties to raise **soft money**—unlimited amounts of money for general purposes, not designated to particular candidates. By law this money was supposed to be used for general party-building purposes, such as voter registration drives or direct mailings on behalf of the party.

Running an Election Campaign

Step 3: Getting Out the Vote Students create a 30-second radio commercial designed to get out the vote.

Directions Explain that short radio commercials are an effective way to reach potential voters and that they are much less expensive than television ads.

Remind students of the importance of reaching voters they think will support their candidate. Ask them to write a 30-second radio message to be broadcast to these voters. Stress that they should have two aims: **(1)** to get registered voters to vote, and **(2)** to convince those voters to vote for their candidate. Encourage them to include the candidate's stand on issues, experience, and personal qualities that they admire. Give

students time to plan their message and to write the script.

Suggest that students take turns reading the message aloud and making suggestions for change. One person in the group could time the message to make sure it fits into a 30-second time slot. When the message has been revised, suggest that they "broadcast" it to the rest of the class. **OL**

(Project continued on the Visual Summary page)

Soft money could come from individuals or PACs. FECA placed no limits on these contributions, and in the 2002 national elections, they totaled about $500 million.

Spending on Media There is also the issue of money spent by interest groups for radio and television ads that support the groups' positions on issues. These ads do not ask people to vote for or against a specific candidate, but they might show a candidate's name or image. They are powerful tools for interest groups to help candidates they like. FECA placed no limits on how much money could be spent on such ads.

A Reluctance for Reform In response to these developments, Congress repeatedly discussed reforming campaign finance laws. Changes, though, were difficult to achieve. PACs gave most of their money to incumbents—politicians who have already been elected to office. As a result, many of these incumbent lawmakers were reluctant to change the rules in ways that might help their opponents in the next election.

Campaign Reform

Change came in 2002, however, when Congress passed legislation aimed at better controlling the money flowing into national campaigns. The Bipartisan Campaign Reform Act—also known as the McCain-Feingold Act—prohibits national political parties, federal officeholders, and federal candidates from raising soft money.

The law also places time restrictions on broadcasting political ads. Corporations, unions, and interest groups are banned from running ads aimed at a candidate for federal office within 60 days of a general election or 30 days of a primary election. Finally, the law raises the limits on hard money contributions, stating that candidates may collect up to $2,000 per donor in each election. Political parties can collect $25,000 per donor in each year.

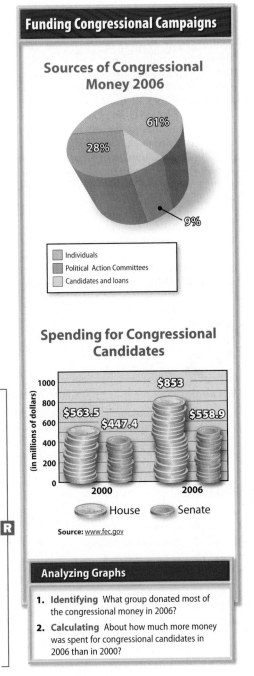

Funding Congressional Campaigns

Sources of Congressional Money 2006

- 61%
- 28%
- 9%

- Individuals
- Political Action Committees
- Candidates and loans

Spending for Congressional Candidates

(in millions of dollars)

- $563.5
- $447.4
- $853
- $558.9

2000 — 2006

House — Senate

Source: www.fec.gov

Analyzing Graphs

1. **Identifying** What group donated most of the congressional money in 2006?
2. **Calculating** About how much more money was spent for congressional candidates in 2006 than in 2000?

C Critical Thinking

Drawing Conclusions Ask: What effect will the McCain-Feingold Act have on how political campaigns are funded? *(The flow of soft money to political parties, federal officeholders, and federal candidates will stop. The limit on hard-money contributions will be stricter.)* **OL**

R Reading Strategy

Inferring Ask: Why are candidates running for office for the first time more likely to benefit from the McCain-Feingold Act than candidates who are running for reelection? *(Political action committees gave most of their soft money to candidates up for reelection. The act stopped this flow of soft money, which benefits first-time candidates because their opponents will receive less money to spend on their campaigns.)* **AL**

Analyzing Graphs

Answers:
1. individuals
2. about $289.5 million more for congressional candidates for the House and $111.5 million more for congressional candidates for the Senate

Differentiated Instruction

Chapter 10 **309**

Leveled Activities

W Writing Support

Persuasive Writing Ask students to decide whether they are for or against candidates spending unlimited amounts of their own money on their campaigns. Ask them to write a paragraph to persuade others to agree with their opinions. *(Answers will vary, but student compositions should include reasons or examples to back up their opinions.)* **OL**

✓ **Reading Check** **Answer:** It prohibited soft-money funding, set limits on ads for candidates, and raised limits on hard-money contributions.

Assess

Civics ONLINE

Study Central™ provides summaries, interactive games, and online graphic organizers to help students review content.

Close

Analyzing Discuss campaign funding issues. **Ask:** Do you think that today only the very rich can afford to run for office? **OL**

Section 3 Review

New Law Upheld

Critics of the new law immediately challenged it as a violation of the First Amendment rights of free speech. In 2003 the Supreme Court case of *McConnell v. Federal Election Commission* upheld all the major provisions of the McCain-Feingold Act as constitutional. The Court stated that it was in the public interest for Congress to limit the size of campaign contributions. Without limits, there would always be the appearance that big donors were able to buy influence with policymakers in ways not available to ordinary citizens.

The majority opinion, written by Justices John Paul Stevens and Sandra Day O'Connor, upheld the ban on corporations, unions, and interest groups from running advertisements for or against a candidate for federal office within a certain period of time before general and primary elections, The Court also supported the McCain-Feingold Act's setting restrictions on campaign advertisements disguised as "issue ads."

Looking to the Future

The Court's decision set the rules for the 2004 elections and beyond. It will affect how candidates go about raising funds. For example, there will be a new emphasis on getting many small donations rather than a few large ones. As a result, the Internet will play a larger role in political fund-raising. The Internet gives politicians and their supporters an inexpensive way to quickly reach millions of people who might be willing to make the smaller contributions.

✓ **Reading Check** **Identifying** How did the McCain-Feingold Act change campaign finance?

Section 3 Review

Vocabulary

1. **Write** sentences related to campaign finance using the following terms: *propaganda, political action committee (PAC), soft money, incumbent.*

Main Ideas

2. **Describing** What is the purpose of a political campaign?

3. **Describing** Why was there some reluctance to reform campaign financing? What groups were most in favor of this reform?

Critical Thinking

4. **BIG Ideas** Explain the two sides in the campaign spending reform issue. With which side do you agree? Explain your position.

5. **Summarizing** On a graphic organizer like the one below, list the different private sources of campaign contributions.

6. **Evaluating** What qualities of competence and leadership do you think are important in a presidential candidate?

CITIZENSHIP Activity

7. **Persuasive Writing** Should the media be required to provide equal coverage for all candidates and for all political parties? Is it fair that the two major political parties can obtain greater coverage in the news than the minor parties? Write a one-page paper explaining your view on these issues.

Civics ONLINE

Study Central™ **To review this section, go to** glencoe.com.

Answers

1. Sentences should use vocabulary words according to their definitions in the section and in the Glossary.

2. Its purpose is to gain votes for a certain candidate.

3. It would mean reducing campaign contributions for some groups. Federal officials up for reelection, for example, would find their campaign funding reduced if soft money contributions were not allowed.

4. Those in favor of finance reform say that it is in the public interest for Congress to limit the size of campaign contributions. Those opposed say that limitations imposed by Congress are a violation of the First Amendment.

5.

6. Students should back up their opinions with reasons, facts, or examples.

7. Essays should clearly express the writer's views on both issues. It should try to persuade the reader with reasons, facts, or examples.

Visual Summary

Voting

Voting is a basic political right of all citizens in a democracy who meet certain qualifications set by law.

Voting allows citizens to take positive actions to influence or control government.

You are qualified to vote if you are not a convicted felon or legally insane, and you are:

- a citizen of the United States
- at least 18 years old
- Most states also require that you be a resident of the state for a specified period and that you register to vote.

Registering to Vote

Registration requirements are set by state law and differ from state to state.

When you register to vote for the first time, you must show proof of citizenship, address, and age.

President John F. Kennedy votes

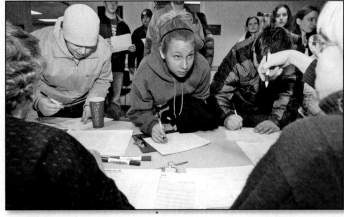

Students register to vote

Voting Procedures

- You vote at a polling place in your home precinct. A precinct is a voting district.
- You will cast your ballot by using a voting machine.
- Citizens who cannot get to the polling place on Election Day can vote by absentee ballot.

The Electoral College

Presidents are not chosen by direct popular vote but by a body known as the Electoral College.

While the presidential candidates' names are printed on the ballot, the voters are not actually voting directly for president and vice president. Rather, they are voting for all of their party's electors in their state.

Political Campaigns

- Running for office costs money.
- Campaigns are funded privately and publicly.
- Campaign finance reform remains an important issue.

Campaign worker monitors voters

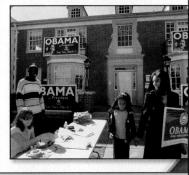

STUDY TO GO Study anywhere, anytime! Download quizzes and flash cards to your PDA from glencoe.com.

Visual Summary 10

Summarizing Information Ask: What is the purpose of this page? *(It aims to present a clear summary of the chapter through the use of boldface heads, photographs, and bulleted lists.)* Explain that summarizing a chapter you've just read is a valuable study skill that helps you recognize and remember what is important—it is helpful to reread a summary just before a test. Call attention to the headings, and ask volunteers to supply a supporting detail they remember from the text. **OL**

This **Reading Skill** (Summarizing Information) was introduced in this unit.

Predicting Remind students of how voting procedures and laws have changed over time. Then lead a discussion of how they might change in the future. **Ask:** What campaign funding issues still need to be resolved? How might voting machines change in the future? Could we cast our votes over the Internet? If so, what problems would it solve? What problems might it create? After the discussion, ask students to choose one aspect of the topic "Voting in the Future" and write a short paper that states their predictions. **OL**

For additional practice on this skill (Predicting), see the **Skills Handbook**.

Hands-On Chapter Project

Step 4: Wrap-Up

Running an Election Campaign

Step 4: Holding the Election Each group will give a presentation designed to "sell" their candidate to prospective voters.

Directions Tell students that they will now plan a presentation designed to capture votes for their candidate. Give them time to prepare their presentation and to decide how to incorporate their campaign posters, radio messages, and songs.

When the groups are ready, have them give their presentations. Ask them to keep their posters visible so that voters can see their candidates' names. Then distribute paper ballots and have students write the name of the candidate for whom they are voting.

Finally, collect the ballots, count the votes, and announce the winner. **OL**

Answers and Analyses
Reviewing Vocabulary

1. A The key word in this question is "results." All the answer options refer to an election, but only one, "returns," fits the definition. Students may be confused by "ballots," since ballots, as well as returns are taken to the election board. They should realize, however, that ballots need to be counted in order to determine election results.

2. B Three of the answers (B, C, and D) refer to ways citizens propose, or vote on a law. Answer A, "recall," can be eliminated by considering the meanings of its prefix and root, "to call back," which would apply to removing an official from office but not to proposing something new. One way to remember the meaning of the correct answer, "initiative," is to think, "Take the *initiative* and propose a new law." Help students make similar connections for the remaining choices. For example: A *proposed* law, or *proposition,* is put on the ballot in a general election; a law is *referred,* or sent back, to voters for approval in a *referendum.*

3. C Questions 2 and 3 give the same answer choices. In answering question 2, students eliminated one choice. Referendum is the logical choice, since a law is referred to voters for a vote in a referendum.

4. D Students should recognize that the answer is probably a person or group of people. This narrows the choices to the last three answers. Since political action committees are formed to collect money for candidates, that is the obvious choice.

Reviewing Main Ideas

5. D The National Voter Registration Act was formed to make it easier for people to vote and to maintain registration.

6. A If students think about how statistics on voter turnout could be obtained, they would realize that there is no way to determine if a voter is disgruntled, has a low income, or is a high-school dropout. Those items are not included on voter registration forms. Date of birth is, however. Thus the correct answer is "middle-aged people."

TEST-TAKING TIP

> Neatness counts even in objective questions. Fill in ovals carefully and print legibly.

Reviewing Vocabulary
Directions: Choose the word(s) that best completes the sentence.

1. The results of an election are called _____.
- **A** returns
- **B** ballots
- **C** exit polls
- **D** electorates

2. Citizens can propose a new law through a(n) _____.
- **A** recall
- **B** initiative
- **C** referendum
- **D** proposition

3. Citizens can approve or reject a local or state law with a(n) _____.
- **A** recall
- **B** initiative
- **C** referendum
- **D** proposition

4. Much of the money from election campaigns comes from _____.
- **A** returns
- **B** electors
- **C** incumbents
- **D** political action committees

Reviewing Main Ideas
Directions: Choose the best answer for each question.

Section 1 *(pp. 292–299)*

5. What does the National Voter Registration Act require states to do?
- **A** deny felons the right to vote
- **B** give the vote to citizens 18 and older
- **C** record voters' party affiliation when they register
- **D** allow people to register when renewing their licenses

6. Which group has the highest rate of voter turnout?
- **A** middle-aged people
- **B** disgruntled citizens
- **C** low-income earners
- **D** high school dropouts

Section 2 *(pp. 300–304)*

7. How many electoral votes does a presidential candidate need to win?
- **A** 100
- **B** 270
- **C** 435
- **D** 538

8. Why is a runoff election held?
- **A** citizens want to remove an elected official
- **B** parties want to narrow a field of candidates
- **C** no candidate in a state election wins a majority
- **D** no presidential candidate wins enough electoral votes

Section 3 *(pp. 305–310)*

9. How do campaign organizations canvass on a national level?
- **A** by going door to door
- **B** by advertising on television
- **C** by conducting frequent polls
- **D** by seeking celebrity endorsements

10. Why does the federal government set limits on direct campaign contributions?
- **A** to limit candidates' free speech
- **B** to keep corruption out of elections
- **C** to create public funding for third parties
- **D** to increase the soft money contributions

GO ON

---

7. B The total number of electoral votes is 538. Since a presidential candidate must win a majority of those votes, a candidate would need at least 270 votes to win.

8. C Students may connect the term "runoff election" with a "playoff game" in sports, which is held to break a tie. Keeping that in mind narrows the answer choices to C and D. If there is a tie in a presidential election, however, the House of Representatives elects the president. Thus, the correct answer is C.

9. C A key word in the question is "national." National elections are too large to rely on door-to-door canvassing, so campaign organizations conduct frequent public opinion polls.

Critical Thinking

Directions: Base your answers to questions 11 and 12 on the diagram below and your knowledge of Chapter 10.

Table 1: Voter Turnout Among Citizens November 2000 and 2004		
	2000	2004
18–24	36%	47%
25–34	51%	56%
35–44	60%	64%
45–54	66%	69%
55–64	70%	73%
65–74	72%	73%
75+	67%	69%
All ages	60%	64%

Source: Authors' Tabulations from the CPS Nov. Voting and Registration Supplements, 1972-2004.

11. Compare the percentage point differences between the 2000 and 2004 elections. Which age group showed the greatest increase in its rate of voter turnout?

A 18–24

B 25–34

C 35–44

D 45–54

12. What can you conclude based on data in the chart?

A More people 65–74 years old voted in 2000 than in 2004.

B Voters 75 and older outnumbered voters between 25 and 34.

C Voters between 18 and 24 had the lowest rates of voter turnout.

D Voters between 45 and 74 made up 72% of the total voters in 2004.

Document-Based Questions

Directions: Analyze the following document and answer the short-answer questions that follow.

The following passage is from a campaign debate between presidential candidates Al Gore and George Bush in 2000.

> *GORE: One of the serious problems, hear me well, is that our system of government is being undermined by too much influence coming from special-interest money. We have to get a handle on it. And like John McCain, I have learned from experience, and it's not a new position for me. Twenty-four years ago I supported full public financing of all federal elections. And anybody who thinks I'm just saying it, it will be the first bill I send to the Congress. . . .*
>
> *BUSH: All right, let me just say one thing!*
>
> *GORE: I care passionately about this, and I will fight until it becomes law.*
>
> *BUSH: I want people to hear what he just said! He is for full public financing of Congressional elections! I'm absolutely, adamantly opposed to that! I don't want the government financing Congressional elections!*
>
> —Presidential Debate, October 3, 2000

13. What are Gore's and Bush's positions on full public financing of federal elections?

14. Why might wealthy special-interest groups object to candidates using only federal funding for their campaigns?

Extended Response

15. Write a brief essay about the kinds of activities that political campaigns include. Also explain why candidates need large amounts of money to run their campaigns.

For additional test practice, use Self-Check Quizzes—Chapter 10 on glencoe.com.

Document-Based Questions

13. Gore passionately supports full public financing of federal elections; Bush is adamantly opposed to it.

14. Supporting only federal funding would prevent groups from using campaign contributions to influence those who will be in a position to help and support them.

Extended Response

15. Essays may include activities such as door-to-door canvassing, conducting public opinion polls, obtaining endorsements, and advertising in the print media and on television. Explanatory examples may include the tens of thousands of dollars per minute paid for a television commercial, the cost of airfare and other transportation, salaries of campaign staff members, and payments made to campaign consultants, such as public-opinion pollsters. In addition there are computer, telephone, postage, and printing costs.

Need Extra Help?

If you missed question. . .	1	2	3	4	5	6	7	8	9	10	11	12	13	14	15
Go to Page. . .	297	301	301	308	295	299	303	301	306	308	299	299	303	303	306

---

10. B Answer B is correct because direct contributions of large sums of money could be used to influence a candidate's decisions if that candidate is elected.

Critical Thinking

11. A The 18–24 age group showed the greatest percentage gain, 11 percent. The gains of the other age groups ranged from 2 percent to 5 percent.

12. C The only answer supported by data in the chart is that the 18–24 age group had the lowest rate of voter turnout. The other answers depend on knowing the number of voters in each age group. The chart does not give that information.

Civics ONLINE

Have students visit the Web site at glencoe.com to review Chapter 10 and take the **Self-Check Quiz**.

Need Extra Help?

Have students refer to the pages listed if they miss any of the questions.

TIME REPORTS

Teach

D ### Differentiated Instruction

Verbal/Linguistic Ask: What do you think is the purpose of this article? (*Its purpose is to alert readers to a problem: The lack of a national balloting system has serious consequences that might include affecting a presidential election.*) **Ask:** What are some of the phrases in the article to persuade the reader that the problem should be corrected? (*Answers may include the following: "patchwork of voting methods …imperfect patchwork … causes hundreds of thousands of ballots to be discarded … voter confusion … serious consequences … has changed the course of U.S. history."*) **AL**

C ### Critical Thinking

Drawing Conclusions Ask: Why do you think the Constitution left election procedures up to the states? (*Answers may include that the states might disagree about election procedures and that it would be difficult to reach a national consensus. For some states, the cost of voting machines and other costs of running an election would have to be addressed in choosing a national voting system.*) **OL**

Additional Support

TIME REPORTS

The Machinery of Democracy

With no national balloting system, the U.S. is a patchwork of voting methods

Unlike India and Canada, America does not have a national system for running elections or counting votes. That's because the Constitution left election procedures to the states. They in turn have passed the responsibility down to counties and cities—some 13,000 of them—which choose and pay for their preferred methods of counting ballots.

The imperfect patchwork of voting methods in use around the U.S. causes hundreds of thousands of ballots to be discarded each year. About 2% of all votes in presidential elections are marked for more than one candidate or for none, mostly as a consequence of voter confusion. Sometimes that confusion has serious consequences. In 2000, George W. Bush was declared President based on a 537-vote lead in Florida. Later analysis revealed that Al Gore lost more than 6,000 votes—and the White House—because some Florida voters marked more than one name on Palm Beach County's "butterfly ballot." On that ballot, the names of 10 presidential candidates alternated on two pages. "Voters' confusion with ballot instruction and design and voting machines appears to have changed the course of U.S. history," concluded a post-election analysis by a group of newspapers.

Courtesy TIME

Tim Boyles/Stringer/Getty Images

314

How Americans Vote: An imperfect system
A look at the various methods used throughout the United States*

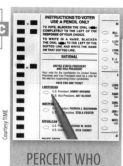

Optical Scan **1**

HOW IT WORKS: Voters fill in rectangles, circles, ovals, or incomplete arrows next to their candidate. A computer selects the darkest mark as the choice.

PROS/CONS: Easy for voters to use, and double-marked ballots are immediately rejected, allowing voters to revise their ballots. But the equipment is expensive and can have problems reading sloppily marked forms.

PERCENT WHO VOTE THIS WAY: **35%**

Electronic **2**

HOW IT WORKS: Voters directly enter choices into the machine using a touchscreen or push buttons. Votes are stored via a memory cartridge.

PROS/CONS: Though as easy as using an ATM, this technology is still fairly expensive. There is no "paper trail" in the event of a recount. And the machines are subject to programming error, malfunction, and tampering.

PERCENT WHO VOTE THIS WAY: **29%**

Background

The 2000 Election The battle for votes did not end on Election Day. At first Gore conceded the election but then retracted his concession when Bush's slim lead in Florida triggered an automatic recount. Gore asked that 1.8 million votes be recounted by hand in four counties that were considered to be Democratic. The Bush team sued to block Gore's request.

The counting of votes had to be completed by November 26 in order for the votes to count. Two counties missed the date to submit their results. Therefore, Florida's secretary of state certified Bush as the winner. After more lawsuits, the counts resumed.

On December 12 the U.S. Supreme Court ruled that since recounts for certain counties were not treating all ballots equally, they were unconstitutional. On December 18, the electorates cast their votes. On January 20, George W. Bush became the 43rd president of the United States.

Punch Card ③

Charles Bennett—AP

HOW IT WORKS: Voters insert blank cards into clipboard-size devices, then punch the hole opposite their choice. Ballots are read by a computer tabulator.

PROS/CONS: An economical method, but holes are often incompletely punched. The dangling bits of cardboard, known as "chads," can lead to inaccurate tabulation of votes. And the notorious "butterfly ballot" caused massive confusion among Florida voters in 2000.

PERCENT WHO VOTE THIS WAY:
14%

Lever Machine ④

Stuart Ramson

HOW IT WORKS: Each candidate is assigned a lever, which voters push down to indicate their choices.

PROS/CONS: Once the most popular form of voting, lever machines are simple to use but heavy, old, and no longer manufactured. There is no paper trail if recounts are necessary.

PERCENT WHO VOTE THIS WAY:
14%

Paper Ballot ⑤

Vincent Letz—AP

HOW IT WORKS: Voters record their choices in private by marking the boxes next to the candidate and then drop ballots in a sealed box.

PROS/CONS: An inexpensive and straightforward method that dates back to 1889. Counting and recounting can be slow.

PERCENT WHO VOTE THIS WAY:
1%

✱ Note: Figures are for the presidential election held in November 2004. Additional 7% is made up of voters in counties where more than one voting method is used. **Sources:** Election Data Services, Federal Election Commission.

Is There a Better Way of Balloting Ahead?

A UNIFORM BALLOT
Some think there should be a single ballot design for all federal elections—same type, style, and size, with ballot marks in the same place.

MOVE ELECTION DAY
Should it be a holiday or moved to the weekend so more people don't have to squeeze in their civic responsibility around work? It's a nice idea, but voters might just take a vacation.

VOTING BY MAIL
Oregon has tried this concept, with mixed success. If the kinks can be worked out, though, it could relieve the crowding on Election Day and boost turnout by giving people more time to vote.

COMPUTERIZED VOTING
Some experts see elections being eventually held entirely over the Internet. Security problems have to be solved first, though. And what about voters who are not computer-literate?

Comstock

C Critical Thinking

Analyzing Ask students to analyze the solutions proposed to institute a better way of balloting. Have them choose one of those solutions and write a short paper in which they list its pros and cons and then state their conclusion about whether or not it would improve voting procedures. *(Answers will vary but should follow the directions to list the pros and cons of the proposed solution and to state their conclusions about it.)* **OL**

📖 Reading Strategy ⟩ Read to Write

Comparing and Contrasting Have students read the explanations of the five voting methods shown. Ask them to look for any general problem concerned with voting, as well as the pros and cons of each voting method. Suggest that they take notes on their observations in preparation for writing.

Ask students to choose two of the voting procedures described and write a composition discussing their similarities and their differences. Suggest that they include the pros and cons of each in solving problems concerned with voting. *(Essays will vary. They should be organized to compare and contrast two voting methods and may include the pros and cons of each.)* **OL**

Key to Ability Levels

BL Below level	**AL** Above level
OL On level	**ELL** English Language Learners

Key to Teaching Resources

Print Material Transparency
CD-ROM or DVD

Levels					Resources	Chapter Opener	Section 1	Section 2	Section 3	Chapter Assess
BL	OL	AL	ELL							
					FOCUS					
BL	OL	AL	ELL		Daily Focus Skills Transparencies		11–1	11–2	11–3	
					TEACH					
BL	OL		ELL		Reading Essentials and Note-Taking Guide*		p. 102	p. 105	p. 108	
BL	OL		ELL		Reading Skills Activity, URB		p. 7			
BL	OL	AL	ELL		Speaking and Listening Skills Activity, URB			p. 9		
	OL	AL			Primary Source Reading, URB		p. 15	p. 15		
BL	OL	AL	ELL		Content Vocabulary Activity, URB*	p. 65	p. 65	p. 65	p. 65	
BL	OL	AL	ELL		Academic Vocabulary Activity, URB	p. 67	p. 67	p. 67	p. 67	
	OL				Biography Activity, URB			p. 69		
BL	OL	AL	ELL		Writing Skills Activity, URB				p. 71	
	OL	AL			Critical Thinking Skills Activity, URB		p. 73			
BL	OL	AL	ELL		Chart, Graph, and Map Skills Activity, URB			p. 75		
BL	OL	AL	ELL		Differentiated Instruction, URB				p. 77	
BL	OL	AL	ELL		School-to-Home Connection Activity, URB*	p. 79	p. 79	p. 79	p. 79	
BL	OL		ELL		Guided Reading Activities, URB*		p. 83	p. 84	p. 85	
	OL	AL			Supreme Court Cases		pp. 105, 131			
BL	OL	AL	ELL		Writer's Guidebook	✓	✓	✓	✓	✓
	OL	AL			Primary Source Document Library	✓	✓	✓	✓	✓
BL	OL	AL	ELL		Daily Lecture & Discussion Notes (in Pres. Plus)		✓	✓	✓	✓
BL	OL	AL	ELL		StudentWorks™ Plus		✓	✓	✓	✓
BL	OL	AL	ELL		Section Spotlight Videos		✓	✓	✓	
BL	OL	AL	ELL		TIME Interpreting Political Cartoons Transp.				Ch. 11	
BL	OL	AL	ELL		Writing Process Transparencies	✓	✓	✓	✓	✓

Note: Please refer to the *Unit 3 Resource Book* for this chapter's URB materials.

* Also available in Spanish

- Interactive Lesson Planner
- Interactive Teacher Edition
- Fully editable blackline masters
- Section Spotlight Videos Launch
- Differentiated Lesson Plans
- Printable reports of daily assignments
- Standards Tracking System

Levels					Resources	Chapter Opener	Section 1	Section 2	Section 3	Chapter Assess
BL	OL	AL	ELL							
					TEACH (continued)					
\multicolumn{4}{c}{**Teacher Resources**}					Building Academic Vocabulary	✓	✓	✓	✓	✓
					Strategies for Success	✓	✓	✓	✓	✓
					Teacher's Guide to Differentiated Instruction	✓	✓	✓	✓	✓
					Graphing Tool	✓	✓	✓	✓	✓
					Presentation Plus! with MindJogger CheckPoint	✓	✓	✓	✓	✓
					ASSESS					
BL	OL	AL	ELL		Quizzes and Tests*		p. 125	p. 126	p. 127	p. 128
BL	OL	AL	ELL		Authentic Assessment with Rubrics				p. 15	
BL	OL	AL	ELL		Standardized Test Practice		p. 21	p. 21	p. 21	p. 21
BL	OL	AL	ELL		*ExamView® Assessment Suite* CD-ROM		11–1	11–2	11–3	Ch. 11
					CLOSE					
BL			ELL		Reteaching Activity, URB*		p. 81	p. 81	p. 81	
BL	OL		ELL		Reading and Study Skills Foldables™ Activity	p. 70		p. 71	p. 71	
BL	OL	AL	ELL		*Civics Today* in Graphic Novel			p. 37		
BL	OL	AL	ELL		Graphic Organizer Transparencies & Strategies	✓	✓	✓	✓	✓

✓ Chapter- or unit-based activities applicable to all sections in this chapter

Using TechCONNECT™

Creating Databases

What is TechCONNECT™?

Glencoe's TechCONNECT™ is a flexible online program that makes it easy to integrate computer technology into the classroom.

How can TechCONNECT™ help my students?

The activities offered in Glencoe's TechCONNECT™ will help students research and create a database in the process of writing a letter concerning a political or social issue. TechCONNECT™ allows students to:

- see online activities related to the creation and management of databases
- complete a self-assessment rubric
- complete a TechCheck quiz

For more information or to get a free 30-day trial of Glencoe TechCONNECT™ for your classroom, visit techconnect.glencoe.com and click the **Free Trial** button. Once you have accessed TechCONNECT™, students can enter code AC067 to begin the project.

Civics ONLINE

Visit glencoe.com and enter *QuickPass*™ code CIV1360c11T for Chapter 11 resources.

You can easily launch a wide range of digital products from your computer's desktop with the McGraw-Hill Social Studies widget.

	Student	Teacher	Parent
Media Library			
• Student Edition Section Audio	●		●
• Spanish Audio Summaries	●		●
• Section Spotlight Videos	●	●	●
***Civics Today* Online Learning Center (Web Site)**			
• Chapter Overviews	●	●	●
• Study Central™	●	●	●
• Study-to-Go	●	●	●
• Student Web Activities	●	●	●
• In Motion Animation	●	●	●
• Self-Check Quizzes	●	●	●
• ePuzzles and Games	●	●	●
• StudentWorks™ Plus Online	●	●	●
• Vocabulary eFlashcards	●	●	●
• Web Activity Lesson Plans		●	
• Vocabulary PuzzleMaker	●	●	●
Classroom Tools			
• Multilingual Glossary	●	●	●
• Beyond the Textbook	●	●	●
• NGS MapMachine	●	●	●

Use this database to search more than 30,000 titles to create a customized reading list for your students.

- Reading lists can be organized by students' reading level, author, genre, theme, or area of interest.
- The database provides Degrees of Reading Power™ (DRP) and Lexile™ readability scores for all selections.
- A brief summary of each selection is included.

Leveled reading suggestions for this chapter:

For students at a Grade 7 reading level:
- *César Chávez,* by Mary Olmstead

For students at a Grade 8 reading level:
- *The Jungle,* by Upton Sinclair

For students at a Grade 9 reading level:
- *Tom Paine: Freedom's Apostle,* by Leo Gurko

For students at a Grade 10 reading level:
- *Walter Lippman and the American Century,* by Ronald Steel

For students at a Grade 11 reading level:
- *Voices of Protest: Huey Long, Father Coughlin and the Great Depression,* by Alan Brinkley

- **Timed Readings Plus in Social Studies** helps students increase their reading rate and fluency while maintaining comprehension. The 400-word passages are similar to those found on state and national assessments.

- **Reading in the Content Area: Social Studies** concentrates on six essential reading skills that help students better comprehend what they read. The book includes 75 high-interest nonfiction passages written at increasing levels of difficulty.

- **Reading Social Studies** includes strategic reading instruction and vocabulary support in Social Studies content for both ELLs and native speakers of English.

- **Content Vocabulary Workout** (Grades 6–8) accelerates reading comprehension through focused vocabulary development. Social Studies content vocabulary comes from the glossaries of Glencoe's Middle School Social Studies texts. www.jamestowneducation.com

KEY Teacher Wraparound

Use this key to help you identify the different types of prompts found in the Teacher Wraparound Edition.

R **Reading Strategies** activities help you teach reading skills and vocabulary.

C **Critical Thinking** strategies help students apply and extend what they have learned.

D **Differentiated Instruction** activities provide instruction for students learning to speak English, along with suggestions for teaching various types of learners.

S **Skill Practice** strategies help students practice historical analysis and geography skills.

W **Writing Support** activities provide writing opportunities to help students comprehend the text.

Teaching strategies and activities have been coded for ability level appropriateness.

AL Activities for students working above grade level

OL Activities for students working on grade level

BL Activities for students working below grade level

ELL Activities for English Language Learners

Focus

Why It Matters

Ask: What are some current issues that different interest groups try to persuade government to support? *(Answers may include issues concerning the environment, the Iraq war, taxes, reproductive rights, education, and so on.)*

More About the Photo

Visual Literacy On September 24, 2005, between 150,000 and 200,000 Americans from around the country rallied in Washington, D.C. to protest the war in Iraq. As they marched around the White House they displayed signs with antiwar slogans and listened to speeches. One of the speakers, Cindy Sheehan, is the mother of a 24-year-old American soldier killed in Iraq. She criticized those members of Congress that supported President Bush's war efforts and led the crowd in demands that no more soldiers be sacrificed. Organizers and participants of the protest hoped their efforts would influence the government to end our involvement the war.

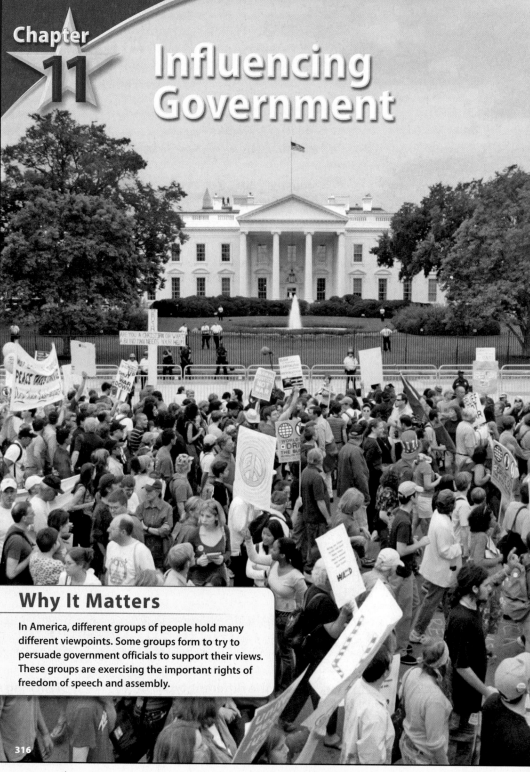

Chapter
11

Influencing Government

Why It Matters

In America, different groups of people hold many different viewpoints. Some groups form to try to persuade government officials to support their views. These groups are exercising the important rights of freedom of speech and assembly.

316

Teach

BIG Ideas *As you begin teaching each section, use these questions and activities to help students focus on the Big Ideas.*

Section 1

Forming Public Opinion Ask: What is public opinion and why does it matter? *(It is the viewpoint held by most people on an issue. It can have a major impact on government policies.)* Point out that in Section 1, students will learn how public opinion is formed. **OL**

Section 2

The Mass Media Ask: What are the mass media? *(Sources of information reaching large groups of people; they include print and electronic media.)* Tell students that in Section 2, they will learn about the different forms of media and how they shape public opinion. **BL**

Section 3

Interest Groups Ask: What are some examples of interest groups? *(Answers may include labor unions, business organizations, civil rights groups, and so on.)* Explain that in Section 3, students will learn how interest groups try to persuade government to support specific policies. **OL**

Chapter Audio

Civics ONLINE
Visit glencoe.com and enter
QuickPass™ code
CIV3093c11 for
Chapter 11
resources.

Chapter Introduction
11

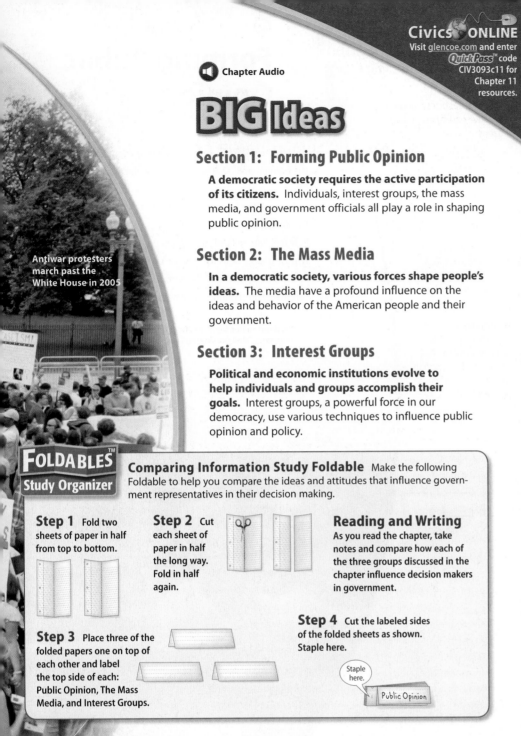

Antiwar protesters march past the White House in 2005

BIG Ideas

Section 1: Forming Public Opinion

A democratic society requires the active participation of its citizens. Individuals, interest groups, the mass media, and government officials all play a role in shaping public opinion.

Section 2: The Mass Media

In a democratic society, various forces shape people's ideas. The media have a profound influence on the ideas and behavior of the American people and their government.

Section 3: Interest Groups

Political and economic institutions evolve to help individuals and groups accomplish their goals. Interest groups, a powerful force in our democracy, use various techniques to influence public opinion and policy.

FOLDABLES™ Study Organizer

Comparing Information Study Foldable Make the following Foldable to help you compare the ideas and attitudes that influence government representatives in their decision making.

Step 1 Fold two sheets of paper in half from top to bottom.

Step 2 Cut each sheet of paper in half the long way. Fold in half again.

Reading and Writing
As you read the chapter, take notes and compare how each of the three groups discussed in the chapter influence decision makers in government.

Step 3 Place three of the folded papers one on top of each other and label the top side of each: Public Opinion, The Mass Media, and Interest Groups.

Step 4 Cut the labeled sides of the folded sheets as shown. Staple here.

Staple here.

Public Opinion

FOLDABLES™ Study Organizer
Dinah Zike's **Foldables**

Purpose This Foldable guides the student to understand influences upon government representatives. The completed Foldable will use tabs to help them compare the effects of public opinion, the mass media, and interest groups. **OL**

More Foldables activities for this chapter can be found in the *Dinah Zike's Reading and Study Skills Foldables* ancillary.

Civics ONLINE

Visit glencoe.com and enter *QuickPass*™ code CIV1360c11T for Chapter 11 resources, including a Chapter Overview, Study Central™, Study-to-Go, Student Web Activity, Self-Check Quiz, and other materials.

Chapter 11 **317**

Focus

Guide to Reading
Answers to Graphic:

```
        Public
        Opinion
       /   |   \
Direction Intensity Stability
```

Section Spotlight Video

To generate student interest and provide a springboard for class discussion, access the Chapter 11, Section 1 video at glencoe.com or on the video DVD.

Guide to Reading

Big Idea
A democratic society requires the active participation of its citizens.

Content Vocabulary
- public opinion *(p. 319)*
- mass media *(p. 320)*
- interest group *(p. 321)*
- public opinion poll *(p. 323)*
- pollster *(p. 323)*

Academic Vocabulary
- uniform *(p. 319)*
- gender *(p. 319)*
- survey *(p. 323)*

Reading Strategy
Identifying As you read, complete a graphic organizer like the one below by identifying the three features of public opinion.

```
   Public
   Opinion
  /   |   \
[  ] [  ] [  ]
```

🔊 Section Audio   🎬 Spotlight Video

Forming Public Opinion

Section 1

Real World Civics Have you heard about all the opinion polls that roll out during election time? Internet blogs are everywhere. In politics, voter opinion is constantly monitored. Students are often part of these polls, as during the Kerry-Bush debates in their 2004 race for president. Pollsters gathered information in pre-debate polls and then in post-debate polls to evaluate shifts in opinion as a result of the debate. Overnight approval ratings of the candidates can rise or drop dramatically because of these polls.

▼ **Students in Pennsylvania post online opinions following 2004 presidential debates**

R Reading Strategies	**C** Critical Thinking	**D** Differentiated Instruction	**W** Writing Support	**S** Skill Practice
Teacher Edition • Inferring, p. 319 • Making Connections pp. 320, 325 • Explaining, p. 321 • Identifying, p. 321 • Questioning, p. 322 • Defining, p. 323 **Additional Resources** • Cont. Vocab., URB p. 65 • Guide. Read., URB p. 83	**Teacher Edition** • Analyzing Info., p. 319 • Making Inferences, p. 320 • Comparing/Contrasting, p. 322 • Distinguishing Fact/ Opinion, p. 324 **Additional Resources** • Crit. Think., URB p. 73	**Teacher Edition** • Interpersonal, p. 319 • Auditory/Musical, p. 321 **Additional Resources** • School-to-Home Act., URB p. 79 • Reteach. Act., URB p. 81	**Teacher Edition** • Personal Writing, p. 323 **Additional Resources** • Read. Skills, URB p. 7	**Teacher Edition** • Reading Polls, p. 323 **Additional Resources** • Daily Focus Trans., 11–1

Public Opinion

Main Idea Public opinion, the ideas and attitudes most people hold, plays a vital role in our democracy.

Civics & You How often have you heard that a president's popularity is up or down? Whose opinion does this represent? Read to find out how public opinion is created and how it, in turn, shapes the way our country is governed.

Public opinion is a term that refers to the ideas and attitudes that most people hold about a particular issue or person. Public opinion plays a key role in a democracy.

Role of Public Opinion For example, public opinion helps shape the decisions of every president. Presidents know they need the support of the public to carry out presidential programs. They also need the support of Congress. Presidents are more likely to have this support if their popularity with the public is high.

Understanding public opinion can also help presidents make effective, timely decisions. Successful presidents have a good sense of when the public is ready for a new idea and when it is not. Franklin D. Roosevelt expressed this idea when he said, "I cannot go any faster than the people will let me."

Diversity Public opinion is not **uniform,** or alike, however. In fact, most Americans agree on very few issues. On any given issue, different groups of the "public" often hold different viewpoints. For example, some Americans support increasing the nation's military forces, while others strongly disagree and wish to minimize military spending. Between these two positions are many shades of opinions. Enough people must hold a particular opinion, however, to make government officials listen to them.

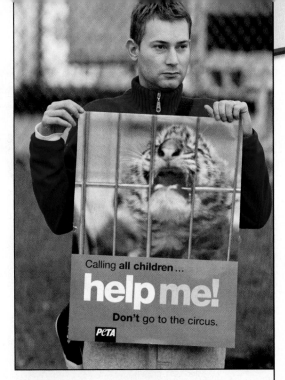

Protecting Animals Activist Tony Madsen protests the treatment of animals by the Ringling Bros. and Barnum & Bailey Circus. **Analyzing** How might a person's age or residence have an effect on his or her opinions?

Sources of Public Opinion

Where does public opinion come from? Why do people often hold widely differing opinions about a particular issue or government action? Among the factors that influence public opinion are a person's background, the mass media, public officials, and interest groups.

Personal Background People's lives and experiences have a major influence on their opinions. Age, **gender,** income, race, religion, occupation, and place of residence play important roles. For example, a wealthy young person who lives in a big city may have very different opinions about the government's role in providing social services than might a poor elderly person who lives in a small town or rural area.

Teach

C Critical Thinking

Analyzing Information Have students reread and explain Franklin D. Roosevelt's quote. *(The quote shows that President Roosevelt believed that government policies need the support of the public.)* **OL**

D Differentiated Instruction

Interpersonal Have students work in small groups and discuss the positions of Americans on current public issues. Encourage them to discuss their individual points of view. Remind students to listen to each other and to discuss their differences respectfully. **OL**

R Reading Strategy

Inferring Ask: Which issue is likely to be a more important concern to a young person: education or Social Security? Why? *(Education is most likely to be a more important concern to a younger person. When they get older, Social Security is more likely to become important.)* **OL**

Caption Answer:

Students may say that people of different ages and locations may have different interests and concerns. Have students list concerns for people of differing backgrounds.

Activity: Collaborative Learning

Identifying Central Issues Remind students that Americans are strongly divided on many important issues. **Ask:** What are some important national or local issues facing our nation? *(the war in Iraq, illegal immigration, taxes, and so on)* Organize the class into small groups and assign each group a different issue. Ask groups to research their issues. The categories students should research include the nature of the issue, its impact on the public, and at least two different points of view about the issue. Have groups script and perform a mock debate that dramatizes their findings. **AL**

Teacher Tip

This activity requires students to do research, to write, and to perform. It allows students with different levels of academic skills and intelligences to work together. As you form groups, consider the needed skills and choose students accordingly.

C Critical Thinking

Making Inferences Have students study the graph of Pre-election Approval Ratings, 1955–2003. **Ask:** Based on the graph, what can we infer about why Lyndon Johnson may have chosen not to run for reelection? *(His approval rating had dropped below 50%.)* **OL**

R Reading Strategy

Making Connections Remind students that public officials use the media to state their views and to influence public opinion. Have students search newspapers and the Internet to find examples of local, state, or national politicians presenting their views. Have students write a quote from three politicians and note the date and source of the quote. **OL**

Analyzing Graphs

Answers:

Jimmy Carter was not reelected despite having approval ratings above 50 percent; Eisenhower and Johnson both had approval ratings above 70 percent; Eisenhower was reelected; Johnson did not run for a second term.

Differentiated Instruction

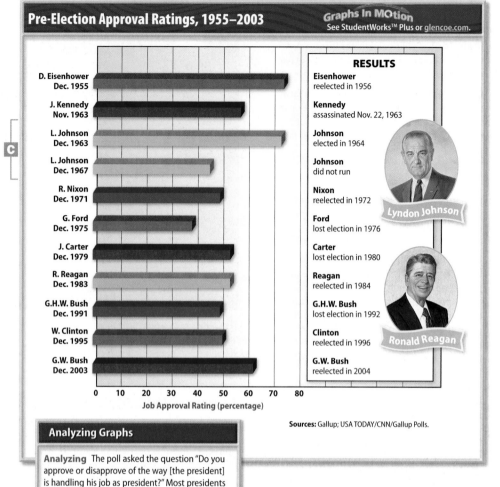

Pre-Election Approval Ratings, 1955–2003

Graphs In MOtion
See StudentWorks™ Plus or glencoe.com.

RESULTS

Eisenhower reelected in 1956

Kennedy assassinated Nov. 22, 1963

Johnson elected in 1964

Johnson did not run

Nixon reelected in 1972

Ford lost election in 1976

Carter lost election in 1980

Reagan reelected in 1984

G.H.W. Bush lost election in 1992

Clinton reelected in 1996

G.W. Bush reelected in 2004

Lyndon Johnson

Ronald Reagan

Sources: Gallup; USA TODAY/CNN/Gallup Polls.

Analyzing Graphs

Analyzing The poll asked the question "Do you approve or disapprove of the way [the president] is handling his job as president?" Most presidents who ended their third year in office with a job approval rating above 50 percent and ran for another term were reelected. Who was not? What presidents had approval ratings of more than 70 percent? Were they reelected?

The Mass Media A medium is a means of communication. (The plural form of the word is *media*.) A letter you send to a friend, for example, is a private medium of communication between the two of you. Television, radio, newspapers, magazines, recordings, movies, Internet Web sites, and books are called the **mass media** because they communicate broadly to masses of people.

Public Officials Political leaders and government officials can influence public opinion. When voters elect people to office, they are indicating that they trust those officials and rely on their opinions. When public officials state their views, they hope to persuade as many people as possible to support their positions.

Leveled Activities

BL Reading Skills Activity 3, URB p. 7

OL Primary Source Reading Activity 3, URB pp. 15–16

AL Critical Thinking Activity 11, URB p. 73

ELL Content Vocabulary Activity 11 , URB p. 65

Interest Groups Individuals who share a point of view about an issue sometimes unite to promote their beliefs. They form what is called an **interest group.** Interest groups work at influencing public opinion by trying to persuade people—including public officials—toward their point of view. Interest groups are sometimes called pressure groups. This refers to their attempts at putting pressure on government to act in their interests.

R4

Features of Public Opinion

Public opinion is often described in terms of three features: *direction, intensity,* and *stability.* These terms are discussed in the following paragraphs.

D

Direction One important question is whether public opinion on any given topic is positive or negative. For example, are people for or against spending more money on national defense? Do people support or oppose a cut in taxes? On most topics, public opinion is mixed, with some people expressing positive opinions and other people holding negative opinions.

Intensity Intensity refers to the strength of an opinion on a given issue. When Americans do have strong feelings, many are often willing to act upon them by voting for or against a candidate, working in an election campaign, or even participating in demonstrations.

R2

Powerful Photos Images shown in the media are often meant to catch attention or change people's opinions about an issue. The baseball player needs funding for a better ballpark. This duck is covered in oil. *Explaining* What interest group would want to publicize this image of the duck?

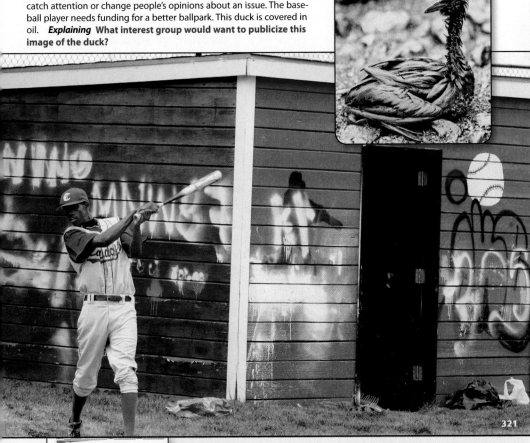

321

George W. Bush's War Speech Reaction Poll

Primary Source Reading 3-B, URB pp. 17–18

Objective: To understand features of public opinion

Focus: Have students discuss the direction, intensity, and stability of public opinion.

Teach: Define categories (Field Date, Population, etc.) at the top of the poll.

Assess: Identify elements of the polls that illustrate the direction, intensity, and stability of public opinion.

Close: Have students summarize public response to President Bush's speech.

C Critical Thinking

Comparing and Contrasting Have students read the American Biography. **Ask:** What were conditions like for retired teachers before and after Andrus formed the National Retired Teachers Association? *(Before the NRTA, retired teachers had no health insurance. After the NRTA, they had health insurance.)* **OL**

R Reading Strategy

Questioning Tell students to read the section on stability. Ask them what questions might reveal that public opinion about a presidential candidate is unstable. *(May include: Do the candidate's policies favor only one class of people? Does he waver in his position on such issues as civil rights? Will his policies harm the economy?)* **AL**

American Biography

Answers: She formed the American Association for Retired Persons that protects the rights of older Americans.

✓ Reading Check Answer: Government officials should form policy with regards to public opinion.

Additional Support

American Biography

Ethel Percy Andrus (1884–1967)

Ethel Percy Andrus spent her life as an educator, becoming the first female principal of a California high school at age 32. When she retired at age 60 in 1944, Andrus volunteered to direct California's Retired Teachers Association. What she discovered troubled her. Many retired teachers struggled to survive on small pensions, often with no health insurance.

Andrus decided to form retired teachers into an alliance that would force lawmakers to listen to them. In 1947 she founded the National Retired Teachers Association.

In 1956 the organization won the first health insurance program for educators over age 65. Two years later, Andrus founded the American Association for Retired Persons, now known as the AARP.

Under the direction of Andrus, the AARP became a powerful lobby, focused on meeting the needs of all Americans over age 50. Today the AARP has more than 34 million members. The AARP advises the government on age-related issues and protects programs like Social Security. Staffed mostly by volunteers, the AARP tries to fulfill the motto given to it by Andrus: "To Serve; Not to be Served!"

Making a Difference CITIZENSHIP

Ethel Andrus was active in education her whole life. **Identifying** What contributions did Andrus make that benefited older Americans?

Stability The stability of public opinion—meaning how firmly people hold to their views—may differ greatly from issue to issue. People's opinions are less likely to change when they have a firm belief. For example, most people's opinions about civil rights are more stable than their opinions about political candidates. Evidence suggests that most Americans hold the strongest convictions about issues that directly affect their lives. It is one thing to support more aid to the poor if you are poor. It is quite another if you are extremely well off. In some campaigns, voters change their minds many times before Election Day. Thus, public opinion on candidates is relatively unstable.

✓ Reading Check Describing Why is public opinion of interest to government officials?

Measuring Public Opinion

Main Idea The most common way of measuring public opinion is with public opinion polls.

Civics & You Have you ever taken part in an opinion poll? Did you think about why the poll was being taken? Read to find out the role of opinion polls in measuring public attitudes.

If public opinion is to affect public policy, then political leaders must be made aware of it. One way to measure public opinion is by looking at election results. If voters elect a candidate, presumably many of them agree with most of the candidate's ideas.

Activity: Collaborative Learning

Making Generalizations Ask students in small groups to research an American who, like Ethel Percy Andrus, worked to meet the needs of a particular group of Americans. Founders of special interest groups such as the Gray Panthers or the American Cancer Society are possible topics. Have them write a one-page report on their subject's work and achievements. Have them combine their reports in a classroom display with illustrations or photos. **OL**

Public Opinion Polls

Measuring public opinion by looking at election results is not always reliable, though. People vote for particular candidates for a variety of reasons. Perhaps they liked how a candidate looked; they supported some, but not all, of the candidate's views; or they voted a straight ticket, that is, for only Republicans or only Democrats. Election results show only a broad measure of public opinion.

R A more accurate measure is to request individuals answer questions in a **survey,** or a **public opinion poll.** Today hundreds of organizations conduct public opinion polls. Every major elected official uses polls to closely monitor public opinion.

What Do Pollsters Do?

Most presidents, for example, have a specialist—a pollster—whose job is to conduct polls regularly. The **pollster** measures the president's popularity or public attitudes toward possible White House proposals, such as a tax increase or change in immigration policy.

Random Samples Pollsters usually question a group of people selected at random from all over the United States. Such a sample, often of about 1,500 people, will usually include both men and women of nearly all races, incomes, ages, and viewpoints. A well-constructed sample will reflect the characteristics of the entire population so that it can present a reasonably accurate picture of public opinion as a whole.

W To find out people's true opinions, pollsters must be careful how they word their questions. By changing the wording of the questions, pollsters can manipulate the process to get nearly any answers they want. For example, the question "Do you favor cutting taxes?" might produce one kind of answer from a person. "Do you favor cutting taxes if it means letting poor people go hungry?" might make the same person respond differently.

TIME™ Teens in *Action*

Alix Olian

Alix Olian, 17, of Highland Park, Illinois, knows that public awareness of an issue is often the key to change. She was one of three students in charge of the annual Highland Park High School (HPHS) Charity Drive. The month-long drive raised $162,000 for the Children's Neuroblastoma Cancer Foundation (CNCF).

QUESTION: What is neuroblastoma?

ANSWER: It is one of the most common childhood cancers. As of now, there is no cure. Yet it gets almost no government funding.

Q: Why is awareness of this form of cancer so important?

A: When leukemia research first began, it was at the point where neuroblastoma is today in terms

Alix Olian with other fundraisers

of its mortality rate and lack of research. Then government funding for leukemia research increased, and doctors made strides toward finding a cure. We hope that by raising awareness, we will inspire the government to take similar action with neuroblastoma research.

Q: What happened at the school assembly at the end of the charity drive?

A: We announced the amount of money we had raised. The mothers of children who had died from neuroblastoma were in tears, and so were a number of students and teachers. It was a moment I will never forget.

Making a Difference CITIZENSHIP

Analyzing What do you think led Alix to provide her time and efforts to support the CNCF cause?

R Reading Strategy

Defining Ask: What is a synonym for "survey"? *(n. public opinion poll; v. examine, view, scrutinize)* **OL**

S Skill Practice

Reading Polls Ask students to find a poll in the newspaper or on the Internet. Help students identify the issue that the poll explores *(what question it asks)*; the poll's sample *(number of people polled)*; the poll's breakdown *(respondents' age, race, income and so on)*; and the results of the poll *(answer to the poll's question)*. **OL**

W Writing Support

Personal Writing Ask students to write a paragraph describing whether or not they think polls are an accurate judge of people's true opinions. **OL**

TIME™ Teens in *Action*

Answer: She wanted the government to increase funding for neuroblastoma research to support doctors' attempts to find a cure for the disease.

Hands-On Chapter Project
Step 1

Creating a Public Interest Campaign

Step 1: Identifying the Issues Have groups of students identify and select an issue of either school, local, or national interest to them.

Directions Write the Big Idea on the board. Tell student groups to prepare a short statement expressing their viewpoint about the issue they selected. The statement should explain what their issue of concern is. It should describe the group's viewpoint about the issue. It should also express why the group holds its particular viewpoint.

Summarizing Have groups share what they learned about the Big Idea while identifying their issues. Ask volunteers to read each group's statements to the class. Encourage the class to question groups about their positions. **OL**

(Project continued in Section 2)

C Critical Thinking

Distinguishing Fact from Opinion Have students read the section on push polls. **Ask:** What fact does the text tell us about push polls? *(Push polls are worded in such a way as to get a desired answer.)* What opinion might this fact elicit? *(Push polls are not fair.)* **OL**

Reading Check **Answer:** They feel that polls can discourage voting if one candidate is far ahead of the others. Some also believe that politicians are too influenced by polls.

Assess

Civics ONLINE

Study Central™ provides summaries, interactive games, and online graphic organizers to help students review content.

Close

Summarizing Ask: What are the influences that shape public opinion? *(The mass media, interest groups, public officials, and personal background all shape public opinion.)* **OL**

Section 1 Review

Push Polls Polls in which the questions are worded so as to influence a person's responses one way or another are called push polls. Push polls are condemned by responsible scientific pollsters. When they are considering poll results, thoughtful citizens should ask themselves whether the questions were, in fact, fair and unbiased.

Support for Polls Some people believe that public-opinion polling serves a useful purpose. Polling, they argue, allows office-holders to keep in touch with citizens' changing ideas about issues. With polls, officials do not have to wait until the next election to see if the people approve or disapprove of government policies.

Problems With Polls Some claim polling makes our elected officials more concerned with pleasing the public rather than exercising political leadership and making wise decisions. Many people also worry that polls affect elections. The media conduct polls constantly during campaigns so they can report who is ahead. Critics argue that these polls treat an election like a horse race, ignoring the candidates' views on issues to concentrate on who is winning or losing at the moment. Furthermore, polls may discourage voting. If they show one candidate far ahead of another, some people may decide not to bother voting because they think the election has already been won or lost.

Our government is responsive to public opinion—to the wishes of the people. However, public opinion is not the only influence on public policy. Interest groups, political parties, the mass media, other institutions of government, and individuals also shape public policy.

Reading Check Explaining Why do some people criticize public opinion polls?

 Section 1 Review

Vocabulary

1. **Define** the following terms and use them correctly in a paragraph about a recent election: *public opinion, mass media, interest group, public opinion poll,* and *pollster.*

Main Ideas

2. **Explaining** What are three components of public opinion and what do they describe?

3. **Describing** In polling, what are random samples?

Critical Thinking

4. **BIG Ideas** Do you think political polling provides accurate results? Useful results? Explain your opinion.

5. **Identifying** In a graphic organizer like the one below, list different forms of mass media.

6. **Analyzing Visuals** Examine the graph—Pre-Election Approval Ratings—on page 320. Write a paragraph summarizing the general trends you feel the results indicate.

CITIZENSHIP Activity

7. **Persuasive Writing** Supporters of polling argue that it is a tool for democracy. Critics of polling think that it makes politicians into reactors rather than leaders. In a short essay, explain which opinion you agree with and why.

Civics ONLINE

Study Central™ To review this section, go to glencoe.com.

Answers

1. Sentences should use vocabulary words according to their definitions in the section and in the Glossary.

2. Direction—agrees or disagrees with stated issue; Intensity—level of feeling about an issue; Stability—likelihood of maintaining or changing opinion.

3. A random sample is a group of people selected by chance, or randomly, to answer questions.

4. Students may point out that the results often depend on the type of poll.

5. Answers may include the Internet, television, radio, magazines, and books.

6. Answers should mention that presidents need at least a 50% approval rating to be reelected.

7. Answers may express the opinion that polls help officials understand and respond to the needs of the public. Students may express the opinion that politicians become too concerned about polls and this interferes with their roles as leaders.

Hazelwood School District v. Kuhlmeier

The Supreme Court's 1969 ruling in Tinker v. Des Moines *affirmed students' First Amendment rights to freedom of expression in public schools (see the* Tinker *decision in Chapter 4, page 132). How far did those rights extend?*

Background of the Case

Hazelwood East High School near St. Louis, Missouri, sponsored a student newspaper as part of its journalism classes. Before each issue, principal Robert Reynolds reviewed the pages.

Reynolds objected to two articles he read in the pages for an issue. One article discussed three pregnant students. The other described a certain student's experience with divorcing parents. Although actual names were not used, Reynolds felt readers could easily identify the featured individuals. Reynolds cancelled the two pages on which the articles appeared.

Kathy Kuhlmeier and two other students who worked on the newspaper sued the school claiming their First Amendment rights had been denied. Many others wore armbands in support.

The Decision

Relying on the Supreme Court's earlier *Tinker* decision, a lower court upheld Kuhlmeier's claim. On January 8, 1988, however, the Supreme Court reversed this ruling. The Court did not overturn the *Tinker* decision. Instead it drew a sharp line between individual expression—as in the wearing of armbands in *Tinker*—and the content of a school-sponsored newspaper. Justice Byron R. White wrote:

> ❝ *A school must be able to set high standards for the student speech that is disseminated [distributed] under its [sponsorship] . . . and may refuse to disseminate student speech that does not meet those standards.* ❞
>
> —Justice Byron R. White

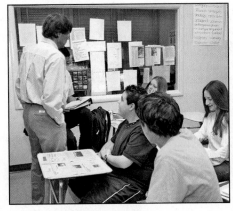

High school students all over the country learn about freedom of the press rights as they publish their school newspapers.

Why It Matters

Although students still have some First Amendment protections, the Hazelwood decision brought on cries of censorship among advocates of free speech and student interest groups. The Student Press Law Center reports that a number of schools, fearing lawsuits, have done away with student newspapers. Schools have also applied the Hazelwood decision to prevent the publication of student yearbooks, to stop stage performances, and to censor the content of student-based Internet Web pages.

Analyzing the Court Decision

1. **Analyzing** Why did the students on the school newspaper sue their school?

2. **Concluding** How do you think Hazelwood could affect a school's responsibility to educate?

Teach

R Reading Strategy

Making Connections Tell students that Supreme Court decisions have sometimes assumed that Amendment IX in the U.S. Constitution guarantees U.S. citizens the right to privacy. **Ask:** How might the newspaper articles have violated their subjects' right to privacy? *(They discussed the personal lives of people that could have been easily identified.)* **OL**

W Writing Support

Persuasive Writing Encourage students to discuss the consequences of the Supreme Court decision. Have them write a brief essay intended to persuade an audience that the decision was either right or wrong. **OL**

ANALYZING THE COURT DECISION

Answers:

1. **Analyzing** They believed their First Amendment right to free speech had been denied.

2. **Concluding** Answers may include: It could influence schools to restrict student access to information and free expression.

Additional Support

Background

Hazelwood School District v. Kuhlmeier
Freedom of speech is considered a fundamental American right. However, when the Constitution was first drafted, this right was not stated. The Constitution set forth the role and powers of government. It did not state what government could not do. The Americans had just won their freedom from a tyrannical king and wanted assurances that their new government would respect the rights of its citizens. They wanted a bill of rights.

The American Bill of Rights was written by James Madison and adopted in 1791. These rights make up the first ten amendments to the Constitution. The high value Americans place on free speech is indicated by its inclusion in the very first amendment. It states that "Congress shall make no law... abridging the freedom of speech."

Focus

Bellringer
Daily Focus Transparency 11–2

Guide to Reading
Answers to Graphic:

Most Powerful Media
1. Television
2. Internet
3. Radio
4. Newspapers
5. Books

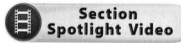

Section Spotlight Video

To generate student interest and provide a springboard for class discussion, access the Chapter 11, Section 2 video at glencoe.com or on the video DVD.

Resource Manager

Guide to Reading

Big Idea
In a democratic society, various forces shape people's ideas.

Content Vocabulary
• print media (p. 327)
• electronic media (p. 327)
• public agenda (p. 327)
• leak (p. 328)
• prior restraint (p. 329)
• libel (p. 330)
• malice (p. 330)

Academic Vocabulary
• acknowledge (p. 328)
• benefit (p. 328)
• regulatory (p. 330)

Reading Strategy
Organizing As you read, note the impact of each of the types of media and list them on a chart like the one below.

Most Powerful Media
1.
2.
3.
4.
5.

The Mass Media

Real World Civics If you see it on the news, or read it in the newspaper, it must be true—right? News media cameras track politicians' every move. But competition for the best photos and newest news is tremendous. While it is the job of the media to report the facts, there are many ways to see the facts. The media can act as a "watchdog," but they also can "spin" the news to present a specific point of view. Remembering that those in the media have their own viewpoints of government and politics can help citizens better understand the messages the media are sending.

▼ **Photographers and reporters swarm presidential candidates**

R Reading Strategies	**C** Critical Thinking	**D** Differentiated Instruction	**W** Writing Support	**S** Skill Practice
Teacher Edition • Organizing, p. 327 • Making Connections, p. 328 • Inferring, p. 329 • Identifying, pp. 329, 330 **Additional Resources** • Cont. Vocab., URB p. 65 • Ac. Vocab., URB p. 67 • Guid. Read., URB p. 84 • Foldables, p. 71	**Teacher Edition** • Making Generalizations, p. 328 **Additional Resources** • Biography Act., URB p. 69 • Graphic Novel, p. 37 • Quizzes and Tests, p. 126	**Teacher Edition** • English Learners, p. 328 **Additional Resources** • School-to-Home Act., URB p. 79 • Reteach. Act., URB p. 81	**Teacher Edition** • Persuasive Writing, p. 327 • Expository Writing, p. 330	**Teacher Edition** • Reading Charts, p. 329 **Additional Resources** • Chart, Graph, and Map Skills, URB p. 75 • Daily Focus Trans., 11–2

NOT AS SEEN ON TV

You Are There Television reporting of news events, such as the damage done by Hurricane Katrina in 2005, takes people right to the event. *Predicting* **How might television affect people's thoughts about how serious an event is?**

The Media's Impact

Main Idea **The nation's media are an important influence on politics and government and also help set the public agenda.**

Civics & You Where do you get your news? How reliable is this source? Read to find out how Americans depend on the media for information.

In the United States the mass media play an important role in influencing politics and government. They also form a link between the people and elected officials.

Types of Media

Newspapers, magazines, newsletters, and books are examples of **print media.** The **electronic media** are radio, television, and the Internet. In the United States, most media outlets are private businesses, run to make a profit. For that reason, media managers often decide what news to run based on what will attract the most viewers, listeners, or readers. The larger the audience, the more money the media can charge for advertising.

Public Agenda

The government must deal with many problems and issues. The ones that receive the most time, money, and effort from government leaders make up what is often called the **public agenda.**

The media have great influence on which problems governments consider important. When the media publicize a problem, such as immigration, white-collar crime, or pollution, people begin to worry about it and to expect that government officials will deal with the problem.

Teach

R Reading Strategy

Organizing Have students read the section Types of Media to answer the question. **Ask:** What are some examples of print and electronic media? *(Print: newspapers, magazines, books. Electronic: television, Internet, radio)* **BL**

W Writing Support

Persuasive Writing The various kinds of media focus public attention on important issues. Have students write one paragraph stating which current issue they believe deserves the most media attention. **OL**

Caption Answer:

Answers will vary, but students should recognize that TV presents events directly and dramatically.

Hands-On Chapter Project
Step 2

Creating a Public Interest Campaign

Step 2: Speaking Out Have groups of students collaborate on an editorial based on the short statement they prepared in Step 1.

Directions Write the Big Idea on the board. Tell student groups to use their short statements as the basis for an editorial. Have students include at least two statistics and one concrete example that backs up the viewpoint expressed in their editorials. Remind students to include the sources they used for the information in their editorials.

Summarizing Have groups share what they learned about the Big Idea while collaborating on their editorials. Ask volunteers to read each group's editorial. **OL**

(Project continued in Section 3)

327

C Critical Thinking

Making Generalizations Ask: How might politicians use the media to their advantage? *(They might use it to gain the approval of the public and/or to manipulate the public.)* **OL**

D Differentiated Instruction

English Learners Ask: How are journalists like watchdogs? *(Just as a watchdog barks to alert its master of danger or intruders, journalists alert the public about danger and important information.)* **ELL**

Caption Answer:

Answers will vary, but students should note that the media can report positive things when politicians do something positive.

Civics ONLINE

Objectives and answers to the **Student Web Activity** can be found at glencoe.com under the Web Activity Lesson Plan for this chapter.

✔ **Reading Check** **Answer:** to test public support

Differentiated Instruction

Watchdogs The media track and report bad behavior and corruption by politicians. *Explaining* What positive things about politicians do the media report?

Coverage of Candidates

Today's modern media, especially television, make it possible for some people to run for office who might never have done so in an earlier time. Previously, candidates were usually experienced politicians who had spent many years working their way up through their political parties. Today sports, media, and Hollywood celebrities with little or no political experience can quickly move into major political positions, based on the fame they earned in other fields.

Media and Elected Officials

The relationship between journalists and politicians is complicated. They need one another, yet they often clash. One presidential assistant explained it this way: "Politicians live—and sometimes die—by the press. The press lives by politicians."

Politicians may also secretly pass on, or **leak,** information to friendly reporters about proposed actions. Leaks allow them to test public reaction to a proposal without having

---

Civics ONLINE

Student Web Activity Visit glencoe.com and complete the Chapter 11 Web Activity.

to **acknowledge,** or admit, that the government is considering it. If the public reacts favorably, the government might officially move ahead with the idea. If the public reaction is negative, they can quietly drop it. Politicians also use leaks to change public opinion on an issue, or to gain favor with a reporter.

Leaking information is part of politics. Many journalists go along with the practice because they **benefit,** or profit, from being able to report "inside" information. When they can get hot news from politicians and "scoop" their rivals—break a story first—they become more successful as journalists.

Watchdog Role

The mass media also play an important "watchdog" role over government activities. Journalists are eager to expose government waste or corruption. They know that stories about government misconduct will attract a large audience. Throughout American history the media have served both their own interests and the public interest by exposing misconduct in government.

Media and National Security

A tension exists between the American citizens' need for information and the need for the government to keep secrets to protect national security. The government can control information the media reports by classifying information as secret and limiting press coverage of military actions. In the war in Iraq, "embedded," or implanted, journalists went with American troops into battle. They reported live on clashes with the enemy as well as on the daily life of the troops. Most journalists welcomed this opportunity. Some critics, however, felt the arrangement made it too easy for the government to control news reporting on the war.

✔ **Reading Check** **Explaining** Why would a government official leak information to the media?

Biography Activity 11, URB pp. 69–70

Edward R. Murrow

Objective: To gain an understanding of the impact of the media

Focus: Have students study the career of CBS journalist Edward R. Murrow.

Teach: Discuss the role of the media as a "watchdog."

Assess: Review that students clearly demonstrated cause and effect in their answers for question 5 on page 70.

Close: Have students create a time line of Murrow's broadcasting career.

Differentiated Instruction Strategies

BL Identify why Murrow wanted to profile Senator McCarthy on his television program.

AL Find a quote from a contemporary public official in which dissent is labeled as disloyal.

ELL Discuss the meaning of the word "fanaticism" and how it applied to Senator McCarthy.

Media Safeguards

Main Idea Freedom of the press is protected by the U.S. Constitution, although some regulation is permitted.

Civics & You Have you ever seen something on TV or heard something on the radio that you thought "went too far"? What do you think should be done about it? Read to find out what the Constitution says and how courts have interpreted it.

Democracy requires a free flow of information and ideas in order to thrive. In the United States the government plays an important role in protecting the ability of the mass media to operate freely. The Constitution extends freedom of speech to the media.

The First Amendment to the U.S. Constitution states, in part,

" Congress shall make no law . . . abridging the freedom . . . of the press. "

Today, "press" in this usage refers not only to print media but to radio, television, and the Internet as well. In the United States, the First Amendment means that the media are free from **prior restraint,** or government censorship of material *before* it is published. Generally the government cannot tell the media what or what not to publish. This means that reporters and editors are free to decide what they will say, even if it is unpopular or embarrassing to the government or to individual politicians.

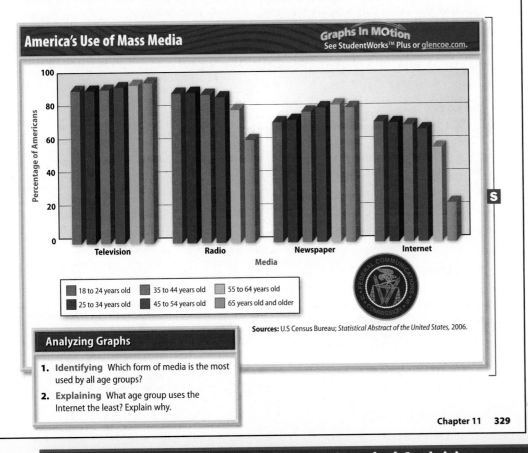

America's Use of Mass Media

Graphs In MOtion See StudentWorks™ Plus or glencoe.com.

Percentage of Americans

Media: Television, Radio, Newspaper, Internet

- 18 to 24 years old
- 25 to 34 years old
- 35 to 44 years old
- 45 to 54 years old
- 55 to 64 years old
- 65 years old and older

Sources: U.S Census Bureau; *Statistical Abstract of the United States,* 2006.

Analyzing Graphs

1. **Identifying** Which form of media is the most used by all age groups?

2. **Explaining** What age group uses the Internet the least? Explain why.

R₁ Reading Strategy

Inferring Ask: What might happen to our democracy without freedom of the press? *(The government would be able to control what the public knows, and citizens would not be able to make informed decisions.)* **OL**

R₂ Reading Strategy

Identifying Have students write a sentence using the word "prior," and a sentence using the word "restraint." Challenge students to define the term "prior restraint" based on the meaning of each of the two words. **BL ELL**

S Skill Practice

Reading Charts Ask: For those aged 55–64, what two media sources do they use in almost equal amounts? *(radio and newspapers)* **OL**

Analyzing Graphs

Answers:
1. television
2. Those 65 years and older use the Internet least of all Americans. They are unfamiliar with the technology since they did not grow up using it.

Leveled Activities

BL Biography Activity 11, URB pp. 69–70

OL Chart/Map/Graph Activity, URB pp. 75–76

AL Speaking and Listening Activity 3, URB pp. 9–12

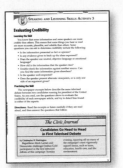

ELL Reteaching Activity 11, URB p. 81

R Reading Strategy

Identifying Ask: What is a synonym for "malice"? *(evil intent)* **BL**

W Writing Support

Expository Writing Tell students that despite shield laws, journalists have at times faced jail to protect the identity of a source. Have students research a case where a journalist refused to reveal his or her source. Ask students to write a one-page report on the case. **AL**

✔ Reading Check Answer: It prevents the government from censoring journalists by telling them what they can or cannot publish.

Assess

Civics ONLINE

Study Central™ provides summaries, interactive games, and online graphic organizers to help students review content.

Close

Personal Journal Ask students what medium is the best source of news. Ask them to write a paragraph in their journals explaining why they prefer it. **OL**

Section ⭐ 2 Review

Freedom Within Limits Freedom of the press is not, however, unlimited. For example, no one is free to publish false information that will harm someone's reputation. This action is called **libel.** Anyone who believes a written story has damaged him or her may sue for libel. Unlike ordinary people, however, government officials rarely win libel lawsuits. In *New York Times Co. v. Sullivan* (1964), the Supreme Court ruled that public officials must prove actual **malice,** or evil intent—meaning that the publisher either knew that the material was false or showed a reckless disregard for the truth.

Protecting Sources Success in gathering news may depend on getting information from those who do not want their names made public. The press and the United States government have fought many battles over the media's right to keep sources secret. Thirty-one states and the District of Columbia have media shield laws to protect reporters from having to reveal their sources.

For the most part, however, reporters have no more right to avoid presenting evidence than do other citizens.

Regulating the Media

The federal government possesses some power to regulate the broadcast media. This is because the government decides who gets access to the limited number of airwaves available for radio and television broadcasting. One way the government regulates broadcasting is through the Federal Communications Commission (FCC). The FCC is a **regulatory,** or managing, commission of the federal bureaucracy. The FCC cannot censor broadcasts, but it can penalize stations that violate its rules. A well-known example is the fine for the broadcast of the 2004 Super Bowl halftime show featuring singer Janet Jackson.

✔ Reading Check Describing How does prior restraint protect the media?

Section Review

Vocabulary

1. **Write** a short paragraph about mass media using each of these terms: *print media, electronic media, public agenda, leak, prior restraint, libel, malice.*

Main Ideas

2. **Explaining** How do the media set the public agenda?

3. **Describing** What are two ways freedom of the press is limited?

Critical Thinking

4. **Analyzing** Explain how the media and public officials are dependent on one another.

5. **BIG Ideas** Describe the roles the media plays in influencing government and politics by completing a graphic organizer like the one below.

Roles of the Media — *watchdog*

6. **Analyzing Visuals** Examine the chart on page 329. What general statements can you make about those 18 to 24 years old?

CITIZENSHIP Activity

7. **Interviewing** Contact a local TV or radio station. Ask them to identify a recent broadcast that drew criticism. Have the station describe its procedure for handling such complaints.

Civics ONLINE

Study Central™ To review this section, go to glencoe.com.

Answers

1. Paragraphs should incorporate definitions for the vocabulary words that are found in the section and in the Glossary.

2. By deciding what stories to cover they influence the public's focus on issues.

3. The law prohibits media from publishing false information about individuals, as well as government classified secrets.

4. Public officials rely on the media to get their message out. Journalist careers benefit from

being the first to report "inside" information.

5. **Roles of Media:** Watchdog; Help Set Public Agenda; Report the News; Cover Government Officials

6. The chart shows that 18–24 year olds use television and radio more than other media. They read newspapers less than older Americans. They use the Internet more than older Americans.

7. Interviews will vary. Students should share the station's explanation of the incident with the class.

Do the media have a political bias?

In the past, most Americans watched the major television networks—CBS, NBC, and ABC—for their news. Today fewer Americans rely on the three major networks and their local newspapers. Many receive their news from a wide variety of sources, including cable television and the Internet. The issue of bias—or prejudice—in the news has become a topic for debate. Interest groups have organized to report on media bias. Some groups report that the media are generally liberal; others say they are more often conservative. Obviously, the bias of the interest group helps determine how it sees the media. Is news reporting in America generally biased?

C₁

"Next...an in-depth report on corporate corruption - excluding, of course, our parent company."

A cartoon shows that it seems the media produced slanted or biased reports.

C₂

C₁ Critical Thinking

Making Inferences Ask: How can you protect yourself from bias in the news? *(Get the news from more than one source. Recognize and sort fact from opinion.)* **OL**

C₂ Critical Thinking

Making Inferences Ask: What does the cartoon suggest about news bias? *(Corporate sponsors of news programs may influence what stories are reported and how they are presented.)* **OL**

YES

The nonpartisan Center for Media and Public Affairs published a study in 1981 showing that the majority of network journalists identified themselves as liberal. Rupert Murdoch founded the Fox News cable channel to counterbalance what he saw as liberal bias at the big three networks. More recently, a CBS broadcast journalist, Bernard Goldberg, wrote a book called *Bias* in which he claimed that a one-sided opinion dominates the mainstream news media. He identified three network anchors: "I said out loud what millions of TV news viewers all over America know and have been complaining about for years: that too often, Dan (Rather) and Peter (Jennings) and Tom (Brokaw) and a lot of their foot soldiers don't deliver the news straight, that they have a liberal bias."

—Bernard Goldberg, Center for American Progress

NO

Network anchors, like former CBS anchorman Dan Rather, claim to be unbiased and above politics. In 1995, Rather said that most reporters did not know whether they were Republican or Democrat. He thought that most were probably moderates. In his recent book *What Liberal Media?* Eric Alterman accused conservatives of using the myth of liberal bias to gain a political advantage. "The myth of the 'liberal media' empowers conservatives to control debate in the United States to the point where liberals cannot even hope for a fair shake anymore. However immodest my goal, I aim to change that." He added that the 47 percent of people polled who believed that the media are "too liberal" were influenced by the myth of liberal bias.

—Eric Alterman, *What Liberal Media?*

 Debating the Issue

1. **Identifying** What three networks captured most of the news viewers in the past?

2. **Recalling** How has the way Americans receive their news changed in recent years?

3. **Contrasting** Explain the difference between Goldberg's and Rather's views of network anchors.

4. **Evaluating** Why do many people believe news reporting is biased?

 Debating the Issue

Answers:
1. ABC, CBS, NBC
2. Americans now get their news from a greater variety of sources that include cable television and the Internet.
3. Goldberg believes that journalists have a liberal bias. Rather feels that most journalists are moderates.
4. Different interest groups evaluate the media's presentation of the news from their own viewpoints. They then convey their assessments to the public.

Additional Support

Chapter 11   **331**

Activity: U.S./World Connections

Comparing and Contrasting Point out to students that other countries have the same concerns about their media's bias. Ask them to read two newspapers from a country whose native tongue is English, such as Australia or Canada. Tell them to choose a national issue that is covered by both papers.

Have the class discuss how each newspaper covers the issue. Ask volunteers to suggest phrases in each paper that reveal a different point of view. List these phrases on the board under the name of the paper in which it appears. Then have the class discuss whether the phrases reveal a political bias. **AL**

Focus

Bellringer
Daily Focus Transparency 11–3

Guide to Reading
Answers to Graphic:

How Interest Groups Influence Government
- Going to Court
- Election Activities
- Lobbying, Peaceful Demonstrations

Section Spotlight Video

To generate student interest and provide a springboard for class discussion, access the Chapter 11, Section 3 video at glencoe.com or on the video DVD.

Resource Manager

Guide to Reading

Big Idea
Political and economic institutions evolve to help individuals and groups accomplish their goals.

Content Vocabulary
- public interest group (p. 334)
- nonpartisan (p. 334)
- political action committee (PAC) (p. 334)
- lobbyist (p. 335)

Academic Vocabulary
- primary (p. 334)
- guarantee (p. 337)

Reading Strategy
Summarizing As you read, complete a web diagram like the one below to show how interest groups influence governmental decision making.

How Interest Groups Influence Government
- election activities

Section 3
Interest Groups

Real World Civics Since our country began, the right to assemble has been a basic freedom. When labor union members such as those in the AFL-CIO get together to support issues, they hope people listen. Labor unions formed early in America to give workers a more powerful voice. Although not all Americans agree with unions, all people have a right to be heard. The AFL-CIO was formed in the 1950s to give labor unions its most powerful voice.

▼ **Steelworkers and postal workers at an AFL-CIO Solidarity rally**

332

R Reading Strategies	**C** Critical Thinking	**D** Differentiated Instruction	**W** Writing Support	**S** Skill Practice
Teacher Edition • Identifying, pp. 333, 334 • Summarizing, pp. 334, 335, 336 • Making Connections, p. 338 • Predicting, p. 342 **Additional Resources** • Cont. Vocab., URB p. 66 • Guid. Read., URB p. 85 • RENTG, p. 128	**Teacher Edition** • Making Inferences, pp. 333, 334, 337 **Additional Resources** • Quizzes and Tests, p. 127	**Teacher Edition** • Gifted & Talented, p. 333 • Below Grade Level, p. 336 • Gifted & Talented, p. 337 **Additional Resources** • Diff. Instr. Act., p. 77 • Reteach. Act., URB p. 81	**Teacher Edition** • Personal Writing, p. 335 **Additional Resources** • Writing Skills Act., URB p. 72	**Teacher Edition** • Analyzing Charts, p. 336 **Additional Resources** • Daily Focus Trans., 11–3 • Pol. Cartoons Trans. 11

Types of Interest Groups

Main Idea Interest groups are an important part of our democratic process because they influence public policy.

Civics & You If you wanted to change a policy at your school, do you think you would have more influence as an individual or as a part of a large group? Read to see how many Americans have answered this question on the national level.

As you learned earlier, interest groups are organizations of people who unite to promote their ideas. People form, join, or support interest groups, also called special-interest groups, because they believe that by pooling their resources, they can increase **C** their influence on decision makers. The First Amendment protects your right to belong to interest groups by guaranteeing "the right of the people peaceably to assemble and to petition the government."

Economic Interest Groups

Some of the most powerful interest groups are based on economic interests. The U.S. Chamber of Commerce, which promotes free enterprise, is one of the largest. Others represent specific types of businesses, such as the **R** Tobacco Institute, which represents cigarette manufacturers. Such groups try to influence government decisions on issues that affect their industries.

Interest groups representing workers have been some of the most influential. They are concerned with wages, working conditions, and benefits. The American Federation of Labor and Congress of Industrial Organizations (AFL-CIO), an alliance of labor unions, is the largest of these groups. Professionals such as lawyers, doctors, and accountants have their own interest groups. The American Medical Association, for instance, represents doctors.

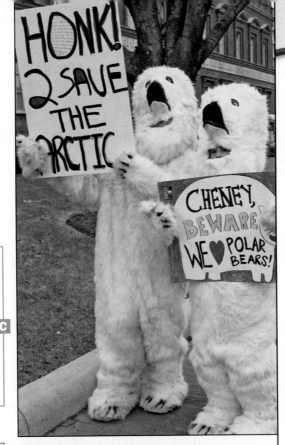

Energy Protest Demonstrators protest President Bush's energy policy in 2003. **Comparing** How are public interest groups different than economic interest groups who protest?

Other Interest Groups

People have also organized to promote an ethnic group, age group, religious group, or gender. The National Association for the Advancement of Colored People (NAACP) works to improve the lives of African Americans. The National Organization for Women (NOW) represents women's interests. AARP **D** promotes the interests of older Americans.

Another category of interest groups works for special causes. For example, the Sierra Club is concerned with protecting nature. The National Rifle Association (NRA) looks after the interests of gun owners.

Chapter 11 333

Teach

C Critical Thinking

Making Inferences Ask: What assumption can we make about people in an interest group? *(They share a common goal or interest.)* What does the phrase, "strength in numbers," tell us about interest groups? *(Interest groups recognize that working with others gives them more power than working as individuals.)* **OL**

R Reading Strategy

Identifying Have students name two economic interest groups. *(Answers may include the U.S. Chamber of Congress, the Tobacco Institute, and the AFL-CIO.)* **BL**

D Differentiated Instruction

Gifted and Talented Have students research the history of a special interest group and its influence on government. Have them present an oral report to the class, using a timeline. **AL**

Caption Answer:
Public interest groups work to benefit all of society. Economic interest groups work to benefit the interests of a particular industry.

Differentiated Instruction

Writing Skill Activity 11, URB pp. 71–72

Writing a Strong Lead

Objective: To understand techniques for engaging readers' interest

Focus: Students will write strong lead sentences.

Teach: Review how writers engage readers.

Assess: Have students rewrite the lead sentence of their chosen article to engage readers' interest.

Close: Have students read a news Web site and identify the type of lead sentence used in an article.

Differentiated Instruction Strategies

BL Ask: Which technique hints about what will happen?

AL Ask: Which technique do you think would best motivate readers to continue reading a scientific explanation of global warming?

ELL Ask: What type of lead sentence includes information about how something looks, sounds, feels, smells, or tastes?

C Critical Thinking

Making Inferences Encourage students to discuss problems that affect them and their families, such as determining the safety of the food sold in grocery stores. **Ask:** Which kind of interest group would you turn to for help with this problem and why? *(Students should recognize that one of the public interest groups would be the best source of help because such a group works for the common good not just the good of a special group.)* **OL**

R₁ Reading Strategy

Identifying Ask: What is a PAC? *(A political action group; these organizations raise money in support of candidates.)* **BL**

R₂ Reading Strategy

Summarizing Have students explain the goals and methods of interest groups. Have them list in outline form what they have learned on this page about interest groups. **OL**

Caption Answer:
Public interest groups work to influence public policy.

Additional Support

Public Interest Groups All the interest groups described earlier are private groups because they promote only the special interests of their own members. Some groups, however, work to benefit all, or at least most, of society. These are **public interest groups.** These groups support causes that affect the lives of Americans in general. For example, the League of Women Voters is a **nonpartisan,** or impartial, group that educates voters about candidates and issues. Other public interest groups have worked for consumer rights and the rights of the disabled.

Interest Groups and Government

Interest groups are an important part of our democratic process because their **primary,** or first, goal is to influence public policy. To do this, interest groups focus their efforts on elections, the courts, and lawmakers.

Elections Some interest groups use political resources to support certain candidates at election time. For example, the Sierra Club might back candidates who support laws to protect nature and oppose those who disagree with its beliefs. Many interest groups, including most labor unions and many corporations and trade associations, have formed **political action committees (PACs).** PACs collect money from the members of their groups and use it to support some candidates and oppose others.

Going to Court Trying to influence public policy by bringing cases to court is another option. For example, when a law—in the opinion of an interest group—is not being properly enforced, the group may sue the party who is breaking the law. A group may also use the courts to argue that a law or government policy is unconstitutional.

Peaceful Demonstrations Many special-interest groups protest peacefully, just asking citizens to read materials or sign petitions. *Describing* What kinds of actions by the government are special-interest groups hoping for?

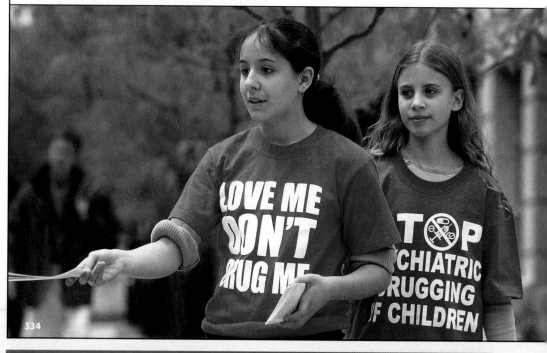

334

Activity: Collaborative Learning

Formulating Questions Help students see that public interest groups can change government policies that affect their daily lives. Tell them that interviewing an official that works in such an organization can acquaint them with that group's activities.

Have students choose an organization that deals with a problem important to them. Then have them research that group. Organize students into three groups. Have each group generate a list of questions based on their research that they would like to ask an official in a public interest group. Then have each group read their questions to the class. The class as a whole will vote on the questions to be asked. Students will then elect a student to conduct the interview. Have that student interview an official from the chosen organization and report back to class. **OL**

TIME™

Political Cartoons

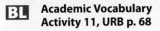

NOW THIS IS A COMPLEX LOVE STORY...

CONGRESS

SPECIAL INTERESTS

—Steve Breen/Copley News Service

Every year, more than half of all Americans do volunteer work ... role in it. One of the responsibilities of citizens is to help make their ... of volunteer grou... small. Perhap... ... dad wh...

In this cartoon, Steve Breen comments on the relationship between special interests and Congress by making reference to the movie *King Kong*.

1. Define special interests.
2. Why do you think the cartoonist represents special interests as a giant?
3. How does Breen portray Congress?
4. Do you think Breen views this relationship as positive or negative? Explain.

Lobbying Government

Interest groups use lobbyists to help them influence government officials, especially at the national and state levels. **Lobbyists** are **W** representatives of interest groups who contact lawmakers or other government officials directly. Lobbyists operate at all levels of government—local, state, and national.

The term *lobbyist* was first used in the 1830s to describe people who waited in the lobbies of statehouses to ask politicians for favors. Today lobbyists use a variety of strategies to influence lawmakers. Lobbyists have a good understanding of how the government functions. Good lobbyists know which government department to contact about a particular concern. They are also talented public relations agents who know how to make friends and talk persuasively.

One of the lobbyist's most important resources is information. The most effective **R** lobbyists are able to supply to lawmakers useful information that helps their own cases. They suggest solutions to problems and issues. Lobbyists sometimes prepare their own drafts of bills for lawmakers to consider and even testify in legislative hearings on bills. All of these activities provide lawmakers with a tremendous amount of information. This is important because lawmakers deal with thousands of bills each year.

The work of lobbyists does not end once a law is passed. Their interest groups also try to make sure the laws are enforced and upheld in court. For example, if an oil exploration bill is approved, environmental groups are likely to watch the whole operation carefully. If oil companies do not observe provisions aimed at protecting the environment, lobbyists for the environmental groups will lobby various government departments or agencies to see that the law is enforced.

✓ Reading Check **Explaining** Why do some people form interest groups?

W Writing Support

Personal Writing Have students write one paragraph describing their opinions about the influence of special interest groups on government. **OL**

R Reading Strategy

Summarizing Have students identify the ways that lobbyists use information to aid lawmakers. *(They provide useful information in support of their own causes. They suggest solutions to problems. They testify in legislative hearings.)* **OL**

TIME™ Political Cartoons

Answers:

1. the desires of a particular group
2. Some people feel that special interest groups have too much power.
3. as being controlled by special interests
4. probably views this relationship as negative; a frightening and out-of-control power

✓ Reading Check **Answer:** to influence government policy about a specific issue or a specific group

Differentiated Instruction

Leveled Activities

R Reading Strategy

Summarizing Have students list techniques that interest groups use to influence public opinion. *(They use direct-mail campaigns to recruit and advertise, stage protests, and organize public events.)* **OL**

C Critical Thinking

Making Inferences Ask: Why are some people more likely to vote for a candidate who has been endorsed by a famous person? *(Answers may include that people feel they can trust the opinion of someone they know and like.)* **BL**

D Differentiated Instruction

Below Grade Level Have students create a Venn diagram listing differences and similarities between the different propaganda techniques. **BL ELL**

Analyzing Charts

Answers:
1. Name-calling uses personal attacks against a candidate.
2. Answers will vary, but students will most likely say the "Stacked Cards" because at least it gives information about a candidate's record, also "Just Plain Folks" because it gives a candidate's background.

Hands-On
Chapter Project
Step 3

Propaganda Techniques

THE BANDWAGON
We're Sure to Win!
"Polls show our candidate is pulling ahead, and we expect to win in a landslide."

NAME-CALLING
DO NOT VOTE FOR "A"
"Candidate A is a dangerous extremist."

ENDORSEMENT
MISS OHIO SAYS... "VOTE FOR B"
Popular beauty queen says, "I'm voting for Candidate B and so should you."

STACKED CARDS
"Candidate C has the best record on the environment."

GLITTERING GENERALITY
"Candidate B is the one who will bring us peace and prosperity."

JUST PLAIN FOLKS
"My parents were ordinary, hardworking people, and they taught me those values."

TRANSFER
Associating a patriotic symbol with a candidate.

Analyzing Charts

1. **Explaining** How does name-calling differ from the other techniques?
2. **Evaluating** In your opinion, which propaganda techniques, if any, are more acceptable than others in political campaigns?

Techniques Interest Groups Use

Main Idea Interest groups use various techniques to influence public opinion and policy.

Civics & You Are you more likely to support a cause because a famous singer supports it? Read to find out how groups and office seekers try to gain your support.

All interest groups want to influence public opinion, both to gain members and to convince people of the importance of their causes. Many use direct-mail campaigns to recruit. Interest groups also advertise. Maybe you have seen ads urging you to drink milk, use ethanol in your car, or buy American-made products. Trade associations sponsor these types of ads. Interest groups also stage protests and organize public events to get coverage in the media.

Beware Propaganda!

Interest groups use propaganda techniques to promote a particular viewpoint or idea. Citizens need to recognize the different types of propaganda described in the chart on this page. Many political and special-interest groups apply the same techniques used to market products to consumers.

Creating a Public Interest Campaign

Step 3: Working Together Have groups of students create their own public interest group on behalf of the issue they identified in Step 1.

Directions Write the Big Idea on the board. Discuss the ways that interest groups attempt to influence government policy. Have students create a name for their interest group and have them plan a peaceful demonstration to promote their agenda. Ask students to consider to whom they most want to communicate their concerns: the government and/or the public. They should consider what activity and location would best communicate their concerns.

Summarizing Have groups share their demonstration plans in class. Then have volunteers share what they learned about the Big Idea while collaborating on their plans. **AL**

(Project continued on the Visual Summary page)

Regulating Interest Groups

Although the Constitution **guarantees,** or promises, Americans the right to participate in interest groups, state and federal governments regulate their activities. Laws have limited the amount of money PACs may contribute to candidates and have required lobbyists to register with congressional officials who have authority to monitor them. Lobbyists must also disclose who hired them, how much they are paid, and how they spend money related to their work.

Federal and state laws also require a waiting period before former government officials can become lobbyists. For example, a person who just ended a term as a representative cannot immediately become a lobbyist for some special-interest group or organization that wants to hire that person. These laws are meant to prevent ex-public officials from taking unfair advantage of inside knowledge and friendships with former associates on behalf of interest groups. Laws regulating lobbyists have had only limited success.

Pros and Cons Interest groups have both their critics and their defenders. Some people argue that interest groups and lobbyists have too much say in government. Critics claim that campaign contributions give interest groups improper influence over officeholders. Many critics point to the example of Jack Abramoff, one of Washington's most powerful lobbyists. In January 2006, Abramoff admitted corrupting government officials and stealing millions of dollars from his lobbying clients.

Those who defend interest groups say that they make government more responsive. They provide necessary and important services by communicating the people's wishes to their representatives. They also enable Americans to organize and participate in the political system, and pressure the government to follow policies they want.

✔ **Reading Check** Explaining What are the main tasks of lobbyists?

Section 3 Review

Vocabulary

1. **Define** the following terms and use them in sentences related to interest groups: *public interest group, nonpartisan, political action committee (PAC), lobbyist.*

Main Ideas

2. **Describing** What are three ways interest groups can be organized?

3. **Explaining** How have laws regulated the activities of interest groups, PACs, and lobbyists?

Critical Thinking

4. **Making Judgments** Which of the marketing techniques discussed in this section do you think is the most effective among consumers and citizens? Why?

5. **BIG Ideas** On a graphic organizer like the one below, compare and contrast the benefits and dangers of interest groups and lobbyists in our political system.

Benefits	Dangers

6. **Analyzing Visuals** Examine the chart of propaganda techniques on page 336. Work with a partner to list an example you have seen, heard, or read in the media of each.

CITIZENSHIP Activity

7. **Expository Writing** You have studied about political parties and about interest groups. Write a one-page paper in which you compare interest groups and political parties. How are they similar? How are they different?

Civics ONLINE

Study Central™ To review this section, go to glencoe.com.

C Critical Thinking

Making Inferences Ask: Why is it important to know for whom lobbyists work? *(to understand whose interests the lobbyist is serving.)* **OL**

D Differentiated Instruction

Gifted and Talented Have students research the Jack Abramoff case—its effects on government and special interest groups. Have them present an oral report to the class. **AL**

✔ **Reading Check** **Answer:** to communicate the desires of interest groups; to pressure government to support policies favorable to interest groups

Assess

Civics ONLINE

Study Central™ provides summaries, interactive games, and online graphic organizers to help students review content.

Close

Predicting Have students discuss what effect banning interest groups might have on a democracy. **OL**

Section 3 Review

Answers

1. Sentences should use vocabulary words according to their definitions in the section and in the Glossary.

2. Answers may include: by economic interest, by characteristics (ethnicity, gender, age), by cause.

3. The law requires that lobbyists register with the government. PACs are limited in the amount of money they can contribute to candidates. Interest groups must report how they spend their money.

4. Answers will vary. Students should give reasons for their judgments.

5. **Benefits:** Allows citizens to organize and participate in political system; communicates needs of citizens for representation; makes government more responsive.

   Dangers: Uses contributions to candidates to gain unfair influence over government policies.

6. Answers will vary but students should provide the media they referenced.

7. Students can review Chapter 9 to find information about political parties.

Financial Literacy

R Reading Strategy

Making Connections Have students discuss shopping on the Internet. **Ask:** Why is information about Internet shopping important for Internet consumers? *(It will help them protect themselves from theft and fraud when using the Internet.)* **OL**

S Skill Practice

Using the Internet Have students search the Internet for an item of their choice. Ask them to list the steps it takes to choose and order an item on each site that they visit. Encourage them to note any information about each company's shipping and return policies. **BL**

Analyzing Economics

Answer:

1. Answers will vary, but arguments should include facts to back up student opinions.
2. Don't send your credit card number by e-mail. Shop only at secure sites. Keep a record of all transactions. Check your credit card statements.

Additional Support

Shopping on the Internet

Shopping on the Internet has become increasingly popular because of the ease with which it can be done. Anybody with access to the Internet and a valid credit card can order on the Web.

Shop Online?
- **Price:** items less expensive because warehouse and staff costs are lower, and online shops want to attract customers
- **Convenience:** shopping can be done at home and at the best time for you
- **Wide choice:** compare from many different sites

Avoid Computer Fraud
- Never send your credit card number by e-mail.
- If buying online, make sure the site is secure—look for symbols such as the closed padlock. If that lock is broken do not send your credit card information.
- Keep a record of the transaction.
- Check your credit card statements to ensure that there are no irregularities.
- If you are buying from a company, the Web site should include the seller's shipping charges and its return, refund, and warranty policies.
- Check for a company's policy on returning goods—most goods have a seven day cancellation period.

Analyzing Economics

1. **Comparing and Contrasting** Make a chart comparing the advantages and disadvantages of shopping on the Internet. In your opinion, do the advantages outweigh the disadvantages or vice versa? Why?

2. **Applying** What are three ways that you and your family can make shopping on the Internet safer for yourselves?

Activity: Economics Connection

Making Connections Discuss how the Internet has changed the way Americans live and work. **Ask:** How have Americans' jobs changed since the development of the Internet? *(More workers are able to work from home, workers can be connected to offices 24 hours a day everyday; new jobs have been created from webmaster to designing and selling virtual clothes; homes, and furniture for virtual characters.)* Organize students into groups. Have each group select and research an Internet career. Then have each group write an employment advertisement for an Internet job specifying the job's duties, requirements, and salary. Students should use at least three Internet sources in their research. **AL**

Visual Summary

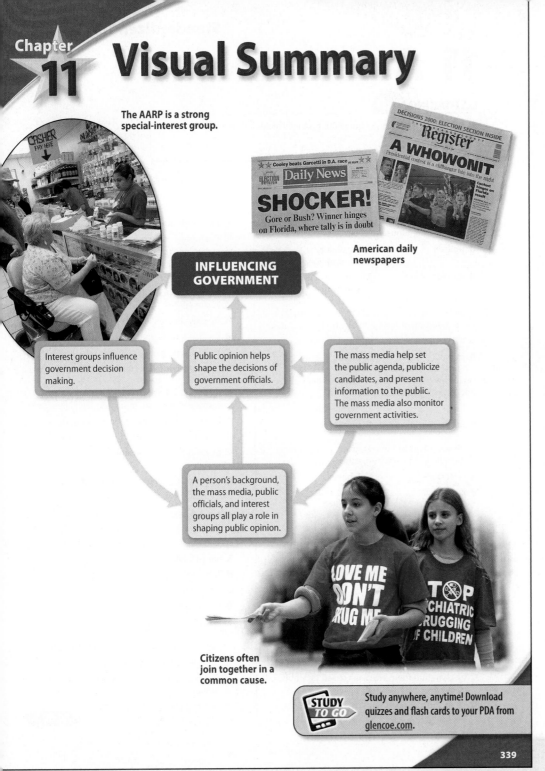

The AARP is a strong special-interest group.

American daily newspapers

INFLUENCING GOVERNMENT

Interest groups influence government decision making.

Public opinion helps shape the decisions of government officials.

The mass media help set the public agenda, publicize candidates, and present information to the public. The mass media also monitor government activities.

A person's background, the mass media, public officials, and interest groups all play a role in shaping public opinion.

Citizens often join together in a common cause.

STUDY TO GO Study anywhere, anytime! Download quizzes and flash cards to your PDA from glencoe.com.

Comparing and Contrasting Have students research opinion polls about public issues most important to voters in the most recent national elections. Then have the students contribute to a group summary of their findings. Next have students choose states. The students will use www.senate.gov to research the views of a senator from their chosen state and compare and contrast the senator's views with public opinion. **Ask:** What were the three most important issues for voters? Which senators agreed with those views and which senators disagreed with those views? Did those senators who disagreed win a recent election? Have students create a chart listing which senators supported and which senators disagreed with public opinion. Have students indicate whether the senators won election or were defeated. Students may present their findings to the class. **AL**

Drawing Conclusions Have students go on the Internet and find three editorials on the same subject from three different newspapers around the country. Then have students list the point of view of each newspaper. Have students determine the direction and intensity of the editorial. Have students discuss what factors may have influenced the point of view of each newspaper editorial. Remind students to consider the locations of each paper and their local industries and populations. **OL**

Hands-On Chapter Project
Step 4: Wrap-Up

Creating a Public Interest Campaign

Step 4: Demonstrating Concern Have students stage a protest using the plan they developed in Step 3.

Directions Write the Big Idea on the board. Using the plan they developed in Step 3, have students incorporate posters, music, movement, and/or a skit that dramatizes their cause.

Summarizing Have groups stage their protests in class. Then have volunteers share what they learned about the Big Idea. Encourage the class to discuss whether or not the protests successfully communicated the concerns of each interest group. **OL**

11 ASSESSMENT

Answers and Analyses

Reviewing Vocabulary

1. A Students will have read about pollsters in Section 1 in a section entitled What Do Pollsters Do?

2. C In this question, the most confusing distracter will most likely be answer B, public opinion. The phrase most time and money in the question should direct students to the correct answer.

3. D The definition of prior restraint can be found in the Media Safeguards portion of Section 2. Understanding that censorship and prior restraint are synonymous will help students answer this question.

4. C All of the answers for this question may seem plausible if students do not read carefully. Remember that lobbyists got their name because they hung around the lobbies of official buildings in order to meet the politician they wished to influence.

Reviewing Main Ideas

5. B Public opinion polls are aimed at helping officials understand the views of the public, and not at persuading the public to support officials. The public official who changes his position based on public opinion is not trying to persuade others to support him. Similarly, it is not necessary to persuade those who share the same belief. This leaves B as the only possible correct answer.

6. B While all of the options here are important issues in polling, only one is discussed in the Push Polls segment of Section 1. Students should recall from their reading that push polls use questions that are worded in order to sway the respondent's answer to the pollster's particular bias.

7. C This question presents a challenge in that all the answers are functions of the media. However, the student should understand that the "watchdog" role of the media refers to its role in exposing public officials' misconduct.

---

11 ASSESSMENT

TEST-TAKING TIP

> When answering an essay question, give specific details to support your main ideas.

Reviewing Vocabulary

Directions: Choose the word(s) that best completes the sentence.

1. A(n) _____ measures public attitudes toward possible White House proposals.

  A pollster   **C** regulatory commission

  B interest group   **D** political action committee

2. Issues that receive the most time and money from government leaders make up the _____.

  A mass media   **C** public agenda

  B public opinion   **D** public interest group

3. Government censorship of material before it is published is called _____.

  A libel   **C** partisanship

  B malice   **D** prior restraint

4. Representatives of interest groups who contact public officials directly are called _____.

  A celebrities   **C** lobbyists

  B journalists   **D** white-collar criminals

Reviewing Main Ideas

Directions: Choose the best answer for each question.

Section 1 *(pp. 318–324)*

5. How do public officials try to persuade as many people as possible to support their positions?

  A by conducting public opinion polls

  B by promoting their views in the mass media

  C by changing their positions based on public opinion

  D by forming groups with others who share their beliefs

6. Why do responsible pollsters condemn push polls?

  A Push polls discourage voting.

  B Push poll questions are biased.

  C Push polls use too few respondents.

  D Push poll samples are seldom random.

Section 2 *(pp. 326–330)*

7. How do mass media act as a "watchdog" over government?

  A by covering leaks from public officials

  B by airing news that attracts more viewers

  C by exposing public officials' misconduct

  D by publicizing entertainers running for office

8. How does the Federal Communications Commission regulate radio and television?

  A by penalizing stations for breaking rules

  B by suing scriptwriters for committing libel

  C by monitoring programmers suspected of malice

  D by censoring objectionable material in broadcasts

Section 3 *(pp. 332–337)*

9. What interest group would most likely back a candidate who supports laws to protect nature?

  A Sierra Club

  B Tobacco Institute

  C Chamber of Commerce

  D League of Women Voters

10. What do critics of interest groups claim?

  A Interest groups have too much influence.

  B Interest groups provide necessary services.

  C Interest groups enable Americans to organize.

  D Interest groups communicate the people's wishes.

GO ON

---

8. A Students should reread the section "Media Safeguards" in Section 2. Here they will learn about the freedoms enjoyed by and the limits placed upon the media. A reading of the section will show that the FCC regulates media by penalizing stations that violate its rules.

9. A In the section Types of Interest Groups, students learned about special and public interest groups. The names of the interest groups in the answers provide clues to the correct answer. For example, the Tobacco Institute is an economic interest group focused on the concerns of the tobacco industry. Sierra refers to a beautiful mountain environment in California. Since it refers to something in nature, students should be able to select the most likely answer A, the Sierra Club.

10. A The word "critics" indicates that the correct answer makes a negative claim about interest groups. Since all of the other

Critical Thinking

Directions: Base your answers to questions 11 and 12 on the diagram below and your knowledge of Chapter 11.

Techniques	How to Recognize It
Name-calling	Referring to an opponent with an unpleasant label or description, such as "un-American"
Glittering generality	Vague or broad statement containing little substance
Card stacking	Giving only one side of the facts to support a position
Transfer of symbol	Associating a patriotic symbol with a point of view or person
Just plain folks	Identifying a person as "just one of the common people"
Testimonial or endorsement	A celebrity endorses a person or point of view
The bandwagon	Urging people to support a position or person because everyone else is

11. Analyze the following passages from special-interest Web sites. Which uses glittering generalities?

A The Sierra Club's members are more than 750,000 of your friends and neighbors.

B Hispanic-American Soldiers have embodied the army's core values for generations.

C The arrogance of anti-gun politicians and their hate of freedom will churn your stomach.

D Robert Redford urges Americans to call on their representative to vote against any bill that would plunder the Arctic Refuge.

12. Which passage uses name-calling?

A The Sierra Club's members are more than 750,000 of your friends and neighbors.

B Hispanic-American Soldiers have embodied the Army's core values for generations.

C The arrogance of anti-gun politicians and their hate of freedom will churn your stomach.

D Robert Redford urges Americans to call on their representative to vote against any bill that would plunder the Arctic Refuge.

Document-Based Questions

Directions: Analyze the following document and answer the short-answer questions that follow.

The following passage discusses reporting on the occupation of Iraq.

> There were photos of the platoon, guns over shoulders, praying for the fallen buddy. The Times *is* careful not to ruin the heroic mood, so there is no photograph of pieces of corporal Smith's shattered head. Instead, there's an old, smiling photo of the wounded soldier.
>
> The reporter, undoubtedly wearing the Kevlar armor of the troop in which he's "embedded," quotes at length the thoughts of the military medic: "I would like to say that I am a good man. But seeing this now, what happened to Smith, I want to hurt people. You know what I mean?"
>
> The reporter does not bother — or dare — to record a single word from any Iraqi in the town of Karma where Smith's platoon was, "performing a hard hit on a house."
>
> And if we asked, I'm sure the sniper would tell us, "I am a good man, but seeing what happened, I want to hurt people."
>
> —Greg Palast, "I Want to Hurt Somebody"

13. Why do you think the author mentions that the reporter is "embedded"?

14. In the third paragraph, the author implies that the reporter used a propaganda technique. Which one?

Extended Response

15. Write a brief essay about requirements for a well-constructed public opinion poll.

For additional test practice, use Self-Check Quizzes— Chapter 11 on glencoe.com.

ASSESSMENT

Document-Based Questions

13. Students' answers will vary. A possible answer is that the author is implying that the reporter will view events from the troops' perspective.

14. card-stacking

Extended Response

15. Students' essays will vary. Look for supporting details from the chapter.

If you missed question...	1	2	3	4	5	6	7	8	9	10	11	12	13	14	15
Go to page...	323	327	329	335	320	324	328	330	333	336	336	336	328	336	323

Need Extra Help?

choices are positive, students should choose the answer A, "Interest groups have too much influence."

Critical Thinking

11. B The student should review the chart to understand the definition of each propaganda technique used by interest groups. Students should compare the statements in the answers to find the technique they most closely match. For question 11, stu-dents should find the passage that contains the broadest statement. Since Answer B gives no specific information, it is a glittering generality.

12. C The student should review the chart to understand the definition of each propaganda technique used by interest groups. For this answer, students should choose the passage that uses name-calling—answer C.

Have students visit the Web site at glencoe.com to review Chapter 11 and take the **Self-Check Quiz**.

Need Extra Help?

Have students refer to the pages listed if they miss any of the questions.

Focus

Extending the Right to Vote

R₁ Reading Strategy

Predicting Remind students that Americans such as Susan B. Anthony and Dr. Martin Luther King, Jr. worked on behalf of special interests. **Ask: What can we assume about the methods of special interest groups in which Susan B. Anthony and Dr. Martin Luther King, Jr. worked?** *(Answers may include, they wrote editorials, lobbied government officials, and staged demonstrations.)* **BL**

R₂ Reading Strategy

Inferring Remind students that the right of citizens to choose their leaders by voting is what makes our nation a democracy. **Ask: Why might some citizens want to keep others from voting?** *(Answers may include, to prevent them from gaining power and for protection.)* **OL**

Reading Focus

On Election Day, every citizen over the age of 18 is able to cast a vote. It is a right that defines our nation as a democracy. But universal suffrage—letting everyone vote—did not appear overnight with the ratification of our Constitution. Many Americans struggled to gain the right to vote.

Read to Discover

As you read, think about the following:

* Why did it take so long for many people to win voting rights?
* How were voting rights extended?

Reader's Dictionary

peer: a person who has equal standing with another or others

comply: meet the terms

The Fight for Woman Suffrage

Susan B. Anthony was a leader in the fight for legal rights for women.

It may be delayed longer than we think; it may be here sooner than we expect; but the day will come when man will recognize woman as his **peer,** not only at the fireside but in the councils of the nation. Then, and not until then, will there be . . . the ideal union between the sexes that shall result in the highest development of the race. What this shall be we may not attempt to define, but this we know, that only good can come to the individual or to the nation through the rendering of exact justice.

—Susan B. Anthony, article on woman suffrage

Promoting Voting Rights

Martin Luther King, Jr., explains why the right to vote is vital.

"We know that Americans of good will have learned that no nation can long continue to flourish or to find its way to a better society while it allows any one of its citizens . . . to be denied the right to participate in the most fundamental of all privileges of democracy—the right to vote."

—Dr. Martin Luther King, Jr., "Civil Rights No. 1: The Right to Vote"

Native American Suffrage

Native Americans also were denied equal rights.

The Indian Citizenship Act of 1924 granted Native Americans citizenship. However, it still took more than 40 years for all 50 states to allow Native Americans to vote.

In order to exercise the right of suffrage, Indians must of course **comply** with the conditions equally required of other voters, and may be denied the privilege of voting if they fail to comply with the requirements of the law as to registration, payment of poll tax, or do not meet the educational or other qualifications for electors, etc., as provided by the State laws.

—Indian Citizenship Act of 1924

Additional Reading

Review suggested books before assigning them.

Anarchy, State, and Utopia, by Robert Nozick discusses the political and social views of liberals, socialists, and conservatives.

Leader by Destiny, by Jeanette Eaton details the life of George Washington, who served in the Revolutionary War and became the first president of the United States.

Martin Luther King, Jr. and the Freedom Movement by Lillie Patterson traces Martin Luther King, Jr., on his march for equal rights, from the Montgomery bus boycott of 1955 to the Selma protest of 1965.

The Voting Rights Act

The purpose of this Act is to ensure that the right of all citizens to vote, including the right to register to vote and cast meaningful votes, is preserved and protected as guaranteed by the Constitution. . . .

The record compiled by Congress demonstrates that, without the continuation of the Voting Rights Act of 1965 protections, racial and language minority citizens will be deprived of the opportunity to exercise their right to vote, or will have their votes diluted, undermining the significant gains made by minorities in the last 40 years.

—H. R. 9, the bill to extend the 1965 Voting Rights Act

Civil rights leader John Lewis, who helped organize voter registration drives in the 1960s, spoke out in favor of extending the Voting Rights Act.

"The Voting Rights Act is the heart and soul of our Democracy. The Voting Rights Act literally ushered in the possibility of transforming electoral politics. In the American South, you had millions who could not vote because of the color of their skin."

—John Lewis on the renewal of the Voting Rights Act

Why I Vote

A college student explains why voting is important.

As a child growing up with parents who were immigrants and had no voice in their country, I was able to see the importance of voting. When my parents became American citizens they took me and my siblings into the voting booth with them every time.

—Sonia Zobdeh, student at Brooklyn College

Photographs as Primary Sources What can you learn from the photo about the people who demonstrated in Selma, Alabama, in the 1950s? What kind of demonstration did they hold?

Document-Based Questions

1. **Interpreting** What did Anthony mean when she argued that women should be recognized as peers to men "not only at the fireside but in the councils of the nation"?

2. **Explaining** What did King mean when he called the right to vote "the most fundamental of all privileges of a democracy"?

3. **Explaining** Why was the right to vote not extended to all Native Americans, despite passage of the Indian Citizenship Act?

4. **Evaluating and Connecting** If Susan B. Anthony and Martin Luther King, Jr., were alive today, what issues do you think they might be addressing? Why?

343

Did You Know?

Woman Suffrage Born into a Quaker family in 1885, American Alice Paul was raised to believe in equality of the sexes. Inspired by Susan B. Anthony, as a young woman she visited England and observed the actions of English suffragists and joined in their struggle.

On her return home, Paul used what she had learned in England to fight for votes for American women. Paul organized women to picket the White House. Eventually, the shocked public came to admire the bravery of Paul and her fellow pickets who faced violent mobs, false imprisonment, and horrific prison conditions. As public sentiment turned, President Woodrow Wilson endorsed a suffrage amendment. Finally, on August 18, 1920 the 19th Amendment was ratified and American women gained the right to vote.

Unit ★ Planning Guide
4

	Unit 4	Chapter 12	Chapter 13	Chapter 14
Day 1	Unit Opener, Reading Social Studies	Chapter Opener, Section 1, Financial Literacy	Chapter Opener, Section 1	Chapter Opener, Section 1
Day 2		Section 2, Issues to Debate	Section 2	Section 2, Financial Literacy
Day 3		Section 3	Section 3	Section 3, Visual Summary, Chapter Review
Day 4		Section 4, Landmark Supreme Court Case Studies	Chapter Review, Visual Summary	Chapter Assessment
Day 5		Visual Summary, Chapter Review	Chapter Assessment	TIME Reports
Day 6		Chapter Assessment		Analyzing Primary Sources

Teacher to Teacher

Vanessa Lal Steinkamp, Adlai Stevenson High School, Chicago, Illinois

Tackling Community Issues This activity will increase student awareness in local government and community issues. Organize students into groups of three or four. After a brief discussion in each group, tell students to choose a community problem dealing with an educational, social or environmental issue that is of interest to their group. Then have students create a plan of action to affect change regarding their issue of interest. Each group should first discuss the various elements of state and local government and determine if their issue is a state or local issue. Students will then prepare a proposal to present to the proper state, city, town, township or village for review indicating why this issue is so important, and why they believe that facet of government should tackle their issue. Students should then present their proposals to the class for discussion.

Author Note

Dear Social Studies Teacher:

Headlines in our daily newspapers inform us about public policy issues that our state and local governments confront. They draw the attention of readers to dramatic stories about controversies pertaining to environmental pollution, school choice, crime prevention, civil rights, public health, and many other community concerns.

We depend upon our state and local governments to authoritatively resolve such public policy issues through interaction with engaged citizens. Thus, we expect good citizens to raise and monitor issues of concern to them and to influence policy decisions by their representatives in government about these issues. Political participation in response to public policy issues is democracy in action.

In order to prepare your students for democratic citizenship, I urge you to teach them how to use newspapers, television, and the Internet to identify pressing public policy issues in your community. You also should help them recognize when and how these issues become occasions for local and state governments to make public policy decisions. Finally, I advise you to involve students individually and collectively in the investigation and discussion of public policy issues and the process of decision making about them.

Make issues-based teaching and learning a staple of civic education in your classroom. If you do it, your classroom will become a living laboratory in which students learn democracy by doing it.

Teaching about hot topics and pressing public issues of your state and local governments, which prompt constructive critical thinking and careful decision making by your students, is an essential element of civic education. This is the way to develop responsible and reflective citizens, who can maintain and improve constitutional government in our democratic republic.

John J. Patrick

Author

Unit Objectives

After studying this unit, students will be able to:

- Explain the powers and responsibilities of state governments.

- Identify various systems of local governments.

- Recognize how state and local governments deal with community issues.

Did You Know?

According to the Center for Information and Research on Civic Learning and Engagement (CIRCLE), a survey of 14-year-olds showed that those who feel involved in running their school are more interested in current events than other youth. Students who participate in classroom current events discussions have a greater interest in politics, improved critical thinking and communication skills, more civic knowledge, and greater interest in discussing public affairs outside school than those who do not participate.

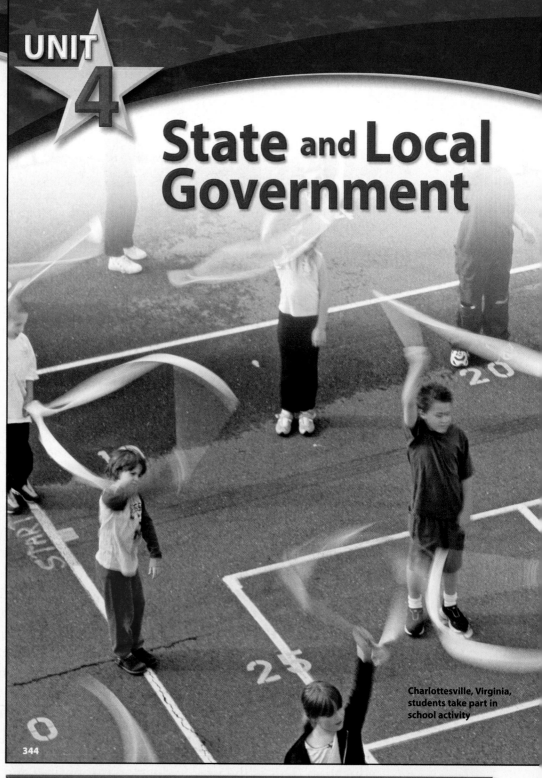

UNIT ★ 4

State and Local Government

Charlottesville, Virginia, students take part in school activity

344

Activity: Launching the Unit

Why Study State and Local Government? Ask: How does the U.S. Constitution make state government powerful? What state and local power affects the life of every student in the United States? *(According to the Tenth Amendment of the Constitution, all powers not specifically given to the federal government or prohibited to state governments are reserved to the states or to the people. Public education is administered by state and local governments. While each state's Department of Public Instruction establishes and oversees educational requirements within their states, local school boards create and administer policies within their communities. At the state level, educational standards are set for each curriculum area, such as social studies and science. Teachers and administrators work to apply these standards as they educate students.)* **OL**

Be an Active Citizen

CITIZENSHIP State and local government issues are closest to citizens. Identify a local issue in your community that concerns you. Find out facts about it, and form an opinion about it. Make a poster expressing this opinion to put in your classroom.

345

Be an Active Citizen

CITIZENSHIP Are your students aware of community issues of concern? Invite a panel of community leaders to your classroom: the managing editor of the local newspaper, the school district superintendent, the mayor or city manager, the chairperson of the county board of supervisors, and one or more representatives of nonprofit social-issue organizations. Ask students to direct questions to the panel to define local concerns about broad topics such as education, poverty, hunger, homelessness, and so on. Have students take notes on their responses and use the information to create posters on a single issue of concern.

Online Current Events Update

Visit Glencoe's *Online Current Events Update* at www.glencoe.com to find news reports, features, maps, graphs, and photos of current events that shape our lives. Students can also make connections between historical events and current events by using the interactive time line.

More About the Photo

Visual Literacy Just as these students from Charlottesville, Virginia, work together to produce the flag show, so Americans work with local government to resolve community issues. To encourage civic participation, Theodore Roosevelt helped found the National Civic League in 1894. The NCL, a nonpartisan, nonprofit organization, seeks to build communities and to promote local government reform. Its All-American City Award program annually recognizes communities in which citizens, businesses, government, and nonprofit organizations work together on social and civic issues. Since 1949, more than 4,000 communities have competed and nearly 500 have earned the title of All-American City.

Why Distinguishing Fact from Opinion **Is Important**

Much of what people read is a mixture of fact (truth) and opinion (personal views on an issue, person, or event). When students are able to distinguish fact from opinion, they are better able to critically question and evaluate what they read. Readers are better able to detect writer bias, which may influence how the readers then think or act. As writers, students can distinguish between expository and persuasive writing. As citizens, they are better able to interact with diverse peoples without prejudice and preconceptions.

 Learn It!

Read the following statement aloud: "Because students have different interests, there should be no required courses in school curriculum." Have students identify the statement as fact or opinion. Discuss signal words that help students identify opinions, such as "should," "ought," "think," "feel," and "believe." Ask students to work in groups to list reasons that support or contradict the statement. **OL**

Distinguishing Fact from Opinion

 Learn It!

A fact is something that can be proven or documented and does not change unless new evidence disproves it. On the other hand, an opinion is what you believe based upon your own viewpoints or feelings. Opinions can change from person to person, but everyone agrees that facts are true. When you read, it is important to distinguish fact from opinion.

- Read the paragraph below.
- Identify the facts in the paragraph.
- Read how one student used the facts to form an opinion about state lotteries.

> In a recent year Americans spent $50 billion on state lotteries—more money than on reading materials or attending movies. Half of that money was returned to the winners. After paying their other costs, the states kept about $15 billion. Many states use the money to help finance education.
>
> *—from page 361*

Chart

Reading Tip
To distinguish fact from opinion, look for phrases such as I believe or I think to note statements that are opinions.

Facts	Opinion
1. Americans spent $50 billon on state lotteries. 2. Half of the money was returned to the winners. 3. States kept about $15 billion. 4. Many states use the money to help finance education.	Lotteries are a good way to raise money for education. People like to play the lottery, and at the same time they are helping their state with education costs.

Reading Strategy ⟩ Determining Importance

Distinguishing Fact from Opinion Students encounter both facts and opinions in their everyday lives. Organize students into groups. List the following real-life situations on the board under the sentence opener

You are: serving on a jury; a state legislator; a municipal court judge. Have students discuss why the ability to distinguish fact from opinion is important in each position. **BL**

② Practice It!

Read the following paragraph from this unit.

- Draw a chart like the one shown below.
- Write facts from the paragraph in the column on the left.
- Write your opinion about cities in the paragraph in the column on the right.

> . . . City leaders [in Galveston] decided that a commission government was the best way to handle the emergency.
>
> Since that time, however, other cities have found that a commission government is not always efficient in running a city. Without clear leadership, a commission is often unable to set and meet goals. Each commissioner is likely to concentrate primarily on his or her own department, without considering the problems of the city as a whole.
>
> —*From page 381*

Facts	Opinion

③ Apply It!

There are many facts presented in Chapters 12, 13, and 14 about state government. You may have no opinion about some of the facts, but others may cause you to think about your own beliefs or feelings. At least three times in each chapter, stop reading and write your opinion about a fact in the text. Share your opinions with others in the class.

Read to Write Activity

Read *Teens in Action* on page 354. Jot down facts about Prateek Peres-da-Silva. Then, write a paragraph in which you express your opinion about his activities in the Governor's Page Program.

② Practice It!

On the board, write the following statements taken directly or modified from the text of Chapter 12: *Because the states created the national government, all of the national government's powers should be limited.* (opinion) *The "necessary and proper" clause in Article I of the Constitution means that Congress has the right to adopt any means it needs to carry out its delegated powers.* (fact) *A state cannot legally punish a person for breaking the laws of another state.* (fact) *States need to cooperate and share responsibilities for maintaining common services, such as transportation facilities.* (opinion) Have students work in pairs to distinguish factual from opinion statements. **OL**

③ Apply It!

Bring a collection of newspaper and magazine articles and editorials to class. Remove headings and salutations that would reveal that the selection is an opinion, such as *To the Editor, Editorial,* and so on. Have students work in pairs to distinguish fact from opinion in their selection. Ask students to underline facts and to circle opinions. **OL**

Reading Strategy · Read to Write

Writing Editorials When writing persuasive pieces such as editorials, students need to clearly state their opinions while supporting them with facts. Have students write an editorial about a controversial issue in Chapter 12, such as the federal government's elimination of many grants-in-aid, the "necessary and proper clause" in the Constitution, mandatory deductions from workers' gross pay, and so on. Remind students to support their opinion with facts. Have students exchange their editorials with partners and comment on how well their partners expressed and supported their opinions. **OL**

Chapter Planning Guide

12

Key to Ability Levels
BL Below Level   **AL** Above Level
OL On Level   **ELL** English Language Learners

Key to Teaching Resources
Print Material   Transparency
CD-ROM or DVD

Levels BL	OL	AL	ELL		Resources	Chapter Opener	Section 1	Section 2	Section 3	Section 4	Chapter Assess
					FOCUS						
BL	OL	AL	ELL	🖨	**Daily Focus Skills Transparencies**		12–1	12–2	12–3	12–4	
					TEACH						
BL	OL		ELL	📁	**Reading Essentials and Note-Taking Guide***		p. 111	p. 114	p. 117	p. 120	
		AL		📁	**Enrichment Activity, URB**		p. 13				
	OL	AL		📁	**Primary Source Reading, URB**		p. 15				
BL	OL	AL	ELL	📁	**Content Vocabulary Activity, URB***	p. 20	p. 20	p. 20	p. 20	p. 20	
BL	OL	AL	ELL	📁	**Academic Vocabulary Activity, URB**	p. 21	p. 21	p. 21	p. 21	p. 21	
	OL			📁	**Biography Activity, URB**				p. 23		
BL	OL	AL	ELL	📁	**Writing Skills Activity, URB**				p. 25		
	OL	AL		📁	**Critical Thinking Skills Activity, URB**		p. 27				
BL	OL	AL	ELL	📁	**Chart, Graph, and Map Skills Activity, URB**		p. 29		p. 29		
BL	OL	AL	ELL	📁	**Differentiated Instruction, URB**		p. 31				
BL	OL	AL	ELL	📁	**School-to-Home Connection Activity, URB***	p. 33	p. 33	p. 33	p. 33	p. 33	
BL	OL		ELL	📁	**Guided Reading Activities, URB***		p. 37	p. 38	p. 39	p. 40	
	OL	AL		📁	**Supreme Court Cases**				p. 81		
BL	OL	AL	ELL	📁	**Writer's Guidebook**	✓	✓	✓	✓	✓	✓
	OL	AL		💿	**Primary Source Document Library**	✓	✓	✓	✓	✓	✓
BL	OL	AL	ELL	💿	**Daily Lecture & Discussion Notes (in Pres. Plus)**		✓	✓	✓	✓	✓
BL	OL	AL	ELL	💿	**StudentWorks™ Plus**		✓	✓	✓	✓	✓
BL	OL	AL	ELL	💿	**Section Spotlight Videos**		✓	✓	✓	✓	
BL	OL	AL	ELL	🖨	**TIME Interpreting Political Cartoons Transp.**			Ch. 12			
BL	OL	AL	ELL	🖨	**Writing Process Transparencies**	✓	✓	✓	✓	✓	✓

Note: Please refer to the *Unit 4 Resource Book* for this chapter's URB materials.

* Also available in Spanish

TeacherWorks Plus
All-In-One Planner and Resource Center

- Interactive Lesson Planner
- Interactive Teacher Edition
- Fully editable blackline masters
- Section Spotlight Videos Launch
- Differentiated Lesson Plans
- Printable reports of daily assignments
- Standards Tracking System

Levels					Resources	Chapter Opener	Section 1	Section 2	Section 3	Section 4	Chapter Assess
BL	OL	AL	ELL								
					TEACH (continued)						
				📁	**Building Academic Vocabulary**	✓	✓	✓	✓	✓	✓
Teacher Resources				📁	**Strategies for Success**	✓	✓	✓	✓	✓	✓
				📁	**Teacher's Guide to Differentiated Instruction**	✓	✓	✓	✓	✓	✓
				💿	**Graphing Tool**	✓	✓	✓	✓	✓	✓
				💿	**Presentation Plus! with MindJogger CheckPoint**	✓	✓	✓	✓	✓	✓
					ASSESS						
BL	OL	AL	ELL	📁	**Quizzes and Tests***		p. 140	p. 141	p. 142	p. 143	p. 144
BL	OL	AL	ELL	📁	**Authentic Assessment with Rubrics**		p. 16	p. 16	p. 16	p. 16	
BL	OL	AL	ELL	📁	**Standardized Test Practice**		p. 23	p. 23	p. 23	p. 23	p. 23
BL	OL	AL	ELL	💿	**ExamView® Assessment Suite CD-ROM**		12–1	12–2	12–3	12–4	Ch. 12
					CLOSE						
BL			ELL	📁	**Reteaching Activity, URB***		p. 35	p. 35	p. 35	p. 35	
BL	OL		ELL	📁	**Reading and Study Skills Foldables™ Activity**	p. 72	p. 73			p. 73	
BL	OL	AL	ELL	🖥️	**Graphic Organizer Transparencies & Strategies**	✓	✓	✓	✓	✓	✓

✓ Chapter- or unit-based activities applicable to all sections in this chapter

12

Searching by Keyword, Author, or Title

What is the Primary Source Document Library Database?

Glencoe's *American History Primary Source Document Library CD-ROMs* includes more than 200 primary source documents to help supplement various lesson plans.

How can the Primary Source Document Library Database help my students?

By allowing students to perform searches using a Keyword, Author, or Title, the *American History Primary Source Document Library* provides versatile access to new sources of knowledge that encourage students to think critically about history and historical concepts. After performing a search, students can:

- choose documents from the results list to read and/or listen to
- utilize Teaching Strategies, Questions/Answers, and Blackline Masters resources in conjunction with the primary source document to maximize student learning

Civics ONLINE
Visit glencoe.com and enter *QuickPass*™ code CIV1360c12T for Chapter 12 resources.

You can easily launch a wide range of digital products from your computer's desktop with the McGraw-Hill Social Studies widget.

	Student	Teacher	Parent
Media Library			
• Student Edition Section Audio	●		●
• Spanish Audio Summaries	●		●
• Section Spotlight Videos	●	●	●
***Civics Today* Online Learning Center (Web Site)**			
• Chapter Overviews	●	●	●
• Study Central™	●	●	●
• Study-to-Go	●	●	●
• Student Web Activities	●	●	●
• In Motion Animation	●	●	●
• Self-Check Quizzes	●	●	●
• ePuzzles and Games	●	●	●
• StudentWorks™ Plus Online	●	●	●
• Vocabulary eFlashcards	●	●	●
• Web Activity Lesson Plans		●	
• Vocabulary PuzzleMaker	●	●	●
Classroom Tools			
• Multilingual Glossary	●	●	●
• Beyond the Textbook	●	●	●
• NGS MapMachine	●	●	●

Use this database to search more than 30,000 titles to create a customized reading list for your students.

- Reading lists can be organized by students' reading level, author, genre, theme, or area of interest.
- The database provides Degrees of Reading Power™ (DRP) and Lexile™ readability scores for all selections.
- A brief summary of each selection is included.

Leveled reading suggestions for this chapter:

For students at a Grade 7 reading level:
- *The Iroquois Constitution,* by Dekanawida

For students at a Grade 8 reading level:
- *The Helping Hands Handbook,* by Patricia Adams and Jean Marzollo

For students at a Grade 9 reading level:
- *The United States v. The Amistad: The Question of Slavery in a Free Country,* by David Hulm

For students at a Grade 10 reading level:
- *God and Government: The Separation of Church and State,* by Ann E. Weiss

For students at a Grade 11 reading level:
- *National Defense,* by James Fallows

- **Timed Readings Plus in Social Studies** helps students increase their reading rate and fluency while maintaining comprehension. The 400-word passages are similar to those found on state and national assessments.

- **Reading in the Content Area: Social Studies** concentrates on six essential reading skills that help students better comprehend what they read. The book includes 75 high-interest nonfiction passages written at increasing levels of difficulty.

- **Reading Social Studies** includes strategic reading instruction and vocabulary support in Social Studies content for both ELLs and native speakers of English.

- **Content Vocabulary Workout** (Grades 6–8) accelerates reading comprehension through focused vocabulary development. Social Studies content vocabulary comes from the glossaries of Glencoe's Middle School Social Studies texts. www.jamestowneducation.com

KEY Teacher Wraparound

Use this key to help you identify the different types of prompts found in the Teacher Wraparound Edition.

R **Reading Strategies** activities help you teach reading skills and vocabulary.

C **Critical Thinking** strategies help students apply and extend what they have learned.

D **Differentiated Instruction** activities provide instruction for students learning to speak English, along with suggestions for teaching various types of learners.

S **Skill Practice** strategies help students practice historical analysis and geography skills.

W **Writing Support** activities provide writing opportunities to help students comprehend the text.

Teaching strategies and activities have been coded for ability level appropriateness.

AL Activities for students working above grade level

OL Activities for students working on grade level

BL Activities for students working below grade level

ELL Activities for English Language Learners

Focus

Why It Matters

Ask: How is the structure of state government similar to that of the federal government? *(Both levels of government have three branches: legislative, executive, and judicial. Each level has a chief executive: the president and a state's governor. With the exception of Nebraska, all states have bicameral legislatures similar to Congress. Both levels have court systems, with the top court in both systems called the Supreme Court.)*

More About the Photo

Visual Literacy Troopers of the Texas Highway patrol are responsible for enforcing traffic and criminal law, usually in unincorporated areas. They also serve as the Texas state police. State troopers also serve in management and administrative positions at Driver License Division offices. Every division office has at least 2 uniformed troopers assigned to it. One plain-clothes trooper also serves as the office's administrator.

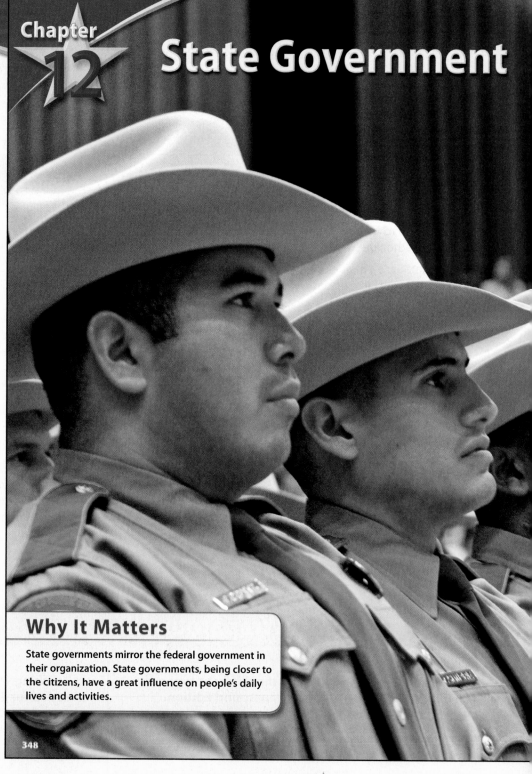

Chapter
12
State Government

Why It Matters

State governments mirror the federal government in their organization. State governments, being closer to the citizens, have a great influence on people's daily lives and activities.

348

Teach

BIG Ideas *As you begin teaching each section, use these questions and activities to help students focus on the Big Ideas.*

Section 1

The Federal System **Ask:** Which powers do state governments share with the federal government? *(Answers may include any of the following: collect taxes, charter corporations and banks, borrow money, build roads, establish courts, make and enforce laws, and spend money for the general welfare.)* Point out that in Section 1 students will examine how state governments work with each other and with the national government. **OL**

Section 2

The State Legislative Branch **Ask:** What limit is placed on state legislation? *(It may not violate the Constitution or previously established federal law.)* Tell students that in Section 2 they will learn how state legislatures function and address problems such as funding public services. **OL**

Civics **ONLINE**
Visit glencoe.com and enter
QuickPass™ code
CIV3093c12 for
Chapter 12
resources.

BIG Ideas

Section 1: The Federal System

Under our federal system, power is shared between the national government and the state governments. Our federal system also establishes a special relationship between the national government and those of the individual states.

Section 2: The State Legislative Branch

The Constitution gives the legislative branch— Congress—the power to make laws. State governments, which generally mirror the federal government in organization, address problems closer to citizens.

Section 3: The State Executive Branch

The Constitution gives the executive branch the power to execute, or implement, the law. Like the president on the national level, governors are the chief executives of the states.

Section 4: The State Judicial Branch

The judicial branch is charged with interpreting the law. Different levels of state courts administer justice.

Texas State troopers receive their commission

FOLDABLES Dinah Zike's
Study Organizer Foldables

Purpose This Foldable guides the student to understand the branches of the state government system in comparison to the federal system. The completed Foldable will use tabs to help them identify the different branches. **OL**

More Foldables activities for this chapter can be found in the *Dinah Zike's Reading and Study Skills Foldables* ancillary.

Civics **ONLINE**
Visit glencoe.com and enter
QuickPass™ code CIV1360c12T for Chapter 12 resources, including a Chapter Overview, Study Central™, Study-to-Go, Student Web Activity, Self-Check Quiz, and other materials.

FOLDABLES
Study Organizer

Organizing Information Study Foldable Make the following Foldable to organize information about the branches of state government.

Step 1 Mark the midpoint of the side edge of one sheet of paper. Then fold in the outside edges to touch the midpoint.

Cut along the fold lines on both sides.

Step 2 Fold the paper in half from side to side.

Step 3 Open and cut along the inside fold lines to form four tabs. Label the Foldable as shown.

Reading and Writing Fill out your Foldable as you read the chapter. You will organize information about the federal system and the three branches of state government.

Federal System | State Legislative Branch
State Executive Branch | State Judicial Branch

Section 3

The State Executive Branch Ask: What are the qualities of a successful governor? *(Answers may include the abilities to lead, to enlist the cooperation of diverse groups, to listen and respond to citizens' needs, to effectively represent state interests on the national scene, and to make decisions that are in the best welfare of the state.)* Explain that in Section 3 students will learn about the roles played by state governors. **OL**

Section 4

The State Judicial Branch Ask: Why is it necessary for state courts to settle the majority of legal matters? *(Answers may include the idea that federal courts are reserved for interstate or treaty disputes, for violations of federal law, and for cases in which local, state, or federal laws may oppose the U.S. Constitution.)* Explain that in Section 4 students will learn about the courts of the state judicial system. **OL**

Focus

Bellringer
Daily Focus Transparency 12–1

Guide to Reading
Answers to Graphic:

- federal government given delegated powers
- remaining powers reserved to states and individuals
- certain powers denied governments
- national law supremacy
- specific national-state shared powers
- governmental cooperation constitutionally provided

Federalism

Section Spotlight Video

Have students watch the Chapter 12, Section 1 video at glencoe.com.

Resource Manager

Guide to Reading

Big Idea
Under our federal system, power is shared between the national government and the state governments.

Content Vocabulary
- federal system (p. 351)
- reserved powers (p. 352)
- concurrent powers (p. 353)
- grants-in-aid (p. 353)

Academic Vocabulary
- consent (p. 351)
- expanded (p. 353)

Reading Strategy
Summarizing On a web diagram like the one below, summarize the important features of the federal system of government.

Federalism

Section 1

The Federal System

Real World Civics Did you know that your state has its own military force? The National Guard of each state, like these troops from Louisiana, is commanded by the governor of that state. The Framers established the National Guard as a way to balance state and federal power. A governor may call up the Guard during a natural disaster, such as Hurricane Katrina, or activate it to keep the peace during a civil disturbance. But the president can also federalize the Guard when needed for national interests.

▼ **National Guard patrols New Orleans, 2006**

R Reading Strategies	**C** Critical Thinking	**D** Differentiated Instruction	**W** Writing Support	**S** Skill Practice
Teacher Edition • Using Context Clues, p. 351 • Making Connections, p. 351 • Act. Prior Know., p. 353 **Additional Resources** • Pri. Source Read Act., URB p. 15 • Cont. Voc., URB p. 20 • Foldables, p. 73	**Teacher Edition** • Ident. Cent. Issues, p. 351 • Det. Cause/Effect, p. 354 **Additional Resources** • Critical Think. Act., URB p. 27	**Teacher Edition** • Visual/Spatial, p. 352 **Additional Resources** • Diff. Instr. Act., URB p. 31 • Reteaching Activity, URB p. 35	**Teacher Edition** • Persuasive Writing, p. 353 **Additional Resources** • Enrichment Activities, URB p. 13	**Teacher Edition** • Categorizing, p. 352 • Diagramming, p. 353 **Additional Resources** • Daily Focus Trans., 12–1 • Chart, Graph, and Map Skills, URB p. 29

Public Safety The states have the power to build and regulate roads as part of guarding the welfare of citizens. *Hypothesizing* Why do you think control of roadways was not left with the federal government?

Constitutional Basis for Federalism

Main Idea The U.S. Constitution created a federal system of government in which the central government and the state governments share power.

Civics & You Can you think of a way the state government affects your daily activities? Read more to find out what these state activities are and why the state pursues them.

The Constitution created a **federal system** of government, or federalism. The Constitution established an arrangement that gives the national government certain powers and reserves others for the states. There are also powers that the Constitution denies to each level of government. In addition, there are some powers that are shared by the national government and by the state governments. The sharing, however, is not equal. If a state law conflicts with a national law, the national law must be followed. Federalism is a middle position between having an all-powerful central government and a system in which the states dominate. The writers of the Constitution wanted to place some limits on national power and yet not allow the states to be so strong that the central government would be ineffective.

Protecting States

The Constitution protects states in several ways. For example, no state can be divided or merged with another state without the states' **consent,** or approval. States can maintain a militia—a military force called the National Guard—under the control of each state's governor. In a national emergency, however, the president may federalize the National Guard, putting it under control of the U.S. armed forces.

Chapter 12 **351**

D Differentiated Instruction

Visual/Spatial Have students work in pairs to create posters illustrating powers prohibited to states. **ELL**

S Skill Practice

Categorizing Ask: Of the powers reserved to states, which protect the safety of citizens? *(Most students will name establishment of police forces and law enforcement operations as well as the building of roads and bridges.)*

For additional practice on this activity, see the **Skills Handbook**. **BL**

Analyzing Charts

Answers:

1. protect the public's health, welfare, and morals
2. Answers may include the idea that both levels of government need revenue to fund programs and operations.

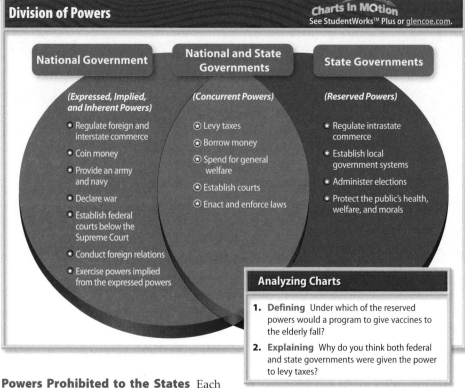

Division of Powers

Charts In MOtion
See StudentWorks™ Plus or glencoe.com.

National Government
(Expressed, Implied, and Inherent Powers)
- Regulate foreign and interstate commerce
- Coin money
- Provide an army and navy
- Declare war
- Establish federal courts below the Supreme Court
- Conduct foreign relations
- Exercise powers implied from the expressed powers

National and State Governments
(Concurrent Powers)
- Levy taxes
- Borrow money
- Spend for general welfare
- Establish courts
- Enact and enforce laws

State Governments
(Reserved Powers)
- Regulate intrastate commerce
- Establish local government systems
- Administer elections
- Protect the public's health, welfare, and morals

Analyzing Charts

1. **Defining** Under which of the reserved powers would a program to give vaccines to the elderly fall?
2. **Explaining** Why do you think both federal and state governments were given the power to levy taxes?

Powers Prohibited to the States Each state is largely free to govern itself the way its citizens consider best. Just as the U. S. Constitution denies certain powers to the national government, it also specifies what the state governments may not do. The explicit prohibitions are found in Article I, Section 10, as well as in many of the amendments to the Constitution. For example, the **D** Constitution forbids states to declare war, to issue their own money, or to impose taxes on imports from other countries or states. The Constitution forbids any state from entering into a treaty on its own with another country. In addition, several constitutional amendments prevent state governments from taking away rights granted by the federal government. The most important of these is the Fourteenth Amendment, which guarantees all Americans equal protection of the laws.

Reserved Powers

The Tenth Amendment to the U.S. Constitution establishes that state governments may exercise *all* powers *not* given to the federal government or denied to the states. These powers are called **reserved powers** because they are reserved to the states. Among them are the powers to make marriage laws, to regulate education, and to hold elections.

In general, each state is responsible for the public health, safety, and welfare of its **S** citizens. States and their governments set up police forces and other law enforcement operations. They build roads and bridges. They set educational requirements and provide money to run the schools. They organize local governments.

Using a T-Chart

Chart, Graph, and Map Activity 12, URB pp. 29–30

Objective:	To organize information by using T-charts
Focus:	Discuss with students when T-charts can help organize information.
Teach:	Ask why the details have been assigned to each column on page 29.
Assess:	Ask students how the information is organized in each of the T-charts.
Close:	Create a T-chart comparing the powers and responsibilities of the governor and the state legislature.

Differentiated Instruction Strategies

BL Make a T-chart to compare and contrast the rules at an elementary school and the rules at a middle school class.

AL What does the T-chart on page 30 tell you about the responsibilities and powers of the president as compared with those of the governor?

ELL Why is this method of organizing information called a T-chart?

Differentiated Instruction

Federal Supremacy

The Constitution grants some **concurrent powers**—those shared by state governments and the federal government. Both, for example, may impose taxes and borrow money. If, however, conflicts arise between the states and the federal government, the Supreme Court decides the case. Article VI of the Constitution states that the laws that Congress makes shall be the "supreme law of the land." This clause is called the supremacy clause.

States' Rights v. Nationalists Throughout history, Americans have argued over how federalism should operate. One view—the states' rights position—argues that because the states created the national government, all of the national government's powers should be limited. Those who favor states' rights believe that state governments are closer to the people and better reflect the people's wishes than the national government can. On the other hand, Americans who support the nationalist position argue that the people, not the states, created the national government and the states. Therefore, the powers granted to the national government should be **expanded,** or developed, as needed to carry out the people's will.

Supporters of this nationalist position argue that the "necessary and proper" clause in Article I of the Constitution means that Congress has the right to adopt any means it needs to carry out its delegated powers. Supporters of the nationalist position look to the national government to take the lead in solving major social and economic problems.

A Balancing Act The balance of powers between the national and state governments has shifted through the years. The national government's ability to wage war, to regulate commerce, and to levy taxes has strengthened the national government's authority. However, some people believe that state and local governments will always be important because Americans identify more closely with their local communities and look to these communities to understand their needs.

Governmental Cooperation

Since the 1930s, state governments and the federal government have increasingly cooperated to fund and administer a wide variety of programs. Although the money is allotted by Congress, the funds are meant to aid state and community citizens. These include funds for highways, education, and welfare. Usually the federal government provides **grants-in-aid**—awards of money—to the states to help them pay for some of their programs. States must contribute some of their own money, and they must obey rules set by Congress in order to receive these grants. The federal government gives some *grants-in-aid* directly to cities and counties. In other cases federal grants "pass through" state governments to cities.

States Provide State agencies provide things such as special telephones for physically challenged citizens. *Explaining* How do states pay for programs to help the disabled?

353

353

C Critical Thinking

Determining Cause and Effect Ask:
Why might a governor refuse extradition of a person charged with a major crime? *(Answers may include the idea that the other state has produced insufficient evidence to show that a crime has been committed or that the accused is involved.)* **AL**

TIME™ Teens in *Action*

Answer:

Answers may include careers in government as elected, appointed, or Civil Service employees.

✓ **Reading Check Answer:** Reserved powers are powers that the U.S. Constitution gives neither to the federal government nor denies to the states. Thus, they are reserved to the states.

Civics ONLINE

Objectives and answers to the **Student Web Activity** can be found at glencoe.com under the Web Activity Lesson Plan for this chapter.

Hands-On Chapter Project
Step 1

National Governors' Conference

Step 1: Research and Petition Student partners research the duties of one state governor and issues that affect that state. Pairs will present their state's concerns and petition for help from the federal government at a mock national governors' conference.

TIME™ Teens in *Action*

Prateek Peres-da-Silva

Paging all future politicians! Check out this story about Prateek Peres-da-Silva, 16, of Carrboro, North Carolina. He spent one week in the North Carolina Governor's Page Program.

QUESTION: What's the Governor's Page Program all about?
ANSWER: High school students get the chance to spend a week in the state capital and learn about how government functions. Pages, students in the program, are assigned to help state workers with various tasks.
Q: How many pages are there?
A: About 1,000 kids from different counties around the state participate each year—20 each week. In addition to the daily responsibilities, pages attend press conferences, tour historic landmarks like the capitol and the legislative building—and they can meet the governor.
Q: Speaking of the governor, did you work with elected officials?
A: Yes! I attended meetings at the senate and spoke to several state senators. I also delivered mail and filed documents in the State Office of Management and Budget.
Q: How were you chosen for the program?
A: I filled out an application form and requested a reference letter from my district senator.
ACTION FACT: A music and sports lover, Peres-da-Silva was born in Goa, India.

North Carolina state legislature

Making a Difference — CITIZENSHIP
1. **Describing** What might be some of the goals of students who take part in the page program?

Cooperation Among States The Constitution ensures that states cooperate with one another. Article IV encourages interstate cooperation by requiring states to give "full faith and credit" to the public laws and court decisions of other states. For example, a car registration or corporation charter issued by one state must be accepted in all other states.

Form of Government Article IV also requires every state to have a "republican form of government." The federal government will protect each state against invasion and domestic violence. When a state or local police force cannot control violent incidents within a state, the governor may call for the assistance of federal troops. In return, states provide certain services to the federal government, such as conducting elections for state officials.

Extradition Article IV also ensures another type of cooperation. Often, someone who breaks the law in one state will flee to another state to avoid punishment. A state cannot legally punish a person for breaking the laws of another state. If requested to do so, however, a governor usually orders that a person charged with a crime be returned to the state where the crime was committed. Returning a suspected criminal is called extradition. **C**

Sharing Responsibilities States cooperate in other ways as well, especially when they share a border. The neighboring states of New York and New Jersey, for example, are partners in an agency called the Port Authority. The Port Authority manages bridges, airports, and other transportation facilities that serve both states.

✓ **Reading Check Defining** What are reserved powers?

Civics ONLINE
Student Web Activity Visit glencoe.com and complete the Chapter 12 Web Activity.

Directions Have each pair of students choose one state to research. Ask students to use the Internet to obtain current information from state government Web sites about the duties of the governor of their chosen state.

Organizing Have student partners chart four or five specific duties of their selected state's governor under the appropriate column headings: *Executive, Legislative,* and *Judicial.* Students will use their charts in Step 2 of this activity. **OL**

(Project continued in Section 2)

State Constitutions

Main Idea While differing in details, all state constitutions share many characteristics.

Civics & You Did you know that your state has a constitution that is similar to the U.S. Constitution? Read to find out how this document can affect your life.

Each state has its own constitution. Like the United States Constitution, a state constitution is a plan of government.

Typical Form and Content

State constitutions are similar in many ways to the U.S. Constitution. Every state constitution provides for separation of powers among three branches of government—legislative, executive, and judicial. The state constitutions outline the organization of each branch, the powers and terms of various offices, and the method of election for state officials. States have also included their own bills of rights in their constitutions, which include all or most of the protections of the Bill of Rights in the U.S. Constitution.

Often, they also include rights not provided in the national Constitution, such as workers' right to join unions and protections for the physically challenged.

State constitutions also establish different types of local governments, including counties, townships, municipalities, special districts, parishes, and boroughs. State constitutions also regulate the ways state and local governments can raise and spend money. Finally, state constitutions establish independent state agencies and boards.

Just as the U.S. Constitution is the highest law in the nation, a state's constitution is the highest law in that state. State constitutions, however, cannot include provisions that clash with the U.S. Constitution.

 Reading Check **Comparing** What do all state constitutions have in common?

 Reading Check **Answer:** All provide for separation of powers, outline how each branch is organized, describe the powers and terms of various offices, specify the method of election of state officials, and include a bill of rights.

Assess

Civics ONLINE

Study Central™ provides summaries, interactive games, and online graphic organizers to help students review content.

Close

Differentiating Have students work in pairs to differentiate reserved powers from delegated powers. Ask students to create a T-chart to list powers in one of two columns headed *State Powers* and *Federal Powers.* **OL**

 Section 1 Review

Vocabulary

1. **Define** the following terms and use them in complete sentences related to the way state and federal governments work together: *federal system, reserved powers, concurrent powers, grants-in-aid.*

Main Ideas

2. **Describing** What happens in a federal system, like that of the United States, if a state law conflicts with a national law?

3. **Identifying** What are three areas usually covered in state constitutions?

Critical Thinking

4. **BIG Ideas** How are reserved powers different from concurrent powers?

5. **Identifying** On a chart like the one below, identify the reserved powers given to states.

Reserved Powers
1.
2.
3.
4.

CITIZENSHIP Activity

6. **Persuasive Writing** Do you think there should be term limitations for every elected government official at all levels—local, state, and federal? Why or why not? Express your views in an essay.

Civics ONLINE

Study Central™ To review this section, go to glencoe.com.

Section 1 Review

Answers

1. Sentences should use vocabulary words according to their definitions in the section and in the Glossary.

2. The national law takes precedence (national supremacy).

3. State constitutions provide for the separation of powers between branches and outline the organization of each branch, designate the powers and terms of various offices and the method of election of state officials, and include a bill of rights.

4. Reserved powers belong only to states, while concurrent powers are shared by both national and state governments.

5.

Reserved Powers
1. Regulate intrastate commerce
2. Establish local government systems
3. Administer elections
4. Protect the public health, welfare, and morals

6. Student essays will vary. Some students may write that terms for all officials should be limited to avoid abuses of power such as those demonstrated during the days of party machines. Others will argue that term limits are necessary at certain levels, such as federal and state, or in certain positions, such as the chief executive officers of the national and state governments. Still others may state that term limits are unnecessary as the people should decide who best will serve the country, state, or local area.

D Differentiated Instruction

Logical/Mathematical Ask: What math term can be used in place of the word "deductions"? *(subtractions)* **BL**

R Reading Strategy

Making Connections Ask: When might you personally benefit from Medicare? *(at age 65 or, if disabled, before age 65)* **AL**

Analyzing Economics

Answers:

1. Net pay represents "take home" pay, or the amount workers receive after all deductions have been subtracted from their gross, or full, pay.
2. Answers may include the idea that workers should monitor deductions to be sure they are accurate.

Additional Support

What Information Is on Your Paycheck?

If you work 40 hours a week and receive $15 an hour, you earn $600. When you get your paycheck, one thing is obvious: Your net pay—the amount of money you take home—is not the same amount as your earnings. Your take-home pay is total earnings minus the deductions.

Period Ending: June 15, 2006

Name: Olivia Detwiler

	This Period
Gross pay	$1,041.60
Deductions:	
Federal Income Tax	-$82.19
Social Security Tax	-$64.59
Medicare Tax	-$15.11
State Income Tax	-$34.27
City Income Tax	-$3.14
Net Pay	$842.30

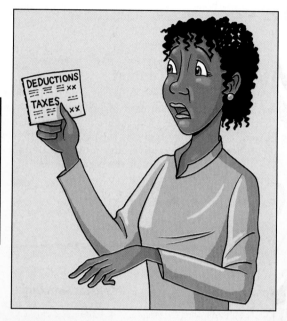

Confirming your net pay is important, but what other information is provided on a typical pay stub?

- Pay period is how often you are paid.
- Gross pay is your pay before deductions.
- Net pay is your pay after deductions.
- Federal income tax withheld is shown.
- You might also choose to withhold a percentage of your gross income to put into a retirement account.

Analyzing Economics

1. **Explaining** How does net pay differ from gross pay?
2. **Analyzing** Why is it important to keep track of all the amounts on your pay stub?

Activity: Economics Learning

Federal Taxes Organize students into six groups. Have two groups research the history and reasoning behind federal tax on personal income. Have two groups do the same for the Social Security tax. Have the final two groups research Medicare and Medicaid taxation. Students can find information on these forms of taxation on the Internet at www.ustreas.gov/education/fact-sheets/taxes/ustax.shtml.

Have one group from each pair support its tax, while the other group disagrees with it. Ask groups to illustrate the evolution of their assigned tax in cartoon form. Cartoons should show both facts and the group's opinion of the tax. **OL**

Guide to Reading

Big Idea
The Constitution gives the legislative branch—Congress—the power to make laws.

Content Vocabulary
• unicameral (p. 358)
• bicameral (p. 358)
• census (p. 359)
• apportion (p. 359)
• malapportionment (p. 359)

Academic Vocabulary
• revise (p. 359)
• whereas (p. 360)

Reading Strategy
Summarizing As you read, take notes by completing a web diagram like the one below by adding details under each of the three secondary heads.

State Legislature
Makeup
Function
Apportionment

Section Audio **Spotlight Video**

The State Legislative Branch

Real World Civics
As a country of immigrants, people who represent you in government come from many different backgrounds. Pedro Colón is the first Latino representative in the Wisconsin State Legislature. His district is 39 percent Latino, making it the majority ethnic group in that district. Colón's job is to represent all Wisconsin citizens in his district, however. Who represents your interests in your state?

▼ **Pedro Colón speaks in Wisconsin**

357

Focus

Guide to Reading
Answers to Graphic:

State Legislature:
Makeup: bicameral with the exception of Nebraska; upper house—senate; lower house—house of representatives **Function:** introduce bills; study bills in committees; pass or defeat bills; work out compromise bills in conference committees; pass compromise bills
Apportionment: congressional districts set up or reexamined after each census; now apportioned based on equal population

 Section Spotlight Video

Have students watch the Chapter 12, Section 2 video at glencoe.com.

Resource Manager

Reading Strategies	C Critical Thinking	D Differentiated Instruction	W Writing Support	S Skill Practice
Teacher Edition • Identifying, p. 358 **Additional Resources** • Cont. Vocab., URB p. 20 • Acad. Vocab., URB p. 21 • Guided Read., URB p. 38	**Teacher Edition** • Comparing/Contrasting, p. 358 **Additional Resources** • Quizzes and Tests, p. 141	**Teacher Edition** • Logical/Math., p. 358 **Additional Resources** • Reteaching Activity, URB p. 35 • School-to-Home Connection Activity, URB p. 33	**Teacher Edition** • Personal Writing, p. 360 **Additional Resources** • Stan. Test Practice, p. 23	**Teacher Edition** • Using Geo. Skills, p. 359 **Additional Resources** • Daily Focus Trans., 12–2 • Pol. Cartoons Trans. 12

Teach

R Reading Strategy

Identifying Ask: What names are given to state lawmaking bodies? *(general assemblies or legislatures)* BL

D Differentiated Instruction

Logical/Mathematical Ask: Why might the minimum age for any state legislator be 18? *(Citizens of the United States must be 18 years old in order to vote.)* OL

C Critical Thinking

Comparing and Contrasting Ask: In what ways are the presiding officers of the senate both the same and different on the national and state levels? *(Both are called senate president; however, the vice president of the United States leads the U.S. Senate, while the lieutenant governors of states lead state senates.)* OL

Caption Answer:

A bicameral legislature is a two-house legislature.

Differentiated Instruction

Legislative Sessions The New Jersey legislature gives Governor Corzine a standing ovation following his speech about budget issues in 2006. **Describing** What is a bicameral legislature?

How Legislatures Function

Main Idea State legislatures pass the laws that govern the states.

Civics & You Can you name your state representative or senator? Read to find out what these important people do for your state's government.

R State lawmaking bodies vary in name and size. In some states the legislature is called the general assembly. Most states, however, call it the legislature. New Hampshire, one of the nation's smallest states in area and population, has the largest legislature—more than 400 members. Nebraska has the smallest, with only 49 members.

Organization

Except for Nebraska's **unicameral,** or one-house, legislature, every state has a **bicameral** legislature, with an upper house, called the senate, and a lower house, usually called the house of representatives. Senators typically serve four-year terms, and representatives two-year terms. Generally, members must be American citizens and live in the district they represent. In most states, representatives **D** must be at least 18 years old, while the minimum age for senators ranges from 18 to 30.

Originally, service in the state legislature required little time. As state governments have gained ever-growing responsibilities, however, membership in the legislature has become a far more demanding job. Some legislatures meet year-round, and pay for members is becoming more suited to the level of work.

What Do Legislatures Do?

State legislatures operate much like the U.S. Congress. Each house has a leader. A speaker of the house directs business in the house of representatives, and a president does the same in the senate. The majority **C** political party selects the house speaker, and in states where the lieutenant governor does not preside over the senate, the majority party picks the senate president. Leaders have great influence over what happens to proposed legislation.

358 Chapter 12

Formulating Questions

Critical Thinking Skills Activity 12, URB pp. 27–28

Objective: To formulate questions

Focus: Discuss how formulating questions can increase understanding.

Teach: Review the terms "concurrent powers" and "reserved powers."

Assess: As a class, discuss how student questions increase understanding of the information on the chart.

Close: Have students write a header for the table to help use it in a discussion of concurrent and reserved powers.

Differentiated Instruction Strategies

BL How could a table such as this one help you study for a quiz or test?

AL Where in a book can students look to find information about the source and authors of a graphic such as this table?

ELL Have students rephrase the powers in their own words before formulating their questions.

How Bills Become State Law Ideas for bills come from many sources, including the governor, individuals, and the legislators themselves. After a member in either house introduces a bill, it goes to the appropriate committee of that house.

The committees study bills, hold hearings, and **revise,** or change, the bills if necessary. In many cases, bills die in committee, never making it to a vote. Otherwise, a committee may send a bill to the full house, with a recommendation that it be passed or rejected. If the two houses pass differing versions of the same bill, it goes to a conference committee, which works out agreeable language. Both houses must approve the final version of a bill, and the governor must sign it before it becomes a law.

Legislative Districts Representatives to the U.S. Congress and the state legislatures are elected from districts. In most states, legislatures draw the boundary lines for each election district.

The U.S. Census Bureau takes a national **census,** or population count, every 10 years. So every 10 years, state legislatures set up or reexamine congressional districts.

Unequal Representation For many years, state senate districts were based roughly on land area, and state house districts were **apportioned,** or divided into districts, based on population. Area-based districts often produced **malapportionment,** or unequal representation, in many state legislatures. For example, a city district and a rural district might each have had one senator, even though the city district had 10 times as many people. U.S. Supreme Court rulings in the 1960s established that state legislatures must be apportioned on the basis of equal population. As a result, many states had to reapportion their legislatures.

Reading Check Defining What is a census?

Political Cartoons

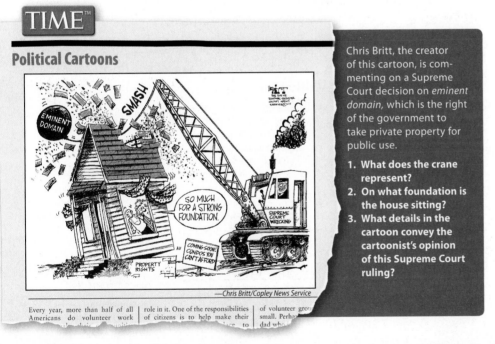

Chris Britt, the creator of this cartoon, is commenting on a Supreme Court decision on *eminent domain,* which is the right of the government to take private property for public use.

1. **What does the crane represent?**
2. **On what foundation is the house sitting?**
3. **What details in the cartoon convey the cartoonist's opinion of this Supreme Court ruling?**

—Chris Britt/Copley News Service

Every year, more than half of all Americans do volunteer work ... role in it. One of the responsibilities of citizens is to help make their ... of volunteer grou... small. Perha... dad who...

National Governors' Conference

Step 2: Identifying Issues of State Concern Student partners continue to prepare for the National Governors' Conference.

Directions Have student partners use the Internet to research current issues of concern in their assigned states. Explain that state newspapers are a good source of online information about problems state and local governments face. Ask students to identify three issues and to categorize them as either executive, legislative, or judicial problems for the state.

Focusing on a Problem Have student partners select one state problem that could be resolved with help from the federal government. Ask partners to list solutions the state has tried and barriers to the solutions, such as funding, federal regulations, and so on. Students will use the problem information in Step 3 of the activity. **OL**

(Project continued in Section 3)

W Writing Support

Personal Writing Have students write a letter to one of their state legislators about a problem the state government is failing to address or addressing ineffectively. Remind students to clearly state the problem, explain why current state measures are ineffective or inadequate, and how their ideas could help the state resolve the issue. **AL**

✓**Reading Check** **Answer:** State legislators face issues such as crime, drug abuse, and raising taxes or cutting programs.

Assess

Civics ONLINE

Study Central™ provides summaries, interactive games, and online graphic organizers to help students review.

Close

Paraphrasing Have students work in pairs to write a paraphrase of the section. Ask pairs of students to exchange written paraphrases with another pair of students and assess how the other pair represented each major idea in their own words. **OL** **ELL**

Section ★ **2** **Review**

Problems Facing States

Main Idea Today's state governments face many difficult challenges.

Civics & You When you do not have enough money to do or buy everything you want, how do you decide what to spend your money on? Read to find out how state legislators address this thorny problem.

Americans expect a great deal from their state governments. They demand better public transportation, better schools, and better services for disabled and disadvantaged people. They also expect state governments to protect the environment, regulate business, and reduce crime and drug abuse.

Paying for Service State governments, however, are finding it difficult to pay for these services. Many legislators refuse to vote to raise taxes. Also, **whereas** federal grants paid for many of these services in the past, the federal government has eliminated many grants because of its own budget concerns.

A Tough Choice

As a result, state governments face a difficult choice: Should they cut programs or raise taxes to pay for them? Legislators fear they may be defeated in the next election if they raise taxes. They also want to avoid cutting essential services. Cutting services at a time when challenges are mounting may be considered irresponsible.

The U.S. Supreme Court's rulings of the 1960s also increased the representation of city dwellers in state legislatures. Since the larger cities are where crime, drug abuse, and unemployment are often highest, today's state legislators face great pressure in dealing with these issues.

✓**Reading Check** **Describing** What issues face state legislators today?

Section Review

2

Vocabulary

1. **Write** complete sentences for each of the following terms related to state legislatures: *unicameral, bicameral, census, apportion, malapportionment.*

Main Ideas

2. **Concluding** Who are the leaders in state legislatures and what do they do?

3. **Evaluating** Which problem facing your state do you feel is the most serious? Why? What do you think the state government should do about the problem?

Critical Thinking

4. **BIG Ideas** Originally most state legislatures required only part-time lawmakers. Today many state legislators work full time. Do you think this is a good development? Why or why not?

5. **Sequencing** On a graphic organizer like the one below, write the steps a bill takes on its way to becoming a law.

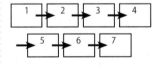

6. **Inferring** What is one problem the legislature of New Hampshire might face because of its large size? Nebraska's because of its small size?

CITIZENSHIP Activity

7. **Expository Writing** Choose one of your state representatives or senators to research. Write a brief biography of the person, focusing on his or her legislative priorities.

Civics ONLINE

Study Central™ To review this section, go to glencoe.com.

Answers

1. Sentences should use vocabulary words according to their definitions in the section and in the Glossary.

2. Answers may include the idea that state governments are closer to their citizens and, thus, better able to make laws necessary for their welfare and protection.

3. Answers will vary but should accurately reflect a current state problem and propose a reasonable government solution.

4. Most students might state that full-time legislators are needed because of an expanded population.

5. **1:** Bill is introduced by a legislator; **2:** Bill is considered in committee; **3:** Bill is voted on by full house; **4:** Bill is sent to other house for consideration; **5:** Other house revises the bill; **6:** Compromise bill is worked out in joint committee, **7:** Both houses pass the compromise bill; **8:** Bill is sent to the Governor for signature

6. Answers may include the ideas that New Hampshire's large legislature may have difficulty reaching a consensus on an issue, while Nebraska's small legislature may be easily influenced by special interest groups or may not represent diverse opinions.

7. Student biographies will vary but should focus on a state legislator and present accurate, verifiable information on the legislator's life and legislative priorities.

Is a lottery a good way to raise state revenue?

In a recent year Americans spent $50 billion on state lotteries—more money than on reading materials or attending movies. Half of that money was returned to the winners. After paying their other costs, the states kept about $15 billion. Many states use the money to help finance education. Although gambling is a controversial way to raise money, about four of every five states today uses the lottery. Some states feel pressure to use a lottery because of the fear that their citizens will gamble in a neighboring state. Studies have shown that the poor spend a higher portion of their income on lotteries than do middle- and upper-income people. Because the lottery is a substitute for other forms of taxation, the question has been raised, "Is a lottery a good way to raise state revenue?"

An attendant rings up lottery ticket sales in Indiana for the multistate lottery drawing.

YES

State lotteries are not new. Between 1790 and 1860 more than half the states used them to finance things such as hospitals, libraries, jails, and schools. Usually, states adopt the lottery as a way to avoid raising taxes. State legislators consider the lottery a voluntary tax because people do not have to play. Executive Director Alan R. Yandow's report on the Vermont lottery is typical of many states: "As much fun as our games are, and as much fun as we have bringing them to you, we're just as serious about the good we do for Vermont. Every year since 1998, all Vermont Lottery profits go exclusively to support the Vermont Education Fund. Last year alone, that meant more than $19 million for the state's Education Fund."

—Alan R. Yandow, Executive Director of Vermont Lottery Commission

NO

Opponents of state lotteries cite the rising number of people addicted to gambling and studies that show the lottery hurts people with low incomes. Andy Rooney of CBS *60 Minutes* said, "There ought to be a law making it compulsory for anyone who reports the name of the winner of a lottery, to also give the name of all the losers. . . . Lower income people in Massachusetts . . . spent 15 times as much on gambling as people who make a decent living. . . . We approve of using some of our tax money for welfare to help the helpless. What I don't approve of is any government agency buying radio commercials to encourage the poor to waste what we give them on lottery tickets."

—Andy Rooney, CBS *60 Minutes*

Debating the Issue

1. **Identifying** About how many states use the lottery to raise money?

2. **Recalling** What income group spends the greatest percentage of its money on lottery tickets?

3. **Explaining** Why do legislators and governors often support the lottery as a means of raising state money?

4. **Concluding** What arguments for and against the lottery are most convincing?

Chapter 12 361

D Differentiated Instruction

Logical/Mathematical Ask: Why can readers *not* conclude that poor people spend more total dollars on lottery tickets than people of higher incomes? *(Although poorer people spend a higher percentage of their incomes, their incomes are much lower than those in average- or high-income brackets. Therefore, the percentage does not necessarily reflect more dollars spent.)* **AL**

C Critical Thinking

Making Inferences Ask: What might be inferred about Andy Rooney's feelings based on the last sentence of his quote? *(Rooney resents poor people spending public assistance money to play lotteries.)* **OL**

Debating the Issue

Answers:
1. approximately 40
2. the poor
3. Many consider lotteries to be a voluntary tax since people can choose whether they wish to participate.
4. Answers will vary. **Pro-lottery:** idea of a voluntary tax or the use of funds for education; **Anti-lottery:** gambling addiction and the harm caused to the poor

Additional Support

Activity: U.S./World Connections

Lottery Fraud Explain the concepts of "fraud" and "scam" (an act meant to deceive or trick). Tell students that many people receive notification through Internet e-mail, by phone, or by mail that they have won an international lottery. Have students work in pairs to research rules regarding the participation of American citizens in international lotteries. Direct students to the following Internet site for their research: www.ftc.gov/bcp/conline/pubs/alerts/intlalrt.htm. Have students create a poster for display in the school or in the community that alerts others about international lottery fraud. **OL**

Focus

Bellringer

Daily Focus Transparency 12–3

Guide to Reading

Answers to Graphic:

American citizen
at least 30 years old
Governor
a minimum state residency of 5 years

Section Spotlight Video

Have students watch the Chapter 12, Section 3 video at glencoe.com.

Resource Manager

Guide to Reading

Big Idea
The Constitution gives the executive branch the power to execute, or implement, the law.

Content Vocabulary
- line-item veto *(p. 364)*
- commute *(p. 364)*
- parole *(p. 364)*

Academic Vocabulary
- issue *(p. 363)*
- guideline *(p. 364)*

Reading Strategy
Organizing As you read, identify three qualifications for governor required by most states.

Governor

 Section Audio   **Spotlight Video**

Section **3**

The State Executive Branch

Real World Civics The most powerful job in your state is the office of governor. Who runs for this office? In the past it was men, with wives sometimes taking over the office if their husbands died while serving. In 2002, Jennifer Granholm became the first female governor elected in Michigan. Like the president of the United States, Governor Granholm runs a large government with budgets and a bicameral legislature. A major focus of her successful campaign was a "Jobs Today, Jobs Tomorrow" plan, which she promotes across the state.

▼ **Governor Granholm promotes her agenda across Michigan**

 R Reading Strategies	 **C** Critical Thinking	 **D** Differentiated Instruction	 **W** Writing Support	 **S** Skill Practice
Teacher Edition • Using Context Clues, p. 363 **Additional Resources** • Content Vocab., URB p. 20 • Acad. Vocab, URB p. 22 • Guide Read., URB p. 39	**Teacher Edition** • Drawing Con., p. 363 • Comparing/Contrasting, p. 365 **Additional Resources** • Biography Activity, URB p. 23	**Teacher Edition** • Logical/Math., p. 364 **Additional Resources** • Reteaching Activity, URB p. 35 • School-to-Home Connection Activity, URB p. 34	**Teacher Edition** • Personal Writing, p. 364 **Additional Resources** • Writing Skills Activity, URB p. 25	**Teacher Edition** • Assessing Value, p. 363 **Additional Resources** • Chart, Graph, and Map Skills, URB p. 29 • Daily Focus Trans., 12–3

Governors Meet Governors from Iowa, Delaware, Virginia, and Arkansas grill meat at the national governors' meeting in Iowa. *Comparing* What do the offices of president and governor have in common?

Powers and Duties of the Governor

Main Idea Governors are the chief executives in all state governments.

Civics & You What do you know about your state's governor? Read to find out how he or she got the job.

Like the federal government, every state has an executive branch consisting of a chief executive—the governor—and a number of departments and agencies.

Becoming a Governor

Each state constitution lists the qualifications for the office of governor. In most states a governor must be an American citizen, at least 30 years old, and a resident of the state for at least 5 years. Most governors have previously been elected to other public offices or been active in state politics.

Almost all potential governors begin by gaining the nomination of a major political party, usually by winning a primary. Then that party nominee runs in the general election, usually with a lieutenant governor. Most governors serve four-year terms. In nearly every state, a governor can be impeached and removed from office for committing a crime. In some of the states, the voters themselves can take steps to unseat their governor by demanding a special "recall" election. In 2003, California voters recalled their governor and replaced him with actor Arnold Schwarzenegger.

Head of the Executive Branch

Like the president of the United States, a governor heads the executive branch of state government and fills many of the same kinds of roles. A governor is the state's chief executive, responsible for carrying out the laws of the state. To help with this job, the governor **issues,** or distributes, executive orders to a large state bureaucracy.

Chapter 12   **363**

S **Skill Practice**

Assessing Value **Ask:** Why might it be helpful for gubernatorial candidates to have experience in other public offices or in state politics? *(Answers may include the idea that candidates would then be well-known within the state or the party and that they would be familiar with state government operations.)* **OL**

C **Critical Thinking**

Drawing Conclusions **Ask:** What conclusion can be drawn about the party affiliation of the lieutenant governor candidate? *(Both the lieutenant governor and governor candidates belong to the same political party.)* **BL**

R **Reading Strategy**

Using Context Clues **Ask:** Which synonym for the word "issues" does the text provide? *(distributes)* **ELL**

Caption Answer:

both are chief executive officers and are responsible for carrying out the laws of their branch of government

Hands-On Chapter Project
Step 3

National Governors' Conference

Step 3: Preparing Computer Presentations Student partners will prepare their issues of concern for presentation at the National Governors' Conference.

Directions Ask partners to create a computer presentation that focuses on the state problem identified in Step 2 of this activity. Student presentations should include a minimum of five slides with a title slide and a closing slide. The title slide should include a visual that displays what the governor would like the federal government to do to help the state with its problem. The following slides should present the problem, explain how it affects citizens of the state, and suggest a federal government solution. The closing slide should summarize the presentation in a dramatic, effective way. **OL**

(Project continued in Section 4)

A New Bridge for Our State

Powers/Duties of Governor

Judicial Leader
Offers pardons and reprieves; Grants parole

Ceremonial Leader
Greets important visitors; Represents the state

Chief Executive
Carries out state laws; Appoints officials; Prepares a budget

Chief Legislator
Proposes legislation; Approves or vetoes legislation

Commander in Chief
In charge of the National Guard (state militia)

Party Leader
Leads the political party in the state

Analyzing Charts

1. **Explaining** What connection does the governor have to the National Guard?

2. **Comparing** Which role of the governor would probably take the most time? Why?

The governor appoints some of the state's top officials. In most states the governor is also responsible for preparing a budget and winning its approval from the legislature. Governors also exercise various legislative and judicial duties and responsibilities.

Legislative and Judicial Duties The governor can suggest new bills and try to persuade the legislature to pass them. All governors have the power to veto bills the legislature has passed. Governors in 43 states have the power to veto specific parts of a bill—an action called a **line-item veto.** State legislatures may override governors' vetoes. Usually, however, overrides require a two-thirds ratio and are rare.

Governors also have judicial powers. A governor may grant pardons to criminals or **commute**—reduce—a sentence. Governors also have the power to grant prisoners **parole,** an early release from prison, within certain **guidelines,** or rules.

One Office, Many Roles Governors play other roles as well. Every governor heads the state National Guard. The governor is the state leader of his or her political party. The governor also serves as ceremonial leader of the state.

Until recently nearly all governors were white males. Since the 1960s, more than half the states have elected female governors. Several Southwestern states have elected Latino governors. Washington State and Hawaii have had Asian American governors. The first Asian American governor was George R. Ariyoshi of Hawaii, elected in 1974. The nation's first elected African American governor was Lawrence Douglas Wilder. He served as governor of Virginia from 1990 to 1994.

Reading Check Recalling What judicial powers does a governor have?

Jennifer Granholm

Objective: To learn about the political life of Jennifer Granholm

Focus: Have students review the duties of a governor.

Teach: Discuss why women are underrepresented in political offices.

Assess: Summarize Granholm's career path and list her accomplishments.

Close: Create a reelection campaign ad for Granholm.

Differentiated Instruction Strategies

BL Explain why Granholm went to college and how she paid for her education.

AL Ask students to discuss Granholm's chances of becoming president. Have them describe what they think might be her qualifications.

ELL Name one important change Granholm made to improve citizens' health.

Executive Departments

Main Idea Top officials in charge of executive departments assist the governor.

Civics & You Have you ever needed help doing a tough job? Read to find out about the people who help the governor run the state.

Not every governor has a cabinet, but every state has a number of top officials who are in charge of executive departments and who advise the governor on important issues. Governors appoint many of these officials. In most states, however, some of these officials are elected.

While the top officials vary from state to state, most states have a few in common. In most states, a secretary of state manages elections and maintains the state's official records. An attorney general represents the state in lawsuits and gives legal advice to the governor, state agencies, and the legislature. A superintendent of public instruc-

tion (sometimes called a commissioner of education) sets educational standards and oversees the state's public schools. A treasurer collects taxes and invests state funds. An auditor reviews the record-keeping of state agencies to make certain that money is used according to state law.

In addition, every state has a number of executive departments, agencies, boards, and commissions. Some, such as departments of justice, agriculture, and labor, are like their federal counterparts. Others exist only at the state level. Most states have a department or board of health, which runs programs in disease prevention and health education. Most of the states also have departments of public works and highways, which are responsible for building and maintaining roads, bridges, and public buildings. Many states have a state welfare board to help the unemployed and people living in poverty.

✓ **Reading Check** **Describing** What does a secretary of state do?

C Critical Thinking

Comparing and Contrasting **Ask:** Which state departments also exist in the national government? *(justice, agriculture, and labor)* **ELL**

✓ **Reading Check** **Answer:** A secretary of a state manages elections and maintains state records.

Assess

Civics ONLINE

Study Central™ provides summaries, interactive games, and online graphic organizers to help students review content.

Close

Organizing Have student groups create a day-planner page detailing one day in the life of a state governor. Ask groups to include at least one activity from each of the governor's roles. Ask groups to exchange schedules and to compare the scheduled activities to the roles described in the text. **OL**

Section 3 Review

Vocabulary

1. **Define** the following terms and use each in a sentence or short paragraph related to state governors: *line-item veto, commute, parole.*

Main Ideas

2. **Identifying** What legislative powers do governors have?

3. **Describing** What role does an attorney general perform in state governments?

Critical Thinking

4. **BIG Ideas** Do you think a governor should have the power to pardon or commute the sentence of a person convicted of a crime? Why or why not?

5. In a graphic organizer like the one below, list the major roles a governor must fill.

CiTIZENSHIP Activity

6. **Expository Writing** Some people consider that the governorship is excellent preparation for the presidency. In what ways do you think it would prepare someone for the presidency? In what ways do you think it would not? Answer these questions in a one-page essay.

Civics ONLINE

Study Central™ To review this section, go to glencoe.com.

Chapter 12 365

Section 3 Review

Answers

1. Sentences should use vocabulary words according to their definitions in the section and in the Glossary.

2. Governors can suggest new bills and veto or line-item-veto bills.

3. A state attorney general represents the state in lawsuits and gives legal advice to the governor, legislature, and state agencies.

4. Answers will vary. Students may feel one person should not have this much power; others may argue that a harsh sentence needed to be overturned.

5.

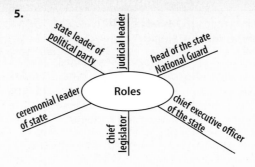

6. Essays may include the following reasons in support of the idea that serving as governor prepares an individual for the presidency: governors become familiar with working with a bureaucracy, governors learn how to influence legislation, and governors have experience with pardons and sentence commutations. Essays may include on the reverse side: state issues may be vastly different from national and international issues, and governors are inexperienced in dealing with other nations.

Focus

Bellringer
Daily Focus Transparency 12–4

Guide to Reading
Answers to Graphic:

Appeals Courts	→	a case charging that the general trial court was unfair
General Trial Courts	→	a felony case, such as murder, armed robbery, drug trafficking
Lower Courts	→	a misdemeanor case, such as traffic, juvenile, or small claims

Section Spotlight Video

To generate student interest and provide a springboard for class discussion, access the Chapter 12, Section 4 video at glencoe.com or on the video DVD.

Resource Manager

Guide to Reading

Big Idea
The judicial branch is charged with interpreting the law.

Content Vocabulary
- justice of the peace *(p. 367)*
- misdemeanor *(p. 367)*
- magistrate court *(p. 367)*
- civil case *(p. 367)*
- plaintiff *(p. 368)*
- defendant *(p. 368)*
- felony *(p. 368)*

Academic Vocabulary
- portion *(p. 367)*
- intermediate *(p. 368)*
- confirm *(p. 369)*

Reading Strategy
Classifying As you read, identify each level of state courts and an example of a type of case heard in each. Write your information on a diagram like the one below.

Section 4

The State Judicial Branch

Real World Civics Most state courts are organized in the same way as the federal courts. The highest position is the chief justice of the state supreme court. When Henry Frye was appointed to that position by the governor of North Carolina in 1999, he became the first African American to serve as chief justice in the state's history. Like the U.S. Supreme Court, the North Carolina Supreme Court does not make law or rule on the facts of a case, but it does rule on errors in legal procedures and on judicial decisions regarding existing law. Chief Justice Frye presided for two years alongside six other justices in reviewing cases.

▼ **Chief Justice Henry Frye congratulated by granddaughters**

R Reading Strategies	**C** Critical Thinking	**D** Differentiated Instruction	**W** Writing Support	**S** Skill Practice
Teacher Edition • Defining, p. 367 • Explaining, p. 367 **Additional Resources** • Content Vocab., URB p. 20 • Ac. Vocab., URB p. 22 • Foldables, p. 73	**Teacher Edition** • Comparing/Contrasting, p. 367 **Additional Resources** • Quizzes and Tests, p. 143	**Teacher Edition** • English Learners, p. 368 **Additional Resources** • School-to-Home Connection Activity, URB p. 33 • Reteaching Activity, URB p. 35	**Teacher Edition** • Personal Writing, p. 369 **Additional Resources** • STSP, p. 24	**Teacher Edition** • Visual Literacy, p. 368 **Additional Resources** • Daily Focus Trans., 12–4

Courtroom Judges Judges are in charge of their courtrooms whether they are dealing with municipal, state, civil, or criminal cases. *Speculating* **Is this courtroom most likely a city or state court? Why?**

The State Court System

Main Idea Most legal matters within a state are handled by the state's court system.

Civics & You Would you like to serve on a trial jury? Why or why not? Read to find out how your state's court system operates.

The federal court system handles only a small **portion,** or part, of the nation's judicial business. The overwhelming majority of legal matters are settled in state courts.

How State Courts Are Organized

Most state courts are organized like the federal court system. They have a three-level system that includes courts for minor law violations and lawsuits, courts for serious crimes and large-scale civil cases, and appeals courts.

Rural Areas and Small Towns In many rural areas and small towns, the local court is called a justice court, and the judge is called a **justice of the peace.** These courts almost always handle less serious crimes, known as **misdemeanors.** An example of such a crime would be a minor theft or breaking and entering. Justice courts operate without juries. Instead, a judge or justice of the peace hears and decides each case. In most communities the voters elect these judges.

Larger Towns and Cities Larger towns may have police courts or **magistrate courts.** These courts handle minor cases such as traffic violations or disturbing the peace. They may also hear civil cases involving small sums of money, usually less than $1,000. **Civil cases** occur when a person or group takes legal action against another person or group. People convicted in these courts usually receive a small fine or a short jail term.

Chapter 12 367

Teach

R1 Reading Strategy

Defining Ask: What are misdemeanors? *(less serious crimes)* **ELL**

R2 Reading Strategy

Explaining Ask: How do justice courts operate? *(No juries hear cases; instead, the judge or justice of the peace hears and decides each case.)* **ELL**

C Critical Thinking

Comparing and Contrasting Ask: In what way are police, or magistrate, courts different from justice courts? *(They hear civil cases.)* **OL**

Caption Answer:

The photo most likely represents a city courtroom because judges usually decide civil or misdemeanor cases without jury hearings.

Differentiated Instruction

Ohio Smoking Ban and Law

Primary Source Reading 4-B, URB pp. 17–18

Objective: To understand how voters shape state and local law

Focus: Explain how a ballot initiative works.

Teach: Have students read the initiative aloud and then paraphrase it.

Assess: Explain why voters must take time to read ballot initiatives carefully and thoughtfully.

Close: Cast private ballots to decide on this initiative as a class.

Differentiated Instruction Strategies

BL Locate each Reader's Dictionary word in a sentence in the text. Explain what the word means in that sentence.

AL Discuss the positive and negative effects that a ban on smoking in public places might have.

ELL Define these legal terms: "prohibit," "retroactively," and "exempted."

Hands-On Chapter Project
Step 4

National Governors' Conference

Step 4: Presenting State Issues at the National Governors' Conference Student partners represent their states at the National Governors' Conference.

State Judicial System

STATE SUPREME COURT
- Panel of judges hears appeals from lower courts

APPELLATE COURTS
- Panel of judges hears appeals from lower courts

GENERAL TRIAL COURTS
- Judges or judge and jury hear criminal and civil cases

LOWER COURTS
- Justice Courts—rural and small towns
- Magistrate Courts—larger towns, smaller cities
- Municipal Courts: traffic, juvenile, misdemeanors—larger cities

Analyzing Charts

1. **Identifying** Which court would handle a case of a teen being out after curfew?
2. **Explaining** Why are there two levels of the courts that hear appeals?

Municipal Courts Large cities may have municipal courts that serve the same purpose. These are often divided into specialized areas, such as traffic, juvenile, and small claims courts. Small claims courts decide civil cases usually involving less than $1,000. **Plaintiffs** (people filing lawsuits) and **defendants** (people being sued) speak for themselves with no lawyers present for either side.

Higher State Courts

The second level of state courts deals with more serious crimes, called felonies, and with civil cases involving large amounts of money. The third level of state courts consists of courts that consider appeals of lower-court decisions.

General Trial Court Defendants charged with **felonies**—murder, armed robbery, drug trafficking, and other major crimes—go on trial in general trial courts. Depending on the state, such a court may be called a district court, county court, common pleas court, circuit court, or superior court.

Trials in these courts may be held before a jury. In such cases, the judge's job is to make sure the trial is conducted fairly and lawfully. The judge does this by ruling on whether certain evidence or testimony is permissible, ruling on objections by attorneys in the case, and guiding the jury on points of law. In many states, the judge also decides on the penalty in case of a guilty verdict.

Appellate Courts Most states have a level of **intermediate** appeals courts. These courts review decisions made by trial courts. Appeals courts do not have juries. Instead, a panel of judges decides cases by a majority vote. If the judges find evidence that the defendant did not have a fair trial, they can overturn the lower court's decision.

Supreme Court The court of last resort in most states is the state supreme court. It reviews decisions of appeals courts and is responsible for supervising all courts in the state. State supreme courts also interpret the state's constitution and laws. A successful appeal at this level requires a majority vote of the judges hearing the case. Except for cases involving federal law or the United States Constitution, the decisions of the state supreme courts are final.

✔ Reading Check **Explaining** Why do you think state supreme courts are called courts of last resort?

Selection of Judges

Main Idea State judges can be elected, appointed, or chosen in a way that combines both methods.

Civics & You Have you ever heard someone described as having good judgment? What does that phrase mean to you?

State judges are selected in different ways. Some are elected by popular vote in either partisan elections (affiliated with a political party) or nonpartisan elections (unaffiliated with a political party). Others are elected by the state legislature or appointed by the governor. Some states appoint judges for life; others for a set number of years. Still other states select judges through a combination of appointment and popular election. Under this plan, the governor appoints a judge from a list prepared by a commission, and voters either reject or **confirm** (approve) the appointed judge.

Many people think judges should not be elected. These critics fear that judges may be more concerned with pleasing voters than administering the law impartially. Other people argue that popular election of judges ensures a government "of the people, by the people, and for the people." Popular election is still commonly used to select judges. According to the American Bar Association, 38 states use some form of election at the highest level of state judiciary.

State judges usually have longer terms of office—6 to 12 years—than legislators or governors. In theory, the longer their terms, the more independent they can be.

Judges can be removed from office by impeachment. Impeachment, though, can be time-consuming. Most states have created boards to investigate any complaints about judges. If the board finds that a judge has acted improperly, it makes a recommendation to the state supreme court. The court may then suspend or remove the judge.

Reading Check Explaining How can state judges be removed from office?

Section 4 Review

Vocabulary

1. **Use** all of the following terms to write a paragraph that summarizes the main points of this section: *justice of the peace, misdemeanor, magistrate court, civil cases, plaintiff, defendant, felony.*

Main Ideas

2. **Identifying** Of the three tiers of state courts, which one uses juries to decide guilt or innocence or to settle civil suits?

3. **Describing** What are three ways state judges are chosen in this country?

Critical Thinking

4. **BIG Ideas** In your opinion, should judges be elected, as they usually are at the state level, or appointed, as they are at the federal level? Explain.

5. **Organizing Information** On a diagram like the one below, note the three types of lower courts and where each is found.

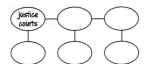

CITIZENSHIP Activity

6. **Reporting** On the Internet, do a search to find opinions on the election-versus-the-selection-of-judges argument. Summarize the main points of both sides and share your findings with the class.

Study Central™ To review this section, go to glencoe.com.

W Writing Support

Personal Writing Have students research how local judges are selected and write their opinions of whether that is the fairest selection method. **OL**

Reading Check **Answer:** State judges can be impeached, but judges are more often removed when state boards investigate misconduct and recommend a removal to the Supreme Court.

Assess

Civics ONLINE

Study Central™ provides summaries, interactive games, and online graphic organizers to help students review content.

Close

Categorizing On slips of paper, write six case descriptions such as jaywalking, burglary, and so on. Organize the class into six groups. Have each group select one slip of paper. Ask groups to identify the type of court that will hear their "case" and to explain their choices. **OL**

Section 4 ★ Review

Answers

1. Sentences should use vocabulary words according to their definitions in the section and in the Glossary.

2. general trial courts

3. Judges are elected by popular vote, appointed by governors, or elected by state legislatures.

4. Answers will vary but may include supporting arguments given in the text on this page.

5.

6. Reports will vary but should summarize opinions from reputable Internet sites on both sides of the issue of election versus selection of judges.

Teach

R1 Reading Strategy

Activating Prior Knowledge Ask: What is a search warrant? *(a document signed by a judge that authorizes a search of an individual's property by law enforcement officials)* **OL**

C Critical Thinking

Drawing Conclusions Ask: How many justices are on the Supreme Court of the United States? *(nine)* **ELL**

R2 Reading Strategy

Summarizing Ask: How can the ruling of the Supreme Court in the case of *Mapp v. Ohio* be summarized? *(Evidence obtained through improper police searches cannot be presented in state criminal courts.)* **OL**

ANALYZING THE COURT DECISION

Answers:
1. the Fourth Amendment
2. Answers may include the idea that law enforcement is a service of government, which is supposed to protect the rights of its citizens, as well as their welfare and safety.

Additional Support

Mapp v. Ohio

The Fourth Amendment aims to protect citizens from unreasonable searches by requiring government officials to first obtain search warrants. In 1914 the U.S. Supreme Court declared that any evidence obtained without this protection cannot be used in federal court trials. How did this "exclusionary" rule find its way into state courts as well?

Background of the Case

In 1957 police officers arrived at the Cleveland, Ohio, apartment of Dollree Mapp. They were looking for evidence linking her with a gambling operation. Mapp asked to see a search warrant. The police flashed a piece of paper, but it never became clear whether the paper was actually a warrant. Although the police found no evidence of gambling, they did discover some pieces of alleged pornography. Ohio courts sentenced Mapp to prison for possession of illegal goods. They held that the pornography could be used against her in court even though the police were not searching for it under their supposed warrant.

Police arrested Dollree Mapp in 1957 for possession of illegal goods found during a questioned search.

The Decision

With Justice Tom C. Clark writing the 5–4 decision, the Supreme Court issued its ruling on June 19, 1961. Clark first called on the Fourteenth Amendment's protection against certain state actions. From there he argued:

 Having once recognized that the right to privacy embodied in the Fourth Amendment is enforceable against the States, and that the right to be secure against rude invasions of privacy by state officers is, therefore, constitutional . . . we can no longer permit it to be revocable [able to be canceled] at the whim of any police officer who . . . chooses to suspend [it]. . . .

—Justice Clark, 1961

The Court declared that the presentation of evidence obtained through improper police searches is unconstitutional in state criminal courts.

Why It Matters

The *Mapp* case marked a shift in Supreme Court thinking. The Court had argued that the Bill of Rights governed only the actions of the federal government. During the 1960s, though, the Court included the states in more protections under the Bill of Rights as implied under the Fourteenth Amendment. After this case, evidence seized in violation of the Fourth Amendment could not be used by the prosecution as evidence of a defendant's guilt in any court—federal, state, or local.

Analyzing the Court Decision

1. **Explaining** On what basis did Justice Clark establish citizens' right to privacy?

2. **Concluding** How might you answer the criticism that the *Mapp* decision could hamper law enforcement?

---

370 Chapter 12

Background

Mapp v. Ohio Within the provisions of the U.S. Constitution, no mention was made of admissibility requirements for evidence presented in state courts. With this Supreme Court decision, the Court reinforced the need for proper police procedures in obtaining and handling evidence. However, this ruling does not require police to always obtain search warrants. If an individual voluntarily agrees to a search in his or her presence, no warrant is necessary. Police officers may also confiscate evidence that is in "plain view" as long as they are authorized to be in the area of the evidence. Following an arrest, police may search the immediate area as long it is necessary to search for the presence of another criminal. Finally, police may search a car without a warrant provided that they stopped the car for "probable cause," or good reason. Their search is limited, however, to objects connected with the reason for stopping the car.

The Federal System

- We live in a federal system in which there are 50 separate state governments and one federal government.
- The U.S. Constitution gives a broad range of powers to state governments.

Connecticut state capitol

State Constitutions

State constitutions are similar in structure to the U.S. Constitution. They include the following:
- A preamble
- A bill of rights
- An outline of the framework of government
- A listing of state powers and responsibilities
- A provision for local government
- The methods of amending the constitution

Florida state seal

State Legislative Branch

- State legislators are chosen by popular vote.
- The lawmaking machinery in the state legislatures is similar to that used in the U.S. Congress.
- All state legislatures, except Nebraska's, are bicameral.

State Executive Branch

- The governor is the chief executive officer in each of the 50 states.
- Important executive powers of the governor include appointing and removing officials, administering laws, planning and carrying out the budget, and commanding the National Guard.

State Judicial Branch

- State courts interpret and apply state and local laws.
- State judges are selected by the governor, by the legislature, or by the people.
- Crimes are defined by state statutes, which are laws enacted by state legislatures.

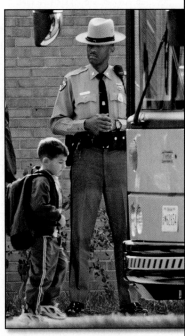

Maryland state trooper guards children

STUDY TO GO Study anywhere, anytime! Download quizzes and flash cards to your PDA from glencoe.com.

371

Visual Literacy Ask: What is the function of a state capitol? *(It houses legislative and judicial sessions as well as the executive offices of state officials.)* **AL**

Making Inferences Ask: Why are both powers and responsibilities of government listed in state constitutions? *(Although governments need specific powers to function, they have duties to the citizens who grant them their powers.)* Have students work in groups to list at least five responsibilities of state government. **OL**

Explaining Ask: What is the function of a state seal? *(It displays the state motto, or guiding principle.)* Have students investigate their state seal on the Internet. Have students work in pairs to design an alternate state seal. **ELL**

Hands-On Chapter Project
Step 5: Wrap-Up

National Governors' Conference

Step 5: Communicating State Needs Students will finish process begun in Step 1.

Directions Explain that the National Governors' Conference will call their concerns to the attention of the president of the United States by proclamation. Organize the class into groups. Create a proclamation form to give each group to complete. **OL**

Proclamation Form Information

WHEREAS, the governors of these United States have met to discuss individual and common state issues, and
WHEREAS, the states enjoy a cooperative relationship with the government of the United States of America, and

WHEREAS, the national government has historically granted monies to promote the welfare of these states and their citizens, THEREFORE, these states do declare these issues to be of pressing concern:

1.

2.

3.

4.

Answers and Analyses

Reviewing Vocabulary

1. A Students will have read about the federal system and the concept of delegated, reserved, and concurrent powers in Section 1. Although the Constitution gives states both reserved and concurrent powers, only reserved powers reside solely with states. A student could analyze word parts to reject answers C and D.

2. D Students will have studied how boundaries are established for state election districts in the text under the Section 2 subheads Legislative Districts and Unequal Representation. A student can eliminate answers A through C by recalling court jurisdictions in the Section 4 opening segment, How State Courts Are Organized. The student can verify that answer D is correct by defining "apportionment" as "division" and the prefix "mal–" as "bad" or "harmful."

3. A Students will recognize answers A, B, and D as powers of the governor after reading about the legislative and judicial duties of the office in Section 3. A student can eliminate the line-item veto as a legislative function. To determine the correct answer, "parole," a student can identify which term applies to prisoners and which term relates to prison sentences.

4. C Students will recognize all answers as court-related terms. By reading about municipal courts in Section 4, a student can eliminate answer choices B and D because they are not linked to civil cases. The student can determine the correct answer by associating familiar terms, such as "complain" and "complaint," with "plaintiff."

Reviewing Main Ideas

5. B Students will have studied concurrent powers in Section 1 of this chapter. By linking each answer to real-life experience and by applying logical thinking, a student can eliminate all answers but the correct answer—the power to collect taxes.

6. C Students will have studied the problem of malapportionment and the Supreme Court's subsequent ruling regarding election district apportion-

---

TEST-TAKING **TIP**

> To prepare for a major exam, save weekly tests and review the questions.

Reviewing Vocabulary

Directions: Choose the word(s) that best completes the sentence.

1. _____ powers belong to the state and are NOT shared with the federal government.

  A reserved   **C** bicameral

  B concurrent   **D** unicameral

2. Area-based legislative districts often produce _____.

  A civil cases   **C** felonies

  B misdemeanors   **D** malapportionment

3. Governors have the power to _____ prisoners.

  A parole   **C** apportion

  B commute   **D** line-item veto

4. A _____ is a person who files a lawsuit.

  A defendant   **C** plaintiff

  B magistrate   **D** justice of the peace

Reviewing Main Ideas

Directions: Choose the best answer for each question.

Section 1 *(pp. 350–355)*

5. What power do the state and national governments share?

  A the power to declare war

  B the power to collect taxes

  C the power to issue money

  D the power to administer elections

Section 2 *(pp. 357–360)*

6. On what basis do states today apportion their legislatures?

  A area

  B parties

  C population

  D legislation

Section 3 *(pp. 362–365)*

7. Which of the following is a legislative duty of the governor?

  A preparing a budget

  B suggesting new bills

  C commanding the National Guard

  D all of the above

8. What state official manages elections?

  A auditor

  B treasurer

  C attorney general

  D secretary of state

Section 4 *(pp. 366–369)*

9. What courts handle traffic violations?

  A trial courts

  B appeals courts

  C magistrate courts

  D state supreme courts

10. Who selects state judges in many states?

  A voters

  B governors

  C legislatures

  D all of the above

GO ON ➡

---

ment in Section 2. To select the correct answer—"population"—a student can use logic to determine which method of apportionment is more logical and fair.

7. B Students will have learned how to categorize gubernatorial duties in Section 3. A student can eliminate incorrect answers by defining the keyword "legislative" in the question. The student can then link the ideas of "legislation" and "bills" to arrive at the correct answer, "suggesting new bills."

8. D Students will recognize all answer choices as state official positions through their study of Section 3. To eliminate incorrect answers, a student can associate meaningful ideas with the first three answer choices. For example, an auditor audits, or checks, financial records, while a treasurer manages the state's treasury, or money. An attorney deals with legal or court, matters.

Critical Thinking

Directions: Base your answers to questions 11 and 12 on the cartoon below and your knowledge of Chapter 12.

11. Which of the following statements best expresses the cartoon's main idea?

   A Joblessness is the root cause of most problems in society.

   B States lack the resources to handle essential social services.

   C Too many federal dollars are dumped into job programs.

   D States farm out their job programs to small-time entrepreneurs.

12. What caused the dilemma illustrated in the cartoon?

   A an increase in state taxes

   B an elimination of grants-in-aid

   C the outsourcing of manufacturing jobs

   D the Supreme Court rulings of the 1960s

Document-Based Questions

Directions: Analyze the following document and answer the short-answer questions that follow.

The following principles are guidelines for child welfare workers in North Carolina.

- Enhancing a parent's safety enhances the child's safety.
- Domestic violence perpetrators may cause serious harm to children.
- Domestic violence perpetrators, and not their victims, should be held accountable for their action and the impact on the well-being of the adult and child victims.
- Appropriate services, tailored to the degree of violence and risk, should be available for adult victims leaving, returning to, or staying in abusive relationships and for child victims and perpetrators of domestic violence.
- Children should remain in the care of their non-offending parent whenever possible.
- When the risk of harm to the children outweighs the detriment of being separated from non-offending parents, alternative placement should be considered.

—North Carolina Well-Being and Domestic Violence Task Force

13. Which problems facing states do you think contribute to domestic violence?

14. How do you think cutting social services in North Carolina might affect children in homes with domestic violence?

Extended Response

15. Write a brief essay about the pros and cons of long terms for state judges. Include a discussion of how most states handle complaints about judges' improper conduct.

STOP

Civics ONLINE

For additional test practice, use Self-Check Quizzes—Chapter 12 on glencoe.com.

Need Extra Help?															
If you missed question. . .	1	2	3	4	5	6	7	8	9	10	11	12	13	14	15
Go to page. . .	352	359	364	368	353	359	364	365	367	369	353	353	360	360	369

ASSESSMENT

dent can verify the correct answer by equating the key term "essential social services" with the label "welfare loads" in the cartoon.

12. B Students can eliminate answer C since outsourcing was not mentioned in Section 2. A student can eliminate answer A since the text of Problems Facing States presents increasing taxes as a solution, rather than a problem. Although both reductions in grants-in-aid and increased pressure from the Supreme Court to address urban problems present dilemmas, the student can associate the money pictured in the cartoon with grants-in-aid to identify the correct answer.

Document-Based Questions

13. Answers may include the following: poverty, unemployment, drug and alcohol abuse, and lack of education.

14. Answers may include the idea that children in abusive situations will more likely remain in these harmful situations and will likely sustain serious injuries.

Extended Response

15. Student essays will vary but should present the benefits and drawbacks of long terms for state judges, as well as a discussion of the review board concept versus impeachment for investigating charges of misconduct and referring removal recommendations to the state's Supreme Court.

---

9. C Although all answers are types of courts explained in Section 4, students can use their knowledge of the difference between trial courts and appeals courts to eliminate answers B and D. A student can further eliminate trial courts by identifying traffic violations as misdemeanors, not felonies.

10. D After reading the body of the Selection of Judges text in Section 4, students will recognize that states use one or more of all three methods to select state judges.

Critical Thinking

11. B In Section 2's Problems Facing States, students will have read about current issues plaguing state legislatures. Careful examination of the cartoon will help a student eliminate answers A, C, and D since the cartoonist makes no mention of jobs. The stu-

Civics ONLINE

Have students visit the Web site at glencoe.com to review Chapter 12 and take the **Self-Check Quiz**.

Need Extra Help?

Have students refer to the pages listed if they miss any of the questions.

Key to Ability Levels

BL	Below level	AL	Above level
OL	On level	ELL	English Language Learners

Key to Teaching Resources

- 📁 Print Material
- 💿 CD-ROM or DVD
- 🖨 Transparency

Levels					Resources	Chapter Opener	Section 1	Section 2	Section 3	Chapter Assess
BL	OL	AL	ELL							
					FOCUS					
BL	OL	AL	ELL	🖨	Daily Focus Skills Transparencies		13–1	13–2	13–3	
					TEACH					
BL	OL		ELL	📁	Reading Essentials and Note-Taking Guide*		p. 123	p. 126	p. 129	
	OL	AL		📁	Citizenship/Decision-Making Activity, URB		p. 3	p. 3	p. 3	
	OL	AL		📁	Economics Activity, URB		p. 5			
BL	OL	AL	ELL	📁	Content Vocabulary Activity, URB*	p. 43	p. 43	p. 43	p. 43	
BL	OL	AL	ELL	📁	Academic Vocabulary Activity, URB	p. 45	p. 45	p. 45	p. 45	
	OL			📁	Biography Activity, URB		p. 47			
BL	OL	AL	ELL	📁	Writing Skills Activity, URB		p. 49			
	OL	AL		📁	Critical Thinking Skills Activity, URB		p. 53	p. 53		
BL	OL	AL	ELL	📁	Chart, Graph, and Map Skills Activity, URB		p. 55			
BL	OL	AL	ELL	📁	Differentiated Instruction, URB		p. 57			
BL	OL	AL	ELL	📁	School-to-Home Connection Activity, URB*	p. 59	p. 59	p. 59	p. 59	
BL	OL		ELL	📁	Guided Reading Activities, URB*		p. 63	p. 64	p. 65	
BL	OL	AL	ELL	📁	Writer's Guidebook	✓	✓	✓	✓	✓
	OL	AL		💿	Primary Source Document Library	✓	✓	✓	✓	✓
BL	OL	AL	ELL	💿	Daily Lecture & Discussion Notes (in Pres. Plus)		✓	✓	✓	✓
BL	OL	AL	ELL	💿	StudentWorks™ Plus		✓	✓	✓	✓
BL	OL	AL	ELL	💿	Section Spotlight Videos		✓	✓	✓	
BL	OL	AL	ELL	🖨	TIME Interpreting Political Cartoons Transp.				Ch. 13	
BL	OL	AL	ELL	🖨	Writing Process Transparencies	✓	✓	✓	✓	✓

Note: Please refer to the *Unit 4 Resource Book* for this chapter's URB materials.

* Also available in Spanish

- Interactive Lesson Planner
- Interactive Teacher Edition
- Fully editable blackline masters
- Section Spotlight Videos Launch
- Differentiated Lesson Plans
- Printable reports of daily assignments
- Standards Tracking System

Levels BL OL AL ELL		Resources	Chapter Opener	Section 1	Section 2	Section 3	Chapter Assess
		TEACH (continued)					
Teacher Resources	📁	**Building Academic Vocabulary**	✓	✓	✓	✓	✓
	📁	**Strategies for Success**	✓	✓	✓	✓	✓
	📁	**Teacher's Guide to Differentiated Instruction**	✓	✓	✓	✓	✓
	💿	**Graphing Tool**	✓	✓	✓	✓	✓
	💿	**Presentation Plus! with MindJogger CheckPoint**	✓	✓	✓	✓	✓
		ASSESS					
BL OL AL ELL	📁	**Quizzes and Tests***		p. 152	p. 153	p. 154	p. 155
BL OL AL ELL	📁	**Authentic Assessment with Rubrics**				p. 17	
BL OL AL ELL	📁	**Standardized Test Practice**		p. 25	p. 25	p. 25	p. 25
BL OL AL ELL	💿	*ExamView® Assessment Suite* CD-ROM		13–1	13–2	13–3	Ch. 13
		CLOSE					
BL ELL	📁	**Reteaching Activity, URB***		p. 61	p. 61	p. 61	
BL OL ELL	📁	**Reading and Study Skills Foldables™ Activity**	p. 74	p. 75		p. 75	
BL OL AL ELL	📁	*Civics Today* in Graphic Novel	p. 45	p. 45	p. 45	p. 45	
BL OL AL ELL	🖨	**Graphic Organizer Transparencies & Strategies**	✓	✓	✓	✓	✓

✓ Chapter- or unit-based activities applicable to all sections in this chapter

Using Study Central™

Main Ideas

What is Study Central™?

Study Central™ is an interactive, online tool that lists the main ideas for each section of a chapter to help highlight key points and provide focus for class discussion.

How can Study Central™ help my students?

Study Central™ contains fun activities that students can use to review important content and reinforce effective study habits. By using the format of the Guide to Reading that opens each section in the textbook, Study Central™ has students write main idea statements as questions, which helps students to:

- build comprehension and study skills
- practice developing and answering questions

Visit glencoe.com and enter a *QuickPass*™ code to go directly to resources for each chapter.

Civics ONLINE

Visit glencoe.com and enter *QuickPass*™ code CIV1360c13T for Chapter 13 resources.

You can easily launch a wide range of digital products from your computer's desktop with the McGraw-Hill Social Studies widget.

	Student	Teacher	Parent
Media Library			
• Student Edition Section Audio	●		●
• Spanish Audio Summaries	●		●
• Section Spotlight Videos	●	●	●
***Civics Today* Online Learning Center (Web Site)**			
• Chapter Overviews	●	●	●
• Study Central™	●	●	●
• Study-to-Go	●	●	●
• Student Web Activities	●	●	●
• In Motion Animation	●	●	●
• Self-Check Quizzes	●	●	●
• ePuzzles and Games	●	●	●
• StudentWorks™ Plus Online	●	●	●
• Vocabulary eFlashcards	●	●	●
• Web Activity Lesson Plans		●	
• Vocabulary PuzzleMaker	●	●	●
Classroom Tools			
• Multilingual Glossary	●	●	●
• Beyond the Textbook	●	●	●
• NGS MapMachine	●	●	●

GLENCOE BOOKLINK 3

Use this database to search more than 30,000 titles to create a customized reading list for your students.

- Reading lists can be organized by students' reading level, author, genre, theme, or area of interest.
- The database provides Degrees of Reading Power™ (DRP) and Lexile™ readability scores for all selections.
- A brief summary of each selection is included.

Leveled reading suggestions for this chapter:

For students at a Grade 7 reading level:
- *The City and Its People: The Story of One City's Government,* by Alvin Schwartz

For students at a Grade 8 reading level:
- *Puritans, Pilgrims, and Merchants: Founders of the Northeastern Colonies,* by Kiernan Doherty

For students at a Grade 9 reading level:
- *Adlai E. Stevenson,* by Stuart G. Brown

For students at a Grade 10 reading level:
- *The City in History: Its Origins, Its Transformations, and Its Prospects,* by Lewis Mumford

For students at a Grade 11 reading level:
- *The Rise of the West: A History of the Human Community,* by William H. McNeill

READING SUPPORT FROM JAMESTOWN EDUCATION

- **Timed Readings Plus in Social Studies** helps students increase their reading rate and fluency while maintaining comprehension. The 400-word passages are similar to those found on state and national assessments.

- **Reading in the Content Area: Social Studies** concentrates on six essential reading skills that help students better comprehend what they read. The book includes 75 high-interest nonfiction passages written at increasing levels of difficulty.

- **Reading Social Studies** includes strategic reading instruction and vocabulary support in Social Studies content for both ELLs and native speakers of English.

- **Content Vocabulary Workout** (Grades 6–8) accelerates reading comprehension through focused vocabulary development. Social Studies content vocabulary comes from the glossaries of Glencoe's Middle School Social Studies texts. www.jamestowneducation.com

KEY Teacher Wraparound

Use this key to help you identify the different types of prompts found in the Teacher Wraparound Edition.

R **Reading Strategies** activities help you teach reading skills and vocabulary.

C **Critical Thinking** strategies help students apply and extend what they have learned.

D **Differentiated Instruction** activities provide instruction for students learning to speak English, along with suggestions for teaching various types of learners.

S **Skill Practice** strategies help students practice historical analysis and geography skills.

W **Writing Support** activities provide writing opportunities to help students comprehend the text.

Teaching strategies and activities have been coded for ability level appropriateness.

AL Activities for students working above grade level

OL Activities for students working on grade level

BL Activities for students working below grade level

ELL Activities for English Language Learners

Focus

Why It Matters

Ask: What daily activities do you think are governed by local government? *(Answers may include attending school, riding on the school bus, placement of stop signs, playing soccer in the park, drinking clean water, and so on.)*

More About the Photo

Visual Literacy Northampton, Massachusetts, was settled in 1654 by Puritan farmers who were attracted to the rich farmland and its location near the Connecticut River. Northampton is known not only for its witch trials and stern preachings from Jonathan Edwards but also for its revolutionary reforms. After the Revolutionary War, farmers were struggling financially and could not pay their taxes. When the state asserted its authority to confiscate farms from delinquent taxpayers, the people spoke up. A group of farmers led by Daniel Shays marched down to the courthouse and let the politicians know this act was unacceptable. This rebellion, known as Shays's Rebellion (1789), was instrumental in prompting a revision of the Articles of Confederation.

Teach

 As you begin teaching each section, use these questions and activities to help students focus on the Big Ideas.

Section 1

City Governments Ask: If national and state governments legislate and enforce laws, what do city governments do? *(They ensure that people receive the services they need, provide local legislation, and protect the people.)* Tell students that

Local Government

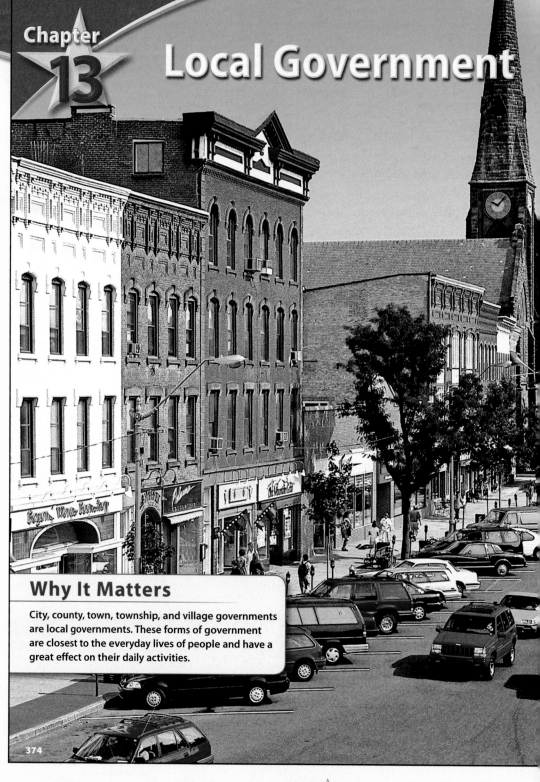

Why It Matters

City, county, town, township, and village governments are local governments. These forms of government are closest to the everyday lives of people and have a great effect on their daily activities.

374

Section 1 provides an overview of how local governments are formed and what their duties are. **OL**

Section 2

County Governments Ask: Who do you think runs the county? *(Answers will vary depending on the county. Usually an elected board runs a county, and the county sheriff enforces local mandates.)* Point out that county governments are just as important as city governments, especially in rural areas. Students will learn about the formation of county governments and the services provided by county officials in Section 2. **OL**

🔊 **Chapter Audio**

BIG Ideas

Section 1: City Governments

People form governments to establish order, provide security, and accomplish common goals. A variety of forms of city government has been developed to meet different needs.

Section 2: County Governments

People form governments to establish order, provide security, and accomplish common goals. County governments somewhat mirror city governments but also meet different needs and provide different services.

Section 3: Towns, Townships, and Villages

Political and economic institutions evolve to help individuals and groups accomplish their goals. Town meetings and township governments developed early in U.S. history and have remained active to the present.

Main Street,
Northampton,
Massachusetts

FOLDABLES™
Study Organizer

Identifying Main Ideas Foldable Make the following Foldable to help you identify the main ideas about city, county, and township governments and their responsibilities and roles.

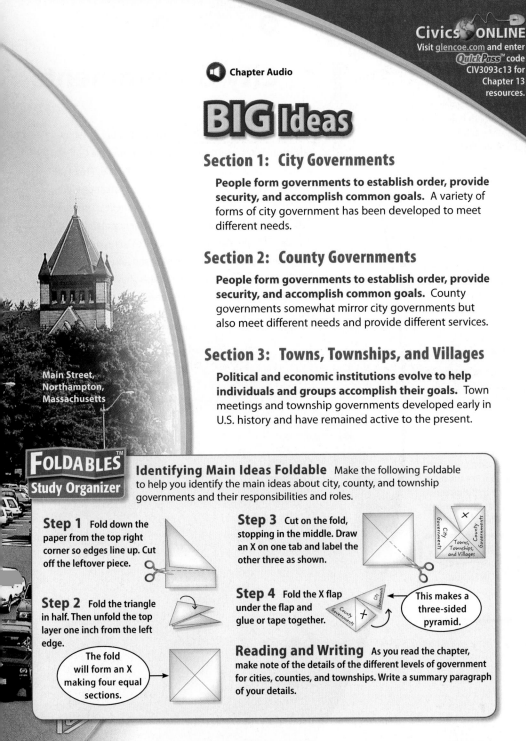

Step 1 Fold down the paper from the top right corner so edges line up. Cut off the leftover piece.

Step 2 Fold the triangle in half. Then unfold the top layer one inch from the left edge.

The fold will form an X making four equal sections.

Step 3 Cut on the fold, stopping in the middle. Draw an X on one tab and label the other three as shown.

Step 4 Fold the X flap under the flap and glue or tape together.

This makes a three-sided pyramid.

Reading and Writing As you read the chapter, make note of the details of the different levels of government for cities, counties, and townships. Write a summary paragraph of your details.

FOLDABLES™
Study Organizer **Dinah Zike's Foldables**

Purpose This Foldable guides the student to understand specific details about local governments. The completed Foldable creates a pyramid to help students identify the details for each different type of local government: city, county, township, and village. **OL**

📁 More Foldables activities for this chapter can be found in the *Dinah Zike's Reading and Study Skills Foldables* ancillary.

Chapter 13   375

Section 3 ⭐

Towns, Townships, and Villages Ask: What kind of government would you expect to find in a small town or village? *(Students may answer that small towns have fewer people in power. For example, they may just have a mayor who assumes many roles.)* In Section 3, students will learn the differences between towns, townships, and villages and what a small community government does. **OL**

Focus

Bellringer
Daily Focus Transparency 13–1

Guide to Reading
Answers to Graphic:

law enforcement
fire protection
schools
City Services
parks and recreation
water and sewage, garbage pick-up

Section Spotlight Video

Have students watch the Chapter 13, Section 1 video at glencoe.com.

Resource Manager

Guide to Reading

Big Idea
People form governments to establish order, provide security, and accomplish common goals.

Content Vocabulary
- incorporate *(p. 377)*
- city charter *(p. 377)*
- home rule *(p. 377)*
- ordinance *(p. 378)*
- strong-mayor system *(p. 379)*
- weak-mayor system *(p. 379)*
- at-large election *(p. 380)*
- special district *(p. 382)*
- metropolitan area *(p. 382)*
- suburb *(p. 382)*

Academic Vocabulary
- dominate *(p. 379)*
- furthermore *(p. 379)*
- reluctant *(p. 379)*

Reading Strategy
Organizing As you read, complete a web diagram like the one below by listing services that city governments provide.

schools
City Services

City Governments

Real World Civics On September 8, 1900, Galveston, Texas, was overrun with water from the Gulf of Mexico. Hurricane winds traveling over 100 miles (161 km) per hour swept through Galveston Island in what residents have often called the "worst disaster" in America. Thousands died. The city rallied immediately. Emergency meetings were called to provide necessary services to residents. The city government then built a seawall and raised the entire city. Engineers and construction workers have made every effort to ensure that this tragedy never happens again.

▼ **Topsy-turvy destruction in Galveston, Texas**

R Reading Strategies	**C** Critical Thinking	**D** Differentiated Instruction	**W** Writing Support	**S** Skill Practice
Teacher Edition • Identifying, p. 377 • Inferring, p. 379 • Defining, p. 382 **Additional Resources** • Cont. Vocab., URB p. 43 • Ac. Vocab., URB p. 45 • Guid. Read., URB p. 63	**Teacher Edition** • Making Inferences, p. 377, 378 • Drawing Con., p. 380 • Analyzing, p. 381 **Additional Resources** • Econ. Act., URB p. 5 • Biographies, URB p. 47 • Crit. Think., URB p. 53	**Teacher Edition** • English Learners, p. 380 **Additional Resources** • Diff. Instr., URB p. 57 • Graphic Novel, p. 45	**Teacher Edition** • Personal Writing, p. 381 **Additional Resources** • Cit./Dec. Making, URB p. 3 • Writing Skills Act., URB p. 49	**Teacher Edition** • Interpreting a Chart, p. 378 **Additional Resources** • Chart, Graph, and Map Skills, URB p. 55 • Daily Focus Trans., 13–1

Chokoloskee, Florida This city hall houses the various departments of city government. *Identifying* **What document grants the power of a local government to become a city?**

How Are Local Governments Formed?

Main Idea Local governments are created by the states.

Civics & You What has your city or town government done for you lately? Read more to find out how local governments are created.

The United States has become a mostly urban nation over the past century. In 1900 only about one-third of the nation's 76 million people lived in urban areas. Today about three-fourths of the 300 million Americans do. Although they are the closest units of government to the people, local governments have no legal independence. The U.S. Constitution does not even mention the existence of local governments. They are created by, and are entirely dependent on, the state. State constitutions usually establish the powers and duties of local governments.

The City Charter Most states define a municipality as an **incorporated** place—a locality with an officially organized government that provides services to residents. A city is a municipal government. New cities are created every year as people who live in urban communities incorporate. They do this by applying to the state legislature for a **city charter,** a document that grants power to a local government. A community must meet certain general requirements to obtain a charter. For example, the community may be required to have a population of a certain minimum size. A city charter is much like a constitution, describing the type of city government, its structure, and its powers.

Home Rule For many decades there has been a movement to grant home rule to cities. **Home rule** allows cities to write their own charters, to choose their own type of government, and to manage their own affairs, although they still have to follow state laws.

✔ **Reading Check** Summarizing How are city governments created?

R Reading Strategy

Identifying Ask: Under what authority do local governments operate? *(state constitutions)* **BL**

C Critical Thinking

Making Inferences Ask: Why would cities benefit from home rule? *(Many cities are large and populous and would benefit from autonomy. Each city's structure could be different based on its needs.)* **AL**

Caption Answer:

a city charter

✔ **Reading Check Answer:** Cities are created after residents apply for and receive a city charter from the state legislature.

Differentiated Instruction

Housing Booms

ECONOMICS ACTIVITY 4

Housing Booms

Economics Activity 4, URB pp. 5–6

Objective:	To see the housing market as an economic indicator
Focus:	Analyze the information in the charts.
Teach:	Discuss how new housing benefits the economy.
Assess:	Write a paragraph explaining the House Price Index.
Close:	Create a chart comparing the number of houses built in a Metropolitan Statistical Area.

Differentiated Instruction Strategies

BL Explain why major cities have surrounding suburbs.

AL Explain why housing prices are higher in Washington, D.C., than in other parts of the United States.

ELL Define the phrase "Metropolitan Statistical Areas."

C Critical Thinking

Making Inferences Ask: Why did most cities prior to the twentieth century use a mayor-council form of government? *(The people wanted to make sure they had a voice in electing members of the council as well as their city's mayor and more control over local issues.)* **OL**

S Skill Practice

Interpreting a Chart Ask students to explain what the arrow from the City Council box to the Mayor box represents in the weak-mayor system. *(The arrow illustrates that the city council makes most of the decisions and defers to the mayor only when he or she needs to break a tie.)* **OL**

For additional practice on this Skill (Interpreting a Chart), see the **Skills Handbook**.

Analyzing Charts

Answers:
1. the weak-mayor system
2. If the mayor appoints the heads of departments, they answer to him or her. If the department heads are answerable to the council, they have many bosses. This could lead to duplication of effort, uneven management, or favoritism.

Hands-On Chapter Project
Step 1

Forming a Local Government

Step 1: Running for City Government Organize the class into two groups: a strong-mayor system and a weak-mayor system.

Directions Write the Big Idea on the board. Tell each group that they will choose two students to run for mayor, and four students to run for city council. Only two members will be elected. Students not running for office will serve as campaign volunteers and help create posters, make a TV or radio ad, and write speeches to be presented to the class in Section 2.

Have students read current newspapers to learn about local concerns such as environmental issues; educational issues; ambulance, firefighter, or police services; and so on. Within each group, one or two students will be reporters. They will write an article that outlines the pros and cons of each candidate. Each student in a group should have an assignment. **OL**
(Project continued in Section 2)

The Mayor-Council Form

Main Idea A common form of city government features an executive and a legislature.

Civics & You Can you name your mayor or a council member? Read to find out what these officials do.

Every municipal charter provides for the type of government the community will have. Today urban areas in the United States use one of three basic forms of municipal government. These are the mayor-council form, the commission form, and the council-manager form.

A Division of Power

Until the early twentieth century, almost all American cities had a mayor-council form of government, which remains a common form of government today. It is the form of government preferred by the largest cities.

The mayor-council form follows the traditional concept of separation of powers.

Executive power belongs to a mayor, and legislative power to a council. Voters elect a mayor and the members of a city council. The mayor is the chief executive of the city government and is responsible for overseeing the operation of administrative offices. Often the mayor appoints the heads of departments, such as public works, planning, police and fire protection, and other offices.

The City's Legislature The council acts as the legislature, approving the city budget and passing city laws, which are usually known as **ordinances**. Most city councils have fewer than 10 members, who usually serve four-year terms. Some cities are divided into voting districts called wards. Each ward elects a representative to the city council. In other cities, some or all of the council members are known as members-at-large, elected by the entire city.

Strong Mayors Two main types of mayor-council government exist, depending on the power given to the mayor. These two types are the strong-mayor system and the weak-mayor system.

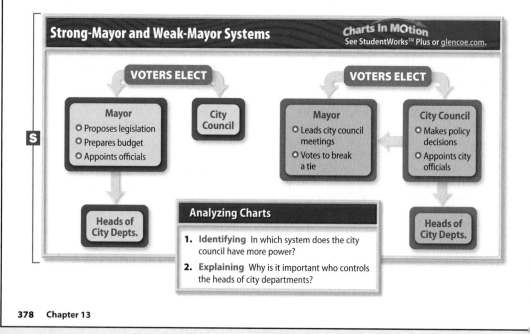

Strong-Mayor and Weak-Mayor Systems

Charts In MOtion See StudentWorks™ Plus or glencoe.com.

VOTERS ELECT

Mayor
- Proposes legislation
- Prepares budget
- Appoints officials

City Council

Heads of City Depts.

VOTERS ELECT

Mayor
- Leads city council meetings
- Votes to break a tie

City Council
- Makes policy decisions
- Appoints city officials

Heads of City Depts.

Analyzing Charts

1. **Identifying** In which system does the city council have more power?
2. **Explaining** Why is it important who controls the heads of city departments?

Most large cities operate under a **strong-mayor system.** The mayor has strong executive powers, such as the power to veto ordinances the city council passes, appoint various city officials, and write the city budget. Strong mayors tend to **dominate,** or control, city government because membership on the city council, even in large cities, is usually a part-time job. **Furthermore,** because council members are elected by wards, they focus on issues that are important to their parts of town. By contrast, a strong mayor usually works full-time, has assistants, and represents the entire city.

Weak Mayors Under a **weak-mayor system,** the mayor's authority is limited. The council, not the mayor, appoints department heads and makes most policy decisions. The mayor usually presides over council meetings but votes only in case of a tie. The weak-mayor system dates from the nation's earliest days. Former colonists, tired of the injustices they suffered at the hands of the British government, were **reluctant,** or unwilling, to grant any official too much power.

Successful Mayor-Council Governments The success of the mayor-council form of government depends to a large extent on the individual who serves as mayor. In the strong-mayor system, a politically skillful mayor can provide effective leadership. Under the weak-mayor plan, because official responsibility is in many hands, success depends upon the cooperation of the mayor and the council.

✔ **Reading Check** Analyzing What are the mayor and council's roles in decision-making under a weak-mayor form of government?

Civics ONLINE
Student Web Activity Visit glencoe.com and complete the Chapter 13 Web Activity.

A Mayor with Class

Michael Sessions, 18, has a new after-school activity: he is running a small town! Sessions was sworn in as the mayor of Hillsdale, Michigan, in 2005. He joined the race as a write-in candidate and beat the former mayor by just two votes.

The young mayor has been involved in politics ever since a fourth-grade trip to the state capitol in Lansing. But it was not until 2003, when his dad lost his job when the auto plant he worked for moved to Mexico, that Michael was moved to take action. "The people of Hillsdale are hard-working, and I knew I had to try to bring jobs here and retain them," he says. "I ran because I wanted to get involved."

When Sessions walks the halls of Hillsdale High School, kids greet him with "Hello, Mayor" and high fives. He is managing to keep a 3.25 GPA in courses that include Spanish, computer science, and accounting, while working as a part-time teacher's aide. All that, plus he is running a town with a $20 million annual budget. "I'll be a student from 7:50 to 2:30," Sessions says. "And then I'll work on mayor stuff from 3 to 6."

Among his duties are signing off on the budget, running Hillsdale's city council meetings, and exercising emergency powers in the event of a crisis.

Sessions serving as mayor

Making a Difference **CITIZENSHIP**

Explaining Why did Michael decide to run for mayor?

R Reading Strategy

Inferring Ask: Why are council members in large cities often part-time officials? *(They are often prominent businessmen or women who have other jobs; city council jobs do not pay enough; there is not enough work for them to make it a full-time job.)* **AL**

✔ **Reading Check** **Answer:** The mayor's role is to run the meetings and be a tiebreaker. The council's role is to appoint department heads and make policy.

Civics ONLINE

Objectives and answers to the **Student Web Activity** can be found at glencoe.com under the Web Activity Lesson Plan for this chapter.

TIME™ Teens in Action

Answer: He wanted to become actively involved in his community and help bring jobs to the people.

Additional Support

Activity: Collaborative Learning

Identifying Central Issues Help students understand that the city council is one of the first places they can go to initiate a change. Divide the class into groups and have each group find out about a local ordinance, service, or issue that affects students personally. For example, does the city have a curfew? Are students allowed to skateboard in the downtown? Can they be absent from school to attend a political demonstration? Are only two or three teens at a time allowed in small stores? Is loud music in a moving vehicle allowed? Have each group report its findings to the class. **OL**

Teacher Tip

This activity requires students to understand local ordinances. Discuss that any proposed law must not conflict with state legislation. Explain that watchdog groups attend meetings to make sure civil liberties are not being violated.

C Critical Thinking

Drawing Conclusions Ask students to discuss the benefits of hiring a professional to create budgets and to manage departments rather than electing someone with political ambitions. **Ask:** In what way can a hired manager be more efficient than an elected mayor? *(Students may say that a professional manager focuses on the job. He or she does not have to worry about promises made during elections or to try to please constituents. A professional who is hired does not owe anyone any favors.)* **OL**

D Differentiated Instruction

English Learners Explain to students that candidates can be elected in two ways. They can be elected by the people whom they will represent within an area. (Only the people who live in that area can vote.) Or a candidate can be elected "at-large," meaning that all the voters can vote and the candidate must represent all of those voters. **ELL**

American Biography

Answer:
He became the first Asian American to win elected office in New York City.

Additional Support

American Biography

John Liu (1967–)

In the Flushing, Queens, section of New York City, voters made history in 2001. They elected John C. Liu to represent their district on the City Council. Liu became the first Asian American to win elected office in New York City—or anyplace else in New York State. "We are in a new era," Liu declared in his victory speech.

Liu, who describes himself as a "Flushing boy," immigrated to Queens from Taiwan at age 5. He attended New York City public schools and, later, State University of New York, before taking a job at an accounting firm. Public service paved his way to the city council. Liu did volunteer work in junior high and high school. In college, he took part in student government. As an adult, Liu worked to improve Flushing by forming community action groups.

As a member of the city council, Liu faced the task of not only representing Flushing but of uniting one of the city's most diverse districts. In a post-election pep talk, Liu told supporters, "The issues facing this district affect us all, and we will solve these issues together." As a member of the Council's Committee on Education, Liu worked to raise standards in public schools and invest city resources in the students. He also instituted programs to fund high-tech upgrades to local schools.

Making a Difference — CiTIZENSHIP

John Liu has lived most of his life and participated in public service in the New York City area.
Explaining How did Liu make history in 2001?

The Council-Manager and Commission Forms

Main Idea Two other local government types are the council-manager and the commission.

Civics & You Do you think a town can be run like a business? Read to find out what form of government adopts this idea.

C Two forms of government that started in the early 1900s are the council-manager and commission forms. The council-manager form of government is a popular form of city government today. When it first appeared in 1912, it was seen as a way to reform corrupt or inefficient mayor-council governments.

Under the council-manager form, the city council, as the legislative body, appoints the manager in much the same way that a school board might appoint a superintendent. The manager recommends a budget, oversees city departments, and deals with personnel matters. The manager reports to the council as a whole. The council can hire and remove the manager by a majority vote. Most managers have specialized training in areas such as budgeting, financial management, and planning.

D In many smaller cities with managers, council members are elected in **at-large elections.** This means they run in citywide elections rather than representing only one district. Some people believe this system forces members to consider the interests of the entire city instead of only looking out for the concerns of their own neighborhoods.

Activity: Collaborative Learning

Setting a Purpose Discuss that in many urban and suburban areas, citizens form groups to improve the quality of their neighborhoods. They may want to ensure that no businesses may move in, for instance. Have students find out about the bylaws, goals, and activities of a neighborhood association in their area. Students may want to attend an association meeting and take notes on how the meeting was conducted. They might invite an officer to speak to the class about what they do and the process involved in making changes. If students live in an area with a neighborhood or homeowners' association, have them read the restrictions and discuss what they mean with the class. **OL**

The Commission Form

The commission form of government was invented a few years before the council-manager form. Only a handful of cities continue to use it.

Executives and Legislators A commission government has no separation of legislative and executive powers. Instead, separate departments, each of which handles a different set of responsibilities, govern the city. Some of the most common departments are police, fire, finance, and health.

The elected heads of these departments, called commissioners, perform executive duties for their particular departments. They also meet together as a commission, with legislative power to pass city ordinances and make policy decisions.

Serious Flaws The commission form of municipal government developed after a devastating hurricane struck Galveston, Texas, in 1900. Thousands died and the city was nearly destroyed. City leaders decided that a commission government was the best way to handle the emergency.

Since that time, however, other cities have found that a commission government is not always efficient in running a city. Without clear leadership, a commission is often unable to set and meet goals. Each commissioner is likely to concentrate primarily on his or her own department, without considering the problems of the city as a whole.

Recognizing its drawbacks, most cities that once used a commission system have switched to a council-manager or mayor-council form of government.

C **Critical Thinking**

Analyzing Ask students to state reasons why the commission form of government was successful in Galveston, Texas. Write their reasons on the board. Then discuss why this system of government would not be as effective on a routine basis. *(Students may offer that in a crisis, a leader in each of those departments would know best what to do. There would be no red tape, and the people could do their jobs fast and efficiently. On a routine basis, there would be too many leaders which could cause confusion.)* **OL**

W **Writing Support**

Personal Writing Have students reflect and write about meetings they have attended in school or in their communities. Have them answer the following questions: What kind of meeting was it? Was it productive? Who was in charge? What kind of system allows for more success in discussions? **OL**

Analyzing Charts

Answers:
1. the board of commissioners
2. the city manager

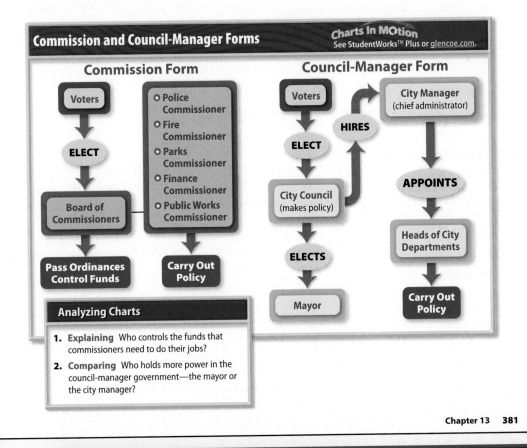

Commission and Council-Manager Forms

Charts In MOtion
See StudentWorks™ Plus or glencoe.com.

Commission Form

Voters → ELECT → Board of Commissioners → Pass Ordinances Control Funds

Police Commissioner, Fire Commissioner, Parks Commissioner, Finance Commissioner, Public Works Commissioner → Carry Out Policy

Council-Manager Form

Voters → ELECT → City Council (makes policy) → ELECTS → Mayor

HIRES → City Manager (chief administrator) → APPOINTS → Heads of City Departments → Carry Out Policy

Analyzing Charts

1. **Explaining** Who controls the funds that commissioners need to do their jobs?
2. **Comparing** Who holds more power in the council-manager government—the mayor or the city manager?

Differentiated Instruction

Leveled Activities

BL Writing Skills Activity 13, URB pp. 49–52

OL Biography Activity 13, URB pp. 47–48

AL Chart/Graph/Map Skills Activity 13, URB pp. 55–56

ELL Guided Reading 13-1, URB p. 63

R Reading Strategy

Defining Have students define "metropolitan area," "city," and "suburb." *(A metropolitan area includes the city and surrounding suburbs; a city is an urban area with a city charter; a suburb is a community that lies just outside of a city.)* **BL**

✔ **Reading Check** **Answer:** In a council-manager government, the executive powers go to the hired city manager. In a mayor-council government, the elected mayor has power.

Assess

Civics ONLINE

Study Central™ provides summaries, interactive games, and online graphic organizers to help students review content.

Close

Summarizing Write headings on the board: mayor-council, commission, and council-manager. Have students vote for and discuss which system of government is the most effective and why. **OL**

Section 1 Review

Other Units of Government

Two other important concepts in municipal government are the special district and the metropolitan area. The **special district** is a unit of government that deals with a specific function, such as education, water supply, or transportation. A board or commission, which may be elected or appointed, runs a special district. Special districts are the most numerous types of local government, because in some states several kinds of special districts overlap most cities. The local school district is the most common example of a special district.

R A **metropolitan area** is a central city and its surrounding suburbs. **Suburbs** are communities near or around cities. A metropolitan area may also include small towns that lie beyond the suburbs. The U.S. Census Bureau has an official name for urban concentrations made up of a central city and suburbs with a combined population of 50,000 or more—Metropolitan Statistical Areas.

Growing Suburbs In the United States since the 1950s, suburbs have expanded around central cities. As a result, often the suburban population has become much greater than that of the central city. For example, Detroit's population dropped from nearly 2 million in 1950 to about 870,000 in 2006, while its suburbs now have more than 3 million people.

The growth in population and the expansion of business in metropolitan areas have created problems in transportation, pollution, law enforcement, and land management. Some metropolitan areas have created a council whereby the central city joins with its suburbs to make area-wide decisions about growth and services, such as mass transit. Today, with fuel supplies and costs at issue, mass transit systems are under consideration in many cities.

✔ **Reading Check** **Contrasting** How does the council-manager government differ from the mayor-council government?

Section 1 Review

Vocabulary

1. **Write** complete sentences related to city government: *incorporate, city charter, home rule, ordinance, strong-mayor system, weak-mayor system, at-large election, special district, metropolitan area, suburb.*

Main Ideas

2. **Describing** What is the purpose of city charters?

3. **Explaining** In the commission form of government, who holds legislative power?

4. **Explaining** Why was the council-manager form of city government developed?

Critical Thinking

5. **BIG Ideas** If you created a city government, what form would you use and why?

6. **Identifying** Use a graphic organizer like the one below to identify the duties of a mayor in a strong-mayor government.

Mayor — Directs dept. heads

CITIZENSHIP Activity

7. **Expository Writing** What is an important issue in your community that you would like to bring before the city council for action? What kind of action would you recommend that the council take? Write a letter to the council addressing the issue.

Civics ONLINE

Study Central™ To review this section, go to glencoe.com.

Answers

1. Sentences should use vocabulary words according to their definitions in the section and in the Glossary.

2. It grants power to a local government, describing a city's type of government, structure, and powers.

3. the board of commissioners

4. to reform corrupt and ineffective mayor-council governments

5. Answers will vary. Students should explain their choices.

6.

Mayor — proposes legislation, prepares a budget, appoints officials, directs dept. heads

7. Letters should mention a community issue and suggested action to take.

Guide to Reading

Big Idea
People form governments to establish order, provide security, and accomplish common goals.

Content Vocabulary
- county *(p. 384)*
- county seat *(p. 384)*

Academic Vocabulary
- levy *(p. 385)*
- estimate *(p. 386)*

Reading Strategy
Identifying As you read, identify the county officials elected by voters in most counties on a graphic organizer like the one below.

Section 2

🔊 Section Audio   🎬 Spotlight Video

County Governments

Real World Civics Counties provide many enjoyable moments and services to their residents—especially the elderly. County departments that serve seniors often have Web sites that allow residents to browse through a list of helpful resources such as long-term care facilities, transportation options, hotlines, and other services. County departments also provide access to information about laws that affect the lives of seniors. In addition, counties provide a wealth of recreational outlets for older citizens, from field trips to classes that offer lifelong learning opportunities.

▼ **Seniors share activities at a county-run senior center**

383

Focus

Guide to Reading
Answers to Graphic:

🎬 **Section Spotlight Video**

To generate student interest and provide a springboard for class discussion, access the Chapter 13, Section 2 video at glencoe.com or on the video DVD.

Resource Manager

R **Reading Strategies**	C **Critical Thinking**	D **Differentiated Instruction**	W **Writing Support**	S **Skill Practice**
Teacher Edition • Explaining, p. 385 • Identifying, p. 386 **Additional Resources** • Cont. Vocab., URB p. 43 • Ac. Vocab., URB p. 45 • Guid. Read., URB p. 64 • RENTG, p. 126	**Teacher Edition** • Comparing, p. 386 **Additional Resources** • Crit. Think., URB p. 53 • Quizzes and Tests, p. 153	**Teacher Edition** • Interpersonal, p. 384 **Additional Resources** • School-to-Home Conn., URB p. 59 • Graphic Novel, p. 45 • Teacher's Guide to Differentiated Instruction, p. 17	**Teacher Edition** • Descriptive Writing, p. 385 **Additional Resources** • Cit./Dec. Making, URB p. 3	**Teacher Edition** • Using Geo. Skills, p. 384 **Additional Resources** • Daily Focus Trans., 13–2

Teach

S Skill Practice

Using Geography Skills Have students use a county map of your state to identify the number of counties, the largest county, the smallest county, and the county in which they live. Students who live in Connecticut and Rhode Island should research why their states are not divided into counties. **OL**

D Differentiated Instruction

Interpersonal Have students attend a county board meeting and describe the courthouse, how business was conducted, and the items that were discussed. **OL**

Caption Answer:

The county sheriff can travel outside city limits and manage county jails.

✓ Reading Check **Answer:** They were located in towns most people could reach and return home by horse and buggy within one day.

Hands-On Chapter Project
Step 2

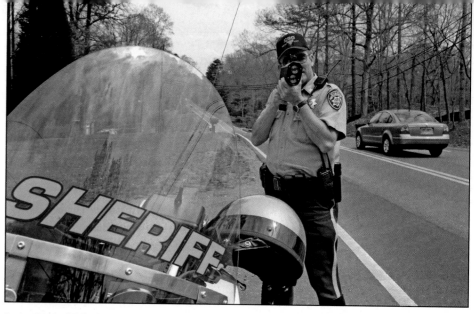

Protection and Safety County sheriffs provide protection and enforce laws meant to keep residents safe. Highway patrol is one protection. *Speculating* Why do you think it is necessary to have county sheriffs in addition to city police?

Organization

Main Idea The nation's more than 3,000 counties show great variety in size, population, and government.

Civics & You Have you ever had to call 911 or buy a license for your dog? Read to find out what level of government handles these activities in most states.

The **county** is normally a state's largest territorial and political subdivision. The U.S. Census Bureau recognizes more than 3,000 counties or countylike units in the nation. All states, except Connecticut and Rhode Island, are divided into counties. There is great variety among American counties. Los Angeles County, California, for example, has about 10 million residents, while 67 people live in Loving County, Texas, according to the 2000 census. San Bernardino County, California, has more land area than the states of Vermont and New Hampshire combined. Texas has 254 counties, and Delaware and Hawaii have 3 each. Alaska and Louisiana do not even use the word *county*. In Alaska, counties are called boroughs; in Louisiana, they are known as parishes.

What Is a County Seat?

When many Midwestern and Southern states were mapping out counties during the nineteenth century, officials were concerned that all citizens would have access to county services. The idea was that residents who lived in the farthest corners of a county should be able to get to the county courthouse and back by horse and buggy in the same day. That is why states in these regions have so many relatively small counties. The county courthouse was the center of government, serving as a headquarters for law enforcement, record keeping, and road construction as well as courts. The towns where the county courthouse is located are called **county seats.**

✓ Reading Check Explaining How were county seats originally chosen?

Forming a Local Government

Step 2: Investigating County Officers' Jobs Groups from Step 1 will present posters, ads, and make speeches for the class. Have all students vote for candidates in each group and announce the winners.

Directions Have students break into the two groups again. This time, each group will research the jobs of county officials: county treasurer, sheriff, tax assessor, district attorney, coroner, and county clerk. Have groups prepare a bulleted list of employment requirements for each position. Students may search the Internet and call county offices to find out about officials' responsibilities and qualifications. Have groups discuss their results and state if any of these positions would interest them as possible career choices. Encourage groups to invite a county officer to visit the class to discuss job opportunities. **OL**

(Project continued in Section 3)

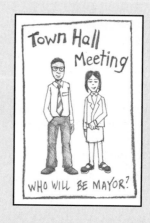

Functions

Main Idea County governments perform many different duties and provide an array of services to residents.

Civics & You What does the word *sheriff* mean to you? Read to find out what a modern-day sheriff does.

With modern transportation and the growth of cities, county government has changed. In some areas, cities now provide many of the services that counties once handled. However, county governments have grown in importance and assumed functions that city governments once handled, from sewer and water service to mass transit systems.

Who Runs a County?

A board of three to five elected commissioners, or supervisors, governs most counties. Most board members serve four-year terms. The board acts as a legislature, adopting ordinances and the annual budget, **levying** taxes, and enforcing laws. County governments have a variety of organizations. These include the commission-manager, commission-elected executive, and strong commission forms.

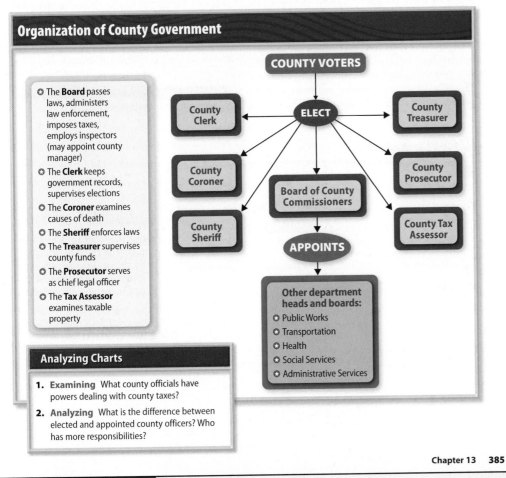

Organization of County Government

- The **Board** passes laws, administers law enforcement, imposes taxes, employs inspectors (may appoint county manager)
- The **Clerk** keeps government records, supervises elections
- The **Coroner** examines causes of death
- The **Sheriff** enforces laws
- The **Treasurer** supervises county funds
- The **Prosecutor** serves as chief legal officer
- The **Tax Assessor** examines taxable property

COUNTY VOTERS

ELECT

County Clerk

County Coroner

County Sheriff

Board of County Commissioners

County Treasurer

County Prosecutor

County Tax Assessor

APPOINTS

Other department heads and boards:
- Public Works
- Transportation
- Health
- Social Services
- Administrative Services

Analyzing Charts

1. **Examining** What county officials have powers dealing with county taxes?

2. **Analyzing** What is the difference between elected and appointed county officers? Who has more responsibilities?

Chapter 13 **385**

W Writing Support

Descriptive Writing Have students write two paragraphs. In the first paragraph, have students describe the many services that city dwellers need. In the second paragraph, have them describe services that people rely on in rural areas. **OL**

R Reading Strategy

Explaining Point out the word "levying." Tell students that in this sentence, levy is a verb, which means "to impose a fine or tax." **Ask:** Do tax assessors always collect the taxes they levy? *(No; sometimes people do not pay their taxes.)* **BL ELL**

Analyzing Charts

Answers:
1. the treasurer and tax assessor
2. The elected officers govern the county. The appointed officers manage specialized departments. The elected officers have more responsibilities because their job descriptions are broader.

Differentiated Instruction

Drawing Conclusions

Critical Thinking Skills Activity 13, URB pp. 53–54

Objective:	To draw conclusions about an ordinance proposal
Focus:	Interpret information about the cost of living, minimum wage, and taxes.
Teach:	Discuss how wage increases affect all citizens.
Assess:	Develop a plan to help the workers and the businesses.
Close:	List the pros and cons of the ordinance.

Differentiated Instruction Strategies

BL List two reasons workers need a pay raise.

AL Write a letter to the editor supporting or opposing the ordinance.

ELL Draw a flowchart illustrating the proposals of the ordinance.

C Critical Thinking

Comparing **Ask:** How have county governments become more like city governments? *(As more people move to rural areas, the responsibilities of the officers have grown. Some have decided to appoint a county manager.)* **AL**

R Reading Strategy

Identifying **Ask:** What does a DA do? *(investigates crimes, brings charges, and prosecutes cases in court)* **OL**

✔ **Reading Check** **Answer:** a board of three to five elected county commissioners

Assess

Civics ONLINE

Study Central™ provides summaries, interactive games, and online graphic organizers to help students review content.

Close

Summarizing Have students write a brief summary stating the services their county provides to its citizens. **OL**

Section **2** Review

Like a City—but Different As their responsibilities have grown, many counties have adopted a form of government in which the county board operates only as a legislature. In some cases, the board of commissioners appoints a county manager, who acts much like a city manager in running the county government.

In other cases, counties have created a new elective office, that of a chief administrative official. This person, often called the county executive, handles all executive responsibilities. Whether appointed or elected, the county manager or executive appoints top officials and manages the organization. The board of commissioners functions alongside this leader, but only as a legislative body.

Sheriffs, DAs, and More

Separately elected officials run some county administrative offices. The sheriff is a county's chief law enforcement officer. The sheriff's department enforces court orders and manages the county jail. In some counties, the sheriff's department shares law enforcement duties with a separate police department. The district attorney (DA) is the county's prosecutor. The DA investigates crimes, brings charges against suspected lawbreakers, and prosecutes the cases in court.

Other county functions are led by officials who may be appointed or elected. The assessor examines all taxable property within the county and **estimates,** or approximately values, how much it is worth. The county's property tax is based on the assessor's estimate. The county finance director or treasurer supervises the county's funds. An auditor makes sure that the county's money is spent within the requirements of state and local law. A county clerk keeps official government records. A coroner works closely with the police department to establish the causes of unusual or suspicious deaths.

✔ **Reading Check** **Identifying** What body governs most counties in the United States?

Section **2** Review

Vocabulary

1. **Write** complete sentences related to county government using the following terms: *county, county seat.*

Main Ideas

2. **Explaining** Why are counties relatively small in the South and Midwest?

3. **Identifying** Many counties today provide services that cities used to handle. What are some services counties often provide today?

Critical Thinking

4. **BIG Ideas** Do you think the United States needs both city and county governments today? Give reasons to support your answer.

5. **Identifying** In a graphic organizer like the one below, list the other boards the county commissioners appoint.

CITIZENSHIP Activity

6. **Expository Writing** Should a county executive be elected or appointed? In a one-page paper explain the advantages and disadvantages of the two methods.

Civics ONLINE

Study Central™ To review this section, go to glencoe.com.

Answers

1. Sentences should use vocabulary words according to their definitions in the section and in the Glossary.

2. They were designed long ago so that residents in the farthest corners of the county could travel to and from the county courthouse in one day.

3. sewer and water service, mass transit systems, health and social services

4. Answers will vary. Students should provide reasons for their positions.

5.

County Commissioners — public works, transportation, social services, administrative services, health

6. Essays should include advantages and disadvantages of both methods. Suggest that students use a graphic organizer, such as a T-chart, to help solidify their ideas before they begin writing.

Guide to Reading

Big Idea
Political and economic institutions evolve to help individuals and groups accomplish their goals.

Content Vocabulary
- town (p. 388)
- town meeting (p. 388)
- township (p. 389)
- village (p. 390)

Academic Vocabulary
- complex (p. 389)
- similar (p. 389)
- decline (p. 390)

Reading Strategy
Identifying As you read, name the different forms of government below the county level by completing a graphic organizer like the one below.

Forms of Government

🔊 **Section Audio**   🎬 **Spotlight Video**

Towns, Townships, and Villages

Real World Civics Neither snow nor hail nor sleet can stop the people of Woodbury, Vermont, from casting their votes in a town meeting. The citizens here have a history of participation in local government that started in 1806. The town meeting provides a forum for community members to voice their feelings on matters ranging from local issues—such as school budgets—to world events. Vermonters are known for their strong sense of civic duty as well as military service during wartime, dating back to the Revolutionary War.

▼ **Citizens of Woodbury, Vermont**

387

Focus

Bellringer
Daily Focus Transparency 13–3

Guide to Reading
Answers to Graphic:

village   town

Forms of Government

township

Section Spotlight Video

To generate student interest and provide a springboard for class discussion, access the Chapter 13, Section 3 video at glencoe.com or on the video DVD.

Resource Manager

R Reading Strategies	**C** Critical Thinking	**D** Differentiated Instruction	**W** Writing Support	**S** Skill Practice
Teacher Edition • Identifying, p. 388 **Additional Resources** • Cont. Vocab., URB p. 43 • Ac. Vocab., URB p. 45 • Guid. Read., URB p. 65 • RENTG, p. 129 • Foldables, p. 75	**Teacher Edition** • Comparing, p. 388 **Additional Resources** • Quizzes and Tests, p. 154	**Teacher Edition** • Visual/Spatial, p. 389 **Additional Resources** • School-to-Home Conn., URB p. 59 • Reteach. Act., URB p. 61 • Graphic Novel, p. 45	**Teacher Edition** • Expository Writing, p. 390 **Additional Resources** • Cit./Dec. Making, URB p. 3	**Teacher Edition** • Using Geo. Skills, p. 390 **Additional Resources** • Daily Focus Trans., 13–3 • Pol. Cartoons Trans. 13

C Critical Thinking

Comparing Ask: Which is smaller, a county or a town? *(a town)* **BL**

R Reading Strategy

Identifying Ask: What is the purpose of a town meeting? *(to discuss and make important decisions that affect the town's citizens)* What topics are discussed at town meetings? *(local ordinances, taxes, and budgets)* **OL**

Caption Answer:

Everyone wants the opportunity to voice his or her opinion and to assist in creating policy, as there are no representatives to do it.

Town Government

Main Idea New England town government is one of the oldest forms of government in the United States.

Civics & You Think about a meeting you attended recently. Was it well organized and productive? Read to learn about a meeting that served as a government.

In 1654 a group of men in Sudbury, Massachusetts, gathered to discuss how to divide the land. The town has seen many changes since that day, but some things have not changed. Today people in Sudbury still meet to discuss issues.

Towns in New England

Just as most states are divided into counties, counties are often divided into smaller political units. In the New England states, these units are called **towns.** In many other states, especially in the Midwest, they are called townships. Like county and city governments, town governments receive their authority from the state.

The relationship between town or township governments and their surrounding counties varies. In New England, town governments handle the needs of most small communities, while counties are mainly judicial districts. In all other states that have townships, county and township governments share authority. County governments tend to be more important in the South and the West where there may be no townships.

New England town government is one of the oldest forms of government in the United States. In early **town meetings,** citizens—rather than elected representatives—made the important decisions. Town meetings are an exercise in direct democracy—as opposed to the representative democracy common throughout most of the United States. Residents in New England still come together once a year to discuss and vote on local ordinances, taxes, and budgets.

Citizens Speak A town meeting in Grafton, New Hampshire, is held in a fire station because of the huge crowd. *Hypothesizing* **Why do you think so many people want to attend town meetings?**

Differentiated Instruction

**Citizenship and Decision-Making Activity 4
URB pp. 3–4**

Making Connections: Getting to Know Local Government

Objective: To create a brochure about local government

Focus: Discuss the services provided by local government.

Teach: Review how local ordinances vary in different towns.

Assess: Have students present their brochures.

Close: Write a paragraph describing new information discovered while creating the brochure.

Differentiated Instruction Strategies

BL List two services your local government provides.

AL Write a short paragraph highlighting qualities of those who work in your local government.

ELL Name one important ordinance in your town.

TIME™

Political Cartoons

In this image, cartoonist Jeff Parker focuses on turnout for local elections.

1. **Whom do the two men wearing neckties represent?**
2. **What do all the performers symbolize?**
3. **How is the voter depicted?**
4. **What do you think explains the voter's attitude?**

—Jeff Parker, Florida Today

Every year, more than half of all Americans do volunteer work | role in it. One of the responsibilities of citizens is to help make their | of volunteer grou... small. Perha... dad who...

Limitations Because town meetings occur so rarely, they are useful only for broad policy making, not the everyday details of government. So each New England town elects a group of officials called "selectmen" to run local government. Selectman, a very old title, now applies to women as well as to men. Towns may also elect executives such as a clerk and a treasurer.

Over the years, as New England towns grew and their governments became more **complex,** or involved, direct democracy became impractical. Some New England towns have replaced the traditional town meetings with representative town meetings. In these meetings, elected representatives make the decisions instead of the people as a whole. Other towns have eliminated the meetings altogether and instead have a town council that runs the local government.

✔ **Reading Check** Defining What are town meetings?

Townships and Villages

Main Idea Townships and villages are the smallest units of local government.

Civics & You Did you know that there are villages all over America? Read to find out more about this type of government.

New York, New Jersey, and Pennsylvania **D** were organized somewhat differently from New England. Their counties are divided into **townships,** which are smaller than New England towns but have **similar,** or almost the same, governments.

As the United States expanded westward, it acquired new land. Congress divided the land into uniform square blocks, usually six miles wide and six miles long—originally designed to be an hour's buggy ride to the township hall for any resident.

Chapter 13   389

D **Differentiated Instruction**

Visual/Spatial Have students draw a graphic organizer or a drawing that illustrates the differences between a town, township, and a village. Have students use keywords or phrases to help explicate their drawings. **OL**

TIME™ Political Cartoons

Answers:
1. The men represent campaign workers or elections officials.
2. The performers symbolize all the media efforts used to get voters to go to the polls to vote.
3. The voter is depicted as bored, inattentive, and apathetic.
4. Answers may vary, but students may say the voters are only concerned about private matters or that voters have become immune to an overexposure to ads and campaign efforts.

✔ **Reading Check** **Answer:** They are a form of direct democracy in which community residents meet to discuss public policy.

Hands-On Chapter Project
Step 3

Forming a Local Government

Step 3: Holding a Town Meeting Have students return to their original groups. Students will conduct a town meeting, discussing policies or rules that relate to the classroom or their school.

Directions Write the Big Idea on the board. Have one group create an agenda, a list of topics that concern the class or school rules and/or policies. Have the other group create a town hall meeting poster that tells when and where the meeting will take place. Once the meeting begins, both groups will elect a moderator, a person to help direct the meeting when it gets off topic. Also assign a secretary, a person to take notes on the board and to count votes.

Summary At the end of the meeting, have students discuss the pros and cons of town meetings. **Ask:** Is a direct democracy or a representative democracy more efficient? Why? **OL**

(Project continued on the Visual Summary page)

Section 3 Review

W Writing Support

Expository Writing Have students research a nearby village and write a brief history of it and its current leaders. **OL**

S Skill Practice

Using Geography Skills Have students draw a map of your state and identify large cities, and several villages and discuss the location of them to each other. **OL**

Reading Check **Answer:** to get better services and to upgrade the community's status

Assess

Civics ONLINE

Study Central™ provides summaries, interactive games, and online graphic organizers to help students review.

Close

Identify Have students create note cards that describe the details of a town, a township, and a village and discuss why they seldom use direct democracy. **BL**

Responsibilities As settlers moved west, they set up local governments called civil townships. Midwestern townships kept the borders established by Congress, so today many appear perfectly square on a map.

Most townships elect a small body of officials known as a township committee, board of supervisors, or board of trustees. They have legislative responsibilities and usually hold regular meetings citizens may attend.

Townships have **declined,** or become less, in importance as cities and counties have taken on more of township functions. In some instances, county and township governments work together to provide local services.

Village Government

A **village** is the smallest unit of local government. Villages almost always lie within the boundaries of other local governments, such as townships or counties. Communities with small populations often have no need for their own government; county or township governments provide for most of their needs. Occasionally, however, community members may be dissatisfied with the services the county provides, or they may want to set up their own school system. In that case, they may organize the community as a village and request permission from the state to set up a village government.

The Village Board The government of most villages consists of a small board of trustees elected by the voters. Some villages also elect an executive. This official is known as the chief burgess, president of the board, or mayor. Large villages might hire a professional city manager. The village board has the power to collect taxes and to spend money on projects that benefit the community, such as maintaining streets or sewer and water systems.

Advantages and Disadvantages The main drawback of becoming a village is that residents often have to pay higher taxes to support the extra layer of government. In return, however, they usually receive better services. Becoming a village also tends to upgrade the community's status, making it more attractive to visitors and potential new residents and businesses.

Reading Check **Explaining** What is an advantage in setting up a village government?

Section 3 Review

Vocabulary

1. **Explain** how the following terms differ: *town, town meeting, township, village.*

Main Ideas

2. **Describing** How did town government begin in the United States?

3. **Explaining** What are the basic responsibilities of village government?

Critical Thinking

4. **BIG Ideas** If you lived in a small community, would you support the establishment of a village government? Why or why not?

5. **Comparing** On a Venn diagram like the one below, compare township and village governments.

Township — Both — Village

CITIZENSHIP Activity

6. **Expository Writing** Do you think that too many smaller local governments, such as townships and villages, in an area reduces or improves the quality of services residents receive? Explain your answer in a short paper.

Civics ONLINE

Study Central™ To review this section, go to glencoe.com.

Answers

1. Comparisons should use vocabulary words according to their definitions in the section and in the Glossary.

2. It began when a group of men in Sudbury, Massachusetts, met to discuss how to divide their land.

3. A village government works on improving services or projects that will help the community and may set up their own school district.

4. Answers will vary. If no, students may say village government requires higher taxes. If yes, students may say a village can offer better services.

5. **Township:** borders established by Congress, citizens elect small body of officials; **Both:** receive authority from state, small units of government; **Village:** lies within boundary of township or county, people elected board of trustees, an executive oversees board, has power to collect taxes

6. Essays will vary. Some students may say more layers of government do not improve services; in fact, it just makes them more expensive because of higher taxes. Others may say that smaller governments are effective in providing services to people who might otherwise not get them.

Local Government

- Local governments provide many important services.
- When residents of a community find some particular reason to organize legally, they seek to incorporate a municipality, which may be called a village, city, or town.

City Governments

- Cities develop local governments when they are granted special legal status by the state legislature through incorporation.
- The major forms of city government are the mayor-council form, the council-manager form, and the commission form.

Buying a house in a town

- A special district is a unit of government created to deal with a specific function, such as education or transportation.
- A metropolitan area is a central city and its surrounding suburbs.

County Governments

- County governments were first set up to provide a few basic services that residents could not provide for themselves.
- The responsibilities of a county are usually determined by the state constitution and state laws.

Towns and Villages

- Counties are often divided into smaller political units. These units are called towns or townships.
- A village is the smallest unit of local government.

Cityscape of Chicago, Illinois

Fire departments serve townships

STUDY TO GO Study anywhere, anytime! Download quizzes and flash cards to your PDA from glencoe.com.

Listing Have students work with a partners and use their Foldables and notes to create a chart like the following:

	Strong-Mayor	Weak-Mayor	Commission Form	Council-Manager Form
Mayor	Elected, Prepares budget			
City Council				
Dept. Heads				
Board of Commissioners				
City Manager				

Have students display their charts and provide an explanation to the class. **OL**

Diagramming Have students create a diagram of a county government. Students may use the diagram on page 385 as a springboard to create their own visual. **OL**

Descriptive Writing Have students describe a small town or village they have visited, read about, or seen on television. Have them use sensory details to describe what they saw or heard in the town. Did the town appeal to them? Did they find it too old-fashioned? What kinds of issues were people talking about? What made the town memorable? **AL**

Hands-On Chapter Project
Step 4: Wrap-Up

Forming a Local Government

Step 4: Discussing the Democratic Process Groups analyze the process of forming local governments.

Directions Have students return to their original groups. Let them discuss what they enjoyed about city government and what they felt could be improved. Students should also discuss the different people that help run a county and what the town meeting accomplished.

Once the groups have analyzed local governments in action, have them create a bulleted list, noting what they liked about city and town governments and what they felt was frustrating. **OL**

Reviewing Vocabulary

1. D In this question, students may choose B, home rule because they might associate rules with laws. They have also seen the phrase "city charter" and may mistakenly choose C.

2. C Choices A, B, and D all deal with geographical areas, not units of government.

3. B Choices A, B, and D all deal with geographical areas. A suburb is not a large territorial subdivision, and a metropolitan area consists of a city and the surrounding suburbs.

4. A This question will require that students know the difference between a town, a village, and a township and which are most prevalent in New England. Most students will be able to eliminate C, a city, as it is not a small community.

Reviewing Main Ideas

5. B This question is challenging, as students need to know how each form of government functions. In the commission form, each commissioner heads a major department. In the strong-mayor system, the mayor appoints department heads. In the council-manager form, the city manager appoints department heads.

6. C This question requires that students read carefully. They may choose B, thinking the question is asking about a document that grants power to a local government. It is the state constitution, and not the U.S. Constitution, that establishes the power and duties of local government, although the Constitution is the supreme law of the land.

7. B This question requires that students recall details about individual states. Texas has many counties of varying sizes. California has some counties with millions of people, and the counties in Louisiana are called parishes.

TEST-TAKING TIP

When taking an exam, follow instructions exactly.

Reviewing Vocabulary

Directions: Choose the word(s) that best completes the sentence.

1. A city law is known as a(n) _____.

  A council   **C** charter

  B home rule   **D** ordinance

2. A unit of government that deals with a specific function is called a(n) _____.

  A suburb   **C** special district

  B county   **D** metropolitan area

3. A state's largest territorial and political subdivision is normally a(n) _____.

  A suburb   **C** special district

  B county   **D** metropolitan area

4. _____ governments handle the needs of most small communities in New England.

  A town   **C** city

  B village   **D** township

Reviewing Main Ideas

Directions: Choose the best answer for each question.

Section 1 (pp. 376–382)

5. In which form of city government does the city council appoint department heads?

  A commission form

  B weak-mayor system

  C strong-mayor system

  D council-manager form

6. What has established the power and duties of most local governments?

  A home rule

  B city charters

  C state constitutions

  D the United States Constitution

Section 2 (pp. 383–386)

7. Which state has boroughs rather than counties?

  A Texas

  B Alaska

  C California

  D Louisiana

8. Which county official enforces court orders?

  A sheriff

  B coroner

  C assessor

  D district attorney

Section 3 (pp. 387–390)

9. What are New England town meetings used for?

  A trying civil cases

  B governing day-to-day

  C making general policy

  D electing representatives

10. Which of the following is the smallest unit of local government?

  A city

  B village

  C township

  D board of trustees

GO ON

---

8. A Students must recall the job requirements of each county official. The coroner establishes the cause of suspicious deaths. The assessor examines taxable property. The district attorney charges and prosecutes lawbreakers.

9. C Students need to remember that the town meeting is the oldest form of government in the United States. Given that the public participates in town meetings and that they occur rarely, students should conclude that people are there to make policy concerning their town.

Critical Thinking

Directions: Base your answers to questions 11 and 12 on the cartoon below and your knowledge of Chapter 13.

11. Based on the cartoon and facts in Chapter 13, who most likely enacted the ban in the headline?

   A a city council

   B a county sheriff

   C a county assessor

   D a board of trustees

12. Which of the following statements best reflects the cartoonist's viewpoint?

   A He objects to the ban on cell phone use.

   B He thinks the ban will prevent accidents.

   C He is undecided about the need for the ban.

   D He believes citizens should know local laws.

Document-Based Questions

Directions: Analyze the document and answer the short-answer questions that follow.

The following passage is from the 2006 State of the City address by Salt Lake City's Mayor Ross C. "Rocky" Anderson.

> *In its 6th edition,* Places Rated Almanac *rated Salt Lake City as the best place to live in North America. That is as true today as in 1999, when the rating was published. As part of a dazzlingly vibrant and diverse community, we benefit from a strong economy and myriad cultural and artistic opportunities. With its captivating scenery, brilliant vistas, and incomparable recreational opportunities, Salt Lake City has long been an international destination for outdoor enthusiasts. We are unique in having such convenient access to so many remarkable, different aspects of life.*
>
> *People around the country are taking note of our extraordinary quality of life. Just a few months ago,* Outside *magazine listed Salt Lake City as one of 18 "new American Dream Towns." The Sierra Club commended our efforts to preserve the character of our neighborhoods and prevent sprawl development. Moreover,* Men's Health *magazine named Salt Lake City the most smoke-free city in the country, and ranked Salt Lake City as the 5th best city in the nation for men, with an A+ ranking.*
>
> —Mayor Ross C. "Rocky" Anderson

13. What qualities do the mayor, magazines, and the Sierra Club attribute to Salt Lake City?

14. How might these qualities benefit the city's economy?

Extended-Response Question

15. Compare and contrast the strong-mayor and weak-mayor systems of city government. Mention a benefit of each system.

STOP

Civics ONLINE

For additional test practice, use Self-Check Quizzes—Chapter 13 on glencoe.com.

Need Extra Help?

If you missed question...	1	2	3	4	5	6	7	8	9	10	11	12	13	14	15
Go to page...	378	382	384	388	378	377	384	386	388	390	378	378	378	378	378

Chapter 13   393

ASSESSMENT

Document-Based Questions

13. Students' answers will vary. Possible answers are a strong economy, cultural and artistic opportunities, captivating scenery, brilliant vistas, incomparable recreational opportunities, extraordinary quality of life, neighborhood preservation, restrictions on sprawl, and smoke-free zones.

14. Students' answers will vary. A possible answer is by attracting tourists, retirees, businesses, and artists to Salt Lake City.

Extended Response

15. Students' comparisons and contrasts will vary. Look for supporting details from the chapter.

---

10. B Students must recall that a village is the smallest unit of government and that it lies within a township or county. The only challenging distractor is C, and students must recall that a township refers to a division of property in New York, New Jersey, and Pennsylvania.

Critical Thinking

11. A This question requires that students assess the situation in the cartoon. A man is reading the headlines and comments that it is "ridiculous." They must notice that the newspaper is from New York and notice the city skyscrapers. Based on these details, students can eliminate choices B–D. A city council is the body that sets ordinances in large cities.

12. B The student should focus on the car. If the cartoonist thought the ban was objectionable, the driver would **not** be driving carelessly. The cartoonist does have an opinion: based on his depiction of the driver, he thinks the ban is a good idea. Choice D is a misreading of the cartoon.

Civics ONLINE

Have students visit the Web site at glencoe.com to review Chapter 13 and take the **Self-Check Quiz**.

Need Extra Help?

Have students refer to the pages listed if they miss any of the questions.

393

Chapter Planning Guide

14

Levels					Resources	Chapter Opener	Section 1	Section 2	Section 3	Chapter Assess
BL	OL	AL	ELL							
FOCUS										
BL	OL	AL	ELL	📠	Daily Focus Skills Transparencies		14–1	14–2	14–3	
TEACH										
BL	OL		ELL	📁	Reading Essentials and Note-Taking Guide*		p. 132	p. 135	p. 138	
BL	OL		ELL	📁	Reading Skills Activity, URB		p. 7	p. 7		
BL	OL	AL	ELL	📁	Speaking and Listening Skills Activity, URB				p. 9	
	OL	AL		📁	Primary Source Reading, URB				p. 15	
BL	OL	AL	ELL	📁	Content Vocabulary Activity, URB*	p. 67	p. 67	p. 67	p. 67	
BL	OL	AL	ELL	📁	Academic Vocabulary Activity, URB	p. 69	p. 69	p. 69	p. 69	
	OL			📁	Biography Activity, URB			p. 71		
BL	OL	AL	ELL	📁	Writing Skills Activity, URB			p. 73		
	OL	AL		📁	Critical Thinking Skills Activity, URB			p. 75		
BL	OL	AL	ELL	📁	Chart, Graph, and Map Skills Activity, URB				p. 77	
BL	OL	AL	ELL	📁	Differentiated Instruction, URB			p. 79		
BL	OL	AL	ELL	📁	School-to-Home Connection Activity, URB*	p. 81	p. 81	p. 81	p. 81	
BL	OL		ELL	📁	Guided Reading Activities, URB*		p. 85	p. 86	p. 87	
BL	OL	AL	ELL	📁	Writer's Guidebook	✓	✓	✓	✓	✓
	OL	AL		💿	Primary Source Document Library	✓	✓	✓	✓	✓
BL	OL	AL	ELL	💿	Daily Lecture & Discussion Notes (in Pres. Plus)		✓	✓	✓	✓
BL	OL	AL	ELL	💿	StudentWorks™ Plus		✓	✓	✓	✓
BL	OL	AL	ELL	💿	Section Spotlight Videos		✓	✓	✓	
BL	OL	AL	ELL	📠	TIME Interpreting Political Cartoons Transp.			Ch. 14		
BL	OL	AL	ELL	📠	Writing Process Transparencies	✓	✓	✓	✓	✓

Note: Please refer to the *Unit 4 Resource Book* for this chapter's URB materials.

* Also available in Spanish

Plus
TeacherWorks
All-In-One Planner and Resource Center

- Interactive Lesson Planner
- Interactive Teacher Edition
- Fully editable blackline masters
- Section Spotlight Videos Launch
- Differentiated Lesson Plans
- Printable reports of daily assignments
- Standards Tracking System

Levels					Resources	Chapter Opener	Section 1	Section 2	Section 3	Chapter Assess
BL	OL	AL	ELL							
					TEACH (continued)					
				📁	**Building Academic Vocabulary**	✓	✓	✓	✓	✓
Teacher Resources				📁	**Strategies for Success**	✓	✓	✓	✓	✓
				📁	**Teacher's Guide to Differentiated Instruction**	✓	✓	✓	✓	✓
				💿	**Graphing Tool**	✓	✓	✓	✓	✓
				💿	**Presentation Plus! with MindJogger CheckPoint**	✓	✓	✓	✓	✓
					ASSESS					
BL	OL	AL	ELL	📁	**Quizzes and Tests***		p. 163	p. 164	p. 165	p. 166
BL	OL	AL	ELL	📁	**Authentic Assessment with Rubrics**			p. 18		
BL	OL	AL	ELL	📁	**Standardized Test Practice**		p. 27	p. 27	p. 27	p. 27
BL	OL	AL	ELL	💿	*ExamView®* **Assessment Suite CD-ROM**		14–1	14–2	14–3	14–4
					CLOSE					
BL			ELL	📁	**Reteaching Activity, URB***		p. 83	p. 83	p. 83	
BL	OL		ELL	📁	**Reading and Study Skills Foldables™ Activity**	p. 76	p. 77		p. 77	
BL	OL	AL	ELL	📁	*Civics Today* **in Graphic Novel**	p. 77	p. 77			
BL	OL	AL	ELL	🖨	**Graphic Organizer Transparencies & Strategies**	✓	✓	✓	✓	✓

✓ Chapter- or unit-based activities applicable to all sections in this chapter

Using PuzzleMaker™ 3.1

Online Word Search Puzzles

What is PuzzleMaker™ 3.1?

Glencoe's PuzzleMaker™ 3.1 is an interactive online tool that lets you create your own puzzles for classroom use based on the glossary and using either content vocabulary or academic vocabulary.

How can PuzzleMaker™ 3.1 help my students?

Completing the word search puzzles helps students to:

- recall important vocabulary terms from the chapter
- reinforce their understanding of the vocabulary

Visit glencoe.com and enter a *QuickPass*™ code to go directly to resources for each chapter.

Civics ONLINE

Visit glencoe.com and enter *QuickPass*™ code CIV1360c14T for Chapter 14 resources.

You can easily launch a wide range of digital products from your computer's desktop with the McGraw-Hill Social Studies widget.

	Student	Teacher	Parent
Media Library			
• Student Edition Section Audio	●		●
• Spanish Audio Summaries	●		●
• Section Spotlight Videos	●	●	●
***Civics Today* Online Learning Center (Web Site)**			
• Chapter Overviews	●	●	●
• Study Central™	●	●	●
• Study-to-Go	●	●	●
• Student Web Activities	●	●	●
• In Motion Animation	●	●	●
• Self-Check Quizzes	●	●	●
• ePuzzles and Games	●	●	●
• StudentWorks™ Plus Online	●	●	●
• Vocabulary eFlashcards	●	●	●
• Web Activity Lesson Plans		●	
• Vocabulary PuzzleMaker	●	●	●
Classroom Tools			
• Multilingual Glossary	●	●	●
• Beyond the Textbook	●	●	●
• NGS MapMachine	●	●	●

Reading List Generator CD-ROM

GLENCOE BookLink 3

Use this database to search more than 30,000 titles to create a customized reading list for your students.

- Reading lists can be organized by students' reading level, author, genre, theme, or area of interest.
- The database provides Degrees of Reading Power™ (DRP) and Lexile™ readability scores for all selections.
- A brief summary of each selection is included.

Leveled reading suggestions for this chapter:

For students at a Grade 7 reading level:
- *Sojourner Truth: Ain't I a Woman?* by Patricia C. McKissack and Fredrick McKissack

For students at a Grade 8 reading level:
- *The Race to Save the Lord God Bird,* by Phillip Hoose

For students at a Grade 9 reading level:
- *Arc of Justice: A Saga of Race, Civil Rights, and Murder in the Jazz Age,* by Kevin Boyle

For students at a Grade 10 reading level:
- *Andrew Young: Man with a Mission,* by James Haskins

For students at a Grade 11 reading level:
- *The Blue Whale,* by George L. Small

READING SUPPORT FROM JAMESTOWN EDUCATION

- **Timed Readings Plus in Social Studies** helps students increase their reading rate and fluency while maintaining comprehension. The 400-word passages are similar to those found on state and national assessments.

- **Reading in the Content Area: Social Studies** concentrates on six essential reading skills that help students better comprehend what they read. The book includes 75 high-interest nonfiction passages written at increasing levels of difficulty.

- **Reading Social Studies** includes strategic reading instruction and vocabulary support in Social Studies content for both ELLs and native speakers of English.

- **Content Vocabulary Workout** (Grades 6–8) accelerates reading comprehension through focused vocabulary development. Social Studies content vocabulary comes from the glossaries of Glencoe's Middle School Social Studies texts. www.jamestowneducation.com

KEY Teacher Wraparound

Use this key to help you identify the different types of prompts found in the Teacher Wraparound Edition.

R **Reading Strategies** activities help you teach reading skills and vocabulary.

C **Critical Thinking** strategies help students apply and extend what they have learned.

D **Differentiated Instruction** activities provide instruction for students learning to speak English, along with suggestions for teaching various types of learners.

S **Skill Practice** strategies help students practice historical analysis and geography skills.

W **Writing Support** activities provide writing opportunities to help students comprehend the text.

Teaching strategies and activities have been coded for ability level appropriateness.

AL Activities for students working above grade level

OL Activities for students working on grade level

BL Activities for students working below grade level

ELL Activities for English Language Learners

Focus

Why It Matters

Ask: Which critical policy issue is the most important in your community? *(Answers may include any of the four topics: education, crime prevention, social programs for the needy, or environmental issues. Ask students to explain their answers.)*

More About the Photo

Visual Literacy Marching bands are the pride of many communities and schools. They usually consist of brass, woodwind, and percussion instruments and incorporate rhythmic movements into their performances. Ask students to describe their experiences with school and community marching bands. **Ask:** How do marching bands add to school and community celebrations? *(Answers may include the idea that bands offer a chance for self-expression, provide pleasure for audiences, and produce pride in school or community.)*

Dealing With Community Issues

Why It Matters

Communities across America face a variety of public policy issues every day. Among the most critical are those involving education; crime prevention; social programs to help poor, elderly, sick, and disabled citizens; and environmental issues.

394

Teach

BIG Ideas As you begin teaching each section, use these questions and activities to help students focus on the Big Ideas.

Section 1

How a Community Handles Issues Ask: How can ordinary citizens influence their community government? *(by voting for leaders who support their views, by lobbying or communicating with commu-*nity leaders, by running for office themselves, or by serving on local governmental committees)* Point out that in Section 1 students will learn how public policy is formed on the community level and how citizens can influence policy. **OL**

Section 2

Education and Social Issues Ask: How can members of a community fight crime? *(by voting for specific laws, by forming neighborhood watch groups, by supporting law enforcement, and so forth)* How can community members determine whether or not

Civics ONLINE
Visit glencoe.com and enter
QuickPass™ code
CIV3093c14 for
Chapter 14
resources.

Chapter Introduction
14

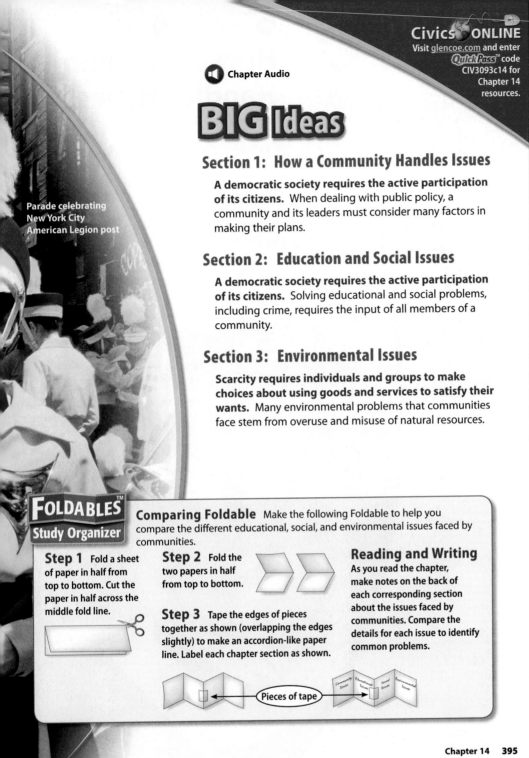

Parade celebrating
New York City
American Legion post

🔊 Chapter Audio

BIG Ideas

Section 1: How a Community Handles Issues

A democratic society requires the active participation of its citizens. When dealing with public policy, a community and its leaders must consider many factors in making their plans.

Section 2: Education and Social Issues

A democratic society requires the active participation of its citizens. Solving educational and social problems, including crime, requires the input of all members of a community.

Section 3: Environmental Issues

Scarcity requires individuals and groups to make choices about using goods and services to satisfy their wants. Many environmental problems that communities face stem from overuse and misuse of natural resources.

FOLDABLES Dinah Zike's
Study Organizer Foldables

Purpose This Foldable helps the student compare the different issues faced by communities. The completed Foldable will be used to take notes on these issues as students read each section. **OL**

📁 More Foldables activities for this chapter can be found in the *Dinah Zike's Reading and Study Skills Foldables* ancillary.

Civics ONLINE

Visit glencoe.com and enter *QuickPass™* code CIV1360c14T for Chapter 14 resources, including a Chapter Overview, Study Central™, Study-to-Go, Student Web Activity, Self-Check Quiz, and other materials.

FOLDABLES
Study Organizer

Comparing Foldable Make the following Foldable to help you compare the different educational, social, and environmental issues faced by communities.

Step 1 Fold a sheet of paper in half from top to bottom. Cut the paper in half across the middle fold line.

Step 2 Fold the two papers in half from top to bottom.

Step 3 Tape the edges of pieces together as shown (overlapping the edges slightly) to make an accordion-like paper line. Label each chapter section as shown.

Reading and Writing As you read the chapter, make notes on the back of each corresponding section about the issues faced by communities. Compare the details for each issue to identify common problems.

Pieces of tape

public schools are doing their job? *(by looking at test scores; by speaking to students, teachers, and administrators; and by joining the parent-teacher association or serving on the school board)* Tell students that in Section 2 they will learn about issues in current public school education, issues in social program policies, and ways in which citizens of communities can help fight crime. **OL**

Section 3

Environmental Issues Ask: What types of environmental problems might any community face? *(Answers may include pollution of air, land, and water; excessive noise or garbage; lack of open spaces; and so forth.)* Explain that in Section 3 students will learn about current environmental problems and how local governments, businesses, and individuals deal with them. **OL**

Focus

Bellringer

Daily Focus Transparency 14–1

Guide to Reading
Answers to Graphic:

Planning Commission
- local residents
- business-people
- government leaders
- architects
- traffic engineers

Section Spotlight Video

Have students watch the Chapter 14, Section 1 video at glencoe.com.

Resource Manager

Guide to Reading

Big Idea
A democratic society requires the active participation of its citizens.

Content Vocabulary
- policy *(p. 397)*
- public policy *(p. 397)*
- planning commission *(p. 398)*
- short-term plan *(p. 398)*
- long-term plan *(p. 398)*
- infrastructure *(p. 399)*
- priority *(p. 399)*
- resource *(p. 399)*
- master plan *(p. 399)*

Academic Vocabulary
- convince *(p. 397)*
- professional *(p. 398)*
- specific *(p. 399)*

Reading Strategy
Analyzing As you read, list on a web diagram like the one below the people who might serve on a community planning commission.

Planning Commission — government leaders

Section 1

How a Community Handles Issues

Real World Civics If you disagree with laws, you can change them. Wendy Hamilton lost her sister and nephew in a car accident with a drunk driver more than 20 years ago. Even before that, she lost an 18-year-old cousin who was riding with a friend who had been drinking. Since then, Hamilton has worked to lower the blood alcohol level that indicates drunkenness and to raise the legal drinking age. She has served as president of MADD (Mothers Against Drunk Driving).

▼ **Activist Wendy Hamilton**

 R **Reading Strategies**	**C** **Critical Thinking**	**D** **Differentiated Instruction**	**W** **Writing Support**	**S** **Skill Practice**
Teacher Edition • Inferring, p. 398	**Teacher Edition** • Contrasting, p. 398	**Teacher Edition** • English Learners, p. 397	**Teacher Edition** • Personal Writing, p. 399	**Teacher Edition** • Analyzing Visuals, p. 397
Additional Resources • Read. Skills, URB p. 7 • Cont. Vocab., URB p. 67 • Ac. Vocab., URB p. 69 • Guid. Read., URB p. 85 • Foldables, p. 77	**Additional Resources** • Quizzes and Tests, p. 163 • Graphic Novel, p. 53	**Additional Resources** • School-to-Home Conn., URB p. 81 • Teacher's Guide to Differentiated Instruction, p. 18		**Additional Resources** • Daily Focus Trans., 14–1

Public Policy

Main Idea Public policy, or how a community deals with issues, has many sources.

Civics & You Do you disagree with something your community has decided that affects your life? Read to find out how some people worked to change their communities' approaches to problems.

S

Do you think going to school should make you sick? A group of families in Sugar Hill, Georgia, did not think so. When they found out a new school would be built between two garbage landfills, the families began to study possible health risks. They formed a group called Community Awareness Regarding Education and Safety (CARES).

The organization sets up committees to continue research and contact the media. Although the school did open, the organization **convinced**, or persuaded, the school board to monitor toxic substances in the building. Mindy Clark, a cofounder of CARES, explained, "We're going to fight. We know too much to walk away."

Mindy Clark and CARES worked to change a policy. All organizations, such as schools, businesses, and governments, have **policies**, or sets of rules or guidelines they follow when making decisions and carrying out actions. Most businesses, for example, have policies about hiring, promoting, and firing employees.

What Is Public Policy? **Public policy** is concerned with the decisions and actions of government as it deals with issues and problems that affect the entire community. Public policy may deal with a specific issue; the decision to build or not build a road is an example. Public policy also deals with issues that are wider in scope, such as health care and the environment. A public policy is not necessarily a law. It may not even be written down.

D

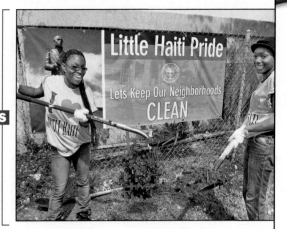

Volunteering Citizens, such as these volunteers in Miami, support many public cleanup programs. *Identifying* **What issues need volunteer support in your community?**

Sources of Public Policy

Where do ideas for public policy originate? They may come from the government. Political parties, interest groups, or the media may suggest them. Another important source of policy ideas, especially at the local level, is private citizens.

Often a single person can have a great impact on government policies. In 1980, after a drunk driver killed her 13-year-old daughter, Cari, a California woman named Candy Lightner launched a campaign to change government policy toward drunk driving. Lightner explained, "I promised myself on the day of Cari's death that I would fight to make this needless homicide count for something positive in the years ahead." She founded Mothers Against Drunk Driving (MADD), which soon became a nationwide organization. Lightner helped MADD bring about the passage of more than 1,000 tough new laws against drunk driving.

✓ Reading Check **Contrasting** What is the difference between a law and public policy?

Teach

S Skill Practice

Analyzing Visuals **Ask:** What are these volunteers doing? *(picking up litter in their neighborhood)* What do you think "Little Haiti Pride" means? *(Little Haiti was probably named by people originally from Haiti. They or their descendants live in this neighborhood and want to show pride in it by cleaning it up.)* **BL** **ELL**

D Differentiated Instruction

English Learners **Ask:** Why is it called "public" policy? *(The policies are developed by members of the public—government officials, political parties, interest groups, media, and private citizens.)* **ELL**

Caption Answer:
Encourage students to provide specific examples of issues that need volunteer help in their community.

✓ Reading Check **Answer:** A law is a rule, usually written, that carries penalties for disobedience. A policy is a set of rules or guidelines for making decisions or taking action. Policies may not be written down or carry penalties for disobedience.

Hands-On Chapter Project
Step 1

Influencing Public Policy

Step 1: Choosing and Researching an Issue Each student group will select an issue to research and influence. They will narrow their issue to a single realistic and achievable goal. Each group will create a pamphlet to educate the public and to influence local government to achieve this goal.

Directions Organize the class into groups. Assign or have each group select an issue to research in educational (general community or in-school focus), social (poor, elderly, crime, health), or environmental (pollution, conservation, wildlife) areas. Allow time for each group to choose a specific problem within their issue. Groups should divide into pairs to research aspects of the problem and solutions using Internet and library sources.

Summarizing Have pairs share what they learned about the problem and possible solutions (tried and untried) with their groups. The group will use this information in Section 2 to decide on a goal for its pamphlet. **OL**

(Project continued in Section 2)

R Reading Strategy

Inferring Ask: What do Amelia's actions reveal about her values and character? *(Answers should include that she believes in helping others and that she exhibits determination, organization, and leadership qualities.)* **BL**

C Critical Thinking

Contrasting Ask: How are long- and short-term plans different? *(Long-term plans are broad guides meant to cover 10, 20, or even 50 years. Short-term plans cover only a few years and are more specific.)* **OL**

TIME™ Teens in *Action*

Answer:

In the first year, Amelia collected 3,000 pairs of socks, 1,000 hats, and 450 pairs of mittens.

Civics ONLINE

Objectives and answers to the **Student Web Activity** can be found at glencoe.com under the Web Activity Lesson Plan for this chapter.

Differentiated Instruction

Reading Skills Activity 4, URB pp. 7–8

TIME™ Teens in *Action*

Amelia Pennewell

When it comes to helping her community, Amelia Pennewell, 16, of Livermore, California, believes in jumping in feet first.

QUESTION: You started an organization called Amelia's Socks. How did you get started?

ANSWER: When I was nine, I was on my way to my aunt's for Thanksgiving dinner. We drove past people who were lined up outside a building. Some people didn't have socks. My mom explained that they were homeless or hungry, and when the doors opened they would get a hot meal. I wanted to help. I thought I could use my money to buy them some socks to help keep them warm. I asked my teacher, Mr. Menendez, to help. I started Amelia's Socks, which is now a nonprofit organization. People help by donating clothing to the group.

Q: How has it worked out?

A: The first year I collected more than 3,000 pairs of new socks, about 1,000 hats, and 450 pairs of mittens. I have given more than 80,000 pairs of new socks over the past seven years. And I've sent socks to Iraq, Mexico, Afghanistan, and to victims of Hurricane Katrina.

Amelia and her volunteers

ACTION FACT: Pennewell was a finalist in the Do Something 2005 Brick Awards. When she's not collecting socks and mittens, Pennewell runs track and plays soccer.

Making a Difference   **CITIZENSHIP**

What was the result of Amelia's efforts in the first year?

Future Plans

Main Idea When ideas for public policy come before a community, leaders must consider many factors.

Civics & You Have you ever had to decide between two things you wanted to do or buy? How did you make your decision? Read to find out how many communities approach this dilemma.

Many who formulate public policy look at what is likely to happen in the future and plan for it now. A growing number of local governments have planning commissions to oversee community growth. A **planning commission** is an advisory group that may include government leaders, businesspeople, local residents, and **professionals,** or skilled people, such as architects and traffic engineers.

Short-Term and Long-Term Plans

Local governments and their planning commissions make both short-term and long-term plans. A **short-term plan** is a policy meant to be carried out over the next few years. For example, granting a builder a permit to construct apartments is a short-term plan.

A **long-term plan** is a broader policy meant to serve as a guide over the next 10, 20, or even 50 years. To make long-term plans, a planning commission makes educated guesses about a community's future needs.

For example, the population of a community is growing, and forecasts show great growth in the future. A situation like this one raises questions for local government. Will heavier traffic overload roads? Should the town build new highways or promote public transportation?

Civics ONLINE

Student Web Activity Visit glencoe.com and complete the Chapter 14 Web Activity.

Making Inferences

Objective: To apply techniques for making inferences

Focus: Review the steps on page 7.

Teach: Discuss prior knowledge of landfills and how students used it to make inferences.

Assess: Assess understanding of the metaphor in the second passage.

Close: Have students write a paragraph about applying the steps to making inferences in the second passage.

Differentiated Instruction Strategies

BL Name two steps that were useful in answering the questions and tell how you used them.

AL Write your opinion of welfare programs. Include a simile, metaphor, or analogy.

ELL Create a simile, metaphor, or analogy to describe poverty.

What other demands will the growing population put on the town's **infrastructure**—its systems of roads, bridges, water, and sewers? How will the town pay for needed improvements?

Evaluating Priorities and Resources

The answers to these questions about planning usually depend on two things—priorities and resources.

Priorities are the goals a community considers most important or most urgent. In setting priorities, a community must decide what it values most. For example, is it more important to have a thriving commerce center or a peaceful place to live? A community must also determine its **specific,** or exact, goals and rank them in order of importance. It may decide, for example, that its top goal is to attract new businesses. Lesser goals may include improving services, preserving open spaces, and upgrading schools.

After a community sets its priorities, it must determine what resources it has and how to use them. **Resources** are the money, people, and materials available to accomplish the community's goals. Suppose, for example, that a community has decided to improve its public transportation system. Is there enough money to build and maintain a new fleet of buses for busy routes?

Creating a Master Plan

After setting priorities and calculating resources, a planning commission makes concrete decisions about the community's future. It usually spells these out in a **master plan.** This plan states a set of goals and explains how the government will carry them out to meet changing needs over time. If the local government accepts the plan, it becomes public policy, and the government is responsible for carrying it out.

Reading Check Explaining What should be considered when deciding on the priorities of a community?

W **Writing Support**

Personal Writing Have students make a list of goals for the coming year and then prioritize them. Tell them to write about how they prioritized their goals. **OL**

Reading Check **Answer:** Planners should consider the relative importance of the goals in order to prioritize them. Next, they consider the resources—money, people, and materials—available to achieve the goals.

Assess

Civics ONLINE

Study Central™ provides summaries, interactive games, and online graphic organizers to help students review content.

Close

Analyzing a Newspaper Article Have students write a summary of a current newspaper article on how local, state, or federal government is dealing with an issue they consider important. Encourage them to tell why they agree or disagree with the government's policy. **OL**

Section 1 Review

Section 1 Review

Vocabulary

1. Define the following terms and use them in sentences related to public policy: *planning commission, short-term plan, long-term plan, infrastructure, priority, resource, master plan.*

Main Ideas

2. Identifying Provide two examples of public policies that deal with specific issues.

3. Explaining What is the purpose of a master plan?

Critical Thinking

4. Discussing What role does setting priorities play in planning for the future?

5. BIG Ideas In a graphic organizer like the one below, identify four ways that ideas for public policy are initiated.

private citizens

Public policy comes from

CITIZENSHIP Activity

6. Descriptive Writing Imagine you are a community leader creating a master plan for a city park. You want to plan for new attractions. You also want to ensure that the park retains its natural beauty. How do you balance the two goals? Describe your plan in a one- to two-page paper.

Civics ONLINE

Study Central™ To review this section, go to glencoe.com.

Answers

1. Sentences should use vocabulary words according to their definitions in the section and in the Glossary.
2. Answers will vary but may include policies such as encouraging recycling to deal with environmental problems or preventing traffic accidents through driver education.
3. The purpose of a master plan is to state specific goals and to describe how they will be achieved. The public can provide input about the master plan. They can also hold the government accountable for putting the policy into practice.
4. Priorities are the goals a community considers most important. Importance is often determined by health or safety reasons or based on the number of people impacted.
5. Answers should include any four of the following: government, political parties, interest groups, the media, private citizens.
6. Answers should include specific actions to be taken to balance the two goals. For example, new attractions may be given limited space in the park and the balance of the land left in its natural state.

Focus

Guide to Reading
Answers to Graphic:

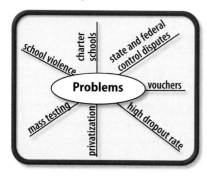

charter schools, state and federal control disputes, vouchers, high dropout rate, privatization, mass testing, school violence — **Problems**

Resource Manager

Guide to Reading

Big Idea
A democratic society requires the active participation of its citizens.

Content Vocabulary
- charter school *(p. 402)*
- tuition voucher *(p. 403)*
- community policing *(p. 405)*
- welfare *(p. 406)*

Academic Vocabulary
- role *(p. 401)*
- impose *(p. 401)*
- ratio *(p. 404)*

Reading Strategy
Summarizing As you read, on a web diagram like the one below, list four challenges that schools face.

Problems — high dropout rate

Education and Social Issues

Real World Civics Community issues usually affect all citizens and sometimes include education. The Navajo Nation chose President Joe Shirley and his wife, Vikki Shirley, to guide the largest Native American tribe in the United States. Many issues are on President Shirley's agenda, including alcohol education in the Navajo Nation. Vikki Shirley lost her 29-year-old daughter to a drunk driver. Using her status as a Navajo leader, Vikki Shirley has devoted much of her time to touring other tribes' reservations with her anti-drunk-driving message and encouraging a ban on drinking on the reservations.

▼ Vikki Shirley speaks to Navajo groups

R Reading Strategies	**C** Critical Thinking	**D** Differentiated Instruction	**W** Writing Support	**S** Skill Practice
Teacher Edition • Academic Voc., p. 402 • Inferring, p. 403 **Additional Resources** • Read. Skills, URB, p. 7 • Cont. Vocab., URB p. 67 • Ac. Vocab., URB p. 69 • Guid. Read., URB p. 86 • RENTG, p. 135	**Teacher Edition** • Drawing Conc., pp. 401, 406 • Det. Cause/Effect., p. 405 **Additional Resources** • Biographies, URB p. 71 • Crit. Think., URB p. 75 • Quizzes and Tests, p. 164	**Teacher Edition** • Below Grade Level, p. 403 • Gifted and Talented, p. 404 **Additional Resources** • Diff. Instr., URB p. 79 • School-to-Home Conn., URB p. 81	**Teacher Edition** • Persuasive Writing, pp. 401, 402 • Personal Writing, p. 407 **Additional Resources** • Writing Skills Act., URB p. 73	**Teacher Edition** • Analyzing Charts and Graphs, p. 402 • Analyzing Charts, p. 407 **Additional Resources** • Daily Focus Trans., 14–2 • Pol. Cartoons Trans. 14

TIME

Political Cartoons

—Marshall Ramsey/Copley News Service

HEY, KIDS, IT AIN'T CALLED HIGHER EDUCATION FOR NOTHIN'..

Marshall Ramsey, the creator of this cartoon, is making a comment on higher education.

1. **What does the yellow crane stand for, and what impact is it having?**
2. **How is this situation affecting students?**
3. **Does Ramsey support or oppose increases in college tuition? How do you know?**

Every year, more than half of all Americans do volunteer work ... role in it. One of the responsibilities of citizens is to help make their ... of volunteer grou... small. Perha... dad who ...

Public Education

Main Idea Schools today are trying to solve a variety of difficult challenges with innovative solutions.

Civics & You Is your school doing a good job of educating students? How do you know? Read to find out how the federal government is trying to grade schools like yours.

Since the U.S. Constitution does not mention education, public education has always been under the general control of the individual states. In colonial times, some local governments took the lead and began offering free public education to children. The [C] practice spread until it became almost universal after the Civil War. Today about 55 million students attend the nation's public elementary and secondary schools. Some 7 million other students go to private schools.

As public education grew, local school districts raised most of the money for schools and determined how students would be taught. In 1816, Indiana set up the first modern public school system. Today in most states, elementary and secondary education remains a local responsibility under state guidelines. The basic administrative unit for public schools is the local school district.

The federal government, though, plays an important **role,** or function, in education, providing aid to local schools in several forms. Its share of the total funding is less than 10 percent, but it **imposes,** or demands, certain rules on local schools. These rules include prohibiting gender discrimination in school activities and saying how schools must meet [W] the needs of students with disabilities.

The steadily increasing role of the federal government in public education has been a source of controversy. Some critics claim that the federal government is overstepping its constitutional bounds.

Chapter 14   401

Teach

[C] Critical Thinking

Drawing Conclusions Ask: Which groups were educated before free public education became available? *(The wealthy were educated; the poor were not.)* How did free public education change American society? *(More of the population became educated.)*

[W] Writing Support

Persuasive Writing Have students write about who they believe should grade public schools for success or failure. They should include reasons for each choice. Encourage students to share their ideas with the class. **OL**

TIME™ Political Cartoons

Answers:
1. The yellow crane stands for federal budget cuts for higher education. The result is higher tuition costs at colleges and universities.
2. The cost of higher education is out of reach for many students.
3. Ramsey is against increases in college tuition. Answers will vary but may include that his cartoon displays his point of view by showing the reactions of the students.

Differentiated Instruction

Analyzing Visual Information

Objective:	To analyze a graph to obtain information
Focus:	Have students identify the graph's title, topic, key, and labels.
Teach:	Discuss the crime rate and what each bar represents.
Assess:	Have pairs answer the questions on page 76. Review answers with class.
Close:	Compare this graph with the one on page 405 of the textbook. Identify the information and patterns shown.

Differentiated Instruction Strategies

BL Describe how each graph presents similar information in a different way.

AL Apply the questions on page 76 to the line graphs on page 405 of the textbook.

ELL Identify the parts of the graph and the information they present.

R Reading Strategy

Academic Vocabulary Ask: What does it mean when someone is "accountable" for something? *(To be accountable is to be held responsible for something.)* **How would you define accountability?** *(the willingness or obligation to take responsibility for something)* **BL ELL**

S Skill Practice

Analyzing Charts and Graphs Ask: What might be the other sources of funding for public education as shown on the pie chart? *(Students may mention businesses in the schools and funding from charitable foundations.)* **AL**

W Writing Support

Persuasive Writing Have students write a one-page paper explaining to the school board why they should grant or deny permission to a fast food restaurant that wants to open a branch inside the school. **OL**

Analyzing Charts

Answers:
1. state government
2. State funds provide $4.75 and local funds provide $4.15 for a total of $8.90.

Hands-On Chapter Project

Step 2

Influencing Public Policy

Step 2: Planning the Pamphlet Student groups will decide on the goals that will be the topic of their pamphlets and what information to include about their goals.

A Landmark Law

In 2001 President George W. Bush signed a landmark education bill known as the "No Child Left Behind Act." This law authorized $26.5 billion in federal spending on education, but it also added to the rules that local schools must follow. For example, all students in grades three through eight must take a series of state tests in reading, science, and math. Bush hoped this law would establish a system of new accountability measures for schools that do not perform well. Bush claimed that "[t]he fundamental principle of this bill is that every child can learn. We expect every child to learn, and you must show us whether or not every child is learning."

Closing the Gap The biggest education issue facing state governments is how to equally provide high-quality schooling to all students. Currently there is a large spending gap between wealthy and poor school districts. The gap occurs because many districts depend heavily on property taxes to fund the schools, and property values vary greatly from one district to another. A community with a healthy, expanding tax base, for example, has far more to spend per student than a community that has not benefited from the same growth in property tax values.

To raise more money, some schools have turned to businesses. The placement of soft drink vending machines in schools is a controversial example of alternative ways to raise money for education.

Challenges to Schools and Teachers

Among the nonfinancial problems facing schools today are low test scores, high dropout rates, and crime and violence on school property. Dealing with dropout rates and violence requires a wide range of remedies, many of which necessarily occur outside the schools. Remedies must take place outside schools because the problems are rooted in broader social problems of poverty, broken families, drug abuse and alcoholism, and crime and violence in the streets.

Charter Schools To combat poor academic performance, more than 30 states now permit the creation of charter schools. These schools receive state funding, but they are excused from meeting many public school regulations. Some educators believe that this freedom will encourage charter schools to be more innovative than conventional public schools. Former public school teachers and community groups may establish and run charter schools.

Funding Elementary and Secondary School Education

41.5%
2.9%
47.5%
8.1%

- Federal Funds
- State Funds
- Local Funds
- Other

Source: U.S. Census Bureau, *Statistical Abstract of the United States,* 2006.

Analyzing Charts

1. **Identifying** Which source contributes the most funds for elementary and secondary education?
2. **Calculating** Out of every 10 dollars of funds for public school, how much comes from local and state sources?

Directions Tell student groups to each decide on one goal about which to educate the public. They will next decide on the information to include in their pamphlets and how to present that information: in text, graphs, charts, and other visuals. You may wish to provide examples of promotional pamphlets on various issues (for example, health) for students to use as models. Encourage students with computer and art abilities to help others with the design of their pamphlets. **OL**

(Project continued in Section 3)

American Biography

Charlotte Hawkins Brown (1883–1961)

The life of **Charlotte Hawkins Brown** from her birth in Henderson, North Carolina, until her death, was centered on education and helping others. The granddaughter of slaves, Brown and her family moved to Massachusetts, where she attended Massachusetts public schools in Cambridge and the State Normal School in Salem.

In 1900, Charlotte Brown met Alice Freeman Palmer, the president of Wellesley College, who became her lifelong trusted friend and adviser. Palmer provided funds for Brown's education to become a teacher. In 1901 Charlotte Brown, just 18 years old,

began her teaching career in a missionary school, the Bethany Institute, in Sedalia, North Carolina. When the mission school closed because of a lack of money, the town's residents asked her to stay and start a new school.

Brown agreed and opened the Palmer Memorial Institute. Through her efforts, the Palmer Institute became one of the leading academies for African American children in the nation.

Beyond being a pioneer of African American education, Brown was an eloquent spokesperson for equal rights and woman suffrage.

Making a Difference

Charlotte Hawkins Brown made important contributions in many fields. **Comparing** What do you think was Brown's most important accomplishment? Explain.

Pros and Cons Opponents of charter schools argue that they take away funds from public schools and that they are likely to enroll many of the better students, leaving "problem" students behind in the public schools. Supporters of charter schools, however, claim that charter schools simply offer alternatives to public schools, and there seems to be no sign that they are luring away the best students from public schools.

The Voucher Controversy Another educational alternative is for cities and states to give parents **tuition vouchers**—a kind of government money order. Parents can use these vouchers to pay for their children to attend private schools. Only a few places, such as Cleveland (Ohio), Milwaukee (Wisconsin), and the state of Vermont, have experimented with vouchers.

Teachers' unions oppose vouchers because they feel vouchers funnel education funds out of the public school system and into private schools. Other opponents contend that vouchers violate the First Amendment because they can be used to pay tuition at religious schools. The Supreme Court has ruled that it is constitutional to use public money (vouchers) at religious schools as long as the funds are granted directly to the parents or guardians, and are not used to promote the religious mission of the school.

Privatization A more extreme alternative to the traditional management of schools by school boards is for private companies to contract with local districts to run the schools. These corporations promise to improve the quality of education and to do it more cheaply than public school administrations, while making a profit for themselves.

Chapter 14   **403**

Activity: Collaborative Learning

Researching Have students form a collaborative group to research the education budget for their local school district. They will divide up and research the following topics: what items are in the school budget and how much is allocated for each. Have the group create a pie chart for allocations by categories. They should then interview a school board member and a school administrator for their opinions on budget allocations and suggestions for changes and improvements. Have students present a summary of their findings to the class and lead a discussion on how education funds should be spent. **OL**

R Reading Strategy

Inferring Have students read the biography of Charlotte Hawkins Brown. **Ask:** Why do you think the townspeople chose Brown to start a new school? *(She had proven to be an excellent teacher.)* Why do you think Brown named the school the Palmer Memorial Institute? *(to honor the woman who had helped her become a teacher)* **OL**

D Differentiated Instruction

Below Grade Level Have students organize the pros and cons of charter schools, vouchers, and mass testing in a chart with those headings. Encourage them to add their own opinions. **BL**

American Biography

Answer: Student answers will vary, but most should focus on her making Palmer Institute one of the leading academies in the nation for African American children.

Additional Support

Teacher Tip

When grouping students for this project, you may choose to mix all four levels of learners in each group so that below-level students and English-language learners can benefit from working with more competent learners.

Section **CHAPTER 14**
2

Community Center "Drums not Drugs" is the theme of this teen performance in Seymour, Connecticut. **Explaining** What teen programs do community centers offer?

D Differentiated Instruction

Gifted and Talented Have students work in pairs to write an opinion about whether or not they think mass testing helps students learn more at school. **AL**

Caption Answer:

Answers may include sports, homework help, trips, art, and social activities.

✔ **Reading Check** **Answer:** A school voucher is a type of money order for a set amount of money that the government gives to parents to pay for their children to attend private schools.

The Rise of Mass Testing As mentioned earlier, the 2001 federal education bill requires states to test all students in reading, math, and science, in grades three through eight. Some states also require students to pass competency tests in order to be promoted to the next grade or to receive a high school diploma at the end of the 12th grade.

Competency tests and other forms of mass testing are given to provide certain measures. These tests are used to:

- provide comparative scores for individual students
- indicate a student's strengths or weaknesses
- assess the effectiveness of teachers, schools, and even entire districts.

D Supporters of competency testing claim that it holds schools and teachers to high levels of accountability, but many teachers' organizations oppose such testing. They claim that it forces teachers to spend valuable classroom time teaching students how to pass tests instead of how to understand the subjects they are supposed to be learning.

✔ **Reading Check** **Describing** What is a school voucher?

Crime and Social Programs

Main Idea Battling crime and ending social problems associated with poverty are two of the biggest challenges governments face.

Civics & You Think about how crime affects the community where you live. What do you believe should be done about it?

Federal and state prisons hold more than 2 million inmates. The **ratio,** or percentage, of prisoners per 100,000 population in the United States is among the highest in the world.

Crime and Poverty

Crime rates are usually highest in large cities, where poverty and crime often go hand in hand. For poor people who have struggled with dead-end, minimum-wage jobs, robbery or drug dealing may seem like an easier way to make a living. For others, having a normal job may not seem possible.

Differentiated Instruction

Leveled Activities

BL **Guided Reading Activity 14–2, URB p. 86**

OL **Biography Activity 14, URB pp. 71–72**

AL **Differentiated Instruction Activity 14, URB pp. 79–80**

ELL **Content Vocabulary, Activity 14, URB p. 68**

Many of the poorest inner-city residents drop out of school early and spend much of their time on the streets. Crime is often the **C** only way of life they know.

Police Forces

America's large cities have many more police officers than in all the nation's state, county, and small-town law enforcement units combined. As a result, urban police are the main crime-fighting force in the nation.

Police Functions More than 3,000 county sheriffs and their deputies are the main law enforcement presence in rural areas. In addition, every state has a law enforcement agency known as the highway patrol or state police. These agencies' main responsibility is highway safety, but they often play an important role in investigating crimes and capturing suspects.

A major function of police departments is to enforce the law, but most of the daily work of uniformed police officers involves keeping the peace. Peacekeeping activities might include handling neighborhood disputes and providing services, such as directing traffic. Much of the credit for the recent drop in crime is given to the use of **community policing.** Under this program, police become a visible presence in neighborhoods, walking or riding bicycles, and getting to know local residents. The program also works to get residents involved in neighborhood watch efforts.

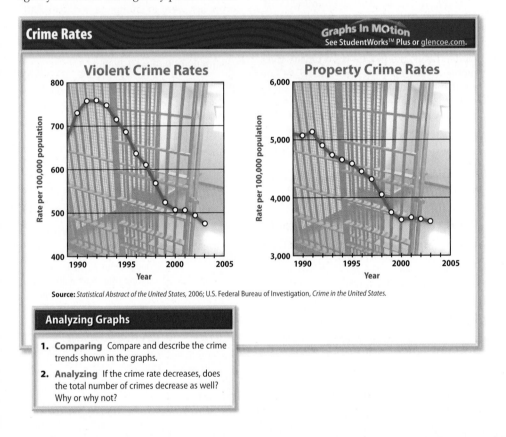

Crime Rates

Graphs In MOtion
See StudentWorks™ Plus or glencoe.com.

Violent Crime Rates

Property Crime Rates

Source: *Statistical Abstract of the United States,* 2006; U.S. Federal Bureau of Investigation, *Crime in the United States.*

Analyzing Graphs

1. **Comparing** Compare and describe the crime trends shown in the graphs.
2. **Analyzing** If the crime rate decreases, does the total number of crimes decrease as well? Why or why not?

Chapter 14 **405**

Activity: Technology Connection

Summarizing and Analyzing Information Discuss how crime prevention and social welfare programs are evaluated. **Ask:** How do we judge their success or failure? Have students work in groups to research a crime prevention or social welfare program on the Internet and in library sources. Each group should read at least three sources on its selected program to determine how it is being evaluated. The group should then make a chart of the positive and negative results of the program and present a summary of its research to the class in the form of a PowerPoint® presentation. Each presentation should be followed by a short question-and-answer period. **AL**

C Critical Thinking

Drawing Conclusions Explain that the new, reformed welfare program, TANF, has a five-year lifetime limit on receiving welfare benefits. **ASK:** What can you conclude about the old welfare program, AFDC? (*It had no time limitations on receipt of benefits.*) **BL**

✔Reading Check **Answer:** Poor families benefit most from welfare programs.

Assess

Civics ONLINE

Study Central™ provides summaries, interactive games, and online graphic organizers to help students review content.

Close

Summarizing Using their graphic organizers, have students write a one-page summary of the most important information in this section. **OL**

Section ⭐ **Review**
2

Social Programs

Our government tries to help Americans who suffer from ill health, old age, poverty, and physical disabilities with **welfare** programs. Policymakers have long struggled over the problems of reducing poverty and administering government financial aid to the best effect. Critics of welfare claim that it undermines self-respect among the poor and encourages dependency. Defenders of welfare assert that it is the only way many poor families can avoid homelessness and hunger.

Welfare Reform After years of debate, in 1996 Congress created a program called Temporary Assistance for Needy Families (TANF). It ended Aid to Families with Dependent Children, a 60-year-old federal program, and gave more power to the states to set the rules for future welfare eligibility. Under TANF, the federal government gives money to the states to pass on as welfare payments. Each state has considerable authority to decide who is eligible for welfare and how much money each person gets, but there are some federal rules attached. There is a five-year lifetime limit on receiving welfare, and states are required to develop job-training programs for the poor to help them leave the welfare rolls.

The number of people on welfare dropped tremendously following passage of TANF. In 1995 about 14.2 million people received welfare benefits. By 2007 there were slightly fewer than 4 million recipients. In 45 states, welfare caseloads dropped by more than 50 percent.

Some critics of the law claim, however, that its successes result mostly from the booming economy of the late 1990s. The labor shortage of the period made it relatively easy for unemployed welfare recipients to find work. Some observers fear that if the economy were to slump, as it did in 2001, people being forced off the welfare rolls will be helpless—without jobs *and* without the so-called safety net of welfare to at least ensure them food and shelter.

✔Reading Check **Explaining** According to defenders of welfare, who benefits most from welfare programs?

Section Review
2

Vocabulary

1. **Define** the following terms and use them in sentences related to public education: *charter school, tuition voucher, community policing, welfare.*

Main Ideas

2. **Defining** What is the privatization of schools?

3. **Explaining** Why do some critics believe the voucher program violates the First Amendment?

Critical Thinking

4. **BIG Ideas** Do you think the federal government plays too great a role in education? Explain.

5. **Making Comparisons** In a chart like the one below, compare the argument for and against charter schools.

CITIZENSHIP Activity

6. **Expository Writing** What is the most significant social issue facing your community? In a one-page paper, discuss how you would address the issue.

Civics ONLINE

Study Central™ To review this section, go to glencoe.com.

Answers

1. Sentences should use vocabulary words according to their definitions in the section and in the Glossary.

2. Privatization is the takeover of the management of a public school by a business for the purpose of improving education at a profit for the business.

3. Some critics believe that the voucher system violates the First Amendment (separation of government from the influence of religion) when vouchers are used to send children to religious schools. Vouchers are paid with taxpayer money.

4. Some students may agree and argue that public education should be locally controlled. Others may argue that the federal government sets important standards, protects minorities, and attempts to give all students an equal education.

5. **Arguments for charter schools:** They may be more innovative and successful than local public schools.

Arguments against charter schools: They may take the best students from the public schools. They also take away needed funds from public schools and may not be more successful.

6. Papers should present the problem clearly and offer specific suggestions for solving it.

College Costs: Planning Ahead

If you want to go to college, it pays to plan ahead. The cost of tuition, fees, and room and board for a year of undergraduate education ranges from $12,127 at the average four-year public university to $29,026 at private universities.

How can I meet the cost of college? A scholarship and other financial aid can help, but most of us still need to save more and spend less. Here are some possibilities to consider:

W

- **Create a budget and keep to it** Budget the items that are under your control.
- **Work** You can attend school full-time and still work part-time, or work full-time and attend school part-time.
- **Get your degree in less than four years** Completing a bachelor's degree in less than four years is difficult, but it is possible.
- **Save regularly** Set a goal to put a specific amount in a savings account monthly.
- **Federal student aid** If you do not have the resources to pay for college, you may apply for financial aid. Different forms include federal grants, student loans, and college work-study. Check with your school to find out which programs are available.

Average Annual College Costs

Public Institutions	
Tuition and mandatory fees	$5,491
Room and board	$6,636
Total College Base Costs	**$12,127**
Books and supplies	$894
Transportation	$852
Other expenses	$1,693
Total College Expenses	**$15,566**

S

Source: The College Board, Trends in College Pricing 2005.

Analyzing Economics

Researching Select a college you would like to attend and contact the financial aid office. Through the office, gather information on all types of financial aid available to incoming freshmen students. Report your findings.

W Writing Support

Personal Writing Have students write in a journal the expenses that should be part of their personal budgets at the present time. Then have them each estimate their income and plan how to increase it, if necessary, to both meet expenses and to save. Refer them to Chapter 20, "Personal Finance and Economics," for information.

S Skill Practice

Analyzing Charts Discuss the expense categories on the chart. **Ask:** What might "other expenses" include? *(Students may list meals at school, clothes, supplies, equipment, and so on.)* **OL**

Analyzing Economics

Answer: Student responses will vary, but should include information on their college of choice.

Additional Support

Activity: Economics Connection

Researching Have a collaborative group divide the following research topics. The group will contact a local community college and research the cost of full-time (12–18 credits) and half-time (6–9 credits) attendance. Researchers should estimate the actual cost of attendance by including all the categories on the Average Annual Costs chart. The group will then produce a chart similar to the model and present its findings to the class in a brief oral report. **OL**

Focus

Bellringer
Daily Focus Transparency 14–3

Guide to Reading
Answers to Graphic:

rainwater runoff

solid waste

automobile exhaust

Pollution

smoking

incinerators

chemical waste

Section
Spotlight Video

To generate student interest and provide a springboard for class discussion, access the Chapter 14, Section 3 video at glencoe.com or on the video DVD.

Resource Manager

Section
3

Environmental Issues

Guide to Reading

Big Idea
Scarcity requires individuals and groups to make choices about using goods and services to satisfy their wants.

Content Vocabulary
- environmentalism *(p. 409)*
- solid waste *(p. 409)*
- landfill *(p. 409)*
- NIMBY *(p. 409)*
- toxic *(p. 409)*
- recycle *(p. 410)*
- conservation *(p. 410)*

Academic Vocabulary
- authority *(p. 409)*
- attitude *(p. 409)*
- federal *(p. 411)*

Reading Strategy
Identifying As you read, use a diagram like the one below to identify three sources of air and water pollution.

Pollution

Real World Civics Can you breathe easily every morning when you leave your home? Does the air around you look clear? The people living in the San Francisco Bay area face many days that look smoggy and polluted. Much has been done by the county and city to try to limit air pollution for citizens and protect the environment. During the summer, the city and county of San Francisco sponsor "Spare the Air" days. On days when dangerous smog levels exist, bay area residents and companies are urged to refrain from activities that cause pollution, such as burning wood, and are asked to take public transportation.

▼ **San Francisco skyline at dawn**

R **Reading Strategies**	C **Critical Thinking**	D **Differentiated Instruction**	W **Writing Support**	S **Skill Practice**
Teacher Edition • Inferring pp. 411, 412 **Additional Resources** • Pri. Source Read., URB p. 17 • Cont. Vocab., URB p. 67 • Ac. Vocab., URB p. 69 • Guid. Read., URB p. 87 • Foldables, p. 77	**Teacher Edition** • Making Inferences, p. 409 **Additional Resources** • Quizzes and Tests, p. 165	**Teacher Edition** • Visual/Spatial, p. 410 **Additional Resources** • School-to-Home Conn., URB p. 81 • Reteach. Act., URB p. 83	**Teacher Edition** • Expository Writing, p. 410 **Additional Resources** • Speak/Listen Skills Act., URB p. 9	**Teacher Edition** • Analyzing Visuals, p. 411 **Additional Resources** • Chart, Map, and Graph Skills, URB p. 77 • Daily Focus Trans., 14–3

Dealing With Concerns

Main Idea Protecting the environment is an important issue with which community leaders must deal.

Civics & You Can a single individual like you make a difference in protecting the environment? Read more to find out some ways you can.

Matt Bell lives near the Cincinnati-Northern Kentucky Airport. The stream behind his home, he explained, "used to be crystal clear." Now the stream is filled with a thick white haze and no aquatic life can live in it.

This was caused by the runoff of de-icing fluid from the nearby airport. Around 600 planes a day take off from the busy transportation hub, and in the winter, they must be deiced with a special chemical. This chemical has found its way into the creek behind Matt Bell's home. No one disagrees that airplanes need to be deiced—but could it be done without destroying a nearby stream?

What Is Environmentalism?

We pay a high price for living in an industrialized society. Every time we turn on a light or throw away trash, we may harm our environment. **Environmentalism,** or protecting our environment, is a national and worldwide concern, but most often it is up to local communities to address environmental problems.

Until the 1970s, state and local **authorities,** or experts, paid little attention to environmental problems. The focus changed in 1970 when Congress passed the Clean Air Act and established the Environmental Protection Agency (EPA). While the EPA has taken the lead in setting goals and standards, the states have implemented the programs by monitoring air and water quality and inspecting industrial facilities.

Dumping Garbage Landfills of solid waste are filling up across the country. *Analyzing* Why is it difficult to find new sites for waste landfills?

Solid Waste

Managing the disposing of solid waste—the technical name for garbage—is a huge problem for cities. Americans produce about 250 million tons of solid waste each year, and most places where it can be dumped, called landfills, are filling up fast. Some landfills have been closed because rainwater seeping through them has damaged underground water reservoirs and streams.

Complicating the search for new landfill sites is the fact that no one wants a garbage dump in his or her general area. Indeed, there is a name for this **attitude—NIMBY,** meaning "not in my backyard." Opposition from citizens' groups makes it difficult to find new landfill sites.

Incineration As an alternative to landfills, much solid waste is burned in huge incinerators. These, however, cause problems of their own: **toxic,** or poisonous, substances in the smoke from incineration can cause serious air pollution. New ways to "scrub" pollutants from incinerator stacks are being developed. Current pollution-control devices for incinerator smokestacks are expensive.

Chapter 14   409

Teach

C Critical Thinking

Making Inferences Ask: Why is local community action vital to environmentalism? *(Communities are aware of local problems and the best means to solve them. Protecting the environment requires individuals to act on a local level.)* **OL**

Caption Answer:

Rainwater seeps through landfills and pollutes underground water sources. For this reason, many citizens groups oppose landfills in their neighborhoods.

Differentiated Instruction

Indicating the Relationship Between Ideas

SPEAKING AND LISTENING SKILLS ACTIVITY 4

Indicating the Relationship Between Ideas

Learning the Skill

It would be frustrating and boring to read an essay consisting of nothing but short, simple sentences that jump quickly from one idea to the next. Creative writers vary their sentence structure to make reading more enjoyable. Careful writers help readers understand the relationships between ideas. This goal can be accomplished through grammatical devices such as subordination, coordination, and apposition.

• **Subordination** is a way of writing that makes one sentence or idea more important than another. The relationship between the ideas in the sentences can often be expressed by using a subordinating conjunction:
Time: when, whenever, after, as, before, once, since, till, until, now that, while, as long as, as soon as
Concession: though, although, even though, if, whereas
Contingency: if, once
Condition: if, in case, as long as, unless, provided that
Reason: because, since, as long as
Result: so, so that
Comparison: as, just as, as if
Contrast: while, whereas

• **Coordination** is a way of writing in which each sentence or idea is equally important. Conjunctive adverbs such as the following are commonly used to express a relationship between two sentences:
Result: therefore, consequently, as a result
Concession: nevertheless, yet, still, after all, of course
Apposition: for example, for instance, that is, in other words
Addition: moreover, furthermore, also, in addition, likewise
Time: meanwhile, in the meantime
Contrast: however, instead, on the contrary, in contrast, but
Summary: thus, in conclusion, then
Reinforcement: further, in particular, indeed, above, in fact

• **Apposition** is a word or phrase placed in a parallel position to a noun in the sentence. An appositive may be set off by commas or dashes:
Kirsten, the best employee in the company, always meets her deadlines.
Appositives necessary to the sense of a sentence are not set off in any way:
The song "Angel" was the crowd's favorite.

Speaking and Listening Skills, Activity 4, URB pp. 9–12

Objective:	To understand subordination, coordination, and apposition
Focus:	Have students read "Learning the Skill" on page 9.
Teach:	Give examples of the three grammatical devices in the excerpt.
Assess:	Review students' examples from page 11.
Close:	The listening group will assess the use of subordination, coordination, and apposition in the oral report.

Differentiated Instruction Strategies

BL Write a summary of the environmental views of your group's candidate.

AL Watch a television newsmagazine report and write a summary using the three devices studied in this activity.

ELL Listen to the tape and pause it after a main idea has been explained. Orally identify each main idea.

W

W Writing Support

Expository Writing Have students research how one material (paper, plastic soda bottles, metal cans, and so forth) is recycled into a new item or reused. They should write a one- or two-page report on this topic. **AL**

D Differentiated Instruction

Visual/Spatial Have students find an example of unnecessary packaging of an item in a store and devise a way for the item to be sold with less packaging. Students may create a visual to display their idea. **OL**

Caption Answer:

They may be using tools made from recycled metal and containers made from recycled plastic. They may use wood scraps in the garden as mulch or for plant stakes and fences.

Reading Check **Answer:** They are encouraged to conserve in shopping by using fewer bags, at home by buying energy-efficient appliances and lighting, in their vehicles by conserving fuel, and in their homes by using less water and less fuel.

Hands-On Chapter Project

Step 3

Recycling

A second alternative to landfills is **recycling,** which means reusing old materials to make new ones. Most communities across the United States have recycling programs. Many Americans recycle materials such as paper, metal cans, plastic and glass bottles, and plastic bags in their homes, schools, and workplaces.

Paper is the number one material that we throw away. For every 100 pounds (45 kg) of trash we throw away, about 35 pounds (16 kg) is paper. When paper is recycled, it saves our forests and reduces our air and water pollution. Recycling paper also means lower disposal costs. Unfortunately, not all waste is recyclable. Furthermore, many people do not bother to participate in recycling efforts.

Conservation **Conservation** is the preservation and protection of our natural resources. For example, some stores offer customers a rebate when they return bags or use their own shopping bags. Businesses are encouraged, and sometimes required by law, to eliminate unnecessary packaging of products.

Many communities depend on private citizens and local businesses to promote conservation. People can conserve electricity by buying energy-efficient appliances and turning off unnecessary lights. They can conserve oil and natural gas by adjusting thermostats, installing more efficient furnaces, and insulating their homes. Many gas companies also offer competitive fees. Similarly, water use in many communities is being reduced significantly through the efforts of private citizens. As conservation becomes a way of life for more Americans, the nation may come closer to solving its environmental problems.

Reading Check **Explaining** What elements of daily life are people encouraged to conserve?

Motor City Makeover This Detroit, Michigan, family spends time cleaning city park grounds and planting flowers. *Speculating* **What recycled products might they be using in their tasks?**

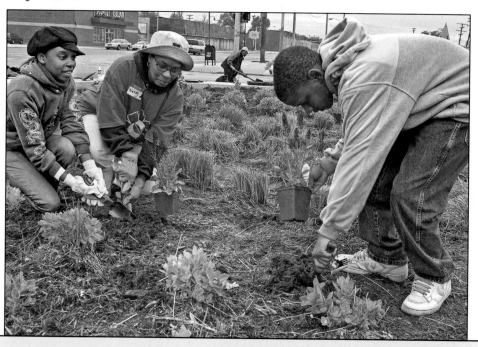

410

Influencing Public Policy

Step 3: Completing the Pamphlet Collaborative groups of students complete their pamphlets and plan their presentations.

Directions Group members complete their pamphlets and plan presentations on the goals that the pamphlets promote. Their presentations should include an explanation of the goals and why they chose them and ways in which the pamphlets can help achieve their goals. They might display the pamphlets on an overhead projector or create copies for class and teacher. Each group member should have a specific role in this presentation and be prepared to answer class questions. **OL**

(Project continued on the Visual Summary page)

Protecting the Air, Water, and Land

Main Idea Sources of pollution include the activities of both industries and individuals.

Civics & You Has a parent or teacher ever reminded you to clean up after yourself? Read to find out how the same good advice applies to communities as well.

Much air, water, and land pollution comes from industrial sources. However, individuals are responsible for pollution as well.

Industrial Pollution

Water pollution comes mainly from factories, which produce all sorts of chemical waste. For generations, some factories pumped this waste directly into rivers and streams. Others buried it, which allowed it to seep into underground water supplies. Factory smokestacks emit many different toxic gases into the air. The EPA has done much to stop industrial pollution of air and water. **Federal,** or national, regulations limit the amounts and kinds of waste that factories may discharge. However, budget limitations keep many of these regulations from being strictly enforced. **R**

Pollution from Individuals

Pollution from factories, nevertheless, is far easier to regulate than pollution from the activities of individuals. In most cities, cars and trucks are the worst air polluters. To reduce the pollution they cause, the federal government mandated the removal of lead from gasoline. It also required the automobile industry to develop more efficient engines and to equip cars with devices to remove pollutants from exhaust gases.

Another important way to reduce urban air pollution is to persuade people to drive less. Many local governments are trying to

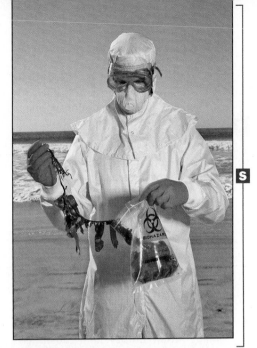
S

Controlling Pollution Constant monitoring of seawater helps scientists trying to ease pollution. *Comparing* Whom do you think pollutes more—individuals or industries? Why?

build or improve public transportation systems to get more people to use subways and buses. They encourage drivers to carpool by creating carpool lanes.

A serious threat to *indoor* air quality is smoking. Many cities and counties have passed no-smoking ordinances. Almost all states regulate smoking in public buildings.

Threat of Hazardous Waste

Hazardous waste is a major environmental danger. Perhaps the most serious form is radioactive waste from nuclear power plants. Hazardous waste also includes runoff from pesticides that farmers and gardeners spray on plants and residues from improperly discarded motor oil, auto engine coolant, and batteries. Until 1970, much toxic waste was put in metal containers, which were then encased in concrete and dumped into the ocean.

Chapter 14 **411**

R Reading Strategy

Inferring Ask: Why is hazardous waste no longer disposed of in the ocean? *(Answers should include that scientists concluded that the containers have leaked and caused pollution and poisoning of living creatures or that they might do so in the future.)* Since there is no safe way to dispose of hazardous waste, what can be done about it? *(Answers may include reducing the creation of this waste.)* **OL**

✔ **Reading Check Answer:** Individual citizens formed environmental protection groups such as the Sierra Club, the Audubon Society, and the Wilderness Society.

Assess

Civics ONLINE

Study Central™ provides summaries, interactive games, and online graphic organizers to help students review content.

Close

Summarizing Summarize how grassroots efforts to protect the environment led to government actions and regulations. **OL**

Section 3 Review

Today, land disposal is the only way to dispose of hazardous waste. Disposal facilities are filling up fast. There is currently no completely safe method of disposing of hazardous waste. Sometimes entire communities are affected by a site. The town of Love Canal, New York, had to be abandoned because residents had so many serious health problems as a result of exposure to toxic waste that began in 1978.

A Grassroots Effort

Beginning in the 1960s, citizens formed groups to do something about protecting the environment. The Sierra Club, the Audubon Society, and the Wilderness Society gained prominence. These organizations worked to protect the environment and promote the conservation of natural resources.

Many communities and businesses responded to the efforts of these organizations and started including sustainable development in their planning. City planners tried to reduce urban sprawl and expand green spaces, builders included energy efficiency in their designs, and the forestry industry started reforestation programs.

Government Actions With the environmental movement gaining support, the federal government took action. The National Environmental Policy Act, which created the Environmental Protection Agency (EPA), was signed into law in 1970. The EPA took on the job of setting and enforcing pollution standards and coordinating antipollution activities with state and local governments.

The Clean Air Act of 1970 established emissions standards for factories and automobiles. In following years, Congress passed two more pieces of important environmental legislation. The Clean Water Act (1972) restricted the discharge of pollutants into the nation's lakes and rivers. The Endangered Species Act (1973) established measures for saving threatened animal species.

✔ **Reading Check Identifying** What have individual citizens done to protect the environment?

Section 3 Review

Vocabulary

1. **Define** the following terms and use them in sentences related to environmental problems in American communities: *environmentalism, solid waste, landfill, NIMBY, toxic, recycle, conservation.*

Main Ideas

2. **Defining** What is environmentalism?

3. **Explaining** Why is the threat of hazardous waste a serious problem?

Critical Thinking

4. **Evaluating** Which of the environmental issues discussed do you think is most critical today? Explain.

5. **BIG Ideas** In a graphic organizer like the one below, describe three ways to limit pollution caused by individuals.

Fighting Pollution
drive less

CITIZENSHIP Activity

6. **Expository Writing** Make a list of five ways that you could change your everyday activities to reduce the amount of waste you create.

Civics ONLINE

Study Central™ To review this section, go to glencoe.com.

Answers

1. Sentences should use vocabulary words according to their definitions in the section and in the Glossary.

2. Environmentalism is the effort to protect the environment.

3. There is no safe way to dispose of hazardous waste.

4. Answers will vary. Students should support their choice with facts from the chapter.

5. Answers may include any of the following: reduce garbage by recycling, reuse, and conservation; conserve water and fuel; stop smoking; buy energy-efficient cars and appliances; stop using pesticides on lawns and gardens.

6. Students' lists should reflect the actions listed in the answer to question 5.

Public Policy

- Government leaders make public policy, which is a general agreement among leaders about how to deal with particular issues.

- One goal of public policy is to anticipate and prevent problems.

- Governments and planning commissions make both short-term and long-term plans.

- Priorities are the goals a community considers most important or most urgent.

- A master plan spells out decisions about a community's future.

Education

- Elementary and secondary education is a local responsibility under state guidelines.

Even so, the federal government plays an important role in education, providing aid to local schools in several forms.

- Local school leaders face funding issues, low test scores, high dropout rates, and crime and violence on school property.

Community volunteers clean up their neighborhood

Crime and Social Issues

- Crime rates are usually highest in large cities, where poverty and crime often go hand in hand.

- Federal, state, and local law enforcement agencies fight crime, although most of the daily work is done by uniformed police officers.

- Policymakers have long struggled over the problems of how to reduce poverty and to best administer government financial aid.

The Environment

- Environmentalism is the concern that our environment must be protected.

- Through the EPA, the government tries to reduce air and water pollution.

North Carolina students work to earn college math credits

Factory wastes cause pollution

STUDY TO GO Study anywhere, anytime! Download quizzes and flash cards to your PDA from glencoe.com.

413

Visual Summary 14

Categorizing and Analyzing Information Have students research information about how their local community government works. **Ask:** How does local government set public policy? Is there a planning commission? Is there a master plan for the community's future? Then, have the students contribute to a group summary of their findings. Next, students will choose an issue that is or should be addressed by their community's master plan. They will research this issue and create a presentation on the issue that they will share with the class. They might also choose to make the presentation to local community government leaders. **AL**

For additional practice on this skill (Categorizing and Analyzing Information), see the **Skills Handbook**.

Comparing and Contrasting Have students select an issue from this chapter and research how their community is currently dealing with the issue. Encourage students to interview local legislators and other community leaders to find out their opinions on how to best deal with the issue. Students will create a chart or other visual to summarize the different points of view. They will present their summary to the class and lead a discussion on the merits of various solutions to the problem they researched. **OL**

Hands-On Chapter Project
Step 4: Wrap-Up

Influencing Public Policy

Step 4: Making a Class Presentation Students will finish the process they started in Step 1.

Directions Each group will make a presentation on its issue to the class. They will display and/or distribute their pamphlets to class members. They will lead a class discussion on the issue. Ask class members to write an evaluation of the presentation and pamphlet.

Group members will have a final meeting in which they self-evaluate their presentation and their pamphlet. At this time, they may decide to make changes in the presentation and to revise the pamphlet. To finalize the project, they may decide to give their presentation and to share their pamphlet with a citizen group that advocates for this issue. **OL**

14 ASSESSMENT

Answers and Analyses
Reviewing Vocabulary

1. D All the other answers involve long-term decisions about the future of a community. This example of a short-term plan is given on page 398.

2. B On page 399, "resources" are defined as money, people, and materials. Also, the clue word "accomplish" should signal that "resources" is the correct answer. The most confusing distractor may be "priorities." However, the difference between priorities and resources is clearly explained on page 399.

3. C The claim that welfare programs may undermine self-respect among the poor is stated on page 406 under Social Programs. Charter schools and tuition vouchers would probably raise, not lower, self-esteem. Community policing programs, as described, would not affect self-esteem among the poor and would exist in prosperous as well as poor neighborhoods.

4. A Although recycling is the most environmentally friendly way to deal with solid waste that already exists, some students may choose D, "conservation." Conservationists argue that through reusing rather than recycling materials and that through eliminating unnecessary packaging and the use of materials that will end up as solid waste, less garbage will be produced. Recycling and conservation are discussed on page 410.

Reviewing Main Ideas

5. D This information can be found under Sources of Public Policy on page 397.

6. D This information can be found under Creating a Master Plan on page 399.

7. C On page 403, under Pros and Cons, it is stated that opponents of charter schools argue that these schools take away funds from public schools. Students can easily eliminate choice A, which is never mentioned, and choice B, which is contradicted directly by the claim that charter schools don't take "problem" students. Choice C, that charter schools pro-

---

14 ASSESSMENT

TEST-TAKING TIP

When answering an essay question on a test, set off lists of facts with numbers or bullets.

Reviewing Vocabulary

Directions: Choose the word(s) that best completes the sentence.

1. Granting a builder a permit to construct apartments is an example of a _____.

  A master plan   **C** public policy

  B long-term plan   **D** short-term plan

2. The money, people, and materials available to accomplish a community's plan are its _____.

  A policies   **C** priorities

  B resources   **D** infrastructure

3. Critics of _____ claim they undermine self-respect among the poor.

  A charter schools   **C** welfare programs

  B tuition vouchers   **D** community policing programs

4. _____ is environmentally friendly because it requires reusing solid waste.

  A recycling   **C** landfills

  B incineration   **D** conservation

Reviewing Main Ideas

Directions: Choose the best answer for each question.

Section 1 (pp. 396–399)

5. Who suggests public policy ideas?

  A media

  B interest groups

  C political parties

  D all of the above

6. What do members of a planning committee consider when formulating a master plan?

  A priorities

  B resources

  C future needs

  D all of the above

Section 2 (pp. 400–406)

7. What do opponents of charter schools claim?

  A Charter schools have high dropout rates.

  B Charter schools only enroll problem students.

  C Charter schools take funds from public schools.

  D Charter schools produce poor academic performance.

8. Which program set a five-year lifetime limit on receiving welfare?

  A Drums not Drugs

  B No Child Left Behind

  C Temporary Assistance to Needy Families

  D Aid to Families with Dependent Children

Section 3 (pp. 408–412)

9. How can businesses help conserve forests?

  A by adjusting thermostats in stores

  B by selling energy-efficient furnaces

  C by eliminating unnecessary packaging

  D by accepting cans and bottles for recycling

10. How can cities reduce air pollution?

  A by improving public transportation

  B by dumping toxic waste in the ocean

  C by eliminating runoff from pesticides

  D by mandating the use of lead in gasoline

GO ON ➡

---

duce poor academic performance, is not supported by evidence in the chapter.

8. C This information is stated on page 406 under the heading Welfare Reform. It states that the five-year limit on receiving welfare is part of the program called Temporary Assistance for Needy Families, which supplanted Aid to Families with Dependent Children in 1996.

9. C Since much packaging is paper, businesses can best conserve forests by limiting packing materials. Choices A and B would result in less use of fuels such as oil, kerosene, and gas, not wood. Choice D would save metal and glass.

10. A Improving public transportation would lead to less driving in private cars and reduce emissions that pollute the air. Choices B and C have nothing to do with air pollution. Choice D would result in the opposite effect of increasing air pollution from cars. These issues are discussed on page 411.

Critical Thinking

Directions: Base your answers to questions 11 and 12 on the graph below and your knowledge of Chapter 14.

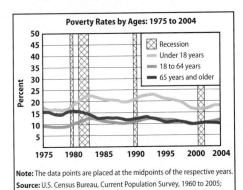

Poverty Rates by Ages: 1975 to 2004

Legend:
- Recession
- Under 18 years
- 18 to 64 years
- 65 years and older

Note: The data points are placed at the midpoints of the respective years.

Source: U.S. Census Bureau, Current Population Survey, 1960 to 2005; Annual Social and Economic Supplements.

11. Which of the following conclusions might you draw based on the graph?

A The percentage of elderly poor has increased since 1965.

B Poverty among working age people has increased since 1975.

C Poverty among children has been greatly reduced since 1975.

D Recessions have no effect on poverty among children.

12. During which period did poverty increase among children and people between 18 and 65?

A 1985–1990

B 1975–1979

C 1996–2000

D 2000–2004

Civics ONLINE

For additional test practice, use Self-Check Quizzes—Chapter 14 on glencoe.com.

Document-Based Questions

Directions: Analyze the document and answer the short-answer questions that follow.

The following passage is from the Clean Air Act.

> *(b) The purposes of this title are -*
>
> *(1) to protect and enhance the quality of the Nation's air resources so as to promote the public health and welfare and the productive capacity of its population;*
>
> *(2) to initiate and accelerate a national research and development program to achieve the prevention and control of air pollution;*
>
> *(3) to provide technical and financial assistance to State and local governments in connection with the development and execution of their air pollution prevention and control programs; and*
>
> *(4) to encourage and assist the development and operation of regional air pollution prevention and control programs.*
>
> *(c) Pollution Prevention—A primary goal of this Act is to encourage or otherwise promote reasonable Federal, State, and local governmental actions, consistent with the provisions of this Act, for pollution prevention.*
>
> —[42 U.S.C. 7401]

13. According to the passage, how does the federal government help state and local governments clean their air?

14. Refer to the first part of the passage. What goal in the preamble to the U.S. Constitution does the Clean Air Act help to achieve?

Extended-Response Question

15. Briefly explain why providing equal education to all students presents a challenge in many states.

STOP

Need Extra Help?

If you missed question...	1	2	3	4	5	6	7	8	9	10	11	12	13	14	15
Go to page...	398	399	406	410	397	399	403	406	410	411	406	406	411	412	401

ASSESSMENT

Document-Based Questions

13. The federal government provides technical and financial assistance to state and local governments to develop and enforce air pollution prevention and to control programs. (article b3)

14. The Clean Air Act protects the public health and welfare.

Extended Response

15. Students' essays will vary. Look for supporting details from the chapter. Students should mention the challenges of adequate school budgets and mandates to provide special services for disabled and challenged children.

Critical Thinking

11. B The percentage of working-age people who are poor has increased from 1970 (about 9 percent) to 2004 (11.3 percent). Choice A is incorrect because the graph shows that the percentage of elderly poor has decreased since 1965. Poverty among children has increased since 1970, so choice C is incorrect. There is no information on the effect of recessions included on the chart, so choice D is irrelevant.

12. D Choice A is incorrect because poverty in these groups declined between 1985 and 1990. Choice B is incorrect because poverty in these groups stayed about the same between 1975 and 1979. Choice C is incorrect because poverty went down in those groups between 1996 and 2000.

Civics ONLINE

Have students visit the Web site at glencoe.com to review Chapter 14 and take the **Self-Check Quiz**.

Need Extra Help?

Have students refer to the pages listed if they miss any of the questions.

415

Focus

R Reading Strategy

Inferring Ask: What values made Bob Anastas create a plan to help students avoid destructive lifestyles? *(belief in the value of education; values of self-reliance, motivation, and self-esteem; the values of compassion, helping others, and improving society)*

Making A Difference

Reading Focus

Recall an individual who made a difference in your life or a group that inspired you. The efforts of Rosa Parks, Rachel Carson, and Bob Anastas spurred action on a large scale.

Read to Discover

As you read, think about the following:

- What encourages individuals to take action?
- What values are important to those individuals who want to improve society?

Reader's Dictionary

moribund: approaching death

The Founding of SADD

Students Against Destructive Decisions (SADD) is a school-based organization dedicated to preventing behaviors that are harmful to young people.

Bob Anastas was direct with students when telling them why he created Students Against Drunk Driving.

"I lost two of my students to drunk driving four days apart," Anastas said. "After two kids died, I said 'Never again.' It is not a game. There is no instant replay."

That was in 1981 when two Wayland [Mass.] High School students died in separate drunk driving auto accidents. Anastas taught and coached both students. He said he has dedicated himself to spreading the word on the evils of drunk driving ever since. . . .

Anastas founded SADD in 1981. The name changed to Students Against Destructive Decisions in 1997 to broaden the organization's mission.

R The problem at Wayland, Anastas said, was the lack of a plan for young students. He said 28 percent of the school sent students to college while most schools in the area were sending 98 percent.

"The only difference was that my students believed they couldn't get there," Anastas said. "Seventy-five percent of the student population would drink, do drugs, be depressed and not motivated and I said we're going to fight this."

Anastas sent another message to the students. He told them to be in the top 25 percent of students instead of the bottom 75 percent that take the easy way out and find excuses. He said students who are partying and drinking instead of studying are in a bad position.

—Steve Lettau, "SADD Founder Visits Campus"

Additional Reading

Review suggested books before assigning them.

Elizabeth Cady Stanton: The Right Is Ours, by Harriet Sigerman highlights the life of Stanton, a staunch activist for women's rights and a mother of seven children.

White House Years, by Henry Kissinger expounds on Dr. Henry Kissinger's first four years as President Nixon's adviser on Foreign Policy and as Assistant to the President for National Security Affairs. He recounts his involvement in the 1971 India-Pakistan War and the Jordan Crisis.

Mississippi Challenge by Mildred Pitts Walter tells a history of the Civil Rights movement in the state of Mississippi. Jailings, bombings, economic reprisals—find out what it was like to be a civil rights worker in the 1960s, to sit in at an all-white lunch counter, and to be threatened by guns and dogs.

Challenging Segregation

Rosa Parks was arrested and fined for refusing to give up her seat on a Montgomery, Alabama, bus. Her simple act of protest sparked a new chapter of the civil rights movement.

One evening in early December 1955 I was sitting in the front seat of the colored section of a bus in Montgomery, Alabama. The white people were sitting in the white section. More white people got on, and they filled up all the seats in the white section. When that happened, we black people were supposed to give up our seats to the whites. But I didn't move. The white driver said, "Let me have those front seats." I didn't get up. I was tired of giving in to white people.

"I'm going to have you arrested," the driver said.

"You may do that," I answered.

Two white policemen came. I asked one of them, "Why do you push us around?"

He answered, "I don't know, but the law is the law and you're under arrest."

—Rosa Parks, *Rosa Parks: My Story*

Photographs as Primary Sources After the Supreme Court decision outlawing segregation on city buses, Rosa Parks rides at the front of the bus. Who are the people in the photograph? What are they doing? What is the photographer trying to communicate to the viewer?

The Beginnings of Environmentalism

In the early 1960s, Rachel Carson warned about the dangers of environmental pollution.

There was a strange stillness. The birds, for example—where had they gone? . . . The feeding stations in the backyards were deserted. The few birds seen anywhere were **moribund**; they trembled violently and could not fly. It was a spring without voices. . . only silence lay over the fields and woods and marsh.

—Rachel Carson, *Silent Spring*

Environmentalist Rachel Carson

DBQ Document-Based Questions

1. **Explaining** How did Anastas's personal experience lead to action?

2. **Connecting** What is a boycott and what effect did the bus boycott have on Alabama's business community?

3. **Examining** How do you think that Rosa Parks, an individual who was relatively uninvolved in the civil rights movement, could have become such an important figure in that movement?

4. **Analyzing** What environmental problem do you think is the most pressing problem we face today? Explain your response.

5. **Evaluating and Connecting** Think about the actions these individuals took to effect change. What is your opinion of their approaches to instituting political and social change? Give reasons for your opinion.

417

Did You Know?

Rachel Carson and *Silent Spring* After World War II, synthetic chemical pesticides were being widely used on farms and gardens, with the approval of agricultural scientists and government agencies. Science writer and trained biologist Rachel Carson became alarmed about the effects of "indiscriminate spraying" of these pesticides. In her groundbreaking book, *Silent Spring* (1962), she challenged these practices and warned against the long-term effects of misuse of chemical pesticides. The chemical industry and some government officials attacked her. In 1963, she was called to testify before Congress, where she urged new policies to protect human health and the environment. She is credited with changes in government policies and public awareness of dangers to the environment.

Teach

S Skill Practice

Analyzing Visuals **Ask:** List all the ways that heat enters the house shown in the diagram on these pages. *(solar panels, south-facing windows, and ceramic tile and concrete floors)* List all the features that cool the house. *(attic fan, trees and bushes, and wooden overhang)* Have students make a flowchart showing how solar energy is converted into electricity and heats different parts of this house. **BL**

C Critical Thinking

Drawing Conclusions **Ask:** How might this house produce extra energy to sell back to the utility company? *(Answers may include that the solar panels can produce electricity while heating and lighting is turned off in the house, as when occupants are not home. This extra electricity would be sent back to the grid, and the utility company could credit it to the home-owner.)* **OL AL**

Additional Support

The House of the Future

S

By harnessing the power of the sun, new designs can save money—and the planet

It sounds like a far-off dream: The home that heats and cools itself for free and actually generates more energy than it consumes, so that the local utility company might even send families a check for supplying power to the community grid. But with commonsense design principles and a little help from the sun, the house of the future can be yours. **C**

Solar energy is the key to the system shown here, which could power a three-bedroom house. The sun's heat is captured in special panels on the home's roof. Pipes carry liquid heated by the solar panels into the house. This heated liquid, a water-alcohol mixture to prevent freezing, is then used to warm the home's air and water.

The hefty up-front cost of this system—about $20,000—is eased by state and federal rebates, and typically pays for itself in 10 years. In the long run, energy-efficient houses like this one would free cash for home improvements and consumer spending, providing a big—and sunny—boost to the economy. **D**

Fast Facts on Solar Power

- All the energy stored in the Earth's reserves of oil, coal, and natural gas is equivalent to the energy from 20 days of sunshine.

- All new homes and apartments in Israel are required to use solar power to heat their water.

- In the U.S., residential and commercial buildings account for one-third of all energy use. Solar power, improved insulation, and more efficient appliances could reduce this demand by up to 80%.

Source: Union of Concerned Scientists

In from grid

Out to grid

Inverter converts direct current produced to 120-volt alternating current.

Utility grid allows users to sell extra power they produce and to buy more as needed.

Utility meter

Circuit-breaker box

To grid

To house

Walls made from straw—a cheap agricultural waste product—provide excellent insulation, as long as the straw is handled with care and treated to make it moisture-resistant.

Floors made of ceramic tiles and concrete soak up the winter sun and release heat at night.

South-facing windows and solar panels take full advantage of the sun's heat in winter.

Landscaping with trees and bushes is a great way to shade eastern and western exposures. Deciduous varieties lose their leaves in winter, allowing the sun to warm the house.

Background

Solar Power in the Northeast According to current research, solar power can benefit homeowners in the densely populated northeastern states almost as much as it does in places with more sunshine and open spaces. This is due to increases in the efficiency of solar panels, decreases in their cost, and financial incentives from the government. But another surprising incentive has emerged. Power companies are willing to "buy back" surplus energy produced by solar power and to credit it to the homeowner's account. As one advocate describes it, "Your meter actually runs backward." The power is sent directly from the home into the power grid and collected by the utility company. It is credited at the same rate charged to the consumer. Surplus electricity is produced whenever the heating and lighting systems are not being used. These electricity credits can be used to pay for electricity to run appliances. With all these benefits, solar power is becoming an attractive option, even in less sunny climates.

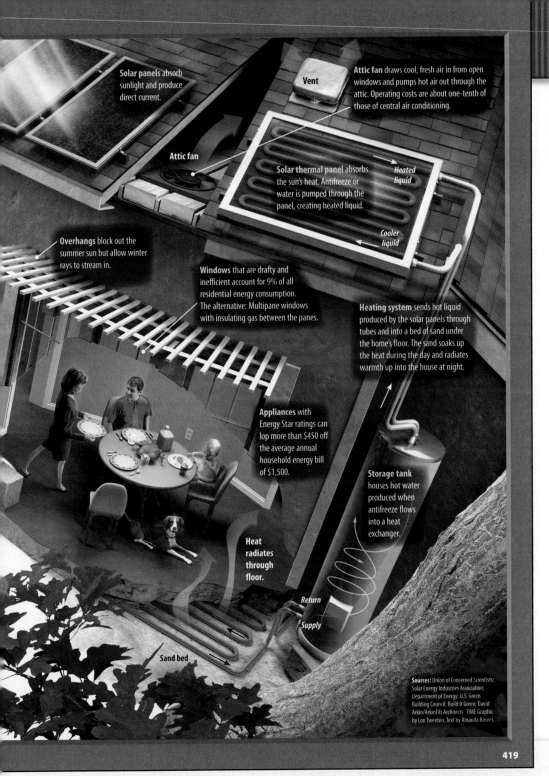

Solar panels absorb sunlight and produce direct current.

Vent

Attic fan draws cool, fresh air in from open windows and pumps hot air out through the attic. Operating costs are about one-tenth of those of central air conditioning.

Attic fan

Solar thermal panel absorbs the sun's heat. Antifreeze or water is pumped through the panel, creating heated liquid.

Heated liquid

Cooler liquid

Overhangs block out the summer sun but allow winter rays to stream in.

Windows that are drafty and inefficient account for 9% of all residential energy consumption. The alternative: Multipane windows with insulating gas between the panes.

Heating system sends hot liquid produced by the solar panels through tubes and into a bed of sand under the home's floor. The sand soaks up the heat during the day and radiates warmth up into the house at night.

Appliances with Energy Star ratings can lop more than $450 off the average annual household energy bill of $1,500.

Storage tank houses hot water produced when antifreeze flows into a heat exchanger.

Heat radiates through floor.

Return

Supply

Sand bed

Sources: Union of Concerned Scientists; Solar Energy Industries Association; Department of Energy; U.S. Green Building Council; Build It Green; David Arkin/ArkinTilt Architects TIME Graphic by Lon Tweeten. Text by Amanda Bower.

419

Reading Strategy ▶ Read to Write

Selling a Solar House Have students discuss how this solar house will have a positive effect on the environment. List all the features and materials that save energy and create less pollution. Then, have students work in pairs to create a magazine advertisement for the sale of this solar house. **OL**

5

UNIT PACING CHART

	Unit 5	Chapter 15	Chapter 16	Chapter 17
Day 1	Unit Opener, Reading Social Studies	Chapter Opener, Section 1	Chapter Opener, Section 1	Chapter Opener, Section 1
Day 2		Section 2	Section 2, Landmark Supreme Court Case Studies	Section 2, Financial Literacy
Day 3		Section 3, Chapter Review, Visual Summary	Section 3, Issues to Debate	Section 3, Chapter Review, Visual Summary
Day 4		Chapter Assessment	Chapter Review, Visual Summary	Chapter Assessment
Day 5		TIME Reports	Chapter Assessment	Analyzing Primary Sources

Teacher to Teacher

**Stephen Venezia,
Marblehead
High School,
Marblehead,
Massachusetts**

Protecting the Accused Divide the class into groups of three. Distribute a copy of the Bill of Rights and a numbered list of the following Constitutional protections: protection from testifying against yourself; speedy public trial; right to an impartial jury; no excessive fines; right to confront witnesses; protection from warrantless searches; right to a lawyer; right to due process; protection from being charged twice for the same crime; and protection from cruel punishment.

Have student groups match each protection with the proper Bill of Rights Amendment. The student groups will rate from 1 to 10 (1 being the most important) which protection is most important. After each group has presented their lists, have the entire class vote to create a class hierarchy of which protections are the most important. Encourage students to research a court case dealing with the highest-rated protection.

Author Note

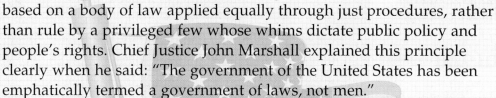

Dear Social Studies Teacher:

This unit presents key ideas about some of the oldest and some of the newest features of our political life. As for the oldest, the concept that we are a nation governed by the rule of law is at the very heart of our democracy. The rule of law means that government is based on a body of law applied equally through just procedures, rather than rule by a privileged few whose whims dictate public policy and people's rights. Chief Justice John Marshall explained this principle clearly when he said: "The government of the United States has been emphatically termed a government of laws, not men."

As for a new feature of American politics, when designing this textbook we believed it was essential to pay special attention to the rapidly growing role of the Internet in politics. It was clear the Internet was dramatically changing how politicians and citizens alike were going to participate in the nation's political life. Today's elected officials likely resemble your students with respect to embracing the latest cyber innovations; the moment a new web activity appears, politicians are adapting it for use in their election campaigns. Many candidates have created their own personal Web sites. Sadly we are also learning that the Internet can also be terribly misused; thereby creating entirely new challenges for elected officials and the American legal system described in this unit.

As for citizens, the opportunities the Internet gives us to gather information about issues and to participate directly in the political process are continually expanding. The "blogosphere," chat rooms, online petitions and the like give citizens of all ages more chances to get involved in everything from presidential elections to selection of the proverbial local dogcatcher. While these new opportunities pose serious challenges for totalitarian regimes, they are the very lifeblood of our participatory democracy.

Richard C. Remy
Author

Unit Objectives

The Individual, the Law and the Internet

After studying this unit, students will be able to:

- Describe how law systems have developed over time and state the legal rights and responsibilities of Americans.

- Explain the differences between civil cases and criminal cases.

- Discuss the rights the Constitution grants to those who are accused of a crime.

- Explain the challenges Americans face with the development of technology.

Did You Know?

Most American citizens obey the law, but many think that criminal activity has increased over the years. But did you know that criminal activity in major U.S. cities is decreasing? After reaching a historic low in 2000, crime rates have continued to drop yearly, thanks to more effective policing and citizen involvement. However, illegal drug activity and related crimes are on the increase. Special government agencies are trying to stop drug-related crimes and to teach students about the dangers of drugs.

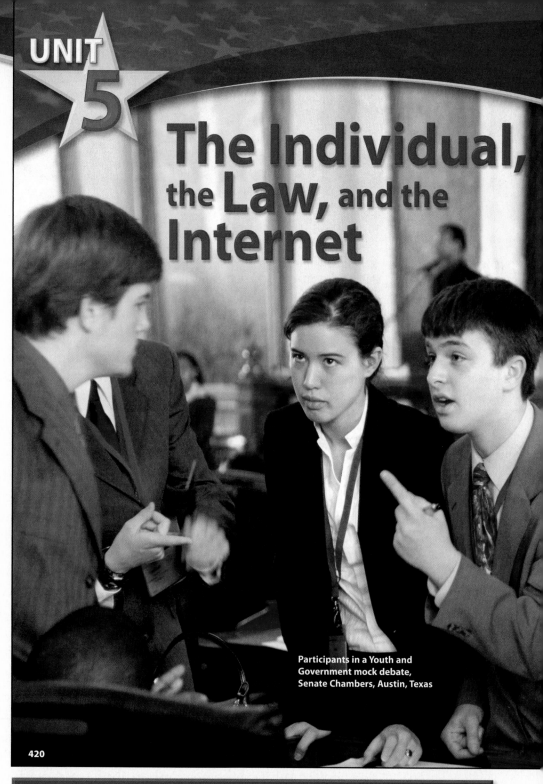

UNIT
5

The Individual, the Law, and the Internet

Participants in a Youth and Government mock debate, Senate Chambers, Austin, Texas

420

Activity: Launching the Unit

The Individual, the Law, and the Internet Ask: Why are laws important? *(Laws are important because they provide a list of rules by which society must abide. Without laws, people are on their own to protect their property and life. Without laws, people who take advantage of others could be shot or hung without any hesitation about whether they are guilty or innocent. Laws protect people who want to be productive citizens of a* community.) Students know about rules and laws and often like to complain about how unfair they are. Have your students make a list of rules they have at home and at school. Then, have them write a list of laws they think are necessary to ensure a successful community. As you read each chapter, have students review their lists and discuss why laws are important to all societies. **OL**

Be An Active Citizen

CITIZENSHIP What laws protect property owners in your community? With a group of students, imagine you are all part owners of a grocery store. Someone slips and is injured in your store. Research the Internet and community laws to find out what problems you might or might not face in this situation. Report your findings to the class.

421

Be an Active Citizen

CITIZENSHIP What happens if someone is seriously injured at your home? Are you responsible for that harm? What rights does the injured party have? How are you protected? Have your students research the Internet to find out about personal injury laws in your state and to find answers to the following questions. How does one initiate a lawsuit? What proof does the victim need? How is the defendant protected? Do most personal injury cases go to court or get settled out of court? Encourage students to define the difference between an accident and negligent behavior.

Online Current Events Update

Visit Glencoe's *Online Current Events Update* at www.glencoe.com to find news reports, features, maps, graphs, and photos of current events that shape our lives. Students can also make connections between historical events and current events by using the interactive time line.

More About the Photo

Visual Literacy Most schools have debate teams who participate in mock debates. When students act the roles of lawyer, prosecutor, defendant, and victim, perspectives can change. Ask students how a defense attorney must view crimes differently than a prosecutor.

Why Identifying Cause and Effect Is Important

As students read, they may note that the author has used a special text structure. One text structure writers use is the cause-and-effect pattern. This pattern shows the reader the impact one event has on another. Writers also use the pattern to examine the reasons why something happened and to analyze the results of the event. The cause-and-effect structure often answers the question "Why?"

 # Learn It!

Have students create a sentence or two that explains the current weather conditions. Then, have them think about weather: Why is it raining/snowing/hot? Tell them to write one effect the weather has, such as "The snow has cancelled our game," or "The rain is helping the corn grow." Then have them combine their sentences into a small paragraph that uses the text structure of cause and effect. Tell students that signal words, such as *because, so,* and *therefore,* can indicate cause-and-effect relationships. **OL**

Reading Social Studies

Identifying Cause and Effect

① Learn It!

Almost everything that happens in life is based upon cause and effect. For example, if you strike a match (cause) a flame appears (effect). Clue words to look for are: *as a result* or *due to.*

- Read the sentences below.
- Identify the cause of the expansion of Roman Law.
- Identify one effect Napoleon had on Louisiana.

> Napoleon updated the Justinian Code and called it the Napoleonic Code. Like the ancient Romans, Napoleon carried his laws to all the lands he controlled. One of those lands was Louisiana, an American territory which France eventually sold to the United States in 1803. The laws of the state of Louisiana are still based on the Napoleonic Code.
>
> —*from page 429*

A chart like the one below will help you identify cause and effect.

Cause: Napoleon conquered lands and brought the Napoleonic Code with him. → **Effect:** Louisiana adopted the Napoleonic Code

Reading Tip
If you can restate the ideas in a sentence using the word *because,* the writer is probably using cause and effect to explain what happened.

Reading Strategy   Analyzing Text Structure

Identifying Cause and Effect Write the following signal words and phrases on the board: *so, since, because,* and *consequently.* Explain to students that some writers provide clue words and phrases that suggest a cause-and-effect relationship. Sometimes this pattern shows a causal chain, how one thing leads to the next. The writer may then comment if the event had a positive or neg- ative effect. Have students reread the second sentence. Point out that the writer describes how Napoleon imposed his laws onto his conquests. One event—Napoleon's conquests—led to another: the spread of Napoleonic law. However, the writer does not describe the result. Ask students to find a paragraph in Chapter 15 that illustrates cause-and-effect. **OL**

② Practice It!

Read the following paragraph from this unit.

- Draw a chart like the one shown below.
- Identify one cause and effect from the paragraph to write in the chart.

In November 2000, residents of Palm Beach County in Florida filed, or registered, a civil lawsuit against the Palm Beach County Canvassing Board, their election authority. The residents argued that a flaw in the ballot format caused them to vote for candidates other than the candidate for whom they intended to vote. This civil suit led to a recounting of votes and reached the Supreme Court. The Court's ruling led to George W. Bush's winning the presidency in 2000.

—from page 449

Cause → Effect

③ Apply It!

Identify a cause and the resulting effects you can find in:

- **Chapter 16, Section 2**
- **Chapter 17, Section 1**

Read to Write Activity

Read the section titled "What Happens in a Civil Case" in Chapter 15, Section 2. Write a paragraph where you provide examples of actions people may take (*causes*) that might result in a civil law case (*effect*).

② Practice It!

Cause: Civil cases filed in Florida over presidential votes.
Effect: Supreme Court supported recounting of votes. President Bush's victory was upheld.

Now have students draw a T-chart and list a few historical events from the past year in the left-hand column. In the right-hand column, have them describe the result or effect of those events. **OL**

③ Apply It!

Bring to class a collection of scientific and historical articles. Organize the class into small groups and have each group analyze a different piece of writing by creating a cause-and-effect chart or causal chain. After they have finished the work, have each group answer the following questions: *Why did it happen?* and *What is the result?* **OL**

 Reading Strategy   **Read to Write**

Sequencing Events After students read Chapter 15, have them write a brief explanation of what happens to someone when they are arrested. Before students begin writing, have them create a flowchart. After students complete their explanations, have them work with partners to review the steps. Partners should check to see if any steps were left out. The order or sequence of events is important too, so have them correct any events that are out of order. **AL**

Chapter Planning Guide

15

Levels					Resources	Chapter Opener	Section 1	Section 2	Section 3	Chapter Assess
BL	OL	AL	ELL							
					FOCUS					
BL	OL	AL	ELL	🖌	Daily Focus Skills Transparencies		15–1	15–2	15–3	
					TEACH					
BL	OL		ELL	📁	Reading Essentials and Note-Taking Guide*		p. 141	p. 144	p. 147	
BL	OL		ELL	📁	Reading Skills Activity, URB			p. 7		
BL	OL	AL	ELL	📁	Content Vocabulary Activity, URB*	p. 21	p. 21	p. 21	p. 21	
BL	OL	AL	ELL	📁	Academic Vocabulary Activity, URB	p. 23	p. 23	p. 23	p. 23	
	OL			📁	Biography Activity, URB				p. 25	
BL	OL	AL	ELL	📁	Writing Skills Activity, URB		p. 27		p. 27	
	OL	AL		📁	Critical Thinking Skills Activity, URB			p. 29		
BL	OL	AL	ELL	📁	Chart, Graph, and Map Skills Activity, URB				p. 31	
BL	OL	AL	ELL	📁	Differentiated Instruction, URB				p. 33	
BL	OL	AL	ELL	📁	School-to-Home Connection Activity, URB*	p. 35	p. 35	p. 35	p. 35	
BL	OL		ELL	📁	Guided Reading Activities, URB*		p. 39	p. 40	p. 41	
	OL	AL		📁	Supreme Court Cases				pp. 81, 89, 99	
BL	OL	AL	ELL	📁	Writer's Guidebook	✓	✓	✓	✓	✓
	OL	AL		💿	Primary Source Document Library	✓	✓	✓	✓	✓
BL	OL	AL	ELL	💿	Daily Lecture & Discussion Notes (in Pres. Plus)		✓	✓	✓	✓
BL	OL	AL	ELL	💿	StudentWorks™ Plus		✓	✓	✓	✓
BL	OL	AL	ELL	💿	Section Spotlight Videos		✓	✓	✓	
BL	OL	AL	ELL	🖌	TIME Interpreting Political Cartoons Transp.				Ch. 15	
BL	OL	AL	ELL	🖌	Writing Process Transparencies	✓	✓	✓	✓	✓

Note: Please refer to the *Unit 5 Resource Book* for this chapter's URB materials.

* Also available in Spanish

TeacherWorks *Plus*
All-In-One Planner and Resource Center

- Interactive Lesson Planner
- Interactive Teacher Edition
- Fully editable blackline masters
- Section Spotlight Videos Launch
- Differentiated Lesson Plans
- Printable reports of daily assignments
- Standards Tracking System

Levels BL	OL	AL	ELL		Resources	Chapter Opener	Section 1	Section 2	Section 3	Chapter Assess
					TEACH *(continued)*					
				📁	**Building Academic Vocabulary**	✓	✓	✓	✓	✓
				📁	**Strategies for Success**	✓	✓	✓	✓	✓
Teacher Resources				📁	**Teacher's Guide to Differentiated Instruction**	✓	✓	✓	✓	✓
				💿	**Graphing Tool**	✓	✓	✓	✓	✓
				💿	**Presentation Plus! with MindJogger CheckPoint**	✓	✓	✓	✓	✓
					ASSESS					
BL	OL	AL	ELL	📁	**Quizzes and Tests***		p. 178	p. 179	p. 180	p. 181
BL	OL	AL	ELL	📁	**Authentic Assessment with Rubrics**				p. 19	
BL	OL	AL	ELL	📁	**Standardized Test Practice**		p. 29	p. 29	p. 29	p. 29
BL	OL	AL	ELL	💿	*ExamView®* **Assessment Suite CD-ROM**		15–1	15–2	15–3	Ch. 15
					CLOSE					
BL			ELL	📁	**Reteaching Activity, URB***		p. 37	p. 37	p. 37	
BL	OL		ELL	📁	**Reading and Study Skills Foldables™ Activity**	p. 78	p. 79		p. 79	
BL	OL	AL	ELL	📁	*Civics Today* **in Graphic Novel**	p. 61	p. 61			
BL	OL	AL	ELL	🖐	**Graphic Organizer Transparencies & Strategies**	✓	✓	✓	✓	✓

✓ Chapter- or unit-based activities applicable to all sections in this chapter

424B

Integrating Technology

15

Using TechCONNECT™

Using a Web Browser

What is TechCONNECT™?

Glencoe TechCONNECT™ is a flexible online program that makes it easy to integrate computer technology into the classroom.

How can TechCONNECT™ help my students?

TechCONNECT™ shows students how to use a Web browser to find credible information online for research projects, and aids classroom learning by:

- reinforcing, supporting, and extending standards-based learning
- instructing students to create real-world products using computer application skills
- enabling students to exercise research, study, and writing skills

For more information or to get a free 30-day trial of Glencoe TechCONNECT™ for your classroom, visit techconnect.glencoe.com and click the **Free Trial** button. Once you have accessed TechCONNECT™, students can enter code AC068 to begin the project.

Civics ONLINE
Visit glencoe.com and enter *QuickPass*™ code CIV1360c15T for Chapter 15 resources.

You can easily launch a wide range of digital products from your computer's desktop with the McGraw-Hill Social Studies widget.

	Student	Teacher	Parent
Media Library			
• Student Edition Section Audio	●		●
• Spanish Audio Summaries	●		●
• Section Spotlight Videos	●	●	●
***Civics Today* Online Learning Center (Web Site)**			
• Chapter Overviews	●	●	●
• Study Central™	●	●	●
• Study-to-Go	●	●	●
• Student Web Activities	●	●	●
• In Motion Animation	●	●	●
• Self-Check Quizzes	●	●	●
• ePuzzles and Games	●	●	●
• StudentWorks™ Plus Online	●	●	●
• Vocabulary eFlashcards	●	●	●
• Web Activity Lesson Plans		●	
• Vocabulary PuzzleMaker	●	●	●
Classroom Tools			
• Multilingual Glossary	●	●	●
• Beyond the Textbook	●	●	●
• NGS MapMachine	●	●	●

GLENCOE BOOKLINK 3

Use this database to search more than 30,000 titles to create a customized reading list for your students.

- Reading lists can be organized by students' reading level, author, genre, theme, or area of interest.
- The database provides Degrees of Reading Power™ (DRP) and Lexile™ readability scores for all selections.
- A brief summary of each selection is included.

Leveled reading suggestions for this chapter:

For students at a Grade 7 reading level:
- *Andrew Young: A Matter of Choice,* by Jan Simpson

For students at a Grade 8 reading level:
- *Crime and Punishment,* by Fyodor Dostoevsky

For students at a Grade 9 reading level:
- *The Legal System: Opposing Viewpoints,* by Tamara L. Roleff

For students at a Grade 10 reading level:
- *Computer Crime,* by Robert L. Perry

For students at a Grade 11 reading level:
- *Malcolm X: By Any Means Necessary,* by Walter Dean Myers

READING SUPPORT FROM JAMESTOWN EDUCATION

- **Timed Readings Plus in Social Studies** helps students increase their reading rate and fluency while maintaining comprehension. The 400-word passages are similar to those found on state and national assessments.

- **Reading in the Content Area: Social Studies** concentrates on six essential reading skills that help students better comprehend what they read. The book includes 75 high-interest nonfiction passages written at increasing levels of difficulty.

- **Reading Social Studies** includes strategic reading instruction and vocabulary support in Social Studies content for both ELLs and native speakers of English.

- **Content Vocabulary Workout** (Grades 6–8) accelerates reading comprehension through focused vocabulary development. Social Studies content vocabulary comes from the glossaries of Glencoe's Middle School Social Studies texts. www.jamestowneducation.com

KEY Teacher Wraparound

Use this key to help you identify the different types of prompts found in the Teacher Wraparound Edition.

R **Reading Strategies** activities help you teach reading skills and vocabulary.

C **Critical Thinking** strategies help students apply and extend what they have learned.

D **Differentiated Instruction** activities provide instruction for students learning to speak English, along with suggestions for teaching various types of learners.

S **Skill Practice** strategies help students practice historical analysis and geography skills.

W **Writing Support** activities provide writing opportunities to help students comprehend the text.

Teaching strategies and activities have been coded for ability level appropriateness.

AL Activities for students working above grade level

OL Activities for students working on grade level

BL Activities for students working below grade level

ELL Activities for English Language Learners

Focus

Why It Matters

Ask: Besides driving within the speed limit, what legal responsibilities do American citizens have? *(Answers may include: obeying all laws, respecting the rights of others, reporting crimes.)*

More About the Photo

Visual Literacy This police officer is ticketing a driver for some traffic violation. Many drivers looking at this photo might remember feeling resentment when an officer stopped them for a similar reason. Drivers often do not consider that the officer may have saved their lives, the lives of their passengers, and/or the lives of the other drivers around them. Some people believe that careless or aggressive drivers should be even more carefully monitored than they are at present. Traffic accidents are a major cause of death in the United States. According to the National Safety Council, a person's "chances of dying in an automobile crash is one in 84 over his or her lifetime. But his or her chances of winning the Mega Million lottery are one in 175 million."

Teach

 As you begin teaching each section, use these questions and activities to help students focus on the Big Ideas.

Section 1

Sources of Our Laws Ask: How might laws and punishment be different today than they were 4,000 years ago? *(Answers may include that we live in a very different world today than 4,000 years ago.*

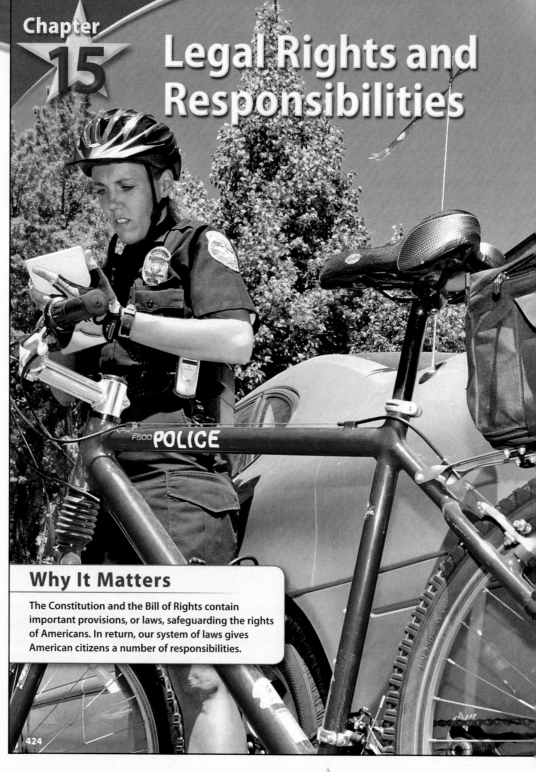

Chapter 15
Legal Rights and Responsibilities

Why It Matters

The Constitution and the Bill of Rights contain important provisions, or laws, safeguarding the rights of Americans. In return, our system of laws gives American citizens a number of responsibilities.

424

Students may suggest that laws were simpler and the punishments were more severe 4,000 years ago.) Tell students that Section 1 provides a brief history of laws. **OL**

Section 2

Types of Laws Ask: What is the difference between criminal law and civil law? Can you provide an example of a crime and a civil dispute? *(Criminal laws were written to prevent people from harming one another. Civil laws were written to regulate noncriminal disputes, such as breaking a contract.)* Section 2 describes various U.S. laws. **OL**

Chapter Audio

Civics ONLINE
Visit glencoe.com and enter *QuickPass*™ code CIV3093c15 for Chapter 15 resources.

Chapter Introduction
15

BIG Ideas

Section 1: Sources of Our Laws

Throughout history, civilizations have developed systems of laws to meet their needs. Our laws today can be traced back to early legal systems such as the Code of Hammurabi and English common law.

Section 2: Types of Laws

The Constitution of the United States establishes and protects the individual's fundamental rights and liberties. A variety of laws protects people and their property, and helps settle disputes between parties.

Section 3: The American Legal System

The Constitution of the United States establishes and protects the individual's fundamental rights and liberties. All Americans have basic constitutional legal rights and responsibilities as well as important protections if they are accused of a crime.

Durango, Colorado, police officer writes a traffic ticket

FOLDABLES Dinah Zike's
Study Organizer Foldables

Purpose This Foldable guides students to analyze and sequence key influences and responsibilities within the judicial branch. The completed Foldable will use a chart to help them compare and contrast the different aspects of laws and how they are applied. **OL**

More Foldables activities for this chapter can be found in the *Dinah Zike's Reading and Study Skills Foldables* ancillary.

Civics ONLINE
Visit glencoe.com and enter *QuickPass*™ code CIV1360c15T for Chapter 15 resources, including a Chapter Overview, Study Central™, Study-to-Go, Student Web Activity, Self-Check Quiz, and other materials.

FOLDABLES
Study Organizer

Evaluating Information Study Foldable Make the following Foldable to help you evaluate the sources and types of American laws, and the rights and responsibilities they protect.

Step 1 Mark a point in the middle of the paper top to bottom. Fold in each side of the paper to meet that point.

Chapter 15: Legal Rights and Responsibilities

Step 2 Unfold the paper and in the center section draw a T diagram.

Sources of Our Laws | The American Legal System | Types of Laws
Rights | Responsibilities

Reading and Writing
As you read the chapter, make notes under each heading about main ideas, key terms, and supporting facts for each topic. Write a paragraph summarizing the types of laws in America.

Step 3 Label all three sections as shown.

Section 3

The American Legal System Ask: What rights does the Constitution guarantee people accused of crimes? *(Possible answers: It guarantees the right to counsel, the right to avoid self-incrimination, and the right to a trial by jury.)* In Section 3, students will learn about the rights of people accused of crimes and the responsibilities citizens owe to society. **OL**

Focus

Bellringer
Daily Focus Transparency 15–1

Guide to Reading
Answers to Graphic:

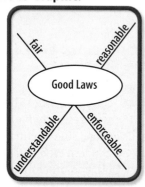

Good Laws
- fair
- reasonable
- understandable
- enforceable

Section Spotlight Video

To generate student interest and provide a springboard for class discussion, access the Chapter 15, Section 1 video at glencoe.com or on the video DVD.

Resource Manager

Guide to Reading

Big Idea
Throughout history, civilizations have developed systems of laws to meet their needs.

Content Vocabulary
- common law *(p. 429)*
- precedent *(p. 429)*
- statute *(p. 429)*

Academic Vocabulary
- potential *(p. 427)*
- resolve *(p. 427)*
- tradition *(p. 427)*

Reading Strategy
Identifying As you read, identify the characteristics of good laws.

Good Laws

Sources of Our Laws

Real World Civics In 2003 Kamala Harris made history, becoming the first woman and the first person of African and East Indian American descent to become a district attorney in the state of California. Now working as the district attorney in San Francisco, Harris represents activism in government. In addition to fighting crime, she works to protect children and improve their lives by pairing them with mentors. She also strives to protect the rights of immigrants, people living in poverty, women, and people of all races.

▼ **Kamala Harris uses her public office to improve the lives of citizens**

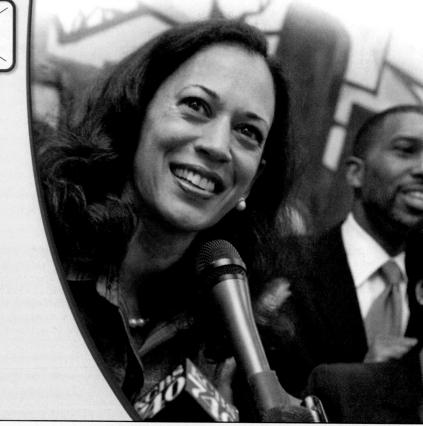

R Reading Strategies	**C** Critical Thinking	**D** Differentiated Instruction	**W** Writing Support	**S** Skill Practice
Teacher Edition • Making Connections, p. 427 • Act. Prior Know., p. 428 **Additional Resources** • Cont. Vocab., URB p. 21 • Ac. Voc., URB p. 23 • Guid. Read., URB p. 39 • RENTG, p. 141 • Foldables, p. 79	**Teacher Edition** • Analyzing Pri. Sources, p. 427 **Additional Resources** • Quizzes and Tests, p. 178	**Teacher Edition** • Gifted and Talented, p. 428 **Additional Resources** • Reteach. Act., URB p. 37 • Graphic Novel, p. 61	**Teacher Edition** • Expository Writing, p. 429	**Teacher Edition** • Reading a Time Line, p. 428 **Additional Resources** • Daily Focus Trans., 15–1

Functions of Laws

Main Idea Laws are sets of rules that allow people in a society to live together.

Civics & You Have you ever wondered why certain laws exist? Read to learn their purpose.

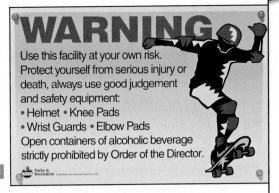

> " *If fire break[s] out in a house, and some one . . . take[s] the property of the master of the house, he shall be thrown into that self-same fire.* "
>
> —Code of Hammurabi, c. 1780 B.C.E.

Does this law strike you as harsh? It comes from the Code of Hammurabi, the first known system of written law.

What Should Laws Do?

Laws are sets of rules that allow people to live together. Laws affect nearly everything we do—the food we eat, how we drive our cars, how we buy and sell things, and even what happens when we are born and when we die. People, organizations, and governments can deal with one another because everyone knows which actions are permissible and which are not.

A major purpose of laws is to keep the peace and prevent violent acts. Laws set punishments that are meant to discourage **potential,** or future, criminals. Laws include the administration of justice in the form of law enforcement agencies (police) and courts. Laws also set the rules for **resolving,** or answering, disagreements over money, property, contracts, and other noncriminal matters.

What Makes a Law a Good Law?

Although not all laws are beneficial, good laws share certain characteristics. Good laws are fair. People in similar circumstances will be treated equally under the law.

WARNING

Use this facility at your own risk. Protect yourself from serious injury or death, always use good judgement and safety equipment:
- Helmet • Knee Pads
- Wrist Guards • Elbow Pads

Open containers of alcoholic beverage strictly prohibited by Order of the Director.

Parks & Recreation

Laws Protect This skateboarding sign in a park in Idaho suggests rules for the use of skateboards. **Comparing** What is the difference between a warning and a law?

Good laws are also reasonable. In England in the 1700s, a person who stole a loaf of bread might have had his or her hand cut off. Today such harsh punishment for a similar crime would be considered unreasonable.

Good laws must be understandable. If laws are too complicated, people may break them without meaning to or realizing it. Ignorance of a law is no excuse for not obeying it. If most people understand the laws and believe they are reasonable and fair, then they will tend to obey the laws.

Finally, good laws are enforceable by communities, state authorities, or federal authorities. The government's ability to enforce a law often depends on the people's willingness to obey it.

A Nation of Laws

When the writers of the Constitution created our government, they based the nation's system of laws on ideas, **traditions** (customs), and laws passed down from generation to generation. Some of these ideas date back thousands of years.

✔ **Reading Check** Explaining What are fair laws?

Teach

C Critical Thinking

Analyzing Primary Sources Discuss with students the quote from the Code of Hammurabi. **Ask:** Why do you think ancient laws were so harsh? *(Students may answer that the authoritarian rulers of the time felt that harsh laws would help them control their realms.)* **AL**

R Reading Strategy

Making Connections Have students discuss the four characteristics of a good law. Ask them to provide an example of each. They may use family, classroom, or school rules as examples. **OL**

Caption Answer:

A warning is advice to act responsibly or to conform to a code of conduct. A law is a rule established by society. Breaking it can lead to formal punishment.

✔ **Reading Check** **Answer:** Laws are fair when all people in similar situations are treated equally.

Hands-On Chapter Project
Step 1

Learning About the Legal System

Step 1: Creating Good Laws In this project, students will create a game in which a defendant will move through the legal system. In each step, groups will create cards to be used to advance the player or defendant through the system. You may vary game rules to meet students' abilities.

Directions Begin by organizing the class into four groups and assigning them to a color: red, yellow, blue, and green. Provide colored note cards to each group. In this step, have each group brainstorm the most common crimes people commit. Then, have them write four good laws to address these crimes. Ask them to discuss if their laws are good, meeting all the characteristics listed in the text. In addition, have them research the typical punishment for breaking each

law. Groups will write each law and its punishment on their colored note cards that will be used in Step 4.

Summary Have groups share their information and discuss if the punishment fits the crime. **OL**

(Project continued in Section 2)

Teach

R Reading Strategy

Activating Prior Knowledge Ask students to recall what they know about prehistoric societies. Encourage them to discuss the difficulty of governing such societies without written laws. **OL**

D Differentiated Instruction

Gifted and Talented Have students research two laws from the Code of Hammurabi and two from the Justinian Code. Ask them to compare the laws from each of these systems in a panel discussion. They might discuss the punishments, why the punishments are different, and whether they think the laws are fair. **AL**

S Skill Practice

Reading a Time Line Have students calculate the approximate number of years between the Justinian Code and the Code of Hammurabi. *(about 2,290 years.)* **OL**

Analyzing Time Lines

Answers:
1. the Code of Hammurabi
2. the Justinian Code

Differentiated Instruction

History of Law

Main Idea Law systems of early societies influence us today.

Civics & You Have you ever seen a courtroom trial? Read more to find out how the judges' rulings also help make law.

Legal scholars believe that some kind of law existed in even the earliest human societies. They trace its beginnings to prehistoric people, who used unwritten rules of behavior to help people avoid or cope with social conflict. These earliest laws were probably passed orally from one generation to the next. Later, people began to write down their laws.

Code of Hammurabi

The first known system of written law was the Code of Hammurabi. King Hammurabi of Babylonia, an ancient Middle Eastern empire, compiled his code in about 1760 B.C. By today's standards, the Code of Hammurabi prescribed very harsh penalties.

Another set of early laws is the Ten Commandments found in the Hebrew Bible. Hebrews living in ancient Palestine followed these laws. Moral rules of the Commandments, such as "thou shalt not steal" and "thou shalt not kill," are reflected in our laws today.

Roman Law

The first code of Roman law was published in 450 B.C. As in the Code of Hammurabi, Roman penalties for offenses were drastic by later standards. Over centuries the Roman senate adopted a great many laws, and Roman judges wrote commentaries on them, which often became part of the law.

Roman Law Spreads As the Roman Empire grew, its laws spread to Europe, Africa, and Asia. In A.D. 533 Emperor Justinian I, ruler of the Byzantine Empire, also known as the Eastern Roman Empire, boiled down the confusing mass of Roman laws into an orderly body of rules called the Justinian Code. This code became the basis of law for the Byzantine Empire. Roman law also became part of the laws of the Roman Catholic Church, known as canon law.

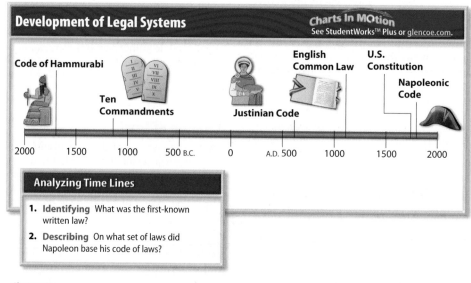

Development of Legal Systems

Charts In MOtion
See StudentWorks™ Plus or glencoe.com.

Code of Hammurabi — Ten Commandments — Justinian Code — English Common Law — U.S. Constitution — Napoleonic Code

2000 | 1500 | 1000 | 500 B.C. | 0 | A.D. 500 | 1000 | 1500 | 2000

Analyzing Time Lines

1. **Identifying** What was the first-known written law?
2. **Describing** On what set of laws did Napoleon base his code of laws?

Understanding and Clarifying Word Meanings

Objective: To determine word meanings

Focus: Have students use a dictionary to find definitions of legal terms.

Teach: Review how knowing Latin root words can help determine word meaning.

Assess: Have students use the words in sentences.

Close: Create a class chart of common Latin roots.

Differentiated Instruction Strategies

BL List two other words with the Latin root "evidens" (clear). Define them.

AL Make a list of five other legal terms from the text and find the words' origins. Write sentences using the terms.

ELL Write the antonym for "innocent" and look up the word's origin.

More than twelve hundred years after the Justinian Code was written, its ideas were taken over by the French emperor Napoleon Bonaparte. Napoleon updated the Justinian Code and called it the Napoleonic Code. Like the ancient Romans, Napoleon carried his laws to all the lands he controlled. One of those lands was Louisiana, an American territory which France eventually sold to the United States in 1803. The laws of the state of Louisiana are still based on the Napoleonic Code.

English Law

The most important source of American laws is English law. Perhaps the greatest contribution is the English system of **common law,** or law based on court decisions rather than on a legal code. In other words, it is a system of analyzing how a previous judge applied a law, and using it later in the same manner. After the Norman conquest of England in 1066, English kings sent judges into the countryside to hold trials and administer the law. When judges decided a new case, they looked in the books for a similar case and followed the earlier ruling, or **precedent.** Precedents are legal opinions that became part of the common law. English judges were familiar with Roman law and canon law, and they blended these into the body of common law. The law came to include basic principles of individual's rights, such as trial by jury and the concept that people are considered innocent until proven guilty.

Although acts of Parliament—written **statutes**—came to dominate the English legal system, common law continued to have a strong influence. When English settlers came to North America in the 1600s and 1700s, they brought with them their traditions of common law and individual's rights. The common-law tradition of following precedents still survives in our U.S. courts.

✔ **Reading Check** Concluding Why was the Justinian Code important?

Teach

W Writing Support

Expository Writing Have students write a few paragraphs relating how the Napoleonic Code and English law came to influence law in the United States. **OL**

✔ **Reading Check Answer:** The Justinian Code organized the Roman laws and became the law system of the Byzantine Empire. Napoleon based his Napoleonic Code on the Justinian Code.

Assess

Civics ONLINE

Study Central™ provides summaries, interactive games, and online graphic organizers to help students review content.

Close

Visual/Spatial Have students create a brochure that includes a bulleted list of the laws that have influenced modern day laws. Have them provide an illustration for each type of law. **BL**

Section 1 Review

Vocabulary

1. **Define** the following terms and use them in sentences related to law and legal systems: *common law, precedent, statute.*

Main Ideas

2. **Explaining** What is the purpose of laws?

3. **Identifying** What are two early legal systems that have influenced the development of our laws?

Critical Thinking

4. **BIG Ideas** How did English law influence the development of American law?

5. **Making Comparisons** Using a graphic organizer like the one below, compare early systems of law.

Examples of Kinds of Laws

6. **Analyzing Visuals** Look at the time line on page 428. The U.S. Constitution was written about how many years after the Justinian Code was written?

CITIZENSHIP Activity

7. **Expository Writing** John Adams wrote in 1779 that Massachusetts should have "a government of laws, and not of men." What do you think he meant by this?

Civics ONLINE

Study Central™ To review this section, go to glencoe.com.

Answers

1. Sentences should use vocabulary words according to their definitions in the section and in the Glossary.
2. Laws set rules for living in a secure and orderly way and enforce these rules with penalties.
3. the Ten Commandments and English law
4. American law stills follows the tradition of precedents, individual rights, and trial by jury.

5.
Examples of Kinds of Laws

Code of Hammurabi: first written laws, established code of behavior for society

English laws: based on court decisions, individual's rights, and trial by jury

Ten Commandments: basic moral rules

Roman law (Justinian and canon law): established orderly body of rules

6. about 1,250 years later
7. Answers will vary. Students may mention that the government should operate according to established rules rather than the will of self-serving officials.

Focus

Bellringer
Daily Focus Transparency 15–2

Guide to Reading
Answers to Graphic:

```
            Types of
              Law
    ┌───────────┼───────────┐
```

| constitutional law: laws that concern the interpretation of constitutions, such as limits of government's power and rights of individuals | administrative law: laws that deal with rules and regulations of government agencies within the executive branch, such as FAA laws | statutory law: laws regulated by the state, such as speed limits |

Section Spotlight Video

Have students watch the Chapter 15, Section 2 video at glencoe.com.

Resource Manager

 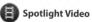
Guide to Reading

Big Idea
The Constitution of the United States establishes and protects the individual's fundamental rights and liberties.

Content Vocabulary
- plaintiff *(p. 431)*
- defendant *(p. 431)*
- felony *(p. 432)*
- misdemeanor *(p. 432)*
- larceny *(p. 432)*
- robbery *(p. 432)*
- burglary *(p. 432)*
- lawsuit *(p. 432)*
- tort *(p. 433)*
- libel *(p. 433)*
- constitutional law *(p. 434)*

Academic Vocabulary
- prohibition *(p. 431)*
- recover *(p. 433)*

Reading Strategy
Comparing As you read, explain on a graphic organizer like the one below the difference between constitutional, administrative, and statutory law.

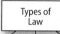
```
  Types of
    Law
┌────┬────┬────┐
```

Section 2
Types of Laws

Real World Civics Moviegoers are thrilled to watch a car chase on the screen . . . but real-life speeding is a crime. The state and federal governments set laws to help protect people from such crimes. In 1995 the national interstate speed limit of 55 miles per hour—which had been federally imposed in 1974 to save fuel—was lifted, and each state set its own speed limits. Most states raised their interstate limits to 65 or 70 miles per hour. Safety is an issue, but motorists have supported the higher speed limits.

▼ **A South Carolina highway crew "ups" the speed limit**

R Reading Strategies	**C** Critical Thinking	**D** Differentiated Instruction	**W** Writing Support	**S** Skill Practice
Teacher Edition • Summarizing, p. 431 **Additional Resources** • Read. Skills, URB p. 7 • Cont. Vocab., URB p. 21 • Ac. Vocab., URB p. 23 • Guid. Read., URB p. 40 • RENTG, p. 144	**Teacher Edition** • Ident. Points of View, p. 431 • Contrasting, p. 432 **Additional Resources** • Crit. Think., URB p. 29 • Quizzes and Tests, p. 179	**Teacher Edition** • Kinesthetic, p. 434 **Additional Resources** • School to Home Conn., URB p. 35	**Teacher Edition** • Personal Writing, p. 432 • Persuasive Writing, p. 433	**Teacher Edition** • Making a Cause/Effect Chart, p. 433 **Additional Resources** • Daily Focus Trans., 15–2

Criminal and Civil Law

Main Idea Criminal laws help maintain a peaceful and orderly society, while civil laws involve disputes between people or groups.

Civics & You What would you do if your bicycle were stolen? Read more to find out how our legal system handles such a case.

Most people are familiar with criminal laws, such as **prohibitions,** or bans, against drunk driving, robbing a store, or selling drugs. Other kinds of laws exist as well. Civil law is concerned with disputes between people (or groups of people) or between the government and its citizens. Public law concerns alleged violations of constitutional rights and disputes involving the actions of government agencies.

Two types of law affect Americans directly—criminal law and civil law. These laws help maintain a peaceful and orderly society. People who break these laws are likely to find themselves in a courtroom.

Criminal Law

Criminal laws seek to prevent people from deliberately or recklessly harming one another or one another's property. American courts operate on an adversary system. Under this system, the courtroom serves as an arena in which lawyers for opposing sides try to present their strongest cases. The judge has an impartial role and should be fair to both sides. Critics of the adversary system argue that it encourages lawyers to ignore evidence that is not favorable to their sides. Supporters, though, claim that it is the best system to bring out the facts of a case.

In criminal cases, the government is always the **plaintiff**—the party that brings the charges against the accused. The basis for this tradition is that the American system of justice assumes that society—everyone—is the victim when a crime is committed.

We Are All Victims The individual or group accused of a crime is the **defendant.** About 95 percent of criminal trials in the United States are for violations of state laws. Most criminal cases are titled in terms of the

Felonies Serious crimes, such as arson, burglary, and murder, are considered felonies. Arson is also categorized as a crime against property. *Identifying* What are other examples of crimes against property?

431

Teach

R Reading Strategy

Summarizing Have students create a T-chart. Label one column Criminal Law and the other Civil Law. As students read, have them write a brief definition for each and provide examples of crimes in each column. Ask them to keep their charts and to continue to fill them in as they read more about criminal and civil law. **OL**

C Critical Thinking

Identifying Points of View Ask students to explain why some people support the adversary system. Then have them explain why others feel that this system is faulty. *(Supporters point out that the adversary system brings out the facts of a case. Other people consider it faulty because it encourages lawyers to ignore evidence unfavorable to their sides.)* **OL**

Caption Answer:

Vandalism, larceny, and robbery are examples of crimes against property.

Differentiated Instruction

Summarizing Information

Critical Thinking Skills Activity 15, URB pp. 29–30

Objective: To summarize a document

Focus: Have students read the complaint about copyright issues over a song.

Teach: Identify the main idea in order to write a summary.

Assess: Check for essential information in summaries.

Close: Create a bulleted list of essential information from the text as a class.

Differentiated Instruction Strategies

BL List two details that you did not include in the summary and explain why you did not include them

AL Explain the meaning of the legal term "intellectual property." Use it in a sentence.

ELL Write one sentence that explains why this complaint was filed.

Teach

C Critical Thinking

Contrasting Ask students to add the terms "felonies" and "misdemeanors" to their T-charts. Have students discuss the difference between felonies and misdemeanors. **OL**

W Writing Support

Personal Writing Have students work with partners and discuss causes of lawsuits with which they are familiar. Ask pairs to discuss kinds of lawsuits they feel are justifiable. Have students write a paragraph or two and share their ideas with the class. **OL**

TIME™ Teens in Action

Answer:

to provide responsible role models to young students and to promote an alcohol-free lifestyle

---

Hands-On Chapter Project
Step 2

Learning About the Legal System

Step 2: Describing the Players In this step, groups will continue to devise note cards to play their game. The same groups from Step 1 will create different scenarios in which a defendant can progress through the legal system.

Directions In this step, each group will describe the progress a defendant makes while attending court. For example, a group might write, "Your trial is delayed due to jury tampering. Skip a turn" or "You plea-bargain your case. Move ahead four spaces." Each group will write four or five scenarios on their color-coded cards. Encourage groups to talk with local attorneys and judges to glean ideas for their scenarios.

Summary Have students keep their cards from both Step 1 and Step 2. In Step 3, students will design the board game. **OL**

(Project continued in Section 3)

TIME™ Teens in Action

Jeremy Verbit

Jeremy Verbit, 18, of Warren, Michigan, was saddened and angry over deaths caused by drunk drivers in his community and decided to take action. Jeremy, who believes, "We're not born with responsibility; it is learned," decided to join Students Against Destructive Decisions (SADD). Now he is spreading an important message.

SADD meeting

QUESTION: How did you turn your anger into something positive?

ANSWER: I became a freshman representative with SADD. My school's chapter works to prevent drunk driving. We wanted to help tomorrow's high school students by starting Peer Resistance Training.

Q: Peer Resistance Training? What's that?

A: It's a program designed to train high school students to go to local fifth-grade classrooms. The older kids serve as role models to promote an alcohol-free lifestyle and let kids know there are lots of ways to have fun that don't involve drinking.

Q: How many younger kids do you speak to?

A: Each year, the program reaches about 300 fifth graders and trains around 20 high school students as role models. And it's working. When we leave the school after our presentations, we can hear fifth graders talking to their friends about how underage drinking is "irresponsible."

ACTION FACT: Verbit's other interests include computers and the Detroit Pistons basketball team.

Making a Difference CiTIZENSHIP

What is the purpose of Peer Resistance Training?

---

state against the defendant—for example, *State of California* v. *John Jones*. This way of naming cases shows that the government, rather than an individual crime victim, is bringing action against the defendant.

C Felonies and Misdemeanors Crimes are graded as either **felonies** or **misdemeanors.** Murder, rape, arson, robbery, and other serious crimes are felonies because they have serious consequences for the victim and the criminal. Misdemeanors are offenses such as vandalism or stealing inexpensive items. Typically, misdemeanors are punishable with a fine or a jail sentence of less than one year.

Crimes Against Property Crimes against property are the most common type of crime. The category of crimes against property includes crimes in which property is destroyed and crimes in which property is stolen or taken against the owner's will. Arson and vandalism are examples of crimes involving the destruction of property.

There are other categories of crimes that involve taking property against the will of the owner. **Larceny** is the unlawful taking away of another person's property with the intent never to return it. **Robbery** is the taking of property from a person's possession by using force or threats, while **burglary** is the unlawful entry into any dwelling or structure with the intention to commit a crime.

Civil Law

Civil law is concerned with disputes between people or groups in which no criminal laws have been broken. These disputes are not viewed as a threat to the social order, so the state will not take legal action. When a civil case goes to court, it is called a **lawsuit.** A lawsuit is a legal action whereby a person or group sues to collect damages for some harm that is done. Individuals who think they have been wronged must take action themselves by filing a lawsuit. The person suing is the plaintiff, while the person or organization being sued is the defendant.

What Happens in a Civil Case? Individuals believe they have lost something of value or suffered some damage because of someone else's blameworthy actions. A case may be a dispute over a contract in which one party believes that the other has not fulfilled the terms of an agreement.

Suppose, for example, that you order something from a mail-order catalog and charge it to your credit card. The mail-order company has, in effect, made a contract with you. If you do not receive the merchandise, the mail-order company has broken the contract. If the company fails to return your money, you can take it to court.

Tort Law Civil law also covers **torts,** or civil wrongs. In tort law a person may suffer an injury and claim that another party is responsible because of negligence. Suppose, for example, that you slip on ice on your neighbor's sidewalk and break a leg. According to your local law, property owners are responsible for keeping their sidewalks clear of ice. If your neighbor does not do this and you are injured as a result, you have a right to sue and **recover,** or get back, the costs of your medical treatment and other damages.

Family Law The basic social unit is the family. Not surprisingly, much civil law involves rules applied to the relationship between members of the family unit. The legality of marriage is regulated by state law. Typically, a state requires a person to be at least 18 years of age to be married unless there is parental consent. Typical family law cases involve divorce, child custody, adoption, alimony, child support, and spousal and child abuse.

Battles for Legal Rights

One of the earliest individuals to fight for people's rights was John Peter Zenger (1697–1746). Zenger was a New York newspaper editor who, in 1732, published stories about the colony's corrupt royal governor. At the time no newspapers had the freedom to criticize government officials. The gov-

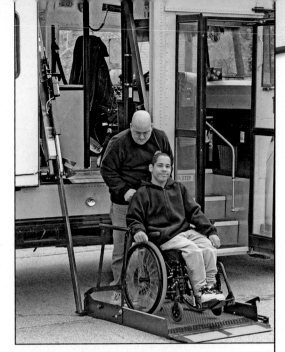

Statutory Law Statutes are the source of many of our rights. The Americans with Disabilities Act states that employees are to be provided "reasonable accommodations" necessary to assist them in doing their jobs. ***Analyzing*** What would be "reasonable accommodations" for a person in a wheelchair?

ernor charged Zenger with **libel,** the printing of false and damaging information, and threw him into jail. When the case came to trial in 1735, however, it took the jurors just 10 minutes to reach a "not guilty" verdict.

Another journalistic trailblazer was Ida Wells-Barnett (1862–1931). The daughter of slaves, she crusaded against lynching and for equal rights for all Americans. Her career was launched when she was forcibly removed from a railroad car reserved for whites in Memphis in 1884. For the rest of her life, she fought against segregation and for women's rights. In 1909 she helped found the National Association for the Advancement of Colored People (NAACP).

✓ **Reading Check** *Comparing* What is the difference between a felony and a misdemeanor?

Chapter 15 433

Teach

W Writing Support

Persuasive Writing Have students write letters to the editor of a local newspaper explaining their opinions about whether the government should legislate the actions of a family. **OL**

S Skill Practice

Making a Cause-and-Effect Chart Have students research why it was illegal to criticize the government in the 1730s and why this law was changed. Have them make a cause-and-effect chart showing the reasons for Zenger's imprisonment and for his release as "not guilty." **AL**

Caption Answer:

Answers may include outside ramps and larger elevators and bathrooms.

✓ **Reading Check** **Answer:** A felony is a serious crime. A misdemeanor is a less serious offense.

Differentiated Instruction

Leveled Activities

BL Academic Vocabulary Activity 15, URB pp. 23–24

OL Reading Activity 5, URB pp. 7–8

AL Critical Thinking Skills Activity 15, URB pp. 29–30

ELL School-to-Home Activity 15, URB pp. 35–36

Teach

D Differentiated Instruction

Kinesthetic Have groups research unusual laws your state still has on record. For example, in Michigan, a person may not tie an alligator to a fire hydrant. Then have groups perform skits that illustrate these peculiar laws. **OL**

 Reading Check **Answer:** speeding laws, food safety regulations, getting a driver's license, and so on

Assess

Civics ONLINE

Study Central™ provides summaries, interactive games, and online graphic organizers to help students review content.

Close

Analyzing Information Have students read the newspaper and locate examples of criminal, civil, constitutional, administrative, and statutory law. Ask students to analyze the information by creating a chart, noting which kind of law was most often in the news. **OL**

Section 2 Review

Other Types of Law

Main Idea Laws protect your rights and enforce rules and statutes.

Civics & You When you buy a snack, do you ever worry it might contain ingredients that could make you sick? Read to find out what kind of law ensures that your snack is safe to eat.

Laws that govern our lives and protect our rights come from many sources. These are state and federal constitutions, administrative agencies, and lawmaking bodies.

Constitutional Law The Constitution is the most fundamental and important source of law in the United States. The term constitutional law applies to that branch of the law dealing with the formation, construction, and interpretation of constitutions. For the most part, cases involving constitutional law decide the limits of the government's power and the rights of the individual.

Administrative Law If the Federal Aviation Administration issued an order requiring commercial airlines to install a new type of safety device, that would be an example of administrative law. Administrative law refers to the rules and regulations that the executive branch must make to carry out its job. It might include an individual charging a government agency with wrongdoing.

Statutory Law Recall from Section 1 that a statute is a law written by a legislative branch of government. The U.S. Congress, state legislatures, and local legislatures write thousands of these laws. Statutes regulate our behavior by setting speed limits and specifying rules for inspecting food products. Statutes are also the source of many of the rights and benefits we take for granted, such as the right to get a Social Security check, to enter a veterans' hospital, to get a driver's license, and to return merchandise you bought at a store.

 Reading Check **Identifying** What is an example of a statutory law?

 Section 2 Review

Vocabulary

1. **Define** the following terms and use them in sentences related to different kinds of laws: *plaintiff, defendant, felony, misdemeanor, larceny, robbery, burglary, lawsuit, tort, libel, constitutional law.*

Main Ideas

2. **Describing** Give at least two reasons a person might file a civil lawsuit.

3. **Classifying** What does administrative law deal with? Why is administrative law considered part of public law?

Critical Thinking

4. **BIG Ideas** Which type of law that you have read about in this section do you feel has the greatest influence on your daily life? Why?

5. **Organizing Information** In a graphic organizer like the one below, give two examples of each kind of law.

Criminal Laws	Civil Laws
Drunk driving	

6. **Evaluating** Describe the contribution of either John Peter Zenger or Ida Wells-Barnett to the rights you enjoy today as an American.

CITIZENSHIP Activity

7. **Creative Writing** Write a newspaper article about an imaginary case involving one of the types of laws you read about in this section.

Civics ONLINE

Study Central™ To review this section, go to glencoe.com.

Answers

1. Sentences should use vocabulary words according to their definitions in the section and in the Glossary.

2. A person might sue someone for damaging them in some way or for causing them to lose something valuable.

3. Administrative law deals with rules and regulations that government agencies of the executive branch issue to carry out their jobs. The laws affect the general welfare of the public.

4. Answers will vary. Students should provide reasons for their positions.

5.

Criminal Laws	Civil Laws
drunk driving	negligence
armed robbery	child custody

6. Answers should include these points: Zenger's contribution has made it possible for U.S. citizens to enjoy freedom of the press. Wells-Barnett challenged segregation and helped promote the rights of African Americans and women.

7. Articles should clearly identity one type of law and provide an accurate portrayal of it.

Guide to Reading

Big Idea
The Constitution of the United States establishes and protects the individual's fundamental rights and liberties.

Content Vocabulary
- stare decisis *(p. 436)*
- writ of habeas corpus *(p. 436)*
- bill of attainder *(p. 436)*
- ex post facto law *(p. 436)*
- due process of law *(p. 437)*
- search warrant *(p. 438)*
- double jeopardy *(p. 439)*
- grand jury *(p. 439)*
- plea bargain *(p. 440)*
- bail *(p. 440)*

Academic Vocabulary
- interpret *(p. 436)*
- factor *(p. 437)*
- presume *(p. 438)*

Reading Strategy
Identifying On a diagram like the one below, list three rights that help ensure a fair trial.

Section Audio   **Spotlight Video**

Section **3**

The American Legal System

Real World Civics From watching television and movies, nearly everyone knows they have the right to remain silent when arrested. Do you know why it is called the Miranda warning? In 1963, Ernesto Miranda was arrested for kidnap and rape. During a two-hour interrogation, he confessed to the crime. He was never told that he could remain silent or that he had the right to an attorney, as provided by the Fifth and Sixth Amendments in the Bill of Rights. Miranda appealed his conviction, and in 1966 the Supreme Court ruled that his rights had been violated. Do you know your other rights that are guaranteed by the Constitution?

▼ **Defendant Ernesto Miranda (left) speaks with his attorney, 1967**

435

Focus

Guide to Reading
Answers to Graphic:

Fair Trial — right to counsel — right to impartial jury — right to grand jury hearing

Section Spotlight Video

To generate student interest and provide a springboard for class discussion, access the Chapter 15, Section 3 video at glencoe.com or on the video DVD.

Resource Manager

R **Reading Strategies**	C **Critical Thinking**	D **Differentiated Instruction**	W **Writing Support**	S **Skill Practice**
Teacher Edition • Questioning, p. 436 **Additional Resources** • Cont. Vocab., URB p. 22 • Ac. Vocab., URB p. 24 • Guid. Read., URB p. 47 • RENTG, p. 147	**Teacher Edition** • Drawing Con., p. 436 • Specifying, p. 437 • Interpreting, p. 438 **Additional Resources** • Biography Act., URB p. 25 • Quizzes and Tests, p. 180	**Teacher Edition** • Visual/Spatial, p. 440 **Additional Resources** • Diff. Instr., URB p. 33 • Reteach. Act., URB p. 37	**Teacher Edition** • Personal Writing, p. 438 **Additional Resources** • Writing Skills Act., URB p. 27	**Teacher Edition** • Interpreting a Chart, p. 439 **Additional Resources** • Chart, Graph, and Map Skills Activity, URB p. 31 • Daily Focus Trans., 15–3 • Pol. Cartoons Trans. 15

Teach

R Reading Strategy

Questioning After students read the introduction, direct their attention to the chart. Have them create a list of questions they have about the rights of the accused. After you complete Section 3, discuss students' questions and make sure they are all answered. **BL**

C Critical Thinking

Drawing Conclusions Ask: Why do you think it was important to the Framers of the Constitution to include the right to a writ of habeas corpus? *(They wanted to ensure that no person was held unlawfully and ignorant of the charges against him or her.)* **OL**

Analyzing Charts

Answers:
1. due process of law and equal protection of the laws
2. The government cannot take an individual's life, liberty, or property without proper exercise of the law.

Differentiated Instruction

Biography Activity 15, URB pp. 25–26

Protections in the U.S. Constitution

Main Idea All Americans have basic legal rights and responsibilities.

Civics & You Have you ever thought a law was wrong or unfair? Read to find out what you can do about it.

Early settlers in the American colonies enjoyed a degree of liberty found in few countries in the eighteenth century. They owed their rights to legal principles that developed in England and were transferred to America with the colonists. Colonial lawyers studied from English law books, and judges used English common law as the basis for their decisions.

As in England, however, American law increasingly became a law of written statutes, which are the work of Congress and state legislatures. Although legislation has replaced common law, courts still refer to common-law principles when no statutes exist to deal with a given legal issue.

Individual Rights

The U.S. Constitution is the basic law of our nation. It gives each branch of government a role in making, enforcing, and **interpreting,** or defining, the law. The legislative branch of government makes the laws of the nation. The executive branch carries out these laws and, in doing so, makes laws as well. The judicial branch applies the law to specific cases. Courts base their rulings on written laws and on the precedents of earlier cases. The rulings are then used to build decisions about similar cases in the future. This process is called **stare decisis,** which is Latin for "let the decision stand."

Several basic legal rights that belong to Americans are included in Article I of the Constitution. One of the most important is

Constitutional Rights of the Accused

ARTICLE I, SECTION 9
• to be granted habeas corpus (released until trial)

FIFTH AMENDMENT
• to have a grand jury hearing
• to be protected from double jeopardy
• to refuse to answer questions that may be incriminating

SIXTH AMENDMENT
• to be informed of the accusation
• to hear and question witnesses
• to be able to subpoena witnesses
• to be represented by an attorney
• to have a speedy and public trial by an impartial jury
• to be represented by a lawyer

FOURTEENTH AMENDMENT
• to have due process of law
• to have equal protection of the laws

Analyzing Charts

1. **Describing** What protections does the Fourteenth Amendment guarantee?
2. **Analyzing** How does due process of law limit what government can do?

the **writ of habeas corpus.** A writ is a written legal order; *habeas corpus* is a Latin phrase that roughly means "you should have the body." The writ of habeas corpus requires an official who has arrested someone to bring that person to court and explain why he or she is being held. This writ is a safeguard against being kept in jail unlawfully.

Article I also forbids enactment of **bills of attainder** and **ex post facto laws.** A bill of attainder is a law that punishes a person

---

Gustavo Garcia and Carlos Cadena

Objective: To explain a Supreme Court case

Focus: Have students restate the Fourteenth Amendment.

Teach: Discuss struggles that American minorities have had.

Assess: Have students explain why this case was a landmark judgment.

Close: Have students write a summary of the case.

Differentiated Instruction Strategies

BL Explain the meaning of "jury of your peers." Why didn't Hernandez have this in Texas?

AL Reread the Fourteenth Amendment and explain why Chief Justice Earl Warren and the state of Texas disagreed on its interpretation.

ELL Define the term "civil rights." Explain how it applies to this case.

accused of a crime without a trial or a fair hearing in court. An ex post facto law is a law that would allow a person to be punished for an action that was not against the law when it was committed.

A Guarantee of Rights The Constitution's Bill of Rights further guarantees the freedoms of individuals. Several of these amendments spell out the rights of Americans in relation to the administration of justice. After the Civil War, Congress proposed and the states ratified the Fourteenth Amendment, extending these rights to formerly enslaved persons. The amendment also requires the states to provide equal protection under the law to all persons.

The Fifth and Fourteenth Amendments guarantee **due process of law.** Due process means, in part, that government may not take our lives, liberty, or property except according to the proper exercise of law. The law requires, for example, that accused people have the opportunity for a trial by jury.

The equal-protection clause in the Fourteenth Amendment requires governments to treat all people equally. It forbids unfair or unequal treatment based on **factors,** or influences such as gender, race, and religion. Since the 1950s, this clause has been the major civil rights tool of minorities and women when challenging laws or government policies that discriminate against them.

Legal Responsibilities

The Declaration of Independence states, "All men are created equal." This democratic ideal of equality means that all people are entitled to equal rights and treatment before the law. Americans have a number of legal responsibilities. By fulfilling them, we ensure that our legal system works as it should and that our legal rights are protected.

C

✓ **Reading Check** Explaining What two amendments guarantee the due process of law?

Teach

C **Critical Thinking**

Specifying Ask: What are some of the legal responsibilities that we must practice as American citizens? *(Answers may include to abide by laws set forth by our government; to serve on a jury; to testify in court; to speak up to defend the innocent, the helpless; and the community; to report criminal activity; and to stay informed about the law.)* **OL**

✓ **Reading Check** **Answer:** the Fifth and Fourteenth Amendments

---

TIME™ Political Cartoons

Political Cartoons

CUT IT OUT!

AFTER YOU.

U.S. CONSTITUTION
FREEDOM OF RELIGION
FREEDOM OF SPEECH
FREEDOM OF THE PRESS
FREEDOM OF ASSEMBLY

—Steve Breen/Copley News Service

With this cartoon, Steve Breen is making a statement on the movement to amend the U.S. Constitution to prohibit flag burning.

1. What do the scissors represent?
2. Why is the man with the flag saying, "After you"?
3. Do you think the cartoonist supports or opposes the proposed amendment? Explain.

Every year, more than half of all Americans do volunteer work ... role in it. One of the responsibilities of citizens is to help make their ... of volunteer grou... small. Perha... dad who...

TIME™ Political Cartoons

Answers:
1. The scissors represent cutting the right to freedom of speech from the Constitution.
2. He is suggesting that he will stop burning the flag only when his freedom of speech has been rescinded.
3. Answers may vary, but students may say the cartoonist opposes changing the Bill of Rights.

Chapter 15 437

Hands-On Chapter Project
Step 3

Learning About the Legal System

Step 3: Journey Through the Legal System Four groups together will create a game about the criminal justice system.

Directions Each group creates four cards about the accused's rights. For example, "Police have taken evidence without a search warrant. Move ahead three spaces."

Next, have students as a class create a board game design. For example, they might design a wheel with spokes, a winding path, or a square. Encourage students to be creative. The spaces or steps will be color coordinated. The spaces should also have a number 2 or 3. Explain that when a player (defendant) lands on a particular color, he or she will pick one of the cards the groups created in Steps 2 and 3. **OL**
(Project continued on the Visual Summary page)

JAIL! ACQUITTED!!
ARRESTED!!

Teach

W Writing Support

Personal Writing Have students write a paragraph explaining why they think that the assumption that accused people are "innocent until proven guilty" is or is not important. Explain that the defendant does not have to prove his or her innocence; the prosecutor has to prove his or her guilt. Invite students to share their responses with the class. **OL**

C Critical Thinking

Interpreting Discuss with students that sometimes a search warrant is not needed, for example, if evidence is in "plain view." Have students research and identify other circumstances in which a search warrant is not required. *(when a person consents to a search without a warrant, when police are in pursuit of a suspect, when public safety is involved, when police officers believe evidence will be removed before a search warrant is obtained)* **AL**

Caption Answer: to refuse to answer questions that may be incriminating, to be protected from double jeopardy, and to have a grand jury hearing

Differentiated Instruction

Guaranteed Rights of Those Accused

Main Idea The U.S. Constitution includes several protections for Americans accused of a crime.

Civics & You Have you ever received a punishment that seemed too drastic for what you did wrong? Read to find out what the Constitution says about this.

The Constitution includes several specific rights that protect citizens accused of crimes. These rights make sure that accused people are treated fairly and receive every chance to defend themselves. Each right is based on the idea that a person is **presumed,** or believed to be, innocent until proven guilty in a court of law.

The Fourth Amendment

The Fourth Amendment protects citizens against "unreasonable searches and seizures." It gives Americans a fundamental right to be secure in their homes and property. Police seeking to intrude on this security must first get a **search warrant**—a judge's authorization—specifying the exact place to be searched and describing what objects may be seized. Police must show the judge that they have probable cause—a good reason—that their search will prove useful. In the 1961 case *Mapp* v. *Ohio*, the Supreme Court adopted what is called the exclusionary rule. This rule says that if the police gain evidence in a way that violates the Fourth Amendment, that evidence may not be used in a trial.

The Fifth Amendment

The Fifth Amendment states that "no person . . . shall be compelled in any criminal case to be a witness against himself." This means that a person does not have to answer questions that may incriminate that person, or show his or her involvement in a crime. Before the 1960s, police often questioned suspects, sometimes under great pressure, to push them to confess to a crime before they saw a lawyer or appeared in court.

In 1966, in *Miranda* v. *Arizona*, the Supreme Court held that police must inform suspects that they have the right to "remain silent"—to refuse to answer police questions. Ernesto Miranda claimed he had not realized he had the right to remain silent or to have a lawyer present during police questioning. Now every person who is arrested hears the Miranda warnings, familiar from TV police programs.

Enforcing Laws An arrested person is taken to a police station where the charges are recorded. At this time, the suspect may be fingerprinted, photographed, or put in a lineup to be identified by witnesses. *Explaining* What are the Fifth Amendment rights of a person accused of a crime?

Leveled Activities

OL Writing Activity 15, URB pp. 27–28

OL Biography Activity 15, URB pp. 25–26

AL Differentiated Instruction Activity 15, URB pp. 33–34

ELL Chart/Graph/Map Activity 15, URB p. 31–32

The Fifth Amendment also protects an accused person from **double jeopardy.** This means that a person who is tried for a crime and found not guilty may not be placed in jeopardy—put at risk of criminal penalty—a second time by being retried for the same crime.

What Is a Grand Jury? The Fifth Amendment says, furthermore, that people accused of serious federal crimes must be brought before a **grand jury** to decide whether the government has enough evidence to bring them to trial. (In some states, a preliminary hearing is used instead of a grand jury indictment.) A grand jury is a group of 12 to 23 citizens that hears evidence presented by a prosecutor. It decides whether there is enough evidence to indicate that the accused has committed a crime. If the grand jury finds sufficient evidence to proceed to trial, it indicts the accused person, or issues a formal charge that names the suspect and states the charges against him or her.

The Sixth Amendment

The Sixth Amendment grants an accused person the right to be defended by a lawyer. In 1963 the Supreme Court, in *Gideon v. Wainwright,* interpreted the amendment to mean that if a defendant cannot afford a lawyer, the state must provide one. Previously the federal government provided lawyers for poor defendants, but some states did not if the case did not involve capital punishment.

The Sixth Amendment also guarantees that accused people must be informed of the nature and cause of the accusations against them and have "the right to a speedy and public trial, by an impartial jury" and the right to confront, or question, witnesses against them. This right protects defendants against

Civics ONLINE

Student Web Activity Visit glencoe.com and complete the Chapter 15 Web Activity.

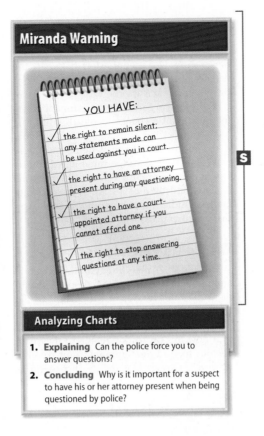

Miranda Warning

YOU HAVE:

✓ the right to remain silent; any statements made can be used against you in court.

✓ the right to have an attorney present during any questioning.

✓ the right to have a court-appointed attorney if you cannot afford one.

✓ the right to stop answering questions at any time.

Analyzing Charts

1. **Explaining** Can the police force you to answer questions?

2. **Concluding** Why is it important for a suspect to have his or her attorney present when being questioned by police?

being held in jail for an unreasonably long time. It also means that trials usually may not be closed to the public or the news media.

Right to a Trial A person accused of a crime also has the right to a trial by an impartial jury. *Impartial* means that jury members will be people who do not know anyone involved in the case and have not already made up their minds about the case. Jury members usually must be drawn from the area where the crime was committed.

Although everyone charged with a crime has a right to a jury trial, defendants may choose to appear before only a judge, without a jury. This kind of trial is called a bench trial.

Chapter 15 439

Teach

S Skill Practice

Interpreting a Chart Explain to students that the Miranda warning was instituted after Ernesto Miranda confessed to a crime while in police custody. **Ask:** Which of the rights included in the Miranda warning do you think is most important? *(Answers will vary.)* **OL**

Civics ONLINE

Objectives and answers to the **Student Web Activity** can be found at glencoe.com under the Web Activity Lesson Plan for this chapter.

Analyzing Charts

Answers:

1. no
2. so that he or she will not inadvertently admit to the crime or say something incriminating

Additional Support

Activity: Collaborative Learning

Naming Group students in small groups, and have them use the note cards they created on page 437 to learn the rights of the accused as guaranteed by the Fourth, Fifth, Sixth, Eighth, and Fourteenth Amendments.

Once groups have memorized the material, organize the class into two teams. Have the teams take turns reading a right aloud. The opposing team must identify the correct amendment. **OL**

Teacher Tip

This activity requires students to remember which rights are protected under different amendments. Group students so that they feel comfortable learning the material. Encourage students to share memory devices, such as songs or mnemonic devices, that help them remember.

Teach

D Differentiated Instruction

Visual/Spatial Have small groups research their state laws and create a poster that ranks at least ten offenses from the most serious to the least serious. For each offense, have them decide on an appropriate bail. **OL**

✓ Reading Check **Answer:** It forced states to examine death penalty laws to make them impartial.

Assess

Civics ONLINE

Study Central™ provides summaries, interactive games, and online graphic organizers to help students review content.

Close

Summarize Have students review the graphic organizer they completed for Section 3. Using their notes and graphic organizers, have students write a summary of the Constitutional Rights of the Accused. **OL**

Section 3 Review

Even so, many criminal prosecutions do not come to trial at all—with or without a jury—because of plea bargains. **Plea bargaining** is a negotiation between the defense attorney and the prosecutor, who is the government's attorney.

In a plea bargain, the government offers the defendant a chance to plead guilty to a less serious crime in exchange for receiving a less severe penalty than he or she might receive at trial. A judge must agree to any bargain. Plea bargains can cut down on the expense and time of a trial. They also help judges handle the volume of criminal cases that courts process.

The Eighth Amendment

The Eighth Amendment outlaws "cruel and unusual punishments." Also, a punishment may not be out of proportion to the crime, such as imposing a life sentence for shoplifting. There is controversy, however, over how this protection relates to the death penalty. In 1972 the Supreme Court ruled in *Furman* v. *Georgia* that the death penalty as

then administered was not constitutional. The Court found that the death penalty was being imposed in unfair ways, for a wide variety of crimes, and mainly on African Americans and poor people.

After the *Furman* decision, most states revised their death penalty laws to comply with the Supreme Court's guidelines. Some states have established a two-stage process to deal with death penalty cases. First, a jury trial determines the guilt or innocence of the defendant. A separate hearing then determines the degree of punishment.

What Is Bail? The Eighth Amendment also prohibits "excessive bail." **Bail** is a sum of money an arrested person pays to a court to win release from jail while awaiting trial.

In determining the amount of bail, the judge considers the seriousness of the case, the criminal record of the accused, and the ability of the accused to post bail.

✓ Reading Check **Explaining** What effect did the *Furman* decision have?

 Review

Vocabulary

1. **Define** the following terms and use them in sentences related to constitutional legal protections and rights of the accused: *writ of habeas corpus, bill of attainder, ex post facto law, double jeopardy, bail.*

Main Ideas

2. **Describing** How is the Bill of Rights related to protecting citizens?

3. **Explaining** Why is a writ of habeas corpus an important right?

Critical Thinking

4. **BIG Ideas** Why do you think it is important for arrested persons to be informed of their Miranda rights?

5. **Summarizing** On a web diagram like the one below, list four legal protections that are included in the Bill of Rights and in the Fourteenth Amendment of the Constitution.

Legal Protections

6. **Analyzing Visuals** Review the chart on page 436. Which part of the U.S. Constitution includes the guarantee that if you are arrested you must be informed of the charges against you?

CITIZENSHIP Activity

7. **Persuasive Writing** Which of the rights guaranteed to people accused of a crime do you think is the most important? Explain.

Civics ONLINE

Study Central™ To review this section, go to glencoe.com.

Answers

1. Sentences should use vocabulary words according to their definitions in the section and in the Glossary.

2. Several amendments in the Bill of Rights protect all U.S. citizens' legal rights before the law.

3. It guarantees U.S. citizens the right to know why they have been arrested and safeguards them from being held in prison indefinitely.

4. The Miranda Rights ensure that all citizens know that they have the opportunity to have a lawyer and a trial and will not be forced to confess.

5. Answers will vary but may include: the right to a grand jury, the right to due process under the law, protection from illegal searches, and the right to a speedy trial.

6. the Sixth Amendment

7. Responses will vary. Students should explain which right they think is most important for the accused and why.

Sources of Our Laws

- The set of rules and standards by which a society governs itself is known as law.
- Laws keep the peace and prevent violent acts.
- Laws set punishments and rules for resolving disputes.
- To be fully effective, laws must be fair and must treat all people equally.

Emergency personnel provide help at an accident scene

Early Systems of Law

- The earliest laws were probably passed from one generation to the next by word of mouth.
- Early laws, such as the Code of Hammurabi, the Ten Commandments, Roman law, and English law, have influenced our laws today.

Lady Justice symbolizes impartiality

The American Legal System

- The Constitution is our most fundamental and important source of law.
- Many types of law exist, including criminal and civil law.
- Whereas criminal law deals with criminal acts, civil law deals with disputes between people or groups.
- Article I of the U.S. Constitution and the Bill of Rights include several protections for those accused of a crime.

STUDY TO GO Study anywhere, anytime! Download quizzes and flash cards to your PDA from glencoe.com.

441

Determining Importance Have students work with partners and list reasons why laws are written. Have them use the details to write a paragraph stating why people need laws. **Ask:** Do you think laws help prevent crimes? Why or why not? Suggest that students find out which communities in your area have the lowest crime rates and why. **OL**

Illustrating Have students create a montage of symbols for the laws that have influenced American laws. Students can use the symbols pictured in this section. Encourage students to use different formats and mediums. Allow students to discuss their work with the class and to display it in the classroom. **OL**

Descriptive Writing Have students review the legal rights provided for under the U.S. Constitution. Have them create bumper stickers that describe these rights. Bumper stickers might involve a play on words or include rhymes. Students may provide a visual for each bumper sticker. **AL**

Hands-On Chapter Project
Step 4: Wrap-Up

Learning About the Legal System

Step 4: Analyzing the Legal Rights and the Legal System Groups will join together to play a board game that illustrates some of the maneuvers of the criminal justice system.

Directions Students will now play their board game. Each group may have a player (defendant) on the board. Defendants will begin by choosing a card from Step 1 to determine what kind of law they broke and their punishment. Next, the defendants must go through the legal system. The cards from Step 2 and 3 will help each defendant progress. The winner is the defendant who exits the legal system first.

At the end of the game, have students discuss how difficult or easy it is to navigate through the criminal justice system. **OL**

Answers and Analyses

Reviewing Vocabulary

1. D In this question, the student has to differentiate between types of laws, which are represented by answer choices A, B, and C, and a system of law. Common law is considered a system of law.

2. A Students must remember that civil law concerns disputes between people. Felonies are serious crimes. Students might mistakenly choose C, thinking libel is part of civil law. Choice D describes a person, not a type of law.

3. B Students will most probably choose between A and B. The plaintiff is the one bringing charges against the accused. The defendant is the accused.

4. C This question requires that students know how attorneys can agree to settle a case without going through the court system. A verdict is the decision the jury or judge offers to the defendant. Due process of law is a right guaranteed by the Constitution.

Reviewing Main Ideas

5. C This question requires that students think about how our laws were created. They are not new. Some students may think they were created as a protest against King George III, but many English laws had a strong influence in the U.S. Constitution.

6. D In this question, students must recall which laws were developed first. Although some of the penalties were harsh, the Code of Hammurabi is the first-known system of written laws.

7. A This question requires that students can differentiate between two types of crimes: felonies and misdemeanors. A felony is a crime such as murder, and the consequence is serious. Choices C and D are legal terms but are not related to crimes.

TEST-TAKING TIP

Make sure the number of answer spaces on the answer sheet matches the number of questions on the test you are taking.

Reviewing Vocabulary

Directions: Choose the word(s) that best completes the sentence.

1. The system of _____ law is based on court decisions rather than on a legal code.

  A criminal   **C** administrative

  B constitutional   **D** common

2. The system of civil law dealing with civil wrongs, or _____, has a long history.

  A torts   **C** libels

  B felonies   **D** plaintiffs

3. A person charged with a crime and tried in court is the _____.

  A plaintiff   **C** tort

  B defendant   **D** judge

4. A _____ is a negotiation between the prosecutor and defense attorney to avoid a trial.

  A verdict   **C** plea bargain

  B due process of law   **D** search warrant

Reviewing Main Ideas

Directions: Choose the best answer for each question.

Section 1 (pp. 426–429)

5. On which of the following did the writers of the U.S. Constitution base the system of laws?

  A Russian law

  B new laws they created

  C ancient laws passed down through generations

  D warnings from King George

6. The oldest system of laws known to the modern world is the _____.

  A Justinian Code

  B Napoleonic Code

  C Roman Code

  D Code of Hammurabi

Section 2 (pp. 430–434)

7. A crime that is considered less serious and requires a short jail sentence is a _____.

  A misdemeanor

  B felony

  C plaintiff

  D lawsuit

8. Which of the following might result in a lawsuit?

  A A person is attacked and a wallet is stolen.

  B A person has his or her garage painted with graffiti.

  C A company breaks a contract to build someone's house.

  D A person is hit by a hit-and-run driver.

Section 3 (pp. 435–440)

9. With a writ of habeas corpus, the person arrested has a right to know _____.

  A why he or she is being held

  B who the prosecutor is

  C who brought the lawsuit against him or her

  D how many people will be on his or her jury

GO ON

8. C This question requires that students apply what they learned about lawsuits. Students must recall that a lawsuit is a legal action in which a person sues to collect damages. Of all the choices, C is the only one in which the individual was wronged. The other choices provide more serious offenses against property, and formal charges would be filed.

9. A Students need to remember the phrase "habeas corpus" means "you should have the body." Students might mistakenly choose choice C, a right protected under the Sixth Amendment.

Critical Thinking

Directions: Choose the best answer for each question.

Base your answers to questions 10 and 11 on the chart below and your knowledge of Chapter 15.

Misdemeanors and Felonies
Minor crimes and misdemeanors are tried in the lower state courts.
• Running a red light • Littering • Shoplifting small items • Vandalism
Felonies are tried in the higher state courts.
• Murder • Arson • Robbery • Drug trafficking

10. What type of law deals with the examples in this chart?

  A civil law

  B criminal law

  C constitutional law

  D administrative law

11. Which of the following offenses would most likely be punished with a fine?

  A arson

  B murder

  C robbery

  D littering

Document-Based Questions

Directions: Analyze the following document and answer the short-answer questions that follow.

Justice Oliver Wendell Holmes, Jr., who served 30 years on the U.S. Supreme Court stated the following about evidence against the accused in his dissenting opinion to the court ruling in *Olmstead* v. *United States*, 1928.

> The government ought not to use evidence obtained and only obtainable by a criminal act. . . For my part I think it is a less evil that some criminals should escape than that the Government should play some ignoble [corrupt] part.
>
> —Justice Oliver Wendell Holmes, Jr.

12. To which Constitutional amendment is Justice Holmes referring in this statement?

  A First Amendment

  B Fourth Amendment

  C Fifth Amendment

  D Sixth Amendment

13. Do you agree with Justice Holmes in his statement? Why or why not?

Extended-Response Question

14. Briefly explain what makes a law a good law. Give at least three characteristics.

Civics ONLINE

For additional test practice, use Self-Check Quizzes—Chapter 15 on glencoe.com.

Need Extra Help?														
If you missed question. . .	1	2	3	4	5	6	7	8	9	10	11	12	13	14
Go to page. . .	429	433	431	440	428	428	432	432	436	431	432	438	438	427

Chapter 15   443

Document-Based Questions

12. B The question requires that students know which rights are guaranteed under each of the amendments listed. The Fourth Amendment concerns search and seizure rights, which Justice Holmes is referring to.

13. Students' answers will vary. Answers should include sound reasoning using supporting details from the chapter.

Extended Response

14. Students' answers will vary. Students should mention that good laws are fair, understandable, and enforceable. Look for supporting details from the chapter.

Critical Thinking

10. B In this question, students need to recall that crimes are categorized as either felonies or misdemeanors, so these content vocabulary words refer to criminal law.

11. D Choices A–C are all crimes that would require jail time. Answer choice D, "littering," is the only offense in this group for which a person could be fined.

Civics ONLINE

Have students visit the Web site at glencoe.com to review Chapter 15 and take the **Self-Check Quiz**.

Need Extra Help?

Have students refer to the pages listed if they miss any of the questions.

Teach

C Critical Thinking

Identifying Central Issues Have students discuss why local officials have decided to take the illegal immigration situation into their own hands. **Ask:** Why do local lawmakers want to pass legislation on immigrants that the federal government is unwilling to pass? (*Local communities feel that they can judge better than the federal government how illegal immigrants affect their quality of life.*) **OL**

S Skill Practice

Interpreting a Chart Have students look at the pie chart. **Ask:** Besides Mexico, where are most illegal immigrants from? (*other Latin American countries*) Ask students to explain how an influx of illegal workers affects the U.S. economy. Have them study the income numbers mentioned on the right, discuss if they think illegal workers help or hinder the economy, and explain their reasons. **OL**

For additional practice on this skill (Interpreting a Chart), see the **Skills Handbook**.

Additional Support

New Laws on Immigration

In the absence of national legislation, lawmakers are formulating local statutes

Fed up with all the Congressional talk and the lack of national legislation on immigration, lawmakers in cities across the U.S. have been taking matters into their own hands. To deter illegal immigrants from coming to town, they've been passing local laws. In Vista, California, a new ordinance requires employers to register with the city before using day laborers, many of whom are illegal immigrants. They must also report whom they hire. The coal town of Hazleton, Pennsylvania (population 31,000), passed the nation's toughest illegal-immigration law in 2006. Hazleton's regulations impose fines on employers who knowingly hire illegal immigrants and on landlords who rent to them. "Our quality of life is at stake, and I'm not going to sit back and wait for the Federal Government to do something about it," said Mayor Louis Barletta. "I know that other cities across the country feel the same way."

The Puerto Rican Legal Defense and Education Fund filed a lawsuit to overturn Hazleton's ordinance, which Cesar Perales, president of the New York City-based advocacy group, calls "unconstitutional and discriminatory." Perales cites a legal analysis by the bipartisan Congressional Research Service that suggests Hazleton's ordinance, by creating penalties for those who aid immigrants, may be trampling on an area of law that is under federal jurisdiction. "You can't have every little town deciding the conditions under which illegal immigrants are going to live there," he says. For now, at least, some communities seem determined to try.

ON THE JOB Landscaping attracts immigrants, both legal and illegal, in East Hampton, New York, a wealthy community on Long Island.

How the Influx Is Changing the U.S.

Illegal immigrants in the U.S. are largely from Mexico ...

Country or region of birth of illegal immigrants in the U.S., March 2004

MEXICO 57%
OTHER LATIN AMERICA 24%
ALL OTHER 19%

Estimates

... Their numbers are growing ...

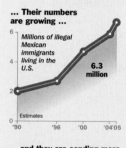

Millions of illegal Mexican immigrants living in the U.S.

6.3 million

Estimates

'90 '96 '00 '04'05

... and they are sending more and more money back home

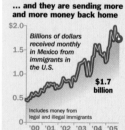

Billions of dollars received monthly in Mexico from immigrants in the U.S.

$1.7 billion

Includes money from legal and illegal immigrants

'00 '01 '02 '03 '04 '05

PROFILE OF IMMIGRATION

1 in 10
Proportion of Mexicans born in Mexico who now reside in the U.S.

80% to 85%
Percentage of new immigrants from Mexico who lack legal documentation

$9
Median hourly wage of Mexican-born workers in the U.S. in 2004

$1.86 (21 pesos)
Median hourly wage in Mexico in 2004

$450 billion
Estimated combined annual gross income of all U.S. workers born in Latin America, of both legal and illegal immigration status, according to a 2004 report*

93%
Percentage of that $450 billion that was spent in the U.S.*

*From the Inter-American Development Bank

Sources: Pew Hispanic Center; National Immigration Law Center; National Conference of State Legislatures; INEGI (Instituto Nacional de Estadística, Geografía e Informática)

Background

Illegal immigration from Mexico is not new, nor are worker programs and amnesty reforms. In 1942, the U.S. government signed an agreement legalizing entry of Mexican migrant workers to states on the southern U.S. border. The Mexican Farm Labor Program Agreement was initiated to supply workers to farms during World War II. The "Bracero Program" set the minimum wage at thirty cents an hour. In addition, farm owners had to provide shelter and food to Mexican farmworkers.

Over four million *braceros* entered the country between 1942 and 1964. While many returned to Mexico after their services were no longer needed, many stayed in the United States illegally. The Immigration and Naturalization Service expelled approximately 3.8 million illegal Mexican workers. In 1964, the program was not renewed. Mechanization, infringement on U.S. workers' employment opportunities, and rising wages led Congress to give up the program.

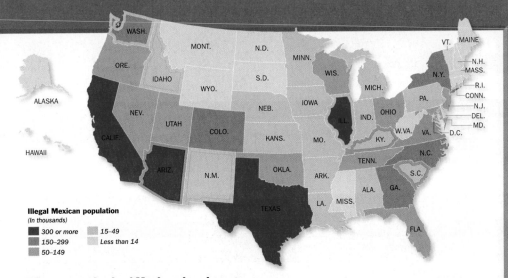

Where unauthorized Mexican immigrants go

Illegal Mexican population
(In thousands)

- ■ 300 or more
- ■ 150–299
- ■ 50–149
- ■ 15–49
- ■ Less than 14

C About 6.3 million illegal immigrants from Mexico live in the U.S., according to the Pew Hispanic Center, and an average of 485,000 more arrive every year. In response, state legislatures considered nearly 300 bills on immigration policy in the first half of 2005 alone, but passed just 47. While some states address the challenges facing migrant workers with families, others are trying to crack down on illegal immigration.

W

SUPPORTIVE LEGISLATION		CRACKING DOWN	
Washington State Reversed a 2002 measure and restored health-care coverage to children regardless of their immigration status.	**Illinois** Governor Rod Blagojevich set up an office to study immigrants' contributions and needs; a new law allows illegal immigrant children to obtain health insurance.	**Virginia** A recent bill would make it the first state to prohibit illegal immigrants from attending state colleges; a new law restricts other benefits.	**South Carolina** A bill passed the state house and senate requiring Medicaid applicants to present proof of legal residency if asked.
Idaho Rejected a bill that would have required counties to pay for transportation of undocumented workers back to their home countries.	**New Mexico** Became the ninth state to extend in-state tuition benefits to undocumented immigrant students.	**Kentucky** Enacted a law requiring anyone seeking licenses for various professions to show proof of immigration status.	**Arizona** Passed a law prohibiting cities from maintaining public day-laborer centers, where migrant workers congregate to seek employment.

TIME POLL

A majority say illegals are a real problem …

How serious a problem is illegal immigration into the U.S.?

Extremely	30%
Very	33%	**63%**
Somewhat	26%
Not very	8%	**34%**

83% are concerned that providing social services for illegal immigrants costs taxpayers too much

71% are concerned that illegal immigrants increase crime

56% think illegal immigrants are taking jobs that citizens don't want

… although few say they are personally affected …

Do you pay less for some items or services because of low-wage illegal-immigrant labor?

Yes	17%
No	71%

61% said they have had some kind of contact with people they believed to be illegal immigrants

5% said they had hired someone they thought might be illegal to work around the house

14% said they had hired a contractor or company that may have used illegal immigrants

… they still want more done about it

Is the government doing enough to keep illegal immigrants from entering the U.S.?

Yes	21%*
No	74%

50% said all illegal immigrants should be deported, but:

76% think illegal immigrants should be able to earn citizenship

73% favor guest-worker registration for those already here

64% favor issuing temporary work visas for seasonal work

*Includes 7% who think the government is doing "too much"

This TIME poll was conducted by telephone Jan. 24-26, 2006 among 1,002 adult Americans by SRBI Public Affairs. The margin of error is 3 percentage points. "Don't know" answers omitted

Teach

C Critical Thinking

Making Inferences Ask: Why might a majority of U.S. citizens feel that illegal immigrants are a real problem when only a few say that they are not personally affected by their presence? *(Answers will vary. Students may mention that many people are prejudiced against people from other countries, fear that low-wage earners will take jobs from U.S. workers, and resent sharing social services with people who do not pay taxes.)* **OL**

W Writing Support

Persuasive Writing After students read about legislation that is both supportive and obstructive, discuss what kinds of rights non-U.S. citizens have. **Ask:** Should people who enter the country illegally have the same rights as those who are here legally? Do you think illegal immigrants share the same responsibilities as U.S. citizens? Have students write their opinions about the topic as letters, addressed to the president of the United States. **OL**

 Reading Strategy | **Read to Write**

Making Decisions Begin a discussion on how students feel about illegal immigrants. To encourage discussion, ask the following questions: Do you think illegal immigration is a serious problem? Do border states have a responsibility to tighten their borders or should the federal government intervene? Is building a wall a viable solution? Will stricter laws deter the influx? Should illegal immigrants who are caught be returned to their country of origin or placed in jail?

Next, have students form small groups and discuss ways in which they think lawmakers should deal with illegal immigration. Have groups come up with one or more solutions and write their proposals. They may use chart paper with bulleted solutions or present a "road map" to border security. Have groups share their proposals with the class. **OL**

<table>
<tr><td colspan="2">**Key to Ability Levels**</td></tr>
<tr><td>**BL** Below level</td><td>**AL** Above level</td></tr>
<tr><td>**OL** On level</td><td>**ELL** English Language Learners</td></tr>
</table>

Key to Teaching Resources

Print Material Transparency
CD-ROM or DVD

Levels				Resources	Chapter Opener	Section 1	Section 2	Section 3	Chapter Assess
BL	OL	AL	ELL						
				FOCUS					
BL	OL	AL	ELL	Daily Focus Skills Transparencies		16–1	16–2	16–3	
				TEACH					
BL	OL		ELL	Reading Essentials and Note-Taking Guide*		p. 150	p. 153	p. 156	
	OL	AL		Economic Activity, URB		p. 5			
	OL	AL		Primary Source Reading, URB			p. 15		
BL	OL	AL	ELL	Content Vocabulary Activity, URB*	p. 43	p. 43	p. 43	p. 43	
BL	OL	AL	ELL	Academic Vocabulary Activity, URB	p. 45	p. 45	p. 45	p. 45	
	OL			Biography Activity, URB		p. 47	p. 47	p. 47	
BL	OL	AL	ELL	Writing Skills Activity, URB			p. 49		
	OL	AL		Critical Thinking Skills Activity, URB			p. 51		
BL	OL	AL	ELL	Chart, Graph, and Map Skills Activity, URB		p. 53			
BL	OL	AL	ELL	Differentiated Instruction, URB			p. 55		
BL	OL	AL	ELL	School-to-Home Connection Activity, URB*	p. 57	p. 57	p. 57	p. 57	
BL	OL		ELL	Guided Reading Activities, URB*		p. 61	p. 62	p. 63	
	OL	AL		Supreme Court Cases			pp. 57, 89		
BL	OL	AL	ELL	Writer's Guidebook	✓	✓	✓	✓	✓
	OL	AL		Primary Source Document Library	✓	✓	✓	✓	✓
BL	OL	AL	ELL	Daily Lecture & Discussion Notes (in Pres. Plus)		✓	✓	✓	✓
BL	OL	AL	ELL	StudentWorks™ Plus		✓	✓	✓	✓
BL	OL	AL	ELL	Section Spotlight Videos		✓	✓	✓	
BL	OL	AL	ELL	TIME Interpreting Political Cartoons Transp.		Ch. 16			
BL	OL	AL	ELL	Writing Process Transparencies	✓	✓	✓	✓	✓

Note: Please refer to the *Unit 5 Resource Book* for this chapter's URB materials.

* Also available in Spanish

- Interactive Lesson Planner
- Interactive Teacher Edition
- Fully editable blackline masters
- Section Spotlight Videos Launch
- Differentiated Lesson Plans
- Printable reports of daily assignments
- Standards Tracking System

Levels					Resources	Chapter Opener	Section 1	Section 2	Section 3	Chapter Assess
BL	OL	AL	ELL							
					TEACH (continued)					
				📁	**Building Academic Vocabulary**	✓	✓	✓	✓	✓
				📁	**Strategies for Success**	✓	✓	✓	✓	✓
Teacher Resources				📁	**Teacher's Guide to Differentiated Instruction**	✓	✓	✓	✓	✓
				💿	**Graphing Tool**	✓	✓	✓	✓	✓
				💿	**Presentation Plus! with MindJogger CheckPoint**	✓	✓	✓	✓	✓
					ASSESS					
BL	OL	AL	ELL	📁	**Quizzes and Tests***		p. 189	p. 190	p. 191	p. 192
BL	OL	AL	ELL	📁	**Authentic Assessment with Rubrics**		p. 20	p. 20	p. 20	p. 20
BL	OL	AL	ELL	📁	**Standardized Test Practice**			p. 31		p. 31
BL	OL	AL	ELL	💿	*ExamView® Assessment Suite* **CD-ROM**		16–1	16–2	16–3	Ch. 16
					CLOSE					
BL			ELL	📁	**Reteaching Activity, URB***		p. 59	p. 59	p. 59	
BL	OL		ELL	📁	**Reading and Study Skills Foldables Activity**	p. 80		p. 81	p. 81	
BL	OL	AL	ELL	📁	*Civics Today* **in Graphic Novel**	p. 69			p. 69	
BL	OL	AL	ELL	🖨	**Graphic Organizer Transparencies & Strategies**	✓	✓	✓	✓	✓

✓ Chapter- or unit-based activities applicable to all sections in this chapter

Using PuzzleMaker™ 3.1

Online Jumble Puzzles

What is PuzzleMaker™ 3.1?
Glencoe's PuzzleMaker™ 3.1 is an interactive online tool that lets you create your own crossword puzzles based on the glossary and using either content vocabulary, academic vocabulary, or both, for classroom use.

How can Glencoe's PuzzleMaker™ 3.1 help my students?
After students complete the jumble puzzles, they will be able to:
- recall and identify scrambled terms with the help of clues
- reinforce their understanding of the vocabulary

Visit glencoe.com and enter a **QuickPass**™ code to go directly to resources for each chapter.

Civics ONLINE
Visit glencoe.com and enter **QuickPass**™ code CIV1360c16T for Chapter 16 resources.

You can easily launch a wide range of digital products from your computer's desktop with the McGraw-Hill Social Studies widget.

	Student	Teacher	Parent
Media Library			
• Student Edition Section Audio	●		●
• Spanish Audio Summaries	●		●
• Section Spotlight Videos	●	●	●
***Civics Today* Online Learning Center (Web Site)**			
• Chapter Overviews	●	●	●
• Study Central™	●	●	●
• Study-to-Go	●	●	●
• Student Web Activities	●	●	●
• In Motion Animation	●	●	●
• Self-Check Quizzes	●	●	●
• ePuzzles and Games	●	●	●
• StudentWorks™ Plus Online	●	●	●
• Vocabulary eFlashcards	●	●	●
• Web Activity Lesson Plans		●	
• Vocabulary PuzzleMaker	●	●	●
Classroom Tools			
• Multilingual Glossary	●	●	●
• Beyond the Textbook	●	●	●
• NGS MapMachine	●	●	●

Reading List Generator CD-ROM

BookLink 3

Use this database to search more than 30,000 titles to create a customized reading list for your students.

- Reading lists can be organized by students' reading level, author, genre, theme, or area of interest.
- The database provides Degrees of Reading Power™ (DRP) and Lexile™ readability scores for all selections.
- A brief summary of each selection is included.

Leveled reading suggestions for this chapter:

For students at a Grade 7 reading level:
- *Penn,* by Elizabeth Janet Gray

For students at a Grade 8 reading level:
- **Miranda v. Arizona: *The Rights of the Accused,*** by Liz Sonneborn

For students at a Grade 9 reading level:
- *The Supreme Court,* by Gerald W. Johnson

For students at a Grade 10 reading level:
- *Mary Ann Shadd Cary: The Black Press and Protest in the Nineteenth Century,* by Jane Rhodes

For students at a Grade 11 reading level:
- **Brown v. Board of Education: *The Case Against School Segregation,*** by Wayne Anderson

Reading Support From Jamestown Education

- **Timed Readings Plus in Social Studies** helps students increase their reading rate and fluency while maintaining comprehension. The 400-word passages are similar to those found on state and national assessments.

- **Reading in the Content Area: Social Studies** concentrates on six essential reading skills that help students better comprehend what they read. The book includes 75 high-interest nonfiction passages written at increasing levels of difficulty.

- **Reading Social Studies** includes strategic reading instruction and vocabulary support in Social Studies content for both ELLs and native speakers of English.

- **Content Vocabulary Workout** (Grades 6–8) accelerates reading comprehension through focused vocabulary development. Social Studies content vocabulary comes from the glossaries of Glencoe's Middle School Social Studies texts. www.jamestowneducation.com

KEY Teacher Wraparound

Use this key to help you identify the different types of prompts found in the Teacher Wraparound Edition.

R **Reading Strategies** activities help you teach reading skills and vocabulary.

C **Critical Thinking** strategies help students apply and extend what they have learned.

D **Differentiated Instruction** activities provide instruction for students learning to speak English, along with suggestions for teaching various types of learners.

S **Skill Practice** strategies help students practice historical analysis and geography skills.

W **Writing Support** activities provide writing opportunities to help students comprehend the text.

Teaching strategies and activities have been coded for ability level appropriateness.

AL Activities for students working above grade level

OL Activities for students working on grade level

BL Activities for students working below grade level

ELL Activities for English Language Learners

Focus

Why It Matters

Ask: What does it mean when we say, "The judicial branch of government is charged with interpreting the law"? *(To help students realize that the law requires interpretation, remind them of the First Amendment, which says, "Congress shall make no law . . . abridging the freedom of speech . . . .")* **Ask:** Does this mean that we can say anything we want to about someone else? If not, then where is the line drawn? *(The judiciary makes these decisions.)*

More About the Photo

Visual Literacy During the late 1800s, many counties across the country built large, beautiful courthouses, like this one in New Bern, North Carolina. These buildings were important symbols of self-government and the rule of law. The Americans who built them believed their grandeur would help to impress all who entered the courts with the majesty and sovereignty of the law.

Teach

BIG Ideas *As you begin teaching each section, use these questions and activities to help students focus on the Big Ideas.*

Section 1

Civil Cases Ask: Why is it important for the legal system to provide ways for citizens to settle private disputes? If there were no civil courts, how might people try to settle such disputes? *(The legal system provides a safe and orga-nized way for people to settle their disputes. If not for the courts, people may perform rash or irrational actions to "prove" they are right.)* In Section 1, students will learn how the civil courts help to settle disputes between citizens or between a citizen and the government. **OL**

Civil and Criminal Law

CRAVEN
COUNTY
COURT
HOUSE

Why It Matters

When is a legal issue a criminal problem, and when is it a civil problem? Civil law concerns disputes between two or more individuals or between individuals and the government. In criminal law, by contrast, the government charges someone with a crime and is always the prosecutor.

446

Section 2

Criminal Cases Ask: What kinds of crimes harm another person? *(robbery, kidnapping, murder)* What kinds of crimes might be seen as harming society as a whole? *(arson, drug dealing, counterfeiting)* Explain to students that in Section 2 they will learn about criminal law, in which the government can charge a citizen with a crime if a law that harms another person or society as a whole has been broken. **OL**

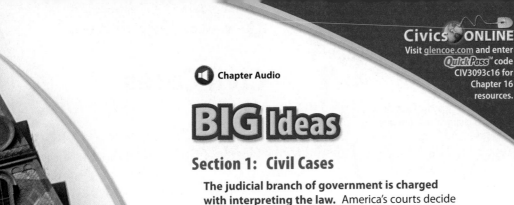

Chapter Audio

Civics ONLINE
Visit glencoe.com and enter
QuickPass™ code
CIV3093c16 for
Chapter 16
resources.

BIG Ideas

Section 1: Civil Cases

The judicial branch of government is charged with interpreting the law. America's courts decide thousands of civil cases each year.

Section 2: Criminal Cases

The Constitution of the United States establishes and protects the individual's fundamental rights and liberties. Thousands of criminal cases each year help define Americans' rights and enforce law and order.

Section 3: Young People and the Courts

The Constitution of the United States establishes and protects the individual's fundamental rights and liberties. A separate legal system, the juvenile justice system, handles the cases of young people in trouble with the law.

Craven County Courthouse, New Bern, North Carolina

FOLDABLES Dinah Zike's
Study Organizer Foldables

Purpose This Foldable helps students to organize and compare information about the procedures of the adult and the juvenile justice systems. The completed Foldable will include a Venn diagram showing procedures unique to each system and procedures shared by both systems. **OL**

More Foldables activities for this chapter can be found in the *Dinah Zike's Reading and Study Skills Foldables* ancillary.

Civics ONLINE
Visit glencoe.com and enter
QuickPass™ code CIV1360c16T for
Chapter 16 resources, including a
Chapter Overview, Study Central™,
Study-to-Go, Student Web Activity,
Self-Check Quiz, and other materials.

FOLDABLES™
Study Organizer

Comparing Foldable Make the following Foldable to help you compare the details and procedures of the juvenile and adult justice systems.

Step 1 Fold a sheet of paper in half from side to side.

Step 2 Fold into thirds. Unfold the paper.

Reading and Writing
As you read the chapter, make notes under each flap about the processes of the different justice systems. Under the flap labeled "both," put anything the two justice systems have in common.

Step 3 Draw intersecting circles on the front as shown. Cut along the fold lines to make three flaps.

Step 4 Label the circles as shown.

Adult Justice System   Both   Juvenile Justice System

Chapter 16   447

Section 3

Young People and the Courts Ask: Why does the legal system treat juvenile offenders differently? *(Juveniles often commit crimes for very different reasons than adults and, thus, need to be treated differently.)* Explain to students that in Section 3 they will learn about the juvenile justice system and ways that young people who are charged with crimes are treated differently than adults. **OL**

Focus

Guide to Reading
Answers to Graphic:

Suit is filed / Defendant responds / Trial / **Civil Lawsuit** / Appeal / Verdict

Section Spotlight Video

To generate student interest and provide a springboard for class discussion, access the Chapter 16, Section 1 video at glencoe.com or on the video DVD.

Resource Manager

Guide to Reading

Big Idea
The judicial branch of government is charged with interpreting the law.

Content Vocabulary
- complaint *(p. 450)*
- summons *(p. 450)*
- discovery *(p. 450)*
- settlement *(p. 450)*

Academic Vocabulary
- file *(p. 449)*
- retain *(p. 450)*
- respond *(p. 450)*

Reading Strategy
Sequencing Use a graphic organizer like the one below to show the steps in a civil lawsuit.

suit is filed / **Civil Lawsuit**

Civil Cases

Real World Civics Would you like to be judged for some wrongdoing by a group of your peers . . . people your own age? Students all over the world see what it is like to be in a court of law by engaging in a mock trial competition in the YMCA Youth and Government program. The mock trials give young people a chance to practice resolving problems in a democratic manner and to learn about the court system. Over 44 teams across the nation compete, along with high school students from Guam, the Marianna Islands, and South Korea.

▼ **Teens argue a mock trial case**

R Reading Strategies	**C** Critical Thinking	**D** Differentiated Instruction	**W** Writing Support	**S** Skill Practice
Teacher Edition • Using Word Parts, p. 449 • Identifying, p. 450 **Additional Resources** • Cont. Vocab., URB p. 43 • Ac. Vocab., URB p. 45 • Guid. Read., URB p. 61	**Teacher Edition** • Det. Cause/Effect, p. 449 • Making Inferences, p. 450 **Additional Resources** • Econ. Act., URB p. 5 • Biographies, URB p. 47 • Quizzes and Tests, p. 189	**Teacher Edition** • English Learners, p. 451 **Additional Resources** • Reteach. Act., URB p. 59	**Teacher Edition** • Expository Writing, p. 451 **Additional Resources** • Authentic Assessment, p. 20	**Teacher Edition** • Analyzing Visuals, p. 450 **Additional Resources** • Chart, Graph, and Map Skills, URB p. 53 • Daily Focus Trans., 16–1 • Pol. Cartoons Trans. 16

TIME

Political Cartoons

AHAAA

NOW, WHAT WERE YOU SAYING ABOUT THE SEAT-BELT LAW BEING SUCH A STUPID IDEA?

STOP

—Chris Britt/Copley News Service

Chris Britt, the creator of this cartoon, is making a comment on laws that require drivers to wear seatbelts.

1. Why might the driver consider the seatbelt law "a stupid idea"?
2. What proves him wrong?
3. Does the cartoonist favor or oppose seat-belt laws?
4. What is your position on seatbelt laws? Explain.

Every year, more than half of all Americans do volunteer work | role in it. One of the responsibilities of citizens is to help make their | of volunteer grou... small. Perha... ... to | dad wh...

Civil Lawsuits

Main Idea Civil lawsuits may involve property disputes, a breach of contract, family matters, or personal injury.

Civics & You The presidential election of 2000 was a disputed election. Read to find out why it ended up in the Supreme Court.

In November 2000, residents of Palm Beach County in Florida **filed,** or registered, a civil lawsuit against the Palm Beach County Canvassing Board, their election authority. The residents argued that a flaw in the ballot format caused them to vote for candidates other than the candidate for whom they intended to vote. This civil suit led to a recounting of votes and reached the Supreme Court. The Court's ruling led to George W. Bush's winning the presidency in 2000.

Why Do People File Civil Suits?

In civil cases the plaintiff—the party bringing a lawsuit—claims to have suffered a loss or injury to themselves and usually seeks damages, an award of money from the defendant. The defendant—the party being sued—argues either that the loss or injury did not occur or that the defendant is not responsible for it. The court's job is to provide a place to resolve the differences between the plaintiff and the defendant.

Courts hear many different kinds of civil lawsuits. Lawsuits may involve property disputes, breaches of contract, or family matters involving two or more parties. Many lawsuits deal with negligence, or personal injury. A negligence suit is filed when someone has been injured or killed or when property has been destroyed because someone else has been careless, or negligent.

✓ Reading Check Identifying Who is the plaintiff in a civil lawsuit?

Chapter 16   449

Teach

R Reading Strategy

Using Word Parts To help students understand the terms "plaintiff" and "defendant," have them look up those terms in a dictionary that includes word derivations. *(The root of "plaintiff" is Old French, "plaintif"—aggrieved or injured. The root of "defendant" is from the Latin, "defendere"—to ward off.)* **AL**

C Critical Thinking

Determining Cause and Effect Ask: What might cause a person to file a civil lawsuit? *(an accident or injury in which there was negligence or because of a property, family, or contract dipute)* **OL**

TIME Political Cartoons

1. Students may say that the driver didn't think the government should tell people what to do.
2. He is thrown through the windshield as a result of an accident.
3. The cartoonist favors seatbelt laws.
4. Answers will vary. Students should give reasons for their positions.

✓ Reading Check Answer: the person who brings, or starts, the suit and seeks damages for some wrongdoing

Differentiated Instruction

Interpreting a Diagram

CHART, GRAPH, AND MAP SKILLS ACTIVITY 16

Interpreting a Diagram

Civil Lawsuit

Objective: To understand the steps of and impacts of civil lawsuits

Focus: Have students identify the format of the diagram on page 53.

Teach: Discuss how to read the diagram.

Assess: Have students interpret the diagram on page 54.

Close: Discuss the impact of landmark rulings.

Chart, Graph, and Map Skills Activity 16, URB pp. 53–54

Differentiated Instruction Strategies

BL Read the diagram aloud. Tell what "process of discovery" means.

AL Explain how civil lawsuits can find defendants guilty of crimes for which they had been acquitted in criminal proceedings.

ELL Define "arbitration," "process of discovery," and "verdict." Write a sentence for each word.

R   Reading Strategy

Identifying **Ask:** What are some examples of discoveries? *(scientific or geographic evidence)* **Ask:** Why is the process during which lawyers for each side seek information called "discovery"? *(They can check facts, gather evidence, and interview witnesses.)* **OL**

C   Critical Thinking

Making Inferences **Ask:** What makes a case weak or strong? *(Answers should indicate an understanding that a strong case means the other side was clearly at fault.)* **OL**

S   Skill Practice

Analyzing Visuals **Ask:** Why do some of the arrows on the chart go both ways? *(to indicate communication back and forth between attorneys on a case)* **OL**

Analyzing Charts

Answers:
1. The plaintiff's attorney files a complaint.
2. Attorneys for both sides argue cases in court.

Hands-On Chapter Project
Step 1

Understanding the Legal System

Step 1: Persuasive Writing Students will learn more about the different aspects of the legal system of the United States by writing complaints and answers.

Directions: Organize the class into groups of four. Have pairs of students work together

The Process in a Civil Case

Main Idea Civil lawsuits follow a specified legal procedure.

Civics & You Despite what you see on TV, lawsuits do not always end up dramatically in court. Read to find out what happens to most of them.

Let us look at how a lawsuit proceeds through the court system. Suppose you are riding in a city bus one day and suffer head injuries and a broken arm when the bus is in an accident. You decide to file a lawsuit against the city to recover the costs of hospital and doctor bills, lost income from days missed at work, and other expenses. You become the plaintiff, or person filing the lawsuit. The party you are suing, in this case the city, is the defendant.

Bringing Suit

You start the process by **retaining,** or hiring, a lawyer, who files a **complaint** with the court. The complaint is a statement naming the plaintiff and the defendant and describing the lawsuit. The court sends the defendant (the city) a **summons,** a document that announces that the defendant is being sued, and sets a date and time for an appearance in court.

The Defendant's Response The defendant's attorneys may **respond,** or react, to the charges by filing an "answer" to the complaint. The answer will either admit to the charges or offer reasons the defendant is not responsible for the injuries the plaintiff is claiming. The complaint and the answer together are referred to as pleadings. Before going to trial, the lawyers on each side have an opportunity to check facts and to gather evidence by questioning the other party and possible witnesses. This process is called **discovery.**

Civil Cases   **Charts In MOtion** See StudentWorks™ Plus or glencoe.com

1. Plaintiff's attorney files a complaint
2. Court sends a summons to defendant
3. Defendant's attorney files a written answer
4. Attorneys for both sides exchange pleadings documents
5. Attorneys for plaintiff and defendant argue cases in court
6. Court gives a verdict

Analyzing Charts

1. **Explaining** What action starts the process of a civil suit?
2. **Describing** What is the last step in the civil case procedure before the court gives a verdict?

Pretrial Hearing Before the trial, the judge might call a conference to help clarify differences between the two sides. At this stage you and your lawyer might decide that your case looks weak, and you may want to drop the suit. Or the city may conclude that your case is very strong and that you are likely to win your suit. The city may, therefore, offer you a **settlement,** in which the parties agree on an amount of money that the defendant will pay to the plaintiff.

Another way to resolve disputes is by a process called mediation. During mediation, each side is given the opportunity to explain

to search for information on the Internet or in the print media about a civil case they find interesting. Have them provide two copies of all the information they find. Pairs should continue working in their groups of four to write both the plaintiff's complaint in their case or to write the defendant's response, or answer.

Class discussion: Have a volunteer from each group read the documents aloud to the class. Lead a discussion of the strong and weak points of each party's case. **OL**

(Project continued in Section 2)

its side of the dispute and must listen to the other side. A trained mediator helps the two sides find a solution.

The two sides may also agree to submit their dispute to arbitration. This is a process conducted by a professional arbitrator who acts somewhat like a judge by reviewing the case and resolving the dispute.

Most civil cases are settled before trial. Because trials are time-consuming and expensive, all the major participants—the defendant, the insurer, the plaintiff, the judge, and the attorneys—are likely to prefer a settlement.

Trial

If the parties do not reach a settlement, the case goes to trial. There may be a jury, or more likely, a judge who will hear the case alone. Both sides present their cases.

In criminal trials the prosecution must prove the defendant guilty "beyond a reasonable doubt." In a civil case the plaintiff has to present only a "preponderance of evidence"—enough to convince the judge or jury that the defendant *more likely than not* was responsible for the incident that caused the damages or injury.

After all evidence has been presented, the judge or jury considers the case and decides on a verdict, or decision, in favor of one party. If the plaintiff wins, a remedy is set. In the case of the bus accident, the remedy might be for the defendant—the city—to pay your medical costs, replace your lost earnings, and compensate you for your pain and suffering with a cash payment. If the defendant wins, the plaintiff—you—gets nothing and must pay court costs for both sides of the lawsuit.

Appeal If the losing side believes the judge made errors during the trial or that some other type of injustice took place, it may appeal the verdict to a higher court. Remember that in the hierarchy of the court system, each district has Courts of Appeals to hear local disputes of this nature. In cases in which the plaintiff wins a large cash award, the defendant or the defendant's insurance company often appeals to have the award reduced. As a result, a winning plaintiff may have to wait years before seeing any of the money the court awarded or, depending on the outcome of the appeals, may end up with nothing.

✓ **Reading Check** Explaining When can the defendant appeal a verdict of a civil lawsuit?

Section 1 Review

Vocabulary

1. **Write** complete sentences using each of the following terms: *complaint, summons, discovery, settlement.*

Main Ideas

2. **Describing** In civil cases, what is the plaintiff usually seeking?

3. **Identifying** What is the purpose of the discovery phase of a civil trial?

Critical Thinking

4. **BIG Ideas** In your opinion, should civil cases be tried before a jury? Why or why not?

5. **Sequencing** Use a graphic organizer similar to the one below to summarize the reasons that most civil cases are settled before trial.

CITIZENSHIP Activity

6. **Expository Writing** Find a newspaper story about a civil lawsuit. Write a summary about the nature of the dispute and the way the lawsuit was resolved. Use the information in this section to make sure the details of your summary are accurate.

Civics ONLINE

Study Central™ To review this section, go to glencoe.com.

D ## Differentiated Instruction

English Learners   Ask: What does "more likely than not" mean when trying to prove a defendant's fault? *(It means that the defendant probably is at fault.)* **ELL**

W ## Writing Support

Expository Writing Have students write a paragraph explaining why the law would force the plaintiff to pay court costs if he/she loses the case. Include a benefit and a drawback to this requirement. **OL**

✓ **Reading Check   Answer:** A defendant can appeal the verdict in a civil lawsuit if the judge made errors in the trial or if an injustice occurred.

Assess

Civics ONLINE

Study Central™ provides summaries, interactive games, and online graphic organizers to help students review content.

Close

Narrative Have students write an account of an imaginary civil suit, as the plaintiff or the defendant. **OL**

Section 1 Review

Answers

1. Sentences should use vocabulary words according to their definitions in the section and in the Glossary.

2. The plaintiff usually seeks a cash award.

3. The purpose of discovery is to allow each side to check facts, to secure evidence, and to question the other party and possible witnesses.

4. Responses will vary. Some students may feel a civil trial would receive a fair result from a jury; others may feel it would be better to have a judge decide the outcome.

5. The graphic should show the following three reasons that cases are often settled before trial: mediation, arbitration, or settlement.

6. Students may find a wide variety of newspaper stories. Make sure that their summaries reflect an accurate understanding of the legal process in civil cases.

Focus

Bellringer
Daily Focus Transparency 16–2

Guide to Reading
Answers to Graphic:

1. hearing
2. arraignment
3. trial
4. verdict
5. sentencing

Section Spotlight Video

To generate student interest and provide a springboard for class discussion, access the Chapter 16, Section 2 video at glencoe.com or on the video DVD.

Resource Manager

Guide to Reading

Big Idea
The Constitution of the United States establishes and protects the individual's fundamental rights and liberties.

Content Vocabulary
- prosecution *(p. 453)*
- crime *(p. 453)*
- penal code *(p. 453)*
- parole *(p. 454)*
- mandatory sentencing *(p. 454)*
- arraignment *(p. 456)*
- testimony *(p. 457)*
- cross-examine *(p. 457)*
- acquittal *(p. 458)*
- hung jury *(p. 458)*

Academic Vocabulary
- function *(p. 453)*
- confine *(p. 453)*
- sufficient *(p. 456)*

Reading Strategy
Sequencing Outline the procedures that take place in a criminal case after an arrest is made.

1. hearing
2.
3.
4.
5.

Section 2

Criminal Cases

Real World Civics Those serving time in prison do not have a lot of choices, but most can get their high school diplomas if they take courses offered. Almost half the inmates in state prisons do not have a high school degree. These Arkansas prisoners received their GED diplomas through a tutoring program provided by the state prison system. Why is this an important service for the state governments to provide?

▼ **Inmates achieve high school graduation**

R Reading Strategies	**C** Critical Thinking	**D** Differentiated Instruction	**W** Writing Support	**S** Skill Practice
Teacher Edition • Skimming, p. 453 • Act. Prior Know., p. 456 • Using Word Parts, p. 456 **Additional Resources** • Pri. Source Read., URB p. 15 • Cont. Vocab., URB p. 43 • Ac. Vocab., URB p. 45 • Guid. Read., URB p. 62	**Teacher Edition** • Drawing Conclusions, pp. 453, 454 • Comparing, p. 457 **Additional Resources** • Biographies, URB p. 47 • Crit. Think., URB p. 51 • Quizzes and Tests, p. 190	**Teacher Edition** • Verbal/Linguistic, p. 457 • Interpersonal, p. 458 **Additional Resources** • Diff. Instr., URB p. 55 • School-to-Home Conn., URB p. 57 • Reteach Act., URB p. 59	**Teacher Edition** • Personal Writing, p. 455 • Expository Writing, p. 455 **Additional Resources** • Writing Skills Act., URB p. 49 • Authentic Assessment, p. 20	**Teacher Edition** • Analyzing Graphs, p. 454 **Additional Resources** • Daily Focus Trans., 16–2

What Is a Criminal Case?

Main Idea In criminal cases, defendants are charged with crimes, and if convicted, they are sentenced as punishment.

Civics & You Have you ever received a punishment for something you did? Read to find out how society deals with punishment.

Criminal law cases are those in which the state or federal government charges someone with a crime. The government is always the prosecution—the party who starts the legal proceedings against another party for a violation of the law. The person accused of the crime is the defendant. A **crime** is an act that breaks a federal or state criminal law and causes harm to people or society.

The Criminal Justice System The state and federal courts, judges, lawyers, police, and prisons that have the responsibility for enforcing criminal law make up the criminal justice system. There is a separate juvenile justice system with special rules and procedures for handling cases dealing with juveniles, who in most states are people under the age of 18. You will read about the juvenile justice system in Section 3.

The Penal Code Crimes are defined in each state's written criminal laws, called the penal code. A state's penal code also spells out the punishments that go with each crime. In general, the more serious the crime, the harsher the punishment will be. The federal government also has a penal code that defines federal crimes such as income tax evasion, kidnapping, and drug smuggling.

Types of Crime

Persons convicted of misdemeanors may be fined or sentenced to one year or less in jail. Some misdemeanors, such as illegal gambling, are considered victimless crimes—no

one individual has been harmed, and often no direct punishment is enacted. Serious crimes, such as burglary, kidnapping, arson, manslaughter, and murder, are considered felonies. These crimes are punishable by imprisonment for a year or more. In the case of murder, the punishment could be death.

People convicted of felonies may also lose certain civil rights such as the right to vote, possess a firearm, and serve on a jury. Further, they may lose employment opportunities in some careers such as the military, law, teaching, and law enforcement.

Misdemeanors may sometimes be treated as felonies. Drunk driving, for example, is often a misdemeanor. However, if a person has been arrested for drunk driving before and has been convicted of the same offense, that person may be charged with a felony.

Penalties for Crimes

Criminal penalties serve several **functions,** or purposes. They provide punishment so that a criminal pays for an offense. They help protect society by keeping dangerous lawbreakers **confined,** or enclosed, in prison. Criminal penalties can also keep other people from committing the same crimes by serving as warnings to deter others.

GPS Global Positioning Systems, electronic devices such as the one being attached below, monitor those under house arrest and are often attached to the ankle. *Speculating* **What kinds of crimes are punished by this method?**

453

Activity: Interdisciplinary Connection

Law Have an attorney or an American history teacher visit your classroom and talk with students about how laws have changed over the course of our nation's history. Some examples of laws that have changed might include immigration laws; laws that restricted voting, such as the poll tax; Prohibition; drunk driving laws; the juvenile justice system; divorce and child custody laws;

laws that allowed people to buy their way out of the draft; laws that segregated or allowed segregation of citizens by race or gender; and so on.

If time permits, have students choose one of these areas and write a report about how laws and attitudes have changed based on library or Internet research. **OL**

S Skill Practice

Analyzing Graphs Ask: Based on this map and bar graph, rank the regions of the country, from highest violent crime rate to lowest. *(the South, the West, the Midwest, the Northeast)* **Ask:** What crimes would not be called either property crimes or violent crimes? *(underage drinking, drug dealing)* **AL**

C Critical Thinking

Drawing Conclusions Ask: Because of the growing support for mandatory sentencing laws that strip judges and parole boards of the power to make sentences lighter, what can you conclude about jails and prisons? *(They are filled to capacity or overflowing.)* **OL**

Analyzing Graphs and Maps

Answers:

1. The highest property crime rate is in the South.
2. The Northeast and the Midwest probably have similar violent crime rates because of a similarity in populations.

Differentiated Instruction

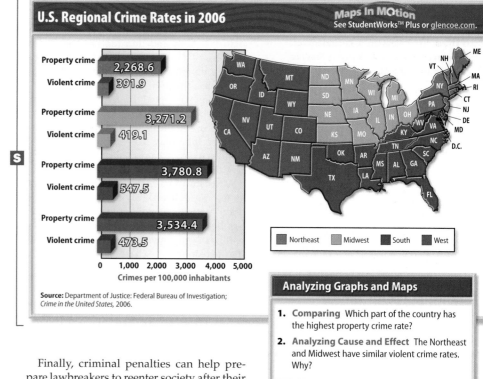

U.S. Regional Crime Rates in 2006

Maps In MOtion
See StudentWorks™ Plus or glencoe.com.

Property crime 2,268.6
Violent crime 391.9
Property crime 3,271.2
Violent crime 419.1
Property crime 3,780.8
Violent crime 547.5
Property crime 3,534.4
Violent crime 473.5

0 1,000 2,000 3,000 4,000 5,000
Crimes per 100,000 inhabitants

■ Northeast ■ Midwest ■ South ■ West

Source: Department of Justice: Federal Bureau of Investigation; *Crime in the United States, 2006.*

Analyzing Graphs and Maps

1. **Comparing** Which part of the country has the highest property crime rate?
2. **Analyzing Cause and Effect** The Northeast and Midwest have similar violent crime rates. Why?

Finally, criminal penalties can help prepare lawbreakers to reenter society after their prison terms have ended. Through counseling, education, and job training, some prisons help inmates learn skills that will help them lead productive, noncriminal lives after prison. Some prisons even support money-making businesses from inmate-made items prisoners have been trained to produce.

Sentencing Determining the sentence, or punishment, of a person convicted of a crime is one of the more complicated and difficult aspects of the criminal justice system. Because the circumstances in each case are different, judges may hand down very different sentences for similar crimes.

In the past, many states used a system of indeterminate sentences in penalizing criminals. An indeterminate sentence is one in which a judge gives a minimum and maximum sentence.

Some prisoners become eligible for **parole** after serving part of their sentences. A parole board decides whether or not to grant a prisoner early release from prison. If parole is granted, the person must report to a parole officer until the sentence expires.

Mandatory Sentencing Critics of the parole system claim that many sentences end up much shorter than intended. In answer to this criticism, some states have established **mandatory sentencing,** which means that judges must impose whatever sentence the law directs. Opponents of mandatory sentencing, though, claim that in some cases, the judge should be able to impose harsher sentences than the law directs.

Distinguishing Relevant from Irrelevant Information

Objective:	To determine important parts of a police report
Focus:	Students learn to distinguish relevant from irrelevant information.
Teach:	On the board, list the details under the headings "Relevant" and "Irrelevant."
Assess:	Have students cite the most important details from the report.
Close:	Have students explain why these details are relevant.

**Critical Thinking Skills Activity 16,
URB pp. 51–52**

Differentiated Instruction Strategies

BL Tell where the car was stolen and how you know that information.

AL Explain what information on the police report a prosecuting attorney would find most essential. Explain your reasoning.

ELL Tell what "dispatch," "event location," and "vehicle" mean. Write a sentence for each word.

Sentencing Options Judges follow basic sentencing options (from least serious to most serious): suspended sentence—a sentence is given but not served at that time; probation—the defendant has supervised release; home confinement—defendant is required to serve his or her sentence at home, closely monitored; a monetary fine—damages are paid; restitution—the defendant is required W1 to pay back or make up for damages; work release—the defendant is allowed to work but must return to prison at night and on weekends; imprisonment—the defendant is confined to an institution to serve the sentence; death—the defendant is sentenced to die for his or her crime in the state where this is mandated.

Many states are giving judges more sentencing options. Among these are shock incarceration, intensive-supervision probation or parole, and house arrest. Shock incarceration involves shorter sentences in a highly structured environment where offenders participate in work, community service, education, and counseling. W2

Intensive-supervision probation or parole keeps high-risk offenders in the community but remaining under close supervision that involves frequent home visits or even nightly curfew checks. The offender often wears an electronic device that continually signals his or her location. A related alternative sentence is house arrest, which requires an offender to stay at home except for certain functions the court permits.

✓ **Reading Check** **Explaining** Why have some states established mandatory sentencing?

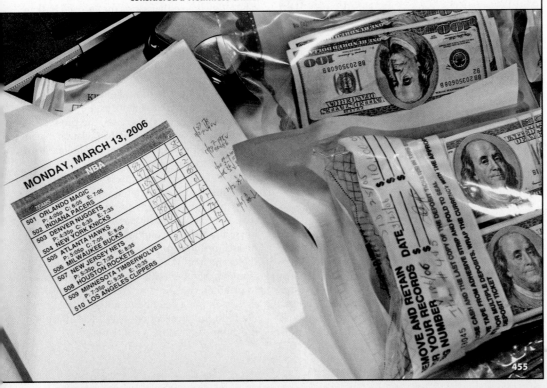

Criminal Evidence Brooklyn, New York, authorities collected evidence of criminal gambling activities that will be presented in court. **Explaining** Why is illegal gambling considered a victimless crime?

Activity: Economics Connection

Making Connections **Ask:** Why are judges permitted so many sentencing options that do not include prison time? Explain to students that one important reason is the economics of incarceration. It is very expensive to operate a prison and to provide food, clothes, and a safe and secure environment for prisoners. Tell students that the U.S. has the highest incarceration rate in the world and, in many states, "corrections" expenditures have become the single largest item in the budget.

Organize the class into three groups. Ask one group to research and report on each of the following: (1) causes of growing prison costs, (2) efforts that are being made to reduce costs, and (3) recommendations to keep prison costs affordable for state and federal governments.

Have groups present their findings to the class in the form of oral reports. **OL**

R₁ **Reading Strategy**

Activating Prior Knowledge **Ask:** What parts of the Bill of Rights address issues related to criminal procedure? *(the 1st, 4th, 5th, 6th, and 8th Amendments.)* **OL**

R₂ **Reading Strategy**

Using Word Parts The terms "indictment" and "arraignment" may be unfamiliar to many students. To help them understand these terms, have them look for each term in a dictionary that gives word origins. *("Arraignment" comes from the Latin adrationare, to call to account. "Indictment" comes from Middle English enditen, to accuse.)* **OL**

Caption Answer:

Police have databases of fingerprints to which each arrested person's fingerprints are added. Fingerprints are matched to others that have been discovered at crime scenes or belong to those arrested for other crimes.

Criminal Case Procedure

Main Idea Criminal cases follow several steps, including arrest, hearing, indictment, arraignment, verdict, sentencing, and appeal.

Civics & You Do you ever have trouble making up your mind? Read to find out what happens when a jury in a criminal trial has this problem.

R₁ **Y**ou learned earlier that the criminal justice system has the responsibility for enforcing criminal law. Criminal cases follow several steps. At each step defendants are entitled to the protections of due process guaranteed in the Bill of Rights.

Fingerprinting Once a criminal suspect is arrested, fingerprints and photographs of them are taken. *Analyzing* Why do the police take fingerprints and what do you think they use the fingerprints for?

Arrest

Criminal cases begin when police or other law enforcement officers arrest a person on suspicion of having committed a crime. Officers make arrests if they have witnessed a suspected crime, if a citizen has made a complaint or a report of a crime, or if a judge has issued an arrest warrant. When they make the arrest, the officers are required to read the suspect his or her Miranda rights, which you learned about in Chapter 15.

The suspect is taken to a local police station and booked, or charged with a crime. As part of the booking process, the police fingerprint and photograph the suspect. During that time he or she is allowed to call a lawyer. If the suspect cannot afford a lawyer, the state must provide one.

Hearing, Indictment, and Arraignment

A few hours after being booked, the suspect appears in court and is informed of the charges against him or her. At this time the prosecution must show the judge that there is probable cause—a good reason—for believing the accused committed the crime. The judge then either sends the accused back to jail, sets bail, or releases the accused on his or her own recognizance, or control.

As noted in Chapter 15, in federal courts and many state courts, grand juries decide whether a person should be indicted—formally charged with a crime. Some states use a preliminary hearing instead of a grand jury indictment. In some cases, the prosecutor files an "information," which claims that there is **sufficient,** or enough, evidence to bring the accused person to trial.

R₂ The defendant then appears in court for a procedure called an **arraignment.** He or she is formally presented with the charges and asked to enter a plea. If the defendant pleads not guilty, the case continues. If the defendant pleads guilty, he or she stands convicted of the crime, and the judge determines a punishment. Another option is for the defendant to plead no contest. A no contest plea means that he or she does not admit guilt but will not fight the prosecution's case. The effect is much the same as for a guilty plea.

Differentiated Instruction

Leveled Activities

BL Writing Skills Activity 16, URB pp. 49–50

OL Crit. Think. Skills Act. 16, URB pp. 51–52

AL Primary Source Reading 5A, URB pp. 15–16

ELL Content Vocabulary Activity 16, URB p. 43

Trial

If the case goes to trial, the defense lawyer interviews witnesses, studies the laws affecting the case, and gathers information. Although criminal defendants have a constitutional right to a jury trial, many give up that right and have their cases tried before a judge alone in what is called a bench trial.

If the defense asks for a jury trial, the first step when the trial starts is to choose the jurors. Both sides select potential jurors from a large pool of residents within the court's jurisdiction. In most states, residents are called randomly for jury duty. A specific excuse or acceptable reason must be presented for a person to be excused from jury duty. Both sides try to avoid jurors who might be unfavorable to their side. Either side can reject a certain number of jury candidates without giving reasons and can ask the judge to dismiss others for various causes.

Presenting the Case After the jury has been selected, the lawyers for each side make opening statements in which they outline the cases they will present. The prosecution and defense then present their cases in turn. Each side calls witnesses who swear that their **testimony**—the answers they give while under oath—will be "the truth, the whole truth, and nothing but the truth."

After a witness testifies for one side, the other side is allowed to **cross-examine.** The questions asked in cross-examination are meant to clarify testimony but are usually designed to make the witness's original testimony appear unreliable or untrue. Finally, each side makes a closing statement highlighting the testimony and evidence that support it and questioning the other side's testimony and evidence. The judge then "instructs" the jury, or explains the law that relates to the case.

Civics ONLINE

Student Web Activity Visit glencoe.com and complete the Chapter 16 Web Activity.

Criminal Cases Charts In MOtion
See StudentWorks™ Plus or glencoe.com.

Arrest
- Police arrest and book a suspect

Preliminary Hearing
- Suspect appears before a judge
- Bail is set

Indictment
- Grand jury (or judge) hears evidence and formally charges the suspect with the crime

Arraignment

- Defendant pleads not guilty
- Trial date is set

- Defendant pleads guilty and accepts a plea bargain

Trial
- Prosecution and defense present cases to jury (or judge)
- Jury (or judge) reaches verdict

Acquittal
- Defendant found not guilty and goes free

Sentencing
- Defendant found guilty
- Judge sentences defendant

Analyzing Charts

1. **Explaining** What is the purpose of a preliminary hearing?
2. **Describing** What are two possible outcomes of an arraignment?

C Critical Thinking

Comparing Ask: What is the difference between a jury trial and a bench trial? *(A jury trial has 12 people deciding a case; a bench trial has only the judge.)* **BL**

D Differentiated Instruction

Verbal/Linguistic Ask: How does repetition in the oath "Do you swear to tell the truth, the whole truth, and nothing but the truth" add to its meaning? *(The repetition of "truth" emphasizes its importance.)* **ELL**

Civics ONLINE

Objectives and answers to the **Student Web Activity** can be found at glencoe.com under the Web Activity Lesson Plan for this chapter.

Analyzing Charts

Answer:
1. prosecutor must show judge probable cause to believe the accused person committed the crime
2. defendant pleads "guilty" and is sentenced or "not guilty" and the case continues

Hands-On Chapter Project
Step 2

Understand the Legal System

Step 2: Mock Trial Ask students to choose a criminal case (use the "Landmark Supreme Court Cases" feature on page 459 of the student text or have students find another case on the Internet). Have them break into groups and write skits that show each phase of the procedures in a criminal case after the arrest and booking: hearing, arraignment, trial, verdict, and sentencing.

Directions: Have students volunteer to play each of the roles they have written and enact the skits, in chronological order, to show the process of a criminal trial. Tell the "audience" to watch for any inaccuracies based on what they have learned in Section 2 and to discuss these as a group after the presentations. **OL**

(Project continued in Section 3)

Section 2 Review

D Differentiated Instruction

Interpersonal Have students reread the factors a judge takes into account when sentencing: the defendant's family situation, criminal record, employment, and victim statements. **Ask:** How might these factors affect the severity of the sentence? *(The judge can give a severe sentence if the defendant has been in trouble before or a lighter sentence if there is family need or a first offense.)* **BL**

✔Reading Check Answer: The judge usually decides the sentence or takes jury recommendations.

Assess

Civics ONLINE

Study Central™ provides summaries, interactive games, and online graphic organizers to help students review.

Close

Outlining Have students review this section by outlining its contents. **OL**

Section 2 Review

The Verdict, Sentencing, and Appeal

After the judge gives the jury a set of instructions, the jury goes to the jury room to discuss the case and reach a verdict. After choosing a foreperson to lead the discussion, the jurors review the evidence and legal arguments. Jury deliberations are secret and have no set time limit. Finally, the jurors vote on whether the defendant is guilty or not guilty. To decide that a person is guilty, the jury must find the evidence convincing "beyond a reasonable doubt." In nearly all criminal cases, the verdict must be unanimous. If a jury feels the prosecution has not proven its case, it can decide on acquittal. **Acquittal** is a vote of not guilty, after which the defendant is immediately released.

Sometimes a jury cannot agree on a verdict, even after many votes. Then the judge declares a **hung jury** and rules the trial a mistrial. With a mistrial, the prosecution must decide whether to ask for a retrial.

Sentencing If a defendant is found guilty, the judge sets a court date for sentencing. In some cases, a jury recommends a sentence. More often, however, the judge decides on the sentence after considering the defendant's family situation, previous criminal record, employment status, and other information. Sentences often specify a period of time to be spent in prison. Victims of the crime are often allowed to make statements about the sentence, and judges may take those statements into account. Sentences may include a variety of options as discussed earlier in this chapter.

Appeal If the defendant is found guilty, the defense may, and often does, appeal the verdict to a higher court. (If the case is a capital case, or one involving the death penalty, the appeal could go directly to the state supreme court.) Usually an appeal contends that the judge made errors or that the defendant's constitutional rights were violated.

✔Reading Check Explaining If a defendant is found guilty, who or what decides his or her sentence?

Section 2 Review

Vocabulary

1. **Write** a paragraph using six of the following key terms in a paragraph that relates to criminal cases: *prosecution, crime, penal code, parole, mandatory sentencing, arraignment, testimony, cross-examine, acquittal, hung jury.*

Main Ideas

2. **Describing** What is included in a state's penal code?

3. **Identifying** What are the seven basic steps in a criminal case?

Critical Thinking

4. **Concluding** Why do you think judges allow some suspects to be released on their own recognizance?

5. **BIG Ideas** Using a graphic organizer like the one below, list the major participants in a trial.

Trial Participants — defendant

6. **Analyzing Visuals** Review the crime rate map/graph on page 454. How does your region compare with others?

CITIZENSHIP Activity

7. **Persuasive Writing** Should judges be allowed to hand down sentences based on the characteristics of individual cases and defendants, or should they follow mandatory sentencing guidelines? Write a newspaper editorial on the subject.

Civics ONLINE

Study Central™ To review this section, go to glencoe.com.

Answers

1. Paragraphs should use vocabulary words according to their definitions in the section and in the Glossary.

2. A penal code sets out the state or federal criminal laws and the punishments that go with each crime.

3. The seven steps are arrest; hearing, or indictment; arraignment; trial; verdict; sentencing; and appeal.

4. Student answers may vary but may include the idea that people are innocent until proven guilty, and if the defendant is not likely to flee or commit other crimes while waiting for trial, there is no justification for charging bail or locking him or her up.

5. This web diagram should be identical to the one in the student text, with arms labeled: defendant, judge, prosecutor, jury.

6. Students' answers will vary based on region.

7. Editorials should supply reasoning that supports their positions.

LANDMARK SUPREME COURT CASE STUDIES

Gideon v. Wainwright

In the 1930s, the Supreme Court ruled that the Sixth Amendment requires the government to supply lawyers for defendants who cannot otherwise afford one in all federal cases. How did poor defendants acquire Sixth Amendment rights in state courts?

Background of the Case

In 1942 the Supreme Court, in *Betts* v. *Brady,* ruled that the Sixth Amendment did not require states to appoint attorneys for people who could not afford them. By way of the Fourteenth Amendment, however, it held that states were required to supply lawyers in cases that held the death penalty.

In June 1961, Clarence Earl Gideon of Florida was accused of theft, a nondeath-penalty crime. Gideon mistakenly believed the Supreme Court had entitled him to court-appointed counsel and so asked for a lawyer. His request was denied, so Gideon defended himself in an intelligent but inadequate manner. The jury found him guilty and the judge sentenced him to five years in prison.

Clarence Earl Gideon

Gideon appealed his conviction claiming, "I knew the Constitution guaranteed me a fair trial, but I didn't see how a man could get one without a lawyer to defend him." The state supreme court refused to review Gideon's case. Gideon appealed his case to the U. S. Supreme Court.

The Supreme Court heard the case after Gideon sent his own petition claiming his Sixth and Fourteenth Amendment rights were violated. Because only lawyers may speak before the Supreme Court, a Washington, D.C., attorney was appointed for Gideon. A Florida lawyer represented Louie Wainwright, head of the state's prisons.

The Decision

The Supreme Court's ruling came on March 18, 1963. Justice Hugo L. Black wrote the unanimous decision:

> ❝ *We accept* Betts *v.* Brady's *assumption . . . that a provision of the Bill of Rights which is 'fundamental and essential to a fair trial' is made obligatory upon the States by the Fourteenth Amendment. We think the Court in* Betts *was wrong, however, in concluding that the Sixth Amendment's guarantee of counsel is not one of these fundamental rights. . . . [A]ny person hauled into court, who is too poor to hire a lawyer, cannot be assured a fair trial unless counsel is provided for him.* ❞

—Justice Hugo L. Black

The Court thus overturned *Betts*. Under the "due process" clause of the Fourteenth Amendment, it found the Sixth Amendment guarantee of counsel binding on state as well as federal courts.

Why It Matters

Although some states by 1963 already had court-appointed lawyers in nondeath-penalty cases, the *Gideon* decision assured this protection for all. Gideon was retried and found not guilty.

Analyzing the Court Decision

1. **Explaining** What protection did the *Gideon* decision guarantee?
2. **Describing** How would you summarize the importance of the decision?

Teach

The decision in *Gideon* v. *Wainwright* was made by the Warren Court as part of a series of dramatic decisions that changed everyday life in the U.S. and moved social institutions in a more liberal direction. Many liberals and civil libertarians hailed these decisions as closing an unjust gap between the rights of the majority and the rights of the poor and minorities. But many other Americans believed that the Supreme Court was overstepping its proper role. The debate over the legacy of the Warren Court continues to this day.

ANALYZING THE COURT DECISION

Answers:
1. The decision in *Gideon* guaranteed that all defendants would have legal counsel.
2. The case was important because poor people, who had sometimes been wrongly convicted because they could not afford to hire a lawyer, were for the first time guaranteed legal representation in all the nation's courts.

Additional Support

Background

Gideon v. Wainwright In his first trial, in which Gideon was denied legal representation and had to defend himself, one piece of testimony that was damaging to him was from a taxi driver who had picked up Gideon at the pool hall on the night of the break-in. He testified that Gideon had said to him, "Don't tell anyone you picked me up."

When this same taxi driver was questioned at Gideon's second trial, Gideon's lawyer asked the driver whether Gideon had ever made the same request of him at other times. The driver said yes, Gideon always made the same request. Point out how different the driver's testimony looks once you know that Gideon said the same thing every time he took a cab.

Ask: What problems might a person have in trying to defend himself or herself in court? (*A defendant may not know about proper court procedures, legal precedents, or the importance of various pieces of evidence.*) **OL**

Focus

Bellringer
Daily Focus Transparency 16–3

Guide to Reading
Answers to Graphic:

Section Spotlight Video

To generate student interest and provide a springboard for class discussion, access the Chapter 16, Section 3 video at glencoe.com or on the video DVD.

Resource Manager

Guide to Reading

Big Idea
The Constitution of the United States establishes and protects the individual's fundamental rights and liberties.

Content Vocabulary
- juvenile *(p. 461)*
- juvenile delinquent *(p. 461)*
- rehabilitate *(p. 462)*

Academic Vocabulary
- emphasis *(p. 463)*
- preliminary *(p. 463)*
- equivalent *(p. 463)*

Reading Strategy
Summarizing Judges have options when sentencing juvenile offenders. List these options in a graphic organizer like the one below.

 Section Audio   **Spotlight Video**

Young People and the Courts

Citizens in Action California Youth Authority Juvenile boot camps are one approach to the problem of dealing with teens in trouble. Sent to a boot camp as the result of a court decision, teens here are taught techniques for managing anger and receive treatment for emotional problems. This alternative sentence is meant to help teens who need counseling and education as well as discipline. They are called boot camps due to their similarity to military organizations.

▼ **Juvenile offenders line up at California boot camp**

R Reading Strategies	**C** Critical Thinking	**D** Differentiated Instruction	**W** Writing Support	**S** Skill Practice
Teacher Edition • Identifying, pp. 461, 462 • Outlining, p. 463 **Additional Resources** • Cont. Vocab., URB p. 43 • Ac. Vocab., URB p. 45 • Guid. Read., URB p. 63 • RENTG, p. 156	**Teacher Edition** • Compare/Contrast, p. 463 • Ident. Cent. Issues, p. 464 **Additional Resources** • Biographies, URB p. 47 • Quizzes and Tests, p. 191	**Teacher Edition** • English Learners, p. 462 **Additional Resources** • Reteach. Act., URB p. 59 • Graphic Novel, p. 69	**Teacher Edition** • Expository Writing, p. 463 **Additional Resources** • Authentic Assessment, p. 20	**Teacher Edition** • Assessing Value, p. 461 **Additional Resources** • Daily Focus Trans., 16–3

Causes of Juvenile Delinquency

Main Idea All states and the federal government have a separate justice system for young people.

Civics & You Have you heard the term *juvenile delinquent*? Read to find out what this term means.

Every state establishes a certain age at which people are considered adults in the eyes of the criminal justice system. Anyone under that age—18 in most states—is considered a **juvenile**. Our system treats young people who commit crimes—called **juvenile delinquents**—somewhat differently from adults. All states and the federal government, however, allow older juveniles who are charged with very serious crimes or already have criminal records to be tried as adults.

This treatment of juveniles was not always the case historically. Even in the late 1800s children were thrown into jail with adults. Long prison terms and physical punishment—such as striking the individual—were common for children and adults, often for crimes we consider minor today.

Children and teenagers currently commit many crimes each year. Some of these crimes are misdemeanors, such as shoplifting. Others, however, are serious crimes, such as armed robbery, rape, and murder. Studies show that children who are abused or neglected, or who suffer emotional or mental problems, are more likely than others to get into trouble with the law. The studies also show that children who grow up in poverty, in overcrowded and rundown neighborhoods where drug and alcohol abuse are common, are more likely to become delinquents.

Although these factors may contribute to juvenile delinquency, they do not explain

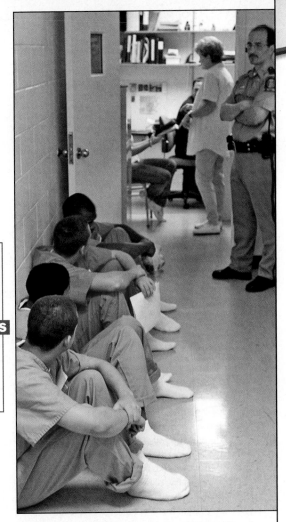

Counseling Services Texas youth offenders await psychological testing before being assigned to specific institutions. ***Analyzing*** Why are young offenders kept separate from adult offenders?

why some young people commit crimes. Many children who suffer abuse and live amid poverty never have trouble with the law, whereas children from all backgrounds can become juvenile delinquents.

✔ **Reading Check** **Explaining** What effect can abuse and neglect have on young people?

Chapter 16   461

Teach

S Skill Practice

Assessing Value Ask: How does it help society to handle juvenile offenders in a system with different procedures than the regular criminal courts? *(Lawmakers hope that society will benefit because young people will be rehabilitated instead of going on to commit more crimes.)* **OL**

R Reading Strategy

Identifying Ask: What are some causes of juvenile delinquency described in this section? *(Some juveniles are abused or neglected; some have emotional or mental problems; some live in overcrowded, poor neighborhoods where crime is common.)* **BL**

Caption Answer:

because they are in danger of being victimized by adult criminals

✔ **Reading Check** **Answer:** Abuse and neglect can make children more likely to get into trouble with the law.

Differentiated Instruction

BIOGRAPHY ACTIVITY 16

Leah Ward Sears (1955–)

Before her swearing-in ceremony, newly elected Chief Justice of the Georgia Supreme Court Leah Ward Sears spoke about her goals for the future. "People no longer understand what the judicial branch is all about," she said. According to Sears, the court is nonpolitical. It is a judge's duty to decide cases on the basis of evidence, not political considerations.

Sears's tenure on the Georgia Supreme Court is historic for several reasons. When she was appointed to the Georgia Supreme Court in 1992, she was both the first woman and the youngest person to sit on that court. Later that year, she ran in an election to keep her appointed seat, and her victory made her Georgia's first woman to win a competitive statewide election. When Sears was elected to the position of chief justice, she became the only African American female chief justice in the United States.

A Judicial Rising Star

The daughter of an Army colonel, Sears was born in Heidelberg, Germany. She graduated from Cornell University and Emory University School of Law. She also received her master's of law from the University of Virginia School of Law.

Sears practiced at a private law firm before Mayor Andrew Young appointed her a judge in Atlanta's Traffic Court in 1985. Three years later, she moved to Georgia's Superior Court and served there until her supreme court appointment.

In her current role as a supreme court justice, Sears has highlighted the need to improve access of the poor to the courts, where they may need help with Social

Security or child support payments. She has noted that indigent people receive financial help to have their cases tried in federal court, but that they receive no money from the state for cases in Georgia's jurisdiction.

Sears has observed that domestic problems make up 65 percent of Georgia's civil cases and looks to reduce that statistic. Sears urges people to accept personal responsibility and work to resolve the underlying domestic issues that lead to these cases.

"The Neutral Branch"

Finally, Sears wants to help people understand the judiciary system. She emphasizes that courts should be removed from "political games." "Judges don't need to 'espouse a platform.' We are not like the governor or the legislature. We are a separate, independent branch of government. We are the neutral branch."

Biography Activity 16, URB pp. 47–48

Leah Ward Sears

Objective: To learn about the first African American woman to lead a state Supreme Court

Focus: Discuss how Sears became Georgia's Chief Justice.

Teach: Read aloud "The Neutral Branch."

Assess: Have students answer the questions on page 48.

Close: Lead a discussion on the pros and cons of electing judges.

Differentiated Instruction Strategies

BL Tell why you think Chief Justice Sears urges people to accept personal responsibility.

AL Write a paragraph explaining the irony of Sears' comment on the political neutrality of the court.

ELL Define the terms "espouse a platform" and "neutral branch."

D Differentiated Instruction

English Learners Have students use a dictionary look up the origin of the word "juvenile." It comes from the Latin word *juvenis*, which means young. Tell students that sometimes juvenile is used as an insult of sorts, as when an older sister says to a younger sibling about his or her annoying behavior, "That's so juvenile!" And note that, when they hear an ad for rejuvenating shampoo or face cream, the same root is being used. **ELL**

R Reading Strategy

Identifying Ask: What two main functions are served by juvenile courts?
(Courts deal with children whose families abuse and neglect them and with young people who have broken the law.) **OL**

TIME™ Teens in *Action*

Answer:

Answers will vary but should include the idea that because participants must undergo eight weeks of training and must stay in the program for a year, it is a major commitment.

Hands-On Chapter Project
Step 3

Understanding the Legal System

Step 3: Designing a Rehabilitation Program Students will create a rehabilitation plan for a juvenile.

Directions: Organize the class into three groups and give them the history of Tina that follows. Each group's task will be to come up with a plan for rehabilitation and present its findings in the form of a poster.

TIME™ Teens in *Action*

The Real Thing

Sarah Carr

Teens around the United States are acting as official judges, jurors, and lawyers.

Hear ye! Hear ye! Youth Court in Colonie, New York, is in session. Prosecutor Sarah Carr, 16, is questioning Andrew G., 17, the defendant. Carr asks, "Didn't you know it was wrong?" Andrew G. nods shyly. He knows that shoplifting a $4.97 popular action figure is not only a petty crime but also a geeky one in the eyes of his high school peers, some of whom are serving on the jury.

In this youth court, the jurors, judge, and lawyers are all teens. The real defendants are limited to first-time offenders who are under the age of 19 and who admit guilt to minor crimes. Sentences are generally creative forms of community service—such as washing police cars—but never jail terms. The record shows that 99 percent of those sentenced complete the required tasks. Doing so keeps their criminal records clean, which is advantageous when completing college and job applications.

Volunteer defenders and prosecutors, like Carr, undergo eight weeks of training to learn about the judicial process. They serve for at least a year and rotate among the other court roles: judge, bailiff, and jury foreperson. Jurors are untrained volunteers in grades 7 through 12.

Many experts say youth court, which is becoming an institution across the U.S., is helping to relieve the clogged criminal-court systems. Some are run by schools, others by police departments or nonprofit groups.

Making a Difference **CITIZENSHIP**
Explain why it takes a strong commitment to take part in this program.

The Juvenile Justice System

Main Idea The juvenile justice system is similar to the adult system, with some important differences.

Civics & You The juvenile court system is modeled after the adult court system. Read on to find out how justice is administered in the juvenile court system.

D When juveniles are charged with violating the law, their cases are handled in separate courts called juvenile courts. The primary goal of juvenile courts is to try to **rehabilitate,** or correct a person's behavior, rather than punish a person. Juvenile courts aim to do whatever is in the best interests of the young people.

Most juvenile court cases begin when police make an arrest. Other cases result from petitions to the courts that school administrators, store managers, or others in contact with children have filed. Parents who cannot control their children's behavior also may petition a court for help.

Neglect and Delinquency

Juvenile courts handle two types of cases. Cases of *neglect* involve juveniles whose caregivers neglect or abuse them. A juvenile court has the power to place these youths with other **R** families in foster homes. *Delinquency* cases involve juveniles who commit crimes. Juvenile courts also handle cases in which juveniles perform acts that are illegal for juveniles but not for adults, such as running away from home or violating curfew laws.

Diversion or Detention?

Most police departments have officers who handle juvenile cases. These officers often have the authority to divert juveniles away from court and into special programs.

Tina, a 15-year-old high school student, was arrested for assault after she got into a fight with another girl at a late-night party at which many of the underage guests were using alcohol. When police took her home, they found three younger siblings asleep and no adult at home. Tina had disciplinary problems at school, including truancy and arguments with teachers. Her mother said that Tina had seemed to be angry and depressed. **OL**
(Project continued on the Visual Summary page)

TINA

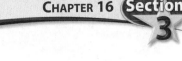

Because the **emphasis,** or importance, is on rehabilitation rather than punishment, the juvenile system offers counseling, job training, and drug-treatment programs to which young people can be diverted.

The Trial

For juveniles who continue to be held for a crime, the next stage is a **preliminary** hearing, as in the adult system. The court procedure for juveniles is similar to adult trials, but with important differences. First, juveniles are not entitled to a jury trial. The judge alone makes the determination as to whether the juvenile is delinquent. Secondly, juvenile cases are normally closed to the public.

The juvenile court system keeps offenders' identities and criminal records secret. In addition, juveniles are not fingerprinted or photographed when they are arrested.

Sentencing If a juvenile is found delinquent, or guilty, the court holds another hearing—the **equivalent,** or equal, to sentencing. Juvenile court judges can sentence offenders in different ways. They may send them home with a stern lecture, or they may place offenders with a previous history of delinquency in a special training school, reformatory, treatment center, or teen shelter.

If the young person successfully completes probation, the charges will be dropped and removed from the record. Juveniles who are neglected may become wards of the court. The court becomes their guardian and can supervise them until adulthood.

Supreme Court Rules

The Supreme Court has established several rules for juvenile criminal cases. In general, juveniles have the same or similar rights as adults accused of crimes: the right to counsel, the right to confront witnesses, and the right not to be forced to incriminate themselves. In 1967, the Court stated, ". . . neither the Fourteenth Amendment nor the Bill of Rights is for adults alone."

Reading Check Describing What does it mean to "divert" a juvenile from the court system?

Section 3 Review

Vocabulary

1. **Define** the following terms and use them in a paragraph about the justice system for young people: *juvenile, juvenile delinquent, rehabilitate.*

Main Ideas

2. **Explaining** Can juveniles be tried as adults?

3. **Describing** What is the primary goal of juvenile courts?

Critical Thinking

4. **BIG Ideas** Do you agree that some young people should be tried as adults? Why or why not?

5. **Describing** Rehabilitation is the goal of the juvenile justice system. On a graphic organizer like the one below, list the programs youths can be diverted into to reach this goal.

Rehabilitation Options

CITIZENSHIP Activity

6. **Creative Writing** Write a series of journal entries from the point of view of someone involved in the juvenile justice system: a young person, a police officer, a parent or caregiver, a crime victim, a judge, or a parole officer. Use details from this chapter to make sure your entries are accurate with regard to the juvenile justice system.

Civics ONLINE

Study Central™ To review this section, go to glencoe.com.

Chapter 16   463

Answers

1. Paragraphs should use vocabulary words according to their definitions in the section and in the Glossary.

2. Yes, all states allow juveniles to be tried as adults if juveniles are older teens and have criminal records or have committed a serious crime.

3. rehabilitation

4. Students' answers will vary but include students' reasons.

5.

counseling — job training — Rehabilitation Options — drug treatment — reform school

6 Student answers will vary. Their account of procedures, however, should be accurate based on the student text.

C Critical Thinking

Identifying Central Issues Ask: Does the side that says schools should be allowed to punish blog speech take the view that adults and teenagers have different rights? *(Students should recognize that this is a central issue of disagreement between the two sides.)* **AL**

Answers:

1. A "blog" is a web log—commentary posted on the Internet for anyone to read and respond to.

2. Association of School Administrators, American Civil Liberties Union, and Student Press Law Center

3. that it constitutes a material disruption to class work or involves a substantial disorder or invasion of the rights of others

4. Students may come up with a variety of ideas, including the idea that blog speech occurs outside of classroom activities, so it is less likely to be disruptive to education than speech in the classroom.

Additional Support

Can schools punish students for undesirable blog speech?

The word *blog* is a blend of *web* and *log*. Individuals with access to the Internet can post comments on blog pages for anyone to read and respond to. In the last few years "blogging" has exploded in popularity for all age groups, especially young people. Today millions of blogs are posted around the world. Blogging was in its early stages when a Missouri school district suspended a student for posting a personal Web page criticizing his school. Since then, the courts have decided a number of cases involving student use of the Internet from locations outside their schools. Should a school be allowed to punish blog speech?

Computer blog speech has become more sophisticated and harder to monitor.

YES

A federal district court ruled a Missouri high school student blogger's criticism of school officials was protected speech. However, not all such speech is protected by the First Amendment. Advising the Association of School Administrators, attorneys Robert Ashmore and Brian Herman noted that, "Student blogs are protected by the First Amendment as long as their content does not constitute a material disruption to classwork or involve substantial disorder or invasion of the rights of others. . . . [T]he U.S. District Court for the Western District of Pennsylvania recently refused to stop a school district from suspending a student, placing him in an alternative school. . . . "The student's Web site had mocked his principal. The court said that, at trial, the Web site probably would be considered a material disruption.

—Robert Ashmore and Brian Herman,
"Abuse in Cyberspace"

NO

The American Civil Liberties Union (ACLU) and the Student Press Law Center (SPLC) often come to the defense of student bloggers who believe their free speech is being violated. With their support, students often win court cases against their schools. In a 1999 case U.S. District Judge Barbara Jacobs Rothstein ruled that a school had violated the First Amendment rights of a student when it expelled him for the content of a poem he wrote about school violence. "'Last Words' was not a sincere expression of intent to harm or assault, and the poem therefore falls squarely within the purview of the First Amendment's core protections," Rothstein said in her decision. "The Supreme Court has repeatedly held that both teachers and students retain their Constitutional rights to freedom of speech and expression. . . . Poetry . . . falls within the core speech protected by the Constitution."

—U.S. District Judge Barbara Jacobs Rothstein,
LaVine v. *Blaine School District*, 2000

Debating the Issue

1. **Defining** What is a blog?

2. **Identifying** What are three organizations that have an interest in student blog speech?

3. **Explaining** What does a school have to prove in order to punish a student for blog speech?

4. **Analyzing** Why would courts rule that content on a personal blog is protected by the First Amendment but that classroom speech is less likely to be?

Activity: U.S./World Connections

China and the Internet As of June 2005, the Chinese government has required all Internet bloggers to register with the government. And many topics, such as independence for Taiwan, are off limits for bloggers The government strictly controls what Web users see through technology known as the "Great Firewall of China."

Have groups research Chinese Internet usage and how strict controls affects it. One group should find topics and ideas that are restricted. A second group should research the measures the Chinese government takes to ensure Internet content is censored. A third group should research how the rest of the world views China's restrictive Internet policies and how this may affect China's economy. **AL**

Civil Law

- Civil law includes disputes over rights, property, and agreements.

- In a civil lawsuit, the plaintiff files a complaint against the defendant, and the defendant responds.

- The legal system has established a procedure that everyone must follow to settle civil disputes.

Criminal Law

- In criminal law cases, the government charges someone with a crime.

Divorce and family law is part of civil law

- A crime is an act that breaks a federal or state criminal law and causes harm to people or society in general.

- Criminal cases are divided into two main groups—felonies and misdemeanors.

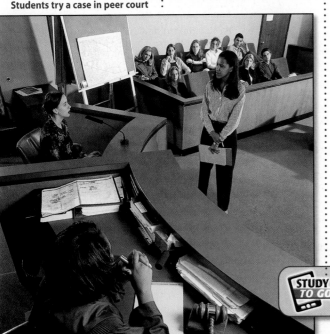

Students try a case in peer court

Juveniles and the Court System

- When a juvenile is arrested, the police must notify his or her parents or caregivers.

- A preliminary hearing is held, followed by a court appearance.

Offender gets tracking device

- At sentencing, juveniles may be sent home, put on probation, made a ward of the court, or sent to a reformatory.

- There is no jury in juvenile court cases.

- The primary goal of juvenile courts is to try to rehabilitate, or correct the behavior of, offenders.

STUDY TO GO Study anywhere, anytime! Download quizzes and flash cards to your PDA from glencoe.com.

465

Diagramming Have students work with a partner to create a diagram of civil or criminal lawsuits. Students may use the charts on page 450 or page 457 as a springboard for their own ideas. **OL**

Making Connections Because television cameras are often not permitted in courtrooms, an illustrator will sketch scenes from notable trials. Have students draw a courtroom scene that they have either experienced or seen on TV. **ELL**

Evaluating Ask: If you were in trouble and a judge were to give a punishment, what would be the most effective punishment for you to keep you from getting into trouble again? Have students get into small groups to discuss the question. **OL**

Hands-On Chapter Project
Step 4: Wrap-Up

Understanding the Legal System

Step 4: Reflecting In this chapter, students have learned about three very different aspects of America's legal system. Ask students to think back over the activities they completed in Steps 1 through 3, as well as what they read in the chapter text itself, and to write down three things they learned that were surprising or troubling to them.

Directions Lead a discussion, asking first about the surprises. Students often form ideas about the legal system based on television shows or news stories that do not give an accurate or balanced picture. Next, discuss with students the things that they found troubling or that seemed unfair. Ask what changes they would like to consider making to improve the legal system as they understand it. **OL**

Answers and Analyses
Reviewing Vocabulary

1. B Students will have read about each of these terms in Section 1 under Bringing Suit and Section 2 under The Penal Code. They should be able to answer the question correctly by process of elimination: Only the complaint is a statement filed with the court to describe the lawsuit. A summons is sent by the court to the defendant telling him to appear in court because he is being sued. A settlement describes the terms of the agreement reached by plaintiff and defendant that ends the lawsuit. The penal code is a set of written laws.

2. D Students have read about penal codes under the heading, What Is a Criminal Case? in Section 2. The other distractors are procedures used in lawsuits and do not spell out penalties for crimes.

3. A Students have read about parole under Sentencing Options in Section 2. The other options are not related to prisoners who have served part of their sentences.

4. D Students have read about the goals of juvenile courts in Section 3 under The Juvenile Justice System, which explicitly contrasts the goal of rehabilitation with that of punishment.

Reviewing Main Idea

5. D Under the heading, Why Do People File Civil Suits, in Section 1, the text singles out negligence as a cause of many civil suits. The family of a worker killed because of equipment failure might well believe that the failure was due to the employer's negligence in keeping it in good repair.

6. D Students will have read about indeterminate sentencing under Sentencing in Section 2. The most confusing distracter here will probably be C, different sentences for similar crimes under different circumstances. Students should recognize that, under indeterminate sentencing, the judge gives a range of time for a prison term, allowing the

parole board to decide when the prisoner will be released. This is different from the judge making that decision at trial based on the particular circumstances of the case.

7. C Students will have read about the defendant being required to enter a plea at arraignment under the heading Hearing, Indictment, and Arraignment in Section 2.

8. B Students have read about risk factors for juvenile crime under Causes of Juvenile Delinquency in Section 3. Poverty, drug and alcohol abuse, and mental or emotional problems are also cited as increasing risk factors.

TEST-TAKING TIP

When reviewing for a civics exam, divide material into easy-to-remember categories such as civic duties, civil rights, and types of law.

Reviewing Vocabulary

Directions: Choose the word(s) that best completes the sentence.

1. A statement naming the defendant and plaintiff and announcing the lawsuit is called a _____.

A summons **C** settlement

B complaint **D** penal code

2. A _____ spells out the punishments that go with each crime.

A summons **C** settlement

B complaint **D** penal code

3. After serving parts of their sentences, some prisoners become eligible for early release, or _____.

A parole **C** discovery

B acquittal **D** arraignment

4. The primary role of juvenile courts is to _____.

A punish **C** acquit

B arraign **D** rehabilitate

Reviewing Main Ideas

Directions: Choose the best answer for each question.

Section 1 *(pp. 448–451)*

5. Which of the following situations may lead to a negligence suit?

A parents argue over custody of their children

B neighboring farmers disagree over boundaries

C a football player quits before his contract expires

D a worker is killed on the job when equipment fails

Section 2 *(pp. 452–458)*

6. What is meant by indeterminate sentencing?

A a set amount of time that the law directs for a specific crime

B probation with intensive supervision

C different sentences for similar crimes under different circumstances

D a sentence that ranges from a minimum to a maximum term

7. When does an accused person enter his or her plea of guilt or innocence?

A on being arrested

B during booking

C at the arraignment

D during cross examination

Section 3 *(pp. 460–463)*

8. According to studies, which young people are most likely to get in trouble with the law?

A older juveniles

B abused children

C mediocre students

D middle-class teenagers

9. What right do accused juveniles NOT share with adults?

A the right to counsel

B the right to a jury trial

C the right to confront witnesses

D the right to refuse to incriminate themselves

GO ON

Critical Thinking

Directions: Base your answers to questions 10 and 11 on the chart below and your knowledge of Chapter 16.

Average Prison Sentences and Time Served for Criminal Cases		
Type of offense	Average sentence given	Percent of sentence served
Murder	12.4 years	48%
Kidnapping	8.7 years	50%
Robbery	8 years	46%
Assault	5.1 years	48%
Other	5 years	47%

10. What conclusion can you draw from the chart?

A More than half of all convicted felons serve their full sentences.

B On average, convicted robbers are sentenced to four years.

C Criminals serve only about half their sentences in prison.

D Convicted murderers spend the rest of their life in prison.

11. What judgment might you make based on the chart?

A Murderers should be in prison for life.

B Robbery is a more serious crime than assault.

C All felonies are equally detrimental to society.

D Society considers kidnapping the most heinous crime.

Document-Based Questions

Directions: Analyze the following document and answer the short-answer questions that follow.

The federal government and 38 states allow the death penalty for certain crimes such as murder and kidnapping. The following passage is by Sister Helen Prejean, the author of Dead Man Walking and an advocate for abolition of the death penalty.

To shackle conscious, imaginative human beings and bring them to the death house with the clock ticking away the days and hours of their lives is mental torture. To prepare human beings for execution by diapering them, shackling them, and forcibly injecting them with valium to lower resistance, then strapping them onto a gurney and injecting them with chemicals that first paralyze them so they can't cry out and then throw them into cardiac arrest is mental torture and in all probability physical torture too. We've been trying over the last 30 years to sanitize death, make it look like we're not really killing them, we're "putting them to sleep."

The death penalty always involves torture. There's no way to kill a human being without causing them extreme pain. Legalizing death doesn't change anything.

—Sister Helen Prejean

12. According to Helen Prejean's characterization, which constitutional freedom does the death penalty negate?

13. What is the main idea of the passage?

Extended-Response Question

14. Describe mediation and arbitration in civil cases, and point out the differences between the two.

Civics ONLINE

For additional test practice, use Self-Check Quizzes—Chapter 16 on glencoe.com.

Need Extra Help?														
If you missed question...	1	2	3	4	5	6	7	8	9	10	11	12	13	14
Go to page...	450	450	454	462	449	454	456	461	463	454	454	453	453	450

ASSESSMENT

that society considers kidnapping the most heinous crime. But although kidnappers on average serve slightly more (2%) of their original sentence than any other group of criminals, the average length of the sentence for kidnappers is almost four years shorter than the average sentence for murderers.

Document-Based Questions

12. freedom from cruel and unusual punishment

13. Students' answers may vary. A possible answer is that Sister Helen Prejean believes that the death penalty is torture and that legalization does not make it less cruel.

Extended Response

14. During mediation, both sides in a disagreement explain their arguments to a mediator in hopes of resolving the issues. In arbitration, two differing sides submit formal arguments to a judge who comes to an opinion about which side wins. Mediation is a less formal process, less expensive and less time consuming for those involved and the court system.

9. B Under the heading The Trial in Section 3 students have read that jury trials are not a right accorded to juveniles. The other major difference in juvenile trials is that the courtroom is ordinarily closed to the public as part of the effort to keep juvenile records and identities private.

Critical Thinking

10. C The third column of the chart clearly shows that in each type of criminal case, the amount of the sentence actually served is 50% or less.

11. B Based on the average length of the sentence for each crime, shown in the second column of the chart, students can deduce that robbery is considered a more serious crime than assault. The distractor that might confuse some students is D—

Civics ONLINE

Have students visit the Web site at glencoe.com to review Chapter 16 and take the **Self-Check Quiz**.

Need Extra Help?

Have students refer to the pages listed if they miss any of the questions.

Chapter Planning Guide

17

Key to Ability Levels
BL Below level   **AL** Above level
OL On level   **ELL** English Language Learners

Key to Teaching Resources
Print Material
CD-ROM or DVD
Transparency

Levels					Resources	Chapter Opener	Section 1	Section 2	Section 3	Chapter Assess
BL	OL	AL	ELL							
					FOCUS					
BL	OL	AL	ELL	🖨	**Daily Focus Skills Transparencies**		17–1	17–2	17–3	
					TEACH					
BL	OL		ELL	📁	**Reading Essentials and Note-Taking Guide***		p. 159	p. 162	p. 165	
	OL	AL		📁	**Citizenship/Decision-Making Activity, URB**			p. 3	p. 3	
BL	OL	AL	ELL	📁	**Speaking and Listening Skills Activity, URB**				p. 9	
		AL		📁	**Enrichment Activity, URB**		p. 13			
	OL	AL		📁	**Primary Source Reading, URB**			p. 15		
BL	OL	AL	ELL	📁	**Content Vocabulary Activity, URB***	p. 65	p. 65	p. 65	p. 65	
BL	OL	AL	ELL	📁	**Academic Vocabulary Activity, URB**	p. 67	p. 67	p. 67	p. 67	
	OL			📁	**Biography Activity, URB**		p. 69			
BL	OL	AL	ELL	📁	**Writing Skills Activity, URB**				p. 71	
	OL	AL		📁	**Critical Thinking Skills Activity, URB**		p. 73			
BL	OL	AL	ELL	📁	**Chart, Graph, and Map Skills Activity, URB**			p. 75		
BL	OL	AL	ELL	📁	**Differentiated Instruction, URB**		p. 77	p. 77	p. 77	
BL	OL	AL	ELL	📁	**School-to-Home Connection Activity, URB***	p. 79	p. 79	p. 79	p. 79	
BL	OL		ELL	📁	**Guided Reading Activities, URB***		p. 83	p. 84	p. 85	
	OL	AL		📁	**Supreme Court Cases**				p. 131	
BL	OL	AL	ELL	📁	**Writer's Guidebook**	✓	✓	✓	✓	✓
	OL	AL		💿	**Primary Source Document Library**	✓	✓	✓	✓	✓
BL	OL	AL	ELL	💿	**Daily Lecture & Discussion Notes (in Pres. Plus)**		✓	✓	✓	✓
BL	OL	AL	ELL	💿	**StudentWorks™ Plus**		✓	✓	✓	✓
BL	OL	AL	ELL	💿	**Section Spotlight Videos**		✓	✓	✓	
BL	OL	AL	ELL	🖨	**TIME Interpreting Political Cartoons Transp.**				Ch. 17	
BL	OL	AL	ELL	🖨	**Writing Process Transparencies**	✓	✓	✓	✓	✓

Note: Please refer to the *Unit 5 Resource Book* for this chapter's URB materials.

*Also available in Spanish

TeacherWorks Plus
All-In-One Planner and Resource Center

- Interactive Lesson Planner
- Interactive Teacher Edition
- Fully editable blackline masters
- Section Spotlight Videos Launch
- Differentiated Lesson Plans
- Printable reports of daily assignments
- Standards Tracking System

Levels					Resources	Chapter Opener	Section 1	Section 2	Section 3	Chapter Assess
BL	OL	AL	ELL							
					TEACH (continued)					
				📁	**Building Academic Vocabulary**	✓	✓	✓	✓	✓
Teacher Resources				📁	**Strategies for Success**	✓	✓	✓	✓	✓
				📁	**Teacher's Guide to Differentiated Instruction**	✓	✓	✓	✓	✓
				💿	**Graphing Tool**	✓	✓	✓	✓	✓
				💿	**Presentation Plus! with MindJogger CheckPoint**	✓	✓	✓	✓	✓
					ASSESS					
BL	OL	AL	ELL	📁	**Quizzes and Tests***		p. 200	p. 201	p. 202	p. 203
BL	OL	AL	ELL	📁	**Authentic Assessment with Rubrics**		p. 21	p. 21	p. 21	p. 21
BL	OL	AL	ELL	📁	**Standardized Test Practice**		p. 33	p. 33	p. 33	p. 33
BL	OL	AL	ELL	💿	*ExamView® Assessment Suite* **CD-ROM**		17–1	17–2	17–3	Ch. 17
					CLOSE					
BL			ELL	📁	**Reteaching Activity, URB***		p. 81	p. 81	p. 81	
BL	OL		ELL	📁	**Reading and Study Skills Foldables™ Activity**	p. 82	p. 83		p. 83	
BL	OL	AL	ELL	🖨	**Graphic Organizer Transparencies & Strategies**	✓	✓	✓	✓	✓

✓ Chapter- or unit-based activities applicable to all sections in this chapter

17

Using Study Central™

Online Quiz

What is Study Central™?

Study Central™ is an interactive, online tool that allows students to check their comprehension of section content with quizzes on the Study Central™ Web site.

How can Study Central™ help my students?

The quizzes on the Study Central™ Web site help students:

- assess their comprehension of chapter content
- build study skills
- identify areas for additional study and reinforcement

Visit glencoe.com and enter a **QuickPass**™ code to go directly to resources for each chapter.

Civics ONLINE
Visit glencoe.com and enter **QuickPass**™ code CIV1360c17T for Chapter 17 resources.

You can easily launch a wide range of digital products from your computer's desktop with the McGraw-Hill Social Studies widget.

	Student	Teacher	Parent
Media Library			
• Student Edition Section Audio	●		●
• Spanish Audio Summaries	●		●
• Section Spotlight Videos	●	●	●
Civics Today **Online Learning Center (Web Site)**			
• Chapter Overviews	●	●	●
• Study Central™	●	●	●
• Study-to-Go	●	●	●
• Student Web Activities	●	●	●
• In Motion Animation	●	●	●
• Self-Check Quizzes	●	●	●
• ePuzzles and Games	●	●	●
• StudentWorks™ Plus Online	●	●	●
• Vocabulary eFlashcards	●	●	●
• Web Activity Lesson Plans		●	
• Vocabulary PuzzleMaker	●	●	●
Classroom Tools			
• Multilingual Glossary	●	●	●
• Beyond the Textbook	●	●	●
• NGS MapMachine	●	●	●

Reading List Generator CD-ROM

GLENCOE BOOKLINK 3

Use this database to search more than 30,000 titles to create a customized reading list for your students.

- Reading lists can be organized by students' reading level, author, genre, theme, or area of interest.
- The database provides Degrees of Reading Power™ (DRP) and Lexile™ readability scores for all selections.
- A brief summary of each selection is included.

Leveled reading suggestions for this chapter:

For students at a Grade 7 reading level:
- *The Cuckoo's Egg: Tracking a Spy through the Maze of Computer Espionage,* by Clifford Stoll

For students at a Grade 8 reading level:
- *The Soul of a New Machine,* by Tracy Kidder

For students at a Grade 9 reading level:
- *How Did We Find Out About Computers?* by Isaac Asimov

For students at a Grade 10 reading level:
- *The Black Press and the Struggle for Civil Rights,* by Carl Senna

For students at a Grade 11 reading level:
- *The Internet,* by Helen Cothran

READING SUPPORT FROM JAMESTOWN EDUCATION

- **Timed Readings Plus in Social Studies** helps students increase their reading rate and fluency while maintaining comprehension. The 400-word passages are similar to those found on state and national assessments.

- **Reading in the Content Area: Social Studies** concentrates on six essential reading skills that help students better comprehend what they read. The book includes 75 high-interest nonfiction passages written at increasing levels of difficulty.

- **Reading Social Studies** includes strategic reading instruction and vocabulary support in Social Studies content for both ELLs and native speakers of English.

- **Content Vocabulary Workout** (Grades 6–8) accelerates reading comprehension through focused vocabulary development. Social Studies content vocabulary comes from the glossaries of Glencoe's Middle School Social Studies texts. www.jamestowneducation.com

KEY Teacher Wraparound

Use this key to help you identify the different types of prompts found in the Teacher Wraparound Edition.

R **Reading Strategies** activities help you teach reading skills and vocabulary.

C **Critical Thinking** strategies help students apply and extend what they have learned.

D **Differentiated Instruction** activities provide instruction for students learning to speak English, along with suggestions for teaching various types of learners.

S **Skill Practice** strategies help students practice historical analysis and geography skills.

W **Writing Support** activities provide writing opportunities to help students comprehend the text.

Teaching strategies and activities have been coded for ability level appropriateness.

AL Activities for students working above grade level

OL Activities for students working on grade level

BL Activities for students working below grade level

ELL Activities for English Language Learners

Focus

Why It Matters

Ask: How does the Internet help citizens take part in civic life? *(Answers may include: the Internet helps citizens get important information; it allows many points of view to be heard; it makes it easier to contact government officials; it helps citizens raise awareness and funds for causes.)*

More About the Photo

Visual Literacy Computer technology camps, such as the one in the photograph, can be found around the country. In these camps, youngsters are introduced to computer concepts and techniques. They receive hands-on experience in computer programming, video game designing, writing a home page, digital video production, and other computer skills. Campers are also encouraged to think about the social implications of computers. Computers and the Internet have changed the way we live. Computer technology camps allow campers to gain important knowledge about the use and role of computers in society.

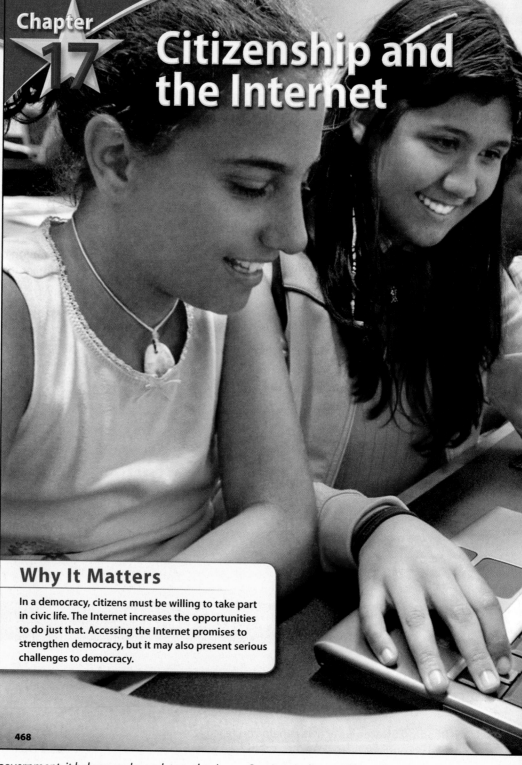

Chapter
17

Citizenship and the Internet

Why It Matters

In a democracy, citizens must be willing to take part in civic life. The Internet increases the opportunities to do just that. Accessing the Internet promises to strengthen democracy, but it may also present serious challenges to democracy.

468

Teach

BIG Ideas *As you begin teaching each section, use these questions and activities to help students focus on the Big Ideas.*

Section 1

Civic Participation Ask: What do you think are the Internet's most important contributions to civic life? *(Answers include: it gives access to information; it enables the homebound to participate in*

government; it helps people work together.) Point out that in Section 1, students will learn how the Internet influences civic life. **OL**

Section 2

Challenges for Democracy Ask: How might the Internet be dangerous to a democracy? *(Answers include: causing an information gap between those with Internet access and those without access, spreading undemocratic ideas.)* Tell students that in

Section 2, they will learn how the Internet both supports and challenges democracy. **OL**

Civics ONLINE
Visit glencoe.com and enter
QuickPass™ code
CIV3093c17 for
Chapter 17
resources.

Chapter Introduction
17

Chapter Audio

BIG Ideas

Section 1: Civic Participation

A democratic society requires the active participation of its citizens. The Internet has changed the way people communicate, get information, and participate in democracy.

Section 2: Challenges for Democracy

A democratic society requires the active participation of its citizens. The Internet can both strengthen and threaten our democracy.

Section 3: Regulating the Internet

Citizens possess certain rights. Citizenship also carries certain responsibilities that all Americans are expected to fulfill. The Internet has become a battleground over the issue of free speech, both in society and in America's schools.

◄ **Students take part in computer technology camp in Fairfield, Connnecticut**

FOLDABLES™
Study Organizer
Dinah Zike's Foldables

Purpose This Foldable guides the student to understand what they read by using a study organizer. The completed Foldable will form a chart to help them organize information about the Internet, its applications, and use. **OL**

More Foldables activities for this chapter can be found in the *Dinah Zike's Reading and Study Skills Foldables* ancillary.

Civics ONLINE
Visit glencoe.com and enter *QuickPass*™ code CIV1360c17T for Chapter 17 resources, including a Chapter Overview, Study Central™, Study-to-Go, Student Web Activity, Self-Check Quiz, and other materials.

FOLDABLES™
Study Organizer

Organizing Foldable Make the following organizing Foldable to help you identify and organize information about each application of the Internet and who would use each.

Step 1 Fold a sheet of paper in thirds from top to bottom. This forms three rows.

Step 2 Open the paper and refold it into fourths from side to side.

This forms four rows.

Reading and Writing
As you read the chapter, make notes about how the Internet can be used for each of these civic issues.

Step 3 Unfold the paper and draw lines along the folds.

Step 4 Label your table as shown.

Internet	Who	What
Civic Participation		
Challenges for Democracy		
Regulating the Internet		

Section 3

Regulating the Internet Ask: Should schools regulate student use of the Internet? *(Answers will vary.)* Explain that in Section 3, students will learn how use of the Internet is being balanced to provide equal access and protections under the law. **OL**

Focus

Bellringer
Daily Focus Transparency 17–1

Guide to Reading
Answers to Graphic:

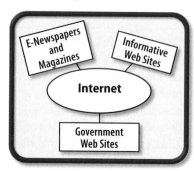

E-Newspapers and Magazines → Internet ← Informative Web Sites

Internet → Government Web Sites

Section
Spotlight Video

To generate student interest and provide a springboard for class discussion, access the Chapter 17, Section 1 video at glencoe.com or on the video DVD.

Resource Manager

Guide to Reading

Big Idea
A democratic society requires the active participation of its citizens.

Content Vocabulary
- Internet *(p. 471)*
- World Wide Web *(p. 471)*
- Web site *(p. 471)*
- archives *(p. 471)*
- nonpartisan *(p. 471)*
- newsgroup *(p. 472)*

Academic Vocabulary
- network *(p. 471)*
- interact *(p. 471)*
- version *(p. 473)*

Reading Strategy
Describing As you read, complete a graphic organizer like the one below, listing ways the Internet helps citizens become well informed.

Internet

Civic Participation

Real World Civics First-time national convention bloggers—online journal writers—worked on their Web log stories at the 2004 Democratic National Convention, revolutionizing campaigning forever. Bloggers posted their reports to the Web audience, providing instant images and thoughts to their readers. Many consider this use of the Internet a type of online "town meeting." It also provides a way for thousands of disabled and homebound voters to participate in politics. One thing is certain: As bloggers continue to express themselves, citizens will have more unfiltered access to information.

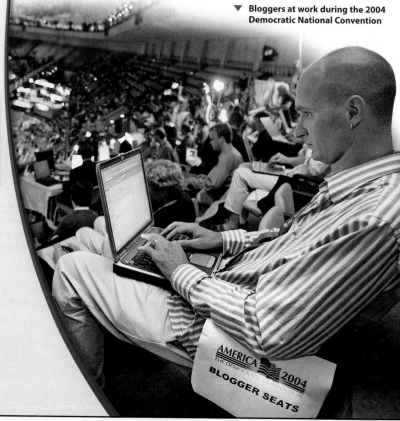

▼ **Bloggers at work during the 2004 Democratic National Convention**

R Reading Strategies	**C** Critical Thinking	**D** Differentiated Instruction	**W** Writing Support	**S** Skill Practice
Teacher Edition • Inferring, p. 471 • Identifying, p. 471 • Predicting, p. 472 **Additional Resources** • Cont. Vocab., URB p. 65 • Ac. Vocab., URB p. 67 • Guide. Read., URB p. 83 • RENTG, p. 159	**Teacher Edition** • Making Generalizations, p. 471 **Additional Resources** • Biographies, URB p. 69 • Crit. Think., URB p. 73 • Quizzes and Tests, p. 200	**Teacher Edition** • Interpersonal, p. 472 **Additional Resources** • Diff. Instr. Act., URB p. 77 • School-to-Home Act., URB p. 79 • Reteach. Act., URB p. 81	**Teacher Edition** • Expository Writing, p. 473 **Additional Resources** • Enrich. Act., URB p. 13 • Auth. Assess., p. 21	**Teacher Edition** • Making a Venn Diagram, p. 473 **Additional Resources** • Daily Focus Trans., 17–1

A Tool for Action

Main Idea The Internet has changed the way people communicate, get information, and participate in democracy.

Civics & You What was the last Web site you visited? Read to find out how Web sites have changed the way we communicate.

The **Internet** and the **World Wide Web** allow people to communicate and collaborate across borders. The Internet is a mass communication system of millions of **networked,** or connected, computers and databases all over the world. The World Wide Web is a system for browsing Internet sites, allowing users to **interact,** or work, with the billions of documents stored on computers across the Internet. These include the vast array of **Web sites**—"pages" on the World Wide Web that contain text, images, audio, and video.

A Billion Users

Currently the Internet has more than a billion users, and more are added daily. The first Web sites started in 1993. Today there are many millions, with the number doubling every few months. Almost three-fourths of the U.S. population has access to the Web. Soon half the population of the world will access the Web, many through wireless devices.

The Internet has created opportunities for citizens to stay informed and to participate thoughtfully in their democracy. Much of what is posted on the Internet is not accurate, however. Before believing what you read, be sure to evaluate the credibility of the source.

Gathering Information

Many citizens use the Internet for information about current events. Most national newspapers and newsmagazines publish online every day and keep **archives,** or files

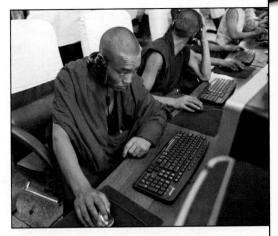

The Internet Monks surf the World Wide Web at an Internet café in Lhasa, Tibet. Millions of people obtain information from the Internet. *Explaining* Why is it important to assess the reliability of the sources of Internet information?

of older stories. Your hometown newspaper may have a Web site as well, as do television and radio networks. Research and educational institutes also have informative Web sites. Be aware, though, that not all "think tanks" are **nonpartisan;** that is, they are not free from political party ties or bias. Many, like the Brookings Institution (liberal) and the Heritage Foundation (conservative), have an ideological bias.

E-Government

Many agencies of government at all levels—federal, state, county, and local—have their own Web sites. E-government makes it easy for citizens to learn about public policy, to check on elected officials, to request services, and to directly participate in government.

Government Web sites help people do everything from obtain marriage licenses to comment on public services. North Carolina's citizens, for example, can use their state government's Web site to register to vote, request an absentee ballot, and learn how their representatives voted on an issue.

Chapter 17   471

Teach

C Critical Thinking

Making Generalizations **Ask:** How might the Internet be said to have made the world smaller? *(The Internet connects computers and databases all over the world, making it easier for people around the world to communicate and to get information.)* **OL**

R₁ Reading Strategy

Inferring **Ask:** Which Web site is probably most likely to have video of candidates' speeches: a newspaper or a television network Web site? *(a television network Web site)* **BL**

R₂ Reading Strategy

Identifying **Ask:** What kinds of things can citizens do using E-government services? *(obtain marriage licenses, register to vote, get information, request services)* **OL**

Caption Answer:

All Internet information is not equal; some Web sites provide incorrect or biased information.

Differentiated Instruction

ENRICHMENT ACTIVITY 5

Citizenship and the Internet

Enrichment Activity 5, URB pp. 13–14

Citizenship and the Internet

Objective: To learn how to identify legitimate sites for grassroots organizations

Focus: Have students search for grassroots organizations' Web sites.

Teach: Discuss characteristics of legitimate Web sites.

Assess: Have students list the kind of information found on Web sites.

Close: Create a class directory of ten Web sites for grassroots organizations.

Differentiated Instruction Strategies

BL Where, on its Web site, might you find information about an organization's history?

AL Select a grassroots organization and create a list of links to the Web sites of other organizations with similar goals.

ELL Identify a grassroots organization dedicated to community service.

D Differentiated Instruction

Interpersonal Have students work in small groups and discuss how they have used the Internet to get information. Some students may keep in touch with distant family members through e-mail. Some may have used the Internet to follow news stories of special interest to them. Encourage them to discuss why this information is important. Invite students to share Web sites they have found to be valuable. **OL**

R Reading Strategy

Predicting Ask: Why would a citizen create a political blog? *(to express personal opinions about candidates, issues, and politics in general)* **OL**

✓ **Reading Check Answer:** The Internet is a system of millions of connected computers. The World Wide Web is a system that allows users to access information on computers across the Internet.

Caption Answer:

The goal is to support political causes. Viewers need to use caution because these sites provide a biased point of view.

Hands-On Chapter Project
Step 1

Group Action Online

One way to influence government is by supporting a special-interest group. The Internet can help you find groups with goals and values similar to your own. Most significant interest groups today have Web sites. Examples of these groups are the Sierra Club, the American Society for the Prevention of Cruelty to Animals (ASPCA), and the National Education Association (NEA). **News-groups,** or Internet discussion forums, provide another way to exchange information and ideas with people who share your concerns. Whether you want to protect the environment, curb TV violence, or help homeless children, you can find a related newsgroup.

✓ **Reading Check** **Explaining** What is the relationship between the Internet and the World Wide Web?

Political Monitoring A member of a political action group uses a computer to tally contributions. Many political action groups as well as many political parties and candidates have Web sites. **Analyzing** What is the goal of these Web sites? Why do viewers need to exercise caution when viewing them?

Election Campaigns

Main Idea The Internet has become a key tool in politics.

Civics & You Have you ever read a blog? Read to find out how they are changing elections.

The Internet is also changing elections. A campaign manager recently said, "We see the Web as the best campaign tool since the phone and the television."

Political Parties and the Web

The Republican and Democratic Parties, along with many minor parties, have Web sites, as does nearly every candidate for higher political office. Many sites feature an electronic newsletter about the candidate's activities. Some candidates even list their campaign contributors online and answer e-mail questions.

When you visit these Web sites, though, you must use caution, because political party and candidate Web sites do not present a wide range of opinions. The goal of these Web sites is to build support for their own ideas and candidates, not to explain both sides of an issue.

Political Blogs

Blogging has become a widely used way for citizens to take part in politics both during and between elections. Blog is short for Web log. "Bloggers" are people who have their own publicly accessible Web sites. Blogs are their personal online journals, a kind of electronic diary that allows others to comment. Bloggers publish their own ideas —more or less continuously—on any topic of interest to them. Political blogs have quickly become popular with people who are trying to express opinions about candidates, issues, and politics in general.

Exploring the "Blogosphere"

Step 1: Making a Blog Chart Groups of students will use a blog search engine to search the Internet and identify a variety of blogs. They will chart the information.

Directions Tell groups of students to use a blog search engine to find blogs on different topics. Groups will then chart the information they have collected in three columns. The first column will give the name and Web address of the site. The second column will describe the topic of site information. Topics may cover a range of subjects—from politics to pop culture. The third column will show what kind of blog it is (private, political, or commercial) and its creator's name.

Summarizing Have students share what they learned about how people use the Internet to communicate. Encourage the class to speculate about the goals of each of the blogs on their charts. **OL**

(Project continued in Section 2)

Bloggers have begun to be recognized as a political influence. Keep in mind anyone can create a blog. Bloggers can, and do, post any messages they want—true or false.

Grassroots Web Sites

Another use of the Internet in politics is grassroots Web sites: citizens set up independent Web sites to support candidates. These sites are the cyberspace **version,** or form, of people putting political signs in their yards. Grassroots Web sites provide an easy way for citizens to get directly involved in an election.

Grassroots Web sites raise some concerns for the major parties and their candidates. The sites may contain misinformation or have links to extremist groups that a candidate would not want to be associated with. Further, it can be hard to tell the difference between official and unofficial sites.

Students at many schools across the country have begun using the Internet to vote in school elections. Using a computer at home or school, students vote online for class officers, student government issues, and prom and homecoming courts. Students are given identification and passwords that prevent them from voting twice in an election.

In most systems, students go online to view an election information page. This page allows student voters to review information about each candidate's background and campaign platform. Students then make their choices, review them, and vote. After organizing her school's first e-election, one California teacher said, "It was very easy to use. . . . The students liked being able to vote anywhere. And it was our most accurate election."

Reading Check Concluding What role do grassroots Web sites play in elections?

Section 1 Review

Vocabulary

1. **Write** a paragraph related to electronic communication using the following terms: *Internet, World Wide Web, Web site, archives, nonpartisan, newsgroup.*

Main Ideas

2. **Explaining** How does e-government allow citizens easier access to government services?

3. **Analyzing** What is a political blog? Why do some people criticize political blogs?

Critical Thinking

4. **BIG Ideas** The Internet offers many advantages for gathering information. What do you think is the biggest disadvantage or danger?

5. **Analyzing** In a graphic organizer like the one below, describe how the Internet and electronic communication have become part of political campaigning.

Campaigning

6. **Researching** Look up the Web site of your representative to Congress or one of your senators. What kind of information can you gather from the site? Share your findings with the class.

CITIZENSHIP Activity

7. **Descriptive Writing** Write a paragraph about your recent use of the Internet to find some information. Describe what you wanted to find out, how you searched for it, and where you found it.

Civics ONLINE

Study Central™ To review this section, go to glencoe.com.

S Skill Practice

Making a Venn Diagram Ask students to make a Venn diagram showing how political Web sites are similar to and different from political signs that people put in their yards. *(Similarity: citizens endorse candidates. Difference: Web sites reach many more people.)* **OL**

W Writing Support

Expository Writing Some schools use the Internet in school elections. Have students write a report describing an election in your school. **OL**

Reading Check **Answer:** allow citizens to get involved in an election

Assess

Civics ONLINE

Study Central™ provides summaries, interactive games, and online graphic organizers to help students review.

Close

Summarizing Ask: What have been some influences of the Internet? *(It has changed the way people communicate and get information.)* **OL**

Section 1 Review

Answers

1. Paragraphs should use vocabulary words according to their definitions in the section and in the Glossary.

2. E-government allows citizens with a computer to access information and services from anywhere.

3. Political blogs are Web logs that express opinions about candidates, issues, and politics in general. Some criticize blogs for false or misleading information.

4. Answers may include that it can be difficult to assess the accuracy of information on the Internet, and it can be difficult to tell the difference between official and unofficial sites.

5. provide information about candidates, list campaign contributors, build support for candidates and issues, answer e-mail questions

6. Answers may include information about representative activities, information about issues, and information about accessing public services.

7. Answers may include researching school projects, searching for products, and sending a question to an expert via e-mail.

Focus

Bellringer
Daily Focus Transparency 17–2

Guide to Reading
Answers to Graphic:

- Don't Give Out Personal Information
- Use Caution Shopping Online
- **Protecting Privacy**
- Use Caution in Chat Rooms

Section Spotlight Video

To generate student interest and provide a springboard for class discussion, access the Chapter 17, Section 2 video at glencoe.com or on the video DVD.

Resource Manager

Guide to Reading

Big Idea
A democratic society requires the active participation of its citizens.

Content Vocabulary
- authoritarian *(p. 475)*
- dissident *(p. 475)*
- extremist group *(p. 476)*
- propaganda *(p. 476)*

Academic Vocabulary
- contrary *(p. 476)*
- isolate *(p. 476)*
- enable *(p. 476)*

Reading Strategy
Summarizing As you read, list on a diagram like the one below three ways to protect your privacy when you use the Internet.

Protecting Privacy

Challenges for Democracy

Real World Civics It has been said that the law is a living, breathing animal, but can it keep up with the Internet? Can privacy be protected? What about national security? In today's climate of fighting terrorism, the debate of privacy versus security is at its peak. Bryan Martin runs an Internet phone service that is seeking the same protections of Internet communication as of private phone services. During times of national crisis, national security has often won out over individual privacy. Online communication has opened up new ways to communicate, and many believe the law has not kept pace.

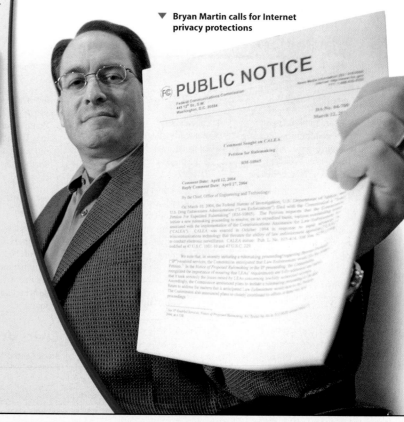

▼ **Bryan Martin calls for Internet privacy protections**

R **Reading Strategies**	C **Critical Thinking**	D **Differentiated Instruction**	W **Writing Support**	S **Skill Practice**
Teacher Edition • Outlining, p. 475 • Summarizing, p. 476 • Identifying, p. 477 **Additional Resources** • Pri. Source Act., URB p. 17 • Guid. Read., URB p. 84 • RENTG, p. 162	**Teacher Edition** • Cause and Effect, p. 476 **Additional Resources** • Crit. Think. Act., URB p. 73 • Quizzes and Tests, p. 201	**Teacher Edition** • English Learners, p. 477 **Additional Resources** • Diff. Instr., URB p. 77 • Reteach. Act., URB p. 81	**Teacher Edition** • Expository Writing, p. 475 • Persuasive Writing, p. 475 **Additional Resources** • Cit./Dec. Making, URB p. 3	**Teacher Edition** • Making a Fact/Opinion Chart, p. 478 **Additional Resources** • Chart, Graph, and Map Skills, URB p. 75 • Daily Focus Trans., 17–2

Divisions in Society

Main Idea The Internet can both strengthen and threaten our democracy.

Civics & You Have you ever used a computer whose access to the Internet was restricted in some way? How do you feel about such restrictions?

When the Internet and the World Wide Web started, many people assumed innovations like these would promote the expansion of democracy. Information and opinions would flow freely across national borders. By spreading democratic ideas worldwide, the Internet would help undermine **authoritarian** regimes. An authoritarian regime is a government in which one leader or group of people holds absolute power.

Restricting Internet Access

Authoritarian governments, however, are finding ways to limit online political communications. They have begun building electronic borders similar to the "firewalls" that protect business networks from intruders.

China, for example, encourages its citizens to get on the Internet. However, the government strictly controls access to the Web sites of human rights groups, foreign newspapers, and similar organizations. Messages that Chinese users post online are closely watched. Furthermore, the government has shut down the Web sites of some dissident groups. A **dissident** group includes people who disagree with the established political or religious system.

Two Dangers

For Americans, the Internet aids the free exchange of knowledge and ideas. Yet the Internet may still pose challenges to democracy. Some people fear that the Internet is widening the gap between the "haves" and "have-nots" and empowering intolerant extremist groups that seek to splinter society. Another concern is that the Internet leaves citizens vulnerable to invasions of privacy.

Democracy does not guarantee everyone equal wealth. It does aim to give all citizens an equal opportunity to develop their talents, though. It also emphasizes equality before the law for all Americans, regardless of gender, race, or religion. How does the Internet affect these two key ingredients of a democratic community?

A Digital Divide

The Internet is becoming a necessity in today's world. People who do not have effective access to the Internet risk being shut out of a key method of gathering information, participating in civic life, and earning money. A report released in 2006 found striking—but shrinking—differences in access by race, education, and family income level.

Impact of the Internet The Internet is becoming a necessity in economics, helping small business owners establish an online presence. *Explaining* What is the risk of not being "wired"?

475

Teach

W1 Writing Support

Expository Writing The Internet has the ability to strengthen our democracy. Have students write one paragraph about the Internet, stating what they believe is its greatest benefit to democracy. **OL**

R Reading Strategy

Outlining Have students use the information in this section to make a list of ways that China restricts Internet access among its citizens. **Ask:** What kinds of Internet sites does China restrict? *(human rights groups, foreign newspapers, and similar organizations)* **BL**

W2 Writing Support

Persuasive Writing The Internet can also threaten our democracy. Have students write one paragraph about the Internet, stating what they believe are its greatest dangers to democracy. **OL**

Caption Answer:

Answers will vary, but most students will say Internet access is necessary to keep up with gathering information and connecting with consumers.

Hands-On Chapter Project
Step 2

Exploring the "Blogosphere"

Step 2: Blog Quotes Students will make posters using quotes from blogs selected from the chart they compiled in Step 1.

Directions Write the Big Idea on the board. Have student groups select a quote from three of the blogs found on their charts. Ask students to make a poster for each quote. Each poster should include the quote in large enough type to be easily read. The posters should also include photographs from newspapers, magazines, and the Internet that illustrate the meaning of the quote.

Summarizing Have students present their posters to the class. Ask the class to match the posters to blogs on the charts compiled in Step 1. Have them discuss in what ways, if any, the blogs from which they have quoted strengthen or threaten democracy. **OL**

(Project continued in Section 3)

R Reading Strategy

R Reading Strategy

Summarizing Have students read the paragraph labeled Access at School. Ask students to make a list of the different ways that schools, the business community, and political leaders are attempting to address the technology gap. **OL**

C Critical Thinking

Cause and Effect Ask: How might the Internet help cause a weaker sense of national unity? *(The Internet can be used by extremist groups to communicate messages of hate and to spread disunity.)* **OL**

Caption Answer:

Schools, public libraries, and nonprofit organizations help provide equal access to computers.

✔ **Reading Check Answer:** They fear the spread of democratic ideas will encourage their citizens to challenge their authoritarian rule

World Wide Web Chinese police inspect an Internet café crowded with students in Guangzhou, the capital of China's southern Guangdong province. *Identifying* What institutions help provide equal access to computers?

The wealthiest families were more likely to have computers and Internet access at home than were households at the lowest income level. Still, a 2006 survey by the Pew Memorial Trust found that almost three-fourths of all Americans report they are Internet users.

Access at School Schools and public libraries help equalize access to computers. Almost all schoolchildren, in every ethnic and income group, now use computers at school. Some have access to the Internet with fast broadband connections. Business, community, and political leaders have also begun to address the technology gap. Some suggest creating nonprofit organizations to provide training and Internet access to millions of low-income Americans. Congress is considering legislation that would support a number of programs.

Extremist Groups

Just as the Internet can communicate and advance democratic values, it can also aid the spread of ideas that are **contrary,** or opposed, to democracy. The Internet has become an important tool for many hate groups and extremist political organizations. **Extremist** **groups** are those whose ideas are the farthest from the political center. In the past, these people might have been **isolated,** or set apart, from one another. The Internet **enables,** or allows, extremists to find one another, band together electronically, spread propaganda, and recruit new members. **Propaganda** is the spreading and promoting of certain ideas and may involve misleading messages designed to manipulate people. (See the descriptions of propaganda techniques in Chapter 11.)

To the extent that the Internet helps strengthen intolerant extremist movements, it may weaken our sense of national unity. Most Americans, however, still take pride in our country's diversity and believe in freedom of speech and expression and equal rights for all Americans.

Terrorists also use the Internet. U.S. Army officials explain that al-Qaeda is making very effective use of the Internet to conduct the war on terror, especially its activities in Iraq. Al-Qaeda raises money, gets recruits, and coordinates attacks through Web sites and blogs. Army officials say such online activities are nearly impossible to shut down.

✔ **Reading Check** Explaining Why do authoritarian regimes limit Internet communication?

Differentiated Instruction

Chart, Graph, and Map Skills Activity 17, URB pp. 75–76

Interpreting a Line Graph

Objective:	To interpret line graphs
Focus:	Students interpret information on three graphs.
Teach:	Discuss how to read a line graph.
Assess:	Have students identify and locate information on the *x* and *y* axes of the graphs.
Close:	Students should write paragraphs interpreting the information on the three graphs.

Differentiated Instruction Strategies

BL Study the graphs on page 75. Why might you conclude that the federal government values telecommunications in schools more than in libraries?

AL Write an editorial about the importance of technology in a democracy.

ELL Which graph shows the percentage of households with Internet access?

Threats to Privacy

Main Idea The Internet poses some significant threats to Americans' privacy.

Civics & You Did you know that businesses and government agencies can keep records of Web sites you visit? Read to find out more about these activities.

The Internet is creating a growing number of threats to privacy. In our digital world, governments, businesses, and even your neighbor can watch what you are doing online.

Personal Information You need to be cautious with information about yourself whenever you go online to make purchases or visit sites with advertisements. You also need to be very careful when e-mailing, blogging, and visiting chat rooms—social network Web sites.

Businesses and the government are able to mix information about you from different sources to create huge "data warehouses." These detailed profiles of people may include your address, income, age, health, what you buy and read, and much more. All of this information can be for sale to nearly anybody willing to pay for it.

D

Some Legal Protection Current privacy laws provide only limited safeguards and are hard to enforce. Congress tried to protect younger Web users by passing the Children's Online Privacy Protection Act (1998). This law requires Web site companies to establish a privacy policy describing the information they are collecting from children and how they will use it. The companies must also get permission from parents to collect information from children under 13 years of age.

R

Government Surveillance

The Internet has become a tool for all kinds of crime and for terrorism. As a result, the federal government conducts a great deal of online surveillance. Online data is being used to solve crimes. In St. Louis, for example, records of a suspect's online searches led to his arrest for a series of murders. The government also monitors electronic communications in an effort to stop terrorist attacks before they occur.

Federal government agencies like the Department of Justice or the National Security Agency collect electronic information in two ways. First, they work with companies that provide Internet services and run Web sites. Second, they develop and operate their own surveillance technology.

Internet Companies Many Web sites keep a log of all user activity and record the Internet Protocol (IP) address of each. Internet companies regularly hand over information about users in response to requests from police and from attorneys involved in lawsuits. The online provider America Online®, for example, receives nearly 1,000 requests a month for information in civil and criminal cases.

In January 2006, the U.S. Justice Department asked search engine companies to turn over records on searches made by millions of their users. The government was collecting data on how often Web searches turn up material harmful to children. In this instance, the government did not ask companies to provide the names of the people making the searches. Three companies—Yahoo!®, MSN®, and AOL® Internet Services—provided some information. Google™ resisted.

Privacy experts warned that search engines could become mechanisms that allow the government to spy on citizens. Some Internet users worried that in the age of terrorism innocent searches related to Islam or

Civics ONLINE
Student Web Activity Visit glencoe.com and complete the Chapter 17 Web Activity.

D Differentiated Instruction

English Learners Have students read the phrase "data warehouse" in the second paragraph of the section Personal Information. Tell them that "data" means information and that a "warehouse" is a place business owners store the things they need to run their businesses. Point out that "warehouse" is made of "ware" and "house." Help them see that other phrases such as "Web site" and "database" are also metaphors for locations on the Internet. **ELL**

R Reading Strategy

Identifying Ask: How has Congress tried to protect the privacy of younger Web users? *(Congress passed the Children's Online Privacy Protection Act in 1998.)* **OL**

Civics ONLINE
Objectives and answers to the **Student Web Activity** can be found at glencoe.com under the Web Activity Lesson Plan for this chapter.

Differentiated Instruction

Leveled Activities

BL Citizenship/Decision-Making Activity 5, URB pp. 3–4

OL Chart/Graph/Map Activity 17, URB pp. 75–76

AL Primary Source Activity 5B, URB pp. 17–18

ELL Guided Reading Activity 17–2, URB p. 84

S Skill Practice

Making a Fact/Opinion Chart Have students make a chart that identifies statements in the "Government Tools" heading as facts or opinions. *(Facts: NSA can monitor e-mail. NSA allowed to eavesdrop on U.S. citizens. Opinions: The government infringed on citizens' privacy. These tools are needed to fight terrorists.)* **OL**

✓ **Reading Check** **Answer:** They must identify the information they collect from children and how they use it. They must get the parents' permission to collect information from children under 13 years of age.

Assess

Civics ONLINE

Study Central™ provides summaries, interactive games, and online graphic organizers to help students review content.

Close

Summarizing Ask: How may the Internet both strengthen and weaken our democracy? *(It allows for the free flow of information and services. It can help extremists spread destabilizing messages.)* **OL**

Section 2 Review

Middle Eastern countries could be misinterpreted by government officials. On the other hand, supporters said the request for user information was for a good cause. One user argued, "For the government to catch people that prey on children, or fight the war on terror, they are going to need the help of search engines."

Government Tools The federal government has also been developing its own techniques for monitoring electronic communications. The National Security Agency (NSA), for example, has technology that can silently monitor millions of e-mail messages an hour. Not long after the terrorist attacks of September 11, 2001, President Bush secretly ordered the NSA to eavesdrop on Americans and others in the United States without getting court-approved search warrants.

Such activities illustrate the tension in a democracy between the need for the government to protect our national security and the need to guard citizens' constitutional rights. Former House Majority Leader Dick Armey of Texas worried that surveillance infringes on basic "constitutional protections against unwarranted search." Others argue that powerful tools are needed to fight terrorists and criminals using cyberspace. "You can't outlaw this technology," one expert stated. "All you can do is set strict legal standards."

Legal Limits Standards for government online surveillance are not clear. The Fourth Amendment protects citizens against "unreasonable searches." However, to what extent does that amendment apply to Internet activities? The 1996 Electronic Communications Privacy Act sets forth some legal standards for protecting online information. For example, the law generally requires a court order for investigators to read e-mail. At the same time, the USA Patriot Act allows some protections to be waived if lives are at risk.

✓ **Reading Check** **Explaining** What does the Children's Online Privacy Protection Act require Web site companies to do?

Section 2 Review

Vocabulary

1. **Define** the following terms and use them in sentences related to the Internet and democracy: *authoritarian, dissident, extremist group, propaganda.*

Main Ideas

2. **Explaining** What is meant by the "digital divide"? Why is it a problem?

3. **Explaining** Why does the government monitor electronic communications? Why do some Americans criticize this action?

Critical Thinking

4. **BIG Ideas** How do you think our society should balance the need for fighting terrorism through activities such as Internet wiretapping against the need to protect the privacy of innocent individuals?

5. **Analyzing Information** In a chart like the one below, describe three effects of threats to privacy posed by the Internet.

Internet: Threat to Privacy

CITIZENSHIP Activity

6. **Creative Writing** Research and write a letter to the editor of your local newspaper about one of the issues raised in this section. Explain your opinion on the issue and discuss what you believe should be done.

Civics ONLINE

Study Central™ To review this section, go to glencoe.com.

Answers

1. Definitions for the vocabulary words are found in the section and in the Glossary.

2. The "digital divide" describes the difficulty of poorer Americans to access the Internet. This causes a widening economic and information gap between classes of Americans.

3. It monitors electronic communications to thwart crime and acts of terrorism. They feel that these actions are illegal invasions of privacy.

4. Answers will vary, but might include stating government controls are needed.

5. Identity Theft, Data Warehousing, Government Surveillance

6. Answers will vary, but students should explain their opinions and propose solutions in their letters to the editor.

Protecting Yourself Against Identity Theft

What is the nation's fastest-growing crime? According to the U.S. Federal Trade Commission, it is identity theft. Identity theft is a crime in which an imposter obtains key pieces of information, such as Social Security and driver's license numbers, and uses it for personal gain. Nearly 10 million U.S. adults were victims in 2005.

What does the identity thief want?
- Your Social Security card
- Your driver's license
- Your account numbers (bank, credit card, and others), PIN(s), and passwords

Even if you never use a computer, you can fall victim to identity theft. Others may be able to get personal information (such as credit card numbers, phone numbers, account numbers, and addresses) by stealing your wallet, overhearing a phone conversation, poking through your trash (a practice known as Dumpster diving), or "phishing"—an e-mail scam that aims to steal personal information.

Tips for Preventing Identity Theft
- Protect your Social Security number (SSN).
- Always take credit card receipts with you. Never toss them into a public trash container.
- Do not give out personal information on the phone, through the mail, or over the Internet unless you know with whom you are dealing.
- Carry only the identification information and the credit and debit cards you will actually need when you go out. If your wallet is stolen or if you lose it, report it immediately to the card issuers and the local police.

Identity Theft Is Affecting Online Shopping

more cautious when they buy online

more careful when they enter personal data

buying fewer items

0 10 20 30 40 50 60 70 80 90 100
Percentage of Respondents

Source: *Business Week*, March 20, 2006; Gartner, Inc.

Analyzing Economics

1. **Explaining** A friend says, "No one can steal my identity because I don't use a computer." Is your friend correct?

2. **Summarizing** How has the increase in identity theft affected online shoppers?

Chapter 17 **479**

Teach

D Differentiated Instruction

English Learners Ask the class to describe what a person does when trying to catch fish. **Ask:** Why do we call e-mail scams aimed at stealing personal information "phishing"? (*Just as fishers cast their rods into the sea hoping to catch fish, criminals send e-mails on the chance they will trick a person into revealing personal information.*) **ELL**

S Skill Practice

Reading Graphs Ask: To protect themselves from identity theft, what percentage of shoppers buy fewer items online? (*30 percent*) **OL**

Analyzing Economics

Answers:
1. Incorrect. Information can be stolen from a wallet, overheard in a conversation, and found in the trash.
2. Seventy percent of shoppers are more cautious when buying online. Sixty percent are more careful when they enter personal data. Thirty percent are buying fewer items online.

Additional Support

Activity: U.S./World Connections

Comparing and Contrasting Point out to students that other countries also have concerns about identity theft. Ask them to research how the United States and the European Union attempt to stop identity theft.

Have the class discuss the similarities and differences between the methods the United States and the European Union use to combat identity theft. List the methods on the board. Ask volunteers to identify the most effective methods. Have the class discuss which of the European Union's methods (if any) they believe the United States should adopt. **AL**

Focus

Bellringer
Daily Focus Transparency 17–3

Guide to Reading
Answers to Graphic:

Online School Newspapers

Filtering Software

File-Sharing Battles

Free Speech

Section Spotlight Video

To generate student interest and provide a springboard for class discussion, access the Chapter 17, Section 3 video at glencoe.com or on the video DVD.

Resource Manager

Guide to Reading

Big Idea
Citizens possess certain rights. Citizenship also carries certain responsibilities that all Americans are expected to fulfill.

Content Vocabulary
• intellectual property *(p. 482)*
• copyright *(p. 483)*
• revenue *(p. 485)*

Academic Vocabulary
• nonetheless *(p. 482)*
• erode *(p. 483)*

Reading Strategy
Summarizing The Internet raises many issues that the Framers of the Constitution could not have imagined. As you read, discuss three free-speech issues that are associated with the Internet. Place your answers on a web diagram like the one below.

Free Speech

 Section Audio   **Spotlight Video**

Regulating the Internet

Real World Civics Are modern-day pirates threatening what may be available on the Internet? Today many people listen to music and play movies on their computers. Sometimes, users download entertainment for free, without paying any fee to the people who created it. Is this fair use? The Senate Government Affairs Committee is acting as watchdog, holding hearings to determine what is fair use of movies, music, and videos on the Internet. The unfair use of such media has been labeled computer "piracy" because it goes against traditional copyright laws.

▼ **Recording and film representatives testify against unauthorized downloading**

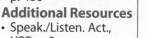
MR. VALENTI
Motion Picture Association

L.L. COOL J
Recording Artist

480

	C Critical Thinking	**D** Differentiated Instruction	**W** Writing Support	**S** Skill Practice
Teacher Edition • Setting a Purpose, p. 481 • Content Vocab., p. 482 • Identifying, pp. 483, 484 • Summarizing, p. 485 **Additional Resources** • Guid. Read., URB p. 85 • RENTG, p. 165	**Teacher Edition** • Making Inferences, p. 483 **Additional Resources** • Cit/Dec. Making Act., URB p. 3 • Quizzes and Tests, p. 202	**Teacher Edition** • Kinesthetic, p. 482 • Gifted and Talented, p. 485 **Additional Resources** • Diff. Instr., URB p. 77 • Reteach Act., URB p. 81	**Teacher Edition** • Personal Writing, p. 481 • Expository Writing, p. 483 • Persuasive Writing, p. 486 **Additional Resources** • Speak./Listen. Act., URB p. 9 • Writing Skills Act., URB p. 71	**Teacher Edition** • Reading Graphs, p. 484 **Additional Resources** • Daily Focus Trans., 17–3 • Pol. Cartoons Trans. 17

TIME™
Political Cartoons

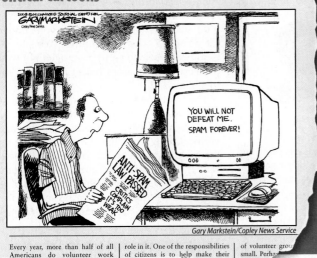

GARY MARKSTEIN
Copley News Service

YOU WILL NOT DEFEAT ME. SPAM FOREVER!

ANTI-SPAM LAW PASSED
CRITICS COMPLAIN IT'S TOO WEAK

Gary Markstein/Copley News Service

This cartoon, drawn by Gary Markstein, makes a comment on efforts to control spam on the Internet.

1. What is Internet spam?
2. Does the cartoonist consider the antispam law effective?
3. What details in the image reveal the cartoonist's point of view?

Every year, more than half of all Americans do volunteer work role in it. One of the responsibilities of citizens is to help make their of volunteer grou small. Perha dad who

---

Internet Speech

Main Idea The Internet has become a battleground over the issue of free speech.

Civics & You Do you know someone who has downloaded music from an Internet site? Read to find out how this activity has been at the eye of a huge storm.

Free speech is a key democratic right, spelled out in the First Amendment to the Constitution. The Internet promotes free speech by giving anyone with a computer the chance to spread his or her views across the world. Unfortunately, this freedom has also enabled hate groups and others to fill the Internet with offensive material.

For more than a decade, governments from your local school board to the U.S. Congress have been scrambling for some control over speech on the Internet. In regulating the Internet, though, does the government infringe on the right of free speech?

Safeguards Computer users can block objectionable Web sites by installing filtering software. Lawmakers have also enacted laws to censor some online speech. In 1996 Congress passed the Communications Decency Act. This law made it a federal crime to send or display indecent or obscene material over the Internet "in a manner available" to those under the age of 18.

Challenge to Internet Censorship Several groups challenged the law in court. They argued that it violated the rights of adults, who can lawfully view graphic material considered inappropriate for children. In *Reno* v. *American Civil Liberties Union* (1997), the Supreme Court declared the indecency portions of the law unconstitutional. The Court held that speech on the Internet should have the highest level of First Amendment protection, similar to the protection given to books and newspapers. This decision was a strong endorsement of free speech on the Internet.

Chapter 17   481

Teach

R Reading Strategy

Setting a Purpose Ask: How have users and the government attempted to regulate the Internet? *(Users have installed filtering software on their computers. The government has passed laws to censor some speech online.)* **OL**

W Writing Support

Personal Writing Have students write one paragraph describing their opinions about the Supreme Court decision declaring the indecency portions of the Communications Decency Act unconstitutional. **Ask:** Do students agree or disagree with the Court's decision? Why? **OL**

TIME™ Political Cartoons

Answers:
1. Spam is unsolicited, usually commercial, e-mail.
2. The cartoonist does not consider the antispam law effective.
3. The man is reading a newspaper with a headline announcing a new antispam law. On his computer screen is a spam message.

Additional Support

Teacher Tip

This activity requires students to make an oral presentation. Remind students to speak clearly and to make eye contact with their audience.

Activity: Collaborative Learning

Verbal/Linguistic Have students work in groups and use the Internet to search for three examples of political cartoons about spam or other Internet issues. Have the groups write and present an oral report describing the viewpoint of the cartoon and pointing out details in the cartoon that convey its message. Have students make large copies of the cartoons or print copies of their cartoons to distribute to the class for their presentations. **OL**

D Differentiated Instruction

Kinesthetic Remind students that courts have ruled that schools can censor student print and online publications. Ask students who agree with the courts to stand at the front left side of the classroom. Ask those students who disagree with the courts to stand at the front right side of the classroom. Have students who are undecided stand between the two groups. Encourage students to explain their positions. **BL** **ELL**

R Reading Strategy

Content Vocabulary Ask: What term best completes this sentence? *Just as carpenters own and can sell what they make, songwriters own and can sell their music; it is their _____. (intellectual property)* **OL**

TIME™ Teens in *Action*

Answer:

Keegan asked for donations by posting a request in the Rye High School E-news.

Hands-On Chapter Project
Step 3

TIME™ Teens in *Action*

Keegan Flynn

The Internet can be a powerful tool to get people involved in good causes. Just ask Keegan Flynn, 14, of Port Chester, New York.

QUESTION: You've said that Hurricane Katrina changed your life. How?

ANSWER: The hurricane, which destroyed much of New Orleans and the Gulf Coast, was very personal for my family. My mom's college roommate and some of our cousins lost their homes and their businesses. They had resources to start over, but I wondered what was going to happen to all those other people who didn't have the same resources. My mom saw on the news that backpacks were needed in Houston, Texas. I decided that this could be a way for me to make a difference.

Q: What happened next?

A: I collected and assembled "school-ready" backpacks for kids in Houston who were victims of Hurricane Katrina who didn't have the ability or funds to gather their own supplies.

Q: How did other people know where to make donations?

A: My mother writes and edits Rye [New York] High School's E-news. I got the word out by posting an announcement there. My mom has a list with over 600 e-mail addresses—all belonging to Rye High School faculty and parents. It was amazing the way people responded to my electronic request.

Flynn's efforts make a difference

Making a Difference   CITIZENSHIP

What steps did Keegan take to request help from volunteers?

In response to the Court's decision, Congress passed the Child Online Protection Act (COPA) in 1998. This law made it a crime for a commercial Web site to knowingly make indecent material available to anyone under the age of 17. The law required Web sites to require all users to verify their ages as a way to keep children from harmful material on their sites.

The Supreme Court stopped enforcement of this law in 2004. In *Ashcroft* v. *American Civil Liberties Union,* the Court ruled that age verification was too harsh of a restriction on the free-speech rights of adults. The justices said filtering software on home computers might be a way to keep children from viewing offensive material while preserving the right of adults to view whatever they want.

Limiting Free Speech in Schools

Although the Supreme Court has ruled that Internet speech is protected by the First Amendment, this protection is not applicable everywhere. **Nonetheless,** restrictions may apply to school-sponsored newspapers on the World Wide Web.

In 1988 the Supreme Court ruled that school administrators can regulate the content of student print publications if doing so serves an educational purpose (see the **D** *Hazelwood School District* v. *Kuhlmeier* case on page 325). Several lower courts have found that students who produce online papers in school with school equipment may be subject to regulation.

Intellectual Property

Americans have always believed in the right of individuals to own property and to use it as they see fit. You can freely sell your old bike, loan your jacket to a friend, or trade away part of your baseball card collection if you so choose. However, special rules apply to **intellectual property**—things that people create, such as songs, movies, books, poetry, art, and software. **R**

Exploring the "Blogosphere"

Step 3: Blogging Students will work in groups to create their own blog.

Directions Write the Big Idea on the board. Remind students that they have the responsibility to practice free speech in a constructive manner. Any criticism they make should be useful and not abusive. Have student

groups use the charts and posters they created in Steps 1 and 2 to brainstorm ideas for a blog topic. Remind students that the content of their blogs must meet school standards. When students have selected a topic and a name for their blogs, have them collaborate on writing the first entries for their blogs.

Summarizing Have students read their blog entries to the class. Encourage the class to discuss how they chose their blog topics and how school standards influenced what they wrote. **OL**

(Project continued on the Visual Summary page)

American Biography

The Birth of Yahoo!®

In 1994, two Stanford University graduate students wanted a better way to keep track of their favorite Internet sites. The students, **Jerry Yang** and **David Filo**, started keeping lists on a computer. Other students began logging on to check out their lists and using them to find their way around the World Wide Web.

The two students named their site "Jerry and David's Guide to the World Wide Web." They understood that others wanted a single "point of entry" to the quickly growing Web. In the fall of 1994, the site had its first one millionth hit, and Yang and Filo decided to start a business. Yahoo!® was born in March 1995, and the pair raised money to expand their idea. The name they chose for their new business appealed to them because it meant "a rude, unsophisticated person." They hired employees and sold stock to raise more money. Today, Yahoo!®

receives about 350 million visits every day, making it the most popular site on the Web.

Jerry Yang recently explained how his company's focus has changed:

"Ten years ago, we were focused on a simple yet vast problem: finding better ways to aggregate and organize information so people can find it. [Today,] ... it's no longer enough to simply provide a structure for users to find what they want on the Web. Today, people expect to find precisely what they're looking for exactly as it relates to them."

—Jerry Yang, "Jerry's Take on What's Next in Search"

Jerry Yang

C Making a Difference **CITIZENSHIP**

Describing In a sentence, express what you think is the key to the success of Yahoo!®

The Power of Copyright When you purchase a CD by Christina Aguilera or a *Harry Potter* book, you do not gain ownership rights to the artistic product. Only the artist or author who created the work has a right to sell it or let others use it.

Over the years, many traditions, court decisions, and legal devices such as copyrights have developed to protect the creators of intellectual property. A **copyright** is the owner's exclusive right to control, publish, and sell an original work. Copyrights are designed to prevent people from taking or copying someone else's creation without permission. Computers and the Internet, however, make it easy to copy and widely distribute all kinds of intellectual property, thus threatening to **erode,** or wear away, copyright protection. As a result, the Internet has become a major battleground for intellectual property rights.

R

In 1998 Congress passed a law aimed at protecting the holders of intellectual property in the Internet age. The Digital Millennium Copyright Act (DMCA) makes it a crime for someone to develop or spread software that will bypass computer codes that protect copyrighted material.

File-Sharing Battles The fight over using file sharing to download music and movies illustrates how the Internet is challenging old rules protecting intellectual property. Grokster and StreamCast Internetworks developed software that allowed Internet users to share computer files on "peer to peer" networks. Such networks connect computers across the globe, making it easy for people to download copyrighted songs and movies without paying for them. Billions of files were being shared over Grokster and similar networks every month.

W

C Critical Thinking

Making Inferences The creators of Yahoo! said the name appealed to them because it means a "rude, unsophisticated person." **Ask:** Why is this name a good fit for the site? *(Even an unsophisticated person can use Yahoo! to help them find what they want on the Web.)* **OL**

R Reading Strategy

Identifying Name three developments that protect creators of intellectual property. *(traditions, court decisions, and legal devices, such as copyrights)* **OL**

W Writing Support

Expository Writing Have students interview their peers about file sharing. Then have students write one paragraph describing what they learned about file-sharing habits, motives, and beliefs. **AL**

American Biography

Answer: Answers may vary, but most students will say that Yahoo is effective in helping people find the precise information they need.

Differentiated Instruction

Writing Skills Activity 17, URB pp. 71–72

Employing Descriptive Strategies

Objective:	To understand the Digital Millennium Act
Focus:	Students will write a dialogue illustrating an aspect of the Digital Millennium Act.
Teach:	Review effective use of description and examples of dialogue.
Assess:	Have students summarize the Digital Millennium Act.
Close:	Write a one-page dialogue that explains the Digital Millennium Act.

Differentiated Instruction Strategies

BL Identify the descriptive words in the second description.

AL Write an essay about the Digital Millennium Act using dialogue, sensory details, actions, thoughts, and creative language.

ELL Write a sentence describing an action that violates the Digital Millennium Copyright Act.

R Reading Strategy

Identifying Ask: What legal principle did the Supreme Court establish in its ruling in the *Metro-Goldwyn-Mayer* v. *Grokster* 2005 case? *(It is not illegal to create technology that can be used for copyright theft, but it is illegal to encourage copyright theft.)* **OL**

S₁ Skill Practice

Reading Graphs According to the graph, which two ethnic groups have approximately the same amount of computer access at home? *(African Americans and Latinos)* **OL**

S₂ Skill Practice

Reading Graphs Ask: How many variables about computer access among schoolchildren do the graphs include? *(Four: the graphs give information about the percentage of users by age at home and at school. They also give information about the percentage of users by ethnicity at home and at school.)* **OL**

Analyzing Graphs

Answers:
1. 11 to 14 years old
2. African Americans, Latinos

Differentiated Instruction

Metro-Goldwyn-Mayer and other entertainment companies sued Grokster. MGM claimed Grokster encouraged people to use its free software to download copyrighted music without paying for it. Grokster argued its software could be used to swap any kind of computer file and thus had many legitimate uses. It was not responsible for those who used its technology to violate copyrights.

The Supreme Court ruled unanimously against Grokster and StreamCast (*Metro-Goldwyn-Mayer* v. *Grokster*, 2005). The justices found the companies "clearly voiced the objective that recipients use the software to download copyrighted works." The ruling set forth a basic legal principle that will govern intellectual property law for some time. It is not illegal to create an Internet technol-ogy that makes copyright theft possible. However, encouraging people to use such technology for copyright violation is prohibited. Companies that promote copyright violations can be held liable for the result.

The music industry said the ruling was a major victory. Still, the Court's decision did not mean the end of online swapping, a global practice. Rather, it is only the latest example of a continuing battle between copyright holders and Internet users. Even as Grokster announced it was stopping distribution of its software, other companies across the world were developing new types of file sharing networks. So-called darknets, for example, allow groups of users to share information without revealing their identity to outsiders who are not part of the group.

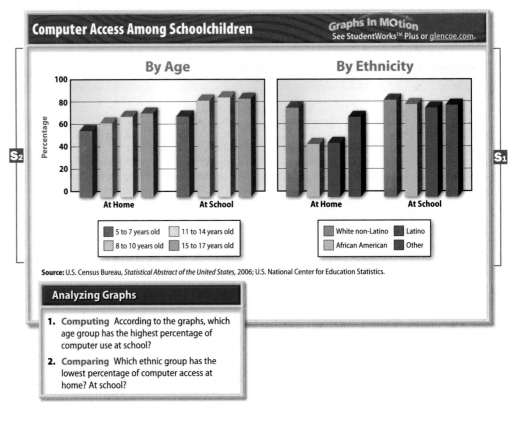

Computer Access Among Schoolchildren

Graphs In MOtion See StudentWorks™ Plus or glencoe.com.

By Age

By Ethnicity

- 5 to 7 years old
- 8 to 10 years old
- 11 to 14 years old
- 15 to 17 years old

- White non-Latino
- African American
- Latino
- Other

Source: U.S. Census Bureau, *Statistical Abstract of the United States,* 2006; U.S. National Center for Education Statistics.

Analyzing Graphs

1. **Computing** According to the graphs, which age group has the highest percentage of computer use at school?

2. **Comparing** Which ethnic group has the lowest percentage of computer access at home? At school?

Leveled Activities

BL Differentiated Instruction Activity 17, URB pp. 77–78

OL Speaking and Listening Activity 5, URB pp. 9–12

AL Writing Skills Activity 17, URB pp. 71–72

ELL Guided Reading Activity 17–3, URB p. 85

Taxing E-Commerce

E-commerce involves using the Internet for purchase and sales transactions. Because e-commerce involves numerous computers communicating, purchase and sales transactions occur very quickly and are often unidentified. How to tax goods and services purchased over the Internet is another important issue. Each year, consumers spend billions of dollars buying goods and services over the Internet. Online shopping is not only convenient, but it also allows customers to avoid paying local sales taxes. Although many states require online consumers to report purchase amounts on income tax forms, state and local governments often lose out on a prime source of **revenue.** Revenue is the income that a government or business collects.

An Unfair Burden? Many state governors and other politicians favor taxation of e-commerce; so do traditional retail stores. After all, the stores lose business if you shop online instead of at your local mall. Many Internet merchants and policy analysts, however, believe that collecting sales taxes would unfairly burden online companies. Because sales taxes vary from state to state, online businesses would have to charge different rates depending on where customers live and then send the funds back to different state governments. Collecting taxes would thus be unusually costly for Internet companies. Furthermore, unlike local merchants, they would share in none of the benefits those taxes pay for, such as police and fire protection, roads, and other government services.

An advisory group created by Congress recently proposed that all state and local tax systems be simplified and made more uniform. Efforts could then be made to develop a fair Internet sales tax.

Reading Check Explaining Why may people who hold copyrights be concerned about Internet use?

School and the Internet Teachers and students use laptop computers at the Mary McDowell Center for Learning in Brooklyn, New York. The Center is a Quaker independent school for children with learning disabilities. **Explaining** Why do many schools use filtering software?

The Internet at School

Main Idea Growing use of the Internet in schools is creating new controversies.

Civics & You Have you used the Internet at school? Read to find out why this issue has become a focus of intense debate.

Tens of millions of American students spend classroom time online. Use of the Internet at school is creating new issues for lawmakers and educators.

School Filters

In 2000 Congress passed the Children's Internet Protection Act. This law requires nearly all schools in the United States to install technology that blocks student access to offensive or dangerous Web materials.

Did You Know?

No Laughing Matter Besides filtering Web content, some schools try to curb student expression on the Internet. After discovering a satiric profile of a school administrator published by Jessica Schoch of Holland, Ohio, on MySpace.com, school officials barred her from attending school and extracurricular activities.

Attorney Arnold Gottlieb of the American Civil Liberties Union represented Jessica at a school board meeting in April of 2006. Gottlieb argued that Jessica's parody was an example of free speech. He stated that various courts have ruled that students may write about their schools as long as it is not done with school equipment or during class

hours. Since Jessica had created the profile at home, her parents, not the school, should deal with her behavior. The school board reinstated Jessica. Attorney Gottleib hoped that "this is a clear signal that schools may not punish students for exercising their free speech rights outside of the school on their own time."

W Writing Support

Persuasive Writing Have students read the section on the use of filtering software in schools. Ask students to write a paragraph stating whether they agree or disagree that school officials should prevent students from visiting sites deemed objectionable. The paragraph should attempt to persuade readers to share the writer's opinion. **OL**

 Reading Check Answer: right of parents to see records of students' use of the Internet; *Issues:* student privacy, censorship, and the safety of young users

Assess

Civics ONLINE

Study Central™ provides summaries, interactive games, and online graphic organizers to help students review content.

Close

Comparing and Contrasting Have students discuss similarities and differences between Internet issues in schools and in society in general. **OL**

Section 3 ★ Review

Many schools use filtering software that allows school officials to decide what material is harmful. The software also monitors the school's Internet traffic. It can identify anyone who tries to use the Internet for prohibited activities, such as drug dealing. One school official reported that since his town installed the filtering software, "access of unauthorized Internet sites probably dropped by 98 percent."

The Issue of Parental Review

Many schools also keep records of the Web sites that students and staff visit. Should parents be able to look at these records? James Knight, the father of four students in New Hampshire, sued his local school district to win that right. Knight said, "If we can find out what books are on the shelves of the school library or what textbooks are being used in the classroom, it seems consistent that we should be able to know where kids are going on the Internet."

Knight's attorneys argued that the school was not doing enough to keep students away from questionable Web sites. School officials argued that releasing students' Internet records would violate their right to privacy. A New Hampshire judge ruled, however, that a parent could inspect the school district's Internet records as long as administrators removed any information that would identify individual students.

As the Internet becomes more fully integrated into American schools, policies and regulations for its use will continue to evolve. School leaders must determine what level of disclosure of student information is safe and appropriate while maintaining their instructional goals. Parents must then approve or disapprove of the disclosure standards. School officials and lawmakers will keep trying to balance concerns about privacy, censorship, and the safety of young Internet users.

 Reading Check Explaining What is parental review? What issues are at stake?

Section 3 Review

Vocabulary

1. **Define** the following terms and use them in sentences related to the Internet: *intellectual property, copyright, revenue.*

Main Ideas

2. **Describing** What is e-commerce?

3. **Explaining** What is the purpose of the Children's Internet Protection Act of 2000?

Critical Thinking

4. **Analyzing** Why have issues such as taxing e-commerce and regulating the Internet in schools arisen?

5. **BIG Ideas** In a diagram like the one below, identify examples of intellectual property.

Intellectual Property

CITIZENSHIP Activity

6. **Expository Writing** Contact your school's computer teacher. Interview him or her about what your school does to monitor Internet use of school computers. Share your findings with the class. Summarize the highlights of your interview in a one-page paper. Then lead a discussion about how your school's policies might be improved.

 Civics ONLINE

Study Central™ To review this section, go to glencoe.com.

Answers

1. Sentences should use vocabulary words according to their definitions in the section and in the Glossary.

2. E-commerce involves using the Internet for purchase and sales transactions.

3. The purpose of the Children's Internet Protection Act of 2000 is to block student access to offensive or dangerous Web materials.

4. These issues have arisen because of the competing interests of e-merchants and state and local tax systems and of parents, school officials, and students.

5. Examples of intellectual property are music, software, books, movies, artwork, and games.

6. Answers will vary. Remind students that their papers should be statements of facts, not their own opinions.

Visual Summary

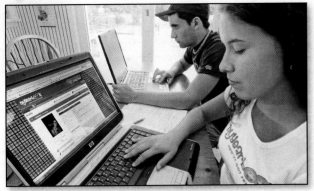

David and Catherine Cook, creators of MyYearbook.com

Regulating the Internet

Many issues surround Internet usage, including the following:
- limits on free speech
- protection of intellectual property
- taxation of e-commerce
- regulation of the Internet in schools

Effects of the Internet

- Millions of people have access to computers, the Internet, and the World Wide Web.
- Electronic communications enable us to instantly access information, to purchase goods and services, and to share ideas around the globe.
- The Internet can help us increase our knowledge about political and social issues.

Issues

- People who do not have access to the Internet cannot enjoy the opportunities it offers.
- Internet users' privacy can be threatened by government and business surveillance.
- Just as the Internet can help advance democratic values, it can also aid the spread of ideas that may run counter to democracy.

Internet café, China

California business owner using the Internet

STUDY TO GO Study anywhere, anytime! Download quizzes and flash cards to your PDA from glencoe.com.

Identifying Central Issues Have students make a list of the issues surrounding Internet use. **Ask:** Which issue do you think is most critical to our democracy? Why? Have students create a poster stating the issue and explaining why it is important to our democracy. Ask students to search online to find news headlines and photographs to include on their posters. **OL**

Drawing Conclusions Have students thoroughly research a court case involving free speech on the Internet. Ask students to act out the case in a mock courtroom. Assign the roles of attorneys, witnesses, judge, and jury, and play the case out in class. After all arguments are presented, have the jury reach a decision. Students should feel free to reach their own decisions in the case. Make time to discuss what students learned by role-playing the case. **AL**

Hands-On Chapter Project
Step 4: Wrap-Up

Exploring the "Blogosphere"

Step 4: Responding to Blogs Student groups respond to blog entries created in Step 3.

Directions Have student groups trade the blogs they created in Step 3. As a group, have students write a response to the blog entry. Remind students that readers contribute to blogs in many ways. They may rebut opinions stated in blogs. They sometimes add helpful information such as links. They may point out errors in information and make corrections. Sometimes, they may simply express admiration for the blog. Have students weigh their rights to free speech with their responsibility to civility as they respond to each other's blogs.

Summarizing Have groups share their blog responses with the class. Encourage the class to discuss what they learned about the Big Ideas of this chapter as they explored the "blogosphere." **OL**

Answers and Analyses
Reviewing Vocabulary

1. C Students will have read about newsgroups in Section 1 in the section entitled Group Action Online.

2. D In this question, the most confusing distractor will most likely be answer B, "extremist." Remembering that extremists are those whose ideas are farthest from the political center will help students avoid this mistake.

3. B The definition of "propaganda" can be found in the section Extremist Groups portion of Section 2. Understanding that misleading information is a central tactic of propaganda will help students answer this question.

4. A A process of elimination will help students answer this question. "Software filters" are used by parents and schools to prevent unauthorized access to inappropriate Web sites. "Revenue" is synonymous with "income." And "intellectual property" is another term for creations such as songs and books. This leaves A, "copyright," as the only possible answer.

Reviewing Main Ideas

5. D Students who are aware that all but one answer for this question provides false information about the Internet should have no trouble answering this question.

6. B Information about political candidates' Web sites can be found in Section 1 on page 472. Understanding the work of politicians will help students answer this question.

7. A Understanding that al-Qaeda is a terrorist organization, students may immediately eliminate answer C, "to spread democratic ideas worldwide." Likewise, answer D, "to widen the gap between haves and have nots," may be eliminated. Students should realize that a training program for terrorists could not be carried out effectively over the Internet. The most sensible answer is A, "to recruit new members."

TEST-TAKING TIP

Learn the meanings of certain words—such as evaluate, enumerate, and illustrate—that appear in many exam questions.

Reviewing Vocabulary

Directions: Choose the word(s) that best completes the sentence.

1. An Internet discussion forum is called a _____.

  A Web site   **C** newsgroup

  B data warehouse   **D** think tank

2. A government in which a leader or group holds absolute power is _____.

  A dissident   **C** nonpartisan

  B extremist   **D** authoritarian

3. Misleading messages designed to misinform people are known as _____.

  A cookies   **C** surveillance

  B propaganda   **D** broadband connections

4. A(n) _____ bars people from using someone else's creation without permission.

  A copyright   **C** revenue

  B software filter   **D** intellectual property

Reviewing Main Ideas

Directions: Choose the best answer for each question.

Section 1 *(pp. 470–473)*

5. What is a disadvantage of using the Internet for information?

  A It offers few sources on most topics.

  B The Internet lacks a diversity of viewpoints.

  C Internet access is limited to computer experts.

  D Facts from the Internet are sometimes inaccurate.

6. Why do political candidates have Web sites?

  A to hold elections online

  B to build support for their ideas

  C to present diverse opinions on issues

  D to exchange information with opponents

Section 2 *(pp. 474–478)*

7. According to the U.S. Army, how does al-Qaeda use the Internet?

  A to recruit new members

  B to conduct training programs

  C to spread democratic ideas worldwide

  D to widen the gap between haves and have-nots

8. Who monitors millions of e-mail messages and other online communications?

  A Chinese dissidents

  B al-Qaeda terrorists

  C National Security Agency

  D eighth graders in New York

Section 3 *(pp. 480–486)*

9. What did the Supreme Court declare in *Reno* v. *American Civil Liberties Union* (1997)?

  A Users can install filters to block Web sites.

  B Indecent material on the Internet is unlawful.

  C The First Amendment protects speech on the Internet.

  D Users must verify their age to view certain Web sites.

GO ON →

---

8. C The question states that millions of e-mails are monitored. This large number should be a clue that only a large organization, such as the National Security Agency, could be the correct answer.

9. C Students should reread the section Internet Speech in Section 3. Here they will learn about the court case *Reno* v. *American Civil Liberties Union* (1997).

10. A Students should remember that Grokster was a company that developed software that made it easy for people to download copyrighted materials without paying for them. This information should help students answer the question correctly.

10. In which case did the Supreme Court decision prohibit companies from encouraging people to use their technology for copyright violations?

  A *Metro-Goldwyn-Mayer* v. *Grokster*

  B *Reno* v. *American Civil Liberties Union*

  C *Hazelwood School District* v. *Kuhlmeier*

  D *Ashcroft* v. *American Civil Liberties Union*

Critical Thinking

Directions: Base your answers to questions 11 and 12 on the cartoon below and your knowledge of Chapter 17.

Tribune Media Services, Inc.

11. What does the highway in the cartoon represent?

  A Internet traffic

  B corporate America

  C government censorship

  D interstate expressways

12. Which of the following statements best expresses the cartoonist's point of view?

  A Some citizen protections need to be waived if lives are at risk.

  B Surveillance of online communications endangers people's privacy.

  C Powerful tools are needed to fight terrorists and criminals using cyberspace.

  D The government needs to catch people who use the Internet to prey on children.

Document-Based Questions

Directions: Analyze the following document and answer the short-answer questions that follow.

> On February 15, 2006, the Senate discussed amending parts of the USA Patriot Act that violate citizens' constitutional rights in the name of the war on terrorism. During the discussion, Senator Robert Byrd from West Virginia made the following statement:
>
> *Attorney General Gonzales refused to divulge whether purely domestic communications have also been caught up in this warrantless surveillance, and he refused to assure the Senate Judiciary Committee and the American public that the administration has not deliberately tapped Americans' telephone calls and computers or searched their homes without warrants. Nor would he reveal whether even a single arrest has resulted from the program.*
>
> *What about the first amendment? What about the chilling effect that warrantless eavesdropping is already having on those law-abiding American citizens who may not support the war in Iraq, or who may simply communicate with friends or relatives overseas? Eventually, the feeling that no conversation is private will cause perfectly innocent people to think carefully before they candidly express opinions or even say something in jest.*
>
> —Senator Byrd

13. How would you sum up Senator Byrd's objections to the government's warrantless surveillance program in the first paragraph?

14. Senator Byrd suggests that warrantless eavesdropping permitted by the USA Patriot Act violates First Amendment freedoms. According to the chapter, what other amendment and freedom may be violated by warrantless searches?

Extended-Response Question

15. Explain why standards for government online surveillance are not clear. **STOP**

For additional test practice, use Self-Check Quizzes—Chapter 17 on glencoe.com.

Need Extra Help?															
If you missed question...	1	2	3	4	5	6	7	8	9	10	11	12	13	14	15
Go to page...	472	475	476	483	471	472	476	477	481	484	471	477	477	478	477

Chapter 17 489

ASSESSMENT

Document-Based Questions

13. Students' answers may vary. A possible answer is that Senator Byrd considers the government's warrantless surveillance secretive and ineffective in capturing terrorists.

14. the Fourth Amendment and freedom from unreasonable searches

Extended Response

15. Students' explanations will vary. Their answers should note that the 1996 Electronic Communications Privacy Act sets standards for protecting online information while the USA Patriot Act allows some citizen protections to be waived.

Critical Thinking

11. A Remind students that in political cartoons symbols are often used—familiar items often stand for something else or have a dual meaning. Remembering that many people refer to the Internet as an "information highway" will help students answer this question.

12. B Paying attention to the details in the cartoon will help students answer this question. The license plate on the car spells out "privacy." Behind this small car looms a large truck with cameras and satellite dishes. These clues lead us to choose B, "surveillance of online communications endangers people's privacy."

Have students visit the Web site at glencoe.com to review Chapter 17 and take the **Self-Check Quiz.**

Need Extra Help?

Have students refer to the pages listed if they miss any of the questions.

Focus

R₁ Reading Strategy

Identifying Ask: What purposes do laws serve? (*Laws resolve conflicts, protect rights, limit government, promote general welfare, set social goals, and control crime.*) **OL**

R₂ Reading Strategy

Organizing Ask: Which law(s) in the Code of Hammurabi falls under the category of family law? (*142*) Which law(s) in the Code of Hammurabi falls under the category of criminal law? (*22, 196*) **OL**

Additional Reading

Analyzing Primary Sources

Sources of American Law

Reading Focus

The set of rules and standards by which a society governs itself is known as law. Laws serve several functions in every society. The law is used to resolve conflict, to protect rights, to limit government, to promote general welfare, to set social goals, and to control crime. **R₁**

Read to Discover

As you read, think about the following:

• How has early law influenced American law?

• What is the importance of common law?

Reader's Dictionary

proprietor: an owner

dowry: the money and goods that a woman brings to her husband in marriage

maxim: a general truth

heretofore: up to this time

repugnant: hostile or opposed to

Code of Hammurabi

The most well-known of the earliest written laws was the Code of Hammurabi, assembled in the 1700s B.C. This code was made up of 282 legal cases that spelled out relationships among individuals as well as punishments in areas that we would now call property law, family law, civil law, and criminal law.

22. If any one is committing a robbery and is caught, then he shall be put to death. . . .

117. If any one fail to meet a claim for debt, and sell himself, his wife, his son, and daughter for money or give them away to forced labor: they shall work for three years in the house of the man who bought them, or the **proprietor,** and in the fourth year they shall be set free. . . .

R₂ 142. If a woman quarrels with her husband . . . the reasons for her prejudice must be presented. If she is guiltless, and there is no fault on her part, but he leaves and neglects her, then no guilt attaches to this woman, she shall take her **dowry** and go back to her father's house. . . .

196. If a man put out the eye of another man, his eye shall be put out. . . .

—"Code of Hammurabi," L.W. King, trans.

The Ten Commandments

An early set of written laws that has influenced our legal system is the Ten Commandments found in the Hebrew Bible and Christian Bible.

1. Do not worship any god except me.
2. Do not . . . bow down and worship idols.
3. Do not misuse my name.
4. Remember that the Sabbath Day belongs to me.
5. Respect your father and your mother.
6. Do not murder.
7. Be faithful in marriage.
8. Do not steal.
9. Do not tell lies about others.
10. Do not want anything that belongs to someone else.

—Exodus 20:3–17

Review suggested books before assigning them.

The Black Press and the Struggle for Civil Rights, by Carl Senna traces the history of the black press in America, starting with the founding of the first black newspaper in 1827.

Business Builders in Computers, by Nathan Aaseng notes that in recent decades, the computer business has boomed! Find out about Bill Gates, An Wang, Steve Jobs, and other computer industry giants.

Not Guilty, by George Sullivan accounts the trials of five people who were wrongly punished for crimes, including Leonard Peltier, whose ordeal inspired a movie, and Johnson Whittaker, who was expelled from West Point for a racist attack on himself.

The Justinian Code

In the A.D. 530s, the Roman emperor Justinian had scholars reorganize and simplify all the laws into a Roman legal code called the Justinian Code.

Book I. Of Persons
I. Justice and Law.

 3. The **maxims** of law are these: to live honestly, to hurt no one, to give every one his due.

 4. The study of law is divided into two branches; that of public and that of private law. Public law regards the government of the Roman empire; private law, the interest of the individuals.

II. Natural, Common, and Civil Law.

 1. Civil law is thus distinguished from the law of nations. Every community governed by laws and customs uses partly its own law, partly laws common to all mankind. The law which a people makes for its own government belongs exclusively to that state and is called the civil law. . . .

—"The Institutes," 535 C.E.

Common Law

The law of the United States was largely derived from the common law of the system of English law. Common law is law based on the concept of precedence—on how the courts have interpreted the law previously—rather than on a legal code. By A.D. 1776 common law was being used throughout the American colonies along with laws created there.

Constitution

ART. 25. The common law of England, as-well as so much of the statute law as has been **heretofore** adopted in practice in this State, shall remain in force, unless they shall be altered by a future law of the legislature; such parts only excepted as are **repugnant** to the rights and privileges contained in this constitution, and the declaration of rights, . . . agreed to by this convention.

—Constitution of Delaware, 1776

Monuments as Primary Sources
This stone monument shows Hammurabi (standing) holding his code. What does the monument tell you about the place and time it was created? What do you think was the artist's purpose in creating this monument?

DBQ Document-Based Questions

1. **Connecting** Consider this statement: Whether Hammurabi's laws were fair or cruel, the culture benefited from having a written code that applied to everyone. Do you agree or disagree? What would it be like to live in a society with no written rules?

2. **Connecting** How does common law differ from statutory law?

3. **Analyzing** How many of the commandments tell people how to interact with other people? How many tell them how to worship and show respect for God?

4. **Evaluating and Connecting** Consider this statement: Liberty depends upon the power of laws. Write a paragraph explaining what the statement means to you.

491

Did You Know?

Contemplation of Justice As have other cultures, the United States has created monuments to honor those values it holds dear. One such monument is the statue *Contemplation of Justice* by James Earle Fraser. The statue stands on the steps leading to the main entrance of the Supreme Court Building in Washington, D.C. It shows a seated woman looking at a smaller statue of Justice, which she holds in her right hand.

The statue of Justice is blindfolded and carries a set of scales. These details are cherished symbols representing important elements of justice. In our legal system we believe that the courts should be blind to the status of individuals. The law must treat the powerful and weak equally. It is also the duty of the courts to weigh carefully every case before it. The scales carried by Justice symbolizes this important value.

Unit **6** Planning Guide

UNIT PACING CHART

	Unit 1	Chapter 18	Chapter 19	Chapter 20	Chapter 21	Chapter 22
Day 1	Unit Opener, Reading Social Studies	Chapter Opener, Section 1	Chapter Opener, Section 1	Chapter Opener, Section 1	Chapter Opener, Section 1	Chapter Opener, Section 1
Day 2		Section 2, Financial Literacy	Section 2, Financial Literacy	Section 2, Financial Literacy	Section 2, Financial Literacy	Section 2, Issues to Debate
Day 3		Chapter Review, Visual Summary	Section 2, Landmark Supreme Court Case Studies	Section 3	Section 3	Section 3, Chapter Review, Visual Summary
Day 4		Chapter Assessment	Chapter Review, Visual Summary	Section 4, Chapter Review, Visual Summary	Section 4, Chapter Review, Visual Summary	Chapter Assessment
Day 5			Chapter Assessment	Chapter Assessment	Chapter Assessment	Analyzing Primary Sources
Day 5					TIME Reports	

Teacher to Teacher

Tony Pottorff, Columbus East High School, Columbus, Indiana

On the first day of class I have students listen to the song "If I Had $1,000,000". They have to listen to the song and make a list of what the singers say they would purchase. I then ask the students to create their own $1,000,000 list. After a few minutes, I ask the students to create a $10,000 list using the items from their previous list. Following that, students create a $1000 list, again using the original list as inspiration.

After some discussion of what students kept and eliminated from their lists at each step of the process, I then ask if students would have any trouble creating a $10,000,000 list, a $100,000,000 list, and so on. We then launch into a discussion of unlimited wants and how we try to meet them in a world of scarcity.

Author Note

Dear Social Studies Teacher:

In college, it may surprise you to learn that there was a time when I was not very interested in economics—and this is coming from the *economics* author of your book! All of that changed when I visited the city of Budapest, Hungary, during the height of the Cold War in the early 1970s.

I was on a study abroad program, and our professor had just taken us to a nearby park that overlooked the city. It was a cold mid-December evening, several inches of snow had just fallen, and a full moon lit up the landscape. By all accounts, the view should have been beautiful, even spectacular perhaps—but it wasn't.

Instead, the landscape was cold, alien, and downright dreary. Even now I can remember asking myself: What is wrong with this scene? Why is it so depressing? Then it dawned on me: *there was no color in the landscape.* Here was a major European city, but everything was in shades black and white. Instead of looking out at a sea of bright red, green, and blue lights at Christmas, all I saw were the dreary white streetlights and faded yellow reflections coming through the windows from inside the buildings and apartments.

Then I remembered what my economics teacher had told me: Hungary had a command economy where consumer goods were so scarce that people had to wait in line to make a purchase. People even had to get on a waiting list to buy a car, and sometimes they had to wait several years before one became available. Outdoor advertising as we know it—with the brightly colored lights that are used to advertise products and attract consumers—was unheard of because of the type of economy that Hungary had.

There were many other differences as well, but for the first time in my life I understood that the economy—and even the study of economics—actually matters.

Gary Clayton

Author

Unit Objectives

After studying this unit, students will be able to:

- Distinguish between wants and needs and identify how scarcity forces people to make economic choices.

- Identify how democratic capitalism and free enterprise work in the American economy.

- Relate personal financial choices and decisions to principles of economics.

- Explain the relationship between demand and supply in an economic system.

- Analyze and comprehend the relationship between management and labor.

Did You Know?

The National Council on Economic Education (NCEE) sponsors a summer institute for students entering their senior year in high school. At this institute—EntrePrep—young people learn the basics of starting a business, or *entrepreneurship*. During their senior year, students then become nonpaid interns in start-up firms. They attend educational seminars and make economic recommendations to improve the firm's business.

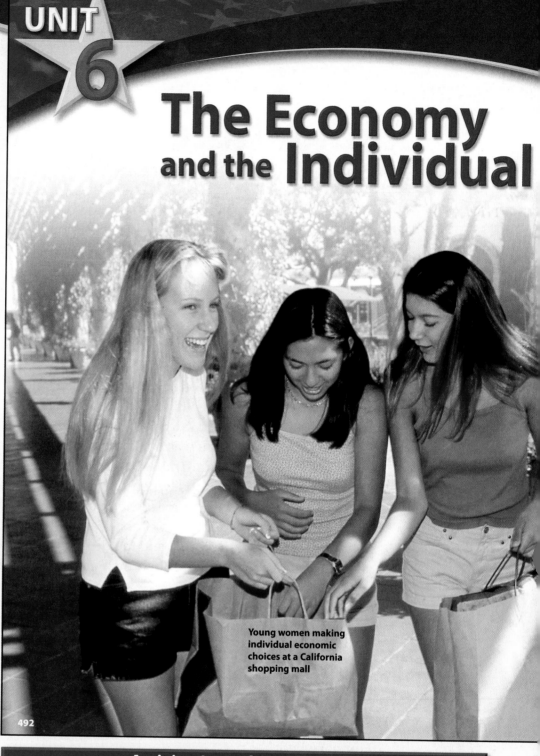

UNIT

6

The Economy
and the Individual

Young women making individual economic choices at a California shopping mall

492

Activity: Launching the Unit

The Economy and the Individual Ask: What part does economics play in education? *(Public schools are supported primarily with money from local and state taxes. Since tax monies are limited, school districts must decide how to use the money available to them. Those decisions include the number of teachers, administrators, and other school personnel. Districts must decide what to spend on hands-on learning centers, such as auto shops. They must find monies to erect and maintain school buildings. Sometimes economic decisions eliminate extra- and cocurricular activities. Some students may want more money spent on music programs, while others might want expanded athletic, debate, or drama programs. Only through a careful study of wants, needs, and available resources can districts make sound economic decisions.)* **OL**

Be An Active Citizen

CITIZENSHIP What do you think economics is? Describe how, in your opinion, economics affects you. After you complete your study of Unit 6, compare your initial ideas with the new information you learn.

493

Be an Active Citizen

CITIZENSHIP How well do your students understand the economic decisions they make every day? Ask students to estimate and write down the cost of the clothes they are wearing; the school supplies they have in their backpacks, desks, or lockers; the food they have eaten that day; the energy costs of transporting them to and from school; and the musical or sports equipment they will use at school that day. Then have students list five wants or needs they could not afford and assign cost values to these items. Ask students to create posters to illustrate these economic decisions in their lives. Encourage them to be creative in illustrating each category of "haves" and each of "have nots." Display and discuss the posters.

Online Current Events Update

Visit Glencoe's *Online Current Events Update* **at** www.glencoe.com **to find news reports, features, maps, graphs, and photos of current events that shape our lives. Students can also make connections between historical events and current events by using the interactive time line.**

More About the Photo

Visual Literacy What economic choices might these girls have considered? Every day, American shoppers using their own criteria select from several brands of the same item. Some brands may offer extra features or be made of better materials. Product prices may vary; some might reflect a discounted, or sale, price. Shoppers also frequently consider the manufacturers' reputations. Some may be known for making products that last longer or work better. The girls may also ask themselves, *Do I need this, or do I simply want it? Am I willing to go without something else so that I can buy it?* Shopping can be fun and educational, too!

Why Comparing and Contrasting Is Important

Making comparisons is an automatic process, even in early childhood. While a young child might compare the size of his scoop of ice cream to that of a sibling, a teen might compare his or her exam score to a classmate's, and an adult might compare his or her wage statement to a coworker's. By comparing and contrasting, people assess how things are similar and how they are different. Based on these comparisons, it is possible to assess which is better, more difficult, more complete, faster, and so on. Comparing and contrasting helps students make better choices and more completely understand ideas, objects, and options presented to them.

① Learn It!

Ask students to draw a Venn diagram. As they recall a recent shopping trip, have students describe something they purchased in the left circle of the diagram. In the right circle, have students describe something they considered but did not buy. Have students list ways in which the items were different in their respective circles. Similarities between the two items should be written in the overlap section of the diagram. As a class, discuss how comparing and contrasting helped students choose the items they purchased. **OL**

Comparing and Contrasting

① Learn It!

When you compare people, things, or ideas you show the similarities among them. When you contrast these things you point out their differences.

- Read the following paragraph. Note how the writer compares fixed costs to variable costs.
- How does the writer contrast fixed costs to variable costs?

> The first kind of cost is fixed costs—costs, or expenses, that are the same no matter how many units of a good are produced. Mortgage payments and property taxes are two examples of fixed costs. It makes no difference whether your company produces one bicycle helmet or a very large number. Your fixed costs, such as your mortgage and property taxes, remain the same. . . . Another kind of cost is variable costs. Variable costs are expenses that change with the number of items produced. Wages and raw materials are examples of variable costs.
>
> —*from page 506*

People, Things, or Ideas	Compare	Contrast
Fixed costs and variable costs	*Both are expenses	*Fixed costs remain the same *Variable costs change with the number of items produced

Reading Tip

As you read, look for signal words such as <u>like, but, however, in contrast,</u> or <u>on the other hand</u> to help you find comparisons and contrasts.

Reading Strategy ⟨ Questioning

Comparing and Contrasting Students compare and contrast every day. Divide students into groups. List the following real-life school situations on the board: *passing through the lunch line, registering for* *classes, selecting what to wear to school.* Have students volunteer questions that would help them use comparing and contrasting to make a decision in each situation. **BL**

② Practice It!

Read the following sentences from this unit that compare and contrast microeconomics to macroeconomics. Draw a chart like the one shown below.

> . . . economics is divided into two branches. In microeconomics, economists look at the small picture. They study the behavior and decision making of small (the meaning of the prefix *micro-*) units such as individuals and businesses. . . . On the other hand, macroeconomics looks at the big (the meaning of the prefix *macro-*) picture. It deals with the economy as a whole and decision making by large units such as governments or whole industries or societies.
>
> —*from page 500*

People, Things, or Ideas	Compare	Contrast
Microeconomics Macroeconomics		

Read to Write Activity

Read the section titled "Circular Flow of Economic Activity" in Chapter 19, Section 2. Choose any two of the sectors (consumer, business, government, or foreign) to compare and contrast. Once you decide which two sectors you will write about, jot down facts about each and write a few sentences to show how they compare or contrast.

② Practice It!

Compare: both are branches of economics; study economic decision making

Contrast: microeconomics looks at behavior on a small scale, such as individuals and businesses; macroeconomics looks at the economy as a whole on a large scale, such as governments or whole industries or societies

③ Apply It!

Bring to class five sets of three or four newspaper or magazine ads that promote different cereals, chewing gums, tires, or other consumer goods. Organize students into five groups, giving each group a set of ads for one type of product. Ask student groups to compare and contrast ad information to decide which products they would most likely purchase. **OL**

③ Apply It!

As you read look for people, things, or ideas that you can compare and contrast in:

- **Chapter 20, Section 1**
- **Chapter 21, Section 2**

Reading Strategy ◄ Read to Write

Writing Product Reviews When writing comparisons such as product reviews, students first need to determine which product features will be compared and contrasted. Have students write a review of several brands of a product, such as cosmetics, pizza, shoes, sporting gear, and so on. Explain that the reviews can be organized by product or by feature. Have students exchange their reviews with a partner and comment on how well their partners used comparing and contrasting to evaluate the products. **OL**

18

Key to Ability Levels

BL	Below level	AL	Above level
OL	On level	ELL	English Language Learners

Key to Teaching Resources

Print Material
CD-ROM or DVD
Transparency

Levels					Resources	Chapter Opener	Section 1	Section 2	Chapter Assess
BL	OL	AL	ELL						
					FOCUS				
BL	OL	AL	ELL		Daily Focus Skills Transparencies		18–1	18–2	
					TEACH				
BL	OL		ELL		Reading Essentials and Note-Taking Guide*		p. 168	p. 171	
	OL	AL			Economics Activity, URB		p. 5		
BL	OL	AL	ELL		Content Vocabulary Activity, URB*	p. 21	p. 21	p. 21	
BL	OL	AL	ELL		Academic Vocabulary Activity, URB	p. 23	p. 23	p. 23	
	OL				Biography Activity, URB			p. 25	
BL	OL	AL	ELL		Writing Skills Activity, URB		p. 27		
	OL	AL			Critical Thinking Skills Activity, URB		p. 29	p. 29	
BL	OL	AL	ELL		Chart, Graph, and Map Skills Activity, URB			p. 31	
BL	OL	AL	ELL		Differentiated Instruction, URB		p. 33	p. 33	
BL	OL	AL	ELL		School-to-Home Connection Activity, URB*	p. 35	p. 35	p. 35	
BL	OL		ELL		Guided Reading Activities, URB*		p. 39	p. 40	
BL	OL	AL	ELL		Writer's Guidebook	✓	✓	✓	✓
	OL	AL			Primary Source Document Library	✓	✓	✓	✓
BL	OL	AL	ELL		Daily Lecture & Discussion Notes (in Pres. Plus)		✓	✓	✓
BL	OL	AL	ELL		StudentWorks™ Plus		✓	✓	✓
BL	OL	AL	ELL		Section Spotlight Videos		✓	✓	
BL	OL	AL	ELL		TIME Interpreting Political Cartoons Transp.			Ch. 18	
BL	OL	AL	ELL		Writing Process Transparencies	✓	✓	✓	✓

Note: Please refer to the *Unit 6 Resource Book* for this chapter's URB materials.

* Also available in Spanish

TeacherWorks *Plus*
All-In-One Planner and Resource Center

- Interactive Lesson Planner
- Interactive Teacher Edition
- Fully editable blackline masters
- Section Spotlight Videos Launch
- Differentiated Lesson Plans
- Printable reports of daily assignments
- Standards Tracking System

Levels					Resources	Chapter Opener	Section 1	Section 2	Chapter Assess
BL	OL	AL	ELL						
TEACH *(continued)*									
				📁	**Building Academic Vocabulary**	✓	✓	✓	✓
Teacher Resources				📁	**Strategies for Success**	✓	✓	✓	✓
				📁	**Teacher's Guide to Differentiated Instruction**	✓	✓	✓	✓
				💿	**Graphing Tool**	✓	✓	✓	✓
				💿	**Presentation Plus! with MindJogger CheckPoint**	✓	✓	✓	✓
ASSESS									
BL	OL	AL	ELL	📁	**Quizzes and Tests***		p. 215	p. 216	p. 217
BL	OL	AL	ELL	📁	**Authentic Assessment with Rubrics**			p. 22	
BL	OL	AL	ELL	📁	**Standardized Test Practice**			p. 35	p. 35
BL	OL	AL	ELL	💿	*ExamView®* **Assessment Suite CD-ROM**		18–1	18–2	Ch. 18
CLOSE									
BL			ELL	📁	**Reteaching Activity, URB***		p. 37	p. 37	
BL	OL		ELL	📁	**Reading and Study Skills Foldables™ Activity**	p. 84		p. 85	
BL	OL	AL	ELL	🖼	**Graphic Organizer Transparencies & Strategies**	✓	✓	✓	✓

✓ Chapter- or unit-based activities applicable to all sections in this chapter

18

Using StudentWorks™ Plus

Read and Listen

What is StudentWorks™ Plus?

Glencoe's StudentWorks™ Plus contains the complete Student Edition in an interactive format, full audio of the text, student workbooks, and links to online activities and resources.

How can StudentWorks™ Plus help my students?

When using StudentWorks™ Plus, students can view the text's pages on screen as they listen to an audio reading of the text. StudentWorks™ Plus helps students with independent study skills by allowing them to:

- practice their reading skills
- improve their comprehension

Civics ONLINE

Visit glencoe.com and enter *QuickPass*™ code CIV1360c18T for Chapter 18 resources.

You can easily launch a wide range of digital products from your computer's desktop with the McGraw-Hill Social Studies widget.

TeacherWorks

	Student	Teacher	Parent
Media Library			
• Student Edition Section Audio	●		●
• Spanish Audio Summaries	●		●
• Section Spotlight Videos	●	●	●
***Civics Today* Online Learning Center (Web Site)**			
• Chapter Overviews	●	●	●
• Study Central™	●	●	●
• Study-to-Go	●	●	●
• Student Web Activities	●	●	●
• In Motion Animation	●	●	●
• Self-Check Quizzes	●	●	●
• ePuzzles and Games	●	●	●
• StudentWorks™ Plus Online	●	●	●
• Vocabulary eFlashcards	●	●	●
• Web Activity Lesson Plans		●	
• Vocabulary PuzzleMaker	●	●	●
Classroom Tools			
• Multilingual Glossary	●	●	●
• Beyond the Textbook	●	●	●
• NGS MapMachine	●	●	●

Reading List Generator CD-ROM

GLENCOE BookLink 3

Use this database to search more than 30,000 titles to create a customized reading list for your students.

- Reading lists can be organized by students' reading level, author, genre, theme, or area of interest.
- The database provides Degrees of Reading Power™ (DRP) and Lexile™ readability scores for all selections.
- A brief summary of each selection is included.

Leveled reading suggestions for this chapter:

For students at a Grade 7 reading level:
- *China: A Study of an Economically Developing Country,* by Julia Waterlow

For students at a Grade 8 reading level:
- *The Great Depression and the New Deal: America's Economic Collapse and Recovery,* by Anne E. Schraff

For students at a Grade 9 reading level:
- *The New Freedom of the New Deal: 1913–1939,* by William Loren Katz

For students at a Grade 10 reading level:
- *Korea: A Story of an Economically Developing Country,* by Sung-Hoon Jung

For students at a Grade 11 reading level:
- *Small is Beautiful: Economics as if People Mattered,* by E.F. Schumacher

READING SUPPORT FROM JAMESTOWN EDUCATION

- **Timed Readings Plus in Social Studies** helps students increase their reading rate and fluency while maintaining comprehension. The 400-word passages are similar to those found on state and national assessments.

- **Reading in the Content Area: Social Studies** concentrates on six essential reading skills that help students better comprehend what they read. The book includes 75 high-interest nonfiction passages written at increasing levels of difficulty.

- **Reading Social Studies** includes strategic reading instruction and vocabulary support in Social Studies content for both ELLs and native speakers of English.

- **Content Vocabulary Workout** (Grades 6–8) accelerates reading comprehension through focused vocabulary development. Social Studies content vocabulary comes from the glossaries of Glencoe's Middle School Social Studies texts. www.jamestowneducation.com

KEY Teacher Wraparound

Use this key to help you identify the different types of prompts found in the Teacher Wraparound Edition.

R **Reading Strategies** activities help you teach reading skills and vocabulary.

C **Critical Thinking** strategies help students apply and extend what they have learned.

D **Differentiated Instruction** activities provide instruction for students learning to speak English, along with suggestions for teaching various types of learners.

S **Skill Practice** strategies help students practice historical analysis and geography skills.

W **Writing Support** activities provide writing opportunities to help students comprehend the text.

Teaching strategies and activities have been coded for ability level appropriateness.

AL Activities for students working above grade level

OL Activities for students working on grade level

BL Activities for students working below grade level

ELL Activities for English Language Learners

Focus

Why It Matters

Ask: How do consumers influence decisions made by producers? *(Consumers have needs and wants. In order to sell their products, producers must identify what consumers need and want or, in other words, what they are willing to buy.)*

More About the Photo

Visual Literacy The American economic system, with its wealth of economic opportunities and choices, owes a great deal to an eighteenth-century economist named Adam Smith. In his *Wealth of Nations*, Smith explained that a large part of a nation's economic health depended on the skill, judgments, and efforts of its citizens to produce goods. Britain's efforts to limit what the colonies could produce or to whom they could sell their goods was a contributing factor in the American Revolution. Today, American businesses—small and large—produce and sell a wide variety of goods locally, nationally, and globally.

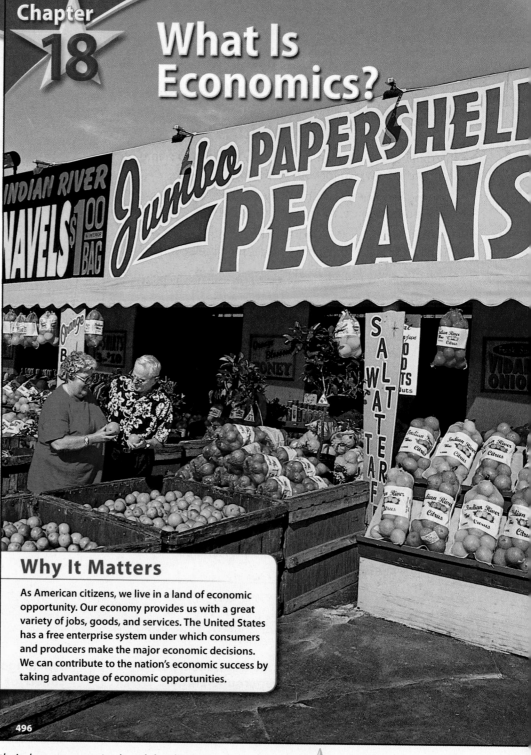

What Is Economics?

Why It Matters

As American citizens, we live in a land of economic opportunity. Our economy provides us with a great variety of jobs, goods, and services. The United States has a free enterprise system under which consumers and producers make the major economic decisions. We can contribute to the nation's economic success by taking advantage of economic opportunities.

496

Teach

BIG Ideas As you begin teaching each section, use these questions and activities to help students focus on the Big Ideas.

Section 1

How Economic Systems Work Ask: How do limited resources affect the decisions you make? *(Answers may include the ideas that limited money determines what students purchase or do, that limited time forces them to choose how* their days are organized, and that limited access to transportation determines their recreational activities and sites.) Point out that in Section 1, students will analyze how scarcity, or limited resources, affects economic decisions made by individuals, businesses, and nations. **OL**

Section 2

Making Economic Decisions Ask: What are the benefits and costs of choosing to play sports? *(Benefits may include the ideas of physical activity and fitness; college athletic scholarships; high-paying professional sport careers; skill development in terms of teamwork and cooperation; personal development in terms of sense of sportsmanship and fair play; avoidance of boredom and*

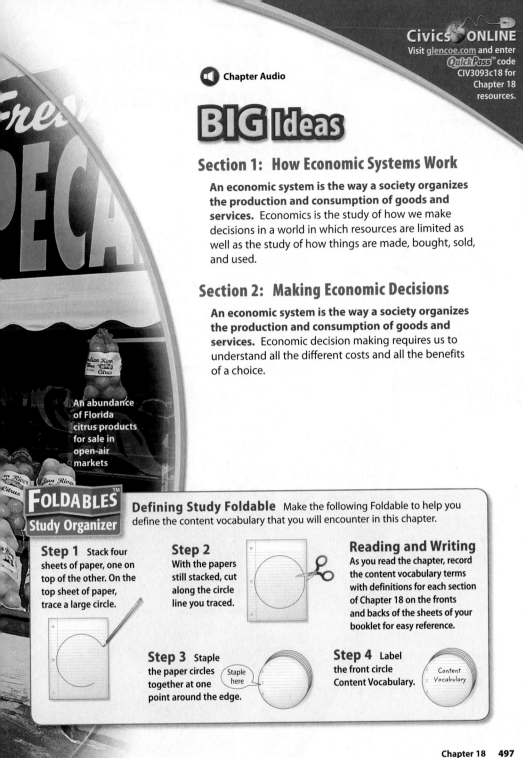

Chapter Audio

BIG Ideas

Section 1: How Economic Systems Work

An economic system is the way a society organizes the production and consumption of goods and services. Economics is the study of how we make decisions in a world in which resources are limited as well as the study of how things are made, bought, sold, and used.

Section 2: Making Economic Decisions

An economic system is the way a society organizes the production and consumption of goods and services. Economic decision making requires us to understand all the different costs and all the benefits of a choice.

An abundance of Florida citrus products for sale in open-air markets

FOLDABLES Dinah Zike's
Study Organizer Foldables

Purpose This Foldable guides the student to understand the content vocabulary associated with basic principles of economics. The completed Foldable will use a circle book of vocabulary definitions to help students understand what they are reading. **OL**

📁 More Foldables activities for this chapter can be found in the *Dinah Zike's Reading and Study Skills Foldables* ancillary.

Civics ONLINE

Visit glencoe.com and enter *QuickPass*™ code CIV1360c18T for Chapter 18 resources, including a Chapter Overview, Study Central™, Study-to-Go, Student Web Activity, Self-Check Quiz, and other materials.

Civics ONLINE
Visit glencoe.com and enter *QuickPass*™ code CIV3093c18 for Chapter 18 resources.

FOLDABLES
Study Organizer

Defining Study Foldable Make the following Foldable to help you define the content vocabulary that you will encounter in this chapter.

Step 1 Stack four sheets of paper, one on top of the other. On the top sheet of paper, trace a large circle.

Step 2 With the papers still stacked, cut along the circle line you traced.

Reading and Writing As you read the chapter, record the content vocabulary terms with definitions for each section of Chapter 18 on the fronts and backs of the sheets of your booklet for easy reference.

Step 3 Staple the paper circles together at one point around the edge. *Staple here*

Step 4 Label the front circle Content Vocabulary. *Content Vocabulary*

negative activities/practices such as substance abuse, gang activities, and criminal activities; and so on. Costs may include the ideas of injuries, overdeveloped sense of competitiveness or self-importance, financial burdens, loss of interest or attention to academic studies, and so on.) Tell students that in Section 2, they will learn how individuals and businesses can use cost-benefit analysis to make sound economic decisions. **OL**

Focus

Section 1

Bellringer

Daily Focus Transparency 18–1

Guide to Reading

Answers to Graphic:

Economics
- Micro — the study of the behavior and decision making of small units, such as individuals and businesses
- Macro — the study of the economy as a whole and decision making by large units, such as governments or whole industries or societies

Section Spotlight Video

To generate student interest and provide a springboard for class discussion, access the Chapter 18, Section 1 video at glencoe.com or on the video DVD.

Resource Manager

Guide to Reading

Big Idea
An economic system is the way a society organizes the production and consumption of goods and services.

Content Vocabulary
- need *(p. 499)*
- want *(p. 499)*
- economics *(p. 499)*
- microeconomics *(p. 500)*
- macroeconomics *(p. 500)*
- economic model *(p. 500)*
- economic system *(p. 500)*
- resource *(p. 501)*
- scarcity *(p. 501)*

Academic Vocabulary
- rational *(p. 499)*
- capable *(p. 501)*
- generate *(p. 502)*

Reading Strategy
Comparing As you read the section, compare the two ways of defining economics: microeconomics and macroeconomics.

Economics
- Micro
- Macro

 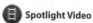

How Economic Systems Work

Real World Economics Have you ever gone to the grocery store and found the shelves empty? Sometimes natural disasters can cause huge economic problems from food shortages to the disruption of gas supplies. Hurricane Rita, on the heels of 2005's Hurricane Katrina, shook the economic roots of not only the South but the entire United States. Because Louisiana and Texas are producers of oil and gas, energy needs all across the nation were affected. Both national and state governments provided help in the form of emergency services, health care, information, and supplies.

▼ **Scarcity of products determines purchase prices following a disaster**

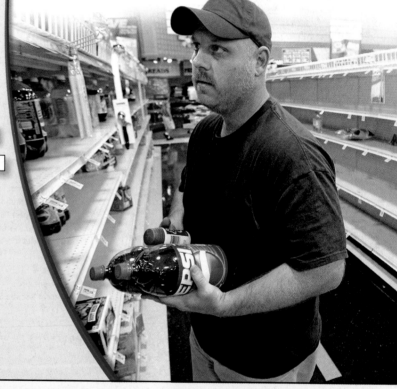

R Reading Strategies	C Critical Thinking	D Differentiated Instruction	W Writing Support	S Skill Practice
Teacher Edition • Act. Prior Know., pp. 499, 501 • Making Connections, p. 501 **Additional Resources** • Cont. Vocab., URB p. 21 • Ac. Vocab., URB p. 23 • Guid. Read., URB p. 39 • RENTG, p. 168	**Teacher Edition** • Drawing Con., p. 499 • Det. Cause/Effect, p. 501 **Additional Resources** • Econ. Act., URB p. 5 • Quizzes and Tests, p. 215	**Teacher Edition** • Logical/Math., p. 500 **Additional Resources** • Diff. Instr., URB p. 33 • School-to-Home Conn., URB p. 35	**Teacher Edition** • Persuasive Writing, p. 499 **Additional Resources** • Writing Skills Act., URB p. 27	**Teacher Edition** • Categorizing, p. 500 **Additional Resources** • Daily Focus Trans., 18-1

Foreign-Made Products Needs and wants are often satisfied by products made in other countries. These auto imports have just been unloaded at the port in Portland, Oregon. **Contrasting** What is the difference between an economic need and a want?

Economic Choices

Main Idea Economics is the study of how we make decisions in a world in which resources are limited as well as the study of how things are made, bought, sold, and used.

Economics & You Have you ever found it difficult to tell the difference between something you wanted and something you needed? Read to find out how these two ideas influence the science of economics.

To be a well-informed citizen, it is important to have a good understanding of economics and the American economic system. Well-informed citizens do more than make choices in the voting booth. They also make **rational**, or reasonable, economic choices, and they make these choices every day. For example, imagine you have $10 to spend on Saturday night. Do you rent a movie, go to a movie, order a pizza, go to a restaurant, buy snacks for a party, put gas in the car, or make any of a dozen other possible choices? You will quickly discover that your $10 will not cover everything you might want to do. Therefore, you must choose.

Needs and Wants

As individuals, we have many **needs** that are required for survival, such as food, clothing, and shelter. In addition, we also have an enormous number of **wants,** or things we would like to have, such as entertainment, vacations, and other items that make life more comfortable and enjoyable.

The choices we face, as individuals and as a society, are based on the fact that we do not have enough productive resources to satisfy all our wants and needs. Even a seemingly plentiful resource such as water is considered scarce because it is not free; we pay to use it.

Economics: A Definition

Economics is the study of how we make decisions in a world in which resources are limited. The study of economics will help you think about the process of making decisions.

Economics is also the study of how things are made, bought, sold, and used. It helps answer questions such as these: Where do these products come from? Who makes them? How do they get to the stores? Who buys them? Why do people buy them?

Teach

W Writing Support

Persuasive Writing Have students write a letter to a parent, guardian, or teacher explaining that something the adult sees as the student's *want* is actually a *need*. Remind students to support their arguments with logical reasoning and facts. **OL**

C Critical Thinking

Drawing Conclusions Ask: What conclusion about scarce resources can be drawn from the idea that people must pay for them? *(When a resource is scarce, it is more valuable.)* **BL**

R Reading Strategy

Activating Prior Knowledge Tell students that suppliers are also known as producers. **Ask:** What term is used to describe buyers, or product users, in an economic system? *(consumers)* **AL**

Caption Answer:

Needs are required for survival; wants are things we'd like to have.

Differentiated Instruction

Environment and the Economy

Economics Activity 6, URB pp. 5–6

Objective: To understand economic choices

Focus: Discuss the uses of petroleum.

Teach: Have students locate each quote's claim(s). Discuss each claim's validity.

Assess: Have students summarize the problem and its solution.

Close: Debate the issue as a class. Then have students cast votes to express their opinions on the issue.

Differentiated Instruction Strategies

BL Which position puts humans first? Which position puts other living things first?

AL Discuss the advantages and disadvantages of drilling for oil in this nation rather than importing oil.

ELL Discuss the value of wilderness areas to this nation or another nation you have experience with.

499

S Skill Practice

Categorizing Ask: Would global economic interdependence focus on micro- or macroeconomics? Why? *(It would focus on macroeconomics, or the study of decision making by large units such as governments, whole industries, or societies.)*
OL

D Differentiated Instruction

Logical/Mathematical Profit is calculated by subtracting expenses from income. Write the following information on the board: *DVD Production Costs:* materials—$2.13; labor—$0.90; energy and equipment—$0.37; advertising—$0.03; packaging and shipping—$0.07; *DVD Income:* $7.00. Have students calculate the profit from the sale of one DVD *($3.50).*
ELL

American Biography

Answer: determination, creativity, industry knowledge, courage

---

✓ **Reading Check Answer:** the decision making of individuals and businesses

---

Differentiated Instruction

American Biography

John H. Johnson (1918–2005)

John H. Johnson began his career in 1942 at the age of 24. He used a $500 loan on his mother's furniture to start *Negro Digest*, a magazine devoted to the accomplishments of African Americans. Today, Johnson Publishing Company, Inc., is the world's largest African American-owned publishing company. This media empire includes many magazines, such as *Ebony* and *Jet*, and Johnson Publishing Company Book Division. Like many minority-owned companies, Johnson faced many hurdles:

"[The difficulties include] trying to get circulation and to break through in advertising to get large companies to recognize that black consumers had money and would respond to advertising directed to them. . . . The first 20 years or so in business, we couldn't get a bank loan."

Many start-up companies face the same hurdles, but in his autobiography, Johnson expressed a message of hope.

In 1995 Johnson received the Presidential Medal of Freedom, America's highest civilian honor, from former president Bill Clinton. Clinton said Johnson gave "African-Americans a voice and a face, in his words, 'a new sense of somebody-ness,' of who they were and what they could do, at a time when they were virtually invisible in mainstream American culture."

Making a Difference CITIZENSHIP

Johnson's businesses support all minorities.
Analyzing What qualities did Johnson possess that made him a leader and a success in business?

Micro and Macro As you read, keep in mind that economics is divided into two branches. In **microeconomics,** economists look at the small picture. They study the behavior and decision making of small (the meaning of the prefix *micro-*) units such as individuals and businesses. Microeconomics helps explain how individual economic decisions are made. On the other hand, **macroeconomics** looks at the big (the meaning of the prefix *macro-*) picture. It deals with the economy as a whole and decision making by large units such as governments or whole industries or societies. Think of other terms you know that start with the prefixes *micro-* and *macro-*.

Micro- and macroeconomics are examples of economic models. An **economic model** is a theory that tries to explain human economic behavior.

Economic Systems

Every country has its own **economic system,** or way of producing the things its people want and need. A country's economic system helps determine how basic economic decisions will be made. In the United States and many other countries, the economic system is called free enterprise capitalism. All free enterprise systems use more or less the same general methods of making economic decisions and producing things their people want and need. Under this system, businesses are allowed to compete for profit with a minimum of government interference. You will learn more about our economic system, along with other economic systems, later in this unit.

✓ **Reading Check Explaining** On what does microeconomics focus?

Leveled Activities

BL Content Vocabulary Activity 18, URB p. 21

OL Critical Thinking Activity 18, URB pp. 29–30

AL School-to-Home Activity 18, URB pp. 35–36

ELL Guided Reading Activity 18–1, URB p. 39

The Problem of Scarcity

Main Idea The limits on, or scarcity of, resources forces people to make careful economic choices.

Economics & You Have you ever wondered why we do not have more schools, parks, and highways? Read to find out why we have to make choices.

The goods and services a country can produce depend on its resources. **Resources** are the things used in making goods and providing services. They include tools; natural resources such as wood, soil, and water; and human resources—the people who provide the necessary labor, skills, and knowledge to produce the country's goods and services.

A country with many resources is **capable,** or able, of satisfying its people's wants and needs better than a country with few resources. A scarcity of resources affects the economic decisions a country and its people make. Scarcity affects decisions concerning what and how much to produce, how goods and services will be produced, and who will get what is produced.

Scarcity and the Need to Choose

Scarcity occurs whenever we do not have enough resources to produce all the things we would like to have. The United States possesses abundant resources such as fertile soil, trained workers, forests, and water. No country, however, has all the resources it needs. Even a country as rich as the United States does not have enough productive resources to produce all the goods and services it needs.

Scarcity is the result. Because of scarcity, we have to make choices among alternatives. For example, a rational consumer compares prices and makes choices based on his or her limited resources. A rational consumer asks whether or not he or she can afford to buy a small car or a big car, own a home or rent, purchase brand-name items or generic ones, and so on.

What to Produce

One of the choices a society has to face is that of *what* to produce. As you have learned, we live in a world of scarcity. If more of one particular item is produced, then less of something else will be produced.

A Variety of Options For example, if resources are limited, we may have to choose between making weapons for defense or producing services for people who are retired or are too ill to work. Or we may have to choose between improving our roads or schools or even a nearby stadium for athletic events. Any civic leader in any community in the United States could extend this list almost indefinitely, given the wants and needs people have in their own communities.

Choices All Societies Face

UNLIMITED WANTS → LIMITED RESOURCES

→ Scarcity →

Choices All Societies Face

→ WHAT to produce   HOW to produce   FOR WHOM to produce

Analyzing Charts

1. **Explaining** How are unlimited wants and limited resources related to scarcity?
2. **Identifying** In a world of scarcity, choices have to be made. What are the three basic economic questions?

C Critical Thinking

Determining Cause and Effect
Ask: How does its citizens' level of education and training affect a country's resources? *(Workers with more knowledge and greater skills are able to contribute more to the work force, enabling a country to produce more goods and services.)* **ELL**

R₁ Reading Strategy

Activating Prior Knowledge Ask: In general, what is the difference in price between brand-name items and generic ones? Why? *(Brand-name items are usually more expensive partly due to advertising costs.)* **OL**

R₂ Reading Strategy

Making Connections Ask: What economic choice has your school district made that affects your life as a student? *(Answers may include that cocurricular and extracurricular programs have received less funding, that after-hour heating of school buildings has been cut.)* **BL**

Analyzing Charts

Answers:
1. Limited resources, or scarcity, cannot satisfy unlimited wants.
2. What to produce? How to produce? For whom to produce?

Hands-On Chapter Project
Step 1

Making Economic Trade-Offs

Step 1: What's Best for Our Community? Student groups will analyze current economic issues in their community, identify trade-offs in proposed solutions, and offer alternative economic decisions.

Directions Bring issues highlighted in recent local newspapers to class. Divide students into groups. Ask groups to clip articles that describe four economic issues currently affecting the local community. Have each group prepare a list of questions concerning one issue; be sure that groups do not select the same issue. Remind students that governments must consider costs, available resources, needs, and wants when making economic decisions.

An Interview with Local Government Invite the head of local government (city mayor or manager, town or village president, county executive) to your classroom. In advance, provide the official with a list of the issues on which students will be asking questions. Students will use information received in Step 2. **OL**

(Project continued in Section 2.)

Section 1 Review

Reading Check **Answer:** Scarcity forces suppliers and consumers to choose among alternatives and to arrive at affordable decisions.

Assess

Civics ONLINE

Study Central™ provides summaries, interactive games, and online graphic organizers to help students review content.

Close

Differentiating List the following items on the board: heat, cake, health care, shelter, computer, and pet. Have students work in pairs to analyze and differentiate the listed items between needs and wants, placing their findings in a two-column chart under the headings *Needs* and *Wants*. **ELL**

How to Produce

After deciding what to produce, a society must then decide *how* these goods and services will be produced. If we need more crude oil to satisfy our energy needs, should we allow drilling in an Alaskan wildlife sanctuary? Or should we restrict oil recovery to less fragile areas? How much pollution should we allow manufacturing firms to **generate,** or create? After all, businesses like to produce as cheaply as possible, and that sometimes means leaving waste behind that may pollute the environment. As you can see, every producer of a good or service faces the question of *how* to produce.

For Whom to Produce

After goods and services are produced, a society must determine how the goods and services will be distributed among its members. *Who* receives the new cars? *Who* benefits from a new school? Will anyone who is able and willing to pay the prices for the goods be able to obtain them, or will government decide who will have the goods?

As you will read, most goods and services in the United States are distributed to individuals and businesses through a price system. Other economies may distribute products through majority rule, a lottery, on a first-come-first-served basis, by sharing equally, by military force, and in a variety of other ways.

These questions concerning what, how, and for whom to produce are not easy for any society to answer. Nevertheless, as long as there are not enough resources to satisfy people's unlimited wants, they must be answered.

Reading Check **Explaining** Why does scarcity lead to the need for making choices?

Section Review

Vocabulary

1. **Write** sentences using each of the following terms that will help explain its meaning: *need, want, economics, microeconomics, macroeconomics, economic model, economic system, resource, scarcity.*

Main Ideas

2. **Defining** What is the difference, in economic terms, between needs and wants? Give two examples of each.

3. **Explain** why scarcity and choice are basic problems of economics.

Critical Thinking

4. **Evaluating** In what ways can the study of economics help you and your family in your daily lives?

5. **BIG Ideas** On a graphic organizer like the one below, identify the three economic choices every society must make.

Economic Choices

CITIZENSHIP Activity

6. **Analyzing** Interview a parent or adult about how the ideas in this section (needs, wants, and scarcity) influence his or her economic decision making. Share your findings in a short essay.

7. **Creative Writing** Write a short story, poem, or song about one of the economic ideas discussed in this section. For example, you might write a humorous song about someone choosing between a need and a want. Share your writing with the class.

Civics ONLINE

Study Central™ To review this section, go to glencoe.com.

502 Chapter 18

Answers

1. Sentences should use vocabulary words according to their definitions in the section and in the Glossary.

2. Needs are items and services that are required for survival, while wants are things people desire. Examples will vary but should accurately reflect the definitions of *needs* and *wants*.

3. Scarcity of resources requires producers and consumers to make choices in what, how, and how many items will be provided or purchased. Scarcity forces both groups to consider alternatives before making choices.

4. Answers may include that economics can help the student's family establish a workable budget that considers both income and expenses, wants and needs.

5. what to produce; how to produce; for whom to produce

6. Student essays will vary. Essays may include that parents must consider their incomes when deciding what they can afford to purchase and that parents must differentiate between their family's needs and wants to prioritize what they can afford to buy.

7. Student responses will vary but should accurately reflect an economic idea discussed in this section.

Guide to Reading

Big Idea
An economic system is the way a society organizes the production and consumption of goods and services.

Content Vocabulary
- trade-off *(p. 504)*
- opportunity cost *(p. 505)*
- marginal cost *(p. 507)*
- marginal benefit *(p. 508)*
- cost-benefit analysis *(p. 508)*

Academic Vocabulary
- previous *(p. 504)*
- compute *(p. 506)*
- diminish *(p. 509)*

Reading Strategy
Identifying As you read, identify the four types of costs and an example of each on a graphic organizer like the one below.

🔊 **Section Audio**   🎞 **Spotlight Video**

Making Economic Decisions

Real World Economics Have you heard the saying "Necessity is the mother of invention"? As the supply of fuel for automobiles becomes more scarce and citizens become more concerned about global warming, the push for developing new energy sources becomes ever stronger. These Wisconsin high school students explored new ideas for fuel efficiency in a contest called the "High Mileage Vehicle Challenge" sponsored by the University of Wisconsin. The team of Eau Claire North High School electronics students competed with a car of their own design and achieved 1,610 miles (2,591 km) per gallon— which propelled them into first place.

▼ **The North High School Hybrid Vehicle Team**

503

Focus

Bellringer
Daily Focus Transparency 18–2

Guide to Reading
Answers to Graphic:

🎞 **Section Spotlight Video**

To generate student interest and provide a springboard for class discussion, access the Chapter 18, Section 2 video at glencoe.com or on the video DVD.

Resource Manager

R Reading Strategies	**C** Critical Thinking	**D** Differentiated Instruction	**W** Writing Support	**S** Skill Practice
Teacher Edition • Making Connections, p. 505 • Using Word Parts, p. 506 • Act. Prior Know., pp. 507, 510 **Additional Resources** • Cont. Vocab., URB p. 21 • Ac. Vocab., URB p. 23	**Teacher Edition** • Pred. Consequences, pp. 504, 506 • Compare/Contrast, p. 507 • Det. Cause/Effect, p. 508 **Additional Resources** • Biographies, URB p. 25 • Crit. Think., URB p. 29 • Quizzes and Tests, p. 216	**Teacher Edition** • Visual/Spatial, p. 504 • Gifted and Talented, p. 507 • Logical/Math., p. 510 **Additional Resources** • Diff. Instr., URB p. 33 • Reteach. Act., URB p. 37	**Teacher Edition** • Personal Writing, p. 508 **Additional Resources** • Authentic Assessment, p. 22	**Teacher Edition** • Inferring, p. 505 • Hypothesizing, pp. 506, 509 **Additional Resources** • Chart, Graph, and Map Skills, URB p. 31 • Daily Focus Trans. 18-2 • Pol. Cartoons Trans. 18

Teach

D Differentiated Instruction

Visual/Spatial Draw a word web on the board. In the center circle write "Scarcity of Fossil Fuels." Draw four circles leading from the center circle and a circle from each of the four circles. Have students list in the inner circles four alternative choices to fuel scarcity. In the outer circles have students write a cost of each choice. **OL**

C Critical Thinking

Predicting Consequences **Ask:** What is a potential, negative consequence of each choice? *(Answers may include: sleeping—poor test grade; partying—poor test grade, overtired; studying—overtired; endangered friendships.)* **OL**

Caption Answer:

In trade-offs, people exchange one good, service, or opportunity for another. With an after-school job, trade-offs to increased income may be the inability to be with friends.

Differentiated Instruction

Chart, Graph, and Map Act. 18, URB pp. 31–32

Trade-Offs

Main Idea Economic decision making requires us to understand all the costs and all the benefits of a choice.

Economics & You Have you ever had to choose one thing instead of another? Read to find out what economists call this common dilemma.

Economic decision making is surprisingly simple. It involves only a few terms and rules. In fact, you probably already think about many problems in the same way that economists do. As you learned **previously**, or earlier, scarcity forces people to make choices about how they will use their resources. Economic decision making requires that we take into account all the costs and all the benefits of an action.

Part-Time Jobs Many young people need to have jobs after school so they have some money with which to make economic choices. *Explaining* Why is a type of economic choice called a trade-off?

Making Trade-Offs

The economic choices people make involve exchanging one good or service for another. If you choose to buy a DVD player, you are exchanging your money for the right to own the DVD player rather than something else that might cost the same amount. A **trade-off** is the alternative you face if you decide to do one thing rather than another.

It is important to remember that a trade-off does not apply only to decisions involving money. Here is an example: Suppose you have an economics test tomorrow. Your friends invite you to a party at their house. Total time at the party and traveling to and from your house is four hours. You calculate you need at least three hours to study for the test. You also need to sleep eight hours that night. How do you make trade-offs with your time—what do you give up—studying time, time with friends, or sleep?

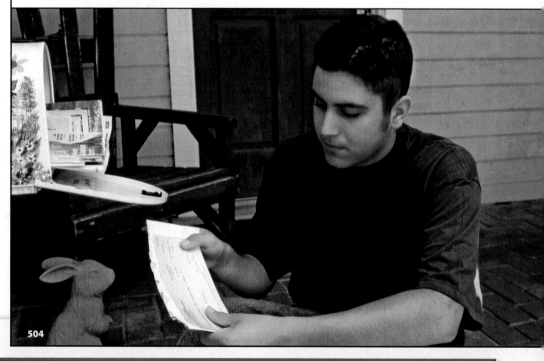

504

Creating a Cost-Benefit Analysis Model

Objective:	To understand a cost-benefit analysis
Focus:	Review the definitions of key terms in this activity.
Teach:	Explain the marginal costs/benefits of cheap items when many are produced.
Assess:	Have students define the term "marginal cost/benefit."
Close:	Discuss why families might analyze the costs-benefits of their financial decisions.

Differentiated Instruction Strategies

BL What do the numbers on the *y*-axis show? What do the numbers on the *x*-axis show?

AL Think of an economic decision your family might make. Create a cost-benefit analysis graph to help your family make the decision.

ELL The graphs in this activity are models. Explain what they represent.

TIME Political Cartoons

Steve Breen/Copley News Service

The creator of this cartoon, Steve Breen, is making a statement on consumers' decisions regarding methods of transportation.

1. **What is the setting for this cartoon?**
2. **What "new interest" is the man on the right pursuing?**
3. **What is the primary factor that prompted this interest?**
4. **Do you think there might be benefits to society if people drive less and cycle more? Explain.**

Every year, more than half of all Americans do volunteer work ... role in it. One of the responsibilities of citizens is to help make their ... to ... of volunteer grou... small. Perha... dad who ...

Think about a trade-off on a larger scale. A country wants to put more money into education. This strategy may be a good one, but putting more money into education means having less money available for space exploration or national defense. Individuals, families, businesses, and societies make trade-offs every time they choose to use their resources in one way and not in another.

Opportunity Cost

S Suppose you decide to go to college after you graduate from high school. If you do, you will quickly discover that the cost of college is more than the cost of books, transportation, tuition, and other fees. One of the biggest costs is the full-time income that you will not be able to earn because of the time you will spend studying and going to classes.

Economists have a term for this broad measure of cost. **Opportunity cost** is the cost of the next best use of your time or money when you choose to do one thing rather than another.

People tend to think of *cost* only in terms of dollars and cents. Note that opportunity cost includes more than just money. It also involves all the possible discomforts and inconveniences linked to the choice. The opportunity cost of cleaning the house, for example, is not just the price of cleaning products. It also includes the time you could spend doing other things, such as listening to music or visiting with your friends.

A good way to think about opportunity cost is to realize that when you make a trade-off, you lose. What do you lose? You lose **R** the ability to engage in your next highest valued alternative. In economics, therefore, opportunity cost is always an opportunity that is given up.

Reading Check Explaining What does making a trade-off require you to do?

Chapter 18 505

S **Skill Practice**

Inferring Ask: Why might a post-high school education be a wise economic choice? (*Often, jobs requiring post-high school education or training pay better wages than others.*) **ELL**

R **Reading Strategy**

Making Connections Ask: What opportunity costs are linked to participation in after-school activities? (*Answers may include reduced time for homework and friends, financial burdens, fatigue, and inability to get a part-time job.*) **BL**

TIME Political Cartoons

Answers:
1. a bicycle shop
2. cycling
3. high gas prices
4. Answers may include fewer and less serious traffic accidents, less air and noise pollution, and a more physically fit population.

Reading Check Answer: pay an opportunity cost

Additional Support

Teacher Tip

When implementing a collaborative learning activity, be sure that the activity is level-appropriate, clearly explained, and allows all group members to play an active role. Consider letting students choose their partners or groups.

Activity: Collaborative Learning

Understanding the Decision-Making Process Have students form groups for this activity. Ask groups to identify a situation in which an economic decision must be made by a group, such as a family, government, school, or society. Be sure that groups do not duplicate issues. Ask each group to write and perform a skit in which a group of people uses cost-benefit analysis to examine possible choices of action and to arrive at a rational economic decision. Remind students that people often disagree on economic decisions based on their individual needs and wants. **OL**

C Critical Thinking

Predicting Consequences Ask: What are the consequences of producing too few products? Too many? *(Answers may include that too few products will not produce enough income for the manufacturer and that consumer demand will not be met, while too many products will exceed consumer demand, and products will sit on the store shelves or drive prices down.)* **BL**

S Skill Practice

Hypothesizing Ask: How might a company reduce its fixed costs? *(Answers may include the ideas of downsizing the store building, renegotiating mortgage rates, or relocating to a community with lower property taxes.)* **OL**

R Reading Strategy

Using Word Parts Ask: How does the base word of "variable" help you understand its meaning? *(The word "vary" means to change. Variable costs change with the number of items produced.)* **ELL**

Caption Answer:

Farmland is a fixed cost, while equipment and fuel are variable costs because they change depending on the amount of crops that are planted and harvested.

Differentiated Instruction

Costs Businesses, such as this farm, incur both fixed costs and variable costs. ***Describing*** Is the farmland used for crops a fixed or a variable cost? How about equipment such as tractors, combines, and plows? Is the fuel to operate the machinery a fixed or a variable cost?

Costs and Revenues

Main Idea Economists have developed ways of measuring different types of costs and revenues.

Economics & You Have you wondered why goods from places like China usually cost less than goods made in the United States? Read to discover why this is so.

Suppose you are in the business of producing bicycle helmets. Do you know how many helmets you would produce? Would it be 100, 500, or 10,000? You may have a feeling that you should not produce too few or too many, but how would you know what were too few and what were too many? To begin to answer these questions, we need to look more closely at costs and revenues.

Types of Costs

All businesses have costs, but not all costs are the same type. Anyone in business must understand several different ways of **computing,** or figuring, cost.

Fixed Costs The first kind of cost is fixed costs—costs, or expenses, that are the same no matter how many units of a good are produced. Mortgage payments and property taxes are two examples of fixed costs. It makes no difference whether your company produces one bicycle helmet or a very large number. Your fixed costs, such as your mortgage and property taxes, remain the same.

Variable Costs Another kind of cost is variable costs. Variable costs are expenses that change with the number of items produced. Wages and raw materials are examples of variable costs.

Leveled Activities

BL Academic Vocabulary Activity 18, URB p. 24

OL Differentiated Instruction Activity 18, URB pp. 33–34

AL Chart, Graph, and Map Activity 18, URB pp. 31–32

ELL Guided Reading Activity 18–2, URB p. 40

Variable costs increase as production grows. Conversely, these expenses will decrease when production decreases. For example, the more helmets you make, the more plastic you must buy.

Total Costs When we add fixed costs to variable costs, we arrive at total costs. Suppose you want to compute total costs for a month. If fixed costs are $1,000 for the month and variable costs are $500, then total costs are $1,500 for the month. Many businesses focus on average total cost. To arrive at average total cost, simply divide the total cost by the quantity produced. For example, if the total cost of making bicycle helmets is $1,500 and the company produces 50, then average total cost is $30 ($1,500/50 = $30).

Marginal Costs One final cost concept remains—**marginal cost.** Marginal cost is the additional cost of producing one additional unit of output. Suppose total cost is $1,500 to produce 30 bicycle helmets and $1,550 to produce 31 helmets. What is the marginal cost of the additional (31st) unit? The change in total cost is $50 and the change in the number of units is 1, so the marginal cost is $50.

Types of Revenue

Businesses use two key measures of revenue to decide what amount of output will produce the greatest profits. The first is total revenue, and the second is marginal revenue.

Total revenue is the number of units sold multiplied by the average price per unit. If 42 units of a product are sold at $2 each, the total revenue is $84.

When a business is thinking about a change in output, it considers how its revenue will change as a result of that change in output. What will be the additional revenue from selling another unit of output? Marginal revenue is the change in total revenue—the extra revenue—that results from selling one more unit of output.

TIME™ Teens in *Action*

Jessica Painter

Jessica Painter, 18, of Yucaipa, California, shares her coupon-clipping know-how with people in need.

QUESTION: How did you become a "coupon queen"?

ANSWER: When my mom was out of work and pregnant with me, stretching cash with coupons was a necessity. Stores nearby doubled the value of coupons, and Mom matched coupons with their weekly sales, and items became free or almost free.

Q: How did this lead to your group Food For Love?

A: Growing up, we had more than we could use. We'd donate the extra items to other needy individuals and families. This was the start of the food program. When I was seven, my mom became ill and couldn't do a lot of things that she needed to do to continue with the program. I didn't want to let the people who depended on us down. I helped with shopping, sorting, and deliveries. I became a community leader and a "coupon queen" to help carry on Food For Love.

Q: What would you tell other teens interested in helping out?

A: Action volunteering is about changing the way people live. I'm hoping to help young people see they can make a difference at any age. Passing volunteerism on to future generations is the goal of my Web Site www.actionvolunteering.com.

ACTION FACT: Painter and her family go to animal shelters and cheer up the animals. At one time the family had nine cats!

Delivering goods to a food bank

Making a Difference — CITIZENSHIP

Why is volunteer work an important part of Jessica's life?

C Critical Thinking

Comparing and Contrasting Ask: How do the variable costs of a large manufacturer compare to those of a small one? *(Because variable costs increase as production grows a large manufacturer's variable costs will be greater.)* **BL**

D Differentiated Instruction

Gifted/Talented Ask: Suppose increased production requires workers to put in overtime hours. How will this affect a company's marginal costs? *(Because workers are paid more when they work overtime, the labor costs of producing additional products will drive up marginal costs.)* **AL**

R Reading Strategy

Activating Prior Knowledge Ask: How do weekly sales affect the prices of products? *(Sale prices are lower than regular prices.)* **ELL**

TIME™ Teens in *Action*

Answer:

Because Jessica and her family had experienced financial difficulties, she wanted to share solutions with others.

Additional Support

Activity: Economic Connection

Lessons from the Lives of American Entrepreneurs Provide students with biographies of Madame C.J. Walker, James Cash Penney, and other American entrepreneurs. Ask students to work with a partner to read one of the biographies and identify economic decisions that served as turning points in the lives of the American businessperson. Have student partners write an interview that may have taken place between their entrepreneur and a reporter from a magazine or newspaper of the time. Explain that the interviews should allow the entrepreneur to "talk about" his or her personal background, experiences, financial challenges, economic philosophy, and attitudes toward financial success. Ask students to share their interviews with the class. As a class, discuss common traits that successful entrepreneurs possess. **OL**

C Critical Thinking

Determining Cause and Effect Ask: Why do marginal revenues decrease as more units are sold? *(At some point, most consumers will have purchased the items; demand drops, sales drop, and marginal revenues drop.)* **AL**

W Writing Support

Personal Writing Have students write a journal entry in which they explain a personal economic decision they later reversed because marginal costs grew too high. Suggested decisions are building a collection, taking private lessons, and participating in outside activities. **OL**

Analyzing Graphs

Answers: The farmer should plant only 15 acres because, after that point, marginal costs exceed marginal benefits.

Civics ONLINE

Objectives and answers to the **Student Web Activity** can be found at glencoe.com under the Web Activity Lesson Plan for this chapter.

Hands-On Chapter Project
Step 2

Measuring Revenue

On page 507, you learned that total revenue is defined as the price of a good multiplied by the quantity sold. For example, if the price of a book at your local bookstore is $5 and 100 are sold, then total revenue is $500. Consider another example:

- MRT is a retail store that sells DVDs for a price of $10 each.
- MRT currently sells 100 DVDs a month.
- This means that MRT's total revenue is $1,000.

If MRT sells one more DVD for $10, what is the change in total revenue that results from the change in output sold?

To answer this question, we first calculate what the total revenue is when MRT sells 101 DVDs instead of 100: it is $1,010. We conclude that the total revenue changes from $1,000 to $1,010 when an additional DVD is sold. In other words, there is a change in total revenue of $10.

The change in total revenue that results from selling an additional DVD is marginal revenue. In the example, $10 is the marginal revenue. If the company sells 2 additional DVDs, the marginal revenue is $20.

This situation provides an example in which marginal revenue is constant (marginal revenue = $10 per DVD sold). This will not always be the case. Businesses often find that marginal revenues start high and then decrease as more and more units are produced and sold.

Marginal Benefit Finally, we usually do something because we expect to achieve some benefit. In other words, we are concerned with the **marginal benefit**, the *additional* satisfaction or benefit received when one more unit is produced.

Cost-Benefit Analysis

Oftentimes, the best decision is made by comparing the *marginal* benefits against the *marginal* costs. To do so, economists use a type of decision making called **cost-benefit analysis.** Rational economic decision making tells us to choose an action when the benefits are greater than the costs. If the costs outweigh the benefits, we should reject the chosen option.

Using Cost-Benefit Analysis The graph on this page shows a sample cost-benefit analysis. Suppose you are a farmer trying to decide how much of your 25 acres to plant with wheat. Assume that the marginal (or extra) cost of planting and harvesting the wheat is the same for all 25 acres. As a result, the line showing marginal cost would be a horizontal line.

Cost-Benefit Analysis

Marginal Benefits

Marginal Costs

| Acres | 0 | 5 | 10 | 15 | 20 | 25 |

Analyzing Graphs

Calculating As long as the marginal benefit of farming more acres exceeds the marginal cost, the farmer is better off farming more acres. At what point should the farmer stop farming more acres?

Civics ONLINE

Student Web Activity Visit glencoe.com and complete the Chapter 18 Web Activity.

Making Economic Trade-Offs

Step 2: Determining Alternative Economic Choices Student groups continue to analyze current local economic issues, identify trade-offs, and to offer alternatives.

Directions Have student groups write one trade-off for each solution proposed either in the newspaper articles or the interview. Ask them to brainstorm economic choices

that may prove more effective in satisfying the wants and needs.

Presenting an Alternative Economic Choice Have groups use computer presentation programs to present their alternative economic choices. Presentations should include an explanation of the issue, presentation of proposed solutions together with their trade-offs, and the group's recommended economic choice. **OL**

(Project continued on the Visual Summary page.)

Diminishing Marginal Benefit Assume, though, that some of your land is better than the rest. As a result, the size of the harvest you can expect from each acre goes down as the number of acres increases. After all, you would plant the most fertile land first.

As more land is planted, you must use land that is less productive. As the graph on page 508 shows, the line representing marginal benefit would be downward-sloping, indicating **diminishing,** or declining, marginal benefits.

How Much Should You Plant? The information in the graph makes it easy to decide how much land you should plant. Clearly, you should plant the first 5 acres, because the marginal cost is low when compared to the marginal benefits to be gained. It would also be beneficial to plant 10 acres, even though the benefits are a bit lower. In fact, it would make sense to plant up to 15 acres, because to that point the marginal

benefit is greater than the marginal cost. You would not, however, want to plant more than 15 acres. After 15 acres, the extra cost is greater than the extra benefit.

Answering the Basic Questions The previous example represents how to use cost-benefit analysis to answer the question of how much to produce. This is an issue all businesses must deal with—not just farmers. The same method can be used to answer other basic economic questions.

For instance, you can also use this method to decide *for whom* to produce. Think of the costs and benefits of selling your wheat in a town that is close to your farm, compared to selling it in a town 100 miles away. Shipping the wheat farther will probably cost more than trucking it locally, so that makes the marginal benefit of selling it nearby greater.

Reading Check Explaining What economic model helps answer the question of *what* to produce?

Skill Practice

Hypothesizing Ask: What economic factor might change a grower's mind about selling crops locally? *(Answers may include low local demand for wheat and low wheat prices as well as less expensive methods of transporting wheat.)* **OL**

Reading Check **Answer:** cost-benefit analysis

Assess

Civics ONLINE

Study Central™ provides summaries, interactive games, and online graphic organizers to help students review content.

Close

Applying Organize students into groups. Have groups use cost-benefit analysis to analyze an economic decision teens face, such as choosing a college or university, buying a clothing item, or saving for a game system or car. Students should use a T-chart to display the costs and benefits. **OL**

Section 2 Review

Vocabulary

1. **Write** sentences that demonstrate the meanings of *trade-off, opportunity cost, marginal cost, marginal benefit, cost-benefit analysis.*

Main Ideas

2. **Explaining** Give two examples of an economic trade-off decision.

3. **Explaining** What is the purpose of cost-benefit analysis?

Critical Thinking

4. **Describe** the relationship between trade-offs and opportunity costs.

5. **BIG Ideas** Identify a large purchase you would like to make. What opportunity costs can you identify if you go ahead with the choice? What is your final decision, based on analyzing the opportunity costs? Illustrate your decision on a grid like the one below.

Choice	Opportunity Cost	Final Decision

Writing

6. **Expository Writing** Because your time is limited, you are constantly facing trade-offs. Write a paragraph or two about the trade-offs you have made in choosing how to use your time during a one-week period. What activities did you choose to do? What were the opportunity costs involved in your choices?

Study Central™ To review this section, go to glencoe.com.

Section 2 Review

Chapter 18 **509**

Answers

1. Sentences should use vocabulary words according to their definitions in the section and in the Glossary.

2. Answers will vary but should describe two trade-off examples, such as buying a computer for schoolwork rather than a used car for recreational use, volunteering for a community organization rather than working at a part-time job, renting DVDs rather than watching movies at theaters, and so on.

3. Cost-benefit analysis helps producers determine how much and for whom to produce, as well as answer other economic questions.

4. In a trade-off, an individual or business makes an economic decision in which there is both benefit or satisfaction as well as drawback or opportunity cost.

5. Answers will vary, but should identify possible opportunity costs of student purchases.

6. Essays will vary but should describe logical trade-offs teens experience over the period of a week, as well as the opportunity costs involved in their decisions.

 Financial Literacy

R Reading Strategy

Activating Prior Knowledge Ask: From your understanding of compound words, how can you infer that compound interest involves added interest? *(In a compound word, one word is combined with another. Similarly, compound interest combines interest calculated on both principal and interest.)* **AL**

D Differentiated Instruction

Logical/Mathematical Have students work in pairs to calculate the account balance after five years with both interest payment methods. **Ask:** Why might people with small account balances may be less likely to notice the difference between the two methods than those with large account balances? *(Interest received will be similar.)* **OL**

 Analyzing Economics

Answers:
1. $54
2. Banks use deposited monies to fund long-term loans, such as home mortgages and business loans. Deposited funds that are committed for long periods of time help banks set profitable loan rates.

Additional Support

Simple and Compound Interest

When you deposit money in a savings account, the bank pays you interest for the use of your money. The amount of interest is expressed as a percentage, such as 6 percent, for a time period, such as a year. One type of interest is simple interest. **Simple interest** is figured on only the principal, or original deposit, not on any interest earned. **Compound interest** is **R** paid on the principal plus any interest that has been earned. In other words, you are earning interest on interest. Over time, there is a significant difference in earnings between simple and compound interest.

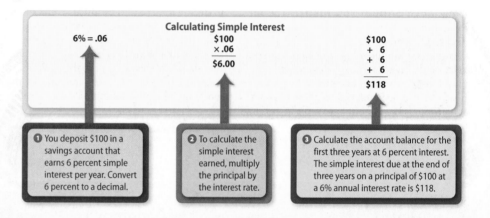

Calculating Simple Interest

6% = .06

$100
× .06
‾‾‾‾‾
$6.00

$100
+ 6
+ 6
+ 6
‾‾‾‾‾
$118

❶ You deposit $100 in a savings account that earns 6 percent simple interest per year. Convert 6 percent to a decimal.

❷ To calculate the simple interest earned, multiply the principal by the interest rate.

❸ Calculate the account balance for the first three years at 6 percent interest. The simple interest due at the end of three years on a principal of $100 at a 6% annual interest rate is $118.

D	Simple Interest	Compound Interest
Principal	$1,000	$1,000
Account Balance After One Year	1,100	1,100
Account Balance After Two Years	1,200	1,210 ($1,100 plus 10% of $1,100)
Account Balance After Three Years	1,300	1,331 ($1,210 plus 10% of $1,210)

 Analyzing Economics

1. **Calculating** How much interest would you earn if you deposited $300 at 6 percent simple interest for three years?

2. **Concluding** Banks often pay higher rates of interest on money you agree to keep in the bank for longer periods of time. Explain why this might be.

Activity: U.S./World Connections

Resource Comparison Have students work with a partner to compare the resources of the United States to those of two economically developing countries. Explain that a developing country is defined as one in which the average income of its citizens is low. Remind students that resources are the things used in making goods and providing services and include tools (natural resources) and the labor, skills, and knowledge of a country's people. Student partners should display their findings in a chart. Column headings should reflect the names of the three countries. Row heads should list the individual resource being compared. Have partners write a brief paragraph explaining a way in which the three countries could help each other through shared resources. **OL**

Crowded college campus

Economics

Economics is the study of how we make decisions in a world in which resources are limited.

Microeconomics deals with decision making by small units such as individuals and firms.

Macroeconomics deals with the economy as a whole and decision making by large units such as government.

Assembly-line worker in Taiwan

Making Economic Decisions

Individuals satisfy their unlimited wants in a world of limited resources by making choices.

The need to make choices arises because of scarcity, the basic problem in economics.

Every society must answer the three basic economic questions:

- What to produce
- How to produce
- For whom to produce

Individuals are forced to make trade-offs every time they use their resources in one way and not in another.

The cost of making a trade-off is known as opportunity cost—the value of the next best alternative that has to be given up to do the action that is chosen.

Shoppers look for bargains

Costs and Revenue

Four important measures of cost are total cost, fixed cost, variable cost, and marginal cost.

A key measure of revenue is marginal revenue, which is the change in total revenue when one more unit of output is sold.

Economic Systems

Every type of economic system must answer the three basic economic questions.

The United States has a free enterprise, or capitalist, economic system.

STUDY TO GO Study anywhere, anytime! Download quizzes and flash cards to your PDA from glencoe.com.

Visual Literacy **Ask:** Why is the use of assembly lines a wise economic decision? *(By assigning workers only one step of a process, production time is reduced, which, in turn, reduces production costs.)* **OL**

Interpersonal Divide the class into groups. List controversial school economic decisions on the board, such as charging user fees to cover the cost of music and athletic programs, charging groups for the use of school facilities for dances and other social events, and increasing school lunch fees. Have groups list the reasons for and benefits and drawbacks of each decision. Ask groups to tally how members feel about the decision. As groups report their tallies, record them on the board. Discuss why individuals may disagree on economic choices made by entities such as school boards or governments. **OL**

Assessing **Ask:** For whom would manufacturers most often produce convenience foods, personal planners, and cell phones? *(busy working people)* Have students work in pairs to design an ad for another product that would appeal to a busy working person. Ask groups to share their ads with the class. **OL**

Hands-On Chapter Project
Step 3: Wrap-Up

Making Economic Trade-Offs

Step 3: Assessing Economic Decisions Students will finish the process they started in Step 1.

Directions As the class views the computer presentations, ask them to jot down questions and comments about the proposed economic decision. Allow class time for students to direct questions to the presenting group. Provide students with an evaluation form in which they assess each proposed economic choice. The form should have headings such as *Issue, Proposed Decision, Trade-Offs, Agree/Disagree,* and *Reason.* Include columns to allow for student writing. **OL**

18 ASSESSMENT

Answers and Analyses

Reviewing Vocabulary

1. D Students will have read about the concept of scarcity, in which limited resources force people to make economic choices.

2. C Although all terms relate to economics, only capitalism is an economic system, or way of producing things people want and need. In Section 2, students will have read about the economic model of cost-benefit analysis. Throughout the chapter, students will have analyzed economic decisions, or choices, made as a result of scarcity of resources. Economics itself is a branch of social sciences; capitalism is not a branch of economics.

3. B While both answers A and B include the idea of loss when making an economic decision, students can use the keyword "opportunity" to choose the correct answer. An opportunity is an available chance or option. An opportunity cost is, therefore, a missed or lost opportunity because another alternative was selected. A trade-off displays the exchange between the benefit of a decision and the drawback, or opportunity cost. Marginal cost and marginal benefit are the features compared during the process of cost-benefit analysis.

4. D Although both answers, C and D, include the idea of changing production quantities, students can focus on the question's keyword "profit" to select marginal benefit as the correct answer. Neither trade-off nor opportunity cost refers to changing production quantities.

Reviewing Main Ideas

5. C The prefix "micro-" prompts students to locate the answer that refers to the smallest entity, individuals. Keywords in the remaining answer choices signal large groups or entities—industries, worldwide, governments.

6. B Students will have studied the difference between needs, or things needed for survival, and wants, or things that make life more enjoyable. By asking, *Which of these is not needed for survival?* students can eliminate the incorrect answers— food, shelter, and clothing.

Standardized Test Practice

18 ASSESSMENT

TEST-TAKING TIP

When you come across an unfamiliar word in an exam, look at the word's parts—root, prefix, and/or suffix—to figure out its meaning.

Reviewing Vocabulary

Directions: Choose the word(s) that best completes the sentence.

1. Economics is the study of how we make decisions in a world of limited _____.

  A needs   **C** choices

  B wants   **D** resources

2. Capitalism is an example of a(n) _____.

  A economic model   **C** economic system

  B economic decision   **D** branch of economics

3. The income from a full time job that you give up when you go to college is called a(n) _____.

  A trade-off   **C** marginal cost

  B opportunity cost   **D** marginal benefit

4. The additional profit obtained from producing one more unit in a factory is called a(n) _____.

  A trade-off   **C** marginal cost

  B opportunity cost   **D** marginal benefit

Reviewing Main Ideas

Directions: Choose the best answer for each question.

Section 1 *(pp. 498–502)*

5. What does microeconomics deal with?

  A the production of whole industries

  B the distribution of goods worldwide

  C the economic decisions of individuals

  D the allocation of resources by governments

6. Which of the following items is a want?

  A food

  B videos

  C shelter

  D clothing

7. Which of the following is a natural resource?

  A water

  B skills

  C machinery

  D knowledge

Section 2 *(pp. 503–509)*

8. What is an example of a fixed cost of doing business?

  A wages

  B cost of fuel

  C price of materials

  D mortgage payment

9. What is the formula for total costs?

  A fixed costs + variable costs

  B fixed costs + marginal costs

  C variable costs + marginal costs

  D fixed costs + variable costs + marginal costs

10. Why do businesses use cost-benefit analysis?

  A to compute total costs

  B to measure total revenues

  C to decide how much to produce

  D to compare marginal cost and marginal revenue

GO ON →

---

7. A Students will have recognized that all answers are resources that are used to produce goods and services. However, the keyword "natural" suggests that the correct answer exists in nature. Skills and knowledge are acquired by people through experience, education, and training. Machinery is built by people with skills and knowledge.

8. D Students will have studied the difference between fixed, or unchanging, costs and variable, or changing, costs. By relating the answer choices to personal experiences and prior knowledge, students will realize that wages change over time, as does the cost of fuel and the price of materials. Students who recognize that a mortgage payment is usually fixed for the term of the loan will select the correct answer.

Critical Thinking

Directions: Base your answers to questions 11 and 12 on the pie graph below and your knowledge of Chapter 18.

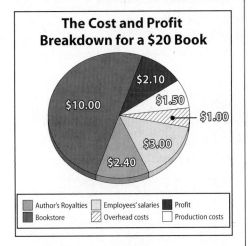

The Cost and Profit Breakdown for a $20 Book

$2.10
$1.50
$10.00
$1.00
$3.00
$2.40

- Author's Royalties
- Employees' salaries
- Profit
- Bookstore
- Overhead costs
- Production costs

11. The publisher is thinking about printing one thousand more books but would have to hire another employee to do so. What would help her decide?

A tabulating the fixed and variable costs of new books

B comparing her marginal benefit to her marginal cost

C determining the marginal revenue for one more book

D calculating the total revenue from the sale of new books

12. What fixed cost paid by the bookstore owner comes in part from his share of the book's price?

A property tax payment

B the author's royalties

C wages for store clerks

D profit for the storeowner

Document-Based Questions

Directions: Analyze the document and answer the short-answer questions that follow.

In the following excerpt from his book *Capitalism and Freedom,* well-known economist Milton Friedman speaks about capitalism and the free enterprise system in the United States.

> *History suggests only that capitalism is a necessary condition for political freedom. Clearly it is not a sufficient condition. . . .*
>
> *Freedom in economic arrangements is itself a component of freedom broadly understood, so economic freedom is an end in itself. . . . Economic freedom is also an indispensable means toward the achievement of political freedom.*
>
> —Milton Friedman

13. What does Friedman say is the connection between capitalism and political freedom?

14. What is the main idea of the second paragraph?

15. What do you think Friedman would expect to happen to the United States if it were not a capitalist country?

Extended-Response Question

16. Compare and contrast microeconomics and macroeconomics.

Civics ONLINE

For additional test practice, use Self-Check Quizzes—Chapter 18 on glencoe.com.

Need Extra Help?

If you missed question...	1	2	3	4	5	6	7	8	9	10	11	12	13	14	15	16
Go to page...	499	500	505	508	500	499	501	506	507	508	507	506	500	500	500	500

ASSESSMENT

Determining only the marginal revenue for one more book, Answer C, does not account for the marginal cost of an additional employee. Only answer B considers both marginal benefit and marginal cost.

12. A Prior knowledge will help students to realize that royalties are paid by publishers, not bookstore owners. Personal experience will help students eliminate D, as profit is net income, not a cost or expense. Students can also eliminate C because wages are variable costs, not fixed costs. A variable cost, such as wages, commissions, and raw materials, varies directly with sales. Fixed costs include property taxes and rent.

Document-Based Questions

13. Friedman states that for political freedom to exist, economic freedom, or capital, must also exist. One cannot exist without the other.

14. Friedman is theorizing that economic freedom in itself is part of a broader concept of freedom, as implemented in a political system.

15. Friedman would probably expect political and other freedoms to break down if capitalism were not the economic process in the United States.

Extended Response

16. Responses should include the ideas that microeconomics is the study of the behavior and decision making of small units, such as individuals and business; macroeconomics deals with the economy as a whole and decision making by large units, such as governments, large industries, or societies.

---

9. A Students can eliminate answers B, C, and D when they recognize that marginal costs occur only when production quantities change. Students who understand the concept of fixed and variable costs recognize that the two categories cover all types of costs associated with doing business.

10. C Students will recognize that both total costs and total revenues must be known before cost-benefit analysis can occur, which helps students eliminate answer choices A and B. They will also identify D as a description of the process of cost-benefit analysis, not its application. Only C describes an application of cost-benefit analysis.

Critical Thinking

11. B The keyword "marginal" in answers B and C both describe increased production, while answers A and D make no mention of production quantities. The question's situation involves an additional 1,000 new books and the hiring of an additional employee.

Civics ONLINE

Have students visit the Web site at glencoe.com to review Chapter 18 and take the **Self-Check Quiz**.

Need Extra Help?

Have students refer to the pages listed if they miss any of the questions.

Chapter Planning Guide

19

Levels					Resources	Chapter Opener	Section 1	Section 2	Section 3	Chapter Assess
BL	OL	AL	ELL		**FOCUS**					
BL	OL	AL	ELL	🖼	**Daily Focus Skills Transparencies**		19–1	19–2	19–3	
					TEACH					
BL	OL		ELL	📁	**Reading Essentials and Note-Taking Guide***		p. 174	p. 177	p. 180	
	OL	AL		📁	**Citizenship/Decision-Making Activity, URB**		p. 3		p. 3	
	OL	AL		📁	**Primary Source Reading, URB**			p. 15	p. 15	
BL	OL	AL	ELL	📁	**Content Vocabulary Activity, URB***	p. 43	p. 43	p. 43	p. 43	
BL	OL	AL	ELL	📁	**Academic Vocabulary Activity, URB**	p. 45	p. 45	p. 45	p. 45	
	OL			📁	**Biography Activity, URB**		p. 47		p. 47	
BL	OL	AL	ELL	📁	**Writing Skills Activity, URB**			p. 49		
	OL	AL		📁	**Critical Thinking Skills Activity, URB**		p. 51			
BL	OL	AL	ELL	📁	**Chart, Graph, and Map Skills Activity, URB**		p. 53			
BL	OL	AL	ELL	📁	**Differentiated Instruction, URB**			p. 55		
BL	OL	AL	ELL	📁	**School-to-Home Connection Activity, URB***	p. 57	p. 57	p. 57	p. 57	
BL	OL		ELL	📁	**Guided Reading Activities, URB***		p. 61	p. 62	p. 63	
	OL	AL		📁	**Supreme Court Cases**				p. 7	
BL	OL	AL	ELL	📁	**Writer's Guidebook**	✓	✓	✓	✓	✓
	OL	AL		💿	**Primary Source Document Library**	✓	✓	✓	✓	✓
BL	OL	AL	ELL	💿	**Daily Lecture & Discussion Notes (in Pres. Plus)**		✓	✓	✓	✓
BL	OL	AL	ELL	💿	**StudentWorks™ Plus**		✓	✓	✓	✓
BL	OL	AL	ELL	💿	**Section Spotlight Videos**		✓	✓	✓	
BL	OL	AL	ELL	🖼	**TIME Interpreting Political Cartoons Transp.**				Ch. 19	
BL	OL	AL	ELL	🖼	**Writing Process Transparencies**	✓	✓	✓	✓	✓

Note: Please refer to the *Unit 6 Resource Book* for this chapter's URB materials.

* Also available in Spanish

- Interactive Lesson Planner
- Interactive Teacher Edition
- Fully editable blackline masters
- Section Spotlight Videos Launch
- Differentiated Lesson Plans
- Printable reports of daily assignments
- Standards Tracking System

Levels					Resources	Chapter Opener	Section 1	Section 2	Section 3	Chapter Assess
BL	OL	AL	ELL							
					TEACH (continued)					
				📁	**Building Academic Vocabulary**	✓	✓	✓	✓	✓
	Teacher Resources			📁	**Strategies for Success**	✓	✓	✓	✓	✓
				📁	**Teacher's Guide to Differentiated Instruction**	✓	✓	✓	✓	✓
				💿	**Graphing Tool**	✓	✓	✓	✓	✓
				💿	**Presentation Plus! with MindJogger CheckPoint**	✓	✓	✓	✓	✓
					ASSESS					
BL	OL	AL	ELL	📁	**Quizzes and Tests***		p. 225	p. 226	p. 227	p. 228
BL	OL	AL	ELL	📁	**Authentic Assessment with Rubrics**		p. 23	p. 23	p. 23	p. 23
BL	OL	AL	ELL	📁	**Standardized Test Practice**		p. 37	p. 37	p. 37	p. 37
BL	OL	AL	ELL	💿	*ExamView® Assessment Suite* CD-ROM		19–1	19–2	19–3	Ch. 19
					CLOSE					
BL			ELL	📁	**Reteaching Activity, URB***		p. 59	p. 59	p. 59	
BL	OL		ELL	📁	**Reading and Study Skills Foldables™ Activity**	p. 86		p. 87	p. 87	
BL	OL	AL	ELL	🖥	**Graphic Organizer Transparencies & Strategies**	✓	✓	✓	✓	✓

✓ Chapter- or unit-based activities applicable to all sections in this chapter

Using a Whiteboard

Teaching with Technology

What is a Whiteboard?

A whiteboard is an interactive computer touch-screen that allows multiple users to interact with a display by touching, writing, or drawing on the board.

How can a Whiteboard help my students?

Whiteboards promote interactive classroom participation and help to:

- actively engage students in the learning process
- increase motivation and enthusiasm for learning
- support various learning styles and levels

Civics ONLINE

Visit glencoe.com and enter **QuickPass**™ code CIV1360c19T for Chapter 19 resources.

You can easily launch a wide range of digital products from your computer's desktop with the McGraw-Hill Social Studies widget.

	Student	Teacher	Parent
Media Library			
• Student Edition Section Audio	●		●
• Spanish Audio Summaries	●		●
• Section Spotlight Videos	●	●	●
***Civics Today* Online Learning Center (Web Site)**			
• Chapter Overviews	●	●	●
• Study Central™	●	●	●
• Study-to-Go	●	●	●
• Student Web Activities	●	●	●
• In Motion Animation	●	●	●
• Self-Check Quizzes	●	●	●
• ePuzzles and Games	●	●	●
• StudentWorks™ Plus Online	●	●	●
• Vocabulary eFlashcards	●	●	●
• Web Activity Lesson Plans		●	
• Vocabulary PuzzleMaker	●	●	●
Classroom Tools			
• Multilingual Glossary	●	●	●
• Beyond the Textbook	●	●	●
• NGS MapMachine	●	●	●

GLENCOE
BookLink 3

Use this database to search more than 30,000 titles to create a customized reading list for your students.

- Reading lists can be organized by students' reading level, author, genre, theme, or area of interest.
- The database provides Degrees of Reading Power™ (DRP) and Lexile™ readability scores for all selections.
- A brief summary of each selection is included.

Leveled reading suggestions for this chapter:

For students at a Grade 7 reading level:
- *The Emperors of Chocolate: Inside the Secret World of Hershey and Mars,* by Joel Glenn Brenner

For students at a Grade 8 reading level:
- *You Are the Corporate Executive,* by Nathan Aaseng

For students at a Grade 9 reading level:
- *Foreign Oil Dependence,* by James Haley

For students at a Grade 10 reading level:
- *Food, Inc.: Mendel to Monsanto—The Promises and Perils of the Biotech Harvest,* by Peter Pringle

For students at a Grade 11 reading level:
- *Poverty: Opposing Viewpoints,* by Karen Baklin

READING SUPPORT FROM JAMESTOWN EDUCATION

- **Timed Readings Plus in Social Studies** helps students increase their reading rate and fluency while maintaining comprehension. The 400-word passages are similar to those found on state and national assessments.

- **Reading in the Content Area: Social Studies** concentrates on six essential reading skills that help students better comprehend what they read. The book includes 75 high-interest nonfiction passages written at increasing levels of difficulty.

- **Reading Social Studies** includes strategic reading instruction and vocabulary support in Social Studies content for both ELLs and native speakers of English.

- **Content Vocabulary Workout** (Grades 6–8) accelerates reading comprehension through focused vocabulary development. Social Studies content vocabulary comes from the glossaries of Glencoe's Middle School Social Studies texts. www.jamestowneducation.com

KEY Teacher Wraparound

Use this key to help you identify the different types of prompts found in the Teacher Wraparound Edition.

R **Reading Strategies** activities help you teach reading skills and vocabulary.

C **Critical Thinking** strategies help students apply and extend what they have learned.

D **Differentiated Instruction** activities provide instruction for students learning to speak English, along with suggestions for teaching various types of learners.

S **Skill Practice** strategies help students practice historical analysis and geography skills.

W **Writing Support** activities provide writing opportunities to help students comprehend the text.

Teaching strategies and activities have been coded for ability level appropriateness.

AL Activities for students working above grade level

OL Activities for students working on grade level

BL Activities for students working below grade level

ELL Activities for English Language Learners

Focus

Why It Matters

Ask: How does America's economic system affect you? *(Answers may include: that students are consumers in the economic system and that resources, prices, and availability of products and services impact their lives directly.)*

More About the Photo

Visual Literacy This photograph shows a farmer checking a crop. **Ask:** How is this farmer both a producer of goods and a consumer of resources? *(The farmer grows and sells a needed food; he also requires machinery, labor, and natural resources to grow his crops.)* Preview with students the interconnectedness of economic resources, products, and activities as they discuss the photograph.

Teach

BIG Ideas *As you begin teaching each section, use these questions and activities to help students focus on the Big Ideas.*

Section 1

Economic Resources Ask: What is a resource? What are the four factors of production? *(A resource is anything needed to produce a product or to make a service available; the four factors of production are natural resources, labor, capi-*

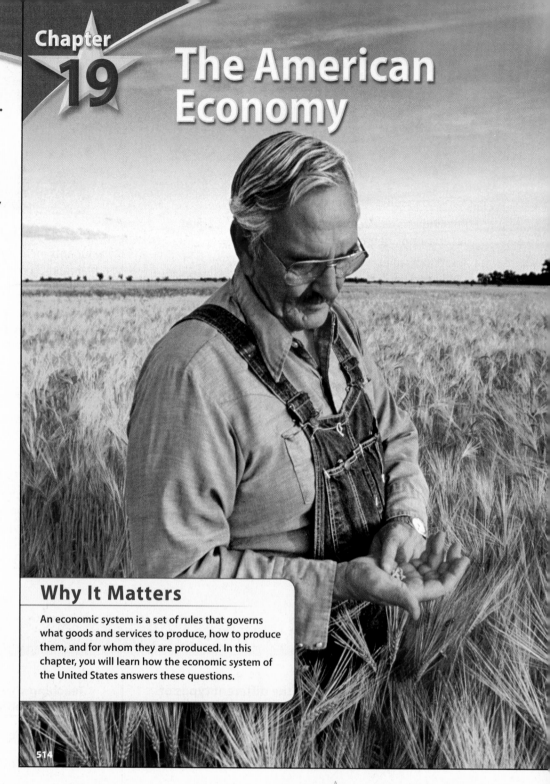

Chapter
19

The American Economy

Why It Matters

An economic system is a set of rules that governs what goods and services to produce, how to produce them, and for whom they are produced. In this chapter, you will learn how the economic system of the United States answers these questions.

514

tal, and entrepreneurship.) Point out that Section 1 discusses the four key factors of production in any economic system. **OL**

Section 2

Economic Activity Ask: What are some of the consequences of economic growth? Of economic decline? *(Economic growth: more jobs, more income for citizens, and more products and services to buy; decline: fewer jobs, less income, and less access to products and services)* Tell students that Section 2 explains how the parts of an economic system must work together for a nation to thrive. **AL**

Civics ONLINE
Visit glencoe.com and enter QuickPass™ code CIV3093c19 for Chapter 19 resources.

Chapter Audio

BIG Ideas

Section 1: Economic Resources

An economic system is the way a society organizes the production and consumption of goods and services. Four different key factors of production are necessary to produce goods and services.

Section 2: Economic Activity

The basis of the market economy is voluntary exchange. In the American economy, the exchange usually involves money in return for a good or service. Economic growth occurs when a nation's total output of goods and services, flowing in a circular motion among several sectors, increases.

Section 3: Capitalism and Free Enterprise

Free enterprise is the freedom of individuals and businesses to operate and compete with a minimum of government interference or regulation. The American economic system is the most successful in the history of the world.

Grain farmer checks barley crop in East Grand Forks, Minnesota

---

FOLDABLES Dinah Zike's
Study Organizer **Foldables**

Purpose This Foldable helps students learn and categorize information about the different sectors of economic activity. The completed Foldable will allow students to review the sectors and understand how the sectors interrelate in economic activity. **OL**

More Foldables activities for this chapter can be found in the *Dinah Zike's Reading and Study Skills Foldables* ancillary.

Civics ONLINE

Visit glencoe.com and enter **QuickPass™** code CIV1360c19T for Chapter 19 resources, including a Chapter Overview, Study Central™, Study-to-Go, Student Web Activity, Self-Check Quiz, and other materials.

FOLDABLES™
Study Organizer

Categorizing Information Study Foldable Make the following Foldable to help you categorize information about the different sectors of economic activity.

Step 1 Fold a sheet of paper from side to side, leaving a 2-inch tab uncovered along the side.

Step 2 Turn the paper and fold it in half once and once again, creating fourths.

Reading and Writing As you read the chapter about economic activity, categorize information about each part of the economy under each flap.

Step 3 Unfold and cut along the three fold lines through the top side of the paper.

Step 4 Label the flaps as shown.

Economic Activity

Section 3

Capitalism and Free Enterprise

Ask: Why might people decide to start a business? *(Answers include that they might want to be their own bosses, to make unique or superior products, and to make money.)* Tell students that Section 3 explains how America's economic system promotes and encourages business. **ELL BL OL**

Focus

Bellringer

Daily Focus Transparency 19–1

Guide to Reading
Answers to Graphic:

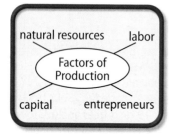

natural resources — labor
Factors of Production
capital — entrepreneurs

Section Spotlight Video

To generate student interest and provide a springboard for class discussion, access the Chapter 19, Section 1 video at glencoe.com or on the video DVD.

Resource Manager

Guide to Reading

Big Idea
An economic system is the way a society organizes the production and consumption of goods and services.

Content Vocabulary
- goods (p. 517)
- services (p. 517)
- factors of production (p. 517)
- natural resources (p. 517)
- labor (p. 517)
- capital (p. 517)
- entrepreneur (p. 517)
- Gross Domestic Product (GDP) (p. 518)
- standard of living (p. 518)

Academic Vocabulary
- output (p. 517)
- innovate (p. 517)

Reading Strategy
Categorizing As you read the section, complete a diagram like the one below by identifying the four factors of production.

Factors of Production

Economic Resources

Real World Economics Do you know what an entrepreneur is? Mylan Murphy knows, because he became one when he started his own line of sports-themed clothing while still in the eighth grade. Mylan turned his love of basketball and his talent as an artist into a real business. Although he is too young to sign a contract, Mylan has enlisted his older brother, Mark, to be his business partner. The American economy depends on entrepreneurs, like the Murphys, as one of the four essential factors of production that keep the economy running.

▼ **Athlete Mylan Murphy is also a sports apparel entrepreneur**

R Reading Strategies	C Critical Thinking	D Differentiated Instruction	W Writing Support	S Skill Practice
Teacher Edition • Academic Vocab., p. 517 **Additional Resources** • Cont. Vocab., URB p. 43 • Ac. Vocab., URB p. 45 • Guid. Read., URB p. 61 • RENTG, p. 174	**Teacher Edition** • Pred. Consequences, p. 518 **Additional Resources** • Crit. Thinking, URB p. 51 • Quizzes and Tests, p. 225	**Teacher Edition** • Logical/Math., p. 517 **Additional Resources** • Reteach. Act., URB p. 59	**Teacher Edition** • Persuasive Writing, p. 519 **Additional Resources** • Cit./Decision-Making, URB p. 3	**Teacher Edition** • Analyzing Charts, p. 518 **Additional Resources** • Chart, Map, and Graph Skills, URB p. 53 • Daily Focus Trans., 19–1

Goods and Services

Main Idea Four factors of production are necessary to produce goods and services.

Economics & You What goes into making your CD player or your backpack? Read to find out what four production elements are necessary.

In 2007, the United States's annual **output**, or amount produced, totaled nearly 25 percent of the world's total output. Some of this production is in the form of **goods**, such as books and automobiles. More of this production is in the form of **services**, or work performed for someone else. Services include haircuts, home repairs, and entertainment.

Factors of Production

There are four **factors of production**, or resources necessary to produce goods and services. These are natural resources, labor, capital, and entrepreneurs.

Natural Resources The first factor, **natural resources**, refers to all the "gifts of nature" that make production possible. Natural resources include actual surface land and water as well as fish, animals, forests, and mineral deposits.

Labor The nation's workforce, **labor**, is its human resources. Labor includes anyone who works to produce goods and services.

Capital Another factor of production is **capital**, which are the manufactured goods used to make other goods and services. The machines, buildings, and tools used to assemble automobiles, for example, are *capital goods*.

Capital goods are unique in that they are the *result* of production. For example, we cannot find a hammer in the forest the way we can find a tree—someone actually has to make a hammer. Capital goods differ from

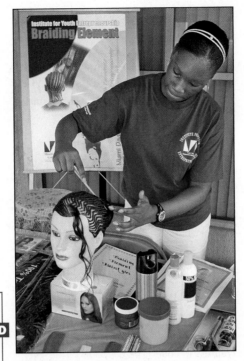

Entrepreneurs A Miami, Florida, teenage entrepreneur owns and operates a hair care business. *Explaining* Why do entrepreneurs start new businesses?

consumer goods. Consumer goods directly satisfy wants—things such as clothes, clocks, foods, and radios. Capital goods satisfy wants indirectly by aiding production of consumer goods.

Entrepreneurs The **entrepreneur** is the fourth factor of production. This is an individual who starts a new business, introduces new products, and improves processes. Being an entrepreneur involves being **innovative**, or original, and being willing to take risks in order to make profits.

✓ **Reading Check** Classifying Under what factor of production would you classify oil deposits? A diamond-cutting machine?

Chapter 19 517

Teach

D Differentiated Instruction

Logical/Mathematical Ask: What is a "factor" in a math equation? How can this information help you understand what an economic factor is? *(A mathematical factor is a number that is combined with other numbers to arrive at the product, or answer. Changing the factor changes the product. In the same way, economic factors help generate a product. That product changes as the factors change.)* **AL**

R Reading Strategy

Academic Vocabulary Ask: What does the root of "innovative" mean? *(The root is "-nov-," meaning "new.")* Explain that to be innovative is to do something original. Students who speak Spanish may be able to supply the cognate "innovar." **ELL OL**

Caption Answer:
Possible answer: entrepreneurs enjoy the challenge of running their own businesses.

✓ **Reading Check Answer:** natural resources; capital good

Differentiated Instruction

Oprah Winfrey

Biography Activity 19, URB pp. 47–48

Objective:	To analyze Winfrey's entrepreneurial decisions
Focus:	Have students relate their prior knowledge about Winfrey.
Teach:	Ask students to read parts of the biography aloud.
Assess:	Have students name the important events in Winfrey's life to contribute to a class list.
Close:	Have two students role-play a TV interview with Winfrey.

Differentiated Instruction Strategies

BL Who started Winfrey on her path to success? What did Winfrey focus on to turn her life around as a teen?

AL Research Winfrey's support of a school for African girls, and report your findings to the class.

ELL What might Winfrey advise young, ambitious students to do? Name two things.

Teach

C Critical Thinking

Predicting Consequences Ask: What would happen to the calculation of GDP if the sale of used products were included? *(GDP would become less accurate because counting used goods would artificially inflate the value of products made that year in the nation.)* **AL**

S Skill Practice

Analyzing Charts Ask: What kinds of products are represented in the chart? Why aren't the parts needed to make bicycles, computers, and watches included? *(Only final goods are represented. No services or intermediate goods are represented. Intermediate goods are not included in the calculation of GDP.)* **OL**

Analyzing Charts

Answers:

1. GDP is calculated by adding up the value of all final goods and services produced in a country in a single year.
2. About 11% (1/9) of GDP comes from the production of bicycles.

Hands-On Chapter Project
Step 1

Making a Business Plan

Step 1: Deciding on a Product or Service The class will research possible products or services to offer for sale.

Directions Tell students that later in the chapter they will write a business plan for their own business. As entrepreneurs, they will determine a need in the community that they are able to meet. In the next step, they will identify resources for meeting the need.

Interpersonal Have students work in groups to list products or services they could sell to their community. For example, one morning a week, students could run a small school-supply shop, set up a tutoring group, or work as a yard-cleaning team. Have students identify each idea as a product, a service, or a combination of both. Finally, ask students to share their ideas, and guide a discussion as the class chooses the need they feel most ready to meet. **OL**

(Project continued in Section 2)

Gross Domestic Product

Main Idea GDP is the total value of all the *final* goods and services produced in a country in one year.

Economics & You Have you ever heard the United States described as a rich country? Read to find out how a nation's wealth is measured.

People often measure their economic well-being by the amount of their incomes and their ability to provide for themselves and their families. The success of the overall economy is measured in a similar way. One measure of the economy's size is **Gross Domestic Product (GDP).** This is the total value, in dollars, of all the *final* goods and services produced in a country during a single year. A final good is a good, such as a loaf of bread, that is sold to its user. The intermediate goods that go into making a loaf of bread—flour or wheat, sugar—are not counted in GDP.

In addition, the sale of used goods is not counted as part of GDP. When ownership of products already produced is transferred from one person or group to another, no new production is generated. Although the sale of a used car, chair, or CD player may give someone cash, only the original sale is included in GDP.

Measuring GDP

Remember that GDP is a measure based on money. If we are to compare the number of goods and services produced, it is helpful to get a meaningful idea of their relative worth. Look at the diagram at the top of the page for an example. Suppose there is a tiny economy in which only three goods are produced, in these quantities: 10 bicycles, 10 computers, and 10 watches. Furthermore, suppose the price of a bicycle is $200, the price of a computer is $1,500, and the price of a watch is $100. To find

---

Measuring GDP

GDP is the total dollar value of all final goods and services produced in a nation in a single year.

10 bicycles	10 computers	10 watch...
at $200 each = $2,000	at $1,500 each = $15,000	at $100 ea... = $1,000...

Gross Domestic Product = $18,000

Analyzing Charts

1. **Explaining** How is GDP calculated?
2. **Calculating** In this example, what percentage of GDP comes from the production of bicycles?

GDP of this economy, we multiply the price of each good by the quantity of that good produced and then add the amounts.

How Is GDP Used? Economists study GDP figures regularly to analyze how the economy is doing. GDP is an important indicator of **standard of living,** the quality of life based on the possession of necessities and luxuries that make life easier.

Weaknesses of GDP GDP is a reasonably accurate and useful measure of economic performance. It is not a measure of society's overall well-being, though. Many things might make a country better off without raising GDP, such as reductions in crime or in drug and alcohol abuse.

Keep in mind that the statistics used in computing GDP are accurate only to a point. Statistics about easily measurable things,

---

such as government purchases, are reliable. Some workers, however, are given food, fuel, or housing as part of their wages. To minimize error in calculating GDP, economists must take into account that GDP can include only an estimate of the value of such goods and services.

Quantity vs. Quality Remember that GDP measures *quantity*. It does not reflect improvements in the *quality* of products. There is a great difference between a $1,000 computer purchased today and a computer costing the same amount just a few years ago. Because of this, economists must take great care to account for quality improvement. Greater production of goods and services is only one of the many factors that contribute to raising the standard of living of any country.

Net Domestic Product

The loss of value because of wear and tear to durable goods, such as automobiles and refrigerators, is called depreciation. The same concept applies to capital goods—machinery and equipment. GDP does not take into account that some production merely keeps machines and equipment in working order and replaces them when they wear out.

Net domestic product (NDP)—another way of measuring the economy—accounts for the fact that some production is only due to depreciation. NDP takes GDP and subtracts the total loss in value of capital goods caused by depreciation.

Reading Check Contrasting What is the difference between final goods and intermediate goods?

Teach

W Writing Support

Persuasive Writing Ask students to state the meaning of "depreciation." Then have them write a paragraph about how this term relates to measuring the economy. **OL**

Reading Check **Answer:** Final goods are what consumers purchase to use. Intermediate goods are the parts and supplies needed to produce final goods.

Assess

Civics ONLINE

Study Central™ provides summaries, interactive games, and online graphic organizers to help students review content.

Close

Making Connections Have students discuss how a year in which many entrepreneurs begin new businesses affects GDP. **OL**

Section 1 Review

Vocabulary

1. **Write** a paragraph in which you use these key terms: *goods, services, factors of production, natural resources, labor, capital, entrepreneur, Gross Domestic Product (GDP), standard of living.*

Main Ideas

2. **Identify** each of the following as one of the four factors of production:
   • carpenter
   • hammer
   • forest

3. **Describing** What is gross domestic product and how is it measured?

Critical Thinking

4. **Comparing** How does the factor of production of entrepreneurship differ from the factor of labor?

5. **BIG Ideas** Create a diagram like the one below and label the center oval as shown. Fill in an example of each factor of production that went into developing this service.

Producing a Movie

6. **Applying** Think like an entrepreneur. Identify a new product or service that you believe many people will want to buy. Outline the details of the new product or service. Then explain why you think people will want to buy it.

CITIZENSHIP Activity

7. **Persuasive Writing** Which of the four factors of production do you think has had the greatest impact on the development and enduring strength of the U.S. economy? Why? Write a position paper stating and supporting your reasons.

Civics ONLINE

Study Central™ To review this section, go to glencoe.com.

Section 1 Review

Answers

1. Paragraphs should use vocabulary words according to their definitions in the section and in the Glossary.

2. Carpenter: labor; hammer: capital good; forest: natural resource

3. Gross Domestic Product is the total value in dollars of all the final goods and services produced in a country in a single year. It is measured by multiplying the price of each good by the number of those produced and then adding together these results.

4. Entrepreneurship creates new jobs and new products. Labor produces goods and services.

5. Answers may include the labor of actors, set designers, writers; the capital goods of machines and delivery methods (DVDs, reels); money invested by producers; the entrepreneurship of the director and producer; and the natural resources of locales.

6. Answers will vary, but should identify and explain the product or service.

7. Papers should identify a single factor of production and provide reasons for its importance to a strong U.S. economy.

Focus

Bellringer

Daily Focus Transparency 19–2

Guide to Reading
Answers to Graphic:

consumers

business

Economic Sectors

government

foreign

Section Spotlight Video

To generate student interest and provide a springboard for class discussion, access the Chapter 19, Section 2 video at glencoe.com or on the video DVD.

Resource Manager

Guide to Reading

Big Idea
The basis of the market economy is voluntary exchange. In the American economy, the exchange usually involves money in return for a good or service.

Content Vocabulary
- market *(p. 521)*
- factor market *(p. 521)*
- product market *(p. 522)*
- productivity *(p. 524)*
- specialization *(p. 524)*
- division of labor *(p. 524)*
- economic interdependence *(p. 525)*

Academic Vocabulary
- sector *(p. 521)*
- consume *(p. 522)*
- input *(p. 523)*

Reading Strategy
Categorizing As you read the section, complete a diagram like the one below by identifying the four sectors of the economy.

consumers

Economic Sectors

Economic Activity

Real World Economics Would you know to shop on the Internet for shoes if you had really large feet? When Neil Moncrief started www.2bigfeet.com, specializing in large-sized shoes, the search engine Google listed his site first on searches for "big feet." Soon Moncrief was getting 95 percent of his business from the Internet. Later Google changed the way its search engines worked and sales decreased dramatically. Moncrief's experience is an example of how business success is based on many factors, including economic interdependence.

▼ **Neil Moncrief stands outside his Albany, Georgia, store**

R Reading Strategies	**C** Critical Thinking	**D** Differentiated Instruction	**W** Writing Support	**S** Skill Practice
Teacher Edition • Act. Prior Know., pp. 521, 523 • Making Connections, p. 525 **Additional Resources** • Cont. Vocab., URB p. 43 • Ac. Vocab., URB p. 45 • Guid. Read., URB p. 62 • RENTG, p. 177	**Teacher Edition** • Pred. Consequences, p. 523 • Making Inferences, p. 524 **Additional Resources** • Quizzes and Tests, p. 226	**Teacher Edition** • EL, p. 521 • Visual/Spatial, p. 522 **Additional Resources** • Diff. Instr., URB p. 55 • School-to-Home Connect., URB p. 57 • Reteach. Act., URB p. 59	**Teacher Edition** • Expository Writing, p. 524 **Additional Resources** • Writing Skills Act., URB p. 49	**Teacher Edition** • Analyzing Diagrams, p. 522 **Additional Resources** • Daily Focus Trans., 19–2

Economic Sectors and Circular Flow

Main Idea Resources, goods and services, and money flow in a circular motion among several sectors.

Economics & You The term *market* may mean to you a place to buy fresh fruits and vegetables, but it has a special meaning to economists. Read to find out more.

In the study of economics, a **market** is not necessarily a place. Rather, it is the free and willing exchange of goods and services between buyers and sellers. In other words, markets are places where people come together. Markets may be local, regional, national, or global. In this section, you will learn about the major groups of decision makers and the major markets in the market system. For example, a market exchange may take place in a worldwide market for a good such as crude oil. It may also take place in a neighborhood market for services such as paper delivery, snow shoveling, and babysitting.

Circular Flow of Economic Activity

In a market system, the flow of resources, goods and services, and money is actually circular, as shown in the diagram on page 522. Economists use this model to show how economic decision making in the market system works. The consumer **sector**, or part, makes up one group of economic decision makers, but there are others—the business, government, and foreign sectors.

The Consumer Sector

What role do consumers play in the circular flow? Consumers earn their income in **factor markets**—the markets where productive resources are bought and sold. Here, workers earn wages, salaries, and tips in exchange for their labor. People who own land may loan it in return for a type of income called rent. Finally, people who own capital exchange it for interest.

Economic Activity Within the circular flow of economic activity, consumers buy goods from businesses, and sell resources to businesses. *Explaining* Is the house builder a member of the consumer sector, the business sector, or both?

521

Teach

R Reading Strategy

Activating Prior Knowledge **Say:** Give a specific example of each kind of market. *(Answers may include local farmers markets, regional restaurant chains, national retail giants, and Internet sites that link consumers around the globe.)* **OL**

D Differentiated Instruction

English Learners Explain that interest is money paid to investors for the use of their capital resources. Give an example: a young entrepreneur has a great idea for a new business but no start-up capital (money) with which to work. A wealthy investor gives money to a young entrepreneur to start a business. Ten years later, the entrepreneur pays the money back to the investor along with 4 percent interest—money the entrepreneur pays for the use of the wealthy investor's capital. **ELL**

Caption Answer:
The house builder is a member of the consumer sector because he earns wages in exchange for his labor. He is a member of the business sector because he receives money for the houses he builds.

Differentiated Instruction

Leveled Activities

BL **Guided Reading Activity 19-2, URB p. 62**

OL **Differentiated Instruction Activity 19, URB pp. 55–56**

ELL **Content Vocabulary Activity 19, URB pp. 43–44**

Teach

D Differentiated Instruction

Visual/Spatial Ask: Which visual element of the diagram indicates the circular nature of the market? *(The arrows that together form an oval around and among the market sectors indicate the circular nature of the market.)* **OL**

S Skill Practice

Analyzing Diagrams Ask students to explain the meaning of the two small inset charts, Product Markets and Factor Markets. *(The vertical axis is labeled P for Price, and the horizontal axis is labeled Q for Quantity. "Supply" is the available amount of a product, a natural resource, or capital and labor. As demand rises, quantity should rise to match it. Otherwise, its price will rise.)* **OL**

Analyzing Diagrams

Answers:

1. It represents all the countries in the world other than the United States.
2. Factor markets are where productive resources are bought and sold. Product markets are where producers offer goods and services for sale to consumers.

Differentiated Instruction

Writing Skills Activity 19, URB pp. 49–50

The Business Sector

After individuals receive their incomes, they spend them in **product markets**—markets where producers offer goods and services for sale. The business sector receives payments in the product markets where they sell goods and services to consumers. Businesses use these payments to pay for the natural resources, labor, and capital they use. These resources are then used to manufacture additional products that are sold in the product markets.

As the diagram shows, the business sector purchases some of the output it produces—primarily capital goods—so that it can continue to produce more goods and services. These purchases include things such as tools, factories, and other goods needed for current production. In actual practice, the business sector is much smaller than the consumer sector. While the consumer sector purchases about two-thirds of all output, the business sector usually **consumes,** or uses, only about 15 to 20 percent of our GDP.

The Government Sector

The government sector is another sector that plays a part in economic decision making. This sector is made up of all three levels of government—federal, state, and

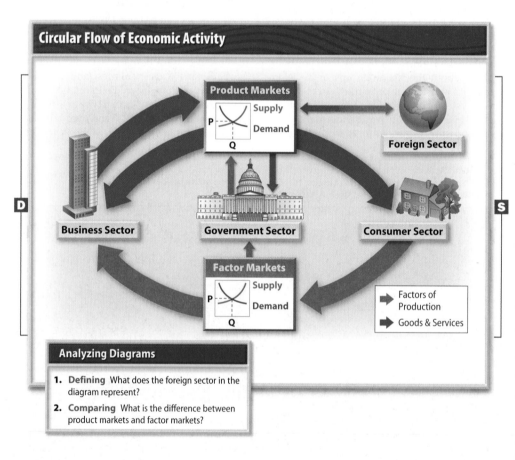

Circular Flow of Economic Activity

Product Markets

Supply
Demand
P
Q

Foreign Sector

Business Sector

Government Sector

Consumer Sector

Factor Markets

Supply
Demand
P
Q

Factors of Production

Goods & Services

Analyzing Diagrams

1. **Defining** What does the foreign sector in the diagram represent?
2. **Comparing** What is the difference between product markets and factor markets?

Objective:	To use cause-and-effect organization in an essay
Focus:	Have students complete the chart on page 49.
Teach:	Review Section 2's discussion of specialization and division of labor.
Assess:	Make sure students understand the relationship between specialization and production.
Close:	Have students compare their charts to correct problems in their summaries.

Differentiated Instruction Strategies

BL Draw a chart that shows several causes leading to a single effect.

AL Discuss why the quality of some products is negatively affected by specialization.

ELL How might one cause lead to a chain of causes and effects? Illustrate an example of this.

local. Because the government sector also produces goods and services, it purchases productive **inputs,** or resources, in the factor markets. Since the time of World War II, the government has become a bigger part of the economy.

Revenues and Expenditures The government receives revenue from the services it sells. For example, public universities charge tuition, public hospitals charge fees, and city buses charge fares. The total cost of government services is seldom covered by fees alone, however. The government sector receives most of its revenues from taxes on businesses and individuals.

Government also uses its revenue to purchase final goods and services in the product markets. School systems, for example, purchase books, buses, and computers while the military purchases trucks, fighter planes, and ships. Historically, the government is the second-largest sector in our economy, purchasing approximately 20 percent of our GDP.

The Foreign Sector

The foreign sector in the diagram represents all the countries in the world. Notice on the diagram on page 522 that this sector is the only one with a line that has an arrow at both ends. The reason is that we both sell products to and buy products from other countries.

The value of the goods and services the United States purchases from other countries and the value of the goods and services it sells to other countries tend to offset one another. As a result, the foreign sector generally accounts for less than 4 percent of our nation's GDP.

Reading Check Describing In the circular flow of activity, in what economic activities is the consumer involved?

Civics ONLINE
Student Web Activity Visit glencoe.com and complete the Chapter 19 Web Activity.

TIME Teens in Action

Erika Fields

Erika Fields, 17, of Cleveland, Ohio, wondered why public schools in some urban areas get less state money than some schools in suburban areas. To help bring about change, and to make school funding more fair, Fields combined her voice with others in "Our Voice."

QUESTION: What is Our Voice?

ANSWER: Our Voice is a group of students who study school funding issues. We try to make a difference by testifying before education committees, holding rallies, and speaking out for fairness in how tax money is distributed to schools.

Q: Tell us about your newspaper.

A: *Our Voices: Students Speak Out* is a student-produced, statewide paper that talks about funding for public schools in Ohio.

Q: Do only teens from your school work on the paper?

A: No. Students from different schools contribute articles and illustrations. We open it up to everyone who has something to say about public schools—negative or positive.

Q: What is the paper's goal?

A: We are working to get our state lawmakers to produce an equal school funding system—to make sure that each and every student has an equal education.

ACTION FACT: Fields enjoys singing— and is planning to become a doctor.

"Our Voice" teens speak out

Making a Difference 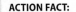 **CITIZENSHIP**
What is the purpose and goal of Our Voice, the group?

C Critical Thinking

Predicting Consequences Ask: What impact might a sudden slowdown in government purchasing have on the nation's economy? (*The economy would slow down, because the government is the second-largest market sector.*) **AL**

R Reading Strategy

Activating Prior Knowledge Ask: With which countries does the United States mainly trade? (*Answers may include nations such as China, Mexico, Canada.*) **OL ELL**

Reading Check Answer: Consumers earn income in the factor markets and spend their income in the product markets.

Civics ONLINE
Objectives and answers to the **Student Web Activity** can be found at glencoe.com under the Web Activity Lesson Plan for this chapter.

TIME Teens in Action

Answer:
to get state lawmakers to produce an equal school funding system

Hands-On Chapter Project
Step 2

Making a Business Plan

Step 2: Assessing Needed Resources Groups of students will consider the resource factors needed for their new business to succeed.

Directions Remind students of the business idea the class has decided to pursue. Review the four factors of production in Section 1, and tell students that they are the entrepreneurs. Then organize them into three groups.

Analyzing Assign each group one of the remaining three factors of production: natural resources, labor, and capital/capital goods. Tell each group to think about the class's business idea and to determine, as accurately as possible, what is needed from each factor of production. Will start-up funds be needed? How many hours of labor will be involved? What machines or supplies will be required? Tell students that they will use their answers to these and related questions as they write their business plan in Step 3. **OL AL**

(Project continued in Section 3)

W Writing Support

Expository Writing Have students write a paragraph responding to the following questions. What are some scarce natural resources, and why is efficient use of these resources especially important? *(Paragraphs should list scarce resources—such as timber, water, fossil fuels, and minerals—and explain that efficient use of these resources is important because they are not easily renewable.)* **OL**

C Critical Thinking

Making Inferences Ask: Why does specialization improve productivity? Give an example. *(Specialists can work quickly and effectively at the task that they have mastered. For example, not all surgeons have studied all parts of the body. Neurosurgeons specialize in brain surgery, while orthopedists specialize in working with joints. Each specialist would have to spend large amounts of time to master another field.)* **BL**

Caption Answer:
The engineer did not make the parts that go into the fan or put them together, nor does he run the fan. His job is to ensure that the fan is correctly built and installed and that it is functioning as it should.

Additional Support

Teacher Tip

If necessary, use a reputable source, such as *Encyclopaedia Britannica*, to review the trade terms before completing this activity with students.

Promoting Economic Growth

Main Idea Economic growth occurs when a nation's total output of goods and services from all economic areas increases.

Economics & You You have probably told yourself at some time or another that you need to be more productive. Find out what productivity means in our nation's economy.

Economic growth occurs when a nation's total output of goods and services increases over time. This increase means that the circular flow becomes larger. Economic growth is important because it raises people's standard of living. This growth is a major goal of our economy and is a way officials can tell if our economy is healthy.

Division of Labor A quality control engineer at a South Carolina plant inspects the fan assembly of a gas-fired turbine. *Explaining* In what way is the engineer's job an example of the division of labor?

524

Productivity

W When scarce resources are used efficiently, everyone benefits. Efficient use of resources is described by the term **productivity**. This is a measure of the amount of output (goods and services) produced by a given level of inputs (land, labor, capital, and entrepreneurship) in a specific period of time. Productivity goes up whenever more output can be produced with the same amount of input in the same amount of time, or when the same output can be produced with less input.

Productivity is often discussed in terms of labor, but it applies to all factors of production. For this reason, business owners try to buy the most efficient capital goods, and farmers try to use the most fertile land for their crops.

Specialization

Specialization takes place when people, businesses, regions, or even countries concentrate on goods or services that they can produce better than anyone else. As a result, nearly everyone depends upon others to produce many of the things that he or she consumes. Specialization is important because it improves productivity.

Few individuals or households seriously consider producing their own food, shelter, and clothing. When people specialize, they are usually far more productive than if they attempt to do many things. For example, Maria is a carpenter who wants to build a house. Even if Maria is capable of building the entire house without any help, she would likely be better off to hire other workers who specialize in foundations, plumbing, and electrical wiring.

Division of Labor

Division of labor is breaking down a job into small tasks performed by different workers. Division of labor makes use of differences in skills and abilities.

Activity: U.S./World Connections

Categorizing and Analyzing Information Remind students that the foreign sector generally accounts for less than 4 percent of the United States' or U.S. GDP. Nevertheless, international trade is important and requires the cooperation of many government offices to manage it well. Guide students to use library and Internet resources to define these international trade terms: *balance of trade, imports/exports, most*

favored nation status, tariffs, trade barriers, trade deficit/surplus.

Then ask students to look at items around the classroom, making a list of the countries of origin of these items. Have students discuss how their purchasing habits and opportunities would change if the United States cut back on imports from other nations. **OL**

For example, you and your coworker would each do the tasks for which you are best suited. Even if your abilities are identical, specialization can be advantageous. By applying all your time to a single task, you are more likely to discover better techniques. Division of labor improves productivity.

Human Capital

Productivity also tends to increase when businesses invest in human capital—the sum of people's skills, abilities, and motivation. Employers are usually rewarded with higher-quality products and higher profits. Workers often benefit from higher pay, better jobs, greater motivation, and more satisfaction with their work.

Economic Interdependence

Because of specialization, our economy displays a strong degree of **economic interdependence.** This means that we rely on others, and others rely on us, to provide goods and services.

Events in one region of the country or the world often have a dramatic impact elsewhere. For example, bad weather in a country where sugarcane is grown can affect sugar prices in the United States, which in turn can affect the demand for sugar substitutes elsewhere.

Interdependence and Trade-Offs Today, economic technology usually describes the use of science to develop new products and new methods of producing and distributing goods and services. Without satellite technology, for example, it would be impossible to buy and sell goods and services with nations around the world.

This example does not mean that economic interdependence is necessarily bad. The gain in productivity and income that results from increased specialization usually offsets the cost associated with the loss of self-sufficiency.

Reading Check Explaining What are the benefits of specialization?

 Review

Vocabulary

1. **Write** a paragraph in which you use the following terms: *productivity, specialization, division of labor, economic interdependence.* Then, write a second paragraph using these terms: *market, factor market, product market.*

Main Ideas

2. **Describing** What is a factor market?

3. **Explain** Why is productivity important to economic growth?

Critical Thinking

4. **BIG Ideas** Describe how either you or a relative of yours who has a job fits into the circular-flow model. Be sure to discuss both the factor market and the product market.

5. **Explaining** On a chart like the one below, define *division of labor* and explain how it improves the efficiency of production.

Division of Labor	
Definition	Results

CITIZENSHIP Activity

6. **Expository Writing** Use the information in this section to write a short speech you could give to fourth graders on the topic "Why Economic Growth Is Important." Remember to make your explanation simple enough for younger students to understand.

Civics ONLINE

Study Central™ To review this section, go to glencoe.com.

Making Connections Ask: What recent events have occurred in one region or nation but impacted the economies of other regions or nations? *(Answers will include any recent event that impacted the economy.)* **OL**

Reading Check Answer: Specialization allows people to master a task so that they can work efficiently.

Assess

Civics ONLINE

Study Central™ provides summaries, interactive games, and online graphic organizers to help students review content.

Close

Personal Writing Have students write about their status as human capital. **OL**

Section 2 Review

Answers

1. Paragraphs should use vocabulary words according to their definitions in the section and in the Glossary.

2. A factor market is a market where production factors—natural resources, labor, and capital—are bought and sold.

3. When productivity is high, resources are used efficiently to produce many goods and services. The economy grows when businesses preserve scarce resources while maintaining high levels of productivity.

4. Answers should focus on an individual's role in both the factor market and the product market and should demonstrate understanding of both markets.

5. **Definition:** breaking down a job into small tasks performed by different workers; **Results:** efficient use is made of differences in skills and abilities

6. Speeches should use audience-appropriate language, define difficult terms, and accurately explain the importance of economic growth.

S Skill Practice

Analyzing Charts Ask: What do you notice about the difference between men's and women's salaries as their levels of education increase? *(Men's salaries lead women's salaries at every educational level; but as the level of education increases, the difference between men's and women's salaries increases as well, from a roughly $7,500 difference to a roughly $20,000 difference.)* Encourage students to consider why this might be. **AL**

C Critical Thinking

Analyzing Primary Sources Read aloud the attribution for this quotation to students. **Ask:** How does this information affect what you think about the quotation? *(As Secretary of Labor, a cabinet position, Elaine Chao was the leading expert on employment in the nation. This information tells readers to take the quotation seriously.)* **OL**

Analyzing Economics

Answers:

1. The median income for men is $41,939; the median income for women is $31,565.
2. The difference is $15,253.

Additional Support

Education and Earning Power

As you probably already know, levels of education and income are related. High-income workers generally have more education than low-income workers. For example,

- high school dropouts earn less than high school graduates;
- high school graduates earn less than college graduates;
- college graduates with bachelor's degrees earn less than those with advanced degrees.

Not only is it likely that income will rise with further education, but also the chances of becoming unemployed are reduced. Unemployment rates for high school graduates are twice that for college graduates. For example, in April 2006, the unemployment rate for workers with a bachelor's degree or higher was 2.2 percent, 3.8 percent for workers with some college or an associate degree, 4.4 percent for those with a high school diploma, and 7 percent for workers with less than a high school diploma.

Level of Education	Median Income*	
	Female	**Male**
Not a high school graduate	$18,938	$26,468
High school graduate	26,074	35,412
Some college	30,142	41,348
Bachelor's degree	41,327	56,502
Master's degree	50,163	70,640
All full-time workers	**$31,565**	**$41,939**

*The median income is the middle income in a series of incomes ranked from smallest to largest.

Source: National Center for Education Statistics.

Did You Know?

"*More than two-thirds of the new jobs being created in our economy are in occupations that require some kind of post-secondary education.*"

—Secretary of Labor Elaine Chao, May 31, 2006

Source: US Dept of Labor: www.dol.gov/sec/media/speeches/20060531_miami.htm

Analyzing Economics

1. **Comparing** What are the median incomes for men and for women who are employed full-time?
2. **Calculating** What is the difference in median income between female high school graduates and females who attain bachelor's degrees?

Activity: Economics Connections

Logical/Mathematical Point out to students that as they think about their futures, they must set the cost of college against the advantages of the higher salaries that come with greater levels of education. Have students use the Internet to learn how much the following degrees currently cost:

- a two-year associate's degree from a community college
- a four-year bachelor's degree from a state college or university
- a four-year bachelor's degree from a private college or university.

Then, refer students to the chart. Have students divide the cost of their desired educational degree into the annual median income for that degree to determine in how many years the degree would pay for itself. **OL**

Guide to Reading

Big Idea
Free enterprise is the freedom of individuals and businesses to operate and compete with a minimum of government interference or regulation.

Content Vocabulary
- capitalism (p. 528)
- free enterprise (p. 528)
- consumer sovereignty (p. 529)
- private property rights (p. 529)
- competition (p. 530)
- profit (p. 530)
- profit motive (p. 530)
- voluntary exchange (p. 530)
- laissez-faire economics (p. 531)

Academic Vocabulary
- accumulate (p. 528)
- dispose (p. 529)
- incentive (p. 529)

Reading Strategy
Organizing As you read the section, complete a diagram like the one below by identifying the features of capitalism. Then provide an example of each feature.

markets — Capitalism

Section 3

🔊 Section Audio 🎬 Spotlight Video

Capitalism and Free Enterprise

Real World Economics Where would you guess the world's busiest McDonald's restaurant is located? Los Angeles? New York? Tokyo? The answer is Moscow, in the former Soviet Union. How does this American restaurant do so well in a former Communist country? In Russian cities, McDonald's caters to the local citizens, not to American tourists. Teens in Moscow hang out at fast-food places in the same way teens in other countries do. Economic reforms in Russia have moved the country more toward a capitalistic, market-oriented system.

▼ **A McDonald's on St. Petersburg's main avenue, Nevsky Prospekt**

527

Focus

Bellringer
Daily Focus Transparency 19–3

Guide to Reading
Answers to Graphic:

markets — economic freedom — private property rights — Capitalism — competition — profit motive — voluntary exchange

🎬 Section Spotlight Video

To generate student interest and provide a springboard for class discussion, access the Chapter 19, Section 3 video at glencoe.com or on the video DVD.

Resource Manager

R Reading Strategies	**C** Critical Thinking	**D** Differentiated Instruction	**W** Writing Support	**S** Skill Practice
Teacher Edition • Making Connections, p. 528 • Questioning, p. 529 **Additional Resources** • Cont. Vocab., URB p. 44 • Ac. Vocab., URB p. 46 • Guid. Read., URB p. 63 • Foldables, p. 87	**Teacher Edition** • Drawing Con., p. 531 **Additional Resources** • Biography, URB p. 47 • Quizzes and Tests, p. 227	**Teacher Edition** • EL, p. 529 **Additional Resources** • School-to-Home Connect, URB p. 58 • Reteach. Act., URB p. 59	**Teacher Edition** • Descriptive Writing, p. 530 **Additional Resources** • Cit./Decision-Making, URB p. 3	**Teacher Edition** • Visual Literacy, p. 528 • Creating a T-Chart, p. 530 **Additional Resources** • Daily Focus Trans., 19–3 • Pol. Cartoon Trans. 19

R Reading Strategy

Making Connections Ask: What is the connection between the market factor called capital and the economic system called capitalism? *(Capitalism is based on the free use of capital—the funds needed to equip and run businesses.)* **AL**

S Skill Practice

Visual Literacy Ask students to describe how the man on the right side of the cartoon is dressed. **Ask:** What does a business suit suggest about the person wearing it? Is this impression of the credit card company representative accurate? *(Usually, a business suit suggests that the person wearing it is professional and responsible. The representative of the credit card company seems to be behaving like a scam artist.)* **OL**

TIME™ Political Cartoons

Answers:

1. He should pay off his debt and improve his credit.
2. They are depicted as willing to exploit consumers already in financial trouble.
3. Credit card companies know that these consumers need ready funds and that they will probably use the card to run up more debt.

Differentiated Instruction

Primary Source Reading 6-A, URB pp. 15–16

Capitalism

Main Idea The economic system of the United States is known as capitalism, in which private citizens own and use the factors of production to seek a profit.

Economics & You Do you feel that the products you want to buy are available? Read to find out what power you have as a consumer.

R The economy of the United States is built largely on free markets and private ownership. It is known as **capitalism,** an economic system in which private citizens own and use the factors of production in order to seek a profit.

Free enterprise is another term to describe the American economy. In a free enterprise economy, competition is allowed to flourish with a minimum of government interference. One of the most remarkable characteristics of our nation's economy is its ability to grow and **accumulate,** or collect, wealth. No other economic system in the history of the world has been as successful.

What Makes Capitalism Work?

Several unique features of capitalism combine to contribute to its success in the United States and in other countries. These features are the use of markets, economic freedom, private property rights, competition, profit motive, and voluntary exchange.

Markets Markets are one important part of our economic system. Markets are the places where the prices of goods and services are determined as exchange takes place. Markets may be local, regional, national, or global. Markets also connect the different sectors of the economy. To illustrate, review the chart on page 522. It shows that consumers and businesses interact primarily in the product and factor markets.

TIME™

Political Cartoons

Gary Markstein/Copley News Service

With this cartoon, Gary Markstein is making a point about consumer credit. Examine the first panel of the cartoon.

1. What "immediate action" would it be logical for the consumer to take in light of his financial situation?
2. Now look at the second panel. How are credit card companies depicted?
3. Why might credit card companies offer high-interest cards to consumers who are already in debt?

Finance Conference on the New Economy

Objective: To connect technology to the economy

Focus: Review the definitions of "market" and "global economy."

Teach: Read the speech aloud, stopping to check comprehension.

Assess: Have students paraphrase and discuss Summers' quote.

Close: Have students predict how communications technologies will shape the new economy.

Differentiated Instruction Strategies

BL Name a technology that you notice more often when it is absent.

AL Explain Summers' comparison of the growth in the new economy to growth during the Industrial Revolution and the Renaissance.

ELL Create word maps that link the Reader's Dictionary words to words you already know.

American Biography

David Hernandez (1969 –)

David Hernandez was only 5 years old when his family left their home in Cuba and moved to the United States. When Hernandez's father died, David delivered newspapers, mowed lawns, and took on odd jobs to help his family. It would have been easy for him to give up on his dream to attend college. Instead, he worked his way through college and graduated magna cum laude from Palm Beach Atlantic University with a degree in accounting. He later earned an MBA from New York University.

When his employer, the energy giant Enron, collapsed, David Hernandez lost his job and his 401(K), but not his entrepreneurial spirit. Along with his brother, Eliezer, and two former colleagues, Hernandez saw an opportunity to build his own company. His plan was to provide small- and mid-sized businesses, with low-cost electric power and great customer support. In less than 4 years, Liberty Power grew from grossing less than $1 million in its first year to more than $100 million in 2005, making it the largest Latino-owned electricity provider in the country.

The company's corporate responsibility does not end with its customers. In January 2004 Hernandez created the Liberty Power Foundation to support education in the communities the company serves.

Making a Difference — CITIZENSHIP

"It's not only important to do well; philosophically, I believe that it's important to do good." **Discuss the meaning of this quote by David Hernandez.**

When you go to work, your labor is being sold in the factor markets. When you go shopping, the goods and services you buy are being purchased in product markets. In our economic system, the consumer is especially important because businesses usually try to produce the products that people want most. Because of the effort to match products to wants, we use the term **consumer sovereignty** to describe the consumer as the "king," or ruler, of the market, the one who determines what products will be produced.

Economic Freedom In the United States, we place a high value on the freedom to make our own economic decisions. Each of us can choose the type of job or occupation we would like to have, and we can choose when and where we would like to work.

As consumers, we have the right to choose the products we will buy. Businesses have the right to choose the products they will produce and offer for sale. However, along with this freedom come certain costs. In particular, individuals must normally accept the consequences of their decisions in our free enterprise system. If an entrepreneur starts a business that fails, the government usually does not help out.

Private Property Rights Another major feature of capitalism is **private property rights.** These rights mean that we have the freedom to own and use, or **dispose** of, or throw away, our own property as we choose as long as we do not interfere with the rights of others. Private property rights give us the **incentive,** or drive, to work, save, and invest because we know we can keep any gains that we might earn. In addition, people tend to take better care of things if they actually own them.

Chapter 19 **529**

R **Reading Strategy**

Questioning Ask: What questions could the owner of a coffee shop ask to determine what consumers need and want and what an attractive price to both the shop and the consumers would be? *(Possible answers: Are there other coffee shops nearby? What are the prices of supplies such as coffee, tea, and paper goods? At what prices are other coffee shops selling their beverages? How far are consumers willing to travel to patronize the shop?)* **OL**

D **Differentiated Instruction**

English Learners Invite students who have lived in other countries to describe the options for employment and property rights in those countries. For instance, in some countries, property is passed down in a family from generation to generation; to sell it is to break with tradition. **ELL**

American Biography

Answers:
Guide students to discuss how doing well is different from doing good. Ask them to provide examples from Hernandez's life and from the lives of other people who have both done well and done good.

Leveled Activities

BL **Academic Vocabulary Activity 19, URB pp. 45–46**

OL **Biography Activity 19, URB pp. 47–48**

AL **Primary Source Reading 6A, URB pp. 15–16**

ELL **Reteaching Activity 19, URB p. 59**

W Writing Support

Descriptive Writing Have students write a couple of paragraphs to answer the following questions: What is a monopoly, and why are monopolies bad for competition? *(Student paragraphs should explain what a monopoly is and why they are bad for competition.)* **OL**

S Skill Practice

Creating a T-Chart Have students create a T-chart to keep track of the rewards and risks involved in the system of capitalism. Encourage them to look back at previous sections of the chapter to gather notes for the chart. Then ask them to write a brief journal entry about whether they would seek the rewards of free enterprise or be put off by the risks. **OL**

Caption Answer:
Competition causes efficient production, higher-quality products, lower prices, and more satisfied consumers.

✓ **Reading Check** **Answer:** efficient production, higher quality products, and more satisfied customers.

Hands-On Chapter Project
Step 3

Competition Cloth making was primarily a home-based craft during colonial times. By the early 1800s, power-loom technology mechanized cloth making, and prices for cloth came down. *Explaining* **What are the benefits of competition?**

Competition Capitalism thrives on **competition**—the struggle between buyers and sellers to get the best products at the lowest prices. The competition between sellers keeps the cost of production low and the quality of the goods higher than they would otherwise be. Buyers likewise compete among themselves to find the best products at the lowest prices.

Competition thus rewards the most efficient producers. Competition also forces the least efficient producers out of business or into other industries. The result is that competition makes for efficient production, higher-quality products, and more satisfied customers.

The Profit Motive Under free enterprise and capitalism, people are free to risk their savings or any part of their wealth in a business venture. If the venture goes well, the people will earn rewards for their efforts. If things go poorly, they could lose part or even all of the investment. The possibility of financial gain, however, leads many to take risks in hopes of earning a profit.

Profit is the amount of money left over after all the costs of production have been paid. The **profit motive**—the driving force that encourages individuals and organizations to improve their material well-being—is largely responsible for the growth of a free enterprise system based on capitalism.

Voluntary Exchange Voluntary exchange is the act of buyers and sellers freely and willingly engaging in market transactions. Who benefits when you buy something—you or the seller? Both are giving something up to gain something else. As long as the transaction involves a voluntary exchange, both you and the seller benefit—or the exchange would not have happened in the first place.

The exchange takes place because both parties feel they will make a profit. Voluntary exchange, then, is both a characteristic of capitalism and a way for us to improve our economic well-being.

✓ **Reading Check** **Explaining** What force pushes people to improve their financial well-being?

Making a Business Plan

Step 3: Developing a Business Plan Groups of students will write a plan for the businesses they have chosen.

Directions Before beginning this step, choose a simple business plan model from the Small Business Association's Web site at www.bplans.com/samples/sba.cfm. Select one that most closely matches the students' business venture idea. Provide copies of this plan for students.

Writing a Business Plan Explain to students that a good business plan will encourage investment in the business. A typical plan will have a summary, objective and mission statement, description of product or service, market analysis, implementation plan, and financial plan. Organize students into groups, each group concentrating on writing one segment of the plan. **OL AL**

(Project continued on the Visual Summary page)

History of Capitalism

Main Idea Capitalism developed gradually in Europe and had a powerful influence on America's constitutional Framers.

Economics & You If you have a job, why do you work? Read to find out how a famous economist answers this question.

In 1776 Adam Smith, a Scottish philosopher and economist, provided a philosophy for the capitalist system in his book *The Wealth of Nations*. Smith's book offered a detailed description of life and trade in British society. It also scientifically described the basic principles of economics for the first time.

Smith wrote that individuals left on their own would work for their own self-interest. In doing so, they would be guided as if by an "invisible hand" to use resources efficiently. From the writings of Smith and others came the idea of **laissez-faire economics.** Laissez-faire, a French term, means "to let alone." According to this philosophy, government should not interfere in the marketplace. The government's role is confined to those actions necessary to ensure free competition.

Many of America's Framers were influenced by *The Wealth of Nations*. James Madison read it, and Alexander Hamilton borrowed heavily from it in his writings. In a 1790 letter he sent, Thomas Jefferson wrote, "... in political economy I think Smith's *Wealth of Nations* is the best book extant [in existence] ..."

✓ **Reading Check** **Explaining** What is the role of government, according to the laissez-faire philosophy?

Critical Thinking

Drawing Conclusions **Ask:** What forms might Adam Smith's "invisible hand" take, given what you have learned in this chapter? *(Answers include: any of the market factors and forces, such as availability of capital and stress of competition, discussed in the chapter.)* **AL**

✓ **Reading Check** **Answer:** The role of government in a laissez-faire economy is to ensure free competition in the marketplace.

Assess

Civics ONLINE

Study Central provides summaries, interactive games, and online graphic organizers to help students review content.

Close

Predicting Drawing on what they have learned about the history of capitalism and on their own ideas about the actions a government might need to take, have students discuss the ways in which a government can ensure free competition in the marketplace. **OL**

Section 3 Review

Vocabulary

1. **Explain** what *free enterprise* means, then explain how each of the following terms relates to free enterprise: *capitalism, consumer sovereignty, private property rights, competition, profit, profit motive, voluntary exchange, laissez-faire economics.*

Main Ideas

2. **Describing** What does the idea of consumer sovereignty express?

3. **Explaining** What are the limits of private property rights?

Critical Thinking

4. **Explaining** According to Adam Smith, what are the results of individuals working for their own self-interest?

5. **Determining** Under capitalism, how would you answer the question: For whom are goods produced?

6. **BIG Ideas** There are six features of capitalism mentioned in this section. On a diagram like the one below, identify the two features that you think are most important. Explain your answer.

CITIZENSHIP Activity

7. **Analyzing** Survey five fellow students, friends, and neighbors to discover what the term *free enterprise* means to them. Review your findings and analyze why people might have different views of free enterprise.

8. **Descriptive Writing** Adam Smith said that people work for self-interest. Do you agree? Write a paragraph describing someone who works for this reason or for another reason.

Civics ONLINE

Study Central™ To review this section, go to glencoe.com.

Answers

1. Free enterprise is based on competition with a minimum of government interference. Explanations for the terms are found in the section and in the Glossary.

2. Consumer sovereignty expresses the idea that the consumer determines what products will be produced and what services will be provided.

3. Property rights apply as long as they do not interfere with the rights of others.

4. They would use resources efficiently.

5. Goods are produced for the consumer.

6. Students may identify any two features of capitalism as long as they support their choices with reasons based on the text.

7. Students should present the findings of five people and then base their analyses on these findings.

8. Paragraphs should include descriptive details about the subject and should either agree or disagree with Smith's claim.

Teach

C1 Critical Thinking

Making Generalizations Ask: In general, why might it weaken the United States if each state set its own trade barriers? *(Possible answer: because the U.S. central government would not have the power to settle commercial disputes between states and to establish a strong economy)* **OL**

C2 Critical Thinking

Predicting Consequences Ask: What might happen if one business controlled access to the most important freeway within a state's limits? *(Possible answer: the controlling business might limit transportation along that freeway for rival businesses.)* **AL**

ANALYZING THE COURT DECISION

Answers:
1. He defined it to apply to all forms of commercial activity.
2. After this ruling, a state could regulate only that trade that occurred within the state itself. Congress now regulates all trade among states or among the United States and foreign nations.

Additional Support

Gibbons v. Ogden

C1 *In the early years of the nation, each state jealously guarded its own commerce. Trade barriers among the states restricted commerce and stood in the way of a strong national economy. What changed this situation?*

Background of the Case

C2 In the early 1800s, the state of New York licensed Robert Fulton and his partner to operate a steamboat monopoly along its waterway. The partners then used their license to grant Aaron Ogden a monopoly on ferryboat travel between New York City and Elizabethtown, New Jersey. Thomas Gibbons, however, had a federal license to run boats between New York and New Jersey.

Ogden wanted to shut down his competition. He sued to close down Gibbons' operation. It was up to the Supreme Court to decide which would prevail—Ogden's state license or Gibbons' federal license.

The Decision

John Marshall delivered the Court's unanimous opinion on March 4, 1824. His decision rested on the power of Congress to "regulate commerce," as granted in Article I, Section 8, of the U.S. Constitution. Marshall interpreted *commerce* to mean "every species of commercial [interaction]," including navigation.

> 66 *This power [to regulate commerce], like all others vested in Congress, is complete in itself, may be exercised to its utmost extent, and acknowledges no limitations other than are prescribed in the Constitution. . . . [However, this rule does not apply to] . . . commerce, which is completely internal, which is carried on between man and man in a State, or between different parts of the same State. . . .* 99
>
> —Justice John Marshall

New York Harbor, painted by Thomas Birch, 1827

The decision gave the federal government sole power to regulate all possible forms of commerce between states. It also affirmed Congress's right to regulate trade with foreign nations. States retained the right to regulate trade entirely inside their borders, and Ogden lost his license.

Why It Matters

The *Gibbons* decision took on more significance in later years than it did at the time. Marshall's broad interpretation of the commerce clause, in fact, helped pave the way for today's strong national government. It allowed Congress to prevent companies from fixing prices. In 1964, Congress was able to prohibit racial discrimination in businesses serving the public because such discrimination was seen as affecting interstate commerce.

Analyzing the Court Decision

1. **Describing** How did Marshall define the commerce clause?
2. **Analyzing** How did this Supreme Court ruling affect states' control of economic activities?

Background

Gibbons v. Ogden When this case was brought before the Supreme Court, the United States was still a young nation. The federal government had not yet decided how much regulation of interstate commerce was necessary. Instead, a patchwork of state rules made interstate trade inefficient, expensive, and in some cases unfair. The Framers of the Constitution had written the Commerce Clause in Article 1, Section 8, of the Constitution so that the federal government could regularize interstate trade. Before this case, however, the extent of federal power had not been tested.

Justice John Marshall favored a strong national government and recognized that this case gave the court the opportunity to define the federal government's power to replace the states' often contradictory and counterproductive trade policies with a more unified and effective policy.

Economic Resources

- The four factors of production (natural resources, labor, capital, and entrepreneurs) provide the means for a society to produce its goods and services.
- Gross Domestic Product (GDP) is the total value of all the *final* goods and services produced in a country in one year.

Economic Activity

- Productivity relates to the efficient use of resources, and tends to go up when workers specialize in the things they do best.

Twin sisters check items on sale

- Resources, goods and services, and money flow in a circular motion among several sectors, and economic growth occurs when a nation's total output of goods and services increases.

Capitalism and Free Enterprise

- The economic system of the United States is based on capitalism and free enterprise.
- Important characteristics are markets, economic freedom, competition, private property rights, the profit motive, and voluntary exchange.

Mother and daughter shop for clothes

Worker stitches American flags onto baseball caps at a Buffalo, New York, factory

STUDY TO GO Study anywhere, anytime! Download quizzes and flash cards to your PDA from glencoe.com.

Identifying Cause and Effect
Ask: Why is it important to understand how the four factors of production affect the nation's economy? *(The nation's economy determines the quality of life for individuals. A strong economy leads to a higher standard of living, while a weak economy leads to a lower standard of living. To participate effectively in the economy, individuals must understand their role in production and consumption.)* **OL AL**

Analyzing Visuals Ask: Which images on the page provide visual examples of these chapter concepts: capital, consumer sovereignty, competition? *(The image of the worker making caps shows human capital [labor] and capital goods. The image of the mother and daughter shopping shows consumer sovereignty. The image of the sisters checking sale items shows competition.)* **AL**

Hands-On Chapter Project
Step 4: Wrap-Up

Making a Business Plan

Step 4: Extending the Project Students will submit their plans to adult advisors for feedback. Students may choose to put their business plan into operation.

Directions Explore your community to find businesspeople who volunteer to mentor young entrepreneurs. Groups such as Junior Achievement and Rotary provide such resources. Arrange a time for students to discuss their business plan with these mentors and to receive feedback.

Interpersonal Before the meeting, encourage students to discuss the dress code for professional meetings. Have students submit a clean copy of their business plan to their mentors before the meeting.

After the meeting, have students summarize the changes they want to make to their business plan based on the feedback they received. Ask students to write a formal letter of thanks to each mentor. **OL**

19 ASSESSMENT

Answers and Analyses
Reviewing Vocabulary

1. B Review the definition of each option with students. Remind them that although these goods may in fact be manufactured, they are used to create final goods for sale. This makes them capital goods.

2. C Encourage students to substitute the full names for the acronyms before they answer. When they recall that GDP means Gross Domestic Product, they can connect "product" and "produced."

3. A Remind students that income is earned in exchange for labor and that labor is one of the four factors in the factor, or consumer, market.

4. D Guide students to recall the definition of each term listed in the options and then to match the definition in the incomplete statement to the correct option. Students may rephrase the statement as a question: What occurs between sellers to keep the cost of production low and the quality of goods high?

Reviewing Main Ideas

5. A Make sure students remember what the four factors of production work together to do: to start, run, and maintain businesses. Students can ask this question: Which of the options starts, runs, and maintains businesses?

6. C Help students see that quantity of products and quality of products are related concepts: standard of living depends not only on products being available (quantity) but on their being of high quality. Quality of life is the measure of standard of living.

7. C Students can rule out options A and D because these exclude the foreign sector. Then they will need to recall the four factors of production to see that these are part of the four sectors. Option C is the logical choice.

8. B Remind students that another word for human capital is labor, the work a person does to earn an income. A better-trained labor force is more valuable than

an untrained labor force because it can do better work. Therefore, additional training increases human capital.

9. A Point out to students that three of the options—voluntary exchange, specialization, and division of labor—should be maximized for free enterprise to succeed. The incomplete statement needs a phrase that identifies the element that should be minimized in a free enterprise economy: government interference.

10. D Students can quickly rule out options A and B because businesses do not produce these. They may be drawn to option C because it uses the word "production," but they must recall that the factors of production make production possible; they do not guide decisions about what to offer on the market. Consumers guide these decisions.

---

19 ASSESSMENT

TEST-TAKING TIP

> Skim through a test before you start to answer questions. That way you can decide how to pace yourself.

Reviewing Vocabulary

Directions: Choose the word(s) that best completes the sentence.

1. Machines, buildings, and tools used to make other goods and services are _____ goods.

  A consumer   **C** factor

  B capital   **D** manufactured

2. The total value of all the final goods and services produced in a country in one year is its _____.

  A income   **C** GDP

  B VAT   **D** resources

3. Consumers earn their income in _____ markets where productive resources are bought and sold.

  A factor   **C** resource

  B product   **D** consumer

4. The _____ between sellers keeps the cost of production low and quality of goods high.

  A profit motive   **C** exchange

  B interdependence   **D** competition

Reviewing Main Ideas

Directions: Choose the best answer for each question.

Section 1 *(pp. 516–519)*

5. The four factors of production are natural resources, labor, capital and

  A entrepreneurs.

  B services.

  C goods.

  D specialization.

6. A nation's standard of living is a measure of not only the quantity of its products, but also

  A the value of its resources.

  B of its people.

  C the quality of its goods and services.

  D of how the products are produced.

Section 2 *(pp. 520–525)*

7. The four sectors, business, consumer, government, and foreign are all part of

  A the GDP.

  B the factors of production.

  C the circular flow of economic activity.

  D a nation's standard of living.

8. When workers receive additional training for their jobs, this increases

  A the cost of production.

  B human capital.

  C economic interdependence.

  D the division of labor.

Section 3 *(pp. 527–531)*

9. In a free enterprise economy, competition is allowed to flourish with a minimum of

  A government interference.

  B voluntary exchange.

  C specialization.

  D division of labor.

10. In our economy businesses try to produce goods and services that people want most; this is an example of

  A private property rights.

  B specialization.

  C the factors of production.

  D consumer sovereignty.

GO ON →

Critical Thinking

Directions: Choose the best answer for each question.

Base your answers to questions 11 and 12 on the chart below and your knowledge of Chapter 19.

Level of Education	Median Income*	
	Female	Male
Not a high school graduate	$18,938	$26,468
High school graduate	26,074	35,412
Some college	30,142	41,348
Bachelor's degree	41,327	56,502
Master's degree	50,163	70,640
All full-time workers	**$31,565**	**$41,939**

Source: National Center for Education Statistics.

*The median income is the middle income in a series of incomes ranked from smallest to largest.

11. If most of the new jobs being created in our economy require a post-secondary education, it is likely that

A higher education will reduce your chances of unemployment.

B the cost of education will continue to fall.

C unemployment will continue to decrease in the larger cities.

D capital goods production will not keep up with consumer goods production.

12. The chart shows that education improves the earning power of almost everyone, but

A it benefits all full time workers equally.

B advanced degrees are very expensive.

C males benefit more than females.

D fewer females work fulltime.

Document-Based Questions

Directions: Analyze the following document and answer the short-answer questions that follow.

In 1776 Adam Smith wrote *The Wealth of Nations*, explaining the foundations of capitalism. Here he describes the advantages of a division of labor.

> *The greatest improvements in the productive powers of labour, and the greater part of the skill, dexterity, and judgment, with which it is anywhere directed, or applied, seem to have been the effects of the division of labour.*
>
> *... This great increase in the quantity of work, which, in consequence of the division of labour, the same number of people are capable of performing, is owing to three different circumstances; first, to the increase of dexterity in every particular workman; secondly, to the saving of the time which is commonly lost in passing from one species of work to another; and lastly, to the invention of a great number of machines which facilitate and abridge labour, and enable one man to do the work of many.*
>
> —Adam Smith

13. According to Adam Smith, what are two advantages that are gained when a task is divided among different workers?

14. Why does the invention of machines depend on the division of labor?

Extended-Response Question

15. A division of labor also assumes that the workers will produce an excess of goods—more than they can use. Write an essay explaining how this excess production relates to free markets.

Civics ONLINE

For additional test practice, use Self-Check Quizzes—Chapter 19 on glencoe.com.

Need Extra Help?															
If you missed question...	1	2	3	4	5	6	7	8	9	10	11	12	13	14	15
Go to page...	517	518	521	530	517	518	521	525	528	529	525	525	524	524	524

ASSESSMENT

Extended Response

15. Essays should note that when workers produce more than they can use, the excess must be sold or traded. Markets facilitate the exchange of goods for other goods. Free markets work best because buyers and sellers may determine their own needs and set their own terms of free exchange. In free markets, prices and wages reflect the needs of both buyers and sellers.

Critical Thinking

11. A Use this unit's reading skill, Identifying Cause and Effect, to explain that each option is a cause-and-effect relationship. Only option A has a logical causal relation that agrees with the information in the chart.

12. C Direct students' attention to the specific numbers in the chart. Guide students to see that the numbers consistently rise with higher levels of education but that males' salaries lead females' salaries at every level of education.

Document-Based Questions

13. Each worker's dexterity improves, and time that would be lost when passing from one task to the next is saved.

14. A machine is usually designed to perform a limited number of tasks, not to complete the whole manufacturing process. To use machinery efficiently, labor must be divided into steps or tasks.

Civics ONLINE

Have students visit the Web site at glencoe.com to review Chapter 19 and take the **Self-Check Quiz**.

Need Extra Help?

Have students refer to the pages listed if they miss any of the questions.

Key to Ability Levels

BL Below level   **AL** Above level
OL On level   **ELL** English Language Learners

Key to Teaching Resources

📁 Print Material   ♦ Transparency
💿 CD-ROM or DVD

Levels					Resources	Chapter Opener	Section 1	Section 2	Section 3	Section 4	Chapter Assess
BL	OL	AL	ELL		**FOCUS**						
BL	OL	AL	ELL	♦	**Daily Focus Skills Transparencies**		20–1	20–2	20–3	20–4	
					TEACH						
BL	OL		ELL	📁	**Reading Essentials and Note-Taking Guide***		p. 183	p. 186	p. 189	p. 192	
BL	OL	AL	ELL	📁	**Content Vocabulary Activity, URB***	p. 65	p. 65	p. 65	p. 65	p. 65	
BL	OL	AL	ELL	📁	**Academic Vocabulary Activity, URB**	p. 67	p. 67	p. 67	p. 67	p. 67	
	OL			📁	**Biography Activity, URB**			p. 69			
BL	OL	AL	ELL	📁	**Writing Skills Activity, URB**		p. 71	p. 71			
	OL	AL		📁	**Critical Thinking Skills Activity, URB**				p. 73		
BL	OL	AL	ELL	📁	**Chart, Graph, and Map Skills Activity, URB**				p. 75		
BL	OL	AL	ELL	📁	**Differentiated Instruction, URB**			p. 77			
BL	OL	AL	ELL	📁	**School-to-Home Connection Activity, URB***	p. 79	p. 79	p. 79	p. 79	p. 79	
BL	OL		ELL	📁	**Guided Reading Activities, URB***		p. 83	p. 84	p. 85	p. 86	
BL	OL	AL	ELL	📁	**Writer's Guidebook**	✓	✓	✓	✓	✓	✓
	OL	AL		💿	**Primary Source Document Library**	✓	✓	✓	✓	✓	✓
BL	OL	AL	ELL	💿	**Daily Lecture & Discussion Notes (in Pres. Plus)**		✓	✓	✓	✓	✓
BL	OL	AL	ELL	💿	**StudentWorks™ Plus**		✓	✓	✓	✓	✓
BL	OL	AL	ELL	💿	**Section Spotlight Videos**		✓	✓	✓	✓	
BL	OL	AL	ELL	♦	**TIME Interpreting Political Cartoons Transp.**			Ch. 20			
BL	OL	AL	ELL	♦	**Writing Process Transparencies**	✓	✓	✓	✓	✓	✓

Note: Please refer to the *Unit 6 Resource Book* for this chapter's URB materials.

* Also available in Spanish

TeacherWorks *Plus*
All-In-One Planner and Resource Center

- Interactive Lesson Planner
- Interactive Teacher Edition
- Fully editable blackline masters
- Section Spotlight Videos Launch
- Differentiated Lesson Plans
- Printable reports of daily assignments
- Standards Tracking System

Levels					Resources	Chapter Opener	Section 1	Section 2	Section 3	Section 4	Chapter Assess
BL	OL	AL	ELL								
					TEACH (continued)						
Teacher Resources				📁	**Building Academic Vocabulary**	✓	✓	✓	✓	✓	✓
				📁	**Strategies for Success**	✓	✓	✓	✓	✓	✓
				📁	**Teacher's Guide to Differentiated Instruction**	✓	✓	✓	✓	✓	✓
				💿	**Graphing Tool**	✓	✓	✓	✓	✓	✓
				💿	**Presentation Plus! with MindJogger CheckPoint**	✓	✓	✓	✓	✓	✓
					ASSESS						
BL	OL	AL	ELL	📁	**Quizzes and Tests***		p. 236	p. 237	p. 238	p. 239	p. 240
BL	OL	AL	ELL	📁	**Authentic Assessment with Rubrics**				p. 24		
BL	OL	AL	ELL	📁	**Standardized Test Practice**		p. 39	p. 39	p. 39	p. 39	p. 39
BL	OL	AL	ELL	💿	*ExamView® Assessment Suite* **CD-ROM**		20–1	20–2	20–3	20–4	Ch. 20
					CLOSE						
BL			ELL	📁	**Reteaching Activity, URB***		p. 81	p. 81	p. 81	p. 81	
BL	OL		ELL	📁	**Reading and Study Skills Foldables™ Activity**	p. 88	p. 89	p. 89			
BL	OL	AL	ELL	📁	*Civics Today* **in Graphic Novel**	p. 77		p. 77			
BL	OL	AL	ELL	🖫	**Graphic Organizer Transparencies & Strategies**	✓	✓	✓	✓	✓	✓

✓ Chapter- or unit-based activities applicable to all sections in this chapter

20

Using TechCONNECT™

Using a Spreadsheet

What is TechCONNECT™?

TechCONNECT™ is a flexible, activities-based program that makes it easy to integrate computer technology into the classroom.

How can TechCONNECT™ help my students?

TechCONNECT™ helps students apply a spreadsheet application to a project dealing with planning and budgeting. TechCONNECT™ supports classroom learning by allowing students to:

- create real-world products
- use computer application skills

For more information or to get a free 30-day trial of Glencoe TechCONNECT™ for your classroom, visit techconnect.glencoe.com and click the **Free Trial** button. Once you have accessed TechCONNECT™, students can enter code AC101 to begin the project.

Civics ONLINE

Visit glencoe.com and enter *QuickPass*™ code CIV1360c20T for Chapter 20 resources.

You can easily launch a wide range of digital products from your computer's desktop with the McGraw-Hill Social Studies widget.

	Student	Teacher	Parent
Media Library			
• Student Edition Section Audio	●		●
• Spanish Audio Summaries	●		●
• Section Spotlight Videos	●	●	●
***Civics Today* Online Learning Center (Web Site)**			
• Chapter Overviews	●	●	●
• Study Central™	●	●	●
• Study-to-Go	●	●	●
• Student Web Activities	●	●	●
• In Motion Animation	●	●	●
• Self-Check Quizzes	●	●	●
• ePuzzles and Games	●	●	●
• StudentWorks™ Plus Online	●	●	●
• Vocabulary eFlashcards	●	●	●
• Web Activity Lesson Plans		●	
• Vocabulary PuzzleMaker	●	●	●
Classroom Tools			
• Multilingual Glossary	●	●	●
• Beyond the Textbook	●	●	●
• NGS MapMachine	●	●	●

Reading List Generator CD-ROM

GLENCOE BookLink 3

Use this database to search more than 30,000 titles to create a customized reading list for your students.

- Reading lists can be organized by students' reading level, author, genre, theme, or area of interest.
- The database provides Degrees of Reading Power™ (DRP) and Lexile™ readability scores for all selections.
- A brief summary of each selection is included.

Leveled reading suggestions for this chapter:

For students at a Grade 7 reading level:
- *Earning Money,* by Stuart Schwartz and Craig Conley

For students at a Grade 8 reading level:
- *Brother, Can You Spare a Dime?: The Great Depression, 1929–1933,* by Milton Meltzer

For students at a Grade 9 reading level:
- *Nickel and Dimed: On (Not) Getting By in America,* by Barbara Ehrenreich

For students at a Grade 10 reading level:
- *A Woman Unafraid: The Achievements of Frances Perkins,* by Penny Colman

For students at a Grade 11 reading level:
- *Influential Economists,* by Marie Bussing-Burks

READING SUPPORT FROM JAMESTOWN EDUCATION

- **Timed Readings Plus in Social Studies** helps students increase their reading rate and fluency while maintaining comprehension. The 400-word passages are similar to those found on state and national assessments.

- **Reading in the Content Area: Social Studies** concentrates on six essential reading skills that help students better comprehend what they read. The book includes 75 high-interest nonfiction passages written at increasing levels of difficulty.

- **Reading Social Studies** includes strategic reading instruction and vocabulary support in Social Studies content for both ELLs and native speakers of English.

- **Content Vocabulary Workout** (Grades 6–8) accelerates reading comprehension through focused vocabulary development. Social Studies content vocabulary comes from the glossaries of Glencoe's Middle School Social Studies texts. www.jamestowneducation.com

KEY Teacher Wraparound

Use this key to help you identify the different types of prompts found in the Teacher Wraparound Edition.

R **Reading Strategies** activities help you teach reading skills and vocabulary.

C **Critical Thinking** strategies help students apply and extend what they have learned.

D **Differentiated Instruction** activities provide instruction for students learning to speak English, along with suggestions for teaching various types of learners.

S **Skill Practice** strategies help students practice historical analysis and geography skills.

W **Writing Support** activities provide writing opportunities to help students comprehend the text.

Teaching strategies and activities have been coded for ability level appropriateness.

AL Activities for students working above grade level

OL Activities for students working on grade level

BL Activities for students working below grade level

ELL Activities for English Language Learners

Focus

Why It Matters

Ask: Why is it important for you to make rational buying decisions? *(Answers may include the idea that if you do not use your money wisely, you will not be able to buy the things you need and to achieve your goals.)*

More About the Photo

Visual Literacy Being able to take a vacation is one of the rewards of knowing how to manage personal finances. Camping is a vacation bargain, which may explain why 28 percent of the population went camping in a recent year. Escaping into luxury is not everyone's idea of a dream vacation. Interest in taking a volunteer or service-based vacation is growing, especially among those who are 35–54 years old. Taking an eco-vacation is also a growing trend being catered to by eco-resorts that buy electricity from wind farms, that serve locally grown food, and that recycle waste. It is not only the kind of vacation you take but where you take it that determines its effect on your budget. The American Automobile Association recently reported that North Dakota, Nebraska, Kansas, Iowa, and Oklahoma had the lowest rates for food and lodging, whereas Hawaii had the highest.

Teach

BIG Ideas *As you begin teaching each section, use these questions and activities to help students focus on the Big Ideas.*

Section 1

Managing Your Money Ask: As a consumer, what should you know before you buy something? *(Answers may include knowledge about a product, whether you need it, whether you can afford it, and if you can return or exchange it.)* Tell students that in Section 1 they will

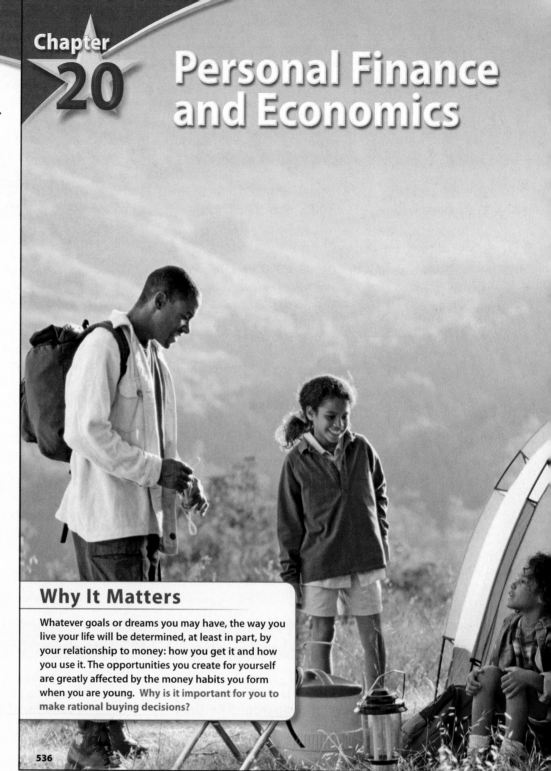

Chapter 20

Personal Finance and Economics

Why It Matters

Whatever goals or dreams you may have, the way you live your life will be determined, at least in part, by your relationship to money: how you get it and how you use it. The opportunities you create for yourself are greatly affected by the money habits you form when you are young. **Why is it important for you to make rational buying decisions?**

536

learn about consumer rights, buying strategies, and how to report a faulty product or service. **OL**

Section 2

Planning and Budgeting Ask: How does having a budget help you control your money? *(Having a budget shows you exactly how you are spending your money, including your credit card expenses.)* Explain that in this section students will learn how to make a budget and how to use credit cards. **OL**

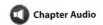

BIG Ideas

Section 1: Managing Your Money

You and everyone around you are consumers and, as such, play an important role in the economic system. As a consumer and a citizen, you will make many economic decisions every day.

Section 2: Planning and Budgeting

We all make economic choices. Opportunity cost, scarcity, and supply and demand influence the decisions we make. Following a budget can be valuable to you.

Section 3: Saving and Investing

We all make economic choices. Opportunity cost, scarcity, and supply and demand influence the decisions we make. It is important for financial security to start the habit of saving.

Section 4: Achieving Your Financial Goals

We all make economic choices. Opportunity cost, scarcity, and supply and demand influence the decisions we make. Our personal interests, wants, and abilities affect our career choices.

◄ Family spending their vacation dollars camping

FOLDABLES™ Study Organizer **Dinah Zike's Foldables**

Purpose This Foldable guides the students to compare the rights and responsibilities of consumers. The completed Foldable will use tabs to help them compare various consumers' rights versus responsibilities. **OL**

📂 More Foldables activities for this chapter can be found in the *Dinah Zike's Reading and Study Skills Foldables* ancillary.

FOLDABLES™ Study Organizer

Comparing Information Study Foldable Make the following Foldable to help you compare the rights and responsibilities of consumers with regards to their personal finances.

Step 1 Lay three sheets of paper on top of one another, about one inch apart at the top.

Step 2 Fold up the bottom edges of the paper to form 6 tabs.

consumer number
consumer income
consumer task
consumer expectations
substitutes
complements

Step 3 When the tabs are all the same size, crease the paper to hold the tabs in place and staple the sheets together. Label the Tabs as shown.

Staple together along the fold.

Reading and Writing As you read the chapter, organize information about the different forces that affect the impact of demand on the economy. Write facts under each appropriate tab.

Section 3

Saving and Investing Ask: Why should you save? Where can you invest your savings? *(Answers may include savings are for a large purchase or for an emergency. Savings may be invested in savings accounts, certificates of deposit, money market funds, stocks, bonds, and mutual funds.)* Explain that this section discusses savings plans and options for investing. **OL**

Section 4

Achieving Your Financial Goals Ask: Why is impulse buying unwise? *(Answers may include that buying on impulse can result in your buying products you do not need.)* Tell students that this section deals with how to control impulse buying. **OL**

Focus

Bellringer
Daily Focus Transparency 20–1

Guide to Reading
Answers to Graphic:

Section Spotlight Video

To generate student interest and provide a springboard for class discussion, access the Chapter 20, Section 1 video at glencoe.com or on the video DVD.

Resource Manager

Guide to Reading

Big Idea
You and everyone around you are consumers and, as such, play an important role in the economic system.

Content Vocabulary
- consumer *(p. 539)*
- disposable income *(p. 539)*
- discretionary income *(p. 539)*
- consumerism *(p. 540)*
- comparison shopping *(p. 541)*
- warranty *(p. 542)*

Academic Vocabulary
- reject *(p. 539)*
- alternative *(p. 541)*

Reading Strategy
Identifying As you read, create a diagram like the one below to list your rights as a consumer.

Section
1

Managing Your Money

Real World Economics Do you make smart decisions when you shop? Making the best use of your money is a skill you can learn and practice throughout your life. Food shopping is a prime example of a way to shop economically. This young woman is looking at two different brands of cereal. This strategy, called comparison shopping, can help a consumer find the best product for the price. As it becomes more difficult for families to meet their basic budgetary needs, smart shopping techniques become more necessary to stretch the family dollar.

▼ **Comparing prices can help you find the best buy**

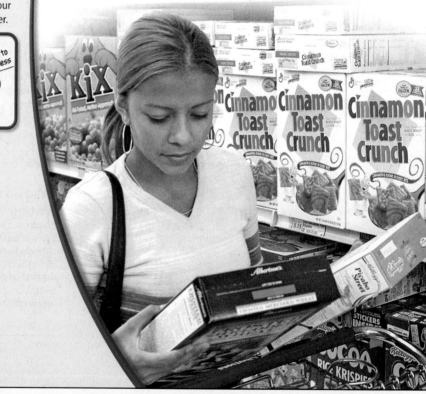

R Reading Strategies	**C** Critical Thinking	**D** Differentiated Instruction	**W** Writing Support	**S** Skill Practice
Teacher Edition • Using Context Clues, p. 541 • Summarizing, p. 543 **Additional Resources** • Cont. Vocab., URB p. 65 • Guid. Read., URB p. 83 • RENTG, p. 183 • Foldables, p. 89	**Teacher Edition** • Contrasting, p. 539 • Analyzing Info., p. 539 • Comparing, p. 541 • Drawing Con., p. 541 **Additional Resources** • Quizzes and Tests, p. 236	**Teacher Edition** • English Learners, p. 540 **Additional Resources** • Reteach. Act., URB p. 81	**Teacher Edition** • Expository Writing, p. 543 **Additional Resources** • Writing Skills Act., URB p. 71	**Teacher Edition** • Using Research Skills, p. 542 **Additional Resources** • Daily Focus Trans., 20–1

Right to a Safe Product A new worker gets on-the-job training at a California restaurant. Restaurants must meet standards of cleanliness and quality assurance for the protection of their clientele. *Analyzing* What is the purpose of the Consumer Bill of Rights?

Consumer Rights

Main Idea To make good economic decisions as consumers, we need to be aware of our rights and responsibilities.

Economics & You Have you ever bought a product or service that did not work the way it was advertised? What did you do? Read to find out more about your rights as a consumer.

The American free enterprise system gives numerous economic rights and protections to individuals such as you, your teachers, your relatives, and your friends. You have the right to enter into just about any profession or business in which you are interested. You have the right to buy the products and brands that you like and to **reject,** or pass on, others. As a **consumer,** or someone who buys a product or service, you also have responsibilities.

Two Types of Income

One of your fundamental rights as a consumer is to spend the money you earn as you wish. Your role as a consumer depends on your available income and how much of it you choose to spend or save. There are two basic types of income: disposable income and discretionary income.

Disposable income is the money that remains after all taxes on it have been paid. People spend their disposable income on many kinds of goods and services. First, they usually buy necessities, such as food, clothing, and housing.

Discretionary income is the money remaining after paying for necessities. Discretionary income can be used to satisfy wants, including luxury items and savings accounts. Regardless of the size of a person's income, spending one's income requires, or needs, constant decision making. As a consumer, each person has choices to make.

Chapter 20   539

Teach

C₁ Critical Thinking

Contrasting Ask: What is the difference between disposable income and discretionary income? *(Disposable income is what is left after taxes have been paid. It is used to buy necessities. Discretionary income is what is left after paying for necessities. It is used to buy items and services that people want but that are not necessities.)* **OL**

C₂ Critical Thinking

Analyzing Information Pair students who are working below grade level with those who are at grade level or above. Have them take turns naming a product or service and deciding if it would be bought with disposable or discretionary income. *(Students should recognize that necessary items and services are bought with disposable income and nonessentials are bought with discretionary income.)* **BL**

Caption Answer:
Its purpose is to help protect consumer rights in regard to product safety, truth in advertising and labeling, product choice, consumer legislation, and obtaining redress for faulty products.

Hands-On Chapter Project
Step 1

Investing in Stocks

Step 1: Researching Stocks Students will use Internet and media resources to research stocks in order to recommend two stocks to their groups, a mock stock-investment club.

Directions Have students work in five groups. Explain that each group will act as a stock-investment club that has $10,000 to invest in five stocks. Club members will then choose two stocks to recommend to the club.

Have groups plan how to conduct their research so that members do not research the same stock. For example, they might agree in advance on which stocks each will investigate; or they might decide to have each person research stocks in one sector, such as energy. Each group will use the research to choose two stocks to present to the club for its consideration.

Summarizing Ask representatives from each group to explain its research plan and to share ideas on where to find information on stocks. **OL**

(Project continued in Section 2)

Differentiated Instruction

English Learners Pair ELL students with student helpers that are proficient in English. Have the helpers work with their ELL partners to paraphrase the information in Protecting Consumer Rights. Suggest that they proceed a sentence at a time. Before they begin, make sure they understand the meaning of the word "paraphrase." **Ask:** How might you paraphrase the first sentence? *(Answers will vary. For example: The Latin phrase Caveat emptor, "let the buyer beware," sums up the rights of consumers throughout much of history.)* **ELL**

Caption Answer:

It aids consumers in comparing products; the list of ingredients on the label helps those who have allergies, and the expiration date indicates product safety.

✔Reading Check **Answer:** to provide information about local businesses and warn consumers about dishonest businesses

Differentiated Instruction

Protecting Consumer Rights

Throughout much of history, consumer rights could be summed up in one Latin phrase: *caveat emptor,* or "let the buyer beware." In this section, you will learn how **consumerism**—a movement to educate buyers about the purchases they make and to demand better and safer products from manufacturers—affects you personally.

Over the years, Congress has passed a number of laws to protect consumer rights. Many of the laws involve labeling. For example, the Fair Packaging and Labeling Act requires every package to have a label identifying its contents and its weight. The Food, Drug, and Cosmetic Act requires packages to list their ingredients according to the amount of each. Other laws protect consumers' health and safety. An early example is the Pure Food and Drug Act, passed in 1906. It requires manufacturers of foods, cosmetics, and drugs to prove that their products are safe.

Many private groups and organizations have taken on the task of protecting individual consumers. One of the oldest groups is the Better Business Bureau (BBB). In 2005, there were more than 120 Better Business Bureaus located in principal cities in the United States. Surprisingly, business groups rather than consumers run these organizations. These businesspeople recognize that the key to success lies in earning the trust of their customers. They provide information about local businesses and warn consumers about dishonest business practices. They also investigate consumer complaints.

Consumer Bill of Rights

In the 1960s, a special effort was made to help consumers. President John F. Kennedy and, later, President Richard Nixon emphasized five consumer rights:

1. Consumers have the *right to a safe product,* one that will not harm their health or lives.
2. Consumers have the *right to be informed* for protection against fraudulent, deceitful, or grossly misleading information, advertising, labeling, or other practices, and to be given the facts necessary for making informed choices.
3. Consumers have the *right to choose* to have available a variety of products and services at competitive prices.
4. Consumers have the *right to be heard*—the guarantee that consumer interests will be listened to when laws are being written.
5. Consumers have the *right to redress*—the ability to obtain from the manufacturer adequate payment if a product causes financial or physical damage.

✔Reading Check **Summarizing** What is the purpose of the Better Business Bureau?

Food Labels The U.S. Food and Drug Administration requires packaged foods to display labels giving key information about their contents. *Explaining* How does this information help consumers?

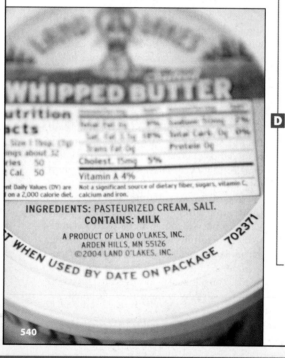

INGREDIENTS: PASTEURIZED CREAM, SALT.
CONTAINS: MILK

A PRODUCT OF LAND O'LAKES, INC.
ARDEN HILLS, MN 55126
©2004 LAND O'LAKES, INC.

540

Writing Skills Activity 20, URB pp. 71–72

Anticipating and Answering Readers' Concerns

Objective:	To write a monthly personal budget
Focus:	Students use a chart to prepare a personal monthly budget.
Teach:	Discuss the expenses listed.
Assess:	Check that students have followed directions to write a budget.
Close:	Have students discuss the benefits of preparing a personal budget.

Differentiated Instruction Strategies

BL What questions might your family ask if you said you wanted to get a job?

AL Explain how you could use a budget to convince others that you would spend your job income wisely.

ELL Tell how preparing a budget can help save money.

Consumer Responsibilities

Main Idea In addition to rights, consumers also have responsibilities.

Economics & You Have you ever regretted spending money on something? Read more to find out how you can make sure you do not make mistakes when it comes to making purchases.

In earlier chapters, you discovered that with every right comes certain responsibilities. With the right to vote, for example, comes the responsibility of staying informed. In the same way, our rights as consumers require some responsibilities on our part.

Smart Buying Strategies

Many consumer responsibilities might also be described as smart buying strategies. These are among the most important:

- Gathering information and finding out as much as we can about the products we buy so that we recognize good quality. Consumer magazines and Web sites often provide trustworthy information about product quality and other consumers' experiences.

- Using advertising carefully to help us learn about products and services and the best places to buy them. At the same time, we must be sure we are not swayed by advertising that appeals to our emotions, tries to get us to buy things we do not need or want, or uses questionable techniques to convince us to buy certain products.

- After you have gathered the information about the product you want, you must decide *where* to buy it. It is generally worthwhile to get information on the types and prices of products available from different stores or companies.

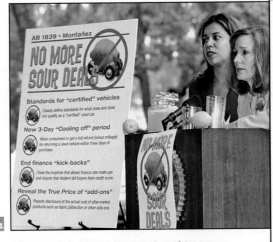

Protecting Consumers The president of Consumers for Auto Reliability, Rosemary Shahan (right), and Assemblywoman Cindy Montanez of San Fernando, California, promote a bill designed to protect used car buyers. ***Describing*** What is your first step if you purchase a faulty product?

This process is known as **comparison shopping.** To comparison shop effectively, read newspaper advertisements, make telephone calls, and visit different stores.

- Looking at both brand-name and usually cheaper but nearly identical generic products

- Balancing the costs and benefits of buying used items, ordering by mail, and **alternative,** or different, methods of making purchases

We cannot always rely on stores and businesses to protect us. We must take steps to protect ourselves.

Other Responsibilities

What are some other consumer responsibilities? Here is an important one: If a product or service is faulty, it is the consumer's responsibility to initiate the problem-solving process.

C1 Critical Thinking

Comparing Ask: How are the rights and responsibilities of a consumer like those of a voter? (*Both have the right to choose and to make a decision that will be of benefit to them. They both have a responsibility to stay informed so that they can make intelligent decisions. Just as voters have the responsibility to vote a corrupt official out of office, consumers have the responsibility to report or complain about defective products in order to protect other consumers as well as themselves.*) **AL**

C2 Critical Thinking

Drawing Conclusions Ask: Why might an advertisement not be the most accurate source of information about a product? (*Since advertising is meant to sell the product, it is apt to present only its positive features.*) **OL**

R Reading Strategy

Using Context Clues Point out the boldface term "comparison shopping." **Ask:** What words in the paragraph give clues to its meaning? (*"get information on the types and prices of products available from different stores or companies"*) **BL**

Caption Answer:
Report the problem immediately.

Leveled Activities

BL Guided Reading Activity 20–1, URB p. 83

OL Content Vocabulary Activity 20, URB p. 65

AL Writing Skill Activity 20, URB pp. 71–72

Reporting a Faulty Product If you purchase a faulty product or service, you should do the following:

- Report the problem immediately.
- Do not try to fix a product yourself; home repair may cancel the **warranty,** the promise of a manufacturer or a seller to repair or replace a faulty product within a certain time period.
- Contact the seller or manufacturer, state the problem, and suggest a fair solution.
- Keep an accurate record of your efforts to get the problem solved. Include the names of the people you speak or write to.

Making Purchases Shopping online or by telephone saves time. *Evaluating* **What do you think is the main disadvantage of shopping from home?**

- Allow each person reasonable time, such as three weeks, to solve the problem before contacting another source.
- If you need to contact the manufacturer in writing, type your letter or send an e-mail directly.
- Keep a copy of all communications.
- Keep your composure. The person who will help you solve your problem is probably not responsible for the problem.

Making Fair Complaints Another responsibility of consumers is to exhibit ethical behavior by respecting the rights of producers and sellers. For example, a responsible consumer does not try to return a used item because it has been advertised elsewhere for a lower price or claim it is faulty if he or she has broken it.

Buyers feel they have a right to expect honesty from sellers. In turn, sellers feel they have a right to expect honesty from buyers. For example, suppose you purchase a DVD player from a store but drop it on the way to your house. Because you dropped it, it does not play as well as it would have. You could, of course, go back to the store and tell the seller that the DVD player you bought does not work properly—without mentioning the fact that you dropped it—but that would be dishonest. You have a responsibility when making a complaint to provide the seller with the whole truth as you know it.

Seeking Help If you have a complaint that you cannot settle with the seller, you have a responsibility to report this fact to the appropriate government agency. Remember, as a consumer, you have the right to voice your complaints, and you also have a responsibility to exercise your rights.

✔ **Reading Check Explaining** What is a warranty and why is it important to consumers?

Civics ONLINE
Student Web Activity Visit glencoe.com and complete the Chapter 20 Web Activity.

Activity: Collaborative Learning

Comparing and Contrasting Ask: What should you consider when you compare two competing products? *(examples: price, quality, reliability, and warranty)* Organize the class into small groups, and have each group select a product and compare two competing brands. Ask them to research each brand's specifications and to record their findings on a chart, listing the brands on the left to form two rows and the specifications across the top to form columns. They then record each product's specifications in the appropriate spaces on its row. Thus, if the first column is "Price," they would record the price for each brand in the first space on its row. **OL**

Making Buying Decisions

Main Idea Buying a product or service costs more than money; it also costs the time it takes to make the purchase and the opportunity cost of *not* buying something else.

Economics & You How do you make the decision about whether to buy a product or service? Read to find out what factors consumers should take into account when making a purchase.

The first decision a consumer must make is whether or not to buy an item. How many times do you actually think about the reasons for the purchase you are about to make? Do you think about whether you really need the item? Should you wait until there is a sale on the item you want? Do you consider the trade-offs involved?

After you have decided to make a purchase, at least two scarce resources are involved—income and time. Before you spend your discretionary income, you need to invest time in obtaining information about the product you wish to buy. Suppose you decide to buy a mountain bike. The time you spend visiting stores and checking models and prices is a cost to you.

Second, virtually all the steps in consumer decision making involve an opportunity cost. Remember that opportunity cost is the value of the highest alternative choice you did *not* make. Suppose your friend recently purchased athletic shoes. You want to buy a pair yourself. Before you do, however, ask yourself, "What can't I buy or do if I buy these shoes?" In other words, you must decide if the shoes are worth what you must give up to buy them.

✓**Reading Check** **Explaining** How does opportunity cost affect the decision to buy something?

Section 1 Review

Vocabulary

1. **Define** the following terms and use them to write a short essay about making buying decisions: *consumer, disposable income, discretionary income, consumerism, comparison shopping, warranty.*

Main Ideas

2. **Explaining** What is the right to redress?

3. **Describing** How does comparison shopping help the consumer?

4. **Explaining** What scarce resources are involved in making a buying decision?

Critical Thinking

5. **BIG Ideas** Describe two examples of how you educate yourself about a product before buying it.

6. **Identifying** As you read, create a diagram like the one below to list your responsibilities as a consumer.

CITIZENSHIP Activity

7. **Expository Writing** Which of the consumer responsibilities do you think is the most important? Why? Explain your choice in a one-page essay.

Civics ONLINE

Study Central™ To review this section, go to glencoe.com.

Expository Writing Review with students the factors involved in making a buying decision. Then ask them to write an article for consumers titled, "What to Ask Yourself Before You Buy." As a prewriting activity, they could write the self-questions they plan to include in their article. *(Answers will vary. They may include opportunity cost and the scarce resources of income and time.)* **OL**

✓**Reading Check** **Answer:** It helps the consumer decide whether or not the potential purchase is worth what must be given up in order to buy it.

Assess

Civics ONLINE

Study Central™ provides summaries, interactive games, and online graphic organizers to help students review content.

Close

Summarizing Have students write several paragraphs to sum up the rights and responsibilities of consumers. **OL**

Section 1 Review

Answers

1. Essays should use vocabulary words according to their definitions in the section and in the Glossary.

2. The right to redress is the right to obtain adequate payment from the manufacturer if a product causes financial or physical damage.

3. It helps the consumer find the best product for the price.

4. Income and time are the scarce resources involved in a buying decision.

5. Answer will vary. They may include doing research through consumer magazines and the Internet, checking advertisements, and comparison shopping.

6. The remaining consumer responsibilities to be included on the diagram are using advertising carefully, doing comparison shopping, checking both brand-name and generic products, and balancing the costs and benefits of alternative buying methods.

7. Essays will vary regarding consumer responsibilities, but students should support their opinions with reasons or examples.

Focus

Bellringer
Daily Focus Transparency 20–2

Guide to Reading
Answers to Graphic:

My Budget

1. my expenses
2. earnings
3. analyze
4. surplus
5. monitor

Section Spotlight Video

To generate student interest and provide a springboard for class discussion, access the Chapter 20, Section 2 video at glencoe.com or on the video DVD.

Resource Manager

Guide to Reading

Big Idea
We all make economic choices. Opportunity cost, scarcity, and supply and demand influence the decisions we make.

Content Vocabulary
- budget *(p. 545)*
- income *(p. 545)*
- expense *(p. 546)*
- credit *(p. 547)*
- annual percentage rate (APR) *(p. 547)*
- collateral *(p. 547)*
- bankruptcy *(p. 549)*

Academic Vocabulary
- exceed *(p. 545)*
- status *(p. 547)*

Reading Strategy
Describing As you read, use a graphic organizer like the one below to describe the steps in making a budget.

1. my expenses

My Budget

🔊 Section Audio   🎞 Spotlight Video

Planning and Budgeting

Real World Economics Do you know how to create a budget? College students often have to learn to budget for the first time in their lives. This Clemson University student is shocked by the cost of his textbooks. Over the last twenty years, the price of textbooks has risen at twice the rate of inflation. With textbooks becoming so much more expensive, many students resort to using credit cards to purchase their books. That can add to their accumulating debt.

▼ Freshman student Noel Cole of Asheville, North Carolina

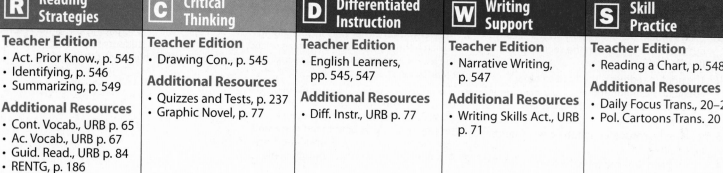

R Reading Strategies	**C** Critical Thinking	**D** Differentiated Instruction	**W** Writing Support	**S** Skill Practice
Teacher Edition • Act. Prior Know., p. 545 • Identifying, p. 546 • Summarizing, p. 549 **Additional Resources** • Cont. Vocab., URB p. 65 • Ac. Vocab., URB p. 67 • Guid. Read., URB p. 84 • RENTG, p. 186 • Foldables, p. 89	**Teacher Edition** • Drawing Con., p. 545 **Additional Resources** • Quizzes and Tests, p. 237 • Graphic Novel, p. 77	**Teacher Edition** • English Learners, pp. 545, 547 **Additional Resources** • Diff. Instr., URB p. 77	**Teacher Edition** • Narrative Writing, p. 547 **Additional Resources** • Writing Skills Act., URB p. 71	**Teacher Edition** • Reading a Chart, p. 548 **Additional Resources** • Daily Focus Trans., 20–2 • Pol. Cartoons Trans. 20

Making a Budget— and Sticking to It!

Main Idea Making and following a budget can help you organize your financial life.

Economics & You Have you ever had to say no to a concert, dance, game, or other event because you did not have enough money? If so, learning more about budgets can help you make sure there is enough money in your wallet for the things you would really like to do. **R**

The best way to get a handle on your spending is to make a **budget.** What is a budget? It is a careful record of all the money you earn and spend. A budget tells you exactly where your money goes. Using a budget can help you make your expenses match your income. **D**

Mr. Micawber, a famous character from Charles Dickens' novel *David Copperfield*, made it very clear to young David why a budget is important: "Annual income twenty pounds, annual expenditure nineteen six, result happiness. Annual income twenty pounds, annual expenditure twenty pounds ought and six, result misery." Mr. Micawber meant that if your expenses **exceed,** or go beyond, your income by even sixpence [six pennies], you are in big trouble. **D**

A budget is more than a record. It can also be a tool. It can help you plan and cut down on unwise spending and provide a road map toward saving for things you really want. **C**

Basic Budgeting Terms The basic terms used in making and using a budget are the same, whether you are a high school student or the president of a giant company. Your **income** is the money you earn. **D**

Budgeting A family works out their monthly budget. As a student, you might think you do not earn enough money to need a budget. You might be surprised to learn how much further your money goes when you budget. **Defining** What is income?

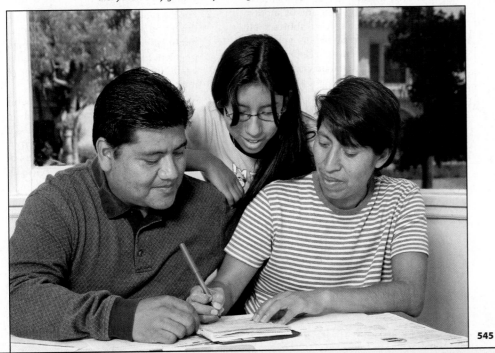

545

R **Reading Strategy**

Activating Prior Knowledge **Ask:** What do you already know about budgets? Have you heard the term used in connection with government or business? *(Answers will vary. Students may mention federal, state, or local budgets, and budgets of companies or other organizations.)* **OL**

D **Differentiated Instruction**

English Learners Call attention to the terms in boldface type. **Ask:** What words in the text help you understand the meaning of "budget"? *("It is a careful record of all the money you earn and spend.")* Have students find context clues for "exceed" and "income." *(exceed: go beyond; income: money you earn)* **ELL**

C **Critical Thinking**

Drawing Conclusions **Ask:** How can recording what you earn and spend also help you save for things you want? *(Answers may include that it will enable you to see how much you have left for savings and where you can cut back on your spending to save more.)* **OL**

Caption Answer:

Income is the money you earn.

Additional Support

Activity: Economics Connection

Making Connections Ask: What are the sources of income for the federal government? *(Answers will vary but should include taxes.)* Discuss taxes that individuals pay to the federal government, including sales taxes on products. Explain that each year, individuals pay federal income tax on their income. Income is not limited to a salary or paycheck.

List the following income sources on the board, and encourage student discussion of each: 1. wages and salaries; 2. tips; 3. Reserve Officers' Training Corp (ROTC); (4) self employment, for example, from mowing lawns or babysitting; (5) newspaper carriers and distributors over the age of 18; (6) interest from financial institutions; (7) interest from U.S. savings bonds and U.S. Treasury

bills, notes, and bonds; (8) dividends; (9) taxable scholarships and grants; (10) contest prizes that do not have to be used for education. **OL**

R Reading Strategy

Identifying Call attention to the terms "expenses" and "balance." **Ask:** What does "balance" mean as it is used here? *(the amount of money left after subtracting expenses)* Ask students to give a synonym for "a negative balance"*(deficit)* and antonyms for "income" *(expenses)* and for "surplus," *(deficit)* **BL**

TIME™ Political Cartoons

Answers:
1. the loan office of a bank.
2. by suggesting that the cost of filling up an SUV is equal to that of buying an expensive house or condo
3. SUVs are known to use a lot of gas.
4. Both. The cartoonist implies that the price of gas is too high and that SUVs are gas-guzzlers.

✓ **Reading Check** **Answer:** It is a careful record of all the money you earn and spend.

Political Cartoons

Chris Britt/Copley News Service

The high cost of gasoline was the inspiration for this cartoon by Chris Britt.

1. **What is the setting for this cartoon?**
2. **How does the cartoonist use exaggeration to help make his point?**
3. **Why do you think Britt decided to have the driver own an SUV?**
4. **Do you think the cartoonist is making a statement about high gas prices, SUVs, or both?**

Every year, more than half of all Americans do volunteer work ... role in it. One of the responsibilities of citizens is to help make their ... of volunteer grou small. Perha ... dad wh

---

Your **expenses** are the money you spend on everything, including what you choose to save. Balance is the amount of money you have left over after you subtract all your expenses. A surplus means you have more income than expenses; a deficit means you have more expenses than income. This unhappy situation—deficit—is also known as a negative balance.

How to Make a Budget

Creating and organizing a personal budget is not difficult. Anyone who knows addition, subtraction, multiplication, and division, can accomplish it. Follow these steps to organize a budget:

1. Make a list of everything you spend for a couple of weeks. Include entertainment, clothing, food, personal items, gifts, transportation, contributions and donations, and savings. You might also want to have a category, or group listing, for other or miscellaneous expenses.

It is important to record *everything* you spend.

2. For the same time period, record everything you earn and its source. Sources might be your allowance, job earnings, payment for household chores, or gifts; again, include a category for other or miscellaneous income.

3. Now that you have recorded your data, analyze it. Do you need to reduce expenses? Where could you cut costs? Would you rather increase your income? Can you work extra hours at your job or advertise your services to neighbors?

4. It is a good idea to have a little surplus for emergency expenses or extra contributions to your savings account.

5. Monitor your spending; use your budget data as a tool for taming any unruly finances. Make changes as needed.

✓ **Reading Check** **Defining** What is a budget?

Differentiated Instruction

Differentiated Instruction Activity 20, URB pp. 77–78

The Power and Danger of "Plastic"

Objective: To interpret a credit card statement

Focus: Ask what effect making the minimum monthly payment has on the balance.

Teach: Go over elements on the statement.

Assess: Discuss students' answers to questions 1 and 2.

Close: Have students calculate the annual finance charge on the current balance.

Differentiated Instruction Strategies

BL How much of the $250 paid last month went to pay finance charges? (*$51.31*)

AL Why is it hard to eliminate credit card debt by making minimum payments when the APR is 23.99%?

ELL Discuss additional meanings for the following terms: "statement," "balance," "credit," and "line."

Credit

Main Idea Credit can be a valuable item in your financial toolbox; however, as with all tools, you have to know how to use it correctly.

Economics & You Have you ever received a credit card offer in the mail? Did you know how to evaluate it? Read more to find out what to look for the next time an offer for a credit card shows up.

A character in a play by William Shakespeare gave some famous advice when he warned, "Neither a borrower nor a lender be." However, it is not very practical today; in fact, almost everyone, along with almost all businesses, sometimes borrows money.

Offers Through the Mail Do you receive "pre-approved" credit card offers in the mail, some with low introductory rates? *Speculating* Is it important to compare terms and fees before you agree to open a credit card account? Explain.

Many of us also lend it. The key is using **credit**—borrowing money to pay for something now while promising to repay it later.

Recognizing Credit Terms

Understanding how credit works in our society requires knowing some important terms.

- A lender is the person who loans someone the money to buy an item.
- A borrower receives the loaned money.
- Interest is the cost for the use of the money.
- The **annual percentage rate (APR)** is the annual cost of credit expressed as a percentage of the amount borrowed.
- A credit rating is an evaluation of the likelihood of a borrower to default on, or be unable to repay, a loan. It is based on the borrower's previous credit experiences, financial situation, job history, **status,** or rank, and other information.
- **Collateral** is property, such as a house, car, or other valuable item, that a borrower pledges as security for a loan. If a borrower fails to repay a loan, the lender can seize the collateral as payment.

Sources of Credit

Banks, credit unions, and finance companies all offer credit to consumers. So do stores that sell relatively expensive merchandise, such as clothing, electronics, appliances, or furniture. Home mortgages and car loans are other popular types of credit. Large credit purchases usually require a down payment, or a part of the purchase price, when you make the purchase. The remaining unpaid balance is then divided into equal monthly payments.

Credit Cards Perhaps the most common type of credit today is the credit card. Issued by banks, credit card companies, and stores, a credit card allows you to charge, or pay using borrowed money, for goods and services up to the value of a preset monthly limit.

Chapter 20 547

Differentiated Instruction

English Learners Tell students that if a word they know does not seem make sense in a passage, the word may have more than one meaning. **Ask:** How can you figure out a word's meaning? *(Look for context clues or think of what word would make sense in the sentence.)* Call on volunteers to give alternate meanings for the following terms: "credit," "interest," "terms," "balance." *(Answers will vary, but should show the words have several different meanings.)* **OL**

Writing Support

Narrative Writing Using the cartoon on page 546 as a springboard, challenge students to write a conversation between a potential borrower and a lender (the banker). Challenge them to include these terms: "lender," "borrower," "interest," "annual percentage rate," "credit rating," and "collateral." *(Compositions should indicate that students know the meanings of the terms.)* **OL**

Caption Answer:

It is important to compare credit terms because they vary and might not be explained well.

Hands-On Chapter Project
Step 2

Investing in Stocks

Step 2: Buying Stocks Groups of students continue the work they began in Section 1.

Directions Have students meet with their investment clubs. Write today's agenda on the board: 1. Give stock presentations to the club. 2. Discuss five stocks. 3. Vote to decide on two stocks to buy and decide how many shares to buy of each stock. 4. Record the club's purchases on a chart.

Remind students that each group has $10,000. After students have evaluated the stocks, have them choose two stocks. The group now must decide how many shares of each stock to buy. Remind them to include a $10 fee in the total cost of each. Explain that they will have money left. In preparation for their next meeting, have groups assign members to keep track of specific stocks and to record their daily prices.

Wrapping Up Have each group make a chart that shows: each stock; its price per share; the number of shares, and its total cost, including the $10 fee. Each day, have them calculate the value of their portfolio and the total cash. **OL**

(Project continued in Section 3)

S Skill Practice

Reading a Chart Refer students to the chart. **Ask:** What is the projected trend in the use of credit and debit cards between 2005 and 2010? *(The number of credit and debit cards issued and the billions of dollars charged to those cards are predicted to increase.)* **BL**

Analyzing Graphs and Charts

Answers:

1. Cash and debit cards were most often used to pay for in-store purchases.
2. The bar graph should illustrate the projected increases in credit and debit card transactions between 2005 and 2010.

Differentiated Instruction

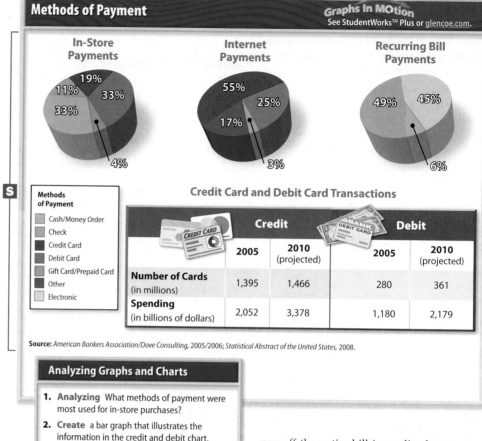

Methods of Payment

Graphs In MOtion See StudentWorks™ Plus or glencoe.com.

In-Store Payments: 19%, 33%, 4%, 33%, 11%

Internet Payments: 55%, 25%, 3%, 17%

Recurring Bill Payments: 45%, 6%, 49%

Methods of Payment: Cash/Money Order, Check, Credit Card, Debit Card, Gift Card/Prepaid Card, Other, Electronic

Credit Card and Debit Card Transactions

	Credit 2005	Credit 2010 (projected)	Debit 2005	Debit 2010 (projected)
Number of Cards (in millions)	1,395	1,466	280	361
Spending (in billions of dollars)	2,052	3,378	1,180	2,179

Source: *American Bankers Association/Dove Consulting, 2005/2006; Statistical Abstract of the United States, 2008.*

Analyzing Graphs and Charts

1. **Analyzing** What methods of payment were most used for in-store purchases?
2. **Create** a bar graph that illustrates the information in the credit and debit chart.

When you apply for a credit card, the issuer checks your credit rating and assigns a dollar limit based on what it thinks you can afford to pay back. To avoid interest charges, you must pay off your full credit balance each month. You are charged a fee if your monthly payment is late. High interest charges on unpaid balances add up quickly and have even brought financial ruin to some unlucky or careless consumers.

Here is an eye-opening example: Say you buy an item that costs $2,000 with a credit card that charges 18 percent interest. If you pay off the entire bill immediately, you pay $0 in interest. If you make only the minimum 4 percent payment, over time, it will take you more than 10 years to pay for the item, and you will have paid $1,142 in interest. Thus, the $2,000 item will have cost you $3,142.

Credit: Benefits and Drawbacks

Americans use credit to make many purchases. The total amount of funds borrowed and lent each year is enormous. Used wisely, credit can be a valuable tool for consumers. It allows you to obtain something you want without waiting until you can save the entire purchase price.

Leveled Activities

Making monthly payments on time can teach you financial discipline. Analyzing your financial situation to see if you can afford to use credit for something you want is an important life skill.

However, credit also carries serious dangers. Many people have gotten in over their heads because they bought more than they could afford. The easy availability of credit, followed by lack of income to pay back the borrowed money, has left millions of people in **bankruptcy,** or the inability to pay debts. A bankruptcy judgment remains on your credit rating from seven to ten years, making it almost impossible for you to get a loan or to receive credit during that time.

Your Responsibilities as a Borrower

Being a responsible borrower means having a plan to make all the payments on your loan or credit purchase in a timely manner.

Your budgeting skills will help make sure you can afford a monthly loan or credit payment, along with other necessities. The time to make sure you can afford a credit purchase is *before* you close the deal. You also need to understand all aspects of the agreement: What is the APR? How long will you make payments? What are the penalties for late payments? Are there extra fees?

Tips for Students As long as they are over 18 years old, students can get a credit card without asking their parents to cosign. Debt advisers say students should hold a credit card on which they can carry only a small balance and must pay off monthly. They should pay more than the minimum on credit cards. Furthermore, they should not charge purchases they can pay for in cash, such as food and gas.

✓ **Reading Check** **Explaining** Why do you need to know the APR of your loan or credit purchase?

Vocabulary

1. **Write** a paragraph about planning and budgeting in which you use at least five of these terms: *budget, income, expense, credit, annual percentage rate (APR), collateral, bankruptcy.*

Main Ideas

2. **Explain** the difference between a surplus and a deficit.

3. **Identify** three sources of credit.

Critical Thinking

4. **Describing** What can a budget help you do?

5. **BIG Ideas** Create a table like the one below to list three questions you should consider when deciding whether to use credit.

Decision to Use Credit
1.
2.
3.

6. **Explaining** Why is it important to maintain a good credit rating?

 Activity

7. **Expository Writing** Think of an item for which you have been saving. How long will it take you to save the funds needed to purchase this item? What are you not buying in the meantime? Explain what you are giving up to buy that particular item. Answer these questions in a one-page paper.

Civics ONLINE

Study Central™ To review this section, go to glencoe.com.

R **Reading Strategy**

Summarizing Ask: What should you know before you make a purchase with a credit card? *(You should know if you can afford the monthly payments, what the APR is, the length of time you will be making the payments, the penalties for late payments, and if there are any additional fees.)* **OL**

✓ **Reading Check** **Answer:** You need to know the APR of a loan or credit card purchase because it shows you the cost of buying on credit.

Assess

Civics ONLINE

Study Central™ provides summaries, interactive games, and online graphic organizers to help students review content.

Close

Summarizing Have students write a short paper on the benefits and the drawbacks of buying on credit. **OL**

Section 2 Review

Answers

1. Paragraphs should use vocabulary words according to their definitions in the section and in the Glossary.

2. **surplus:** more income than expenses. **deficit:** more expenses than income.

3. Three sources of credit are banks, credit unions, and finance companies.

4. It can help you match your expenses to your income and develop a savings plan for things you want.

5. Answers will vary but should include three of these ideas: Can I afford the monthly payment? What is the APR? How long will I be making payments? What are the penalties for late payments? Are there any extra fees?

6. Answers may include that a good credit rating enables you to borrow money and to obtain a favorable interest rate.

7. Papers will vary but should include an explanation of what the writer wants to buy, how long it will take to save for it, and what the writer cannot buy while saving.

R Reading Strategy

Analyzing Text Structure Have students preview the selection. **Ask:** What kind of selection is it, and what is its purpose? *(It is an informational, how-to selection; its purpose is to give instructions on how to make a monthly budget.)* Have students identify the two major steps involved in making a budget. *(Obtain the necessary tools and follow the set of procedures listed under Step B.)* Call attention to the chart on page 551 and point out that a copy of the chart is one of the tools they will use as they make their budget. **OL**

D Differentiated Instruction

Logical/Mathematical Ask: In the first procedure for Step B, does the monthly earnings of $1,236.66 include the amount taken out for taxes? *(Taxes have already been deducted.)* Ask comprehension questions about the remaining procedures, and answer any questions students have. **OL**

Additional Support

Making a Budget

A good budget is a useful tool. It can help you
- understand your actual financial situation.
- fill your basic and material needs.
- gradually achieve your objectives.
- avoid debt.
- save.

In this activity, you will design a strategy for earning, spending, and investing your resources.

Step A: Tools Needed

√ Copies of Table "My Monthly Budget"
√ Newspapers with advertisements for apartment rentals and auto sales
√ Ads from local grocery stores
√ Magazines with photos of apartments, automobiles, and furniture
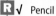 **R** √ Pencil
√ Calculator

Step B: Procedures to Follow

1. Annually you make $16,640, of which $1,800 goes to pay taxes. Monthly you earn **D** $1,236.66. Your total expenditures will include the items listed in the table.

2. Analyze the newspaper ads to select an apartment to rent. List the rental fee in the table. Also consider the cost of rental insurance.

3. Plan your weekly menus. Then multiply supplies by 4 to budget your food expenses for one month. Use the ads from grocery stores to select and price the food products needed for your menus.

4. Decide on a type of car to buy. Analyze the newspaper ads to obtain the approximate monthly payment for an automobile.

5. From the magazines, select items of furniture to furnish your apartment.

6. Call the following places or ask family members to obtain prices or monthly fees for other necessities: phone company, electric company, gas company, auto insurance, furniture store, medical insurance, and other costs.

7. Fill in your costs in the table. When you complete the table, subtract the total expenses from your earnings for the month to find out how much money you have remaining.

Activity: Collaborative Learning

Analyzing Information Ask: How can students cut down on their spending or increase their earnings? Organize students into small groups to discuss those questions and to suggest answers. Have some groups list suggestions on how students can cut down on spending and others list ideas on how students can increase their earnings.

Suggest that groups first brainstorm to generate ideas, offering as many ideas as they can in a short period of time without pausing to consider each one. One person in each group can act as recorder and jot down their ideas. After brainstorming, groups should discuss and evaluate the ideas they generated and list those they feel are helpful. Encourage groups to share their lists with the class. **OL**

My Monthly Budget

CATEGORIES OF EXPENSES	MONTHLY COST
Rent	
Rental insurance	
Telephone	
Electricity	
Gas heat	
Car payment	
Car insurance	
Car expenses (gas and repairs)	
Furniture expenses	
Clothing expenses	
Groceries	

CATEGORIES OF EXPENSES	MONTHLY COST
Medical insurance	
Medical expenses	
Credit card bill	
Entertainment and dining out	
Laundry and toiletries	
Other	
Monthly earnings	$ 1,236.66
Subtract total monthly expenses	
Total remaining	

Analyzing Economics

1. **Identifying** What is your largest monthly expense?
2. **Calculating** How much money did you have left at the end of the month?
3. **Explaining** What expense(s) surprised you the most? Why?
4. **Calculating** What expenditures did you have to reduce to be able to pay your other monthly expenses?

S Skill Practice

Reading a Chart Call attention to the chart's title and discuss how the chart is set up. Make sure students understand that the expenses listed for each category are for an entire month. **Ask:** Where do you enter the sum total of expenses for the month? *(in the next-to-last box in the right-hand column)* How do you find out if you have a surplus or a deficit? *(Subtract monthly expenses from monthly earnings.)* **OL**

Analyzing Economics

Answers:

Answers for Questions 1, 2, 3, 4, will vary, depending on the entries students make in their charts. Question 3 requires an explanation; Question 4 requires students to tell the expenditures they had to reduce in order to pay monthly expenses.

Activity: Economics Connection

Interpersonal Encourage students to form a support group for following a budget, similar to a Weight Watcher's group. Suggest that they meet for about fifteen minutes each week.

During the first meeting, they can help each other plan a budget using the form on page 551. Have them choose a secretary to take notes on each meeting.

At subsequent meetings, they can compare each other's progress as they feel comfortable and award prizes to those that have successfully kept to their budgets. They can also share suggestions for saving money and news about sales and bargains.

Help them develop the idea that it is more desirable to buy inexpensive, durable clothes, sports equipment, and accessories than to spend a lot of money on famous-brand products. Introduce them to a good consumer's guide.

Each week, the secretary can submit a written report on the club members' tips on how to save money. **OL**

Focus

Bellringer
Daily Focus Transparency 20–3

Guide to Reading
Answers to Graphic:

Savings accounts: can make deposits; fairly low interest rate; can withdraw at any time; interest added automatically to account

Checking accounts: can make deposits; money withdrawn for checks you write; some pay small amount of interest; some charge fees; some offer debit cards

Money Market accounts: can make deposits; can write checks; pays interest, often a little higher than savings accounts

Section Spotlight Video

Have students watch the Chapter 20, Section 3 video at glencoe.com.

Resource Manager

Guide to Reading

Big Idea
We all make economic choices. Opportunity cost, scarcity, and supply and demand influence the decisions we make.

Content Vocabulary
- save *(p. 553)*
- interest *(p. 554)*
- principal *(p. 555)*
- return *(p. 557)*
- stock *(p. 557)*
- dividend *(p. 557)*
- bond *(p. 557)*
- mutual fund *(p. 558)*

Academic Vocabulary
- establish *(p. 553)*
- fund *(p. 553)*
- interval *(p. 557)*

Reading Strategy
Comparing and Contrasting
As you read, use a chart like the one below to explain how savings accounts, checking accounts, and money market accounts are similar and how they differ.

Type of Account	Similarities/ Differences
Savings accounts	
Checking accounts	
Money Market accounts	

Saving and Investing

Real World Economics For most teenagers, getting a driver's license and a first car marks a major move into adulthood. But how will they pay for that car? Heather Kimble's mother, Lorene, helped Heather get a debit card, a checking account, and a savings account to learn how to manage the money she earns from an after-school job in Corning, New York. Buying a car was her goal. Learning to save money can be hard, but this is one lesson from which most people will benefit.

▼ **Heather Kimble gets backup from mother, Lorene**

Reading Strategies	**C** **Critical Thinking**	**D** **Differentiated Instruction**	**W** **Writing Support**	**S** **Skill Practice**
Teacher Edition	**Teacher Edition**	**Teacher Edition**	**Teacher Edition**	**Teacher Edition**
• Summarizing, p. 554 • Identifying, p. 555 • Making Connections, p. 557 • Identifying, p. 558	• Pred. Consequences, p. 553 • Making Inferences, pp. 554, 555 • Analyzing Info., p. 555	• Auditory/Musical, p. 553	• Expository Writing, p. 557	• Reading Graphs, p. 555 • Reading Charts, p. 556
Additional Resources	**Additional Resources**	**Additional Resources**		**Additional Resources**
• Cont. Vocab., URB p. 66 • Guid. Read., URB, p. 85 • RENTG, p. 189	• Critical Thinking Skills, URB p. 73 • Quizzes and Tests, p. 238	• School-to-Home Connection Activity, URB p. 79 • Reteach. Act., URB p. 81		• Chart, Map, and Graph Skills, URB p. 75 • Daily Focus Trans., 20–3

Saving for the Future

Main Idea Saving part of your income is the key to meeting many of your short-term and long-term financial goals.

Economics & You Do you know the old fable of the grasshopper and the ants? Unlike the industrious ants, the grasshopper did not bother to put aside food for the winter, and he was left hungry. Read more to find out how you can avoid being a financial grasshopper.

Everyone has long-term goals: what you want to do, where you want to live, how you want to spend your time. One way to help you reach your long-term *purchasing* goals is to save. To **save** means to set aside income for a time so you have it to use later. It is that part of your income that you do not spend. You may already be saving some of your income for a future use, such as buying a car or continuing your education.

Think of saving as a regular "expenditure" item; think of what you "buy" with it. Many people simply save what is left over at the end of the month. This attitude downgrades saving to a less important position than purchasing goods and services.

Why Save?

Saving money can be a difficult habit to **establish,** or create. There are many good reasons for saving. Most people cannot make major purchases, such as a car or a house, without putting aside money to help pay for them. Saving also comes in handy in emergencies. In addition, people can save for luxuries, such as a nicer car or a vacation.

When individuals save, the economy as a whole benefits. Your saving makes money available for others to invest or spend. Saving also allows businesses to borrow from a savings bank to expand, which provides greater income for consumers and raises the standard of living.

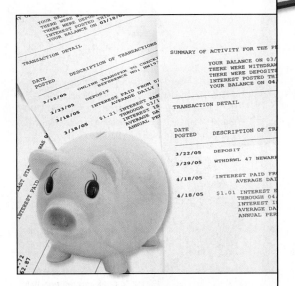

Deciding to Save No matter how you do it, it is important to save some of your money. *Explaining* What is an advantage of making regular deposits to a savings account?

Saving Regularly

To make it easier for people to save, some employers will withhold a fixed amount from employees' paychecks. This money is automatically deposited into the participating employees' savings accounts. Many people, however, handle the responsibility themselves. Each week or month, they budget a specific amount of money to put aside for savings. There is a budget line for savings right next to the lines for food, movies, gas, and other necessities.

Easy Availability Generally, when people think of saving, they think of putting their **funds,** or money, in a savings bank or a similar financial institution. A major appeal of savings accounts is that they offer easy availability of funds. The depositor can usually withdraw funds at any time without paying a penalty—forfeiting any money.

Chapter 20 553

Teach

C Critical Thinking

Predicting Consequences Ask: Why should you consider making regular savings a part of your budget? *(Answers may include that saving regularly will help you have money for emergencies and will enable you to make major purchases in the future.)* **BL**

D Differentiated Instruction

Auditory/Musical Encourage students to discuss reasons why they and their friends should establish savings. In groups have them create jingles that could be set to music that encourage students to save. Encourage them to share their jingles, put them to music if possible, and post them on school bulletin boards. **OL**

> **Caption Answer:**
>
> Making regular savings deposits makes it easier to save and helps ensure that your savings will grow.

Hands-On Chapter Project
Step 3

Investing in Stocks

Step 3: Evaluating Stock Performance Groups of students continue the work they began in Section 2.

Directions At this meeting, explain that they will check on the performance of each of their stocks since the last meeting. They will then calculate the current value of their portfolio.

Have students report to their groups on the stocks they have been tracking. Ask them to give each stock's day-to-day price and to predict the direction of its price in the next two weeks. Suggest that they consider whether the performance of all their stocks indicates a trend in the stock market. Does the performance of a single stock indicate a trend in its sector of the market?

Finally, have the group write its prediction of the direction stocks will take in the interval between today and its next meeting.
Summarizing Have a group representative report to the class on the performance of the group's stocks and what the group's prediction is for the performance of the stock market in the near future. **OL**

(Project continued in Section 4)

C Critical Thinking

Making Inferences Ask: How are lending institutions able to pay interest on depositors' money? *(They lend money at a higher interest rate than they pay to depositors.)* **BL**

R Reading Strategy

Summarizing Ask: What factors should you consider when you are deciding how much to save? *(Answers may include your everyday expenses, why you are saving, how much interest you will earn, and your expectations for your future income.)* **OL**

American Biography

Answers: Student answers might suggest that Otero was motivated to help poor people get capital to start businesses and to develop their own wealth. The study of political economics relates directly to that goal; literature does not.

✔ **Reading Check** **Answer:** Individual savings make money available to be invested in business and enterprises whose growth will expand the economy.

Differentiated Instruction

Critical Thinking Skills Activity 20, URB pp. 73–74

American Biography

María Otero (1950–)

María Otero joined ACCIÓN International in 1986 and has served as president and CEO of the private, nonprofit organization since 2000. ACCIÓN provides loans and business training to poor women and men who start their own businesses. Since 1996, ACCIÓN-affiliated programs have issued $9.4 billion in loans to nearly 4 million people.

"We don't need to give people charity," says Otero. "We need to give people opportunity and access."

Otero believes the programs not only help businesses get started now, but will "manifest . . . in the education and choices that will open up for their children. . . . The power of putting capital in the hands of poor people enables them to create their own wealth and invest in their children."

Born in La Paz, Bolivia, Otero and her family moved to Washington, D.C., when she was 12. After attending Johns Hopkins University, Otero returned to Bolivia to work. She says, "I really had to determine who I was. Living in Bolivia as an adult and preparing myself to then come back and do more graduate work in economics was very significant. That's what helped me accept that I could be both Bolivian and American."

Making a Difference ★ **CITIZENSHIP**

At first, Otero studied literature but decided to give up literature for political economics. *Speculating* Why do you think she made this decision?

Earning Interest Another advantage of depositing your money in a savings account is that it will earn interest. **Interest** is the payment people receive when they lend money, or allow someone else to use their money. In this case, the financial institution pays interest to the person with the savings account. The institution can lend these funds to someone else, who will in turn pay interest to the financial institution for the use of the money. A person receives interest on his or her savings for as long as funds are in the account.

Deciding About Your Saving

It is important to remember that the more money you put in a savings account, and the longer you keep the money deposited, the more interest you will earn, and the larger your account will grow.

Saving and Trade-Off Saving involves a trade-off, as does every other activity. The more you save today, the more you can buy a year from now, 10 years from now, or 30 years from now. You will, however, have less to spend today.

Deciding how much to save depends on your answer to several questions: How much do you spend on your everyday expenses? What are your reasons for saving? How much interest can you earn on your savings and, therefore, how fast will your savings grow? How much income do you think you will be earning in the future? If you expect to make a much higher income tomorrow, you have less reason to save a large percentage of your income today. It is a good idea, however, to have some type of savings plan.

✔ **Reading Check** **Explaining** How do the savings of individuals benefit the entire economy?

Categorizing Information

? CRITICAL THINKING SKILLS ACTIVITY 20

Objective:	To categorize types of savings and investment accounts
Focus:	Students sort information about different kinds of accounts.
Teach:	Review how to read a table.
Assess:	Use the questions on page 74 to check students' categorizing skills.
Close:	Have students categorize the accounts according to their minimum deposits.

Differentiated Instruction Strategies

BL Which accounts let you withdraw money without paying a penalty? List them.

AL Explain why CDs are good investment choices if you think interest rates are going down.

ELL Choose one account from the table and tell its features in your own words.

Types of Savings

Main Idea A variety of options is available to allow you to save money.

Economics & You Benjamin Franklin said, "A penny saved is a penny earned." Read to find out how this advice applies to you and your financial future.

While savings accounts are probably the best-known way to save, there are other ways, too.

Saving and Checking Accounts

You can open a savings account at a bank, savings and loan, or credit union. These institutions accept people's money, pay them a fairly low rate of interest, and loan the money on deposit to other customers of the institution. You can withdraw your money at any time, and the interest you earn is added automatically to your **principal**, or the amount you initially deposited. You cannot write a check on a savings account. To do that, you will need a checking account.

Just as with a savings account, you make deposits into a checking account. When you write a check, the banking institution pays out of the funds in your checking account. You must be careful not to write checks that exceed the amount of money in your checking account. The way to protect yourself from "bouncing" a check is to keep a record of each check you write.

Some institutions pay a small amount of interest on checking accounts, but most do not. Some charge you a per-check or monthly fee, while others do not. Some institutions require you to keep a minimum amount in your checking account.

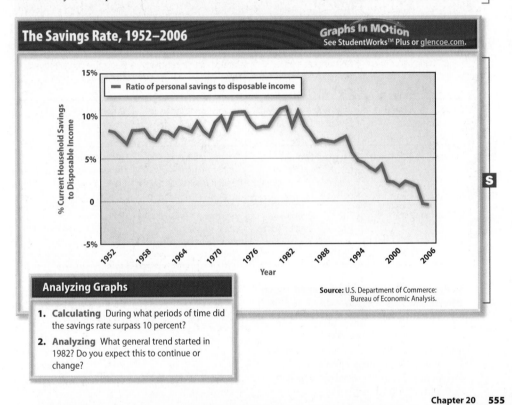

The Savings Rate, 1952–2006

Graphs In MOtion
See StudentWorks™ Plus or glencoe.com.

Ratio of personal savings to disposable income

% Current Household Savings to Disposable Income

Year

Source: U.S. Department of Commerce: Bureau of Economic Analysis.

Analyzing Graphs

1. **Calculating** During what periods of time did the savings rate surpass 10 percent?

2. **Analyzing** What general trend started in 1982? Do you expect this to continue or change?

C Critical Thinking

Making Inferences **Ask:** Why might someone decide to open both a savings and checking account? *(a savings account to earn interest on money they do not need right away and a checking account to pay their bills)* **BL**

S Skill Practice

Reading Graphs **Ask:** During what time period did the savings rate show a gradual rise? *(It was on the rise between 1952 and 1970, approximately.)* **OL**

R Reading Strategy

Identifying **Ask:** What kinds of fees might be applied to a checking account? *(Checking accounts may charge a per-check or monthly fee or require you to keep a minimum balance.)* **OL**

Analyzing Graphs

Answers:

1. Rates surpassed 10% for short time between 1974 and 1976, between 1980 and 1981, and in 1983, approximately.

2. A downward trend started in 1982. Students' opinions on the continuation of that trend will vary.

Additional Support

Activity: Technology Connection

Analyzing Information Tell students that they will use the Internet to do research on new cars and decide which make and model to buy. Then they will find out what their monthly payments would be if they put 20% down and took out a 3-year loan on the balance.

Before students begin their Internet research, discuss where they intend to shop for cars that might interest them.

After students have completed their research and summaries, have them meet in groups to compare notes. Suggest that they discuss questions such as, *What helpful* *websites did you find? Did anyone find an exceptionally good car loan offer? What did you find out when you compared offers from different car dealers? Did you search for new cars on any auction sites?* After groups have exchanged their findings, call on volunteers to summarize them for the class. **OL**

555

S Skill Practice

Reading Charts **Ask:** According to the chart, which account gives the lowest return on savings? *(the savings account)* **OL**

✓**Reading Check** **Answer:** Checking accounts allow you to write checks but charge fees and pay little interest. Savings accounts pay interest but do not allow check writing.

Analyzing Charts

Answers:

1. Savings accounts pay low interest, but you can withdraw money. CDs pay higher interest but often must be held for more than a year.
2. Money market accounts let you write checks but require a higher minimum balance.

Differentiated Instruction

If your funds fall below the minimum, they charge you a monthly fee. Many institutions now offer a debit card. This allows you to pay for a purchase directly from your checking account instead of writing a paper check.

Money Market Funds and Certificates of Deposit

A money market account is similar to a checking account in that it allows you to write checks, usually for larger amounts, against the money you have deposited. It is like a savings account because it pays interest, often a little higher than that on savings accounts. Yet another way to save is with certificates of deposit (CDs).

CDs are a kind of time deposit, in which you agree to deposit a sum of money with a financial institution for a certain amount of time, usually at least a year. In return, the institution guarantees you a set rate of interest that will be added to your principal when the CD matures, or comes due. The rate of interest on a CD is almost always higher than that on a savings account. Why? You have less flexibility to withdraw your money; if you want to withdraw it before the stated date, you must pay a substantial penalty. In general, longer-term CDs pay you a higher rate of interest as a reward for locking up your money for a longer period of time.

✓**Reading Check** **Contrasting** What are some differences between checking and savings accounts?

Types of Savings Accounts

	DEFINITION	RETURN	TIME FRAME
Bank Savings Accounts	Accounts at a bank, savings association, or credit union	Interest rate is relatively low	Depositor can withdraw money at any time
Certificates of Deposit	Bank notes for a set period of time at a fixed rate of interest	Interest rates are usually higher than rates for bank savings accounts	Vary, generally from 6 months to 5 years
Money Market Accounts	Savings accounts offered by banks that require a high minimum balance	Interest rates are usually higher than rates for regular bank savings accounts	Depositor may withdraw funds at any time
U.S. Savings Bonds	The U.S. government issues savings bonds as one of its ways of borrowing money.	Interest rate is usually higher than rates on bank savings accounts	Good for medium- and long-term savings goals

Analyzing Charts

1. **Comparing** How do bank savings accounts and certificates of deposit differ?
2. **Explaining** What is an advantage of a money market account? What is a disadvantage?

Leveled Activities

BL **School-to-Home Activity**
20, URB p. 79

OL **Chart/Graph/Map Activity**
20, URB pp. 75–76

AL **Critical Thinking Activity**
20, URB pp. 73–74

ELL **Guided Reading Activity**
20–3, URB p. 85

Investments

Main Idea Making wise investments in a variety of stocks and bonds is an important part of achieving long-term financial goals.

Economics & You Have you ever gone together with friends and pooled your money to buy something you could all use? Read to find out how this idea is the foundation for many key investment practices.

Savings accounts, money market accounts, and CDs are considered investments, but their **return,** or profit earned by the investor, is usually low. Almost all investors also invest in stocks and bonds, which have averaged a higher return over the years than savings accounts, money market accounts, and CDs. If people are willing to take a chance on earning a higher rate of return, however, they can invest their savings in other ways, such as in stocks and bonds. **W**

Stocks

When you buy shares of **stock,** you are buying partial ownership in a company. If the company does well, the value of your share will probably go up. If the company does not do well, your share will likely be worth less than you paid for it. You can sell it at any time, hopefully for more than you paid, and the difference is your profit.

Dividends Some companies also pay **R** shareholders a portion of company earnings at regular **intervals,** or periods, based on the number of shares people hold. This payment, called a **dividend,** can substantially increase your profit from owning stock.

Greater Risk Stocks generally earn a higher return than other investments because they carry greater risk. There is no guarantee, as with government-protected savings accounts (protected by the Federal Deposit Insurance Corporation [FDIC]) and CDs, that you will make money on your stock investment. In fact, if the company goes out of business, you will lose your entire investment.

Bonds

Whereas stocks represent ownership of a company, buying a **bond** is lending money to a company or government. Unlike buying stock, buying a bond does not make a bondholder part owner of the company or government that issued the bond.

Company Bonds Companies issue bonds to raise money for new equipment, research, or other business expenses. Companies pay bondholders a certain rate of interest over a set number of years. Bonds also carry risk; the company could become unable to pay you your interest or make final repayment of the principal.

Stock as an Investment Millions of people all over the world buy and sell shares of stock every day. Stock certificates like these are issued to people who have invested in a corporation. **Describing** What are two ways stockholders can make money from their investments?

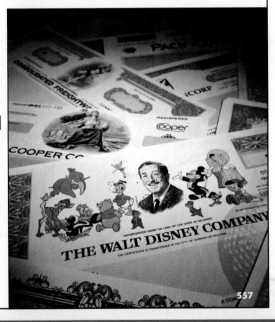

THE WALT DISNEY COMPANY

557

W **Writing Support**

Expository Writing Have students write a paper that examines investment choices and determines which one is best for a high-school senior who will need the money for college in six months. *(Answers will vary, but students should consider the student's 6-month time limit and the need for a safe investment.)* **OL**

R **Reading Strategy**

Making Connections Explain that business owners often need to invest for their retirement. **Ask:** Where should a young business owner invest funds for retirement? *(Answers will vary, but students should be able to explain their reasoning. Some might recognize that the investor's long time frame helps lessen the risk of losing all in the stock market and helps make stocks an attractive choice.)* **AL**

Caption Answer: They make money if their stocks go up and if the stocks pay dividends.

Activity: Collaborative Learning

Analyzing Information Ask: What are some of the sectors, or categories, of businesses? *(Answers may include energy, utilities, retail sales, manufacturing, finance, health care, transportation, technology, consumer staples, manufacturing, communication, basic materials, construction, real estate, arts and entertainment, and education.)*

Explain that stocks are grouped into sectors to make it easy to compare them. Organize the class into small groups, and have each investigate one sector of the economy. Ask them to find answers to questions such as: *What is the function of this sector in the economy? What are its major companies? How did the stocks in this sector perform last year? How are they performing today?*

Ask students to write a summary of what their group learned through its research. Explain that they will do this as a group activity and produce a written summary to share with the class. They may print their completed summaries to share with the class. **OL**

R Reading Strategy

Identifying Ask: How does a mutual fund work? *(A group of people pools their money to buy a collection of stocks or bonds and to hire a fund manager. The investors share the fund's profits. Spreading their investments among many stocks and bonds limits the investors' loss if a stock or bond loses money.)* **OL**

✔Reading Check Answer: Investments that have a high return have a higher-than-average risk.

Assess

Civics ONLINE

Study Central™ provides summaries, interactive games, and online graphic organizers to help students review content.

Close

Analyzing Information Ask: What kinds of investments are best suited for investors who do not like to take a risk? *(Savings accounts, U.S. government bonds, Treasury bills, and notes are backed by the U.S. government.)* **OL**

Section 3 Review

Government Bonds The U.S. government, along with cities and states, also borrows money to pay for its expenses. The United States issues savings bonds, along with other bonds called Treasury bills, notes, and bonds. U.S. government bonds are considered among the safest of all investments because they are backed by the financial strength of the U.S. government. The government pays interest on these bonds, but it builds the interest into the redemption price rather than sending checks on a regular basis.

A person buying a savings bond pays half the bond's face value. You could purchase a $50 bond for only $25. The bond increases in value every six months until its full face value is reached. (The *Rule of 72* tells you how long it takes for the bond to mature: Divide the number 72 by the interest rate.) If you redeem a U.S. savings bond before it matures you are guaranteed the interest rate, which changes depending on the rates of interest in the economy.

Mutual Funds

Many investors find it easier to invest in stocks and bonds using **mutual funds.** Mutual funds are pools of money from many people. Their money is invested in a selection of individual stocks and/or bonds chosen by financial experts. Your return is based on the experts' choices of investments. Mutual funds are less risky than investments in individual stocks and bonds. Mutual **R** funds usually own several hundreds—or thousands—of different stocks and bonds. Spreading your investment among many stocks or bonds limits the loss if one individual stock or bond performs poorly.

Many popular mutual funds are tracked by a government regulated index. An index is a measuring system that tracks stock prices over the long term. The Dow Jones Industrial Average (DJIA) and the Standard & Poor's (S&P) are the two most common indexes.

✔Reading Check Explaining What is the relationship of an investment's risk to its potential return?

Section Review

3

Vocabulary

1. **Write** a paragraph about saving and investing in which you use at least five of these terms: *save, interest, principal, return, stock, dividend, bond, mutual fund.*

Main Ideas

2. **Explain** how the decision to save involves trade-offs.

3. **Comparing** How is a money market account similar to a checking account?

4. **Contrasting** What is the basic difference between a stock and a bond?

Critical Thinking

5. **BIG Ideas** Saving affects you as well as others. On a graphic organizer like the one below, list three results of saving.

6. **Explaining** Why are certificates of deposit described as time deposits?

7. **Explaining** How does buying a U.S. savings bond increase the United States government's debt?

CITIZENSHIP Activity

8. **Expository Writing** List your short-term savings goals, such as saving to buy a new iPOD. Then list your long-term savings goals, such as saving for a house. In a short essay, explain the major differences between the two kinds of saving.

Civics ONLINE

Study Central™ To review this section, go to glencoe.com.

Answers

1. Sentences should use vocabulary words according to their definitions in the section and in the Glossary.

2. The more you save today, the more you can spend in the future; but the less you can spend now

3. Money market accounts and checking accounts are similar in that they both permit you to write checks on your account.

4. With a stock, you own a share in a company. With a bond, you lend money to a company or the government.

5.

6. They are deposits you agree to keep in the financial institution for a set period of time.

7. The U.S. government both repays the bonds and pays interest on them. This increases government debt.

8. Essays will vary but should include examples of students' short-term and long-term savings goals and the difference between those two kinds of savings.

Guide to Reading

Big Idea
We all make economic choices. Opportunity cost, scarcity, and supply and demand influence the decisions we make.

Content Vocabulary
• impulse buying (p. 561)

Academic Vocabulary
• evaluate (p. 560)
• commit (p. 562)
• eliminate (p. 562)

Reading Strategy
Describing As you read, use a diagram like the one below to describe three ways to keep impulse buying in check.

Section 4

Achieving Your Financial Goals

Real World Economics James Meredith struggled to be admitted to the University of Mississippi in 1962, at that time an all-white school in the South. It took a federal court order to get him into the segregated college of his choice. Forty years later, his son, Joseph, completed a PhD in business administration at the same school. But race was not the big problem anymore. It was rather how to pay for this college education. With tuition costs increasing as much as 50 percent over three years in some states, saving to pay for college requires financial planning.

▼ **James and Joseph Meredith**

559

Focus

Guide to Reading
Answers to Graphic:

Section Spotlight Video

To generate student interest and provide a springboard for class discussion, access the Chapter 20, Section 4 video at glencoe.com or on the video DVD.

Resource Manager

R Reading Strategies	**C** Critical Thinking	**D** Differentiated Instruction	**W** Writing Support	**S** Skill Practice
Teacher Edition	**Teacher Edition**	**Teacher Edition**	**Teacher Edition**	**Teacher Edition**
• Inferring, p. 561	• Det. Cause/Effect, p. 561	• English Learners p. 560	• Persuasive Writing, p. 560	• Reading Charts, p. 560
Additional Resources	• Drawing Con., p. 562	**Additional Resources**		**Additional Resources**
• Cont. Vocab., URB p. 66	**Additional Resources**	• School-to-Home Act., URB p. 80		• Daily Focus Trans., 20–4
• Academic Vocab., URB p. 67	• Quizzes and Tests, p. 239	• Reteach. Act., URB p. 81		
• Guid. Read., URB p. 86				
• RENTG, p. 192				

Teach

D Differentiated Instruction

English Learners Remind students that a word they do not know may be defined if they read a little further. Ask them to read "Impulse Buying" to find the meaning of the term "impulse." *(It is defined as "acting on feelings or emotions without thinking about consequences.")* **ELL** **BL**

S Skill Practice

Reading Charts **Ask:** Which advertising techniques focus on people's vanity rather on the product's features? *(the snob appeal and testimonial techniques)* **OL**

W Writing Support

Persuasive Writing Have students choose one of the advertising techniques and write an advertisement that illustrates how it is used to appeal to buyers. **OL**

Analyzing Charts

Answers:
1. the testimonial
2. Answers may include that many people look up to public figures.

Differentiated Instruction

What Kind of Spender Are You?

Main Idea Careful spenders avoid pitfalls, such as impulse buying, on their way to meeting their financial goals.

Economics & You Have you ever bought something expensive on the spur of the moment and regretted it later? Read to find out more about how to avoid budget breakers like this.

As you learned, managing your money, budgeting, and saving and investing money are aimed at the same target: helping you reach your financial goals. These goals today may be modest—things such as being able to afford a movie every weekend, taking a skiing or rafting trip, or saving ten dollars a week. However, as you get older, you can be sure that your goals will get bigger. You may want to buy a car or a house or to continue your education. All of these things take a lot of money. That is why, when setting and monitoring, or examining, your current financial goals, it is useful to **evaluate**, or review, your spending habits.

Impulse Buying

Do you know what it means to be impulsive? One definition is "acting on feelings or emotions without thinking about consequences." When it is paired with buying, it is easy to see how the combination can ruin a carefully organized budget.

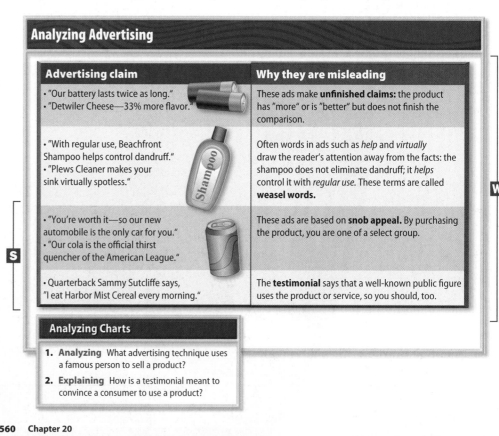

Analyzing Advertising

Advertising claim	Why they are misleading
• "Our battery lasts twice as long." • "Detwiler Cheese—33% more flavor."	These ads make **unfinished claims:** the product has "more" or is "better" but does not finish the comparison.
• "With regular use, Beachfront Shampoo helps control dandruff." • "Plews Cleaner makes your sink virtually spotless."	Often words in ads such as *help* and *virtually* draw the reader's attention away from the facts: the shampoo does not eliminate dandruff; it *helps* control it with *regular use*. These terms are called **weasel words.**
• "You're worth it—so our new automobile is the only car for you." • "Our cola is the official thirst quencher of the American League."	These ads are based on **snob appeal.** By purchasing the product, you are one of a select group.
• Quarterback Sammy Sutcliffe says, "I eat Harbor Mist Cereal every morning."	The **testimonial** says that a well-known public figure uses the product or service, so you should, too.

Analyzing Charts

1. **Analyzing** What advertising technique uses a famous person to sell a product?
2. **Explaining** How is a testimonial meant to convince a consumer to use a product?

560 Chapter 20

Interpreting a Bar Graph

Chart, Graph, and Map Skills Activity 20, URB pp. 75–76

Objective:	To use a bar graph to make comparisons and identify trends
Focus:	Students interpret a bar graph.
Teach:	Review the directions on page 75.
Assess:	Use the questions on page 76 to assess students' interpretation of bar graphs.
Close:	Have students explain the use of graphs in making comparisons.

Differentiated Instruction Strategies

BL What information is given by the length of the bars?

AL Make a graph that combines the information on investments shown in the graphs on pages 75–76.

ELL What information is shown on the *x*-axis and on the *y*-axis of each graph?

Marketers know that many consumers buy on impulse. That is why there is such a dazzling display of inexpensive items near the checkout line at the grocery or department store. One of your greatest challenges as a careful consumer is to avoid **impulse buying.**

Danger Signals Here are signals you may be an impulse buyer:

- You buy lots of things you do not really want and do not need.
- Buying things makes you feel better.
- You are always borrowing money from friends because you have spent yours.
- You quickly lose interest in something you have bought.

Even rational consumers can fall prey to the danger of impulse buying.

Tips Here are some tips to keep your impulse buying under control and keep it from ruining your budget.

- Have a line in your spending budget for impulse items of any kind. You will then know how much you have to spend—if anything—on impulse purchases.
- Make a list of things you really need—and take the list when you shop.
- If you see something very tempting, take a break. Leave the store, walk around, and decide whether you really need the item. Better yet, go away and come back tomorrow, after thinking hard about the purchase.
- If you have decided you really do need something, comparison-shop. You may find a better price somewhere else.
- Be careful with online buying. It is easy to charge things online.
- Record all impulse purchases in the spending part of your budget. You need to know how much you are spending on impulse items so you can try to control it.

✓ **Reading Check** Explaining How can impulse buying ruin your budget?

TIME™ Teens in *Action*

Fuel for Thought

Looking for a little "fuel" for thought? Jon Russell, 17, of Scarborough, Maine, might have just what you are looking for!

QUESTION: Your club is called ECOS. What does it stand for?

ANSWER: Environmental Club of Scarborough. I started the group three years ago with four friends to promote environmental awareness.

Q: How are you doing that?

A: We traveled through our school with a rolling Dumpster on Friday afternoons, collecting paper waste and bottles for recycling. With the steadily increasing price of oil, we will soon need a cheaper form of fuel. So ECOS is converting a small school bus to run on waste vegetable oil.

Q: Did you say vegetable oil?

A: Yes. At a fraction of the cost per gallon of gasoline, it's a very thrifty solution. Our nation is too dependent on oil and other nonrenewable sources of energy. I hope our biofuel bus will help others understand that change toward renewable sources of energy is both possible and economical. We'll use data collected from the biofuel bus to introduce our project to local and state governments.

We hope our work will have an impact on their lawmaking decisions.

ECOS members work on school bus

Making a Difference   CITIZENSHIP

Why does Jon believe we should use renewable energy sources?

Chapter 20   561

C Critical Thinking

Determining Cause and Effect Ask: What are the effects of impulse buying on financial goals and on how buyers feel about themselves? *(Answers may include that impulse buying destroys financial goals or delays reaching them. The impulse buyer loses sight of future goals. Impulse buyers may feel guilty when they realize they wasted money they had planned to save.)* **AL**

R Reading Strategy

Inferring Ask: Why do you think it might be a good idea to leave the store and come back the next day when you are tempted to buy something? *(Answers may include that you will lose the impulse to buy the item and will not return for it.)* **OL**

✓ **Reading Check** **Answer:** by wasting money you had planned to save

TIME™ Teens in *Action*

Answer:

He believes that we are too dependent on nonrenewable energy sources, such as oil.

Hands-On Chapter Project
Step 4

Investing in Stocks

Step 4: Evaluating Stock Portfolios Groups of students continue the investment activity they began in Section 3.

Directions Have students meet with their groups to report on the stocks they have been following. Give them time to discuss the reports. Then explain that today they will 1. Compute the value of the club's portfolio (the current price of the stocks plus the money left after buying them); 2. Make a chart to track the portfolio's value; 3. On the chart, record the portfolio's initial value and current value.

Have students work with their club members to chart the portfolio. Tell them to continue tracking their individual stocks until the next meeting. **OL**

(Project continued on the Visual Summary page)

Our Stock Portfolio

10/6   10/11

C Critical Thinking

Drawing Conclusions Ask: How can budgeting help reach long-term financial goals without delaying current buying? *(if you include a place in your budget for impulse purchases, you can spend that money without feeling guilty or deprived, and meet your long-term goals)* **OL**

✓ Reading Check Answer: Saving to meet your long-term goals might mean having to give up what you want now; buying what you want to buy now might mean having to give up your long-term financial goals.

Assess

Civics ONLINE

Study Central™ provides summaries, interactive games, and online graphic organizers to help students review content.

Close

Summarizing Have students write a paper on how advertisers tempt buyers to ignore their budgets and what buyers can do to avoid this. **OL**

Section 4 Review

Your Goals and Your Buying Decisions

Main Idea The buying decisions you make can have a major impact on your life and career choices.

Economics & You Do you have a long-term plan for meeting your financial goals? Read to find out how the decisions you make can play a key role in achieving these goals.

It is important to consider your economic goals when you make buying decisions. The kinds of buying decisions you make help reveal what kind of a decision-maker you are and how **committed,** or dedicated, you are to your goals.

Now or Later?

Suppose you work after school and on weekends to save money for a new computer. That is your long-term goal. You also see many things that you would like to buy now. If you buy these things, you will find it harder to accomplish your long-term goal. Which option do you choose? You could buy what you want now and reduce, postpone, or even **eliminate,** or throw out, the chances of buying the computer. Or you could buy less of what you want now and increase the chances of buying the computer later. Long-term goals often conflict with short-term spending decisions.

Long-term planning becomes even more crucial the farther out you go. For example, many students need to save as well as borrow money to further their education. Statistics show that people with more post-high school education earn significantly more money over their working lives than those who complete only high school. Therefore, making the financial sacrifices necessary to continue your education is likely to pay off in a big way later.

✓ Reading Check Explaining In what way can long-term goals conflict with short-term spending decisions?

Section 4 Review

Vocabulary

1. **Define** *impulse buying.* Provide an example of impulse buying.

Main Ideas

2. **Identify** three ways you can cut down on impulse buying.

3. **Explaining** Why is it important to consider your goals when making a buying decision?

Critical Thinking

4. **Concluding** Explain whether you think impulse buying is more common when purchasing expensive or inexpensive items.

5. **BIG Ideas** "You should always shop until you find exactly what you are looking for at the lowest possible price." Do you agree or disagree? Explain your answer.

6. **Classifying** On a chart like the one below, provide two examples of short-term buying goals and two examples of long-term buying goals.

Short Term	Long Term
1.	1.
2.	2.

CITIZENSHIP Activity

7. **Creative Writing** Write a conversation between you and a telemarketer who is trying to sell you something you do not want or need. What does the telemarketer say? What do you say?

Civics ONLINE

Study Central™ To review this section, go to glencoe.com.

Answers

1. Sentences should use vocabulary word according to its definition in the section and in the Glossary.

2. Ways to cut down include having a place in your budget for impulse buying, making a shopping list of things you need, and leaving the store when you are tempted to buy something on impulse.

3. You might buy things you do not really want and may not save enough to meet your goals.

4. Answers will vary. Some students might suggest that it is more difficult to buy expensive things on impulse.

5. Student opinions will vary. Students should, however, give details to support their opinions.

6. Student answers will vary but should follow the directions.

7. Student scripts will vary but should indicate that students have an understanding of the persuasive tactics telemarketers use to tempt impulse buyers.

Buying Strategy

- Making consumer decisions involves deciding the following:
  - whether to spend your money
  - what you will purchase
  - how to use your purchase.
- Comparison shopping involves making comparisons among brands, sizes, and stores.

Consumerism

Consumer rights include
- the right to safety
- the right to be informed
- the right to choose
- the right to be heard
- the right to redress

Negotiation to purchase a car

Budget

- A budget is an organized plan for spending and saving money.
- What you do with the information in a budget is up to you. No one can force you to spend less and save more unless you want to.

Credit

- When buying on credit, the amount you will owe is equal to the principal plus interest.
- Financial institutions that provide credit include commercial banks, savings and loan associations, and credit unions.

Saving and Investing

- It is important to get into the habit of saving.
- Individuals have many places to invest their savings, including savings accounts and certificates of deposit.
- Shares of stock entitle the buyer to a certain part of the future profits and assets of the corporation that is selling the stock.

Entertainment spending

Department store shopping in Paris

STUDY TO GO Study anywhere, anytime! Download quizzes and flash cards to your PDA from glencoe.com.

563

Visual Summary 20

Questioning Have students review the chapter by supplying an example or detail for every bulleted item in the visual summary. For example, call attention to the section Buying Strategy. **Ask:** How do you make a decision on which product you will buy? Encourage students to give examples of what to consider when making a buying decision. Continue by having students supply supporting details or examples for the remaining sections summarized on the page. **OL**

Summarizing Conclude by asking volunteers to tell what new information they learned as they read the chapter focusing on managing savings. **BL**

Hands-On Chapter Project
Step 5: Wrap-Up

Investing in Stocks

Step 5: Reporting on Investments Students finish the process begun in Step 4.

Directions Have students meet with their investment-club group. Ask them to speculate on whether or not they would make any changes in the portfolio. Would they have purchased a stock another group purchased but they did not?

Have each group choose a member to report to the class on the club's investments. Explain that the presenter will show the chart made at the last meeting and then give the portfolio's current value.

Summarizing After the presentations, hold a class discussion to review the results and to see which clubs (if any) made a profit. Emphasize that they made a short-term investment. The results might be quite different a few months or a year from now. Finally, call on volunteers to comment on their investment-club experience and tell whether or not they plan on continuing to keep track of their club's portfolio. **OL**

1. B Answer options B and D are both connected with the cost of credit and are expressed as percentages. However, B is specifically "the cost of credit expressed as a percentage of the amount borrowed."

2. D The key phrase here is "credit rating." The only answer choice that applies to a credit rating is "bankruptcy."

3. C The phrase "amount initially deposited" points to "principal" as the only logical choice. Choice D is the only other possible answer, and it is incorrect because a "loan" earns interest for the bank, not the depositor.

4. A Answer choices A and B both apply to money that shareholders earn on their investments, but only a dividend is paid by companies at regular intervals.

Reviewing Main Ideas

5. C If students know the meanings of the terms given in the answer choices, the only possible answer is C. Students should recognize that governmental "Acts" are not buying strategies, warranties, or comparison shopping.

6. D Choices B–D are connected to choices consumers make, but only "opportunity cost" refers to a choice *not* made.

7. A Although all the answer options are related to credit card terms, students should realize that the only way to avoid interest charges is to keep a zero balance. Thus, A is the only logical answer.

8. B Answer options A and D can be eliminated because they may be results of bankruptcy but are not causes. Choice C could be a contributing factor to bankruptcy, but only for people already it debt. Thus, B is the best choice because it can cause someone to be led into bankruptcy.

TEST-TAKING TIP

> Pay attention to other test questions as you read. Sometimes the information in one question contains help for another.

Reviewing Vocabulary

Directions: Choose the word(s) that best completes the sentence.

1. The cost of credit expressed as a percentage of the amount borrowed is the _____.

  A surplus   **C** credit rating

  B APR   **D** interest

2. A _____ remains on a person's credit rating for at least seven years, making it almost impossible to get a loan.

  A warranty   **C** charge

  B deficit   **D** bankruptcy

3. A bank adds the interest you earn to your _____, the amount you initially deposited.

  A mortgage   **C** principal

  B debit card   **D** loan

4. Some companies pay shareholders a _____ at regular intervals, based on the number of shares they hold.

  A dividend   **C** time deposit

  B return   **D** bond

Reviewing Main Ideas

Directions: Choose the best answer for each question.

Section 1 *(pp. 538–543)*

5. The Pure Food and Drug Act and the Fair Packaging and Labeling Act are examples of _____.

  A smart buying strategies

  B extended warranties

  C protecting consumer rights

  D comparison shopping

6. The value of the highest alternative choice that a consumer did not make is the _____.

  A time deposit

  B down payment

  C balance of payments

  D opportunity cost

Section 2 *(pp. 544–549)*

7. To avoid interest charges on a credit card, a consumer must _____.

  A pay off the full balance each month

  B make no charges at the end of the month

  C pay the minimum monthly amount

  D pay half the monthly balance

8. Millions of people have been left in bankruptcy by the _____.

  A lack of collateral

  B easy availability of credit

  C annual percentage rate

  D high down payment requirement

Section 3 *(pp. 552–558)*

9. Because certificates of deposit (CDs) require investors to lock up their money for a longer period of time than a regular savings account _____.

  A banks rarely sell CDs

  B there is no penalty for cashing them in

  C CDs pay a higher rate of interest

  D CDs pay lower rates of interest

10. Compared to stocks and bonds, mutual funds are generally _____.

  A less risky investments

  B longer term investments

  C higher risk investments

  D shorter term investments

GO ON ➡

---

9. C Students should recognize that choices A and B are false. Logically, banks can pay more interest on money they know they can invest for a certain length of time. Thus, C is correct, because savings deposits may be withdrawn from the bank at any time.

10. A Answer choices B and D can be eliminated because the term of investment for all three investments is up to the investor. Since individual stocks and bonds may drop in value, having a collection of them spreads the risk, making mutual funds a less risky investment.

11. D Students should recognize that options A–C all describe possible consequences of being an impulse buyer.

Section 4 *(pp. 559–562)*

11. If you are an impulse buyer, you may find that

    A you quickly lose interest in things you buy.

    B you buy things that you do not need.

    C you buy things that make you feel better.

    D all of the above.

Critical Thinking

Directions: Base your answers to questions 12 and 13 on the chart below and your knowledge of Chapter 20.

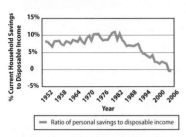

    ■ Ratio of personal savings to disposable income

Source: U.S. Department of Commerce: Bureau of Economic Analysis.

12. Because savings not only benefit investors but also provide capital for businesses to grow, the chart indicates that in the future _____.

    A business will hire more people soon

    B consumers have little money to spend

    C business growth could slow down

    D interest rates will begin to fall

13. Which of the following economic conditions characterized the United States between 1980 and 2006?

    A Consumer credit and savings increased.

    B Savings increased; consumer credit decreased.

    C Consumer credit increased, savings decreased.

    D Savings and consumer credit decreased.

Document-Based Questions

Directions: Analyze the following document and answer the short-answer questions that follow.

Bankrate.com asked economist Joel Naroff whether America's negative savings rate was a problem. The following is his reply.

> *To some extent we're spending way beyond our means. We're drawing down on wealth that has come from equities or, more importantly, our homes. Economists worry because we've gone through an environment where housing prices have soared, and we've spent a lot of the wealth that was generated.*
>
> *The probability that over the next three years we'll see that same increase in property values is pretty low, and there's the possibility that prices will fall. What that says to economists is that the probability that we'll draw that kind of money from equity again is small. If we spend a lot of the wealth and we don't have that money going forward, consumer spending slows and the economy slows.*
>
> —Joel Naroff

14. According to Naroff, where are Americans getting the money to spend that they are not earning? Why are some economists worried?

15. How could spending our wealth today affect tomorrow's economy?

Extended-Response Question

16. Is consumer debt still rising? At what rate? Do research to determine how fast such debt is growing and make some predictions about how it will affect the future.

For additional test practice, use Self-Check Quizzes— Chapter 20 on glencoe.com.

Need Extra Help?

If you missed question...	1	2	3	4	5	6	7	8	9	10	11	12	13	14	15	16
Go to page...	547	549	555	557	540	543	548	549	556	558	560	553	553	553	553	548

Critical Thinking

12. C The chart clearly shows a drop in the savings rate. Since that means there will be less capital available for growth, option C is correct, "business growth could slow down."

13. C Choices A and B are incorrect because savings did not increase. D is incorrect because consumer credit increased. Students should recognize that if people are saving less, they may be borrowing more through their use of credit cards.

Document-Based Questions

14. Americans are using the equity in their homes to get money to spend. Economists are worried because people have spent much of the money that increases in housing prices generated. Housing sales have historically been a good barometer of the general wealth of the economy.

15. Without a lot of wealth and money to spend, consumer spending slows, and the economy slows.

Extended Response

16. Students' essays will vary but should reflect current data that consumer debt continues to rise at a steady rate. Students should also have become aware that no controls are currently in place to radically alter this trend but there are some needed.

Have students visit the Web site at glencoe.com to review Chapter 20 and take the **Self-Check Quiz.**

Need Extra Help?

Have students refer to the pages listed if they miss any of the questions.

Chapter Planning Guide

21

Levels				Resources	Chapter Opener	Section 1	Section 2	Section 3	Section 4	Chapter Assess
BL	OL	AL	ELL							
				FOCUS						
BL	OL	AL	ELL	Daily Focus Skills Transparencies		21-1	21-2	21-3	21-4	
				TEACH						
BL	OL		ELL	Reading Essentials and Note-Taking Guide*		p. 195	p. 198	p. 201	p. 204	
BL	OL		ELL	Reading Skills Activity, URB			p. 7			
BL	OL	AL	ELL	Speaking and Listening Skills Activity, URB		p. 9	p. 9	p. 9	p. 9	
		AL		Enrichment Activity, URB		p. 13	p. 13	p. 13	p. 13	
BL	OL	AL	ELL	Content Vocabulary Activity, URB*	p. 88	p. 88	p. 88	p. 88	p. 88	
BL	OL	AL	ELL	Academic Vocabulary Activity, URB	p. 89	p. 89	p. 89	p. 89	p. 89	
	OL			Biography Activity, URB					p. 91	
BL	OL	AL	ELL	Writing Skills Activity, URB		p. 93	p. 93	p. 93	p. 93	
	OL	AL		Critical Thinking Skills Activity, URB		p. 95	p. 95	p. 95	p. 95	
BL	OL	AL	ELL	Chart, Graph, and Map Skills Activity, URB					p. 97	
BL	OL	AL	ELL	Differentiated Instruction, URB				p. 99	p. 99	
BL	OL	AL	ELL	School-to-Home Connection Activity, URB*	p. 101	p. 101	p. 101	p. 101	p. 101	
BL	OL		ELL	Guided Reading Activities, URB*		p. 105	p. 106	p. 107	p. 108	
BL	OL	AL	ELL	Writer's Guidebook	✓	✓	✓	✓	✓	✓
	OL	AL		Primary Source Document Library	✓	✓	✓	✓	✓	✓
BL	OL	AL	ELL	Daily Lecture & Discussion Notes (in Pres. Plus)		✓	✓	✓	✓	✓
BL	OL	AL	ELL	StudentWorks™ Plus		✓	✓	✓	✓	✓
BL	OL	AL	ELL	Section Spotlight Videos		✓	✓	✓	✓	
BL	OL	AL	ELL	TIME Interpreting Political Cartoons Transp.					Ch. 21	
BL	OL	AL	ELL	Writing Process Transparencies	✓	✓	✓	✓	✓	✓

Note: Please refer to the *Unit 6 Resource Book* for this chapter's URB materials.

* Also available in Spanish

- Interactive Lesson Planner
- Interactive Teacher Edition
- Fully editable blackline masters
- Section Spotlight Videos Launch
- Differentiated Lesson Plans
- Printable reports of daily assignments
- Standards Tracking System

Levels					Resources	Chapter Opener	Section 1	Section 2	Section 3	Section 4	Chapter Assess
BL	OL	AL	ELL								
					TEACH (continued)						
				📁	**Building Academic Vocabulary**	✓	✓	✓	✓	✓	✓
				📁	**Strategies for Success**	✓	✓	✓	✓	✓	✓
Teacher Resources				📁	**Teacher's Guide to Differentiated Instruction**	✓	✓	✓	✓	✓	✓
				💿	**Graphing Tool**	✓	✓	✓	✓	✓	✓
				💿	**Presentation Plus! with MindJogger CheckPoint**	✓	✓	✓	✓	✓	✓
					ASSESS						
BL	OL	AL	ELL	📁	**Quizzes and Tests***		p. 248	p. 249	p. 250	p. 251	p. 252
BL	OL	AL	ELL	📁	**Authentic Assessment with Rubrics**		p. 25	p. 25	p. 25	p. 25	p. 25
BL	OL	AL	ELL	📁	**Standardized Test Practice**					p. 41	p. 41
BL	OL	AL	ELL	💿	*ExamView® Assessment Suite* **CD-ROM**		21-1	21-2	21-3	21-4	Ch. 21
					CLOSE						
BL			ELL	📁	**Reteaching Activity, URB***		p. 103	p. 103	p. 103	p. 103	
BL	OL		ELL	📁	**Reading and Study Skills Foldables™ Activity**	p. 90	p. 91		p. 91		
BL	OL	AL	ELL	📁	*Civics Today* **in Graphic Novel**	p. 83				p. 83	
BL	OL	AL	ELL	🖫	**Graphic Organizer Transparencies & Strategies**	✓	✓	✓	✓	✓	✓

✓ Chapter- or unit-based activities applicable to all sections in this chapter

Using Study Central™

Section Previews

What is Study Central™?

The Study Central™ Web site offers an in-depth, section-based preview that summarizes the content of each section of a chapter.

How can Study Central™ help my students?

The Study Central™ Section Previews summarize content and help students:

- prepare for better understanding of section content
- practice reading and comprehension skills

Visit glencoe.com and enter a *QuickPass*™ code to go directly to resources for each chapter.

Civics ONLINE

Visit glencoe.com and enter *QuickPass*™ code CIV1360c21T for Chapter 21 resources.

You can easily launch a wide range of digital products from your computer's desktop with the McGraw-Hill Social Studies widget.

	Student	Teacher	Parent
Media Library			
• Student Edition Section Audio	●		●
• Spanish Audio Summaries	●		●
• Section Spotlight Videos	●	●	●
***Civics Today* Online Learning Center (Web Site)**			
• Chapter Overviews	●	●	●
• Study Central™	●	●	●
• Study-to-Go	●	●	●
• Student Web Activities	●	●	●
• In Motion Animation	●	●	●
• Self-Check Quizzes	●	●	●
• ePuzzles and Games	●	●	●
• StudentWorks™ Plus Online	●	●	●
• Vocabulary eFlashcards	●	●	●
• Web Activity Lesson Plans		●	
• Vocabulary PuzzleMaker	●	●	●
Classroom Tools			
• Multilingual Glossary	●	●	●
• Beyond the Textbook	●	●	●
• NGS MapMachine	●	●	●

Reading List Generator CD-ROM

GLENCOE BookLink 3

Use this database to search more than 30,000 titles to create a customized reading list for your students.

- Reading lists can be organized by students' reading level, author, genre, theme, or area of interest.
- The database provides Degrees of Reading Power™ (DRP) and Lexile™ readability scores for all selections.
- A brief summary of each selection is included.

Reading suggestions

Leveled reading suggestions for this chapter:

For students at a Grade 7 reading level:
- *Careers Inside the World of Entrepreneurs,* by Sue Hurwitz

For students at a Grade 8 reading level:
- *Eli Whitney: Cotton Gin Genius,* by Kaye Patchett

For students at a Grade 9 reading level:
- *Future Sources of Energy,* by Mark Lambert

For students at a Grade 10 reading level:
- *Business Builders in Fast Food,* by Nathan Aaseng

For students at a Grade 11 reading level:
- *Overpopulation,* by John Zeaman

READING SUPPORT FROM JAMESTOWN EDUCATION

- **Timed Readings Plus in Social Studies** helps students increase their reading rate and fluency while maintaining comprehension. The 400-word passages are similar to those found on state and national assessments.

- **Reading in the Content Area: Social Studies** concentrates on six essential reading skills that help students better comprehend what they read. The book includes 75 high-interest nonfiction passages written at increasing levels of difficulty.

- **Reading Social Studies** includes strategic reading instruction and vocabulary support in Social Studies content for both ELLs and native speakers of English.

- **Content Vocabulary Workout** (Grades 6–8) accelerates reading comprehension through focused vocabulary development. Social Studies content vocabulary comes from the glossaries of Glencoe's Middle School Social Studies texts. www.jamestowneducation.com

KEY Teacher Wraparound

Use this key to help you identify the different types of prompts found in the Teacher Wraparound Edition.

R **Reading Strategies** activities help you teach reading skills and vocabulary.

C **Critical Thinking** strategies help students apply and extend what they have learned.

D **Differentiated Instruction** activities provide instruction for students learning to speak English, along with suggestions for teaching various types of learners.

S **Skill Practice** strategies help students practice historical analysis and geography skills.

W **Writing Support** activities provide writing opportunities to help students comprehend the text.

Teaching strategies and activities have been coded for ability level appropriateness.

AL Activities for students working above grade level

OL Activities for students working on grade level

BL Activities for students working below grade level

ELL Activities for English Language Learners

Focus

Why It Matters

Ask: What happens to the price of goods when supply is less than demand? *(The price increases.)*

More About the Photo

Visual Literacy These San Diego drivers are participating in a type of consumer organization with a long history. Known as cooperatives, these groups are made of individuals banding together to negotiate lower prices for goods and services. The modern consumer cooperative movement began in the United States in the early 1900s. Cooperative groups negotiated lower prices for their members for goods and services ranging from food, clothes, and housing to insurance, health care, and electricity.

Chapter
21

Demand and Supply

GASOLINE

Hours of Operation
Mon - Fri 6:00 AM - 9:30 PM
Saturday 6:00 AM - 8:00 PM
Sunday 6:00 AM - 7:00 PM

OPEN

Self-Serve
Debit and Credit
Cards Only
No Cash Accepted
No Cash On Premises

PLEASE
Pull to
Forward

Why It Matters

Two forces work together in markets to establish prices for all the goods and services we buy. They are demand—the desire, willingness, and ability to buy a good or service—and supply—the quantities of a good or service that producers are willing to sell at all possible market prices.

566

Teach

BIG Ideas *As you begin teaching each section, use these questions and activities to help students focus on the Big Ideas.*

Section 1

Demand Ask: What is demand? *(the desire, willingness, and ability to buy a good or service)* Point out that in Section 1 students will learn the role that demand plays in a market economy. **OL**

Section 2

Factors Affecting Demand Ask: How does price influence demand? *(When prices are high, demand decreases. When prices are low, demand increases.)* Tell students that in Section 2 they will learn about the many factors that affect demand in a market economy. **OL**

Section 3

Supply and the Supply Curve Ask: How does price influence supply? *(When prices are high, producers increase supply. When prices are low, producers do not have any incentive to increase supply.)* Tell students that in Section 3, they will learn about the many factors that affect supply in a market economy. **OL**

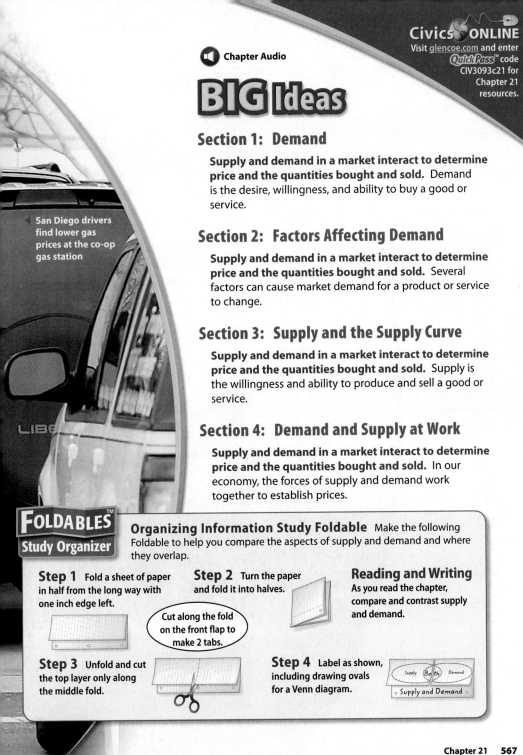

San Diego drivers find lower gas prices at the co-op gas station

Chapter Audio

Civics ONLINE
Visit glencoe.com and enter QuickPass™ code CIV3093c21 for Chapter 21 resources.

Chapter Introduction
21

BIG Ideas

Section 1: Demand

Supply and demand in a market interact to determine price and the quantities bought and sold. Demand is the desire, willingness, and ability to buy a good or service.

Section 2: Factors Affecting Demand

Supply and demand in a market interact to determine price and the quantities bought and sold. Several factors can cause market demand for a product or service to change.

Section 3: Supply and the Supply Curve

Supply and demand in a market interact to determine price and the quantities bought and sold. Supply is the willingness and ability to produce and sell a good or service.

Section 4: Demand and Supply at Work

Supply and demand in a market interact to determine price and the quantities bought and sold. In our economy, the forces of supply and demand work together to establish prices.

FOLDABLES Dinah Zike's
Study Organizer Foldables

Purpose This Foldable helps the students improve their study skills using the information in the chapter. The completed Foldable will use a Venn diagram to help students organize information about factors that influence the impact of demand and supply on the economy. **OL**

📁 More Foldables activities for this chapter can be found in the *Dinah Zike's Reading and Study Skills Foldables* ancillary.

Civics ONLINE

Visit glencoe.com and enter *QuickPass*™ code CIV1360c21T for Chapter 21 resources, including a Chapter Overview, Study Central™, Study-to-Go, Student Web Activity, Self-Check Quiz, and other materials.

FOLDABLES
Study Organizer

Organizing Information Study Foldable Make the following Foldable to help you compare the aspects of supply and demand and where they overlap.

Step 1 Fold a sheet of paper in half from the long way with one inch edge left.

Step 2 Turn the paper and fold it into halves.

Reading and Writing
As you read the chapter, compare and contrast supply and demand.

Cut along the fold on the front flap to make 2 tabs.

Step 3 Unfold and cut the top layer only along the middle fold.

Step 4 Label as shown, including drawing ovals for a Venn diagram.

Supply Both Demand
Supply and Demand

Section 4

Demand and Supply at Work Ask: How does the market signal the interaction between demand and supply? *(Prices act as a signal in the market. They tell producers what, how, and for whom to produce goods and services.)* Tell students that in Section 4 they will learn about the influence of market forces on price. **OL**

Focus

Bellringer
Daily Focus Transparency 21–1

Guide to Reading
Answers to Graphic:

```
                Price
              /       \
          Rises        Falls
            |            |
        Effect:       Effect:
        Demand        Demand
        Falls         Rises
```

Section Spotlight Video

To generate student interest and provide a springboard for class discussion, access the Chapter 21, Section 1 video at glencoe.com or on the video DVD.

Resource Manager

 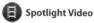

Guide to Reading

Big Idea
Supply and demand in a market interact to determine price and quantities bought and sold.

Content Vocabulary
- demand *(p. 569)*
- demand schedule *(p. 569)*
- demand curve *(p. 569)*
- law of demand *(p. 569)*
- market demand *(p. 570)*
- utility *(p. 570)*
- marginal utility *(p. 572)*

Academic Vocabulary
- identify *(p. 570)*
- illustrate *(p. 572)*
- likewise *(p. 572)*

Reading Strategy
Analyzing As you read the section, complete the diagram below to illustrate how change in prices affects the quantity demanded.

```
         Price:
         /     \
     Rises      Falls
       |          |
    Effect:    Effect:
```

Section **1**

Demand

Real World Economics With recent heating and oil prices at all-time highs, people began to look for alternative sources of heat. All across New England—especially—people are turning to wood as fuel, and the price for it has risen. Reed's Firewood in Durham, Maine, supplies its customers who want to supplement their heating sources and to use wood as backup if their power goes out. As wood use increases over time, its price will rise more, and consequently, its demand will diminish.

▼ **Paul Reed, Sr., loads firewood for customers in Maine**

R Reading Strategies	**C** Critical Thinking	**D** Differentiated Instruction	**W** Writing Support	**S** Skill Practice
Teacher Edition • Identifying, p. 569 • Making Connections, p. 571 **Additional Resources** • Cont. Vocab., URB p. 88 • Ac. Vocab., URB p. 89 • Foldables, p. 91 • RENTG, p. 203	**Teacher Edition** • Making Inferences, p. 569 • Compare/Contrast, p. 570 **Additional Resources** • Crit. Think. Act., URB p. 95 • Quizzes and Tests, p. 248	**Teacher Edition** • Interpersonal, p. 572 **Additional Resources** • Speak./Listen. Act., URB p. 9 • Diff. Instr., URB p. 99	**Teacher Edition** • Personal Writing, p. 570 **Additional Resources** • Writing Skills Act., URB p. 93	**Teacher Edition** • Reading Charts, p. 571 **Additional Resources** • Daily Focus Trans., 21–1

An Introduction to Demand

Main Idea Demand is the desire, willingness, and ability to buy a good or service.

Economics & You Do your ears perk up when something you want goes on sale? Read to find out which economic principle is at work.

What is **demand?** In economics, it refers to the desire, willingness, and ability to buy a good or service. For demand to exist, a consumer must *want* a good or service. The consumer has to be *willing* to buy the good or service. Finally, the consumer needs the *resources* to buy it.

The Individual Demand Schedule

When you buy something, do you wonder why it sells at a particular price? A **demand schedule** is a table that lists the various quantities of a product or service that someone is willing to buy over a range of prices. Look at the demand schedule on page 571. It shows how many video games a person—we will call him Ryan—would be willing to buy at different prices. For example, Ryan would not purchase any video games if they cost $50 each. If the price were $20 per game, though, he would be willing to buy two.

The Individual Demand Curve

Demand can also be shown graphically. A **demand curve** is a graph that shows the amount of a product that would be bought at all possible prices in the market. The curve is drawn with prices on the vertical axis and quantities on the horizontal axis. Each point on the curve shows how many units of the product or service an individual will buy at a particular price.

Look at the demand curve on page 571. Notice that each point on the graph matches the quantity listed in the demand schedule.

Desire to Buy New technology for video games available at computer stores is always in high demand. ***Explaining*** How does the price of an item affect the demand?

Ryan would buy five video games if the price were $5 each, three games at $10 each, and so on.

The Law of Demand

Look at the graph again. As you see, demand curves usually slope downward because people are normally willing to buy less of a product if the price is high and more of it if the price is low. According to the **law of demand,** quantity demanded and price move in opposite directions. This is the way people behave in everyday life. People ordinarily do buy more of a product at a low price than at a high price. All we have to do is to observe the increased traffic and purchases at the mall whenever there is a sale. This is just common sense. Are you not more interested in buying more of something when the price is lower than when the price is higher?

Reading Check ***Comparing*** Describe the relationship between the demand schedule and the demand curve.

Teach

R Reading Strategy

Identifying Ask: What factors are necessary to create demand for goods and services? *(consumer desire, willingness, and ability to buy)* **OL**

C Critical Thinking

Making Inferences Ask: When a store advertises a sale, what can you infer about their goods? *(They have too many.)* **OL**

Caption Answer:
Price affects the ability and willingness of consumers to buy goods and services. Higher prices decrease demand for goods and services. Lower prices increase demand for goods and services.

Reading Check **Answer:** The demand curve is a graphic illustration of the demand schedule.

Differentiated Instruction

Leveled Activities

BL **Academic Vocabulary Activity 21, URB p. 89**

OL **Writing Skills Activity 21, URB pp. 93–94**

AL **Speaking/Listening Activity 6, URB pp. 9–11**

ELL **Content Vocabulary Activity 21, URB p. 88**

C Critical Thinking

Compare and Contrast Ask: What do individual demand and market demand have in common? *(Both measure demand for a product or service.)* How do individual demand and market demand differ? *(Individual demand measures only the demand of a single individual for a product or service. Market demand measures the total demand of all consumers for a product or service.)* **OL**

W Writing Support

Personal Writing Have students write a paragraph about a product from which they get a great deal of enjoyment and a second paragraph about a product from which they get very little enjoyment. Make sure students explain why they do or do not enjoy each product. **OL**

TIME™ Teens in *Action*

Answers: Answers may vary, but most students will probably say that it is important for young readers to see how words are written as well as to hear how they are pronounced.

Hands-On Chapter Project
Step 1

Demand and Supply in a Market Economy

Step 1: Big Sellers of Yesteryear Have groups of students identify and research the history of best-selling products from the past.

Directions Organize students into groups to research the histories of best-selling products from the past, such as the hula hoop or the Model T automobile. Make sure student groups have selected different products. Have students prepare oral reports about their products. Remind students to include information on how the products were first received by consumers, what factors contributed to their appeal, and for how long the products maintained their popularity. **OL**

(Project continued in Section 2)

TIME™ Teens in *Action*

Daniel Lawrence

Daniel Lawrence, 15, of Knoxville, Tennessee, did not have to read between the lines to see that his city had a literacy problem. He decided to help out!

QUESTION: Why did you start "Let Me Read to You"?

ANSWER: Inner-city schools in Knoxville ask parents to read to younger children every night. Many of these students live in homes where this request is not met—either because parents can't read, or they don't have the time or energy to read to their children. "Let Me Read to You" was founded in 2005 to help.

Q: How does it work?

A: Commercial audiobooks already exist—but these families can't afford them. So our organization records early reader books onto CDs and donates the books and CDs to inner-city schools. The students are typically in first through third grades. They can read and hear the books at school or take them home for the night.

Q: How will the CDs help these kids?

A: They help them develop good reading skills—a very important thing in today's world. These students will have a better chance to succeed in life.

Q: What's next?

A: Once in high school I am going to start a program to fight Knoxville's litter problem.

Making a Difference

CITIZENSHIP

Daniel's group helped children look at the books and listen to them. Why do you think both looking and listening are important?

Market Demand

Main Idea Market demand is the total demand of all consumers for a product or service.

Economics & You Does your ninth slice of pizza taste just as good as the first? Read to find out what economic principle this example illustrates.

So far we have been looking at only one person's demand for a product or service. Companies hope to sell to many people, though. They are interested in the **market demand**—the total demand of all consumers for their product or service. Market demand can also be shown as a demand schedule or as a demand curve (see page 571).

An Example of Demand

Imagine you are opening a bicycle repair shop. Before you begin, you need to know where the demand is. You want to set up your shop in a neighborhood with many bicycle riders and few repair shops. After you **identify**, or establish, an area in which to locate the shop, how do you measure the demand for your services? You may visit other shops and gauge the reactions of consumers to different prices. You may poll consumers about prices. You could study data compiled over past years, which would show consumer reactions to prices. All of these methods would give you a general idea as to the desire, willingness, and ability of people to pay.

Marginal Utility

Almost everything that we buy provides **utility**, meaning the pleasure, usefulness, or satisfaction we get from using the product. The utility of a good or service may vary from one person to the next. For example, you may get a great deal of enjoyment from a home computer, but your friend may get very little. A good or service does not have to have utility for everyone, only for some.

The Law of Demand

Individual Demand Schedule	
Price per video game	Quantity
$50	0
$40	1
$30	1
$20	2
$10	3
$ 5	5

Individual Demand Curve

R

Market Demand Schedule	
Price per video game	Total Quantity Demanded
$50	100
$40	150
$30	180
$20	230
$10	300
$ 5	400

Market Demand Curve

S

Analyzing Charts and Graphs

1. **Calculating** How many video games is the market willing to purchase at a price of $30? What happens to market demand if the price falls to $20 per video game?

2. **Explaining** The demand curve is the graphic representation of the law of demand. Why does the demand curve slope downward?

Chapter 21   571

R Reading Strategy

Making Connections Ask: Why would an individual be willing to buy only one video game for $40 but five at $5? (*The individual is able to get more for the money when the video games cost less.*) BL ELL

S Skill Practice

Reading Charts Ask: How many video games is the market willing to purchase at a price of $10? (*300*) OL

Analyzing Charts and Graphs

Answers:

1. 180; market demand for video games increases to 230 if the price drops to $20.

2. Demand curves usually slope downward because people are normally willing to buy less of a product if the price is high and more of it if the price is low.

Differentiated Instruction

Enrichment Activity 6

Enrichment Activity 6,
URB pp. 13–14

Objective: To understand the law of demand and supply

Focus: Explore factors affecting demand in the real estate market.

Teach: Discuss the real estate markets in Detroit and Las Vegas.

Assess: Students should list factors affecting the real estate market in Detroit.

Close: Have students research Detroit's current real estate market, then compare and contrast it with 2005.

Differentiated Instruction Strategies

BL Explain how a rapidly increasing population, such as in Las Vegas, affects an area's housing market.

AL Name a real estate market with high property values and identify the factors supporting those property values.

ELL Explain the differences between a robust real estate market and a volatile one.

D Differentiated Instruction

Interpersonal Have groups of students discuss their experiences with diminishing marginal utility. Do they experience this only when consuming food? When watching a movie more than once? If they purchased the same shirt many times? Have students explain their responses. **OL**

✔ **Reading Check Answer:** Individual demand is the desire and ability of an individual to buy a product or service. Market demand is the total demand of all consumers.

Assess

Civics ONLINE

Study Central™ provides summaries, interactive games, and online graphic organizers to help students review.

Close

Identifying List the following items on the board: my favorite DVD; 2008 passenger cars; Ipods; a new swimsuit; a snack; food for my cat. Ask students to work in pairs to determine if each item represents individual demand or market demand. **OL**

Section 1 Review

Diminishing Marginal Utility

Our satisfaction usually changes as we consume more of a particular product. For example, when eating pizza, you may be very hungry before you eat the first slice, and so it will give you the most satisfaction. Because you are not quite as hungry after eating the first slice, you receive less **marginal utility,** or additional satisfaction, from each additional slice that you eat. This **illustrates,** or shows, diminishing marginal utility—the principle that our additional satisfaction, or our marginal utility, tends to go down as more units are consumed.

This concept is not something you consciously call marginal utility in your mind when you do it, but it is part of your thought processes. If the extra benefits (the marginal utility) to be gained are greater than the marginal cost (the money given up or paid) then we make the purchase. Otherwise we keep our money.

Because our marginal utility diminishes when we consume more of a product, it stands to reason that we would not be as willing to pay as much for the second item as we did for the first. **Likewise,** we would not be willing to pay as much for the third item as we did for the second. When the demand curve slopes downward, it simply tells us that we would be willing to pay the highest price for the first unit we consume, a slightly lower price for the next, an even lower price for the third, and so on.

✔ **Reading Check Comparing** What is the difference between individual demand and market demand?

Section 1 Review

Vocabulary

1. **Write** a sentence for each of these terms that helps explain its meaning: *demand, demand schedule, demand curve, law of demand, market demand, utility, marginal utility.*

Main Ideas

2. **Explaining** What is the law of demand?

3. **Comparing** What is the difference between a demand schedule and a demand curve?

Critical Thinking

4. **Analyzing** Explain how the principle of diminishing marginal utility is related to the law of demand.

5. **BIG Ideas** On a diagram like the one below, identify a relatively rare good or service today that you think will be in very high demand in 20 years. Provide at least two reasons for your prediction.

Good or Service	
Reason 1	
Reason 2	

6. **Analyzing Visuals** Study the schedule and graph illustrating the law of demand on page 571. What is the quantity demanded at $40? What happens to the total quantity demanded as the price increases?

CITIZENSHIP Activity

7. **Interview** a local merchant to determine the demand for a particular product or service at a specific period of time. Present your findings in graph form. Write a paragraph explaining what factors most affected demand for the product or service.

8. **Expository Writing** Suppose the boss of a company you work for has asked you how to estimate the demand for a new product the company is introducing. Write a memo outlining how you would approach this assignment.

Civics ONLINE

Study Central™ To review this section, go to glencoe.com.

Answers

1. Sentences should use vocabulary words according to their definitions in the section and in the Glossary.

2. The law of demand is the principle that overall demand and price move in opposite directions. Higher prices lead to decreased demand, and lower prices lead to increased demand.

3. A demand schedule is a table that lists the various quantities of products or services at the prices that consumers are willing to pay.

A demand curve is a graphic illustration of the demand schedule.

4. Diminishing marginal utility stipulates that consumer satisfaction diminishes with greater consumption of a product or service. This leads to a decrease in demand for the product or service.

5. Answers will vary. Possible answers may include: **Good or Service**—Gasoline. **Reason 1**—It is a limited natural resource for which there is high demand. **Reason 2**—

This resource is found in some politically unstable areas of the world.

6. The Market Demand Schedule shows a demand of 150 video games at a price of $40. As the price per video increases the total quantity demanded decreases.

7. Interview information with graphs and explanatory paragraphs will vary.

8. Memos outlining an approach to this assignment will vary.

Guide to Reading

Main Idea
Supply and demand in a market interact to determine price and the quantities bought and sold.

Content Vocabulary
- substitute *(p. 575)*
- complement *(p. 576)*
- demand elasticity *(p. 577)*

Academic Vocabulary
- immigration *(p. 574)*
- phenomenon *(p. 577)*

Reading Strategy
Organizing As you read the section, complete a diagram like the one below by identifying six factors that affect demand.

Factors Affecting Demand

🔊 **Section Audio**   🎬 **Spotlight Video**

Factors Affecting Demand

Real World Economics "Back-to-school" for college students means big business for some retailers. While sales in some areas of the home furnishings business in America may be weak, companies that cater to back-to-school shoppers do not suffer from the effects of high energy prices or slower housing sales. Each fall, when thousands of students return to school, stores that sell items such as desk supplies, computers, and dorm-room furnishings can count on a high demand.

▼ **College student in Texas tests possible dorm chair's comfort**

573

Focus

Bellringer
Daily Focus Transparency 21–2

Guide to Reading
Answers to Graphic:

Changes in population

Changes in income

Changes in tastes

Factors Affecting Demand

Changes in expectations

Changes in complements

Changes in substitutes

 Section Spotlight Video

To generate student interest and provide a springboard for class discussion, access the Chapter 21, Section 2 video at glencoe.com or on the video DVD.

Resource Manager

R Reading Strategies	**C** Critical Thinking	**D** Differentiated Instruction	**W** Writing Support	**S** Skill Practice
Teacher Edition • Identifying, p. 574 • Content Vocab., pp. 576, 577 • Inferring, p. 579 **Additional Resources** • Reading Skills Act., URB p. 7 • Foldables, p. 91 • RENTG., p. 206	**Teacher Edition** • Making Generalizations, pp. 574, 577 • Drawing Con., p. 574 • Making Inferences, p. 575 • Det. Cause/Effect, p. 576 **Additional Resources** • Crit. Think., URB p. 95 • Quizzes and Tests, p. 249	**Teacher Edition** • Below Grade Level, p. 578 **Additional Resources** • School-to-Home Act., URB p.101 • Reteach. Act., URB p.103	**Teacher Edition** • Narrative Writing, p. 575 **Additional Resources** • Enrich. Act., URB p. 13	**Teacher Edition** • Reading Graphs, p. 575 **Additional Resources** • Daily Focus Trans., 21–2

Teach

R Reading Strategy

Identifying Ask: What factors cause market demand to change? *(changes in the number of consumers, incomes, tastes, expectations, and the prices of related goods)* **OL**

C₁ Critical Thinking

Making Generalizations Ask: How will an area's increase in population influence demand for goods and services in a particular market area? *(It will increase demand for goods and services in the area.)* **OL**

C₂ Critical Thinking

Drawing Conclusions Ask: If the demand for goods and services experienced a sudden increase in one city, what could you conclude? *(The population had risen.)* **BL**

Caption Answer:
Overall market demand for that magazine would increase.

Differentiated Instruction

Changes in Demand

Main Idea Several different factors can cause market demand for a good or service to change.

Economics & You Can you remember a toy that you absolutely had to have when you were younger? Read to find out how a product's popularity affects demand.

The demand for any product or service is not the same over time. Sometimes people are willing to buy higher quantities of a good or a service at a particular price. At other times they are less willing to do so. As a result, demand can increase or decrease.

Why Does Demand Change?

Several factors cause market demand to change. Market demand can change when more consumers enter the market. Market demand can also change when the incomes, tastes, and expectations of the consumers in the market change. Finally, changes in the prices of related goods affect demand.

Demand and Choice The huge variety of magazines produced is made possible by consumer tastes. *Predicting* What would happen to demand if there were only one magazine about a particular topic?

These changes can all be graphed using a market demand curve. When demand goes down, people are willing to buy fewer items at all possible prices (see the graph showing a decrease in demand on page 575). In this case, the demand curve shifts to the left. When demand goes up, people are willing to buy more of the same item at any given price. This pushes the entire demand curve to the right. Look at the graph on page 575 that shows an increase in demand.

What Determines Demand?

Demand curves do not shift to the right or left without cause. They shift because of changes in income, preferences, price of related goods, and changes in population. You as a consumer need to be aware of these factors.

Changes in Population Demand for a good in a particular market area is related to the number of consumers in the area. More people means the higher the demand; the smaller the population, the lower the demand.

For example, suppose a company puts up a new apartment building and the building is soon filled with families. These new residents begin to buy products and services from area businesses. As a result, demand for gasoline, food, and video rentals in this area will go up. In this case, the demand curve will shift to the right.

The same factor can cause a change in the opposite direction. When many people move out of an area, demand in that area for goods and services goes down. Here the demand curve shifts to the left.

Why Population Changes The number of consumers in a particular market area may change for a number of reasons. A higher birthrate or increased **immigration**—the arrival of people from another region—increases the number of consumers. Factors such as a higher death rate or the migration of people out of a region can also cause the number of consumers to fall.

Leveled Activities

BL School-to-Home Activity 21, URB pp. 101–102

OL Crit. Thinking Skills Activity 21, URB pp. 95–96

AL Enrichment Activity 6, URB pp. 13–14

ELL Guided Reading Activity 21-2, URB p. 106

Changes in Income Demand also changes when consumers' incomes change. When the economy is healthy, people receive raises or move to better-paying jobs. With more money to spend, they are willing to buy more of a product at any particular price. **C**

The opposite can happen, too. In hard times, people lose their jobs. They have less money to spend, so demand goes down.

Changes in Tastes Changing tastes and fading popularity of a product can affect demand as well. When a product becomes popular, the demand curve shifts to the right. More people are willing to buy the product at a particular price. We often see this during the holiday shopping season when a new product becomes the "must-buy" of the year. **W**

Many products, though, fade in popularity over time. When that happens, fewer are sold at a particular price, and the demand curve shifts to the left.

Changes in Expectations Expectations refer to the way people think about the future. For example, suppose that a leading maker of audio products announces a technological breakthrough that would allow more music to be recorded on a smaller disk at a lower cost than before. Even if the new product might not be available for another year, some consumers might decide to buy fewer music CDs today because they want to wait for the new product.

Expectations can also affect demand in another way. In late 2001, following the September 11 terrorist attacks, people were worried about the economy. As a result, they were less willing to spend money on holiday gifts. The demand for goods was reduced.

Expectations can also force demand higher. If people expect a shortage of a good, such as gasoline, they tend to stock up and demand increases. This shifts the demand curve to the right.

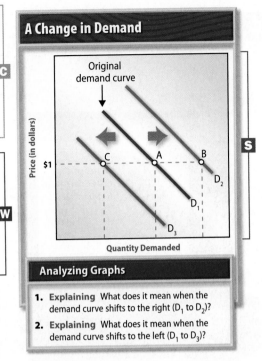

A Change in Demand

Original demand curve

Price (in dollars)

$1

C   A   B

D₂

D₁

D₃

Quantity Demanded

Analyzing Graphs

1. **Explaining** What does it mean when the demand curve shifts to the right (D₁ to D₂)?

2. **Explaining** What does it mean when the demand curve shifts to the left (D₁ to D₃)?

S

Product-Related Changes

You have learned that demand curves do not shift to the right or left without cause. Factors that also affect demand are related to the products themselves.

Demand can be influenced by changes in the price or quality of related products. The demand for older computers falls when new models with faster processors come out. The demand for a certain brand of tire may increase when another tire has safety problems.

Price of Related Goods

The demand for a good is affected by the prices of related goods. There are two types of related goods; substitutes and complements. Competing products are called **substitutes** because consumers can use one in place of the other.

(Project continued in Section 3)

C **Critical Thinking**

Making Inferences Ask: When consumer spending decreases, what can this tell us about general expectations for the economy? (*Reduced consumer spending often indicates a poor economy.*) **OL**

W **Writing Support**

Narrative Writing Have students write a one-page story about a product that became popular at school. Remind students they may write about the subject from many different angles. The stories may detail the rise and fall of the product's popularity. They might illustrate the effect the product had on the school. They might portray a character's effort to obtain the product. Tell students the tone of their stories may be realistic or exaggerated. **AL**

S **Skill Practice**

Reading Graphs Ask: What is the original asking price for the good in the graph? (*$1*) **BL**

Analyzing Graphs

Answers:
1. Demand is increasing.
2. Demand is decreasing.

Hands-On Chapter Project
Step 2

Demand and Supply in a Market Economy

Step 2: The Secret of Their Success Have student groups organize information about factors influencing the success of their best-selling products from the past.

Directions Write the Big Idea on the board. Tell students to research information about factors that may have influenced the popularity of the products they reported on in Step 1. What changes in the population may have influenced demand for their products? What was the state of the general economy at the time of its popularity? What were the overall trends in taste and expectations when the products were popular? Have groups make lists of the most important factors that affected demand for their products from the past.

Summarizing Have each group present its lists to the class. Ask students to compare the factors influencing the success of each group's best-selling product. Have volunteers share what they learned about the Big Idea while preparing their lists. **OL**

(Project continued in Section 3)

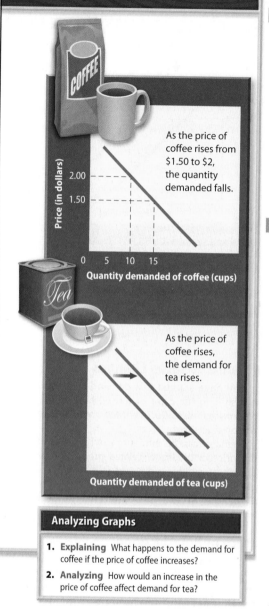

Change in Demand for Substitutes

As the price of coffee rises from $1.50 to $2, the quantity demanded falls.

Price (in dollars)

2.00

1.50

0 5 10 15

Quantity demanded of coffee (cups)

As the price of coffee rises, the demand for tea rises.

Quantity demanded of tea (cups)

Analyzing Graphs

1. **Explaining** What happens to the demand for coffee if the price of coffee increases?
2. **Analyzing** How would an increase in the price of coffee affect demand for tea?

Changes in Substitutes When two goods are substitutes, a change in the price of one good causes the demand for the other good to move in the *same* direction. For example, for many people, butter is a substitute for margarine. If the price of margarine increases, the demand for butter also increases (shifts to the right).

Changes in Complements Some products are **complements**—they are used together. For example, computers and software are complements. With complementary goods, the demand for one moves in the opposite direction as the price of the other. So if computer prices rise, fewer computers will be demanded, and the demand for computer software will go down.

You can also see the same effect when the price goes down instead of up. When the price of DVD players goes down, more DVD players are demanded, which also results in an increase in the demand for DVDs. Other examples of complements (or complementary goods) include cars and gasoline, and lightbulbs and lamps.

A Change in Quantity Demanded

You learned that a change in demand refers to a shift in the *entire* demand curve. You learned that factors that can shift the demand curve include the number of buyers, income, taste, preferences, and price of related goods.

A change in quantity demanded refers to a movement from one point to another along a given demand curve. The only factor that can directly cause a change in the quantity of a good is a change in the price—its own price. For example, as shown here, the price of coffee increased from $1.50 to $2 per cup. The change in the price of coffee brings about a change in the quantity demanded.

Reading Check Comparing Are butter and margarine substitute goods? Why or why not?

Activity: Collaborative Learning

Logical/Mathematical Ask: What affects demand in a market economy? *(price)* Organize the class into small groups and have each group select a single product or service. Ask groups to research the current price for a particular product or service such as laptops or lawn mowing. Have students create a chart that includes information naming the product or service, its available prices, the average price for the product or service, and the greatest price difference. Have each group present their charts to the class. Encourage students to discuss their findings as they relate to the law of demand. **AL**

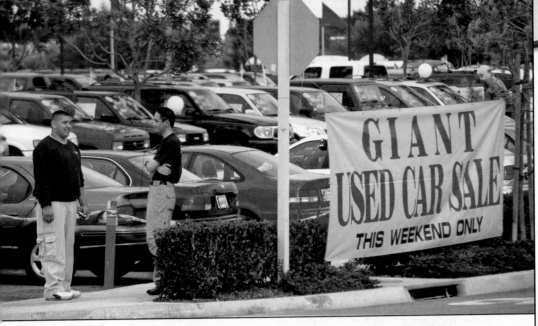

Demand Elasticity Auto sales can be affected by changes in price. *Explaining* If these young men purchase a car at a recently reduced price, how does the purchase illustrate the elasticity of demand?

Elasticity of Demand

Main Idea Demand elasticity is the extent to which a change in price causes a change in the quantity demanded.

Economics & You Does your family always have turkey at Thanksgiving? Read to find out what might happen if stores raised the price of turkey at Thanksgiving.

The law of demand states that price and quantity demanded move in opposite directions. If price goes up, quantity demanded goes down; and if price goes down, quantity demanded goes up.

Now suppose price goes up from $1 to $1.25, a 25 percent increase. We know that quantity demanded will go down, but we do not know by how much. Quantity demanded could go down by 25 percent, by less than 25 percent, or by more than 25 percent.

All products and services are not affected by these factors in the same way. Economists call this **phenomenon,** or rare occurrence, **R** **demand elasticity.** Demand elasticity is the extent to which a change in price causes a change in the quantity demanded.

Elastic Demand

For some goods and services, demand is elastic. This means that each change in price causes a relatively larger percentage of change in quantity demanded. For example, when automakers reduce car prices modestly, the quantity sold goes up greatly. When they raise the price of their cars, the quantity sold goes down a great deal.

When there are attractive substitutes for a good or service, demand tends to be elastic. That is because consumers can choose to buy the substitute. Expensive items generally **C** have elastic demand. That is because consumers are less willing to pay even more for goods that are expensive in the first place.

Chapter 21 577

D **Differentiated Instruction**

D **Differentiated Instruction**

Below Grade Level Tradition creates an inelastic demand for turkey during Thanksgiving. Have students think of other traditional items that may create an inelastic demand. *(roses and candy at Valentine's Day; sparklers and red, white, and blue items for the Fourth of July)* **OL**

✓**Reading Check** **Answer:** Insulin is a necessity. A person with diabetes must have insulin no matter the cost.

Assess

Civics ONLINE

Study Central™ provides summaries, interactive games, and online graphic organizers to help students review.

Close

Outlining Have students work in pairs to outline the various factors affecting demand. *(population changes; income increases or decreases; tastes; expectations; substitutes; complements).* **OL**

Section ★ 2 Review

Finally, demand is usually elastic when a purchase can be postponed until later. In this case, consumers delay buying the good or service in the hopes that the price will go down. Again, this usually happens when consumers are dealing with higher priced items.

Inelastic Demand

You know that demand for a good or service is elastic if it is very responsive to a change in price. For other goods and services, demand is inelastic. This means that price changes have little effect on the quantity demanded. For example, the demand for turkey at Thanksgiving tends to be inelastic. Many people make turkey a central part of their Thanksgiving meal. If supermarkets slightly raise the price of turkey, they would probably not lose many customers. At another time of year, higher turkey prices might cause consumers to purchase other meat products instead.

The demand for goods with very few or no substitutes, such as pepper, electricity, and some medicines, is likely to be inelastic. Heart medicine, for example, has relatively few substitutes; many people must have it to stay well. Even if the price of heart medicine doubled, quantity demanded probably would not fall by much.

Necessities and Luxuries Demand for heart medicine and food is inelastic because these are necessities. Necessities are goods that people need in order to survive. If the price of a necessity increases, people cannot cut back very much on the quantity demanded. However, demand for luxuries is likely to be elastic. If the price of a luxury good increases, buyers are more able to cut back on the quantity demanded.

✓**Reading Check** **Inferring** Why is the demand for insulin, a medicine for people with diabetes, inelastic?

Section 2 Review

Vocabulary

1. **Write** a paragraph in which you use each of these terms correctly: *substitute, complement, demand elasticity.*

Main Ideas

2. **Explaining** If income and population increase, what tends to happen to demand?

3. **Comparing** What is the distinction between elastic and inelastic demand?

Critical Thinking

4. **Concluding** Will products that are very important to us and that have no close substitutes have elastic or inelastic demand? Why? What is an example of such a product?

5. **BIG Ideas** Re-create the diagram below. Use arrows to indicate the direction of movement on the demand curve for tennis balls if the price of tennis rackets increases.

CITIZENSHIP Activity

6. **Research** Find an example of the law of demand or elasticity of demand in a newspaper or magazine article or advertisement. Share your findings with the class.

7. **Creative Writing** Working with a partner, write a dialogue between a store owner and a customer about some aspect of demand, as discussed in this section. Perform your dialogue with a partner for the class.

Study Central™ To review this section, go to glencoe.com.

Answers

1. Paragraphs should use the vocabulary words according to their definitions in the section and in the Glossary.
2. Demand increases.
3. Goods and services for which demand is very responsive to a change in price are those with elastic demand. Goods and services for which price has little effect are those with inelastic demand.

4. Inelastic demand; these products are necessities we must have. Medicines and utilities such as heat and water are examples of products with inelastic demand.
5. Tennis rackets and tennis balls are complementary products. The arrows should indicate movement to the left of the demand curve.

6. Answers will vary; students should explain how their articles or advertisements illustrate the law of demand.
7. Dialogues will vary; all should effectively illustrate an aspect of demand.

Writing a Résumé: Dos and Don'ts

A résumé is a brief summary of your abilities, education, experience, and skills. To get an employer's attention, prepare a one- to two-page résumé that highlights your talents and skills. Prevent it from landing in the recycle bin by keeping these ideas in mind. **R₁**

Résumé Dos

- Include your contact information.
- Make the layout easy to read.
- Highlight your special skills.
- Print your résumé on high-quality paper.
- Review your résumé for any grammar errors or other mistakes.
- Use action words to describe your experience and accomplishments.
- Always include a cover letter with your résumé. Get right to the point in your letter. State your employment goal and highlight reasons that you are qualified for the job. **C**

Résumé Don'ts

- Do not include any personal information such as your race, religion, family, or marital status.
- Do not use inaccurate dates or pad your résumé with things you have not actually done.
- Do not write long paragraphs; use bulleted lists instead.

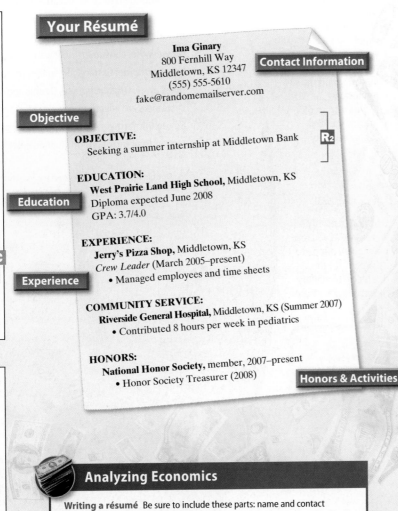

Your Résumé

Contact Information

Ima Ginary
800 Fernhill Way
Middletown, KS 12347
(555) 555-5610
fake@randomemailserver.com

Objective

OBJECTIVE: **R₂**
Seeking a summer internship at Middletown Bank

Education

EDUCATION:
West Prairie Land High School, Middletown, KS
Diploma expected June 2008
GPA: 3.7/4.0

Experience

EXPERIENCE:
Jerry's Pizza Shop, Middletown, KS
Crew Leader (March 2005–present)
- Managed employees and time sheets

COMMUNITY SERVICE:
Riverside General Hospital, Middletown, KS (Summer 2007)
- Contributed 8 hours per week in pediatrics

HONORS:
National Honor Society, member, 2007–present
- Honor Society Treasurer (2008)

Honors & Activities

Analyzing Economics

Writing a résumé Be sure to include these parts: name and contact information, objective statement (your career goals), education, professional experience, and skills.

Teach

R₁ Reading Strategy

Inferring Ask: What can we infer about a résumé that lands in the recycle bin? *(The job seeker did not get the job.)* **OL**

R₂ Reading Strategy

Organizing Ask: Which section of a résumé states the job seeker's career goals? *(objective)* **BL**

C Critical Thinking

Predicting Consequences Ask: What is the likely consequence of a long, rambling cover letter? *(Answers may vary, but many students will say that the employer may be too busy to read the entire letter.)* **OL**

Analyzing Economics

Answer: Résumés will vary, students should include all parts of the résumé and follow a standard format.

Additional Support

Activity: Collaborative Learning

Interpersonal: Ask: What is the key factor in being hired for a job? Remind students that performing well on a job interview is just as important as having an impressive résumé. Organize students into groups. Have each group brainstorm a list of job interview dos and don'ts. After students have compiled their lists, ask each group to write a short scene showing the correct and incorrect way to interview for a job. Have students perform their scenes. Encourage the class to revise their lists of dos and don'ts, incorporating the best ideas from each other's lists and scenes. **OL**

Focus

Bellringer
Daily Focus Transparency 21-3

Guide to Reading
Answers to Graphic:

Why Supply Changes

- Cost of Resources
- Productivity
- Technology
- Government Policies

Section Spotlight Video

To generate student interest and provide a springboard for class discussion, access the Chapter 21, Section 3 video at glencoe.com or on the video DVD.

Resource Manager

Guide to Reading

Big Idea
Supply and demand in a market interact to determine price and the quantities bought and sold.

Content Vocabulary
- supply *(p. 581)*
- law of supply *(p. 581)*
- supply schedule *(p. 581)*
- supply curve *(p. 583)*
- profit *(p. 583)*
- market supply *(p. 584)*
- productivity *(p. 585)*
- technology *(p. 585)*
- subsidy *(p. 585)*
- supply elasticity *(p. 586)*

Academic Vocabulary
- motive *(p. 583)*
- restrict *(p. 585)*

Reading Strategy
Organizing As you read the section, complete a diagram like the one below to identify the factors that affect supply.

Why Supply Changes

 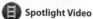
Supply and the Supply Curve

Real World Economics Organic farming is changing the face of American agriculture. Why? Because of the growing demand for its products from customers. In addition to concerns about pesticides that nonorganic growers use, consumers now want to "buy local" to avoid using extra fuel to transport food from thousands of miles away. Organic farmers Dennis and Sandy Dierks find customers are willing to pay extra for their organic produce. So organic farmers are reporting rising profits, which help recoup their increased production costs.

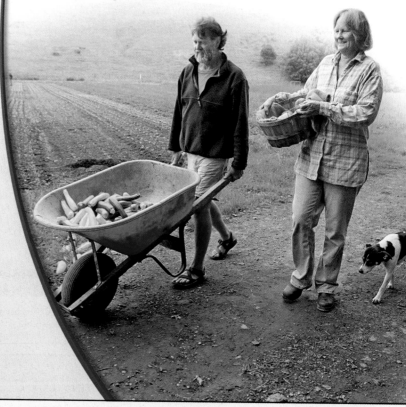

▼ **Dennis and Sandy Dierks harvest vegetables on their organic farm**

R Reading Strategies	**C** Critical Thinking	**D** Differentiated Instruction	**W** Writing Support	**S** Skill Practice
Teacher Edition • Making Connections, p. 581 • Predicting, p. 582 • Setting a Purpose, p. 583 **Additional Resources** • Ac. Vocab., URB p. 90 • Guid. Read., URB p. 107 • Foldables, p. 91	**Teacher Edition** • Drawing Con., p. 581 • Pred. Consequences, p. 584 • Det. Cause/Effect, p. 586 **Additional Resources** • Crit. Think. Act., URB p. 95 • Quizzes and Tests, p. 250	**Teacher Edition** • Logical/Math., p. 584 **Additional Resources** • Diff. Instr., URB p. 99 • Reteach Act., URB p. 103	**Teacher Edition** • Persuasive Writing, p. 585 **Additional Resources** • Enrich. Act., URB p.13 • Writing Skills Act., URB p. 93	**Teacher Edition** • Reading Graphs and Charts, pp. 582, 583 **Additional Resources** • Daily Focus Trans., 21–3

Supply and Choice Consumers must choose from a huge number of snack foods, each with a different price and nutritional value. **Comparing** What do you think affects the supply of snack foods the most—the price or ingredients? Why?

An Introduction to Supply

Main Idea Supply is the quantities of a good or service that producers are willing to sell at all possible market prices.

Economics & You If you were paid overtime, would you want to work extra hours? Read to find out what economic theory is at work.

What is supply? **Supply** refers to the various quantities of a good or service that producers are willing to sell at all possible market prices. Supply normally refers to the output of a single business or producer. However, it is also possible to add together the supply of all producers to get the supply for the entire market.

Supply is the opposite of demand. Buyers demand different quantities of a good depending on the price sellers ask. Suppliers offer different quantities of a product depending on the price buyers are willing to pay.

The Law of Supply

Remember that as the price rises for a good, the quantity demanded goes down. As the price of a good goes down, the quantity demanded rises. The quantity supplied also varies according to price—but in the opposite direction. As the price rises for a good, the quantity supplied rises. As the price falls, the quantity supplied also falls. This is the **law of supply,** the principle that suppliers will normally offer more for sale at higher prices and less at lower prices. The higher the price of a good, the greater the incentive is for a producer to produce more.

We can represent the law of supply with numbers, just as we did with the law of demand. The table at the top left of page 582 shows this. As the price goes up from $5 to $10 to $20 and to $50, the quantity supplied goes up from 1 to 10 to 30 and to 100. Producers create more items in the hopes of selling more at the higher price. A numerical chart that illustrates the law of supply is called a **supply schedule.**

✓ **Reading Check** **Explaining** What does a supply schedule show?

Chapter 21 **581**

Teach

C Critical Thinking

Drawing Conclusions Remind students that as the price of a good rises, consumer demand for the good decreases. However, as the price of a good rises, businesses have an increased incentive to produce the good. **Ask:** How might these two factors interact with each other in a market economy? *(These two factors create a constant fluctuation between price, supply, and demand.)* **OL**

R Reading Strategy

Making Connections **Ask:** Why do suppliers ask different prices for products? *(to determine how much buyers are willing to pay)* **OL**

Caption Answer:
Ingredients. The total cost of ingredients used to make the snack food will affect the overall price of the product.

✓ **Reading Check** **Answer:** A supply schedule is a numerical chart that shows the various quantities of a good or service that producers are willing to sell at all possible market prices.

Differentiated Instruction

Leveled Activities

BL Reteaching Activity 21, URB p. 103

OL Academic Vocabulary Activity 21, URB p. 90

AL Diff. Instruction Activity 21, URB pp. 99–100

ELL Guided Reading Activity 21-3, URB p. 107

581

R Reading Strategy

Predicting Ask: What would most likely happen to the total quantity supplied if the price per video game went from $50 to $100? *(the total quantity would increase)* **BL**

S Skill Practice

Reading Charts Ask: As the price per video game rises from $30 each to $40 each, does the market supply more videos or less? *(more)* How many more videos does the market supply? *(45)* **OL**

Analyzing Charts and Graphs

Answers:

1. Higher prices create more incentive for producers to supply greater quantities of goods and services. Lower prices reduce incentive for producers to supply greater quantities of goods and services.

2. As prices rise, producers supply greater quantities of goods and services.

The Law of Supply

R

Supply Schedule	
Price per video game	Quantity
$50	100
$40	90
$30	70
$20	30
$10	10
$5	1

Software House's Supply Curve

S

Market Supply Schedule	
Price per video game	Total Quantity Supplied
$50	275
$40	225
$30	180
$20	105
$10	55
$5	30

Market Supply Curve

Analyzing Charts and Graphs

1. **Describing** What is the relationship between the price of a good and the quantity supplied?

2. **Explaining** The supply curve is the graphic representation of the law of supply. Why does the supply curve slope upward?

Differentiated Instruction

Diff. Instruction Act. 21, URB pp. 99–100

A Demand for Change

Objective:	To understand the interaction between supply and demand
Focus:	Predict the effect of oil supplies on demand for fuel-efficient vehicles.
Teach:	Review the line graphs on page 99.
Assess:	Have students write two sentences summarizing each graph's information.
Close:	Have students write paragraphs explaining how the two line graphs illustrate supply and demand.

Differentiated Instruction Strategies

BL How does the trend in sales of hybrid vehicles compare with the trend in gasoline prices on the line graphs?

AL Research world supply of oil and demand for oil by major industrial nations. Then create a graph showing supply and demand for oil.

ELL Explain the use of hyphens in compound words such as "gas-electric."

Graphing the Supply Curve

Main Idea As with the law of demand, special tables and graphs can show the law of supply.

Economics & You Suppose you own a company that sells television sets and the price of a set falls from $500 to $400. Would you want to supply more or fewer TV sets? Read on to find how the law of supply operates.

You have learned that we can represent the law of supply in a numerical chart called a supply schedule. We can also illustrate the law of supply with a graph.

The Individual Supply Curve

A **supply curve** is a graph that shows the amount of a product that would be supplied at all possible prices in the market.

Like the demand curve, the supply curve graph is drawn with prices on the vertical axis and quantities on the horizontal axis. In the supply curve on the previous page, the quantities are the amounts of the good or service that the business will supply. Unlike the demand curve, the supply curve slopes upward. This reflects the fact that suppliers are generally willing to offer more goods and services at a higher price and fewer at a lower price.

The Profit Motive

Businesses invest time, money, and other capital resources to make money. Businesses try to set prices at a level that allows them to cover their costs. If they do not, they will lose money.

In our economy, businesses provide goods and services, hoping to make a **profit.** Profit is the money a business receives for its products or services *over and above* its costs. It is a primary **motive,** or purpose, in business.

Changes in Supply When a leak was discovered in this oil pipeline in Prudhoe Bay, Alaska, the BP company shut it down. ***Describing*** How could this shutdown affect the price and supply of oil?

583

Hands-On Chapter Project
Step 3

D Differentiated Instruction

Logical/Mathematical Tell students the Daily Bread Bakery produces a popular whole wheat bread. It costs the bakery 79 cents to make each loaf of bread.
Ask: What is the least amount of money the bakery must charge per loaf to make a profit? *(80 cents)* **OL**

C Critical Thinking

Predicting Consequences Ask: What will happen to a business in which the producers keep all the profits for themselves? *(If some of the profits are not put back into the business, the business will not grow and may eventually fail.)* **OL**

✔ **Reading Check** **Answer:** Price is the most important factor, with suppliers preferring to produce more at a higher price.

Analyzing Charts

Answers:
1. The quantity has decreased.
2. to the right—new technology is usually in demand by consumers

---

Additional Support

D If it costs Software House $40 to make a video game and it sells the game for $40, the company gains nothing from the sale. Making money on the sale requires selling the game for more than $40. The additional money is the owner's profit.

C Producers can choose to use their profits in many different ways. They can increase wages, invest the money in the business, acquire more space, buy new equipment, or hire new workers. They can also keep the money for themselves.

Market Supply

The total of all consumers' demand is called the market demand. If you combine the supply schedules of all the businesses that provide the same good or service, the total is called the **market supply.**

An Upward Slope The figure on page 582 shows the market supply for video games in one community. Notice that the market supply for all producers is larger than the supply for the Software House alone. (Compare the graphs on page 582.) Still, the market supply curve has the same shape as the individual supply curve. The upward slope shows that all of the producers in the market would prefer to sell more video games at higher prices and fewer games at lower prices.

Price and Other Factors Keep in mind that the price is the most significant influence on the quantity supplied of any product. For example, you are offering your services for sale when you look for a job. Your economic product is your labor, and you would probably be willing to supply more labor for a high wage, or price, than you would for a low one.

However, other factors affect supply. The supply curve is drawn assuming that these and other things are fixed and do not change. If any of these factors do change, a change in supply will occur.

✔ **Reading Check** **Explaining** How is market supply determined?

Changes in Supply

Main Idea Supply increases or decreases depending on many different factors.

Economics & You Would you expect to pay a high price for a tomato if it were the only one in the whole grocery store? Read to find out why that tomato would probably be costly.

Just like demand, supply can increase or decrease, depending on many different factors.

Why Does Supply Change?

The profit incentive is a factor that motivates people in a market economy which pushes other factors. For a change in supply to take place, producers must decide to offer a different quantity of output at each possible price in the market.

Shifts in the Supply Curve

Analyzing Charts

1. **Explaining** What does it mean when the supply curve shifts to the left?
2. **Deducing** In what direction would new technology push the supply curve? Explain.

Activity: Economics Connection

Converting a Supply Schedule into a Supply Curve Remind students that price affects supply in a market economy. Ask students to use the information in the supply schedule to create supply curve graphs. Have students use graph paper to create their supply curves. *(Supply curves should resemble model on this page.)* **OL**

Supply Schedule	
Price Per Stereo Shelf System	**Quantity**
$200	300
$150	225
$100	150
$75	80
$50	30
$30	1

When supply goes down, the supply curve moves to the left. When supply goes up, the supply curve is pushed to the right. This means suppliers are willing to sell a larger quantity of goods and services at the original price and all other prices. You can see these changes in the figure on page 584.

Factors that can affect supply include the following:

- **The Cost of Resources** When the prices of resources used to produce goods and services fall, production costs fall. Sellers are able to produce and sell more of the good. When resource prices rise, sellers are less able to produce and sell the same quantities of the good because production costs rise.
- **Productivity** When workers are more productive, a company's costs go down. More products are produced at every price. When productivity falls, it costs more for a company to produce the same amount of goods and services.
- **Technology** Technology refers to the methods, or processes, used to make goods and services. New technology can speed up ways of doing things and cut a business's costs. The business is willing to supply more goods and services at the same price.
- **Government Policies** In general, increased government regulations **restrict**, or limit, supply, causing the supply curve to shift to the left. A rise in the minimum wage or new safety requirements in cars can result in higher production costs, which, in turn, lead to lower production levels. **W**
- **Taxes** To businesses, higher taxes mean higher costs, pushing the supply curve to the left. Lower taxes—lower costs— move the supply curve to the right.

Civics ONLINE

Student Web Activity Visit glencoe.com and complete the Chapter 21 Web Activity.

- **Subsidies** A **subsidy** is a government payment to an individual, business, or other group for certain actions. Subsidies lower the cost of production. When subsidies are repealed, costs go up, and the supply curve shifts to the left.
- **Expectations** If businesses believe that consumer demand will not be very high in the near future, they will produce less of their products. If they expect demand to go up, they will produce more at all possible prices.
- **Number of Suppliers** The larger the number of suppliers, the greater the market supply. If some suppliers leave the market, market supply decreases, shifting the curve to the left.

Reading Check **Explaining** How does productivity affect supply?

Quality Control An inspector at the Indian Motorcycle plant in California works at the end of the assembly line. *Analyzing* **What happens to company costs if workers at the plant are more productive?**

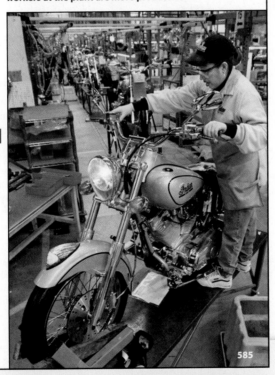

585

W Writing Support

Persuasive Writing Have students research a government business regulation and write an editorial arguing for or against the regulation. If writing in favor, students should explain why the benefits outweigh the costs. If writing against, students should explain why higher production is of greater value than the benefits of the regulation. **AL**

Civics ONLINE

Objectives and answers to the **Student Web Activity** can be found at glencoe.com under the Web Activity Lesson Plan for this chapter.

Reading Check **Answer:** Increased productivity lowers production costs, which leads to increased supply.

Caption Answer:
When workers are more productive, company costs go down.

Additional Support

Activity: Collaborative Learning

Analyzing Information Ask: Why does the U.S. government subsidize oil companies? Have students research the issues around government subsidies for oil companies. Organize students into groups to present information to the class on various aspects of the question: record oil profits; incentives to oil companies to build refiner-

ies and to search for oil; disincentives to create renewable, environmentally friendly energy and energy-efficient products.

After the groups have presented their information, poll the class about whether they agree or disagree that the government should subsidize oil companies. Encourage students to explain their positions. **AL**

C Critical Thinking

Determining Cause and Effect Ask:
What makes a product supply inelastic? *(the inability of producers to quickly increase supply of the product in response to higher demand and increased prices)* OL

✓ **Reading Check Answer:** the ability of producers to quickly increase product supply in response to increased demand and higher prices

Assess

Civics ONLINE

Study Central™ provides summaries, interactive games, and online graphic organizers to help students review.

Close

Determining Importance Have students discuss the role of supply in a market economy. *(It plays an important role in determining the price and quantities of products and services bought and sold.)* OL

Section ★ 3 Review

Elasticity of Supply

Main Idea Supply elasticity measures how the quantity supplied of a good or service changes in response to changes in price.

Economics & You What is the price of a gallon of gasoline right now? Read to find out why gasoline producers react slowly to a change in the price of gas.

Like demand, supply can be elastic or inelastic. **Supply elasticity** is a measure of how the quantity supplied of a good or service changes in response to changes in price. If the quantity changes a great deal when prices go up or down, the product is said to be supply elastic. It is elastic in the sense that like a piece of elastic it can expand out or decrease in size. If the quantity changes very little, the supply is inelastic.

Supply elasticity depends on how quickly a company can change the amount of a product it makes in response to price changes. For example, oil is supply inelastic. When oil prices go up, oil companies cannot quickly dig a new well, build a pipeline to move the oil, and build a refinery to turn it into gasoline. The same is true of other products that require producers to invest large sums of money in order to produce them.

The supply curve is likely to be elastic, however, for kites, candy, and other products that can be made quickly without huge amounts of capital and skilled labor. This is especially true of food items whose production can be quickly increased, and often is during special holiday time during the year. If consumers are willing to pay twice the price for any of these products, most producers will be able to gear up quickly to increase production.

✓ **Reading Check Explaining** What is supply elasticity?

Section 3 Review

Vocabulary

1. **Write** sentences in which you use these key terms: *supply, law of supply, supply schedule, supply curve, profit, market supply, productivity, technology, subsidy, supply elasticity.*

Main Ideas

2. **Explain** the law of supply.
3. **Identify** four factors that can cause changes in supply.
4. **Describing** What kinds of products are considered supply elastic?

Critical Thinking

5. **Describing** What is an example of how business expectations can increase or decrease supply?
6. **BIG Ideas** Use a chart like the one below to illustrate the effect of price on supply.

Price	→	Effect
Increase		
Decrease		

7. **Analyzing Visuals** Study the two supply schedules on page 582. How are they similar? How are they different?

CITIZENSHIP Activity

8. **Research** Make a list of products manufactured in your town, city, or community. Decide if each one is supply elastic or supply inelastic. Share your list with the class.
9. **Descriptive Writing** Write a short chalk talk for first graders in which you explain the law of supply. Be sure to include examples and graphic aids that your audience will understand.

Study Central™ To review this section, go to <u>glencoe.com</u>.

Answers

1. Sentences should use vocabulary words according to their definitions in the section and in the Glossary.
2. The law of supply is the principle that the higher the price of a good, the greater the incentive for a producer to produce it.
3. Answers may include the following: price, cost of resources, productivity, technology, government policies, taxes, subsidies.
4. Elastic products are items that producers can quickly increase or decrease the supply of in response to changes in demand and prices.
5. Answers will vary. Many students may say that expectations about consumer response to a new technology will lead to an increased or a decreased supply of the item.
6. **Price Increase:** Increased Supply; **Price Decrease:** Decreased Supply
7. Both supply schedules provide information on quantities of video games at various prices. The first supply schedule provides information about supply quantities for only the Software House. The second supply schedule provides information about total market supply quantities.
8. Lists will vary. Students should list a variety of products and include both elastic and inelastic products.
9. Chalk talks will vary. Students should remember to tailor their talks to their audiences.

Guide to Reading

Big Idea
Supply and demand in a market interact to determine price and the quantities bought and sold.

Content Vocabulary
- surplus *(p. 588)*
- shortage *(p. 589)*
- equilibrium price *(p. 589)*
- price ceiling *(p. 589)*
- price floor *(p. 589)*
- minimum wage *(p. 589)*

Academic Vocabulary
- mechanism *(p. 588)*
- purchase *(p. 588)*
- focus *(p. 590)*

Reading Strategy
Analyzing Cause and Effect
As you read the section, complete a diagram like the one below by describing three advantages of using prices to distribute goods and services.

🔊 Section Audio   🎬 Spotlight Video

Demand and Supply at Work

Real World Economics In 1974, U.S. gasoline customers waited in line for hours for a chance to buy fuel. At the time, several Middle Eastern nations had decided not to ship any oil to the United States. The resulting oil shortage caused the price for a gallon of gasoline to quadruple and the supply to diminish. Gas stations often could not meet the demand and refused to sell their product to anyone who brought in an empty container rather than the item itself. This forced customers to wait in line with their lawn mowers and other fuel-powered tools.

▼ **A man in San Jose, California, lines up with his lawn mower to buy gas during a fuel shortage**

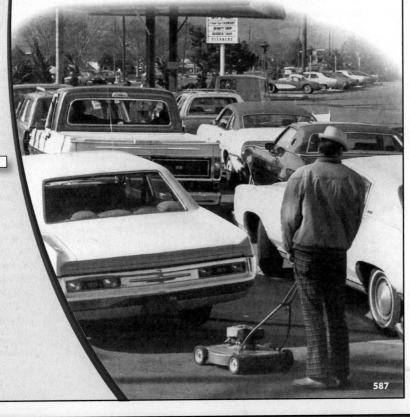

587

Focus

Bellringer
Daily Focus Transparency 21-4

Guide to Reading
Answers to Graphic:

🎬 **Section Spotlight Video**

To generate student interest and provide a springboard for class discussion, access the Chapter 21, Section 4 video at glencoe.com or on the video DVD.

Resource Manager

R **Reading Strategies**	C **Critical Thinking**	D **Differentiated Instruction**	W **Writing Support**	S **Skill Practice**
Teacher Edition • Identifying, pp. 588, 589 • Monitoring, p. 590 • Questioning, p. 591 **Additional Resources** • Cont. Vocab., URB p. 88 • Ac. Vocab., URB p. 90 • Guided Read., URB p. 108 • RENTG, p. 204	**Teacher Edition** • Pred. Consequences, p. 588 • Making Inferences, pp. 589, 590 • Det. Cause/Effect, p. 591 **Additional Resources** • Biographies., URB p. 91 • Crit. Think. Act., URB p. 95 • Quizzes and Tests, p. 251	**Teacher Edition** • Below Grade Level, p. 592 **Additional Resources** • Diff. Instr., URB p. 99 • Reteach Act., URB p. 103 • Graphic Novel, p. 83	**Teacher Edition** • Expository Writing, p. 592 **Additional Resources** • Writing Skills Act., URB p. 93 • Enrich. Act., URB p. 13	**Teacher Edition** • Reading Graphs, p. 589 **Additional Resources** • Chart, Graph, and Map Skills, URB p. 97 • Daily Focus Trans., 21–4 • Pol. Cartoons Trans. 21

Teach

R Reading Strategy

Identifying Ask: In a market economy, what is the basis for making economic decisions? *(price)* **BL**

C Critical Thinking

Predicting Consequences According to the Price Adjustment chart, there is a surplus of 75 video games at a price of $40 each. **Ask:** How will this probably affect the price of the 75 surplus video games? *(The price of the games will go down.)* **OL**

TIME™ Political Cartoons

Answers:

1. The store has a supply surplus.
2. Businesses can reduce the price of their products or withhold some of the products from the market in an attempt to create increased demand.
3. This situation is economically unhealthy for businesses because it causes them to make a smaller profit or even to lose money. It is economically healthy for consumers because it allows them to save money by getting products at a lower price.

Additional Support

Markets and Prices

Main Idea The forces of supply and demand work together in markets to establish prices.

Economics & You Have you ever tried to bargain for a lower price on something you bought? Read to find out how economists view the process of setting prices.

As you learned earlier, a market is any **mechanism,** or place, where buyers and sellers of a good or service get together to exchange that good or service. For example, to buy corn, people might go to a farmers market or a supermarket. Someone who wants to buy stock might use a computer to **purchase,** or buy, it from a stock market. In each case, markets bring buyers and sellers together.

R The forces of supply and demand work together in markets to establish prices. In our economy, prices form the basis for economic decisions.

The Price Adjustment Process

A market consists of all buyers and sellers of a product. To see how supply and demand work together, we need to combine the supply and demand curves. Look at the graph on page 589. It shows the market demand curve for video games (the line marked "D" on the graph) and the market supply curve (marked "S") for those games.

Surplus Suppose we start by watching how buyers and sellers react to a price of $40 in this market for video games. The graph shows **C** that sellers will supply 225 video games to the market at this price. Buyers, however, are willing to buy only 150 games at $40 each. This leaves a surplus of 75 video games.

A **surplus** is the amount by which the quantity supplied is higher than the quantity demanded. The surplus also appears as the horizontal distance between the supply and demand curves at any point above where the demand and supply curves intersect.

TIME™

Political Cartoons

In this cartoon, Sidney Harris is making a comment on supply and demand.

1. **Why is the store shown in the cartoon holding a sale?**
2. **What are some options that businesses have when supply exceeds demand?**
3. **Is this situation economically healthy for businesses? For consumers?**

Sidney Harris/ScienceCartoonsPlus.com

Every year, more than half of all Americans do volunteer work ... role in it. One of the responsibilities of citizens is to help make their ... of volunteer grou... small. Perha... dad wh...

Activity: Collaborative Learning

Visual/Spatial Have students work in pairs to create their own political cartoons illustrating the principles of supply and demand. Have one student create the image (they may draw the image or find an appropriate photograph) and the other student write the caption. Student teams should brainstorm ideas together before coming up with the images or captions. Remind students they may use information from the entire chapter as a basis for the topics of their cartoons. Have students share their cartoons with the class. **Ask:** What principle of supply and demand do each of the cartoons illustrate? **AL**

A surplus signals that the price is too high. In that case, consumers are unwilling to pay the price in large enough numbers to satisfy producers. If the market is competitive, this surplus will not exist for long. Sellers will have to lower their prices if they want to sell their goods.

Shortage What if the price had been $20? Look at the graph again. At this price, suppliers offer only 105 video games for sale. Consumers, though, are willing to buy 230 games. This difference is a shortage. A **shortage** is the amount by which the quantity demanded is higher than the quantity supplied. The shortage is shown as the horizontal distance between the two curves at any price below the point where demand and supply cross.

A shortage signals that the price is too low. In this situation, suppliers are unwilling to sell their goods or services in large enough numbers to meet all the demand. If the market is competitive, the shortage will not last. The price will have to rise.

Market Forces

One of the benefits of the market economy is that it eliminates shortages and surpluses when it operates without restriction. Over time, a surplus forces the price down and a shortage forces the price up. This process goes on until supply and demand are balanced. The point where they achieve balance is the **equilibrium price.** At this price, there is neither a surplus nor a shortage. In the figure on this page, the equilibrium price for video games is $30.

Once the market price reaches equilibrium, it will tend to stay there until either supply or demand changes. Once that happens, the market will have a temporary surplus or shortage. If there is a surplus, the price will be driven down. If there is a temporary shortage, the price will be driven up. The price will move in this way until the market establishes a new equilibrium price.

The Price Adjustment Process

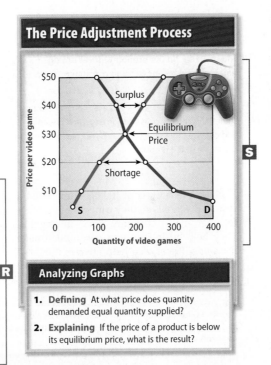

Analyzing Graphs

1. **Defining** At what price does quantity demanded equal quantity supplied?

2. **Explaining** If the price of a product is below its equilibrium price, what is the result?

Price Controls

Occasionally the government sets the price of a product because it believes that the forces of supply and demand are unfair. When this happens, the new price may favor either consumers or producers.

A **price ceiling** is a maximum price set by the government that can be charged for goods and services. For example, city officials might set a price ceiling on what landlords may charge for rent. A **price floor** is a government minimum price that can be charged for goods and services. Price floors—more common than price ceilings—prevent prices from dropping too low. The **minimum wage,** the lowest legal wage that can be paid to most workers, is a price floor.

Reading Check **Explaining** If the price of a product is above its equilibrium price, what is the result?

R Reading Strategy

Identifying **Ask:** What is a market shortage? *(A shortage is the amount by which the quantity demanded is higher than the quantity supplied.)* **Ask:** What happens when there is a product shortage? *(The price of the product rises, giving incentive to producers to increase supply.)* **OL**

C Critical Thinking

Making Inferences **Ask:** What can we assume if, over time, a product surplus does not force down prices? *(The market is not operating freely but is being manipulated.)* **AL**

S Skill Practice

Reading Graphs **Ask:** What is the quantity of video games demanded and supplied when the product reaches its equilibrium price? *(200)* **OL**

Analyzing Graphs

Answers:
1. equilibrium price
2. A shortage exists because of excess demand. The price is too low.

Reading Check **Answer:** A surplus, or excess supply, exists. The price is too high.

Differentiated Instruction

Delivering Biographical and Autobiographical Presentations

Speaking and Listening Skills Activity 6, URB pp. 9–11

Objective:	To understand biographical and autobiographical forms
Focus:	Have students read the excerpt.
Teach:	Review biographical and autobiographical techniques.
Assess:	Have students compare and contrast biographical and autobiographical forms.
Close:	Have students rewrite the excerpt from Walton's autobiography as a biography.

Differentiated Instruction Strategies

BL Use a Venn diagram to compare and contrast biographies and autobiographies.

AL Find a biographical article about Sam Walton on the Internet or in the library. Write a review of what you read.

ELL How do writers of biographies find out information about their subjects? Illustrate two ways.

R Reading Strategy

Monitoring Ask: What three economic questions does price help answer? *(what, how, and for whom to produce)* **OL**

C Critical Thinking

Making Inferences Ask: In what way do prices help businesses decide how to produce? *(In order to make the greatest profit, producers spend the least amount possible making their products. They will select the lowest-priced resources available to make their products. In this way, price helps businesses decide how to produce.)* **OL**

Caption Answer:
equilibrium price

Differentiated Instruction

Prices as Signals

Main Idea In our economy, prices are signals that help businesses and consumers make decisions.

Economics & You Have you ever refused to buy something you thought was too expensive? Read to find out what message you may have been sending to the maker of the product.

The different parts of the economy need a system of signals so they can work smoothly together. In our economy, prices are signals. They help businesses and consumers make decisions. Prices also help answer the basic economic questions—*what* to produce, *how* to produce, and *for whom* to produce.

What Do Prices Tell Us?

For example, consumers' purchases help producers decide *what* to produce. They **focus**, or center, on providing the goods and services that consumers are willing to buy at prices that allow the suppliers to earn profits. A company will make video games as long as consumers are willing to buy them at a price that generates profits. If consumers are not willing to pay that price, the company will not be willing to make video games.

Prices also help businesses and consumers decide the question of *how* to produce. Suppose it costs a hair salon $20 in labor and supplies to provide a haircut. Consumers, though, are willing to pay only $15 for the haircut. To stay in business, the salon needs to find less costly ways of providing that haircut.

Housing Market Even when the sale of houses slows down, price reductions eventually balance supply and demand. *Identifying* What is the term for a price showing there is no surplus or shortage?

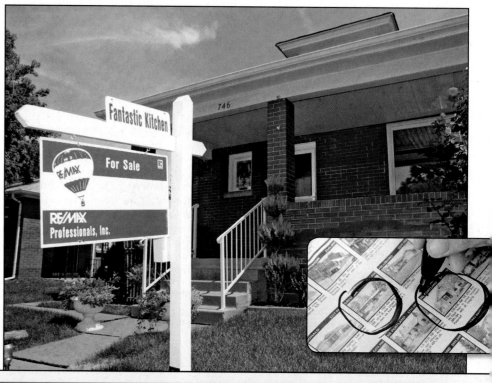

590

Leveled Activities

BL Content Vocabulary 21, URB p. 88

OL Chart/Graph/Map Activity 21, URB pp. 97–98

AL Biography Activity 21, URB pp. 91–92

ELL Reteaching Activity 21, URB p. 103

American Biography

Dick Burke (1935 – 2008)

Like most entrepreneurs, **Dick Burke** started out thinking small. He never dreamed of leading a huge corporation. In fact, his first job at a large equipment manufacturer convinced him otherwise. "I entered a training program in Caterpillar's finance department," he explained. "After 18 months I knew that large corporations were not for me and I was not for them. Just before they fired me, I quit."

In the mid-1970s, Burke was working in Milwaukee, Wisconsin, when two things happened: Gas prices shot up, and Americans began to become more interested in physical fitness. Burke put the two together and started a small business in a red barn in the town of Waterloo, Wisconsin.

What was the product that addressed both issues? Dick Burke began making bicycle frames. He called the company Trek.

Today the company is world famous, thanks to providing the bicycles Lance Armstrong used to win seven Tour de France titles. Today, Trek has about 1,700 employees and annual revenues around $600 million.

Although the company has grown tremendously, some things have not changed. It is still located near that red barn in Waterloo. And the firm's original goals—quality products for our customers at competitive value and deliver them on time—have not changed either.

Making a Difference — CITIZENSHIP

Analyzing What qualities do you think have helped make Trek a success?

Prices also help businesses and consumers decide the question of *for whom* to produce. Some businesses aim their goods or services at those consumers who are willing to pay higher prices. Other businesses aim their goods or services at the larger number of people who want to spend less.

Advantages of Prices

You know that consumers look for the best values for what they spend, while producers seek the best price and profit for what they have to sell. The information that prices provide allows people to work together to get more of the things that people want. Without prices, the economy would not run as smoothly, and decisions about allocating goods and services would have to be made some other way.

Prices Are Neutral First, prices in a competitive market economy are neutral because they favor neither the producer nor the consumer. Prices are the result of competition between buyers and sellers. In this way, prices represent compromises with which both sides can live. The more competitive the market is, the more efficient the price adjustment process.

Prices Are Flexible Second, prices in a market economy are flexible. Unforeseen events such as war and natural disasters affect the supply and demand for items. Buyers and sellers react to the new level of prices and adjust their consumption and production accordingly. Before long, the system functions as smoothly as it had before. The ability of the price system to absorb unexpected "shocks" is one of its strengths.

Chapter 21 591

R Reading Strategy

Questioning Have students read pages 591–592 in Section 4. Tell students to use the headings on the page to help them formulate questions about the function of prices. **OL**

C Critical Thinking

Determining Cause and Effect **Ask:** Why is the price adjustment process more efficient in more competitive markets? (*The more competitive the market, the faster price responds to changes in supply and demand.*) **OL**

American Biography

Answer: Answers will vary, but many students will say being a hard worker, having a commitment to quality, persistence, and determination.

Hands-On Chapter Project
Step 4

Demand and Supply in a Market Economy

Step 4: Selling It! Have student groups develop television commercials to sell the products or services they created in Step 3.

Directions Tell student groups to develop television commercials to sell their products or services. As they brainstorm the best way to persuade consumers to buy their products students should keep in mind to whom they want to sell their products. They should also consider how price, expectations, utility, or satisfaction influences consumers. Remind students to review their research from Step 2 and to consider the sales strate-gies used for the best-selling products from the past. After each group has settled on a sales strategy, they should collaborate on writing a script for their commercials.

Summarizing Have groups trade and review each other's scripts. Encourage groups to explain their strategies. **OL**

(Project continued on the Visual Summary page)

W Writing Support

Expository Writing Have students research and write a one-page report comparing and contrasting the economy of Cuba and that of the United States. **AL**

D Differentiated Instruction

Below Grade Level Have students write from memory the prices of everyday products such as bread, soda, or paper. Ask students to bring in an ad from a supermarket to compare its prices with the prices they listed. **BL**

> ✔**Reading Check** **Answer:** High prices may signal low demand and excess supply.

Assess

Civics ONLINE

Study Central™ provides summaries, interactive games, and online graphic organizers to help students review.

Close

Making Connections Have students discuss an experience when price alone influenced a purchase. Have they ever tried to buy a product in short supply? **OL**

Section **4** Review

Prices and Freedom of Choice Third, the price system provides for freedom of choice. Because a market economy typically provides a variety of products at a wide range of prices, consumers have many choices. If the price is too high, a lower-priced product can usually be found. Even if a suitable alternative cannot be found, no one forces the consumer to pay a certain price for a product in a competitive market economy.

Competitive markets tend to find their own prices without outside help or interference. No bureaucrats need to be hired, no committees formed, no laws passed, or other decisions made. Even when prices adjust from one level to another, the change is usually so gradual that people hardly notice.

W In command economies, such as those found in Cuba and North Korea, consumers face limited choices. Government planners determine the total quantity of goods produced—the number of radios, cars, toasters, and so on. The government then limits the product's variety to keep production costs down. Items such as food, transportation, and housing are offered to citizens at artificially low prices, but seldom are enough produced to satisfy everyone. Many people go without.

Prices Are Familiar Finally, prices are **D** something that we have known about all our lives—from the time we were old enough to ask our parents to buy us something to the age where we were old enough to buy it ourselves. As a result, prices are familiar and easily understood. There is no doubt about a price—if something costs $4.99, then we know exactly what we have to pay for it. This allows people to make decisions quickly and efficiently.

> ✔**Reading Check** **Explaining** What signal does a high price send to buyers and sellers?

Section **4** Review

Vocabulary

1. **Write** a paragraph in which you use these key terms: *surplus, shortage, equilibrium price, price ceiling, price floor, minimum wage.*

Main Ideas

2. **Identifying** What is the point called at which the quantity demanded of a product and the quantity supplied meet?

3. **Explaining** What causes prices to rise—a shortage or a surplus of a good or service? Explain why.

Critical Thinking

4. **Demonstrating** If a firm charges a price below the equilibrium price, what will be the result? Explain.

5. **BIG Ideas** Create a diagram like the one below to show how shortages and surpluses affect prices of goods and services.

Cause	→	Effect

6. **Analyzing Visuals** Study the graph of the price adjustment process on page 589. Does a price of $40 result in a surplus or a shortage? What is the equilibrium price?

CITIZENSHIP Activity

7. **Research** Compare the prices of the same product at three different stores. What conclusion can you draw about the equilibrium price for the product from the individual prices?

8. **Persuasive Writing** Do you think the government should ever set price ceilings or price floors? Write a letter to the editor of your local newspaper stating and supporting your view.

Civics ONLINE

Study Central™ To review this section, go to glencoe.com.

Answers

1. Paragraphs should use vocabulary words according to their definitions in the section and in the Glossary.

2. The point at which the quantity demanded and the quantity supplied meet is known as equilibrium.

3. Shortages cause prices to rise because more consumers are vying for fewer products.

4. A price below the equilibrium will generally cause a shortage.

5. **Cause:** Shortages **Effect:** Higher Prices
   Cause: Surpluses **Effect:** Lower Prices

6. The price of $40 results in a surplus; $30 is the equilibrium price.

7. Answers will vary. Students should research the prices of the same product at three stores and make a conclusion about the equilibrium price.

8. Editorials will vary. Students should state their positions clearly and explain their reasoning.

Visual Summary

Demand and Supply

Farmers market in California

Demand is the desire, willingness, and ability to buy a good or service.

Supply is the quantity of a good or service that producers are willing to sell at all possible market prices.

Market demand is the total demand of all consumers for a product or service.

Supply increases or decreases depending on many different factors.

Several different factors can cause market demand for a product or service to change.

Supply elasticity measures how the quantity supplied of a good or service changes in response to changes in price.

Demand elasticity is the extent to which a change in price causes a change in the quantity demanded.

The forces of supply and demand work together in markets to establish prices. In our economy, prices are signals that help businesses and consumers make decisions.

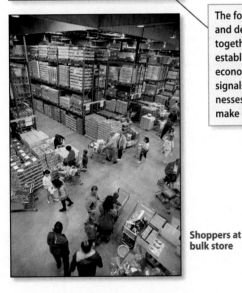

Shoppers at bulk store

Supply of soccer balls for sale

STUDY TO GO Study anywhere, anytime! Download quizzes and flash cards to your PDA from glencoe.com.

Visual Summary 21

Identifying Central Issues Have students demonstrate their understanding of the effect of expectation on supply and demand. Ask students to give one example each of how expectation may affect consumer demand for products and a producer's willingness to supply products. **OL**

Making Connections Have students find a news story about the interaction between supply and demand in a market economy. Then ask students to write summaries of the story, clearly detailing the product and the situation affecting its supply, demand, and price. Finally, students should identify the economic principle illustrated in the news story. **OL**

Hands-On Chapter Project
Step 5: Wrap-Up

Demand and Supply in a Market Economy

Step 5: Show Time! Have student groups present the television commercials they created in Step 4.

Directions Have each group present their commercial to the class. If there are limited roles, some students in the group may introduce the commercial, others may be in charge of props or costumes, and others may be in charge of music or sound effects. Remind students performing commercials to speak slowly, loudly, and to enunciate.

Summarizing Have the class assess the effectiveness of the commercials. **Ask:** What did you learn about the Big Idea while working on the various steps in the Hands-On Project? **OL**

Answers and Analyses
Reviewing Vocabulary

1. C Students will have read about demand curves in Section 1. A demand curve is a graphic representation of the demand schedule. Students will then immediately be able to eliminate answers B and D because they refer to economic principles not graphs. Furthermore, they will have read the description of a demand curve as "a graph that shows the amount of a product that would be bought at all possible prices in the market."

2. D Students will have encountered the economic terms "substitutes", "surplus", "elastic", and "complements" in Section 2 of the chapter. Recalling the definition of complements as products that are used together should help the student answer this question.

3. B At least three of the answers for this question may seem plausible if students do not read carefully. "Resources", "production", and "technology" are all *factors* in creating the supply of goods. However, if students remember that technology refers to the methods in which resources are used to produce goods, they should be able to answer the question. The phrase "methods or services" in the question will be helpful in directing students to the correct answer.

4. D The definition of "equilibrium price" can be found in Section 4. The student should recall that at the equilibrium price there is neither a surplus nor a shortage and that prices are stable. In addition, understanding that the word "equilibrium" is synonymous with a "state of balance" will help students answer this question.

Reviewing Main Ideas

5. C Students will have encountered the fundamental economic principles of supply and demand in Section 1 of the chapter. Remembering the common experience, that consumers are more willing to buy products with a lower price—thus creating higher demand for lower priced goods—will help students.

TEST-TAKING TIP

> When working numerical problems out on scrap paper, make sure you copy numbers correctly, not transposing or dropping any figures.

Reviewing Vocabulary

Directions: Choose the word(s) that best completes the sentence.

1. A _____ is a graph that shows the amount of a product that would be bought at all prices in the market.

  A supply curve   **C** demand curve

  B law of demand   **D** market demand

2. Some products, such as DVD players and DVDs, are called _____ because demand for one moves in the opposite direction as the price of the other.

  A substitutes   **C** elastic

  B surplus   **D** complements

3. The methods or services used to make goods and services are called _____.

  A factors   **C** resources

  B technology   **D** production

4. At the _____ price there is neither a surplus nor a shortage.

  A profitable   **C** exchange

  B ceiling   **D** equilibrium

Reviewing Main Ideas

Directions: Choose the best answer for each question.

Section 1 *(pp. 568–572)*

5. According to the law of demand, quantity demanded and price _____.

  A move in the same direction

  B depend on marginal utility

  C move in opposite directions

  D are not related

6. Diminishing marginal utility is the explanation for the consumer's decision to _____.

  A spend less money for sale items

  B buy only one dessert with a meal

  C purchase more CDs of a favorite singer

  D buy expensive gifts for close friends

Section 2 *(pp. 573–578)*

7. Total demand may change if more consumers enter the market, consumer tastes change, or _____.

  A consumer expectations change

  B substitutes become popular

  C demand is inelastic

  D supply remains the same

Section 3 *(pp. 580–586)*

8. Businesses invest time, money, and other capital resources for the primary motive of _____.

  A paying good wages

  B supplying better products

  C making a profit

  D satisfying customers' needs

Section 4 *(pp. 587–592)*

9. One of the strengths of a market economy is that _____.

  A prices absorb some of the shocks or unexpected changes in the economy

  B most consumers can afford plenty of the goods and services they want

  C producers almost always make a profit

  D demand is never greater than supply

GO ON ➡

---

6. B The definition of "diminishing marginal utility" can be found in Section 1. The example of decreasing enjoyment when eating succeeding slices of pizza illustrates the idea. For students who do not remember this example, breaking down the meaning of the words "diminishing" and "utility"—lessening usefulness—should help answer this question.

7. A Students who have carefully read Section 2 will have no trouble answering this question. Furthermore, the word "consumer" in answer A should help point students to the correct answer.

8. C Students will have read that businesses invest time, money, and other capital resources to make money. Though all the answers may at first seem plausible, keeping in mind the limiting phrase "primary motive," should help students answer this question.

Critical Thinking

Directions: Base your answers to questions 10 and 11 on the graph below and your knowledge of Chapter 21.

Price Adjustment Process

10. The price adjustment graph shows that at a price of more than $30 _____.

   A consumer demand would increase

   B the cost of production would have to be more than $40

   C supply would increase and cause a surplus

   D supply would decrease, causing a shortage

11. The graph illustrates that at the equilibrium price of video games _____.

   A producers will supply nearly 200 units

   B consumers will demand more than 200 units

   C demand will fall

   D there may be a shortage of games

Document-Based Questions

Directions: Analyze the following document and answer the short-answer questions that follow.

A price ceiling is a government-set maximum price that can be charged for goods and services. Below, a city sets such a maximum price for rent in the Washington, D.C., area.

> *No landlord shall charge a monthly rent for any controlled rental unit in an amount more than the fair market rent level established annually by the Department of Housing and Urban Development for the Washington Metropolitan Statistical Area for a four-bedroom unit or 1% of the property's assessed value for property taxes in a given year, whichever is greater.... Beginning in January 2007 and every three years thereafter, the City Council may reconsider the criteria for the establishment of rent ceilings based, among other factors, on the triennial reassessments of properties in the City.*
>
> —City of College Park (Md.)

12. For what period of time will each rent ceiling be set by the city government? Why will the council review the rent ceiling periodically?

13. Does a ceiling benefit renters or landlords? If the price of a product is set below its equilibrium price, what is the likely result?

Extended-Response Question

14. Do you think that the rent ceiling will provide more low cost housing in the area in the long term? Write a paragraph describing the possible results of rent ceilings that are set below the equilibrium price.

STOP

Civics ONLINE

For additional test practice, use Self-Check Quizzes— Chapter 21 on glencoe.com.

Need Extra Help?														
If you missed question...	1	2	3	4	5	6	7	8	9	10	11	12	13	14
Go to page...	569	576	585	589	569	572	574	583	589	589	589	584	584	584

ASSESSMENT

11. A Students should understand how to read the Price Adjustment graph to answer this question. They should know that prices are found on the vertical axis and quantities are found on the horizontal axis. The graph clearly shows the equilibrium price to be $30 so the correct answer must be A, 200 units.

Document-Based Questions

12. The rent ceiling is set every three years. The council will review its rent ceiling based on periodic property assessments.

13. A rent ceiling benefits renters. A shortage of the product would result if the ceilings are set below the equilibrium price.

Extended Response

14. Answers will vary. Students may note that if the rent is below equilibrium price, fewer houses will be offered for rent and a shortage will result. Those people who have obtained rentals will be less likely to move out, and few people will be able to move into the area.

---

9. A Students will have read about prices and market forces in Section 4 of Chapter 21. The section will teach students about the flexible nature of prices and enable students to correctly answer this question. In addition, identifying which of the answer choices is a true statement will lead students to the correct answer.

Critical Thinking

10. C Students should pay careful attention to the Price Adjustment graph. The graph shows that at a price of more than $30, producers increase supply of the product. This illustrates the law of supply and demand that when supply outpaces demand, a surplus is created.

Civics ONLINE

Have students visit the Web site at glencoe.com to review Chapter 21 and take the **Self-Check Quiz.**

Need Extra Help?

Have students refer to the pages listed if they miss any of the questions.

Teach

S Skill Practice

Reading Graphs Ask: From which country does the United States import the second largest percentage of oil? *(Saudi Arabia).* **BL**

C Critical Thinking

Analyzing Ask: About how much of America's oil is imported? *(about 58%)* **Ask:** Does this fact support or negate the arguments of those who want to increase drilling for oil in protected lands of Alaska? *(Answers will vary and could take either side of the argument.)* **OL**

Additional Support

TIME
REPORTS

Oil and Gas Consumption in the U.S.

America's addiction to oil is getting ever more costly for car-loving consumers and energy-dependent industries

1 The U.S. is the world's biggest oil consumer—and importer

WHERE THE U.S. GETS ITS OIL

Canada 11%
U.S.A. 42%
Mexico 11%
Venezuela 8%
Nigeria 7%
Iraq 4%
Saudi Arabia 9%
● 25 other countries: 8%
May 2005 figures

■ Americans account for **4.5%** of the world's population but guzzle **25%** of the planet's petroleum output. On a typical day, the U.S. consumes **21 million barrels** of oil—more than any other country.

■ About **58%** of America's oil is imported from other countries. As the map above shows, most of America's oil imports come from **outside the Middle East**. Canada and Mexico are major suppliers of U.S. oil.

■ The U.S. holds **700 million barrels** of oil in the **Strategic Petroleum Reserve**. That's equivalent to about 70 days' worth of imports. This emergency oil supply is stored at four sites on the Gulf of Mexico.

Activity: U.S./World Connections

Comparing and Contrasting: Tell students that many countries, including the United States, are exploring the use of alternative fuels. Ask students to research the production of, use of, and government policies toward the alternative fuel called ethanol in Brazil and the United States. Students should particularly note similarities and differences in ethanol production, use, and cost in both countries.

Based on what they learned, have the class make recommendations on United States policy regarding ethanol. **Ask:** Should the government make changes in its current policy? If so, in what way? If not, why not? *(Opinions will vary.)* **AL**

Spot Price for a Barrel of Crude Oil
West Texas Intermediate, a widely used benchmark

August 2006: $75.45

November 2001: $17.50

2 Demand for oil is soaring

The U.S. has long been the dominant customer for the world's oil, buying more than China, Japan, and Germany combined in 2005. By 2025, U.S. oil consumption is projected to increase 32%. At current rates of consumption, the known oil supply will be exhausted by the middle of the 21st century.

C₁

3 As oil prices rise, the effects ripple through the economy

Higher oil prices mean higher gasoline prices, since gasoline is produced by refining crude oil. The U.S. consumes nearly 400 million gallons of gasoline every day, most of it going into cars and trucks. The impact of rocketing gas prices stretches well beyond the pump:

C₂

- **Airlines** are among the hardest hit, with each penny increase in the per-gallon price of jet fuel costing the industry $180 million annually. For the first time in decades, major carriers are spending more for fuel than they are for labor. That means higher fares for passengers.

- **Delivery companies** like FedEx and U.P.S. also suffer; many have added surcharges to help cover rising costs.

- **Farmers** from coast to coast are affected as the cost of operating machinery and irrigation systems rises.

- And **retailers** suffer because it costs more for goods—and for customers—to reach stores.

Average U.S. Retail Price for a Gallon of Gasoline

$3.04▸

Price adjusted for inflation

Retail price

Sources: Energy Information Administration; Bureau of Labor Statistics; TIME Graphic by Lon Tweeten, Jackson Dykman, Kristina Dell and Jeremy Caplan.

U.S. Gasoline Production, Demand
Millions of bbl. a day

Demand   Production

Summer

George Hall/Corbis

FEELING THE IMPACT Every dollar jump in the price of oil costs the major U.S. airlines $365 million more in fuel per year.

597

Background

More Miles per Gallon? Corporate Average Fuel Economy (CAFE) standards require automakers to build vehicles that meet a set number of miles per gallon of gasoline. The standards were enacted during the energy crisis of the 1970s as an attempt by Congress to increase fuel efficiency for cars and light trucks. Today, despite higher gasoline prices and popular gas-guzzling vehicles, CAFE requirements have not changed much since they were enacted.

Those in favor of raising CAFE standards argue that increased fuel efficiency would lessen our dependence on foreign oil, reduce air pollution, and fight global warming. They contend that the technology already exists to substantially increase vehicle mileage. United States automakers are prominent among those against higher CAFE standards. They argue their companies are already in a financial crisis and that producing higher fuel-efficient vehicles would be too costly. With high gasoline prices and a dwindling world fuel supply, CAFE standards are bound to remain a topic of debate.

22

Key to Ability Levels

| BL | Below level | AL | Above level |
| OL | On level | ELL | English Language Learners |

Key to Teaching Resources

Print Material
CD-ROM or DVD
Transparency

Levels					Resources	Chapter Opener	Section 1	Section 2	Section 3	Chapter Assess
BL	OL	AL	ELL		**FOCUS**					
BL	OL	AL	ELL	🖨	**Daily Focus Skills Transparencies**		22-1	22-2	22-3	
					TEACH					
BL	OL		ELL	📁	**Reading Essentials and Note-Taking Guide***		p. 207	p. 210	p. 213	
	OL	AL		📁	**Citizenship/Decision-Making Activity, URB**		p. 3			
	OL	AL		📁	**Primary Source Reading, URB**			p. 15		
BL	OL	AL	ELL	📁	**Content Vocabulary Activity, URB***	p. 111	p. 111	p. 111	p. 111	
BL	OL	AL	ELL	📁	**Academic Vocabulary Activity, URB**	p. 113	p. 113	p. 113	p. 113	
	OL			📁	**Biography Activity, URB**		p. 115			
BL	OL	AL	ELL	📁	**Writing Skills Activity, URB**		p. 117			
	OL	AL		📁	**Critical Thinking Skills Activity, URB**	p. 119	p. 119	p. 119	p. 119	
BL	OL	AL	ELL	📁	**Chart, Graph, and Map Skills Activity, URB**	p. 121	p. 121	p. 121	p. 121	
BL	OL	AL	ELL	📁	**Differentiated Instruction, URB**				p. 123	
BL	OL	AL	ELL	📁	**School-to-Home Connection Activity, URB***	p. 125	p. 125	p. 125	p. 125	
BL	OL		ELL	📁	**Guided Reading Activities, URB***		p. 129	p. 130	p. 131	
BL	OL	AL	ELL	📁	**Writer's Guidebook**	✓	✓	✓	✓	✓
	OL	AL		💿	**Primary Source Document Library**	✓	✓	✓	✓	✓
BL	OL	AL	ELL	💿	**Daily Lecture & Discussion Notes (in Pres. Plus)**		✓	✓	✓	✓
BL	OL	AL	ELL	💿	**StudentWorks™ Plus**		✓	✓	✓	✓
BL	OL	AL	ELL	💿	**Section Spotlight Videos**		✓	✓	✓	
BL	OL	AL	ELL	🖨	**TIME Interpreting Political Cartoons Transp.**			Ch. 22		
BL	OL	AL	ELL	🖨	**Writing Process Transparencies**	✓	✓	✓	✓	✓

Note: Please refer to the *Unit 6 Resource Book* for this chapter's URB materials.

* Also available in Spanish

- Interactive Lesson Planner
- Interactive Teacher Edition
- Fully editable blackline masters
- Section Spotlight Videos Launch
- Differentiated Lesson Plans
- Printable reports of daily assignments
- Standards Tracking System

Levels					Resources	Chapter Opener	Section 1	Section 2	Section 3	Chapter Assess
BL	OL	AL	ELL							
					TEACH *(continued)*					
				📁	**Building Academic Vocabulary**	✓	✓	✓	✓	✓
Teacher Resources				📁	**Strategies for Success**	✓	✓	✓	✓	✓
				📁	**Teacher's Guide to Differentiated Instruction**	✓	✓	✓	✓	✓
				💿	**Graphing Tool**	✓	✓	✓	✓	✓
				💿	**Presentation Plus! with MindJogger CheckPoint**	✓	✓	✓	✓	✓
					ASSESS					
BL	OL	AL	ELL	📁	**Quizzes and Tests***		p. 260	p. 261	p. 262	p. 263
BL	OL	AL	ELL	📁	**Authentic Assessment with Rubrics**		p. 26			
BL	OL	AL	ELL	📁	**Standardized Test Practice**		p. 43			
BL	OL	AL	ELL	💿	*ExamView® Assessment Suite* **CD-ROM**		22-1	22-2	22-3	Ch. 22
					CLOSE					
BL			ELL	📁	**Reteaching Activity, URB***		p. 127	p. 127	p. 127	
BL	OL		ELL	📁	**Reading and Study Skills Foldables™ Activity**	p. 92	p. 93	p. 93		
BL	OL	AL	ELL	🖼	**Graphic Organizer Transparencies & Strategies**	✓	✓	✓	✓	✓

✓ Chapter- or unit-based activities applicable to all sections in this chapter

Using the Glencoe Web Site

Chapter Overviews

What is the Glencoe Web site?
The Glencoe Web site offers in-depth overviews that summarize and reinforce the content of each chapter.

How can the Glencoe Web site help my students?
Chapter Overviews on the Glencoe Web site help students:

- prepare to read a chapter
- recognize a chapter's main concepts
- practice reading and comprehension skills

Visit glencoe.com and enter a *QuickPass*™ code to go directly to resources for each chapter.

Civics ONLINE

Visit glencoe.com and enter *QuickPass*™ code CIV1360c22T for Chapter 22 resources.

You can easily launch a wide range of digital products from your computer's desktop with the McGraw-Hill Social Studies widget.

	Student	Teacher	Parent
Media Library			
• Student Edition Section Audio	●		●
• Spanish Audio Summaries	●		●
• Section Spotlight Videos	●	●	●
***Civics Today* Online Learning Center (Web Site)**			
• Chapter Overviews	●	●	●
• Study Central™	●	●	●
• Study-to-Go	●	●	●
• Student Web Activities	●	●	●
• In Motion Animation	●	●	●
• Self-Check Quizzes	●	●	●
• ePuzzles and Games	●	●	●
• StudentWorks™ Plus Online	●	●	●
• Vocabulary eFlashcards	●	●	●
• Web Activity Lesson Plans		●	
• Vocabulary PuzzleMaker	●	●	●
Classroom Tools			
• Multilingual Glossary	●	●	●
• Beyond the Textbook	●	●	●
• NGS MapMachine	●	●	●

Reading List Generator CD-ROM

GLENCOE BOOKLINK 3

Use this database to search more than 30,000 titles to create a customized reading list for your students.

- Reading lists can be organized by students' reading level, author, genre, theme, or area of interest.
- The database provides Degrees of Reading Power™ (DRP) and Lexile™ readability scores for all selections.
- A brief summary of each selection is included.

Reading suggestions
Leveled reading suggestions for this chapter:

For students at a Grade 7 reading level:
- *Rosie the Riveter Revisited: Women, the War, and Social Change,* by Sherna Berger Gluck

For students at a Grade 8 reading level:
- *Top Entrepreneurs and Their Businesses* by Robert B. Pile

For students at a Grade 9 reading level:
- *Interviewing for Information,* by Schwartz, Stuart & Conley, Craig

For students at a Grade 10 reading level:
- *The Dust Bowl and the Depression in American History,* by Debra McArthur

For students at a Grade 11 reading level:
- *Be Your Own Boss: Small Businesses,* by Ernestine Giesecke

READING SUPPORT FROM JAMESTOWN EDUCATION

- **Timed Readings Plus in Social Studies** helps students increase their reading rate and fluency while maintaining comprehension. The 400-word passages are similar to those found on state and national assessments.

- **Reading in the Content Area: Social Studies** concentrates on six essential reading skills that help students better comprehend what they read. The book includes 75 high-interest nonfiction passages written at increasing levels of difficulty.

- **Reading Social Studies** includes strategic reading instruction and vocabulary support in Social Studies content for both ELLs and native speakers of English.

- **Content Vocabulary Workout** (Grades 6–8) accelerates reading comprehension through focused vocabulary development. Social Studies content vocabulary comes from the glossaries of Glencoe's Middle School Social Studies texts. www.jamestowneducation.com

KEY Teacher Wraparound

Use this key to help you identify the different types of prompts found in the Teacher Wraparound Edition.

R **Reading Strategies** activities help you teach reading skills and vocabulary.

C **Critical Thinking** strategies help students apply and extend what they have learned.

D **Differentiated Instruction** activities provide instruction for students learning to speak English, along with suggestions for teaching various types of learners.

S **Skill Practice** strategies help students practice historical analysis and geography skills.

W **Writing Support** activities provide writing opportunities to help students comprehend the text.

Teaching strategies and activities have been coded for ability level appropriateness.

AL Activities for students working above grade level

OL Activities for students working on grade level

BL Activities for students working below grade level

ELL Activities for English Language Learners

Focus

Why It Matters

Ask: What types of businesses do you patronize? What kind of business would you like to work in? Have you ever thought of starting your own business? *(Answers include: fast food restaurants, clothing stores, video stores, and so on. Students may want to work in a small family business or a large corporation. Encourage students to discuss business opportunities they wish to start.)*

More About the Photo

Visual Literacy Many people attend technical schools or college to get a job such as the one pictured. Some businesses require that employees have college degrees. Presidents of large corporation, bankers, and managers typically have business degrees. There are also many family-run businesses that hire both a professional and a service staff. Whether you work in a family bakery, a small office, or a large chain department store, employees have rights. When unions are available, employees often join them in order to protect their jobs and wages.

Teach

BIG Ideas *As you begin teaching each section, use these questions and activities to help students focus on the Big Ideas.*

Section 1

Types of Businesses Ask: How many types of businesses can you name? *(Answers may include a family-owned business, such as a local restaurant; a small business, such as a law firm; and a large corporation, such as a supermarket chain.)*

598

Chapter 22 Business and Labor

Why It Matters

Businesses and labor organizations play a major role in our nation and communities. They work separately, as well as together, to make people's lives better by keeping the economy as healthy as possible.

598

Explain that Section 1 provides an overview of three basic types of businesses and reviews the advantages and disadvantages of each type. **OL**

Section 2

The American Labor Force Ask: What do you know about labor unions? *(Answers will vary. Some students may point out that unions protect workers. Others may state that unions are not needed in today's marketplace.)* Point out that some companies require union membership. Tell students that they will learn about unions and membership requirements in Section 2. **OL**

Civics ONLINE
Visit glencoe.com and enter
QuickPass™ code
CIV3093c22 for
Chapter 22
resources.

Chapter Introduction
22

Technician works on jet engine compressor

🔊 Chapter Audio

BIG Ideas

Section 1: Types of Businesses

Market economies rest upon the fundamental principle of individual freedom for consumers, producers, and workers. The three basic types of business organizations in the United States are sole proprietorship, partnership, and corporation.

Section 2: The American Labor Force

Market economies rest upon the fundamental principle of individual freedom for consumers, producers, and workers. Labor unions represent about 14 percent of U.S. workers and play an important role in the nation's economy and political life. They negotiate wages and workplace agreements with management.

Section 3: Businesses in Our Economy

Market economies rest upon the fundamental principle of individual freedom for consumers, producers, and workers. Businesses play many different roles in our economy, including that of consumer, employer, and producer. Businesses also have responsibilities to their consumers, owners, employees, and communities.

FOLDABLES™ Dinah Zike's
Study Organizer Foldables

Purpose This Foldable allows students to write summaries and review what they know about business and labor. The completed Foldable uses pockets to store note cards in which students can compare the differences and similarities between business and labor practices. **OL**

📁 More Foldables activities for this chapter can be found in the *Dinah Zike's Reading and Study Skills Foldables* ancillary.

Civics ONLINE

Visit glencoe.com and enter *QuickPass*™ code CIV1360c22T for Chapter 22 resources, including a Chapter Overview, Study Central™, Study-to-Go, Student Web Activity, Self-Check Quiz, and other materials.

FOLDABLES™
Study Organizer

Comparing Information Study Foldable Make the following Foldable to help you compare the differences and similarities between business and labor practices.

Step 1 Fold a two inch tab along the long edge of a sheet of paper.

Step 2 Fold the paper in half so the tab is on the inside.

Step 3 Open the paper pocket Foldable and glue or staple the edges together. Store note cards in the pockets.

Business   Labor

Reading and Writing
As you read the chapter, collect information about business and labor practices. Write a summary paragraph about each using your note cards.

Section 3 ★

Businesses in Our Economy Ask: Who protects the consumer? *(Students may answer that the government protects the consumer. Others may suggest that the buyer must beware: it is up to the consumer to protect himself or herself.)* Tell students that in Section 3, they will learn how businesses have many responsibilities, not just to the consumer, but to the community. **OL**

Focus

Bellringer
Daily Focus Transparency 22–1

Guide to Reading
Answers to Graphic:

Partnership
owned by more than one person, not all partners contribute funds to the business, raising money is easier, partners share in decision making

Both
no corporate income tax, owners have unlimited liability, owners take pride in ownership

Sole Proprietorship
owned by one person, raising money is difficult, owner makes all decisions

Section Spotlight Video

To generate student interest and provide a springboard for class discussion, access the Chapter 22, Section 1 video at glencoe.com or on the video DVD.

Resource Manager

Guide to Reading

Big Idea
Market economies rest upon the fundamental principle of individual freedom for consumers, producers, and workers.

Content Vocabulary
- sole proprietorship *(p. 601)*
- financial capital *(p. 601)*
- partnership *(p. 602)*
- articles of partnership *(p. 602)*
- corporation *(p. 603)*
- charter *(p. 604)*
- stock *(p. 604)*
- stockholder *(p. 604)*
- board of directors *(p. 604)*
- cooperative *(p. 606)*

Academic Vocabulary
- sole *(p. 601)*
- consult *(p. 601)*
- clarify *(p. 602)*

Reading Strategy
Organizing Create a diagram like the one below, then analyze the similarities and differences between partnerships and sole proprietorships. Where the ovals overlap, write the characteristics that both share.

Section 1

Types of Businesses

Real World Economics Small businesses are very important to the American economy and employ thousands of young people. Many teens, such as this girl who works in a small market, put in hours on the job after school and on weekends. Without these workers, small businesses could not survive. Support also comes from the U.S. Small Business Administration (SBA). It has been guaranteeing loans to businesses that are high-risk, not traditional, or are competing with much larger competitors.

▼ **New York teen works after school in neighborhood market**

R Reading Strategies	**C** Critical Thinking	**D** Differentiated Instruction	**W** Writing Support	**S** Skill Practice
Teacher Edition	**Teacher Edition**	**Teacher Edition**	**Teacher Edition**	**Teacher Edition**
• Analyzing Text Structure, p. 601	• Evaluating, p. 601	• English Learners, p. 602	• Expository Writing, p. 606	• Interpreting a Graph, p. 601
• Identifying, p. 602	• Making Inferences, p. 602	• Verbal/Linguistic, p. 604		• Interpreting a Chart, p. 604
• Inferring, p. 605	• Drawing Conclusions, p. 603	**Additional Resources**	**Additional Resources**	
Additional Resources	• Speculating, p. 603	• Reteach. Act., URB p. 127	• Cit./Dec. Making, URB p. 3	**Additional Resources**
• Cont. Vocab., URB p. 111	• Determining Cause and Effect, p. 605	• Teacher's Guide to Diff. Instr., p. 28	• Writing Skills Act., URB p. 117	• Daily Focus Trans., 22–1
• Ac. Vocab., URB p. 113	**Additional Resources**		• Authentic Assessment, p. 26	• Stan. Test, p. 43
• Foldables, p. 93	• Crit. Think., URB p. 119			

Proprietorships

Main Idea The most common, and simplest, form of business organization in the United States is the **sole** proprietorship.

Economics & You What kind of business could you start right now? Read to find out how you would organize that business.

There are three main kinds of business organizations in the economy today—the sole proprietorship, the partnership, and the corporation. Each offers its owners important advantages and disadvantages.

The most common form of business organization in the United States is the **sole proprietorship,** or simply, proprietorship—a business owned and operated by a **sole,** or single person. You have seen such businesses in your neighborhood—beauty salons, cleaners, and pizza restaurants.

Have you ever earned money mowing lawns or babysitting? If so, you were a sole proprietor. Important advantages of sole proprietorships are that the proprietor has full pride in owning the business and receives all the profits. The proprietor can make decisions quickly, without having to **consult,** or check with, a co-owner or boss.

The biggest disadvantage is that the proprietor has unlimited liability, or complete legal responsibility for all debts and damages arising from doing business. If the business has debts, the owner's personal assets, such as houses, cars, and jewelry, may be seized to pay the debts.

Sole proprietors also find it difficult to raise **financial capital**—the money needed to run a business or enable it to grow larger. Another disadvantage is the difficulty of attracting qualified employees. Many high school and college graduates are more likely to be attracted to positions with larger firms that can offer better benefits—paid vacations, sick leave, and health and medical insurance.

Reading Check Identifying Who makes the decisions in a sole proprietorship?

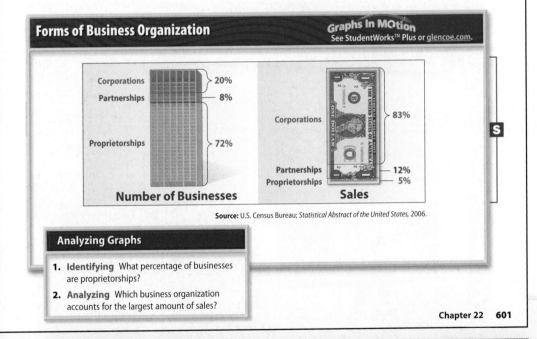

Forms of Business Organization

Graphs In MOtion See StudentWorks™ Plus or glencoe.com.

Corporations — 20%
Partnerships — 8%
Proprietorships — 72%

Number of Businesses

Corporations — 83%
Partnerships — 12%
Proprietorships — 5%

Sales

Source: U.S. Census Bureau; *Statistical Abstract of the United States,* 2006.

Analyzing Graphs

1. **Identifying** What percentage of businesses are proprietorships?

2. **Analyzing** Which business organization accounts for the largest amount of sales?

Chapter 22   601

Activity: Interdisciplinary Connection

Language Arts Discuss with students that opening a business requires a lot of work. Make a list of sole proprietorships in your community. Group students together and have each group choose one proprietorship. Have students interview owners to find out what kind of business plans they created before they decided to go into business.

Remind students that some businesses are family-owned and have been passed down from generation to generation. In such cases, have students interview current owners to discover the pros and cons of running a family business. Have members of each group present their findings to the class in the form of a business article. **OL**

C Critical Thinking

Making Inferences **Ask:** Why should business partners prepare legal ownership documents? *(The documents are a contract. They protect all parties. Legal documents will stand up in a court of law, but a handshake or verbal agreement will not.)* **OL**

R Reading Strategy

Identifying **Ask:** In which kind of partnership do the partners share the work and responsibility? *(a general partnership)* **BL**

D Differentiated Instruction

English Learners Point out that the caption identifies the grocery shown in the photograph as a *bodega*. Ask students to define that word and to identify the language from which it comes. *(Spanish)* Encourage speakers of languages other than Spanish or English to give the word for *store* or *shop* in their own languages. **ELL**

Caption Answer: The owner can share expenses and the workload with someone else.

Partnerships

Main Idea A partnership is a business owned by two or more people.

Economics & You Can you think of someone with whom you would be willing to go into business? Read to find out more about this type of organization.

Suppose you are a proprietor, and your workload increases so much that you have little time to do anything else. You could expand your business by hiring an employee. However, you also need money to buy new equipment, and you would rather not take out a loan. You decide to take on a partner.

The best solution is to look for someone who can keep books, order supplies, handle customers, and invest in the business. You offer to form a **partnership,** a business that two or more people own and operate.

Structure

When you start the business, you and your partner draw up a legal agreement called **articles of partnership.** This document identifies how much money each of you will contribute and what role each partner will play in the business. It **clarifies,** or spells out, how you will share profits or losses. Finally, the document describes how to add or remove partners, or even how to break up the business if you want to close it down.

Kinds of Partnerships There are two kinds of partnerships. The most common form of partnership is a *general* partnership, one in which all partners are responsible for the management and financial obligations of the business. In a *limited* partnership, at least one partner is not active in the daily running of the business, although he or she may have contributed funds to finance the operation.

D **Partnerships** Many small businesses like this New York City bodega are owned by more than one person. *Analyzing* Why would a business owner want to share ownership?

602

Identifying Sequence of Activities

Writing Skills Activity 22, URB pp. 117–118

Objective: To put steps in sequential order

Focus: Students list steps to organizing a corporation and starting a business.

Teach: Discuss how corporations and other businesses are started.

Assess: Check that students have listed steps in the correct order.

Close: Create a class flow chart that illustrates the steps to starting a partnership.

Differentiated Instruction Strategies

BL Explain why initial research is important when starting a business.

AL Make a list of sub-steps for three of the major steps for starting a proprietorship.

ELL Write three steps you might take if you were going to hire a manager for your business.

Differentiated Instruction

Advantages Much like sole proprietorships, an advantage of partnerships is the pride of sharing ownership in a business. Partnerships also overcome some disadvantages of a proprietorship. Because there are multiple owners, partnerships can usually raise more money. If money cannot be borrowed, the partners can always take in new partners to provide funds. Like sole proprietors, partners pay no corporate income tax.

Another advantage of partnerships is that each owner often brings special talent to the business. If, for example, one partner in an advertising agency is better at public relations and another is better at artwork, each can work at the tasks for which he or she is most capable. The ad agency then has a better chance of succeeding than if only one person ran it.

Another advantage of a partnership is the slightly larger size, which often makes for more efficient operations. In some areas, such as medicine and law, a relatively small firm with three or four partners may be just the right size for the market. Other partnerships, such as accounting firms, may have hundreds of partners offering services throughout the United States.

Disadvantages One disadvantage of the partnership is that the legal structure is complex. When a partner is added or removed, a new agreement has to be made.

The main disadvantage is that the owners have unlimited liability. This means that each owner is fully responsible for all the debts of the partnership. Suppose that you and four others form an equal partnership. The articles of partnership state that you own one-fifth of the business and have the right to one-fifth of its profits. Suppose, though, that someone was injured by the company and sued for damages. If the other owners cannot pay, you could be required to pay 100 percent of the damages.

> **Reading Check** **Describing** What is the main disadvantage of a partnership?

Corporations

Main Idea The corporation is a business recognized by law and is the most complicated of the three main types of business.

Economics & You Think of a big company whose name you see everywhere. Chances are, it is organized in the manner you are going to read about.

The **corporation** is an organized business recognized by law that has many of the rights and responsibilities of an individual.

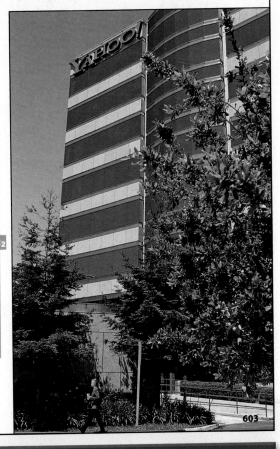

Successful Corporation Yahoo!'s corporate headquarters in California often holds meetings with the board of directors of this fast-growing Web provider. **Explaining** What is the role of a board of directors?

603

S **Skill Practice**

S Skill Practice

Interpreting a Chart Explain to students what the chain of command in a corporation involves. **Ask:** How many people report directly to the president of the corporation? *(three—the VP of sales, the VP of production, and the VP of finance.)* **BL**

D Differentiated Instruction

Verbal/Linguistic Have partners write questions and answers on note cards about the advantages and disadvantages of partnerships and corporations. Collect their cards. Organize the class into two teams and have teams answer the questions. **OL**

Analyzing Charts

Answers:
1. the vice president of production
2. the stockholders

Civics ONLINE

Objectives and answers to the **Student Web Activity** can be found at glencoe.com under the Web Activity Lesson Plan for this chapter.

Hands-On Chapter Project
Step 1

Taking Stock of American Corporations

Step 1: Researching the New York Stock Exchange Students will research several American corporations sold on the New York Stock Exchange (NYSE) and create a financial picture to assess profitability and overall business practices.

Corporate Chain of Command

OWNERS (STOCKHOLDERS) elect the

BOARD OF DIRECTORS who select the

PRESIDENT who hires

VICE PRESIDENT OF SALES
- Domestic
- International

VICE PRESIDENT OF PRODUCTION
- Quality Control
- Research and Development

VICE PRESIDENT OF FINANCE
- Payroll

Analyzing Charts

1. **Identifying** To whom does the Director of Quality Control report?
2. **Analyzing** If the board of directors needed to raise capital, to whom would it appeal?

In fact, a corporation can do anything a person can do—own property, pay taxes, sue or be sued—except vote. One-fifth of all businesses are corporations.

Structure

Someone who wants to start a corporation must get a **charter**—a government document granting permission to organize. The charter includes the name, purpose, address, and other features of the business. The charter also specifies the amount of **stock,** or ownership shares of the corporation, that will be issued. The people who buy this stock—the **stockholders**—become part owners of the corporation. The corporation uses the money received from selling the stock to set up and run the business.

Civics ONLINE

Student Web Activity Visit glencoe.com and complete the Chapter 22 Web Activity.

The stockholders elect a **board of directors** to act on their behalf. The board hires managers to run the corporation on a daily basis. The chart above shows the relationship of these groups. As you can see, the business owners and the managers of a corporation are different groups of people.

Advantages The first advantage of the corporation is the ease of raising financial capital. If it needs additional money to expand, for example, the corporation can sell new shares of stock. Corporations also find it easier than the other types of businesses to borrow large sums of money.

The second advantage results from the ease of raising capital. This allows corporations to grow to be huge. Today's large corporations employ thousands of workers and carry out business around the world.

Directions Organize the class into small groups. Each group will research corporations for which stocks are sold on the NASDAQ and the NSYE. Students can find several Internet sites that evaluate companies. Upon close review, each group will decide on four NASDAQ and four other NYSE companies to research more thoroughly. Groups should collect or print out financial reports or inquire about a prospectus for each of the eight companies they choose. These reports will be used to create a poster in Section 3. **OL**

(Project continued in Section 2)

The Largest Corporations A recent study found that some corporations are bigger than the economies of many countries. Of the world's largest 150 economic entities, 95 are corporations, according to data released in 2005 by *Fortune* magazine and the World Bank. The ranking is based on corporations by revenue and countries by GDP. Wal-Mart is the world's largest corporation and ranks number 22. Other high ranking corporations are BP at 23, Exxon Mobil at 24, and General Motors at 33. Each of these corporations was larger than the domestic economies of Finland (34th), Ireland (35th), and Argentina (48th).

A third advantage of corporations is that the board of directors can hire professional managers to run the business. Many corporations hire professional managers. If those managers do not succeed, the board can replace them.

A fourth advantage is that ownership of the corporation can be easily transferred. If you own shares in one corporation and would rather have shares in another, you simply sell the first stock and buy the second.

A final advantage of the corporation is limited liability. Only the corporation, not its owners, is responsible for the debts of the corporation. For instance, if you paid $1,000 for stock in a corporation that later went bankrupt, you would lose your $1,000 investment—but no more than that. Unlike the proprietorship or the partnership, you would not be liable for the company's debts.

Disadvantages Corporations have their disadvantages as well. First, they often are expensive and complex to set up. In addition, the business owners have very little say in the management of the business. Millions of people own the shares of major corporations, but it is difficult for them to unite to force the managers to act in a particular way.

Third, corporations are subject to more regulation by government than the other forms of business. They must release certain reports on a regular basis. These reports give detailed financial information about the company. The reports are designed to keep potential and current shareholders informed about the state of the business.

Profit Sharing This assembly worker at Ford Motor Company may also be a stockholder in the corporation. *Explaining* How are the funds raised by stock used?

C Critical Thinking

Determining Cause and Effect Ask: How do you think rich and powerful corporations affect the American economy? *(Possible answers: Such corporations can help keep the prices down, allowing all Americans to buy goods at reasonable prices. However, when they lose money, their losses affect everyone. Prices go up, jobs are lost, and personal incomes decrease. Some students may point out that when rich and powerful corporations donate money to political campaigns, they threaten the democratic process.)* **AL**

R Reading Strategy

Inferring Ask: Why do you think the U.S. government regulates corporations more strictly than it does partnerships or proprietorships? *(Corporations are very large and therefore very powerful. The government wants to regulate them and watch over them, making sure they comply with the law. In addition, the government receives twice the amount of taxes from corporations, making corporations a target for close review.)* **OL**

Caption Answer: The funds are used to set up and run the business.

Differentiated Instruction

605

Leveled Activities

BL Guided Reading Activity 22-1, URB p. 129

OL Writing Skills Activity 22, URB pp. 117–118

AL Cit./Decision-Making Activity 6, URB p. 3

ELL Content Vocabulary Activity 22, URB p. 111

Reading Check Answer: The stockholders must pay taxes on profits, and the corporation pays taxes on profits. This is money the business cannot use to reinvest. No one wants to pay taxes twice.

Assess

Civics ONLINE

Study Central™ provides summaries, interactive games, and online graphic organizers to help students review content.

Close

Summarizing Have students review the note cards they wrote for their Foldables. Have them write a brief summary that explains how different types of businesses are important to the American economy. **OL**

Section 1 Review

Finally, stockholders are subject to double taxation, or paying taxes twice on corporate profits. First, the corporation pays a tax on its profits. Then, when the profits are distributed to the stockholders, the stockholders have to pay tax on those earnings. Because of double taxation, corporations are required to keep detailed records of sales and expenses so that it can compute and pay taxes on its profits. Sole proprietors and partners also must pay taxes on the profits they earn. However, proprietorships and partnerships do not pay a separate profit tax.

Other Business Organizations

W Profit-seeking proprietorships, partnerships, and corporations are not the only types of business organizations. Other organizations operate on a "not-for-profit" basis. Examples of nonprofit institutions include churches, hospitals, and social service agencies.

What Are Cooperatives? Another example of a nonprofit organization is the **cooperative,** a voluntary association of people formed to carry on an economic activity that benefits its members. Consumer cooperatives buy bulk amounts of goods on behalf of their members. Members usually help keep the cost of the operation down by devoting several hours a week or month to the operation. Service cooperatives provide services, such as insurance and credit, rather than goods to their members.

Producers can also have cooperatives. A producer cooperative helps members promote or sell their products. For example, farmers cooperatives help members sell their crops directly to central markets or to companies that use the products.

Reading Check Describing Why is double taxation a disadvantage for corporations?

Section 1 Review

Vocabulary

1. **Define** these terms from the section and make a set of flash cards to help you learn them: *sole proprietorship, financial capital, partnership, articles of partnership, corporation, charter, stock, stockholder, board of directors, cooperative.*

Main Ideas

2. **Explaining** Why is a proprietorship the easiest form of business to set up? What is the most complex form?

3. **Comparing** What are the advantages and disadvantages of forming a partnership?

Critical Thinking

4. **Evaluating** If you were planning to open your own business, which form of business organization would you prefer—sole proprietorship, partnership, or corporation? Justify your answer.

5. **BIG Ideas** On a chart similar to the one below, identify the advantages of the corporation.

Corporation Advantages

6. **Analyzing Visuals** Study the graphs on page 601. What can you conclude about the form of business having the largest number of organizations and sales generated by that form of business?

CITIZENSHIP Activity

7. **Persuasive Writing** Write a paragraph either supporting or disagreeing with this statement: The sole proprietorship is the basis of U.S. business. Give reasons for your opinion.

Study Central™ To review this section, go to glencoe.com.

Answers

1. Flash cards should use vocabulary words according to their definitions in the section and in the Glossary.

2. It is easiest because it is a business owned and operated by a single person. The most complex form is the corporation, which involves many people and large amounts of money.

3. Advantages: more people to invest money in the business, to share the workload, and to contribute skills. Disadvantages: complex legal structures; unlimited liability.

4 Answers will vary. Preferences should be based on information from the text.

5.

Corporation Advantages
Ease of raising capital
Limited liability
Professional management
Easily transferred ownership

6. Proprietorships contribute the least amount of sales. It is easy to start a proprietorship, but profits are not large.

7. Paragraphs should include a statement of position and supporting reasons.

The Job Interview: First Impressions Count

If your résumé is what opens the door to job opportunity, keep the door open by making a good first impression. Do your homework by researching information about the company before you arrive. Have specific job goals in mind. Then practice interviewing with a friend or relative.

On the day of the interview, plan to arrive early. Dress to impress—nothing flashy, just well-groomed clothes suitable to the job.

When you meet the interviewer, shake hands firmly. Address the person as Mr., Mrs., or Ms. unless told otherwise. Relax promptly and use good manners. Maintain eye contact throughout the interview, be enthusiastic, and answer questions clearly and honestly. Focus on the training or experience you can bring to the job. Ask questions about the organization and the position. Thank the interviewer when you leave, and as a follow-up, send a thank-you note.

The company offered me the job. Now what?

- Take time to make your decision.
- Consider the salary and benefits of the job. If you have not already done so, research the job turnover of the company. High turnover might reveal employee dissatisfaction or a lack of job stability.
- Confirm the opportunities open to you, such as chances for advancement or additional training.
- Create a balance sheet weighing the pros and cons of the job. If the pros outweigh the cons, take a deep breath and jump into the job market. You are on the way to building your career!

Analyzing Economics

1. **Summarizing** What can you do to prepare for a job interview?
2. **Hypothesizing** What should you do if an employer asks you a question you cannot answer? Explain.

Teach

W Writing Support

Expository Writing Have students write a résumé. If students have a résumé already, ask them to update the information and revise it. Encourage students with no work experience to focus on school achievements and participation in clubs or sports. Students may also describe skills they have, such as using various software programs or repairing equipment. **OL**

D Differentiated Instruction

Interpersonal Have students make a list of different businesses in which they would like to work. Have them research the business and create a "snapshot" of the company. **OL**

Analyzing Economics

Answers:

1. research information about the company, be prepared for the interview by dressing appropriately, be on time, act confident, be courteous
2. State that you do not know the answer but will research the question.

Additional Support

Activity: Collaborative Learning

Preparing for an Interview Encourage students to discuss the interviewing process. Have them make a list of concerns students have about the process. Explain that they are going to role-play interviews for jobs. Students will take turns acting as the interviewer and the person being interviewed. Have students choose a job they would like to get, perhaps one that is in your local newspaper. Provide a list of questions for the interviewers. Set a date and have students dress for an interview and bring in their résumés. Ask students to give each other feedback as to their behavior as job applicants. **OL**

Focus

Bellringer
Daily Focus Transparency 22–2

Guide to Reading
Answers to Graphic:

Bargaining Goals

higher pay   improved benefits

better working conditions

Section Spotlight Video

To generate student interest and provide a springboard for class discussion, access the Chapter 22, Section 2 video at glencoe.com or on the video DVD.

Resource Manager

Guide to Reading

Big Idea
Market economies rest upon the fundamental principle of individual freedom for consumers, producers, and workers.

Content Vocabulary
• labor union *(p. 609)*
• right-to-work law *(p. 610)*
• collective bargaining *(p. 611)*
• mediation *(p. 611)*
• arbitration *(p. 611)*
• strike *(p. 612)*
• boycott *(p. 612)*

Academic Vocabulary
• comprise *(p. 609)*
• technique *(p. 611)*
• option *(p. 611)*

Reading Strategy
Organizing As you read the section, complete a diagram like the one below that shows the goals of collective bargaining.

Bargaining Goals

The American Labor Force

Real World Economics Since the first immigrants came to America and formed a huge labor force, unions have played a part in American industry. These AFL-CIO members are raising their voices in Pittsburgh to draw attention to national union issues. Unions represent more than 15 million workers in the United States and offer a powerful voice for workers to negotiate for better wages and working conditions. Some economists believe that unions are good for the economy, as they produce members who are better trained and stay on the job longer than employees who are not union members.

▼ **Union members showing support at a labor rally**

R Reading Strategies	**C** Critical Thinking	**D** Differentiated Instruction	**W** Writing Support	**S** Skill Practice
Teacher Edition • Identifying, pp. 609, 611 • Summarizing, p. 610 **Additional Resources** • Pri. Source Read., URB p. 17 • Cont. Vocab., URB p. 111 • Ac. Vocab., URB p. 113 • Foldables, p. 93	**Teacher Edition** • Contrasting, p. 611 • Ident. Cent. Issues, p. 612 • Det. Cause/Effect, p. 612 **Additional Resources** • Crit. Think., URB p. 119 • Quizzes and Tests, p. 261	**Teacher Edition** • Logical/Math., p. 609 **Additional Resources** • School-to-Home Conn., URB p. 125 • Teacher's Guide to Diff. Instr., p. 28	**Teacher Edition** • Descriptive Writing, p. 613	**Teacher Edition** • Using Geo. Skills, p. 610 **Additional Resources** • Chart, Graph, and Map Skills, URB p. 121 • Daily Focus Trans., 22–2 • Pol. Cartoons Trans. 22

TIME™ Political Cartoons

This cartoon, by Michael Ramirez, makes a statement about unions in the United States.

1. **What animals does Ramirez use to represent unions?**

2. **Why do you think he selected these symbols?**

3. **Do you think Ramirez believes the SEIU and Teamsters' decision to break away from the AFL-CIO will be effective? Explain.**

Michael Ramirez/Copley News Service

Every year, more than half of all Americans do volunteer work ... role in it. One of the responsibilities of citizens is to help make their ... of volunteer grou... small. Perha... dad wh...

Organized Labor

Main Idea Labor unions play an important role in the nation's economy and political life.

Economics & You Do you think people working together have a greater chance of success than individuals? Read to find out how American workers put this idea into action.

The population of the United States by October 2006 was approximately 300 million people. Slightly more than half, or about 151 million, belonged to the civilian labor force—men and women 16 years old and over who are either working or actively looking for a job.

Some workers choose to organize. They form **labor unions,** groups of workers who band together to have a better chance to obtain higher pay and better working conditions. Only about 14 percent of American workers belong to unions. The percentage of U.S. workers who are union members has fallen since the 1980s. One of the major reasons for the decrease is the shift from a manufacturing to a service economy. Still, unions play an important role in the nation's economy and political life.

Types of Unions

There are two types of unions. Workers who perform the same skills join together in a craft or trade union, such as a printers' union. Industrial unions bring together different types of workers from the same industry. An example is the United Auto Workers. In the past, unions were formed mainly by workers in industry. Today, though, people in jobs as different as airline workers, teachers, and professional athletes join unions.

Local Unions A local union is **comprised** of, or includes, the members of a union in a factory, company, or geographic area. Unions that also have members in Canada or Mexico are often called international unions.

Chapter 22   609

Teach

D Differentiated Instruction

Logical/Mathematical Have students use the 2006 statistics about the labor force to determine approximately how many workers belong to unions. *(approximately 21 million workers)* **OL**

R Reading Strategy

Identifying Have students list the different types of unions. *(craft or trade unions, industrial unions)* **Ask:** Do teachers who join unions belong to a trade union or an industrial union? *(trade union)* **OL**

TIME™ Political Cartoons

Answers:
1. dinosaurs
2. Dinosaurs are extinct. He wants to show that unions are dying out.
3. No. Students may say that because Ramirez identifies the SEIU as a dinosaur as well, he does not think it will be any different than the AFL-CIO. Ramirez's cartoon indicates he thinks that unions are no longer effective.

Differentiated Instruction

Farm Workers' Voices

PRIMARY SOURCE READING 6-B

Farmworkers' Voices

Primary Source Reading 6-B, URB pp. 17–18

Objective:	To identify situations in which workers have benefited from unions
Focus:	Students read factual accounts of mistreatment of workers.
Teach:	Discuss different kinds of work environments and rights of workers in each.
Assess:	List how people can make their work environments safer.
Close:	Create a class list of what students expect from future employers.

Differentiated Instruction Strategies

BL List three reasons why farm workers would want to join the UFW.

AL Why are unions such as the UFW still necessary in today's work environment? Write an essay that explains your reasoning.

ELL Write a short statement that explains the purpose of the UFW.

S Skill Practice

Using Geography Skills Remind students that states without right-to-work laws have a greater union influence. Have students identify regions in which union influence is the strongest. *(the northeastern and west coast states)* **Ask:** Why do workers in these regions require union membership? *(northeastern states are more industrial; west coast states have many dockworkers and farm workers.)* **OL**

R Reading Strategy

Summarizing Have students label three columns: closed shops, union shop, modified union shop. Have students list requirements next to each union arrangement. *(closed shop: mandatory to join union before hiring; union shop: mandatory to join after working; modified union shop: membership optional)* **OL**

Analyzing Maps

Answers:
1. 22
2. Answers will vary. Students may prefer the right to choose to join a union; others may not.

Reading Check **Answer:** Yes

Hands-On Chapter Project
Step 2

Taking Stock of American Corporations

Step 2: Forming Unions in Corporations Students will research their chosen companies from Step 1 to determine which require union memberships and which do not have unions.

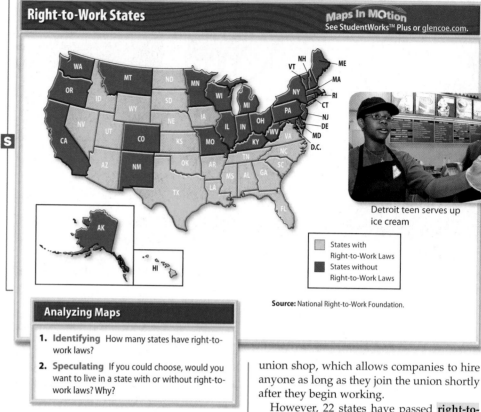

Right-to-Work States

Maps In MOtion See StudentWorks™ Plus or glencoe.com.

Detroit teen serves up ice cream

☐ States with Right-to-Work Laws
■ States without Right-to-Work Laws

Source: National Right-to-Work Foundation.

Analyzing Maps

1. **Identifying** How many states have right-to-work laws?

2. **Speculating** If you could choose, would you want to live in a state with or without right-to-work laws? Why?

National Unions Above the locals are the national unions. These organizations are the individual craft or industrial unions that represent locals on a nationwide level. The American Federation of Labor-Congress of Industrial Organizations, or AFL-CIO, is a national union. The federation represents more than 13 million working men and women nationwide.

Union Arrangements

Before they were declared illegal in 1947, closed shops were one kind of union arrangement. In closed shops, a worker had to first join a union in order to be hired by a company. A common arrangement today is the union shop, which allows companies to hire anyone as long as they join the union shortly after they begin working.

However, 22 states have passed **right-to-work laws,** which prevent mandatory union membership required by the union shop. This led to the modified union shop, which does not require a worker to join a union to be hired or keep the job. Workers must, however, remain in the union if they decide to join. Finally, the agency shop requires workers to pay a fee to the union for representing them even if they do not join the union.

A union cannot be brought into a workplace unless a majority of the workers votes in favor of it. A federal government agency, the National Labor Relations Board (NLRB), makes sure that these union elections are carried out fairly and honestly.

Reading Check **Summarizing** Is the union shop illegal in right-to-work states? Explain.

Directions Write the Big Idea on the board. Have each group research the eight companies they chose in Step 1 to find out which companies have unions. For those companies with unions, ask students to review recent labor-management conflicts and document how they were resolved. For those companies without unions, have students research the kind of benefits that are offered to workers. Have students keep the results to add to the posters they will create in Step 3. **OL**

(Project continued in Section 3)

Negotiations

Main Idea Labor and management negotiate workplace agreements.

Economics & You Have you ever had a third person help you and a friend reach a compromise? Read to find out how labor and management use this method.

Once workers choose to be represented by a union, the union carries out **collective bargaining** for them. Officials from the union and the company meet to discuss the workers' new contract. The negotiations focus on wages and benefits, including health care, holidays, working conditions, and procedures for changing rules.

Getting Outside Help

If the parties cannot agree on the terms for the new contract, they have different **options**, or choices. They might try **mediation,** in which they bring in a third party who tries to help them reach a compromise agreement. In some cases, the two sides choose **arbitration:** A third party listens to both sides, then decides how to settle the disagreement. Both parties agree in advance to accept the arbitrator's decision.

Labor-Management Conflict

Most contracts are settled at the bargaining table. Sometimes, however, negotiations break down. Unions and management use different **techniques,** or methods to pressure the other side to accept their positions.

R Reading Strategy

Identifying Ask: Who meets with management to discuss the workers' concerns? *(union officials)* What topics do they discuss? *(wages, benefits, holidays, working conditions, rule changes)* **OL**

C Critical Thinking

Contrasting Ask students to explain how mediation is different from arbitration. *(In mediation, a third party helps both sides come to an agreement. It is a three-way conversation. In arbitration, the third party decides how to settle the dispute.)* **OL**

American Biography

César Estrada Chávez (1927–1993)

César Chávez knew the suffering of farmworkers. He had labored in the fields since age 10, when his family lost their Arizona farm during the Great Depression. Like thousands of other farmers, the Chávez family became migrant workers, constantly moving to be near work. Chávez attended some 65 schools before dropping out at the end of eighth grade.

After serving in World War II, Chávez took a paid job with a Latino civil rights group to win greater rights for Mexican Americans. However, he could not forget the migrant workers. In 1962, with the support of his wife, Helen Fabela Chávez,

he returned to the fields and his dream of organizing farmworkers into a union.

In 1965, Chávez launched La Huelga—"the strike"— in which he battled the power of grape growers in the San Joaquin Valley. Chávez, who lived on a salary of $5 a week, asked Americans to boycott grapes until growers signed union contracts. Some 17 million Americans stopped buying grapes, and industry profits tumbled. "For the first time," Chávez said, "the farmworker got some power." The power came in the form of the United Farm Workers, the first successful farmworkers union in the nation's history.

Making a Difference CITIZENSHIP

Explaining Chávez spent much of his life trying to help farmworkers. How did Chávez force grape growers to sign union contracts with farmworkers?

American Biography

Answer: He persuaded 17 million Americans to boycott grapes, causing profits for growers to fall.

Differentiated Instruction

Leveled Activities

BL Guided Reading Activity 22-2, URB p. 130

OL Diff. Instruction Activity 22, URB pp. 123–124

AL Chart/Graph/Map Act. 22, URB pp. 121–122

ELL Content Vocabulary Activity 22, URB p. 111

C1 Critical Thinking

Identifying Central Issues Ask: What is the purpose of a strike? *(Workers in a union refuse to work, hoping that the business will shut down or lose money and give in to union demands.)* **What is the purpose of a boycott?** *(to persuade consumers not to buy the business's products so that the business will lose money and negotiate with union members)* **OL**

C2 Critical Thinking

Determining Cause and Effect Ask: When does management initiate a lockout? *(when workers go on strike)* **What effect does a lockout have?** *(Workers cannot work unless they agree to management's terms. Workers lose wages, which affects them more than when the business loses money.)* **OL**

Analyzing Graphs

Answers:
1. about 12 percent to 88 percent
2. The trend decreased. In 1985, union membership was 18 percent. In 2007, it decreased to about 12 percent.

Additional Support

Labor Tools Workers can call a **strike**, in which all workers in the union refuse to go to work. The workers hope that the business will have to shut down without any employees, forcing the company to accept the union's contract terms. Strikers usually walk up and down in front of their workplace carrying picket signs that state their disagreement with the company. Picketing is meant to discourage workers from crossing the picket line to work for the employer. It is also aimed at embarrassing the company and building public support for the strike. Unions can also encourage members and the public to **boycott**, or refuse to buy, the business's products.

Strikes can drag on for months and even years. After a long period of time, strikers sometimes become discouraged. Some may decide to go back to work without gaining what they wanted. In most cases, however, strikes are settled as management and labor return to the negotiating table and work out an agreement.

Management Tools When faced with a strike by its workers, management has methods of its own to use against strikers. Its strongest tool is the lockout. In a lockout, the company prevents workers from entering its buildings until they accept its contract terms. The business hopes that the loss of income will convince workers to accept the company's position.

Injunctions Management sometimes requests a court injunction to limit picketing or to prevent a strike from continuing or even occurring. An injunction is a legal order of a court preventing some activity.

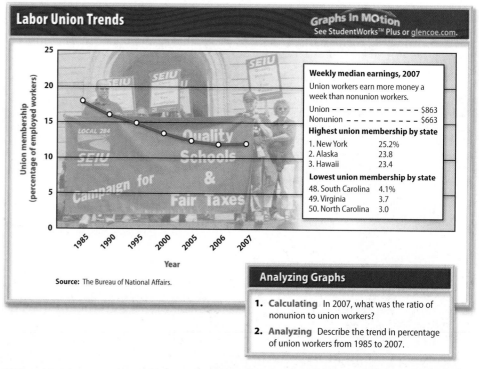

Labor Union Trends

Graphs In MOtion
See StudentWorks™ Plus or glencoe.com.

Weekly median earnings, 2007
Union workers earn more money a week than nonunion workers.
Union – – – – – – – – – – – $863
Nonunion – – – – – – – – – $663

Highest union membership by state
1. New York   25.2%
2. Alaska   23.8
3. Hawaii   23.4

Lowest union membership by state
48. South Carolina   4.1%
49. Virginia   3.7
50. North Carolina   3.0

Source: The Bureau of National Affairs.

Analyzing Graphs

1. **Calculating** In 2007, what was the ratio of nonunion to union workers?
2. **Analyzing** Describe the trend in percentage of union workers from 1985 to 2007.

Activity: U.S./World Connections

Understanding a World Union Discuss how the world economy has made world unions more popular. Have students research the Industrial Workers of the World Union on the Internet at www.iww.org. Have them create a bulletin board that lists the goals of the Industrial Workers of the World Union and shows photographs of recent strikes, both in the U.S. and other parts of the world. The bulletin board might also include a list of companies in which the IWW is present and a short article that describes the effect the IWW has on the world market. **OL**

In the early days of the labor union movement, the courts had treated unions as illegal conspiracies. Union leaders were regularly prosecuted and sued for damages. Even up to the early 1900s, injunctions were used against labor unions to prevent strikes and some other activities. Because of the use of injunctions by employers during this period, labor unions found it very difficult to strike.

Both companies and unions may ask for an injunction. If issued against a union, the injunction may direct the union not to strike. If issued against a company, it may direct the company not to lock out its workers. In 1995, after professional baseball players ended their strike and went back to work, the owners promptly called a lockout. The players then went to court and got an injunction against the owners, and the 1995 baseball season began—without a labor agreement between the two sides.

Seizure Under extreme circumstances, the government may resort to seizure—a temporary takeover of operations—to allow the government to negotiate with the union. This occurred in 1946, when the government seized the bituminous coal industry. The government felt the welfare of the entire country was at stake because of its need for coal. While operating the mines, government officials worked out a settlement with the miners' union.

Public Employee Unions

An important development in the labor movement in the 1960s and 1970s was the growth in public employee union membership. A public employee union is a union whose members work for the local, state, or federal government. The American Federation of Government Employees (AFGE) is the largest federal employee union representing 600,000 workers.

Reading Check Contrasting What is the difference between a strike and a lockout?

W Writing Support

Descriptive Writing Distribute two or three articles about strikes from newspapers, online articles, or magazines. Have each student write a description of one of the labor/management conflicts, either from the point of view of a union member or management. Students should include several content vocabulary words. **OL**

Reading Check **Answer:** In a strike, workers refuse to work until their demands are met. In a lockout, the company prevents workers from working until they accept the offer.

Assess

Civics ONLINE

Study Central™ provides summaries, interactive games, and online graphic organizers to help students review.

Close

Determining Cause and Effect Have students work in small groups and create charts that show why union membership tends to be declining. **OL**

Section 2 Review

Vocabulary

1. **Write** a true statement *and* a false statement for each of the following terms: *labor union, right-to-work law, collective bargaining, mediation, arbitration, strike, boycott.* Indicate which statements are true and which are false. Below each false statement explain why it is false.

Main Ideas

2. **Comparing** What is the difference between a union closed shop and a union shop?

3. **Explaining** When is mediation used with labor unions? What are its goals?

Critical Thinking

4. **Summarizing** How does a right-to-work law protect independent workers?

5. **BIG Ideas** Assume that you have been given the job of mediating a strike between the workers in a print shop and its management. On a diagram like the one below, identify three things you would want to know before you suggested a solution.

What I need to know

CITIZENSHIP Activity

6. **Persuasive Writing** Write a newspaper editorial supporting or opposing one of the following practices: closed shop, right-to-work laws, boycott, or lockout. Give reasons, and if possible, cite examples to support your position.

Civics ONLINE

Study Central™ To review this section, go to glencoe.com.

Answers

1. Statements should use vocabulary words according to their definitions in the section and in the Glossary.

2. In a union closed shop, workers have to join before they are hired. In a union shop, workers are hired with the understanding that they will join the union after they begin working.

3. Mediation: union officials and management bring in a third party to help both sides make compromises so that an agreement can be reached.

4. Workers cannot be required to join a union.

5. Responses will vary.

What I need to know		
How much do the workers currently make?	How much do workers in print shops typically make in your area?	What kind of profits does the print shop make to accommodate a wage increase?

6. Editorials should include an opinion about one of the topics listed and supported by reasons.

C Critical Thinking

Recognizing Bias Have students use the Internet to find out why the AFL-CIO supports a minimum wage increase. *(The AFL-CIO believes the economy is doing well and that the wealth should be passed along to the worker. They do not believe that people would lose jobs if the minimum wage is increased.)* Next, have students research the Heritage Foundation. **Ask:** Why is Tim Kane against raising the minimum wage? *(Kane is director of the Heritage Foundation, a conservative research institute. He states that raising the minimum wage would put poorly educated workers out of work.)* Have students debate the issue. Then have the class discuss which option seems most beneficial to the economy. **OL**

Debating the Issue

Answers:
1. to set the rate of hourly income that employers must pay workers
2. 1938
3. workers who are paid hourly rather than those who earn a salary
4. Answers will vary.

Additional Support

Should Congress raise the minimum wage?

Minimum wage is a term that identifies the hourly income that employers must pay their workers. Congress established a minimum wage of 25 cents per hour in 1938. It applied only to those employees engaged in interstate commerce. Congress revised the law in 1961 and 1968, extending coverage to most workers. Every few years thereafter, Congress raised the rate. For many years, the minimum wage of $5.15 remained unchanged. Some states passed higher minimum wage rates than the federal government. When a minimum wage issue appears on a state ballot, voters often approve it. Should Congress respond to the people's desire for a higher minimum wage?

Minimum wage jobs include retail and service jobs, such as poultry processing, fruit and vegetable picking, and restaurant service.

YES

One reason that the minimum wage should be raised every few years is because inflation gradually erodes the wages of everyone. If the purpose of the minimum wage is to lift the earnings of low-wage workers, the delay in raising it defeats the original intent of the law. The AFL-CIO, a major labor union, reported, "If the minimum wage had just kept pace with inflation since 1968 when it was a $1.60 an hour, minimum wage would have been $8.88 (an hour) in 2005." Supporters believe that raising the minimum wage would help women and children, and also have a ripple effect throughout the whole economy, improving the purchasing power of consumers.

—AFL-CIO, 2006

NO

The main argument against minimum wage laws is that raising minimum wages forces employers to dismiss low-productivity workers. This policy negatively affects those with the least education, job experience, and maturity. Teenagers are likely to face unemployment when the minimum wage is increased. According to Tim Kane of the Heritage Foundation, most economists believe a minimum wage does not work in free markets. Kane says, "Although the minimum wage will not work according to economic theory—and it has not worked in reality—what makes it especially tragic is that it hits poor Americans hardest. . . . Average pay in America has been increasing steadily in recent years, despite the fact that the minimum wage has not changed since 1997. Real wages rise when productivity rises."

—Tim Kane, PhD, March 4, 2005

Debating the Issue

1. **Describing** What is the purpose of a minimum wage law?
2. **Recalling** When did Congress begin passing minimum wage laws?
3. **Explaining** What workers are most likely to be affected by an increase in the minimum wage?
4. **Concluding** Why do you think Congress refused to increase the minimum wage for several years?

Activity: Economics Connections

Exploring Minimum Wage Assign students to small groups. Ask them to use the Internet and to read different opinions from politicians and economists to create a list of the pros and cons of raising the minimum wage. Encourage them to find quotes from members of Congress that support either position. After they have researched the topic, have each group vote on whether the minimum wage should be increased. Have them give reasons for their positions. Groups will present their opinions to the class. They may use line graphs, bar graphs, or other graphics to help support and illustrate their points of view. **OL**

Guide to Reading

Big Idea
Market economies rest upon the fundamental principle of individual freedom for consumers, producers, and workers.

Content Vocabulary
- transparency *(p. 617)*
- discrimination *(p. 618)*
- social responsibility *(p. 618)*

Academic Vocabulary
- foundation *(p. 616)*
- crucial *(p. 617)*
- reveal *(p. 617)*

Reading Strategy
Organizing As you read the section, complete a diagram like the one below by identifying at least one responsibility of business in each category.

Responsibility of Business	
To consumers	To employees

Section Audio **Spotlight Video**

Businesses in Our Economy

Real World Economics Have you ever thought about starting your own business? These plumbers are fulfilling that dream as they service homes in the Miami, Florida, area. They promote their own business and welfare by running an honest company while at the same time being part of America's construction industry—a booming industry that fuels America's economy. Businesses like theirs have a responsibility to provide quality service to consumers. They also have a responsibility when hiring others, to pay a fair wage.

▼ **Adjusting the plumbing on a Florida condominium**

615

Focus

Bellringer
Daily Focus Transparency 22–3

Guide to Reading
Answers to Graphic:

Responsibility of Business	
To consumers	To employees
to provide safe products and truthful advertising	to treat all of them fairly

Section Spotlight Video

To generate student interest and provide a springboard for class discussion, access the Chapter 22, Section 3 video at glencoe.com or on the video DVD.

Resource Manager

R Reading Strategies	**C** Critical Thinking	**D** Differentiated Instruction	**W** Writing Support	**S** Skill Practice
Teacher Edition • Specifying, p. 616 **Additional Resources** • Cont. Vocab., URB p. 111 • Ac. Vocab., URB p. 113 • Guide. Read., URB p. 131	**Teacher Edition** • Making Inferences, p. 616 **Additional Resources** • Biographies, URB p. 115 • Crit. Think., URB p. 119 • Quizzes and Tests, p. 262	**Teacher Edition** • Gifted and Talented, p. 617 **Additional Resources** • Diff. Instruction, URB p. 123 • Reteach. Act., URB p. 127	**Teacher Edition** • Personal Writing, p. 617	**Teacher Edition** • Creating a Table, p. 618 **Additional Resources** • Daily Focus Trans., 22–3

Teach

C Critical Thinking

Making Inferences   Ask: Why do you think many businesses, both large and small, contribute financial donations to foundations, schools, and charities? *(Possible Answers: They believe they have a social responsibility to give back to the community that helps support their businesses; they are compassionate; they receive tax deductions.)* **OL**

R Reading Strategy

Specifying Have students suggest examples of businesses that produce goods that meet people's needs. Write examples on the board. *(Suggestions may include Wendy's, McDonald's, the Gap, Home Depot, Ford, Max Factor, Sony, Dell, and so on.)* **BL**

✔ Reading Check Answer: They buy machines and services from other businesses.

Caption Answer: They can donate money or supplies.

Hands-On Chapter Project
Step 3

Roles of Business

Main Idea Businesses play many different roles in our economy. Businesses also have many responsibilities.

Economics & You Have you ever played in a park that was paid for by a local business? Read to find out other ways businesses assist our economies.

You may have eaten a square, onion-smothered White Castle hamburger. But did you know that the Ingram family, founders of that fast-food chain, have given $11 million to support education through its family **foundation** (an institution created to promote the public good)?

Businesspeople such as the Ingrams can be very generous. This generosity comes not only from major corporate givers like the Ingrams. Many local businesses, also, make similar efforts. They donate money or supplies to school fund-raisers. They give money to support children's athletic teams. This community involvement is just one way that business plays a role in society.

Businesses play many different roles in our economy. Sometimes businesses act as consumers—they buy goods and services from other businesses. Manufacturers buy energy and raw materials, while insurance companies buy office furniture and supplies. Stores purchase computers and software to track sales. Businesses are also employers. They provide jobs to millions of workers.

Of course, businesses are also producers. Businesses large and small produce the food, clothing, and shelter that meet people's basic needs, as well as the cars, movies, and appliances that make life more enjoyable and comfortable.

✔ Reading Check Explaining Businesses are producers. In what way are businesses also consumers?

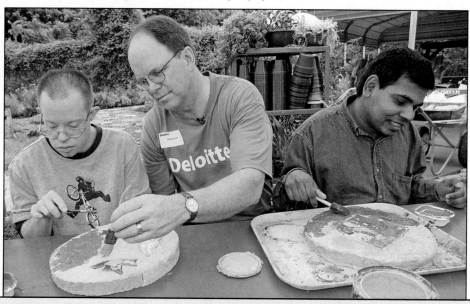

Generosity Many businesspeople, such as James H. Quigley, the CEO of the North Carolina-based Deloitte & Touche USA, participate in community service. ***Describing*** **How else can businesses help a community in addition to donating employees' time?**

616

Taking Stock of American Corporations

Step 3: Preparing a Financial Picture of Corporations Students will use research from Steps 1 and 2 to create posters that provide a financial picture of five companies.

Directions Instruct each group to review the research they collected in Steps 1 and 2 and to choose five companies that they feel are the best, based on financial earnings, labor practices, and social responsibility. After the groups have made their final choices, have them create a poster for each of the five companies. The poster should include information such as the company's product or service, financial earnings, labor relations, and contributions to communities or charities. Encourage students to be creative in their presentations. Groups will share their final products in Step 4. **OL**

(Project continued on the Visual Summary page)

Responsibilities

Main Idea Businesses have responsibilities to their consumers, owners, employees, and communities.

Economics & You Can you think of anything in your school that was donated by a local company? Read to find out why more and more businesses feel a responsibility to their communities.

A s they carry out their roles, businesses have different responsibilities. Sometimes laws spell out those responsibilities. Business managers may suffer serious consequences if they do not act responsibly.

Responsibilities to Consumers

Businesses have the responsibility of selling products that are safe. Products and services should also work as promised. A new video game should run without flaws. An auto mechanic should change a car's oil correctly. Businesses also have the responsibility of being truthful in their advertising. Finally, businesses should treat all customers fairly.

Responsibilities to Owners

Another responsibility is to the owners of the business. This is especially **crucial,** or key, in corporations, in which the managers and owners are different groups of people. To protect stockholders, corporations are required to release important financial information regularly.

Revealing, or making public, this information is called **transparency.** The purpose of publishing this information is to provide investors with full disclosure before they choose to invest, or continue to invest, in the company.

Sometimes the managers of a corporation are not completely honest in what they say about the business. When that happens, the government can prosecute them for breaking the law.

TIME™ Teens in Action

Brittany Clifford

B rittany Clifford, 16, of Scottsdale, Arizona, does not have cold feet when it comes to soliciting businesses for donations. A few companies foot the bill for Fuzzy Feet, Clifford's foundation that provides children with slippers to warm their feet during hospital stays.

QUESTION: Why did you start Fuzzy Feet?

ANSWER: My friend Michael had heart surgery. In the hospital, he always seemed to be cold. I found out that most of the children in the hospital wore only socks, and many had bare feet. I had an idea to establish a program that would donate slippers to sick children to ease their hospital stay.

Q: How many kids have you reached?

A: Through the generosity of businesses that donate slippers, Fuzzy Feet brings comfort and smiles to hospitalized children across the United States. We delivered our first slippers on Valentine's Day, 2002. Since then, Fuzzy Feet has given away more than 8,000 slippers to sick children in Phoenix, Los Angeles, and New York City.

Q: What kind of reaction do you get when you give kids the slippers?

A: Tons of smiles and lots of laughter. Some people have even cried.

Q: What about the future?

A: My goal is to have different chapters all around the U.S. and maybe in other countries. I want to go to Kenya, Africa, and give out slippers to the kids there. I want to go everywhere to give slippers to everyone!

ACTION FACT: Clifford loves to dance and cheerlead. She has a terrier named Tinker Bell.

Making a Difference — CITIZENSHIP

Describing How did Brittany get the idea for Fuzzy Feet?

W Writing Support

Personal Writing Have students write about a personal experience in which a product they purchased was flawed. Ask them to describe the problem and what—if anything—the business did to remedy the situation. Invite students to share their anecdotes with the class. **Ask:** How did the business that produced the flawed product guarantee their product? *(Answers will vary.)* How could word of mouth affect these businesses? *(It might cause them to lose customers.)* **OL**

D Differentiated Instruction

Gifted and Talented Have students research the Enron financial scandal. Have students find out what the crime was, who reported it, and the effect it had on stockholders. *(securities fraud and conspiracy)* Have students report their findings to the class. **AL**

TIME™ Teens in Action

Answer: Her friend, who was hospitalized, always had cold feet. She noticed many children in the hospital also had bare feet. She wanted to help keep children's feet warm.

Differentiated Instruction

Bethany McLean

Biography Activity 22, URB pp. 115–116

Objective:	To identify McLean's role in breaking the Enron scandal
Focus:	Discuss what McLean's job was and how it related to Enron.
Teach:	Discuss the reasons for the declining of stocks in the early 2000s.
Assess:	**Ask:** How could McLean tell Enron's accounting practices were questionable?
Close:	Create a timeline chronicling the fall of Enron.

Differentiated Instruction Strategies

BL **Ask:** Why would a business give misleading information about its earnings?

AL If you had 100 shares of Enron stock at its record-high, how much money would you have lost when the stock hit its lowest point?

ELL Have students define "bookkeeping" and "brokering."

S Skill Practice

Creating a Table Bring in copies of business magazines, such as *BusinessWeek,* *Forbes,* or *Fortune.* Ask students to find articles and to take notes about businesses that provide a safe workplace for employees or contribute to the community. Have students create a table that lists businesses that show civic responsibility. **OL**

Reading Check **Answer:** the sense of duty to pursue goals that benefit society as well as the business

Assess

Civics ONLINE

Study Central™ provides summaries, interactive games, and online graphic organizers to help students review.

Close

Illustrating Have students create a graphic organizer that shows specific examples of the responsibilities that businesses have to the consumers, employees, owners, and the community. **OL**

Section 3 Review

The scandal involving bankrupt energy company Enron showed the damage that can be done to investors when critical financial information is not reported by auditors.

Responsibilities to Employees

Businesses also have responsibilities to their employees. Businesses are required to give their workers a safe workplace and to treat all workers fairly and without **discrimination.** This means that they cannot treat employees differently on the basis of race, religion, color, gender, age, or disability.

S Some companies are recognized for working hard to meet the needs of their employees. Johnson & Johnson, which makes baby and health care products, takes an active role in fulfilling its responsibilities to its employees. *Latina* and *Working Mother* magazines cited Johnson & Johnson as one of the best U.S. companies in this area.

Responsibilities to the Community

More and more businesses are emphasizing their **social responsibility**—the obligation to pursue goals that benefit society as well as themselves. Gifts to charities are one example of how businesses meet this social responsibility. Many businesses take an active role in meeting the needs of their communities. The retail store Target, for example, promotes programs of community and national volunteering.

American Express has a tradition of responding to emergencies and providing assistance to disaster victims through grants to relief agencies. Another company program promotes historical and environmental preservation.

Reading Check **Defining** What is social responsibility?

Section Review
3

Vocabulary

1. **Write** a paragraph describing the social responsibility of businesses using the following terms: *transparency,* *discrimination.*

Main Ideas

2. **Describing** How do businesses act as producers?

3. **Explaining** Why is it important for corporations to publish their financial information regularly?

Critical Thinking

4. **Evaluating** Which of the business responsibilities described in this section do you feel makes the biggest impact on your community? Why?

5. **BIG Ideas** On a diagram like the one below, identify as many of the responsibilities of businesses to consumers as you can.

CITIZENSHIP Activity

6. **Analyzing** Contact a local business and ask how the business contributes to the community. Describe the actions of the business and what you think the effects are. Share your findings with the class.

Writing

7. **Descriptive Writing** Research on the Internet and describe the corporate responsibility program of a large, well-known U.S. company. Share your findings with the class.

Civics ONLINE

Study Central™ To review this section, go to glencoe.com.

Answers

1. Paragraphs should use vocabulary words according to their definitions in the section and in the Glossary.

2. They produce products that help meet people's needs.

3. It is important that a company's stockholders have enough financial information to make decisions about buying or selling their stock.

4. Possible answers: donating time, money, and supplies to charitable organizations; providing safe, reliable products and services; giving stockholders important financial information regularly; giving their employees a safe workplace

5.

6. Remind students to call ahead to set an appointment with the business owner and to state the purpose of their meeting. Students should take notes so that their findings are accurate and thank the business owner for his or her time.

7. Findings should demonstrate an understanding of the concept of social responsibility.

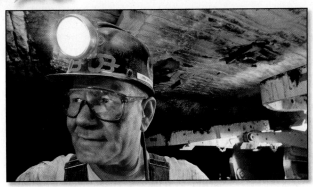

Mine workers support those pursuing safety laws

Business

- Sole proprietorships are small, easy-to-manage enterprises owned by one person.
- Proprietorships are relatively numerous and profitable.
- Disadvantages include raising financial capital and attracting qualified employees.
- Partnerships are owned by two or more persons.
- Corporations are owned by shareholders.

Independent beekeeper in North Carolina

- One of the major advantages of a corporation is limited liability.
- A major disadvantage of corporations is that they are taxed more heavily than other forms of business organizations.

Responsibilities

- Businesses have a responsibility to provide safe, working products to their customers.
- Businesses have an obligation to pursue goals that benefit society as a whole as well as themselves.

Labor

- For much of its history, organized labor in the United States has been split into two groups: craft unions and industrial unions
- Organized labor operates at three levels:
  - local union
  - national union
  - federation
- The closed shop (now illegal) required that employers hire only union members.

Small businesses employ local workers

Collective Bargaining

- Collective bargaining is the process by which unions and employers negotiate the conditions of employment.
- When collective bargaining fails, several other methods are available to settle labor disputes.

STUDY TO GO Study anywhere, anytime! Download quizzes and flash cards to your PDA from glencoe.com.

Visual Summary 22

Making Comparisons Have students create a slide show that depicts the three main types of businesses and describes the advantages and disadvantages of each. Students may draw posters or use magazine photographs as substitutes for slides. The slide show should include a script that explains each visual. **AL**

For additional practice on this skill (Making Comparisons), see the **Skills Handbook**.

Identifying Central Issues Have students create two advertisements. In one, the advertisement will emphasize a company's responsibility to its customers, including a safe product and guaranteed services. In the other, the advertisement will emphasize the product's qualities and selling points. Encourage students to be creative, making up names of companies and products. **OL**

Identifying Points of View Have students create a T-chart with the headings Labor and Management. In each column, have students write a bulleted list that describes the methods each side uses to settle labor disputes. **OL**

Hands-On Chapter Project
Step 4: Wrap-Up

Taking Stock of American Corporations

Step 4: Preparing a Financial Picture of Corporations Groups will present their five posters to the class and evaluate each company.

Directions Have each group present its poster to the class.

Each group should choose a speaker from its members to explain the poster. The speaker's presentation should focus on the financial stability and sound business practices of the selected companies.

After all groups have presented their posters, lead a discussion about companies in which students think it would be wise to invest money. Write their choices on the board. Next, ask students which companies would be good workplaces. Have them explain their choices. Display student posters in class. **OL**

Reviewing Vocabulary

1. C This question requires that students know the five advantages of corporations listed in the text. Students must also remember the difference between unlimited liability and limited liability. Students may mistakenly choose A, thinking that a corporation provides an environment for rapid promotion. However, with so many people working in corporations, the competition is tough.

2. A Students must remember the corporate chain of command to answer this question. The board of directors selects a president, who then hires a vice president. Managers are much lower in the chain of command. Choice D is a term used in small businesses.

3. B Students might hesitate between A and B. However, choice A, "arbitration," refers to including a third party to help settle differences.

4. D This question requires that students remember what responsibilities businesses have to their owners. The key word is "investors". This should help students remember that investors or stockholders are protected when investing in a corporation.

Reviewing Main Ideas

5. A To answer this question, students must recall that a business owned by a single person is the most common in the United States. Students may mistakenly choose D, thinking that because corporations are large and more well known, there are more of them.

6. B Students should notice the stem refers to partners, leaving choices B and C as possible answers. In a general partnership, choice C, all partners manage the business.

7. C This question requires that students differentiate between closed shops, which require workers to join a union *before* getting hired, and a union shop, which allows workers to join the union *after* they are hired.

TEST-TAKING **TIP**

> Question 8 asks you about mediation. Reading all the answer choices may help you remember information about this topic.

Reviewing Vocabulary

Directions: Choose the word(s) that best completes the sentence.

1. Among the advantages of corporations are the ease of raising financial capital, professional management, and _____.

  A rapid promotions   **C** limited liability

  B lower taxes   **D** specialization

2. The stockholders of a corporation elect a _____ to act on their behalf.

  A board of directors   **C** manager

  B vice president   **D** proprietor

3. Union and management discussion about wages and working conditions is an example of _____.

  A arbitration   **C** conflict

  B collective bargaining   **D** open shop

4. The purpose of _____ is to provide investors with full disclosure before they choose to invest.

  A insurance   **C** arbitration

  B insight   **D** transparency

Reviewing Main Ideas

Directions: Choose the best answer for each question.

Section 1 *(pp. 600–606)*

5. The most common form of business organization in the United States is the _____.

  A sole proprietorship

  B limited partnership

  C department store

  D corporation

6. At least one partner is not active in the daily running of the business in a _____.

  A proprietorship

  B limited partnership

  C general partnership

  D corporation

Section 2 *(pp. 608–613)*

7. In a union shop, workers are required to join a union _____.

  A before they begin working

  B after their first paycheck

  C after they begin working

  D before arbitration

8. Mediation is used in negotiations over wages and benefits when _____.

  A a strike is about to occur

  B the parties cannot agree

  C the government orders it

  D everything else has failed

Section 3 *(pp. 615–618)*

9. Businesses have the obligation to pursue goals that benefit society as well as themselves. This is called _____.

  A transparency

  B full disclosure

  C social responsibility

  D unlimited liability

10. Corporations are required to release important financial information regularly to _____.

  A citizens

  B employees

  C competitors

  D stockholders

GO ON

---

8. B Students must recall the process of management negotiation. When the parties cannot agree, they will often opt for mediation. Students may recall how mediation is used in school conflicts. Some students may choose A because strikes typically occur when negotiations break down. Government intervention, choice C, is used under extreme circumstances.

9. C Students need to remember what responsibilities businesses have to their consumers. Products must be safe, services should be performed as promised, and employees must be treated fairly. Choices A and B refer to a company making information available.

Critical Thinking

Directions: Base your answers to questions 11 and 12 on the map below and your knowledge of Chapter 22.

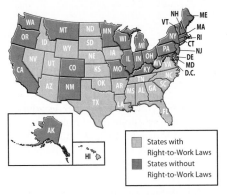

States with Right-to-Work Laws

States without Right-to-Work Laws

Source: National Right to Work Foundation.

11. What statement best explains the map's division of states in the eastern half of the United States?

    A The northern states have more people than the southern states.

    B Right-to-work laws are popular in vacation areas.

    C Union influence is stronger in the industrial Northeast.

    D The closed shop is more popular in the South.

12. Which of the following states does not permit union shops?

    A Idaho

    B Ohio

    C California

    D Missouri

Document-Based Questions

Directions: Analyze the following document and answer the short-answer questions that follow.

The Securities and Exchange Commission is the federal government's agency that regulates the sale of securities, such as stocks and bonds. Recently its chairman, William H. Donaldson, talked about business ethics to the Caux Roundtable in Minnesota.

> *As we all know, much of American business is defined by its dynamism and frequent change—new products, new systems, and vigorous competition. In this climate, business practices will frequently outpace any government regulator's ability to develop specific rules governing these practices. . . .*
>
> *This is where having a culture of doing what is right—in the absence of specific rules and even in the face of your competitors' choosing a different path—is vital. This is where the courage and commitment of the firm's leaders is needed to question whether a particular firm practice—no matter what the lawyers say—is truly ethical or is truly in the best interests of client and customers. . . . What I'm talking about is creating a renewed culture of compliance in American business.*

13. According to William H. Donaldson, why is it difficult for regulators to govern everyday business practices in America?

14. What is a "culture of compliance," and why is it needed?

Extended-Response Question

15. The free market has its own way of weeding out bad businesses. Should government also have a role in that process? Explain your answer.

For additional test practice, use Self-Check Quizzes—Chapter 22 on glencoe.com.

Need Extra Help?															
If you missed question...	1	2	3	4	5	6	7	8	9	10	11	12	13	14	15
Go to page...	605	604	611	617	601	602	610	611	618	617	610	610	617	617	617

ASSESSMENT

12. A Students must remember that a union shop means that an employee must join a union after he or she is hired. Idaho has a right-to-work law, indicating that workers do not have to join a union.

Document-Based Questions

13. America's business climate is one of frequent change. This makes it difficult for regulators to keep up by adopting specific rules for all the new practices.

14. Businesses should take the responsibility of doing what is ethical and fair whether or not the government has passed laws to make them comply.

Extended Response

15. Consumer and other businesses eventually refuse to purchase goods and services from other businesses that develop a bad reputation. However, many people may be hurt or cheated in the short term or may not realize the problem. In such cases, government has the power to investigate and to require accountability.

---

10. D Answering this question requires that students remember what responsibilities corporations have to their stockholders. The financial information allows stockholders to determine if they should continue to hold stock in the company or to sell.

Critical Thinking

11. C Students should notice that the states in the Northeast are states without right-to work laws. This indicates that these states have mandatory union membership. Students may mistakenly choose D, thinking a closed shop refers to a right-to-work state. However, it is a modified union shop that allows a worker to choose whether he or she wishes to join a union.

Have students visit the Web site at glencoe.com to review Chapter 22 and take the **Self-Check Quiz.**

Need Extra Help?

Have students refer to the pages listed if they miss any of the questions.

Focus

R Reading Strategy

Paraphrasing Read all of the excerpts aloud. Remind students that word structure changes over time, just as fashion styles do. To better understand the meaning behind the words of Adam Smith, have students, as a class, work on paraphrasing Smith's excerpt. Write their suggestions on the board. Remind students to emphasize the main idea.

Next, have students work alone to paraphrase the excerpts from Hayek and Hazlitt. Invite volunteers to read their work aloud.

Finally, have students write three sentences: one that summarizes Smith's ideas, one that summarizes "The Free Market" excerpt, and one that summarizes Hazlitt's sentence. **OL**

Additional Reading

Analyzing Primary Sources

Economic Concepts

Reading Focus

Capitalism is a system in which government plays a limited role in the nation's economic activity. Demand and supply have an important effect on production and pricing.

Read to Discover

As you read, think about the following:

- How do freedom of enterprise and freedom of choice apply to the American economy?
- How can prices serve as signals to both producers and consumers?

Reader's Dictionary

endeavours: makes an effort

effectually: fully adequately

monopolist: one who has exclusive control or ownership

affluence: wealth, abundance

brevity: shortness

R

The Invisible Hand

The central principles of capitalism are found in the words of Scottish economist Adam Smith.

[E]very individual, therefore, **endeavours** as much as he can [to direct his resources toward his own business so] that its produce may be of the greatest value; every individual … neither intends to promote the public interest, nor knows how much he is promoting it … he intends only his own gain, and he is in this, as in many other cases, led by an invisible hand to promote an end which was no part of his intention. … By pursuing his own interest he frequently promotes that of the society more **effectually** than when he really intends to promote it.

—from *The Wealth of Nations* by Adam Smith

The Free Market

Economists and political philosophers Friedrich Hayek and Henry Hazlitt were strong defenders of free market capitalism.

Our freedom of choice in a competitive society rests on the fact that, if one person refuses to satisfy our wishes, we can turn to another. But if we face a **monopolist** we are at his mercy. And an authority directing the whole economic system would be the most powerful monopolist imaginable.

—from *Road to Serfdom* by Friedrich A. Hayek

Benefits of Capitalism

Capitalism, the system of private property and free markets, is not only a system of freedom and of natural justice—which tends in spite of exceptions to distribute rewards in accordance with production—but it is a great co-operative and creative system that has produced for our generation an **affluence** that our ancestors did not dare dream of.

—from *Man vs. the Welfare State* by Henry Hazlitt

Review suggested books before assigning them.

Bill Gates: Helping People Use Computers by Charnan Simon is a biography about Bill Gates. Gates's innovative operating system, MS-DOS and Windows, helped create a computer revolution around the world.

The Problem Solvers: People Who Turned Problems into Products by Nathan Aaseng tells the story of nine inventors who turned an existing problem into successful products, such as Astroturf, the Jacuzzi, and the innovative Polaroid camera.

Bubblemania: The Chewy History of Bubble Gum by Lee Wardlaw traces the history of chewing gum from the Stone Age to today. Find out who invented modern bubblegum, what a bubblegum factory looks like, and how to blow a champion-size bubble.

Supply and Demand and Prices

British economist Alfred Marshall popularized the idea that prices are determined by *both* supply and demand.

The remainder of the present volume will be chiefly occupied with interpreting and limiting this doctrine that the value of a thing tends in the long run to correspond to its cost of production. In particular … [we will consider] the controversy whether "cost of production" [supply] or "utility" [demand] governs value.

We might as reasonably dispute whether it is the upper or the under blade of a pair of scissors that cuts a piece of paper, as whether value is governed by utility or cost of production. It is true that when one blade is held still, and the cutting is effected by moving the other, we may say with careless **brevity** that the cutting is done by the second; but the statement is not strictly accurate, and is to be excused only so long as it claims to be merely a popular and not a strictly scientific account of what happens.

In the same way, when a thing already made has to be sold, the price which people will be willing to pay for it will be governed by their desire to have it, together with the amount they can afford to spend on it. Their desire to have it depends partly on the chance that, if they do not buy it, they will be able to get another thing like it at as low a price: this depends on the causes that govern the supply of it, and this again upon cost of production. …

—from *Principles of Economics* by Alfred Marshall

R

Photographs as Primary Sources What do you know for sure by looking at the photograph? What can you infer by looking at the photograph? Write a caption explaining how this photograph can be used to illustrate the effect that supply and demand have on price.

623

DBQ Document-Based Questions

1. **Analyzing** Would Adam Smith agree that the benefits of free enterprise are a consequence of people's desire to make life better for others? Explain.

2. **Explaining** What does Hayek say is an important benefit of a free market economy? What benefit does Hazlitt stress?

3. **Connecting** What example does Marshall use to depict the workings of supply and demand on price? Do you think this is a good example? Explain.

4. **Categorizing** Some prices in our economy very seldom change, whereas others change all the time, even daily. Make a list of products whose prices change slowly, if at all. Make another list of products whose prices you think change quickly. Write a paragraph explaining in your own words why the price of some items is unchanging while the price of others changes often.

Analyzing Primary Sources

Teach

. . . .

R Reading Strategy

Making Connections Have students discuss why people are willing to pay a high price for something scarce. **OL**

Caption Answer: The house is large and is for sale. Inference: With a reduced price, the house was either too expensive or has been on the market for awhile. Sample Caption: Homebuyers are willing to spend more money if supply is low. Too many houses on the market causes prices to go down.

DBQ Document-Based Questions

Answers:
1. No. Smith writes that the entrepreneur intends only his own gain.
2. freedom of choice; wealth
3. a pair of scissors cutting a piece of paper; opinions may vary.
4. Responses will vary. Products whose value does not change include jewelry, expensive cars, gold, houses. Prices fluctuate quickly on fad items such as toys, farm products, and clothes.

Additional Support

Did You Know?

Shortages and Surpluses In 1973, OPEC stopped exporting oil to the United States, thus creating a scarcity of that important energy source. The price of gasoline quadrupled, from 25 cents a gallon to over a dollar. Some gas stations ran out of fuel and had to close. People waited in lines for hours to fill up their cars. In order to save money, Americans lowered their consumption of oil and started building more fuel-efficient cars.

The prices of surplus goods usually drop. For many years, oranges were a surplus crop in Florida, especially if there were no hurricanes or prolonged frosts. Orange growers had to sell oranges at low prices before they rotted. But then the Southern Regional Research Center developed frozen orange juice concentrate. Because the growers now had a use for their surplus oranges, they no longer had to sell them at low prices.

Unit 7 Planning Guide

UNIT PACING CHART

	Unit 7	Chapter 23	Chapter 24	Chapter 25
Day 1	Unit Opener, Reading Social Studies	Chapter Opener, Section 1, Issues to Debate	Chapter Opener, Section 1	Chapter Opener, Section 1
Day 2		Section 2, Financial Literacy	Section 2	Section 2, Financial Literacy
Day 3		Section 3, Landmark Supreme Court Case Studies	Section 3, Financial Literacy	Section 3, Chapter Review, Visual Summary
Day 4		Chapter Review, Visual Summary	Chapter Review, Visual Summary	Chapter Assessment
Day 5		Chapter Assessment	Chapter Assessment	TIME Reports
Day 6				Analyzing Primary Sources

 Teacher to Teacher

Josh Barkeloo, Westland High School, Galloway, Ohio

The Fed The Federal Reserve System can be challenging for students to understand. In my classroom we play a game that helps my students understand how The Federal Reserve operates. Using play money, bank slips, and teacher generated scenario cards, my students work in groups, acting as the banking industry. The goal is to be the best team at responding to The Fed, without triggering a collapse. Groups receive scenario cards from The Fed (the teacher) and must respond to them on a bank slip that will be deposited at the Federal Reserve with their reserve requirements. Example scenarios include: 1)Your Bank did not save enough money to meet your Reserve Requirements. How will you fix this problem before your deadline? 2)The Fed increases reserve requirements 10%. What impact does this have on your bank's lending power?

Author Note

Dear Social Studies Teacher:

Many economists admire the free enterprise system, claiming there is no better way to obtain, organize, and use scarce resources. The free enterprise system, along with private ownership of property, is often hailed as the most prolific weather-generating system the world has ever seen.

At the same time, the free enterprise system does not provide for all of the things we want and need. Free enterprise may be unmatched when it comes to providing personal goods, such as houses and cars; but it does not provide enough of the many public goods, such as education and national defense.

This is where our government comes into play.

Government in the United States is fascinating because it can do many things well. For example, it provides the laws, highways, and public education that set the United States apart from so many other nations. The government also can do many things poorly—as when political leaders succumb to corruption and commit us to courses of action that are not in our best interests.

Because of this dichotomy, there is heated debated between people wanting less government and those wanting more government. To make matters worse, even economists are not sure exactly how much government is necessary, let alone optimal. So, for an author like myself, it comes to this—how to write about something that can be both intensely satisfying as well as deeply infuriating?

The short answer is to be as descriptive as possible, weigh the costs and benefits of different government activities separately—and then let people make up their own minds. As teachers, we have the obligation to challenge our students to evaluate every situation on its own merits. We must give students the tools to help them analyze a problem as well as the information to help them make a decision.

Gary Clayton

Author

Unit Objectives

After studying this unit, students will be able to:

- Identify how government promotes and monitors economic activity in the United States.

- Define voluntary exchange and understand how the federal government and the banking industry function together to help people achieve their financial goals.

- Describe the system by which federal, state, and local governments and institutions manage tax income of citizens and businesses to promote economic goals.

Did You Know?

The value of money today is agreed upon by the people using it. For much of the country's history, the value of money was set by the gold standard. The United States and other nations determined the value of an ounce of gold. A dollar would then be equal to a certain weight of gold, and gold was available to back every dollar. However, it was not practical to carry around gold for buying and selling. Currency took the place of gold—it represented the gold sitting in banks.

The discovery of gold in California and Alaska in the late 1800s and World War I shook the stability of the gold standard. Eventually, in 1971, President Richard Nixon announced that the United States would abandon the gold standard as the method of setting the value of a dollar.

UNIT 7

The Free Enterprise System

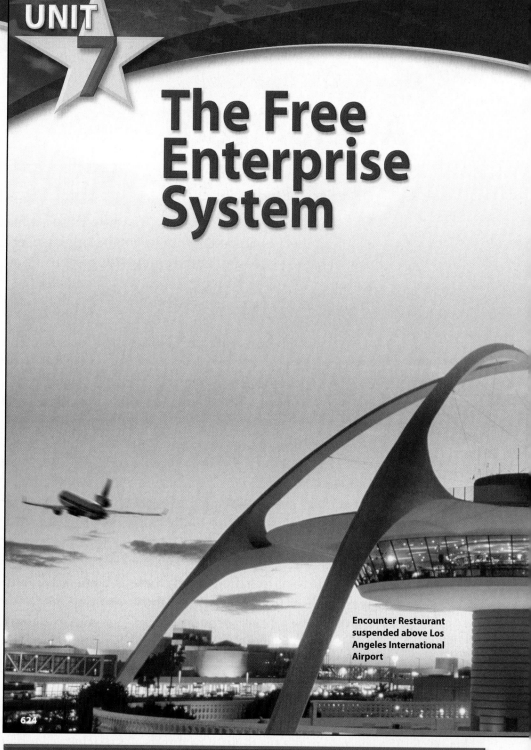

Encounter Restaurant suspended above Los Angeles International Airport

624

Activity: Launching the Unit

The Free Enterprise System Ask: Do you have a personal budget? How do you decide how much money to spend, where to spend it, what to buy, how much to save, and where to save it? *(Answers will include students' various spending plans or lack of plans.)* Explain that students will learn about the decisions that shape a budget. Individuals, families, businesses, states, and the federal government all must decide, based on money coming in, how to spend and what to set aside for later. To do this, people must understand how money works and how banks and other financial institutions invest money. At the end of the unit, have students revise their personal budgets, using what they have learned to shape their spending and saving decisions. **OL**

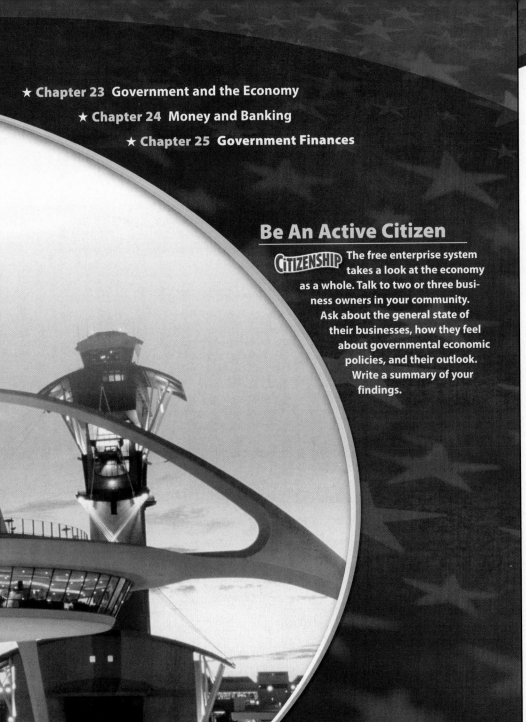

Be An Active Citizen

CITIZENSHIP The free enterprise system takes a look at the economy as a whole. Talk to two or three business owners in your community. Ask about the general state of their businesses, how they feel about governmental economic policies, and their outlook. Write a summary of your findings.

625

Be an Active Citizen

CITIZENSHIP Do your students know the business leaders in their community? Before beginning this activity, contact your city's chamber of commerce to get a list of community business leaders who may be willing to take time to participate in this activity. Before students interview business leaders, have them prepare a list of interview questions based on the instructions. Students may conduct their interviews by phone, by e-mail, or in person. Remind students to write formal thank-you letters to each business leader who participates.

Online Current Events Update

Visit Glencoe's *Online Current Events Update* **at** www.glencoe.com **to find news reports, features, maps, graphs, and photos of current events that shape our lives. Students can also make connections between historical events and current events by using the interactive time line.**

More About the Photo

Visual Literacy Los Angeles International Airport, called LAX, began as a small private landing strip in the early 1920s. The city purchased the land in 1928 and began to build the airport that today is one of the world's busiest for passengers and cargo. The futuristic terminal complex shown in this photo was completed in 1961 and has become a well-known California landmark. Students can view the space-age design of the Encounter Restaurant at www.lawa.org/lax/galleryAirport.cfm. Airports such as LAX are hubs of national and international travel and trade and strong contributors to the economy.

Why Making Inferences Is Important

Making inferences is an important skill for reading social studies and other subjects. Writers do not always connect every idea or draw each conclusion for their readers. Readers must make connections themselves, by using what they are reading and what they have read and experienced in the past. Help students see that they make inferences daily as they "read between the lines" to decide why a friend seems annoyed or when the best time to ask a parent for a favor might be.

Draw this "equation" on the board:

What the writer says
+ (plus)
What I already know or have experienced
= (equals)
An inference

Have students use the equation to make an inference based on the paragraph on inflation. Explain that readers must read closely, think about the information they read, and compare that information to their own knowledge and experiences to make helpful inferences. **OL**

Making Inferences

① Learn It!

Writers do not always state directly what they want to say. Often, they expect readers to make inferences or draw conclusions. Making an inference is "reading between the lines" by using clues and details the author provides to gain additional meaning from the text.

- Read the paragraph below.
- Pay attention to the facts provided by the writer.
- Read the inference that was drawn by the reader.

A chart like the one below can help you identify information you can use to make inferences.

> Suppose that an ice-cream cone that costs you a dollar doubles in price. This price increase causes the purchasing power of your dollar to fall because you have to use twice as many dollars to buy the same item. This is why inflation is particularly hard on people who have fixed incomes. . . . Inflation also reduces the value of money in a savings account because it will buy less after inflation than before.
>
> —*from page 642*

Information from Text

Inflation is an increase in prices.

Inflation is hard on people with fixed incomes.

It is important for a country to keep inflation under control because it hurts its citizens' purchasing power.

Inflation reduces the value of money in a savings account.

📖 Reading Strategy ⟨ Analyzing Information

Making Inferences Students can use an outline to identify and record the claims or assertions a writer makes. They can then study the outline to see how the writer's claims are related to each other—by cause and effect, for example, or by comparison or contrast. If students cannot identify this relationship, then they know that they must make an inference and supply the missing connection between ideas. **OL**

② Practice It!

Read the following paragraph from this unit.

- Draw a chart like the one shown below.
- Write three important facts from the paragraph in the boxes on the left-hand side.
- Make an inference about the sensitivity of the stock market based upon the information from the text and write it in the box on the right.

> The price of a company's stock, like most other things, is determined by supply and demand. Factors such as changes in sales or profits, rumors of a possible takeover, or news of a technological breakthrough can change the demand for a company's stock and, therefore, its price.
>
> —*from page 643*

Read to Write Activity

Read the section titled *Safeguarding Our Financial System* in Chapter 24. Jot down any relevant facts. Then, write a statement in which you make an inference about how safe you feel using the banking system.

② Practice It!

Have students read the paragraph "Why Stock Prices Change" in Chapter 23, Section 2. Explain that a graphic organizer listing *Facts* from which an *Inference* can be made can help readers understand what a writer means. Have students work with partners to make inferences about what companies should do to control stock prices. **OL**

③ Apply It!

Supply students with a page of letters to the editor of a major newspaper in your city and with the article that prompted the letters. Explain that because letters to the editor must be short, the ideas in each are condensed, forcing readers to make inferences. Have students read the article and the letters responding to it and use the information in the article to list inferences about the ideas expressed in the letters. **AL**

Information from Text

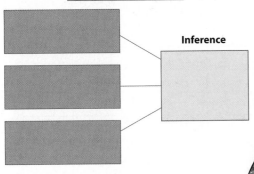

Inference

③ Apply It!

Choose one section from each chapter in this unit and create a chart like the one above. Read your facts to a partner and ask if your partner made a similar inference based on the facts you provided.

📖 Reading Strategy ▸ Read to Write

Writing Reviews Writing a review of a newspaper or magazine article, a section of a book, or a news show gives students the opportunity to use the skill of making inferences to evaluate the usefulness of the source of information. Allow students to choose the source of information they review so that it is in line with their interests: a sports page, for instance, or a description of a new video game from a gaming magazine. As they write their reviews, have them ask these questions to make inferences about the usefulness of the source: What information does the writer communicate? What information does the writer leave out? Can most readers supply the missing information and understand the source? **OL**

<table>
<tr><td colspan="2">Key to Ability Levels</td></tr>
</table>

Key to Ability Levels

BL Below level	**AL** Above level
OL On level	**ELL** English Language Learners

Key to Teaching Resources

Print Material	Transparency
CD-ROM or DVD	

Levels					Resources	Chapter Opener	Section 1	Section 2	Section 3	Chapter Assess
BL	OL	AL	ELL							
					FOCUS					
BL	OL	AL	ELL	🖳	**Daily Focus Skills Transparencies**		23-1	23-2	23-3	
					TEACH					
BL	OL		ELL	📁	**Reading Essentials and Note-Taking Guide***		p. 216	p. 219	p. 222	
	OL	AL		📁	**Citizenship/Decision-Making Activity, URB**		p. 3			
BL	OL		ELL	📁	**Reading Skills Activity, URB**		p. 7			
	OL	AL		📁	**Primary Source Reading, URB**		p. 15			
BL	OL	AL	ELL	📁	**Content Vocabulary Activity, URB***	p. 21	p. 21	p. 21	p. 21	
BL	OL	AL	ELL	📁	**Academic Vocabulary Activity, URB**	p. 23	p. 23	p. 23	p. 23	
	OL			📁	**Biography Activity, URB**		p. 25	p. 25		
BL	OL	AL	ELL	📁	**Writing Skills Activity, URB**				p. 27	
	OL	AL		📁	**Critical Thinking Skills Activity, URB**		p. 31			
BL	OL	AL	ELL	📁	**Chart, Graph, and Map Skills Activity, URB**			p. 33		
BL	OL	AL	ELL	📁	**Differentiated Instruction, URB**				p. 35	
BL	OL	AL	ELL	📁	**School-to-Home Connection Activity, URB***	p. 37	p. 37	p. 37	p. 37	
BL	OL		ELL	📁	**Guided Reading Activities, URB***		p. 41	p. 42	p. 43	
	OL	AL		📁	**Supreme Court Cases**				p. 3	
BL	OL	AL	ELL	📁	**Writer's Guidebook**	✓	✓	✓	✓	✓
	OL	AL		💿	**Primary Source Document Library**	✓	✓	✓	✓	✓
BL	OL	AL	ELL	💿	**Daily Lecture & Discussion Notes (in Pres. Plus)**		✓	✓	✓	✓
BL	OL	AL	ELL	💿	**StudentWorks™ Plus**		✓	✓	✓	✓
BL	OL	AL	ELL	💿	**Section Spotlight Videos**		✓	✓	✓	
BL	OL	AL	ELL	🖳	**TIME Interpreting Political Cartoons Transp.**			Ch. 23		
BL	OL	AL	ELL	🖳	**Writing Process Transparencies**	✓	✓	✓	✓	✓

Note: Please refer to the *Unit 7 Resource Book* for this chapter's URB materials.

* Also available in Spanish

Teacher Works *Plus*
All-In-One Planner and Resource Center

- Interactive Lesson Planner
- Interactive Teacher Edition
- Fully editable blackline masters
- Section Spotlight Videos Launch
- Differentiated Lesson Plans
- Printable reports of daily assignments
- Standards Tracking System

Levels					Resources	Chapter Opener	Section 1	Section 2	Section 3	Chapter Assess
BL	OL	AL	ELL							
					TEACH *(continued)*					
Teacher Resources				📁	Building Academic Vocabulary	✓	✓	✓	✓	✓
				📁	Strategies for Success	✓	✓	✓	✓	✓
				📁	Teacher's Guide to Differentiated Instruction	✓	✓	✓	✓	✓
				💿	Graphing Tool	✓	✓	✓	✓	✓
				💿	Presentation Plus! with MindJogger CheckPoint	✓	✓	✓	✓	✓
					ASSESS					
BL	OL	AL	ELL	📁	Quizzes and Tests*		p. 275	p. 276	p. 277	p. 278
BL	OL	AL	ELL	📁	Authentic Assessment with Rubrics			p. 27		
BL	OL	AL	ELL	📁	Standardized Test Practice		p. 45	p. 45	p. 45	p. 45
BL	OL	AL	ELL	💿	*ExamView® Assessment Suite* CD-ROM		23-1	23-2	23-3	Ch. 23
					CLOSE					
BL			ELL	📁	Reteaching Activity, URB*		p. 39	p. 39	p. 39	
BL	OL		ELL	📁	Reading and Study Skills Foldables™ Activity	p. 94	p. 95	p. 95		
BL	OL	AL	ELL	🖨	Graphic Organizer Transparencies & Strategies	✓	✓	✓	✓	✓

✓ Chapter- or unit-based activities applicable to all sections in this chapter

Using Study Central™

Take Notes

What is Study Central™?

Study Central™ is an interactive, online tool that provides students with a variety of ways to study and to check their comprehension of section content.

How can Study Central™ help my students?

The Take Notes portion of the Study Central™ Web site allows students to take notes related to an important section concept using an interactive graphic organizer and helps students:

- assess their comprehension of section content
- build study skills
- identify areas for additional study and reinforcement

Visit glencoe.com and enter a *QuickPass*™ code to go directly to resources for each chapter.

Civics ONLINE

Visit glencoe.com and enter *QuickPass*™ code CIV1360c23T for Chapter 23 resources.

You can easily launch a wide range of digital products from your computer's desktop with the McGraw-Hill Social Studies widget.

	Student	Teacher	Parent
Media Library			
• Student Edition Section Audio	●		●
• Spanish Audio Summaries	●		●
• Section Spotlight Videos	●	●	●
***Civics Today* Online Learning Center (Web Site)**			
• Chapter Overviews	●	●	●
• Study Central™	●	●	●
• Study-to-Go	●	●	●
• Student Web Activities	●	●	●
• In Motion Animation	●	●	●
• Self-Check Quizzes	●	●	●
• ePuzzles and Games	●	●	●
• StudentWorks™ Plus Online	●	●	●
• Vocabulary eFlashcards	●	●	●
• Web Activity Lesson Plans		●	
• Vocabulary PuzzleMaker	●	●	●
Classroom Tools			
• Multilingual Glossary	●	●	●
• Beyond the Textbook	●	●	●
• NGS MapMachine	●	●	●

GLENCOE BookLink 3

Use this database to search more than 30,000 titles to create a customized reading list for your students.

- Reading lists can be organized by students' reading level, author, genre, theme, or area of interest.
- The database provides Degrees of Reading Power™ (DRP) and Lexile™ readability scores for all selections.
- A brief summary of each selection is included.

Leveled reading suggestions for this chapter:

For students at a Grade 7 reading level:
- *The Problem Solvers: People Who Turned Problems into Products,* by Nathan Aaseng

For students at a Grade 8 reading level:
- *They All Laughed . . . From Light Bulbs to Lasers,* by Ira Flatow

For students at a Grade 9 reading level:
- *Business Builders in Cosmetics,* by Nathan Aaseng

For students at a Grade 10 reading level:
- *The Information Revolution: Opposing Viewpoints,* by Laura K. Egendorf

For students at a Grade 11 reading level:
- *Is Air Pollution a Serious Threat to Health?* by Andrea C. Nakaya

READING SUPPORT FROM JAMESTOWN EDUCATION

- **Timed Readings Plus in Social Studies** helps students increase their reading rate and fluency while maintaining comprehension. The 400-word passages are similar to those found on state and national assessments.

- **Reading in the Content Area: Social Studies** concentrates on six essential reading skills that help students better comprehend what they read. The book includes 75 high-interest nonfiction passages written at increasing levels of difficulty.

- **Reading Social Studies** includes strategic reading instruction and vocabulary support in Social Studies content for both ELLs and native speakers of English.

- **Content Vocabulary Workout** (Grades 6–8) accelerates reading comprehension through focused vocabulary development. Social Studies content vocabulary comes from the glossaries of Glencoe's Middle School Social Studies texts. www.jamestowneducation.com

KEY Teacher Wraparound

Use this key to help you identify the different types of prompts found in the Teacher Wraparound Edition.

R **Reading Strategies** activities help you teach reading skills and vocabulary.

C **Critical Thinking** strategies help students apply and extend what they have learned.

D **Differentiated Instruction** activities provide instruction for students learning to speak English, along with suggestions for teaching various types of learners.

S **Skill Practice** strategies help students practice historical analysis and geography skills.

W **Writing Support** activities provide writing opportunities to help students comprehend the text.

Teaching strategies and activities have been coded for ability level appropriateness.

AL Activities for students working above grade level

OL Activities for students working on grade level

BL Activities for students working below grade level

ELL Activities for English Language Learners

Focus

Why It Matters

Ask: Why is a strong economy important to you, your family, and the nation as a whole? *(Answers may include the idea that a strong economy means a better standard of living for students and their families and more choices of how people across the nation work, live, and enjoy themselves.)*

More About the Photo

Visual Literacy The Houston Ship Channel, in use since steamboats first navigated it in 1837, plays a major role in the economy of the Houston area and of Texas. More than 150 businesses provide over 250,000 jobs and pump billions of dollars into the economy as 200 million tons of cargo enter the United States through the port each year. The Port of Houston Authority oversees the ship channel's operations.

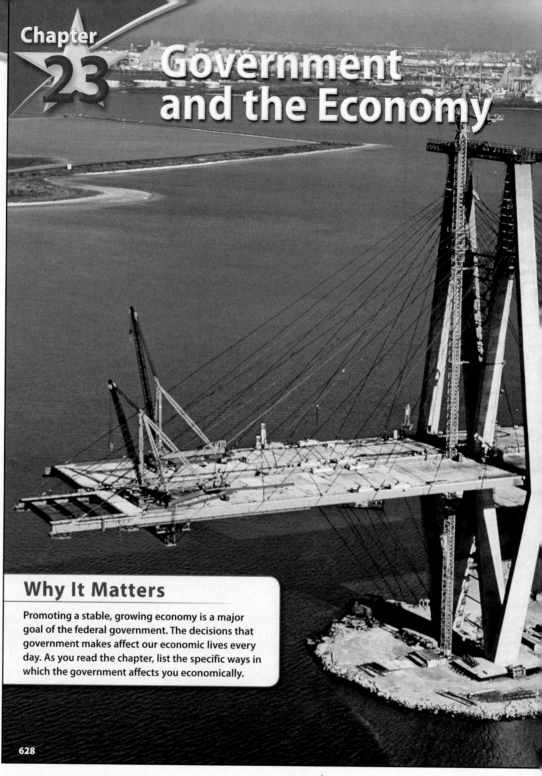

Chapter
23
Government and the Economy

Why It Matters

Promoting a stable, growing economy is a major goal of the federal government. The decisions that government makes affect our economic lives every day. As you read the chapter, list the specific ways in which the government affects you economically.

628

Teach

BIG Ideas *As you begin teaching each section, use these questions and activities to help students focus on the Big Ideas.*

Section 1

The Role of Government Ask: Where do you see government influence in how you earn and spend your money? *(Answers may include government rating systems, which place age restrictions on products, and age, driving, and time limitations for some teen jobs.)* Point out that in Section 1 students will learn how government intervention encourages a healthy and competitive business environment in the nation. **OL**

Section 2

Measuring the Economy Ask: Do you ever hear or read about the daily gains and losses of the stock market? What does this information mean? *(Answers may include an awareness of the Dow Jones, NASDAQ, or S&P highs and lows and an understanding that when the stock market goes up, it is often an indicator of a healthy economy.)* Tell students that in Section 2 they will learn how economists determine the health of the nation's economy. **OL**

Civics ONLINE
Visit glencoe.com and enter
QuickPass™ code
CIV3093c23 for
Chapter 23
resources.

Chapter Introduction
23

🔊 Chapter Audio

BIG Ideas

Section 1: The Role of Government

Free enterprise is the freedom of individuals and businesses to operate and compete with a minimum of government interference or regulation. In order to encourage competition and prevent monopolies, governments take steps to regulate economies.

Section 2: Measuring the Economy

An economic system is the way a society organizes the production and consumption of goods and services. Our government plays a limited, but important, role in measuring and trying to balance the alternating periods of growth and decline called the business cycle.

Section 3: Government, the Economy, and You

People form governments to establish order, provide security, and accomplish common goals. A major focus of government programs is to help people in poverty.

Suspension bridge construction across the Houston, Texas, ship channel

FOLDABLES™
Study Organizer

Summarizing Information Study Foldable Make the following Foldable to help you summarize what you read about the role of government, how it measures the economy, and how you are involved.

Step 1 Mark the midpoint of the side edge of a sheet of paper.

Step 2 Fold the outside edges in to touch at the midpoint.

Step 3 Unfold the paper and label the three columns as shown.

Reading and Writing As you read the chapter, note information about the three economics topics in each of the columns. Then write a summary of each topic using the information you noted.

FOLDABLES™
Study Organizer

Dinah Zike's Foldables

Purpose This Foldable helps students summarize information about the interaction of the government, the individual, and the economy and their respective roles in this interaction. The completed Foldable will help students review the key concepts in the chapter and apply them to their own lives. **OL**

📁 More Foldables activities for this chapter can be found in the *Dinah Zike's Reading and Study Skills Foldables* ancillary.

Civics ONLINE

Visit glencoe.com and enter *QuickPass*™ code CIV1360c23T for Chapter 23 resources, including a Chapter Overview, Study Central™, Study-to-Go, Student Web Activity, Self-Check Quiz, and other materials.

Chapter 23   629

Section 3

Government, the Economy, and You Ask: What programs exist in your community to assist people in financial need? *(Answers may include local food pantries, school lunch programs, homeless shelters, or counseling programs.)* Explain that in Section 3 students will learn what steps local, state, and federal governments take to aid people in times of financial difficulty. **OL**

Focus

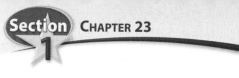

Bellringer
Daily Focus Transparency 23–1

Guide to Reading
Answers to Graphic:

```
        Cause:
       Antitrust
         Laws

Effect:              Effect:
encourage            prohibit
competition          business
by banning           practices
monopolies           that limit
                     competition
```

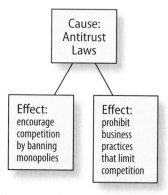

Section Spotlight Video

Have students watch the Chapter 23, Section 1 video at glencoe.com.

Resource Manager

Guide to Reading

Big Idea
Free enterprise is the freedom of individuals and businesses to operate and compete with a minimum of government interference or regulation.

Content Vocabulary
- private good *(p. 631)*
- public good *(p. 631)*
- externality *(p. 631)*
- monopoly *(p. 633)*
- antitrust law *(p. 633)*
- merger *(p. 633)*
- natural monopoly *(p. 634)*
- recall *(p. 635)*

Academic Vocabulary
- exclude *(p. 631)*
- achieve *(p. 632)*
- minimize *(p. 634)*

Reading Strategy
Analyzing Cause and Effect As you read, record the results of the government passing antitrust laws on a graphic organizer like the one below.

```
       Cause:
      Antitrust
        Laws

Effect:        Effect:
```

The Role of Government

Real World Economics Fuels of the future are brought to life at a government-sponsored design exposition in Washington, DC. Scientists, businesspeople, and students are brought together to compete against each other with new ideas about technology and design. This student from Appalachian State University won an award for building a production facility that makes biodiesel fuel from used cooking oil and then recycles the oil's waste to make soap.

▼ **Award-winning student with biodiesel fuel**

R Reading Strategies	**C** Critical Thinking	**D** Differentiated Instruction	**W** Writing Support	**S** Skill Practice
Teacher Edition • Academic Vocab., p. 631 • Making Connect., p. 632 • Act. Prior Know., p. 634 **Additional Resources** • Read. Skills, URB p. 7 • Pri. Source Read., URB p. 15 • Foldables, URB p. 95	**Teacher Edition** • Contrasting, p. 631 • Det. Cause/Effect, p. 633 • Ident. Cent. Issues, p. 634 **Additional Resources** • Biography Act., URB p. 25 • Crit. Think. Act., URB p. 31	**Teacher Edition** • Visual/Spatial, p. 633 **Additional Resources** • School-to-Home Act., URB p. 37 • Reteach. Act., URB p. 39	**Teacher Edition** • Persuasive Writing, p. 635 **Additional Resources** • Citizenship/Decision-Making, URB p. 3	**Teacher Edition** • Analyzing Visuals, p. 632 **Additional Resources** • Daily Focus Trans., 23–1

Providing Public Goods

Main Idea Governments usually provide public goods, while businesses usually provide private goods.

Economics & You Would you like to live near an airport? Read to find out what economic idea might influence your decision.

Government plays several important roles in the economy. One role is providing goods and services—such as national defense—that private businesses do not provide.

What Are Private Goods? Most goods and services that businesses produce are private goods, or goods that, when consumed by one individual, cannot be consumed by another. Consumption of private goods and services is subject to the exclusion principle. This means that a person is **excluded**, or prevented, from using that good or service unless he or she pays for it. Private goods are the items we buy and replace, for example, clothes and food. Private services include such things as insurance, haircuts, medical services, auto care, and telephone services.

What Are Public Goods? This is in contrast to public goods, or goods that can be consumed by one person without preventing the consumption of the good by another. Consumption of public goods is subject to the nonexclusion principle. This means that no one is excluded from consuming the benefits of a public good whether or not he or she pays. Examples of public goods include public parks, public libraries, museums, highways, and street lighting.

Because of the difficulty of charging for public goods, the government usually provides them. If government did not provide these public goods and services, then the private sector would not provide them in adequate amounts because it is so difficult to get people to pay for them.

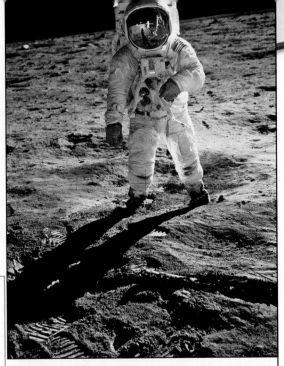

Public Goods Public goods include the highway system, national defense, and space exploration. *Analyzing* Would the private sector provide these goods and services if the government did not?

As a result, the production of public goods is one of the responsibilities of government. The government still has to pay for them, but it raises the money through taxes and then provides the products to everyone.

Dealing with Externalities

The government also plays a role in handling externalities. An **externality** is the unintended side effect of an action that affects someone not involved in the action. Suppose a company pays end-of-year bonuses to its workers. Restaurants and stores in the area will probably see their sales go up because the workers have more money to spend. These businesses experience externalities. They were not involved in the paying of bonuses, but they were affected by it.

Chapter 23   631

Teach

R Reading Strategy

Academic Vocabulary Ask: What other words or phrases mean nearly the same as "excluded"? *(Answers may include synonyms such as "left out", "omitted", "barred", "prohibited", and "kept out".)* **ELL**

C Critical Thinking

Contrasting Ask: How do private goods differ from public goods? *(Private goods must be paid for by the individual consumer; public goods are provided by the government for all to use without a transfer of money. Private goods are often items that are used up and replaced; public goods are often used over a long period of time.)* **OL**

Caption Answer:
Answers may include the idea that some of these public goods, such as the highway and defense systems, are necessary and might be provided by private companies. The space program, though not essential, might also hold great interest for private companies.

Differentiated Instruction

Free Enterprise and You

Cit./Decision-Making Act. 7, URB pp. 3–4

Objective:	To discuss big-box chains
Focus:	Have students explain why they shop at certain stores.
Teach:	Have students describe big-box stores near them.
Assess:	Have students debate the pros and cons of big-box stores.
Close:	Invite a local businessperson to describe the impact of big-box stores on him or her.

Differentiated Instruction Strategies

BL Ask big-box store employees about their jobs. Report your findings to the class.

AL Research a community that has tried to keep a big-box store from moving in. Report your findings to the class.

ELL Discuss U.S. big-box stores that operate in other countries.

S Skill Practice

Analyzing Visuals Ask: Of the federal agencies described, which is the most vital? *(Answers will vary but immediate medical care will probably be mentioned.)* **OL**

R Reading Strategy

Making Connections Ask: How does the government work to prevent negative externalities? *(through agencies such as the Environmental Protection Agency and Food and Drug Administration)* **OL**

Analyzing Charts

Answers:
1. the EPA
2. Answers may include the idea that health concerns are usually national, not statewide, and researchers work in every part of the nation.

Civics ONLINE

Objectives and answers to the **Student Web Activity** can be found at glencoe.com under the Web Activity Lesson Plan for this chapter.

Reading Check Answer: taxes

Hands-On Chapter Project
Step 1

An Economic History of Our Community

Step 1: Locating Sources of Information Students will research sources of information about the community's economic development.

Directions Write the Big Idea of Section 3 on the board. Remind students that an

---

Federal Regulatory Agencies

Federal Agency	Responsibility
Environmental Protection Agency (EPA)	Prevents air and water pollution
Centers for Disease Control and Prevention (CDC)	Considers all factors that affect the health of the nation
Occupational Safety and Health Administration (OSHA)	Makes sure that workplaces are safe and healthful
National Institutes of Health (NIH)	Serves as the nation's medical research agency
Food and Drug Administration (FDA)	Makes sure that food, drugs, and cosmetics are pure, effective, and truthfully labeled

Analyzing Charts

1. **Identifying** Which agency would regulate a kind of filtering system on a factory smokestack?
2. **Analyzing** Why do you think the National Institutes of Health is a national agency rather than a state-run agency?

Positive Externalities One reason that governments provide public goods is that these goods produce positive externalities. Everyone—not just drivers—benefits from good roads. Good roads make it cheaper to transport goods. As a result, those transported goods can sell for lower prices, which benefits everybody.

Governments can also take actions that indirectly lead to positive externalities. In the 1960s, the government wanted to put a man on the moon. The space program needed someone to develop smaller computers to **achieve,** or reach, this goal. The government provided money to researchers who developed tiny computer chips. Today, those chips are found in calculators, cars, household appliances, and cell phones, benefiting many people. Many government activities encourage positive externalities.

Negative Externalities Some externalities can be negative. That happens when an action harms an uninvolved third party. Suppose a chemical company tried to cut costs by dumping poisonous waste into a river. People who relied on the river water would suffer a negative externality from this pollution. One of the roles of government is to prevent these and other kinds of negative externalities.

Civics ONLINE
Student Web Activity Visit glencoe.com and complete the Chapter 23 Web Activity.

Reading Check Describing How does a government usually pay for public goods and services?

---

orderly, secure community is one in which a strong economy provides work for people to do and goods and services for consumers to use. Tell students that they will learn about the economy in their community and assess its health. They will use their research to produce a brochure about their community's economic history and its future.

Gathering Information Divide students into groups to research libraries, newspaper archives, historical societies, and Web sites or local offices for information about the history of small and large businesses in their community. Each group should take notes from their assigned source. **OL**

(Project continued in Section 2)

Maintaining Competition

Main Idea One government role is to ensure competition in the economy.

Economics & You Have you ever played the game Monopoly? Read to find out for which economic idea this game is named.

Markets work best when there are large numbers of buyers and sellers. Sometimes, however, a market becomes controlled by a **monopoly**, a sole provider of a good or service. With no competition, a monopoly can charge any price it wants, and consumers may suffer.

Antitrust Laws

Historically, one of the goals of government in the United States has been to encourage competition in the economy. The government tries to meet this objective through its **antitrust laws,** or laws to control monopoly power and to preserve and promote competition.

Sherman Antitrust Act In 1890, the federal government passed the Sherman Antitrust Act. This law banned monopolies and other forms of business that prevented competition. In 1911, the government used it to break up the Standard Oil Company, which had a monopoly on oil. More than 70 years later, the government used the act again to regulate American Telephone and Telegraph (AT&T). This action created more competition in telephone service.

Clayton Act In 1914 Congress passed the Clayton Act to clarify the Sherman Act. The Clayton Act prohibited or limited a number of business practices that lessened competition; for example, charging high prices in an area where little competition existed. Another part of the Clayton Act restricted the use of the injunction against labor unions. It also gave legal support to peaceful strikes and boycotts.

Mergers

Whenever a **merger,** a combination of two or more companies to form a single business, threatens competition, government may step in to prevent it. For example, when the two leading office-supply stores, Staples and OfficeMax, wanted to merge, the federal government prevented it, arguing that a merger of these two giant firms would result in less competition and higher prices for consumers. On the other hand, the government did not prevent the 2001 merger of Hewlett-Packard and Compaq Computer, two leading personal-computer makers.

Oil Trust John D. Rockefeller took almost total control of the oil industry in the late 1800s until the government broke up his Standard Oil empire. *Explaining* **Why did the government want the Standard Oil Company broken up?**

633

C Critical Thinking

Identifying Central Issues Ask: How do governments reduce negative externalities? *(by regulating some activities of businesses)* **BL**

R Reading Strategy

Activating Prior Knowledge Ask: Why is the telecommunications industry no longer a natural monopoly? *(There are now many companies competing for consumers with a variety of telecommunications products.)* **OL**

American Biography

Answer:
Chao has worked in the Office of Policy Development, the Department of Transportation, the Federal Maritime Commission, the Peace Corps, and the Department of Labor.

Additional Support

Teacher Tip

As you guide the discussion, ascertain whether students' understanding of the connection between natural monopolies and the need for government regulation is clear.

American Biography

Elaine L. Chao (1953 –)

Elaine Chao is the first Asian American to hold the position of Secretary of Labor. She was named to the position in 2001 by President George W. Bush.

Chao's father came to the United States in 1958 as an employee of a Chinese shipping company and later opened his own shipping business. He brought his family to America three years later. Elaine graduated from Syosset High School in Westchester County, New York, and earned her bachelor's degree in economics from Mount Holyoke College. She was awarded an MBA from Harvard Business School and also studied at Columbia University, MIT, and Dartmouth College.

Before entering government service, Chao worked for Gulf Oil Corporation and as a loan specialist in the ship financing department of Citicorp. She was accepted as a White House Fellow in 1983 as a special assistant in the Office of Policy Development in the Ronald Reagan administration. Chao's other government positions include Deputy Secretary at the U.S. Department of Transportation, Chairman of the Federal Maritime Commission, and Deputy Maritime Administrator in the U.S. Department of Transportation. President George H. W. Bush nominated her to head the Peace Corps in 1991.

Chao, the mother of three daughters, is married to the former Assistant Majority Leader of the United States Senate, Senator Mitch McConnell of Kentucky.

Making a Difference CITIZENSHIP

Describing In what departments of government has Chao worked?

Regulating Market Activities

C Recall that governments want to reduce negative externalities. To carry out this work, they regulate some activities by businesses. That is, government agencies make sure that businesses act fairly and follow the laws. Some of the federal agencies that regulate businesses are shown on the chart on page 632. Government regulation is needed in three important areas.

Natural Monopolies Sometimes it makes sense to have a single firm produce all of a particular good or service for a market. For example, it would not make sense to have three or four telephone companies compete in a local community if each company had to put up its own set of telephone poles.

This often leads to a **natural monopoly,** a market situation in which the costs of production are **minimized,** or lessened, by having a single firm produce the product. In exchange for having the market all to itself, the firm agrees to government regulation. This is why many public services such as natural gas and water are delivered by a single firm.

R In the past, the telecommunications industry was usually considered a natural monopoly. Like water companies and railway companies, the existence of several telecommunications companies serving the same area would result in inefficiency.

The large size, or scale, of most natural monopolies seemed to give them economies of scale—by which they could produce the largest amount for the lowest cost. However, advances in technology are making these industries more competitive. The government is making moves to deregulate and open natural monopolies up for competition.

Activity: Technology Connection

Considering New Natural Monopolies Ask: What new technologies might fall under government regulation as natural monopolies? Which will thrive in a competitive market instead? Have students brainstorm a list of new technologies for producing energy that are slowly entering the energy market. Students might think of technologies that utilize wind, solar, or wave power. Have students work in groups to research what is required to produce these new kinds of energy. **OL**

Advertising and Product Labels

Government is also involved when it comes to truth in advertising and product labeling information. For example, some sellers may be tempted to give misleading information about a product in order to sell it. Even the content of food labels is important because some people are allergic to certain products such as eggs, milk, and peanuts.

The Food and Drug Administration (FDA) is the agency that deals with the purity, effectiveness, and labeling of food, drugs, and cosmetics. The Federal Trade Commission (FTC) deals with problems of false advertising and product claims. The FTC also administers antitrust laws forbidding unfair competition and price fixing.

The FTC has the power to review the advertising claims made about all products sold in interstate commerce. It may determine whether an advertisement for a product is false or unfair. If it is, the FTC can order the company to change the ad to comply with FTC standards. As a result of one ruling, cigarette manufacturers must place a health warning on cigarette packages.

Product Safety Product safety is another important area of regulation. From time to time, the Consumer Product Safety Commission recalls products that pose a safety hazard. In a **recall,** a company pulls a product off the market or agrees to change it to make it safe. In September 2006 producers needed to recall fresh spinach because of suspected E-coli contamination. That same month, 7 million Sony laptop batteries were recalled.

✓ Reading Check Explaining What is a recall? Why are some products recalled?

W **Writing Support**

Persuasive Writing Have students select an ad from a magazine or newspaper for a product with which they are familiar. Ask them to write an assessment of the ad as though they are from the FTC and must review all advertising claims. **AL**

✓ Reading Check Answer: A recall is the removal of a product from the market due to safety or health concerns.

Assess

Civics ONLINE

Study Central™ provides summaries, interactive games, and online graphic organizers to help students review content.

Close

Predicting Consequences Have students discuss what the consequences might be with the end of government oversight of the nation's business practices. **OL**

Section 1 Review

Vocabulary

1. Write a paragraph related to government's role in the economy using the following terms: *private good, public good, externality, monopoly, antitrust law, merger, natural monopoly, recall.*

Main Ideas

2. Explaining What is a positive externality?

3. Describing How can a monopoly control the price of a product?

Critical Thinking

4. Concluding Think about something that your local government provides for citizens. Could this good or service be supplied by a private business? Why or why not?

5. BIG Ideas On a diagram like the one below, give an example of a negative externality and a positive externality of having an airport built near your home.

Airport	
Negative Externality	Positive Externality

CITIZENSHIP Activity

6. Research Interview a local business owner. Find out what he or she feels about government regulations that affect his or her business. Ask how the business owner would change government policies and programs.

7. Persuasive Writing Write a paragraph either supporting or disagreeing with this statement: Private businesses can do a better job than government of supplying water, sewer, and electricity to our community. Give reasons for your opinion.

Civics ONLINE

Study Central™ To review this section, go to glencoe.com.

Chapter 23 635

Section 1 Review

Answers

1. Paragraphs should use the vocabulary words according to their definitions in the section and in the Glossary.

2. A positive externality is a benefit from a product or service to people who do not use that product or service.

3. A monopoly is the only source of a product or service, so it can set the price of that product or service and not fear any competition.

4. Answers may include any good or service provided by the community, such as parks, hiking trails, and water and sewer services.

5.

Airport	
Negative Externalities	Positive Externalities
More noise, traffic, and air pollution	New businesses such as restaurants and motels for travelers

6. Students should report the interviewed business owner's ideas accurately and completely.

7. Paragraphs should be governed by a clear position supporting or disagreeing with the statement and should include specific support for that position.

S Skill Practice

Debating the Issue

Answers:

1. Outsourcing is moving jobs from the United States to other countries, where workers are paid less.

2. Jobs requiring specialized training and education—skilled labor— were once secure.

3. Madigan suggests that training to help workers gain skills and financial support for those whose jobs are outsourced are needed. Mandel says that U.S. businesses must continue to produce new technologies and thus new and better jobs.

4. The stockholder is interested in increasing profits, and outsourcing can increase profits by decreasing labor costs. The worker wants to protect a job.

Additional Support

Issues to Debate

Does outsourcing jobs to other countries hurt America?

How would you feel if you had a good job for several years, then your company closed its American office and opened a new branch in another country? National news media often report the number of "jobs lost" in the United States from this outsourcing of jobs. Outsourcing is a controversial issue because it causes plant closings and unemployment in the United States. The number of jobs being outsourced has been growing. Who supports outsourcing? Not only do businesses like the idea, but some economists support it because it helps American business to be competitive in world markets. Outsourcing also helps consumers by lowering prices. So, does outsourcing hurt the American economy?

The Vietnamese workers at a Nike plant help the company export about 22 million pairs of shoes each year.

YES

Kathleen Madigan, a Business Outlook editor for *BusinessWeek,* warns that outsourcing is not only growing, but it is now hitting skilled and service jobs. Former jobs such as writing computer code are no longer complex enough to be secure, and American technology companies are moving them to other continents. What can be done? Madigan says, "The only way the U.S. will keep one rung ahead of the rest of the world is to ensure that we have a broadly educated workforce that keeps learning. At the corporate level, training programs would help current employees move up to better positions. And the government should overhaul jobless benefits to allow displaced workers the time and money to enter new careers."

—Kathleen Madigan, August 25, 2003

NO

Michael J. Mandel, *BusinessWeek* chief economist, believes that the United States should not fear outsourcing as long as we continue to be the most innovative economy. Our new technologies are providing more jobs than we are losing. "Despite anecdotes of well-paying jobs being sucked overseas, there's little evidence that educated workers, overall, are worse off than they were after the last recession." Mandel believes the key is staying at the top of the innovation ladder. "The biggest danger to U.S. workers isn't overseas competition. It's that we worry too much about other countries climbing up the ladder and not enough about finding the next higher rung for ourselves."

—Michael J. Mandel, August 25, 2003

Debating the Issue

1. **Defining** What is outsourcing?

2. **Identifying** What kind of jobs used to be secure from outsourcing?

3. **Comparing** What do the authors quoted above suggest the United States should do about outsourcing?

4. **Analyzing** Why might a stockholder or owner of an American company disagree with a worker in that company about outsourcing?

Activity: U.S./World Connections

Training for Call Centers **Ask:** What is it like to take a job at a call center and deal with phone calls from Americans? Tell students that one kind of job that has often been outsourced is that of call center worker. These workers take catalogue orders, deal with computer service issues, handle customer complaints, and do other jobs that can be done on the phone. Have students use the Internet to see what call center workers in other countries must learn before they can work for U.S. businesses. Allow students to discuss their findings and to consider the challenges of this type of job. **OL**

Guide to Reading

Big Idea
An economic system is the way a society organizes the production and consumption of goods and services.

Content Vocabulary
- real GDP *(p. 638)*
- business cycle *(p. 638)*
- civilian labor force *(p. 640)*
- unemployment rate *(p. 640)*
- fiscal policy *(p. 641)*
- inflation *(p. 641)*
- consumer price index (CPI) *(p. 642)*

Academic Vocabulary
- period *(p. 638)*
- implement *(p. 641)*

Reading Strategy
Organizing Information
Create a graphic organizer like the one below to describe the expansion and recession that can take place in an economy.

```
        Economy
       /        \
  Expansion    Recession
```

🔊 **Section Audio**   🎬 **Spotlight Video**

Measuring the Economy

Real World Economics Traders at the Chicago Stock Exchange cheer after receiving encouraging news from the Federal Reserve. Organized in 1848, the Chicago Board of Trade was the first grain futures exchange in the United States. In its early history, the CBOT monitored only the business of agriculture. Today, cotton, grain, soy, and silver are just some of the items bought and sold in the electronic hubbub of the Chicago Board of Trade.

▼ **Traders in the Dow Pit of The Chicago Board of Trade**

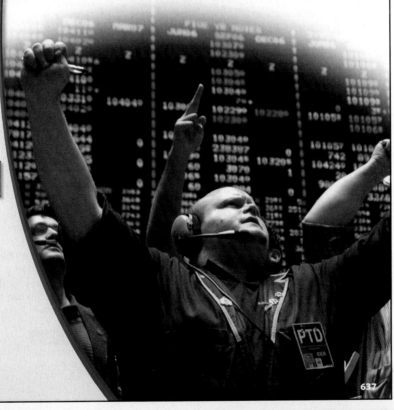

637

Focus

Bellringer
Daily Focus Transparency 23–2

Guide to Reading
Answers to Graphic:

```
        Economy
       /        \
```

Expansion:	Recession:
real GDP goes up; reaches a peak and then declines; normally lasts longer than recession	real GDP goes down; tends to be shorter than expansion; job losses; may worsen into depression

🎬 **Section Spotlight Video**

Have students watch the Chapter 23, Section 2 video at <u>glencoe.com</u>.

Resource Manager

R **Reading Strategies**	**C** **Critical Thinking**	**D** **Differentiated Instruction**	**W** **Writing Support**	**S** **Skill Practice**
Teacher Edition	**Teacher Edition**	**Teacher Edition**	**Teacher Edition**	**Teacher Edition**
• Making Connections, pp. 638, 643	• Drawing Con., p. 639	• English Learners, p. 639	• Personal Writing, p. 644	• Visual Literacy, p. 638
• Reading Graphs, p. 640	• Det. Cause/Effect, p. 640	• Adv. Learners, p. 641		**Additional Resources**
• Identifying, p. 641	• Ident. Cent. Issues, p. 642	• Logical/Math., p. 642		• Chart, Graph, and Map Act., URB p. 33
• Set. a Purpose, p. 643		• Visual/Spatial, p. 644		• Daily Focus Trans., 23–2
• Monitoring, p. 645	**Additional Resources**			• Pol. Cartoons Trans. 23
Additional Resources	• Biography, URB p. 25	**Additional Resources**		
• Acad. Vocab, URB p. 23	• Quizzes and Tests, p. 276	• School-to-Home Act., URB p. 37		
• Foldables, p. 95		• Reteach Act., URB p.39		

Teach

R Reading Strategy

Making Connections Ask: What are two advantages of a growing economy? *(Businesses hire more workers, and people have more money to spend.)* **OL**

S Skill Practice

Visual Literacy Ask: In what way does the representation of the business cycle, the wave graph, fail to represent an actual business cycle? *(The wave components are equal in length and height, whereas a real business cycle will exhibit variation in the lengths of expansion and recession and in the heights of peaks and depths of troughs.)* **AL**

Analyzing Graphs

Answers:
1. a trough
2. the peak; expansion leads to the peak

✓ Reading Check Answer: The phases of a business cycle are expansion leading to a peak in growth, followed by a contraction or recession of growth, leading to a trough.

Differentiated Instruction

Measuring Growth

Main Idea The real gross domestic product is the most accurate measure of an economy's performance.

Economics & You Have you ever found that an item you wanted to buy had gone up in price? Read to find out how we have to adjust for this phenomenon when we measure economic growth.

Sometimes the economy grows, but sometimes it falters. How do economists decide which **period,** or phase, the economy is in? How do government leaders decide what to do about these changes in economic performance? You will learn the answers to these questions.

R One measure of an economy's performance is whether or not it is growing. Economic growth is beneficial to nearly everyone. When the economy grows, businesses are producing more goods and services, and they usually have to hire more workers. People then have more money and buy more.

Model of the Business Cycle

S

Peak — Expansion — Contraction or Recession — Peak — Expansion — Contraction or Recession — Trough (Lowest Point)

Analyzing Graphs

1. **Identifying** What is the lowest point of the cycle called?

2. **Explaining** At what point in the cycle is the economy the strongest? What leads up to this point?

The gross domestic product (GDP) is a measure of the economy's output. GDP is the dollar value of all final goods and services produced in a country in a year.

Real GDP

Even if the country produces the same amount of goods and services from one year to the next, the gross domestic product could go up simply because prices increase. That would make it *seem* that the economy was growing even though it really was not. To avoid being misled in this way, another measure, **real GDP,** is used. Real GDP shows an economy's production after the distortions of price increases have been removed. This eliminates the false impression that output has gone up when prices go up.

The Business Cycle

The economy tends to grow over time, but it does not grow at a constant rate. Instead it goes through alternating intervals of growth and decline that we call the **business cycle.** The graph on this page shows an idealized business cycle. The line on the graph tracks real GDP. When the line moves upward, real GDP is growing. A downward slope shows a decline in real GDP.

According to this model, the phases of a business cycle begin with expansion leading to an economic peak—a period of prosperity. New businesses open, factories are producing at full capacity, and most people can find work. Eventually, however, real GDP levels off and begins to decline. During this part of the cycle, a contraction of the economy occurs. Business activity begins to slow down. At some point, the downward direction of the economy levels off in a trough. A trough is the lowest point in the business cycle. It occurs when real GDP levels off and slowly begins to increase.

✓ Reading Check **Explaining** What are the phases of a business cycle?

Leveled Activities

BL Biography Activity 23, URB pp. 25–26

OL Chart, Graph, and Map Act. 23, URB pp. 33–34

ELL Guided Reading Activity 23-2, URB p. 42

TIME™
Political Cartoons

Gary Markstein/Copley News Service

Wages for American workers are the topic of this cartoon by Gary Markstein.

1. What railroad symbolism do you see in this image?
2. How does Markstein use these symbols to comment on wages and on the economy?
3. Do you think Markstein is optimistic or pessimistic about higher wages for American workers? Explain.

Every year, more than half of all Americans do volunteer work ... role in it. One of the responsibilities of citizens is to help make their ... of volunteer grou... small. Perha... dad who...

Business Fluctuations

Main Idea The economy goes through alternating periods of growth and decline.

Economics & You What did you do the last time you were a little short of cash? Read to find out one way our country copes with economic ups and downs.

In the real world, the business cycles are not as regular as the model shows. An entire business cycle is measured from peak to peak.

Expansions

An economic expansion takes place when real GDP goes up. It does not matter whether the economy is growing by a little or by a lot. As long as the real GDP is higher from one period to the next, the economy is expanding. At some point, real GDP reaches its highest point in an expansion. Then it starts to decline.

Expansions are normally longer than recessions. The longest peacetime expansion in U.S. history lasted from March of 1991 until March of 2001, exactly 10 years.

Recession

A recession takes place when real GDP goes down for six straight months, although most last longer than that. On the business cycle graph, the recessions are shown by a colored background. Fortunately, recessions tend to be shorter than expansions, with the average recession lasting about one year. Even so, recessions are painful times. When the economy declines, many people lose their jobs.

If a recession becomes severe, it may turn into a depression—a state of the economy with large numbers of people out of work, acute shortages, and excess capacity in manufacturing plants.

Chapter 23　**639**

C Critical Thinking

Drawing Conclusions Ask: Why do economists look for six straight months of decline in GDP before declaring the economy in recession? *(Six straight months of decline is good evidence of an economic trend.)* **OL**

D Differentiated Instruction

English Learners Ask: What is the difference between a depression and a recession? *(A recession is a slowing of the economy with some job losses. A depression is worse; large numbers of people are out of work and there are severe shortages.)* **ELL**

TIME™ Political Cartoons

Answers:
1. The engine, representing the economy, has become detached from the car it should pull, representing wages.
2. Markstein uses the symbols to assert that economic growth is not resulting in higher wages.
3. He is pessimistic. The economy engine is steaming down the track, unconcerned about having left the car of wage earners behind.

Differentiated Instruction

BIOGRAPHY ACTIVITY 23

Alexander Hamilton (1755–1804)

Biography Activity 23, URB pp. 25–26

Alexander Hamilton

Objective:	To learn Hamilton's advice for strengthening the U.S. economy
Focus:	Discuss the possible costs of the American Revolution.
Teach:	Point out Hamilton's consistently pro-federal government decisions.
Assess:	Have students list the important events in Hamilton's life.
Close:	Have students write obituaries for Hamilton that stress his contributions to the nation.

Differentiated Instruction Strategies

BL Have students list and describe two roles Hamilton played in the U.S. government.

AL Why is the metaphor in the last line of the biography particularly appropriate, given Hamilton's career?

ELL What was Hamilton's country of birth? Why did he come to New York?

C **Critical Thinking**

Determining Cause and Effect Ask:
What are two reasons that businesses would rather be hiring people than having to lay them off? *(Businesses benefit from a growing economy; employed people have money to spend on goods and services, and businesses can expand when more people are purchasing their goods and services.)* **OL**

R **Reading Strategy**

Reading Graphs Ask: According to this graph, how does the economy fare during times of war? *(The economy fares well during times of war; the graph shows an increase in economic growth coinciding with the wars listed.)* **OL**

Unemployment

Another way of measuring the economy is to look at employment. Economists start by identifying the civilian labor force, which includes all civilians 16 years old or older who are either working or are looking for work. In the United States, about half of all people belong to the civilian labor force.

The unemployment rate is the percentage of people in the civilian labor force who are not working but are looking for jobs. As the graph on page 642 shows, the unemployment rate tends to rise sharply during recessions and then comes down slowly afterward.

Changes in the unemployment rate are important in terms of the economy as a whole.

A 1 percent drop in the unemployment rate results in a 2 percent rise in total income in the economy. In 2006, total income in the American economy was about $13.3 trillion. As a result, a 1 percent drop in unemployment would increase total income by about $266 *billion*.

Of course, the personal impact of unemployment and lost income can be tremendous. Some people cut back on luxuries, while others must cut back on basic needs such as health care. Some families go deeper into debt by buying more goods on credit.

Times of high unemployment create stress for many people. High unemployment becomes a problem that requires some government action.

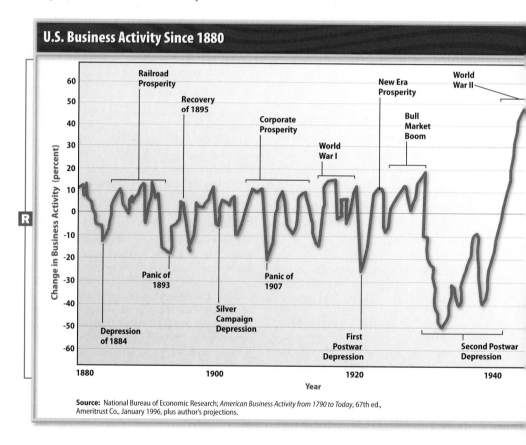

U.S. Business Activity Since 1880

Source: National Bureau of Economic Research; *American Business Activity from 1790 to Today*, 67th ed., Ameritrust Co., January 1996, plus author's projections.

Hands-On Chapter Project
Step 2

An Economic History of Our Community

Step 2: Compiling and Organizing Information About the Community's Economic Development Students will share the information they have learned and decide on an organizational strategy for presenting the information.

Directions Have students type or scan their research into a common file on the class computer or make copies of each group's research to distribute. Tell students that they will now compare their findings and decide on an organizational plan.

Organizing Information Guide students to check for overlapping information first so that they don't work with the same set of facts more than once. Then, have them sort

the information they have gathered either by time periods, by business types, by area of the community, or by some other organizational strategy. Create student groups to continue working on sections of the decided organizational strategy. In Step 3, students will create a brochure to publish their information. **OL**

(Project continued in Section 3)

Fiscal Policy

When the government does step in, it **D** uses **fiscal policy,** or changes in government spending or taxation. The government might cut taxes, expecting people to spend more and businesses to hire more workers. Sometimes, it increases spending to spur businesses to hire workers and boost production. Fiscal policy is a key tool because it can affect the total amount of output—gross domestic product.

Unfortunately, political differences often prevent the best use of fiscal policy. Effective fiscal policies are difficult to **implement,** or carry out, when politicians differ about whether to cut taxes or to increase spending.

When crises are especially severe, the government may take drastic action. In 2008, turmoil hit financial markets. Investment banks collapsed or faced bankruptcy due to bad loans and a housing slump. With the economic crisis spreading globally, Congress passed a gigantic rescue plan that called for pumping 700 billion dollars into the shattered U.S. financial system.

R Price Stability

Another important indicator of an economy's performance is **inflation.** This is a sustained increase in the general level of prices. Inflation hurts the economy because it reduces the purchasing power of money and may alter the decisions people make.

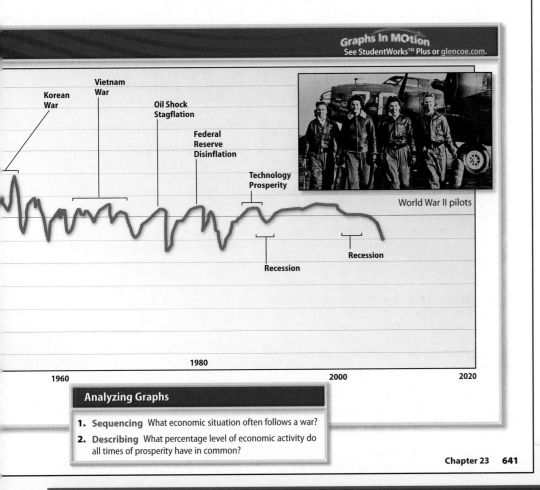

Graphs In MOtion
See StudentWorks™ Plus or glencoe.com.

Korean War

Vietnam War

Oil Shock Stagflation

Federal Reserve Disinflation

Technology Prosperity

Recession

Recession

World War II pilots

1960   1980   2000   2020

Analyzing Graphs

1. **Sequencing** What economic situation often follows a war?

2. **Describing** What percentage level of economic activity do all times of prosperity have in common?

Activity: U.S./World Connection

Making Connections **Ask:** What may have caused the dramatic spike in business activity during World War II? Write students' suggestions on the board. Explain to them that during the years of World War II, U.S. manufacturers had to meet a worldwide demand for military material. After the attack on Pearl Harbor, the United States also had to rebuild its own military forces. With so many men and women in uniform, the need for labor in U.S. manufacturing was so great that unemployment was minimal and salaries rose. Women and minorities entered the workforce in greater numbers than ever before to fill the jobs left by soldiers. By 1944, U.S. productivity had far surpassed the productivity of all the enemy nations combined. New products and technologies arose from the effort to win the war. **OL**

C Critical Thinking

Identifying Central Issues Ask: How is the rate of inflation defined? *(by the change in the average level of prices as measured by the CPI)* **ELL**

D Differentiated Instruction

Logical/Mathematical Ask: Why do people on fixed incomes have problems during times of inflation? *(The value of the dollar falls, requiring more dollars to buy the same amount of goods.)* **OL**

Analyzing Graphs

Answers:
1. 5 percent
2. Unemployment is high during periods of recession.

Reading Check Answer: A drop in the unemployment rate improves the economy because more people are earning wages. They can then return those wages to the economy by purchasing goods and services.

Additional Support

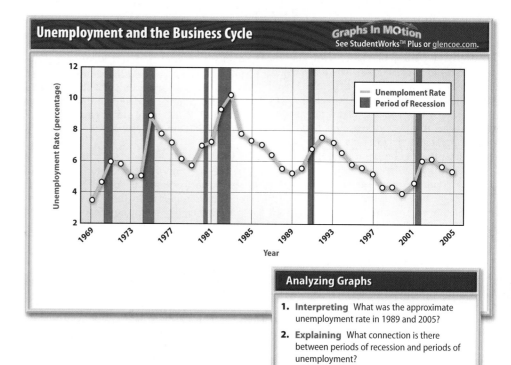

Unemployment and the Business Cycle

Graphs In MOtion
See StudentWorks™ Plus or glencoe.com.

Legend: Unemployment Rate / Period of Recession

Analyzing Graphs

1. **Interpreting** What was the approximate unemployment rate in 1989 and 2005?
2. **Explaining** What connection is there between periods of recession and periods of unemployment?

Consumer Price Index To keep track of inflation, the government samples prices every month for about 400 products commonly used by consumers. The prices of these 400 items make up the **consumer price index (CPI)**, which is a popular measure of the price level. Typically, the prices of some items in the CPI go up every month, and the prices of others go down. However, the change in the average level of prices as measured by the CPI defines the rate of inflation.

Inflation and the Value of Money Suppose that an ice-cream cone that costs you a dollar doubles in price. This price increase causes the purchasing power of your dollar to fall because you have to use twice as many dollars to buy the same item. This is why inflation is particularly hard on people who have fixed incomes—people who get a pension or other fixed amount of money. Inflation also reduces the value of money in a savings account because it will buy less after inflation than before.

Prices provide the signals that help individuals and businesses make the economic decisions that allocate the factors of production. High rates of inflation distort this process because people begin to speculate, or buy things such as land or works of art they think will go up in value.

When speculation takes the place of investment in capital goods or services such as education, the economy begins to suffer. Unfortunately, the government itself can do very little to prevent inflation because inflation results from monetary policy decisions. You will read about monetary policy and how the Federal Reserve System implements monetary policy in the next chapter.

Reading Check Describing How does a drop in the unemployment rate affect the nation's economy?

Did You Know?

Ask: Why is there a Consumer Price Index? *(to determine how much consumers are getting for their money)* The Consumer Price Index measures the costs of many necessities such as food, fuel, and medical care, as well as luxuries. Wealthier nations, whose productivity is diverse, might measure the costs of several hundred items; nations with lower productivity might measure only those items people must have, not those items people may want or choose to buy. The formula for measuring the cost of the items is not precise. A gallon of milk, for example, might cost more in a rural grocery store than in a city supermarket. Still, the CPI provides a method of determining whether individuals and families are getting more— or less—for each dollar spent. **OL**

Stocks and Stock Markets

Main Idea Stock markets are usually good indicators of the health of the economy.

Economics & You You have probably heard a statement like this on the news: "The Dow Jones Industrial Average rose 2 percent today." Read to find out what statements like these tell us about the economy.

Investors normally want to buy stock if they think they will make money on it. Profits from stock come in two ways—from dividends or from capital gains. Dividends are a share of the corporation's profits that are distributed to shareholders. A capital gain occurs when stock can be sold for more than it originally cost to buy. Suppose a person buys stock at $20 a share and sells it for $30. The person has had an increase in his or her capital, or wealth, of $10 a share. Of course, the value of stock may also fall. If a person decides to sell stock at a lower price than he or she paid for it, that person suffers a capital loss. Money may be made or lost on government bonds in much the same way.

Why Stock Prices Change

The price of a company's stock, like most other things, is determined by supply and demand. Factors such as changes in sales or profits, rumors of a possible takeover, or news of a technological breakthrough can change the demand for a company's stock and, therefore, its price.

The NYSE To be listed on the New York Stock Exchange, a corporation must prove to the exchange that it is in good financial condition. *Analyzing* How does inflation affect the value of stocks sold on the NYSE?

643

Activity: Economics Connection

Identifying Ask: What are the major stock indexes? *(the Dow-Jones Industrial Average, Standard and Poor's, and NASDAQ)* Have students use library or Internet sources to research basic facts about the stock indexes. Students should answer these questions about each index: What does its name mean, or what is it named after? When did it come into use as a measure of the economy? What kinds of stocks does it measure? Have students present their findings in a chart or other graphic organizer. **OL**

Writing Support

Personal Writing Have students write a paragraph about their feelings on stock market investments. Would they buy stocks or not? **OL**

Differentiated Instruction

Visual/Spatial Remind students that a bull market is headed up, but a bear market is headed down. Have students illustrate their interpretations of bull and bear markets. **ELL BL**

✓ **Reading Check** **Answer:** by receiving dividends as shareholders or by buying stocks at one price and selling them at a higher price.

Assess

Civics ONLINE

Study Central™ provides summaries, interactive games, and online graphic organizers to help students review.

Close

Taking Notes Have students use the Reading Essentials and Note-taking Guide for the chapter to take notes, and quiz each other. **OL**

Section 2 Review

Stock Market Indexes Because most investors are concerned about the performance of their stocks, they often consult stock indexes. These are statistical measures that track stock prices over time and give us an idea of the well-being of the stock market as a whole. The Dow-Jones Industrial Average (DJIA) and Standard and Poor's (S&P) are the two most popular indexes. The DJIA tracks prices of 30 representative stocks. The S&P 500 index tracks the prices of 500 large stocks.

Stock Exchanges Stocks in publicly traded companies are bought and sold in a stock market, or a stock exchange, a specific location where shares of stock are bought and sold. The exchange makes buying and selling easy, but you do not have to actually travel to a stock exchange in order to buy or sell stock. Instead, you can call a stockbroker, who can buy or sell your stocks.

Most stocks in the United States are traded on the New York Stock Exchange (NYSE), the American Stock Exchange, or an electronic stock market like the NASDAQ. Computer technology and electronic trading allow investors to trade major stocks around the clock, anywhere in the world.

The Stock Market and the Economy

Indexes like the DJIA and the S&P 500 do more than tell us about the level of stock prices—they reveal investors' expectations about the future. If investors expect economic growth to be rapid, profits high, and unemployment low, then stock prices tend to rise in what is referred to as a "bull market." If investors are pessimistic, stock prices could fall in what is called a "bear market."

✓ **Reading Check** **Explaining** What are two ways investors make money on stocks?

Section 2 Review

Vocabulary

1. **Write** complete sentences using each of the following terms that will help explain its meaning: *real GDP, business cycle, civilian labor force, unemployment rate, fiscal policy, inflation, consumer price index (CPI).*

Main Ideas

2. **Comparing** How do GDP and real GDP differ?

3. **Describing** How is the unemployment rate computed?

4. **Explaining** How does supply and demand affect a stock's price?

Critical Thinking

5. **Evaluating** Do you think it is the government's responsibility to try to balance the ups and downs of the business cycle? Justify your answer.

6. **BIG Ideas** On a chart like the one below, evaluate how a sharp increase in inflation might affect people.

Cause: Sharp Increase in Inflation		
effect	effect	effect

7. **Analyzing Visuals** Study the graph showing the phases of the business cycle on page 638. How are the recessionary periods in this graph illustrated?

CITIZENSHIP Activity

8. **Creative Writing** Write a play, short story, poem, or song about a family coping with a down period in the business cycle or a time of high inflation. Share your creative work with the class.

Civics ONLINE

Study Central™ To review this section, go to <u>glencoe.com</u>.

Answers

1. Sentences should use vocabulary words according to their definitions in the section and in the Glossary.

2. GDP measures the dollar worth of all final goods and services produced in a country in one year. Real GDP adjusts that value by removing the distortions of price increases from the GDP.

3. Economists identify the numbers of civilians in the labor force who are working or looking for work. Then, they calculate the percentage of civilians in the labor force who are not working but are looking for work.

4. Whatever affects the supply or demand for a company's services or goods—new technologies, rumors of a takeover, and so on—also affects the price of its stock as investors consider whether that company's stock will increase in value.

5. Students may agree or disagree but should provide evidence for their positions based on the chapter.

6. Effects of a sharp increase: the purchasing power of money decreases; the value of money in savings accounts decreases; people on fixed incomes have less money to spend on necessities.

7. The recessionary periods are illustrated by sharp dips heading for a trough.

8. Students' creative works will vary but should describe the results from times of recession, depression, or high inflation.

How Much Does It Cost?

If something cost $64 in 1965, what would be the equivalent price in 2008 dollars? Using the Consumer Price Index (CPI) provides an answer. The CPI is a measure of the average change in prices over time for a specific collection of goods and services.

Average Gas Prices, 1950-2008

Year	Price Per Gallon	Price Per Gallon (adjusted for inflation)
1950	$0.23	$2.06
1955	$0.24	$1.85
1960	$0.26	$1.89
1965	$0.26	$1.78
1970	$0.30	$1.67
1975	$0.48	$1.92
1980	$1.05	$2.75
1985	$1.01	$2.02
1990	$0.97	$1.60
1995	$0.96	$1.36
2001	$1.45	$1.77
2002	$1.31	$1.60
2003	$1.38	$1.62
2004	$1.67	$1.92
2005	$2.20	$2.43
2006	$3.03	$3.24
2007	$3.26	$3.39
2008*	$3.94	$3.94

Source: U.S. Department of Energy.   *May 2008

Measuring Price Changes

The CPI can be used to compare the price level in one year with price levels in earlier or later periods.

Use this formula to calculate:

2008 Price = 1965 Price x (2008 CPI/1965 CPI)

Here's the calculation:

2008 Price = $64 x (216.5/31.5)

2008 Price = $64 x 6.87

2008 Price = $439.68

If something cost $64 in 2008, what would be the equivalent price in 1965? To calculate, use this formula:

1965 price = 2008 price x (1965 CPI/2008 CPI)

Here's the calculation:

1965 Price = $64 x (31.5/216.5)

1965 Price = $64 x .145

1965 Price = $9.28

Analyzing Economics

1. **Analyzing** What, if anything, surprises you about the average price of gasoline over time?
2. **Calculating** From one year to the next, which year shows the biggest increase in the actual price?
3. **Calculating** From one year to the next, which year shows the biggest increase in price adjusted for inflation?

 C **Critical Thinking**

Identifying Central Issues Ask: Why is the price of gasoline and other transportation fuels a key to understanding the health of the economy? *(Gasoline is necessary for people to get to their jobs, for factories to run their machines, for the shipment of goods to points of sales, and for heating homes in winter. When fuel prices rise, the prices of goods rise, and simultaneously, people must cut back on spending to pay for their commutes to work.)* **OL**

R **Reading Strategy**

Monitoring Ask: Who supplies the information on gas prices? *(the Department of Energy)* **BL**

Analyzing Economics

Answers:

1. Answers may vary but might include that the price has not increased as much as it seems to have when adjusted for inflation. In addition, prices decreased for years before beginning to climb.

2. The biggest increase in actual price occurred in 2006.

3. The biggest increase in price adjusted for inflation occurred in 1980.

Additional Support

Activity: U.S./World Connection

Determining Cause and Effect Ask: What happened between 1975 and 1980 to cause the sharp increase in the price of gas? Have students use library sources, interviews with older family members and friends, and the Internet to research the oil crisis, or oil shock, that began in 1973. Questions students should answer include: What is OPEC, and how does OPEC influence oil prices? What happened in 1973 to cause a shortage of oil in the United States? How did the oil embargo affect the U.S. economy? How did these events affect research into alternative sources of power? Have students then write a summary of the events that led to the crisis, its effects on American citizens, and the resolution of the crisis. **OL**

Focus

Bellringer
Daily Focus Transparency 23–3

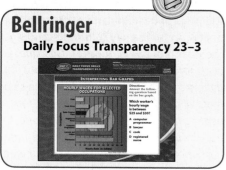

Guide to Reading
Answers to Graphic:

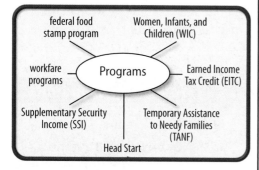

- federal food stamp program
- Women, Infants, and Children (WIC)
- workfare programs
- **Programs**
- Earned Income Tax Credit (EITC)
- Supplementary Security Income (SSI)
- Temporary Assistance to Needy Families (TANF)
- Head Start

Section Spotlight Video

To generate student interest and provide a springboard for class discussion, access the Chapter 23, Section 3 video at glencoe.com or on the video DVD.

Resource Manager

Guide to Reading

Big Idea
People form governments to establish order, provide security, and accomplish common goals.

Content Vocabulary
- food stamps *(p. 648)*
- Women, Infants, and Children (WIC) *(p. 648)*
- workfare *(p. 649)*
- progressive income tax *(p. 649)*
- Earned Income Tax Credit (EITC) *(p. 649)*

Academic Vocabulary
- survive *(p. 648)*
- supplement *(p. 649)*

Reading Strategy
Comparing Information
On a diagram like the one below, identify four major government programs or policies that are meant to ease the problem of poverty.

Programs

Government, the Economy, and You

Real World Economics "Give me a head start!" exclaims this student enrolled in the federally funded preschool program Head Start. For over 40 years, the Head Start program has been a vital educational resource for lower-income families and their preschoolers. It provides educational support to improve children's readiness level for public school. Additional programs are offered in the areas of health, nutrition, and family support. Today, Head Start supporters are urging Congress to increase funding.

▼ **Louisiana 5-year-old successfully finishes lesson with Head Start teacher**

R Reading Strategies	C Critical Thinking	D Differentiated Instruction	W Writing Support	S Skill Practice
Teacher Edition	**Teacher Edition**	**Teacher Edition**	**Teacher Edition**	**Teacher Edition**
• Inferring, p. 648	• Drawing Con., pp. 648, 650	• Interpersonal, p. 647	• Personal Writing, p. 647	• Analyzing, p. 648
Additional Resources	• Pred. Consequences, p. 649	**Additional Resources**	**Additional Resources**	**Additional Resources**
• Cont. Vocab., URB p. 21		• Diff. Instr. Act., URB p. 35	• Writing Skills Activi-ties, URB p. 27	• Daily Focus Trans., 23–3
• Acad. Vocab., URB p. 23	**Additional Resources**	• Reteach. Act., URB p. 39		
• Guide Read, URB p. 43	• Quizzes and Tests, p. 277			
• RENTG, p. 222				

Income Inequality

Main Idea Education, family wealth, and discrimination are reasons for income differences.

Economics & You Think of a wealthy family in your community. How did they earn their wealth? Read to find out three key factors that can influence a person's income.

Though the United States is a wealthy country, not all Americans are personally wealthy. Income levels vary for many reasons. Some people—such as Tiger Woods, Beyoncé, and Stephen King—have special talents that enable them to earn huge amounts of money.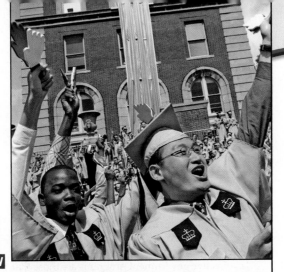

Education Opportunities Students from Columbia University in New York City celebrate graduation. ***Explaining*** **What other factors besides education determine a person's future income?**

Three Influences on Income

Incomes differ for several reasons. Education, family wealth, and discrimination are common reasons for income differences.

Education Level of education has a major impact on a person's income. The average income of a college graduate—someone with a bachelor's degree—is nearly twice the average income of a high school graduate. More advanced degrees increase income even more. Education puts people in a better position to get the higher-paying jobs that require a higher level of skills.

Because education contributes so much to income, the federal government tries to encourage people to improve their education. This is why there are many programs that encourage education, from free or subsidized lunches to college grants and low-interest loans.

Family Wealth Some people are born into wealth. Having wealthy parents often gives people access to excellent colleges. In addition, wealthy parents can set up their children in a business or pass on their own business.

Discrimination Discrimination is one of the reasons some people do not receive higher incomes. Women and members of minority groups may not be hired into jobs that pay well, or they may not receive promotions for which they are eligible. In addition, salaries for men are normally higher than those for women. This difference is partly a result of discrimination against women.

The government has passed several laws to reduce discrimination. The Equal Pay Act of 1963 requires equal pay for jobs that require equivalent skills and responsibilities. The Civil Rights Act of 1964 bans discrimination on the basis of gender, race, color, religion, and national origin. The Equal Employment Opportunity Act of 1972 strengthened earlier laws. The Americans with Disabilities Act of 1990 extended this protection to people with physical and mental disabilities. People who suffer discrimination can use the courts to enforce these laws.

Reading Check Explaining How does the government encourage people to obtain an education?

Teach

W Writing Support

Personal Writing Direct students to write about a U.S. citizen who has inspired them by achieving career successes and also wealth. The person might be an entertainer or someone in business, research, sports, or philanthropy. **OL**

D Differentiated Instruction

Interpersonal Bring in job applications that students will have to complete. Point out the sections that require applicants to list education and the Equal Employment Opportunity Commission (EEOC) compliance statement commonly found. Tie the discussion of the applications to the information about influences on income. **OL**

Caption Answer:
family wealth, opportunities or the lack of opportunities (discrimination), and the determination to achieve

Reading Check Answer: The government provides free or reduced-price lunches for children in public schools as well as grants and low-interest loans to college students.

Differentiated Instruction

Analyzing Effects of Literary Works

Writing Skills Act. 23, URB pp. 27–30

Objective:	To analyze the impact of the excerpts
Focus:	Discuss familiar minimum-wage jobs.
Teach:	As you read the excerpts aloud, check comprehension and encourage discussion.
Assess:	Have students record their reactions to the excerpts in their journals.
Close:	Have students base their essays on their journal entries.

Differentiated Instruction Strategies

BL What do the jobs that Ehrenreich mentions have in common?

AL What does Ehrenreich mean by "secret economies" and "special costs" in the first excerpt? Give examples.

ELL Check how the definitions "health insurance," "routine care," "prescription drugs," and "antibiotics" relate to the excerpts.

R Reading Strategy

Inferring Ask: Because the most effective programs for helping people in poverty are those that encourage people to go back to work, what can you infer about a leading cause of poverty? *(Lack of work or unwillingness to work is a leading cause of poverty.)* **BL**

C Critical Thinking

Drawing Conclusions Ask: What does it mean for impoverished families that the guidelines are based on "conservative estimates" of the costs of necessities? *(Conservative estimates will allow just enough to cover the basics, and careful budgeting will be critical.)* **OL**

S Skill Practice

Analyzing Ask: If poverty guidelines are revised annually, when inflation is factored in, would you expect the poverty level of $9,800 for a single person to go up or down in 2007? *(up)* **AL**

TIME™ Teens in *Action*

Answer:
She means that when people read the works written by homeless people, they will see that homeless people have the same hopes and fears that all people have, rather than thinking of them in a stereotypical way.

Hands-On Chapter Project
Step 3

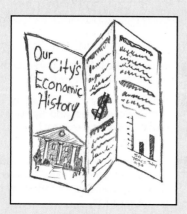

Poverty

Main Idea Poverty is a major problem in America.

Economics & You Do you know a person with a disability who receives money from the government? Read to find out why government helps support people with disabilities.

People living in poverty or those who are at the bottom of the income scale receive special attention from the government. The most effective government programs are those that have incentives that encourage people to go back to work.

Poverty Guidelines and Programs

The government uses poverty guidelines to determine whether someone is eligible for certain programs. These guidelines are revised annually and are based on conservative estimates of how much it costs to buy enough food, clothing, and shelter to **survive**, or exist.

People in Poverty In 2006, a single person was considered to be in poverty if his or her annual income was $9,800, or about $27 a day. Today, there are almost 37 million people who fall *below* this income guideline.

Welfare Programs Most welfare programs are federal programs. The federal **food stamp** program serves millions of Americans. The goal of the food stamp program is to alleviate hunger and malnutrition by allowing low-income households to obtain a more healthful diet. Some states use electronic debit systems in place of coupons. The program gives low-income families the opportunity to buy food with Electronic Benefits Transfer (EBT) cards.

Another federal welfare program is the **Women, Infants, and Children (WIC)** program. It provides help with nutrition and health care to low-income women, infants, and children up to age 5.

TIME™ Teens in *Action*

Erika Herman

Erika Herman, 18, of Bethesda, Maryland, sees potential in people—that is why she started Project Hidden GEMS (Giving, Educating, Making Solutions).

QUESTION: Why did you create Hidden GEMS?

ANSWER: The idea clicked in 2004 at a conference about poverty that I attended in Washington, D.C. I met a homeless man who said poetry was his passion but that no one was ever willing to publish his work. I talked to my friend Emily Grunewald about creating a magazine [Hidden GEMS] for people like him. Our goals are to provide an outlet for expression for homeless and inner-city writers; to break down stereotypes and promote awareness among diverse groups of people; and to raise money for individuals and organizations in need.

Q: Have you seen changes in people that work on the magazine?

A: It gives hope to many homeless individuals whose talents would otherwise be ignored. In one case, a homeless man gained enough self-confidence from seeing that people cared about his writing that he worked hard to get a job. Now he's supporting himself in his own apartment.

Making a Difference ——— **CITIZENSHIP**

Explaining What does Erika mean by breaking down stereotypes?

An Economic History of Our Community

Step 3: Creating a Brochure Students will use their research to publish the city's economic history in a brochure.

Directions The final brochure should be as professional as students have the ability and technology to make it.

Expository Writing Show students several examples of brochures so that they can see how the brochures are folded and how information in them is divided among the pages. Students can use the brochures as models for their own design and layout. If the community is large or has a long economic history, each group can produce their own brochure. Have students write the text and lay out their brochures. **OL**

(Project continued on the Visual Summary page)

Income Assistance Other programs pay cash to certain people. Additional, or **Supplemental** Security Income (SSI), for instance, gives payments to blind or disabled people and to persons age 65 and older. Temporary Assistance to Needy Families (TANF) is another direct cash program. TANF makes payments to families who need help because a parent is dead, disabled, or absent. The number of months that a recipient can receive benefits is limited. The intent of this limit is to make sure that people do not rely on the program but look for paying work.

Workfare **Workfare** is a term used to describe programs that require welfare recipients to exchange some of their labor in exchange for benefits. Most of the programs are run at the state level, and most are designed to teach people the skills they need to succeed in a job. Many states also require some form of workfare if families want to receive TANF benefits. People who are part of workfare often assist law enforcement officials, sanitation and highway crews, or perform other community service work.

Tax Policies Another way the government helps poor people is with a **progressive income tax.** That means that the tax rate is lower at lower incomes and higher for higher incomes. This helps lower-income people by taking a smaller proportion of their income in taxes. The federal government provides additional help for low-income families and individuals. Many workers use the federal **Earned Income Tax Credit (EITC),** which gives tax credits and even cash payments to qualified workers. This program benefits about 20 million working families every year.

✓ **Reading Check** **Summarizing** How does the government use poverty guidelines?

C Critical Thinking

Predicting Consequences Ask: What might happen if the government did not offer assistance such as SSI, WIC, and TANF? *(Answers may include there would probably be more hungry, homeless, and poor people. The economy would also be damaged by a loss of buying power within this group.)* **OL**

✓ **Reading Check** **Answer:** to determine at what income an individual or family can no longer afford basic necessities of food, clothing, and shelter and to determine the cost of these necessities

Assess

Civics ONLINE

Study Central™ provides summaries, interactive games, and online graphic organizers to help students review content.

Close

Predicting Have students discuss: What can individuals do to avoid poverty? What situations beyond individuals' control might lead to poverty? **OL**

Section 3 Review

Vocabulary

1. **Define** these terms from the section and make a set of flash cards to help you learn them: *food stamps; Women, Infants, and Children (WIC); workfare; progressive income tax; Earned Income Tax Credit (EITC).*

Main Ideas

2. **Describing** What does the Americans with Disabilities Act provide?

3. **Describing** What does Supplemental Security Income provide?

Critical Thinking

4. **BIG Ideas** Which of the anti-poverty programs do you think is the most effective? Explain your answer.

5. **Identifying** On a graphic organizer like the one below, identify the groups of people who are helped by government income assistance programs.

low-income families

Programs

CITIZENSHIP Activity

6. **Summarizing** Scan a local newspaper for a short editorial or article about income. Take notes by writing down the main idea and supporting facts. Summarize the article using only your notes.

7. **Persuasive Writing** Write a paragraph either supporting or disagreeing with this statement: Welfare programs have a negative effect on poor people and should be eliminated. Give reasons for your opinion.

Civics ONLINE

Study Central™ To review this section, go to glencoe.com.

Section 3 **Review**

Answers

1. Flash cards should use vocabulary words according to their definitions in the section and in the Glossary.

2. The Americans with Disabilities Act extends protection from discrimination to people with mental and physical disabilities.

3. SSI provides payments to blind or disabled people and to people age 65 or older.

4. Answers will vary, but students should refer to a program from this section.

5. Programs: people with disabilities; low-income families; women, infants, and children; people age 65 or older; people in temporary need of financial assistance due to death or disability.

6. Students' summaries should accurately summarize the main idea and supporting facts of the editorial or article they selected.

7. Students' paragraphs should state a clear position for or against the statement and include reasons for the position.

C Critical Thinking

Drawing Conclusions Ask: Why was the Supreme Court decision, *McCulloch v. Maryland*, unpopular? (*The decision limited states' rights to increase revenue by taxing the national banks.*) OL

ANALYZING THE COURT DECISION

Answers:

1. Marshall argued that the Constitution gives Congress power to "make all laws . . . necessary and proper" for carrying out its duties and that the national bank fell under the implied powers that this wording permits.

2. Answers may include the idea that some people viewed the federal system as intruding on states' rights and responsibilities while other people viewed the federal system as providing strongly for the nation's well-being.

Additional Support

McCulloch v. Maryland

How did the national government expand its financial powers to meet the needs of a growing nation?

Background of the Case

Alexander Hamilton, the nation's first secretary of the Treasury, urged Congress to pass a law establishing a national bank. With the backing of President George Washington, Congress did so in 1791. The bank's funds were used to build roads, canals, and other projects that would help the nation grow. The first bank lasted until 1811; a second bank was chartered in 1816.

Many citizens withdrew deposits from state banks and reinvested them in the new national bank. Angry over the competition from the national bank, states worked to weaken it. Some states, including Maryland, taxed national bank branches operating inside their boundaries. James McCulloch of the Baltimore branch bank refused to pay the state's $15,000 tax. Maryland sued him and won in a state court. McCulloch appealed to the Supreme Court.

The Decision

The Court had to decide if the national bank was constitutional, even though not mentioned in the Constitution. Chief Justice John Marshall wrote the unanimous decision on March 6, 1819:

> **❝** [T]here is no phrase . . . [that] excludes incidental or implied powers; and which requires that everything granted shall be expressly and minutely described. . . . [T]he states have no power, by taxation or otherwise . . . to impede the . . . operations of the constitutional laws enacted by Congress. **❞**
>
> —Justice John Marshall

Federal Reserve Bank, Washington, D.C.

Marshall based the ruling on Article I, Section 8, which gives Congress powers to "make all laws . . . necessary and proper" for carrying out its duties.

Why It Matters

C The Court's unpopular decision upheld the national bank and denied states the power to tax it. The modern Federal Reserve System eventually grew out of the national bank concept.

The case established the implied powers doctrine, which meant Congress had, under the "necessary and proper" clause, a wide range of powers to carry out the powers that the Constitution *expressly* gave it. *McCulloch v. Maryland* also established the principle of national supremacy, which forbids the states from intruding into the constitutional operations of the national government.

Analyzing the Court Decision

1. **Describing** How did Marshall justify the *McCulloch* decision?

2. **Analyzing** Do you think the decision affected the ways Americans viewed our federal system?

Background

McCulloch v. Maryland The court's ruling in this case, handed down in 1819, went beyond the enumerated (explicit) powers granted to Congress by the Constitution. It was controversial at the time and continues to raise issues today. Marshall reasoned that, "Although, among the enumerated powers of government, we do not find the word 'bank' or 'incorporation,' we find the great powers to lay and collect taxes; to borrow money; to regulate commerce; to declare and conduct a war; and to raise and support armies and navies." The federal government could carry out these responsibilities more easily through its own central bank.

This ruling strengthened the federal government's ability to set fiscal policy and to guide the nation's economy.

Visual Summary

Government and the Economy

Government's Role

- Government provides public goods.
- Government regulates the economy to ensure competition.

Measuring the Economy

- Real GDP is GDP that has been adjusted for inflation.
- The real gross domestic product is the most accurate measure of an economy's performance.

Workers with more education earn more money

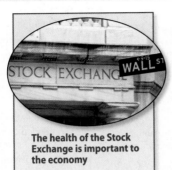

The health of the Stock Exchange is important to the economy

- Government must deal with unemployment, inflation, and periods of growth and decline called the business cycle.
- Stock markets are usually good indicators of the health of the economy.

The Problem of Poverty

- Education, family wealth, and discrimination are reasons for income differences.
- Government uses several different programs and policies to combat poverty.

Laborers benefit from working for government-funded programs

STUDY TO GO Study anywhere, anytime! Download quizzes and flash cards to your PDA from glencoe.com.

651

Making Inferences Ask: In general, what are the government's goals for individuals and families in our nation? *(The government's goals include promoting economic development and offering programs and services that help individuals and families get educations and find jobs that pay an adequate wage.)* **OL**

This **Reading Skill** (Making Inferences) was introduced in this unit.

Analyzing Visuals Ask: Look at the image of the students at the bottom of the page. What impression of college does this photograph create? *(The impression is one of relaxed studying, friendly communication, and an attractive outdoor setting.)* **BL**

Hands-On Chapter Project
Step 4: Wrap-Up

An Economic History of Our Community

Step 4: Publishing the Brochure Students will present their brochures to the Chamber of Commerce or similar organization.

Directions If possible, contact a member of the Chamber of Commerce or other organization and arrange a time when students can describe their project and present their brochure. Students may also submit a copy of the brochures with a formal letter by mail to the chamber. In either case, students should offer the brochure for printing and distribution.

Organizing Information Prepare students to present their brochure by having them draft what they will say about the project they have just completed. (Students may use this draft to write the formal letter if they choose to mail their brochures.) Students should be able to explain how their researched brochure would be useful to people considering doing business in or with the city. **OL**

Reviewing Vocabulary

1. C This question describes two companies becoming one. Point out that when two things become a single thing, they have merged. Then have students look for the related word "merger" among the options. Students might be confused by answer B, "monopoly," because a monopoly also affects competition negatively. Today, the government prevents monopolies from forming by preventing mergers that could eliminate competition.

2. B Point out answers A and B. Guide students to replace TANF and GDP with the phrases for which these abbreviations stand. When students substitute "Gross Domestic Product" for GDP, they can easily make the connection between the correct answer and the word "production" in the question.

3. B Help students reason through the options by identifying the causal relationship: What affects the rate of inflation? Fiscal policy is policy the government carries out to direct the economy; the stock market tracks and trades in the economy but, again, does not determine the rate of inflation. The unemployment rate, likewise, is more an effect than a cause of inflation. Only answer B, "consumer price index," helps economists determine the rate of inflation.

4. B Students should see that answers A and D do not name taxes and can be safely ignored. Then, students can use their knowledge of prefixes and roots to see that "progressive" (moving forward or upward) is the opposite of "regressive" (moving backward or downward).

Reviewing Main Ideas

5. B Ask students to identify the two options that do not name or describe a good. They should exclude answers C and D. Now, help them see the connection between the word "private," meaning "for one only," and the nature of private goods, which, once consumed by one person, cannot be consumed by another.

6. D This is a difficult question if students are not clear about the role of the FTC. Have students quiz themselves: What or who produces goods? Commis-

---

TEST-TAKING TIP

> Stay focused on your own test. Do not be distracted if others are finishing early.

Reviewing Vocabulary

Directions: Choose the word(s) that best completes the sentence.

1. Whenever two or more companies try to form a(n) _____ that threatens competition, the government may take action to stop it.

  A antitrust   **C** merger

  B monopoly   **D** externality

2. What is the term for a nation's economic production that has been adjusted for price changes?

  A TANF   **C** business cycle

  B real GDP   **D** inflation

3. Changes in the _____ determine inflation.

  A fiscal policy   **C** stock market

  B consumer price index   **D** unemployment rate

4. What is the term for an income tax whose rate increases as income level rises?

  A public good

  B progressive tax

  C regressive tax

  D real GDP

Reviewing Main Ideas

Directions: Choose the best answer for each question.

Section 1 *(pp. 630–635)*

5. A(n) _____ is a good in which one person's consumption takes away from another person's consumption.

  A public good

  B private good

  C monopoly

  D externality

6. One of the roles of the Federal Trade Commission is to _____.

  A produce public goods

  B reduce negative externalities

  C supervise corporate mergers

  D deal with the problems of false advertising

Section 2 *(pp. 637–644)*

7. A period of business recovery when economic activity increases is called _____.

  A a recession   **C** the business cycle

  B real GDP   **D** an expansion

8. Which explanation best explains the effects of inflation?

  A Consumers have more products to choose from.

  B Inflation erodes the purchasing power of the dollar.

  C Inflation results in lower prices.

  D Demand increases because prices are higher.

Section 3 *(pp. 646–649)*

9. What law provides protection for people with physical and mental disabilities?

  A Clayton Act

  B Sherman Antitrust Act

  C Americans with Disabilities Act

  D Supplemental Security Income

10. What program provides help for nutrition and health care to low-income families?

  A Clayton Act

  B Federal Trade Commission

  C Americans with Disabilities Act

  D Women, Infants, and Children (WIC) program   **GO ON**

---

sions usually do not produce goods. What or who reduces negative externalities? All business decisions should try to reduce negative externalities. Now remind students that for trade to be beneficial to the nation as a whole, it must be handled fairly. False advertising is an unfair trade practice.

7. D Tell students that they can use what they learn from other questions. Students can rule out answer A. They also know that real GDP involves productivity. Ask students

to recall and describe the chart showing a business cycle, with its wave that has peaks and troughs. Then point out to students the related meanings of the word "increases" in the question and the word "expansion" in answer D.

8. B Students can rule out answer A by describing the economic environment in which it could occur. Answer C states the opposite of the effect of inflation. Though answer D does mention higher prices, it also

Critical Thinking

Directions: Choose the best answer for each question.

2006 Poverty Guidelines

Size of Family Unit	Poverty Guidelines
1	$ 9,800
2	$13,200
3	$16,600
4	$20,000
5	$23,400
6	$26,800
7	$30,200
8	$33,600

Source: Department of Health and Human Services.

Poverty guidelines help the government determine financial eligibility for certain federal programs.

11. What was the measure of poverty in 2006 for a family of four?

A $13,200

B $16,600

C $20,000

D $41,000

12. For family units with more than eight members, how much must be added for each additional member to meet the poverty guidelines?

A $1,000

B $2,200

C $3,400

D $9,800

Document-Based Questions

Directions: Analyze the following document and answer the short-answer questions that follow.

In speaking before Congress, former U.S. Treasury secretary John W. Snow discusses inflation.

> **Government and Inflation**
>
> *But clearly an economy that's growing and expanding like this one—and it certainly is doing that with a high GDP output, employment numbers strong, capacity utilization strong—that's an environment in which the Fed needs to continually be alert to early signs of inflation.*
>
> —John W. Snow, Secretary of the Treasury

13. What things about the economy does Snow recognize are strong?

14. Evaluate how a sharp increase in inflation might affect the following people:

- a person who has just withdrawn a considerable amount from a savings account
- a doctor on staff at a large hospital
- a retired autoworker on a fixed pension

Extended-Response Question

15. If we were to enter a period of recession, what would likely happen to demand? What would likely happen to the unemployment rate? The poverty rate? Write an essay in which you answer these questions and provide the reasons for your answers.

STOP

For additional test practice, use Self-Check Quizzes—Chapter 23 on glencoe.com.

Need Extra Help?

If you missed question...	1	2	3	4	5	6	7	8	9	10	11	12	13	14	15
Go to page...	633	638	642	649	631	635	639	641	647	648	648	648	642	642	639

Chapter 23   653

ASSESSMENT

income level at or below which poverty is defined. Demonstrate how to locate the row for a family of four in the left column and the income row in the right column.

12. C Subtracting the dollar amount for a family of one from the dollar amount for a family of two, for example, yields a difference of $3,400.

Document-Based Questions

13. He cites that the economy is growing and has a high GDP output, strong employment numbers, and strong capacity utilization.

14. Possible Answers: This person will find that the money he or she saved has less purchasing power than it did when it was initially saved; a doctor's work will be largely unaffected because the need for basic medical services is relatively inelastic; however, doctors who specialize in elective procedures such as cosmetic surgery will face decreased demand for such services; or people living on fixed incomes will experience a loss of purchasing power.

Extended Response

15. Possible Answer: Students' essays will vary but should explain: Demand would likely decrease as people had fewer dollars to spend on goods and services. Unemployment and the poverty rate would increase as businesses had to lay off workers to cut costs in response to falling demand.

mentions higher demand. Only answer B both fits the definition of inflation and correctly predicts its effect on consumers.

9. C Remind students that answers A and B refer to acts that prevent monopolies. Answer D, "Supplemental Security Income," provides payments to people who are blind or disabled. However, the question asks about "protection" for disabled people, not payments to them; so the correct answer is C.

10. D Encourage students to use the information in question 6 to rule out the options here. Students might be drawn to answer C because they assume that all ADA people are also low-income. Then help students see the connection between the "families" in the question and answer D, the "Women, Infants, and Children program."

Critical Thinking

11. C Guide students to understand the layout of the chart. The left column gives family size, and the right column gives the

Have students visit the Web site at glencoe.com to review Chapter 23 and take the **Self-Check Quiz.**

Need Extra Help?

Have students refer to the pages listed if they miss any of the questions.

653

Levels					Resources	Chapter Opener	Section 1	Section 2	Section 3	Chapter Assess
BL	OL	AL	ELL		**FOCUS**					
BL	OL	AL	ELL	📠	**Daily Focus Skills Transparencies**		24–1	24–2	24–3	
					TEACH					
BL	OL		ELL	📁	**Reading Essentials and Note-Taking Guide***		p. 225	p. 228	p. 231	
	OL	AL		📁	**Economics Activity, URB**			p. 5		
BL	OL	AL	ELL	📁	**Speaking and Listening Skills Activity, URB**				p. 9	
	OL	AL		📁	**Primary Source Reading, URB**				p. 15	
BL	OL	AL	ELL	📁	**Content Vocabulary Activity, URB***	p. 45	p. 45	p. 45	p. 45	
BL	OL	AL	ELL	📁	**Academic Vocabulary Activity, URB**	p. 47	p. 47	p. 47	p. 47	
	OL			📁	**Biography Activity, URB**		p. 49			
BL	OL	AL	ELL	📁	**Writing Skills Activity, URB**			p. 51		
	OL	AL		📁	**Critical Thinking Skills Activity, URB**		p. 53	p. 53	p. 53	
BL	OL	AL	ELL	📁	**Chart, Graph, and Map Skills Activity, URB**				p. 55	
BL	OL	AL	ELL	📁	**Differentiated Instruction, URB**			p. 57		
BL	OL	AL	ELL	📁	**School-to-Home Connection Activity, URB***	p. 59	p. 59	p. 59	p. 59	
BL	OL		ELL	📁	**Guided Reading Activities, URB***		p. 63	p. 64	p. 65	
BL	OL	AL	ELL	📁	**Writer's Guidebook**	✓	✓	✓	✓	✓
	OL	AL		💿	**Primary Source Document Library**	✓	✓	✓	✓	✓
BL	OL	AL	ELL	💿	**Daily Lecture & Discussion Notes (in Pres. Plus)**		✓	✓	✓	✓
BL	OL	AL	ELL	💿	**StudentWorks™ Plus**		✓	✓	✓	✓
BL	OL	AL	ELL	💿	**Section Spotlight Videos**		✓	✓	✓	
BL	OL	AL	ELL	📠	**TIME Interpreting Political Cartoons Transp.**			Ch. 24		
BL	OL	AL	ELL	📠	**Writing Process Transparencies**	✓	✓	✓	✓	✓

Note: Please refer to the *Unit 7 Resource Book* for this chapter's URB materials.

* Also available in Spanish

TeacherWorks Plus
All-In-One Planner and Resource Center

- Interactive Lesson Planner
- Interactive Teacher Edition
- Fully editable blackline masters
- Section Spotlight Videos Launch
- Differentiated Lesson Plans
- Printable reports of daily assignments
- Standards Tracking System

Levels					Resources	Chapter Opener	Section 1	Section 2	Section 3	Chapter Assess
BL	OL	AL	ELL							
					TEACH (continued)					
				📁	**Building Academic Vocabulary**	✓	✓	✓	✓	✓
				📁	**Strategies for Success**	✓	✓	✓	✓	✓
Teacher Resources				📁	**Teacher's Guide to Differentiated Instruction**	✓	✓	✓	✓	✓
				💿	**Graphing Tool**	✓	✓	✓	✓	✓
				💿	**Presentation Plus! with MindJogger CheckPoint**	✓	✓	✓	✓	✓
					ASSESS					
BL	OL	AL	ELL	📁	**Quizzes and Tests***		p. 286	p. 287	p. 288	p. 289
BL	OL	AL	ELL	📁	**Authentic Assessment with Rubrics**		p. 28			
BL	OL	AL	ELL	📁	**Standardized Test Practice**		p. 47	p. 47	p. 47	p. 47
BL	OL	AL	ELL	💿	*ExamView®* **Assessment Suite** CD-ROM		24–1	24–2	24–3	Ch. 24
					CLOSE					
BL			ELL	📁	**Reteaching Activity, URB***		p. 61	p. 61	p. 61	
BL	OL		ELL	📁	**Reading and Study Skills Foldables™ Activity**	p. 97		p. 97	p. 97	
BL	OL	AL	ELL	📁	*Civics Today* **in Graphic Novel**	p. 89	p. 89			
BL	OL	AL	ELL	🗂	**Graphic Organizer Transparencies & Strategies**	✓	✓	✓	✓	✓

✓ Chapter- or unit-based activities applicable to all sections in this chapter

Using TechCONNECT™

Using a Scanner

What is TechCONNECT™?

TechCONNECT™ is a flexible, activities-based program that makes it easy to integrate computer technology into the classroom.

How can TechCONNECT™ help my students?

TechCONNECT™ helps students create a presentation using a scanner to enter graphics found in various sources, along with a presentation application, and the Internet. TechCONNECT™ supports classroom learning by allowing students to:

- create real-world products
- use computer application skills

For more information or to get a free 30-day trial of Glencoe TechCONNECT™ for your classroom, visit techconnect.glencoe.com and click the **Free Trial** button. Once you have accessed TechCONNECT™, students can enter code AC012 to begin the project.

Civics ONLINE

Visit glencoe.com and enter *QuickPass*™ code CIV1360c24T for Chapter 24 resources.

You can easily launch a wide range of digital products from your computer's desktop with the McGraw-Hill Social Studies widget.

	Student	Teacher	Parent
Media Library			
• Student Edition Section Audio	●		●
• Spanish Audio Summaries	●		●
• Section Spotlight Videos	●	●	●
***Civics Today* Online Learning Center (Web Site)**			
• Chapter Overviews	●	●	●
• Study Central™	●	●	●
• Study-to-Go	●	●	●
• Student Web Activities	●	●	●
• In Motion Animation	●	●	●
• Self-Check Quizzes	●	●	●
• ePuzzles and Games	●	●	●
• StudentWorks™ Plus Online	●	●	●
• Vocabulary eFlashcards	●	●	●
• Web Activity Lesson Plans		●	
• Vocabulary PuzzleMaker	●	●	●
Classroom Tools			
• Multilingual Glossary	●	●	●
• Beyond the Textbook	●	●	●
• NGS MapMachine	●	●	●

Reading List Generator CD-ROM

GLENCOE BookLink 3

Use this database to search more than 30,000 titles to create a customized reading list for your students.

- Reading lists can be organized by students' reading level, author, genre, theme, or area of interest.
- The database provides Degrees of Reading Power™ (DRP) and Lexile™ readability scores for all selections.
- A brief summary of each selection is included.

Leveled reading suggestions for this chapter:

For students at a Grade 7 reading level:
- *Opening a Bank Account,* by Stuart Schwartz and Craig Conley

For students at a Grade 8 reading level:
- *Dollars and Sense: Managing Your Money,* by Ernestine Giesecke

For students at a Grade 9 reading level:
- *The House of Morgan: An American Banking Dynasty and the Rise of Modern Finance,* by Ron Chernow

For students at a Grade 10 reading level:
- *Martin Van Buren: 8th President of the United States,* by Rafaela Ellis

For students at a Grade 11 reading level:
- *Alexander Hamilton,* by Ron Chernow

READING SUPPORT FROM JAMESTOWN EDUCATION

- **Timed Readings Plus in Social Studies** helps students increase their reading rate and fluency while maintaining comprehension. The 400-word passages are similar to those found on state and national assessments.

- **Reading in the Content Area: Social Studies** concentrates on six essential reading skills that help students better comprehend what they read. The book includes 75 high-interest nonfiction passages written at increasing levels of difficulty.

- **Reading Social Studies** includes strategic reading instruction and vocabulary support in Social Studies content for both ELLs and native speakers of English.

- **Content Vocabulary Workout** (Grades 6–8) accelerates reading comprehension through focused vocabulary development. Social Studies content vocabulary comes from the glossaries of Glencoe's Middle School Social Studies texts. www.jamestowneducation.com

KEY   Teacher Wraparound

Use this key to help you identify the different types of prompts found in the Teacher Wraparound Edition.

R **Reading Strategies** activities help you teach reading skills and vocabulary.

C **Critical Thinking** strategies help students apply and extend what they have learned.

D **Differentiated Instruction** activities provide instruction for students learning to speak English, along with suggestions for teaching various types of learners.

S **Skill Practice** strategies help students practice historical analysis and geography skills.

W **Writing Support** activities provide writing opportunities to help students comprehend the text.

Teaching strategies and activities have been coded for ability level appropriateness.

AL Activities for students working above grade level

OL Activities for students working on grade level

BL Activities for students working below grade level

ELL Activities for English Language Learners

Focus

Why It Matters

Ask: What are the advantages of using money as the primary form of exchange for goods and services? *(Answers should include that paper money and coins are issued by governments and have a definite value backed by governments and that money is easily carried or accessed.)*

More About the Photo

Visual Literacy The photograph shows a machine that sorts money at the United States Department of the Treasury. The Bureau of Engraving and Printing makes paper currency. The Mint makes coins. The Treasury produces more than 30 million paper notes each day. A large amount of this currency replaces paper notes that are going out of circulation because they are torn or worn. The new paper notes are sent to the banks and branches of the Federal Reserve and from there to commercial banks and then to individuals and businesses. (Students can learn more from Economics Activity 7, How Does Money Get to Banks?, URB p. 5.)

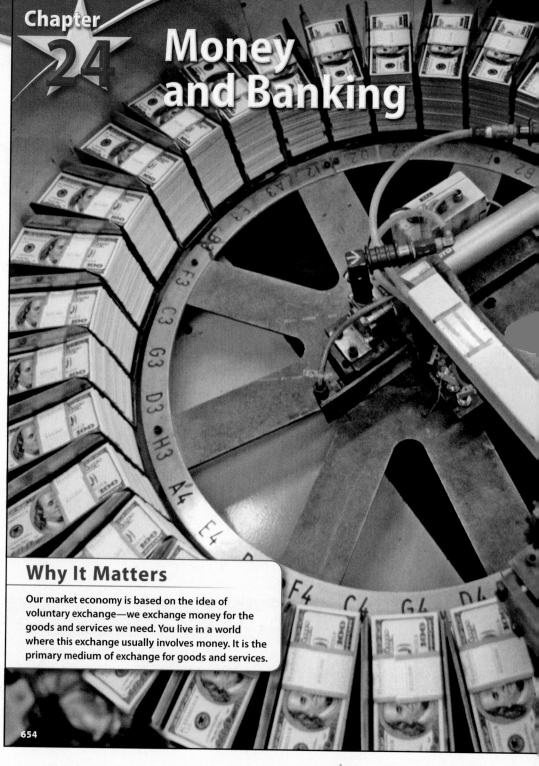

Chapter
24 Money and Banking

Why It Matters

Our market economy is based on the idea of voluntary exchange—we exchange money for the goods and services we need. You live in a world where this exchange usually involves money. It is the primary medium of exchange for goods and services.

654

Teach

BIG Ideas *As you begin teaching each section, use these questions and activities to help students focus on the Big Ideas.*

Section 1

What Is Money? **Ask:** Why do people deposit their money into banks or other financial institutions? *(These are safe places to keep money, and depositors can earn interest. Depositing money also establishes credit and makes it easier to take out a loan.)* Point out that in Section 1 students will learn about the functions of money, what gives money value, the different kinds of financial institutions available to depositors, and how the federal government protects depositors. **OL**

Section 2

The Federal Reserve System **Ask:** What do you know about the Federal Reserve System? *(Answers will vary and may include that it controls the money supply and serves as the government's bank.)* Tell students that in Section 2 they will learn about the organization and functions of the Federal Reserve System, including how it conducts monetary policy. **OL**

Chapter Audio

Civics ONLINE
Visit glencoe.com and enter
QuickPass™ code
CIV3093c24 for
Chapter 24
resources.

Chapter Introduction
24

Sorting $100 bills at the U.S. Department of the Treasury

BIG Ideas

Section 1: What Is Money?

The basis of the market economy is voluntary exchange. In the American economy, the exchange usually involves money in return for a good or service. People are willing to accept money in exchange for goods, and financial institutions give people a safe place to deposit their money or take out loans.

Section 2: The Federal Reserve System

Political and economic institutions evolve to help individuals and groups accomplish their goals. The central bank of the United States is the Federal Reserve System. It controls the money supply, serves as the government's bank, and watches over the banking industry.

Section 3: How Banks Operate

Political and economic institutions evolve to help individuals and groups accomplish their goals. Banks offer important financial services to millions of people.

FOLDABLES Dinah Zike's
Study Organizer Foldables

Purpose This Foldable is meant to help students evaluate the workings of the Federal Reserve. As they read Section 2, students should take notes about the Federal Reserve under the appropriate tab on their Foldable. **OL**

More Foldables activities for this chapter can be found in the *Dinah Zike's Reading and Study Skills Foldables* ancillary.

Civics ONLINE
Visit glencoe.com and enter *QuickPass*™ code CIV1360c24T for Chapter 24 resources, including a Chapter Overview, Study Central™, Study-to-Go, Student Web Activity, Self-Check Quiz, and other materials.

FOLDABLES™
Study Organizer

Evaluating Information Study Foldable Make the following Foldable to help you evaluate the workings of the Federal Reserve.

Step 1 Mark the midpoint of the side edge of a sheet of paper. Then fold in the outside edges to meet at the midpoint.

Step 2 Fold in half from side to side.

Step 3 Open and cut the inside fold lines to form four tabs. Label the tabs *what, when, where* and *why.*

Reading and Writing As you read the chapter, note information about the Federal Reserve under the appropriate tab.

What: The Federal Reserve	When:
Where:	Why/How:

Chapter 24   655

Section 3

How Banks Operate Ask: What banking services have you used? *(Answers will vary and may include savings and checking accounts, certificates of deposit, and loans for cars and other expenses.)* Explain that in Section 3 students will learn about banking services, the history of banking in the United States, and recent developments in banking. **OL**

Focus

Bellringer
Daily Focus Transparency 24–1

Guide to Reading
Answers to Graphic:

What Is Money?
- Medium of Exchange
- Store of Value
- Measure of Value

Section Spotlight Video

To generate student interest and provide a springboard for class discussion, access the Chapter 24, Section 1 video at glencoe.com or on the video DVD.

Guide to Reading

Big Idea
The basis of the market economy is voluntary exchange. In the American economy, the exchange usually involves money in return for a good or service.

Content Vocabulary
- coin (p. 657)
- currency (p. 657)
- commercial bank (p. 658)
- savings and loan association (S&L) (p. 658)
- credit union (p. 658)

Academic Vocabulary
- obvious (p. 657)
- medium (p. 657)

Reading Strategy
Describing As you read the section, complete a graphic organizer like the one below that illustrates three functions of money.

What Is Money?

What Is Money?

Real World Economics No flaws allowed here. This Treasury Department expert examines new sheets of $100 bills as they shoot off the presses. The money is actually made at the Bureau of Engraving and Printing. The first $100 bills, issued in 1862, were called "legal tenders." Benjamin Franklin became the face on the $100 bill in 1914. Today this bill, which may stay in circulation for up to five years, is the largest denomination in use.

▼ **U.S. Treasury worker inspects newly printed $100 bills**

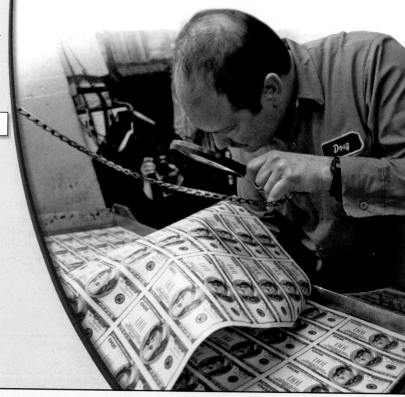

Resource Manager

R **Reading Strategies**	C **Critical Thinking**	D **Differentiated Instruction**	W **Writing Support**	S **Skill Practice**
Teacher Edition • Academic Vocab., p. 657 • Synthesizing, p. 658 **Additional Resources** • Content Vocab., URB p. 45 • Ac. Vocab., URB p. 47 • Guid. Read., URB p. 63 • RENTG, p. 225	**Teacher Edition** • Drawing Con. p. 659 **Additional Resources** • Biography Act., URB p. 49 • Graphic Novel, p. 89	**Teacher Edition** • Visual/Spatial, p. 658 **Additional Resources** • Reteach. Act., URB, p. 61	**Teacher Edition** • Expository Writing, p. 659 **Additional Resources** • Auth Assess., p. 24	**Teacher Edition** • Visual Literacy, p. 658 **Additional Resources** • Daily Focus Trans., 24–1

Money

Main Idea People are willing to accept money in exchange for goods.

Economics & You How much money do you have in your pocket or purse? Read to find out why this money has value to you and everyone else.

Money is more interesting than you might think. It serves different functions, comes in several different forms, and has value for reasons that are not immediately **obvious,** or clear.

Functions and Types of Money

Money has three functions. First, it serves as a **medium,** or form, of exchange—we can trade money for goods and services. Without money, people would have to barter—exchange goods and services for other goods and services. Second, money serves as a store of value. We can hold our wealth in the form of money until we are ready to use it. Third, money serves as a measure of value. Money is like a measuring stick that can be used to assign value to a good or service. When somebody says that something costs $10, we know exactly what that means.

Types of Money How would you define money? According to economists, money is anything that people are willing to accept in exchange for goods. At various times in history, salt, animal hides, gems, and tobacco have been used as mediums of exchange.

The most familiar types of money today are coins and currency. **Coins** are metallic forms of money such as pennies and nickels. **Currency** includes both coins and paper money. There are other forms of money as well.

Civics ONLINE

Student Web Activity Visit glencoe.com and complete the Chapter 24 Web Activity.

What Gives Money Value?

Why do we value and accept money? The simple reason is that we are absolutely sure that someone else will accept its value as well. Without this confidence in money, we would not accept it from someone else for payment in the first place.

Money by itself generally has no other value. A $10 bill costs only a few cents to make and has no alternative use. Coins contain only small amounts of precious metal. The same is true of checking and savings accounts—they have value only because we accept that they have value.

Reading Check **Explaining** Why does money have value?

Bartering People have used different goods for buying or trading. Kyle MacDonald from Montreal, Quebec, spent a year trading items on the Internet through Craigslist. He started trading with a red paper clip and ended up trading for a home. **Identifying** What two types of money are most commonly used today?

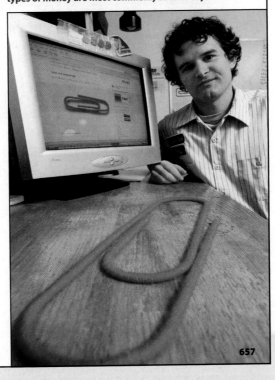

657

Teach

R Reading Strategy

Academic Vocabulary English-language learners may be confused by the use of the word "medium" in "Money is a *medium* of exchange." Have students find this meaning of medium in a dictionary. Ask students if they know the word "media." Tell them that "media" is the plural of "medium." Of what do the media consist? *(newspapers, magazines, television, radio)* What do money and the media have in common? *(Both are means of conveying something. The media convey information; money conveys value. Therefore it can be exchanged for goods.)* **ELL**

Reading Check **Answer:** We accept that money has value and know that others also will accept it for the value it bears.

Caption Answer:

The two most used types of money are paper money and coins. Some students may add that credit and debit cards, checks, and money orders are also widely used.

Hands-On Chapter Project Step 1

Achieving a Financial Goal

Step 1: Choosing a Goal Groups will choose a financial goal to research. They may create their own or choose one from the following six topics: 1) getting a loan for college; 2) getting a loan to start a business; 3) getting a mortgage to buy a home; 4) investing in government bonds and treasury bills; 5) investing in certificates of deposit; 6) qualifying for jobs in banking.

Directions Have students form small groups based on their choices of goals. They should discuss which financial institutions might help them achieve their goals. They will find and list research sources on the Internet and in the library and divide research tasks among the group members. A helpful Web site is www.federalreserveeducation.org (click on personal financial education). They will also brainstorm a list of advisers, such as bank managers, financial planners, school counselors, and business owners. **OL**

(Project continued in Section 2)

The Financial System

Main Idea Financial institutions give people a safe place to deposit their money or take out loans.

Economics & You Do you have a savings account? Read to find out what happens to your money when you make a deposit.

R Do you know what happens when people and businesses with money to save take it to financial institutions? These institutions do not simply put the money in a safe and leave it there. Instead, they put the money to work by lending it to other people or businesses that need funds. They use the money to make more money. The financial institution covers its costs—and makes a profit—from the interest, or fees, it charges for those loans.

Financial Institutions

Commercial banks are financial institutions that offer full banking services to individuals and businesses. They are probably the most important part of our financial system because of their large areas of influence. Most people have their checking and savings accounts in commercial banks.

Savings and loan associations (S&L) are financial institutions that traditionally loaned money to people buying homes. They also take deposits and issue savings accounts in return. Today, S&Ls perform many of the activities that commercial banks do.

Credit unions work on a not-for-profit basis. They are open only to members of the group that sponsors them, usually businesses, labor unions, and government institutions. Generally, credit unions offer better rates on savings and loans than do other financial institutions.

D **Features of U.S. Currency**

Federal Reserve indicators

Microprinting

Portrait

Serial number

Color-shifting ink

Security thread

Watermark

S

Analyzing Charts

1. **Predicting** What security features of this bill would be most difficult to duplicate for a counterfeiter?

2. **Explaining** Why is counterfeit money in the monetary system a problem for the economy?

Reading Strategy

R **Reading Strategy**

Synthesizing How do borrowers, depositors, and the bank all benefit from the loans the bank provides? *(Borrowers benefit from loans for personal and business needs. The bank receives interest on loans from borrowers and uses some of this money to pay interest to depositors on their savings and checking accounts.)* **BL** **OL**

Differentiated Instruction

D **Differentiated Instruction**

Visual/Spatial Students who are visually or spatially oriented may wish to research how microprinting, color-shifting ink, and a security thread are used to create hard-to-copy paper money. Encourage them to present their findings to the class using visuals. **OL** **AL**

Skill Practice

S **Skill Practice**

Visual Literacy Ask students to find each of the features labeled on the bill in the chart on a bill of any denomination. **OL**

Analyzing Charts

Answers:

1. Microprinting, color-shifting ink, and the security thread would be the most difficult to copy.
2. Nothing backs the counterfeited currency, so it is worthless.

Differentiated Instruction

Biography Activity 24, URB pp. 49–50

Anna Escobedo Cabral

Objective: To discover the cause and effects surrounding Cabral's education

Focus: Have students locate Cabral's signature on a dollar bill.

Teach: Discuss the causes for Cabral's attending college and their effects.

Assess: Have student pairs research financial aids available for college.

Close: Have students write letters requesting financial aid information.

Differentiated Instruction Strategies

BL Research two sources of financial aid offered at a local community or technical college.

AL Research cost of a four-year college they wish to attend and devise a financial plan to meet the cost.

ELL Research scholarships and aid available to various ethnic groups.

Each of these types of banking institutions performs a similar function. They all act to bring together savers and borrowers. They give people a safe place to deposit their money when they want to save it and a source for borrowing when they need a loan. You will learn more about this system in Section 3.

Safeguarding Our Financial System

The financial system of the United States is one of the safest in the world. This safety results from two factors—regulation and insurance.

Banking is one of the most regulated industries in the country primarily because of the banking disaster of the 1920s. Most financial institutions have to report to one or more regulatory agencies. They are required to follow rules and accounting practices that minimize unnecessary risk.

The FDIC When financial institutions fail, federal deposit insurance protects consumers' deposits. The most important insurance agency is the Federal Deposit Insurance Corporation (FDIC), a national corporation that insures individual accounts in financial institutions for up to $100,000. The collapse of the banking system during the Great Depression of the 1930s wiped out people's entire savings. Now if a bank fails, depositors do not lose their savings.

Consumer Confidence Because accounts in financial institutions have some type of government insurance, consumers feel safer wherever they deposit their money. As a result, they continue to make deposits—and those deposits give financial institutions the funds they need to make loans that help fuel economic growth.

Reading Check **Explaining** How do financial institutions make a profit?

C Critical Thinking

Drawing Conclusions **Ask:** If you had $300,000 to deposit at a bank, how would you make sure all of the money was covered by FDIC insurance? *(Answers might include having three accounts of $100,000 apiece at one bank or different banks.)* **OL**

W Writing Support

Expository Writing Have students write a paragraph explaining how regulation and insurance of the banking system helps fuel financial growth. **OL**

Reading Check **Answer:** by charging interest on loans and by fees paid by borrowers and depositors

Assess

Civics ONLINE

Study Central™ provides summaries, interactive games, and online graphic organizers to help students review content.

Close

Lecture Invite a bank official to speak to the class about saving opportunities provided by financial institutions. **OL**

Section 1 Review

Section 1 Review

Vocabulary

1. **Write** a paragraph about the U.S. financial system that uses each of these terms: *coin, currency, commercial bank, savings and loan association (S&L), credit union.*

Main Ideas

2. **Name** two forms of money in addition to currency and coin.

3. **Describing** What is the purpose of the FDIC?

Critical Thinking

4. **Explaining** What advantage do credit unions offer their customers? Why?

5. **BIG Ideas** In a graphic organizer like the one below, describe the types of institutions in the American financial system.

American Financial System		

CITIZENSHIP Activity

6. **Comparing** Obtain brochures from several banks, credit unions, and savings and loans. Compare their services and fees. If you had $1,000 to deposit, which institution would you choose? Explain your choice.

7. **Descriptive Writing** Write a paragraph describing which financial institution services you expect to use over the next five years.

Study Central™ To review this section, go to glencoe.com.

Chapter 24   659

Answers

1. Paragraphs should use vocabulary words according to their definitions in the section and in the Glossary.

2. Answers may include gold, gems, credit and debit cards, checks, and money orders.

3. The purpose of the FDIC is to protect consumers against the loss of their bank deposits when a financial institution fails.

4. Credit unions offer their customers better rates on savings and loans. They can do this because they are not-for-profit institutions.

5. **commercial banks**—offer full banking services to individuals and businesses; **savings and loan associations**—traditionally loaned money to home buyers but now perform many of the activities that commercial banks do; **credit unions**—not-for-profit organizations open only to the groups that sponsor them

6. Students should support their choices with information from the text and prior knowledge.

7. Answers will vary and may include loans for college, automobiles, home ownership, starting a business, and so forth.

Focus

Guide to Reading
Answers to Graphic:

Section Spotlight Video

To generate student interest and provide a springboard for class discussion, access the Chapter 24, Section 2 video at glencoe.com or on the video DVD.

Resource Manager

Guide to Reading

Big Idea
Political and economic institutions evolve to help individuals and groups accomplish their goals.

Content Vocabulary
- central bank (p. 661)
- Federal Open Market Committee (FOMC) (p. 661)
- monetary policy (p. 664)
- discount rate (p. 664)
- reserve (p. 665)
- open market operations (p. 665)

Academic Vocabulary
- manipulate (p. 661)
- contract (p. 664)

Reading Strategy
Classifying As you read this section, complete a graphic organizer like the one below by listing the components that make up the Federal Reserve System.

The Federal Reserve System

Real World Economics The Federal Reserve System, usually known as the Fed, is the United States bank from which all other banks borrow. Chairperson Ben Bernanke is shown here with the president of the European Central Bank at an international monetary conference. Previously a professor and economic analyst, Bernanke replaced Alan Greenspan, long-time chairperson of the Fed. The Fed enters your life every day as the agency that controls interest rates on loans and controls the money supply, affecting inflation in America.

▼ **Ben Bernanke, right, became the Fed chairperson in February 2006**

BERNAN

R **Reading Strategies**	C **Critical Thinking**	D **Differentiated Instruction**	W **Writing Support**	S **Skill Practice**
Teacher Edition • Content Vocab., p. 664 **Additional Resources** • Content Vocab. URB p. 45 • Ac. Vocab., URB p. 47 • Guid. Read., URB p. 64 • RENTG, p. 228 • Foldables, p. 97	**Teacher Edition** • Making Inferences, p. 661 • Comparing, p. 661 • Drawing Con., p. 662 • Det. Cause/Effect, p. 664 • Pred. Consequences, p. 665 **Additional Resources** • Economics Act., URB p. 5 • Crit. Think., URB p. 53	**Teacher Edition** • Below Grade Level, p. 663 **Additional Resources** • Diff. Instr., URB p. 57 • Reteach. Act., URB p. 61	**Teacher Edition** • Expository Writing, p. 665 **Additional Resources** • Speak./Listen. Skills URB p. 9 • Writing Skills Act. URB p. 51	**Teacher Edition** • Read. Chart/Map, p. 662 **Additional Resources** • Daily Focus Trans., 24–2 • Pol. Cartoons Trans. 24

Structure and Organization

Main Idea The central bank of the United States is the Federal Reserve System.

Economics & You Do you remember hearing about "the Fed" raising interest rates? Read to find out what this important body does.

The **central bank** of the United States is the Federal Reserve System, known as the Fed. When people or corporations need money, they borrow from banks. When banks need money, they borrow from the Fed. The Federal Reserve System is a banker's bank.

The United States is divided into 12 Federal Reserve districts. Each district has one main Federal Reserve Bank, along with branch banks. Thousands of banks in the United States are members of the Federal Reserve System. Member banks are owners of the Fed because they buy stock in the Fed and earn dividends from it.

Board of Governors

The Fed was established in 1913. At that time the largest banks were required to buy stock in the Fed. To prevent these banks from having too great an influence over the Fed, the law also required that the president appoint and the Senate ratify the seven members who make up the Board of Governors. The president selects one of the board members to chair the Board of Governors for a four-year term.

The Board of Governors controls and coordinates the Fed's activities. It sets general policies for the Federal Reserve and its member banks to follow. Board members and the chairperson are independent of both the president and the Congress. This allows the Board of Governors to make economic decisions independent of political pressure.

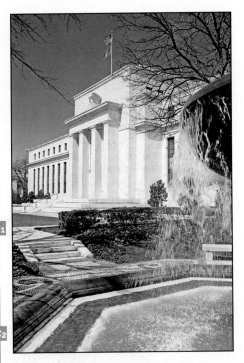

The Fed The headquarters of the Federal Reserve System is in Washington, D.C. The Board of Governors sets the Fed's policies. **Explaining** Why is it important that the Board remain independent of the legislative and executive branches?

Advisory Councils

The Fed has several advisory councils. One council reports on the general condition of the economy in each district. Another reports on financial institutions. A third reports on issues related to consumer loans. Officials of the district banks serve on these councils.

The FOMC A major policy-making group within the Fed is the **Federal Open Market Committee (FOMC).** The FOMC makes the decisions that affect the economy as a whole by **manipulating,** or controlling, the money supply. The FOMC has 12 members.

✓ **Reading Check** **Explaining** How is the Fed's Board of Governors chosen?

Chapter 24 661

S Skill Practice

Reading a Chart and Map Have students read the names of the cities in which Federal Reserve Banks are located. Then have them locate the cities on the map. **Ask:** Why do you think these particular cities were chosen as sites for these banks? *(Each city is a major economic center in its district.)* **BL** **ELL**

C Critical Thinking

Drawing Conclusions **Ask:** Why do you think the Federal Reserve System's Board of Governors is located in Washington, D.C.? *(The Federal Reserve System's Board of Governors needs to be near the seat of the U.S. government in order to communicate with U.S. leaders.)* **OL**

Analyzing Charts and Maps

Answers:

1. Twelve; Answers will vary.

2. The twelve members of the FOMC are the seven members of the Board of Governors and five Reserve Bank presidents.

Hands-On Chapter Project

Step 2

Achieving a Financial Goal

Step 2: Interviewing Financial Advisors Group members will interview financial advisers who can provide information on how to achieve the financial goals. They will use the lists they brainstormed in Step 1.

Directions Group members will discuss whom they will interview and form pairs to interview one or more advisers together. Pairs will devise a list of questions and arrange interviews by phone, email, or in person. They will write a summary of the interview to share with the group. **OL**

(Project continued in Section 3)

The Federal Reserve System

The Organization

PARTICIPATES

Board of Governors
7 members appointed by the president and confirmed by Congress to serve 14-year terms

ADVISES

Federal Open Market Committee
7 Board members
5 District bank presidents

12 District Banks

Federal Advisory Committees

| Atlanta | Boston | Chicago | Cleveland | Dallas | Kansas City |
| Minneapolis | New York City | Philadelphia | Richmond | St. Louis | San Francisco |

Federal Reserve Districts

Board of Governors
Federal Reserve Bank Cities
Federal Reserve Bank Districts

Analyzing Charts and Maps

1. **Identifying** How many Federal Reserve districts are there? In which district do you live?

2. **Identifying** Who makes up the membership of the FOMC?

662 Chapter 24

TIME Political Cartoons

RAMIREZ

ECONOMY

LETS JUST RAISE THESE A LITTLE MORE...

INTEREST RATES

Michael Ramirez/Copley News Service

In this cartoon, Michael Ramirez makes a comment on the U.S. economy and on the former chairperson of the Federal Reserve, Alan Greenspan.

1. **What action is Greenspan taking?**
2. **What symbol does the cartoonist use to represent the economy?**
3. **Why do you think the cartoonist chose this symbol?**
4. **Do you think the artist approves of Greenspan's action? Explain.**

Every year, more than half of all Americans do volunteer work ... role in it. One of the responsibilities of citizens is to help make their ... of volunteer grou... small. Perha... dad wh...

Functions of the Fed

Main Idea The Fed controls the money supply, serves as the government's bank, and watches over the banking industry.

Economics & You Can money ever be "cheap" or "expensive"? Read to find out how the Fed can raise or lower the "price" of money.

The Fed has two main regulatory functions: it deals with banking regulation and consumer credit.

The Fed as Regulator

The Fed oversees and regulates large commercial banks. If two national banks wish to merge, the Fed will decide whether the action will lessen competition. If so, the Fed could block the merger. It also regulates connections between American and foreign banking and oversees the international business of banks that operate in this country.

The Fed also enforces many laws that deal with consumer borrowing. For example, lenders must spell out the details of a loan before a consumer borrows money. The Fed specifies what information lenders must provide.

Acting as the Government's Bank

The Fed also acts as the government's bank. First, it holds the government's money. Government revenues are deposited in the Fed. When the government buys goods, it draws on these accounts. Second, the Fed sells U.S. government bonds and Treasury bills, which the government utilizes to borrow money. Third, the Fed manages the nation's currency, including paper money and coins. This money is produced by government agencies, but the Fed controls its circulation. When coins and currency become damaged, banks send them to the Fed for replacement.

Chapter 24 663

D Differentiated Instruction

Below Grade Level Help below-level students take notes on the functions of the Fed, using the Evaluating Information Study Foldable. Work with students as a group to identify main ideas and important details. Encourage students to create organizational charts and flowcharts about the Fed and how it functions and how monetary policy works. Remind them to use these visuals as study aids. **BL**

TIME Political Cartoons

Answers:
1. He is raising the tracks on the roller coaster.
2. a roller coaster
3. The economy has periods of expansion followed by periods of contraction, similar to the ups and downs of a roller coaster.
4. Student answers will vary, but should be backed by evidence from the cartoon.

Differentiated Instruction

Leveled Activities

BL Guided Reading Activity 24-2, URB p. 64

OL Criti. Thinking Skills Activity 24, URB pp. 53–54

AL Economics Activity 7, URB pp. 5–6

ELL Writing Skills Activity 24, URB pp. 51–52

Content Vocabulary Review content vocabulary before students read about monetary policy. Have them review the concept of inflation in Chapter 23, page 641. **Ask:** What is the money supply? *(the amount of money available for borrowing)* What phrase means the same as "the price of credit"? *(interest rates)* What is inflation? *(Inflation occurs when prices rise. This makes currency worth less because it buys less.)* Pair below-level and English-language learners with competent partners and have them discuss how monetary policy works. **BL** **ELL**

C **Critical Thinking**

Determining Cause and Effect **Ask:** Why does lowering the discount rate stimulate the economy? *(Banks borrow more from the Fed and give out more loans. Businesses expand; people spend more.)* What happens when it raises the rate? *(Banks borrow less and have less money to lend, which slows the economy.)*

Analyzing Graphs

Answers:
1. Interest rates go up.
2. Banks make more loans and collect more interest. Therefore they can afford to lower interest rates.

Additional Support

Teacher Tip

Before beginning this activity, have students discuss the ways in which flowcharts can make a process clearer and easier to remember. Ask them to design their charts to clarify the information they wish to display.

How Monetary Policy Works

One of the Fed's major tasks is to conduct monetary policy. **Monetary policy** is the controlling of the supply of money and the cost of borrowing money—credit—according to the needs of the economy. The Fed can increase or decrease the supply of money.

Changing the Supply of Money The **R** supply and demand diagrams on this page help explain monetary policy. Because the amount of money is fixed at any given time, the money supply is shown as a vertical line. In the diagrams, the point where supply of money and demand for money meet sets the interest rate—the rate that people and businesses must pay to borrow money. The Fed can change the interest rate by changing the money supply. So, if the Fed wants a *lower* interest rate, it must expand the money supply by moving the supply curve to the right. This is shown in diagram A. If the Fed wants to *raise* the interest rate, it has to **contract**, or reduce, the money supply by shifting the supply curve to the left (see diagram B).

Monetary Policy Tools Several tools help the Fed manipulate the money supply. First, the Fed can raise or lower the **discount rate.** The discount rate is the rate the Fed charges member banks for loans. If the Fed wants to stimulate the economy, it lowers the dis**C** count rate. Low discount rates encourage banks to borrow money from the Fed to make loans to their customers. If the Fed wants to slow down the economy's rate of growth, it raises the discount rate to discourage borrowing. This contracts the money supply and raises interest rates. High discount rates mean banks will borrow less money from the Fed.

Monetary Policy and Interest Rates

(A) Effects of Buying Bonds

Expansion of Money Supply

New Money Supply

Interest Rate

7%
6%

Demand for Money

Quantity of Money

(B) Effects of Selling Bonds

Contraction of Money Supply

8%
7%

Interest Rate

New Money Supply

Demand for Money

Quantity of Money

Analyzing Graphs

1. **Describing** What happens to interest rates when the money supply contracts?

2. **Inferring** Why does the price of credit fall when the money supply increases?

Activity: Collaborative Learning

Synthesizing and Displaying Information Organize students into three groups. Write the following questions on the board: 1) How does money flow from the Federal Reserve to member banks and into the community? 2) Where does the Federal Reserve get its money and how does it increase its supply of money? 3) Where does the money come from to give investors in the banking system returns on their investment? Have each group research a different question, using the text and other sources such as the Internet to create a flowchart that answers its question. Each group will present its chart to the class and explain its meaning. **BL**

Second, the Fed may raise or lower the reserve requirement for member banks. Member banks must keep a certain percentage of their money in Federal Reserve Banks as a reserve against their deposits. This money is called the reserve. If the Fed raises the reserve requirement, banks must leave more money with the Fed, and they have less money to lend. When the Fed lowers the reserve requirement, member banks have more money to lend.

Finally, the Fed can change the money supply through **open market operations.** These are the purchase or sale of U.S. government bonds and Treasury bills. Buying bonds from investors puts more cash in investors' hands, increasing the money supply. This shifts the supply curve of money to the right, which lowers interest rates. Consumers and businesses then borrow more money, which increases consumer demand and business production. As a result, the economy grows. If the Fed decides that interest rates are too low, the Fed can sell bonds.

When people buy those bonds, money comes out of the economy. This shifts the supply curve to the left, and raises interest rates.

Why Is Monetary Policy Effective?

Monetary policy can be implemented quickly and Fed officials can also easily fine-tune its policy. They can watch the results of selling bonds or raising the discount rate. If the desired result has not occurred, they can act again, selling more or fewer bonds or raising or lowering the discount rate.

Interest Rates and Business Interest rates influence business investment and consumer spending. The Fed can affect these activities by manipulating interest rates. For example, if the Fed wants to encourage business investment, it can lower interest rates. Raising rates will have the opposite effect.

Reading Check Describing How does the Fed protect consumer borrowers?

C Critical Thinking

Predicting Consequences Ask: Why does the Fed require banks to keep a certain percentage of deposits in the Federal Reserve? *(The reserve gives the Fed money to lend to banks. The money in reserve also protects deposits in banks so that banks can cover withdrawals.)* **OL**

W Writing Support

Expository Writing Have students write an explanation of how and why the Federal Reserve controls the money supply and the cost of borrowing money. **OL**

Reading Check **Answer:** The Fed requires lenders to spell out details of a loan before a consumer borrows.

Assess

Civics ONLINE

Study Central™ provides summaries, interactive games, and online graphic organizers to help students review content.

Close

Summarizing Have students write a one-page summary of the section. **OL**

Section ★ Review

Section 2 Review

Vocabulary

1. **Create** a fill-in-the-blank quiz for a partner using these words: *central bank, Federal Open Market Committee (FOMC), monetary policy, discount rate, reserve, open market operations.*

Main Ideas

2. **Describing** In what way are member banks the owners of the Fed?

3. **Explaining** In what ways does the Fed act as the government's bank?

Critical Thinking

4. **Concluding** What would Fed officials likely do if prices rise too quickly?

5. **BIG Ideas** On a diagram like the one below, list five of the functions of the Federal Reserve System.

The Fed

CITIZENSHIP Activity

6. **Comparing** Contact three banks in your community. Find out what interest rate they are charging on loans for a three-year loan on a new car. Compare this to the current Fed discount rate. Which is higher or lower?

7. **Expository Writing** Write a short newspaper article that explains how the Fed can use its powers to encourage or discourage business activity.

Civics ONLINE

Study Central™ To review this section, go to glencoe.com.

Chapter 24 **665**

Answers

1. Definitions for the vocabulary words are found in the section and in the Glossary.

2. Member banks own stock in the Federal Reserve and earn dividends.

3. As the government's bank, the Fed holds the government's revenue from taxes and from the sale of government bonds and treasury bills. The government withdraws this money to meet its expenses.

4. It would contract the money supply by raising discount rates to member banks. This would raise interest rates for consumers. These steps would slow or halt inflation.

5. oversees and regulates commercial banks; enforces borrower protection laws; acts as the government's bank; conducts monetary policy; buys and sells government bonds and treasury bills.

6. Students should find that the current Fed discount rate is lower than interest rates charged by commercial banks.

7. Students should demonstrate understanding of how the Fed increases and decreases the money available for loans and the interest rates charged.

Focus

Bellringer

Daily Focus Transparency 24–3

Guide to Reading
Answers to Graphic:

The three types are: certificates of deposit, savings accounts, and checking accounts.

Section Spotlight Video

To generate student interest and provide a springboard for class discussion, access the Chapter 24, Section 3 video at glencoe.com or on the video DVD.

Resource Manager

Guide to Reading

Big Idea
Political and economic institutions evolve to help individuals and groups accomplish their goals.

Content Vocabulary
- checking account (p. 667)
- savings account (p. 667)
- certificate of deposit (CD) (p. 667)

Academic Vocabulary
- initial (p. 667)
- principal (p. 667)
- behalf (p. 668)

Reading Strategy
Classifying On a graphic organizer like the one below, identify three types of bank deposits.

Deposits — CDs

 Section Audio 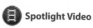 **Spotlight Video**

How Banks Operate

Real World Economics Imagine what might happen if all your money were held in a bank that went bankrupt. This is what happened during the Great Depression in 1929. When the stock market crashed, stock prices fell nearly 25 percent in two days. As banks tried to collect the money investors had borrowed and invested in the stock market, many people lost everything that they owned. Banks went bankrupt, too.

▼ **Wall Street speculator tries to sell his car to make up for losses**

R Reading Strategies	**C** Critical Thinking	**D** Differentiated Instruction	**W** Writing Support	**S** Skill Practice
Teacher Edition • Making Connections, p. 668 **Additional Resources** • Content Vocab., URB p. 46 • Ac. Vocab., URB p. 48 • Guid. Read., URB p. 65 • RENTG, p. 232 • Foldables, p. 97	**Teacher Edition** • Drawing Con. p. 668 **Additional Resources** • Primary Source Reading, URB p. 15 • Crit. Think., URB p. 53	**Teacher Edition** • Logical/Math., p. 667 • Below Level, p. 669 **Additional Resources** • School-to-Home Conn. URB p. 59 • Reteach. Act., URB p. 61	**Teacher Edition** • Descriptive Writing, p. 668 **Additional Resources** • Speak./Listen. Skills, URB p. 9	**Teacher Edition** • Making Comparisons, p. 667 **Additional Resources** • Chart, Graph, and Map Skills, URB p. 55 • Daily Focus Trans., 24–3

Banking Services

Main Idea Banks offer important financial services to millions of people.

Economics & You Do you know the difference between a savings and a checking account? Read to find out how these accounts differ.

Banks are started by investors. They pool financial investments, money, property, and other funds to provide banking services to people in their communities. If 10 investors each put up $10,000, the new bank would have $100,000 in funds.

A bank that relied on only the funds raised by its **initial,** or first, investors would not grow. It would have a limited amount of money available for loans. Banks need to attract depositors to survive.

What Banks Do

To earn money, banks accept deposits to create different types of accounts and then use these deposited funds to make loans.

Accepting Deposits Banks hope to attract customers who make deposits. They offer **checking accounts,** which allow customers to write checks or to use check or debit cards. Checks can be used to pay bills or to transfer money from one person to another. These accounts, however, usually pay no or only a low rate of interest. People do not keep money in checking accounts for very long. They deposit the money and then use the funds to meet their regular expenses.

Sometimes people have some money that they can leave untouched for longer periods of time. With **savings accounts,** banks pay interest to customers based on how much money they have deposited. Because the bank pays interest, the money grows larger the longer it is left in a savings account.

Banks also offer **certificates of deposit (CDs)** to customers. CDs require a saver to

Banking Transactions A New York City bank in the early 1930s handles the day-to-day transactions of its customers. *Explaining* What are the advantages of a checking account?

deposit his or her funds for a certain period of time. CDs offer higher interest rates than checking accounts or savings accounts. The longer the maturity—the period of time—the higher the interest rate that the bank pays. Depositors cannot withdraw their money any sooner unless they pay a substantial penalty. Thus they lose control of their money for some time.

Making Loans One of the **principal,** or main, activities of banks is to lend money to businesses and consumers. Loans can actually increase the supply of money.

Suppose that Maria deposits $1,000 in the bank. The bank can use some of that money to make loans to other customers. Those people then deposit the money they have borrowed, and that money, too, can be loaned to new customers. In that way, the amount of money in circulation continues to accumulate.

✓ **Reading Check** *Explaining* Where do banks get the money they loan to customers?

Achieving a Financial Goal

Step 3: Creating a How-to Pamphlet The groups will share information and plan how-to pamphlets on achieving their financial goals. They will work together to complete the pamphlets.

Directions The group will produce a short pamphlet on how to achieve the financial

goals they have chosen. They should include quotes from the advisors that they interview as well as explanatory text. They may include flowcharts or lists of steps on how to achieve the goals. Students with design and computer experience can help the groups produce the pamphlets. **OL**

(Project continued on the Visual Summary page)

Teach

S Skill Practice

Making Comparisons Have students look at the photo of a 1930s bank. **Ask:** How is this scene different from a modern bank? **BL ELL**

D Differentiated Instruction

Logical/Mathematical Have students research the best rate they could obtain locally on a certificate of deposit for $500 for a 12-month period. **Ask:** If you renewed the CD for a total of three years, how much money would you have, based on current rates? *(Answers will vary according to local rates.)* **OL**

Caption Answer:

Advantages include: People don't have to carry around large sums of money; they may earn interest on their checking account; they can pay bills by check; they can deposit their paycheck and other checks and can cash checks written to them.

✓ **Reading Check Answer:** Money comes from investors and depositors. Interest also is collected from borrowers.

Hands-On Chapter Project

Step 3

C Critical Thinking

Drawing Conclusions Ask: Why do you think Andres signed up for Washington Business Week? *(Answers should include that he probably wants to start his own business someday.)* **OL**

R Reading Strategy

Making Connections What was the result of the closing of the National Bank in 1836? *(With no outside control, each state bank issued its own currency. Because the banks printed too much money, inflation occurred and money had less value.)* **OL**

W Writing Support

Descriptive Writing Have students research the history of national banks in the United States. Then have them write a short description of how national banks affect the U.S. economy. **OL**

TIME™ Teens in Action

Answers:
Students should support their answers with reasonable arguments.

Differentiated Instruction

Chart, Graph, and Map Activity 24,
URB pp. 55–56

TIME™ Teens in Action

Andres Mendoza

Andres Mendoza, 16, of George, in the state of Washington, is all business when it comes to . . . well, business. So he signed up for a weeklong camp called Washington Business Week (WBW), which was hosted by Gonzaga University in Spokane.

QUESTION: You're originally from Oaxaca, Mexico?
ANSWER: My family moved to the United States four years ago. We didn't speak English, but luckily we learn really fast; it wasn't as difficult as it seemed.

Q: What's up with WBW?
A: WBW shows what's involved in working for a business—or running your own.

Q: What did you do there?
A: We formed mock companies. I was named Chief Executive Officer—or CEO—of my company. Everyone had to develop ideas for new products—ours was a microwave that not only warmed but also *froze* the food.

Before going to WBW, I really had no idea what went into running a business. I thought everything was about making money. But at WBW, you learn there's so much more to it—like behaving ethically.

For more info on Washington Business Week go to www.wbw.org.

Making a Difference CITIZENSHIP

Analyzing Do you think there is a market for Mendoza's product? Explain.

Changes in Banking

Main Idea Throughout American history, banking has become safer and more efficient.

Economics & You Look closely at a dollar bill. Who issued it? Read to find out why this was not always the case in the United States.

The banking system of the United States has changed through the years. Often, crises led to key developments that helped strengthen American banks and safeguard the rights of citizens.

Early Banking

In the early days of our nation, leaders found that the country needed a central bank to bring order to the nation's finances. The Bank of the United States, chartered in 1791, collected fees and made payments on **behalf** of, or on the part of, the federal government. In 1816, the Second Bank of the United States was chartered for 20 years. The Bank, however, aroused much opposition, and when its charter lapsed, it was allowed to go out of business.

After that, the only banks in the nation were those chartered by the states. Because the federal government did not print paper currency until the Civil War, most of the money supply was paper currency that privately owned, state-chartered banks issued.

The end of the Bank of the United States removed a vital check on the activities of state-chartered banks. Freed from the Bank's regulations, private banks expanded the volume of bank notes, leading to an increased money supply and inflation.

The National Banking Act In 1863, Congress passed the National Banking Act. Federally chartered private banks issued national banknotes, or national currency, which were uniform in appearance and backed by U.S. government bonds.

Reading a Bank Statement

Chart, Graph, and Map Skills Activity 24

Reading a Bank Statement

Your Bank Statement

Objective: To understand bank statements

Focus: Discuss the accounts available at commercial banks, savings and loan associations, and credit unions.

Teach: Discuss how bank statements display information.

Assess: Have groups research the features of checking and savings accounts at various financial institutions.

Close: Have groups present charts displaying their research.

Differentiated Instruction Strategies

BL Based on the charts, which financial institution would you choose for checking and savings? Write a paragraph explaining your choice.

AL Learn how to balance a checking account and demonstrate for the class.

ELL Write a paragraph describing what services you or family members use or would like to use at a financial institution.

The Federal Reserve The National Banking Act corrected some of the weaknesses of the pre-Civil War banking system. Bank crises, however, did not disappear. The Panic of 1907 resulted in the passage of the Federal Reserve Act of 1913, which you read about earlier in this chapter.

The Great Depression The Great Depression of the 1930s dealt a severe blow to the banking industry. When Franklin D. Roosevelt became president, he closed all banks. Each bank was allowed to reopen only after it proved it was financially sound. Congress established the Federal Deposit Insurance Corporation (FDIC), which insured funds of individual depositors.

Recent Developments

Several more recent developments have also changed the face of American banking. Among these were the savings and loan crisis and congressional legislation.

The Savings and Loan Crisis In the late 1970s Congress began to ease regulation of banking activities. Savings and Loans (S&Ls) were allowed to make higher-risk loans and investments. When these investments went bad, hundreds of S&Ls failed in the late 1980s and early 1990s. Because the federal government insured the savings of most depositors, the cost of bailing out these institutions cost taxpayers an estimated $200 billion. As a result, the FDIC intervened and took over regulation of the S&L industry.

The Gramm-Leach-Bliley Act The Gramm-Leach-Bliley Act, passed in 1999, permits bank holding companies greater freedom to engage in a full range of financial services, including banking, insurance, and securities. The act also requires all financial institutions to establish safeguards to protect their customers' personal financial information.

Reading Check Identifying Which banks issued paper currency before the Civil War?

Section 3 Review

Vocabulary

1. **Write** a paragraph about the activities of a bank using each of these terms: *checking account, savings account, certificate of deposit (CD).*

Main Ideas

2. **Describing** How do bank loans increase the supply of money?

3. **Explaining** What effect did the National Banking Act of 1863 have on banking in the United States?

Critical Thinking

4. **Predicting** What do you think would happen if everyone who had money deposited at a bank wanted to withdraw it at the same time?

5. **BIG Ideas** Using a diagram like the one below for certificates of deposit, compare the advantages and disadvantages of putting money into CDs.

Certificates of Deposit	
Advantage:	Disadvantage:

CITIZENSHIP Activity

6. **Comparing** Obtain brochures from at least three banks that explain the banks' services to customers. How are the services alike? How are they different?

7. **Creative Writing** Use what you learned in this section to write a TV or radio commercial for a bank, stressing its services.

Civics ONLINE

Study Central™ To review this section, go to glencoe.com.

D **Differentiated Instruction**

Below Grade Level Have students create a vertical time line of the changes in banking in the United States using information from pages 668–669. Have students work as a group to make a list of significant dates and summaries of the most important changes that occurred. Encourage them to share their time lines with the class. **BL**

Reading Check **Answer:** State chartered banks issued their own paper currency.

Assess

Civics ONLINE

Study Central™ provides summaries, interactive games, and online graphic organizers to help students review content.

Close

Analyzing Information Have students write a paragraph explaining why a national banking system is needed. **OL**

Section 3 Review

Answers

1. Paragraphs should use vocabulary words according to their definitions in the section and in the Glossary.

2. Bank loans put deposited money into circulation through loans. The borrowers spend the money and the economy gains.

3. The Banking Act created a national currency backed by U.S. government bonds.

4. Possible answer: The bank would probably not be able to pay everyone all the money in his or her account. The bank would have to borrow from the Federal Reserve in order to cover withdrawals or ask the FDIC for help.

5. **Advantage:** pay more interest than savings; **Disadvantage:** money not available for a set time

6. Answers will vary.

7. Commercials should promote the bank's services and fit the medium of radio or TV.

Financial Literacy

S Skill Practice

Analyzing a Flowchart Ask: What does the Federal Reserve do with Jennifer's check? *(It credits the company account the check is paid to and sends the check back to Jennifer's bank.)* **OL**

R Reading Strategy

Summarizing Remind students that a summary contains the main ideas and most important details of a piece of information. Have students read the flowchart and summarize each step in a phrase or short sentence on a bulleted list. Then have them write a summary of "The Life of a Check" in one paragraph of not more than six sentences using the information on their lists. **BL ELL**

Analyzing Economics

Answers:

1. The check has gone through the Federal Reserve banking system and has been credited and debited to accounts.
2. Read your bank statement. Students may also mention calling or going to the bank.

Additional Support

Life of a Check

A check is a written order directing your bank to transfer money from your account to the account of whomever receives your check. Millions of checks are moved around the country, sorted, tabulated, and credited or debited to the accounts of financial institutions. This is known as check clearing.

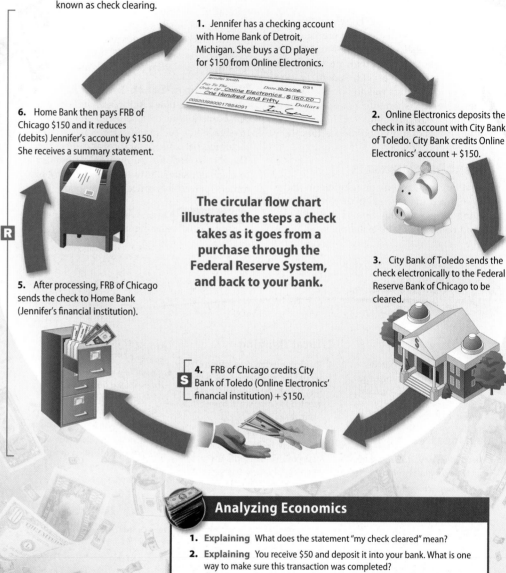

1. Jennifer has a checking account with Home Bank of Detroit, Michigan. She buys a CD player for $150 from Online Electronics.

2. Online Electronics deposits the check in its account with City Bank of Toledo. City Bank credits Online Electronics' account + $150.

3. City Bank of Toledo sends the check electronically to the Federal Reserve Bank of Chicago to be cleared.

4. FRB of Chicago credits City Bank of Toledo (Online Electronics' financial institution) + $150.

5. After processing, FRB of Chicago sends the check to Home Bank (Jennifer's financial institution).

6. Home Bank then pays FRB of Chicago $150 and it reduces (debits) Jennifer's account by $150. She receives a summary statement.

The circular flow chart illustrates the steps a check takes as it goes from a purchase through the Federal Reserve System, and back to your bank.

Analyzing Economics

1. **Explaining** What does the statement "my check cleared" mean?
2. **Explaining** You receive $50 and deposit it into your bank. What is one way to make sure this transaction was completed?

670 Chapter 24

Did You Know?

Checking on History Checks came into use around the early 1500s in Amsterdam, Holland, a major shipping and trading center. Some people deposited their cash with cashiers for a fee because it was safer than keeping it at home. Depositors wrote a note or written order permitting the cashiers to pay their debts from the money in their accounts. Checking spread to England. The first U.S. checks were used in Boston in 1681. The first printed checks were made in England in 1762. They may have been called "checks" because the serial numbers on them were used to keep track of them.

Visual Summary

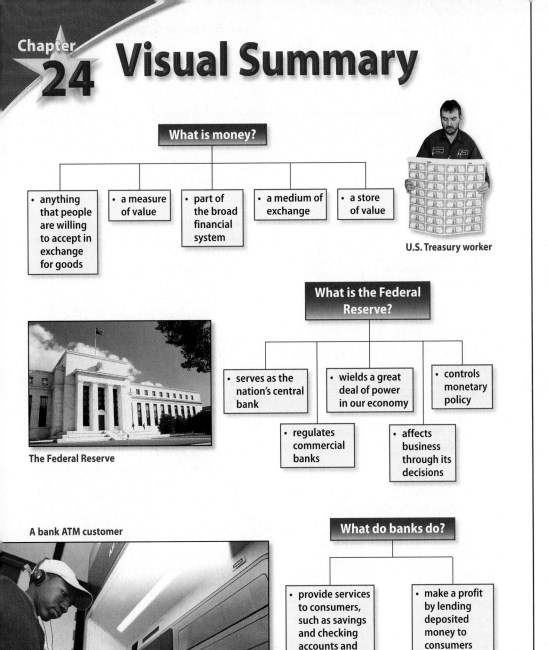

What is money?

- anything that people are willing to accept in exchange for goods
- a measure of value
- part of the broad financial system
- a medium of exchange
- a store of value

U.S. Treasury worker

What is the Federal Reserve?

- serves as the nation's central bank
- wields a great deal of power in our economy
- controls monetary policy
- regulates commercial banks
- affects business through its decisions

The Federal Reserve

A bank ATM customer

What do banks do?

- provide services to consumers, such as savings and checking accounts and CDs
- make a profit by lending deposited money to consumers

STUDY TO GO Study anywhere, anytime! Download quizzes and flash cards to your PDA from glencoe.com.

671

Visual Summary 24

Categorizing and Analyzing Information Have students research current information about how the Federal Reserve is making monetary policy at this time. Helpful Web sites include www.federalreserve.gov (see News & Events; Monetary Policy) and www.federalreserveonline.org. **Ask:** What is the current state of the economy? What has the Fed done recently to manipulate the economy? Have students create a flowchart answering these questions and showing the results of the Fed's actions. Students should present their findings to the class. **OL AL**

For additional practice on this skill (Categorizing and Analyzing Information), see the **Skills Handbook**.

Organizing Have students create a flowchart or charts illustrating how money flows to and from federal, state, and local banks. **BL**

Hands-On Chapter Project
Step 4: Wrap-Up

Achieving a Financial Goal

Step 4: Making a Presentation Students will make presentations about the federal and state governments' roles in the financial goals their groups have chosen.

Directions Group members will research how the federal government and their state government regulates the loan, mortgage, or security goals they have chosen. For example, they can research regulations regarding mortgages, government lending for mortgages, and consumer protections for mortgage holders. Each group should consult at least four credible sources, including two governmental sources. Helpful Web sites include www.federalreserve.gov. and www.federalreserveeducation.org. To wrap up the project, students will discuss how their findings have defined their personal financial goals. **OL**

Answers and Analyses

Reviewing Vocabulary

1. B Students will have read about currency in Section 1 under "Types of Money," where it is defined as "coins and paper money." One distractor, answer C, might confuse students. Checking accounts, however, are not forms of money. Using the clue "coins," students should be able to eliminate answer A, bank notes, because these were used as paper money but did not include coins. Federal Reserve notes are not mentioned in the chapter.

2. A Only credit unions are owned and operated by their members. None of the other choices are institutions owned by depositors.

3. C In Section 2, under "Monetary Policy Tools," the discount rate is defined as the rate the Fed charges to member banks for loans. If students chose answer A, dividend, point out dividends are returns on investments such as stocks and are paid to the investor.

4. B The clue word "account" and the phrase "writing an order" should lead students to the correct answer. Orders cannot be written on savings accounts or certificates of deposit.

Reviewing Main Ideas

5. A The clue words "make a profit" should steer students away from answers B and C, which describe borrowing activities, not profit-making ones. Regarding "promissory notes," define these as IOUs and have students find the definition in a dictionary. Students can eliminate answer C when they recall that only the Department of the Treasury prints currency.

6. C Students should recall that the FDIC was created to insure individual checking and savings deposits. If students choose answer A, they might be mistaking the FDIC for the FOMC. If they choose answers B or D, they might be mistaking the FDIC for the Federal Reserve.

7. B Only answer B is a banking system. If students make another choice, they may need to review the functions of these other institutions.

8. A Some students might not understand what the reserve requirement of the Federal Reserve means. Information on the reserve requirement for member banks in the Federal Reserve appears under the heading "Monetary Policy Tools" in Section 2.

9. A To answer this question, students must know that the money invested in certificates of deposit cannot be withdrawn (without large penalties) during the period of investment. If students eliminate answers C and D because neither are accounts, they can then rely on their previous knowledge as well as information in the text to lead them to answer A, "savings accounts."

TEST-TAKING TIP

Try not to go back and change your answers unless you are very sure they are wrong. Usually your first thought is your best thought.

Reviewing Vocabulary

Directions: Choose the word(s) that best completes the sentence.

1. _____ includes both coins and paper money.
   - **A** Bank notes
   - **B** Currency
   - **C** Checking accounts
   - **D** Federal Reserve notes

2. An institution owned and operated by its members that provides low-interest loans to its members is called a _____.
   - **A** credit union
   - **B** commercial bank
   - **C** state bank
   - **D** board of governors

3. The interest rate that the Federal Reserve charges on loans to its member banks is the _____.
   - **A** dividend
   - **B** money supply
   - **C** discount rate
   - **D** medium of exchange

4. An account in which deposited money can be withdrawn at any time by writing an order is called a _____.
   - **A** savings account
   - **B** checking account
   - **C** discount rate
   - **D** certificate of deposit

Reviewing Main Ideas

Directions: Choose the best answer for each question.

Section 1 *(pp. 656–659)*

5. How do banks and other financial institutions that lend money make a profit?
   - **A** by charging interest
   - **B** by borrowing money
   - **C** by printing currency
   - **D** through promissory notes

6. What is the main purpose of the Federal Deposit Insurance Corporation?
   - **A** buy and sell for investors
   - **B** approve changes in the interest rate
   - **C** insure checking and savings deposits
   - **D** make decisions that affect the economy as a whole

Section 2 *(pp. 660–665)*

7. The central bank of the United States is the ___.
   - **A** Board of Governors
   - **B** Federal Reserve System
   - **C** Federal Open Market Committee
   - **D** Federal Deposit Insurance Corporation

8. The Fed requires banks to keep a ___, or a percentage of their money.
   - **A** reserve
   - **B** discount rate
   - **C** interest rate
   - **D** growth rate

Section 3 *(pp. 666–669)*

9. In what kind of account do savers have the most control over their money?
   - **A** savings accounts
   - **B** certificates of deposit
   - **C** open market operation
   - **D** legal tender

GO ON ▶

10. A deposit account that requires savers to deposit their money for a certain period of time is a _____.

   A savings account

   B certificate of deposit

   C open market operation

   D legal tender

Critical Thinking

Directions: Base your answers to questions 11 and 12 on the chart below and your knowledge of Chapter 24.

Functions of Money
Medium of exchange
Store of value
Measure of value

11. If you read in the newspaper that the Federal Reserve had just lowered the discount rate, what might you conclude about the economy?

   A The nation is in a financial crisis.

   B The economy is operating at full capacity.

   C The Fed wants to discourage bank loans.

   D The economy is sluggish and needs to be stimulated.

12. Money serves as a measure of value. What does this mean?

   A Your money is safe in a savings account.

   B Money is a value medium everyone understands.

   C Money owed must be paid.

   D CDs are a good investment.

13. To say that money is a medium of exchange means that _____.

   A money is durable

   B an item for sale is marked with a price

   C money can be deposited in a bank

   D a seller will accept it in exchange for a good or service

Document-Based Questions

Directions: Analyze the document and answer the short-answer questions that follow.

Ben S. Bernanke was sworn in on February 1, 2006, as chairman of the Board of Governors of the Federal Reserve System. This passage is from a speech given by Bernanke in November 2006.

> *Inflation, which picked up earlier this year, has been somewhat better behaved of late. Overall inflation was pushed up this spring by a surge in energy prices, but the recent declines in energy prices have largely reversed those effects. Price inflation for consumer goods and services excluding energy and food, the so-called core inflation rate, has also moderated a bit in the past few months. But the level of the core inflation rate remains uncomfortably high.*
>
> —Ben S. Bernanke

14. How does Bernanke characterize the rate of inflation—in positive terms, negative terms, or both? Explain.

15. Is Bernanke calling for any specific action or policy to combat inflation? Based on your reading, what could cause the Fed to take action?

Extended-Response Question

16. When the Federal Reserve was started, it was to serve the function of a "lender of last resorts." Do you think banks need the Federal Reserve to act as a lender of last resorts more often during good economic times or bad economic times? Explain. **STOP**

For additional test practice, use Self-Check Quizzes—Chapter 24 on glencoe.com.

ASSESSMENT

13. D To answer the question, students must understand that medium is being used to mean "a way or a form of exchange." Answer A is the easiest to eliminate because it does not deal with this function of money. Regarding answer C, money deposited in a bank is *not* exchanged for goods or services. Answer B might be confusing because the price of an item for sale is related to money's function as a medium of exchange.

Document-Based Questions

14. Bernanke characterizes the rate of inflation in both positive and negative terms. The positive news is that the inflation rate has moderated or lowered slightly. However, the negative news is that the inflation rate remains high.

15. Bernanke feels that although the inflation rate is "uncomfortably high," no action is needed at this time. The Fed might take action if inflation continues or worsens.

Extended Response

16. Students should note that most likely banks would need the Fed as a "lender of last resort" during bad economic times. If people and businesses cannot repay their loans, banks lose money and need assistance from the Fed in order to have the money on hand to pay interest and withdrawals to depositors.

Need Extra Help?																
If you missed question...	1	2	3	4	5	6	7	8	9	10	11	12	13	14	15	16
Go to page...	657	658	664	667	658	659	661	665	667	667	664	657	657	660	660	660

10. B This question also requires students to recall information about certificates of deposit. If students pay careful attention to the clue words "deposit accounts," they will eliminate answers C and D, which have nothing to do with deposit accounts.

Critical Thinking

11. D This question requires a careful reading of how the Fed uses monetary policy to manage the economy. The text on monetary policy states that more borrowing can lead to business expansion, more jobs, and more money for consumers to spend, thereby stimulating the economy.

12. B To answer this question, students must infer that "measure of value" means "a way of assigning value to goods and services." When it is said that a good or service costs $20, we know exactly what that means.

Have students visit the Web site at glencoe.com to review Chapter 24 and take the **Self-Check Quiz.**

Need Extra Help?

Have students refer to the pages listed if they miss any of the questions.

Key to Ability Levels
- **BL** Below level
- **OL** On level
- **AL** Above level
- **ELL** English Language Learners

Key to Teaching Resources
- Print Material
- CD-ROM or DVD
- Transparency

Levels (BL / OL / AL / ELL)		Resources	Chapter Opener	Section 1	Section 2	Section 3	Chapter Assess
		FOCUS					
BL OL AL ELL	🖨	Daily Focus Skills Transparencies		25-1	25-2	25-3	
		TEACH					
BL OL __ ELL	📁	Reading Essentials and Note-Taking Guide*		p. 234	p. 237	p. 240	
__ __ AL __	📁	Enrichment Activity, URB			p. 13		
BL OL AL ELL	📁	Content Vocabulary Activity, URB*	p. 67	p. 67	p. 67	p. 67	
BL OL AL ELL	📁	Academic Vocabulary Activity, URB	p. 69	p. 69	p. 69	p. 69	
__ OL __ __	📁	Biography Activity, URB			p. 71		
BL OL AL ELL	📁	Writing Skills Activity, URB			p. 73		
__ OL AL __	📁	Critical Thinking Skills Activity, URB			p. 75		
BL OL AL ELL	📁	Chart, Graph, and Map Skills Activity, URB		p. 77			
BL OL AL ELL	📁	Differentiated Instruction, URB		p. 79		p. 79	
BL OL AL ELL	📁	School-to-Home Connection Activity, URB*	p. 81	p. 81	p. 81	p. 81	
BL OL __ ELL	📁	Guided Reading Activities, URB*		p. 85	p. 86	p. 87	
BL OL AL ELL	📁	Writer's Guidebook	✓	✓	✓	✓	✓
__ OL AL __	💿	Primary Source Document Library	✓	✓	✓	✓	✓
BL OL AL ELL	💿	Daily Lecture & Discussion Notes (in Pres. Plus)		✓	✓	✓	✓
BL OL AL ELL	💿	StudentWorks™ Plus		✓	✓	✓	✓
BL OL AL ELL	💿	Section Spotlight Videos		✓	✓	✓	
BL OL AL ELL	🖨	TIME Interpreting Political Cartoons Transp.				Ch. 25	
BL OL AL ELL	🖨	Writing Process Transparencies	✓	✓	✓	✓	✓

Note: Please refer to the *Unit 7 Resource Book* for this chapter's URB materials.

* Also available in Spanish

TeacherWorks *Plus*
All-In-One Planner and Resource Center

- Interactive Lesson Planner
- Interactive Teacher Edition
- Fully editable blackline masters
- Section Spotlight Videos Launch

- Differentiated Lesson Plans
- Printable reports of daily assignments
- Standards Tracking System

Levels					Resources	Chapter Opener	Section 1	Section 2	Section 3	Chapter Assess
BL	OL	AL	ELL							
					TEACH *(continued)*					
				📁	**Building Academic Vocabulary**	✓	✓	✓	✓	✓
Teacher Resources				📁	**Strategies for Success**	✓	✓	✓	✓	✓
				📁	**Teacher's Guide to Differentiated Instruction**	✓	✓	✓	✓	✓
				💿	**Graphing Tool**	✓	✓	✓	✓	✓
				💿	**Presentation Plus! with MindJogger CheckPoint**	✓	✓	✓	✓	✓
					ASSESS					
BL	OL	AL	ELL	📁	**Quizzes and Tests***		p. 297	p. 298	p. 299	p. 300
BL	OL	AL	ELL	📁	**Authentic Assessment with Rubrics**			p. 29		
BL	OL	AL	ELL	📁	**Standardized Test Practice**		p. 49	p. 49	p. 49	p. 49
BL	OL	AL	ELL	💿	*ExamView®* **Assessment Suite CD-ROM**		25–1	25-2	25-3	Ch. 25
					CLOSE					
BL			ELL	📁	**Reteaching Activity, URB***		p. 83	p. 83	p. 83	
BL	OL		ELL	📁	**Reading and Study Skills Foldables™ Activity**	p. 98	p. 99		p. 99	
BL	OL	AL	ELL	🖱	**Graphic Organizer Transparencies & Strategies**	✓	✓	✓	✓	✓

✓ Chapter- or unit-based activities applicable to all sections in this chapter

Using the Glencoe Web Site

Student Web Activity

What is the Glencoe Web site?

The Glencoe Web site offers in-depth overviews and activities that summarize and reinforce the content of each chapter.

How can the Glencoe Web site help my students?

The Glencoe Web site offers a Student Web Activity for each of the book's chapters. A Student Web Activity contains a link to an interesting, appropriate Web site related to the chapter content, along with a series of questions for students to answer. The Student Web Activity will help students:

- extend their knowledge beyond the content provided in the textbook
- strengthen their online research skills
- check their understanding of chapter content

Visit glencoe.com and enter a *QuickPass*™ code to go directly to resources for each chapter.

Civics ONLINE

Visit glencoe.com and enter *QuickPass*™ code CIV1360c25T for Chapter 25 resources.

You can easily launch a wide range of digital products from your computer's desktop with the McGraw-Hill Social Studies widget.

	Student	Teacher	Parent
Media Library			
• Student Edition Section Audio	●		●
• Spanish Audio Summaries	●		●
• Section Spotlight Videos	●	●	●
***Civics Today* Online Learning Center (Web Site)**			
• Chapter Overviews	●	●	●
• Study Central™	●	●	●
• Study-to-Go	●	●	●
• Student Web Activities	●	●	●
• In Motion Animation	●	●	●
• Self-Check Quizzes	●	●	●
• ePuzzles and Games	●	●	●
• StudentWorks™ Plus Online	●	●	●
• Vocabulary eFlashcards	●	●	●
• Web Activity Lesson Plans		●	
• Vocabulary PuzzleMaker	●	●	●
Classroom Tools			
• Multilingual Glossary	●	●	●
• Beyond the Textbook	●	●	●
• NGS MapMachine	●	●	●

GLENCOE BookLink 3

Use this database to search more than 30,000 titles to create a customized reading list for your students.

- Reading lists can be organized by students' reading level, author, genre, theme, or area of interest.
- The database provides Degrees of Reading Power™ (DRP) and Lexile™ readability scores for all selections.
- A brief summary of each selection is included.

Leveled reading suggestions for this chapter:

For students at a Grade 7 reading level:
- *Budgeting Your Money,* by Stuart Schwartz and Craig Conley

For students at a Grade 8 reading level:
- *Six Days in October: The Stock Market Crash of 1929,* by Karen Blumenthal

For students at a Grade 9 reading level:
- *Your Money at Work: Taxes,* by Ernestine Giesecke

For students at a Grade 10 reading level:
- *Legendary Labor Leaders,* by Thomas Streissguth

For students at a Grade 11 reading level:
- *Health Care: Opposing Viewpoints,* by Karen Balkin

READING SUPPORT FROM JAMESTOWN EDUCATION

- **Timed Readings Plus in Social Studies** helps students increase their reading rate and fluency while maintaining comprehension. The 400-word passages are similar to those found on state and national assessments.

- **Reading in the Content Area: Social Studies** concentrates on six essential reading skills that help students better comprehend what they read. The book includes 75 high-interest nonfiction passages written at increasing levels of difficulty.

- **Reading Social Studies** includes strategic reading instruction and vocabulary support in Social Studies content for both ELLs and native speakers of English.

- **Content Vocabulary Workout** (Grades 6–8) accelerates reading comprehension through focused vocabulary development. Social Studies content vocabulary comes from the glossaries of Glencoe's Middle School Social Studies texts. www.jamestowneducation.com

KEY Teacher Wraparound

Use this key to help you identify the different types of prompts found in the Teacher Wraparound Edition.

R **Reading Strategies** activities help you teach reading skills and vocabulary.

C **Critical Thinking** strategies help students apply and extend what they have learned.

D **Differentiated Instruction** activities provide instruction for students learning to speak English, along with suggestions for teaching various types of learners.

S **Skill Practice** strategies help students practice historical analysis and geography skills.

W **Writing Support** activities provide writing opportunities to help students comprehend the text.

Teaching strategies and activities have been coded for ability level appropriateness.

AL Activities for students working above grade level

OL Activities for students working on grade level

BL Activities for students working below grade level

ELL Activities for English Language Learners

Focus

Why It Matters

Ask: What are some services funded by taxes? *(education, police and fire protection, entitlement programs, highway construction, national defense)*

More About the Photo

Visual Literacy *Semper Paratus*, the Latin phrase meaning "Always Ready," is the motto of the United States Coast Guard. The Coast Guard was certainly ready during Hurricane Katrina. Upon learning of the storm's path, this maritime branch of the military moved its regional command from New Orleans to St. Louis to prevent its being incapacitated. In preparation for the monstrous storm, Coast Guard officials set up a unified command with state and local industries. As soon as Katrina's winds died down, the military group sprang into action. Rescue helicopters and cutters plucked thousands of people from rooftops in flooded areas, saving lives on dangerous around-the-clock missions. Many hailed the efforts of the Coast Guard during Katrina as a shining light in a dark tragedy.

Teach

BIG Ideas *As you begin teaching each section, use these questions and activities to help students focus on the Big Ideas.*

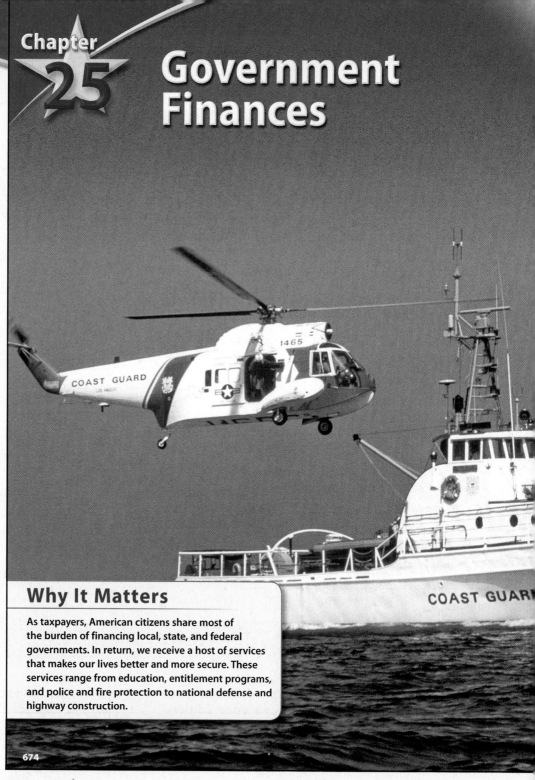

Chapter 25

Government Finances

Why It Matters

As taxpayers, American citizens share most of the burden of financing local, state, and federal governments. In return, we receive a host of services that makes our lives better and more secure. These services range from education, entitlement programs, and police and fire protection to national defense and highway construction.

674

Section 1

The Federal Government Ask: How does the government raise money for the projects in its budget? *(by taxing citizens, residents, tourists, and businesses)* Point out that in Section 1, students will learn about the federal budget process. **OL**

Section 2

State and Local Governments Ask: What are some ways that state and local governments raise revenues? *(intergovernmental funds, sales taxes, income taxes)* Tell students that in Section 2, they will learn about the major forms of revenue and expenditures for state and local governments. **OL**

● Chapter Audio

BIG Ideas

Section 1: The Federal Government

Under our federal system, the executive, legislative, and judicial branches share the responsibility of governing the nation. The president and Congress work together to create the budget—a blueprint for raising and spending the nation's money.

Section 2: State and Local Governments

Political and economic institutions evolve to help individuals and groups accomplish their goals. State and local governments have their own revenue sources and decide how to spend the money they take in.

Section 3: Managing the Economy

Political and economic institutions evolve to help individuals and groups accomplish their goals. Governments use various tools to manage the economy.

◄ Coast Guard helicopter on patrol with Guard cutter

FOLDABLES™
Study Organizer

Dinah Zike's Foldables

Purpose This Foldable guides the student to understand the budget process. The completed Foldable will use a table to help them compare the revenues and expenditures of the different levels of government. **OL**

📁 More Foldables activities for this chapter can be found in the *Dinah Zike's Reading and Study Skills Foldables* ancillary.

FOLDABLES™
Study Organizer

Comparing Information Foldable Make the following Foldable to help you compare the revenues and expenditures of the different levels of government.

Step 1 Fold a sheet of paper into thirds from top to bottom.

Step 2 Open the paper and refold it into thirds from side to side.

Step 3 Unfold the paper and draw lines along the folds.

Government Finances	Federal Government	State and Local Government
Revenues		
Expenditures		

Reading and Writing
As you read the chapter, use your Foldable chart to compare how money is administered among the federal, state, and local governments.

Section 3 ★

Managing the Economy Ask: What tools does the government use to manage the economy? *(Possible answers include tax cuts; spending to make the economy grow; economic stabilizers, such as unemployment benefits and a progressive tax code.)* Explain that in Section 3, students will learn about surpluses, deficits, and fiscal policy. **OL**

Focus

Bellringer
Daily Focus Transparency 25–1

Guide to Reading
Answers to Graphic:

Expenditures	Revenues
1. Social Security	1. Individual income tax
2. National defense	2. Payroll tax
3. Other	3. Corporate profits tax

Section Spotlight Video

To generate student interest and provide a springboard for class discussion, access the Chapter 25, Section 1 video at glencoe.com or on the video DVD.

Resource Manager

Guide to Reading

Big Idea
Under our federal system, the executive, legislative, and judicial branches share the responsibility of governing the nation.

Content Vocabulary
- budget *(p. 677)*
- mandatory spending *(p. 677)*
- discretionary spending *(p. 677)*
- appropriations bill *(p. 677)*
- Social Security *(p. 678)*
- Medicare *(p. 678)*

Academic Vocabulary
- enormous *(p. 677)*

Reading Strategy
Representing Create a diagram like the one below to identify the three largest federal expenditures and the three largest sources of federal revenue.

Expenditures	Revenues
1. Social Security	1.
2.	2.
3.	3.

The Federal Government

Real World Economics Will the money be there when you retire? Social Security, the federal program designed to provide economic security for people once they retire, is often the subject of protest. Today, many younger generations of Americans are afraid they will pay into the system but never reap the benefits. That is because the Social Security system's long-term financial stability is in question, although economists have offered possible solutions.

▼ Protesters rally against changing Social Security

Reading Strategies	**Critical Thinking**	**D Differentiated Instruction**	**W Writing Support**	**S Skill Practice**
Teacher Edition • Identifying, p. 677 • Sequencing Info., p. 677 **Additional Resources** • Cont. Vocab., URB p. 67 • Ac. Vocab., URB p. 69 • Guide. Read., URB p. 85 • Foldables, p. 99	**Teacher Edition** • Analyzing Information, p. 678 • Determining Cause and Effect, p. 679 **Additional Resources** • Quizzes and Tests, p. 297	**Teacher Edition** • English Learners, p. 680 **Additional Resources** • Diff. Instr., URB p. 79	**Teacher Edition** • Personal Writing, p. 678	**Teacher Edition** • Reading Graphs, p. 679 **Additional Resources** • Chart, Graph, and Map Act., URB p. 77 • Daily Focus Trans., 25–1

Preparing the Budget

Main Idea The federal budget, created by the president and Congress, is the government's blueprint for raising and spending money.

Economics & You Does your family spend money on things it must have then spend what is left over on things it wants but does not really need? Read to find out how your family is like the government.

Did you know that total federal government spending accounts for more than 20 percent of our gross domestic product (GDP)? This is an **enormous,** or very large, amount of money. Each year, the president and Congress work together to create a **budget.** This budget is a blueprint of how the government will raise and spend money. 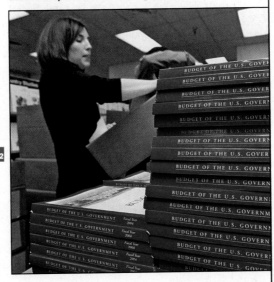 **R1**

The government's budget year differs from a calendar year. The government uses a fiscal year (FY), a 12-month period that may or may not match the calendar year. The federal government's budget year begins October 1 and ends on September 30 of the following year and must be renewed at that time.

The Budget Process

By the first Monday in February, the president proposes a budget to Congress outlining how the government should spend its money. The president then formally sends the proposed budget to Congress along with an annual budget message.

Congress then passes a budget resolution. This document totals revenues and spending for the year and sets targets for how much **R2** will be spent in various categories. Spending is divided into two types: mandatory and discretionary.

Spending that does not need annual approval is called **mandatory spending.** Examples are Social Security benefit checks and interest payments on the government debt, which must be paid every year.

Discretionary spending is government expenditures that must be approved each year. These include things such as money for the Coast Guard, highway construction, and defense. Discretionary spending makes up only about one-third of the federal budget.

Appropriations Bills Another step remains before the government can actually spend any money: Congress must pass **appropriations bills.** These are laws that approve spending for a particular activity. Appropriations bills always begin in the House of Representatives. The Senate then works with the House to pass all appropriations bills by October 1, the beginning of the fiscal year. Appropriations bills must be approved by both houses and either signed into law or vetoed by the president.

✓ Reading Check Explaining How does a fiscal year differ from a calendar year?

Budget of the U.S. Government The federal government publishes a collection of documents that contains the president's budget message and other budget-related publications. *Identifying* What is the first step in the federal budget process?

Chapter 25 **677**

Money Matters

Step 1: Planning a Class Trip Have students work in teams to create proposals for a class trip.

Directions Remind students that part of the government's budget process involves planning projects on which it will spend taxpayer money. Divide students into groups. Have each group plan a class trip to the U.S. capital, Washington, D.C. Have the groups create a trip poster to represent their proposed plans. Posters should have labels describing the trips and images that represent their highlights.

Summarizing Have groups share their posters and plans with the class. **OL**

(Project continued in Section 2)

677

Revenues and Expenditures

Main Idea The federal budget has two main parts—revenues and expenditures.

Economics & You Do you sometimes have trouble matching what you earn to what you spend? Read to find out why the government faces the same challenge.

The federal budget contains two main parts—revenues and expenditures. The main sources of federal revenues are shown in the graph on page 679.

Revenues

Nearly half of the federal government's revenue comes from the income tax paid by individual Americans. Each year, every worker files a tax return, or a report that calculates the tax a worker must pay on his or her income. Corporations also pay income tax on profits they earn.

The second-largest source of federal income is payroll taxes, which are deducted from a worker's paycheck to fund **Social Security** and **Medicare.** Social Security provides money to people who are retired or disabled. Medicare pays some health care costs of elderly people.

Other taxes are also sources of revenue. Consumers pay an excise tax when they purchase goods such as gasoline, tobacco, and telephone services. When wealthy people die, the federal government collects estate taxes on the wealth passed on to their heirs. The government charges a tax on certain gifts. Miscellaneous sources such as entry fees to national parks also add to federal revenues.

Forms of Taxation

Taxes can be classified according to the effect they have on those who are taxed. In the United States today, these classifications

Taxation Whenever we buy gasoline, we not only must pay for the gasoline, but also federal and state taxes on the gasoline. *Identifying* What form of taxation is the tax on gasoline?

include progressive, regressive, and proportional taxes.

Progressive Tax With a *progressive* tax, like our federal income tax, the tax rate (the proportion of earnings taken in taxes) increases as income increases. Therefore, the higher the income, the larger the percentage of income is paid as taxes.

Regressive Tax The opposite of a progressive tax is a *regressive* tax: the percentage you pay goes down as you make more money. One example of regressive taxes is the gasoline tax. Poorer families spend a larger proportion of their income on gasoline. Therefore, the sales tax they pay on gasoline takes up a larger proportion of their total income than a wealthier family pays.

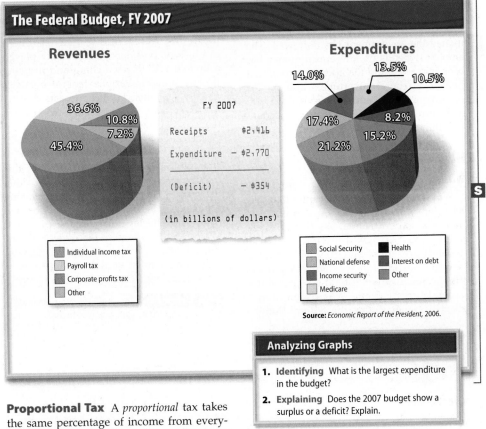

The Federal Budget, FY 2007

Revenues

36.6%
10.8%
7.2%
45.4%

FY 2007

Receipts $2,416

Expenditure – $2,770
_____
(Deficit)   – $354

(in billions of dollars)

Legend:
- Individual income tax
- Payroll tax
- Corporate profits tax
- Other

Expenditures

14.0%   13.5%   10.5%
17.4%   8.2%
21.2%   15.2%

Legend:
- Social Security
- National defense
- Income security
- Medicare
- Health
- Interest on debt
- Other

Source: *Economic Report of the President,* 2006.

S

Analyzing Graphs

1. **Identifying** What is the largest expenditure in the budget?

2. **Explaining** Does the 2007 budget show a surplus or a deficit? Explain.

Proportional Tax A *proportional* tax takes the same percentage of income from everyone, regardless of how much he or she earns. If there is a tax of 10 percent on all income and you earn $1,000, you pay $100 in taxes; if you earn $10,000, you pay $1,000 in taxes, and so on.

Federal Expenditures The graphs above show where the federal government planned to spend its money in 2007. Social Security was the largest single spending category. Because the number of older people in the population is growing, this expense is expected to grow in the future.

Medicare costs are also likely to rise as the population continues to age. Income security includes retirement benefits for some government workers and others, along with

payments to poorer Americans for housing and child nutrition. Health costs include payments for medical research and Medicaid, which pays for health care for people with low incomes.

Defense National defense is the second-largest category of federal expenditures. The original FY 2007 budget set defense spending at more than 17 cents of every federal dollar spent. During times of conflict or war, spending for national defense is increased. Because of the war on terrorism, the 17 percent represents an increase over the percentage of defense spending before September 11, 2001.

C

Chapter 25   679

D Differentiated Instruction

English Learners Give students a hundred pennies or chips and explain the hundred pennies represent a dollar of tax revenues. Ask students to identify and count out which group of pennies represents the amount of the budget spent on defense. *(17)* Students can refer to the graph on the previous page and name other groups of pennies. *(21 Social Security, 15 Other, 14 Income security, 13 Medicare, 10 Health, 8 Debt interest)* **ELL BL**

✔**Reading Check** **Answer:** due to increasing numbers of elderly people in the population

Assess

Civics ONLINE

Study Central™ provides summaries, interactive games, and online graphic organizers to help students review.

Close

Summarizing Ask: What is a government budget? *(A blueprint of how the government will raise and spend money)* **OL**

Section 1 Review

Interest on Debt and Other Expenditures A portion of the federal budget each year goes toward paying interest on the money the government has borrowed. The amount depends on how much money has been borrowed and the interest rates of that debt. The federal government also spends on programs from education to highways to natural resources. These categories account for billions of dollars of spending.

How the Budget Process Has Changed

When the federal government began its operation under the Constitution, it had few expenditures. As the government took on new functions, federal expenditures increased greatly. President George Washington was able to put all the figures for the national government's expenditures for one year on one large sheet of paper. Today the federal budget consists of more than 1,000 pages of small type.

Changing Roles During much of American history, presidents traditionally played a limited role in researching and drawing up the budget. Various federal agencies usually sent their budget requests directly to the secretary of the treasury, who passed them on to Congress.

The Budget and Accounting Act of 1921 changed this procedure in an effort to streamline the process. As a result of this law, the president is responsible for directing the preparation of the budget and making the major decisions about national budget priorities. The law requires the president to propose to Congress the budget for the entire federal government, each fiscal year. This budget must be delivered within 15 days after Congress convenes each January.

✔**Reading Check** **Explaining** Why are Medicare and Social Security costs expected to rise?

Section 1 Review

Vocabulary

1. **Define** the following terms and use them in sentences related to federal budgeting: *budget, mandatory spending, discretionary spending, appropriations bill, Social Security, Medicare.*

Main Ideas

2. **Identifying** What is an example of mandatory government spending?

3. **Contrasting** How does a progressive tax differ from a proportional tax?

4. **Evaluating** If the government needed to increase government revenue, which kind of tax do you think it should increase? Why?

Critical Thinking

5. **BIG Ideas** In a graphic organizer like the one below, show how the president and Congress cooperate to create the federal budget.

1	President sends budget to Congress
2	
3	
4	

6. **Analyzing Visuals** Study the 2007 federal budget on page 679. What two major categories are represented? What percentage of expenditures was budgeted for health?

CITIZENSHIP Activity

7. **Persuasive Writing** Write a newspaper editorial supporting a position for or against this statement: The federal government should be required to balance its budget each year.

Civics ONLINE

Study Central™ To review this section, go to glencoe.com.

Answers

1. Sentences should use vocabulary words according to their definitions in the section and in the Glossary.

2. Social Security, interest payments on government debt

3. Progressive taxes increase as income increases. Proportional taxes take the same percentage of income from everyone.

4. Answers will vary, but students should explain their choices.

5. 1. President sends budget to Congress. 2. Congress passes a budget resolution. 3. Congress passes appropriations bills. 4. The president signs the bills into law.

6. revenues and expenditures; 10.5 percent for health

7. Editorials will vary. Students should clearly express their opinions and reasoning.

Guide to Reading

Big Idea
Political and economic institutions evolve to help individuals and groups accomplish their goals.

Content Vocabulary
- intergovernmental revenue (p. 682)
- sales tax (p. 682)
- property tax (p. 682)
- entitlement program (p. 684)
- subsidize (p. 684)

Academic Vocabulary
- revenue (p. 682)
- utilize (p. 684)
- resource (p. 684)

Reading Strategy
Categorizing As you read, complete a graphic organizer like the one below to show the four major expenditures of local government.

🔊 **Section Audio**   🎬 **Spotlight Video**

Section 2
State and Local Governments

Real World Economics Have you shopped on a "sales tax holiday"? It has been initiated in many states as a day when consumers do not have to pay any sales tax to the state. The sales tax holiday allows shoppers to save as much as 10 percent by eliminating the sales tax on certain products—school supplies, clothing, computers, and other items—for as many as 10 days at a time. In New York City, where the events of September 11th, 2001, caused economic devastation, store owners have looked to the sales tax holiday to help them rebound from difficult times.

▼ **Store manager arranges stock for Alabama's sales tax holiday**

681

Focus

Guide to Reading
Answers to Graphic:

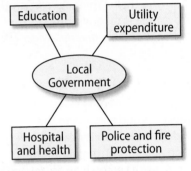

🎬 **Section Spotlight Video**

To generate student interest and provide a springboard for class discussion, access the Chapter 25, Section 2 video at glencoe.com or on the video DVD.

Resource Manager

R Reading Strategies	**C** Critical Thinking	**D** Differentiated Instruction	**W** Writing Support	**S** Skill Practice
Teacher Edition	**Teacher Edition**	**Teacher Edition**	**Teacher Edition**	**Teacher Edition**
• Monitoring, p. 682	• Compare and Contrast, p. 682	• Advanced Learners, p. 685	• Persuasive Writing, p. 684	• Reading Graphs, p. 683
• Identifying, p. 684	• Making Inferences, p. 685			
• Inferring, p. 686		**Additional Resources**	**Additional Resources**	**Additional Resources**
• Identifying, p. 686	**Additional Resources**	• Enrich. Act., URB p. 13	• Writing Skills Act., URB p. 73	• Daily Focus Trans., 25–2
	• Biography, URB p. 71			
Additional Resources	• Crit. Think. Act., URB p. 75			
• Cont. Vocab., URB p. 67	• Quizzes and Tests, p. 298			
• Ac. Vocab., URB p. 69				
• Guide. Read., URB p. 85				
• RENTG, p. 237				

Teach

C Critical Thinking

Compare and Contrast **Ask:** Which revenue sources for states and local governments are the same? *(intergovernmental revenues, sales taxes, and income taxes)* Which sources are different? *(States collect contributions from state workers for their retirement plans. Local governments collect property taxes, fines, and fees.)* **OL**

R Reading Strategy

Monitoring **Ask:** Which type of property do most local governments tax? *(real property—land and buildings)* **OL**

Civics ONLINE

Objectives and answers to the **Student Web Activity** can be found at glencoe.com under the Web Activity Lesson Plan for this chapter.

Reading Check **Answer:** Real property taxes tax land and buildings. Personal property taxes tax portable objects such as stocks and bonds, jewelry, and furniture.

Differentiated Instruction

Revenues

Main Idea State and local governments have their own revenue sources.

Economics & You Sales taxes raise the price of things you buy. Read to find out why this source of revenue is important to cities and states.

• • • • • • • • • • • • • • • • • • • •

State and local governments have their own budget approval processes, **revenues,** and expenditures. The major sources of revenue for each are described below.

State Governments

The most important sources of state government revenues, shown in the graph on page 683, are **intergovernmental revenues.** This revenue is money that one level of government receives from another level. For states, most of this revenue comes from the federal government. The federal government gives states money for welfare, highway construction, hospitals, and other needs.

Sales Tax Next in importance is the state **sales tax.** A sales tax is a general tax levied on consumer purchases of nearly all products. The tax is a percentage of the purchase price, which is added to the final price the consumer pays. The merchant regularly turns over the taxes to the proper state government agency. Five states do not have sales taxes. Rates in the other states range from 2.9 percent to 7.25 percent.

Contributions A third source of state revenue is the contributions that states and state government workers make to their retirement plans. This money is invested until it is needed to pay retirement benefits.

Civics ONLINE

Student Web Activity Visit glencoe.com and complete the Chapter 25 Web Activity.

Income Tax The last major category of revenue is state income taxes. As with sales tax rates, state income tax rates vary a great deal. Some states tax a percentage of the federal income tax. A few states charge a single rate to all taxpayers. In the other states, the rate goes up as income goes up. Seven states have no state income tax.

Local Governments

Intergovernmental revenues are even more important for many local governments than they are for states. The states provide most of this money.

Property Tax The second-largest source of local revenue is local **property taxes.** These are taxes that people pay on the land and houses they own. Property taxes are collected on real property and personal property. Real property includes lands and buildings. Personal property consists of portable objects—things that can be moved—such as stocks and bonds, jewelry, and furniture. Most local governments now tax only real property.

Other Sources Local governments have other revenue sources as well. These include revenue from water and utility systems, sales taxes, local income taxes, and fines and fees.

Many states allow their local governments to impose a local sales tax. Merchants collect these taxes right along with the state sales tax, at the point of sale. As indicated on the graphs on page 683, sales taxes are the fourth most important source of local government revenues. Another source of revenue is the local income tax, a tax on personal income. Fines for traffic and other violations and fees for permits and special services also provide income for local governments. Special assessments are fees that property owners must pay for local services. For example, a city may impose a special assessment when it improves a sidewalk.

Reading Check **Contrasting** How do real property and personal property taxes differ?

Leveled Activities

BL Biography Activity 25, URB pp. 71–72

OL Writing Skills Activity 25, URB pp. 73–74

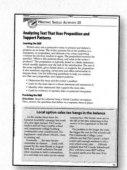

AL Enrichment Activity 7, URB pp. 13–14

AL Crit. Think. Activity 25, URB pp. 75–76

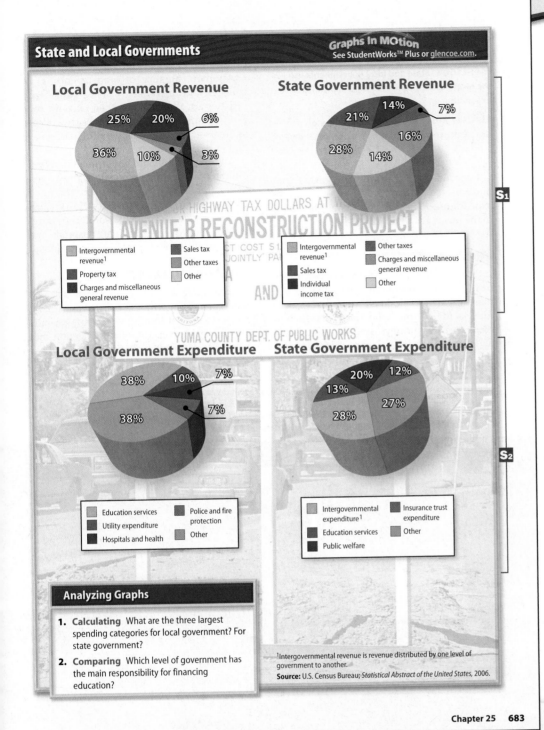

State and Local Governments

Graphs In Motion
See StudentWorks™ Plus or glencoe.com.

Local Government Revenue

25% 20% 6%
36% 10% 3%

Legend:
- Intergovernmental revenue[1]
- Property tax
- Charges and miscellaneous general revenue
- Sales tax
- Other taxes
- Other

State Government Revenue

14% 7%
21% 16%
28% 14%

Legend:
- Intergovernmental revenue[1]
- Sales tax
- Individual income tax
- Other taxes
- Charges and miscellaneous general revenue
- Other

Local Government Expenditure

38% 10% 7%
38% 7%

Legend:
- Education services
- Utility expenditure
- Hospitals and health
- Police and fire protection
- Other

State Government Expenditure

20% 12%
13% 27%
28%

Legend:
- Intergovernmental expenditure[1]
- Education services
- Public welfare
- Insurance trust expenditure
- Other

[1]Intergovernmental revenue is revenue distributed by one level of government to another.

Source: U.S. Census Bureau; *Statistical Abstract of the United States*, 2006.

Analyzing Graphs

1. **Calculating** What are the three largest spending categories for local government? For state government?

2. **Comparing** Which level of government has the main responsibility for financing education?

S₁ Skill Practice

Reading Graphs **Ask:** What is the smallest revenue category for state government revenue? *(taxes other than sales and individual income taxes)* **BL**

S₂ Skill Practice

Reading Graphs **Ask:** What percentage of state revenues is disbursed to local governments? *(28%).* **OL**

Analyzing Graphs

Answers:
1. The three largest spending categories for local government are education services, other, and utility expenditure. The three largest spending categories for state government are intergovernmental expenditure, other, and public welfare.
2. local government

Differentiated Instruction

Introduction to Local Government Finances

Enrichment Activity 7,
URB pp. 13–14

Objective:	To understand how local governments manage finances
Focus:	Students learn how local governments handle difficulties.
Teach:	Discuss the financial difficulties of two cities.
Assess:	Have students identify the causes of the fiscal crises in New York and Cleveland.
Close:	Summarize the financial problems of New York City and Cleveland.

Differentiated Instruction Strategies

BL What is MAC?

AL Explain how New York City was able to avoid defaulting on its loans.

ELL What does the Enrichment Activity describe as the ideal budget scenario?

W Writing Support

Persuasive Writing Remind students that many human services provided by government are entitlement expenditures—programs to help those who qualify. Have students write a paragraph expressing their views about what kinds of entitlements citizens should have. Does the government provide enough or too much entitlement support? What is the proper balance between taxes and entitlements? Remind students to explain their reasoning. **OL**

R Reading Strategy

Identifying **Ask:** Which level of government provides police and fire protection? *(local government)* **BL**

Caption Answer:
state government

Hands-On Chapter Project
Step 2

Money Matters

Step 2: Determining Cost Have students work in teams to break down the cost of their proposed class trips.

Directions Write the Big Idea on the board. Remind students that in order for governments to budget wisely they must keep track of expenditures. Explain that part of

Expenditures

Main Idea State and local governments use the revenues they take in to fund many different expenditures.

Civics & You What do you think is the most important service your local government provides? Why?

State and local governments **utilize**, or make use of, their revenues to fund various expenditures. These expenditures are shown in the lower graph on page 683.

State Governments

Public welfare, or human services, is the name we give to government expenditures that maintain basic health and living conditions for people who have insufficient **resources**, or money, of their own. Most of these expenditures cover **entitlement programs**, such as health, nutritional, or income payments to people who meet established eligibility requirements.

Another category of state spending is colleges and universities. States **subsidize**, or pay part of the cost of, their citizens' college education. Without this subsidy, college students at state schools would have to pay higher tuition and other fees.

Although the federal government pays for building much of the interstate highway system, states are required to maintain those and additional highways. Other categories that take up smaller percentages of expenditures include employee retirement, hospitals and health facilities, and corrections institutions.

Local Governments

Local governments also provide services that they pay for with their revenues. Among the services that local governments provide are education, police and fire protection, and water, sewage, and sanitation services.

Government Services A street sweeper cleans the streets as residents of Trenton, New Jersey, clean up after the Delaware River overflowed its banks in July 2006. Different levels of government must work together to deal with emergencies. **Identifying** Which branch of government has primary responsibility for maintaining highways?

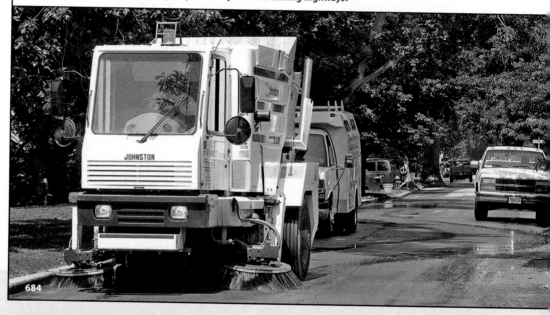

684

the government budget process involves determining the costs of proposed programs. Have students continue working with the proposed class trips they planned in Step 1. Ask each group to research the cost of their trips. Have students create a chart outlining trip expenses. Their charts should include information about the cost of: transportation, attraction ticket prices,

meals, housing, and any special expenses. Encourage them to brainstorm possible unexpected costs or changes of plans.

Summarizing Have each group share its expense charts with the class. Encourage volunteers to share what they learned about the Big Idea while working on their expense charts. **OL**

(Project continued in Section 3)

Education A large share of local tax revenues in many states goes to pay for public schools. Some states pay a large percentage of local public school costs, but local school districts generally provide a large share of the money and make the key decisions regarding operation of the public schools.

Police and Fire Protection Police and fire protection also make up a large part of local budgets. Fire protection is a local function that varies with the size of the community. In small towns, volunteers usually staff the fire department. In large cities, professional, full-time fire departments provide fire protection.

Water Supply Local governments make the vital decisions regarding water service. Smaller communities may contract with privately-owned companies to supply water. The threat of pollution has prompted some local governments to create special water districts. In case of a water shortage, such districts or local governments may try to limit the amount of water used.

Sewage and Sanitation Local governments are responsible for sewage disposal. Proper sewage treatment is vital to the conservation of useful water supplies. Many local governments maintain sewage treatment plants.

In the past, most trash and garbage was buried. Because of environmental concerns, these landfills are no longer the simple solution to sanitation. Some local governments use garbage-processing plants to dispose of a community's solid wastes.

✔ **Reading Check** Identifying What level of government makes most of the key decisions regarding operation of the public schools?

C Critical Thinking

Making Inferences Ask: Why might small towns be likely to have a volunteer fire department? *(Small towns often have less revenue than larger towns.)* **OL**

D Differentiated Instruction

Advanced Learners Have students research and write a one-page report on ways that local governments are using revenues to deal with threats to their water supply, such as pollution. **AL**

✔ **Reading Check** **Answer:** local government

Assess

Civics ONLINE

Study Central™ provides summaries, interactive games, and online graphic organizers to help students review.

Close

Predicting Consequences Ask: What would happen if citizens stopped paying taxes? *(The government would no longer be able to function and to fund programs.)* **OL**

Section 2 Review

Vocabulary

1. **Write** sentences related to state and local governments using the following terms: *intergovernmental revenue, sales tax, property tax, entitlement program, subsidize.*

Main Ideas

2. **Identifying** What are the largest sources of revenue for state and local governments?

3. **Describing** What is the effect of state subsidies on the cost of public colleges and universities?

Critical Thinking

4. **Evaluating** If you needed to raise local government revenues, which source of revenue would you target for an increase? Explain.

5. **BIG Ideas** In a graphic organizer like the one below, explain how a state government gets its revenue.

6. **Analyzing Visuals** Study the two graphs that appear on page 683. Are police and fire protection the responsibility of state or local government?

CITIZENSHIP Activity

7. **Expository Writing** Write a newspaper article that includes your own experiences with local government. Focus on one of these issues: police or fire protection, sewer or water services, trash disposal, or education.

Civics ONLINE

Study Central™ To review this section, go to glencoe.com.

Chapter 25   685

Answers

1. Definitions for the vocabulary words are found in the section and in the Glossary.
2. intergovernmental revenue
3. State subsidies help lower the cost of public colleges and universities.

4. Answers will vary. Students must explain their answers.
5. State Government: Sales Tax, Intergovernmental revenue, Income Tax, Other Taxes

6. local government
7. Articles will vary. Articles should address students' own experiences and be clearly written.

Section 2 Review

C Critical Thinking

Making Inferences Ask: When might a higher-priced product be a better value than a lower-priced similar product? *(when the higher-priced product is of better quality than the lower-priced product)* **OL**

This **Reading Skill** (Making Inferences) was introduced in this unit.

R Reading Strategy

Identifying Ask: What information do you need to compute the unit price of a product? *(the price and the weight or the amount of the product)* **OL**

Analyzing Economics

Answers:

1. The $1.20 loaf is a better buy.

2. Possible answers include the most economical size is too large and would spoil before it could be completely used; the economical size has a larger price and the buyer does not have enough cash to purchase the product.

Additional Support

Financial Literacy

How Do You Calculate Unit Prices?

Trying to compare the prices of different amounts of a product—one pound of Product A versus one-half pound of Product B—can be confusing. To get the most for your money, it is important to compare the price, amount, and quality of similar **C** products. Unit pricing can help. The unit price tells you the costs per "unit" (such as per ounce, per pound, per sheet) to buy the product.

Your supermarket offers three sizes of the same cereal.

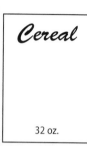

Cereal	*Cereal*	*Cereal*
32 oz.	20 oz.	14 oz.
$5.76	**$3.40**	**$2.52**

R To compute the unit price—the price per ounce, in this case—you need to divide the price of each item by its weight. Here is the formula:

$$\text{Unit price} = \frac{\text{Price}}{\text{Weight}}$$

Which one is the best buy?

$5.76 divided by 32 ounces = 18¢
$3.40 divided by 20 ounces = 17¢
$2.52 divided by 14 ounces = 18¢

In this case, the 20-ounce box offers the best price at 17 cents per ounce.

Analyzing Economics

1. **Calculating** Figure the unit price and compare accuracy to the unit price sticker. For example, which is the better buy: a 16-oz. loaf of bread at $.96 or a 25-oz. loaf at $1.20?

2. **Explaining** Can you think of a situation in which you would *not* buy a product at the most economical price? Explain your reasons.

Activity: Economics Connection

Calculating Unit Prices Have pairs of students work to compile lists of prices and amounts for ten typical grocery store items. They should compare at least two different sizes of the same type of product and include a variety of items, such as milk, rice, and soap. Students may get information from advertisements, store circulars, or on-site research. After they have compiled their lists, have students work separately to calculate the unit price of each item. When students have finished calculating the unit price for the items on their lists, have pairs switch papers and check each other's work. **OL**

Guide to Reading

Big Idea
Political and economic institutions evolve to help individuals and groups accomplish their goals.

Content Vocabulary
- surplus *(p. 688)*
- deficit *(p. 688)*
- bond *(p. 688)*
- debt *(p. 688)*
- balanced budget *(p. 688)*
- automatic stabilizer *(p. 692)*

Academic Vocabulary
- precise *(p. 688)*
- ideological *(p. 691)*

Reading Strategy
Explaining As you read, complete a graphic organizer like the one below to explain the differences between a federal deficit and the federal debt.

🔊 **Section Audio**   📱 **Spotlight Video**

Section 3

Managing the Economy

Real World Economics This clock is the same in all time zones. The National Debt Clock, created by New York City historian Seymour Durst, acts as a wake-up call to citizens in the United States, making them aware of how much the nation has economically overextended itself—how much money it owes. Today, the national debt is approaching the $10 trillion mark, an amount so enormous most people cannot understand it. The clock spells it out.

▼ **National Debt Clock in midtown Manhattan, New York City**

Focus

Guide to Reading
Answers to Web Diagram:

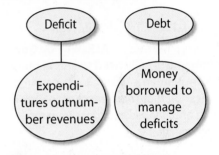

Deficit — Expenditures outnumber revenues

Debt — Money borrowed to manage deficits

 Section Spotlight Video

To generate student interest and provide a springboard for class discussion, access the Chapter 25, Section 3 video at glencoe.com or on the video DVD.

Resource Manager

R Reading Strategies	**C** Critical Thinking	**D** Differentiated Instruction	**W** Writing Support	**S** Skill Practice
Teacher Edition • Making Connections, p. 689 • Monitoring, p. 691 • Summarizing, p. 692 **Additional Resources** • Cont. Vocab., URB p. 67 • Ac. Vocab., URB p. 69 • Guid. Read., URB p. 87 • Foldables, p. 99	**Teacher Edition** • Cause and Effect, p. 688 • Making Inferences, p. 688 • Drawing Conclusions, p. 689 • Comparing and Contrasting, p. 690 **Additional Resources** • Quizzes and Tests, p. 299	**Teacher Edition** • Interpersonal, p. 688 **Additional Resources** • Diff. Instr. Act., URB p. 79 • School-to-Home Act., URB p. 81	**Teacher Edition** • Personal Writing, p. 691	**Teacher Edition** • Reading Graphs, p. 690 **Additional Resources** • Daily Focus Trans., 25–3 • Pol. Cartoons Trans. 25

Teach

D Differentiated Instruction

Interpersonal Organize students into small groups and have them discuss constructive ways that individuals can deal with personal debt. **OL**

C₁ Critical Thinking

Cause and Effect Ask: Why does the government sometimes go into debt? *(When the government has a deficit it must borrow money to pay its bills.)* **OL**

C₂ Critical Thinking

Making Inferences Ask: Why do governments usually need to spend more on entitlements during bad economic times? *(At these times more people are in need of economic assistance from the government.)* **OL**

Surpluses and Deficits

Main Idea Governmental budgeting can result in either a surplus, a deficit, or a balanced budget.

D **Economics & You** Do you find it easy to estimate how much money you will need over a week or a month? Read to find out why estimating is a challenge for most governments.

Governmental budgeting can be difficult. A budget, after all, is built on forecasts, which are not always **precise,** or exact. If tax revenues are lower than expected, the budget is in trouble. The same is true if expenses are higher than anticipated because of some emergency. In this section, you will learn what happens when the government spends more—or collects more—than it planned. You will also see what steps governments can take to try to influence the economy in certain ways.

When a government spends less than it collects in revenues, it enjoys a **surplus.** A government runs a **deficit** when it spends more than it collects in revenues. Review the proposed federal budget from Section 1 on page 679. As you can see, the federal government planned to end the fiscal year with a deficit of $354 billion. Look at graph A on page 690. You will see that the federal government had deficits for almost all the years shown on the graph.

From the Deficit to the Debt

C₁ When the federal government runs a deficit, it must borrow money so it can pay its bills. This borrowing is similar to an individual overspending his or her income and using credit. The government borrows money by selling **bonds.** A bond is a contract to repay the borrowed money with interest at a specific time in the future. When you buy United States savings bonds, you are also lending funds to the federal government.

State and local governments can borrow by selling bonds to finance some of their activities. All the money that has been borrowed over the years and has not yet been paid back is the government's **debt,** also known as the national debt.

When a government runs deficits, its total debt goes up. On the other hand, surpluses can be used to cut the debt. Suppose, for example, that the U.S. government had a deficit of $100 billion in one year, followed by a deficit of $75 billion the next. If the country had no earlier debt, it would have a total debt of $175 billion after two years. Suppose it then had a surplus of $50 billion in the third year. That money could be used to reduce the debt to $125 billion.

How Big Is the Debt? The national debt has grown almost continuously since 1900, when the debt was $1.3 billion. By 1940 it was $50.7 billion. Huge budget deficits in the early 1990s and early 2000s have pushed the national debt held by the public to approximately $4.9 trillion by October 2006. This equals about $16,365 for every man, woman, and child in America.

A Balanced Budget

The government achieves a **balanced budget** when spending equals revenues. The federal government is not required by law to have a balanced budget, but 48 states and many local governments are. In these cases, governments must cut spending when revenues go down.

C₂ During bad economic times, revenues often go down. Yet those are the times when states need to spend more on entitlements. This can make the budgeting process difficult. Many state and local governments are prohibited from borrowing to pay operating expenses. For that reason, they try to maintain an emergency fund balance—a government savings account from which deficits can be paid.

Hands-On Chapter Project
Step 3

Money Matters

Step 3: Dealing with Deficits Have students continue to work in teams to deal with a revenue deficit for their planned class trips.

Directions Remind students that overestimated income and unforeseen expenses can spoil the most carefully drawn budget.

Using the expense charts they created in Step 2, have students deal with a deficit in revenues for their planned class trip. Write different percentages on slips of paper (10%, 25%, 75%, etc.), fold the slips of paper in half, and place them in a paper bag. Have someone from each group select a slip of paper. The percentage on the slip will determine the size of the deficit in the trip bud-

get of each group. Have each group brainstorm a plan for dealing with the deficit. The groups might decide to borrow money or to scale back trip expenses.

Summarizing Have each group share their new plans with the class. **OL**

(Project continued on the Visual Summary page)

TIME™ Political Cartoons

Michael Ramirez/Copley News Service

America's major entitlement programs are the subject of this cartoon by Michael Ramirez.

1. **How are Social Security and Medicare represented?**
2. **What does the wave stand for?**
3. **What do you think the cartoonist's outlook is for the future of Social Security and Medicare?**

Every year, more than half of all Americans do volunteer work ... role in it. One of the responsibilities of citizens is to help make their ... of volunteer grou... small. Perha... dad who ...

Impact of the National Debt

When the government spends more than it collects in tax revenues, it has to borrow the difference. You have learned that deficits lead to debt. But what does debt lead to?

Even though we owe most of the national debt to ourselves—through the purchase of bonds—the debt can affect the economy in several ways.

Paying Interest The national debt's most direct impact on the federal budget is the amount of tax money needed each year to finance past borrowing. Every year the interest on the national debt must be paid. U.S. taxpayers shoulder the responsibility of paying the interest. In fiscal year 2006, interest on the publicly held debt amounted to $218 billion. This total is roughly equal to one-quarter of all personal income tax revenue collected for 2006, and is a larger amount than the federal share of the payments for Medicaid.

The larger the national debt, the larger the interest payments, and, therefore, the more taxes needed to pay them. When people pay more taxes to the government, they have less money to spend on their own needs.

Interest Rate Additionally, when the federal government borrows money, it leaves less for citizens and private business to borrow. According to the law of supply and demand, an increase in the government's demand for credit will push up the price of credit—the interest rate. A Federal Reserve study in 2003 concluded that for every percentage point increase in the deficit as a share of GDP, long-term interest rates will rise by one-quarter percent. For example, you purchase an automobile for $20,000. Based on a four-year loan at 8 percent interest, your cumulative payments total $23,436.48, of which $3,436.48 is interest. If the interest rate is 9 percent, you pay an additional $453.21 in interest over the life of the loan.

Reading Check Explaining How does the federal government get money when it runs a budget deficit?

Paying Income Taxes

Objective: To understand federal income tax

Focus: Students will calculate taxable income.

Teach: Review these terms: "taxable income," "marginal tax rate," "dependency exemption," and "personal exemption."

Assess: Have students define each of the terms reviewed.

Close: Have students calculate the taxable income for earnings of $23,500, $62,750, and $225,000.

C Critical Thinking

Comparing and Contrasting Ask: What do surpluses and deficits have in common? *(They are both related to revenues and expenditures.)* **Ask:** How do they differ? *(Surpluses occur when government revenues are in excess of government expenditures. Deficits occur when government revenues are below government expenditures.)* **OL**

S Skill Practice

Reading Graphs Ask: What percentage of the national debt is held by government accounts? *(52 percent)* **BL**

Analyzing Graphs

Answers:

1. 1998—2001
2. From 1975 until 1980, the national debt rose slightly. From the 1980s to the 1990s, the national debt rose more sharply. It leveled off during the late 1990s but rose dramatically after 2000.

Differentiated Instruction

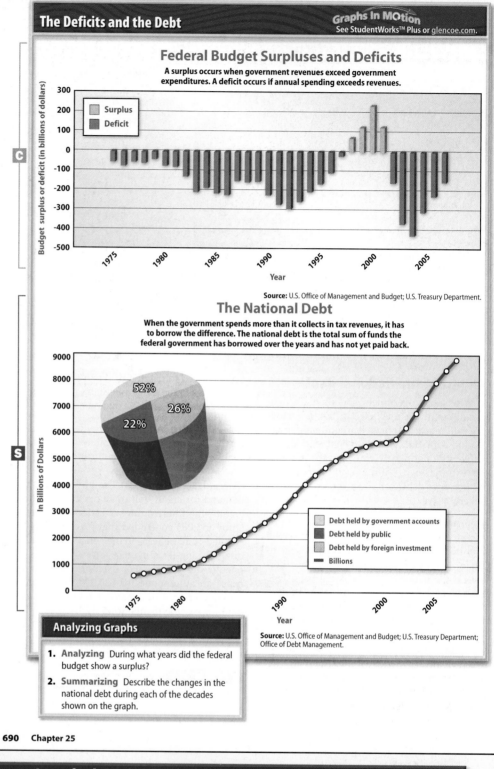

The Deficits and the Debt

Graphs In MOtion
See StudentWorks™ Plus or glencoe.com.

Federal Budget Surpluses and Deficits

A surplus occurs when government revenues exceed government expenditures. A deficit occurs if annual spending exceeds revenues.

Source: U.S. Office of Management and Budget; U.S. Treasury Department.

The National Debt

When the government spends more than it collects in tax revenues, it has to borrow the difference. The national debt is the total sum of funds the federal government has borrowed over the years and has not yet paid back.

- 52%
- 26%
- 22%

Legend:
- Debt held by government accounts
- Debt held by public
- Debt held by foreign investment
- Billions

Source: U.S. Office of Management and Budget; U.S. Treasury Department; Office of Debt Management.

Analyzing Graphs

1. **Analyzing** During what years did the federal budget show a surplus?
2. **Summarizing** Describe the changes in the national debt during each of the decades shown on the graph.

690 Chapter 25

Leveled Activities

BL Reteaching Activity 25, URB p. 83

OL School-to-Home Activity 25, URB p. 81

OL Academic Vocabulary Activity 25, URB p. 69

ELL Guided Reading Activity 25-3, URB p. 87

Fiscal Policy

Main Idea The tool of fiscal policy can help governments control the economy.

Economics & You Do you need to talk your friends into doing something they already want to do? Of course not! Read how this idea applies to fiscal policy.

The role of government in the nation's economy extends beyond its activities as a regulator of specific industries. The government also manages the pace of economic activity. As you learned in Chapter 23, the federal government can try to use taxes and spending to help the economy grow. This practice is known as fiscal policy.

In theory, the government can stimulate the economy during a recession by increasing spending and cutting taxes. When the economy begins to grow again, less stimulus is needed. In those times, the government can reduce spending and increase taxes.

Fiscal Policy in Practice

Nonetheless, these decisions are difficult to make. Many people want lower taxes regardless of the state of the economy. Many people also want government services, so the federal government has a difficult time cutting spending even when the economy is strong.

Does Fiscal Policy Work? Some lawmakers oppose increased spending or tax cuts on **ideological** grounds, or sets of beliefs they hold. Even when leaders agree that a stimulus is needed, they often argue over where and how to spend the money.

Moreover, government action does not always have the desired effect. Sometimes it takes a long time for political leaders to agree on a plan to stimulate the economy. By then, many months may have passed, and the economic situation may have changed.

TIME™ Teens in Action

Katie Anderton

The homeless shelter Bethesda House in Schenectady, New York, has found the perfect volunteer in Katie Anderton. This 16-year-old from the same city says, "A lot of people my age are afraid of anyone different from them, but I don't see differences—I see people."

QUESTION: What is Bethesda House?

ANSWER: It's the lead agency serving the homeless in Schenectady. They're trying to end homelessness and make our community a welcoming place for everyone to live.

Q: What does it do to help?

A: Everything! Bethesda House has things like hot meals, showers, and a laundry. There's a medical clinic for people with no health insurance and case managers to assist people to find affordable housing. The agency also helps to educate the community about homelessness, to advocate for fairness in jobs, salaries, and health insurance.

Q: Wow! How many people does it assist?

A: Almost 8,000 different people come to Bethesda House each year. More than 60,000 meals are served. Over 500 homeless people are placed in emergency shelters and 85 percent of them are helped to move into permanent housing.

Making a Difference CITIZENSHIP

Explaining What is the purpose of Bethesda House?

Monitoring Ask: How can the government stimulate the economy during a recession? *(The government can increase spending and cut taxes.)* **OL**

W Writing Support

Personal Writing Have students write one paragraph expressing their personal opinions about taxes and government spending. How willing are they to pay higher taxes for government services? **OL**

TIME™ Teens in Action

Answer: The purpose of Bethesda House is to serve the homeless in Schenectady.

Additional Support

Teacher Tip

Discuss the importance of being prepared and courteous during an interview. Have students schedule an appointment at a convenient hour for the community volunteer, be on time, and thank the volunteer for his or her time.

Activity: Interdisciplinary Connection

Language Arts Have students interview a community volunteer. Tell students to prepare the following questions: For which organization do you work? What is its mission? How does it attempt to fulfill its mission? What does the volunteer do while working for the organization? How can others interested in volunteering get involved?

In addition, have students ask the volunteer at least two questions of their own devising. One question should be prepared in advance of the interview. The other question should be one that arises during the interview.

Have students share what they learned with the class. **AL**

R Reading Strategy

Summarizing What automatic stabilizers does the economy have and how do they work? *(Unemployment benefits help workers who lose their jobs. The federal progressive income tax lowers tax rates on people when their income goes down and raises it when their income rises.)* **OL**

✓ Reading Check **Answer:** Because policies do not always have the desired effect and because planning takes time, the government cannot always react quickly to economic situations.

Assess

Civics ONLINE

Study Central™ provides summaries, interactive games, and online graphic organizers to help students review content.

Close

Determining Cause and Effect Have students discuss the effects of government surpluses and deficits on the economy. **OL**

Section 3 Review

Automatic Stabilizers

It is difficult for the federal government to use fiscal policy to effectively stabilize the economy. However, the economy has a number of **automatic stabilizers.** These are programs that begin working to stimulate the economy as soon as they are needed. The main advantage of these programs is that they are already in place and do not need further government action to begin.

Unemployment Benefits Unemployment insurance programs are one example of automatic stabilizers. When people lose their jobs—as may happen in a recession—they collect unemployment payments. These payments are not very large. Still, they do give people some help until they can find a new job—or until the economy improves and they are hired back by their former employers.

Income Tax The fact that the federal income tax is progressive is another stabilizer. Remember that a progressive tax is based on a taxpayer's ability to pay. The higher a person's taxable income, the higher the tax rate. Progressive tax rates are lower at lower income levels. When people lose their jobs, their income goes down, pushing them into a lower tax bracket. The lower bracket helps ease the impact of the cut in income.

When the economy recovers, the opposite happens. People make more money and, therefore, need and receive less help from entitlements. Generally, automatic stabilizers go into effect much more rapidly than discretionary fiscal policies—policies that governments *choose* to implement.

✓ Reading Check **Explaining** Why is fiscal policy difficult to implement?

Section 3 Review

Vocabulary

1. **Define** the following terms and use them in sentences related to governmental management of the economy: *surplus, deficit, bond, debt, balanced budget, automatic stabilizer.*

Main Ideas

2. **Explaining** What two situations can cause a budget deficit?

3. **Describing** What is the main advantage of an automatic stabilizer?

Critical Thinking

4. **Concluding** Do you think the federal government should be required, like most state governments, to balance the budget every year? Explain.

5. **BIG Ideas** In a graphic organizer like the one below, explain the effect of a government budget deficit.

Cause: Government spends more than it collects in revenues.	→	Effect:

6. **Analyzing Visuals** Look at the graphs on page 690 that show the deficit and the debt. Describe the deficit in the 1970s compared to that of the 1990s.

CITIZENSHIP Activity

7. **Persuasive Writing** Write a paragraph that supports a position on the following statement: In a free-market system like ours, it should never be the government's job to stimulate the economy.

Civics ONLINE

Study Central™ To review this section, go to glencoe.com.

Answers

1. Sentences should use vocabulary words according to their definitions in the section and in the Glossary.

2. Lower tax revenues and higher expenses than expected can cause a budget deficit.

3. Automatic stabilizers are already in place and can begin to stimulate the economy as soon as they are needed.

4. Answers will vary. Students should explain their reasoning.

5. Effect: The government is forced to borrow money, which leads to increased national debt and higher interest rates.

6. The debt in the 1970s rose slowly. The debt in 1990s increased sharply.

7. Students' positions will vary. They should use the information in this section to support their positions.

Visual Summary

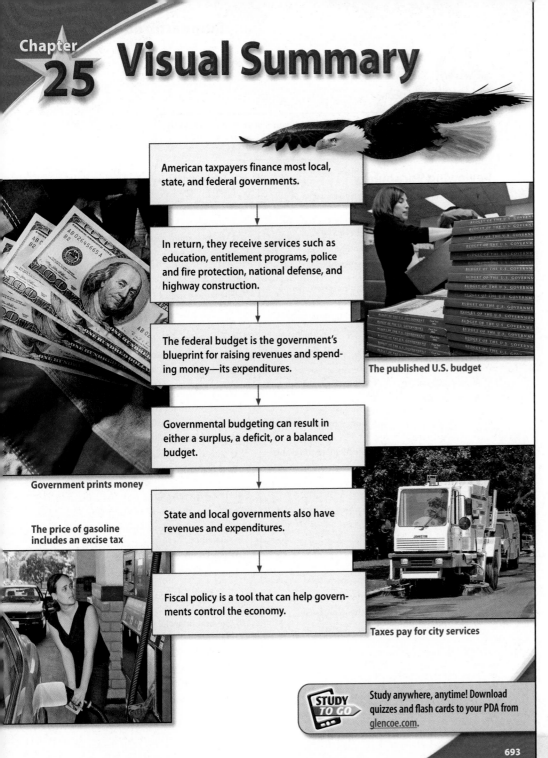

American taxpayers finance most local, state, and federal governments.

In return, they receive services such as education, entitlement programs, police and fire protection, national defense, and highway construction.

The federal budget is the government's blueprint for raising revenues and spending money—its expenditures.

Governmental budgeting can result in either a surplus, a deficit, or a balanced budget.

State and local governments also have revenues and expenditures.

Fiscal policy is a tool that can help governments control the economy.

Government prints money

The price of gasoline includes an excise tax

The published U.S. budget

Taxes pay for city services

STUDY TO GO Study anywhere, anytime! Download quizzes and flash cards to your PDA from glencoe.com.

693

Visual Summary 25

Making Connections The photograph at the bottom right shows a city street sweeper cleaning the streets. For what other types of services do taxes pay? *(Answers may include entitlement programs, highway maintenance, police and fire protection.)* **OL**

Summarizing Have students find an editorial on government fiscal policy on the Internet. Ask students to state the overall position of the editorial, and then summarize it by listing its main points. Have students number each point in their summary. Then have students print out the editorial. Ask them to highlight and number the points in the editorial to match the numbered points in their summary. **OL**

Hands-On Chapter Project
Step 4: Wrap-Up

Money Matters

Step 4: Reviewing the Planning Process Students will present a final report on their class trip.

Directions Write the Big Idea on the board. Ask student groups to prepare short reports about their efforts to deal with their class trip budget deficit. Have students review their initial expense charts from Step 2. Then have the groups collaborate on writing an overview of the steps they took to deal with the deficit. Their reports should include information on: the amount of the original budget, the size of the deficit, the options the group considered, and the choices the group made to deal with their budget deficit.

Summarizing Once again have the groups present the posters they created in Step 1 to the class. Using the posters as a backdrop, have groups present their reports to the class. Encourage students to share what they learned about the Big Idea throughout the Hands-On Project. **OL**

Reviewing Vocabulary

1. C Choices B and D refer to kinds of taxes. Answer A refers to money raised from taxes. Students should understand that the president and Congress work together to create the budget. It is a blueprint of how the government will raise and spend money.

2. A In this question, the most confusing distractor will probably be answer B, "Medicare." Students should be able to note the key differences between Social Security and Medicare after reading about government expenditures. Recognizing that Medicare specifically covers health care should eliminate it as the correct answer and lead students to answer A as the correct choice.

3. D The phrase in the question that most clearly suggests the right answer is "consumer purchases." Students should remember from their reading that sales taxes are levied on products purchased by consumers.

4. B While all of the answer options here are elements of the government's financial processes, only one concerns borrowing money. A deficit is when expenditures exceed revenues. Entitlement programs are a large expenditure by the government. Appropriations are laws passed by Congress to approve spending. Eliminating these answers leaves B, "bonds," as the correct choice.

Reviewing Main Ideas

5. A Choices B and C might be the major distractors. But each refers to a tax rate that decreases in relation to income. One meaning of the word "progressive" is "increasing in extent." It would be applied to a tax that increases as the income increases.

6. D Keeping in mind that interest is a charge for borrowed money will lead students to the correct answer for this question. Interest is not paid by money lenders nor is interest paid on taxes and scientific research. These facts eliminate answers B and C. Students will recall that a portion of each year's federal budget

---

TEST-TAKING TIP

When reading a question, note words that tell you that your answer is to be in the negative, such as *Which of these is NOT. . . or All of these EXCEPT. . . .*

Reviewing Vocabulary

Directions: Choose the word(s) that best completes the sentence.

1. Each year the president and Congress have to agree on a plan for spending called a _____.

  A revenue   **C** budget

  B progressive tax   **D** regressive tax

2. _____ provides government money to people who are retired or disabled.

  A Social Security   **C** Appropriations bill

  B Medicare   **D** Proportional tax

3. A(n) _____ is usually levied on consumer purchases of almost all products.

  A property tax   **C** education tax

  B entitlement   **D** sales tax

4. The government borrows money by selling _____.

  A deficits   **C** entitlement programs

  B bonds   **D** appropriations

Reviewing Main Ideas

Directions: Choose the best answer for each question.

Section 1 *(pp. 676–680)*

5. The federal income tax is a progressive tax, which means the _____.

  A tax rate increases as income increases

  B tax rate decreases as income increases

  C tax rate decreases as income decreases

  D tax rate and income are not related

6. A portion of the federal budget each year pays for the interest on _____.

  A money lent to Great Britain

  B money collected in taxes

  C money spent on scientific research

  D money borrowed by the government

Section 2 *(pp. 681–685)*

7. The largest source of revenues for local governments is _____.

  A property taxes

  B intergovernmental revenues

  C local income taxes

  D fines and fees

8. Which of the following is funding that state governments are NOT responsible for?

  A welfare and health programs

  B universities and colleges

  C interstate highway maintenance

  D water supplies and sewers

Section 3 *(pp. 687–692)*

9. Managing the nation's fiscal policy _____.

  A requires the president and Congress to work together

  B is left entirely to Congress

  C is voted on by the people of Washington, D.C.

  D must be approved by the Supreme Court

10. The best financial situation for the United States is to have _____.

  A deficits exceed surpluses

  B surpluses exceed deficits

  C deficits exceed revenues

  D deficits and surpluses to be equal

GO ON ➡

---

goes toward paying interest on money the government has borrowed.

7. B This question presents a challenge in that all the answers are forms of revenue for local governments. To answer this question, students must review the graph illustrating State and Local Government revenues. The graph shows that intergovernmental revenue is clearly the largest percentage of revenue for local governments.

8. D Students who carefully read the "Expenditures" portion in Section 2 will be able to answer this question.

9. A Students should recognize that managing fiscal policy involves regulating spending and taxes in an attempt to help the economy grow. Students should immediately be able to eliminate answers C and D. Furthermore, students should remember that spending and taxes are elements of the budget process that require coopera-

Critical Thinking

Directions: Choose the best answer for each question.

11. What trend can be seen when looking at the size of the national debt over decades?

  A It gets smaller every year and could be paid off in ten years.

  B It is a very small part of the federal budget.

  C It grows larger every year and will be difficult to pay off.

  D It developed because the government had a revenue surplus every year.

12. What trend is expected with Medicare costs in the future?

  A The costs will go up steadily.

  B The costs will go down dramatically.

  C The costs will remain stable with little change.

  D The government will do away with the Medicare program.

Base your answer to question 13 on the diagram below and your knowledge of Chapter 25.

13. Expenditures for Social Security and national defense best fit under which level of government?

  A Federal

  B State

  C Local

  D Federal and State

Document-Based Questions

Merton Miller was a well-respected American economist and teacher who lived from 1923–2000.

> . . . if you take money out of your left pocket and put it in your right pocket, you're no richer.
>
> —Merton Miller

14. How do you think Miller feels about the government investing its money to make it grow?

  A He would disagree with investing.

  B He thinks saving is the best way to manage funds.

  C He would be in favor of investing funds.

  D He doesn't believe in income taxes for investing.

15. What do you think Miller believed the government's role in managing its money should be?

  A The government should stay out of money management.

  B The government is doing a good job of balancing the budget.

  C The government has to make its funds increase for the country to prosper.

  D The government should ask individual citizens to manage its money.

Extended-Response Question

16. Some people believe more power over spending money should be given to the states rather than the federal government controlling it. What do you think? Write a Pro/Con list for giving the states more power over spending. Conclude with a paragraph about what your list shows.

For additional test practice, use Self-Check Quizzes—Chapter 25 on glencoe.com.

Need Extra Help?															
If you missed question...	1	2	3	4	5	6	7	8	9	10	11	12	13	14	15	16
Go to page...	677	678	682	688	678	680	682	684	691	688	690	680	680	678	678	684

ASSESSMENT

13. A Programs such as Social Security and national defense affect the entire U.S. population. Expenditures for these programs fit under the federal level, since it is concerned with the nation as a whole.

Document-Based Questions

14. C If you take money from one pocket and put it into another, you will have the same amount that you started with. Miller's point is that this procedure will not enrich you. Investment is the only procedure that might lead to an increased amount of money.

15. C Miller is advocating economic growth.

Extended Response

16. Answers will vary. Student's paragraphs should clearly support the information in their pro and con lists.

---

tion between Congress and the president. Therefore, the correct answer is A.

10. B If students know the definitions of surpluses and deficits, they should see that it is better for the government to have excess money rather than insufficient money to meet the needs of the nation.

Critical Thinking

11. C Students should review the graphs on page 690. Since surpluses do not lead to debt, students should eliminate answer D. A quick glance at the graphs shows answers A and B to be false. Therefore, C is the correct answer.

12. A Students will remember from reading Section 1 that Medicare is a program that provides health insurance for the elderly. This fact should lead students to the conclusion that a growing elderly population will lead to higher Medicare costs. This means that A is correct.

Have students visit the Web site at glencoe.com to review Chapter 25 and take the **Self-Check Quiz.**

Need Extra Help?

Have students refer to the pages listed if they miss any of the questions.

Teach

C₁ Critical Thinking

Cause and Effect Ask: What reason does Josh Bolten give for the budget deficit under President George W. Bush? *(He claims that Bush inherited an economy that was in the process of weakening. "Revenues just disappeared.")* **OL**

C₂ Critical Thinking

Predicting Consequences Ask: What is estimated about deficits if Bush's tax cuts are made permanent? *(Deficits will persist for at least 10 years.)* **OL**

Additional Support

TIME
REPORTS

The Federal Deficit

As government spending grows and tax revenues shrink, the United States racks up record-breaking debt

Back in 2000, when Bill Clinton was completing his second term as President, the United States had a budget surplus of $236 billion—meaning that the federal government took in 236 billion more dollars than it spent that year. Under President George W. Bush, the surplus has become an annual deficit of $400 billion. About a quarter of what the government has spent since Bush entered the White House has been borrowed.

In Bush's defense, Josh Bolten— who served as Director of the Office of **C₁** Management and Budget before becoming White House Chief of Staff—points to the economy the President inherited. "We had this burst bubble. Revenues just disappeared, and this was all before the President's tax cuts." But when Bush came into office, the nonpartisan Congressional Budget Office (CBO) was projecting surpluses for years to come, until Bush's tax cuts went into effect. CBO estimates show that if Bush's tax cuts **C₂** are made permanent—as he is advocating— deficits will persist for at least 10 years.

OUR NATIONAL DEBT: $8,200,264,018.46
YOUR *Family share* **$89,521**
THE NATIONAL DEBT CLOCK

ADDING IT UP This electronic clock, located in New York City, shows the total U.S. government debt as of August 2006 (top) and the estimated share for each American family (bottom). The *national debt* is the total amount of money that the government owes; the *deficit* is the yearly amount by which spending exceeds revenue. The clock does not have enough digits to show the debt when it reaches the $10 trillion mark, which is expected to occur by 2008.

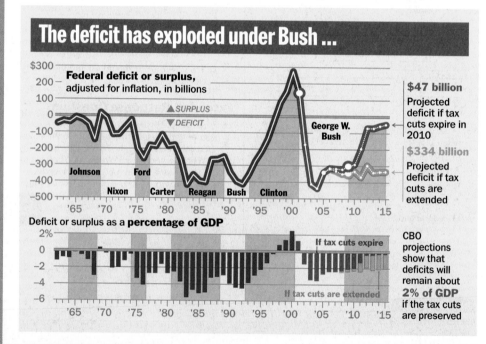

The deficit has exploded under Bush ...

Federal deficit or surplus, adjusted for inflation, in billions

▲ SURPLUS
▼ DEFICIT

George W. Bush

Johnson Ford Nixon Carter Reagan Bush Clinton

'65 '70 '75 '80 '85 '90 '95 '00 '05 '10 '15

$47 billion Projected deficit if tax cuts expire in 2010

$334 billion Projected deficit if tax cuts are extended

Deficit or surplus as a percentage of GDP

If tax cuts expire

If tax cuts are extended

'65 '70 '75 '80 '85 '90 '95 '00 '05 '10 '15

CBO projections show that deficits will remain about **2% of GDP** if the tax cuts are preserved

Background

The Congressional Budget Office The Congressional Budget Office (CBO) was founded on July 12, 1974, and began operating on February 24, 1975. Its mission is to assist Congress in preparing the budget by providing objective and impartial economic reports and analyses. In addition, each year the CBO provides projected estimates of spending and revenue levels for a 10-year period. However, these estimates do not take into account future changes in law (such as changes in tax law) that could affect spending and revenue. For this reason, the CBO routinely updates its information as events influence the economic forecast. To insure the quality of the work of the CBO, a panel of economic advisers meets twice a year to review the CBO's reports and analyses.

... and spending has increased rapidly ...

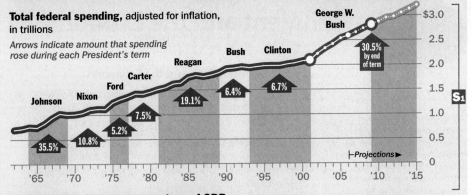

Total federal spending, adjusted for inflation, in trillions

Arrows indicate amount that spending rose during each President's term

Johnson 35.5%
Nixon 10.8%
Ford 5.2%
Carter 7.5%
Reagan 19.1%
Bush 6.4%
Clinton 6.7%
George W. Bush 30.5% by end of term

←Projections►

Total federal spending as a **percentage of GDP**

←Projections►

... across the entire government

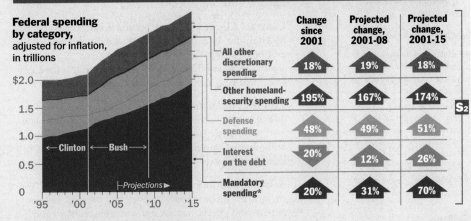

Federal spending by category, adjusted for inflation, in trillions

←Clinton— —Bush→

←Projections►

	Change since 2001	Projected change, 2001-08	Projected change, 2001-15
All other discretionary spending	18%	19%	18%
Other homeland-security spending	195%	167%	174%
Defense spending	48%	49%	51%
Interest on the debt	20%	12%	26%
Mandatory spending*	20%	31%	70%

*Programs such as Social Security, Medicare, Medicaid, veterans' benefits, unemployment, food stamps

Sources: Congressional Budget Office, Bureau of Labor Statistics, Center on Budget and Policy Priorities. All inflation-adjusted figures are 2006 dollars

697

S₁ Skill Practice

Reading Graphs Ask: According to the graph, under which president did federal spending most increase? *(Johnson)* **OL**

S₂ Skill Practice

Reading Graphs Ask: Which federal spending category has increased the most since 2001? *(homeland security spending)* **OL**

Reading Strategy · Read to Write

Expressing Opinions Despite rising security costs and growing entitlement programs, President George W. Bush hopes to make his tax cuts permanent. As you have read, the CBO estimates that if the tax cuts are made permanent, the deficit will persist for at least 10 years. Do you feel it is appropriate to cut taxes when the government is running deficits? Write an editorial expressing your opinion about tax cuts and the deficit. Be sure to explain your reasoning. **OL**

Focus

Analyzing Primary Sources

R₁ **Reading Strategy**

Identify **Ask:** Which clause gives Congress the right to regulate commerce? *(Commerce Clause)* **BL**

R₂ **Reading Strategy**

Making Connections Remind students that critics of President Bush's warrantless wiretapping program, which allowed the government to eavesdrop on the phone conversations of Americans without a warrant, say that it was unconstitutional. **Ask:** Which of these provisions in the Constitution best supports the critic's position? *(Amendment IV, Searches and Seizures)* **OL**

Government and the Economy

Reading Focus

In the nation's early years, most political leaders were reluctant to involve the federal government too heavily in the economic sector. They accepted the idea of laissez-faire, a doctrine opposing government interference. While consumers and producers make most economic decisions, government activities have a powerful effect on the U.S. economy.

Read to Discover

As you read, think about the following:

- Why did the Framers believe it was necessary that the Constitution include the commerce clause?
- How much influence should the government have over the economy?

Reader's Dictionary

Bill of Attainder: a law that punishes a person accused of a crime without a trial or a fair hearing in court

ex post facto law: a law that would allow a person to be punished for an action that was not against the law when it was committed

The Constitution and the Economy

Some provisions in the U.S. Constitution protect private property rights and the freedom to take part in commercial activities free of arbitrary restrictions.

R₁ **Commerce Clause** Article I, Section 8, states that Congress shall have the power "To regulate Commerce with foreign Nations, and among the several States, and with the Indian Tribes; . . ."

Coinage Clause Article I, Section 8, states that Congress shall have the power "To coin Money, regulate the value thereof, . . ." and "To provide for the Punishment of counterfeiting the Securities and current Coin of the United States; . . ." Article I, Section 10, gives Congress this power exclusively by stating that "No State shall . . . coin Money; . . ."

Copyright Clause Article I, Section 8, states that Congress shall have the power "To promote the Progress of Science and useful Arts, by securing for limited Times to Authors and Inventors the exclusive Right to their respective Writing and Discoveries; . . ."

Contract Clauses Article I, Section 9, states that "**No Bill of Attainder** or **ex post facto Law** shall be passed . . ." by Congress. Article I, Section 10, states that "No state shall . . . pass any Bill of Attainder, ex post facto Law, or Law impairing the Obligations of Contracts, . . ."

Export Clauses Article I, Section 9, states that "No Tax or Duty shall be laid on Articles exported from any State . . .", and Article I, Section 10, states that "No State shall, without the Consent of the Congress, lay any Imposts or Duties on Imports or Exports, . . ."

R₂ **Searches and Seizures** Amendment IV states that "The right of the people to be secure in their persons, houses, papers, and effects, against unreasonable searches and seizures, shall not be violated, . . ."

698

Additional Reading

Review suggested books before assigning them.

Small is Beautiful: Economics as if People Mattered by E. F. Schumacher discusses modern economics, recycling, natural resources, growth, and intermediate technology.

Money Business: Banks and Banking by Ernestine Giesecke tells how banks keep track of people's money, describes the services that banks offer, and explains the Federal Reserve System.

Philanthropists and Their Legacies by Carol G. Traub profiles philanthropists such as Alfred Nobel, Andrew Carnegie, and John D. and Catherine T. MacArthur. It describes how the philanthropists made their money and explains why they gave away so much of it.

Due Process Amendment V states that "No person shall . . . be deprived of life, liberty, or property, without due process of the law; . . ." and Amendment XIV, Section 1, states, "nor shall any State deprive any person of life, liberty, or property, without due process of law; . . ."

Reserved Rights and Powers Amendment IX states that "The enumeration in the Constitution, of certain rights, shall not be construed to deny or disparage others retained by the people." And Amendment X states, "The powers not delegated to the United States by the Constitution, nor prohibited by it to the States, are reserved to the States respectively, or to the people."

Role of Government

Two presidents provide their views on the role of government in the economy.

> [A] wise and frugal government, which shall restrain men from injuring one another, which shall leave them otherwise free to regulate their own pursuits of industry and improvement, and shall not take from the mouth of labor the bread it has earned. This is the sum of good government.
>
> —Thomas Jefferson, First Inaugural Address, March 4, 1801

> Government ought to have the right and will have the right, after surveying and planning for an industry to prevent, with the assistance of the overwhelming majority of that industry, unfair practice and to enforce this agreement by the authority of government. The so-called anti-trust laws were intended to prevent the creation of monopolies and to forbid unreasonable profits to those monopolies. That purpose of the anti-trust laws must be continued, but these laws were never intended to encourage the kind of unfair competition that results in long hours, starvation wages and overproduction.
>
> —President Franklin D. Roosevelt, Fireside chat, Sunday, May 7, 1933

Photographs as Primary Sources A new $1 coin was introduced in 2007. The United States Mint will mint and issue four presidential $1 coins per year. Why do you think the coin features the presidents?

DBQ Document-Based Questions

1. **Explaining** What restrictions does the U.S. Constitution place on state and local taxing powers?

2. **Describing** Which excerpt supports a laissez-faire position regarding government and the economy? Explain.

3. **Evaluating and Connecting** Originally the Framers of the Constitution wanted to ensure that

Congress could not involve itself in the states' internal affairs. Yet, the necessary and proper clause has been expanded so that Congress now has some control over virtually all economic activities, even within each state's borders. Do you think this is a fair exercise of congressional power? Give reasons for your answer.

Did You Know?

Antitrust Laws and the FTC As you have read, President Roosevelt stated in a 1933 Fireside Chat: "The so-called antitrust laws were intended to prevent the creation of monopolies…." The first of these laws was the Sherman Antitrust Act of 1890. The Clayton Antitrust Act of 1914 increased the power of antitrust law by prohibiting acts such as price discrimination and binding buyers or sellers to contracts that forced them to do business with a particular firm. In 1915 the Federal Trade Commission (FTC), an independent agency of the government, was formed to enforce antitrust laws. The president and the Senate appoint its five members for seven-year terms. In an effort to maintain a bipartisan FTC, no more than three members may be from the same party. To carry out its mission, the FTC brings federal charges against companies that it believes have violated antitrust laws.

Unit 8 Planning Guide

UNIT PACING CHART		
Unit 8	**Chapter 26**	**Chapter 27**
Day 1 Unit Opener, Reading Social Studies	Chapter Opener, Section 1, Issues to Debate	Chapter Opener, Section 1
Day 2	Section 2, Financial Literacy	Section 2
Day 3	Section 3, Chapter Review, Visual Summary	Section 3
Day 4	Chapter Assessment	Chapter Review, Visual Summary
Day 5	TIME Reports	Chapter Assessment
Day 6		Analyzing Primary Sources

Teacher to Teacher

Dana Mehl, Goshen High School, Goshen, Indiana

How Connected Are We? Have students select a partner, and look at each other's shirt label to determine where it was made. As a class, begin a list of all the countries in the classroom from the shirt labels. Discuss the terms imports and exports. Determine how many of the shirts students are wearing were made in the U.S., and how many of the shirts were imported to the U.S. Have students answer these questions: Why does the United States import more clothes than it makes domestically? As a consumer, do you support importing clothing? As a clothing manufacturer, would you support this? The partners then develop a position on free trade. Explain if they are in favor of or opposed to free trade. Partners turn in their written responses.

Author Note

Dear Social Studies Teacher:

In the mid-1990s, the textbook I used in our Introduction to Political Science course included a short discussion of Francis Fukuyama's *The End of History and the Last Man.* Simplified, Fukuyama's argument is that history can be seen as a struggle of political ideologies. With many nations becoming liberal democracies, Fukuyama suggested that the "end of history," in terms of this struggle, was near. Considering that the Cold War had ended, the Berlin Wall had fallen, and new democratic governments were emerging around the world, my students and I agreed that the "end" appeared to be near.

Now the future looks more clouded. Theocracies, monarchies, and autocratic dictators remain in control throughout the Middle East and Africa. About 20 percent of the world's population lives in communist China, which has changed its economy, but not its politics. The former Soviet Union is, at best, a semi-democracy. In the western hemisphere, leftist authoritarian regimes are in power in Venezuela, Bolivia, and Nicaragua.

Most significantly for the United States, the plan to democratize Iraq and set off a kind of democratic domino effect in the Middle East has yet to materialize.

We need to remind our students that while the number of democratic countries is higher than in 1980, many of the new democracies remain fragile. Several hard core authoritarian regimes seem as intractable as ever. Even with the best intentions, the ability of the United States to move democracy along (even incrementally) is questionable. It can happen only with very careful advance planning that is based on a clear understanding of the society we seek to change. Democratization is a long-term process and, at the present time, it does not seem to be inevitable. In other words, history keeps moving and the ideological struggle continues.

David C. Saffell
Author

Unit Objectives

After studying this unit, students will be able to:

• Understand and identify market, command, and mixed economies throughout the world.

• Relate global economic interdependence to changing traditions, values, and beliefs.

Did You Know?

To promote trade and economic prosperity throughout the world, countries have banded together by region or political philosophy to discuss economic issues. For example, the Big Seven, a consortium of noncommunist countries (Canada, France, Germany, the United Kingdom, Italy, Japan, and the United States), was formed in 1975 to discuss and coordinate major economic policies. The United Nations also concerns itself with world economies. Within its Economic and Social Council (ECOSOC) is the World Trade Organization, which provides a way for members to resolve trade conflicts and to work toward the goal of lowering and possibly eliminating tariffs and other trade barriers.

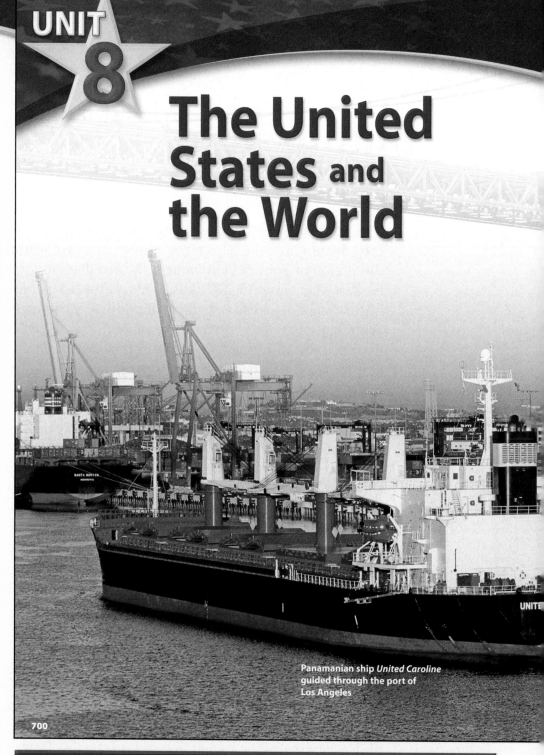

UNIT ★ 8

The United States and the World

Panamanian ship *United Caroline* guided through the port of Los Angeles

700

Activity: Launching the Unit

The United States and the World Ask: What is a global economy? (*In a global economy, the economies of world countries are linked by trade. As goods and information flow between countries, local, national, and world economists study the location of resources, the balance or imbalance of trade, and how trade relationships affect the quality of life of world citizens. For example, when a company relocates its manufacturing plants from a high-wage country to a low-wage country, both countries and their citizens are affected.*) **OL**

Be an Active Citizen

CITIZENSHIP The world seems smaller than it did only 50 years ago. Modern transportation and communication have brought people around the globe closer together. As citizens of the United States and members of the global community, we have a responsibility to stay informed about developments in other nations and the world.

701

Be an Active Citizen

CITIZENSHIP Are your students aware of how political and social issues affect the economies of world countries? Organize students into groups. Give each group one or more issues of a nationally known newspaper or newsmagazine. Ask groups to list events and issues in the United States and other countries that affect their economies, such as drought, war, human rights violations, other social issues, and so on. Beside each event, have groups predict the result of the event or issue on that country's economy.

Online Current Events Update

Visit Glencoe's *Online Current Events Update* **at** www.glencoe.com **to find news reports, features, maps, graphs, and photos of current events that shape our lives. Students can also make connections between historical events and current events by using the interactive time line.**

More About the Photo

Visual Literacy The Port of Los Angeles was officially founded on December 9, 1907, when the Los Angeles City Council created the Los Angeles Board of Harbor Commissioners. That year, the port handled 2 million tons of cargo worth $2 million. Today, port employees annually see nearly $239 billion in cargo with a combined weight of 190 million tons! Although the port depended heavily on the Pacific Northwest region for trade in its early years, today China is the port's main trade partner.

Why Monitoring and Clarifying Is Important

Monitoring and clarifying help students better understand and remember what they read. Questions such as *What did I learn from this example? What clues to this word's meaning does the text provide?* and *What are the main points of this paragraph?* help students distinguish what they understand and what needs clarification. Graphic organizers are another tool of monitoring comprehension. When students organize what they read graphically, they are testing their understanding of the written material.

 Learn It!

Write the following paragraph on the board: "Tariffs are obstacles to international trade because they discourage the importation of foreign goods. However, they are sometimes necessary to protect domestic industries. When tariffs fail, governments often use quotas to limit the amount of goods coming into a country." Have students work in pairs to identify a word that needs clarification and to write two questions that monitor comprehension. **OL**

Monitoring and Clarifying

 Learn It!

When you read something that is difficult, monitor your comprehension to determine when your understanding breaks down. Clarify, or clear up, confusing parts by rereading, defining unfamiliar words, and asking questions.

- Read the following paragraph and look at the chart below. Write what you understand from the text in the column labeled √.
- Write what is confusing in the column labeled **?**.

> The German thinker and writer Karl Marx was a socialist who predicted violent revolution. Marx believed that the population in industrialized nations is divided into capitalists, or bourgeoisie, who own the means of production and workers, or proletariat, who work to produce the goods. Marx interpreted human history as a class struggle between the workers and the capitalists. Eventually, he thought the workers would revolt and overthrow the capitalists.
>
> —*from page 717*

Reading Tip
If you read something confusing, slow down and think about the text. Look at pictures, words in bold, and other hints to figure out the meaning.

Clarifying Text	
√	?
Karl Marx was a socialist who predicted violent revolution.	What is a socialist?
Workers, or the proletariat, work to produce goods.	*Capitalists, or bourgeoisie, own the means of production.* What does it mean to "own the means of production"?
Eventually, the workers would revolt and overthrow the capitalists.	*Marx interpreted human history as a class struggle between the workers and the capitalists.* Does that mean that he thinks every civilization will have a class struggle?

Reading Strategy ❯ **Making Connections**

Mointoring and Clarifying In the course of a normal day, students automatically monitor their own understanding and seek to clarify things they do not understand. To help students connect to this important reading strategy, organize them into groups and list the following real-life situations on the board: *assembling a computer desk, reading a football playbook, completing a job application.* Have students discuss how monitoring and clarifying help them succeed in each situation. **OL**

② Practice It!

- Read the following paragraph. Draw a chart like the one below.
- Write what you understand from the text in the column labeled √.
- Write what is confusing in the column labeled **?**.

> Nevertheless, the United Nations has helped bring about peace in some areas and helped those who live in war-torn countries. In nations such as El Salvador, Cambodia, and Haiti, UN peace-keeping operations have helped sustain cease-fires, conduct free elections, monitor troop withdrawals, and prevent violence.
>
> —*from page 741*

√	?

③ Apply It!

In a paragraph, identify two things you understand and two things that are confusing for:

- **Chapter 27, Section 2**

② Practice It!

Have students read the opening paragraphs in the section Global Interdependence in Chapter 27, Section 1. Explain that graphic organizers are a good tool in monitoring comprehension. Have students work with partners to create word webs around the central word "Drawbacks." Have student complete the web with possible disadvantages of global trade. **OL**

③ Apply It!

Provide students with a recent newspaper or magazine article on a current topic of economic concern, such as oil prices and supply, the trade deficit in the United States, a new trade agreement between countries, and so on. Have students work in groups to read the article aloud, pausing periodically to ask questions that monitor the group's understanding of the article. Ask groups to display their comprehension by rewriting the article with appropriate subheads that describe each section's content. **OL**

Unit 8   703

📖 Reading Strategy ‹ Read to Write

Writing Summaries When summarizing the main ideas in a text, students need to monitor their comprehension as they read and seek to clarify ideas and terms that are unfamiliar or difficult. Have students read Market Economies in Section 2 of Chapter 26. Point out that a good time to monitor and clarify is at the completion of each subsection. Ask students to write summaries and then exchange their summaries with partners. Have them comment on whether their partners' summaries reflect an accurate understanding of ideas and terms. **OL**

Key to Ability Levels

BL Below level AL Above level
OL On level ELL English Language Learners

Key to Teaching Resources

Print Material Transparency
CD-ROM or DVD

Levels					Resources	Chapter Opener	Section 1	Section 2	Section 3	Chapter Assess
BL	OL	AL	ELL							
					FOCUS					
BL	OL	AL	ELL	🖨	**Daily Focus Skills Transparencies**		26–1	26–2	26–3	
					TEACH					
BL	OL		ELL	📁	**Reading Essentials and Note-Taking Guide***		p. 243	p. 246	p. 249	
	OL	AL		📁	**Citizenship/Decision-Making Activity, URB**		p. 3			
	OL	AL		📁	**Economic Activity, URB**				p. 5	
BL	OL		ELL	📁	**Reading Skills Activity, URB**		p. 7			
		AL		📁	**Enrichment Activity, URB**		p. 11			
BL	OL	AL	ELL	📁	**Content Vocabulary Activity, URB***	p. 19	p. 19	p. 19	p. 19	
BL	OL	AL	ELL	📁	**Academic Vocabulary Activity, URB**	p. 21	p. 21	p. 21	p. 21	
	OL			📁	**Biography Activity, URB**		p. 23			
BL	OL	AL	ELL	📁	**Writing Skills Activity, URB**		p. 25			
	OL	AL		📁	**Critical Thinking Skills Activity, URB**		p. 27			
BL	OL	AL	ELL	📁	**Chart, Graph, and Map Skills Activity, URB**		p. 29	p. 29	p. 29	
BL	OL	AL	ELL	📁	**Differentiated Instruction, URB**		p. 31			
BL	OL	AL	ELL	📁	**School-to-Home Connection Activity, URB***	p. 33	p. 33	p. 33	p. 33	
BL	OL		ELL	📁	**Guided Reading Activities, URB***		p. 37	p. 38	p. 39	
BL	OL	AL	ELL	📁	**Writer's Guidebook**	✓	✓	✓	✓	✓
	OL	AL		💿	**Primary Source Document Library**	✓	✓	✓	✓	✓
BL	OL	AL	ELL	💿	**Daily Lecture & Discussion Notes (in Pres. Plus)**		✓	✓	✓	✓
BL	OL	AL	ELL	💿	**StudentWorks™ Plus**		✓	✓	✓	✓
BL	OL	AL	ELL	💿	**Section Spotlight Videos**		✓	✓	✓	
BL	OL	AL	ELL	🖨	**TIME Interpreting Political Cartoons Transp.**		Ch. 26			
BL	OL	AL	ELL	🖨	**Writing Process Transparencies**	✓	✓	✓	✓	✓

Note: Please refer to the *Unit 8 Resource Book* for this chapter's URB materials.

* Also available in Spanish

- Interactive Lesson Planner
- Interactive Teacher Edition
- Fully editable blackline masters
- Section Spotlight Videos Launch
- Differentiated Lesson Plans
- Printable reports of daily assignments
- Standards Tracking System

Levels					Resources	Chapter Opener	Section 1	Section 2	Section 3	Chapter Assess
BL	OL	AL	ELL							
TEACH *(continued)*										
				📁	**Building Academic Vocabulary**	✓	✓	✓	✓	✓
				📁	**Strategies for Success**	✓	✓	✓	✓	✓
Teacher Resources				📁	**Teacher's Guide to Differentiated Instruction**	✓	✓	✓	✓	✓
				💿	**Graphing Tool**	✓	✓	✓	✓	✓
				💿	**Presentation Plus! with MindJogger CheckPoint**	✓	✓	✓	✓	✓
ASSESS										
BL	OL	AL	ELL	📁	**Quizzes and Tests***		p. 312	p. 313	p. 314	p. 315
BL	OL	AL	ELL	📁	**Authentic Assessment with Rubrics**		p. 30			
BL	OL	AL	ELL	📁	**Standardized Test Practice**		p. 51	p. 51	p. 51	p. 51
BL	OL	AL	ELL	💿	*ExamView®* **Assessment Suite CD-ROM**		26–1	26–2	26–3	Ch. 26
CLOSE										
BL			ELL	📁	**Reteaching Activity, URB***		p. 35	p. 35	p. 35	
BL	OL		ELL	📁	**Reading and Study Skills Foldables™ Activity**	p. 100	p. 101	p. 101		
BL	OL	AL	ELL	📁	*Civics Today* **in Graphic Novel**	p. 97			p. 97	
BL	OL	AL	ELL	🖨	**Graphic Organizer Transparencies & Strategies**	✓	✓	✓	✓	✓

✓ Chapter- or unit-based activities applicable to all sections in this chapter

Using the Glencoe Web Site

Interactive Graphic Organizers

What is the Glencoe Web site?

The Glencoe Web site offers in-depth overviews and activities that summarize and reinforce the content of each chapter.

How can the Glencoe Web site help my students?

The Glencoe Web site offers Interactive Graphic Organizers for students to use with each section of the chapter. Each colorful Interactive Graphic Organizer focuses on a concept from the section and allows students to take notes online. The Interactive Graphic Organizers will help students:

- focus their notetaking on specific concepts from the chapter
- take notes in an interactive environment
- reinforce their understanding of key chapter concepts

Visit glencoe.com and enter a **QuickPass**™ code to go directly to resources for each chapter.

Civics ONLINE

Visit glencoe.com and enter **QuickPass**™ code CIV1360c26T for Chapter 26 resources.

You can easily launch a wide range of digital products from your computer's desktop with the McGraw-Hill Social Studies widget.

	Student	Teacher	Parent
Media Library			
• Student Edition Section Audio	●		●
• Spanish Audio Summaries	●		●
• Section Spotlight Videos	●	●	●
***Civics Today* Online Learning Center (Web Site)**			
• Chapter Overviews	●	●	●
• Study Central™	●	●	●
• Study-to-Go	●	●	●
• Student Web Activities	●	●	●
• In Motion Animation	●	●	●
• Self-Check Quizzes	●	●	●
• ePuzzles and Games	●	●	●
• StudentWorks™ Plus Online	●	●	●
• Vocabulary eFlashcards	●	●	●
• Web Activity Lesson Plans		●	
• Vocabulary PuzzleMaker	●	●	●
Classroom Tools			
• Multilingual Glossary	●	●	●
• Beyond the Textbook	●	●	●
• NGS MapMachine	●	●	●

Reading List Generator CD-ROM

GLENCOE BookLink 3

Use this database to search more than 30,000 titles to create a customized reading list for your students.

- Reading lists can be organized by students' reading level, author, genre, theme, or area of interest.
- The database provides Degrees of Reading Power™ (DRP) and Lexile™ readability scores for all selections.
- A brief summary of each selection is included.

Leveled reading suggestions for this chapter:

For students at a Grade 7 reading level:
- *Bangladesh: A Study of an Economically Developing Country,* by Steve Brace

For students at a Grade 8 reading level:
- *The Opening of the Suez Canal,* by Carol Zeman Rothkopf

For students at a Grade 9 reading level:
- *Mexico: A Study of an Economically Developing Country,* by Anna Lewington

For students at a Grade 10 reading level:
- *Handbook of the Former Soviet Union,* by Michael G. Kort

For students at a Grade 11 reading level:
- *Ghana: A Study of an Economically Developing Country,* by Steve Brace

READING SUPPORT FROM JAMESTOWN EDUCATION

- **Timed Readings Plus in Social Studies** helps students increase their reading rate and fluency while maintaining comprehension. The 400-word passages are similar to those found on state and national assessments.

- **Reading in the Content Area: Social Studies** concentrates on six essential reading skills that help students better comprehend what they read. The book includes 75 high-interest nonfiction passages written at increasing levels of difficulty.

- **Reading Social Studies** includes strategic reading instruction and vocabulary support in Social Studies content for both ELLs and native speakers of English.

- **Content Vocabulary Workout** (Grades 6–8) accelerates reading comprehension through focused vocabulary development. Social Studies content vocabulary comes from the glossaries of Glencoe's Middle School Social Studies texts. www.jamestowneducation.com

KEY — Teacher Wraparound

Use this key to help you identify the different types of prompts found in the Teacher Wraparound Edition.

R **Reading Strategies** activities help you teach reading skills and vocabulary.

C Critical Thinking strategies help students apply and extend what they have learned.

D **Differentiated Instruction** activities provide instruction for students learning to speak English, along with suggestions for teaching various types of learners.

S **Skill Practice** strategies help students practice historical analysis and geography skills.

W **Writing Support** activities provide writing opportunities to help students comprehend the text.

Teaching strategies and activities have been coded for ability level appropriateness.

AL Activities for students working above grade level

OL Activities for students working on grade level

BL Activities for students working below grade level

ELL Activities for English Language Learners

Focus

Why It Matters

Ask: What advantages do foreign-made goods give American consumers? *(Answers may include the ideas that imported goods are often less expensive than American goods, may be of better quality because of specialization, and often provide a wide variety of choices for today's shoppers.)*

More About the Photo

Visual Literacy Since its beginning, SAIL has contributed to the small communities of India. The steel company has built houses, schools, community centers, parks, and markets for employees and their families. India has 20 SAIL hospitals staffed by a team of 5,600 workers, including about 800 doctors and 1,700 nurses.

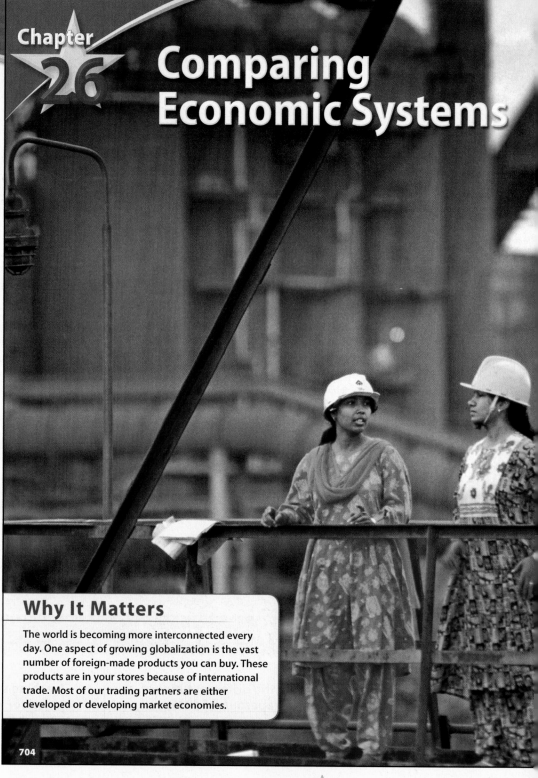

Chapter
26 Comparing Economic Systems

Why It Matters

The world is becoming more interconnected every day. One aspect of growing globalization is the vast number of foreign-made products you can buy. These products are in your stores because of international trade. Most of our trading partners are either developed or developing market economies.

704

Teach

BIG Ideas *As you begin teaching each section, use these questions and activities to help students focus on the Big Ideas.*

Section 1

International Trade Ask: What might prevent countries from producing certain goods? *(Answers may include environmental factors, such as short growing seasons and unsuitable climates; human factors, such as lack of education and train-ing; and inadequate natural resources.)* Point out that in Section 1, students will examine how countries make trade agreements to regulate the flow of goods and services. **OL**

Section 2

Economic Systems Ask: Why do few pure market economies exist? *(In pure market economies, supply and demand dictate all economic decisions. However, it is usually necessary for government to make some marketplace decisions to protect the public interest and to assure free competition.)* Tell students that in Section 2, they will learn the differences between market, command, and mixed economies. **OL**

Civics ONLINE
Visit glencoe.com and enter
QuickPass™ code
CIV3093c26 for
Chapter 26
resources.

🔊 **Chapter Audio**

BIG Ideas

Section 1: International Trade

The exchange of goods and services helps create economic interdependence among peoples in different places and different countries. Nations trade with one another to obtain goods and services they themselves cannot produce efficiently.

Section 2: Economic Systems

An economic system is the way a society organizes the production and consumption of goods and services. Market and command economies approach economic decision making in very different ways.

Section 3: Economies in Transition

An economic system is the way a society organizes the production and consumption of goods and services. Both former command economies and developing nations face severe challenges in creating market economies.

◄ Workers at a plant that is part of Steel Authority of India Limited (SAIL), the leading steelmaking company in India

---

FOLDABLES™ Study Organizer **Dinah Zike's Foldables**

Purpose This Foldable guides the student in comparing the merits of three trade agreements. The completed Foldable will use tabs to help them identify the steps in the process. **OL**

📁 More Foldables activities for this chapter can be found in the *Dinah Zike's Reading and Study Skills Foldables* ancillary.

Civics ONLINE
Visit glencoe.com and enter *QuickPass*™ code CIV1360c26T for Chapter 26 resources, including a Chapter Overview, Study Central™, Study-to-Go, Student Web Activity, Self-Check Quiz, and other materials.

FOLDABLES™ Study Organizer

Analyzing Information Study Foldable Make the following Foldable to help you analyze the purposes and powers of world regional economic trade agreements.

Step 1 Fold a sheet of paper in half from side to side, leaving a two-inch tab at the bottom. Turn the paper and fold it into thirds.

Step 2 Unfold and cut along the top fold lines to create three tabs.

Step 3 Label the three tabs as shown.

European Union | NAFTA | WTO
International Trade Agreements

Reading and Writing
As you read the chapter, note information about the three trade agreements. Then write a paragraph describing the agreement that you think is strongest and explain why.

Section 3

Economies in Transition **Ask:** What prompts countries to change their economic systems? *(Answers may include the ideas that market economies are extremely successful and that command economies often fail to achieve sufficient economic growth to benefit citizens.)* Explain that in Section 3, students will learn about countries with changing and developing economies and the challenges they face. **OL**

Focus

Bellringer
Daily Focus Transparency 26–1

Guide to Reading
Answers to Graphic:

obtains scarce goods | gives comparative advantage

Benefits of Trade

creates jobs

Section Spotlight Video

To generate student interest and provide a springboard for class discussion, access the Chapter 26, Section 1 video at glencoe.com or on the video DVD.

Resource Manager

Guide to Reading

Big Idea
The exchange of goods and services helps create economic interdependence among peoples in different places and different countries.

Content Vocabulary
• export *(p. 707)*
• import *(p. 707)*
• comparative advantage *(p. 708)*
• tariff *(p. 708)*
• quota *(p. 708)*
• free trade *(p. 710)*
• exchange rate *(p. 712)*
• balance of trade *(p. 712)*
• trade surplus *(p. 712)*
• trade deficit *(p. 713)*

Academic Vocabulary
• consequently *(p. 708)*
• eventually *(p. 710)*
• flexible *(p. 712)*

Reading Strategy
Classifying On a graphic organizer like the one below, identify three reasons that nations trade.

Benefits of Trade

creates jobs

Section 1
International Trade

Real World Economics Opening celebrations at the Hong Kong Stock Exchange include the giving of "Lai See," or red packets of lucky money, to the crowd. International trade—which is transacted in this stock exchange—is important to the U.S. economy. China is the second-largest exporter of goods to the United States. It is also the fastest growing market for U.S. goods. U.S. exports to China have grown over 300 percent since China joined the World Trade Organization in 2001.

▼ **Traders at Hong Kong Stock Exchange wave traditional lucky money**

R Reading Strategies	**C** Critical Thinking	**D** Differentiated Instruction	**W** Writing Support	**S** Skill Practice
Teacher Edition • Using Word Parts, p. 707 • Making Connections, pp. 707, 714 • Academic Vocab., p. 713 **Additional Resources** • Read. Skills, URB p. 7 • Cont. Vocab., URB p. 19 • Ac. Vocab., URB p. 21	**Teacher Edition** • Det. Cause/Effect, pp. 708, 714 • Making Generalizations, p. 709 • Making Inf., p. 710 • Drawing Con., p. 711 • Analyzing Info., p. 712 **Additional Resources** • Biographies, URB p. 23 • Crit. Think., URB p. 27	**Teacher Edition** • Visual/Spatial, p. 707 • Logical/Math., pp. 711, 712 **Additional Resources** • Enrich. Act., URB p. 11 • Diff. Instr., URB p. 31 • Teacher's Guide to Diff. Instr., p. 33	**Teacher Edition** • Personal Writing, p. 708 • Persuasive Writing, p. 710 **Additional Resources** • Writing Skills Act., URB p. 25	**Teacher Edition** • Speculating, p. 708 • Using Geo. Skills, p. 709 • Applying Economic Concepts, p. 712 • Diagramming, p. 713 **Additional Resources** • Chart, Graph, and Map Skills, URB p. 29 • Daily Focus Trans., 26–1 • Pol. Cartoons Trans. 26

Industry Workers craft athletic shoes at a factory in South Korea. The nation's major exports include motor vehicles and petrochemicals as well as footwear. *Explaining* Why do nations trade?

Why Nations Trade

Main Idea Nations trade with one another to obtain goods and services they themselves cannot produce efficiently.

Economics & You What do you think would happen if the United States could no longer sell goods to other countries or buy goods in return? Read to find out how this situation might affect our standard of living.

No country produces everything it needs to survive. Every country depends on other countries. Because of international trade, Americans can eat fruit during the winter grown in Central America. Through international trade, American computers are sold in Africa and Asia. More than 12 percent of all the goods produced in the United States are **exported,** or sold to other countries. A larger amount of goods are **imported,** or purchased from abroad. These purchases give Americans products they might not otherwise be able to enjoy.

Obtaining Scarce Goods

Trade is one way that nations solve the problem of scarcity. Nations trade for some goods and services because they could not otherwise have them or have them as cheaply. The United States buys industrial diamonds from other countries because it has almost no deposits of this mineral. Other nations trade for goods they cannot produce but that the United States can produce. Commercial aircraft built in California are sold to other countries that do not have the necessary factories or the skilled workers.

Chapter 26 **707**

Teach

R₁ Reading Strategy

Using Word Parts Ask: How do the prefixes "ex-" and "im-" contribute to the meanings of the words "exports" and "imports"? *(The prefix "ex-" means from, out, or away. An export is a good that is sent out or away from a country. The prefix "im-" means "in" or "on." An import is a good that is brought into the country.)* OL ELL

D Differentiated Instruction

Visual/Spatial Have students use prior knowledge and personal experience to illustrate a poster showing the flow of specific imported and exported goods to and from the United States. AL

R₂ Reading Strategy

Making Connections Ask: What imported items do you have in your home? *(Answers may include clothing, dishes, appliances, decorative items, calculators, computers, and so on.)* OL

Caption Answer:
Trade is one way that nations solve the problem of scarcity.

Additional Support

Activity: Collaborative Learning

Connecting Geography and Imports Ask: How do elements of physical geography, such as climate and landforms, affect a country's imports? To help students better understand why countries import certain goods, have them form groups and study an atlas showing the physical geography of the following countries: Sri Lanka, Norway, Japan, Uganda, and Iceland. Have each group create a three-column chart, indicating in the first column a distinctive geographical feature of each country. Groups should predict two or three products the country might import as a result of geographical limitations and then research the actual imports of each country for the second and third columns. OL

Teacher Tip

This activity requires students to use an atlas. Discuss the many features and types of information and maps available in atlases, including flat views, global views, population, annual rainfall, minerals, vegetation, peoples, and landforms.

S Skill Practice

Speculating Ask: Why might other countries be able to produce certain goods more cheaply than the United States? *(Answers may include the ideas that workers labor for lower wages in some countries and that necessary natural resources are more plentiful or accessible.)* **OL**

C Critical Thinking

Determining Cause and Effect Ask: What is an additional effect of overproduction? *(lower prices)* **OL**

W Writing Support

Personal Writing Have students write brief essays explaining their feelings about the following issue: *Should the United States trade with countries in which workers and other citizens are not treated according to U.S. standards of fairness?* **OL**

✔ **Reading Check** **Answer:** Comparative advantage is the ability of a country to produce a good at a relatively lower cost than another country.

Comparative Advantage

The main reason countries trade with one another is **comparative advantage.** This is the ability of a country to produce a good at a relatively lower cost than another country can. The United States could make color televisions. Other countries, however, can make them at a lower cost. **Consequently,** the United States now buys color televisions that are made abroad.

Specialization Because of comparative advantage, nations can specialize. They use their scarce resources to produce those things that they produce better than other countries. Specialization can lead to overproduction—when a country produces more of a good than all the people in the country could consume. The answer to this problem is to sell the extra amount that is produced to other countries.

Factors of Production Comparative advantage can be based on natural resources. Saudi Arabia's comparative advantage, its huge deposits of oil, allows it to export oil. Sometimes comparative advantage is based on labor and capital. The United States has large supplies of wealth, many highly skilled workers, and advanced technology. As a result, it has a comparative advantage in making expensive products such as airplanes and weapons.

Creating Jobs

Finally, international trade creates jobs. Suppose, for example, that American airplane makers built planes for only American airline companies. If so, they would have a limited market, because each airline needs only so many new planes each year. By exporting the planes, the companies have a chance to win more orders, which leads to the hiring of more workers.

✔ **Reading Check** **Defining** What is comparative advantage?

Restrictions and Integration

Main Idea Countries sometimes try to protect their economies by setting up trade barriers.

Economics & You How important is price to you when you are shopping? If you are like most people, it is pretty important. In this section, you will learn how government actions can raise the price of imported goods.

Many consumers like to buy foreign-produced goods because they are cheaper. When they do so, companies in the consumers' own country lose sales. The companies are then likely to lower production and to lay off workers. When this happens, the affected workers and industries often demand that the government step in on their behalf to remedy the situation. The two most common kinds of barriers to trade that governments can apply are tariffs and quotas.

A tax on imported goods is called a **tariff,** or customs duty. If the United States wants to protect American steel producers, it can put a 20 percent tariff on all imported steel, thus adding 20 percent to its price. The goal of most tariffs is to make the price of imported goods higher than the price of the same goods produced domestically.

Sometimes people want a product so badly that higher prices have little effect—they will purchase it anyway. In this case, countries can block trade by using **quotas,** or limits on the amount of foreign goods imported. For example, during most of the 1970s, Japanese-made automobiles were so popular in the United States that the jobs of American autoworkers were threatened. As a result, President Ronald Reagan placed quotas on Japanese-made automobiles.

Civics ONLINE

Student Web Activity Visit glencoe.com and complete the Chapter 26 Web Activity.

Differentiated Instruction

Biography Activity 26, URB pp. 23–24

Carlos M. Gutierrez

Objective: To identify experiences that allowed Gutierrez to succeed

Focus: Point out Gutierrez's impact on international trade.

Teach: Discuss limited opportunities for Cuban citizens.

Assess: Have students list goals that Gutierrez hopes to achieve.

Close: Create a timeline of events and achievements in Gutierrez's life.

Differentiated Instruction Strategies

BL Explain the responsibilities Gutierrez has as Secretary of Commerce. Make a list of his duties.

AL Explain why you think President Bush appointed Gutierrez to be Secretary of Commerce.

ELL Tell how Gutierrez worked his way to a high-level position in government. List each step in a basic timeline.

Imports and Exports, Selected Nations

Maps In MOtion
See StudentWorks™ Plus or glencoe.com.

Percentage of total exports to trade country

0   1,500   3,000 miles
0   1,500   3,000 kilometers
Robinson projection

Main Export Partners

- Argentina—Brazil
- Australia—Japan
- Chad—U.S.
- China—U.S.
- Europe—U.S.
- India—U.S.
- Mexico—U.S.
- Peru—U.S.
- Saudi Arabia—U.S.
- Taiwan—China & Hong Kong
- Tanzania—India

The Five Leading Exporters

In Trillions of U.S. Dollars

- European Union — $1.318
- Germany — $1.016
- United States — $0.927
- China — $0.752
- Japan — $0.550

The Five Leading Importers

In Trillions of U.S. Dollars

- United States — $1.727
- European Union — $1.402
- Germany — $0.801
- China — $0.631
- United Kingdom — $0.483

Source: *CIA The World Factbook,* 2006.

Analyzing Maps and Graphs

1. **Identifying** What nation is Brazil's chief import partner?
2. **Describing** Identify Mexico's chief export partner. What percentage of Mexico's exports go to that nation?

Chapter 26   709

S Skill Practice

Using Geography Skills   Ask: Why might Australia and Japan have a strong export partnership? *(Answers may include the idea that they are geographically close. This reduces transportation time and expense.)* **ELL BL**

C Critical Thinking

Making Generalizations   Ask: What general statement can be made about the value of the United States as a trade partner? *(Because the United States imports far more than it exports, it is a valued market for many exporters.)* **OL**

Analyzing Maps and Graphs

Answers:
1. Argentina
2. the United States; 87 percent

Additional Support

Activity: Interdisciplinary Connection

Considering Environmental Impact   Ask: How might the exportation of natural resources harm the environment? *(Answers may include the following: the exportation of lumber is eliminating the rain forest and, consequently, depriving many animal species of their habitat and leading to their extinction; mining might cause pollution, destroy local wildlife habitats, and contaminate human water sources.)* Invite a science teacher to the classroom. Ask the teacher to discuss how world trade in natural resources is affecting the environment locally, nationally, and globally. Have students work in groups after the presentation to brainstorm ways in which world countries can solve the problems caused by exportation of natural resources. Ask groups to prepare posters that show how problems connected to the exportation of a specific resource can be resolved. **OL**

C Critical Thinking

Making Inferences Ask: What costs do countries pay for establishing trade barriers? *(Answers may include the ideas that trade barriers create political ill will, deny workers in other countries opportunities for employment, and deny citizens opportunities to purchase goods otherwise unavailable.)* **OL**

W Writing Support

Persuasive Writing Have students write brief persuasive essays supporting or criticizing the elimination of all trade barriers among the NAFTA countries. **AL**

TIME™ Political Cartoons

Answers:

1. as a large ship
2. Ships are used to transport imported and exported goods.
3. Uncle Sam is portrayed as a rowboat operator, unaware of the ship that is close to running him down.
4. The country's huge trade deficit will hurt the U.S. economy.

Reading Check Answer: Quotas protect domestic manufacturers by allowing a limited number of certain types of goods to be imported.

Differentiated Instruction

TIME™ Political Cartoons

In this cartoon, Scott Stantis reflects on America's trade deficit—the difference between the value of goods the U.S. imports and exports.

1. **How is the U.S. trade deficit represented?**
2. **Why do you think Stantis selected this symbol?**
3. **How is Uncle Sam portrayed?**
4. **What warning is Stantis issuing about the U.S. economy?**

Scott Stantis/Copley News Service

Trade Agreements

C Most policymakers agree that the total costs of trade barriers are higher than their benefits. For this reason, most countries now try to reduce trade barriers. They aim to achieve **free trade.** To increase trade, countries can join together with a few key trading partners to set up zones of free trade.

The European Union The European Union (EU) is an organization of independent European nations. There are no trade barriers among these nations. Goods, services, and even workers can move freely among them. In January 2002, these countries became even more closely linked when most began using a common currency, the euro.

NAFTA In the 1990s, the United States, Canada, and Mexico signed the North American Free Trade Agreement (NAFTA). This pact will **eventually** eliminate all barriers to trade among the three countries. Since NAFTA was enacted, trade among the countries has grown twice as fast as the separate economies themselves have grown. Opponents of NAFTA contended that American workers would lose their jobs because U.S. plants would move to Mexico to take advantage of cheaper wages and less stringent enforcement of environmental and workers' rights laws. NAFTA supporters argued that increased trade would stimulate growth and put more low-cost goods on the market.

W

The WTO An international body called the World Trade Organization (WTO) oversees trade among nations. It organizes negotiations about trade rules, provides help to countries that are trying to develop their economies, and settles trade disputes. Critics say that WTO policies favor major corporations at the expense of workers, the environment, and poor countries.

Reading Check Explaining Why do nations sometimes place quotas on an imported good?

Leveled Activities

BL Writing Skills Activity 26, URB pp. 25–26

OL Cit./Decision-Making Act. 8, URB pp. 3–4

AL Diff. Instruction Activity 26, URB pp. 31–32

ELL Academic Vocabulary Activity 26, URB p. 21

The North American Free Trade Agreement (NAFTA)

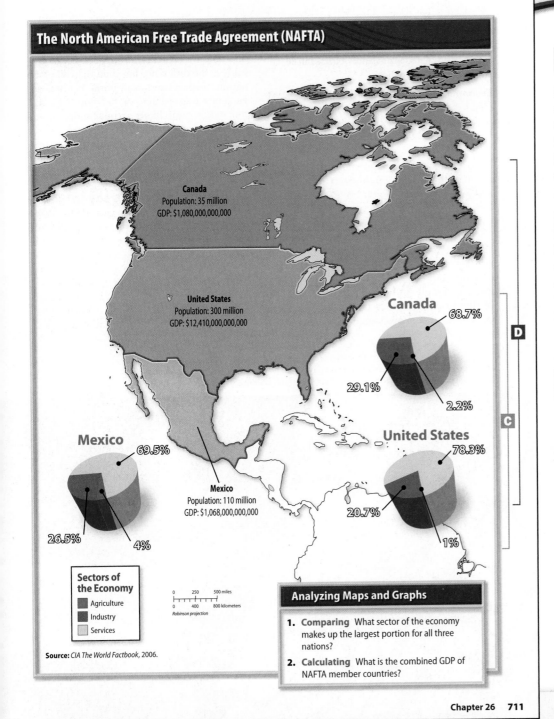

Canada
Population: 35 million
GDP: $1,080,000,000,000

United States
Population: 300 million
GDP: $12,410,000,000,000

Mexico
Population: 110 million
GDP: $1,068,000,000,000

Canada
68.7%
29.1%
2.2%

United States
78.3%
20.7%
1%

Mexico
69.5%
26.5%
4%

Sectors of the Economy
■ Agriculture
■ Industry
□ Services

0   250   500 miles
0   400   800 kilometers
Robinson projection

Source: *CIA The World Factbook*, 2006.

Analyzing Maps and Graphs

1. **Comparing** What sector of the economy makes up the largest portion for all three nations?

2. **Calculating** What is the combined GDP of NAFTA member countries?

D **Differentiated Instruction**

Logical/Mathematical Explain that per capita GDP is calculated by dividing total GDP by the number of people in a country. Have students calculate the per capita GDP for each of the three NAFTA countries. *(Mexico—$9,709.09; U.S.—$41,366.67; Canada—$30,857.14)* **ELL**

C **Critical Thinking**

Drawing Conclusions Ask: From your calculations of per capita GDP, what conclusion can be drawn about the NAFTA countries? *(Despite the free trade agreement, the countries vary widely in standard of living.)* **AL**

Analyzing Maps and Graphs

Answers:
1. services
2. $14,558,000,000,000

Additional Support

Activity: Technology Connection

Examining the North American Free Trade Agreement Ask: When an economic decision is controversial, how should citizens and their governments analyze it to determine whether it is the right decision? *(Individuals, businesses, and the government need to weigh the advantages and disadvantages to determine its net effect. They must also analyze each effect to* determine its importance; a crucial disadvantage might outweigh several advantages, for example.) Have students work in pairs to study the advantages and disadvantages of the North American Free Trade Agreement (NAFTA). The benefits of the trade agreement can be found on the Internet at www. fas.usda.gov/info/factsheets/NAFTA.asp. Information on NAFTA-related unemploy- ment and job losses is available at www. epinet.org/briefingpapers/nafta01/state-losses-table.pdf. Have partners use a computer presentation program to prepare presentations on NAFTA. After students present, engage the class in a problem-solving activity to address the concerns students raised. **AL**

D Differentiated Instruction

Logical/Mathematical Have students use an online currency converter to compare the U.S. dollar to four other world currencies. Ask students to calculate the price of a $50 sweater in these currencies. **OL**

S Skill Practice

Applying Economic Concepts Ask: When supply is scarce and demand is high, what happens to prices? Why? *(Prices rise because competition is greater for the small supply of a good or service.)* **OL**

C Critical Thinking

Analyzing Information Ask: What happens to the prices of a nation's goods when its currency is strong? *(Prices rise.)* **BL**

Caption Answer:
The ratio of imports to exports determines a nation's balance of trade. A nation that exports more than it imports has a positive balance of trade, or trade surplus. Conversely, a nation that imports more than it exports has a negative balance of trade, or trade deficit.

Hands-On Chapter Project
Step 1

Connecting to World Economies

Step 1: You, Your Country, and Your World Student groups will participate in a series of activities that helps them connect to the economies of various countries as well as the world economy.

Financing Trade

Main Idea A nation's balance of trade can be either a surplus or a deficit.

Economics & You Can you name the currencies of some foreign countries? Read to find out how these currencies are valued against our dollar.

- -

The United States uses the dollar as its medium of exchange; Mexico, the peso; and Japan, the yen. If you travel outside the U.S. or invest in foreign business, you will want to know the **exchange rate**—what the price of your nation's currency is in terms of another nation's currency. Most of the world's nations use a **flexible,** or adjustable, exchange rate system. Under this system, the forces of supply and demand are allowed to set the price of various currencies. Thus, a currency's price may change each day.

The Balance of Trade

Exchange rates have an important effect on a nation's balance of trade. The **balance of trade** is the difference between the value of a nation's exports and its imports. If a nation's currency depreciates, or becomes "weak," the nation will likely export more goods because its products will become cheaper for other nations to buy. If a nation's currency appreciates in value, or becomes "strong," the amount of its exports will decline.

Positive Balance of Trade When the value of a nation's exports exceeds the value of its imports, a positive balance of trade exists. For example, if the value of a country's exports is $100 billion and the value of its imports is $50 billion, then the country has a positive balance of trade ($50 billion). In this case, the nation is bringing in more money than it is paying out. A positive balance of trade is known as a **trade surplus.**

Balance of Trade Bananas are the most profitable export fruit in the world. Most bananas imported to the United States are grown on plantations in Latin America. *Explaining* How are exports and imports used to calculate a nation's balance of trade?

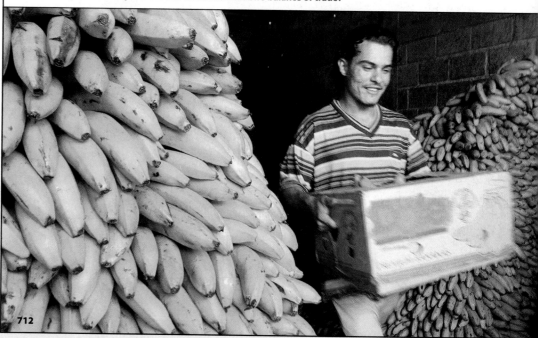

712

Directions Organize the class into four groups. Assign each group a category: self, family, community, or country. On the board, illustrate five rings of economics by drawing concentric circles, labeling them, from innermost to outermost: *self, family, community, country, world.* Explain how each circle depends on the ones inside and outside it. For example, what an individual buys

affects a family, which influences a community, and so on. Have each group list three to six personal or universal ideas or objects that explain their categories.

Sharing Ask groups to share their lists with the class. Discuss students' lists and add to them as a class. **OL**

(Project continued in Section 2)

Negative Balance of Trade A negative balance of trade exists when the value of goods coming into a country is greater than the value of those going out. For example, if the value of a country's exports is $70 billion and the value of its imports is $120 billion, then the country has a negative balance of trade (–$50 billion). A negative balance of trade is known as a **trade deficit**. A trade deficit can affect other factors in a country's economy.

Effects of a Trade Deficit

What are the effects of a trade deficit? A trade imbalance tends to erode the value of a country's currency on foreign exchange markets. The devalued currency then causes a chain reaction that affects income and employment in that country's industries. For example, the large deficit in the United States's balance of payments in late 2006

flooded the foreign exchange markets with dollars. As economists predicted, the rise in the supply of dollars caused the dollar to lose some of its value. The weaker dollar caused unemployment in import industries as imports became more expensive. However, this had an opposite effect in the area of exports. It caused employment to rise in export industries as the prices of these goods became more competitive.

Under flexible exchange rates, trade deficits will correct themselves through the price system. Historically this has been the case with regards to the American economy. A strong currency generally leads to a deficit in the balance of payment and a subsequent decline in the value of the currency. A weak currency tends to cause trade surpluses, which eventually pull up the value of the currency.

Reading Check Describing What is a trade deficit?

Section 1 Review

Vocabulary

1. **Create** a set of flash cards to use when you review the section; write the definitions on the backs of the cards for these terms: *export, import, comparative advantage, tariff, quota, free trade, exchange rate, balance of trade, trade surplus, trade deficit.*

Main Ideas

2. **Identifying** What are three reasons that nations trade among themselves?

3. **Explaining** How can trade barriers raise prices?

4. **Identifying** What is the name for the condition that exists when the value of a nation's exports exceeds the value of its imports?

Critical Thinking

5. **BIG Ideas** In a graphic organizer like the one below, explain the likely effects of weak and strong currencies on a nation's exports.

| Weak Currency | → | Effect |
| Strong Currency | → | Effect |

6. **Evaluating** Is a trade deficit a bad situation for a country? Explain your answer.

CITIZENSHIP Activity

7. **Creative Writing** Write a song, poem, short story, or dialogue about an effect of international trade, such as the demand for cheaper goods or the loss of jobs, on individuals in a community like yours. Share your work with the class.

Civics ONLINE

Study Central™ To review this section, go to glencoe.com.

R Reading Strategy

Academic Vocabulary Ask: Which economic term applies to goods coming into a country? What is the term for goods going out of a country? *(imports; exports)* **BL**

S Skill Practice

Diagramming Have students diagram the chain of events that results from a nation's trade deficit. **OL**

Reading Check Answer: a negative balance of trade, or a situation in which the value of a nation's imports exceeds that of its exports

Assess

Civics ONLINE

Study Central™ provides summaries, interactive games, and online graphic organizers to help students review content.

Close

Summarizing Have students work in groups to write summaries of the key concepts in the chapter. Suggest that students incorporate academic vocabulary into their summaries. **OL**

Section 1 Review

Answers

1. Cards should accurately reflect the definitions of the vocabulary words as explained in the section and in the Glossary.

2. to solve the problem of scarcity, to attain comparative advantage, to create jobs

3. Tariffs add an additional tax on imported items. Quotas limit the number of imported items, which makes competition for them stronger and, consequently, raises the prices of the items.

4. trade surplus

5.

| Weak Currency | → | greater export activity |
| Strong Currency | → | less export activity |

6. Student essays will vary. Some students might argue that a trade deficit erodes the value of a nation's currency and causes unemployment in the import industries. Others might argue that a trade deficit increases employment in export industries and is self-correcting within the price system.

7. Student writing will vary but should address an effect of international trade on individuals of a community.

R Reading Strategy

Making Connections **Ask:** How do highways in your state represent Americas' increased dependence on foreign oil? *(The number of vehicles in use has risen. Also, many vehicles, such as SUVs and pickup trucks, use large amounts of gasoline.)* **OL**

C Critical Thinking

Determining Cause and Effect **Ask:** Why might increased dependence on foreign oil raise gasoline prices? *(Strong demand allows producers to set higher prices.)* **OL**

Answers:
1. Arctic National Wildlife Refuge
2. Northeast Alaska; 19 million acres
3. Drilling in ANWR could reduce American dependence on foreign oil and high gas prices.
4. Answers will vary but will probably reflect the text arguments on one side or the other of the issue.

Additional Support

Should the United States Open ANWR for Oil Drilling?

More than 40 years ago, the United States government set aside lands in northeast Alaska to protect its wildlife, wilderness, and recreation values. The 1980 Alaska National Interest Lands Conservation Act doubled the size of the Arctic Range to 19 million acres and renamed it the Arctic National Wildlife Refuge (ANWR). About 100 miles west of ANWR is Prudhoe Bay, North America's largest oil field. Americans' increasing dependence on foreign oil and the rising price of gasoline has raised the issue of whether the federal government should allow oil companies to drill in ANWR. The issue has sparked heated debate in Congress and among interest groups.

Discovered in 1968, the oil fields at Prudhoe Bay in northern Alaska are the largest in North America.

YES

Supporters of drilling in ANWR claim that only a small area of the wildlife refuge would be affected. New drilling technology would protect the environment, while a major oil discovery would reduce the nation's dependence on foreign oil. Representative Don Young of Alaska, in an open letter to Congress, said, "According to the U.S. Energy Administration, the mean estimate of technically recoverable oil in ANWR is 10.4 billion barrels. That is almost half of the total U.S. proven reserve of 21 billion barrels. So in basic economic terms, if we open up ANWR, we would be increasing our supply, which in turn would lower prices. . . . Getting ANWR passed would provide Congress a tangible answer for its constituents when they want to know what we are doing about the high energy costs. ANWR is American oil. ANWR is 30 years worth of Saudi Arabian imports."

—Representative Don Young, May 24, 2006

NO

Defenders of Wildlife is one of the many environmental interest groups that opposes drilling in ANWR. These groups believe that oil development in the region would require a large web of industrial companies, hundreds of miles of roads and pipelines, refineries, and power plants that would change the environment. The grizzly bears, wolves, caribou, whales, and other species would be at risk. Defenders of Wildlife reports, "At the Prudhoe Bay oil field just west of the Arctic Refuge, spills of oil products and hazardous substances happen *every single day,* and noise and air pollution are rampant. According to Alaska's Department of Environmental Conservation, there are 55 contaminated waste sites already associated with this development." And they add, "Drilling for oil in the Arctic National Wildlife Refuge will not end America's dependence on Persian Gulf or other oil imports."

—Defenders of Wildlife, 2006

Debating the Issue

1. **Identifying** What is ANWR?
2. **Describing** What is the location and size of ANWR?
3. **Explaining** Why has Congress considered drilling for oil in this area?
4. **Concluding** Do the benefits outweigh the risks of drilling for oil in ANWR? Explain.

Activity: U.S./World Connections

Economics and China's Yellow River **Ask:** How can a nation's economic advancements harm its citizens? *(Answers may include the idea that individual wants might be sacrificed for the country's needs, such as sacrificing neighborhood parks for housing developments, and so on.)* To help students comprehend the far-reaching effects of a government's economic decisions, have students work in pairs in the library to research the effects of modernization, industrialization, and economic advancement on China's Yellow River. Information about current problems (which include pollution, overfishing, damming to produce hydroelectric power, and water shortages) can be found in news and environmental magazines as well as on the Internet. Have student partners prepare cause-and-effect diagrams that explain the conflict between economics and environmentalism in China. Students should choose three cause-and-effect pairs to explain in their diagrams. **OL**

🔊 **Section Audio**   🎬 **Spotlight Video**

Economic Systems

Guide to Reading

Big Idea
An economic system is the way a society organizes the production and consumption of goods and services.

Content Vocabulary
- market economy *(p. 716)*
- per capita GDP *(p. 716)*
- command economy *(p. 717)*
- socialism *(p. 717)*
- communism *(p. 718)*
- mixed economy *(p. 719)*

Academic Vocabulary
- intervene *(p. 716)*
- exploit *(p. 717)*

Reading Strategy
Describing As you read, complete a diagram like the one below by describing characteristics of a market economy.

Real World Economics Suppose the government told you that you could not operate your own business. That is exactly what happened to this Cuban woman in 2005. The Cuban government—one of the best-known examples of a command economy—told her that she could no longer sell flowers to make extra money. In Cuba, the government makes all the economic decisions. Many Americans hope that Cuba moves toward a freer market economy.

▼ Havana native Laura Sanchez had her license to sell flowers revoked

715

Focus

Bellringer
Daily Focus Transparency 26-2

Guide to Reading
Answers to Graphic:

competition — individual freedom — Market Economy — dealing with externalities — higher per capita GDPs

🎬 **Section Spotlight Video**

To generate student interest and provide a springboard for class discussion, access the Chapter 26, Section 2 video at glencoe.com or on the video DVD.

Resource Manager

R Reading Strategies	**C** Critical Thinking	**D** Differentiated Instruction	**W** Writing Support	**S** Skill Practice
Teacher Edition • Questioning, p. 717 • Reading Charts, p. 720 **Additional Resources** • Cont. Vocab., URB p. 19 • Ac. Vocab., URB p. 21 • Guid. Read., URB p. 38 • RENTG, p. 246	**Teacher Edition** • Det. Cause/Effect, p. 716 • Making Inferences, p. 716 • Predicting, p. 718 **Additional Resources** • Quizzes and Tests, p. 313	**Teacher Edition** • Interpersonal, p. 719 **Additional Resources** • School-to-Home Conn., URB p. 33 • Reteach. Act., URB p. 35	**Teacher Edition** • Descriptive Writing, p. 716 • Persuasive Writing, p. 717	**Teacher Edition** • Hypothesizing, p. 717 • Theorizing, p. 718 **Additional Resources** • Chart, Graph, and Map Skills, URB p. 29 • Daily Focus Trans., 26–2 • Stan. Test, p. 51

Teach

C1 Critical Thinking

Determining Cause and Effect Ask: Why can individuals in a market economy amass more wealth than is possible in a command economy? *(Individuals own the factors of production in a market economy.)* **OL**

W Writing Support

Descriptive Writing Have students write a description of a typical week in which they benefited from a market economy. **OL**

C2 Critical Thinking

Making Inferences Ask: How do consumers benefit from competition between sellers? *(Answers may include lower prices, greater selection, and better quality of products.)* **OL**

✔**Reading Check** **Answer:** All people in a market economy make the decisions; no one coordinates the decisions.

Differentiated Instruction

Crit. Thinking Activity 26, URB p. 27–28

Market Economies

Main Idea Market economies are characterized by individual freedom, competition, and less government control.

Economics & You Would having more pizza parlors in your town lower pizza prices or improve pizza quality? Read to find out why governments work to ensure competition.

Economic systems around the world vary. Some, like the one in the United States, are based on markets. Others, like China's, feature far greater government control. These different economies deal with scarcity in different ways. All societies face the basic questions of *what* to produce, *how* to produce, and *for whom* to produce. How society answers these questions determines its economic system. In a pure **market economy,** the decisions are made in free markets based on the interaction of supply and demand. Capitalism is another name for this system.

Characteristics of a Market Economy

In a market economy, private citizens—not the government—own the factors of production. As you recall, those factors are natural resources, capital, labor, and entrepreneurship.

Individual Freedom A market economy offers a high degree of individual freedom. Businesses decide *what* to produce, *how* to produce, and *for whom* to produce. Driving those decisions is the business owner's desire to earn a profit. At the same time, consumers decide what to buy. In a market economy, supply and demand interact to set prices, and producers and consumers make their own decisions.

Decisions in a market economy are made by all the people in the economy, not by just a few. Therefore, we say a market economy is decentralized. The economy seems to run by itself because no one coordinates the decisions.

Pure market economies seldom exist. Even in the United States, for example, the government provides public goods such as national defense and a system of justice.

Competition Governments play another role in an economy: they make sure markets stay competitive. As a consumer in a market economy, you are likely to benefit from competition between sellers. Effective competition requires a large number of sellers. The U.S. government can ensure this by regulating businesses. It also **intervenes,** or interferes, to punish businesses that break laws meant to ensure competition.

Dealing with Externalities Governments also influence externalities. These are the unintended side effects that have an influence on third parties. For example, the government works to reduce pollution, which is a negative externality. It also encourages activities that generate positive externalities. For instance, it provides money to fund scientific research, which businesses can then use to develop new products.

Higher Per Capita GDPs Most of the largest economies are market economies. Look at the map on page 718, which shows the per capita gross domestic product (GDP) for selected nations. **Per capita GDP** is the total GDP divided by the country's population. By expressing GDP in terms of each person, we can compare one nation's economic success to another's without regard to the size of the two economies. Most of the countries that have high per capita GDPs, including the United States, have market economies.

✔**Reading Check** **Explaining** Why do we say a market economy runs itself?

Evaluating Information

Objective:	To evaluate an excerpt from a Web site
Focus:	Examine the reliability of Web sources.
Teach:	Review ways of evaluating the reliability of sources.
Assess:	Have students use the Web to verify information from this source.
Close:	Create a checklist to evaluate text and Web sites.

Differentiated Instruction Strategies

BL Explain what the author means when he writes, "A country does not have to be the best at anything to gain from trade."

AL Explain the meaning of "comparative advantage." Why do you think it could be described as "true and non-trivial"?

ELL Explain the difference between imports and exports.

Command Economy North Korean leader Kim Jong Il (far right) inspects a new food processing plant operated by the Korea People's Army (KPA) Unit 543. A factor contributing to the nation's poor economic performance is that North Korea focuses on producing weapons and not consumer goods. *Identifying* Who owns most of North Korea's productive resources?

Command Economies

Main Idea In command economies, the government tells producers what to do.

Economics & You Would you like the government to choose your job for you? In some economies, governments exert vast control over individuals.

Characteristics of a Command Economy

The opposite of a market economy is called a **command economy.** In a pure command economic system, the individual has little, if any, influence over how the basic economy functions. Major economic decisions are made by the central government. The government tells producers what to do—it *commands* what actions they should take. This economic system is also called a controlled economy.

Socialism Starting in the early 1800s, some people came to believe that aiding **exploited,** or oppressed, workers required eliminating capitalism completely. They advocated **socialism,** the belief that the means of production should be owned and controlled by society, either directly or through the government. Socialists felt that this system would distribute wealth more equally among all citizens.

Communism The German thinker and writer Karl Marx was a socialist who predicted violent revolution. Marx believed that the population in industrialized nations is divided into capitalists, or bourgeoisie, who own the means of production and workers, or proletariat, who work to produce the goods. Marx interpreted human history as a class struggle between the workers and the capitalists. Eventually, he thought the workers would revolt and overthrow the capitalists.

Chapter 26 717

S Skill Practice

Theorizing Ask: Why has no world country met the terms of pure communism? *(Answers may include the idea that people by nature wish to own property, want to distinguish themselves from others, and prefer the rules and protection that government provides.)* **AL**

C Critical Thinking

Predicting Ask: What might happen to the quality of work if all people performing the same task earned the same wage? *(Because there is no financial incentive to produce better work, the quality of work might decline.)* **OL**

For additional practice on this skill (Predicting), see the **Skills Handbook**.

Analyzing Maps

Answers:

1. Luxembourg—$55,600; Somalia—$600

2. The per capita GDP would increase because a market economy is more efficient and grows more quickly.

Reading Check Answer: In a pure market economy, citizens own all factors of production; in a pure command economy, the citizen has little influence over the economy.

Differentiated Instruction

Per Capita GDP, Selected Nations

Canada $32,900
United States $42,000
Mexico $10,100
Cuba $3,300
Brazil $8,400
Argentina $13,700
World Average $9,300
Germany $29,800
Luxembourg $55,600
United Kingdom $30,900
France $30,000
Greece $22,800
Israel $22,300
Egypt $4,400
Somalia $600
South Africa $12,100
Russia $10,700
North Korea $1,800
South Korea $20,400
China $6,300
Japan $30,700
India $3,400
Indonesia $3,700
Australia $32,000

Source: *CIA The World Factbook,* 2006.

Analyzing Maps

1. **Comparing** Which nation on the map has the highest per capita GDP? Which has the lowest?

2. **Hypothesizing** If Cuba became a market economy, would the per capita GDP go up or down? Why?

Marx believed socialism would develop into **communism.** Under communism, one **S** class would evolve, all property would be held in common, and there would be no need for government.

Government Control In a command economy, most productive resources—especially land and capital—are owned by government, not by private individuals. The government makes the three basic allocation decisions. It decides *what* to produce; it tells factory managers whether to make cars, buses, or military vehicles. The government also regulates *how* goods will be produced. It tells managers where to buy their raw materials, for example. Finally, the government **C** decides for *whom* to produce. It fixes the wages of all workers and sets prices as well.

Unsurprisingly, governments in command economies have planning agencies with a great deal of power. These organizations make the important decisions for different parts of the economy, such as agriculture, steel production, and consumer products manufacturing.

Slow Growth Because of their inefficiency, command economies tend to grow more slowly and attain a lower per capita GDP than do market economies. Cuba and North Korea are perhaps the two best current examples of command economies. Look at the map on this page to see how low their per capita GDPs are.

Reading Check Contrasting What is the difference between a pure market economy and a pure command economy?

Leveled Activities

BL Content Vocabulary Activity 26, URB pp. 19–20

OL Academic Vocabulary Activity 26, URB pp. 21–22

AL Chart, Graph, and Map Act. 26, URB pp. 29–30

ELL Guided Reading Activity 26-2, URB p. 38

Mixed Economies

Main Idea Today the American economy and others like it are described as mixed economies.

Economics & You Do you think it is possible for a nation to have a pure market economy? Read to find out about how some nations combine elements of different economic systems.

Pure forms of command or market economies are rare. In most cases, a country's economic system combines these principles in what is known as a mixed economy. In a mixed economy, individuals carry on their economic affairs freely, but are subject to some government intervention. Many countries of the world have a mixed economy.

In the United States, free enterprise is combined with and supported by government decisions in the marketplace. The government keeps competition free and fair and protects the public interest.

The United States also promotes the economy by providing services to businesses and consumers. For example, the federal and state governments have built extensive highway systems that have helped promote travel and the transportation of goods.

Many government agencies produce and distribute goods and services to consumers, giving government a direct role in the economy. The role is "direct" because the government supplies a good or service that competes with private businesses. Perhaps the best known is the U.S. Postal Service.

The government plays an indirect role when it acts as an umpire to make sure the economy operates smoothly and efficiently. One such case is the regulation of public utilities, investor- or municipal-owned companies that offer important products to the public, such as water or electric service.

Reading Check Explaining In what ways can mixed economies be considered a combination of other economic systems?

Section 2 Review

Vocabulary

1. **Write** complete sentences about the world economic system using each of the following terms: *market economy, per capita GDP, command economy, socialism, communism, mixed economy.*

Main Ideas

2. **Describing** Why is per capita GDP a good way to compare the economic success of different countries?

3. **Explaining** What did advocates of socialism hope to achieve?

Critical Thinking

4. **Assessing** Why do you think most of the world's most successful economies are market economies? Explain your answer.

5. **BIG Ideas** In a graphic organizer like the one below, compare and contrast market and command economies.

Market Economy	Command Economy

6. **Analyze Visuals** Examine the map on page 718. What five countries had the highest per capita GDPs?

CITIZENSHIP Activity

7. **Persuasive Writing** Write an editorial that supports a position on the following statement: *Any government intervention in the U.S. economy is harmful.* Use your editorial to debate the idea with classmates.

Civics ONLINE

Study Central™ To review this section, go to glencoe.com.

D **Differentiated Instruction**

Interpersonal Have students work in pairs to think of another competitive good or service the government could provide to benefit Americans. Ask students to create a poster advertising the good or service. **OL**

Reading Check **Answer:** Mixed economies combine the individual economic freedom of market economies with the government involvement of command economies.

Assess

Civics ONLINE

Study Central™ provides summaries, interactive games, and online graphic organizers to help students review content.

Close

Illustrating Have students work in pairs to illustrate the benefits of a mixed economy with a scene that is typical of American life, such as a supermarket, a clothing store, a video store, and so on. **OL**

Section 2 Review

Answers

1. Sentences should use vocabulary words according to their definitions in the section and in the Glossary.

2. A comparison of per capita GDPs eliminates disparities in population.

3. more equal distribution of wealth among citizens

4. Market economies are more efficient and produce higher per capita GDPs. They allow greater individual production and consumption freedom, encourage market competition, and use government to deal with externalities.

5.

Market Economy	Command Economy
individual freedom in economic decisions, competition, higher per capita GDPs	government makes all economic decisions, no competition, lower per capita GDPs

6. Luxembourg, the United States, Canada, Australia, the United Kingdom

7. Editorials will vary depending on students' positions on the issue. While some may argue that government intervention in the economy is an unconstitutional expansion of federal powers, others may argue that government has a responsibility to provide for the welfare and protection of its citizens.

Financial Literacy

C Critical Thinking

Making Inferences Ask: What do the projected new job statistics suggest about the future of the U.S. economy? *(It will continue to grow and be strong.)* **BL**

R₁ Reading Strategy

Reading Charts Ask: Which of the fastest-growing occupations are in the medical field? *(home-health aides, medical assistants, physician assistants, registered nurses)* **ELL**

R₂ Reading Strategy

Identifying Ask: Which occupation of those listed requires the most postsecondary education? *(postsecondary teachers—doctoral degree)* **OL**

Analyzing Economics

1. service; The occupations listed as fastest-growing are all in the service sector.

2. Between 2004 and 2014, millions of new jobs will be added, millions will be added to the workforce, and millions of jobs will be filled by young people ages 16–24.

Hands-On Chapter Project
Step 2

Connecting to World Economies

Step 2: Trading Around the World Student groups continue to draw connections to the national and global economies through trade.

Directions Organize the class into six groups, each representing a continent

---

Financial Literacy

Help Wanted: Tomorrow's Job Market

C The Bureau of Labor Statistics (BLS) predicts that more than 18.9 million new jobs will be added between 2004 and 2014, increasing the workforce from 147.4 million to more than 162 million. Young people ages 16–24 are projected to fill more than 22 million jobs.
- Employment growth will be concentrated in the service industries.
- Five of the 10 occupations adding the most jobs are service occupations.
- An associate or bachelor's degree is the major source of postsecondary education or training for 6 of the 10 fastest-growing occupations.

Fastest-Growing Occupations, 2004–2014

Percentage Growth

Occupation	Total employment 2014 (in thousands)	Percentage growth 2004–2014	Most significant source of postsecondary education or training
Home health aides	974	56	On-the-job training
Network systems and data communications analysts	357	55	Bachelor's degree
Medical assistants	589	52	On-the-job training
Physician assistants	93	50	Bachelor's degree
Computer software engineers	682	48	Bachelor's degree

Jobs Gaining the Most Workers

Occupation	Total employment 2014 (in thousands)	Employment growth 2004–2014 (in thousands)	Most significant source of postsecondary education or training
Retail salespersons	4,992	736	On-the-job training
Registered nurses	3,096	703	Associate degree
Postsecondary teachers	2,153	524	Doctoral degree
Customer service representatives	2,534	471	On-the-job training
Janitors and cleaners	2,813	440	On-the-job training

Source: Bureau of Labor Statistics.

Analyzing Economics

1. **Classifying** Is most of the growth concentrated in the service or the manufacturing sector? Explain.
2. **Describing** What are three factors that will change the job market?

---

except Antarctica (Africa, North America, South America, Europe, Asia, and Australia). The objective is for groups to buy and sell as many products as possible using the least amount of currency.

Importing and Exporting Have groups design and name currency for their continent and specify the rate of exchange in U.S. dollars (for example, five European

grunkos might be the equivalent of $1 U.S.). Students should use the Internet to identify two export products from their continents and should price their exports in their units of currencies. After ten minutes of trading, have each group explain its buying and selling strategies, the profit they made or lost, and how they will use their imported items. **OL**

(Project continued in Section 3)

Guide to Reading

Big Idea
An economic system is the way a society organizes the production and consumption of goods and services.

Content Vocabulary
• developing country *(p. 724)*
• traditional economy *(p. 724)*

Academic Vocabulary
• collapse *(p. 722)*
• nevertheless *(p. 723)*

Reading Strategy
Identifying As you read, note the ways developing countries can overcome some of their obstacles.

Overcome obstacles

Section 3

Section Audio | **Spotlight Video**

Economies in Transition

Real World Economics The economy of Vietnam is in a state of transition. This woman sells appliances in an electronics shop in Hanoi that may soon feature products from Japan, China, and the United States. Vietnam, once a fiercely communist country, has been moving toward a market economy, which replaced its earlier command economy. Now, slightly more than 35 years after the Vietnam War ended, Vietnam is a member of the World Trade Organization (WTO).

▼ **Customer and salesperson at a Hanoi electronics store**

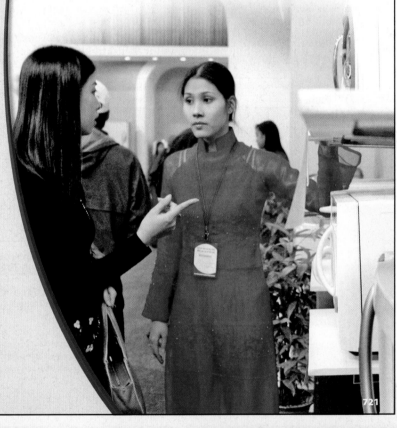

721

Focus

Bellringer
Daily Focus Transparency 26–3

Guide to Reading
Answers to Graphic:

limit population growth — promote the welfare of citizens — remove trade barriers — **Overcome obstacles** — turn away from command economies — allow competitive markets to make production decisions

Section Spotlight Video

To generate student interest and provide a springboard for class discussion, access the Chapter 26, Section 3 video at glencoe.com or on the video DVD.

Resource Manager

R Reading Strategies	**C** Critical Thinking	**D** Differentiated Instruction	**W** Writing Support	**S** Skill Practice
Teacher Edition • Explaining, p. 722 • Using Context Clues, pp. 722, 724 • Act. Prior Know., p. 725 **Additional Resources** • Cont. Vocab., URB p. 19 • Ac. Vocab., URB p. 21 • Guid. Read., URB p. 39 • RENTG, p. 249	**Teacher Edition** • Compare/Contrast, p. 723 • Making Inferences, p. 724 **Additional Resources** • Econ. Act., URB p. 5 • Quizzes and Tests, p. 314	**Teacher Edition** • Kinesthetic, p. 722 • Below Grade Level, p. 726 **Additional Resources** • Reteach. Act., URB p. 35 • Graphic Novel, p. 97 • Teacher's Guide to Diff. Instr., p. 33	**Teacher Edition** • Personal Writing, p. 724	**Teacher Edition** • Defining, p. 723 • Theorizing, p. 725 **Additional Resources** • Chart, Graph, and Map Skills, URB p. 29 • Daily Focus Trans., 26–3

Teach

R Reading Strategy

Explaining Ask: What changes when a nation has changes that are political in nature? *(its government)* **BL**

D Differentiated Instruction

Kinesthetic Have students note on the chart the GDP per capita of the three nations. Have them draw a simple pie graph that compares this data. *(graphs should be divided into 3 pieces in descending size: U.S., Russia, China)* **OL**

Analyzing Charts

Answers:
1. six
2. A nation has a favorable balance of trade when the value of its exports exceeds that of its imports. Russia and China have favorable trade balances.

Changing Economies

Main Idea Russia and China are making the difficult transition from command to market economies.

Civics & You Have you ever decided to make a big change in your life? Major changes are difficult for countries, too.

Many nations in the world are making the transition from one type of economy to another. Some are moving from a traditional economy to a more developed system. Others are shifting from a command economy to a market system. The main reason for the transition is the remarkable success of the major market economies in the world. Many countries hope to bring the same prosperity to their own people.

Failure of Command Economies

In the 1980s, command economies began to seem increasingly unattractive. They were unable to achieve the economic growth that market economies could. The Soviet Union, China, and the countries of Eastern Europe had command economies. By 1991, however, they were all in the process of changing. In Eastern Europe, this economic change was accompanied by political changes. The countries moved toward greater democracy in addition to market economies.

Russia

The same transition took place in the Soviet Union, where change came with the actual breakup of the country. In 1991, the Soviet Union **collapsed,** or fell apart. Communist leaders could no longer keep the economy going. Russia emerged as the largest country to come out of the former Soviet Union.

Comparing Economies: Russia, China, and the U.S.

	Russia	China	United States
Population (July 2006 est.)	142,894,000	1,313,974,000	300,000,000
GDP per capita	$11,000	$6,800	$41,600
Labor Force -Agriculture -Industry -Services	5.4% 21.4% 57.5%	12.5% 47.3% 40.3%	1% 20.4% 78.7%
Exports	$245 billion	$752.2 billion	$927.5 billion
Imports	$125 billion	$631.8 billion	$1.727 trillion

Source: *CIA The World Factbook,* 2006; Statistics based on 2005, 2006 estimates.

Analyzing Charts

1. **Calculating** About how many times larger is the GDP per capita of the United States than of China?

2. **Explaining** What constitutes a favorable balance of trade? Do any of the nations listed show a favorable balance of trade?

Differentiated Instruction

Economics Activity 8, URB pp. 5–6

Command and Market Economies

Objective:	To analyze economic growth
Focus:	Students study information on a line graph.
Teach:	Discuss command and market economies.
Assess:	Have students compare and contrast the two economies.
Close:	Create a bar graph showing the improvement of four countries under a market-based economy.

Differentiated Instruction Strategies

BL Tell why some countries with command economies switched to market economies.

AL Why does politics plays such an important role in a country's economy? Write a paragraph to explain.

ELL Create a bulleted list of countries that have improved using market economies. Locate these countries on a map.

Economic Change in China A worker at a construction site in Yantai, China still uses hand tools. In the background, several cranes are operating. *Describing* What economic problems is China facing?

Economic Change Most economic decisions during Soviet times were made by a central planning body. Soviet production was inefficient. Supplies did not arrive on time, too much or too little of a good was produced, and goods were not always delivered to the places that needed them most. The process became too complicated to work effectively.

Following the breakup of the Soviet Union, Russia's leaders wanted to use some elements of a market-based economy. State-owned factories had to be put in the hands of private ownership. Stock markets had to be created so that people could own the factories. People had to learn to make decisions based on supply and demand and market prices. This ongoing transition has been difficult, and the process will probably continue for many more years.

China

Like Russia, China is trying to incorporate certain elements of a market economy. The Chinese economy had been modeled on the Soviet system of central planning. By the 1980s, China was falling far behind the market-based economies of its neighbors Taiwan, South Korea, Hong Kong, and Singapore. China began introducing market reforms to catch up. For example, it converted many state-owned factories to privately owned factories. The reunification of Hong Kong with China in 1997 gave China further motivation to change. Chinese leaders hoped to learn more about markets from Hong Kong.

China's economy has averaged 10 percent annual, or yearly, growth over the past 20 years—a high level of growth. Many workers in China's cities can now buy goods they were never able to have in the old economy. **Nevertheless,** along with these successes, there are some serious problems. Farmers find it hard to compete with cheaper foreign food. About 160 million Chinese are unemployed. China's leaders must find solutions to these problems.

✓ **Reading Check** Explaining Why did China introduce market reforms?

Chapter 26   723

Hands-On Chapter Project
Step 3

Connecting to World Economies

Step 3: Economic Cooperation and the IMF Student groups will identify the importance of global economic cooperation and international trade.

Directions Ask groups to reflect on how the trading activity required cooperation to determine products to sell and buy as well as their pricing. Ask groups to use the Web site www.imf.org/external/np/exr/facts/ glance.htm to research the International Monetary Fund (IMF) and answer the following questions: *How does the IMF promote global cooperation? Why is cooperation necessary on this level?*

Focusing on Cooperation Have groups create maps showing economic activity in North America through NAFTA. Their maps should illustrate the flow of goods exchanged between the U.S., Canada, and Mexico. **OL**

(Project continued on the Visual Summary page)

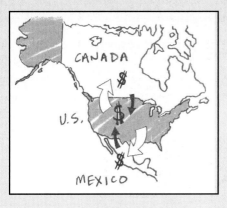

C Critical Thinking

Making Inferences Ask: Based on the ratio of developed to developing world countries, what can be inferred about the standard of living of most people in the world? *(Their standard of living is low; many live in poverty.)* **BL**

R Reading Strategy

Using Context Clues Ask: Which words in this sentence define the term "developed"? *(more industrialized)* **OL**

W Writing Support

Personal Writing Ask: Should the governments of developing countries limit the number of children families can have to improve the economic situation of the country and its citizens? Have students write a one-page personal response to this question. Remind them to support their opinions with sound reasoning. **OL**

TIME™ Teens in *Action*

Answer: Paragraphs will vary but should describe school-based and after-school programs that build young people's understanding of complex global issues, such as ethnic and religious diversity and poverty.

Differentiated Instruction

Developing Countries

Main Idea Developing countries face many problems as they try to create market economies.

Civics & You How do you feel when you owe a friend money? Does your debt nag at you until you pay it back? A similar problem affects developing countries around the world.

Economic Characteristics

Of the nearly 200 countries in the world, only about 35 are considered developed nations. These nations include the United States, Japan, Australia, the Republic of China, and Spain. Dozens of other countries are trying to make the transition to a market-based economy. Most of the countries are **developing countries,** or countries whose average per capita income is only a fraction of that in more industrialized countries.

Many of the countries trying to make this transition have **traditional economies.** Economic decisions are based on custom or habit. For example, if your grandparents and parents fished for a living, you also will fish for a living. Traditional methods and materials are used to make items in this economy.

Problems Developing Countries Face

Developing countries face numerous obstacles that make economic growth difficult. A major obstacle to economic growth is a high rate of population growth. When population grows faster than GDP, per capita GDP declines—each person has a smaller share of what the economy produces. Countries with higher rates of population growth tend to have lower per capita GDPs (see the map on page 718). Countries with high per capita GDPs, on the other hand, have low rates of population growth. Rapid population growth is often the source of many other problems, such as lack of food and housing.

TIME™ Teens in *Action*

Jacorey Patterson

Jacorey Patterson, 17, goes to a local school in his hometown of Brooklyn, New York. But with the help of Global Kids, Inc., Jacorey thinks worldwide.

QUESTION: What is Global Kids?
ANSWER: An educational organization that provides school-based and after-school programs to build young people's understanding of complex global issues.

Q: Like what?
A: Diversity and discrimination, human rights, education, the environment, immigration—and many other issues!

Q: What kinds of kids are involved?
A: They are racially, ethnically, and socio-economically diverse. The majority identify themselves as African American, Latino, South Asian, Middle Eastern, East Asian, or Caribbean.

Q: How does the organization affect the community?
A: In many ways; for example, following September 11, Global Kids youth conducted training for peers on Muslim stereotypes and facilitated an online dialogue for youth to share their fears and concerns about the attacks.

For more information about Global Kids, please visit www.globalkids.org.

Making a Difference — CITIZENSHIP

Describing Write a paragraph describing how you could adapt Jacorey's Global Kids plan to your school.

Leveled Activities

BL Reteaching Activity 26, URB p. 35

OL Chart, Graph, and Map Act. 26, URB pp. 29–30

AL Economics Activity 8, URB pp. 5–6

ELL Guided Reading Activity 26–3, URB p. 39

Social Statistics Comparison, Selected Regions

Legend:
- North Africa
- Africa South of the Sahara
- Latin America & the Caribbean
- Southeastern Asia
- Southern Asia
- Western Asia
- Eastern Asia

	Africa		Asia				Latin America & Caribbean	World
	Northern	South of Sahara	Eastern	Southeastern	Southern	Western		
Mortality Rate								
Deaths per 1,000 live births	33	102	30	35	65	48	27	55
Under 5 years of age mortality rate, per 1,000	38	172	37	46	90	60	32	80
Unemployment rate of young people								
Percentage of females aged 15–24 unemployed	14.2	39.1	5.8	17.7	17.1	22.5	20.8	14.2
Percentage of males aged 15–24 unemployed	14.5	25.5	8.1	15.6	13.5	20.1	14.0	14.5
Literacy								
Literacy rate of 15–24-year-old females	72.5	69.3	98.6	95.1	62.8	80.3	95.9	83.8
Literacy rate of 15–24-year-old males	84.1	79.0	99.2	96.4	81.6	90.7	95.2	90.7

Source: United Nations, 2005.

Analyzing Maps and Charts

1. **Comparing** What region has the lowest percentage of young people employed?
2. **Comparing** How does the literacy rate in Latin America and the Caribbean compare with the world literacy rate?

R Reading Strategy

Activating Prior Knowledge Ask: What factors contribute to high infant and child mortality rates? *(Answers may include inadequate nutrition, polluted water, war, inadequate shelter, and poor medical care.)* **ELL**

S Skill Practice

Theorizing Ask: Why might females have lower literacy rates in some countries than males? *(In some traditional societies, females do not receive the level of formal schooling that males do.)* **OL**

Analyzing Maps and Charts

Answers:
1. Africa South of the Sahara
2. The literacy rate of Latin America and the Caribbean is higher than the world literacy rate.

Additional Support

Activity: Interdisciplinary Connection

Literacy and Economic Prosperity Ask: How does the literacy rate of a country affect its economic health? *(Answers may include that educated citizens are more skilled and can better contribute to a nation's workforce which, in turn, produces more and better goods and services.)* Invite a representative from a literacy program to the classroom. Have students write interview questions in advance to uncover whom the program serves, the services the program provides, how the program is funded, and the measurable results of the program. Have students work in pairs to identify a country with a low literacy rate. Have them research the country to define barriers to literacy as well as existing efforts to improve the education of the nation's citizens. Have students read about UNESCO-Private Sector Partnerships at www.unesco.org. Ask students to design a brochure promoting a new public/private partnership to work toward increasing literacy in their chosen countries. **AL**

Section 3 Review

D Differentiated Instruction

Below Grade Level Give students a political map of Africa. Have students identify sub-Saharan developing countries as to whether they have ocean access or key natural resources. Students should list their inferences in a three-column chart with the headings *Country, Ocean Access,* and *Natural Resources.* **BL**

✔**Reading Check Answer:** high rate of population growth, war, debt, corrupt government, geographical and natural resource obstacles to trade

Assess

Civics ONLINE

Study Central™ provides summaries, interactive games, and online graphic organizers to help students review.

Close

Illustrating Have students work in pairs to inform people of the challenges facing developing countries by writing a poem or a song contrasting their challenges to conditions in the United States. **OL**

D Geography and natural resources present other obstacles. Many developing countries do not have access to ocean trade routes. Others may have ocean access but lack key natural resources.

War, Debt, and Corruption War has left a chilling legacy in many developing countries. Countries such as Afghanistan, Ethiopia, and Vietnam experienced recent wars. Thousands of people have lost their lives since the Darfur conflict in the western region of Sudan erupted in February 2003.

Many countries also face the problem of severe debt. They borrowed large sums of money to spur economic growth. Now many cannot pay off the loans or even the interest on their debt.

Finally, corruption delays the development of some economies. Nigeria, for example, is rich in oil but is still a relatively poor nation because of the alleged corruption of its government officials.

Growth and Development

Developing countries face the responsibility for directing their own economic development and future. The World Bank has created a set of recommendations for developing countries. Governments in developing countries need to invest more in people—education, family planning, nutrition, and health care.

Price controls, subsidies, and other regulations limit the development of markets. The World Bank suggests that competitive markets—not government officials—should make the *what, how,* and for *whom* decisions.

Many developing countries have quotas, tariffs, and other barriers to protect domestic jobs and young industries. At the same time, trade barriers protect inefficient industries. Countries that open their markets to the world can begin to grow economically.

✔**Reading Check Describing** What economic challenges do developing nations face?

Section 3 Review

Vocabulary

1. **Write** complete sentences about two nations of the world using each of the following terms: *developing country, traditional economy.*

Main Ideas

2. **Explaining** Why did the former Soviet Union economy collapse?

3. **Identifying** What problems do developing nations face?

Critical Thinking

4. **Evaluating** Which of the problems that face developing countries do you think is the most challenging? Why?

5. **BIG Ideas** In a graphic organizer like the one below, list some of Russia's and China's achievements in their efforts to change economically.

Russia

China

6. **Analyzing Visuals** Examine the map and chart on page 725. In what region is female literacy the lowest? In what region is the mortality rate the highest?

CITIZENSHIP Activity

7. **Expository Writing** Write a paragraph explaining how large amounts of debt can hamper development in developing nations and what has been proposed to address the problem.

Civics ONLINE

Study Central™ To review this section, go to glencoe.com.

Answers

1. Sentences should accurately apply the terms to two world nations.

2. Communist leaders could no longer keep the economy going.

3. Answers may include any or all of the following: high rates of population growth, geographic obstacles to trade, lack of natural resources, war, severe debt, and government corruption.

4. Answers will vary but should reasonably explain why one of the problems presented in the chapter is more challenging than the rest.

5. **Russia:** privatized ownership of factories; created stock markets

   China: privatized ownership of factories; reunified with Hong Kong

6. Southern Asia; Africa South of the Sahara

7. Paragraphs will vary but should discuss the inability of developing nations with heavy debt loads to provide services to develop their human resources (education, health care, adequate nutrition, and so on).

International Trade

- Nations trade with one another to obtain goods and services that they themselves cannot produce efficiently.
- Comparative advantage is the ability of a country to produce a good at a relatively lower cost than another country can.
- Countries sometimes try to protect their economies by setting up trade barriers, such as tariffs and quotas.
- A nation's balance of trade can be either a surplus or a deficit.
- A nation's currency can be strong or weak.

Flower seller, Havana, Cuba

Economic Systems

South Korean athletic shoe factory

- Market economies, or capitalist systems, are characterized by individual freedom, competition, and less government control.
- In command economies, the government tells producers what to do, resulting in inefficiency and slow economic growth.

Economies in Transition

- Russia and China, two former command economies, with the nations of Eastern Europe, are making the difficult transition from command to market economies.

North Korean leaders inspect newly built food processing plant

- Developing nations are nations with little industrial development and low standards of living.
- Developing countries with traditional economies, many in Africa and Asia, also face problems as they try to create market economies.

STUDY TO GO Study anywhere, anytime! Download quizzes and flash cards to your PDA from glencoe.com.

Determining Cause and Effect **Ask:** What factors contribute to a nation's comparative advantage? *(Answers may include abundance of natural and human resources, advanced technology and mechanization, and high levels of education.)* Have students work in pairs to list reasons why the United States does not always have a comparative advantage over another country. **AL**

Predicting **Ask:** What happens to a country's currency when it consistently has a trade surplus? *(It becomes stronger.)* Have students work in pairs to illustrate the concept of strong currency through trade surplus. **OL**

For additional practice on this skill (Predicting), see the **Skills Handbook**.

Making Inferences **Ask:** Why might people in Africa and Asia resist economic change? *(They have lived in traditional economies that practice the economic customs and values of their ancestors.)* Have students design a poster advocating a market economy approach to citizens of a transitioning economy, such as women in the work force, and so on. **OL**

Hands-On Chapter Project
Step 4: Wrap-Up

Connecting to World Economies

Step 4: Assessing the Importance of Global Economic Cooperation Students will finish the process they started in Step 1.

Directions Explain that the World Trade Organization conducts an annual review of member nations to assess the state of their economies. Tell students to assume that the WTO has asked their groups to evaluate member countries' efforts in working toward sound economies and economic prosperity for their citizens. Ask students to design a "report card" that could be used to assess a developing nation's efforts to improve its economic status. Remind students that reviews should evaluate how well the country addresses its individual challenges, the needs of its citizens, its available natural and human resources, and its government's ability to deal with externalities such as industrial pollution. Display the report cards in the classroom. **OL**

Answers and Analyses

Reviewing Vocabulary

1. B The keyword "imported" in the question will help students eliminate answer A or "export." Students might confuse answer C because countries with trade deficits consider restricting imports to achieve a balanced trade. Students can eliminate answer D, as nations with a trade surplus already have more exports than imports. Students will recognize the correct answer—"quota"—as a trade barrier that limits the amount of an imported good.

2. D From their study of Section 2, students will recognize that socialism and communism are both forms of a command economy in which a government makes all economic decisions. The keyword "pure" will help students reject answer A, a mixed economy. Only in a pure market economy does supply and demand solely dictate economic decisions.

3. C Word parts will help students select the correct answer. Students can link the keyword "society" to "social" in "socialism." Also, students might recognize that the suffix –"ism" refers to a belief. Answers A and B refer to types of economies, not economic beliefs or tenets. Answer D is a facet of a market economy.

4. C Students might confuse answer B, "traditional economy," with the correct answer because traditional economies are often inefficient. Because developed countries are more industrialized, they have higher per capita GDP. The per capita GDP is very low in a developing country, where industrialization is minimal.

Reviewing Main Ideas

5. B Answer A, "free trade," refers to unrestricted trade. Similarly, answer D, "import quota," refers to a trade barrier, not to a comparison of countries' production. "Balance of trade," answer C, is an internal comparison of a country's exports and imports. "Comparative advantage" is the correct answer because it compares the abilities of two countries to produce a product.

TEST-TAKING TIP

> When learning about international topics it helps to look at a world map or globe to see where major countries are located.

Reviewing Vocabulary

Directions: Choose the word(s) that best completes the sentence.

1. A nation may put a limit on the amount of foreign goods imported by placing a(n) _____ on these goods.

 A export   **C** deficit

 B quota   **D** trade surplus

2. In a pure _____ , economic decisions are made based on the interaction of supply and demand.

 A mixed economy   **C** communism

 B socialism   **D** market economy

3. The belief that society should own and control the means of production is part of the philosophy of _____.

 A a traditional economy

 B a mixed economy

 C socialism

 D free enterprise

4. In a _____ the per capita GDP is very low.

 A developed country

 B traditional economy

 C developing country

 D all of the above

Reviewing Main Ideas

Directions: Choose the best answers for each question.

Section 1 (pp. 706–713)

5. The ability of a country to produce a product at a lower cost than another country is called _____.

 A free trade   **C** balance of trade

 B comparative advantage   **D** import quota

6. The NAFTA trade agreement was made among _____.

 A United States, Canada, and Mexico

 B European countries

 C developing countries

 D United States, Russia, and China

Section 2 (pp. 715–719)

7. The way a society organizes the production and consumption of goods and services is its _____.

 A trade economy   **C** communism

 B economic system   **D** socialism

8. In a command economy, trade decisions are made by _____.

 A the individuals in the society

 B factory owners

 C one class of people

 D the government

Section 3 (pp. 721–726)

9. Many command economies have failed because of _____.

 A the greater success of market economies

 B the greater success of socialism

 C the greater success of the Soviet Union's economy

 D the greater success of China's economy

10. A major challenge facing developing countries is _____.

 A below average temperatures

 B huge population growth

 C lack of roadways

 D lack of organized religion

GO ON

---

6. A Students who are able to decode the acronym NAFTA will eliminate the incorrect answers B and D because European countries, Russia, and China are not North American countries. Students will identify that North America has no developing countries and, therefore, eliminate answer C.

7. B Students will eliminate answer A, "trade economy," because it refers to a country's economic activity with other countries, not its internal organization of production and consumption. Both answers C and D, incorporate a particular strategy for organizing production and consumption that involves government control. The way in which any society organizes production and consumption is an economic system.

8. D Students will be able to eliminate "factory owners," B, because command economies seek to remove individual ownership. Students might confuse answers A and C as

Critical Thinking

Directions: Choose the best answer for each question.

11. Why do some countries have trade barriers?

   A to encourage trade

   B to do away with quotas

   C to become communist

   D to protect their economies

Base your answers to questions 12 and 13 on the graph below and your knowledge of Chapter 26.

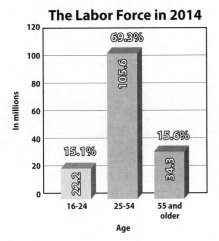

The Labor Force in 2014

In millions

- 16–24: 15.1% — 22.2
- 25–54: 69.3% — 105.6
- 55 and older: 15.6% — 34.3

Age

Source: Monthly Labor Review estimate.

12. What is the projected size of the total U.S. labor force in 2014?

   A 105.6 million

   B 34.3 million

   C 162.1 million

   D 120 million

13. According to the estimates, for every 100 workers in 2014, how many will be between the ages of 16 and 24?

   A 5

   B about 15

   C about 25

   D 22.2

Document-Based Questions

Directions: Analyze the following document and answer the short-answer questions that follow.

Milton Friedman, who died in 2006, was considered one of the greatest economists of the twentieth century. Here he comments on society and economics.

> Freedom requires individuals to be free to use their own resources in their own way, and modern society requires cooperation among a large number of people...The only way that has ever been discovered to have a lot of people cooperate together voluntarily is through the free market.
>
> —Milton Friedman, Nobel Prize-winning economist

14. From this quotation, would you say Friedman is a supporter of capitalism or a non-supporter? Explain.

15. Why do you think Friedman sees a connection between society—people—and economics?

Extended-Response Question

16. Developing countries have several challenges they face in improving their economies. What one thing do you think is the most challenging and what suggestion could you make to help that challenge?

STOP

Civics ONLINE

For additional test practice, use Self-Check Quizzes— Chapter 26 on glencoe.com.

Need Extra Help?

If you missed question. . .	1	2	3	4	5	6	7	8	9	10	11	12	13	14	15	16
Go to page. . .	708	716	717	724	708	710	716	717	722	724	708	720	720	716	716	724

ASSESSMENT

ers will eliminate answer B. After studying Section 2 on command economies, students will recognize that some countries use trade barriers to protect domestic industries.

12. C Students who correctly interpret the graph will calculate the answer by adding 22.2, 105.6, and 34.3, to arrive at the correct answer—162.1 million.

13. B Students who correctly identify a percentage as a fraction of 100 will recognize that the bar representing the 16–24 age group reflects 15.1 percent of the labor force in 2014, or about 15 workers out of every 100.

Document-Based Questions

14. Friedman is a supporter of capitalism because he identifies it as the economic system in which greed is allowed to do the least harm.

15. Answers will vary but may include the following: the decisions made by a nation's economic system affect its citizens. Citizens in unsuccessful economic systems suffer from poverty and lack of government services, such as education, health care, and protection from criminal activity. Those in successful economies attain a standard of living that ensures their welfare.

Extended Response

16. Student answers will vary but should name one of the challenges to developing countries discussed in Section 3 of this chapter, such as high rates of population growth, corrupt governments, lack of government services, war and conflict, and closed markets. Solutions should be logical and viable.

---

correct answers, because they both theorized that society—one-class society—would make economic decisions.

9. A Students will recognize that both the Soviet Union and China were command economies that failed to achieve economic prosperity, in comparison to the successful market economies of other world countries.

10. B Students will eliminate answer D as a factor that is not associated with economic decision-making. Students might confuse

answer C as the correct answer because some developing countries have difficulty transporting goods. Although some students might select answer A which affects the agricultural products, it is huge population growth that is a problem of developing countries.

Critical Thinking

11. D The question keyword "barriers" will help students eliminate answer A. Students who recognize that quotas are trade barri-

Civics ONLINE

Have students visit the Web site at glencoe.com to review Chapter 26 and take the **Self-Check Quiz**.

Need Extra Help?

Have students refer to the pages listed if they miss any of the questions.

TIME REPORTS

Teach

C **Critical Thinking**

Identifying Central Issues Discuss how technology and economic development are interconnected. **Ask:** What are some of the ways that information and communication technologies (**ICTs**) improve the lives of people living in remote rural communities? *(Better communication means better entrepreneurial skills as villagers gain essential information for economic development.)* **AL**

Did You Know?

- Close to 1.5 billion people worldwide—that's almost 1 out of 4 people—use kerosene to light their houses.
- In India, where 100,000 villages have no electricity, 80 million people rely on kerosene lamps.
- The indoor air pollution generated when using fuels such as kerosene for lighting leads to an estimated 1.6 million deaths worldwide each year.
- One LED lamp produces a light that is 200 times more powerful than a kerosene lamp and almost 50 times the amount of a single 100-watt light bulb.

Additional Support

TIME REPORTS

New Technology for the Developing World

C

From pedal-powered laptops to wireless Internet, high-tech tools are reaching those who need them most

The $100 Laptop

When Nicholas Negroponte took a year off from his job as a professor at the Massachusetts Institute of Technology, he launched an ambitious project: to build a laptop so cheap that developing countries could buy them by the millions to help their kids leapfrog into the 21st century.

With the support of the United Nations, the "$100 laptop" quickly found backing from a wide range of corporations. On the latest prototype, a new foot pedal supplies power in areas lacking electricity.

Negroponte hopes to start in seven countries—Nigeria, India, China, Thailand, Brazil, Argentina, and Egypt—with a combined total of at least 5 million orders. "If this makes the industry address low-power, low-cost laptops that can be used in very remote places, that's perfect," he says.

The New Electric Lamp

Artificial lighting may not seem a necessity like food or shelter, but 1.6 billion people around the globe lack access to electricity and the on-off switches we take for granted. Inspired by the Light Up the World Foundation, which promotes the use of energy-efficient light-emitting diodes (LEDs), Matt Scott and Amit Chugh teamed up to devise a replacement for the kerosene lamp.

The result is the Mightylight, a waterproof, shockproof, LED lamp that can

NEW POWER Mightylight is replacing kerosene lamps in India.

be used as a flashlight, reading lamp, or ceiling fixture. Solar-powered, capable of holding an eight-hour charge, and designed to last 100,000 hours, the Mightylight is safer and more cost effective than kerosene lamps. Not only do kerosene lamps start a lot of fires, but they are also a primary source of indoor air pollution, a major killer in developing countries.

More than 4,000 Mightylights have been distributed for earthquake relief in Pakistan and to the poor in Afghanistan, Guatemala, and Kashmir. In India, weavers and fishermen are using the lights to extend their work hours. Says Scott: "The exciting thing—more than just the light itself—is the model of using a sustainable approach to effect social change."

730

Background

One Laptop Per Child Nicholas Negroponte and the team of scientists, inventors, and educators who designed the XO—as the computer is referred to—believe deeply that children learn best by exploring and expressing. Negroponte calls the One Laptop Per Child (OLPC) campaign "an education project, not a laptop project." The goal of the OLPC Foundation is "to provide children around the world with new opportunities to explore, experiment and express themselves." Designed specifically for children of the emerging world, the XO has open-source software that allows the children and teachers who use it to program the computer according to their needs. The software itself is graphics-based with universal symbols. This gives even those who lack reading skills the ability to create and share meaningful forms of communication. Students can check out the software interface online at http://www.laptop.org/laptop/.

Villagewide Wi-Fi

To reach the village of Nyarukamba in western Uganda, visitors have to climb up a thin, almost vertical dirt track. It's not the kind of place you would expect to find farmers surfing the Web with wi-fi computers or making VOIP (voice over Internet protocol) phone calls. But that's exactly what the village's 800 or so inhabitants have been doing—thanks to a wireless, solar-powered communications system installed in the Ruwenzori mountains by Inveneo, a San Francisco nonprofit group.

Inveneo's founders had done enough volunteer work overseas to see how wireless communications could improve and save lives—through phone calls to health clinics, fast reporting of natural disasters, support for trading co-ops, and better educational opportunities. So they designed a solar-powered Internet network that is easy to install, inexpensive, and nearly maintenance-free. At its heart is a regional hub from which wireless relay stations—some bolted to trees—fan out for up to four miles and connect a network of PCs. The total cost, including solar panels, was just $1,995.

Nyarukamba is already reaping the benefits. Village income is rising, buying power has increased, and more people are learning to read. And in case the sun doesn't shine, the system can be powered up with a retrofitted bicycle.

Photosare Courtesy of Inveneo

IT TAKES A VILLAGE Local residents carried equipment to Nyarukamba in the foothills of Uganda's Rwenzori mountains (top) and helped set up the solar panel that powers the village's wireless Internet system (right). An old tree trunk is being used as a mounting pole for the network's antenna (above).

731

R **Reading Strategy**

Inferring **Ask:** How does a lack of sunshine affect Nyarukamba's wireless network? *(The network is solar-powered, so if the sun doesn't shine, the network won't work properly.)* OL

W **Writing Support**

Personal Writing Have students write about which technology piece from this feature most interests them. **Ask:** Which technological development do you think makes the most difference? *(Student responses will vary but should all reflect an understanding of improvement in daily living due to the introduction of each technology.)* OL

Activity: U.S./World Connection

Making Connections Discuss how individuals and nonprofit companies based in the United States can often be far more effective than local government agencies or for-profit corporations when it comes to bettering lives in developing nations. **Ask:** What makes these groups so effective? *(Students might say that many groups are staffed and funded by people who are strongly motivated to make a difference instead of a profit. Unlike governments, these groups have the funds and talent available to focus on one specific issue, instead of all the problems of a country.)* Organize three groups and assign a focus to each in one area—health, energy, or education. Have each group research nongovernmental projects in developing countries, and create a poster to illustrate a project that they would like to support. OL

Chapter Planning Guide

27

Levels					Resources	Chapter Opener	Section 1	Section 2	Section 3	Chapter Assess
BL	OL	AL	ELL		**FOCUS**					
BL	OL	AL	ELL	📽	**Daily Focus Skills Transparencies**		27–1	27–2	27–3	
					TEACH					
BL	OL		ELL	📁	**Reading Essentials and Note-Taking Guide***		p. 252	p. 255	p. 258	
BL	OL	AL	ELL	📁	**Speaking and Listening Skills Activity, URB**				p. 9	
	OL	AL		📁	**Primary Source Reading, URB**		p. 13	p. 13	p. 13	
BL	OL	AL	ELL	📁	**Content Vocabulary Activity, URB***	p. 19	p. 19	p. 19	p. 19	
BL	OL	AL	ELL	📁	**Academic Vocabulary Activity, URB**	p. 43	p. 43	p. 43	p. 43	
	OL			📁	**Biography Activity, URB**		p. 45			
BL	OL	AL	ELL	📁	**Writing Skills Activity, URB**				p. 47	
	OL	AL		📁	**Critical Thinking Skills Activity, URB**		p. 51			
BL	OL	AL	ELL	📁	**Chart, Graph, and Map Skills Activity, URB**		p. 53			
BL	OL	AL	ELL	📁	**Differentiated Instruction, URB**		p. 55			
BL	OL	AL	ELL	📁	**School-to-Home Connection Activity, URB***	p. 57	p. 57	p. 57	p. 57	
BL	OL		ELL	📁	**Guided Reading Activities, URB***		p. 61	p. 62	p. 63	
BL	OL	AL	ELL	📁	**Writer's Guidebook**	✓	✓	✓	✓	✓
	OL	AL		💿	**Primary Source Document Library**	✓	✓	✓	✓	✓
BL	OL	AL	ELL	💿	**Daily Lecture & Discussion Notes (in Pres. Plus)**		✓	✓	✓	✓
BL	OL	AL	ELL	💿	**StudentWorks™ Plus**		✓	✓	✓	✓
BL	OL	AL	ELL	💿	**Section Spotlight Videos**		✓	✓	✓	
BL	OL	AL	ELL	📽	**TIME Interpreting Political Cartoons Transp.**				Ch. 27	
BL	OL	AL	ELL	📽	**Writing Process Transparencies**	✓	✓	✓	✓	✓

Note: Please refer to the *Unit 8 Resource Book* for this chapter's URB materials.

* Also available in Spanish

- Interactive Lesson Planner
- Interactive Teacher Edition
- Fully editable blackline masters
- Section Spotlight Videos Launch
- Differentiated Lesson Plans
- Printable reports of daily assignments
- Standards Tracking System

Levels					Resources	Chapter Opener	Section 1	Section 2	Section 3	Chapter Assess
BL	OL	AL	ELL							
TEACH *(continued)*										
Teacher Resources				📁	**Building Academic Vocabulary**	✓	✓	✓	✓	✓
				📁	**Strategies for Success**	✓	✓	✓	✓	✓
				📁	**Teacher's Guide to Differentiated Instruction**	✓	✓	✓	✓	✓
				💿	**Graphing Tool**	✓	✓	✓	✓	✓
				💿	**Presentation Plus! with MindJogger CheckPoint**	✓	✓	✓	✓	✓
ASSESS										
BL	OL	AL	ELL	📁	**Quizzes and Tests***		p. 323	p. 324	p. 325	p. 326
BL	OL	AL	ELL	📁	**Authentic Assessment with Rubrics**		p. 31			
BL	OL	AL	ELL	📁	**Standardized Test Practice**		p. 54	p. 54	p. 54	p. 54
BL	OL	AL	ELL	💿	*ExamView® Assessment Suite* **CD-ROM**		27–1	27–2	27–3	Ch. 27
CLOSE										
BL			ELL	📁	**Reteaching Activity, URB***		p. 59	p. 59	p. 59	
BL	OL		ELL	📁	**Reading and Study Skills Foldables™ Activity**	p. 102		p. 103	p. 103	
BL	OL	AL	ELL	🖨	**Graphic Organizer Transparencies & Strategies**	✓	✓	✓	✓	✓

✓ Chapter- or unit-based activities applicable to all sections in this chapter

Using Study Central™

Web Links

What is Study Central™?

Study Central™ is an interactive, online tool that provides students with a variety of ways to study and to check their comprehension of section content.

How can Study Central™ help my students?

The Web Links portion of the Study Central™ Web site provides direct links to interesting, appropriate Internet resources related to the section and allows students to:

- prepare for better understanding of section content
- extend their knowledge beyond the content provided in the textbook
- practice research and reading skills

Visit glencoe.com and enter a **QuickPass**™ code to go directly to resources for each chapter.

Civics ONLINE

Visit glencoe.com and enter **QuickPass**™ code CIV1360c27T for Chapter 27 resources.

You can easily launch a wide range of digital products from your computer's desktop with the McGraw-Hill Social Studies widget.

	Student	Teacher	Parent
Media Library			
• Student Edition Section Audio	●		●
• Spanish Audio Summaries	●		●
• Section Spotlight Videos	●	●	●
***Civics Today* Online Learning Center (Web Site)**			
• Chapter Overviews	●	●	●
• Study Central™	●	●	●
• Study-to-Go	●	●	●
• Student Web Activities	●	●	●
• In Motion Animation	●	●	●
• Self-Check Quizzes	●	●	●
• ePuzzles and Games	●	●	●
• StudentWorks™ Plus Online	●	●	●
• Vocabulary eFlashcards	●	●	●
• Web Activity Lesson Plans		●	
• Vocabulary PuzzleMaker	●	●	●
Classroom Tools			
• Multilingual Glossary	●	●	●
• Beyond the Textbook	●	●	●
• NGS MapMachine	●	●	●

Reading List Generator CD-ROM

BookLink 3

Use this database to search more than 30,000 titles to create a customized reading list for your students.

- Reading lists can be organized by students' reading level, author, genre, theme, or area of interest.
- The database provides Degrees of Reading Power™ (DRP) and Lexile™ readability scores for all selections.
- A brief summary of each selection is included.

Reading suggestions
Leveled reading suggestions for this chapter:

For students at a Grade 7 reading level:
- *To Afghanistan and Back,* by Ted Rall

For students at a Grade 8 reading level:
- *Great Lives: Human Rights,* by William Jay Jacobs

For students at a Grade 9 reading level:
- *Democracy in America,* by Alexis de Tocqueville

For students at a Grade 10 reading level:
- *The Story of the United Nations,* by Katharine Savage

For students at a Grade 11 reading level:
- *The Arms Trade,* by Richard Bingley

READING SUPPORT FROM JAMESTOWN EDUCATION

- **Timed Readings Plus in Social Studies** helps students increase their reading rate and fluency while maintaining comprehension. The 400-word passages are similar to those found on state and national assessments.

- **Reading in the Content Area: Social Studies** concentrates on six essential reading skills that help students better comprehend what they read. The book includes 75 high-interest nonfiction passages written at increasing levels of difficulty.

- **Reading Social Studies** includes strategic reading instruction and vocabulary support in Social Studies content for both ELLs and native speakers of English.

- **Content Vocabulary Workout** (Grades 6–8) accelerates reading comprehension through focused vocabulary development. Social Studies content vocabulary comes from the glossaries of Glencoe's Middle School Social Studies texts. www.jamestowneducation.com

KEY Teacher Wraparound

Use this key to help you identify the different types of prompts found in the Teacher Wraparound Edition.

R **Reading Strategies** activities help you teach reading skills and vocabulary.

C **Critical Thinking** strategies help students apply and extend what they have learned.

D **Differentiated Instruction** activities provide instruction for students learning to speak English, along with suggestions for teaching various types of learners.

S **Skill Practice** strategies help students practice historical analysis and geography skills.

W **Writing Support** activities provide writing opportunities to help students comprehend the text.

Teaching strategies and activities have been coded for ability level appropriateness.

AL Activities for students working above grade level

OL Activities for students working on grade level

BL Activities for students working below grade level

ELL Activities for English Language Learners

Focus

Why It Matters

Ask: In what ways is the United States dependent on other countries? *(Answers should include that we buy products made in other countries, that we sell products to the rest of the world, and that we are dependent on other nations for resources such as oil. The photograph may lead students to mention that wars with other countries affect Americans because of military service and homeland security. Others may mention that unrest in other parts of the world may also affect the nation's security and its economy.)*

More About the Photo

Visual Literacy Ask: What do you notice about the refugees in the picture? *(Answers will vary and may include the objects they carry and the expressions on their faces.)* Have students locate Afghanistan and Kabul on a world map. Ask students to share their knowledge of the war in Afghanistan and the part played by the Taliban. Refer students to the following Web site to find out more about the role of the Taliban in Afghanistan: www.infoplease.com/spot/taliban.html. Encourage interested students to research this topic and the conflict in Afghanistan and to report to the class.

Teach

BIG Ideas
As you begin teaching each section, use these questions and activities to help students focus on the Big Ideas.

Section 1

Global Developments Have students examine labels on their clothing and book bags to determine where they were made. **Ask:** What products have you purchased recently that were made in other countries? *(Answers will vary, but should include clothing and electronics.)*

732

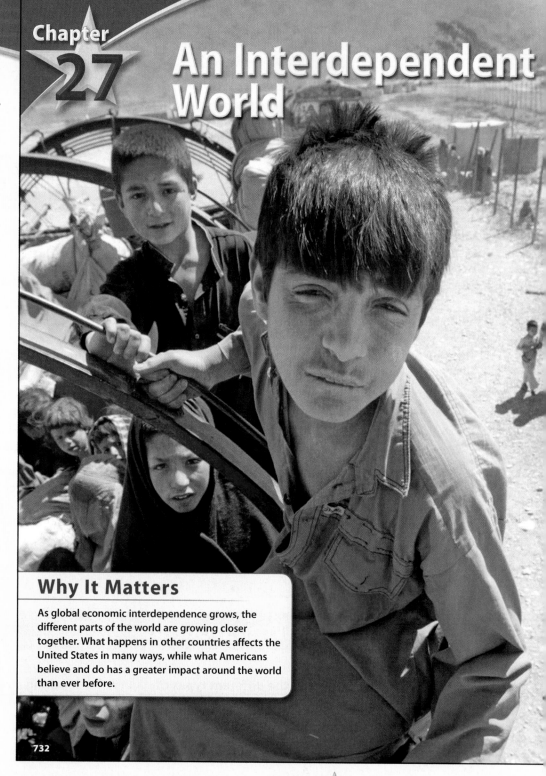

Chapter
27
An Interdependent World

Why It Matters

As global economic interdependence grows, the different parts of the world are growing closer together. What happens in other countries affects the United States in many ways, while what Americans believe and do has a greater impact around the world than ever before.

732

Point out that in Section 1 students will learn about global economic interdependence and the challenges that an interdependent world now faces. **OL**

Section 2

The United Nations Ask: What is the United Nations? What are its goals? *(Answers should include that the United Nations is an international organization that tries to promote peace between nations and works to solve global challenges such as hunger and disease.)* Tell students that in Section 2 they will learn about the United Nations and its efforts to deal with serious global problems. **OL**

Chapter Audio

Civics ONLINE
Visit glencoe.com and enter
QuickPass™ code
CIV3093c27 for
Chapter 27
resources.

Chapter Introduction
27

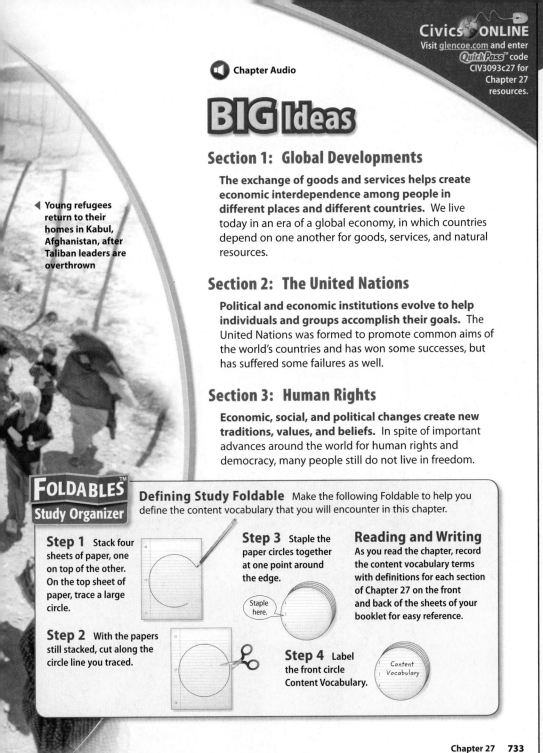

◀ Young refugees
return to their
homes in Kabul,
Afghanistan, after
Taliban leaders are
overthrown

BIG Ideas

Section 1: Global Developments

The exchange of goods and services helps create economic interdependence among people in different places and different countries. We live today in an era of a global economy, in which countries depend on one another for goods, services, and natural resources.

Section 2: The United Nations

Political and economic institutions evolve to help individuals and groups accomplish their goals. The United Nations was formed to promote common aims of the world's countries and has won some successes, but has suffered some failures as well.

Section 3: Human Rights

Economic, social, and political changes create new traditions, values, and beliefs. In spite of important advances around the world for human rights and democracy, many people still do not live in freedom.

FOLDABLES™
Study Organizer

Defining Study Foldable Make the following Foldable to help you define the content vocabulary that you will encounter in this chapter.

Step 1 Stack four sheets of paper, one on top of the other. On the top sheet of paper, trace a large circle.

Step 2 With the papers still stacked, cut along the circle line you traced.

Step 3 Staple the paper circles together at one point around the edge.

Staple here.

Step 4 Label the front circle Content Vocabulary.

Content Vocabulary

Reading and Writing
As you read the chapter, record the content vocabulary terms with definitions for each section of Chapter 27 on the front and back of the sheets of your booklet for easy reference.

Chapter 27 733

FOLDABLES™
Study Organizer
Dinah Zike's **Foldables**

Purpose This Foldable will help students learn the content vocabulary in this chapter. As they read each section, have students write content vocabulary and any other unfamiliar words and their definitions on the booklet pages of this foldable. **OL**

📁 More Foldables activities for this chapter can be found in the *Dinah Zike's Reading and Study Skills Foldables.*

Civics ONLINE
Visit glencoe.com and enter *QuickPass*™ code CIV1360c27T for Chapter 27 resources, including a Chapter Overview, Study Central™, Study-to-Go, Student Web Activity, Self-Check Quiz, and other materials.

Section 3 ⭐

Human Rights Ask: What are some rights that all human beings have? *(Answers will vary and may include "life, liberty and the pursuit of happiness," the right to choose and participate in their government, and freedom of religion.)* Explain that in Section 3 students will learn about human rights and how they are protected. Students will also examine the growth of democracy and liberty in the world today. **OL**

Focus

Guide to Reading
Answers to Graphic:

immigration and refugees
natural disasters
drug trafficking and crime

Global Challenges

environment
wars and terrorism
economic inequality

Section Spotlight Video

To generate student interest and provide a springboard for class discussion, access the Chapter 27, Section 1 video at glencoe.com or on the video DVD.

Resource Manager

Guide to Reading

Big Idea
The exchange of goods and services helps create economic interdependence among people in different places and different countries.

Content Vocabulary
- protectionism *(p. 735)*
- acid rain *(p. 737)*
- conservation *(p. 737)*
- refugee *(p. 738)*

Academic Vocabulary
- cooperate *(p. 735)*
- access *(p. 736)*

Reading Strategy
Explaining As you read, complete a graphic organizer like the one below by identifying three global challenges. Then explain why each of these is a problem.

Global Challenges

environment

 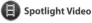
Section 1
Global Developments

Real World Civics Independent workers, such as this tailor surrounded by mounds of fabric in Beijing, China, are part of the American economy. The United States more than doubled its imports of clothing from China and other Asian nations in a five-year period beginning in 1998—and imports continue to grow. International trade, quotas, and imports and exports are powerful tools in the area of American foreign relations.

▼ **Tailor at outdoor market in Beijing**

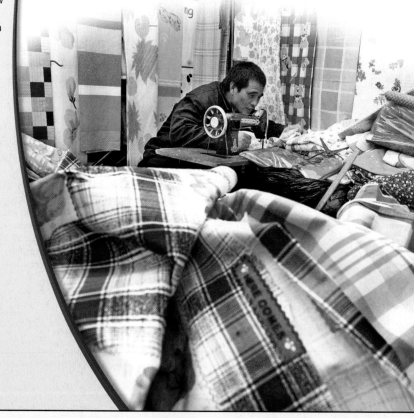

R Reading Strategies	**C** Critical Thinking	**D** Differentiated Instruction	**W** Writing Support	**S** Skill Practice
Teacher Edition • Monitoring/Clarifying, p. 735 **Additional Resources** • Pri. Source Read., URB p. 13 • Cont. Vocab., URB p. 41 • Ac. Vocab., URB p. 43 • Guid. Read., URB p. 61	**Teacher Edition** • Predicting, p. 737 **Additional Resources** • Crit. Think., URB p. 51 • Biographies, URB p. 45 • Quizzes and Tests, p. 323	**Teacher Edition** • Interpersonal, p. 736 • Below Grade Level, p. 736 **Additional Resources** • Diff. Instr., URB p. 55 • Teacher's Guide to Differentiated Instruction, p. 34	**Teacher Edition** • Persuasive Writing, p. 738	**Teacher Edition** • Reading a Graph, p. 736 **Additional Resources** • Chart, Graph, and Map Skills, URB p. 53 • Daily Focus Trans., 27–1

Global Interdependence R

Main Idea We live today in an era of global economic interdependence, in which countries depend on one another for goods, services, and natural resources.

Economics & You Think of five products you use every day. Do you know many of these items were made in a foreign country? Read more to find out how global trade has created an interdependent world.

Global interdependence means that people and nations all over the world now depend on one another for many goods and services. An important part of global interdependence is trade. As you learned in Chapter 26, trade includes both competition and **cooperation,** or assistance. Nations compete to sell their products. They also cooperate to make trade beneficial for everyone.

Global trade has many advantages. Businesses can make more profit. Greater competition may result in lower prices and a wider choice of products. However, global trade can also lead to problems worldwide. Competition may force weak companies out of business, hurting some national economies and costing workers their jobs. Nations sometimes try to protect their industries from foreign competition by placing tariffs on imports. This forces the price of foreign goods up and makes local prices more competitive. This policy, called **protectionism,** can cause harm as well as good. Price increases can lead to trade wars, in which nations set up even greater trade barriers.

The European Union (EU)—an organization that continues to grow—has eliminated most trade and many other barriers in Europe. The North American Free Trade Agreement (NAFTA) will gradually abolish all trade barriers among the United States, Mexico, and Canada.

Interdependence Hyundai autos are loaded for export at the port city of Ulsan. Hyundai, South Korea's largest carmaker, depends on the U.S. market, which accounts for about one-third of Korean vehicle exports. *Explaining* What is global interdependence?

The U.S. and Trade

The fuel to power our cars, planes, trains, trucks, and buses; to heat and light our homes; and to run our factories is an important example of growing interdependence. The United States must import more than two-thirds of the oil it uses, and the percentage is expected to keep rising.

In addition, the United States imports many of the minerals its industries need to keep working. For instance, 98 percent of the manganese, 93 percent of the bauxite, 81 percent of the tin, and 62 percent of the mercury used in American industries comes from other countries.

Global interdependence also means that other countries depend on us. The United States sells wheat, computers, telecommunications equipment, aircraft, medical equipment, machinery, and other high-technology products around the world. American services and entertainment products are also in demand. In addition, many poorer countries look to the United States for food, medicine, and defense weaponry.

Reading Check Explaining Why does the United States trade with other countries?

Teach

R Reading Strategy

Monitoring and Clarifying Tell students to monitor their understanding of the text as they read this chapter. Refer them to the Unit 8 Reading Social Studies lesson, which demonstrates using a chart to monitor and clarify understanding. Have them record confusing text in this section. **BL ELL**

Caption Answer:
People and nations worldwide depend on each other for many goods and services.

Reading Check **Answer:** The United States needs to import oil and minerals used in our industries and by consumers. The products we grow and make are sold around the world.

Hands-On Chapter Project
Step 1

Participating in a Mock United Nations Assembly

Step 1: Choosing an Issue and a Country Class groups will represent different countries at a mock United Nations Assembly and will choose a human rights issue or global challenge to be voted on at an assembly meeting.

Directions Direct class members to choose a global challenge or human rights issue. Organize the class into groups of four to research the selected issue or challenge in newspapers, magazines, and on the Internet. Each group should choose a country that is a member of the United Nations and, if possible, has a stake or an interest in this challenge or issue. Try to have a mix of developed and developing countries. Groups will do research to find out their countries' position on this challenge or issue. Monitor the groups to make sure that students who need support are matched with peers who can help them. **OL**

(Project continued in Section 2)

D₁ Differentiated Instruction

Interpersonal Have students research how NAFTA has affected the United States. In their report, they should compare benefits and challenges for businesses, workers, and consumers. **AL**

D₂ Differentiated Instruction

Below Grade Level Have students copy a world map from the Internet or an atlas. Ask them to color developing countries and developed countries with contrasting colors. Organize the class into pairs, and have each pair choose a developing country and research its resources, industries, and foreign trade. Then, have each present a 5-minute report about that country. **BL**

S Skill Practice

Reading a Graph Ask: Which countries have the highest and lowest compensation costs? *(highest, Denmark; lowest, Mexico)* What country has nearly the same hourly compensation costs as the U.S.? *(France, $23.89)* **BL**

Analyzing Graphs

Answers:
1. Spain at $17.10 per hour
2. $1.99 per hour

Differentiated Instruction

Diff. Instruction Act. 27, URB pp. 55–56

Global Issues

Main Idea The world community faces many serious global problems.

Economics & You What do you think makes a family rich or poor? Read to find out how countries can also be rich or poor and what factors make them so.

One of the biggest global problems is the growing economic inequality among nations. There is a growing divide between the rich and poor nations of the world. As this gap grows, conflicts flare, and the United States faces difficult decisions. On one side of the divide are about 35 rich, industrialized countries, including the United States, Japan, Germany, Canada, Great Britain, and France.

These developed countries have natural resources such as coal and iron, or they have easy **access**, or connection, to such resources. They have many large industries, such as steel, electronics, and carmaking. These countries produce many of the manufactured goods sold around the world. They also consume much of the world's natural resources, enjoying a high standard of living. On the other side of the divide are about 165 poorer and less developed nations. Because most of the poor countries are trying to develop industrial economies, they are called developing countries.

Comparing Developing Nations

Some developing countries, such as Chad, Albania, and Paraguay, are very poor. They have few natural resources and cannot

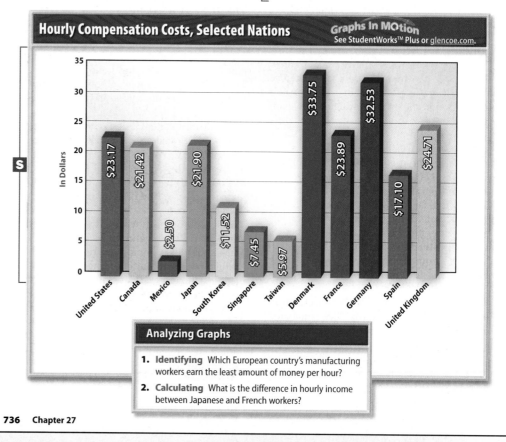

Hourly Compensation Costs, Selected Nations

Graphs In MOtion — See StudentWorks™ Plus or glencoe.com.

Analyzing Graphs

1. **Identifying** Which European country's manufacturing workers earn the least amount of money per hour?
2. **Calculating** What is the difference in hourly income between Japanese and French workers?

736 Chapter 27

Working to Improve Africa

Objective: To draw conclusions about Maathai's work

Focus: Have students identify why Maathai was honored and by which organization.

Teach: Discuss Maathai's contributions to improving Africa's environment.

Assess: Have students write a paragraph explaining how planting trees helped improve the lives of the women in rural Kenya.

Close: Discuss how Americans might adapt Maathai's ideas to improve our environment.

Differentiated Instruction Strategies

BL Describe how planting the trees improved African women's lives.

AL Have students report on causes of rain forest degradation in Africa.

ELL Have students follow along as you read each paragraph aloud. Have them identify the main idea of each paragraph. At the end, have them explain the most important ideas of the speech in their own words.

Projected Water Use, 2025

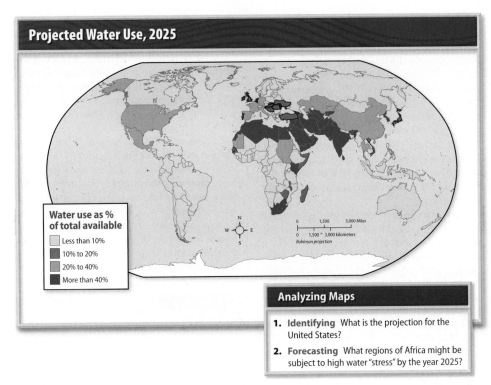

Water use as % of total available

- Less than 10%
- 10% to 20%
- 20% to 40%
- More than 40%

0   1,500   3,000 Miles
0   1,500   3,000 kilometers
Robinson projection

Analyzing Maps

1. **Identifying** What is the projection for the United States?

2. **Forecasting** What regions of Africa might be subject to high water "stress" by the year 2025?

C Critical Thinking

Predicting Have students reread the text under "Environmental Destruction" on pages 737-738. **Ask:** Should developing nations be allowed to pollute in order to build up their industries? Why or why not? *(Students should include information from the text and other sources to support their answers.)* **AL**

For additional practice on this skill (Predicting), see the **Skills Handbook**.

Analyzing Maps

Answers:

1. 20 to 40 percent of total water available will be needed by the United States

2. North Africa and parts of eastern Africa and southeastern Africa

---

produce enough food to feed their populations. They manufacture few products for export. They have high levels of unemployment, disease, and poverty. The average life expectancy in these countries is under 40 years.

Other developing countries have valuable natural resources. Countries such as Saudi Arabia and Venezuela have oil. Colombia grows coffee. The Democratic Republic of the Congo has copper. Some of these countries have little industry, though. Some do not have the governmental, health, and educational facilities to develop their human resources. It generally takes able leaders, scientists, engineers, bankers, and businesspeople to develop industry.

Cooperation Developed and developing nations need each other. Rich nations sell their products to the poorer nations.

Developed nations also get raw materials from developing countries. For their part, the developing nations badly need the food, technology, and money that developed nations can supply.

Environmental Destruction

Another global problem is the destruction of the natural environment. Industries and motor vehicles have pumped poisonous metals, such as mercury and lead, into the air and water. Coal-burning factories release sulfur dioxide gas into the air. Sulfur dioxide mixes with water vapor and later falls to the earth as **acid rain,** damaging forests and lakes. To save the environment, countries must work to end pollution both within their borders and internationally. An important way to reduce pollution is through **conservation**— limiting the use of polluting substances.

C

Chapter 27   737

Leveled Activities

BL Guided Reading Activity 27-1, URB p. 61

OL Chart, Graph, and Map Activity 27, URB p. 53

AL Critical Thinking Activity 27, URB pp. 51–52

ELL Content Vocabulary Activity 27, URB p. 41

W Writing Support

Persuasive Writing Have students choose a global challenge discussed in the chapter, such as pollution or preserving peace, and write a letter to the editor persuading Americans to confront this challenge. **OL**

✔ Reading Check **Answer:** Acid rain damages forests and pollutes lakes and streams, killing fish and other aquatic life. It can negatively affect human and animal health.

Assess

Civics ONLINE

Study Central™ provides summaries, interactive games, and online graphic organizers to help students review.

Close

Summary Have students discuss and then summarize in writing how developed and developing nations are dependent on each other. **OL**

Section ⭐ 1 Review

Conserving gasoline, for example, cuts the amount of gases that pollute the atmosphere. Conserving wood protects forests and wildlife habitats and leaves more trees available to absorb carbon dioxide. Some people oppose conservation efforts, claiming that they slow economic growth. Others argue that lack of conservation may produce short-term gains but long-term problems. Many experts believe that not dealing with air pollution, for example, may lead to dangerous changes in climate, destruction of forests and lakes, and health problems as people breathe polluted air.

Many people in poor nations believe that antipollution regulations are unfair because such rules would make it more difficult for them to develop their own industries. They argue that the developed countries polluted freely while they were becoming rich, but now the developed countries do not want to let poor countries do the same.

Other Global Challenges

An interdependent world community also faces other serious problems. Combating the international traffic in drugs and the influence of cross-border crime requires cooperation, as will repairing the damage caused by natural catastrophes such as the Asian tsunami of 2004.

W Coping with the pressures of greater immigration from poor to rich countries is sure to concern future world leaders. Another growing problem is the plight of millions of **refugees,** people who have unwillingly left their homes to escape war, famine, or other disaster. Preserving peace remains a pressing global issue. The threat of war and other forms of violence continues to grow. Terrorism persists as a major global concern.

✔ Reading Check **Describing** What are the effects of acid rain?

Section 1 Review

Vocabulary

1. **Define** the following terms and use them in sentences related to economic and environmental issues: *protectionism, acid rain, conservation, refugee.*

Reviewing Main Ideas

2. **Explaining** What do industrialized nations have in common?

3. **Comparing** How do developing countries differ from developed countries?

Critical Thinking

4. **Evaluating** What is the most serious problem the world community faces? Why?

5. **BIG Ideas** Create a diagram like the one below to explain four characteristics of developing nations.

Developing
Nations

6. **Analyzing Visuals** Study the graph on page 736. In what country are production workers' costs between $10 and $15 per hour?

CITIZENSHIP Activity

7. **Expository Writing** Select a developing nation and write a research report about its economic and social conditions. Consider including information in your report about the nation's housing, food production, and medical care.

Civics ONLINE

Study Central™ To review this section, go to glencoe.com.

Answers

1. Sentences should use vocabulary words according to their definitions in the section and in the Glossary.

2. Industrialized nations have natural resources or easy access to them. They have many large industries and produce manufactured goods that are sold worldwide. They also consume a lot of natural resources to maintain their high standard of living.

3. Developing countries may be either rich or poor in natural resources. The poor nations export few products and often do not produce enough food for their people. They often have high levels of unemployment, disease, and poverty. Nations rich in natural resources may have poor governmental leadership, health, and educational facilities.

4. Students should support their answers with convincing arguments.

5. **Developing nations:** lack of or inefficient use of natural resources; need for more industrial development; need for better government; need to raise living standards of the people

6. in South Korea at $11.52 an hour

7. Student reports should meet criteria set in the question.

Guide to Reading

Big Idea
Political and economic institutions evolve to help individuals and groups accomplish their goals.

Content Vocabulary
- internationalism *(p. 740)*
- charter *(p. 740)*
- globalization *(p. 742)*
- multinational *(p. 742)*

Academic Vocabulary
- maintain *(p. 740)*
- promote *(p. 740)*
- mutual *(p. 741)*

Reading Strategy
Describing As you read, complete a graphic organizer like the one below by describing how the UN has responded to these global issues.

The United Nations

Real World Civics These Afghan girls are learning to play guitar today in a country—Afghanistan—that until recently banned all music. How is this possible? The United Nations has funded an educational program, which will soon be self-supporting, to provide them with lessons. The girls are now also allowed to attend school under the protection of the United Nations.

▼ **Women of the northern Afghan city of Mazār-e Sharīf playing guitars**

739

Focus

Guide to Reading
Answers to Graphic:

UN
peacekeeping — environment

UN aided cease-fires and free elections–El Salvador, Haiti, and Cambodia; aid for refugees worldwide

Earth Summits: have resulted in treaties to reduce pollution and to protect animals and plant life.

Section Spotlight Video

Have students watch the Chapter 27, Section 2 video at glencoe.com.

Resource Manager

R Reading Strategies	**C** Critical Thinking	**D** Differentiated Instruction	**W** Writing Support	**S** Skill Practice
Teacher Edition • Monitoring/Clarifying, p. 740 • Inferring, p. 741 **Additional Resources** • Pri. Source Act., URB p. 13 • Cont. Vocab., URB p. 41 • Ac. Vocab., URB p. 43 • Guid. Read., URB p. 62 • Foldables, p. 103	**Teacher Edition** • Making Inferences, p. 740 **Additional Resources** • Quizzes and Tests, p. 324	**Teacher Edition** • Gifted/Talented, p. 741 **Additional Resources** • School-to-Home Conn., URB, p. 57 • Teacher's Guide to Diff. Instr., p. 35	**Teacher Edition** • Expository Writing, p. 742	**Teacher Edition** • Analyzing Charts, p. 741 **Additional Resources** • Daily Focus Trans., 27–2

Teach

R Reading Strategy

Monitoring and Clarifying Have students continue monitoring and clarifying their understanding of text in this section. **BL** **ELL**

C Critical Thinking

Making Inferences **Ask:** Why did the United States and its allies start planning for the United Nations during a war? *(The fact that so many countries were at war was proof of the great need for an organization dedicated to peace and to solving global challenges.)* **OL**

TIME™ Teens in *Action*

Answer:
Kevin is more aware of global issues. He has taken responsible actions to confront challenges such as pollution. He sees people from all of the world's countries as "world citizens." His analytic and problem-solving skills have improved.

✓ **Reading Check** **Answer:** 191 nations

Hands-On Chapter Project

Step 2

TIME™ Teens in *Action*

Kevin McGregor

What would it be like to represent the United States at the United Nations? How about China? Or maybe Burkina-Faso? Students like Kevin McGregor, 17, of Russellville, Arkansas, who take part in Model United Nations (MUN), have a pretty good idea. When these American teens get together at MUN conferences, they act as if they are delegates from different countries.

QUESTION: Where can people find MUN?

ANSWER: All over the United States and the globe. The conferences provide an awesome chance to learn about diplomacy and the intricacies of international relations—while developing public speaking and research skills.

Q: How has MUN changed you?

A: I think it's made me a more responsible world citizen. I took up biking to school because I felt it was a more efficient use of resources. It makes you think more about what is going on in the world. You start to see people that look different from you are fellow world citizens.

Q: How will MUN help your future?

A: Students that participate in Model UN are more aware of global issues and adopt more analytical ways of looking at problems. Those same students become voters and leaders in their community, maybe even politicians.

ACTION FACT:
Kevin loves to be outside doing things like backpacking and mountain biking.

Making a Difference **CITIZENSHIP**

Explaining In what way has Kevin changed because of his participation in the program?

R Purpose of the UN

Main Idea The United Nations was formed to promote the common aims of the world's countries.

Civics & You Think about a time you tried to get a group of your friends to agree on a movie or activity. What did you do? Read to find out how the nations of the world succeeded when they decided to form an international organization.

Internationalism is the idea that nations should cooperate to promote common aims, such as supporting economic development and fighting terrorism. They do this through membership in an organization, the United Nations, which is made up of many nations.

UN Goals

The United States and its allies started planning for the United Nations during World War II. In 1944 delegates from the United States, Great Britain, and the Soviet Union drafted a **charter,** or constitution, for the UN. In 1945 representatives from 50 countries—at that time, almost all the independent countries in the world—signed the charter at a meeting in San Francisco. The UN's main purposes are to **maintain**, or preserve, international peace; develop friendly relations among nations; **promote,** or encourage, justice and cooperation; and seek solutions to global problems. On United Nations Day, October 24, 2001, President George W. Bush praised the UN for its commitment to "promoting human rights, protecting the environment, fighting disease, fostering development, and reducing poverty."

The UN now has 192 members. Its main headquarters is in New York City. The different parts of the United Nations are shown on the chart on page 741.

✓ **Reading Check** **Describing** How many nations are members of the UN?

Participating in a Mock United Nations Assembly

Step 2: Create a Position Paper Each group will write a position paper stating its selected country's views on the issue or challenge adopted in Step 1.

Directions Each group will use previous government actions as well as statements by leaders to understand its country's current viewpoint. The position paper of each group should be at least one typed page in length. It should be expository and organized with main ideas supported by details. Remind students that it is NOT their opinion that they are expressing but that of the country they will represent at the mock United Nations Assembly. **OL**

(Project continued in Section 3)

UN Activities

Main Idea The United Nations had some success in solving world problems, but lack of cooperation has hampered its efforts.

Civics & You Do you think it is difficult to get all your friends to agree on something? Read more to find out how the United Nations has struggled with the same problem.

The UN has been successful in several ways. It has served as a meeting place where representatives from many nations can discuss **mutual,** or common, problems. Special agencies of the UN have done a great deal to fight sickness, poverty, and ignorance. However, a lack of cooperation among the Security Council's permanent members has made the UN less effective in settling disputes and preventing conflict.

Efforts to Promote Peace

Nevertheless, the United Nations has helped bring about peace in some areas and helped those who live in war-torn countries. In nations, such as El Salvador, Cambodia, and Haiti, UN peacekeeping operations have helped sustain ceasefires, conduct free elections, monitor troop withdrawals, and prevent violence. The UN has also provided aid for more than 30 million refugees.

Organization of the United Nations

Principal Units

International Court of Justice	Also known as the World Court, this is the main judicial agency of the UN. Consisting of 15 judges selected by the General Assembly and the Security Council, the court decides disputes between countries.
Security Council	The Security Council is the UN's principal agency for maintaining international peace and security. Of the 15 Council members, 5 members—China, France, Russian Federation, the United Kingdom, and the United States—are permanent members. The other 10 are elected by the General Assembly for two-year terms. Decisions of the Council require nine yes votes.
General Assembly	All UN member states are represented in the General Assembly. It meets to consider important matters such as international peace and security, the UN budget, and admission of new members. Each member state has one vote.
Secretariat	The Secretariat carries out the administration work of the United Nations as directed by the General Assembly, the Security Council, and the other agencies. Its head is the secretary-general.
Economic and Social Council	The Economic and Social Council recommends economic and social policies.
Trusteeship Council	The Trusteeship Council was established to ensure the rights of territories as they took the steps toward self-government or independence.

Analyzing Charts

1. **Describing** What are the six main units of the UN?
2. **Explaining** What nations make up the General Assembly?

Chapter 27   741

R **Reading Strategy**

Inferring   Ask: Why might the permanent members of the Security Council find it hard to agree on issues of peace and security? *(Answers will vary, but should include that the foreign policy goals and international commitments of these countries are often quite varied.)* **OL**

S **Skill Practice**

Analyzing Charts   Ask: Who are the permanent members of the Security Council? *(China, France, Russia, the United Kingdom, and the United States)* **BL**

D **Differentiated Instruction**

Gifted and Talented Have these students create a poster or comic book that illustrates the work of the UN Economic and Social Council, the General Assembly, or the World Court. **AL**

Analyzing Charts

Answers:
1. International Court of Justice, Security Council, General Assembly, Secretariat, Economic and Social Council, Trusteeship Council
2. all UN member states

Differentiated Instruction

Pri. Source Reading 8B, URB pp. 15–16

Vladimir Putin's Speech to the UN General Assembly

Objective:	To understand why Putin made this speech
Focus:	Have students read "Interpreting the Source." Elicit prior knowledge of terrorist attacks.
Teach:	Identify and discuss the two actions that Putin advocates for the UN to combat terrorism.
Assess:	Have students write a paragraph explaining how the United Nations might work to solve a particular regional conflict.
Close:	Make a chart of student ideas about UN efforts. Ask for student evaluations.

Differentiated Instruction Strategies

BL Ask students to explain Putin's idea that terrorism today is as severe a threat as Nazism was in the past.

AL Have students research and report on terrorism in Russia.

ELL Read the paragraphs aloud and have students identify the main idea of each. Ask them to explain why Putin made this speech.

W Writing Support

Expository Writing Direct students to research and write a report on one of the areas in which the United Nations works: peacekeeping, providing disaster aid, fighting disease, protecting the environment, or helping refugees. **OL**

Reading Check Answer: Lack of cooperation between members of the Security Council has kept the United Nations from being more effective in settling disputes.

Assess

Civics ONLINE

Study Central™ provides summaries, interactive games, and online graphic organizers to help students review content.

Close

Discussion Haves students reread the quote from Kofi Annan under "Responses to Global Problems." Ask them for suggestions about how globalization might reduce poverty and human suffering. List these suggestions on the board and discuss. **AL**

Section 2 Review

Responses to Global Problems

The United Nations was created in the early twentieth century to respond to global problems. Countries around the world have established progressively closer contacts over time, but recently the pace has increased significantly. This interdependence and interaction among individuals and nations working across barriers of distance, culture, and technology is called **globalization.** Former Secretary-General Kofi A. Annan of Ghana wrote, "Globalization is transforming the world. . . . Our challenge today is to make globalization an engine that lifts people out of hardship and misery, not a force that holds them down."

The Environment In 1992 a major conference on the environment was held in Rio de Janeiro, Brazil. This Earth Summit brought together representatives from 178 nations who discussed ways of protecting the environment. Leaders signed treaties pledging to safeguard animal and plant life and limit the pollution that causes global warming. In 1997 world leaders gathered at the United Nations for Earth Summit II. They agreed that, while some progress had been made, much remained to be done.

Economic Inequality In 2006 the United Nations addressed the problem of growing economic inequality that divides the world into rich and poor nations. The UN found that countries with weak economic structures (laws, institutions, and markets), and low infrastructure (roads, transportation, and water access) gain less from global markets. Globalization has been led by **multinationals,** large firms that do business or have offices in many countries. The UN has called on leaders of private enterprise to play a stronger role in integrating economic, social, and environmental development in the countries in which they operate.

Reading Check Identifying What factor makes the UN less effective in settling disputes than many had hoped?

Section 2 Review

Vocabulary

1. **Write** a short paragraph in which you use the following key terms: *internationalism, charter, globalization, multinational.*

Main Ideas

2. **Explaining** What is the purpose of the UN?

3. **Identifying** To which UN body do all member nations belong?

Critical Thinking

4. **Analyzing** What do you think is the most important role of the UN in the world today? Explain.

5. **BIG Ideas** On a diagram like the one below, describe how the General Assembly operates.

General Assembly

6. **Analyzing Visuals** Study the chart on page 741. How many judges sit on the World Court? How are the judges of the World Court selected?

CITIZENSHIP Activity

7. **Research** Take a poll of several adults in your community. Find out their opinions about the work of the United Nations and about U.S. involvement in that organization.

8. **Persuasive Writing** Every member nation has an equal vote in the UN General Assembly. Do you think this one-nation, one-vote system is fair? Explain in a one-page paper.

Civics ONLINE

Study Central™ To review this section, go to glencoe.com.

Answers

1. Vocabulary words should be used according to their definitions as found in the section and in the Glossary.

2. to promote the common aims of the world's countries, such as supporting economic development, fighting disease and poverty, solving international disputes peacefully, and combating terrorism

3. All member nations belong to the General Assembly.

4. Answers will vary, but should be supported by credible reasons.

5.

General Assembly		
international peace and security	the UN budget	admission of new members

6. Fifteen judges are selected by the General Assembly and the Security Council.

7. Students should write the results of their inquiries.

8. Answers should be supported by reasons and should follow a persuasive writing style.

Guide to Reading

Big Idea
Economic, social, and political changes create new traditions, values, and beliefs.

Content Vocabulary
• human rights *(p. 744)*
• tribunal *(p. 745)*
• genocide *(p. 745)*
• apartheid *(p. 746)*
• sanction *(p. 746)*
• satellite *(p. 747)*
• Cold War *(p. 748)*

Academic Vocabulary
• commission *(p. 744)*
• adequate *(p. 744)*
• policy *(p. 745)*

Reading Strategy
Describing As you read, complete a graphic organizer like the one below by describing how the UN has responded to these global issues.

Section 3
Human Rights

Real World Civics Human rights issues for migrant workers are huge questions in the Dominican Republic and elsewhere in the world. These Haitian children's parents are migrant workers who cut cane in the sugar fields and work in the processing plants in the Dominican Republic. They are allowed to go to school only because a nongovernmental organization associated with the United Nations has intervened and set up the school.

▼ **Young Haitian girls attend school on the grounds of a sugar plantation**

743

Focus

Bellringer
Daily Focus Transparency 27–3

Guide to Reading
Answers to Graphic:

```
       Protecting
       Human Rights
        /        \
   adopting      international
UN Declaration   tribunals to try
of Human Rights  human rights
                 violators
```

Section Spotlight Video

To generate student interest and provide a springboard for class discussion, access the Chapter 27, Section 3 video at glencoe.com or on the video DVD.

Resource Manager

R Reading Strategies	C Critical Thinking	D Differentiated Instruction	W Writing Support	S Skill Practice
Teacher Edition • Monitoring/Clarifying, p. 745 • Act. Prior Know., p. 746 **Additional Resources** • Cont. Vocab., URB p. 41 • Ac. Vocab., URB p. 43 • Guid. Read., URB p. 63 • RENTG, p. 258	**Teacher Edition** • Drawing Con., pp. 744, 748 • Det. Cause/Effect, p. 744 **Additional Resources** • Quizzes and Tests, p. 325	**Teacher Edition** • EL, p. 746 **Additional Resources** • Reteach Act., URB, p. 59	**Teacher Edition** • Persuasive Writing, p. 747 **Additional Resources** • Speak/Listen Skills Act., URB p. 9 • Writ. Skills Act., URB p. 47	**Teacher Edition** • Reading Maps, p. 745 • Reading Graphs, p. 746 **Additional Resources** • Daily Focus Trans., 27–3 • Pol. Cartoons Trans. 27

Teach

Standards for Human Rights

Main Idea Although basic human rights have spread to more countries, they are still not respected in many parts of the world.

Civics & You What basic rights do you think all people should have? Read to find out about the spread of basic human rights around the world.

Human rights are the basic freedoms that all people should enjoy. Human rights include the right to safety, to food, and to shelter, among other things. In democracies like the United States, citizens and noncitizens can worship as they please, and speak, read, and write freely. In recent decades, the issue of human rights has captured world attention.

A Mixed Picture

Despite democratic advances, however, many governments still imprison and abuse people for speaking their minds. Among the

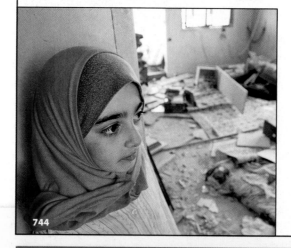

Right to Safety A returning refugee surveys the damage in her family's apartment due to fighting in southern Lebanon. The right to safety is one of the basic freedoms for all people. *Explaining* What are other human rights?

744

countries accused of human rights violations are China, Indonesia, Myanmar (Burma), Iran, Cuba, and Sudan. The good news is that human rights abuses are more carefully monitored than in the past. In South Africa, Haiti, and El Salvador, for example, national **commissions,** or committees, have investigated abuses of past governments. International groups have also called on individuals to account for their war crimes.

The Universal Declaration of Human Rights

In 1948 the United Nations adopted what has become the most important human rights document of the post-World War II years—the Universal Declaration of Human Rights. Addressing social and economic freedoms as well as political rights worldwide, the articles of the Declaration form a statement not of the way things are but of the way they should be with a unified effort.

Protection of Rights Articles 1 and 2 proclaim that "all human beings are born equal in dignity and rights." Articles 3–21 state the civil and political rights of all human beings, including many of the same liberties and protections of the U.S. Constitution. They also include other rights, such as freedom of movement, the right to seek asylum, the right to a nationality, the right to marry and found a family, and the right to own property.

Raising Standards of Living Articles 22 to 27 spell out the economic, social, and cultural rights of all people. These include the right to security, the right to work, the right to receive equal pay for equal work, and the right to form and join trade unions. The Declaration also lists the right to enjoy rest and leisure, the right to have a standard of living **adequate,** or acceptable, for health and well being, the right to education, and the right to participate in the cultural life of the community.

Protecting Human Rights

The UN High Commissioner for Human Rights directs programs that promote and protect human rights. For example, the UN Commission on Human Rights monitors and reports rights violations in all parts of the world. By drawing attention to these abuses, the UN hopes to bring pressure to halt them.

International Tribunals The Security Council has acted to punish human rights violators by establishing international tribunals. These courts have authority from the UN to hear cases and make judgments about violations of international human rights law.

Genocide During the 1990s, ethnic tensions in the East African nations of Rwanda and Burundi led to violent conflict. In a **genocide**, or the deliberate killing of members of a racial or cultural group, Hutu forces killed more than 500,000 people, mostly Tutsis. The International Criminal Tribunal Court for Rwanda began bringing to justice people accused of participating in the genocide.

Working for Human Rights The efforts of individuals make a difference in fighting for human rights. Salih Mahmoud Osman is an attorney from the Darfur region of Sudan. For 20 years, Osman has given free legal aid to people who have been taken into custody unfairly and tortured by the Sudanese government. Now a member of Sudan's parliament, Osman has led investigations of ethnic cleansing and other crimes against the people of Darfur.

Omid Memarian, an Iranian journalist and blogger, was arrested and tortured for his defense of human rights. He was released from prison after the international community campaigned for his freedom. He continues to expose arbitrary imprisonment, torture, and mistreatment of prisoners in Iran.

✓ Reading Check Describing What is genocide? How might an international tribunal deal with a case of genocide?

Spread of Democracy and Liberty

Main Idea Democracy has spread to more countries over the last 50 years, aided by support from democratic nations and the collapse of the Soviet Union.

Civics & You How do you define *freedom*? Read more to find out how freedom is described and encouraged around the world.

The United Nations has encouraged the spread of democracy and human rights throughout the world. So has the United States, which has made these causes an important part of its foreign **policy**, or guidelines.

Growth of Democracy

At the beginning of the twentieth century, only about 12 percent of the world's people lived in a democracy. By 1950 there were 22 democratic nations, with 31 percent of the world's population. Over the next 50 years, democracy grew rapidly, especially after 1980. Today nearly 64 percent of the world's population in 150 countries live under politically democratic conditions. This has all taken place during the time the UN has been established.

A publication called *Freedom in the World* provides an annual evaluation of political rights and civil liberties for more than 190 countries. At a minimum, "a democracy is a political system in which the people choose their authoritative leaders freely in public elections from among competing groups and individuals who were not chosen by the government." Countries that go beyond this standard for democracy offer the broadest range of human rights. These countries are "fully free" democracies. In 2007, there were 90 countries with free and democratic governments.

Chapter 27   745

R Reading Strategy

Monitoring and Clarifying Have students monitor their understanding of the section "Protecting Human Rights" by making a chart of the parts they don't fully understand. Encourage them to reread the text and to do research on the Internet or in the library to answer their questions. **BL ELL**

S Skill Practice

Reading Maps Have volunteers locate Rwanda, Burundi, and the Darfur region of Sudan on a political/physical map in an atlas or other source. **OL**

✓ Reading Check **Answer:** Genocide is the deliberate killing of members of a racial or cultural group. International tribunals would hear the case and make a judgment against those responsible for the genocide.

Hands-On Chapter Project
Step 3

Participating in a Mock United Nations Assembly

Step 3: Learn About a Mock Assembly Session Students will use a Web site to find out how a mock United Nations Assembly is conducted.

Directions Groups will get information about how a mock Assembly is conducted by visiting the Web site www.un.org/cyberschoolbus/modelun/index.asp. On the Web site, they will visit "Getting Started" and "Prepare for a Conference" and use this information to prepare a format for a mock assembly session in which they will present their position papers. Plan the mock assembly as a class. The amount of time needed depends on how many student groups are presenting papers. Two sessions might be needed.

(Project continued on the Visual Summary page)

D Differentiated Instruction

English Learners Have student volunteers point out their country of birth on a map, describe how it is governed, and determine in which category it fits on the graph. **ELL**

R Reading Strategy

Activating Prior Knowledge Ask: What is a totalitarian government? *(a government that controls almost all aspects of the lives of its citizens)* **BL ELL**

S Skill Practice

Reading Graphs Have students find the category "totalitarian" on the graph. **Ask:** How has the number of totalitarian governments changed between 1950 and 2000? *(They have declined.)* **OL**

Analyzing Graphs

Answers:

1. The number of monarchies was reduced by about half.
2. Most people prefer living in a democracy and will work toward achieving one.

D There were 58 "partly free" countries; none of these countries guaranteed a broad range of individual liberties beyond holding free and fair elections, however. In 2006 about 37 percent of the world's population lived in 49 countries that were not free. These nondemocracies often practiced or permitted terrible violations of human rights.

Fight for Rights in South Africa

A success story of the late twentieth century is South Africa. White leaders of South Africa enforced a policy of racial separation between blacks and whites called **apartheid.**

Apartheid laws dictated where blacks could travel, eat, and go to school. Black people could not vote or own property, and they could be jailed indefinitely without cause. For more than 40 years, people inside and outside South Africa protested against apartheid. Both the United States and the European Economic Community (now known as the European Union) ordered economic **sanctions,** or coercive measures, against South Africa. Mounting pressure brought a gradual end to apartheid. In April 1994, South Africa held its first election open to all races. Voters elected antiapartheid leader Nelson Mandela as the first black president.

R **S**

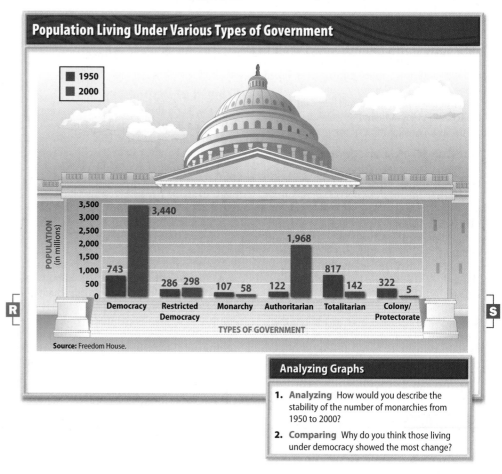

Population Living Under Various Types of Government

■ 1950
■ 2000

Democracy: 743, 3,440
Restricted Democracy: 286, 298
Monarchy: 107, 58
Authoritarian: 122, 1,968
Totalitarian: 817, 142
Colony/Protectorate: 322, 5

POPULATION (in millions)

TYPES OF GOVERNMENT

Source: Freedom House.

Analyzing Graphs

1. **Analyzing** How would you describe the stability of the number of monarchies from 1950 to 2000?
2. **Comparing** Why do you think those living under democracy showed the most change?

Differentiated Instruction

Preparing and Delivering Narrative Presentations

Objective:	To prepare and deliver a presentation
Focus:	Students read and discuss "Learning the Skill."
Teach:	Read the presentation under "Practicing the Skill." Discuss how a storyteller elicits audience interest.
Assess:	Have students work in pairs to write about a person who deserves a citizenship award.
Close:	Pairs will present and assess narratives, using the criteria on page 49.

Differentiated Instruction Strategies

BL Have students listen to the narrative referred to on page 745 a second time. As they listen, they should write transitions that lead from one idea to another.

AL Have students videotape and assess their presentations.

ELL Students can use audiotapes to practice their presentations.

TIME™ Political Cartoons

Michael Ramirez/Copley News Service

This cartoon, drawn by Michael Ramirez, focuses on laws regarding Internet use.

1. What is the setting for this image?
2. In the cartoon, where does the Information Superhighway lead?
3. What does the "great wall" symbolize?
4. What do you think Ramirez's intention was in creating this cartoon?

Every year, more than half of all Americans do volunteer work | role in it. One of the responsibilities of citizens is to help make their | of volunteer grou... small. Perha... dad who...

Fight for Rights in Afghanistan

After Afghanistan collapsed into civil war in the 1990s, many people turned to the Taliban for leadership. By 1996 the Taliban had taken control of about 80 percent of the country. They put in place harsh policies based on a strict interpretation of Islam. Basic freedoms were severely restricted, especially for women. In late 2001 the United States accused the Taliban of supporting terrorists. The U.S. and a coalition of European forces have been waging war on the Taliban ever since. The United Nations began working with the nation's leaders to create a climate that protected human rights.

Safeguarding Democracy

During most of the twentieth century, the global advancement of democracy and liberty was a main objective of the U.S. government. President Woodrow Wilson declared during and after World War I that the United States and its allies should "make the world safe for democracy." During World War II, President Franklin D. Roosevelt said that the United States and its allies were fighting for democracy and freedom in the world. Roosevelt said,

> " Freedom means the supremacy of human rights everywhere. Our support goes to those who struggle to gain those rights or to keep them. "
>
> —Franklin D. Roosevelt

The Cold War After World War II, the Soviet Union dominated Eastern Europe. It forced countries there to become **satellites**—countries politically and economically dominated or controlled by another more powerful country. Soviet actions during these years convinced the United States and its allies that the Soviet goal was to expand its power and influence.

Chapter 27 747

Leveled Activities

C Critical Thinking

Drawing Conclusions Ask: How did the ideas of democracy win the struggle against the ideas of communism? *(through education, economic prosperity, and people's desire for freedom)* **OL**

✓ **Reading Check Answer:** The Cold War was a clash of ideas between democratic nations and communist nations.

Assess

Civics ONLINE

Study Central™ provides summaries, interactive games, and online graphic organizers to help students review content.

Close

Identifying Central Issues Have students bring in newspaper and magazine articles about human rights issues around the world. Identify these issues on a chart and keep the articles for reference for interested students to study. **OL**

Section 3 Review

Most of the world soon divided into two hostile camps—the democratic nations and the Communist nations. This bitter struggle between the two sides was known as the **C Cold War** because it more often involved a clash of ideas than a clash of arms. The struggle was between the American ideas of democracy and freedom and the Soviets' communism and totalitarianism.

Soviet Domination Ends From 1945 until the fall of the Soviet Union in 1991, American presidents declared their commitment to the spread of democracy and liberty. After the collapse of Soviet totalitarianism, American presidents promoted the advance of democracy in the former Soviet Union and in other countries in central and eastern Europe that had suffered under Soviet domination. The spread of democracy elsewhere in the world continued to be a goal of U.S. foreign policy.

War Against Terror In response to the September 11, 2001, terrorist attacks on the United States, President George W. Bush repeated America's commitment to democracy and liberty around the world. He said in a speech to Congress,

❝ *The advance of human freedom—the great achievement of our time, and the hope of every time—now depends on us.*❞

—President George W. Bush

A world that is increasingly democratic and free means that the United States and other nations will have an easier time maintaining peace, prosperity, and national security. Thus, it is in the national interest of the United States to promote the global advancement of democracy and liberty.

✓ **Reading Check Identifying** What was the Cold War?

Section 3 Review

Vocabulary

1. **Write** a paragraph that summarizes key points of this section. Use all of the following terms: *human rights, tribunal, genocide, apartheid, sanction, satellite, Cold War.*

Main Ideas

2. **Explaining** What are human rights? List two important political rights.

3. **Explaining** What actions are being taken to safeguard human rights?

Critical Thinking

4. **BIG Ideas** Why are many nations turning to a more democratic form of government?

5. **Classifying** In a diagram like the one below, describe the characteristics of these types of government.

Characteristics

Fully Free | Partly Free | Not Free

CITIZENSHIP Activity

6. **Expository Writing** Choose a country discussed in this section. Research the country. Imagine that you are traveling to the country. Write a letter to a friend describing the country and the extent to which the government affects people's everyday lives.

Civics ONLINE

Study Central™ To review this section, go to glencoe.com.

Answers

1. Sentences should use vocabulary words according to their definitions in the section and in the Glossary.

2. Human rights are the basic freedoms that all people should enjoy. Political rights include: the right to vote, freedom of speech, freedom of religion, the right to a nationality, the right to assemble peaceably, and the right to participate in government.

3. Actions include reporting on human rights abuses and hearing human rights cases before UN international tribunals.

4. Answers will vary, but should include the idea that most people prefer the freedoms and rights enjoyed in democracies.

5. **Fully free:** offers the fullest range of human rights to its citizens; **partly free:** holds free and fair elections, but individual rights not guaranteed; **not free:** basic human rights are violated

6. Answers will vary. Students should describe the country and the government in terms of people's everyday lives.

Visual Summary

Main Idea	Supporting Details
We live in an era of global economic interdependence, in which countries depend on one another for goods, services, and natural resources.	Trade among nations is a major part of global interdependence.
The world faces many serious global challenges.	Challenges include the growing split between developed and developing nations, destruction of the natural environment, international traffic in drugs and other crime, damage caused by natural catastrophes, greater immigration from poor to rich countries, and the plight of millions of refugees.
The United Nations was established to provide a forum for nations to settle their disputes by peaceful means.	The UN's main purposes are to maintain international peace, develop friendly relations among nations, promote justice and cooperation, and seek solutions to global problems.
The UN has had some success in solving world difficulties, but a lack of cooperation has hampered its efforts.	The UN has battled sickness, poverty, and ignorance around the world, but has had less success in narrowing the gap between rich and poor and in protecting the environment.
Although acknowledgment of basic human rights has spread to more countries, rights are still not respected in many parts of the world.	The Universal Declaration of Human Rights lists basic human rights of all people, but these rights have been limited in places like Rwanda, the former Yugoslavia, China, Indonesia, Myanmar, Iran, Cuba, and Sudan.
Democracy has spread to more countries over the last 50 years, aided by support from democratic nations and the collapse of the Soviet Union.	A growing number of countries have instituted democratic reforms.

STUDY TO GO Study anywhere, anytime! Download quizzes and flash cards to your PDA from glencoe.com.

Visual Summary 27

Monitoring and Clarifying Ask students to report on their experiences with monitoring and clarifying their understanding of the text. **Ask:** What methods did you use to clarify confusing text? Which techniques would you recommend to others? *(Answers will vary.)*

Identifying Central Issues Have students form groups to study one of the global challenges examined in the chapter. **Ask:** What are the central issues? What actions are being taken to resolve these issues? Which actions do you think are most effective? Groups should share their responses with the class. **OL**

Understanding Question-Answer Relationships Have students work in small groups to turn each head in the chapter into a question and then write a one- or two-sentence summary of the main idea and one or two of the most important supporting details. Students can use their summaries to review the chapter for the Chapter Assessment. **BL ELL**

Hands-On Chapter Project
Step 4: Wrap-Up

Participating in a Mock United Nations Assembly

Step 4: Conduct a Mock Assembly Session Each group will present its paper and work on a proposal for UN action on the issue or problem.

Directions At the mock assembly session, groups will present their position papers. Each group should choose one representative to sit on a committee to create a proposal for United Nations action on this issue or problem. Students might not be able to agree on a proposal. If so, they can discuss why and what they learned from this experience. If they agree on a proposal, all assembly members should vote on it, representing their countries' viewpoints. **OL**

Reviewing Vocabulary

1. B Protectionism involves placing tariffs on imports as a way to protect industries. The words "guarding . . . against outside competition" should serve as a clue that protectionism is being defined in this question. Some students may choose answer D, "sanctions," economic weapons used to achieve political ends. The term, however, does not fit the definition.

2. A Tribunals are international courts with UN authority. The clue words "hear cases" and "human rights violations" should alert students to pick the one answer that refers to a court.

3. A During the Cold War, some eastern European countries were economically and politically controlled by the Soviet Union. Answer B, "charters," and answer D, "multinationals," might confuse some students, who will need to review this vocabulary.

4. C The words "people" and "basic freedoms" should be clues to direct students to the correct answer, "human rights."

Reviewing Main Ideas

5. C Developing countries claim that they should be able to set up industries and not be subjected to the pollution controls desired by developed countries. All the other choices are true statements about the relations between developed and developing nations.

6. C High levels of poverty challenge many developing countries. Some students might choose answer A, but an abundance of natural resources is true of only some developing nations.

7. B The clue word "security" should alert students that answer B is correct. Answer D should be eliminated because it is not an agency of the United Nations. Some students might choose C, but the General Assembly considers security among many other matters.

8. B Multinationals are the driving force behind globalization. Students might be confused by answer D, which mentions business leaders from developing

---

TEST-TAKING TIP

> Read through all of the answer choices before choosing the one that provides a general restatement of the information.

Reviewing Vocabulary

Directions: Choose the word(s) that best completes the sentence.

1. The policy of _____ involves a nation guarding its own industries against outside competition.

  A internationalism   **C** globalization

  B protectionism   **D** sanctions

2. _____ are courts with UN authority to hear cases involving international human rights violations.

  A Tribunals   **C** Satellites

  B Sanctions   **D** Charters

3. During the Cold War, many nations became _____ of the Soviet Union.

  A satellites   **C** sanctions

  B charters   **D** multinationals

4. Basic freedoms that should be available to all people are called _____.

  A charters   **C** human rights

  B multinationals   **D** sanctions

Reviewing Main Ideas

Directions: Choose the best answers for each question.

Section 1 (pp. 734–738)

5. Which of the following is NOT a way in which developed and developing nations help one other?

  A Developed nations get raw materials from developing nations.

  B Developed nations sell products to developing nations.

  C Developed nations are less strict with antipollution regulations for developing nations.

  D Developed nations send aid to developing nations.

6. Many developing nations have _____.

  A abundant natural resources

  B low unemployment

  C high levels of poverty

  D many industries

Section 2 (pp. 739–742)

7. The principal agency of the United Nations for maintaining peace and security is the _____.

  A Secretariat

  B Security Council

  C General Assembly

  D Earth Summit

8. An important force that is driving globalization are multinationals, which are _____.

  A UN peacekeeping forces

  B large firms that do business in many countries

  C organizations that promote conservation

  D made up of business leaders from developing countries

Section 3 (pp. 743–748)

9. The deliberate killing of members of a racial or cultural group is called _____.

  A genocide

  B apartheid

  C domestic terror

  D totalitarianism

10. Apartheid laws dictated where blacks could travel, eat, and go to school in _____.

  A Sudan

  B China

  C Myanmar

  D South Africa

GO ON

---

nations. However, if students correctly understand globalization, they should recognize B as the right answer.

9. A Genocide is the deliberate killing of a racial or cultural group. Some students might choose answer B, C, or D, but they do not specifically relate to the deliberate killing of a group.

10. D If students can answer this question correctly, they can eliminate "apartheid" as a choice in the previous question. Apartheid is described on page 746 as a former policy of the government of South Africa.

Critical Thinking

11. B Students can eliminate answers that are disproved by figures on the chart. Comparing figures from 2000 and 2005 in both imports and exports shows an increase in trade in every category. This eliminates

Critical Thinking

Directions: Base your answers to questions 11–13 on the chart and your knowledge of Chapter 27.

U.S. International Trade, 2000 and 2005 (in millions of dollars)		
Exports:	**2000**	**2005**
Goods	$771,994	$894,631
Services	$298,603	$380,614
Imports:	**2000**	**2005**
Goods	$1,224,408	$1,677,371
Services	$223,748	$314,604

Source: U.S. Census Bureau, *U.S. International Trade in Goods and Services*

11. This comparison of U.S. trade statistics shows that _____.

A trade decreased between 2000 and 2005

B the United States imported more goods than it exported

C the United States exported more goods than it imported

D services made up a larger share of U.S. trade than did goods

12. In both 2000 and 2005, the United States imported more goods and services than it exported, which means that the nation had _____.

A a positive balance of trade

B a negative balance of trade

C a system of tariffs in place

D instituted protectionist policies

13. In 2005 the United States exported about _____ times as many goods as it did services.

A two

B five

C ten

D fifteen

Document-Based Questions

Directions: Analyze the document and answer the short-answer questions that follow.

In December 2006, Ban Ki-moon of the Republic of Korea was sworn in as the eighth secretary-general of the United Nations. The excerpt is from a news story.

> [I will do] everything in my power to ensure that our United Nations can live up to its name, and be truly united, so that we can live up to the hopes that so many people around the world place in this institution, which is unique in the annals of human history....
>
> You could say that I am a man on a mission. And my mission could be dubbed 'Operation Restore Trust': trust in the Organization, and trust between Member States and the Secretariat.
>
> I hope this mission is not 'Mission Impossible, ...'
>
> Member States need a dynamic and courageous Secretariat, not one that is passive and risk-averse. The time has come for a new day in relations between the Secretariat and Member States. The dark night of distrust and disrespect has lasted far too long.
>
> —UN News Service

14. What does Ban Ki-moon convey as one of the problems facing the UN? Why do you think he considers this a problem?

15. What is the Secretariat? Do you think Ban is criticizing it? Explain.

Extended Response

16. Why might industrialized nations such as the United States exercise influence on developing nations to develop free market economies and democracy? Express your answer in a one-page essay.

STOP

Civics ONLINE

For additional test practice, use Self-Check Quizzes— Chapter 27 on glencoe.com.

Need Extra Help?

If you missed question...	1	2	3	4	5	6	7	8	9	10	11	12	13	14	15	16
Go to page...	735	745	747	744	736	736	741	742	745	746	735	735	735	741	741	745

Chapter 27 **751**

ASSESSMENT

Document-Based Questions

14. According to Ban Ki-Moon, a major problem is the distrust member nations feel toward the UN Secretariat. Distrust would be a deterrent to accomplishing any of the goals of the organization.

15. The Secretariat is the administrative unit of the United Nations. Ban is criticizing it for being passive and fearful of taking risks. He wants to restore respect for the Secretariat.

Extended Response

16. Students should realize that free market economics is the preferred trade policy of the United States and that American economists believe that it leads to greater competition, lower prices, and a wider choice of products. Many economists believe that eliminating trade barriers will help developing countries. The United States supports the spread of democracy because it believes that democracy allows for the fullest development of people.

---

answer A. Comparing figures for both years shows that imports exceeded exports, so answer C is incorrect. Answer D can be eliminated because in both years goods made up a larger share of trade than did services.

12. B Students who understand balance of trade will realize that when a country imports more than it exports, it is in a negative position. Answer C can be eliminated because if a system of tariffs were in place, imports would have gone down. Answer D can be eliminated because protectionist policies involve high tariffs on imports.

13. A When students compare $380,614 million worth of services exported in 2005 to the $894,631 million worth of goods, they will see that the latter figure is more than twice as much as the former.

Civics ONLINE

Have students visit the Web site at glencoe.com to review Chapter 27 and take the **Self-Check Quiz**.

Need Extra Help?

Have students refer to the pages listed if they miss any of the questions.

751

Analyzing Primary Sources

Focus

R Reading Strategy

Inferring Have students review the Preamble to the U.S. Constitution: *"We the People of the United States, in order to form a more perfect Union, establish Justice, insure domestic Tranquility, provide for the common defense, promote the general Welfare, and secure the Blessings of Liberty, to ourselves and our Posterity, do ordain and establish this Constitution for the United States of America."* **Ask:** What do you think is the purpose of this preamble? *(The purpose is to explain the goals of the Constitution.)*

W Writing Support

Expository Writing Organize the class into four groups and assign each group a preamble. Have each group write answers to the questions under "Read to Discover" and report to the class.

Analyzing Primary Sources

Comparing Constitutions

Reading Focus

The Preamble to the U.S. Constitution sets forth the general purposes for which our government was established. The Preamble also declares that the power of government comes from the people. Have you ever wondered how the Preamble to our Constitution compares to the preambles of other nations' constitutions?

Read to Discover

Each nation has its own unique culture and history. As you read, think about these points:

- How do the words in each preamble relate to the shared experiences of the people who live in that country?

- What values and beliefs expressed in each preamble are similar to the expressions in the other preambles?

Reader's Dictionary

multinational: originating from several countries

immutable: never changing

Constitution of the Russian Federation

The Constitution of the Russian Federation was ratified December 12, 1993.

We, the **multinational** people of the Russian Federation, united by a common destiny on our land, asserting human rights and liberties, civil peace and accord, preserving the historic unity of the state, proceeding from the commonly recognized principles of equality and self-determination of the peoples honoring the memory of our ancestors, who have passed on to us love of and respect for our homeland and faith in good and justice, reviving the sovereign statehood of Russia and asserting its **immutable** democratic foundations, striving to secure the well-being and prosperity of Russia and proceeding from a sense of responsibility for our homeland before the present and future generations, and being aware of ourselves as part of the world community, hereby approve the Constitution of the Russian Federation.

Constitution of the Argentine Nation

This constitution was adopted by the people of Argentina in 1853 and, like the United States Constitution, has had a number of amendments added to it since its adoption.

We, the representatives of the people of the Argentine Nation, gathered in General Constituent Assembly by the will and election of the Provinces which compose it, in fulfillment of pre-existing pacts, in order to form a national union, guarantee justice, secure domestic peace, provide for the common defense, promote the general welfare and secure the blessings of liberty to ourselves, to our posterity, and to all men of the world who wish to dwell on Argentine soil: invoking the protection of God, source of all reason and justice: do ordain, decree, and establish this Constitution for the Argentine Nation.

Additional Reading

752

Review suggested books before assigning them.

How the Garcia Girls Lost Their Accents by Julia Alvarez introduces the Garcia family, who must leave their Caribbean home and settle in the United States. The girls become Americanized, much to the disappointment of their traditional parents.

Footprints on the Planet: A Search for an Environmental Ethic by Robert Cahn is the story of a journalist who chronicles the ongoing struggle between private industry and environmental activists.

Foreign Oil Dependence by James Haley shows the U.S. dependence on foreign oil from different viewpoints.

Constitution of India

India is the world's largest democracy. This constitution became the law of the land on November 26, 1949, shortly after India received its independence from Great Britain.

WE, THE PEOPLE OF INDIA, having solemnly resolved to constitute India into a SOVEREIGN SOCIALIST SECULAR DEMOCRATIC REPUBLIC and to secure to all its citizens:
JUSTICE, social, economic and political
LIBERTY of thought, expression, belief, faith and worship
EQUALITY of status and of opportunity
FRATERNITY, assuring the dignity of the individual and the unity and integrity of the Nation.
IN OUR CONSTITUENT ASSEMBLY this twenty-sixth day of November, 1949, do HEREBY ADOPT, ENACT AND GIVE TO OURSELVES THIS CONSTITUTION.

Constitution of Iraq

In October 2005, more than 63 percent of eligible Iraqi voters went to the polls to decide whether to accept or reject the nation's new constitution. The constitution was overwhelmingly ratified.

We the people of Iraq, newly arisen from our disasters and looking with confidence to the future through a democratic, federal, republican system, are determined—men and women, old and young—to respect the rule of law, reject the policy of aggression, pay attention to women and their rights, the elderly and their cares, the children and their affairs, spread the culture of diversity and defuse terrorism.

[We accept this constitution] which shall preserve for Iraq its free union of people, land and sovereignty.

Photographs as Primary Sources An Iraqi woman displays her ink-stained finger after voting. Why do you think voters' fingers were marked with ink? Some Iraqis call it the "ink of freedom." What does that phrase tell you about what voting means to them?

DBQ Document-Based Questions

1. **Analyzing** What does this statement from the Russian constitution "multinational people . . . united by a common destiny" mean?

2. **Responding** What do you think it means to "promote the general welfare and secure the blessing of liberty"?

3. **Predicting** In what ways do racist and extreme policies affect countries and bring harm to the people?

4. **Connecting** Compare the preambles that are presented in this activity. Describe how they are similar and how they are different. Explain what you believe is the purpose of a preamble to a constitution. Then identify which preamble best expresses that purpose.

753

Did You Know?

Democracy Sweat Lodge The U.S. Constitution was created in the summer of 1787 at a convention in Philadelphia. The convention began on May 25, and delegates from every state met in secret for four months. During this very hot summer, the delegates bolted the doors and sealed the windows of the Pennsylvania State House (Independence Hall) where they met in order to preserve secrecy. Every delegate swore not to discuss the proceedings with any outsider. In fact, George Washington was reported to have become angry with one delegate who lost a page of his notes. The purpose of the secrecy was to ensure that the delegates could debate freely. The Founders saw their task as the creation of a new form of government. According to historians, the delegates wanted to consider what opponents of the Constitution might say before revealing the document to the nation.

Appendix

What Is an Appendix?

By definition, an appendix is supplementary material attached to the end of a piece of writing. Students can use the appendix to help them understand the material in their textbook. Explain that students may use an appendix to find out what a word means, how to pronounce a word, or find additional information about a particular word or topic. **Ask:** What materials are contained in this appendix? *(Skills Handbook, Gazetteer, Glossary/Glosario, Index, and Acknowledgments.)*

Explain what students will learn in the various components of the appendix: the Skills Handbook teaches important social studies skills; the Gazetteer teaches about important geographic locations covered in this textbook; the Glossary/Glosario defines the vocabulary terms found in this chapter in both English and Spanish; the Index can be used to find the page references where many important topics are covered in the textbook; and the Acknowledgments gives credit to the sources for primary sources, artists and agencies, and photos credits. **BL**

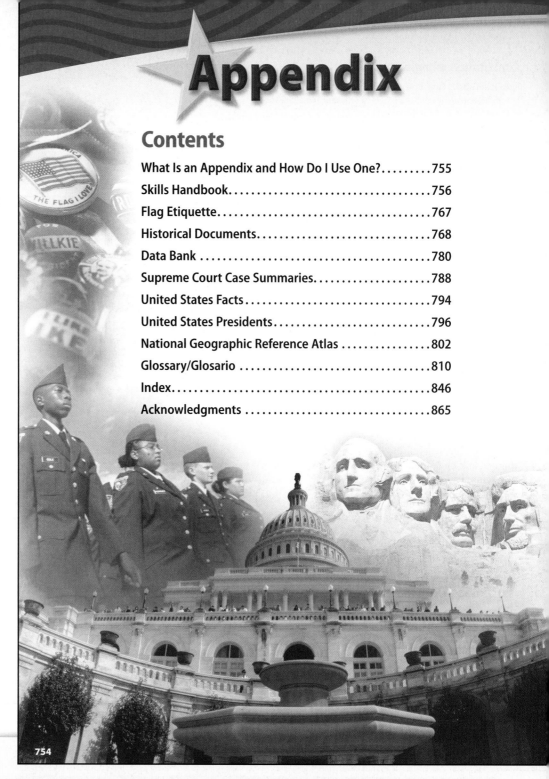

Appendix

Contents

754

What Is an Appendix and How Do I Use One?

An appendix is the additional material you often find at the end of books. The following information will help you learn how to use the appendix in Civics Today: Citizenship, Economics, & You.

Skills Handbook

The Skills Handbook offers you information and practice using critical thinking and social study skills. Mastering these skills will help you in all your courses.

Historical Documents

This is a collection of some of the most important writings in American history. Each document begins with an introduction describing the author and placing the selection within its historical context.

Data Bank

A data bank is a collection of data organized for rapid search and retrieval. This data bank supplies information about the government and economy of the United States. It also includes information about state governments and economies.

Supreme Court Case Summaries

Supreme Court case summaries provide readable discussions of important Supreme Court cases. The summaries are listed in alphabetical order and include a summary of the facts of each case and its impact.

United States Facts

This quick resource lists all the states and territories of the Union along with the year each was admitted and its population, land area, and number of representatives in Congress.

United States Presidents

The presidents have served as our nation's leaders. In this resource you will find information of interest on the nation's presidents, including their terms in office, political affiliations, and occupations before they became president.

National Geographic Reference Atlas

Helpful maps of the United States and world are available for your easy reference.

Glossary/Glosario

A glossary is a list of important or difficult terms found in a textbook. The glossary gives a definition of each term as it is used in the book. The glossary also includes page numbers telling you where in the textbook each term is used. This glossary combines the English term with the Spanish translation and definition to aid Spanish-speaking students.

Index

An index is an alphabetical listing that includes the subjects of the book and the page numbers where those subjects can be found. The index in this book also lets you know that certain pages contain maps, graphs, or photos about the subjects.

Acknowledgments

This section lists photo credits and/or literary credits for the book. You can look at this section to find out where the publisher obtained the permission to use a photograph or to use excerpts from other books.

Test Yourself

Find the answers to these questions by using the Appendix on the following pages.

1. What are "intergovernmental revenues"?
2. Who was the sixth president of the United States and what term did he serve?
3. On what page can I find out about John Peter Zenger?
4. What year was Michigan admitted to the Union?
5. What was the Supreme Court's decision in *Marbury v. Madison*?

Appendix

Using an Appendix

Use the descriptions in the student text to explain the sections in the Appendix. Then instruct students to answer the questions at the bottom of the page. Next, discuss the answer to each question. **Ask:** How can the information in each section help you as you read your textbook? **OL**

Tell students to write five questions similar to those in **Test Yourself** on a sheet of paper. Students should write the answers on the back of the same paper. Then have students exchange questions and quiz each other. Conclude by having students check their responses. **BL**

Additional Support

Test Yourself Answers

1. funds one level of government receives from another level of government
2. John Quincy Adams; 1825–1829
3. pages 123 and 433
4. 1837
5. The Court ruled against Marbury. This case established the Court's power of judicial review.

Skills Handbook

Teach

INTRODUCTION

The following **Skills Handbook** offers opportunities to practice individual critical thinking and social studies skills. Students can benefit in multiple ways from completing the lessons. First, being equipped with these skills makes students' reading more meaningful and supports the content of the text. Second, the lessons give students practice in using skills they will need to complete standardized tests successfully because many of these skills are assessed on standardized tests.

You may use the lessons at any point in the text and in any order that you wish. You also can use these lessons as review for students who need extra practice with these skills.

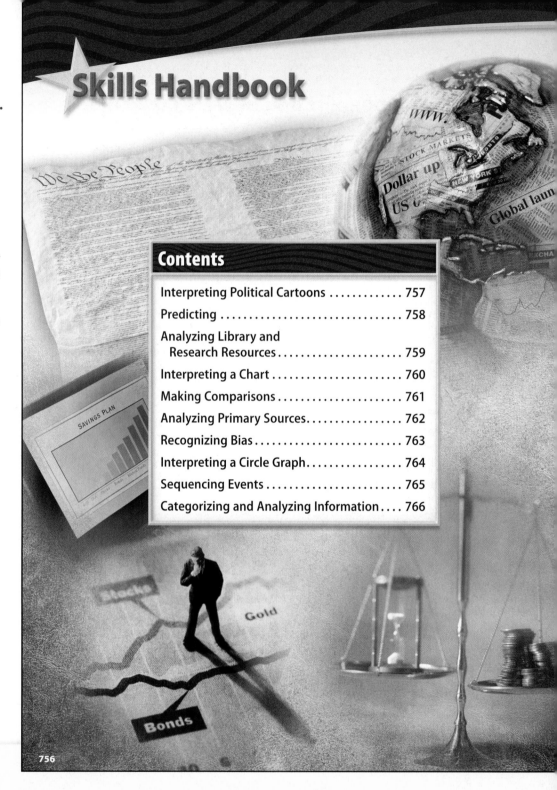

Skills Handbook

Contents

756

Interpreting Political Cartoons

Why Learn This Skill?

Political cartoons express the cartoonist's opinions through art. The cartoons appear in newspapers, magazines and books, and on the Internet. Political cartoons usually focus on public figures, political events, or economic or social conditions. This type of art can give you a summary of an event or circumstance, along with the artist's opinion, sometimes with exaggeration.

① Learn It!

Follow these steps to interpret political cartoons:

- Read the title, caption, or conversation balloons. They help you identify the subject of the cartoon.

- Identify the characters or people in the cartoon. They may be caricatures, or unrealistic drawings that exaggerate the characters' physical features.

- Identify any symbols. Symbols are objects that stand for other things. An example is the American flag, which is a symbol of our country. Commonly recognized symbols may not be labeled. Unusual symbols might be labeled.

- Examine the actions in the cartoon—what is happening and why?

- Identify the cartoonist's purpose. What statement or idea is he or she trying to express? Decide if the cartoonist wants to persuade, criticize, or just make people think.

② Practice It!

On a separate piece of paper, answer these questions about the political cartoon below.
1. What is the subject of the cartoon?
2. What words give clues to the meaning of the cartoon?
3. Why is the picture on a milk carton?
4. What message do you think the cartoonist is trying to send?

③ Apply It!

Bring a newsmagazine to class. With a partner, analyze the message in each political cartoon you find in the magazine.

Political Cartoons

HAVE YOU SEEN ME?

USA

NAME: THE AMERICAN WORKER
AGE: 18-65
LAST SEEN GETTING A PINK SLIP AT MANUFACTURING JOB THAT WAS OUTSOURCED TO ANOTHER COUNTRY.

MILK   OPEN

GARYMARKSTEIN
Copley News Service

Gary Markstein/Copley News Service

Every year, more than half of all Americans do volunteer work ... role in it. One of the responsibilities of citizens is to help make their ... of volunteer grou... small. Perha... dad who...

D Differentiated Instruction

Visual/Spatial Ask students to choose an issue of importance to them. Tell them to choose a school, community, or national issue. Have students create a cartoon that illustrates their opinions about the issue. Display completed cartoons on a bulletin board. **OL**

S Skill Practice

Visual Literacy Before the class reads the lesson, distribute copies of two or three political cartoons to small groups of students. Be sure that the selected cartoons contain examples of some of the characteristics described in the lesson: title, caption, conversation balloons, caricatures or exaggerations, and symbols. Have groups compare their cartoons and list the characteristics of cartoons.
Ask: What is your cartoon's message? What details helped you figure out the message? *(List group replies on the board, grouping similar responses together.)* **OL**

Additional Support

Skills Practice Answers

Practice It! Answers

1. American workers losing jobs to outsourcing

2. "Have You Seen Me?" implies that the American worker is disappearing; the milk carton is labeled with "The American Worker" and mentions outsourcing jobs.

3. It is a play on how milk cartons display missing persons.

4. Students may suggest that the cartoonist is against outsourcing jobs, feeling that it will make American's lose their jobs.

Apply It! Answer

Students should use the information under "Learn It!" to help them interpret the cartoons they find in their magazines.

Skills Handbook

R1 Reading Strategy

Activating Prior Knowledge Ask students what they think would happen if they watch a movie the evening before an important test instead of studying. *(Students likely would perform less well on the test than they would have if they had studied.)* **Ask:** Why do you think this outcome is likely? On what factors are you basing your predictions? *(prior experience, experience of others, common sense, and so on)* **BL**

R2 Reading Strategy

Predicting Have students read these questions, then read the first paragraph from a section in their textbooks. Ask them to think about what might happen next. Then have them read the following paragraphs to see if their predictions are true. **OL**

Additional Support

Predicting

Why Learn This Skill?

You have probably read about people making difficult decisions based on something they think *might* happen. You will have a better understanding of why people make certain choices when you consider the factors that influenced their decisions, or predictions. **R1**

① Learn It!

As you read a paragraph or section in your book, think about what might happen next. What you think will happen is your *prediction*. A prediction does not have a correct or incorrect answer. A prediction is an educated guess of what might happen next based on facts.

To make a prediction, ask yourself:

- What happened in this paragraph or section that I just read?
- What prior knowledge do I have about the information in the text?
- What similar circumstances do I know of?
- What do I think might happen next?
- Test your prediction: read further to see if you were correct.

② Practice It!

To practice the skill, read the following paragraph about a possible case of discrimination. Then answer the questions.

A high school student who uses a wheelchair needs a ramp installed to reach the stage during a graduation ceremony held at an auditorium. The principal says no, the diploma can be awarded down in front of the stage.

1. What action do you predict the student will take? Why?
2. What action do you think the principal will take as a result of your predicted student action?
3. If you were the principal in this situation, what do you predict you would do?

③ Apply It!

Watch a television show or a movie. Halfway through the show, write down your prediction of how it will end. At the end of the show, check your prediction. Were you correct? What clues did you use to make your prediction? What clues did you miss?

Skills Practice Answers

Practice It! Answers

1. Students may suggest that the student may go above the principal or start a petition to get a ramp installed.
2. Answers will vary based on the previous predictions.
3. Answers will vary, but should consist of probable actions taken by a principal.

Apply It! Answer

Answers will vary; students should have logical arguments to explain their predictions.

Analyzing Library and Research Resources

Why Learn This Skill?

Imagine that your teacher has sent you to the library or to the Internet to research and to write a report about the current makeup of the United States Congress. Knowing how to choose sources that contain accurate and current information will help you save time in the library or on the Internet. You will also be able to write a better and more accurate report.

1 Learn It!

Not all sources will be useful for your report on the members of the Senate and House of Representatives. Even some sources that involve topics about government will not always provide the information you want. In analyzing sources for your research project, choose items that are nonfiction and that contain the most information about your topic. Also choose sources based on their depth and how timely they are.

When choosing research resources, ask these questions:

- Is the information up-to-date?

- Does a book's or journal's index have several page references listed for the topic?

- Is the research written in a way that is easy to understand?

- Are there helpful statistical graphs, charts, and photos?

2 Practice It!

Look at the following list of sources. Which would be most helpful in writing a report on the United States Congress? Explain your choices.

(1) The Declaration of Independence
(2) The current *Information Please* Almanac
(3) A children's storybook about the U.S. Congress
(4) A student's notes on the Internet about a family trip to Washington, D.C.
(5) A book about U.S. history
(6) A Web site, www.thomas.loc.gov
(7) A journal article written by the current president of the United States
(8) a biographical dictionary

3 Apply It!

Go to your local library or use the Internet to create a bibliography of sources you might use to write a report on the current membership of the U.S. Congress. Explain why you would choose each source. Make sure you include information about both the House of Representatives and the Senate, including a breakdown of the membership of each.

C Critical Thinking

Making Inferences **Ask:** What does having several pages listed for the topic tell you about the book? *(how much information the book has about the topic)* What other parts of the book could you use to make this judgment? *(the table of contents)* **OL**

R Reading Strategy

Reading Secondary Sources **Ask:** How could you answer this question about a source? *(Students may say that they could read a few paragraphs or a couple of pages of text to judge the source's readability.)* **OL**

Skills Practice Answers

Practice It! Answers

Students should indicate that the most helpful would be 2, 5, and 6, because they would all have specific information about the U.S. Congress. However, they might also get some information from 3, 7, and 8.

Apply It! Answer

Encourage students to review each source to evaluate the comprehensiveness and accuracy of the information presented.

Skills Handbook

R Reading Strategy

Organizing Assign students a section in the textbook and have them look for ideas and facts that are grouped together or have similar characteristics. Tell them to list these characteristics, or categories, as the headings on a chart. Then tell them to look for details as they read and to fill them in under the proper categories on the chart. **OL**

Interpreting a Chart

Why Learn This Skill?

To make learning easier, you can organize information into groups of related facts and ideas. One way to organize information is with a chart. A chart presents written or numerical information in lists, columns, and rows. It helps you remember and compare information more easily. Cross-referencing data is an important comparison that can be made on a chart. **R**

① Learn It!

To organize information in a chart, follow these steps:

- Decide what information you must organize.

- Identify several major categories of ideas or facts about the topic, and use these categories as column headings.

- Find information that fits into each category, and write those facts or ideas under the appropriate column heading.

② Practice It!

On a separate sheet of paper, answer the following questions using the chart on this page.

Time Management Tips for High School Students
1. Make a "To Do" list every day.
2. Use spare minutes wisely.
3. It's okay to say "No!" when keeping your study priorities in mind.
4. Find the right time of the day to work.
5. Review your notes every day.
6. Get a good night's sleep.
7. Communicate your schedule to others so they do not interrupt your study time.
8. Become a taskmaster and budget your time.
9. Don't waste time agonizing over setbacks or procrastinating.
10. Keep things in perspective by setting realistic goals.
Source: collegeboard.com.

1. What type of information does the chart contain?
2. Whom would this chart help?
3. What features of the chart help you read ideas easily?

③ Apply It!

Create a chart to track your school assignments. Work with five areas of information: Subject, Assignment, Description, Due Date, and Completed Assignments. Be sure to keep your chart up-to-date.

Additional Support

Skills Practice Answers

Practice It! Answers

1. helpful time management tips for students

2. students—particularly those who have problems managing their time

3. The chart is numbered, and it uses short, concise sentences

Apply It! Answer

Check that students have constructed their charts properly with the five areas of information as column headings. Encourage them to keep the chart up-to-date.

Making Comparisons

Why Learn This Skill?

Suppose you want to buy a portable CD player, and you must choose among three models. To make this decision, you would probably compare various features of the three models, such as price, sound quality, size, and so on. After you compare the models, you will choose the one that is best for you.

In your studies of civics and economics, you must often compare forms of government and different economic plans, identify patterns, make predictions, and make generalizations about them.

1 Learn It!

When making comparisons, you identify and examine two or more places and their economies, or their forms of government. Then you identify any similarities between two types, or ways the two types are alike. Finally, you also note their differences—the things about them that are not alike.

When making comparisons, apply the following steps:

- Decide what types of government or economies to compare. Clue words such as *also, as well as, like, same as,* and *similar to* can help you identify when topics are being compared.

- Read the information about each type carefully.

- Identify what information is similar for both topics.

- Make note of aspects of both that are different or dissimilar.

2 Practice It!

To practice the skill, analyze the information in the chart at the bottom of this page. Then answer these questions:

1. What types of government are being compared?
2. What categories for each government are being compared?
3. In what ways, if any, are the United States and Cuba similar?
4. Suppose you wanted to compare the two governments in more detail. What other categories might you use?

Democratic vs. Totalitarian		
	Democratic	**Totalitarian**
Country	United States	Cuba
Control of Economy	Individual Development	Government
Control of Laws	Citizens Vote, Government Enforces	Government Dictates
Choice of Leaders	Citizens Vote	Government Selects or Appoints

3 Apply It!

Think about two sports that are played at your school. Make a chart comparing categories such as where the games are played, who plays them, what equipment is used, and so on.

C Critical Thinking

Making Inferences Have students brainstorm some things that citizens or government officials might want to compare. *(Answers may include government programs, volunteer opportunities, civil and criminal law, and so on.)* **OL**

R Reading Strategy

Activating Prior Knowledge Write the words "cat" and "dog" on the board. **Ask:** How are the two animals similar? *(Both are mammals, have fur and four legs, and are popular pets.)* How are they different? *(Cats meow, dogs bark; cats climb trees, dogs do not; cats are felines, dogs are canines; cats are often solitary, dogs like to live in packs.)* Point out to students that the skill of making comparisons includes identifying how things are similar to and different from one another. **BL**

Skills Practice Answers

Practice It! Answers

1. democratic and totalitarian
2. control of economy, control of laws, and choice of leaders
3. Both governments enforce laws, if in a different way.
4. Answers might include individual freedoms, property rights, political parties, and so on.

Apply It! Answer

Answers should show an understanding of the two chosen sports and the similarities and differences between them.

Skills Handbook

S Skill Practice

Visual Literacy Point out to students that images can be primary sources as well. Have them look through their textbook and identify images that are primary sources, and discuss what aspect of history or civics the images teach us. **OL**

C Critical Thinking

Analyzing Primary Sources Ask students to contribute to a class list of questions to ask about a written primary source document to help them determine its reliability. *(Questions might include who wrote it, what biases the author might have had, what the author's purpose was in writing the document, and so on.)* **AL**

Analyzing Primary Sources

Why Learn This Skill?

People who study civics and government examine pieces of evidence to understand their government, laws, and economy. These types of evidence—both written and illustrated—are called *primary sources*. Examining primary sources can help you understand your government. They are called primary sources because a specific source or origin of the information can be identified.

1 Learn It!

Primary sources of civics are firsthand accounts that describe an event, law, or constitutional development. They can include letters, diaries, photographs, pictures, news articles, legal documents, stories, literature, and artwork.

Ask yourself the following questions when analyzing primary sources:

- What is the primary source?
- Who created it?
- What is its original format or source?
- When was it created?
- What does it reveal about the topic I am studying?
- Why was it created and for what audience?

2 Practice It!

The following primary source is the first verse of the song "The Star-Spangled Banner" written by Francis Scott Key during the War of 1812. Read the verse, and then answer the questions that follow.

> *Oh, say, can you see, by the dawn's early light*
> *What so proudly we hailed at the twilight's last gleaming,*
> *Whose broad stripes and bright stars through the perilous fight,*
> *O'er the ramparts we watched were so gallantly streaming?*
> *And the rocket's red glare, the bombs bursting in air,*
> *Gave proof through the night that our flag was still there.*
> *Oh, say, does that star-spangled banner yet wave*
> *O'er the land of the free, and the home of the brave?*
>
> —Excerpt from "The Star-Spangled Banner" by Francis Scott Key, 1812

1. What is the main topic?
2. What details let you know he is talking about the American flag?
3. How do we know there is a war going on?
4. What emotion is the songwriter trying to convey?

3 Apply It!

Find a primary source from your past, such as a photo, newspaper clipping, or diary entry. Explain to the class what it shows about that time in your life.

Skills Practice Answers

Practice It! Answers

1. Key is referring to watching the flag during and after a battle.
2. "Broad stripes and bright stars" refer to the flag, as does the "star-spangled banner."
3. He talks about "the perilous fight," "ramparts," "rocket's red glare," and "bombs bursting in air."
4. He seems proud of the flag and what it represents. He is trying to convey patriotism.

Apply It! Answer

Make sure students know that they will share their primary sources on a voluntary basis. Encourage students to respond based on their interests or likes and dislikes, but not to reveal personal information that they may be uncomfortable sharing.

Additional Support

Recognizing Bias

Why Learn This Skill?

If you say, "Summer is a prettier season of the year than winter," you are stating a bias. A *bias* is an attitude that favors one way of thinking over another. A bias can also be thought of as a form of an opinion. That is someone's personal attitude, but not necessarily a true fact. It can prevent you from looking at a situation in a reasonable or truthful way.

① Learn It!

Most people have feelings and ideas that affect their points of view. Their viewpoints, or *biases,* influence the way they interpret events. For this reason, an idea that is stated as a fact may really be only an opinion. Recognizing bias will help you judge the accuracy of what you read and sort opinions from true facts.

To recognize bias, follow these steps:

- Identify the speaker or writer and examine the views presented. Why did the person speak or write about a particular issue?

- Look for language that shows emotion or opinion. Look for words such as *all, never, best, worst, might,* or *should.*

- Examine the information for imbalances. Is it written from one point of view? Does it take into consideration other points of view?

- Identify statements of fact. Factual statements usually answer the *who, what, where,* and *when* questions.

- Does the writer use facts to support his or her point of view? Statements such as *I think,* or *I believe* often indicate a point of view—not a fact.

② Practice It!

Read the following statement by an author who writes about what goes on in American politics and government.

> *Misusing words is, in politics, an art form. The politician who uses plain English is not likely to be a politician for long. Often it is better to be obscure.*

1. What problem is the speaker addressing?
2. What reason does the speaker give for the problem?
3. What is the speaker's point of view, or bias?
4. What words give clues as to the speaker's bias?

③ Apply It!

Choose a "Letter to the Editor" from a newspaper. Summarize the issue being discussed and the writer's bias about the issue. Describe a possible opposing opinion and who might have that opinion and why.

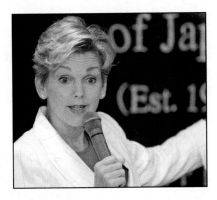

Skills Handbook

C1 Critical Thinking

Analyzing Information Ask: Is this paragraph saying that it is wrong to have opinions? If not, what is the point of the paragraph? *(The paragraph is not warning against having opinions, but against allowing opinions to cloud one's judgment.)* **OL**

C2 Critical Thinking

Comparing and Contrasting Distribute copies of two reviews of the same movie, book, television show, or music CD. After students have read both, ask them what biases are revealed in the reviews. Have them identify words and sentences that reveal those biases. **OL**

Additional Support

Skills Practice Answers

Practice It! Answers

1. how politicians spin words
2. If politicians don't learn how to misuse words, they will lose their positions.
3. the ability to be obscure and to spin words is a good quality for a politician to have
4. The author refers to misusing words as "an art form" and says that it is "better to be obscure."

Apply It! Answer

Summaries and analyses of bias should accurately reflect the letters chosen. Students should also describe an opposing opinion and who might hold this opinion in terms of their age, occupation, and background.

Skills Handbook

R₁ Reading Strategy

Monitoring **Ask:** Why is a circle graph also called a pie chart? *(because the circle is divided into "slices," or wedge-shaped sections representing parts of the whole)* What percentage should all of the slices in a circle graph add up to? *(100 percent)*
BL

R₂ Reading Strategy

Reading Graphs Have students study the circle graph on this page. **Ask:** How does this circle graph indicate what each slice represents? *(by using different shading for each slice)* How does it indicate the exact percentage that each slice represents? *(by labeling each slice with a percent)* **ELL**

Additional Support

Interpreting a Circle Graph

Why Learn This Skill?

Have you ever watched someone serve pieces of pie? When the pie is cut evenly, everyone's slice is the same size. If one slice is cut a little larger, however, someone else gets a smaller piece.

A *circle graph* is like a sliced pie. It is often called a pie chart. In a circle graph, the complete circle represents a whole group—or 100 percent. The circle is divided into "slices," or wedge-shaped sections representing parts of the whole.

R₁

① Learn It!

To read a circle graph, follow these steps:

- Read the title of the circle graph to find the subject.

- Study the labels or the key to see what each "slice" represents.

- Compare the sizes of the circle slices.

- Draw conclusions from your comparison.

② Practice It!

The circle graph below represents that same information shown on this chart, but in a different format. Study the circle graph, and answer the following questions.

1. What is the subject of the circle graph?
2. Which region of the U.S. has produced the most presidents?
3. Which states on the graph produced the fewest presidents?
4. What conclusion could you draw from this circle graph?

③ Apply It!

Quiz some friends about the first names of 10 presidents of which you supply them the last names. Create a circle graph showing percentages of correct and noncorrect results of those who answered your questions.

R₂

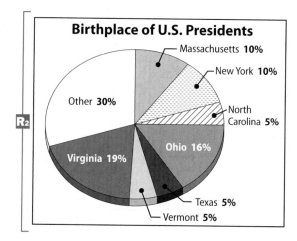

Birthplace of U.S. Presidents

- Massachusetts **10%**
- New York **10%**
- North Carolina **5%**
- Ohio **16%**
- Texas **5%**
- Vermont **5%**
- Virginia **19%**
- Other **30%**

Skills Practice Answers

Practice It! Answers

1. where U.S. Presidents were born
2. the eastern portion of the U.S.
3. North Carolina, Texas, and Vermont
4. A majority of presidents were born in the Midwest or New England area.

Apply It! Answer

The circle graph should have labels or a key to show what each slice represents. The size of the slices should accurately reflect the percentage of friends in each category, and the percentages should add up to 100 percent.

Sequencing Events

Why Learn This Skill?

Have you ever had to remember events and their dates in the order in which they happened? *Sequencing* means listing facts in the correct order that they occurred. A time line helps you do this. A time line is a diagram that shows how dates and events relate to one another. The years are evenly spaced on most time lines. Time lines may be horizontal or vertical. Events on time lines are described beside the date on which they occurred.

① Learn It!

To understand how to sequence events, follow these steps:

* As you read, look for dates or clue words that hint at chronological order, such as *in 2006, the late 1900s, first, then, finally,* and *after.*

* To read a time line, find the dates on the opposite ends of the time line. These dates show the range of time that is covered.

* Note the equal spacing between dates on the time line. These are the time intervals.

* Study the order of events.

* Look to see how the events relate to one another.

② Practice It!

Examine the time line below and answer the questions.

1. When does the time line begin? When does it end?
2. What major event for a UN agency happened in 1965?
3. In what country did the UN monitor a cease-fire in 1991?
4. During what decade did South Africa hold its first free elections?

③ Apply It!

List key events from one of the chapters in Unit 1 of your textbook that covers the history of the United States. Decide what time period to cover and what time intervals you will put on your time line. Create a time line that lists these events in the order they occurred.

United Nations–50 Years

UN Charter ratified — 1945
UNICEF awarded Nobel Peace Prize — 1965
UN monitors cease-fire in Angola
UN 50th anniversary
First UN Environmental Council meets — 1965
UN monitors first free elections in South Africa
1945 | 1955 | 1965 | 1975 | 1985 | 1995

D Differentiated Instruction

Interpersonal Have students work in small groups to gather information about events in the life of a historical figure, an inventor, or a favorite musical group. Ask them to choose significant events and include them in a time line. Remind students to include the correct time period on the time lines and to place events in chronological order with the proper spacing between events. **AL**

S Skill Practice

Reading a Time Line Have students study the time line on this page. **Ask:** What happened first—the first free elections in South Africa or UNICEF being awarded the Nobel Peace Prize? *(UNICEF's Nobel Peace Prize award)* About how many years were there between the two events? *(about 25 years)* **OL**

Additional Support

Skills Practice Answers

Practice It! Answers

1. 1945; 1995
2. UNICEF awarded the Nobel Peace Prize
3. Angola
4. in the 1990s

Apply It! Answer

Time lines should include key events from the chapter placed in the correct sequence. The time lines should also include clear beginning and end dates and have equal spacing between years.

Skills Handbook

SKILLS HANDBOOK

C Critical Thinking

Drawing Conclusions Ask: Based on the reading, which cases are more serious—civil or criminal? *(Answers will vary. Students should realize that both types of cases range from minor to serious.)* **OL**

SKILLS HANDBOOK

C

Categorizing and Analyzing Information

Why Learn This Skill?

If you looked at the season statistics for your favorite football game to decide if they have a chance at the championship, you would be categorizing and analyzing information about the team.

Categorizing information means you sort information into related groups or topics. Then in analyzing that information, you determine its accuracy and reliability. In the case of football statistics, this process would involve looking at scores, player injuries, yards gained rushing, and other data from the past season.

1 Learn It!

To learn to categorize and analyze information, follow these steps:

- As you read, sort information into categories or groups according to related topics.

- Choose headings for your categories to help you identify relationships.

- Look at the source of information to determine its accuracy. Is it a primary or secondary source?

- Compare the same information from different sources to check reliability and look for contradictions.

2 Practice It!

Read the following excerpt describing laws in the United States, and then answer the questions.

Laws fall into two major groups: criminal and civil. Criminal laws regulate public conduct and set duties owed to society. Criminal laws have penalties and offenders can be imprisoned, fined, or punished in some other way. Civil laws regulate relations between individuals or groups of individuals. A civil action is a lawsuit. As a result, the courts may award the injured person money for his or her loss or require the offender to make amends in some other way.

1. What major categories are discussed in the paragraph?
2. Under what subtopics would you list information in each category?
3. Which would be the more reliable source for this information—a textbook or the newspaper? Why?

3 Apply It!

Choose an article from your newspaper describing the details of a crime. Categorize and analyze to explain it to a classmate. Does the information seem complete and accurate? What is the source? Share your findings.

Skills Practice Answers

Practice It! Answers

1. criminal and civil laws

2. each law's domain (what it regulates) and penalties/results

3. Students might suggest a textbook, as newspapers may mention these cases but not define them.

Apply It! Answer

Have students share their articles with the class. Open up class discussion on the accuracy of the articles.

Additional Support

Flag Etiquette

For Americans, the flag has always had a special meaning. It is a symbol of our nation's freedom and democracy. Over the years, Americans have developed rules and customs concerning the use and display of the flag. One of the most important things every American should remember is to treat the flag with respect.

★ The flag should be raised and lowered by hand and displayed only from sunrise to sunset. On special occasions, the flag may be displayed at night, but it should be illuminated.

★ The flag may be displayed on all days, weather permitting, particularly on national and state holidays and on historic and special occasions.

★ No flag may be flown above the American flag or to the right of it at the same height.

★ The flag should never touch the ground or floor beneath it.

★ The flag may be flown at half-staff by order of the president, usually to mourn the death of a public official.

★ The flag may be flown upside down only to signal distress.

★ The flag should never be carried flat or horizontally, but always carried aloft and free.

★ When the flag becomes old and tattered, it should be destroyed by burning. According to an approved custom, the Union (stars on blue field) is first cut from the flag; then the two pieces, which no longer form a flag, are burned.

Historical Documents

The Magna Carta

The Magna Carta, signed by King John in 1215, marked a decisive step forward in the development of constitutional government in England. Later, it became a model for colonists who carried the Magna Carta's guarantees of legal and political rights to America.

1. . . . [T]hat the English Church shall be free, and shall have its rights entire, and its liberties unimpaired. . . . we have also granted for us and our heirs forever, all the liberties written out below, to have and to keep for them and their heirs, of us and our heirs:

39. No free man shall be seized or imprisoned, or stripped of his rights or possessions, or outlawed or exiled, or deprived of his standing in any other way, nor will we proceed with force against him, or send others to do so, except by the lawful judgment of his equals, or by the law of the land.

40. To no one will we sell, to no one deny or delay right or justice.

41. All merchants may enter or leave England unharmed and without fear, and may stay or travel within it, by land or water, for purposes of trade, free from all illegal exactions, in accordance with ancient and lawful customs. This, however, does not apply in time of war to merchants from a country that is at war with us. . . .

42. In future it shall be lawful for any man to leave and return to our kingdom unharmed and without fear, by land or water, preserving his allegiance to us, except in time of war, for some short period, for the common benefit of the realm. . . .

60. All these customs and liberties that we have granted shall be observed in our kingdom in so far as concerns our own relations with our subjects. Let all men of our kingdom, whether clergy or laymen, observe them similarly in their relations with their own men. . . .

63. . . . Both we and the barons have sworn that all this shall be observed in good faith and without deceit. Witness the abovementioned people and many others. Given by our hand in the meadow that is called Runnymede, between Windsor and Staines, on the fifteenth day of June in the seventeenth year of our reign.

Illuminated manuscript, Middle Ages

The Mayflower Compact

On November 21, 1620, 41 colonists aboard the Mayflower drafted this agreement. The Mayflower Compact was the first plan of self-government ever put in force in the English colonies.

In the Name of God, Amen. We, whose names are underwritten, the Loyal Subjects of our dread Sovereign Lord King James, by the Grace of God, of Great Britain, France, and Ireland, King, Defender of the Faith, etc. Having undertaken for the Glory of God, and Advancement of the Christian Faith, and the Honour of our King and Country, a Voyage to plant the first Colony in the northern Parts of Virginia; Do by these Presents, solemnly and mutually, in the Presence of God and one another, covenant and combine ourselves together into a civil Body Politick, for our better Ordering and Preservation, and Furtherance of the Ends aforesaid: And by Virtue hereof do enact, constitute, and frame, such just and equal Laws, Ordinances, Acts, Constitutions, and Officers, from time to time, as shall be thought most meet and convenient for the general Good of the Colony; unto which we promise all due Submission and Obedience. In Witness whereof we have hereunto subscribed our names at Cape-Cod the eleventh of November, in the Reign of our Sovereign Lord King James, of England, France, and Ireland, the eighteenth, and of Scotland, the fifty-fourth, Anno Domini, 1620.

The Federalist, No. 10

James Madison wrote several articles supporting ratification of the Constitution for a New York newspaper. In the excerpt below, Madison argues for the idea of a federal republic.

By a faction, I understand a number of citizens . . . who are united and actuated by some common impulse . . . adverse to the rights of other citizens. . . .

The inference to which we are brought is that the causes of faction cannot be removed and that relief is only to be sought in the means of controlling its effects. . . .

A republic, by which I mean a government in which the scheme of representation takes place . . . promises the cure for which we are seeking. . . .

The two great points of difference between a democracy and a republic are: first, the delegation of the government, in the latter, to a small number of citizens elected by the rest; secondly, the greater number of citizens, and greater sphere of country, over which the latter may be extended.

James Madison

The effect of the first difference is . . . to refine and enlarge the public views, by passing them through the medium of a chosen body of citizens, whose wisdom may best discern the true interest of their country, and whose patriotism and love of justice will be least likely to sacrifice it to temporary or partial considerations. . . .

Washington's Farewell Address

At the end of his second term as president, George Washington spoke of the dangers facing the young nation. He warned against the dangers of political parties and sectionalism, and he advised the nation against permanent alliances with other nations.

. . . Citizens by birth or choice of a common country, that country has a right to concentrate your affections. The name of American, which belongs to you in your national capacity, must always exalt the just pride of patriotism more than any appellation derived from local discriminations. With slight shades of difference, you have the same religion, manners, habits, and political principles. You have in a common cause fought and triumphed together. . . .

In contemplating the causes which may disturb our union it occurs as matter of serious concern that any ground should have been furnished for characterizing parties by geographical discriminations. . . .

George Washington

No alliances, however strict, between the parts can be an adequate substitute. They must inevitably experience the infractions and interruptions which all alliances in all times have experienced. . . .

The great rule of conduct for us in regard to foreign nations is, in extending our commercial relations to have with them as little political connection as possible. . . .

. . . I anticipate with pleasing expectation that retreat in which I promise myself to realize . . . the sweet enjoyment of partaking in the midst of my fellow citizens the benign influence of good laws under a free government—the ever-favorite object of my heart, and the happy reward, as I trust, of our mutual cares, labors, and dangers.

The Star-Spangled Banner

During the British bombardment of Fort McHenry during the War of 1812, a young Baltimore lawyer named Francis Scott Key was inspired to write the words to "The Star-Spangled Banner." Although it became popular immediately, it was not until 1931 that Congress officially declared "The Star-Spangled Banner" as our national anthem.

O! say can you see by the dawn's early light,

What so proudly we hailed at the twilight's last gleaming,

Whose broad stripes and bright stars through the perilous fight,

O'er the ramparts we watch'd, were so gallantly streaming?

And the Rockets' red glare, the Bombs bursting in air,

Gave proof through the night that our Flag was still there;

O! say does that star-spangled Banner yet wave,

O'er the Land of the free, and the home of the brave!

The Monroe Doctrine

In 1823 President James Monroe proclaimed the Monroe Doctrine. Designed to end European influence in the Western Hemisphere, it became a cornerstone of United States foreign policy.

. . . With the existing colonies or dependencies of any European power we have not interfered and shall not interfere. But with the Governments who have declared their independence and maintained it, and whose independence we have, on great consideration and on just principles, acknowledged, we could not view any interposition for the purpose of oppressing them, or controlling in any other manner their destiny, by any European power in any other light than as the manifestation of any unfriendly disposition toward the United States. . . .

Our policy in regard to Europe, which was adopted at an early stage of the wars which have so long agitated that quarter of the globe, nevertheless remains the same, which is, not to interfere in the internal concerns of any of its powers; to consider the government de facto as the legitimate government for us; to cultivate friendly relations with it, and to preserve those relations by a frank, firm, and manly policy, meeting in all instances the just claims of every power, submitting to injuries from none. . . .

James Monroe

Memorial of the Cherokee Nation

The Indian Removal Act of 1830 called for the relocation of Native Americans to territory west of the Mississippi River. Cherokee leaders protested the policy.

We are aware that some persons suppose it will be for our advantage to remove beyond the Mississippi. We think otherwise. Our people universally think otherwise. . . .

We wish to remain on the land of our fathers. We have a perfect and original right to remain without interruption or molestation. The treaties with us, and laws of the United States made in pursuance of treaties, guaranty our residence and our privileges, and secure us against intruders. Our only request is, that these treaties may be fulfilled, and these laws executed. . . .

. . . We have been called a poor, ignorant, and degraded people. We certainly are not rich; nor have we ever boasted of our knowledge, or our moral or intellectual elevation. But there is not a man within our limits so ignorant as not to know that he has a right to live on the land of his fathers, in the possession of his immemorial privileges, and that this right has been acknowledged by the United States; nor is there a man so degraded as not to feel a keen sense of injury, on being deprived of his right and driven into exile. . . .

The Seneca Falls Declaration

One of the first documents to express the desire for equal rights for women is the Declaration of Sentiments and Resolutions, issued in 1848 at the Seneca Falls Convention in Seneca Falls, New York. Led by Lucretia Mott and Elizabeth Cady Stanton, the delegates adopted a set of resolutions that called for woman suffrage and opportunities for women in employment and education. Excerpts from the Declaration follow.

When, in the course of human events, it becomes necessary for one portion of the family of man to assume among the people of the earth a position different from that which they have hitherto occupied, but one to which the laws of nature and of nature's God entitle them, a decent respect to the opinions of mankind requires that they should declare the causes that impel them to such a course.

We hold these truths to be self-evident: that all men and women are created equal; that they are endowed by their Creator with certain inalienable rights; that among these are life, liberty, and the pursuit of happiness; that to secure these rights governments are instituted, deriving their just powers from the consent of the governed. Whenever any form of government becomes destructive of these ends, it is the right of those who suffer from it to refuse allegiance to it, and to insist upon the institution of a new government, laying its foundation on such principles, and organizing its powers in such form as to them shall seem most likely to effect their safety and happiness. Prudence, indeed, will dictate that governments long established should not be changed for light and transient causes; . . . But when a long train of abuses and usurpations, pursuing invariably the same object, evinces a design to reduce them under absolute despotism, it is their duty to throw off such government, and to provide new guards for their future security. . . .

The history of mankind is a history of repeated injuries and usurpations on the part of man toward woman, having in direct object the establishment of an absolute tyranny over her. To prove this, let facts be submitted to a candid world. . . .

Now, in view of the entire disfranchisement of one-half the people of this country, their social and religious degradation—in view of the unjust laws above mentioned, and because women do feel themselves aggrieved, oppressed, and fraudulently deprived of their most sacred rights, we insist that they have immediate admission to all the rights and privileges which belong to them as citizens of these United States. . . .

Elizabeth Cady Stanton

The Emancipation Proclamation

On January 1, 1863, President Abraham Lincoln issued the Emancipation Proclamation, which freed all enslaved people in states under Confederate control. The Proclamation was a step toward the Thirteenth Amendment (1865), which ended slavery in all of the United States.

... That on the 1st day of January, in the year of our Lord 1863, all persons held as slaves within any state or designated part of a state, the people whereof shall then be in rebellion against the United States, shall be then, thenceforward, and forever free; and the Executive Government of the United States, including the military and naval authority thereof, will recognize and maintain the freedom of such persons, and will do no act or acts to repress such persons, or any of them, in any efforts they may make for their actual freedom.

That the Executive will, on the 1st day of January aforesaid, by proclamation, designate the states and parts of states, if any, in which the people thereof, respectively, shall then be in rebellion against the United States; and the fact that any state, or the people thereof, shall on that day be in good faith represented in the Congress of the United States, by members chosen thereto at elections wherein a majority of the qualified voters of such states shall have participated, shall, in the absence of strong countervailing testimony, be deemed conclusive evidence that such state, and the people thereof, are not then in rebellion against the United States. ...

And, by virtue of the power and for the purpose aforesaid, I do order and declare that all persons held as slaves within said designated states and parts of states are, and henceforward shall be, free; and that the Executive Government of the United States, including the military and naval authorities thereof, will recognize and maintain the freedom of said persons.

And I hereby enjoin upon the people so declared to be free to abstain from all violence, unless in necessary self-defense; and I recommend to them that, all cases when allowed, they labor faithfully for reasonable wages.

And I further declare and make known that such persons, of suitable condition, will be received into the armed service of the United States. ...

And upon this act, sincerely believed to be an act of justice, warranted by the Constitution upon military necessity, I invoke the considerate judgement of mankind and the gracious favor of Almighty God. ...

Abraham Lincoln

The Gettysburg Address

On November 19, 1863, President Abraham Lincoln gave a short speech at the dedication of a national cemetery on the battlefield of Gettysburg. His simple yet eloquent words expressed his hopes for a nation divided by civil war.

Four score and seven years ago our fathers brought forth on this continent a new nation, conceived in liberty, and dedicated to the proposition that all men are created equal.

Now we are engaged in a great civil war, testing whether that nation, or any nation so conceived and so dedicated, can long endure. We are met on a great battlefield of that war. We have come to dedicate a portion of that field as a final resting place for those who here gave their lives that that nation might live. It is altogether fitting and proper that we should do this.

But, in a larger sense, we can not dedicate—we can not consecrate—we can not hallow—this ground. The brave men, living and dead, who struggled here, have consecrated it far above our poor power to add or detract. The world will little note nor long remember what we say here, but it can never forget what they did here. It is for us, the living, rather, to be dedicated here to the unfinished work which they who fought here have thus far so nobly advanced. It is rather for us to be here dedicated to the great task remaining before us—that from these honored dead we take increased devotion to that cause for which they gave the last full measure of devotion; that we here highly resolve that these dead shall not have died in vain; that this nation, under God, shall have a new birth of freedom; and that government of the people, by the people, for the people, shall not perish from the earth.

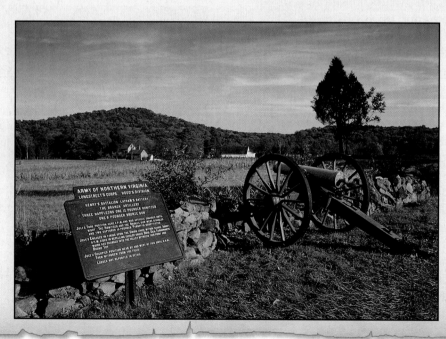

Current day photo of Gettysburg battlefield

I Will Fight No More

In 1877 the Nez Perce fought the government's attempt to move them to a smaller reservation. After a remarkable attempt to escape to Canada, Chief Joseph realized that resistance was hopeless and advised his people to surrender.

Tell General Howard I know his heart. What he told me before I have in my heart.

I am tired of fighting. . . . The old men are all dead. It is the young men who say yes or no. He who led the young men is dead. It is cold and we have no blankets. The little children are freezing to death. My people, some of them have run away to the hills, and have no blankets, no food; no one knows where they are—perhaps freezing to death. I want to have time to look for my children and see how many of them I can find. Maybe I shall find them among the dead. Hear me, my chiefs.

I am tired; my heart is sick and sad. From where the sun now stands I will fight no more forever.

Cheyenne shield

The Pledge of Allegiance

In 1892 the nation celebrated the 400th anniversary of Columbus's landing in America. In connection with this celebration, Francis Bellamy, a magazine editor, wrote and published the Pledge of Allegiance. The words "under God" were added by Congress in 1954 at the urging of President Dwight D. Eisenhower.

I pledge allegiance to the Flag of the United States of America and to the Republic for which it stands, one Nation under God, indivisible, with liberty and justice for all.

Students in a New York City school recite the Pledge of Allegiance

The American's Creed

William Tyler Page of Friendship Heights, Maryland, wrote The American's Creed. This statement of political faith summarizes the true meaning of freedom available to all Americans. The U.S. House of Representatives adopted the creed on behalf of the American people on April 3, 1918.

I believe in the United States of America as a Government of the people, by the people, for the people; whose just powers are derived from the consent of the governed; a democracy in a republic; a sovereign Nation of many sovereign States; a perfect union, one and inseparable; established upon those principles of freedom, equality, justice, and humanity for which American patriots sacrificed their lives and fortunes.

I therefore believe it is my duty to my Country to love it, to support its Constitution, to obey its laws, to respect its flag, and to defend it against all enemies.

The Fourteen Points

On January 8, 1918, President Woodrow Wilson went before Congress to offer a statement of aims called the Fourteen Points. Wilson's plan called for freedom of the seas in peace and war, an end to secret alliances, and equal trading rights for all countries. The excerpt that follows is taken from the president's message.

. . . We entered this war because violations of right had occurred which touched us to the quick and made the life of our own people impossible unless they were corrected and the world secured once for all against their recurrence. What we demand in this war, therefore, is nothing peculiar to ourselves. It is that the world be made fit and safe to live in; and particularly that it be made safe for every peace-loving nation which, like our own, wishes to live its own life, determine its own institutions, be assured of justice and fair dealing by the other peoples of the world as against force and selfish aggression. All the peoples of the world are in effect partners in this interest, and for our own part we see very clearly that unless justice be done to others it will not be done to us. The program of the world's peace, therefore, is our program; and that program, the only possible program, as we see it, is this:

I. Open covenants of peace, openly arrived at, after which there shall be no private international understandings of any kind but diplomacy shall proceed always frankly and in the public view.

II. Absolute freedom of navigation upon the seas, outside territorial waters, alike in peace and in war, except as the seas may be closed in whole or in part by international action for the enforcement of international covenants.

XIV. A general association of nations must be formed under specific covenants for the purpose of affording mutual guarantees of political independence and territorial integrity to great and small states alike. . . .

Brown v. Board of Education

On May 17, 1954, the Supreme Court ruled in Brown v. Board of Education of Topeka, Kansas, that racial segregation in public schools was unconstitutional. This decision provided the legal basis for court challenges to segregation in every aspect of American life.

. . . The plaintiffs contend that segregated public schools are not "equal" and cannot be made "equal" and that hence they are deprived of the equal protection of the laws. Because of the obvious importance of the question presented, the Court took jurisdiction. . . .

Our decision, therefore, cannot turn on merely a comparison of these tangible factors in the Negro and white schools involved in each of the cases. We must look instead to the effect of segregation itself on public education.

In approaching this problem, we cannot turn the clock back to 1868 when the Amendment was adopted, or even to 1896 when Plessy v. Ferguson was written. We must consider public education in the light of its full development and its present place in American life throughout the Nation. Only in this way can it be determined if segregation in public schools deprives these plaintiffs of the equal protection of the laws.

Today, education is perhaps the most important function of state and local governments. Compulsory school attendance laws and the great expenditures for education both demonstrate our recognition of the importance of education to our democratic society. . . . In these days, it is doubtful that any child may reasonably be expected to succeed in life if he is denied the opportunity of an education. Such an opportunity, where the state has undertaken to provide it, is a right which must be made available to all on equal terms.

We come then to the question presented: Does segregation of children in public schools solely on the basis of race, even though the physical facilities and other "tangible" factors may be equal, deprive the children of the minority group of equal educational opportunities? We believe that it does.

. . . We conclude that in the field of public education the doctrine of "separate but equal" has no place. Separate educational facilities are inherently unequal. Therefore, we hold that the plaintiffs and others similarly situated for whom the actions have been brought are, by reason of the segregation complained of, deprived of the equal protection of the laws guaranteed by the Fourteenth Amendment. . . .

Armed guards escort African American students

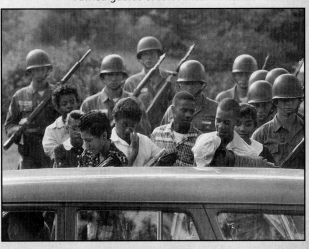

John F. Kennedy's Inaugural Address

President Kennedy's Inaugural Address on January 20, 1961, set the tone for his administration. In his address Kennedy stirred the nation by calling for "a grand and global alliance" to fight tyranny, poverty, disease, and war.

We observe today not a victory of party but a celebration of freedom—symbolizing an end as well as a beginning—signifying renewal as well as change. For I have sworn before you and Almighty God the same solemn oath our forebears prescribed nearly a century and three-quarters ago.

The world is very different now. For man holds in his mortal hands the power to abolish all forms of human poverty and all forms of human life. And yet the same revolutionary beliefs for which our forebears fought are still at issue around the globe—the belief that the rights of man come not from the generosity of the state but from the hand of God.

We dare not forget today that we are the heirs of that first revolution. Let the word go forth from this time and place, to friend and foe alike, that the torch has been passed to a new generation of Americans—born in this century, tempered by war, disciplined by a hard and bitter peace, proud of our ancient heritage—and unwilling to witness or permit the slow undoing of those human rights to which this nation has always been committed, and to which we are committed today at home and around the world.

Let every nation know, whether it wishes us well or ill, that we shall pay any price, bear any burden, meet any hardship, support any friend, oppose any foe to assure the survival and the success of liberty.

This much we pledge—and more.

To those old allies whose cultural and spiritual origins we share, we pledge the loyalty of faithful friends. United, there is little we cannot do in a host of cooperative ventures. Divided, there is little we can do. . . .

Let us never negotiate out of fear. But let us never fear to negotiate.

Let both sides explore what problems unite us instead of belaboring those problems which divide us. . . .

Let both sides seek to invoke the wonders of science instead of its terrors. Together let us explore the stars, conquer the deserts, eradicate disease, tap the ocean depths, and encourage the arts and commerce. . . .

And so, my fellow Americans: ask not what your country can do for you—ask what you can do for your country.

My fellow citizens of the world: ask not what America will do for you, but what together we can do for the freedom of man. . . .

President Kennedy speaking

I Have a Dream

On August 28, 1963, while Congress debated wide-ranging civil rights legislation, Dr. Martin Luther King, Jr., led more than 200,000 people in a march on Washington, D.C. On the steps of the Lincoln Memorial he gave a stirring speech in which he eloquently spoke of his dreams for African Americans and for the United States. Excerpts of the speech follow.

. . . There are those who are asking the devotees of civil rights, "When will you be satisfied?"

We can never be satisfied as long as the Negro is the victim of the unspeakable horrors of police brutality. . . .

We cannot be satisfied as long as the Negro's basic mobility is from a smaller ghetto to a larger one.

We can never be satisfied as long as a Negro in Mississippi cannot vote and a Negro in New York believes he has nothing for which to vote. . . .

I say to you today, my friends, that in spite of the difficulties and frustrations of the moment I still have a dream. It is a dream deeply rooted in the American dream. I have a dream that one day this nation will rise up and live out the true meaning of its creed: "We hold these truths to be self-evident, that all men are created equal."

I have a dream that one day on the red hills of Georgia the sons of former slaves and the sons of former slaveowners will be able to sit down together at the table of brotherhood.

I have a dream that one day even the state of Mississippi, a desert state sweltering with the heat of injustice and oppression, will be transformed into an oasis of freedom and justice.

I have a dream that my four little children will one day live in a nation where they will not be judged by the color of their skin but by the content of their character. . . .

. . . When we let freedom ring, when we let it ring from every village and every hamlet, from every state and every city, we will be able to speed up that day when all of God's children, black men and white men, Jews and Gentiles, Protestants and Catholics, will be able to join hands and sing in the words of the old Negro spiritual: "Free at last! Free at last! Thank God Almighty, we are free at last!"

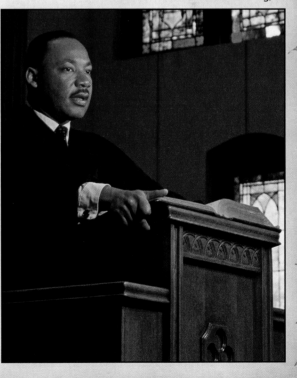

Dr. Martin Luther King, Jr.

Data Bank

Contents

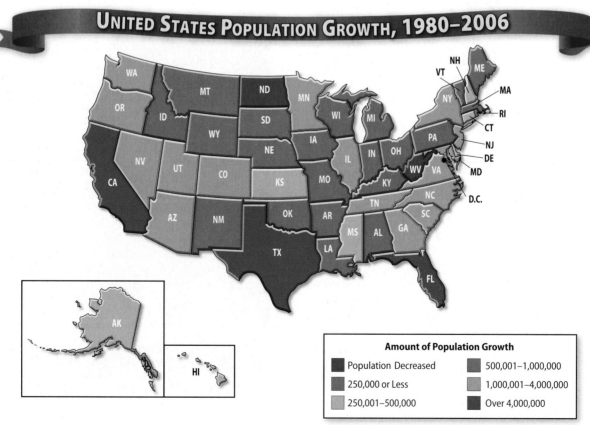

UNITED STATES POPULATION GROWTH, 1980–2006

Amount of Population Growth

- Population Decreased
- 250,000 or Less
- 250,001–500,000
- 500,001–1,000,000
- 1,000,001–4,000,000
- Over 4,000,000

Source: U.S. Bureau of the Census, *Statistical Abstract of the United States,* 2006.

CRIME AND THE JUSTICE SYSTEM

Supreme Court Cases

Supreme Court Decisions

Types of Cases in Federal District Courts, 2007

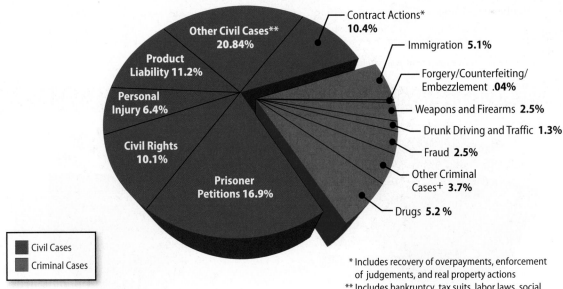

Other Civil Cases** 20.84%

Product Liability 11.2%

Personal Injury 6.4%

Civil Rights 10.1%

Prisoner Petitions 16.9%

Contract Actions* 10.4%

Immigration 5.1%

Forgery/Counterfeiting/ Embezzlement .04%

Weapons and Firearms 2.5%

Drunk Driving and Traffic 1.3%

Fraud 2.5%

Other Criminal Cases+ 3.7%

Drugs 5.2 %

■ Civil Cases
■ Criminal Cases

* Includes recovery of overpayments, enforcement of judgements, and real property actions
** Includes bankruptcy, tax suits, labor laws, social security issues, protected property rights, RICO, other statutory actions, and forfeiture and penalty
+ Includes federal statute violations, sex offenses, larceny/theft, homicide, robbery, assault, and burglary

Sources: U.S. Bureau of the Census, *Statistical Abstract of the United States,* 2008 (Washington, D.C.: 2008); Administrative Office of the U.S. Courts, *Statistical Tables for the Federal Judiciary,* 2007.

BILLS INTRODUCED, PASSED, AND ENACTED BY CONGRESS, 1961–2006

CONGRESS (Years)	BILLS INTRODUCED* House	Senate	BILLS PASSED* House	Senate	BILLS ENACTED
87th (1961–62)	15,751	4,565	2,424	2,345	1,569
88th (1963–64)	15,299	3,937	1,734	1,691	1,026
89th (1965–66)	21,999	4,567	2,148	1,968	1,283
90th (1967–68)	24,227	4,906	1,659	1,731	1,002
91st (1969–70)	23,575	5,466	1,712	1,676	941
92nd (1971–72)	20,458	4,896	1,469	1,371	768
93rd (1973–74)	21,095	5,127	1,524	1,564	774
94th (1975–76)	19,371	4,913	1,624	1,552	729
95th (1977–78)	17,800	4,513	1,615	1,596	803
96th (1979–80)	10,400	4,194	1,478	1,482	736
97th (1981–82)	9,175	3,172	1,058	1,209	528
98th (1983–84)	8,104	4,097	1,348	1,322	677
99th (1985–86)	7,522	4,080	1,368	1,330	690
100th (1987–88)	7,269	4,013	1,502	1,430	758
101st (1989–90)	7,611	4,184	1,370	1,321	666
102nd (1991–92)	7,771	4,245	1,338	1,277	609
103rd (1993–94)	6,647	3,177	1,126	938	473
104th (1995–96)	5,329	2,661	1,012	822	337
105th (1997–98)	5,982	3,161	1,186	891	404
106th (1999–2000)	6,942	3,898	1,534	1,245	604
107th (2001–2002)	7,029	3,770	1,215	948	383
108th (2003–2004)	6,954	3,716	1,421	1,253	281
109th (2005–2006)	7,568	4,543	1,113	972	281

Source: thomas.loc.gov
*Includes House and Senate resolutions, joint resolutions, and concurrent resolutions.

FEDERAL REVENUE BY SOURCE, 2007

2.6%
45.3%
14.4%
33.8%
1.9%
1.0%
1.0%

Corporate Income Taxes
Customs Duties
Estate and Gift Taxes
Excise Taxes
Individual Income Taxes
Other Receipts
Social Insurance Taxes and Contributions

EXPENDITURES BY TYPE, 2007

3.6%
35.6%
9.7%
12.4%
27.0%
11.7%

Income Support
Medicaid
Social Security
Medicare
Other Retirement and Disability
Other Programs

* Percentages may not total 100% due to rounding.

Source: U.S. Congressional Budget Office, U.S. Congress, www.cbo.gov

FEDERAL REVENUES, EXPENDITURES, AND DEBTS, 1960–2006

Federal Revenues and Expenditures, 1965-2005

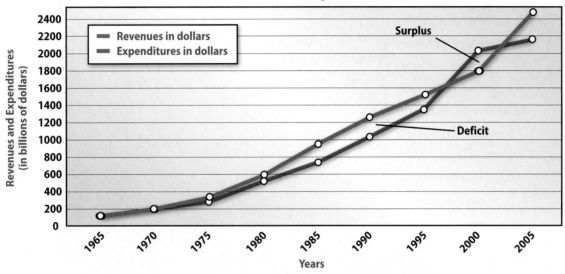

Gross Federal Debt, 1965–2005

National Debt per Capita, 1960–2006*

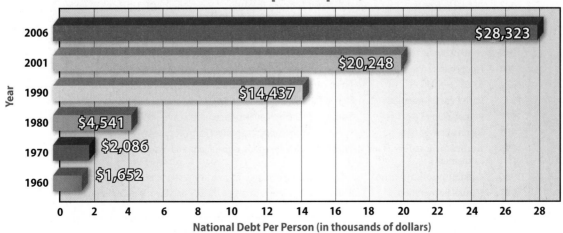

* Includes federal debt held by public and by the federal government.
Source: U.S. Bureau of the Census; U.S. Bureau of Public Debt; *Statistical Abstract of the United States,* 2001.

EXECUTIVE DEPARTMENT CIVILIAN EMPLOYEES*

Department	Number of Employees (in thousands)
Department of Defense	676,452
Department of Veterans Affairs	236,938
Department of Homeland Security	151,771
Department of the Treasury	112,000
Department of Justice	106,159
Department of Agriculture	101,887
Department of Transportation	53,573
Department of the Interior	71,593
Department of Health and Human Services	60,756
Department of Commerce	40,335
Department of State	33,968
Department of Labor	15,434
Department of Energy	14,838
Department of Housing and Urban Development	9,814
Department of Education	4,257

*as of September 2006

Source: U.S. Bureau of the Census, *Statistical Abstract of the United States,* 2008 (Washington, D.C.: 2008).

Number of Employees (in thousands)

MAJOR UNITED STATES TREATIES

Year	Treaty	Major Provisions
1783	**Treaty of Paris**	Great Britain recognized U.S. independence
1795	**Pinckney's Treaty**	Spain granted U.S. navigation rights on Mississippi River
1803	**Louisiana Purchase**	U.S. gained Louisiana Territory from France
1818	**Convention of 1818**	Set border with Canada west from Great Lakes as the 49th parallel
1819	**Adams-Onís Treaty**	Spain ceded Florida; U.S. border set with Spanish territory in West
1846	**Oregon Treaty**	Signed with Great Britain to settle claims to Oregon Country
1848	**Treaty of Guadalupe Hidalgo**	Ended Mexican War; U.S. gained Southwest and California
1867	**Alaska Purchase**	U.S. gained Alaska from Russia
1898	**Treaty of Paris**	Ended Spanish-American War; U.S. gained Puerto Rico and Philippines
1903	**Hay-Buneau-Varilla Treaty**	Signed with Panama to give U.S. right to build Panama Canal
1949	**North Atlantic Treaty**	Multinational agreement for defense of Western Europe; created NATO
1968	**Nonproliferation Treaty**	International agreement to prevent spread of nuclear weapons
1972	**SALT I**	Agreements between U.S. and Soviet Union to limit nuclear weapons
1973	**Paris Peace Agreement**	Signed with North Vietnam to end U.S. involvement in Vietnam War
1977	**Panama Canal Treaties**	Transferred Panama Canal to Panama effective in 1999
1985	**Vienna Convention**	International agreement to protect Earth's ozone layer
1993	**North American Free Trade Agreement**	Established duty-free trade with Canada and Mexico
1996	**Counterterrorism Accord**	Israel and U.S. agreed to cooperate in investigation of terrorist acts
1997	**Mutual Recognition Agreement**	Reduced trade barriers between the U.S. and European Community

Sources: U.S. State Department, *Treaties in Force;* Findling, *Dictionary of American Diplomatic History,* 2nd ed. (New York: Greenwood Press, 1989).

THE WHITE HOUSE . . .
The President's Home

White House Statistics

3 Elevators
5 Major Floors with:
2 Basements
7 Staircases
12 Chimneys
32 Bathrooms
132 Rooms
160 Windows
412 Doors

White House Technology Firsts

1834 Indoor Plumbing
1845 Central Heating
1848 Gas Lighting
1866 Telegraph
1877 Telephone
1891 Electricity
1921 Radio
1926 Electric Refrigerator
1933 Air Conditioning
1942 Bomb Shelter
1947 Television
1979 Computer

Did You Know?

■ *The first baby born in the White House* was Thomas Jefferson's grandson in 1806.

■ *The first White House wedding held* was for Dolley Madison's sister in 1812.

■ *General Lafayette visited the White House in 1825* with his pet alligator, which he kept in the East Room.

■ *Cows grazed on the front lawn of the White House* up until 1913.

■ *The only president married in the White House* was Grover Cleveland, in 1886.

STATE REVENUES AND EXPENDITURES, 2004

Revenue by Category

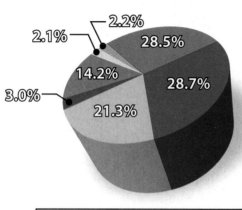

- 28.5%
- 28.7%
- 21.3%
- 14.2%
- 3.0%
- 2.1%
- 2.2%

- Intergovernmental
- Sales Taxes
- Licenses
- Individual Income Taxes
- Corporate Income Taxes
- Other Taxes
- Miscellaneous Revenue

* Percentages may not total 100% due to rounding.

Expenditures by Category

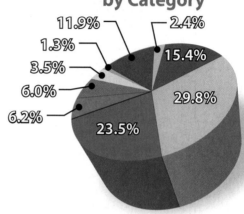

- 11.9%
- 1.3%
- 3.5%
- 6.0%
- 6.2%
- 2.4%
- 15.4%
- 29.8%
- 23.5%

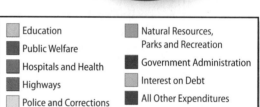

- Education
- Public Welfare
- Hospitals and Health
- Highways
- Police and Corrections
- Natural Resources, Parks and Recreation
- Government Administration
- Interest on Debt
- All Other Expenditures

Source: U.S. Bureau of the Census.

STATE EXPENDITURES FOR PUBLIC EDUCATION

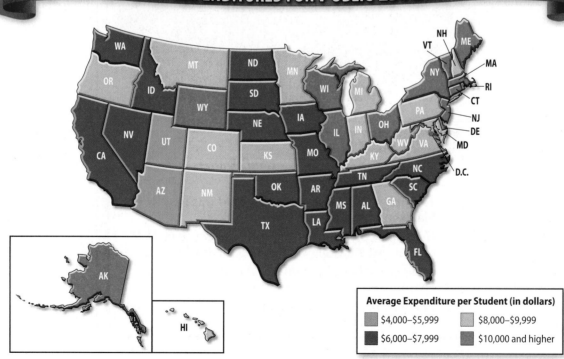

Average Expenditure per Student (in dollars)

- $4,000–$5,999
- $6,000–$7,999
- $8,000–$9,999
- $10,000 and higher

Source: U.S Bureau of the Census.

SIZE OF STATE LEGISLATURES

State	House Members	Senate Members
Alabama	105	35
Alaska	40	20
Arizona	60	30
Arkansas	100	35
California	80	40
Colorado	65	35
Connecticut	151	36
Delaware	41	21
Florida	120	40
Georgia	180	56
Hawaii	51	25
Idaho	70	35
Illinois	118	59
Indiana	100	50
Iowa	100	50
Kansas	125	40
Kentucky	100	38
Louisiana	105	39
Maine	151	35
Maryland	141	47
Massachusetts	160	40
Michigan	110	38
Minnesota	134	67
Mississippi	122	52
Missouri	163	34
Montana	100	50
Nebraska	N/A	49
Nevada	42	21
New Hampshire	400	24
New Jersey	80	40
New Mexico	70	42
New York	150	62
North Carolina	120	50
North Dakota	94	47
Ohio	99	33
Oklahoma	101	48
Oregon	60	30
Pennsylvania	203	50
Rhode Island	75	38
South Carolina	124	46
South Dakota	70	35
Tennessee	99	33
Texas	150	31
Utah	75	29
Vermont	150	30
Virginia	100	40
Washington	98	49
West Virginia	100	34
Wisconsin	99	33
Wyoming	60	30

Source: *The World Almanac and Book of Facts*, 2005.

STATE LEGISLATORS' COMPENSATION

State	Salary	Expense allowance during session
Alabama	$10/day*	$2,280/month
Alaska	$24,012	$163–218/day
Arizona	$24,000	$35–60/day
Arkansas	$14,765	$130/day
California	$113,098	$162/day
Colorado	$30,000	$45–99/day
Connecticut	$28,000	$0
Delaware	$42,000	$0
Florida	$30,996	$126/day
Georgia	$17,342	$173/day
Hawaii	$35,900	$10–120/day
Idaho	$16,116	$49–122/day
Illinois	$57,619	$125/day
Indiana	$11,600	$137/day
Iowa	$25,000	$88–118/day
Kansas	$84.80/day*	$99/day
Kentucky	$180.54/day*	$108.90/day
Louisiana	$16,800	$138/day
Maine	$12,713	$70/day
Maryland	$43,500	$157/day
Massachusetts	$58,237.15	$10–100/day
Michigan	$79,650	$12,000/year
Minnesota	$31,140.90	$77–96/day
Mississippi	$10,000	$91/day
Missouri	$31,351	$79.20/day
Montana	$82.67/day+	$98.75/day
Nebraska	$12,000	$39–99/day
Nevada	$137.90/day*	federal rate
New Hampshire	$200	$0
New Jersey	$49,000	$0
New Mexico	$0	$142/day
New York	$79,500	varies
North Carolina	$13,951	$104/day
North Dakota	$125/day*	up to $900/month
Ohio	$58,933.56	$0
Oklahoma	$38,400	$122/day
Oregon	$18,408	$99/day
Pennsylvania	$73,613	$129/day
Rhode Island	$13,089.44	$0
South Carolina	$10,400	$119/day
South Dakota	$6,000	$110/day
Tennessee	$18,123	$153/day
Texas	$7,200	$139/day
Utah	$130/day*	$144/day
Vermont	$600.78/week+	$51–139/day
Virginia	$18,000	$135–140/day
Washington	$36,311	$90/day
West Virginia	$15,000	$115/day
Wisconsin	$47,413	$88/day
Wyoming	$150/day+	$85/day

* calendar day
+ legislative day
Source: National Conference of State Legislatures, www.ncsl.org ,2007

Supreme Court Case Summaries

CONTENTS

Brown v. Board of Education
1954

In *Brown* v. *Board of Education of Topeka, Kansas,* the Supreme Court overruled *Plessy* v. *Ferguson* (1896) [see p. 259] making the separate-but-equal doctrine in public schools unconstitutional. The Supreme Court rejected the idea that truly equal but separate schools for African American and white students would be constitutional. The Court explained that the Fourteenth Amendment's requirement that all persons be guaranteed equal protection of the law is not met simply by ensuring that African American and white schools "have been equalized . . . with respect to buildings, curricula, qualifications and salaries, and other tangible factors."

The Court then ruled that racial segregation in public schools violates the Equal Protection Clause of the Constitution because it is inherently unequal. In other words, nothing can make racially segregated public schools equal under the Constitution because the very fact of separation marks the separated race as inferior. In practical terms, the Court's decision in this case has been extended beyond public education to virtually all public accommodations and activities.

George E.C. Hayes, Thurgood Marshall, and James Nabrit, Jr., were attorneys who argued the case against segregation in *Brown* v. *Board of Education*.

Bush v. Gore
2000

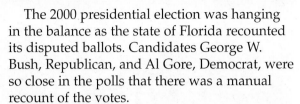

The 2000 presidential election was hanging in the balance as the state of Florida recounted its disputed ballots. Candidates George W. Bush, Republican, and Al Gore, Democrat, were so close in the polls that there was a manual recount of the votes.

Bush went to the Court to stop the recount, stating that it violated the Fourteenth Amendment. The Court ruled that since the manual recount had no uniform way to judge each disputed vote equally, it did violate the Constitution and had to be stopped. As a result, Bush won Florida's electoral votes and became President.

District of Columbia v. Heller
2008

In *District of Columbia* v. *Heller* the Supreme Court for the first time ruled that the Constitution protects an individual's right to have a gun. In a landmark decision, the justices stated that the Second Amendment guaranteed a citizen the right to possess a gun "for traditionally lawful purposes, such as self-defense within the home," in addition to the right of governments to form militias. The case stemmed from protests that the Washington, D.C., strict gun law made it nearly impossible to legally possess a gun within the District of Columbia.

Dred Scott v. Sandford
1857

Dred Scott was taken by slaveholder John Sanford to the free state of Illinois and to the Wisconsin Territory, which had also banned slavery. Later they returned to Missouri, a slave state. Several years later, Scott sued for his freedom under the Missouri legal principle of "once free, always free." In other words, under Missouri law, enslaved people were entitled to freedom if they had lived in a free state at any time. Missouri courts ruled against Scott, but he appealed the case all the way to the United States Supreme Court.

Dred Scott

The Supreme Court decided this case before the Fourteenth Amendment was added to the Constitution. (The Fourteenth Amendment provides that anyone born or naturalized in the United States is a citizen of the nation and of his or her state of residence.) The Court held that enslaved African Americans were property, not citizens, and thus had no rights under the Constitution.

Furman v. Georgia
1972

This decision put a halt to the application of the death penalty under state laws then in effect. For the first time, the Supreme Court ruled that the death penalty amounted to cruel and unusual punishment, which is outlawed in the Constitution. The Court explained that existing death penalty laws did not give juries enough guidance in deciding whether or not to impose the death penalty. As a result, the death penalty in many cases was imposed arbitrarily, that is, without a reasonable basis in the facts and circumstances of the offender or the crime.

The *Furman* decision halted all executions in the 39 states that had death penalty laws at that time. Since the decision, 38 states have rewritten death penalty laws to meet the requirements established in the *Furman* case.

Gibbons v. Ogden
1824

Thomas Gibbons had a federal license to operate a steamboat along the coast, but he did not have a license from the state of New York to travel on New York waters. He wanted to run a steamboat line between Manhattan and New Jersey that would compete with Aaron Ogden's company. Ogden had a New York license. Gibbons sued for the freedom to use his federal license to compete against Ogden on New York waters.

Gibbons won the case. The Supreme Court made it clear that the authority of Congress to regulate interstate commerce (among states) includes the authority to regulate intrastate commerce (within a single state) that bears on, or relates to, interstate commerce.

Gideon v. Wainwright
1963

After being accused of robbery, Clarence Gideon defended himself in a Florida court because the judge in the case refused to appoint a free lawyer. The jury found Gideon guilty. Eventually, Gideon appealed his conviction to the United States Supreme Court, claiming that by failing to appoint a lawyer, the lower court had violated his rights under the Sixth and Fourteenth Amendments.

The Supreme Court agreed with Gideon. In *Gideon* v. *Wainwright* the Supreme Court held for the first time that poor defendants in criminal cases have the right to a state-paid attorney under the Sixth Amendment. The rule announced in this case has been refined to apply whenever the defendant, if convicted, can be sentenced to more than six months in jail or prison.

In 1983 Fred Korematsu (center) won a reversal of his conviction.

Korematsu v. United States
1944

After the Japanese bombing of Pearl Harbor in 1941, thousands of Japanese Americans on the West Coast were forced to abandon their homes and businesses, and they were moved to internment camps in California, Idaho, Utah, Arizona, Wyoming, Colorado, and Arkansas. The prison-like camps offered poor food and cramped quarters.

The Supreme Court's decision in *Korematsu* v. *United States* upheld the authority of the federal government to move Japanese Americans, many of whom were citizens, from designated military areas that included almost the entire West Coast. The government defended the so-called exclusion orders as a necessary response to Japan's attack on Pearl Harbor. Only after his reelection in 1944 did President Franklin Roosevelt rescind the evacuation orders, and by the end of 1945 the camps were closed.

Marbury v. Madison
1803

During his last days in office, President John Adams commissioned William Marbury and several other men as judges. This action by Federalist president Adams angered the incoming Democratic-Republican president Thomas Jefferson. Jefferson then ordered James Madison, his secretary of state, not to deliver the commissions, thus blocking the appointments. William Marbury sued, asking the Supreme Court to order Madison to deliver the commission that would make him a judge.

The Court ruled against Marbury, but more importantly, the decision in this case established one of the most significant principles of American constitutional law. The Supreme Court held that it is the Court itself that has the final say on what the Constitution means. This is known as judicial review. It is also the Supreme Court that has the final say in whether or not an act of government—legislative or executive at the federal, state, or local level—violates the Constitution.

McCulloch v. Maryland
1819

Following the War of 1812, the United States experienced years of high inflation and general economic turmoil. In an attempt to stabilize the economy, the United States Congress chartered a Second Bank of the United States in 1816. Maryland and several other states, however, opposed the competition that the new national bank created and passed laws taxing its branches. In 1818, James McCulloch, head of the Baltimore branch of the Second Bank of the United States, refused to pay the tax to the state of Maryland. The case worked its way through the Maryland state courts all the way to the United States Supreme Court.

The Supreme Court declared the Maryland tax unconstitutional and void. More importantly, the decision established the foundation for expanded congressional authority. The Court held that the necessary and proper clause of the Constitution allows Congress to do more than the Constitution expressly authorizes it to do. The decision allows Congress to enact nearly any law that will help it achieve any of its duties as set forth in the Constitution. For example, Congress has the express authority to regulate interstate commerce. The necessary and proper clause permits Congress to do so in ways not actually specified in the Constitution.

Minnesota v. Mille Lacs Band of Chippewa Indians
1999

An 1855 treaty with the United States set aside lands in present-day Minnesota and Wisconsin to several Chippewa bands as reservations at Mille Lacs, but made no mention of, among other things, whether it abolished rights guaranteed by previous treaties. Minnesota was admitted to the Union in 1858. In 1990, the Mille Lacs Band and several members sued Minnesota, its Department of Natural Resources, and state officials (collectively State), seeking, among other things, a declaratory judgment that they retained their ownership rights to the land without state interference. The District Court ultimately concluded that the Chippewa retained their claim under the 1837 treaty and resolved several resource allocation and regulation issues. The State's argument under the "equal footing doctrine," that Minnesota's entrance into the Union in 1855 extinguished any Indian treaty rights, was considered void. The Supreme Court ruled in favor of the Chippewa and the existing 1837 treaty.

Miranda v. Arizona
1966

In 1963, police in Arizona arrested Ernesto Miranda for kidnapping. The court found Miranda guilty on the basis of a signed confession. The police admitted that neither before nor during the questioning had Miranda been advised of his right to consult with an attorney before answering any questions or of his right to have an attorney present during the interrogation. Miranda appealed his conviction, claiming that police had violated his right against self-incrimination under the Fifth Amendment by not informing him of his legal rights during questioning.

Miranda won the case. The Supreme Court held that a person in police custody cannot be questioned unless told that: 1) he or she has the right to remain silent, 2) he or she has the right to an attorney (at government expense if the accused is unable to pay), and 3) anything the person says after stating that he or she understands these rights can be used as evidence of guilt at trial. These rights have come to be called the Miranda warning. They are intended to ensure that an accused person in custody will not unknowingly give up the Fifth Amendment's protection against self-incrimination.

In 1963, the arrest of Ernesto Miranda (left) led to a landmark decision.

New York Times Company v. United States
1971

In June 1971, the *New York Times* published the "Pentagon Papers," a classified document about government actions in the Vietnam War era. The secret document had been leaked to the *Times* by antiwar activist Daniel Ellsberg. President Richard Nixon went to court to block further publication of the Pentagon Papers. The *New York Times* appealed to the Supreme Court to allow it to continue publishing without government interference.

The Supreme Court's ruling in this case upheld earlier decisions establishing the doctrine of prior restraint. This doctrine protects the press (broadly defined to include newspapers, television and radio, filmmakers and distributors, etc.) from government attempts to block publication. Except in extraordinary circumstances, the press must be allowed to publish.

Plessy v. Ferguson
1896

In the late 1800s, railroad companies in Louisiana were required by state law to provide "separate-but-equal" cars for white and African American passengers. In 1890 a group of citizens in New Orleans selected Homer Plessy to challenge that law. In 1892, Plessy boarded a whites-only car and refused to move. He was arrested. Plessy appealed to the Supreme Court, arguing that the Louisiana separate-but-equal law violated his right to equal protection under the Fourteenth Amendment.

Homer Plessy lost the case. The *Plessy* decision upheld the separate-but-equal doctrine used by Southern states to perpetuate segregation following the Civil War. The court ruled that the Fourteenth Amendment's clause required only equal public facilities for the two races, not equal access to the same facilities. This decision was overruled in 1954 by *Brown v. Board of Education of Topeka, Kansas*.

Roe v. Wade
1973

Roe v. *Wade* challenged restrictive abortion laws in both Texas and Georgia. The suit was brought in the name of Jane Roe, an alias.

In this decision, the Supreme Court ruled that females have a constitutional right under various provisions of the Constitution—most notably, the due process clause—to decide whether or not to terminate a pregnancy. The Court's decision was the most significant in decisions over a period of 50 years that recognized a constitutional right of privacy, even though the word *privacy* is not found in the Constitution.

Tinker v. Des Moines School District
1969

During the Vietnam War, some students in Des Moines, Iowa, wore black armbands to school to protest American involvement in the conflict and were suspended. Two days earlier, school officials had adopted a policy banning the wearing of armbands. The students argued that school officials violated their First Amendment right to free speech.

The Supreme Court sided with the students. The Court said that "it can hardly be argued that either students or teachers shed their constitutional rights of freedom of speech or expression at the schoolhouse gate." It ruled that a public school could not suspend students who wore black armbands to school to symbolize their opposition to the Vietnam War. In so holding, the Court likened the students' conduct to pure speech.

United States v. Nixon
1974

In the early 1970s, President Nixon was named an unindicted co-conspirator in the criminal investigation that arose in the aftermath of a break-in at the offices of the Democratic Party in Washington, D.C. A federal judge had ordered President Nixon to turn over tapes of conversations he had with

President Nixon encounters angry protesters in 1974 during the Watergate scandal.

his advisers about the break-in. Nixon resisted the order, claiming that the conversations were entitled to absolute confidentiality by Article II of the Constitution.

The decision in this case made it clear that the president is not above the law. The Supreme Court held that only those presidential conversations and communications that relate to performing the duties of the office of president are confidential and protected from a judicial order of disclosure. The Court ordered Nixon to give up the tapes, which revealed evidence linking the president to the conspiracy to obstruct justice. He resigned from office shortly thereafter.

Worcester v. Georgia
1832

State officials in Georgia wanted to remove the Cherokees from land that had been guaranteed to them in earlier treaties. Samuel Worcester was a congregational missionary who worked with the Cherokee people. He was arrested for failure to have a license that the state required

to live in Cherokee country and for refusing to obey an order from the Georgia militia to leave Cherokee lands. Worcester then sued the state of Georgia. He claimed that Georgia had no legal authority on Cherokee land because the United States government recognized the Cherokee in Georgia as a separate nation.

The Supreme Court agreed with Worcester by a vote of 5 to 1. Chief Justice John Marshall wrote the majority opinion, which said that Native American nations were a distinct people with the right to have independent political communities and that only the federal government had authority over matters that involved the Cherokee.

President Andrew Jackson supported Georgia's efforts to remove the Cherokee to Indian Territory and refused to enforce the Court's ruling. After the ruling Jackson remarked, "John Marshall has made his decision. Now let him enforce it." As a result of Jackson's refusal to enforce the Court's order, thousands of Cherokees died on the long, forced trek to Indian Territory, known as the "Trail of Tears."

United States Facts

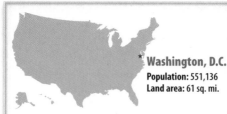

Washington, D.C.
Population: 551,136
Land area: 61 sq. mi.

U.S. Territories

Puerto Rico
Population: 3,912,000
Land area: 3,425 sq. mi.

Guam
Population: 168,564 (est.)
Land area: 209 sq. mi.

U.S. Virgin Islands
Population: 108,708 (est.)
Land area: 134 sq. mi.

American Samoa
Population: 57,881 (est.)
Land area: 77 sq. mi.

The states are listed in the order they were admitted to the Union.

Population figures are based on the U.S. Bureau of the Census projection for July 2005. House of Representatives figures from the 2000 census are from the Clerk of the House of Representatives. States are not drawn to scale.

1 Delaware
Year Admitted: 1787
Population: 836,687
Land area: 1,955 sq. mi.
Representatives: 1

★ Dover

2 Pennsylvania
Year Admitted: 1787
Population: 12,426,603
Land area: 44,820 sq. mi.
Representatives: 19

★ Harrisburg

3 New Jersey
Year Admitted: 1787
Population: 8,745,279
Land area: 7,419 sq. mi.
Representatives: 13

Trenton ★

9 New Hampshire
Year Admitted: 1788
Population: 1,314,821
Land area: 8,969 sq. mi.
Representatives: 2

Concord ★

10 Virginia
Year Admitted: 1788
Population: 7,552,581
Land area: 39,598 sq. mi.
Representatives: 11

Richmond ★

11 New York
Year Admitted: 1788
Population: 19,258,082
Land area: 47,224 sq. mi.
Representatives: 29

★ Albany

17 Ohio
Year Admitted: 1803
Population: 11,477,557
Land area: 40,953 sq. mi.
Representatives: 18

★ Columbus

18 Louisiana
Year Admitted: 1812
Population: 4,534,310
Land area: 43,566 sq. mi.
Representatives: 7

★ Baton Rouge

19 Indiana
Year Admitted: 1816
Population: 6,249,617
Land area: 35,870 sq. mi.
Representatives: 9

Indianapolis ★

24 Missouri
Year Admitted: 1821
Population: 5,765,166
Land area: 68,898 sq. mi.
Representatives: 9

Jefferson City ★

25 Arkansas
Year Admitted: 1836
Population: 2,777,007
Land area: 52,075 sq. mi.
Representatives: 4

Little Rock ★

26 Michigan
Year Admitted: 1837
Population: 10,207,421
Land area: 56,809 sq. mi.
Representatives: 15

Lansing ★

27 Florida
Year Admitted: 1845
Population: 17,509,827
Land area: 53,997 sq. mi.
Representatives: 25

★ Tallahassee

28 Texas
Year Admitted: 1845
Population: 22,775,004
Land area: 261,914 sq. mi.
Representatives: 32

Austin ★

33 Oregon
Year Admitted: 1859
Population: 3,596,083
Land area: 96,003 sq. mi.
Representatives: 5

★ Salem

34 Kansas
Year Admitted: 1861
Population: 2,751,509
Land area: 81,823 sq. mi.
Representatives: 4

Topeka ★

35 West Virginia
Year Admitted: 1863
Population: 1,818,887
Land area: 24,087 sq. mi.
Representatives: 3

★ Charleston

36 Nevada
Year Admitted: 1864
Population: 2,352,086
Land area: 109,806 sq. mi.
Representatives: 3

★ Carson City

37 Nebraska
Year Admitted: 1867
Population: 1,744,370
Land area: 76,878 sq. mi.
Representatives: 3

Lincoln ★

42 Washington
Year Admitted: 1889
Population: 6,204,632
Land area: 66,582 sq. mi.
Representatives: 9

★ Olympia

43 Idaho
Year Admitted: 1890
Population: 1,407,060
Land area: 82,751 sq. mi.
Representatives: 2

★ Boise

44 Wyoming
Year Admitted: 1890
Population: 507,268
Land area: 97,105 sq. mi.
Representatives: 1

Cheyenne ★

45 Utah
Year Admitted: 1896
Population: 2,417,998
Land area: 82,168 sq. mi.
Representatives: 3

★ Salt Lake City

46 Oklahoma
Year Admitted: 1907
Population: 3,521,379
Land area: 68,679 sq. mi.
Representatives: 5

Oklahoma City ★

4 Georgia
Year Admitted: 1788
Population: 8,925,796
Land area: 57,919 sq. mi.
Representatives: 13

★ Atlanta

5 Connecticut
Year Admitted: 1788
Population: 3,503,185
Land area: 4,845 sq. mi.
Representatives: 5

★ Hartford

6 Massachusetts
Year Admitted: 1788
Population: 6,518,868
Land area: 7,838 sq. mi.
Representatives: 10

Boston ★

7 Maryland
Year Admitted: 1788
Population: 5,600,563
Land area: 9,775 sq. mi.
Representatives: 8

Annapolis ★

8 South Carolina
Year Admitted: 1788
Population: 4,239,310
Land area: 30,111 sq. mi.
Representatives: 6

Columbia ★

12 North Carolina
Year Admitted: 1789
Population: 8,702,410
Land area: 48,718 sq. mi.
Representatives: 13-

★ Raleigh

13 Rhode Island
Year Admitted: 1790
Population: 1,086,575
Land area: 1,045 sq. mi.
Representatives: 2

★ Providence

14 Vermont
Year Admitted: 1791
Population: 630,979
Land area: 9,249 sq. mi.
Representatives: 1

★ Montpelier

15 Kentucky
Year Admitted: 1792
Population: 4,163,360
Land area: 39,732 sq. mi.
Representatives: 6

Frankfort ★

16 Tennessee
Year Admitted: 1796
Population: 5,965,317
Land area: 41,220 sq. mi.
Representatives: 9

★ Nashville

20 Mississippi
Year Admitted: 1817
Population: 2,915,696
Land area: 46,914 sq. mi.
Representatives: 4

★ Jackson

21 Illinois
Year Admitted: 1818
Population: 12,699,336
Land area: 55,593 sq. mi.
Representatives: 19

★ Springfield

22 Alabama
Year Admitted: 1819
Population: 4,527,1660
Land area: 50,750 sq. mi.
Representatives: 7

Montgomery ★

23 Maine
Year Admitted: 1820
Population: 1,318,557
Land area: 30,865 sq. mi.
Representatives: 2

★ Augusta

29 Iowa
Year Admitted: 1846
Population: 2,973,700
Land area: 55,875 sq. mi.
Representatives: 5

Des Moines ★

30 Wisconsin
Year Admitted: 1848
Population: 5,554,343
Land area: 54,314 sq. mi.
Representatives: 8

Madison ★

31 California
Year Admitted: 1850
Population: 36,038,859
Land area: 155,973 sq. mi.
Representatives: 53

Sacramento ★

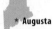

32 Minnesota
Year Admitted: 1858
Population: 5,174,743
Land area: 79,617 sq. mi.
Representatives: 8

Saint Paul ★

38 Colorado
Year Admitted: 1876
Population: 4,617,962
Land area: 103,730 sq. mi.
Representatives: 7

Denver ★

39 North Dakota
Year Admitted: 1889
Population: 635,468
Land area: 68,994 sq. mi.
Representatives: 1

Bismarck ★

40 South Dakota
Year Admitted: 1889
Population: 771,803
Land area: 75,898 sq. mi.
Representatives: 1

Pierre ★

41 Montana
Year Admitted: 1889
Population: 933,005
Land area: 145,556 sq. mi.
Representatives: 1

★ Helena

47 New Mexico
Year Admitted: 1912
Population: 1,902,057
Land area: 121,365 sq. mi.
Representatives: 3

★ Santa Fe

48 Arizona
Year Admitted: 1912
Population: 5,868,004
Land area: 113,642 sq. mi.
Representatives: 8

Phoenix ★

49 Alaska
Year Admitted: 1959
Population: 661,110
Land area: 570,374 sq. mi.
Representatives: 1

Juneau ★

50 Hawaii
Year Admitted: 1959
Population: 1,276,552
Land area: 6,432 sq. mi.
Representatives: 2

Honolulu ★

UNITED STATES FACTS

United States Presidents

In this resource you will find portraits of the individuals who served as presidents of the United States, along with their occupations, political party affiliations, and other interesting facts.

George Washington 1

Presidential term: 1789–1797
Lived: 1732–1799
Born in: Virginia
Elected from: Virginia
Occupations: Soldier, Planter
Party: None
Vice President: John Adams

John Adams 2

Presidential term: 1797–1801
Lived: 1735–1826
Born in: Massachusetts
Elected from: Massachusetts
Occupations: Teacher, Lawyer
Party: Federalist
Vice President: Thomas Jefferson

Thomas Jefferson 3

Presidential term: 1801–1809
Lived: 1743–1826
Born in: Virginia
Elected from: Virginia
Occupations: Planter, Lawyer
Party: Republican**
Vice Presidents: Aaron Burr,
George Clinton

James Madison 4

Presidential term: 1809–1817
Lived: 1751–1836
Born in: Virginia
Elected from: Virginia
Occupation: Planter
Party: Republican**
Vice Presidents: George Clinton,
Elbridge Gerry

James Monroe 5

Presidential term: 1817–1825
Lived: 1758–1831
Born in: Virginia
Elected from: Virginia
Occupation: Lawyer
Party: Republican**
Vice President: Daniel D.
Tompkins

John Quincy Adams 6

Presidential term: 1825–1829
Lived: 1767–1848
Born in: Massachusetts
Elected from: Massachusetts
Occupation: Lawyer
Party: Republican**
Vice President: John C. Calhoun

Andrew Jackson 7

Presidential term: 1829–1837
Lived: 1767–1845
Born in: South Carolina
Elected from: Tennessee
Occupations: Lawyer, Soldier
Party: Democratic
Vice Presidents: John C. Calhoun,
Martin Van Buren

Martin Van Buren 8

Presidential term: 1837–1841
Lived: 1782–1862
Born in: New York
Elected from: New York
Occupation: Lawyer
Party: Democratic
Vice President: Richard M.
Johnson

William H. Harrison 9

Presidential term: 1841
Lived: 1773–1841
Born in: Virginia
Elected from: Ohio
Occupations: Soldier, Planter
Party: Whig
Vice President: John Tyler

*** The Republican Party during this period developed into today's Democratic Party. Today's Republican Party originated in 1854.*

U.S. PRESIDENTS

U.S. Presidents

John Tyler
10

Presidential term: 1841–1845
Lived: 1790–1862
Born in: Virginia
Elected as V.P. from: Virginia
 Succeeded Harrison
Occupation: Lawyer
Party: Whig
Vice President: None

James K. Polk
11

Presidential term: 1845–1849
Lived: 1795–1849
Born in: North Carolina
Elected from: Tennessee
Occupation: Lawyer
Party: Democratic
Vice President: George M. Dallas

Zachary Taylor
12

Presidential term: 1849–1850
Lived: 1784–1850
Born in: Virginia
Elected from: Louisiana
Occupation: Soldier
Party: Whig
Vice President: Millard
 Fillmore

Millard Fillmore
13

Presidential term: 1850–1853
Lived: 1800–1874
Born in: New York
Elected as V.P. from: New York
 Succeeded Taylor
Occupation: Lawyer
Party: Whig
Vice President: None

Franklin Pierce
14

Presidential term: 1853–1857
Lived: 1804–1869
Born in: New Hampshire
Elected from: New Hampshire
Occupation: Lawyer
Party: Democratic
Vice President: William R. King

James Buchanan
15

Presidential term: 1857–1861
Lived: 1791–1868
Born in: Pennsylvania
Elected from: Pennsylvania
Occupation: Lawyer
Party: Democratic
Vice President: John C.
 Breckinridge

Abraham Lincoln
16

Presidential term: 1861–1865
Lived: 1809–1865
Born in: Kentucky
Elected from: Illinois
Occupation: Lawyer
Party: Republican
Vice Presidents: Hannibal Hamlin,
 Andrew Johnson

Andrew Johnson
17

Presidential term: 1865–1869
Lived: 1808–1875
Born in: North Carolina
Elected as V.P. from: Tennessee
 Succeeded Lincoln
Occupation: Tailor
Party: Republican
Vice President: None

Ulysses S. Grant
18

Presidential term: 1869–1877
Lived: 1822–1885
Born in: Ohio
Elected from: Illinois
Occupations: Farmer, Soldier
Party: Republican
Vice Presidents: Schuyler Colfax,
 Henry Wilson

U.S. PRESIDENTS

Rutherford B. Hayes 19

Presidential term: 1877–1881
Lived: 1822–1893
Born in: Ohio
Elected from: Ohio
Occupation: Lawyer
Party: Republican
Vice President: William A.
  Wheeler

James A. Garfield 20

Presidential term: 1881
Lived: 1831–1881
Born in: Ohio
Elected from: Ohio
Occupations: Laborer, Professor
Party: Republican
Vice President: Chester A.
  Arthur

Chester A. Arthur 21

Presidential term: 1881–1885
Lived: 1830–1886
Born in: Vermont
Elected as V.P. from: New York
  Succeeded Garfield
Occupations: Teacher, Lawyer
Party: Republican
Vice President: None

Grover Cleveland 22

Presidential term: 1885–1889
Lived: 1837–1908
Born in: New Jersey
Elected from: New York
Occupation: Lawyer
Party: Democratic
Vice President: Thomas A.
  Hendricks

Benjamin Harrison 23

Presidential term: 1889–1893
Lived: 1833–1901
Born in: Ohio
Elected from: Indiana
Occupation: Lawyer
Party: Republican
Vice President: Levi P. Morton

Grover Cleveland 24

Presidential term: 1893–1897
Lived: 1837–1908
Born in: New Jersey
Elected from: New York
Occupation: Lawyer
Party: Democratic
Vice President: Adlai E.
  Stevenson

William McKinley 25

Presidential term: 1897–1901
Lived: 1843–1901
Born in: Ohio
Elected from: Ohio
Occupations: Teacher, Lawyer
Party: Republican
Vice Presidents: Garret Hobart,
  Theodore Roosevelt

Theodore Roosevelt 26

Presidential term: 1901–1909
Lived: 1858–1919
Born in: New York
Elected as V.P. from: New York
  Succeeded McKinley
Occupations: Historian, Rancher
Party: Republican
Vice President: Charles W. Fairbanks

William H. Taft 27

Presidential term: 1909–1913
Lived: 1857–1930
Born in: Ohio
Elected from: Ohio
Occupation: Lawyer
Party: Republican
Vice President: James S.
  Sherman

U.S. PRESIDENTS

Woodrow Wilson — 28

Presidential term: 1913–1921
Lived: 1856–1924
Born in: Virginia
Elected from: New Jersey
Occupation: College Professor
Party: Democratic
Vice President: Thomas R. Marshall

Warren G. Harding — 29

Presidential term: 1921–1923
Lived: 1865–1923
Born in: Ohio
Elected from: Ohio
Occupations: Newspaper Editor, Publisher
Party: Republican
Vice President: Calvin Coolidge

Calvin Coolidge — 30

Presidential term: 1923–1929
Lived: 1872–1933
Born in: Vermont
Elected as V.P. from:
Massachusetts–Succeeded Harding
Occupation: Lawyer
Party: Republican
Vice President: Charles G. Dawes

Herbert C. Hoover — 31

Presidential term: 1929–1933
Lived: 1874–1964
Born in: Iowa
Elected from: California
Occupation: Engineer
Party: Republican
Vice President: Charles Curtis

Franklin D. Roosevelt — 32

Presidential term: 1933–1945
Lived: 1882–1945
Born in: New York
Elected from: New York
Occupation: Lawyer
Party: Democratic
Vice Presidents: John N. Garner, Henry A. Wallace, Harry S. Truman

Harry S. Truman — 33

Presidential term: 1945–1953
Lived: 1884–1972
Born in: Missouri
Elected as V.P. from: Missouri Succeeded Roosevelt
Occupations: Clerk, Farmer
Party: Democratic
Vice President: Alben W. Barkley

Dwight D. Eisenhower — 34

Presidential term: 1953–1961
Lived: 1890–1969
Born in: Texas
Elected from: New York
Occupation: Soldier
Party: Republican
Vice President: Richard M. Nixon

John F. Kennedy — 35

Presidential term: 1961–1963
Lived: 1917–1963
Born in: Massachusetts
Elected from: Massachusetts
Occupations: Author, Reporter
Party: Democratic
Vice President: Lyndon B. Johnson

Lyndon B. Johnson — 36

Presidential term: 1963–1969
Lived: 1908–1973
Born in: Texas
Elected as V.P. from: Texas Succeeded Kennedy
Occupation: Teacher
Party: Democratic
Vice President: Hubert H. Humphrey

Richard M. Nixon 37

Presidential term: 1969–1974
Lived: 1913–1994
Born in: California
Elected from: New York
Occupation: Lawyer
Party: Republican
Vice Presidents: Spiro T. Agnew,
Gerald R. Ford

Gerald R. Ford 38

Presidential term: 1974–1977
Lived: 1913–2006
Born in: Nebraska
Appointed as V.P. upon Agnew's
resignation; succeeded Nixon
Occupation: Lawyer
Party: Republican
Vice President: Nelson A. Rockefeller

James E. Carter, Jr. 39

Presidential term: 1977–1981
Lived: 1924–
Born in: Georgia
Elected from: Georgia
Occupations: Business, Farmer
Party: Democratic
Vice President: Walter F.
Mondale

Ronald W. Reagan 40

Presidential term: 1981–1989
Lived: 1911–2004
Born in: Illinois
Elected from: California
Occupations: Actor, Lecturer
Party: Republican
Vice President: George H.W.
Bush

George H. W. Bush 41

Presidential term: 1989–1993
Lived: 1924–
Born in: Massachusetts
Elected from: Texas
Occupation: Business
Party: Republican
Vice President: J. Danforth
Quayle

William J. Clinton 42

Presidential term: 1993–2001
Lived: 1946–
Born in: Arkansas
Elected from: Arkansas
Occupation: Lawyer
Party: Democratic
Vice President: Albert Gore, Jr.

George W. Bush 43

Presidential term: 2001–2008
Lived: 1946–
Born in: Connecticut
Elected from: Texas
Occupation: Business
Party: Republican
Vice President: Richard B. Cheney

Barack H. Obama 44

Presidential term: 2009–
Lived: 1961–
Born in: Hawaii
Elected from: Illinois
Occupation: Attorney
Party: Democratic
Vice President: Joseph Biden

U.S. PRESIDENTS

REFERENCE ATLAS

NATIONAL GEOGRAPHIC

ATLAS KEY

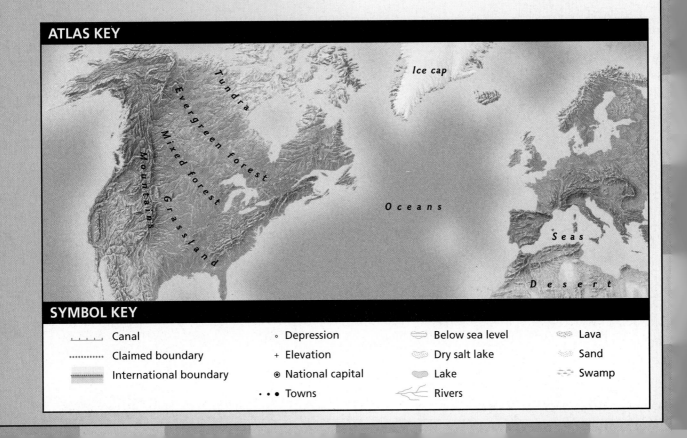

Ice cap

Tundra

Evergreen forest

Mixed forest

Mountains

Grassland

Oceans

Seas

Desert

SYMBOL KEY

Canal	○ Depression	Below sea level	Lava
Claimed boundary	+ Elevation	Dry salt lake	Sand
International boundary	⊛ National capital	Lake	Swamp
• • Towns	Rivers		

130°W 120°W 110°W 100°W 90°W 80°W 70°W 60°W 50°W 40°W 30°W 20°W

70°N

A

GREENLAND
(KALAALLIT NUNAAT)
Den.

N

60°N

B

30°W

ARCTIC CIRCLE

50°N

C

UNITED STATES POLITICAL

0 mi _____ 600

0 km _____ 600

OBLIQUE AZIMUTHAL EQUIDISTANT PROJECTION

NATIONAL GEOGRAPHIC

40°W

D

C A N A D A

E

40°N

40°W

MAINE

MONTANA
Helena

NORTH DAKOTA
Bismarck

MINNESOTA

MICHIGAN

Lake Superior

Lake Huron

Montpelier · Augusta
· Portland
Concord, N.H.
· Boston, MASS.
· Providence, R.I.
Hartford, CONN.

50°W

F

Billings

SOUTH DAKOTA
Pierre

Minneapolis · St. Paul
WISCONSIN
Milwaukee
Madison

Lansing

L. Michigan

NEW YORK
Lake Ontario
Albany

Lake Erie

Detroit · Buffalo
Cleveland PA.
Toledo

New York City

Casper

WYOMING
Cheyenne

NEBRASKA
Lincoln

Sioux City
IOWA
Des Moines
Omaha

Chicago
ILLINOIS
IND.

Columbus
OHIO

Pittsburgh
Harrisburg
Baltimore

Dover, DEL.
Philadelphia
Trenton, N.J.

50°N

ROCKY MOUNTAINS

Denver

COLORADO

Kansas City
Topeka · MISSOURI

KANSAS
Jefferson City

Springfield
St. Louis

Indianapolis · Cincinnati
Dayton W.VA.
Frankfort
Charleston

Louisville
KENTUCKY

Washington, D.C.
Annapolis, MD.
Richmond
VIRGINIA
Virginia Beach

30°N

G

Santa Fe
Albuquerque

NEW MEXICO

El Paso

Oklahoma City
OKLAHOMA

ARKANSAS
Little Rock

TENNESSEE
Nashville
Memphis

Tulsa

Fort Worth · Dallas

TEXAS

Austin

San Antonio

MISS.
Jackson

LOUISIANA

Baton Rouge
New Orleans

Houston

Birmingham
ALABAMA
Montgomery

Atlanta
GEORGIA

NORTH CAROLINA
Charlotte
SOUTH CAROLINA
Columbia
Charleston

Raleigh

Savannah

Jacksonville

Tallahassee

FLORIDA

Tampa

Miami

Bermuda Is.
U.K.

A T L A N T I C   O C E A N

30°N

H

20°N

MEXICO

Rio Grande

Gulf of Mexico

Straits of Florida

BAHAMAS

J

20°N

CUBA

Caribbean Sea

HAITI

DOMINICAN REPUBLIC

PUERTO RICO
U.S.

San Juan

ANTIGUA & BARBUDA

ST. KITTS & NEVIS

DOMINICA

60°W

K

100°W 90°W 80°W JAMAICA 70°W

ARCTIC

150°W 120°W 90°W 60°W 30°W 0°

Queen Elizabeth Islands

GREENLAND
(KALAALLIT NUNAAT)
Den.

Chukchi
Sea

Beaufort
Sea

RUSSIA

Baffin
Bay

Greenland Sea

ALASKA
U.S.

60°N

•Anchorage

Bering
Sea

Gulf of
Alaska

Mackenzie

Great
Bear Lake

Baffin
Island

Nuuk

ARCTIC CIRCLE

Reykjavík
ICELAND

Aleutian Islands

Great
Slave Lake

CANADA

Hudson
Bay

Labrador
Sea

Island of
Newfoundland

UNITED
KINGDOM

Dublin
IRELAND

Vancouver
Seattle•

•Calgary

Great Lakes

London•

NORTH

Missouri

Toronto• ⊕Ottawa

PACIFIC

San Francisco•

UNITED STATES

Chicago•

Ohio

New York City
⊕Washington, D.C.

NORTH

Madrid⊕
PORTUGAL ⊕ SPAIN

30°N

•Los Angeles

Houston•

Mississippi

•Atlanta

ATLANTIC

Azores
Port.

Madeira Is. Rabat
Port. ⊕
MOROCCO

OCEAN

TROPIC OF CANCER

Rio Grande

Gulf of
Mexico

OCEAN

Canary Is.
Sp.

WESTERN
SAHARA
Morocco

Hawaiian
Islands
U.S.

MEXICO

Havana

BAHAMAS

DOMINICAN REP.

Santo Domingo

CAPE
VERDE

MAURITANIA

MALI

•Guadalajara

CUBA

PUERTO RICO U.S.

Mexico City⊕

BELIZE
HAITI

ST. KITTS & NEVIS
ANTIGUA & BARBUDA

JAMAICA

DOMINICA

SENEGAL

GUATEMALA

Caribbean Sea

BARBADOS

GAMBIA

Guatemala⊕
EL SALVADOR

HONDURAS

ST. LUCIA
GRENADA

ST. VINCENT &
THE GRENADINES

GUINEA-
BISSAU

GUINEA

30°N

NICARAGUA

TRINIDAD & TOBAGO

BURKINA FASO

COSTA RICA

⊕Caracas

SIERRA LEONE

LIBERIA

CÔTE
D'IVOIRE

GHANA

PANAMA

VENEZUELA

FRENCH
GUIANA
Fr.

Medellin•

⊕Bogota

GUYANA

Christmas Island
Kiribati

COLOMBIA

SURINAME

EQUATOR

Quito⊕

0°

Galapagos
Islands
Ecua.

⊕ECUADOR

Manaus•

Negro

Amazon

Marquesas
Islands
Fr.

PERU

BRAZIL

Madeira

•Recife

SAMOA

Lima⊕

Salvador
(Bahia)

AMERICAN
SAMOA
U.S.

La Paz⊕
BOLIVIA

Brasilia⊕

São Francisco

SOUTH

FRENCH POLYNESIA
Fr.

Sucre⊕

Rio de
Janeiro

ATLANTIC

TONGA

TROPIC OF CAPRICORN

PARAGUAY

Sao Paulo•

OCEAN

Asuncion⊕

Parana

Porto Alegre•

SOUTH

Cordoba•

URUGUAY

30°S

Santiago⊕

Buenos
Aires

⊕Montevideo

PACIFIC

CHILE

ARGENTINA

OCEAN

PRIME MERIDIAN (MERIDIAN OF GREENWICH)

Falkland Islands
U.K.

Tierra del Fuego

South
Georgia
U.K.

Strait of Magellan

Drake Passage

Antarctic
Peninsula

60°S

ANTARCTIC CIRCLE

Weddell
Sea

Ross
Sea

Berkner
Island

WORLD
POLITICAL

0 mi   2000

0 km   2000

WINKEL TRIPEL PROJECTION

NATIONAL
GEOGRAPHIC

A

O C E A N
30°E 60°E 90°E 120°E 150°E
Franz Josef
Land
Svalbard
Nor.
Barents
Sea
Novaya
Zemlya
Severnaya
Zemlya
New Siberian
Islands
Kara
Sea
Laptev Sea
East
Siberian Sea

B
Norwegian
Sea
NORWAY
SWEDEN
FINLAND
Oslo
DENMARK
NETH.
GERMANY
BELG.
POLAND BELARUS
Paris
SWITZ.
FRANCE
ITALY
Rome
Mediterranean Sea
Algiers
TUNISIA
Tripoli
ALGERIA
LIBYA
NIGER
CHAD
NIGERIA
Niamey
Lagos
BENIN
TOGO
EQ. GUINEA
SAO TOME
& PRINCIPE
CABINDA
Ang.
GABON
CONGO
Luanda
ANGOLA
NAMIBIA
Windhoek
Gaborone
Tshwane (Pretoria)
BOTSWANA
SOUTH
AFRICA
Cape Town
Bloemfontein
LESOTHO
SWAZILAND
Maputo
MOZAMBIQUE
Harare
ZIMBABWE
ZAMBIA
Lusaka
MALAWI

St. Petersburg
EST.
LATVIA
LITH.
Baltic Sea
Moscow
Kyiv (Kiev)
UKRAINE
CZECH
REP.
SLOVAKIA
AUST. HUNG.
SLOV.
CROAT.
ROMANIA
BULGARIA
SERB.
BOS.
KOS.
MACED.
ALBANIA
GREECE
MOLD.
AZERBAIJAN
GEORGIA
ARMENIA
TURKEY
Ankara
CYPRUS
SYRIA
LEBANON
ISRAEL
JORDAN
IRAQ
Baghdad
Cairo
EGYPT
SAUDI
ARABIA
Riyadh
BAHRAIN
QATAR
U.A.E.
KUWAIT
Red Sea
Nile
SUDAN
Khartoum
ERITREA
ETHIOPIA
Addis Ababa
SOMALIA
DJIBOUTI
YEMEN
Sanaa
Socotra
Yemen
Arabian
Sea
Masqat
OMAN
Ashkhabad
TURKMENISTAN
IRAN
Tehran
Caspian Sea
Black Sea

RUSSIA
Samara
Volga
Ural
Yekaterinburg
Omsk
Irtysh
Novosibirsk
Astana
KAZAKHSTAN
Aral Sea
Ob
Yenisey
Tashkent
UZBEKISTAN
Almaty
KYRGYZSTAN
Bishkek
TAJIKISTAN
Dushanbe
Islamabad
AFGHANISTAN
PAKISTAN
Karachi
Delhi
New
Delhi
Lahore
NEPAL
Brahmaputra
BHUTAN
BANGLADESH
Dhaka
Kolkata
(Calcutta)
MYANMAR
(BURMA)
INDIA
Mumbai
(Bombay)
Hyderabad
Bengaluru
(Bangalore)
Chennai
(Madras)
SRI
LANKA
Colombo
MALDIVES
EQUATOR
Bay
of
Bengal
Nay Pyi Taw
LAOS
THAILAND
Bangkok
CAMBODIA
Phnom
Penh
VIETNAM
Hanoi
Hainan
Ho Chi Minh
City
SEYCHELLES

Ulaanbaatar
MONGOLIA
Lake
Baikal
Yakutsk
Lena
Amur
Harbin
Shenyang
NORTH
KOREA
P'yŏngyang
Beijing
Tianjin
Huang
(Yellow)
CHINA
Chengdu
Wuhan
Chang Jiang
(Yangtze)
Guangzhou
Hong Kong
Shanghai
SOUTH
KOREA
Seoul
JAPAN
Tokyo
Osaka
Kyushu
Honshu
Hokkaido
Sapporo
Sea of
Okhotsk
Kamchatka
Peninsula
Bering
Sea
60°N
30°N
Taipei
TAIWAN
The People's Republic
of China claims Taiwan
as its 23rd province.
Philippine
Sea
Luzon
Manila
PHILIPPINES
Mindanao
South
China
Sea
BRUNEI
MALAYSIA
Kuala
Lumpur
SINGAPORE
Sumatra
Borneo
Celebes
INDONESIA
Jakarta
Java
Surabaya
EAST TIMOR
(TIMOR-LESTE)
Arafura Sea
Darwin
New
Guinea
PAPUA
NEW GUINEA
Port
Moresby
PALAU
FEDERATED STATES
OF MICRONESIA
NORTHERN
MARIANA
ISLANDS
U.S.
NORTH
PACIFIC
OCEAN
MARSHALL
ISLANDS
KIRIBATI
NAURU
TUVALU
SOLOMON
ISLANDS
VANUATU
FIJI
ISLANDS
Coral
Sea
New Caledonia
Fr.
SOUTH
PACIFIC
OCEAN
AUSTRALIA
Brisbane
Perth
Darling
Murray
Sydney
Canberra
Melbourne
Tasman
Sea
Tasmania
North
Island
Auckland
NEW ZEALAND
Wellington
South
Island

UGANDA
KENYA
Nairobi
RWANDA
BURUNDI
DEM. REP.
OF THE
CONGO
Brazzaville
Kinshasa
Dodoma
Dar es Salaam
TANZANIA
CENTRAL
AFRICAN
REPUBLIC
Bangui
CAMEROON
N'Djamena
Mogadishu
COMOROS
Antananarivo
MADAGASCAR
MAURITIUS
Reunion
Fr.
INDIAN
OCEAN
Orange

INDIAN
OCEAN
Kerguelen Islands
Fr.
60°S

The Atlantic, Indian, and Pacific Oceans merge around Antarctica. Some define this as an ocean, calling it the Antarctic Ocean, Austral Ocean, or Southern Ocean. While most accept four oceans (including the Arctic Ocean), there is little international agreement on the name and extent of a fifth ocean.

ANTARCTICA
Ross Sea

ABBREVIATIONS

AUST.	AUSTRIA
B.&H.	BOSNIA & HERZEGOVINA
BELG.	BELGIUM
CROAT.	CROATIA
CZECH REP.	CZECH REPUBLIC
DEM. REP. OF THE CONGO	DEMOCRATIC REPUBLIC OF THE CONGO
EQ. GUINEA	EQUATORIAL GUINEA
EST.	ESTONIA
HUNG.	HUNGARY
KOS.	KOSOVO
LITH.	LITHUANIA
MACED.	MACEDONIA
MOLD.	MOLDOVA
NETH.	NETHERLANDS
SERB.	SERBIA
MONT.	MONTENEGRO
SLOV.	SLOVENIA
SWITZ.	SWITZERLAND
U.A.E.	UNITED ARAB EMIRATES

NGS REFERENCE ATLAS

	1	2	3	4	5	6	7	8

130°W   50°N   120°W   110°W   100°W

C   **A**   **N**

A

Seattle
Olympia ⊙   *Columbia*

B   **WASHINGTON**
9

Portland
Salem ⊙   **MONTANA**   **NORTH**
Helena ⊙   1   **DAKOTA**
Eugene   Bismarck
OREGON   **I D A H O**   1
5   *Missouri*

C   Boise ⊙   **SOUTH**
Snake   Pierre   **DAKOTA**
40°N   **WYOMING**   1   Sioux Falls

D   Salt Lake   1   **NEBRASKA**
Sacramento ⊙   Carson City ⊙   City ⊙   Cheyenne ⊙   3   Omaha
San Francisco   **NEVADA**   **UTAH**   Lincoln ⊙
San Jose   3   3   **COLORADO**   Denver
E   **C A L I F O R N I A**   7   Colorado   4
53   Springs   **K A N S A S**
Las   *Arkansas*
PACIFIC   Vegas   Wichita
OCEAN
F   Los Angeles   **ARIZONA**   Santa Fe ⊙   Oklahoma
8   Albuquerque   City ⊙
120°W   Phoenix ⊙   **NEW MEXICO**   Amarillo   **OKLAHOMA**
San Diego   3   *Red*   5
ARCTIC OCEAN
G   68°N   Tucson   El Paso   Dallas
180°   *Rio Grande*   Fort
RUSSIA ARCTIC CIRCLE   68°N   110°W   Worth
Yukon   30°N   32
H   **ALASKA**   **CANADA**   **M E X I C O**   **T E X A S**
172°W   1   Austin ⊙
60°N
Anchorage   San
J   **Bering**   **Antonio**
Sea   Juneau   Corpus
52°N   **PACIFIC**   Christi
0 mi.   300   **OCEAN**
ALASKA
K   0 km   300   52°N

164°W   156°W   148°W   140°W   132°W

	1	2	3	4	5	6	7	8

Legend:
- State gaining 2 seats
- State gaining 1 seat
- No change
- State losing 1 seat
- State losing 2 seats

*Numerals in each state indicate number of representatives the state sends to the House of Representatives

90°W 80°W 50°N 70°W

A A

D A

MINNESOTA
8

Lake Superior

MICHIGAN

Lake Huron

MAINE
2

⊙ Augusta

Montpelier ⊙ N.H.
VT. 2 ⊙ Concord
1

MINNEAPOLIS
Minneapolis
⊙ St. Paul

WISCONSIN
8

Lake Michigan

Lake Ontario

NEW YORK
29

Albany ⊙

Boston

10 MASS.

Mississippi

Milwaukee
Madison ⊙

Lansing ⊙
Detroit

15

Buffalo

Hartford ⊙ 5
CONN.

Providence
RHODE ISLAND
2

40°N

I O W A
5

⊙ Des Moines

Chicago

Lake Erie

Cleveland

PENNSYLVANIA
19

Harrisburg ⊙
Pittsburgh

N.J. New York City
13

Trenton
Philadelphia

ILLINOIS
19

Fort Wayne

OHIO
18

⊙ Columbus

MARYLAND
Dover
DELAWARE
1

INDIANA

Springfield ⊙

Indianapolis ⊙

9

Cincinnati

Ohio

WEST
VIRGINIA

Washington,
D.C. 8

Annapolis

ATLANTIC
OCEAN

Kansas
City

Topeka ⊙

Jefferson ⊙
City

St.
Louis

Louisville ⊙

Frankfort ⊙

KENTUCKY
6

⊙ Charleston

3

11

Richmond ⊙

VIRGINIA

Virginia Beach

MISSOURI
9

13 ⊙ Raleigh

NORTH CAROLINA

Tulsa

9 ⊙ Nashville

TENNESSEE

Charlotte

ARKANSAS

Little ⊙
Rock

Memphis

Tennessee

4

Mississippi

Atlanta ⊙

SOUTH
⊙ Columbia

CAROLINA

6

N

MISSISSIPPI

4

Birmingham

ALABAMA

GEORGIA

Savannah

UNITED
STATES

2000 CONGRESSIONAL
REAPPORTIONMENT

Jackson ⊙

7

Montgomery ⊙

13

Savannah

0 mi. 300

0 km 300

ALBERS CONIC EQUAL-AREA PROJECTION

LOUISIANA
7

Mobile

Tallahassee ⊙

Jacksonville

NATIONAL
GEOGRAPHIC

Baton Rouge ⊙
New Orleans

25

FLORIDA

Houston

Gulf of Mexico

Tampa

Miami

90°W

159°W 156°W

Niihau Kauai

Oahu

Honolulu ⊙ Molokai
Lanai Maui 21°N
Kahoolawe Hawaii

PACIFIC

OCEAN 2

PRINCIPAL HAWAIIAN
ISLANDS

0 mi. 100

0 km 100

156°W

TROPIC OF CANCER

CUBA

80°W

30°N

70°W

20°N

Glossary/Glosario

- Content vocabulary are words that relate to civics and government content. They are highlighted yellow in your text.

- Words below that have an asterisk (*) are academic vocabulary. They help you understand your school subjects and are **boldfaced** in your text.

························· **ENGLISH** ·············

absentee ballot one that allows a person to vote without going to the polls on Election Day (p. 297)

access* as a way or means of approach (p. 736)

accumulate* to increase in quantity or size (p. 528)

achieve* to accomplish or successfully gain (p. 632)

acid rain rain containing high amounts of chemical pollutants (p. 737)

acknowledge* to recognize the existence of or to make something known (pp. 239, 328)

acquire* to gain or get possession of (p. 39)

acquittal a vote of not guilty (p. 458)

adapt* to adjust or become adjusted to a situation or condition (p. 45)

adequate* acceptable (p. 744)

adjacent* neighboring or near (p. 281)

adjust* to change or alter in order to fit or conform (p. 179)

affect* to produce an effect on (p. 244)

affirmative action programs intended to make up for past discrimination by helping minority groups and women gain access to jobs and opportunities (p. 143)

alien a noncitizen (p. 16)

alternative* a choice or possibility (p. 541)

·············· **ESPAÑOL** ··············

absentee ballot/boleta electoral por correspondencia aquélla que permite que una persona vote sin ir al lugar de votación el día de la elección (pág. 297)

access/acceso* una forma o medio de acercamiento (pág. 736)

accumulate/acumular* aumentar en cantidad o tamaño (pág. 528)

achieve/lograr* alcanzar u obtener algo con éxito (pág. 632)

acid rain/lluvia ácida lluvia que contiene grandes cantidades de sustancias químicas contaminantes (pág. 737)

acknowledge/reconocer* aceptar la existencia de o dar a conocer algo (págs. 239, 328)

acquire/adquirir* obtener o conseguir la posesión de (pág. 39)

acquittal/absolución un voto de inocente (pág. 458)

adapt/adaptarse* ajustarse a una situación o condición (pág. 45)

adequate/adecuado* aceptable (pág. 744)

adjacent/adyacente* vecino o cercano (pág. 281)

adjust/ajustar* cambiar o alterar a fin de corresponder o cumplir con algo (pág. 179)

affect/afectar* producir un efecto en (pág. 244)

affirmative action/acción afirmativa programas con el fin de compensar la discriminación pasada al ayudar a los grupos minoritarios y las mujeres a obtener acceso a empleos y oportunidades (pág. 143)

alien/extranjero una persona que no es ciudadana (pág. 16)

alternative/alternativa* una opción o posibilidad (pág. 541)

ambassador

assume

ambassador an official representative of a country's government (p. 222)

amendment any change in the Constitution (p. 82)

amnesty a pardon to a group of people (p. 217)

annual* covering the period of a year or occurring once a year (p. 162)

annual percentage rate (APR) annual cost of credit expressed as a percentage of the amount borrowed (p. 547)

Anti-Federalists those who opposed ratification of the Constitution (p. 78)

antitrust law legislation to prevent new monopolies from forming and police those that already exist (p. 633)

apartheid system of laws that separated racial and ethnic groups and limited the rights of blacks in South Africa (p. 746)

apathy a lack of interest (p. 299)

appeals court a court that reviews decisions made in lower district courts (p. 244)

appellate jurisdiction the authority of a court to hear a case appealed from a lower court (p. 244)

apportion divide among districts (p. 359)

appropriations bill legislation earmarking funds for certain purposes (p. 677)

arbitration situation in which union and company officials submit the issues they cannot agree on to a third party for a final decision (p. 611)

archives files of older stories (p. 471)

area* a region or section (p. 69)

arraignment a hearing in which a suspect is charged and pleads guilty or not guilty (p. 456)

articles of partnership formal legal papers specifying the arrangement between partners (p. 602)

assign* to dole out or give as a task (p. 88)

assist* to help or aid (p. 48)

assume* to take over a job or responsibility (p. 84)

ambassador/embajador un representante oficial del gobierno de un país (pág. 222)

amendment/enmienda cualquier cambio en la Constitución (pág. 82)

amnesty/amnistía un perdón a un grupo de personas (pág. 217)

annual/anual* que cubre el período de un año u ocurre una vez por año (pág. 162)

annual percentage rate (APR)/tasa de interés anual (TPA) costo de crédito anual expresado como un porcentaje de la cantidad tomada en préstamo (pág. 547)

Anti-Federalists/antifederalistas aquéllos que se oponían a la ratificación de la Constitución (pág. 78)

antitrust law/ley antimonopolista ley para evitar la formación de nuevos monopolios y supervisar a aquéllos que ya existen (pág. 633)

apartheid/*apartheid* sistema de leyes que separaba a los grupos raciales y étnicos y limitaba los derechos de los negros en Sudáfrica (pág. 746)

apathy/apatía falta de interés (pág. 299)

appeals court/tribunal de apelación un tribunal que revisa las decisiones tomadas en tribunales de distrito inferiores (pág. 244)

appellate jurisdiction/jurisdicción de apelación la autoridad de un tribunal de ver un caso apelado de un tribunal inferior (pág. 244)

apportion/asignar dividir entre distritos (pág. 359)

appropriations bill/proyecto de ley de apropiación presupuestaria ley que destina fondos para ciertos propósitos (pág. 677)

arbitration/arbitraje situación en la que jefes de sindicatos y compañías presentan las cuestiones sobre las que no pueden llegar a un acuerdo a un tercero para que tome una decisión final (pág. 611)

archives/archivos registros de historias antiguas (pág. 471)

area/área* una región o sección (pág. 69)

arraignment/comparecencia una audiencia en la que un sospechoso es acusado y se declara culpable o inocente (pág. 456)

articles of partnership/artículos de asociación documentos legales formales que especifican el acuerdo entre socios (pág. 602)

assign/asignar* repartir o dar como una tarea (pág. 88)

assist/ayudar* brindar ayuda o asistencia (pág. 48)

assume/asumir* hacerse cargo de un empleo o una responsabilidad (pág. 84)

at-large election an election for an area as a whole; for example, statewide (p. 380)

attitude* a feeling or way of thinking (p. 409)

authoritarian a government in which one leader or group of people holds absolute power (p. 475)

authority* power or influence over other people or groups; person or persons having the power of government (pp. 33, 409)

automatic stabilizer program that when needed provides benefits to offset a change in people's incomes (p. 692)

at-large election/elección general una elección para un área en general; por ejemplo, en todo el estado (pág. 380)

attitude/actitud* una forma de pensar o sentir (pág. 409)

authoritarian/autoritario un gobierno en el que un líder o grupo de personas tiene poder absoluto (pág. 475)

authority/autoridad* poder o influencia sobre otras personas o grupos; persona o personas que tienen el poder del gobierno (págs. 33, 409)

automatic stabilizer/estabilizador automático programa que brinda beneficios automáticamente para compensar un cambio en los ingresos de la gente (pág. 692)

B

bail a sum of money used as a security deposit to ensure that an accused person returns for his or her trial (p. 440)

balance of trade the difference between the value of a nation's exports and its imports (p. 712)

balanced budget annual budget in which expenditures equal revenues (p. 688)

ballot the list of candidates on which you cast your vote (p. 296)

bankruptcy inability to pay debts (p. 549)

behalf* in the interest of (p. 668)

benefit* to be useful or profitable to (p. 328)

bicameral a legislature consisting of two parts, or houses (pp. 67, 177, 358)

bill of attainder a law that punishes a person accused of a crime without a trial or a fair hearing in court (p. 436)

board of directors people elected by the shareholders of a corporation to act on their behalf (p. 604)

bond contract to repay borrowed money with interest at a specific time in the future (pp. 557, 688)

boycott the refusal to purchase certain goods (p. 612)

bail/fianza una suma de dinero usada como depósito de garantía para asegurar que una persona acusada regrese para su juicio (pág. 440)

balance of trade/balanza comercial la diferencia entre el valor de las exportaciones y las importaciones de una nación (pág. 712)

balanced budget/presupuesto equilibrado presupuesto anual en el que los gastos equivalen a los ingresos (pág. 688)

ballot/boleta electoral la lista de candidatos sobre la que emites tu voto (pág. 296)

bankruptcy/quiebra bancarrota imposibilidad para pagar las deudas (pág. 549)

behalf/defensa, favor* en beneficio de (pág. 668)

benefit/beneficio* ser útil o rentable para (pág. 328)

bicameral/bicameral un cuerpo legislativo que consiste en dos partes o cámaras (págs. 67, 177, 358)

bill of attainder/ley de proscripción un ley que castiga a una persona acusada de un delito sin un juicio o una audiencia justa en un tribunal (pág. 436)

board of directors/junta directiva personas elegidas por los accionistas de una corporación para que actúen en su nombre (pág. 604)

bond/bono contrato para devolver el dinero tomado en préstamo con interés en un tiempo específico en el futuro (págs. 557, 688)

boycott/boicot la negativa de comprar ciertos bienes (pág. 612)

brief

certificate of deposit

brief a written document explaining the position of one side or the other in a case (p. 256)

budget a plan for making and spending money (pp. 22, 545, 677)

bureaucracy complex systems with many departments, many rules, and many people in the chain of command (p. 157)

burglary unlawful entry into any dwelling or structure (p. 432)

business cycle alternating periods of growth and decline that the economy goes through (p. 638)

brief/expediente un documento escrito que explica la posición de una parte o la otra en un caso (pág. 256)

budget/presupuesto un plan para generar y gastar dinero (págs. 22, 545, 677)

bureaucracy/burocracia sistemas complejos con muchos departamentos, muchas reglas y muchas personas en la cadena de mando (pág. 157)

burglary/robo ingreso ilegal a una vivienda o estructura (pág. 432)

business cycle/ciclo de negocios períodos alternos de crecimiento y descenso por los que pasa la economía (pág. 638)

cabinet a group of advisers to the president that includes the heads of 15 top-level executive departments (p. 226)

capable* having ability or competence (p. 501)

capital previously manufactured goods used to make other goods and services (p. 517)

capitalism a system in which private citizens own most, if not all, of the means of production and decide how to use them within legislated limits (pp. 500, 528)

casework the work that a lawmaker does to help constituents with a problem (p. 195)

category* a division or grouping used to classify something (p. 198)

caucus a meeting of political party members to conduct party business (p. 279)

censorship the banning of printed materials or films due to alarming or offensive ideas (p. 122)

census a population count taken by the Census Bureau (pp. 179, 359)

central bank an institution that lends money to other banks; also, the place where the government does its banking business (p. 661)

certificate of deposit timed deposit that states the amount of the deposit, maturity, and rate of interest being paid (p. 667)

cabinet/gabinete un grupo de asesores del presidente que incluye a los jefes de 15 departamentos ejecutivos de alto nivel (pág. 226)

capable/capaz* que posee habilidad o competencia (pág. 501)

capital/capital bienes previamente fabricados que se utilizan para hacer otros bienes y servicios (pág. 517)

capitalism/capitalismo un sistema en el que los ciudadanos privados son propietarios de la mayoría de, si no todos, los medios de producción y deciden cómo usarlos dentro de límites legales (págs. 500, 528)

casework/proyecto particular el trabajo que realiza un legislador para ayudar a los electores con un problema (pág. 195)

category/categoría* una división o agrupación usada para clasificar algo (pág. 198)

caucus/*caucus* una reunión de miembros de un partido político para tratar los asuntos del partido (pág. 279)

censorship/censura la prohibición de materiales impresos o películas debido a ideas ofensivas o inquietantes (pág. 122)

census/censo un recuento de la población que realiza la Oficina de Censos (págs. 179, 359)

central bank/banco central una institución que presta dinero a otros bancos; también, el lugar donde el gobierno realiza sus operaciones bancarias (pág. 661)

certificate of deposit/certificado de depósito depósito a plazo que especifica la cantidad del depósito, el vencimiento y la tasa de interés que debe pagarse (pág. 667)

challenge* a demand for justification or a dispute (p. 54)

charter a written document granting land and the authority to set up colonial governments (p. 36); or a government document granting permission to organize a corporation (pp. 604, 740)

charter schools schools that receive state funding, but are excused from meeting many public school regulations (p. 402)

checking account an account in which deposited money can be withdrawn at any time by writing a check (p. 667)

checks and balances a system in which each branch of government is able to check, or restrain, the power of the others (p. 88)

circuit the area of jurisdiction of a federal court of appeals (p. 240)

circumstance* an incident or occurrence (p. 242)

citizen community member who owes loyalty to the government and is entitled to protection from it (p. 7)

citizenship rights and duties of members of a state (p. 7)

city charter a document granting power to a local government (p. 377)

civics the study of the rights and duties of citizens (p. 7)

civil case person or group taking legal action against another person or group (p. 367)

civil liberties freedoms to think and act without government interference or fear of unfair legal treatment (p. 121)

civil rights the rights of full citizenship and equality under the law (p. 140)

civil service system the practice of hiring government workers on the basis of open, competitive examinations and merit (p. 229)

civil service worker person hired into a government position (p. 229)

civilian labor force all civilians 16 years old or older who are either working or are looking for work (p. 640)

challenge/desafío* demanda de justificación o un conflicto (pág. 54)

charter/carta de privilegio un documento escrito que otorga territorio y la autoridad de establecer gobiernos coloniales; o un documento gubernamental que otorga permiso para organizar una corporación (págs. 604, 740)

charter schools/escuelas con carta de privilegio escuelas que reciben financiación del estado, pero se las libera de la obligación de cumplir muchas reglamentaciones de las escuelas públicas (pág. 402)

checking account/cuenta de cheques una cuenta en la que el dinero depositado puede retirarse en cualquier momento al emitir un cheque (pág. 667)

checks and balances/controles y balances un sistema en el que cada poder del gobierno puede controlar, o limitar, el poder de los demás (pág. 88)

circuit/circuito el área de jurisdicción de un tribunal federal de apelación (pág. 240)

circumstance/circunstancia* un incidente o acontecimiento; una condición que acompaña o determina un hecho o evento (pág. 242)

citizen/ciudadano miembro de una comunidad que le deben lealtad al gobierno y tienen derecho a recibir protección de éste (pág. 7)

citizenship/ciudadanía derechos y deberes de los miembros de un estado (pág. 7)

city charter/carta municipal un documento que otorga poder a un gobierno local (pág. 377)

civics/civismo o cívica el estudio de los derechos y las obligaciones de los ciudadanos (pág. 7)

civil case/caso civil persona o grupo que realiza acciones legales contra otra persona o grupo (pág. 367)

civil liberties/libertades civiles libertades para pensar y actuar sin la interferencia del gobierno o miedo a un trato legal injusto (pág. 121)

civil rights/derechos civiles los derechos de ciudadanía e igualdad total según la ley (pág. 140)

civil service system/sistema de servicio civil la práctica de contratar empleados gubernamentales basándose en su mérito y en exámenes abiertos y competitivos (pág. 229)

civil service worker/trabajador de servicio civil persona contratada para un puesto federal (pág. 229)

civilian labor force/fuerza laboral civil todos los civiles mayores de 16 años que están trabajando o buscando un empleo (pág. 640)

clarify

community policing

clarify* to make something more understandable (p. 602)

closed primary an election in which only the declared members of a party are allowed to vote for that party's nominees (p. 283)

cloture a procedure used in the Senate to limit debate on a bill (p. 200)

coin metallic form of money such as pennies, nickels, and dimes (p. 657)

Cold War conflict between the United States and the Soviet Union dating from the later 1940s to the late 1980s, when the two countries competed for world influence without declared military action (p. 748)

collapse* to fall apart (p. 722)

collateral property or valuable item serving as security for a loan (p. 547)

collective bargaining process by which unions and employers negotiate the conditions of employment (p. 611)

colony a group of people in one place who are ruled by a parent country elsewhere (p. 36)

command economy an economic system in which the major economic decisions are made by the central government (p. 717)

commercial bank a financial institution that offers full banking services to individuals and businesses (p. 658)

commission* a special committee (p. 744)

commit* to pledge or assign oneself to a particular action (p. 562)

common law a system of law based on precedent and customs (p. 429)

communicate* to exchange information, thoughts, or feelings (p. 256)

communism economic system in which the central government directs all major economic decisions (p. 718)

community a group of people who share the same interests and concerns (p. 21)

community policing local police force visibly keeping the peace and patrolling neighborhoods (p. 405)

clarify/aclarar* hacer que algo sea más comprensible (pág. 602)

closed primary/elección primaria cerrada una elección en la que sólo los miembros declarados de un partido pueden votar por los candidatos de ese partido (pág. 283)

cloture/clausura un procedimiento usado en el Senado para limitar el debate sobre un proyecto de ley (pág. 200)

coin/moneda forma metálica de dinero como "pennies" (monedas de un centavo), "nickels" (monedas de cinco centavos) y "dimes" (monedas de diez centavos) (pág. 657)

Cold War/Guerra Fría conflicto entre los Estados Unidos y la Unión Soviética desde fines de los años 40 hasta fines de los años 80, cuando los dos países compitieron por la influencia mundial sin acción militar declarada (pág. 748)

collapse/colapsar* desploarse (pág. 722)

collateral/garantía aval propiedad u objeto de valor que sirve como caución para un préstamo (pág. 547)

collective bargaining/negociación colectiva proceso mediante el cual sindicatos y empleadores negocian las condiciones de empleo (pág. 611)

colony/colonia un grupo de personas en un lugar que están gobernados por un país matriz en otro lugar (pág. 36)

command economy/economía de mando un sistema económico en el que las principales decisiones económicas las toma el gobierno central (pág. 717)

commercial bank/banco comercial una institución financiera que ofrece servicios bancarios completos a personas y empresas (pág. 658)

commission/comisón* comité especial (pág. 744)

commit/comprometer commit/cometer* prometer o hacerse cargo de una acción particular (pág. 562)

common law/derecho consuetudinario un sistema legal basado en precedentes y costumbres (pág. 429)

communicate/comunicar* intercambiar información, pensamientos o sentimientos (pág. 256)

communism/comunismo sistema económico en el cual el gobierno central toma todas las decisiones económicas principales (pág. 718)

community/comunidad un grupo de personas que comparten los mismos intereses e inquietudes (pág. 21)

community policing/control de la comunidad fuerza policial local que visiblemente mantiene la paz y patrulla los vecindarios (pág. 405)

commute to reduce a criminal's sentence (p. 364)

compact an agreement, or contract, among a group of people (p. 36)

comparative advantage the ability of a country to produce a good at a lower opportunity cost (p. 708)

comparison shopping buying strategy to get best buy for the money (p. 541)

competition the struggle that goes on between buyers and sellers to get the best products at the lowest prices (p. 530)

complaint a formal notice that a lawsuit is being brought (p. 450)

complement product often used with another product (p. 576)

complex* complicated or intricate (pp. 193, 389)

comprise* to consist or be made up of (p. 609)

compute* to determine or calculate (p. 506)

concurrent jurisdiction authority for both state and federal courts to hear and decide cases (p. 242)

concurrent powers powers shared by the state and federal governments (pp. 89, 353)

concurring opinion a statement written by a justice who votes with the majority, but for different reasons (p. 256)

confederation a group of individuals or state governments (p. 68)

confine* to restrict or imprison (p. 453)

confirm* to approve (p. 369)

conflict* a struggle or disagreement (p. 252)

consent* to express willingness or to agree (p. 351)

consequently* as a result (p. 708)

conservation the careful preservation and protection of natural resources (pp. 410, 737)

consist* to be made up of (p. 80)

constituent a person from a legislator's district (p. 179)

constitution a detailed, written plan for government (p. 67)

commute/conmutar reducir la sentencia de un delincuente (pág. 364)

compact/convenio un acuerdo, o contrato, entre un grupo de personas (pág. 36)

comparative advantage/ventaja comparativa la habilidad de un país de producir un bien a un costo de oportunidad menor (pág. 708)

comparison shopping/comparar antes de comprar estrategia de compras para obtener la mejor compra por el dinero empleado (pág. 541)

competition/competencia la lucha que tiene lugar entre compradores y vendedores para obtener los mejores productos a los precios más bajos (pág. 530)

complaint/queja un aviso formal de que se entabló. Una demanda (pág. 450)

complement/complemento producto a menudo usado con otro producto (pág. 576)

complex/complejo* complicado o intrincado (págs. 193, 389)

comprise/constar* estar compuesto o conformado por (pág. 609)

compute/computar* determinar o calcular (pág. 506)

concurrent jurisdiction/jurisdicción concurrente autoridad de tribunales estatales y federales para ver y decidir casos (pág. 242)

concurrent powers/poderes concurrentes poderes compartidos por los gobiernos estatales y federales (págs. 89, 353)

concurring opinion/opinión concurrente una declaración escrita por un juez que vota con la mayoría, pero por diferentes razones (pág. 256)

confederation/confederación un grupo de personas o gobiernos estatales (pág. 68)

confine/confinar* restringir o encerrar (pág. 453)

confirm/confirmar* aprobar (pág. 369)

conflict/conflicto* una lucha o un desacuerdo (pág. 252)

consent/consentir estar dispuesto o aceptar (pág. 351)

consequently/consiguientemente* como resultado (pág. 708)

conservation/conservación la cuidadosa preservación y protección de los recursos naturales (págs. 410, 737)

consist/consistir* estar compuesto por (pág. 80)

constituent/elector una persona del distrito de un legislador (pág. 179)

constitution/constitución un plan de gobierno escrito y detallado (pág. 67)

constitutional in accordance with the Constitution (p. 252)

Constitutional Convention meeting of state delegates in 1787 leading to adoption of new Constitution (p. 73)

constitutional law branch of law dealing with formation, construction, and interpretation of constitutions (p. 434)

constrain* to force, limit, or hold back (p. 25)

consult* to seek information or advice from a person or resource (p. 601)

consume* to use up (p. 522)

consumer someone who buys a good or service (p. 539)

consumer price index measure of change in price over time of specific group of goods and services (p. 642)

consumer sovereignty the role of consumer as the ruler of the market, determining what products will be produced (p. 529)

consumerism a movement to educate buyers about the purchases they make and to demand better and safer products from manufacturers (p. 540)

contract* to become smaller (p. 664)

contrary* opposite or different (p. 476)

convert* to change from one belief, form, or use to another (p. 67)

convince* to persuade through argument or evidence (p. 397)

cooperative a voluntary association of people formed to carry on some kind of economic activity that will benefit its members (p. 606)

copyright the owner's exclusive right to control, publish, and sell an original work (p. 483)

corporation type of business organization owned by many people but treated by law as though it were a person (p. 603)

cost-benefit analysis economic model that compares the marginal costs and marginal benefits of a decision (p. 508)

constitutional/constitucional de acuerdo con la Constitución (pág. 252)

Constitutional Convention/Convención Constitucional reunión de delegados estatales en 1787 que llevó a la adopción de una nueva Constitución (pág. 73)

constitutional law/ley constitucional rama del derecho que trata de la información, construcción e interpretación de las constituciones. (pág. 434)

constrain/constreñir* forzar, limitar o retener (pág. 25)

consult/consultar* buscar información o consejos de una persona o un recurso (pág. 601)

consume/consumir* agotar (pág. 522)

consumer/consumidor alguien que compra un bien o un servicio (pág. 539)

consumer price index/índice de precios de consumo medida del cambio en el precio con el paso del tiempo de un grupo específico de bienes y servicios (pág. 642)

consumer sovereignty/soberanía del consumidor la función del consumidor como el gobernante del mercado, donde determina qué productos se producirán (pág. 529)

consumerism/protección al consumidor un movimiento para educar a los compradores sobre las compras que hacen y para demandar productos mejores y más seguros a los fabricantes (pág. 540)

contract/contraer* reducir a menor tamaño (pág. 664)

contrary/contrario* opuesto o diferente (pág. 476)

convert/convertir* cambiar de una creencia, forma o uso a otra (pág. 67)

convince/convencer* persuadir mediante argumentos o evidencia (pág. 397)

cooperative/cooperativa una asociación voluntaria de personas formada para realizar algún tipo de actividad económica que beneficie a sus miembros (pág. 606)

copyright/derecho de autor el derecho exclusivo del propietario de controlar, publicar y vender una obra original (pág. 483)

corporation/sociedad anónima tipo de organización comercial propiedad de varias personas pero tratada por la ley como si fuera una persona (pág. 603)

cost-benefit analysis/análisis costo-beneficio modelo económico que compara los costos marginales y los beneficios marginales de una decisión (pág. 508)

county normally the largest territorial and political subdivision of a state (p. 384)

county seat a town where the county courthouse is located (p. 384)

credit money borrowed to pay for a good or service p. 547

credit union nonprofit service cooperative that accepts deposits, makes loans, and provides other financial services (p. 658)

crime an act that breaks a law and causes harm to people or society in general (p. 453)

cross-examine to question a witness at a trial or a hearing to check or discredit the testimony (p. 457)

crucial* of vital importance (p. 617)

currency both coins and paper money (p. 657)

county/condado normalmente, la subdivisión territorial y política más grande de un estado (pág. 384)

county seat/capital del condado una ciudad en la que está ubicado el palacio de justicia del condado (pág. 384)

credit/crédito dinero tomado en préstamo para pagar un bien o un servicio (pág. 547)

credit union/asociación de crédito cooperativa de servicio sin fines de lucro que acepta depósitos, otorga préstamos y presta otros servicios financieros (pág. 658)

crime/delito un acto que viola una ley y provoca un daño la gente o a la sociedad en general (pág. 453)

cross-examine/interrogar hacer preguntas a un testigo en un juicio o una audiencia para confirmar o desacreditar el testimonio (pág. 457)

crucial/crucial* de importancia vital (pág. 617)

currency/moneda dinero en monedas y en papel (pág. 657)

D

debt money borrowed and not yet paid back (p. 688)

decade* a period of 10 years (p. 39)

decline* to lessen or diminish (p. 390)

defendant an individual or group being sued or charged with a crime (pp. 368, 431)

deficit situation in which government spends more than it collects in revenues (p. 688)

delegate a representative to a meeting (p. 54)

demand the desire, willingness, and ability to buy a good or service (p. 569)

demand curve downward-sloping line that graphically shows the quantities demanded at each possible price (p. 569)

demand elasticity measure of responsiveness relating change in quantity demanded to a change in price (p. 577)

demand schedule table showing quantities demanded at different possible prices (p. 569)

democracy a government in which citizens hold the power to rule (p. 23)

deny* refusal to grant, agree, or believe (p. 17)

deport to send an alien or immigrant back to his or her own country (p. 19)

debt/deuda dinero prestado y aún no pagado (pág. 688)

decade/década* un período de 10 años (pág. 39)

decline/declinar* reducir o disminuir (pág. 390)

defendant/acusado una persona o un grupo demandado o acusado de un delito (págs. 368, 431)

deficit/déficit situación en la que el gobierno gasta más de lo que recauda en ingresos (pág. 688)

delegate/delegado un representante en una reunión (pág. 54)

demand/demanda el deseo, la disposición y la habilidad de comprar un bien o servicio (pág. 569)

demand curve/curva de demanda línea en declive que muestra gráficamente las cantidades demandadas a cada precio posible (pág. 569)

demand elasticity/elasticidad de demanda medida de respuesta que relaciona un cambio en la cantidad demandada con un cambio en el precio (pág. 577)

demand schedule/tabla de demanda tabla que muestra las cantidades demandadas a los diferentes precios posibles (pág. 569)

democracy/democracia un gobierno en el que los ciudadanos tienen el poder para gobernar (pág. 23)

deny/negar* negativa de otorgar, aceptar o creer (pág. 17)

deport/deportar enviar a un extranjero o inmigrante a su propio país (pág. 19)

despite* in spite of (p. 73)

developing country a country whose average per capita income is only a fraction of that in more industrialized countries (p. 724)

devote* to dedicate oneself to (p. 297)

diminish* to lessen or reduce (p. 509)

direct democracy a form of democracy in which the people vote firsthand (p. 23)

direct primary an election in which voters choose candidates to represent each party in a general election (p. 283)

discount rate the interest rate the Fed charges on its loans (p. 664)

discovery process by which attorneys have opportunity to check facts and gather evidence (p. 450)

discretionary income money income left after necessities have been bought and paid for (p. 539)

discretionary spending spending for federal programs that must receive annual approval (p. 677)

discrimination unfair treatment based on prejudice against a certain group (pp. 140, 618)

display* to put in plain view (p. 210)

disposable income money income left after all taxes on it have been paid (p. 539)

dispose* to throw away or discard (p. 529)

dissenting opinion a statement written by a justice who disagrees with the majority opinion, presenting his or her opinion (p. 256)

dissident person or group that disagrees with established systems (p. 475)

district court federal court where trials are held and lawsuits are begun (p. 244)

diverse* differing from one another (p. 8)

dividend payment of a portion of a company's earnings (p. 557)

division of labor the breaking down of a job into separate, smaller tasks to be performed individually (p. 524)

docket a court's calendar, showing the schedule of cases it is to hear (p. 255)

despite/a pesar* en contra de (pág. 73)

developing country/país en desarrollo un país cuyo ingreso per cápita promedio es sólo una fracción del valor en países más industrializados (pág. 724)

devote/dedicarse* destinar la atención de uno a (pág. 297)

diminish/disminuir* reducir (pág. 509)

direct democracy/democracia directa una forma de democracia en la que el pueblo vota directamente (pág. 23)

direct primary/elección primaria directa una elección en la que los votantes eligen a los candidatos para representar a cada partido en una elección general (pág. 283)

discount rate/tipo reducido la tasa de interés que el Fed cobra en sus préstamos (pág. 664)

discovery/descubrimiento proceso mediante el que los abogados pueden verificar los hechos y obtener evidencia (pág. 450)

discretionary income/ingresos discrecionales ingreso de dinero restante luego de haber comprado y pagado las necesidades básicas (pág. 539)

discretionary spending/gasto discrecional gastos para programas federales que deben recibir aprobación anual (pág. 677)

discrimination/discriminación trato injusto basado en el prejuicio contra cierto grupo (págs. 140, 618)

display/exhibir* colocar a la vista de todos (pág. 210)

disposable income/ingreso disponible ingreso de dinero restante luego de haber pagado todos los impuestos sobre éste (pág. 539)

dispose/desechar* tirar o descartar (pág. 529)

dissenting opinion/opinión disidente declaración escrita que presenta la opinión de un juez que está en desacuerdo con la opinión mayoritaria (pág. 256)

dissident/disidente persona o grupo que está en desacuerdo con los sistemas establecidos (pág. 475)

district courts/tribunales distrito tribunales federales en los que se llevan a cabo juicios y se inician demandas (pág. 244)

diverse/diverso* que difieren entre sí (pág. 8)

dividend/dividendo pago de una parte de las ganancias de una empresa (pág. 557)

division of labor/división de trabajo la separación de un trabajo en tareas separadas y más pequeñas que deben realizarse de manera individual (pág. 524)

docket/registro el calendario de un tribunal, que detalla el programa de casos que debe ver (pág. 255)

document* a written paper that provides information or proof of something (p. 33)

domestic* relating to or occurring in one's own country (p. 160)

dominate* to have command or control over (p. 379)

double jeopardy putting someone on trial for a crime of which he or she was previously acquitted (p. 128)

draft* to call up (p. 152)

due process following established legal procedures (p. 128)

due process of law procedures established by law and guaranteed by the Constitution (p. 437)

duty a thing we are required to do (p. 151)

document/documento* un documento escrito que brinda información o prueba de algo (pág. 33)

domestic/doméstico* que se relaciona con u ocurre en el país de uno (pág. 160)

dominate/dominar* dirigir o tener el control sobre (pág. 379)

double jeopardy/riesgo doble llevar a una persona a juicio por un delito por el que había sido absuelta anteriormente (pág. 128)

draft/llamamiento* a filas reclutar (pág. 152)

due process/proceso correspondiente seguir los procedimientos legales establecidos (pág. 128)

due process of law/proceso legal correspondiente procedimientos establecidos por la ley y garantizados por la Constitución (pág. 437)

duty/deber una cosa que debemos hacer (pág. 151)

E

Earned Income Tax Credit (EITC) a program that gives tax credits and even cash payments to qualified workers (p. 649)

economic interdependence a reliance on others, as they rely on you, to provide goods and services to be consumed (p. 525)

economic model simplified representation of the real world that economists develop to describe how the economy behaves and is expected to perform in the future (p. 500)

economics the study of how individuals and nations make choices about ways to use scarce resources to fulfill their needs and wants (p. 499)

economic system nation's way of producing things its people want and need (p. 500)

egalitarianism the philosophy or spirit of equality (p. 48)

elastic clause clause in Article I, Section 8 of the Constitution that gives Congress the right to make all laws "necessary and proper" to carry out its expressed powers (p. 185)

elector person appointed to vote in presidential elections for the major candidates (p. 210)

Earned Income Tax Credit (EITC)/crédito fiscal sobre ingresos un programa que otorga créditos fiscales e incluso pagos en efectivo a trabajadores calificados (pág. 649)

economic interdependence/interdependencia económica dependencia en otros, mientras que ellos dependen de ti, a fin de suministrar bienes y servicios para el consumo (pág. 525)

economic model/modelo económico representación simplificada del mundo real que los economistas crean para describir la forma en que la economía se comporta y se espera que actúe en el futuro (pág. 500)

economics/economía el estudio de la forma en que personas y naciones toman decisiones sobre las maneras de usar los recursos escasos, para satisfacer sus necesidades y deseos (pág. 499)

economic system/sistema económico manera de una nación de producir cosas que su población necesita y desea (pág. 500)

egalitarianism/igualitarismo la filosofía o el espíritu de igualdad (pág. 48)

elastic clause/cláusula elástica cláusula en el artículo I, sección 8 de la Constitución que otorga al Congreso el derecho de crear todas las leyes "necesarias y adecuadas" para ejercer sus poderes explícitos (pág. 185)

elector/elector persona designada para votar en elecciones presidenciales por los principales candidatos (pág. 210)

Electoral College a group of people named by each state legislature to select the president and vice president (pp. 76, 210, 301)

electorate all the people who are eligible to vote (p. 299)

electronic media radio, television, and the Internet (p. 327)

element* a component of a whole (p. 198)

eliminate* to get rid of (p. 562)

embargo an agreement among a group of nations that prohibits them all from trading with a target nation (p. 223)

eminent domain the right of government to take private property for public use (p. 128)

emphasis* placing stress or special importance on something (p. 463)

enable* to make able or possible (p. 476)

enforce* to carry out by force or ensure compliance (p. 21)

Enlightenment movement that spread the idea that reason and science could improve society (p. 33)

enormous* very large (p. 677)

ensure* to secure or make sure (p. 87)

entitlement program a program using eligibility requirements to provide health, nutritional, or income supplements to individuals (p. 684)

entrepreneur individual who starts a new business, introduces a new product, and improves a management technique (p. 517)

environmentalism movement concerned with protecting environment (p. 409)

equilibrium price the price at which the amount producers are willing to supply is equal to the amount consumers are willing to buy (p. 589)

equivalent* alike or equal to in number or meaning (p. 463)

erode* to wear away or destroy gradually (p. 483)

establish* to bring into existence or create (p. 553)

estimate* to judge the approximate nature, value, quality, or amount of a thing (pp. 193, 386)

Electoral College/Colegio Electoral un grupo de personas designadas por cada cuerpo legislativo estatal para elegir al presidente y al vicepresidente (págs. 76, 210, 301)

electorate/electorado todas las personas que tienen derecho a votar (pág. 299)

electronic media/medios electrónicos de comunicación radio, televisión e Internet (pág. 327)

element/elemento* un componente de un todo (pág. 198)

eliminate/eliminar* deshacerse de (pág. 562)

embargo/embargo un acuerdo entre un grupo de naciones que les prohíbe a todas comerciar con una nación en particular (pág. 223)

eminent domain/dominio eminente el derecho del gobierno de tomar propiedad privada para uso público (pág. 128)

emphasis/énfasis* hacer hincapié o dar especial importancia a algo (pág. 463)

enable/permitir* hacer posible (pág. 476)

enforce/hacer cumplir* llevar a cabo por fuerza o asegurar la conformidad (pág. 21)

Enlightenment/Iluminismo movimiento que sostenía la idea de que la razón y la ciencia podían mejorar a la sociedad (pág. 33)

enormous/enorme* muy grande (pág. 677)

ensure/asegurar* garantizar (pág. 87)

entitlement program/programa de derechos un programa que utiliza requisitos de elegibilidad para dar suplementos de ingresos, salud o nutricionales a personas (pág. 684)

entrepreneur/empresario persona que inician nuevos negocios, presentan nuevos productos y mejoran las técnicas de administración (pág. 517)

environmentalism/ecología movimiento dedicado a la protección del medio ambiente (pág. 409)

equilibrium price/precio de equilibrio el precio al que los productores están dispuestos a ofertar es igual al monto que los consumidores están dispuestos a comprar (pág. 589)

equivalent/equivalente* similar o igual en número o significado (pág. 463)

erode/desgastar* gastar o destruir gradualmente (pág. 483)

establish/establecer* dar vida o crear (pág. 553)

estimate/estimar* juzgar la naturaleza, el valor, la calidad o la cantidad aproximada de algo (págs. 193, 386)

ethnic* relating to races or groups of people who share common traits and customs (p. 9)

evaluate* to assess or find the value of (p. 560)

eventually* in the end (p. 710)

exceed* to be or go beyond a limit (p. 545)

exchange rate the price of one nation's currency in terms of another nation's currency (p. 712)

exclude* to shut out (p. 631)

exclusive jurisdiction authority of only federal courts to hear and decide cases (p. 242)

executive agreement an agreement between the president and the leader of another country (p. 222)

executive branch the branch of government that carries out laws (p. 80)

executive order a rule or command that has the force of law (p. 216)

exit poll a survey taken at polling places of how people voted (p. 297)

expand* to increase in size or amount (p. 353)

expense money spent on goods and services (p. 546)

exploit* to take advantage of (p. 717)

export to sell goods to other countries; a good produced in one country, then sold to another (p. 707)

ex post facto law a law that would allow a person to be punished for an action that was not against the law when it was committed (p. 188)

expressed powers powers that Congress has that are specifically listed in the Constitution (pp. 89, 185)

externality the unintended side effect of an action that affects someone not involved in the action (p. 631)

extremist group organization that promotes ideas that are farthest from the political center (p. 476)

ethnic/étnico* relativo a razas o grupos de personas que comparten los mismos rasgos y costumbres (pág. 9)

evaluate/evaluar* encontrar el valor de (pág. 560)

eventually/finalmente* por ultimo (pág. 710)

exceed/exceder* estar o ir más allá de un límite (pág. 545)

exchange rate/tipo de cambio el precio de la moneda de una nación en términos de la moneda de otra nación (pág. 712)

exclude/excluir* dejar afuera (pág. 631)

exclusive jurisdiction/jurisdicción exclusiva autoridad de los tribunales federales únicamente de ver y decidir casos (pág. 242)

executive agreement/acuerdo ejecutivo un acuerdo entre el presidente y el líder de otro país (pág. 222)

executive branch/poder ejecutivo el poder del gobierno que crea las leyes (pág. 80)

executive order/orden ejecutiva una regla que tiene la fuerza de una ley (pág. 216)

exit poll/encuesta de votación una encuesta que se realiza en los lugares de votación sobre cómo votó la gente (pág. 297)

expand/expandir* incrementar en tamaño o cantidad (pág. 353)

expense/gasto dinero gastado en bienes y servicios (pág. 546)

exploit/explotar* aprovecharse de (pág. 717)

export/exportar, exportación vender bienes a otros países; un bien producido en un país y luego vendido a otro (pág. 707)

ex post facto law/ley con efecto retroactivo una ley que permitiría que una persona sea castigada por una acción que no era contra la ley cuando la realizó (pág. 188)

expressed powers/poderes explícitos poderes que tiene el Congreso y que están detallados específicamente en la Constitución (págs. 89, 185)

externality/exterioridad el efecto secundario no planificado de una acción que afecta a alguien que no forma parte en la acción (pág. 631)

extremist group/grupo extremista organización que promueve ideas totalmente alejadas del centro político (pág. 476)

F

factor* an element contributing to a result (p. 437)

factor market a market where productive resources are bought and sold (p. 521)

factors of production resources necessary to produce goods and services (p. 517)

federal* of or involving the federal government (p. 411)

federal bureaucracy agencies and the employees of the executive branch of government (p. 228)

federalism a form of government in which power is divided between the federal, or national, government and the states (p. 77)

Federalists supporters of the Constitution (p. 77)

Federal Open Market Committee (FOMC) the most powerful committee of the Fed, because it makes the decisions that affect the economy as a whole by manipulating the money supply (p. 661)

federal system the sharing of power between the central and state governments (p. 351)

fee* a charge (p. 307)

felony a serious crime such as murder, rape, kidnapping, or robbery (pp. 368, 432)

file* to submit or register (p. 449)

filibuster a tactic for defeating a bill in the Senate by talking until the bill's sponsor withdraws it (p. 200)

financial capital money used to buy the tools and equipment used in production (p. 601)

fiscal policy the federal government's use of spending and taxation policies to affect overall business activity (p. 641)

flexible* able to adapt easily (p. 712)

factor/factor* un elemento que contribuye a un resultado (pág. 437)

factor market/mercado de factores un mercado en el que se compran y venden recursos productivos (pág. 521)

factors of production/factores de producción recursos necesarios para producir bienes y servicios (pág. 517)

federal/federal* perteneciente o relacionado con el gobierno federal (pág. 411)

federal bureaucracy/burocracia federal las agencias colectivas y los empleados del poder ejecutivo (pág. 228)

federalism/federalismo una forma de gobierno en la que el poder está dividido entre el gobierno federal, o nacional, y los estados (pág. 77)

Federalists/federalistas defensores de la Constitución (pág. 77)

Federal Open Market Committee (FOMC)/ Comité Federal del Mercado Abierto el comité más poderoso del Fed, ya que toma las decisiones que afectan la economía en general al manipular la oferta monetaria (pág. 661)

federal system/sistema federal la posesión conjunta del poder entre los gobiernos centrales y estatales (pág. 351)

fee/costo* un cargo (pág. 307)

felony/felonía un delito grave como asesinato, violación, secuestro o robo (págs. 368, 432)

file/presentar* enviar o registrar (pág. 449)

filibuster/maniobra obstruccionista una táctica para rechazar un proyecto de ley en el Senado al hablar hasta que el patrocinador del proyecto de ley la retire (pág. 200)

financial capital/capital financiero dinero usado para comprar las herramientas y los equipos usados en la producción (pág. 601)

fiscal policy/política fiscal el uso de políticas sobre gastos e impuestos por parte del gobierno federal para afectar la actividad comercial en general (pág. 641)

flexible/flexible* que se adapta con facilidad (pág. 712)

focus* a central point of attention or activity (p. 590)

food stamps government coupons that can be used to purchase food (p. 648)

foreign policy a nation's overall plan for dealing with other nations (p. 220)

foundation* an organization (p. 616)

franking privilege the right of senators and representatives to send job-related mail without paying postage (p. 192)

free enterprise economic system in which individuals and businesses are allowed to compete for profit with a minimum of government interference (p. 528)

function* to serve a purpose (p. 453)

fund* a sum of money (p. 553)

furthermore* in addition, moreover (p. 379)

focus/centro* un punto central de atención o actividad (pág. 590)

food stamps/estampillas para alimentos cupones del gobierno que pueden usarse para comprar alimentos (pág. 648)

foreign policy/política extranjera el plan global de una nación para el trato con otras naciones (pág. 220)

foundation/fundación* una organización (pág. 616)

franking privilege/privilegio de franqueo el derecho de los senadores y representantes de enviar correo relacionado con el trabajo sin pagar franqueo (pág. 192)

free enterprise/empresa libre sistema económico en el que personas y negocios pueden competir por las ganancias con mínima interferencia del gobierno (pág. 528)

function/función* servir para un propósito (pág. 453)

fund/fondo* una suma de dinero (pág. 553)

furthermore/además* lo que es más, por otra parte (pág. 379)

G

gender* a notation of the sex of a person (pp. 141, 319)

generate* to bring into existence (p. 502)

genocide mass murder of a people because of their race, religion, ethnicity, politics, or culture (p. 745)

gerrymander an oddly-shaped election district designed to increase the voting strength of a particular group (p. 179)

global* relating to the entire world (p. 151)

globalization individuals and nations working across barriers of distance, culture, and technology (p. 742)

good tangible product that we use to satisfy our wants and needs (p. 517)

government the ruling authority for a community (p. 21)

government corporation a business owned and operated by the federal government (p. 229)

grand jury a group of citizens that decides whether there is sufficient evidence to accuse someone of a crime (pp. 128, 439)

gender/género* una notación del sexo de una persona (págs. 141, 319)

generate/generar* dar vida (pág. 502)

genocide/genocidio asesinato en masa de un pueblo debido a su raza, religión, origen étnico, política o cultura (pág. 745)

gerrymander/*gerrymander* un distrito formado de manera extraña para incrementar la fuerza de votación de un grupo particular (pág. 179)

global/global* relativo a todo el mundo (pág. 151)

globalization/globalización personas y naciones que trabajan a través de las barreras de distancia, cultura y tecnología (pág. 742)

good/biene producto tangible que usamos para satisfacer nuestros deseos y necesidades (pág. 517)

government/gobierno la autoridad que gobierna a una comunidad (pág. 21)

government corporation/corporación gubernamental una empresa que es propiedad del gobierno federal y es operada por éste (pág. 229)

grand jury/jurado un grupo de ciudadanos que decide si hay suficiente evidencia para acusar a una persona de un delito (págs. 128, 439)

grant   **implied powers**

grant to allow or permit (p. 33)

grants-in-aid money awarded to the states by the federal government (p. 353)

Great Compromise agreement providing a dual system of congressional representation (p. 75)

Gross Domestic Product (GDP) total dollar value of all final goods and services produced in a country during a single year (p. 518)

guarantee* to promise or give security (p. 337)

guideline* an outline or guide for a future course of action (p. 364)

grant/otorgar permitir (pág. 33)

grants-in-aid/subsidios dinero otorgado a los estados por parte del gobierno federal (pág. 353)

Great Compromise/Gran Compromiso acuerdo que estipula un sistema dual de representación del Congreso (pág. 75)

Gross Domestic Product (GDP)/Producto Interno Bruto (PIB) valor total en dólares de todos los bienes y servicios finales producidos en un país durante un único año (pág. 518)

guarantee/garantizar* prometer o dar seguridad (pág. 337)

guideline/directriz* un esquema o una guía para un curso de acción futuro (pág. 364)

home rule allows cities to write their own charters, choose their own type of government, and manage their own affairs (p. 377)

human rights fundamental freedoms of individuals (p. 744)

hung jury a jury that cannot agree on a verdict (p. 458)

home rule/autonomía política permite que las ciudades redacten sus propias cartas, elijan a su propio tipo de gobierno y administren sus propios asuntos (pág. 377)

human rights/derechos humanos libertades fundamentales de las personas (pág. 744)

hung jury/jurado en desacuerdo un jurado que no puede llegar a un veredicto (pág. 458)

identify* to find or show the identity of (p. 570)

ideological* relating to a body of opinions (p. 691)

illustrate* to show or make clear by example (p. 572)

image* a representation or public perception (p. 307)

immigrant a person who moves permanently to a new country (p. 16)

impact* to influence or affect (pp. 69, 216)

impeach to accuse government officials of misconduct in office (p. 187)

implement* to put into practice (p. 641)

implied powers powers that Congress has that are not stated explicitly in the Constitution (p. 185)

identify/identificar* encontrar o mostrar la identidad de (pág. 570)

ideological/ideólogical* relativo un conjunto de ideas u opiniones (pág. 691)

illustrate/ilustrar* mostrar o aclarar mediante un ejemplo (pág. 572)

image/imagen* una representación o percepción pública (pág. 307)

immigrant/inmigrante una persona que se muda de manera permanente a un nuevo país (pág. 16)

impact/impactar* influir o afectar (págs. 69, 216)

impeach/impugnar acusar a funcionarios del gobierno de mala conducta en el desempeño de su cargo (pág. 187)

implement/implementar* poner en práctica (pág. 641)

implied powers/poderes implícitos poderes que tiene el Congreso y que no están detallados explícitamente en la Constitución (pág. 185)

imply* to suggest something rather than directly state it (p. 123)

import a good purchased from one country by another (p. 707)

impose* to establish as a charge or penalty (p. 401)

impulse buying purchasing an item on the spot because of an emotional rather than planned decision (p. 561)

incentive* reward offered to try to persuade people to take certain economic actions (p. 529)

income* money received from labor, business, or property (pp. 152, 545)

incorporate to receive a state charter, officially recognizing the government of a locality (p. 377)

incumbent a politician who has already been elected to office (p. 309)

indentured servant workers who contracted with American colonists for food and shelter in return for their labor (p. 42)

independence self-reliance and freedom from outside control (p. 54)

independent agency federal board or commission that is not part of any cabinet department (p. 229)

indictment a formal charge by a grand jury (p. 128)

inflation sustained increase in the general level of prices (p. 641)

infrastructure a community's system of roads, bridges, water, and sewers (p. 399)

initial* the very first (p. 667)

initiative a procedure by which citizens can propose new laws or state constitutional amendments (p. 301)

innovate* to introduce or create something new (p. 517)

input* resources factored into the economy (p. 523)

institution sets of ideas that people have about relationships, obligations, roles, and functions of society (p. 13)

intellectual property things that people create, such as songs, movies, books, poetry, art, and software (p. 482)

imply/insinuar* algo sugerido en vez de dicho directamente (pág. 123)

import/importación un bien que compra un país a otro (pág. 707)

impose/imponer* establecer como un cargo o una pena (pág. 401)

impulse buying/comprar por impulso comprar un artículo en el momento debido a una decisión emocional en lugar de una planificada (pág. 561)

incentive/incentivo* recompensa ofrecida para tratar de persuadir a que la gente tome ciertas decisiones económicas (pág. 529)

income/ingresos* dinero recibido del trabajo, negocio o propiedad (págs. 152, 545)

incorporate/incorporar recibir una carta del estado, mediante la que se reconoce oficialmente el gobierno de una localidad (pág. 377)

incumbent/titular un político que ya ha sido elegido para un cargo (pág. 309)

indentured servant/sirvientes por contrato trabajadores que se empleaban con los colonos estadounidenses por alimento y casa a cambio de su trabajo (pág. 42)

independence/independencia dependencia en sí mismo y libertad del control externo (pág. 54)

independent agency/agencia independiente comisión o junta federal que no forma parte de ningún departamento del gabinete (pág. 229)

indictment/acusación un cargo formal de un jurado (pág. 128)

inflation/inflación incremento sostenido en el nivel general de los precios (pág. 641)

infrastructure/infraestructura el sistema de calles, puentes, agua y desagües de una comunidad (pág. 399)

initial/inicial* el primero de todos (pág. 667)

initiative/iniciativa un procedimiento mediante el que los ciudadanos pueden proponer nuevas leyes o exponer enmiendas constitucionales (pág. 301)

innovate/innovar* introducir o crear algo nuevo (pág. 517)

input/insumos* recursos ingresados a la economía (pág. 523)

institution/institución conjuntos de ideas que las personas tienen sobre las relaciones, las obligaciones, los papeles y las funciones de la sociedad (pág. 13)

intellectual property/propiedad intelectual cosas que la gente crea, como canciones, películas, libros, poesía, arte y software (pág. 482)

interact   **justice of the peace**

interact* to act upon one another (p. 471)

interest the payment people receive when they lend money or allow someone else to use their money (p. 554)

interest group a group of people who share a point of view about an issue and unite to promote their beliefs (p. 321)

intergovernmental revenues funds one level of government receives from another level of government (p. 682)

intermediate* being or occurring in the middle or between two points (p. 368)

internationalism involvement in world affairs (p. 740)

Internet a mass communication system of millions of networked computers and databases all over the world (p. 471)

interpret* to explain or translate (p. 436)

interval* a break or period of time between two events (p. 557)

intervene* to come between (p. 716)

involve* to take part in or include as a necessary component (p. 131)

isolate* to separate or keep apart (p. 476)

issue* a matter of debate or dispute (p. 301); to distribute or send out (p. 363)

interact/interactuar* actuar recíprocamente (pág. 471)

interest/interés el pago que recibe la gente cuando presta dinero o permite que otra persona use su dinero (pág. 554)

interest group/grupo de interés un grupo de personas que comparten un punto de vista sobre una cuestión y se unen para promover sus creencias (pág. 321)

intergovernmental revenues/ingresos intergubernamentales fondos que recibe un nivel del gobierno de otro nivel del gobierno (pág. 682)

intermediate/intermedio* que está u ocurre en el medio o entre dos puntos (pág. 368)

internationalism/internacionalismo participación en los asuntos mundiales (pág. 740)

Internet/Internet un sistema de comunicación masiva de millones de computadoras y bases de datos conectados en red en todo el mundo (pág. 471)

interpret/interpretar* explicar o traducir (pág. 436)

interval/intervalo* un descanso o período de tiempo entre dos eventos (pág. 557)

intervene/intervener* interponerse entre (pág. 716)

involve/involucrar* formar parte de o incluir como un componente necesario (pág. 131)

isolate/aislar* separar o mantener alejado (pág. 476)

issue/cuestión* un asunto de debate o conflicto (pág. 301) **issue/expedir*** distribuir o enviar (pág. 363)

J

joint resolution a resolution that is passed by both houses of Congress (p. 198)

joint-stock company investors provide partial ownership in a company organized for profit (p. 36)

judicial branch the branch of government that interprets laws (p. 81)

judicial review the power of the Supreme Court to say whether any federal, state, or local law or government action goes against the Constitution (p. 252)

jurisdiction a court's authority to hear and decide cases (p. 240)

justice of the peace the judge of a small, local court (p. 367)

joint resolution/resolución colectiva una resolución que es aprobada por ambas cámaras del Congreso (pág. 198)

joint-stock company/sociedad anónima inversores con propiedad parcial de una empresa organizada para obtener ganancias (pág. 36)

judicial branch/poder judicial el poder del gobierno que interpreta las leyes (pág. 81)

judicial review/revisión judicial el poder de la Suprema Corte de decir si alguna acción gubernamental o ley federal, estatal o local va en contra de la Constitución (pág. 252)

jurisdiction/jurisdicción la autoridad de un tribunal de ver y decidir casos (pág. 240)

justice of the peace/juez de paz el juez de un tribunal local pequeño (pág. 367)

juvenile a person not yet legally an adult (p. 461)

juvenile delinquent a child or teenager who commits a serious crime or repeatedly breaks the law (p. 461)

juvenile/menor una persona que aún no es legalmente un adulto (pág. 461)

juvenile delinquent/delincuente juvenil un niño o adolescente que comete un delito grave o viola la ley repetidamente (pág. 461)

L

labor human effort directed toward producing goods and services (p. 517)

labor union association of workers organized to improve wages and working conditions (p. 609)

laissez-faire economics economic system where government should not interfere in the marketplace (p. 531)

landfill place where garbage is dumped (p. 409)

larceny the unlawful taking away of another person's property with the intent never to return it (p. 432)

law of demand the concept that people are normally willing to buy less of a product if the price is high and more of it if the price is low (p. 569)

law of supply suppliers will normally offer more for sale at higher prices and less at lower prices (p. 581)

lawsuit a legal action in which a person or group sues to collect damages for some harm that is done (p. 432)

leak the release of secret government information by anonymous government officials to the media (p. 328)

legislative branch the lawmaking branch of government (p. 80)

legislature a group of people that makes laws (p. 33)

levy* to require taxes to be paid (p. 385)

libel written untruths that are harmful to someone's reputation (pp. 124, 330, 433)

likewise* similarly or in addition (p. 572)

line-item veto to veto only a specific part of a bill (p. 364)

labor/trabajo esfuerzo humano con el objetivo de producir bienes y servicios (pág. 517)

labor union/sindicato asociación de trabajadores organizada para mejorar los salarios y las condiciones de trabajo (pág. 609)

laissez-faire economics/economía laissez-faire sistema económico en el que el gobierno no intervendría en el mercado (pág. 531)

landfill/vertedero lugar donde se vierte la basura (pág. 409)

larceny/robo tomar ilegalmente la propiedad de otra persona sin intención alguna de devolverla (pág. 432)

law of demand/ley de demanda el concepto de que la gente normalmente está dispuesta a comprar menos de un producto si el precio es alto y más si el precio es bajo (pág. 569)

law of supply/ley de oferta los proveedores normalmente ofrecen más para la venta a precios más altos y menos a precios más bajos (pág. 581)

lawsuit/pleito una acción legal en la que una persona o un grupo realiza una demanda para cobrar una compensación por algún daño que se le ha hecho (pág. 432)

leak/filtración de información la revelación de información gubernamental confidencial por parte de funcionarios gubernamentales anónimos a los medios de comunicación (pág. 328)

legislative branch/poder legislativo el poder del gobierno que crea las leyes (pág. 80)

legislature/asamblea legislativa un grupo de personas que crea leyes (pág. 33)

levy/recaudar* exigir que se paguen los impuestos (pág. 385)

libel/difamación falsedades escritas que son perjudiciales para la reputación de alguien (págs. 124, 330, 433)

likewise/igualmente* asimismo o también (pág. 572)

line-item veto/veto parcial vetar sólo una parte específica de un proyecto de ley (pág. 364)

lobbyist representative of an interest group who contacts lawmakers or other government officials directly to influence their policy making (pp. 192, 335)

long-term plan a government plan for policy that can span 10 to 50 years (p. 398)

lobbyist/lobista representante de un grupo de interés que contacta a legisladores u otros funcionarios gubernamentales directamente para influir en su creación de políticas (págs. 192, 335)

long-term plan/plan a largo plazo plan del gobierno por política que se puede extender de 10 a 50 años (pág. 398)

M

macroeconomics economic behavior and decision-making by government or whole industries or societies (p. 500)

magistrate courts police courts generally located in larger towns, may handle traffic violations, civil cases involving small amounts of money, etc. (p. 367)

maintain* to keep up (p. 740)

majority a number that is more than 50 percent of the total (p. 284)

majority opinion a statement that presents the views of the majority of Supreme Court justices regarding a case (p. 256)

majority party in both the House of Representatives and the Senate, the political party to which more than half the members belong (p. 180)

majority rule political principle providing that a majority of the members of a community has the power to make laws binding upon all the people (p. 25)

malapportionment unequal representation in state legislatures (p. 359)

malice evil intent (p. 330)

mandatory sentencing punishment that judges must impose according to what the law directs (p. 454)

mandatory spending federal spending required by law that continues without the need for annual approvals by Congress (p. 677)

manipulate* to handle with skill (p. 661)

marginal benefit the additional or extra benefit associated with an action (p. 508)

marginal cost the additional or extra opportunity cost associated with an action (p. 507)

macroeconomics/macroeconomía conducta económica y toma de decisiones por parte de un gobierno, las industrias en conjunto o las sociedades (pág. 500)

magistrate courts/cortes de magistrados juzgados de guardia generalmente ubicados en pueblos más grandes; pueden encargarse de las violaciones de tránsito, casos civiles relacionados con pequeñas cantidades de dinero, etc. (pág. 367)

maintain/mantener* continuar con (pág. 740)

majority/mayoría cantidad que es más del 50 por ciento del total (pág. 284)

majority opinion/opinión mayoritaria declaración que presenta la opinión de la mayoría de los jueces de la Suprema Corte sobre un caso (pág. 256)

majority party/partido mayoritario tanto en la Cámara de Representantes como en el Senado, el partido político al que pertenece más de la mitad de los miembros (pág. 180)

majority rule/principio mayoritario principio político que estipula que una mayoría de los miembros de una comunidad tiene el poder de crear leyes vinculantes para toda la gente (pág. 25)

malapportionment/mala asignación representación desigual en las legislaturas estatales (pág. 359)

malice/malicia propósito maligno (pág. 330)

mandatory sentencing/sentencias obligatorias castigos que los jueces deben imponer de acuerdo a lo que dicta la ley (pág. 454)

mandatory spending/gastos obligatorios gastos federales requeridos por ley que tienen lugar sin la necesidad de aprobaciones anuales del Congreso (pág. 677)

manipulate/manipular* manejar hábilmente (pág. 661)

marginal benefit/beneficio marginal el beneficio extra o adicional asociado con una acción (pág. 508)

marginal cost/costo marginal el costo de oportunidad extra o adicional asociado con una acción (pág. 507)

marginal utility additional use that is derived from each unit acquired (p. 572)

market free and willing exchange of goods and services between buyers and sellers (p. 521)

market demand the total demand of all consumers for a product or service (p. 570)

market economy system in which individuals own the factors of production and make economic decisions through free interaction (p. 716)

market supply the total of the supply schedules of businesses that provide the same good or service (p. 584)

mass media a mechanism of mass communication, including television, radio, newspapers, magazines, recordings, movies, the Internet, and books (p. 320)

master plan a plan that states a set of goals and explains how the government will carry them out to meet changing needs over time (p. 399)

mechanism* the steps that compose a process or activity (p. 588)

media* a means of communication with large influence (p. 122)

mediation situation in which union and company officials bring in a third party to try to help them reach an agreement (p. 611)

Medicare government program that provides health care for the aged (p. 678)

medium* a means of doing (p. 657)

mercantilism the theory that a country should sell more goods to other countries than it buys (p. 51)

merger a combination of two or more companies to form a single business (p. 633)

merit system hiring people into government jobs on the basis of their qualifications (p. 230)

method* a procedure or process of doing something (p. 222)

metropolitan area a large city and its suburbs (p. 382)

marginal utility/utilidad marginal uso adicional que se obtiene de cada unidad adquirida (pág. 572)

market/mercado intercambio de bienes y servicios libre y voluntario entre compradores y vendedores (pág. 521)

market demand/demanda de mercado la demanda total de todos los consumidores para un producto o servicio (pág. 570)

market economy/economía de mercado sistema en el que las personas son propietarias de los factores de producción y toman decisiones económicas a través de una interacción libre (pág. 716)

market supply/oferta de mercado el total de los programas de oferta de los negocios que proporcionan el mismo bien o servicio (pág. 584)

mass media/medios masivos de información un mecanismo de comunicación masiva, que incluye televisión, radio, periódicos, revistas, grabaciones, películas, Internet y libros (pág. 320)

master plan/plan maestro un plan que especifica un conjunto de objetivos y explica la forma en que el gobierno los llevará a cabo para satisfacer las necesidades cambiantes con el tiempo (pág. 399)

mechanism/mecanismo* los pasos que componen un proceso o una actividad (pág. 588)

media/medios de comunicación* un medio de comunicación con gran influencia (pág. 122)

mediation/mediación situación en la que los jefes de compañías y sindicatos requieren a un tercero para que los ayude a llegar a un acuerdo (pág. 611)

Medicare/Medicare programa gubernamental que brinda atención médica a las personas mayores (pág. 678)

medium/medio* cosa que puede servir para un determinado fin (pág. 657)

mercantilism/mercantilismo la teoría de que un país debería vender más bienes a otros países de los que compra (pág. 51)

merger/fusión empresarial una combinación de dos o más compañías para formar un único negocio (pág. 633)

merit system/sistema de méritos la contratación de personas en empleos gubernamentales sobre la base de sus calificaciones (pág. 230)

method/método* un procedimiento o proceso para hacer algo (pág. 222)

metropolitan area/área metropolitana una gran ciudad y sus suburbios (pág. 382)

microeconomics the economic behavior and decision-making by individuals and small businesses (p. 500)

minimize* to make as small as possible (p. 634)

minimum wage lowest legal wage that can be paid to most U.S. workers (p. 589)

minority party in both the House of Representatives and the Senate, the political party to which fewer than half the members belong (p. 180)

misdemeanor a relatively minor offense such as vandalism or stealing inexpensive items (pp. 367, 432)

mixed economy system combining characteristics of more than one type of economy (p. 719)

monarch king or queen (p. 33)

monarchy a government with a hereditary, single leader (p. 24)

monetary policy policy that involves changing the rate of growth of the money supply in circulation in order to affect the cost and availability of credit (p. 664)

monitor* to watch or observe (p. 225)

monopoly when the market creates a sole provider for a good or service (p. 633)

motive* something that causes a person to act (p. 583)

multinational firm that does business or has offices in many countries (p. 742)

mutual* shared feelings (p. 741)

mutual funds pools of money from many people who are invested in a selection of individual stocks and bonds chosen by financial experts (p. 558)

microeconomics/microeconomía conducta económica y toma de decisiones realizada por individuos y pequeñas empresas (pág. 500)

minimize/minimizar* hacer lo más pequeño posible (pág. 634)

minimum wage/salario mínimo el más bajo sueldo legal que se le puede pagar a la mayoría de trabajadores en Estados Unidos (pág. 589)

minority party/partido minoritario tanto en la Cámara de Representantes como en el Senado, el partido político al que pertenece menos de la mitad de los miembros (pág. 180)

misdemeanor/delito menor una falta relativamente menor como vandalismo o el robo de artículos sin valor (págs. 367, 432)

mixed economy/economía mixta sistema que combina características de más de un tipo de economía (pág. 719)

monarch/monarca rey o reina (pág. 33)

monarchy/monarquía gobierno con un único líder hereditario (pág. 24)

monetary policy/política monetaria política que implica el cambio de la tasa de crecimiento de la oferta monetaria en circulación a fin de afectar el costo y la disponibilidad del crédito (pág. 664)

monitor/monitorear* mirar u observar (pág. 225)

monopoly/monopolio situación en la que el mercado crea un solo proveedor para un bien o servicio (pág. 633)

motive/motivo* algo que hace que una persona actúe (pág. 583)

multinational/multinacional empresa que hace negocios o posee oficinas en varios países (pág. 742)

mutual/mutuo* sentimientos compartidos (pág. 741)

mutual funds/fondos mutuos montos de dinero proveniente de muchos individuos que se invierten en una variedad de acciones y bonos individuales seleccionados por expertos financieros. (pág. 558)

N

national committee representatives from the 50 state party organizations who run a political party (p. 279)

national security the ability to keep the country safe from attack or harm (p. 220)

natural monopoly a market situation in which the costs of production are minimized by having a single firm produce the product (p. 634)

national committee/comité nacional representantes de las organizaciones de partidos de los 50 estados que dirigen un partido político (pág. 279)

national security/seguridad nacional la habilidad de mantener al país seguro frente a ataques o daños (pág. 220)

natural monopoly/monopolio natural una situación de mercado en la que los costos de producción se ven minimizados al haber una única empresa que produce el bien (pág. 634)

natural resources gifts of nature that make production possible (p. 517)

natural rights freedoms people possess relating to life, liberty, and property (p. 34)

naturalization a legal process to obtain citizenship (p. 15)

need requirement for survival, such as food, clothing, and shelter (p. 499)

network* a group of broadcasting stations; a system of connected or related parts (p. 471)

nevertheless* even so (p. 723)

newsgroup Internet discussion forum (p. 472)

nonetheless* nevertheless, however (p. 482)

nonpartisan free from party ties or bias (p. 471)

natural resources/recursos naturales regalos de la naturaleza que posibilitan la producción (pág. 517)

natural rights/derechos naturales libertades que las personas poseen relativas a la vida, a la libertad y a la propiedad (pág. 34)

naturalization/naturalización proceso legal para obtener la ciudadanía (pág. 15)

need/necesidad requisito para la supervivencia, como alimentos, vestimenta y alojamiento (pág. 499)

network/red* un grupo de estaciones de radiodifusión; un sistema de partes conectadas o relacionadas (pág. 471)

nevertheless/sin embargo* no obstante, a pesar de ello (pág. 723)

newsgroup/grupo de noticias foro de conversación en Internet (pág. 472)

nonetheless/sin embargo* no obstante, a pesar de ello (pág. 482)

nonpartisan/no partidario libre de vínculos partidarios o parcialidad (pág. 471)

O

obtain* to gain or acquire (p. 17)

obvious* easily found, seen, or understood (p. 657)

occur* to happen or take place (p. 178)

odd* additional to what is usual (p. 301)

open market operations purchase or sale of U.S. government bonds and Treasury bills (p. 665)

open primary an election in which voters need not declare their party preference (p. 283)

opinion a detailed explanation of the legal thinking behind a court's decision in a case (p. 245)

opportunity cost the cost of the next best use of time and money when choosing to do one thing or another (p. 505)

option* an alternative or choice (p. 611)

ordinance a law, usually of a city or county (p. 378)

original jurisdiction the authority to hear cases for the first time (p. 244)

outcome* the result of an action or event (p. 210)

output* something produced (p. 517)

obtain/obtener* ganar o adquirir (pág. 17)

obvious/obvio* fácil de encontrar, ver o entender (pág. 657)

occur/ocurrir* suceder o tener lugar (pág. 178)

odd/impar* adicional a lo que es usual (pág. 301)

open market operations/operaciones de mercado libre compra o venta de letras del Tesoro y bonos del gobierno de los EE. UU. (pág. 665)

open primary/elección primaria abierta una elección en la que los votantes no deben declarar su partido de preferencia (pág. 283)

opinion/opinión una explicación detallada del pensamiento legal detrás de la decisión de un tribunal en un caso (pág. 245)

opportunity cost/costo de oportunidad el costo del próximo mejor uso de tiempo y dinero cuando se elige hacer una cosa u otra (pág. 505)

option/opción* una alternativa (pág. 611)

ordinance/ordenanza una ley, normalmente de una ciudad o un condado (pág. 378)

original jurisdiction/jurisdicción original la autoridad para ver casos por primera vez (pág. 244)

outcome/resultado* las consecuencias de una acción o un evento (pág. 210)

output/producto* algo producido (pág. 517)

pardon

pocket veto

P

pardon a declaration of forgiveness and freedom from punishment (p. 217)

parole to grant a prisoner an early release from prison, with certain restrictions (p. 454)

partnership a business owned by two or more people (p. 602)

penal code a state's written criminal laws (p. 453)

per capita GDP Gross Domestic Product per person (p. 716)

percent* a portion of 100 (p. 158)

period* a length of time (p. 638)

petition a formal request for government action (p. 123); or, a process by which candidates who are not affiliated with one of the two major parties can get on the ballot for the general election in most states (p. 284)

phenomenon* a rare or important fact or event (p. 577)

philosophy* a system of beliefs or principles about practical affairs (p. 250)

Pilgrim colonial Puritans who considered themselves people on a religious journey (p. 41)

plaintiff a person or party filing a lawsuit (pp. 368, 431)

plank each individual part of a political party's platform (p. 277)

planning commission an advisory group to a community (p. 398)

plantation a large estate (p. 43)

platform a series of statements expressing the party's principles, beliefs, and positions on election issues (p. 277)

plea bargain negotiation between the defense attorney and the prosecutor (p. 440)

plurality the most votes among all those running for a political office (p. 284)

pocket veto president's power to kill a bill, if Congress is not in session, by not signing it for 10 days (p. 202)

pardon/indulto una declaración de perdón y liberación de una pena (pág. 217)

parole/libertad condicional otorgar a un prisionero una liberación anticipada de la prisión, con ciertas restricciones (pág. 454)

partnership/asociación un negocio que es propiedad de una o más personas (pág. 602)

penal code/código penal leyes penales escritas de un estado (pág. 453)

per capita GDP/PIB per cápita producto interno bruto por persona (pág. 716)

percent/porcentaje* una porción de 100 (pág. 158)

period/período* un tiempo determinado (pág. 638)

petition/petición una solicitud formal de acción gubernamental (pág. 123); o, un proceso mediante el cual candidatos no que están afiliados a uno de los dos partidos principales pueden ingresar a la boleta electoral para la elección general en la mayoría de los estados (pág. 284)

phenomenon/fenómeno* un hecho o evento raro o importante (pág. 577)

philosophy/filosofía* un sistema de creencias o principios sobre cuestiones prácticas (pág. 250)

Pilgrim/Peregrino puritanos coloniales que se consideraban individuos en un viaje religioso (pág. 41)

plaintiff/demandante una persona o un partido que presenta una demanda (págs. 368, 431)

plank/punto cada parte individual de la plataforma de un partido político (pág. 277)

planning commission/comisión de planificación grupo asesor de una comunidad (pág. 398)

plantation/plantación propiedad extensa (pág. 43)

platform/plataforma una serie de declaraciones que expresan los principios, las creencias y las posiciones del partido político sobre los temas de la elección (pág. 277)

plea bargain/acuerdo de reducción de sentencia negociación entre el abogado defensor y el fiscal (pág. 440)

plurality/pluralidad la mayor cantidad de votos entre aquellas personas que se postulan a un cargo político (pág. 284)

pocket veto/veto indirecto el poder del presidente de acabar con un proyecto de ley, si el Congreso no está en sesión, al no firmarlo durante 10 días (pág. 202)

policy* a guiding course of action (pp. 217, 397, 745)

political action committee (PAC) political organization established by a corporation, labor union, or other special-interest group designed to support candidates by contributing money (pp. 308, 334)

political appointee a person appointed to a federal position by the president (p. 229)

political machine a strong party organization that can control political appointments and deliver votes (p. 282)

political party an association of voters with broad common interests who want to influence or control decision making in government by electing the party's candidates to public office (p. 273)

poll tax a sum of money required of voters before they are permitted to cast a ballot (p. 137)

polling place the location where voting is carried out (p. 295)

pollster a specialist whose job is to conduct polls regularly (p. 323)

popular sovereignty the notion that power lies with the people (pp. 12, 86)

pork-barrel project government project grant that primarily benefits the home district or state (p. 196)

portion* a share or part of a whole (p. 367)

potential* capable of being or becoming (p. 427)

Preamble the opening section of the Constitution (p. 80)

precedent a ruling that is used as the basis for a judicial decision in a later, similar case (pp. 34, 245, 429)

precinct a geographic area that contains a specific number of voters (pp. 281, 295)

precise* to be exact (p. 688)

preliminary* coming before the main part or item (p. 463)

presume* to assume or suppose to be true (p. 438)

previous* coming before or prior (p. 504)

price ceiling maximum price that can be charged for goods and services, set by the government (p. 589)

policy/política* un curso de acción guía (págs. 217, 397, 745)

political action committee (PAC)/comité de acción política organización política establecida por una corporación, un sindicato u otro grupo de interés especial diseñada para apoyar a los candidatos al contribuir con dinero (págs. 308, 334)

political appointee/político asignado una persona asignada a un cargo federal por parte del presidente (pág. 229)

political machine/maquinaria política una fuerte organización partidaria que puede controlar los nombramientos políticos y dar votos (pág. 282)

political party/partido político una asociación de votantes con numerosos intereses comunes que desean influir en o controlar la toma de decisiones en el gobierno al elegir a los candidatos del partido para un cargo público (pág. 273)

poll tax/impuesto de contribución una suma de dinero que deben pagar los votantes antes de que se les permita emitir un voto (pág. 137)

polling place/lugar de votación la ubicación en la que se lleva a cabo la votación (pág. 295)

pollster/encuestador un especialista cuyo trabajo es realizar encuestas con regularidad (pág. 323)

popular sovereignty/soberanía popular la noción de que el poder lo tiene el pueblo (págs. 12, 86)

pork-barrel projects/*proyectos pork-barrel* proyectos y subsidios del gobierno que benefician principalmente al estado o distrito local (pág. 196)

portion/porción* una parte de un todo (pág. 367)

potential/potencial* capaz de ser o convertirse en (pág. 427)

Preamble/Preámbulo la sección de apertura de la Constitución (pág. 80)

precedent/precedente un fallo que se utiliza como base para una decisión judicial de un caso similar posterior (págs. 34, 245, 429)

precinct/precinto un área geográfica que contiene un número específico de votantes (págs. 281, 295)

precise* que es exacto (pág. 688)

preliminary/preliminar* que viene antes de la parte o el artículo principal (pág. 463)

presume/presumir* asumir o suponer que es verdadero (pág. 438)

previous/previo* que viene antes (pág. 504)

price ceiling/precio máximo precio máximo que se puede cobrar por bienes y servicios, establecido por el gobierno (pág. 589)

price floor minimum price that can be charged for goods and services, set by the government (p. 589)

primary* first in time or importance (p. 334)

principal* the most important (p. 667)

principle* a rule of conduct or belief (p. 11)

print media newspapers, magazines, newsletters, and books (p. 327)

prior restraint government censorship of material before it is published (p. 329)

priority* the goals a community considers most important or most urgent (pp. 18, 399)

private good good that, when consumed by one individual, cannot be consumed by another (p. 631)

private property rights the freedom to own and use our own property as we choose as long as we do not interfere with the rights of others (p. 529)

process* an action or a series of actions directed toward a result (p. 72)

product market a market where producers offer goods and services for sale (p. 522)

productivity the degree to which resources are being used efficiently to produce goods and services (pp. 524, 585)

professional* engaging or working in a profession (p. 398)

profit the money a business receives for its products or services over and above its costs (pp. 530, 583)

profit motive the driving force that encourages individuals and organizations to improve their material well-being (p. 530)

progressive income tax a tax that takes a larger percentage of higher incomes than lower incomes (p. 649)

prohibition* an order forbidding something (p. 431)

promote* to encourage the acceptance or recognition of (pp. 274, 740)

price floor/precio mínimo precio mínimo que se puede cobrar por bienes y servicios, establecido por el gobierno (pág. 589)

primary/primario, primero* primero en tiempo o en importancia (pág. 334)

principal/principal* el más importante (pág. 667)

principle/principio* una regla de conducta o creencia (pág. 11)

print media/medios de comunicación impresos periódicos, revistas, boletines informativos y libros (pág. 327)

prior restraint/restricción anterior censura gubernamental de material antes de que se publique (pág. 329)

priority/prioridad* algo a lo que se le da más atención o importancia (págs. 18, 399)

private goods/bienes privados bienes que, cuando los consume una persona, no pueden ser consumidos por otra (pág. 631)

private property rights/derechos de propiedad privada la libertad de ser propietario y usar nuestra propiedad como queramos siempre que no interfiramos con los derechos de otros (pág. 529)

process/proceso* una acción o una serie de acciones con el fin de obtener un resultado (pág. 72)

product market/mercado de productos un mercado en el que los productores ofrecen bienes y servicios para la venta (pág. 522)

productivity/productividad el grado al que se utilizan los recursos de manera eficaz para producir bienes y servicios (págs. 524, 585)

professional/profesional* que participa o trabaja en una profesión (pág. 398)

profit/ganancia el dinero que recibe un negocio por sus productos o servicios y que supera sus costos (págs. 530, 583)

profit motive/motivo lucrativo el impulso que incentiva a las personas y las organizaciones a mejorar su bienestar material (pág. 530)

progressive income tax/impuesto progresivo sobre la renta un impuesto que toma un porcentaje mayor de ingresos superiores que de ingresos inferiores (pág. 649)

prohibition/prohibición* una orden que no permite algo (pág. 431)

promote/promover* incentivar la aceptación o el reconocimiento de (págs. 274, 740)

GLOSSARY/GLOSARIO

propaganda certain ideas that may involve misleading messages designed to manipulate people (pp. 307, 476)

property tax tax on land and property (p. 682)

proportion* the size or amount of something in relation to something else or to a whole (p. 129)

proposition a petition asking for a new law (p. 301)

proprietary colony area with owner-controlled land and government (p. 39)

prosecution party who starts the legal proceedings against another party for a violation of the law (p. 453)

protectionism policy of trade restrictions to protect domestic industries (p. 735)

public agenda issues considered most significant by government officials (p. 327)

public goods economic goods that are consumed collectively, such as highways and national defense (p. 631)

public interest group an organization that supports causes that affect the lives of Americans in general (p. 334)

public opinion the ideas and attitudes that most people hold about elected officials, candidates, government, and political issues (p. 319)

public opinion poll a survey in which individuals are asked to answer questions about a particular issue or person (p. 323)

public policy the course of action the government takes in response to an issue or problem (pp. 22, 397)

purchase* to buy or pay for (p. 588)

Puritan religious dissenter who came to the colonies to purify, or reform, the Anglican Church (p. 41)

propaganda/propaganda ciertas ideas que pueden incluir mensajes falsos o erróneos diseñados para manipular a la gente (págs. 307, 476)

property tax/impuesto a la propiedad impuesto sobre la tierra y la propiedad (pág. 682)

proportion/proporción* el tamaño o la cantidad de algo en relación con otra cosa o con un todo (pág. 129)

proposition/proposición una petición que solicita una nueva ley (pág. 301)

proprietary colony/colonia propietaria zona con la tierra y el gobierno controlados por un propietario (pág. 39)

prosecution/fiscalía parte que inicia los procedimientos legales contra otra parte por una violación a las leyes (pág. 453)

protectionism/proteccionismo política de restricciones comerciales para proteger a las industrias nacionales (pág. 735)

public agenda/agenda pública cuestiones consideradas más importantes por los funcionarios de gobierno (pág. 327)

public goods/bienes públicos bienes económicos que se consumen colectivamente, como las carreteras y la defensa nacional (pág. 631)

public interest group/grupo de interés público una organización que apoya causas que afectan las vidas de los estadounidenses en general (pág. 334)

public opinion/opinión pública las ideas y actitudes que tiene la mayoría de la gente sobre los funcionarios electos, los candidatos, el gobierno y los asuntos políticos (pág. 319)

public opinion poll/encuesta de opinión pública una encuesta en la que se pide a las personas que respondan preguntas sobre un asunto o una persona en particular (pág. 323)

public policy/política pública el curso de acción que toma el gobierno en respuesta a un asunto o problema (págs. 22, 397)

purchase/comprar* adquirir o pagar por (pág. 588)

Puritan/puritano disidente religioso que llegó hasta las colonias para purificar, o reformar, la Iglesia Anglicana (pág. 41)

Q

quota a limit on the amount of foreign goods imported into a country (p. 708)

quota/cupo un límite en la cantidad de bienes extranjeros importados a un país (pág. 708)

R

racial profiling singling out an individual as a suspect due to appearance of ethnicity (p. 143)

range* a variation between limits (p. 279)

ratify to vote approval of (p. 68)

ratio* the relationship between two or more things (p. 404)

rational* showing reason (p. 499)

real GDP GDP after adjustments for inflation (p. 638)

recall a special election in which citizens can vote to remove a public official from office (p. 301); situation in which a company pulls a product off the market or agrees to change it to make it safe (p. 635)

recover* to regain or reclaim (p. 433)

recycle reusing old materials to make new ones (p. 410)

referendum a way for citizens to vote on state or local laws (p. 301)

refugee a person who has unwillingly left his or her home to escape war, famine, or other disaster (p. 738)

register* to record or enroll (p. 160)

regulate* to control or govern (p. 185)

regulatory* used to describe an agency or body whose function is to control or govern (p. 330)

rehabilitate to correct a person's behavior (p. 462)

reject* to refuse or throw away (p. 539)

religious dissenter those who followed a religious faith other than the official religion of England (p. 41)

reluctant* having doubt or unwillingness (p. 379)

remand to send a case back to a lower court to be tried again (p. 245)

repeal to cancel a law (p. 52)

representative democracy a government in which citizens choose a smaller group to govern on their behalf (p. 24)

racial profiling/prácticas discriminatorias raciales señalar a una persona como sospechosa debido al origen étnico (pág. 143)

range/rango* una variación entre límites (pág. 279)

ratify/ratificar votar la aprobación de algo (pág. 68)

ratio/relación* el vínculo entre dos o más cosas (pág. 404)

rational/racional* que muestra razón (pág. 499)

real GDP/PIB real PIB luego de ajustes por inflación (pág. 638)

recall/revocación una elección especial en la que los ciudadanos pueden votar para quitar a un funcionario público de un cargo (pág. 301); **recall/retirada** situación en la que una compañía retira un producto del mercado o acepta cambiarlo para hacerlo seguro (pág. 635)

recover/recuperar* volver a obtener (pág. 433)

recycle/reciclar volver a usar de materiales viejos para hacer nuevos (pág. 410)

referendum/referéndum una forma en que los ciudadanos pueden votar sobre las leyes estatales o locales (pág. 301)

refugee/refugiando persona que ha dejado su hogar de buena voluntad para escaparse de la guerra, la hambre, o de otra desasrte (pág. 738)

register/registrar* anotar o inscribir (pág. 160)

regulate/regular* controlar o determinar (pág. 185)

regulatory/regulatorio* se usa para describir a una agencia o un organismo cuya función es controlar o determinar (pág. 330)

rehabilitate/rehabilitar corregir el comportamiento de una persona (pág. 462)

reject/rechazar* no aceptar o desechar (pág. 539)

religious dissenter/disidente religioso persona que seguía una fe religiosa distinta a la religión oficial de Inglaterra (pág. 41)

reluctant/reacio* que tiene duda o no está dispuesto (pág. 379)

remand/remitir enviar un caso a un tribunal inferior para ser juzgado nuevamente (pág. 245)

repeal/revocar cancelar una ley (pág. 52)

representative democracy/democracia representativa un gobierno en que los ciudadanos escogen un grupo pequeño para gobernar en su representación (pág. 24)

reprieve an order to delay a person's punishment until a higher court can hear the case (p. 217)

republic a representative democracy where citizens choose their lawmakers (p. 24)

require* to have a need for or to order (p. 215)

reserve a certain percentage of deposits that banks have to set aside as cash in their own vaults or as deposits in their Federal Reserve district bank (p. 665)

reserved powers powers that the Constitution does not give to the national government that are kept by the states (pp. 89, 352)

resolve* to find a solution or reach a decision (p. 427)

resource* the money, people, and materials available to accomplish a community's goals (pp. 399, 501, 684)

respond* to answer or react (p. 450)

responsibility an obligation that we fulfill voluntarily (p. 151)

restore* to bring back into existence or put back in an original condition (p. 54)

restrict* to place limits on or keep within bounds (p. 585)

retain* to keep or to hold secure (p. 450)

return profit earned through investing (p. 557)

returns ballots and results of an election (p. 297)

reveal* to make known or show plainly (p. 617)

revenue* the income that a government collects for public use (pp. 485, 682)

revise* to correct or improve (p. 359)

right-to-work laws state laws forbidding unions from forcing workers to join (p. 610)

robbery the taking of property from a person's possession by using force or threats (p. 432)

role* the function of a person or thing (pp. 225, 401)

roll-call vote a voting method in the Senate in which members voice their votes in turn (p. 202)

reprieve/aplazamiento una orden para retrasar la pena de una persona hasta que un tribunal superior pueda ver el caso (pág. 217)

republic/república democracia representativa en la que los ciudadanos eligen a sus legisladores (pág. 24)

require/requerir* tener una necesidad u ordenar (pág. 215)

reserve/reserva cierto porcentaje de los depósitos que los bancos deben separar como dinero en efectivo en sus propias bóvedas o como depósitos en su banco de distrito de la Reserva Federal (pág. 665)

reserved powers/poderes reservados poderes que la Constitución no otorga al gobierno nacional y que mantienen los estados (págs. 89, 352)

resolve/resolver* encontrar una solución o llegar a una decisión (pág. 427)

resource/recurso* el dinero, las personas y los materiales disponibles para alcanzar las metas de una comunidad (págs. 399, 501, 684)

respond/responder* contestar o reaccionar (pág. 450)

responsibility/responsabilidad una obligación que cumplimos voluntariamente (pág. 151)

restore/restaurar* volver a dar vida o colocar en una condición original (pág. 54)

restrict/restringir* colocar límites en o mantener entre límites (pág. 585)

retain/retener* conservar o mantener seguro (pág. 450)

return/rendimiento ganancia que se obtiene mediante la inversión (pág. 557)

returns/resultados boletas electorales y consecuencias de una elección (pág. 297)

reveal/revelar* dar a conocer o mostrar directamente (pág. 617)

revenue/ingreso* la renta que un gobierno recauda para uso público (págs. 485, 682)

revise/revisar* corregir o mejorar (pág. 359)

right-to-work laws/leyes de derecho a trabajar leyes estatales que prohíben a los sindicatos obligar a los trabajadores a unirse (pág. 610)

robbery/robo toma de una propiedad de las posesiones de una persona mediante el uso de fuerza o amenazas (pág. 432)

role/papel* la función de una persona o cosa (págs. 225, 401)

roll-call vote/votación por nómina un método de votación en el Senado en el que cada uno de los miembros expresa su voto (pág. 202)

royal colony a colonial area of land controlled directly by a king or other monarch (p. 39)

rule of law principle that the law applies to everyone, even those who govern (p. 87)

S

sales tax tax levied on a product at the time of sale (p. 682)

sanction measure such as withholding economic aid used to influence a foreign government's actions (p. 746)

satellite nation politically and economically dominated or controlled by another, more powerful country (p. 747)

save to set aside income for a period of time so that it can be used later (p. 553)

savings account an account in which customers receive interest based on how much money they have deposited (p. 667)

savings and loan association (S&L) financial institutions that traditionally loaned money to people buying homes (p. 658)

scarcity not having enough resources to produce all of the things we would like to have (p. 501)

search warrant a court order allowing law enforcement officers to search a suspect's home or business and take specific items as evidence (pp. 127, 438)

section* an area or division (p. 140)

sector* a segment or distinct part (p. 521)

segregation the social separation of the races (p. 140)

seniority years of service, which is used as a consideration for assigning committee members (p. 182)

separation of powers the split of authority among the legislative, executive, and judicial branches (p. 88)

service work performed by a person for someone else (p. 517)

service economy where the majority of people earn their living by providing a service rather than manufacturing a product (p. 10)

royal colony/colonia real zona de tierra colonial controlada directamente por un rey u otro monarca (pág. 39)

rule of law/reglamento de ley principio de que la ley se aplica a todos, incluso a aquéllos que gobiernan (pág. 87)

sales tax/impuesto a las ventas impuesto aplicado a un producto en el momento de la venta (pág. 682)

sanction/sanción medida como la negación de ayuda económica para influir en las acciones de un gobierno extranjero (pág. 746)

satellite/satélite nación dominada o controlada política y económicamente por otro país más poderoso (pág. 747)

save/ahorro separar y acumular ingresos durante un tiempo para poder usarlos luego (pág. 553)

savings account/cuenta de ahorros una cuenta en la que los clientes reciben intereses según la cantidad de dinero que tienen depositado (pág. 667)

savings and loan association (S&L)/asociación de ahorros y préstamos instituciones financieras que tradicionalmente prestaban dinero a personas que compraban viviendas (pág. 658)

scarcity/escasez no tener suficientes recursos para producir todo lo que quisiéramos tener (pág. 501)

search warrant/orden de allanamiento una orden judicial que permite a los agentes de policía revisar la vivienda o el negocio de un sospechoso y tomar ciertos artículos como evidencia (págs. 127, 438)

section/sección* un área o una división (pág. 140)

sector/sector* un segmento o parte diferenciada (pág. 521)

segregation/segregación la separación social de las razas (pág. 140)

seniority/antigüedad años de servicio, que se utilizan como consideración para la designación de miembros del comité (pág. 182)

separation of powers/separación de poderes la división de la autoridad entre los poderes, legislativo, ejecutivo y judicial (pág. 88)

service/servicio trabajo realizado por una persona para otra (pág. 517)

service economy/economía de servicio en la que la mayoría de las personas se ganan la vida al proporcionar un servicio en lugar de fabricar un producto (pág. 10)

settlement in a legal case, the amount of money the defendant agrees to pay the plaintiff (p. 450)

shortage situation in which quantity demanded is greater than quantity supplied (p. 589)

short-term plan a government policy being carried out over the next few years (p. 398)

similar* having qualities in common or resembling (p. 389)

slander spoken untruths that are harmful to someone's reputation (p. 124)

social contract an agreement among people in a society with a government (p. 35)

social responsibility the obligation a business has to pursue goals that benefit society as well as themselves (p. 618)

Social Security federal program that provides monthly payments to people who are retired or unable to work (p. 678)

socialism economic system in which government owns some factors of production and distributes the products and wages (p. 717)

soft money donations given to political parties and not designated for a particular candidate's election campaign (p. 308)

sole* being the only one (p. 601)

sole proprietorship a business owned and operated by a single person (p. 601)

solid waste the technical name for garbage (p. 409)

special district a unit of government that deals with a specific function, such as education, water supply, or transportation (p. 382)

special-interest group an organization of people with some common interest who try to influence government decisions (p. 199)

specialization when people, businesses, regions, and/or nations concentrate on goods and services that they can produce better than anyone else (p. 524)

specific* clearly specified, precise, or explicit (p. 399)

specify* to mention exactly or clearly (p. 137)

settlement/acuerdo en un caso legal, monto de dinero que el acusado acuerda pagar al demandante (pág. 450)

shortage/déficit situación en la que la cantidad demandada es mayor que la cantidad ofertada (pág. 589)

short-term plan/plan a corto plazo política del gobierno que se lleva a cabo durante los próximos siguientes años (pág. 398)

similar/similar* que tienen cualidades en común o se parecen (pág. 389)

slander/calumnia falsedades escritas que son perjudiciales para la reputación de alguien (pág. 124)

social contract/contrato social acuerdo entre las personas en una sociedad con el gobierno (pág. 35)

social responsibility/responsabilidad social la obligación que tiene un negocio de buscar metas que beneficien a la sociedad así como a él mismo (pág. 618)

Social Security/Seguro Social programa federal que proporciona pagos mensuales a la gente jubilada o que no puede trabajar (pág. 678)

socialism/socialismo sistema económico en el que el gobierno es propietario de algunos factores de producción y distribuye los productos y los salarios (pág. 717)

soft money/soft money donaciones otorgadas a los partidos políticos y no designadas para la campaña electoral de un candidato particular (pág. 308)

sole/único* ser exclusivo (pág. 601)

sole proprietorship/propietario único un negocio que es propiedad de una sola persona y es manejado por ésta (pág. 601)

solid waste/desecho sólido el nombre técnico para basura (pág. 409)

special district/distrito especial una unidad de gobierno que trata con una función específica, como educación, suministro de agua o transporte (pág. 382)

special-interest group/grupo de interés especial una organización de personas con algún interés común que intentan influir en las decisiones del gobierno (pág. 199)

specialization/especialización cuando las personas, los negocios, las regiones o las naciones se concentran en los bienes y servicios que pueden producir mejor que cualquier otro (pág. 524)

specific/específico* especificado claramente, preciso o explícito (pág. 399)

specify/especificar* mencionar con exactitud o claridad (pág. 137)

spoils system   **suffrage**

spoils system rewarding people with government jobs on the basis of their political support (p. 230)

standard of living the material well-being of an individual, group, or nation measured by how well their necessities and luxuries are satisfied (p. 518)

standing committee permanent committee that continues its work from session to session in Congress (p. 181)

standing vote in Congress, when members stand to be counted for a vote on a bill (p. 202)

stare decisis the practice of using earlier judicial rulings as a basis for deciding cases (pp. 257, 436)

status* a position or rank (p. 547)

statute a law written by a legislative branch (p. 429)

stock ownership share of a corporation (pp. 557, 604)

stockholder an individual who has invested in a corporation and owns some of its stock (p. 604)

stress* to place special importance or emphasis on something (p. 273)

strike when workers deliberately stop working in order to force an employer to give in to their demands (p. 612)

strong-mayor system a type of government, usually in large cities, under which the mayor has strong executive powers (p. 379)

submit* to present for review or decision (p. 246)

subsidize to aid or promote with money (p. 684)

subsidy a government payment to an individual, business, or group in exchange for certain actions (p. 585)

substitute a competing product that consumers can use in place of another (p. 575)

suburb community that is near or surrounds a larger city (p. 382)

sufficient* to be adequate for a purpose (p. 456)

suffrage the right to vote (p. 135)

spoils system/sistema de despojo recompensar a la gente con empleos gubernamentales sobre la base de su apoyo político (pág. 230)

standard of living/estándar de vida el bienestar material de una persona, un grupo o una nación medido según la eficacia con la que satisfacen sus necesidades y lujos (pág. 518)

standing committee/comité permanente aquéllos que continúan su trabajo de sesión en sesión en el Congreso (pág. 181)

standing vote/voto de pie en el Congreso, cuando los miembros se paran y se los cuenta para votar por una ley (pág. 202)

stare decisis/*stare decisis* la práctica de usar fallos judiciales anteriores como base para decidir casos (págs. 257, 436)

status/estatus* una posición o un rango (pág. 547)

statute/estatuto una ley escrita por un poder legislativo (pág. 429)

stock/acciones participación en la propiedad de una corporación (págs. 557, 604)

stockholder/accionista una persona que ha invertido en una corporación y es propietaria de parte de sus acciones (pág. 604)

stress/hincapié* dar especial importancia o poner énfasis en algo (pág. 273)

strike/huelga cuando los trabajadores dejan de trabajar deliberadamente para obligar a su empleador a satisfacer sus demandas (pág. 612)

strong-mayor system/sistema de alcalde fuerte un tipo de gobierno, normalmente en grandes ciudades, en el que el alcalde posee poderes ejecutivos contundentes (pág. 379)

submit/presentar* enviar para revisión o decisión (pág. 246)

subsidize/subvencionar ayudar o promover con dinero (pág. 684)

subsidy/subvención un pago del gobierno a una persona, un negocio o un grupo a cambio de ciertas acciones (pág. 585)

substitute/sustituto un producto de la competencia que los consumidores pueden usar en lugar de otro (pág. 575)

suburb/suburbio comunidad que se encuentra cerca de una ciudad más grande o la rodea (pág. 382)

sufficient/suficiente* ser adecuado para un propósito (pág. 456)

suffrage/sufragio el derecho al voto (pág. 135)

summons a notice directing someone to appear in court to answer a complaint or a charge (p. 450)

summons/requerimiento judicial un aviso que indica a una persona que debe comparecer ante un tribunal para dar respuesta a una queja o a un cargo (pág. 450)

supplement* something that supplies what is needed or makes an addition (p. 649)

supplement/suplemento* algo que suministra lo que se necesita o que se añade a otra cosa (pág. 649)

supply the amount of goods and services that producers are able and willing to sell at various prices during a specified time period (p. 581)

supply/oferta la cantidad de bienes y servicios que los productores son capaces y están dispuestos a vender a diferentes precios durante un tiempo específico (pág. 581)

supply curve upward-sloping line that graphically shows the quantities supplied at each possible price (p. 583)

supply curve/curva de oferta línea en aumento que muestra gráficamente las cantidades ofertadas a cada precio posible (pág. 583)

supply elasticity responsiveness of quantity supplied to a change in price (p. 586)

supply elasticity/elasticidad de oferta respuesta de la cantidad ofertada a un cambio en el precio (pág. 586)

supply schedule table showing quantities supplied at different possible prices (p. 581)

supply schedule/tabla de oferta tabla que muestra las cantidades ofertadas a los diferentes precios posibles (pág. 581)

surplus situation in which quantity supplied is greater than quantity demanded; situation in which government spends less than it collects in revenues (pp. 588, 688)

surplus/excedente situación en la que la cantidad ofertada es mayor que la cantidad demandada; situación en la que el gobierno gasta menos de lo que recauda en ingresos (págs. 588, 688)

survey* to gather information about, as in a poll (p. 323)

survey/sondear* reunir información sobre, como en una encuesta (pág. 323)

survive* to continue to exist (p. 648)

survive/sobrevivir* continuar existiendo (pág. 648)

T

target* a goal or aim (p. 223)

target/objetivo* una meta o un propósito (pág. 223)

tariff a customs duty; a tax on an imported good (p. 708)

tariff/tarifa un derecho aduanero; un impuesto sobre un producto importado (pág. 708)

technique* procedure or method by which something is done (p. 611)

technique/técnica* procedimiento o método mediante lo que se hace algo (pág. 611)

technology the methods or processes used to make goods and services (p. 585)

technology/tecnología los métodos o procesos usados para producir bienes y servicios (pág. 585)

testimony the statement a witness makes under oath (p. 457)

testimony/testimonio la declaración que hace un testigo bajo juramento (pág. 457)

third party a party that challenges the two major parties (p. 274)

third party/tercer partido un partido que desafía a los dos partidos principales (pág. 274)

Three-fifths Compromise agreement providing that enslaved persons would count as three-fifths of other persons in determining representation in Congress (p. 75)

Three-fifths Compromise/Compromiso de Tres Quintos acuerdo que estipulaba que los esclavos se contarían como tres quintos de otras personas para determinar la representación en el Congreso (pág. 75)

Tidewater areas of low, flat plains near the seacoast of Virginia and North Carolina (p. 46)

Tidewater/región de aguas de marea zonas de planicies llanas y bajas cerca de la costa marina de Virginia y Carolina del Norte (pág. 46)

tolerance respecting and accepting others, regardless of their beliefs, practices, or differences (p. 154)

toleration acceptance of other groups, such as religious groups (p. 41)

torts wrongful acts for which an injured party has the right to sue (p. 433)

totalitarian a system in which government control extends to almost all aspects of people's lives (p. 26)

town political unit that is larger than a village and smaller than a city (p. 388)

town meeting a gathering of local citizens to discuss and vote on important issues (p. 388)

township a subdivision of a county that has its own government (p. 389)

toxic poisonous or deadly (p. 409)

trade deficit situation in which the value of the products imported by a country exceeds the value of its exports (p. 713)

trade sanction an effort to punish another nation by imposing trade barriers (p. 223)

trade surplus situation in which the value of the products exported by a country exceeds the value of its imports (p. 712)

trade-off the alternative you face if you decide to do one thing rather than another (p. 504)

tradition* a way of thinking or acting that is long established (p. 427)

traditional economy an economic system in which the decisions of what, how, and for whom to produce are based on custom or habit (p. 724)

transparency process of making business deals more visible to everyone (p. 617)

treaty a formal agreement between the governments of two or more countries (p. 222)

triangular trade pattern of trade that developed in colonial times among the Americas, Africa, and Europe (p. 43)

tribunal courts established by the UN to hear cases of violations of international human rights laws (p. 745)

tolerance/tolerancia el respeto y la aceptación de los demás, independientemente de sus creencias, prácticas o diferencias (pág. 154)

toleration/tolerancia aceptación de otros grupos, como los grupos religiosos (pág. 41)

torts/agravios actos ilegales por los que la parte perjudicada tiene derecho a demandar (pág. 433)

totalitarian/totalitario un sistema en el que el control del gobierno se extiende a casi todos los aspectos de las vidas de la gente (pág. 26)

town/pueblo unidad política que es más grande que una aldea y más pequeña que una ciudad (pág. 388)

town meeting/reunión municipal asamblea de ciudadanos locales para debatir y votar sobre cuestiones importantes (pág. 388)

township/municipio una subdivisión de un condado que tiene su propio gobierno (pág. 389)

toxic/tóxico pernicioso o mortal (pág. 409)

trade deficit/déficit comercial situación en la que el valor de los productos importados por un país supera el valor de sus exportaciones (pág. 713)

trade sanction/sanción comercial una acción para castigar a otra nación al imponer barreras comerciales (pág. 223)

trade surplus/excedente comercial situación en la que el valor de los productos exportados por un país supera el valor de sus importaciones (pág. 712)

trade-off/*trade-off* la alternativa que uno enfrenta si decide hacer una cosa en vez de otra (pág. 504)

tradition/tradición* una forma de pensar o actuar que está muy arraigada (pág. 427)

traditional economy/economía tradicional un sistema económico en el que las decisiones sobre qué, cómo y para quién producir se basan en costumbres o hábitos (pág. 724)

transparency/transparencia proceso mediante el que los negocios se hacen más visibles para todos (pág. 617)

treaty/tratado un acuerdo formal entre los gobiernos de dos o más países (pág. 222)

triangular trade/comercio triangular patrón de comercio que se desarrolló en la época colonial entre las Américas, África y Europa (pág. 43)

tribunal/tribunal corte establecida por las Naciones Unidas para atender casos internacionales de violaciones a las leyes de derechos humanos (pág. 745)

tuition voucher program providing subsidies for education payments, allowing families the option of sending students to private schools (p. 403)

two-party system a system of government in which two parties compete for power (p. 273)

tuition vouchers/vale educativo programa que otorga subvenciones para pagos educativos, con lo que se las familias pueden enviar a los estudiantes a escuelas privadas (pág. 403)

two-party system/sistema bipartita un sistema de gobierno en el que dos partidos compiten por el poder (pág. 273)

ultimate* the most basic or final (p. 293)

unanimous opinion the Supreme Court rules on a case in which all justices agree on the ruling (p. 256)

unemployment rate the percentage of people in the civilian labor force who are not working but are looking for jobs (p. 640)

unicameral one-house legislature (p. 358)

uniform* consistent or unvarying (p. 319)

utility the amount of satisfaction one gets from a good or service (p. 570)

utilize* to make use of (p. 684)

ultimate/primordial, final* el más básico o en el último lugar (pág. 293)

unanimous opinion/opinión unánime la Suprema Corte dictamina en un caso en el que todos los jueces acuerdan en el fallo (pág. 256)

unemployment rate/tasa de desempleo el porcentaje de personas en la fuerza laboral civil que no trabajan pero que buscan un empleo (pág. 640)

unicameral/unicameral cuerpo legislativo de una cámara (pág. 358)

uniform/uniforme* consistente o sin variación (pág. 319)

utility/utilidad la cantidad de satisfacción que se obtiene de un bien o servicio (pág. 570)

utilize/utilizar* hacer uso de (pág. 684)

value the general principles or beliefs people use to make judgments and decisions (p. 11)

version* a particular form or type (p. 473)

veto refusal to sign a bill or resolution (p. 202)

village smallest unit of local government (p. 390)

violate* to fail to keep or to break, as in a law (p. 134)

voice vote a voting method in which those in favor say "Yea" and those against say "No" (p. 202)

voluntary exchange the act of buyers and sellers freely and willingly engaging in market transactions (p. 530)

volunteerism the practice of offering your time and services to others without payment (p. 158)

value/valor principio o creencia general que las personas utilizan para emitir juicios y tomar decisiones (pág. 11)

version/versión* una forma o un tipo particular de otra ya existente (pág. 473)

veto/veto negativa de firmar un proyecto de ley o una resolución (pág. 202)

village/aldea la unidad más pequeña de gobierno local (pág. 390)

violate/violar* no cumplir o romper, como una ley (pág. 134)

voice vote/voto en voz alta un método de votación en el que aquéllos a favor dicen "Sí" y aquéllos en contra dicen "No" (pág. 202)

voluntary exchange/intercambio voluntario el acto de compradores y vendedores que realizan transacciones de mercado de manera libre y voluntaria (pág. 530)

volunteerism/voluntarismo la práctica de ofrecer tu tiempo y servicios a otros sin pago (pág. 158)

want a thing we would like to have, such as entertainment, vacation, or an item, that makes life comfortable and enjoyable (p. 499)

ward several adjoining precincts making up a larger election unit (p. 281)

warranty the promise made by a manufacturer or a seller to repair or replace a product within a certain time period if it is faulty (p. 542)

weak-mayor system a type of government under which the mayor has limited executive powers (p. 379)

Web site a "page" on the World Wide Web that may contain text, images, audio, and video (p. 471)

welfare the health, prosperity, and happiness of the members of a community (pp. 158, 406)

whereas* while; on the contrary (p. 360)

winner-take-all system a system in which the candidate who wins the popular vote in a state usually receives all of the state's electoral votes (p. 303)

Women, Infants, and Children (WIC) program a program that provides help for nutrition and health care to low-income women, infants, and children up to age 5 (p. 648)

workfare programs that require welfare recipients to exchange some of their labor in return for benefits (p. 649)

World Wide Web operating within the Internet, it allows users to interact with the billions of documents stored on computers across the Net (p. 471)

writ of habeas corpus a court order that requires police to bring a prisoner to court to explain why they are holding the person (pp. 188, 436)

want/deseo cosas que te gustaría tener, como entretenimiento, vacaciones y artículos que hacen que la vida sea cómoda y agradable (pág. 499)

ward/distrito varios precintos contiguos que conforman una unidad electoral más grande (pág. 281)

warranty/garantía la promesa que hace un fabricante o vendedor de reparar o cambiar un producto dentro de un período determinado si éste tiene una falla (pág. 542)

weak-mayor system/sistema de alcalde débil un tipo de gobierno en el que el alcalde tiene poderes ejecutivos limitados (pág. 379)

Web site/página web un sitio en la World Wide Web que puede contener texto, imágenes, audio y vídeo (pág. 471)

welfare/bienestar la salud, prosperidad y felicidad de los miembros de una comunidad (págs. 158, 406)

whereas/mientras que* en tanto que por otro lado (pág. 360)

winner-take-all system/sistema de ganador toma todo un sistema en el cual el candidato que gana el voto popular en un estado normalmente recibe todos los votos electorales del estado (pág. 303)

Women, Infants, and Children (WIC) program/ programa para Mujeres, Bebés y Niños un programa que brinda ayuda para la nutrición y asistencia médica a mujeres de bajos ingresos, bebés y niños de hasta 5 años (pág. 648)

workfare/trabajo requerido programas que requieren que beneficiarios del bienestar social cambien parte de su trabajo por beneficios (pág. 649)

World Wide Web funciona dentro de Internet y permite que los usuarios interactúen con los miles de millones de documentos guardados en las computadoras por la red (pág. 471)

writ of habeas corpus/escrito de hábeas corpus una orden judicial que requiere que la policía lleve a un prisionero a un tribunal para explicar por qué retienen a la persona (págs. 188, 436)

Index

Acknowledgments

Text and Art Credits

361 From "Let's List the Lottery Losers" by Andy Rooney. CBS News, August 6, 2006. Reprinted by permission of Andy Rooney.

Glencoe would like to acknowledge the artists and agencies who participated in illustrating this program: Anthology Inc.; Kenneth Batelman; Bill Dickson, represented by Contact Jupiter.

Photo Credits

Cover (t)CORBIS, (b)Miles Ertman/Masterfile; **iv** (bl)Crittenden Studio/Jupiter Images; (br)Getty Images; **v** Bettmann/CORBIS; **vi** Marleen Cate/Jupiter Images; **vii** Dennis Halliman/Jupiter Images; **viii** Jupiter Images; **xx** BananaStock/PunchStock; **xxi** (l)Don Farrall/Getty Images, (c)The McGraw-Hill Companies Inc./Ken Cavanagh Photographer; (r)Don Farrall/Photodisc/Getty Images; **2** Justin Lane/epa/CORBIS; **4** Carlos Barria/Reuters/CORBIS; **5** Mark Gibson/Index Stock Imagery; **6** Joe Raedle/Getty Images; **7** Panoramic Images; **9** Catherine Karnow/CORBIS; **10** (t)Freeman Patterson/Masterfile, (c)Robert Fried/Alamy, (r)CORBIS, (b)blickwinkel/Alamy; **11** Panoramic Images/Getty Images; **12** Steve Breen/Copley News Service; **14** Denis Poroy/AP Images; **15** John Moore/AP Images; **16** Reuters/CORBIS; **17** (t)Rob O'Neal, (b)WWF/South Florida Program; **18** Jim Sugar/CORBIS; **20** Judy Fahys/AP Images; **21** David Butow/CORBIS SABA; **23** Getty Images; **27** (t)CORBIS, (bl)Marianna Day Massey/ZUMA/CORBIS, (br)Spencer Grant/PhotoEdit; **30** Panoramic Images/Getty Images; **32** Alden Pellett/AP Images; **33** The Granger Collection, New York; **35** Bettmann/CORBIS; **36** Gibson Stock Photography; **38** Chuck Liddy/AP Images; **39** North Wind/North Wind Picture Archives; **40** (t)Ingram Publishing/Alamy, (b)Comstock/SuperStock; **41** The Art Archive/Culver Pictures; **44** AP Images; **46** North Wind/North Wind Picture Archives; **47** Yale University Art Gallery, Bequest of Eugene Phelps Edwards; **48** Bita Emrani; **50** Comstock/Imagestate; **51** The Art Archive/Musée des Arts Africains et Océaniens/Dagli Orti; **52** Library of Congress; **53** Bettmann/CORBIS; **55** Kean Collection/Getty Images; **57** (tcl)The Granger Collection, New York, (tcr)The Colonial Williamsburg Foundation, (tr)File Photo, (cl)The Colonial Williamsburg Foundation, (bc)Military & Historical Image Bank, (c)The Colonial Williamsburg Foundation, (cr)Military & Historical Image Bank, (bl)Lee Snider/Photo Images/CORBIS; **59** Mike Peters, reprinted by permission of UFS, Inc.; **61** CORBIS; **63** (t)CORBIS, (b)Bettmann/CORBIS; **64** Scott Frances/Esto; **66** Leif Skoogfors/CORBIS; **67** James Lemass/Index Stock; **68** CORBIS; **71** Diana Walker/Time Life Pictures/Getty Images; **72** George Widman/AP Images; **73** (t)Bettmann/CORBIS, (c)CORBIS; **74** Dennis Degnan/CORBIS; **75** file photo; **76** Bettmann/CORBIS; **77** National Archives; **79** Rick Bowmer/AP Images; **81** CORBIS; **82** (t)Russ Curtis, (b)Russ Curtis; **85** Gerald Herbert/AP Images; **86** Scott Stantis/Copley News Service; **87** Getty Images; **91** (tl)Art Resource, NY, (tr)Dave Bartruff/CORBIS, (bl)Dennis Degnan/CORBIS, (br)Bettmann/CORBIS; **94** Steve Allen/Brand X Pictures/Jupiter Images; **96** White House Historical Association; **102** Greg Gibson/AP Images; **106** George Widman/AP Images; **112** General Photographic Agency/Getty Images; **116** Bettmann/CORBIS; **117** Sandy Schaeffer/TimePix; **118** Justin Sullivan/Getty Images; **120** Evan Vucci/AP Images; **122** (bl)David Paul Morris/Getty Images, (br)Peter Hvizdak/The Image Works; **123** ANA/The Image Works; **125** BananaStock/PunchStock; **126** David Duprey/AP Images; **127** Teri L. Gilman; **128** Mikael Karlsson/Alamy; **129** Porter Gifford/Liaison Agency/Getty Images; **130** Ann Purcell; **132** Bettmann/CORBIS; **133** AP Images; **134** North Wind/North Wind Picture Archives; **136** Bettmann/CORBIS; **139** Danny Johnston/AP Photo; **140** Mike Thompson/Copley News Service; **141** MPI/Getty Images; **142** David J. & Janice L. Frent Collection/CORBIS; **144** Bettmann/CORBIS; **145** (t)Robert A. Reeder/Pool/Reuters/CORBIS, (c)Bruce Roberts/Photo Researchers, (b)MPI/Getty Images; **148** Dima Gavrysh/AP Images; **150** John Sandy Santucci/AP Images; **151** Bod Daemmrich/PhotoEdit; **152** (t)Nicole Robinson,(b)Ben Baker; **153** (t)Brand X Pictures/PunchStock, (c)Bob Daemmrich; **155** (t)The McGraw-Hill Companies, Inc./Emily and David Tietz, (b)StudiOhio; **156** Marc Lester/AP Images; **157** Ben Sklar/AP Images; **158** Marshall Ramsey/Copley News Service; **159** Getty Images; **160** James L. Amos/CORBIS; **163** (t)Las Cruces Sun-News, Norm Dettlaff/AP Images, (bl)Joe Rowley/AP Images, (br)Peter Turnley/CORBIS; **166 167** Bettmann/CORBIS; **168** (t)Comstock, Culver Pictures, (br)Time Life Pictures/Getty Images; **169** (t)Brooks Kraft/CORBIS, (c)Ethan Miller/Getty Images, (bl)Time Life Pictures/Getty Images, (br)Bettmann/CORBIS; **170** Matthew Borkoski/Index Stock; **174** Lester Lefkowitz/Getty Images; **176** Steve Warmowski/Jacksonville Journal-Courier/The Image Works; **177** Roberto Schmidt/AFP/Getty Images; **180** Mark Wilson/Getty Images; **184** David McNew/Getty Images; **185** U.S. Navy photo; **186** (t)Department of the Army, (b)Department of the Navy; **187** Jason Reed/Reuters/CORBIS; **189** Bob Daemmrich/PhotoEdit; **190** Chip Somodevilla/Getty Images; **191** Mark Humphrey/AP Images; **192** Mike Theiler/Getty Images; **193** (t)Sarah Seufer, (b)Chuck Kennedy/KRT/Newscom; **194** Courtesy Ileana Ros-Lehtinen; **195** Michael Ramirez/Copley News Service; **197** William Lovelace/Express/Getty Images; **198** Richard Broadwell/Alamy; **199** Bettmann/CORBIS; **203** (t)PCL/Alamy, (c)Jurgen Vogt/Getty Images; **205** Mark Cullum; **206** Stan Honda/AFP/Getty Images; **208** Paul J. Richards/AFP/Getty Images; **209** Susan Walsh/AP Images; **211** (inset) Hulton Archive, (others) White House Historical Association; **212** Alex Wong/AFP/Getty Images; **214** Susan Walsh/AP Images; **216** Courtesy AMillionThanks.org; **217** Mandel Ngan/AFP/Getty Images; **219** Tim Graham Picture Library/AP Images; **220** Marshall Ramsey/Copley News Service; **221** Brooks Kraft/CORBIS; **222** Evan F. Sisley-Pool/Getty Images; **224** Jean Louis Atlan/CORBIS; **226** AP Images; **227** Martin H. Simon/CORBIS; **228** Jim Watson AFP/Getty Images; **231** (t)Alex Wong/Getty Images, (cl)John F. Kennedy Presidential Library and Museum, Boston, (c)Bettmann/CORBIS, (b)Terry Ashe/Time Life Pictures/Getty Images; **235** Steven P. Widoff for TIME; **236** Olivier Doubiery/Abaca/Time; **238** National Park Service/AP Images; **239** ART LIEN/AFP/Getty Images; **241** Gary Sargent; **243** Pablo Martinez/CORBIS; **244** Jennifer Altman/Bloomberg News /Landov; **245** Richard Cummins/Lonely Planet Images; **246** NILS JUUL-HANSEN; **248** Mike Theiler/Getty Images; **249** Matthew Cavanaugh/epa/CORBIS; **250** Mark Wilson/Getty Images; **251** Pablo Martinez Monsivais/AP Images; **252** Joseph Mirachi/The Cartoon Bank; **254** Staff/AP Images; **257** Jim Rassol/CORBIS SYGMA; **260** Liza Biganzoli, National Geographic Society Image Collection; **261** (t)Getty Images, (bl)MIKE THEILER/AFP/Getty Images, (br)Richard A. Bloom/CORBIS; **265** Public Domain; **266** Bob Daemmrich/The Image Works; **270** Mark Wilson/Getty Images; **272** Staff/AP Images; **273** Ramin Talaie/CORBIS; **274** (t)National Museum of American History, Smithsonian Institution, Smithsonian Institution, Behring Center, (b)Collection of David J. & Janice L. Frent; **275** Jim Mone/AP Images; **276** David J. & Janice L. Frent Collection/CORBIS; **278** Peter Thompson/Getty Images; **279** George Skadding/Time Life Pictures/Getty Images; **280** (t)Democratic National Committee. All rights reserved, (b)Republican National Committee. All rights reserved; **281** (t)Susan Liebold, **282** Michael Ramirez/Copley News Service; **283** Jim Cole/AP Images; **285** David McNew/Getty Images; **287** (tl)Jim Cole/AP Images, (tr)David Bacon/The Image Works, (b)AP Images; **290** Orjan F. Ellingvag/CORBIS; **292** Kathy Willens/AP Images; **293** Spencer Platt/Getty Images; **294** Jack Star/PhotoLink/Getty Images; **295** CORBIS; **296** William Lovelace/Express/Getty Images; **298** Mike Thompson/Copley News Service; **300** Jon Readle/Getty Images; **302** (b)Nancy Pierce; **305** Kenneth Lambert/AP Images; **306** Herald-Mail, Kevin G. Gilbert/AP Images; **307** Michael Newman/PhotoEdit; **311** (t)B. Ray/Cedar Rapids Gazette/ZUMA/CORBIS, (bl)Bettmann/CORBIS, (br)Marianne Todd/Getty Images; **314** (c)Courtesy TIME, (b)Tim Boyles/Stringer/Getty Images; **315** (t)Charles Bennett/AP Images, (c)Stuart Ramson, (bl)Vincent Lerz/AP Images, (br)Comstock; **316** JIM BOURG/Reuters/Landov; **318** Daniel Shanken/AP Images; **319** Tim Boyle/Getty Images; **320** White House Historical Association; **321** (t)David Joel, (b)David Joel; **322** Bettmann/CORBIS; **323** (inset)AP Images, Larry Downing/Reuters/Landov; **325** Kayte M. Deioma/PhotoEdit; **326** Jim Bourg/Reuters; **327** Alex Brandon/AP Images; **328** Bettmann/CORBIS; **329** Federal Communications Commission; **331** Harley Schwadron/CartoonStock; **332** Brian Kersey/AP Images; **333** Alex Wong/Getty Images; **334** William Thomas Cain/Getty Images; **335** Steve Breen/Copley News Service; **339** (tl)Radhika Chalasani/Getty Images, (tr)David Young-Wolff/PhotoEdit, (b)William Thomas Cain/Getty Images; **342 343** Flip Schulke/CORBIS; **344** Karen Kasmauski/CORBIS; **346** A. Ramey/Stock Boston; **348** Bob Daemmrich/CORBIS; **350** Reuters; **351** George Steinmetz/CORBIS; **353** James W. Porter/CORBIS; **354** (t)Courtesy of Prateek Pere-da-Silva, (b)Gerry Broome/AP Images; **357** Allen Fredrickson/Reuters; **358** Tony Kurdzuk/Star Ledger/CORBIS; **359** Chris Britt/Copley News Service; **361** Scott Olson/Getty Images; **362** Koji Sasahara/AP Images; **363** Mark Kegans/Getty Images; **366** Scott Sharpe/AP Images; **367** Michael Kelley/Getty Images; **370** AP Images; **371** (l)Joseph Sohm, ChromoSohm/CORBIS, (c)Florida Department of State; (r)Reuters/CORBIS; **373** Steve Greenberg courtesy Seattle Post-Intelligencer; **374** Dave L. Ryan/Index Stock; **376** Library of Congress; **377** Charles Shoffner/Index Stock; **379** (t)Christian Science Monitor/Getty Images, (b)Rebecca Cook/Reuters; **380** Courtesy John Liu; **383** David McNew/Getty Images; **384** Robin Nelson/PhotoEdit; **387** Toby Talbot/AP Images; **388** Lee Marriner/AP Images; **389** Jeff Parker, Florida Today; **391** (t)Thinkstock/Jupiter Images, (bl)Scenics of America/PhotoLink/Getty Images, (br)Pete Fisher/911 Pictures; **393** By permission of Steve Breen and Creators Syndicate, Inc.; **394** Ethel Wolvovitz/The Image Works; **396** Bill Haber/AP Images; **397** Jeff Greenberg/The Image Works; **398** Russ Curtis; **400** Ben Chrisman/AP Images; **401** Marshall Ramsey/Copley News Service; **403** Courtesy Charlotte Hawkins Brown Museum at Historic Palmer Memorial Institute; **404** Peter Hvizdak/The Image Works;

405 Design Pics Inc./Alamy; **408** Sylvain Grandadam/Getty Images; **409** Paul Sancya/AP Images; **410** Jim West/The Image Works; **411** CORBIS; **413** (t)Jeff Greenberg/The Image Works, (bl)Gerry Broome/AP Images, (br)Steve Cole/Getty Images; **417** (t)Bettmann/CORBIS, (c)Alfred Eisenstaedt/Time Life Pictures/Getty Images; **419** Lon Tweeten; **420** Bob Daemmrich/PhotoEdit; **424** Nancy Richmond/The Image Works; **426** Kat Wade/San Francisco Chronicle/CORBIS; **427** Gibson Stock Photography; **430** LOU KRASKY/AP Images; **431** Cumberland Times-News, Steve Bittner/AP Images; **432** (t)Lee Anderlite/Stage 3 Productions, (b)Grantpix/Index Stock; **433** Dennis MacDonald/PhotoEdit; **435** Bettmann/CORBIS; **437** Steve Breen/Copley News Service; **438** Fat Chance Productions/CORBIS, (inset)Comstock Images/Alamy; **441** (t)Robertstock, (b)Las Cruces Sun-News, Norm Dettlaff/AP Images; **446** Andre Jenny/Alamy; **448** Michael Newman/PhotoEdit; **449** Chris Britt/Copley News Service; **452** Danny Johnston/AP Images; **453** Bob Daemmrich/The Image Works; **455** Ramin Talaie/CORBIS; **456** Mikael Karlsson/Arresting Images; **459** AP Images; **460** A. Ramey/PhotoEdit; **461** Larry Kolvoord/The Image Works; **462** Katja Heinemann/Aurora Photos; **464** SARGENT ©2005 Austin American-Statesman; **465** (t)Richard Lord/PhotoEdit, (c b)Bob Daemmrich; **468** Peter Hvizdak/The Image Works; **470** Mario Tama/Getty Images; **471** China Photos/Getty Images; **472** The Plain Dealer, Marvin Fong/AP Images; **474** Paul Sakuma/AP Images; **475** Ken James/CORBIS; **476** Reuters/CORBIS; **480** Mannie Garcia/Reuters/CORBIS; **481** Gary Markstein/Copley News Service; **482** Tom Sobolik; **483** Everett Kennedy Brown/epa/CORBIS; **485** Ed Kashi/CORBIS; **487** (t)Mel Evans/AP Images, (c)Ken James/CORBIS, (b)Reuters/CORBIS; **489** Tribune Media Services, Inc.; **491** Photri; **492** Spencer Grant/PhotoEdit; **495** Frank Siteman/PhotoEdit; **496** Wendell Metzen/Index Stock; **498** Paul Sancya/AP Images; **499** Rick Bowmer/AP Images; **500** Cynthia Johnson/Time Life Pictures/Getty Images; **503** Dan Reiland/AP Images; **504** David Young-Wolff/PhotoEdit; **505** Steve Breen/Copley News Service; **506** Author's Image - Celestial Panoramas Ltd/Alamy; **507** (b)Courtesy Jessica Painter; **508** Robert Glusic/Getty Images; **511** (tl)David Frazier/PhotoEdit, (tr)Don Ryan/AP Images, (b)Wally Santana/AP Images; **514** Andy Sacks/Getty Images; **516** Mike Cardew/Akron Beacon Journal/AP Images; **517** Jeff Greenberg/The Image Works; **520** Elliott Minor/AP Images; **521** Justin Sullivan/Getty Images; **523** (t)Anthony Gray, (b)Courtesy Ohio Fair Schools Campaign; **524** Brownie Harris/CORBIS; **527** Catherine Karnow/CORBIS; **528** Gary Markstein/Copley News Service; **529** Courtesy Liberty Power; **530** The Granger Collection, New York; **532** The Art Archive/Museum of the City of New York; **533** (t)Myrleen Ferguson Cate/PhotoEdit, (bl)Spencer Grant/Stock Boston, (br)AP Images; **536** Rob Gage; **538** David Young-Wolff/Photo Edit; **539** Michael Newman/PhotoEdit; **540** Scott Olson/Getty Images; **541** Rich Pedroncelli/AP Images; **542** Mango Productions/CORBIS; **544** Ken Ruinard/AP Images; **545** Bill Aron/PhotoEdit; **546** Chris Britt/Copley News Service; **547** Jerry Arcieri/CORBIS; **550 551** C Squared Studios; **552** David Duprey/AP Images; **553** Creatas/SuperStock, (inset)Thomas Northcut/Getty Images; **554** Rohanna Mertens for ACCION International; **557** Daniel Acker/Bloomberg News/Landov; **559** Robert Jordan/AP Images; **561** (t)Tim Byrne; **563** (t)Barry Austin Photography/Getty Images, (bl)Directphoto.org/Alamy, (br)Spencer Grant/PhotoEdit; **566** Denis Poroy/AP Images; **568** Pat Wellenbach/AP Images; **569** Paul Sakuma/AP Images; **570** Gary Heatherly; **573** Ron Heflin/AP Images; **574** Tom Carter/PhotoEdit; **577** Spencer Grant/PhotoEdit; **580** George Nikitin/AP Images; **581** Spencer Platt/Getty Images; **583** Al Grillo/AP Images; **585** Mike Fiala/AP Images; **587** AP Images; **588** Sidney Harris/ScienceCartoonsPlus.com; **590** David Zalubowski/AP Images, (inset)Don Ryan/AP Images; **591** Trek Bikes;

593 (t)Phil Klein/CORBIS, (bl)Mark Richards/PhotoEdit, (br)CORBIS; **597** George Hall/CORBIS; **598** Jeff Greenberg/Index Stock; **600** Dick Blume/The Image Works; **602** Jeremy Horner/CORBIS; **603** Justin Sullivan/Getty Images; **604** Skip Nall/Getty Images; **605** Carlos Osorio/AP Images; **608** Keith Srakocic/AP Images; **609** Michael Ramirez/Copley News Service; **610** Paul Sancya/AP Images; **611** Arthur Schatz/Time Life Pictures/Getty Images; **612** Michael Siluk/The Image Works; **614** Mike Stewart/Time Life Pictures/Getty Images; **615** Jeff Greenberg/PhotoEdit; **616** Business Wire/Getty Images; **617** Courtesy Fuzzy Feet Foundation; **619** (t)Seth Perlman/AP Images, (c)M. Spencer Green/AP Images, (b)Gerry Broome/AP Images; **622** The Granger Collection, New York; **623** David Duprey/AP Images; **624** Chris Daniels/CORBIS; **627** Sam C. Pierson, Jr./Photo Researchers; **628** Bill Pogue/Getty Images; **630** Chip Somodevilla/Getty Images; **631** NASA; **633** Bettmann/CORBIS; **634** Shawn Thew/epa/CORBIS; **636** Steve Raymer/CORBIS; **637** Joe Tabacca/Bloomberg News/Landov; **639** Gary Markstein/Copley News Service; **641** US Air Force Museum; **643** AP Images; **646** Mario Villafuerte/Getty Images; **647** Spencer Platt/Getty Images; **648** Courtesy Erika Herman; **650** Mark Burnett/Stock Boston; **651** (t)William Manning/CORBIS, (bl)Gary Conner/PhotoEdit, (br)Warren Morgan/CORBIS; **654 656** James Leynse/CORBIS; **657** Canadian Press, David Boily/AP Images; **658** (t)Michael Houghton, StudiOhio; **660** PAUL J. RICHARDS/AFP/Getty Images; **661** Hisham Ibrahim/Getty Images; **663** Michael Ramirez/Copley News Service; **666 667** Bettmann/CORBIS; **668** (t)©Gavin Seim Photography, (b)Courtesy Washington Business Week; **671** (t)Rob Crandall/Stock Boston, (c)Mark Burnett/Stock Boston, (b)AP Images; **674** Michael Newman/PhotoEdit; **676** Manuel Balce Ceneta/AP Images; **677** Kevin Lamarque/Reuters; **678** Spencer Grant/PhotoEdit; **681** Jamie Martin/AP Images; **683** Tony Freeman/PhotoEdit; **684** William Thomas Cain/Getty Images; **687** Stan Honda/AFP/Getty Images; **689** Michael Ramirez/Copley News Service; **691** Fred Ricard; **693** (t)Digital Vision, (cl)JupiterImages/ComStock, (cr)Kevin Lamarque/Reuters, (bl)Spencer Grant/PhotoEdit, (br)William Thomas Cain/Getty Images; **696** AFP/Getty Images; **699** (t)Kevin Wolf/United States Mint/AP Images (c b)Bettmann/CORBIS; **700** Richard Cummins/CORBIS; **703** IT Stock Free/JupiterImages; **704** Indiapicture/Alamy; **706** Mike Clarke/AFP/Getty Images; **707** Ahn Youngjoon/AP Images; **710** Scott Stantis/Copley News Service; **712** Elmer Martinez/AFP/Getty Images; **714** British Petrolium Handout/epa/CORBIS; **715** Jorge Rey/AP Images; **717** KCNA/epa/CORBIS; **721** Kham Kham/CN/Reuters; **723** Reuters/CORBIS; **724** (t)Courtesy Global Kids, (b)Joe Robinson; **727** (t)Ahn Youngjoon/AP Images, (c)KCNA/epa/CORBIS, (b)Jorge Rey/AP Images; **732** Silvia Izquierdo/AP Images; **734** Guang Niu/Reuters/CORBIS; **735** KIM JAE-HWAN/AFP/Getty Images; **736** (t)fuse-project, (b)Courtesy of Cosmos Ignite Innovations; **737** Courtesy Inveneo, **739** Ahmad Masood/REUTERS/Landov; **740** (t)Susan Liebold, (b)Jonathan Nourok/PhotoEdit; **743** Gideon Mendel/CORBIS; **744** Marco Di Lauro/Getty Images; **747** Michael Ramirez/Copley News Service; **749** (t) KIM JAE-HWAN/AFP/Getty Images, (c)IT Stock Free/JupiterImages, (b)Marco Di Lauro/Getty Images; **753** Thaier Al-Sudani/Reuters/CORBIS; **757** By permission of Gary Markstein and Creators Syndicate, Inc.; **758** Dennis MacDonald/PhotoEdit; **760** Michael Newman/PhotoEdit; **763** Koji Sasahara/AP Images; **772** National Portrait Gallery/Smithsonian Institution, Art Resource; **773** Smithsonian Institution; **774** Mark Burnett; **775** (t)Denver Art Museum (b) CORBIS; **777** CORBIS; **778** CORBIS; **779** Flip Schulke/CORBIS; **790** CORBIS; **791** Bettmann/CORBIS; **797 798 799 800** White House Historical Association; **801** White House Historical Association, (bl)Bush 2000 Campaign, (br)Brooks Kraft/CORBIS.